Textbook Chapter Number	Textbook Chapter Title	Discovering Psychology Video Program	Discovering Psychology Video Program Description
Chapter 10	Intelligence and Intelligence Assessment	**Program 16:** Testing and Intelligence	Just as no two fingerprints are alike, no two people have the same set of abilities, aptitudes, interests, and talents. **Program 16** explains the tools psychologists use to measure these differences. It also describes the long-standing controversy over how to define intelligence and how IQ tests have been misused and misapplied. Is it wise, accurate, or fair to reduce intelligence to a number? Researchers are currently debating the value of intelligence and personality tests.
Chapter 11	Human Development Across the Life Span	**Program 5:** The Developing Child	**Program 5** looks at how advances in technology and methodology have revealed the abilities of newborn infants, giving researchers a better understanding of the role infants play in shaping their environment. In contrast to the nature-versus-nurture debates of the past, today's researchers concentrate on how heredity and environment interact to contribute to the developmental process.
		Program 6: Language Development	**Program 6** examines how children acquire language and demonstrates the methods psychologists use to study the role of biology and social interaction in language acquisition. It also looks at the contribution of language to children's cognitive and social development.
		Program 18: Maturing and Aging	Thanks to growing scientific interest in the elderly, research on aging has replaced many myths and fears with facts. **Program 18** focuses on what scientists are learning about life cycle development as they look at how aging is affected by biology, environment, and lifestyle.
Chapter 12	Motivation	**Program 12:** Motivation and Emotion	What moves us to act? Why do we feel the way we do? **Program 12** shows how psychologists study the continuous interactions of mind and body in an effort to explain the enormous variety and complexities of human behaviour.
Chapter 13	Emotion, Stress, and Health	**Program 23:** Health, Mind, and Behaviour	A profound rethinking of the relationship between mind and body has led to an approach to health that assumes that mental and physical processes are constantly interacting. **Program 23** looks at what health psychologists know about the factors that increase our chances of becoming ill and what we can do to improve and maintain our health.
Chapter 14	Understanding Human Personality	**Program 15:** The Self	What makes each of us unique? What traits and experiences make you? **Program 15** describes how psychologists systematically study the origins and development of self-identity, self-esteem, and other aspects of our thoughts, feelings, and behaviours that make up our personalities.
Chapter 15	Psychological Disorders	**Program 21:** Psychopathology	**Program 21** describes the major types of mental illnesses and some of the factors that influence them—both biological and psychological. It also reports on several approaches to classifying and treating mental illness and explains the difficulties of defining abnormal behaviour.
Chapter 16	Therapies for Psychological Disorders	**Program 22:** Psychotherapy	**Program 22** looks at psychotherapy and therapists, the professionals trained to help us solve some of our most critical problems. You will learn about different approaches to the treatment of mental, emotional, and behavioural disorders and the kind of helping relationships that therapists provide.
Chapter 17	Social Psychology	**Program 19:** The Power of the Situation	**Program 19** investigates the social and situational forces that influence our individual and group behaviour and how our beliefs can be manipulated by other people.
		Program 20: Constructing Social Reality	**Program 20** explores our subjective view of reality and how it influences social behaviour. It reveals how our perceptions and reasoning ability can be influenced in positive and negative ways, and it increases our understanding of how psychological processes govern our interpretation of reality.

PEARSON
mypsych︱lab ™

Save Time.

Improve Results.

More than 6 million students have used a Pearson MyLab.

MyPsychLab is an all-in-one learning and testing environment for introductory psychology. This easy-to-navigate site provides students with a variety of resources including

- An interactive Pearson eText

- Audio and video material to view or listen to, whatever your learning style

- Personalized learning opportunities—YOU choose what, where, and when you want to study

- Self-assessment tests that create a personalized study plan to guide you on making the most efficient use of study time

To take advantage of all that MyPsychLab has to offer, you will need an access code. If you do not already have an access code, you can buy one online at **www.mypsychlab.com**.

Personalized Learning

In MyPsychLab you are treated as an individual with specific learning needs.

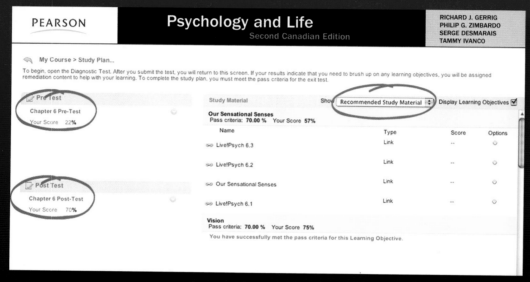

The study and assessment resources that come with your textbook allow you to review content and develop what you need to know, on your own time, and at your own pace.

MyPsychLab provides

- Quizzes with immediate grades

- A personalized study plan that tells you where to study based on your results, and where you can find the key topics you need to review to improve

- A gradebook where you can find your grades to see your progress as the term unfolds

- An opportunity for your instructor to see the gradebook, too

- More than 150 video clips with closed-captioning and activities after you watch

- The Pearson Experiments Tool, a new online activity that gives students the chance to "do psychology"

- The 23 Discovering Psychology videos that are referenced in the text, along with related self-graded quizzes

Save Time. Improve Results. www.mypsychlab.com

Psychology and Life Second Canadian Edition

Psychology and Life Second Canadian Edition

RICHARD J. GERRIG STONY BROOK UNIVERSITY

PHILIP G. ZIMBARDO STANFORD UNIVERSITY

SERGE DESMARAIS UNIVERSITY OF GUELPH

TAMMY IVANCO UNIVERSITY OF MANITOBA

Pearson Canada
Toronto

Library and Archives Canada Cataloguing in Publication

Psychology and life / Richard J. Gerrig . . . [et al.].—2nd Canadian ed.

Includes bibliographical references and indexes.

ISBN 978-0-205-76705-2

1. Psychology—Textbooks.   I. Gerrig, Richard J.

BF121.P838 2011   150   C2010-906855-6

ISBN 978-0-205-76705-2

Vice-President, Editorial Director: Gary Bennett
Editor-in-Chief: Ky Pruesse
Acquisitions Editor: Matthew Christian
Sponsoring Editor: Kathleen McGill
Executive Marketing Manager: Judith Allen
Senior Developmental Editor: Catherine Belshaw
Project Manager: Avinash Chandra
Production Editors: Avivah Wargon, Lila Campbell
Copy Editor: Lenore Latta
Proofreader: Alison Kooistra
Compositor: MPS Limited, a Macmillan Company
Permissions and Photo Researcher: Terri Rothman, M.L.S.
Art Director: Julia Hall
Cover and Interior Designer: Miguel Acevedo
Cover Image: Diana Ong / Superstock / Getty Images

1 2 3 4 5   14 13 12 11 10

Printed and bound in United States of America

We dedicate this book to our daughters Alex, Zara, and Tanya.

My daughter Alex has become a remarkable young woman. She brings an
articulate passion to a broad range of substantial issues. Alex will soon begin
her college career with an interest in political science.
I have no doubt that she will continue to excel — R. J. G.

My wonderful daughters, Zara Maria and Tanya Lucia, have been a source of
endless delight and personal support over the past three decades. They have
always modeled what is best in students, curiosity in knowing why and how things and
behavior work, while never settling for the obvious simple answers to complex issues.
I look forward to the unfolding of their careers as teachers, social activists,
and Zara as a cultural anthropologist, and Tanya as a museum
curator in media arts — P. G. Z.

To Chris — S. D.

To Rayan and the fuzzy kids — T. L. I.

Brief Contents

Contents

Preface

Teaching introductory psychology is one of the greatest challenges facing any academic psychologist. Indeed, because of the range of this subject matter, it is probably the most difficult course to teach effectively in all of academia. We must cover both the micro-level analyses of nerve cell processes and the macro-level analyses of cultural systems, both the vitality of health psychology and the tragedy of lives blighted by mental illness. Our challenge in writing this text—like your challenge in teaching—is to give form and substance to all this information and bring it to life for our students.

More often than not, students come into our course filled with misconceptions about psychology that they have picked up from the infusion of "pop psychology" into our society. They also bring with them high expectations about what they want to get out of a course in psychology—they want to learn much that will be personally valuable, that will help them improve their everyday lives. Indeed, that is a tall order for any teacher to fill. We believe that *Psychology and Life* can help you to fill it.

Our goal has been to design a text that students will enjoy reading as they learn what is so exciting and special about the many fields of psychology. In every chapter and in every sentence, we have tried to make sure that students will want to go on reading. At the same time, we have focused on how our text will work within the syllabi of instructors who value a research-centred, applications-relevant approach to psychology.

This second Canadian edition of *Psychology and Life* is truly a collaborative endeavour. The U.S. authors, Philip Zimbardo and Richard Gerrig, have now co-authored five versions of this book for the U.S. market. The Canadian authors, Serge Desmarais and Tammy Ivanco, began their co-authorship of this book four years ago. The partnership between Canadian and U.S. co-authors was forged because we shared a commitment to teaching psychology as a science relevant to human welfare. We could all bring our teaching experience to bear on a text that balances scientific rigour with psychology's relevance to contemporary life concerns. Furthermore, our respective academic expertise (Richard in cognitive psychology; Tammy in developmental neuroscience and memory; Phil and Serge in social psychology) has helped us achieve a balanced coverage of the various subdisciplines within psychology and keep

pace with its rapid changes, particularly in areas such as neuroscience.

With this second Canadian edition, we also wanted to place the discipline of psychology—a discipline that has no national boundaries—within the proper cultural context for Canadian learners. Our intent was not to overemphasize Canadian research, but to place the discipline of psychology within a context that Canadian learners understand, with examples and illustrations that are part of our common experience.

New in the Second Canadian Edition

Psychology and Life includes a number of new features and is fresh with the most up-to-date coverage and brimming with new references. Our goal is to be the most current, most accurate, and most accessible treatment of our discipline today.

CHAPTER-BY-CHAPTER HIGHLIGHTS

Chapter 1

- New *Psychology in Your Life*: In What Ways Do Psychologists Participate in the Legal System?
- Updated discussion of the history of psychology training in Canada

Chapter 2

- New research studies:
  - "Children's knowledge of deceptive gaze cues and its relation to their actual lying behavior" (McCarthy & Lee, 2009)
  - "The value of believing in free will: Encouraging a belief in determinism increases cheating" (Vohs & Schooler, 2008)
  - "The face of success: Inferences from chief executive officers' appearance predict company profits" (Rule & Ambady, 2008)

- Discussion on the process of research expanded to include more information on peer review and the need to disseminate research results
- Updated research included on free will versus determinism
- Discussion of third variable added to section on correlational methods
- Updated information on ethics of animal rights

Chapter 3

- New *Critical Thinking in Your Life*: What Does "It's Genetic" Mean?
- Broad discussion of why music evolved
- More evidence and discussion of the effect of colour on emotions
- *Psychology In Your Life* revolves around how much media, like movies and books, incorporate genetic engineering as a way to provide suspense and storyline
- Comparison of language and math, providing evidence for why language comes much easier to most than math skills

Chapter 4

- New *Psychology in Your Life*: How Does Your Brain Determine Trust?
- New *Critical Thinking in Your Life*: New Cells in an Old Brain focuses on how the concept of stem cells is revolutionizing how we think about the brain
- Discussion of the brain and its functions reorganized to convey information in a more student-friendly way
- Introduction to new research on the plasticity of the brain, with content on stroke recovery, the generation of new neurons in the brain, and the role of estrogen and menopause

Chapter 5

- New *Critical Thinking in Your Life*: Are Drivers Distracted When They Use Their Cell Phones? discusses how this issue has captured our attention and why it is widely believed that cell phone use during driving is particularly dangerous
- Discussion of the distinctions between sensations and perception revised to convey information in a more student-friendly way
- Research on the sense of taste and more discussion of why some foods are hot and, potentially, painful

Chapter 6

- Updated research added to *Psychology in Your Life*: Do You Get Enough Sleep?
- New *Critical Thinking in Your Life*: What Can We Learn From "the Munchies"?
- New research studies:
  - "Dare to compare: Fact-based versus simulation-based comparison in daily life" (Summerville & Roese, 2007)
  - "Focused analgesia in waking and hypnosis: Effects on pain, memory, and somatosensory event-related potentials" (De Pascalis et al., 2008)
  - "Acute disinhibiting effects of alcohol as a factor in risky driving behavior" (Fillmore et al., 2008)
- Updated information on the impact of alcohol consumption on accidents

- New research investigating the cortical thickness in brains as people grow older
- Updated sections on moral reasoning, nightmares, and night terrors
- Expanded section on the consequences of sleep deprivation
- Updated research on amphetamine use in Canada and of these drugs' impact on our bodies
- Updates made to discussions of cannabinoids, OxyContin, depressants, alcohol, and MDMA

Chapter 7

- Discussion of the return of the habitual response
- New Research Study on Clark's Nutcrackers and how they find food they have cached based on cues from the environment, as well as cues from their own behaviour

Chapter 8

- New Research Study on the relationships between working memory and wandering memory
- New discussion of amnesia and autobiographical memory
- New Research Study on the role of context in memory
- Discussion of flashbulb memories
- Revised discussion of the biology of Alzheimer's disease
- New Research Study on how memories differ if you imagine doing something versus doing it yourself

Chapter 9

- New Research Study on the mismatch that occurs when size and number are not consistent
- Discussion of speech errors
- New Research Study on lexical ambiguity results in context input to determine the correct definition
- Discussion of patterns of errors in English and non-English speakers
- New Research Study on how description influences the map you make of different neighbourhoods
- Discussion of the belief bias
- Additional focus on heuristics in decision making
- Discussion of the ability of framing to influence decision making

Chapter 10

- New *Psychology in Your Life*: How Can You Become More Creative?
- Updated discussion of stereotypes and cultural impact of them on intelligence testing
- Updated section on intellectual disabilities and learning disorders
- New Research Study on assessing emotional intelligence
- Discussion of the genetics of intelligence using twin studies
- Thorough discussion of creativity

Chapter 11

- Updated discussion of the visual system and its development
- Updated discussion of the "use it or lose it" concept in development

Chapter 12

- New *Psychology in Your Life*: How Does the Presence of Others Influence Your Eating?
- New *Critical Thinking in Your Life*: How Does Motivation Affect Academic Achievement?
- New research studies:
  - "Brains of anorexia nervosa patients process self-images differently from non-self-images: An fMRI study" (Sachdev et al., 2008)
  - "A question of belonging: Race, social fit, and achievement" (Walton & Cohen, 2007)
  - "Modern and old-fashioned homonegativity among samples of Canadian and American university students" (Morrison et al., 2009)
- Expanded discussion on drives and incentives
- Updated discussion on obesity, including genetic mechanisms that may predispose some individuals to obesity (Farooqi & O'Rahilly, 2007)
- New discussion on binge eating disorder
- New research on genetic factors causing eating disorders
- Updated discussion on gender and cultural difference in eating disorders
- New research on sexual practices of university students
- Updated research on brain differences between homosexuals and heterosexuals (Savic & Lindström, 2008)
- Updated research on societal perceptions of gays and lesbians

Chapter 13

- New *Psychology in Your Life*: Can You Accurately Predict Your Future Emotions?
- Updated research in Critical Thinking in Your Life: Can Health Psychology Help Your Get More Exercise?
- New research studies:
  - "Do infants show distinct negative facial expressions for fear and anger? Emotional expression in 11-month-old European American, Chinese, and Japanese infants" (Camras et al., 2007)
  - "On being happy and gullible: Mood effects on skepticism and detection of deception" (Forgas & East, 2008)
  - "The role of positive and negative emotions in life satisfaction judgment across nations" (Kuppens et al., 2008)
  - "Lending a hand: Social regulation of the neural response to threat" (Coan et al., 2006)
  - "Patient and physician attitudes in the health care context: Attitudinal symmetry predicts patient satisfaction and adherence" (Cvengros et al., 2007)
- Expanded section on positive psychology
- New research on how life events may affect subjective well-being
- Updates made to Social Readjustment Rating Scale (SRRS)
- New research on how daily hassles may be balanced out by daily positive experiences (Jain et al., 2007)
- New research examining the ways in which women cope with the stress of undergoing surgery for breast cancer (Roussi et al., 2007)
- New research exploring the heritability of why people start smoking (Boardman et al., 2008)
- New research on optimism and immune function (Segerstrom, 2006, 2007)
- Updated data on leading causes of death in Canada

Chapter 14

- New *Critical Thinking in Your Life*: How Is Your Personality Conveyed in Cyberspace?
- New research studies:
  - "Genetic and environmental influences on positive traits of the values in action classification, and biometric covariance with normal personality" (Steger et al., 2007)
  - "Verbal intelligence and self-regulatory competencies: Joint predictors of boys' aggression" (Ayduk et al., 2007)
  - "Using past performance, proxy efficacy, and academic self-efficacy to predict college performance" (Elias & MacDonald, 2007)
  - "She works hard for the money: Valuing effort underlies gender differences in behavioral self-handicapping" (McCrae et al., 2008)
- Extended section on evolutionary perspectives on trait dimensions, with updated research
- New discussion of Rotter's Expectancy Theory
- Updated research on self-esteem
- New information on the MMPI-2-RF

Chapter 15

- New *Critical Thinking in Your Life*: How Do Disorders Enter the DSM?
- New research studies:
  - "Time course of selective attention in clinically depressed young adults: An eye tracking study" (Kellough et al., 2008)
  - "When does the gender difference in rumination begin? Gender and age differences in the use of rumination by adolescents" (Jose & Brown, 2008)
  - "fMRI in patients with motor conversion symptoms and controls with simulated weakness" (Stone et al., 2007)
  - "Life events and high-trait reactivity together predict psychotic symptom increases in schizophrenia" (Docherty et al., 2008)
- New section on the concept of insanity and its application in the Canadian legal system
- Updated section on the biological causes of anxiety disorders
- Updated discussion of gender differences in depression
- Updated section on causes of dissociative disorders
- New discussion of gender differences in ADHD
- Updated discussion and research related to autistic disorder

Chapter 16

- Updated research in *Psychology in Your Life*: Are Lives Haunted by Repressed Memories?
- Updated research in *Critical Thinking in Your Life*: Does Therapy Affect Brain Activity?
- New research studies:
  - "Virtual reality exposure therapy and standard (in vivo) exposure therapy in the treatment of fear of flying" (Rothbaum et al., 2006)
  - "A randomized, controlled trial of group cognitive-behavioral therapy for compulsive buying disorder: Posttreatment and 6-month follow-up results" (Mueller et al., 2008)
- New section on diversity issues in psychotherapy

- New research on how exposure therapy has also been used to combat obsessive-compulsive disorder
- Additional updated research on cognitive behavioural therapy, including a study on how it was used to treat women with binge eating disorder (Cassin et al., 2008)
- New discussion on the debate regarding whether individuals who take antidepressant drugs are at a greater risk for suicide
- Expanded discussion of psychosurgery, including a recent study that evaluated the effectiveness of a cingulotomy (Shields et al., 2008)

Chapter 17

- Chapter 17 updated, restructured, and made more succinct for the 2nd Canadian edition
- New *Psychology in Your Life*: In What Ways Are You Like a Chameleon?
- New research studies:
  - "Going for the gold: Models of agency in Japanese and American contexts" (Markus et al., 2006)
  - "Attributions, deception, and event related potentials: An investigation of self-serving bias" (Krusemark et al., 2008)
  - "Asking questions changes behavior: Mere measurement effects on frequency of blood donation" (Godin et al., 2008)
  - "Biased assimilation and attitude polarization in response to learning about biological explanations of homosexuality" (Boysen & Vogel, 2007)
  - "Kinship and altruism: A cross-cultural experimental study" (Madsen et al., 2007)
- Expanded discussion on the long-term consequences of the Stanford Prison Experiment
- New research examining the types of messages that work most effectively to bring about reductions in people's energy consumption (Nolan et al., 2007)
- New section on suicide cults
- New research on the elaboration likelihood model (Burkley, 2008) and on stereotype threats (Stone & McWhinnie, 2008)
- Updated research on the situational factors that affect aggression

Text Theme:
The Science of Psychology

The aim of *Psychology and Life* is to use solid scientific research to combat psychological misconceptions. In our experience as teachers, one of the most reliable occurrences on the first day of introductory psychology is the throng of students who push forward at the end of class to ask, in essence, "Will this class teach me what I need to know?"

> My mother is taking Prozac: Will we learn what it does?
> Are you going to teach us how to study better?
> I need to put my son in daycare to come back to school. Is that going to be all right for him?
> What should I do if I have a friend talking about suicide?

We take comfort in knowing that each of these questions has been addressed by rigorous empirical research. *Psychology and Life* is devoted to providing students with scientific analyses of their foremost concerns. As a result, the features of *Psychology and Life* support a central theme: psychology as a science, with a focus on *applying* that science to your students' lives.

CRITICAL THINKING IN YOUR LIFE

An important goal of *Psychology and Life* is to teach the scientific basis of psychological reasoning. When our students ask us questions—what they need to know—they quite often have acquired partial answers based on the types of information available in the popular media. Some of that information is accurate, but often students do not know how to make sense of it. How do they learn to interpret and evaluate what they hear in the media? How can they become wiser consumers of the overabundance of research studies and surveys cited? How can they judge the credibility of these sources? To counteract this infusion of so-called reliable research, we provide students with the scientific tools to think critically about the information with which they are surrounded and to draw generalizations appropriate to the goals and methods of research.

With a feature we call *Critical Thinking in Your Life*, we seek to confront students directly with the experimental basis of critical conclusions. Our intention is not to maintain that each of these boxes has the definitive answer to a particular research area, but to invite critical thinking and open the door for further questions.

Critical Thinking in Your Life topics, by chapter:

Why Do Friendships End? (Chapter 1)
How Can You Evaluate Psychological Information on the Web? (Chapter 2)
The Cinderella Effect (Chapter 3)
What Does "It's Genetic" Mean? (Chapter 3)
New Cells in an Old Brain (Chapter 4)

PSYCHOLOGY IN YOUR LIFE

The questions we cited earlier are real questions from real students, and your students will find the answers throughout the book. These questions represent data we collected from students over the years. We told them, "Tell us what you need to know about psychology," and we have placed those questions—your students' own voices—directly into the text in the form of the popular *Psychology in Your Life* sections. Our hope is that your students will see, in each instance, exactly why psychological knowledge is directly relevant to the decisions they make every day of their lives.

Psychology in Your Life topics, by chapter:

RESEARCH STUDIES

Throughout the book, we highlight major studies to showcase the *how* and *why* behind key psychological research. These studies have been expertly integrated into the text itself, allowing students to understand their full impact within the context of the readings. Example topics include plasticity in the visual cortex of adult rats, the impact of meditation on brain structure, the impact of culture on judgments of which category members are typical, the impact of emotions on memory for visual details, individual differences in intimacy goals, family therapy for children's anxiety disorders, cross-cultural differences in cognitive dissonance, and genetic influences on physical and social aggression. Many of the research studies described in detail throughout the text are new or have been revised for this edition.

Research Studies are identified throughout the text by a purple vertical line running along the left margin of the study.

DISCOVERING PSYCHOLOGY VIDEO PROGRAM AND VIEWING GUIDES

We are thrilled to be able to integrate into our textbook the wildly successful video series, *Discovering Psychology: Updated Edition*, produced by WGBH Boston with funding by Annenberg Media. Author Philip Zimbardo narrates the video series, as leading researchers, practitioners, and theorists probe the mysteries of the mind and body and bring psychology to life for introductory students. Most chapters of this textbook end with a Discovering Psychology Viewing Guide containing program review questions that draw attention to key information presented in the video. Answers to these questions are also provided in the Answer Appendix.

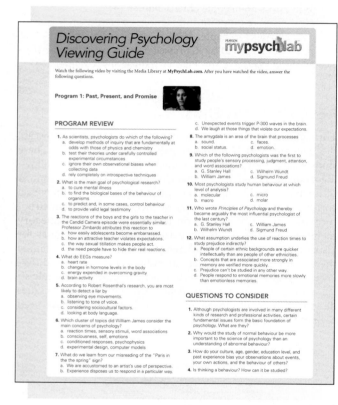

PEDAGOGICAL FEATURES

Psychology and Life presents the science of psychology in a way that is challenging yet accessible to a broad range of students. To enhance students' experience with the book, we include several pedagogical features:

- **Stop and Review.** This feature appears at the end of every major section and provides students with thought-provoking questions to test their mastery of material before moving on. Answers can be found in the Answer Appendix.
- **Recapping Main Points.** Each chapter concludes with a chapter summary, *Recapping Main Points,* which summarizes the chapter content and is organized according

to major section headings. A list of multimedia assets available on MyPsychLab and related to the content in each chapter will help students deepen their understanding of the material.

- **Key Terms.** Key terms are boldfaced in the text as they appear with their definitions at the bottom of each page and are listed, with page references, at the end of each chapter for quick review.
- **Practice Test.** Each chapter concludes with a practice test with multiple-choice questions based on the material in both the main text and the boxes. In addition, we've provided sample essay questions that allow students to think more broadly about the content of each chapter. Multiple-choice answers can be found in the Answer Appendix, and suggested answers for the essay questions can be found in the Instructor's Manual.

The *Psychology and Life* Teaching Program

A good textbook is only one part of the package of educational materials that makes an introductory psychology course valuable for students and effective for instructors. To make the difficult task of teaching introductory psychology easier for you and more interesting for your students, we have prepared a number of valuable ancillary materials in both electronic and print form.

SAVE TIME. IMPROVE RESULTS. *PUT SCIENTIFIC THINKING TO THE TEST*

Across the country, from small community colleges to large universities, a trend is emerging. Psychology enrolments are increasing, and available resources can't keep pace. The result is instructor time stretched to the limit like never before. At the same time, continual feedback is an important component to successful student progress. The APA strongly recommends student self-assessment tools and the use of embedded questions and assignments. In response to these demands, Pearson's MyPsychLab (MPL) offers students useful and engaging self-assessment tools and instructors flexibility in assessing and tracking student progress.

What is MyPsychLab?

MyPsychLab offers instructors and students all of their resources located in one place and organized to accompany this text. MyPsychLab is also a learning and assessment tool that enables instructors to assess student performance and adapt their course—without investing additional time or resources.

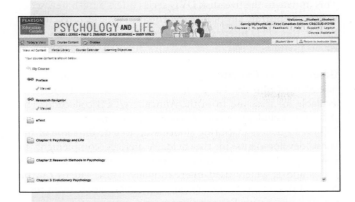

MyPsychLab includes

- An interactive Pearson eText that gives students access to the text whenever and wherever they have access to the internet. eText pages look exactly like the printed text, offering powerful new functionality for students and instructors. Users can create notes, highlight the text, create bookmarks, zoom, click hyperlinked words and phrases, and view in single-page or two-page view. Pearson eText allows for quick navigation to key parts of the eText using a table of contents and provides full text search. The eText also offers links to associated media files, enabling users to access videos, animations, or other activities as they read the text.
- Customized student Study Plans that are dynamically generated when students complete a chapter pre-test. The Study Plan for each student helps to focus his or her efforts where they are needed the most.
- Glossary Flashcards of key terms from the text.
- A Multimedia Library with links to video clips and embedded animations and simulations that dynamically illustrate chapter concepts.
- A Gradebook for instructors and the availability of full course management capabilities for instructors.
- Online access to the *Discovering Psychology* Videos.

MyPsychLab is available to instructors by going to **www.mypsychlab.com** and following the instructions on the page. Students receive a MyPsychLab access code with the purchase of a new text.

New Pearson Psychology Experiments Tool This tool presents a suite of data-generating study demonstrations, self-inventories, and surveys that allow students to experience firsthand some of the main concepts covered in the textbook. Each item in the Experiments Tool generates anonymous class data that instructors can download and use in lectures or as homework assignments. With assignable demonstrations such as

- Ambiguous Figures
- Depth of Processing
- Digit Span
- Emotion and Memory
- Hemispheric Specialization
- and many others,

the Experiments Tool provides opportunities for students to actively participate in doing psychology and for instructors to analyze, interpret, and discuss the results.

MyClassPrep New from Pearson, MyClassPrep makes lecture preparation simpler and less time-consuming. It collects the very best class presentation resources—art and figures from our leading texts, videos, lecture activities, classroom activities, demonstrations, and much more—in one convenient online destination. You may search through MyClassPrep's extensive database of tools by content topic (arranged by standard topics within the psychology curriculum) or by content type (video, audio, simulation, Word documents, etc.). You can select resources appropriate for your lecture, many of which can be downloaded directly. Or you may build your own folder of resources and present from within MyClassPrep. MyClassPrep can be accessed in the Instructor's Resources folder within the Course Content tab in MyPsychLab. Please contact your Pearson representative for access to MyPsychLab.

INSTRUCTOR SUPPLEMENTS

Instructor's Resource CD-ROM (**ISBN** 0205009085) This resource CD includes the following instructor supplements:

Instructor's Manual (Mike Lee, University of Winnipeg) This Instructor's Manual provides a wonderful tool for classroom preparation and management for first-time or experienced instructors. For each chapter, the Instructor's Manual includes a Chapter-at-a-Glance grid linking chapter topics to other available supplements and resources, including learning objectives targeting specific goals for the chapter; detailed chapter outlines; a comprehensive list of discussion questions; lecture extensions; biographical profiles of key figures; a timeline placing important psychological discoveries in historical context; suggestions for further reading; case study lecture launchers; demonstrations and activities for classroom use; updated video, media, and web resources; and other detailed pedagogical information.

Test Item File (Anneke Olthof, University of Guelph, and Katrina E. Gantly, Camosun College) Each chapter of the test bank contains over 100 multiple-choice questions along with up to 20 true/false questions and 5 to 10 fill-in-the-blank questions. The correct answer in each multiple-choice question has an answer justification, and all questions include a page reference, a difficulty rating (easy/medium/difficult), and skill type (conceptual/factual/analytical). Essay questions have also been included, along with sample answers for each. The test item file is available in Word and online through Pearson's MyTest platform.

Secondary Test Item File (Fred Whitford, University of Montana) includes over 1500 additional questions. Item analysis data for these questions is based on actual student performance. Each test item has been classified, and the following summary statistics are presented: correct answer, percent of students who selected the correct answer in each item as well as the percent who selected each alternative answer in the item, and the overall point biserial r for each item.

MyTest The Test Item File is available in a computerized format called MyTest. MyTest is a powerful assessment generation program that helps instructors easily create and print quizzes, tests, exams, as well as homework or practice handouts. Questions and tests can all be authored online, allowing instructors ultimate flexibility and the ability to efficiently manage assessments at anytime, from anywhere.

PowerPoint Presentation The PowerPoint Presentation (Nick Carleton, University of Regina) pairs key points covered in the chapters with images from the textbook to enhance lectures and encourage effective classroom discussions.

Clicker-Ready Personal Response System Questions (Randal Tonks, Camosun College) This edition features the addition of PowerPoint slides suitable for the Personal Response System you use in your classroom. These questions can be used to evaluate students' knowledge of material and to enhance classroom discussions.

Image Library This file offers selected figures and tables from the text that can be incorporated into your PowerPoint presentations, as desired.

Most of these instructor supplements are also available for download from a password-protected section of Pearson Education Canada's online catalogue (**http://vig.pearsoned. ca**). Navigate to your book's catalogue page to view a list of those supplements that are available. See your local sales representative for details and access.

ADDITIONAL SUPPLEMENTS FOR YOUR INTRODUCTORY PSYCHOLOGY COURSE

Pearson Teaching Films: Introductory Psychology, Instructor's Library (**ISBN** 0131754327) This five-disk DVD series includes 82 segments covering all of the major topics in introductory psychology. All of the segments have been selected from ABC News, Films for Humanities & Sciences, Pearson Education's own assets, and SciCentral.

Pearson Teaching Films: Introductory Psychology, Instructor's Library © 2008 UPDATE (**ISBN** 0205652808)

This update to the five-disk DVD series offers a fresh new set of videos to illustrate key points and enhance your lectures. In particular, this DVD offers some new segments addressing science versus pseudoscience!

Discovering Psychology Videos Written, designed, and hosted by Philip Zimbardo, this set of 26 half-hour videos is available for class use from the Annenberg/CPB collection. The collection includes two completely new programs and more than 15 new sequences that bring students up to date on some of the latest developments in the field. A perfect complement to *Psychology and Life*, this course supplement has won numerous prizes and is widely used internationally. These videos can be accessed through MyPsychLab. For more information about these videos, contact your Pearson Canada sales representative.

CourseSmart for Instructors CourseSmart goes beyond traditional expectations—providing instant, online access to the textbooks and course materials you need at a lower cost for students. And even as students save money, you can save time and hassle with a digital eText that allows you to search for the most relevant content at the very moment you need it. Whether it's evaluating textbooks or creating lecture notes to help students with difficult concepts, CourseSmart can make life a little easier. See how when you visit **www.coursesmart.com/instructors**.

Technology Specialists Pearson's Technology Specialists work with faculty and campus course designers to ensure that Pearson technology products, assessment tools, and online course materials are tailored to meet your specific needs. This highly qualified team is dedicated to helping schools take full advantage of a wide range of educational resources, by assisting in the integration of a variety of instructional materials and media formats. Your local Pearson Education sales representative can provide you with more details on this service program.

STUDENT SUPPLEMENTS

MyPsychLab with Discovering Psychology Videos This online all-in-one study resource offers a powerful, electronic version of the *Psychology and Life* textbook with embedded video clips, animations, and simulations that dynamically illustrate chapter concepts. MyPsychLab helps students master the concepts and prepare for exams. After a student completes a chapter pre-test, MyPsychLab generates a customized Study Plan for that student that helps to focus his or her study efforts where they're needed the most. MyPsychLab is available in both course management and website versions, and can be used as an instructor-driven assessment program and/or a student self-study learning program.

MyPsychLab also offers online access to the Discovering Psychology Videos as well as the Grade Aid Study Guide with Practice Tests.

Visit the site at **www.mypsychlab.com** and log in using the Access Code Card provided with this text. If your text did not come with an Access Code Card, ask for one at your campus store.

Grade Aid Study Guide with Practice Tests (**ISBN** 0205018769) (Heather Schellinck, Dalhousie University) A comprehensive and interactive study guide filled with in-depth activities. Each chapter includes "Before You Read," with a brief chapter summary and chapter learning objectives; "As You Read," a collection of demonstrations, activities, and exercises; "After You Read," containing three short practice quizzes and one comprehensive practice test; "When You Have Finished," with web links for further information; and crossword puzzles using key terms from the text. An appendix includes answers to all practice tests and crossword puzzles.

The Grade Aid Study Guide is available in two convenient formats. You can access the electronic version through MyPsychLab for *Psychology and Life*. A customizable printed version of the Grade Aid Study Guide is also available. Please contact your instructor or local Pearson Education Canada sales representative about getting a copy.

CourseSmart for Students CourseSmart goes beyond traditional expectations—providing instant, online access to the textbooks and course materials you need at an average savings of 60%. With instant access from any computer and the ability to search your text, you'll find the content you need quickly, no matter where you are. And with online tools like highlighting and note-taking, you can save time and study efficiently. See all the benefits at **www.coursesmart.com/students**.

Personal Acknowledgments

Although the Beatles may have gotten by with a little help from their friends, the only way we have survived the production of this second Canadian edition of *Psychology and Life* is with a *great deal* of help from many colleagues and friends. We especially thank Erin Allard, Tyler Wereha, and Rayan Horswill.

We would like to thank the following reviewers of this edition who read drafts of the manuscript and provided valuable feedback:

John S. Conklin, Camosun College
Hank Davis, University of Guelph
Zoe Dennison, University of the Fraser Valley
Kathy Foxall, Wilfrid Laurier University
Rick Healey, Memorial University of Newfoundland
Thom Herrmann, University of Guelph-Humber
Kim O'Neil, Carleton University
Heather Poole, University of Ottawa
David E. Reagan, Camosun College
Sean Scott, Heritage College
Donald Sharpe, University of Regina
Jady Wong, University of Manitoba
Kristi D. Wright, University of Regina

The enormous task of writing a book of this scope was possible only with the expert assistance of all these friends and colleagues and that of the editorial staff of Pearson Education Canada. We gratefully acknowledge their invaluable contributions at every stage of this project, collectively and, now, individually. We thank the following people at Pearson Education Canada: Ky Pruesse, Executive Acquisitions Editor; Kathleen McGill, Sponsoring Editor; Matthew Christian, Acquisitions Editor; Catherine Belshaw, Developmental Editor; Judith Allen, Executive Marketing Manager; Avivah Wargon, Production Editor; Avinash Chandra, Project Manager; Lenore Latta, Copy Editor; and Alison Kooistra, Proofreader.

Serge Desmarais is a professor of psychology and the Associate Vice-President (Academic) at the University of Guelph. He joined that university in 1995 following earlier teaching positions at Wilfrid Laurier University in Waterloo, and Saint Mary's University in Halifax. Desmarais is a past recipient of a Canada Research Chair in Applied Social Psychology. His research expertise and interests are varied but are broadly associated with two general themes: (1) the changes and impact of gender norms and (2) issues of justice and personal entitlement. These two research themes often intersect, as is the case of studies of gender differences in pay entitlement, recent work on gender-based perceptions of pay and benefits considerations such as parental leave for child care, studies of gender roles' influence on men's and women's work stress, and the studies of entitlement and justice issues in close relationships. His scholarly activities have recently expanded to include studies on gender and sexuality and the impact of social media, such as Facebook, on relationship development and continuation as well as perceptions of privacy.

Richard J. Gerrig is a professor of psychology at Stony Brook University. Before joining the Stony Brook faculty, Gerrig taught at Yale University, where he was awarded the Lex Hixon Prize for teaching excellence in the social sciences. Gerrig's research on cognitive psychological aspects of language use has been widely published. One line of work examines the mental processes that underlie efficient communication. A second research program considers the cognitive and emotional changes readers experience when they are transported to the worlds of stories. His book *Experiencing Narrative Worlds* was published by Yale University Press. Gerrig is a Fellow of the Society for Text & Discourse, the American Psychological Association, and the Association for Psychological Science. He is also an associate editor of *Psychonomic Bulletin & Review*. Gerrig is the proud father of Alexandra who, at age 18, provides substantial and valuable advice about many aspects of psychology and life. Life on Long Island is greatly enhanced by the guidance and support of Timothy Peterson.

Tammy L. Ivanco is an associate professor of psychology at the University of Manitoba. She joined the University in 2000. She recently completed a term as the Associate Head (Undergraduate) in the Department of Psychology. During her tenure at the University of Manitoba, she was cross-appointed in the Department of Human Anatomy and Cell Science and held an adjunct position in the Department of Physiology in the Faculty of Medicine at the University of Manitoba. Ivanco has been awarded the Department of Psychology Teaching Award. Ivanco's laboratory uses a number of different techniques to investigate mammalian brain plasticity throughout the lifespan. This research is aimed at examining how our brains change in response to experience—particularly how it is that our brains change when we learn new motor skills and how damage influences the brain. Ivanco uses animal models to investigate consequences to the brain of oxygen deprivation and strokes, autism, and Fragile X Mental Retardation Syndrome. Ivanco is a foster mom to a number of dogs that she has been showing in confirmation trials and rally-O, and is training for obedience and tracking.

Philip G. Zimbardo, Stanford University professor emeritus, has taught the introductory psychology course for 50 years and has been writing and coauthoring *Psychology and Life*, as well as the Faculty Guides and Student Workbooks, for the past 38 years. He has been called the "Face and Voice of Psychology" because of his popular PBS-TV series, *Discovering Psychology*, which is used in many high school and university courses both nationally and internationally. Zimbardo also loves to conduct and publish research on a wide variety of subjects, as well as teaching and engaging in public and social service activities. He has published more than 350 professional and popular articles and chapters and 50 books of all kinds. His recent trade book on the psychology of evil, *The Lucifer Effect*, relates his classic Stanford Prison Experiment to the abuses at Iraq's Abu Ghraib Prison. It was a New York Times best seller and William James Prize book of the year. Zimbardo has also just published *The Time Paradox*, a summary of research and applications of the psychology of time perspective. He is currently exploring research and developing new educational materials on the topic of the psychology of ordinary heroes. Please see these websites for more information: **www.zimbardo.com**, **www.prisonexp.org**, **www.lucifereffect.com**, and **www.everydayheroism.com**. Zimbardo now teaches graduate courses at the Pacific Graduate School of Psychology and also at the Naval Postgraduate School in Monterey, CA.

Psychology and Life

1

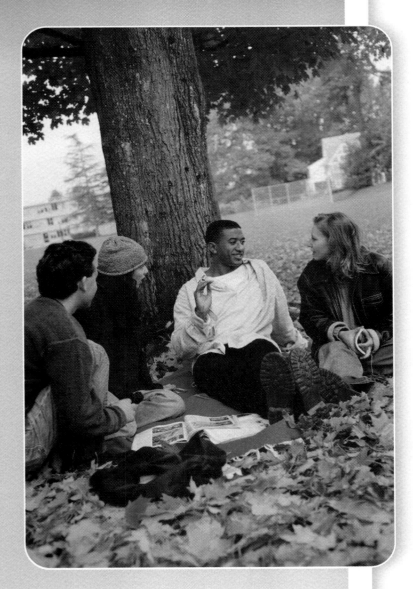

Why should you study psychology? Our answer to that question is quite straightforward: We believe that psychological research has immediate and crucial applications to important issues of everyday experience, including your physical and mental health, your ability to form and sustain close relationships, and your capacity for learning and personal growth. One of the foremost goals of *Psychology and Life* is to highlight the personal relevance and social significance of psychological expertise.

Every semester when we begin to teach, we are faced with students who enter an introductory psychology class with some very specific questions in mind. Sometimes those questions emerge from their own experience ("What should I do if I think my mother is mentally ill?" "Will this course teach me how to improve my grades?"); sometimes the questions emerge from the type of psychological information that is communicated through the popular press ("Is it true that oldest children are the most conservative?" "Are women really always better parents than men are?"). The challenge for us as we teach the course is to bring the products of scientific research to bear on questions that matter to our students.

Research in psychology provides a continuous stream of new information about the basic mechanisms that govern mental and behavioural processes. As new ideas replace or modify old ideas, we are continually intrigued and challenged by the many fascinating pieces of the puzzle of human nature. We hope that, by the end of this journey through psychology, you too will cherish your store of psychological knowledge.

Foremost in the journey will be a scientific quest for understanding. We will inquire about the how, what, when, and why of human behaviour and about the causes and consequences of behaviours you observe in yourself, in other people, and in animals. We will seek to explain why you think, feel, and behave as you do. What makes you uniquely different from all other people? Yet why do you often behave so much like others? Are you moulded by heredity, or are you shaped more by personal experiences? How can aggression and altruism, love and hate, and madness and creativity exist side by side in this complex creature—the human animal? In this opening chapter, we consider how and why all these types of questions have become relevant to psychology's goals as a discipline.

What Makes Psychology Unique?

To appreciate the uniqueness and unity of psychology, you must consider the way psychologists define the field and the goals they bring to their research and applications. By the end of this book, we hope you will think like a psychologist. In this first section, we will give you a strong idea of what that might mean.

---

psychology The scientific study of the behaviour of individuals and their mental processes.

scientific method The set of procedures used for gathering and interpreting objective information in a way that minimizes error and yields dependable generalizations.

behaviour The actions by which an organism adjusts to its environment.

DEFINITIONS

Many psychologists seek answers to this fundamental question: What is human nature? Psychology answers this question by looking at processes that occur within individuals, as well as forces that arise within the physical and social environment. In this light, we formally define **psychology** as the scientific study of the behaviour of individuals and their mental processes. Let's explore the critical parts of this definition: *scientific*, *behaviour*, *individual*, and *mental*.

The scientific aspect of psychology requires that psychological conclusions be based on evidence collected according to the principles of the scientific method. The **scientific method** consists of a set of orderly steps used to analyze and solve problems. This method uses objectively collected information as the factual basis for drawing conclusions. We will elaborate on the features of the scientific method more fully in Chapter 2, when we consider how psychologists conduct their research.

Behaviour is the means by which organisms adjust to their environment. Behaviour is action. The subject matter of psychology largely consists of the observable behaviour of humans and other species of animals. Smiling, crying, running, hitting, talking, and touching are some obvious examples of behaviours you can observe. Psychologists examine what the individual does and how the individual goes about doing it within a given behavioural setting and in the broader social or cultural context.

The subject of psychological analysis is most often an *individual*—a newborn infant, a teenage athlete, a university student adjusting to life in a dormitory, a man facing a midlife career change, or a woman coping with the stress of her husband's deterioration from Alzheimer's disease. However, the subject might also be a chimpanzee learning to use symbols to communicate, a white rat navigating a maze, or a sea slug responding to a danger signal. An individual might be studied in its natural habitat or in the controlled conditions of a research laboratory.

Many researchers in psychology also recognize that they cannot understand human actions without also understanding *mental processes*, the workings of the human mind. Much human activity takes place as private, internal events—thinking, planning, reasoning, creating, and dreaming. Many psychologists believe that mental processes represent the most important aspect of psychological inquiry. As you shall soon see, psychological investigators have devised ingenious techniques to study mental events and processes—to make these private experiences public.

The combination of these concerns defines psychology as a unique field. Within the *social sciences*, psychologists focus largely on behaviour in individuals, whereas sociologists study the behaviour of people in groups or institutions, and anthropologists focus on the broader context of behaviour in different cultures. Even so, psychologists draw broadly from the insights of other scholars. Psychologists share many interests with researchers in *biological sciences*, especially with those who study brain processes and the biochemical bases of behaviour. As part of the emerging area of *cognitive science*, psychologists' questions about how the human mind works are related to research and theory in computer science, artificial intelligence, and applied mathematics. As a *health science*—with links to medicine, education, law, and environmental studies—psychology seeks to improve the quality of each individual's and the collective's well-being.

Most psychological study focuses on individuals—usually human ones, but sometimes those of other species. What aspects of your own life would you like psychologists to study?

Although the remarkable breadth and depth of modern psychology are sources of delight to those who become psychologists, these same attributes make the field a challenge to the student exploring it for the first time. There is so much more to the study of psychology than you might expect initially—and, because of that, there will also be much of value that you can take away from this introduction to psychology. The best way to learn about the field is to learn to share psychologists' goals. Let's consider those goals.

THE GOALS OF PSYCHOLOGY

The goals of the psychologist conducting basic research are to describe, explain, predict, and control behaviour. These goals form the basis of the psychological enterprise. What is involved in trying to achieve each of them?

Describing What Happens The first task in psychology is to make accurate observations about behaviour. Psychologists typically refer to such observations as their *data* (*data* is the plural, *datum* the singular). **Behavioural data** are reports of observations about the behaviour of organisms and the conditions under which the behaviour occurs. When researchers undertake data collection, they must choose an appropriate *level of analysis* and devise measures of behaviour that ensure *objectivity*.

To investigate an individual's behaviour, researchers may use different *levels of analysis*—from the broadest, most global level down to the most minute, specific level. Suppose, for example, you were trying to describe a painting you saw at a museum (see **Figure 1.1**). At a global level, you might describe it by title, *Bathers*, and by artist, Georges Seurat. At a more specific level, you might recount features of the painting: Some people are sunning themselves on a riverbank, others are enjoying the water, and so on. At a very specific level, you might describe the technique Seurat used—tiny points of paint—to create the scene. The description at each level would answer different questions about the painting.

Different levels of psychological description also address different questions. At the broadest level of psychological analysis, researchers investigate the behaviour of the whole person within complex social and cultural contexts. At this level, researchers might study cross-cultural differences in violence, the origins of prejudice, and the consequences of mental illness. At the next level, psychologists focus on narrower, finer units of behaviour, such as speed of reaction to a stop light, eye movements during reading, and grammatical errors made by children acquiring language. Researchers can study even smaller units of behaviour. They might work to discover the biological bases of behaviour by identifying the places in the brain where different types of memories are stored, the biochemical changes that occur during learning, and the sensory paths responsible for vision or hearing. Each level of analysis yields information essential to the final composite portrait of human nature that psychologists hope ultimately to develop.

---

behavioural data Observational reports about the behaviour of organisms and the conditions under which the behaviour occurs or changes.

FIGURE 1.1   Levels of Analysis

Suppose you wanted a friend to meet you in front of this painting. How would you describe it? Suppose your friend wanted to make an exact copy of the painting. How would you describe it?

However tight or broad the focus of the observation, psychologists strive to describe behaviour *objectively*. Collecting the facts as they exist, and not as the researcher expects or hopes them to be, is of utmost importance. Every observer brings to each observation his or her *subjective* point of view—biases, prejudices, and expectations—so these personal factors must be prevented from creeping in and distorting the data. As you will see in the next chapter, psychological researchers have developed a variety of techniques in an effort to maintain objectivity.

Explaining What Happens Whereas *descriptions* must stick to perceivable information, *explanations* deliberately go beyond what can be observed. In many areas of psychology, the central goal is to find regular patterns in behavioural and mental processes. Psychologists want to discover *how* behaviour works. Why do you laugh at situations that differ from your expectations of what is coming next? What conditions could lead someone to attempt suicide or commit rape?

Explanations in psychology usually recognize that most behaviour is influenced by a combination of factors. Some factors operate within the individual, such as genetic makeup, motivation, intelligence level, or self-esteem. These inner determinants reveal something special about the organism. Other factors, however, operate externally. Suppose, for example, that a child tries to please a teacher to win a prize, or that a motorist trapped in a traffic jam becomes frustrated and hostile. These behaviours are largely influenced by events outside the person. When psychologists seek to explain behaviour, they almost always consider both types of explanations. If they want to explain why some people start smoking, for instance, they might examine the possibility that some individuals are particularly prone to risk taking (an internal explanation) or that some individuals experience a lot of peer pressure (an external explanation)—or that both a disposition toward risk taking and situational peer pressure are necessary (a combined explanation).

Often a psychologist's goal is to explain a wide variety of behaviours in terms of one underlying cause. Consider a situation in which your teacher says that to earn a good grade, each student must participate regularly in class discussions. Your roommate, who is always well prepared for class, never raises his hand to answer questions or volunteer information. The teacher chides him for being unmotivated and assumes he is not bright. That same roommate also goes to parties but never asks anyone to dance, does not openly defend his point of view when it is challenged by someone less informed, and rarely engages in small talk at the dinner table. What is your diagnosis? What underlying cause might account for this range of behaviour? How about *shyness*? Like many other people who suffer from intense feelings of shyness, your roommate may be unable to behave in desired ways (Zimbardo & Radl, 1999). We can use the concept of shyness to explain the full pattern of his behaviour.

To forge such causal explanations, researchers must often engage in a creative process of examining a diverse collection of data. Master detective Sherlock Holmes drew shrewd conclusions from scraps of evidence. In a similar fashion, every researcher must use an informed imagination, which creatively *synthesizes* what is known and what is not yet known. Well-trained psychologists can explain observations by using their insight into the human experience along with the facts that previous researchers have uncovered about the phenomenon in question. Much psychological research attempts to determine which of several explanations most accurately accounts for a given behavioural pattern.

Predicting What Will Happen Predictions in psychology are statements about the likelihood that a certain behaviour will occur or that a given relationship will be found. Often an accurate explanation of the causes underlying some form of behaviour will allow a researcher to make accurate predictions about future behaviour. Thus, if we believe your roommate to be shy, we could confidently predict that he would be uncomfortable if asked to converse with a stranger. When different explanations are put forward to account for some behaviour or relationship, they are usually judged by how well they can make accurate and comprehensive predictions. If your roommate were to blossom in contact with a stranger, we would be forced to rethink our diagnosis.

Just as observations must be made objectively, scientific predictions must be worded precisely enough to enable them to be tested and then rejected if the evidence does not support them. Suppose, for example, a researcher predicts that the presence of a stranger will reliably cause human and monkey

A psychological prediction

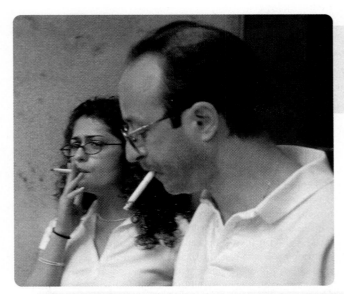

What causes people to smoke? Can psychologists create conditions under which people will be less likely to engage in this behaviour?

Psychology in Your Life

IN WHAT WAYS DO PSYCHOLOGISTS PARTICIPATE IN THE LEGAL SYSTEM?

An important lesson of *Psychology and Life* is that empirical research provides psychologists with a broad range of expertise. As this text unfolds, we will often illustrate how research results are applied to important issues in everyday life. In this opening chapter, we'll take an opportunity to provide a concrete example of how psychological expertise functions in the public forum. We focus our attention on some ways in which forensic psychologists become involved in important legal decisions.

The legal system relies on forensic psychologists to provide assessments for both civil and criminal proceedings (Packer, 2008). On the civil side, for example, forensic psychologists provide evidence that influences decisions about child custody in divorce hearings. They might also testify about the potential psychological harm workers have sustained in a particular place of employment. On the criminal side, forensic psychologists evaluate people's capacity to understand the acts they have committed and their competence to stand trial. The legal system also asks forensic psychologists to assess whether individuals are a danger to themselves or others.

Let's examine that last role more closely.

It's hard to read the news without learning about someone who has committed a violent crime. Suppose that person is sent to prison and, after having served a specified time, he or she arrives at a parole hearing. An important consideration at that hearing will be whether or not the prisoner will reoffend in the future. What is the likelihood that a violent act will occur again?

In recent years, psychologists have attempted to provide increasingly research-based answers to that question (Fabian, 2006). This type of research often begins with a theoretical analysis of the factors in people's lives that make violence more or less likely. Researchers make an important distinction between static and dynamic factors (Douglas & Skeem, 2005). Static factors are those that are relatively stable over time (such as sex and age at first conviction); dynamic variables are those that may change over time (such as substance abuse). The inclusion of dynamic factors suggests why a particular individual's risk of reoffending changes over time. Past history alone does not provide a valid indication of how a person

will behave in the future. It's also important to measure the trajectory of a person's life.

When researchers develop new risk assessment devices, they must provide evidence that those devices are successful at predicting future violence. To do so, researchers often follow groups of individuals over time. For example, Wong and Gordon (2006) evaluated 918 adult male offenders who were incarcerated in Alberta, Saskatchewan, and Manitoba. Each person was evaluated with the Violence Risk Scale (VRS), an instrument that measures 6 static and 20 dynamic variables. To evaluate the validity of the VRS, the researchers followed their participants over several years to see how often they were convicted of new crimes after they had been released into the community. In both the short term (after 1 year) and the longer term (after 4.4 years), men who had obtained higher ratings on the VRS were more likely to be convicted of additional violent crimes.

Research results of this sort are quite important because they help forensic psychologists provide more accurate guidance for legal judgment.

babies beyond a certain age to respond with signs of anxiety. We might want to bring more precision to this prediction by examining the dimension of what we mean by the word "stranger." Would fewer signs of anxiety appear in a human or a monkey baby if the stranger were also a baby rather than an adult, or if the stranger were of the same species rather than a different one? To improve future predictions, a researcher would create systematic variations in environmental conditions and observe their influence on the baby's response.

Controlling What Happens For many psychologists, control is the central, most powerful goal. Control means making behaviour happen or not happen—starting it, maintaining it, stopping it, and influencing its form, strength, or rate of occurrence. A causal explanation of behaviour is convincing if it can create conditions under which the behaviour can be controlled.

The ability to control behaviour is important because it gives psychologists ways of helping people improve the quality of their lives. Throughout *Psychology and Life*, you will see examples of the types of *interventions* psychologists have devised to help people gain control over problematic aspects of their lives. Chapter 16, for example, discusses treatments for mental illness. We also describe how people can harness psychological forces to eliminate unhealthy behaviours, such as smoking, and initiate healthy behaviours, such as regular exercise (see Chapter 13). You will learn what types of parenting practices can help parents maintain solid bonds with their children (Chapter 11) and what forces make strangers reluctant to offer assistance in emergency situations, as well as how those forces can be overcome (Chapter 17). These are just a few examples of the broad range of circumstances in which psychologists use their knowledge to control and improve people's lives. In this respect, psychologists are a rather optimistic group; many believe that virtually any undesired behaviour pattern can be modified by the proper intervention. *Psychology and Life* shares that optimism.

STOP AND REVIEW

❶ What is psychology? How would you define it?

❷ What four goals apply to psychologists who conduct research?

❸ Why is there often a close relationship between the goals of explanation and prediction?

The Evolution of Modern Psychology

Today, it is relatively easy to define psychology and to state the goals of psychological research. As you begin to study psychology, however, it is important to understand the many forces that led to the emergence of modern psychology. At the core of this historical review is one simple principle: *Ideas matter.* Much of the history of psychology has been characterized by heated debates about what constitutes the appropriate subject matter and methodologies for a science of mind and behaviour.

Our historical review will be carried out at two levels of analysis. In the first section, we will consider the period of history in which some of the critical groundwork for modern

psychology was laid down. This focus will enable you to witness at close range the battle of ideas. In the second section, we will describe in a broader fashion seven perspectives that have emerged in modern-day psychology. For both levels of focus, you should allow yourself to imagine the intellectual passion with which the theories evolved.

PSYCHOLOGY'S HISTORICAL FOUNDATIONS

"Psychology has a long past, but only a short history," wrote **Hermann Ebbinghaus** (1908/1973), one of the first experimental psychologists. Scholars had long asked important questions about human nature—about how people perceive reality, the nature of consciousness, and the origins of madness—but they did not possess the means to answer them. Consider the fundamental questions posed in the fourth and fifth centuries B.C. by the classical Greek philosophers Socrates, Plato, and Aristotle. Although forms of psychology existed in ancient Indian Yogic traditions, Western psychology traces its origin to these great thinkers' dialogues about how the mind works, the nature of free will, and the relationship of individual citizens to their community or state. Toward the end of the 19th century, psychology began to emerge as a discipline when researchers applied the laboratory techniques of other sciences—such as physiology and physics—to the study of these fundamental questions of philosophy.

A critical figure in the evolution of modern psychology was **Wilhelm Wundt**, who, in 1879 in Leipzig, Germany, founded the first formal laboratory devoted to experimental psychology. Although Wundt had been trained as a physiologist, over his research career his interest shifted from questions of body to questions of mind: He wished to understand basic processes of sensation and perception as well as the speed of simple mental processes. By the time he established his psychology laboratory, Wundt had already accomplished a range of research and had published the first of several editions of *Principles of Physiological Psychology* (Kendler, 1987). Once Wundt established his laboratory at Leipzig, he began to train the first graduate students specifically devoted to the emerging field of psychology. Many of those students became founders of their own psychology laboratories around the world.

As psychology became established as a separate discipline, psychology laboratories began to appear in universities throughout North America, the first at Johns Hopkins University in 1883. Many of these early laboratories were influenced by Wundt. For example, after studying with Wundt, **Edward Titchener** became one of the first psychologists in the United States, founding a laboratory at Cornell University in 1892. At around the same time (1889), another proponent of Wundt's experimental approach, **James Mark Baldwin**, established the first psychology laboratory in Canada at the University of Toronto (Hoff, 1992). While these new laboratories had a tremendous influence on the development of psychology in North America, it was **William James**—a young Harvard philosophy professor who had studied medicine and had strong interests in literature and religion (and who was the brother of the great novelist Henry James)—who wrote the two-volume work *The Principles of Psychology* (1890/1950), which many experts consider to be the most important psychology text ever written. Shortly after, in 1892, **G. Stanley Hall** founded the American Psychological Association; the Canadian Psychological

In 1879, Wilhelm Wundt founded the first formal laboratory devoted to experimental psychology. Suppose you decided to found your own psychology laboratory. What types of issues would you study?

sensations; (2) it was *elemental* because it sought to combine parts, or elements, into a whole rather than study complex, or whole, behaviours directly; and (3) it was *mentalistic* because it studied only verbal reports of human conscious awareness, ignoring the study of individuals who could not describe their introspections, including animals, children, and the mentally disturbed.

One important alternative to structuralism, pioneered by the Frankfurt University psychologist **Max Wertheimer**, focused on the way in which the mind understands many experiences as *gestalts*—organized wholes—rather than as the sums of simple parts: Your experience of a painting, for example, is more than the sum of the individual daubs of paint. As we see in Chapter 5, *Gestalt psychology* continues to have an impact on the study of perception.

A second major opposition to structuralism came under the banner of *functionalism.*

Functionalism: Minds with a Purpose

William James agreed with Titchener that consciousness was central to the study of psychology, but for James, the study of consciousness was not reduced to elements, contents, and structures. Instead, consciousness was an ongoing stream, a property of mind in continuous interaction with the environment. Human consciousness facilitated one's adjustment to the environment; thus the acts and *functions* of mental processes were of significance, not the contents of the mind.

Functionalism gave primary importance to the learned habits that enable organisms to adapt to their environment and to function effectively. For functionalists, the key question to be answered by research was "What is the function or purpose of any behavioural act?" The founder of the school of functionalism was the American philosopher **John Dewey**. His concern for the practical uses of mental processes led to important advances in education. Dewey's theorizing provided the impetus for *progressive education*—an approach to education that favoured "learning by doing" to encourage intellectual curiosity (Kendler, 1987). To this day, the progressive model remains extremely influential in both the United States and Canada; in this country, Dewey's philosophy of education continues to be the dominant perspective among most of Canada's educational practitioners.

Although James believed in careful observation, he put little value on Wundt's rigorous laboratory methods. In James's view, there was a place for emotions, self, will, values, and even religious and mystical experiences. His "warm-blooded" psychology recognized a uniqueness in each individual that could not be reduced to formulas or numbers from test results. For James, explanation rather than experimental control was the goal of psychology (Arkin, 1990).

The Legacy of These Approaches

Despite their differences, the insights of the practitioners of both structuralism and functionalism created an intellectual context in which contemporary psychology could flourish. To this day, psychologists

Association (CPA) was established more than 40 years later, in 1939. By 1900 there were more than 40 psychology laboratories in North America (Hilgard, 1986).

Almost as soon as psychology emerged, a debate arose about the proper subject matter and methods for the new discipline. This debate isolated some of the issues that still loom large in psychology—specifically, the tension between structuralism and functionalism.

Structuralism: The Contents of the Mind

Psychology's potential to make a unique contribution to knowledge became apparent when psychology became a laboratory science organized around experiments. In Wundt's laboratory, experiment participants made simple responses (saying yes or no, pressing a button) to stimuli they perceived under conditions varied by laboratory instruments. Because the data were collected through systematic, objective procedures, independent observers could replicate the results of these experiments. Emphasis on the scientific method (see Chapter 2), concern for precise measurement, and statistical analysis of data characterized Wundt's psychological tradition.

When Titchener brought Wundt's psychology to North America, he advocated that such scientific methods be used to study consciousness. His method for examining the elements of conscious mental life was *introspection*, the systematic examination by individuals of their own thoughts and feelings about specific sensory experiences. Titchener emphasized the "what" of mental contents rather than the "why" or "how" of thinking. His approach came to be known as **structuralism**, the study of the structure of mind and behaviour.

Structuralism was based on the presumption that all human mental experience could be understood as the combination of basic components. The goal of this approach was to reveal the underlying structure of the human mind by analyzing the component elements of sensations and other experiences that form an individual's mental life. Many psychologists attacked structuralism on three fronts: (1) It was *reductionistic* because it reduced all complex human experience to simple

---

structuralism The study of the structure of mind and behaviour; the view that all human mental experience can be understood as a combination of simple elements or events.

functionalism The perspective on mind and behaviour that focuses on the examination of their functions in an organism's interactions with the environment.

Educational practices in North America were changed through the efforts of the functionalist John Dewey. What can teachers do to encourage "intellectual curiosity"?

examine *both* the structure and the function of behaviour. Consider the process of speech production. Suppose you want to invite a friend to watch the final game of the Stanley Cup. To do so, the words you speak must serve the right function—*watch, Stanley Cup, with me*—but also have the right structure—a listener would not understand if you said, "Would Stanley Cup me watch the with you to like?" To understand how speech production works, researchers study the way that speakers fit meanings (functions) to the grammatical structures of their languages (Bock, 1990). (We will describe some of the processes of language production in Chapter 9.) Throughout *Psychology and Life*, we will emphasize both structure and function as we review classic and contemporary research. Psychologists continue to employ a great variety of methodologies to study the general forces that apply to all humans as well as to the unique aspects of each individual.

PERSPECTIVES ON PSYCHOLOGY

Suppose your friend accepts the invitation to watch the final game of the Stanley Cup. What *perspective* does each of you bring to your viewing of the game? Suppose one of you played hockey in high school, but the other did not. Or suppose one of you has cheered from birth for one of the competing teams, whereas the other has no favourite. You can see how these different perspectives would affect the way in which you evaluate the game as it unfolds.

---

psychodynamic perspective A psychological model in which behaviour is explained in terms of past experiences and motivational forces, and actions are viewed as stemming from inherited instincts, biological drives, and attempts to resolve conflicts between personal needs and social requirements.

In a similar fashion, psychologists' perspectives determine the ways in which they examine behaviour and mental processes. The perspectives influence what psychologists look for, where they look, and what research methods they use. In this section, we define seven perspectives—psychodynamic, behaviourist, humanistic, cognitive, biological, evolutionary, and sociocultural. As you read the section, note how each perspective defines the causes and consequences of behaviour.

A word of caution: Although each perspective represents a different approach to the central issues of psychology, it is important to appreciate why most psychologists borrow and blend concepts from more than one of these perspectives. Each perspective enhances the understanding of the entirety of human experience. In the chapters that follow, we will elaborate in some detail on the contributions of each approach because, taken together, they represent what contemporary psychology is all about.

The Psychodynamic Perspective According to the **psychodynamic perspective**, behaviour is driven, or motivated, by powerful inner forces. In this view, human actions stem from inherited instincts, biological drives, and attempts to resolve conflicts between personal needs and society's demands. States of deprivation, physiological arousal, and conflicts provide the power for behaviour just as coal fuels a steam locomotive. According to this model, the organism stops reacting when its needs are satisfied and its drives reduced. The main purpose of action is to reduce tension.

Psychodynamic principles of motivation were most fully developed by the Viennese physician **Sigmund Freud** (1856–1939) in the late 19th and early 20th centuries. Freud's ideas grew out of his work with mentally disturbed patients, but

Sigmund Freud, photographed with his daughter, Anna, on a trip to the Italian Alps in 1913. Freud suggested that behaviour is often driven by motives outside of conscious awareness. What implications does that perspective have for the ways in which you make life choices?

he believed that the principles he observed applied to both normal and abnormal behaviour. Freud's psychodynamic theory views a person as pulled and pushed by a complex network of inner and outer forces. Freud's model was the first to recognize that human nature is not always rational, and that actions may be driven by motives that are not in conscious awareness.

Many psychologists since Freud have taken the psychodynamic model in new directions. Freud himself emphasized early childhood as the stage at which personality is formed. Neo-Freudian theorists have broadened psychodynamic theory to include social influences and interactions that occur over the individual's entire lifetime. Psychodynamic ideas have had a great influence on many areas of psychology. You will encounter different aspects of Freud's contributions as you read about child development, dreaming, forgetting, unconscious motivation, personality, and psychoanalytic therapy.

The Behaviourist Perspective Those who take the **behaviourist perspective** seek to understand how particular environmental stimuli control particular kinds of behaviour. First, behaviourists analyze the *antecedent* environmental conditions—those that precede the behaviour and set the stage for an organism to make or withhold a response. Next, they look at the *behavioural response*, which is the main object of study—the action to be understood, predicted, and controlled. Finally, they examine the observable *consequences* that follow from the response. A behaviourist, for example, might be interested in the way in which speeding tickets of varying penalties (the consequences of speeding) change the likelihood that motorists will drive with caution or abandon (behavioural responses).

The behaviourist perspective was pioneered by **John Watson** (1878–1958), who argued that psychological research

John Watson was an important pioneer of the behaviourist perspective. Why did Watson seek laws of behaviour that applied across species?

should seek the laws that govern observable behaviour across species. **B. F. Skinner** (1904–1990) extended the influence of behaviourism by expanding its analyses to the consequences of behaviours. Both researchers insisted on precise definitions of the phenomena studied and on rigorous standards of evidence. Both Watson and Skinner believed that the basic processes they investigated with nonhuman animals represented general principles that would hold true for humans as well.

Behaviourism has yielded a critical practical legacy. Its emphasis on the need for rigorous experimentation and carefully defined variables has influenced most areas of psychology. Although behaviourists have conducted much basic research with nonhuman animals, the principles of behaviourism have been widely applied to human problems. Behaviourist principles have yielded a more humane approach to educating children (through positive reinforcement rather than punishment), new therapies for modifying behaviour disorders, and guidelines for creating model utopian communities.

The Humanistic Perspective Humanistic psychology emerged in the 1950s as an alternative to the psychodynamic and the behaviourist models. According to the **humanistic perspective**, people are neither driven by the powerful, instinctive forces postulated by the Freudians nor manipulated by their environments, as proposed by the behaviourists. Instead, people are active creatures who are innately good and capable of choice. Humanistic psychologists study behaviour, but not by reducing it to components, elements, and variables in laboratory experiments. Instead, they look for patterns in people's life histories.

According to the humanistic perspective, the main task for humans is to strive for positive development. For example, **Carl Rogers** (1902–1987) emphasized that individuals have a natural tendency toward psychological growth and health—a process that is aided by the positive regard of those who surround them. **Abraham Maslow** (1908–1970) coined the term *self-actualization* to refer to each individual's drive toward the fullest development of his or her potential. In addition, Rogers, Maslow, and their colleagues defined a perspective that strives to deal with the whole person, practising a *holistic* approach to human psychology. They believed that true understanding requires integrating knowledge of the individual's mind, body, and behaviour with an awareness of social and cultural forces.

The humanistic approach expands the realm of psychology to include valuable lessons from the study of literature, history, and the arts. In this manner, psychology becomes a more complete discipline. Humanists suggest that their view is the yeast that helps psychology rise above its focus on negative forces and on the animal-like aspects of humanity. As we shall see in Chapter 16, the humanistic perspective had a major impact on the development of new approaches to psychotherapy.

---

behaviourist perspective The psychological perspective primarily concerned with observable behaviour that can be objectively recorded and with the relationships of observable behaviour to environmental stimuli.

behaviourism A scientific approach that limits the study of psychology to measurable or observable behaviour.

humanistic perspective A psychological model that emphasizes an individual's phenomenal world and inherent capacity for making rational choices and developing to maximum potential.

The Cognitive Perspective The cognitive revolution in psychology emerged as another challenge to the limits of behaviourism. The centrepiece of the **cognitive perspective** is human thought and all the processes of knowing—attending, thinking, remembering, and understanding. From the cognitive perspective, people act because they think, and people think because they are human beings, exquisitely equipped to do so.

According to the cognitive model, behaviour is only partly determined by preceding environmental events and past behavioural consequences, as behaviourists believe. Some of the most significant behaviour emerges from totally novel ways of thinking, not from predictable ways used in the past. The ability to imagine options and alternatives that are totally different from what is or was enables people to work toward futures that transcend current circumstances. An individual responds to reality not as it is in the objective world of matter, but as it is in the *subjective reality* of the individual's inner world of thoughts and imagination. Cognitive psychologists view thoughts as both results and causes of overt actions. Feeling regret when you have hurt someone is an example of thought as a result. But apologizing for your actions after feeling regret is an example of thought as a cause of behaviour.

Cognitive psychologists study higher mental processes such as perception, memory, language use, problem solving, and decision making at a variety of levels. They may examine patterns of blood flow in the brain during different types of cognitive tasks; a student's recollection of an early childhood event; or changes in memory abilities across the life span. Because of its focus on mental processes, many researchers see the cognitive perspective as the dominant one in psychology today.

The Biological Perspective The **biological perspective** guides psychologists who search for the causes of behaviour in the functioning of genes, the brain, the nervous system, and the endocrine system. An organism's functioning is explained in terms of underlying physical structures and biochemical processes. Experience and behaviours are largely understood as the result of chemical and electrical activities taking place within and between nerve cells.

Researchers who take the biological perspective generally assume that psychological and social phenomena can be ultimately understood in terms of biochemical processes: Even the most complex phenomena can be understood by analysis, or reduction into ever smaller, more specific units. They might,

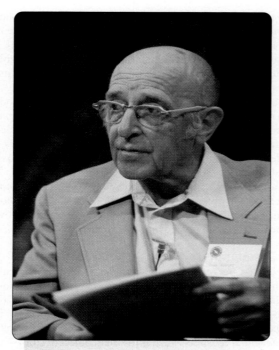

Carl Rogers provided foundational ideas for the humanistic perspective. Why did Rogers place an emphasis on positive regard?

for example, try to explain how you are reading the words of this sentence with respect to the exact physical processes in cells in your brain. According to this perspective, behaviour is determined by physical structures and hereditary processes. Experience can modify behaviour by altering these underlying biological structures and processes. Researchers might ask, "What changes in your brain occurred while you learned to read?" The task of psychobiological researchers is to understand behaviour at the most precise level of analysis.

Many researchers who take the biological perspective contribute to the multidisciplinary field of **behavioural neuroscience**. Neuroscience is the study of brain function; behavioural neuroscience attempts to understand the brain processes underlying behaviours such as sensation, learning, and emotion. The advances in the brain-imaging techniques that we describe in Chapter 4 have led to dramatic breakthroughs in the field of **cognitive neuroscience**. Cognitive neuroscience uses a multidisciplinary research focus to study the brain bases of higher cognitive functions such as memory and language. As we shall see, brain-imaging techniques allow the biological perspective to be extended into a broad range of human experience.

The Evolutionary Perspective The **evolutionary perspective** seeks to connect contemporary psychology to a central idea of the life sciences: Charles Darwin's theory of evolution by natural selection. The idea of natural selection is quite simple: Those organisms that are better suited to their environments tend to produce offspring (and pass on their genes) more successfully than those organisms with poorer adaptations. Over many generations, the species changes in the direction of the privileged adaptation. The evolutionary perspective in psychology suggests that *mental abilities* evolved over millions

---

cognitive perspective The perspective on psychology that stresses human thought and the processes of knowing, such as attending, thinking, remembering, expecting, solving problems, fantasizing, and consciousness.

biological perspective The approach to identifying causes of behaviour that focuses on the functioning of genes, the brain, the nervous system, and the endocrine system.

behavioural neuroscience A multidisciplinary field that attempts to understand the brain processes that underlie behaviour.

cognitive neuroscience A multidisciplinary field that attempts to understand the brain processes that underlie higher cognitive functions in humans.

evolutionary perspective The approach to psychology that stresses the importance of behavioural and mental adaptiveness, based on the assumption that mental capabilities evolved over millions of years to serve particular adaptive purposes.

of years to serve particular adaptive purposes, just as physical abilities did.

To practise evolutionary psychology, researchers focus on the environmental conditions in which the human brain evolved. Humans spent 99 percent of their evolutionary history as hunter-gatherers living in small groups during the Pleistocene era (the roughly 2-million-year period ending 10 000 years ago). Evolutionary psychology uses the rich theoretical framework of evolutionary biology to identify the central adaptive problems that faced this species: avoiding predators and parasites, gathering and exchanging food, finding and retaining mates, and raising healthy children. After identifying the adaptive problems that these early humans faced, evolutionary psychologists generate inferences about the sorts of mental mechanisms, or psychological adaptations, that might have evolved to solve those problems.

Evolutionary psychology differs from other perspectives most fundamentally in its focus on the extremely long process of evolution as a central explanatory principle. Evolutionary psychologists, for example, attempt to understand the different gender roles assumed by men and women as products of evolution, rather than as products of contemporary societal pressures. Evolutionary psychologists must be particularly inventive to provide evidence in favour of their theories because they cannot carry out experiments that vary the course of evolution.

The Sociocultural Perspective Psychologists who take a **sociocultural perspective** study *cross-cultural* differences in the causes and consequences of behaviour. The sociocultural perspective is an important response to the criticism that psychological research has too often been based on a Western conception of human nature and had as its subject population only white, middle-class North Americans and Europeans (Gergen, Gulerce, Lock, & Misra, 1996). A proper consideration of cultural forces may involve comparisons of groups within the same

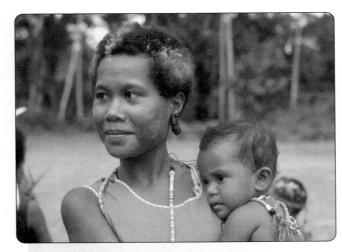

Bronislaw Malinowski documented the important roles women play in the culture of the Trobriand Islands. Why is cross-cultural research critical to the search for universal psychological principles?

national boundaries. For example, researchers may compare the prevalence of eating disorders for white Canadian versus black Canadian or Asian-Canadian teenagers (see Chapter 12). Cultural forces may also be assessed across nationalities, as in comparisons of moral judgments in Canada and India (see Chapter 11). Cross-cultural psychologists want to determine whether the theories that researchers have developed apply to all humans, or only to more narrow, specific populations.

A cross-cultural perspective can be brought to bear on almost every topic of psychological research: Are people's perceptions of the world affected by culture? Do the languages people speak affect the way they experience the world? How does culture affect the way children develop into adults? How do cultural attitudes shape the experience of old age? How does culture affect our sense of self? Does culture influence an individual's likelihood to engage in particular behaviours? Does culture affect the way individuals express emotions? Does culture affect the rates at which people suffer from psychological disorders?

By asking these types of questions, the sociocultural perspective often yields conclusions that directly challenge those generated from the other perspectives. Researchers have claimed, for example, that many aspects of Freud's psychodynamic theories cannot apply to cultures that are very different from Freud's Vienna. This concern was raised as early as 1927 by the anthropologist **Bronislaw Malinowski** (1927), who soundly critiqued Freud's father-centred theory by describing the family practices of the Trobriand Islanders of New Guinea, for whom family authority resided with mothers rather than with fathers. The sociocultural perspective, therefore, suggests that some universal claims of the psychodynamic perspective are incorrect. The sociocultural perspective poses a continual, important

What mental abilities were needed by the *Australopithecus africanus* of 2 to 3 million years ago, and how might these abilities have evolved to the present day?

---

sociocultural perspective The psychological perspective that focuses on cross-cultural differences in the causes and consequences of behaviour.

challenge to generalizations about human experience that ignore the diversity and richness of culture.

Comparing Perspectives: Focus on Aggression

Each of the seven perspectives rests on a different set of assumptions and leads to a different way of looking for answers to questions about behaviour. **Table 1.1** summarizes the perspectives. As an example, let's briefly compare how psychologists using these different models might deal with the question of why people act aggressively. All of the approaches have been used in the effort to understand the nature of aggression and violence. For each perspective, we give examples of the types of claims researchers might make and experiments they might undertake.

- **Psychodynamic**. Analyze aggression as a reaction to frustrations caused by barriers to pleasure, such as unjust authority. View aggression as an adult's displacement of hostility originally felt as a child against his or her parents.
- **Behaviourist**. Identify reinforcements of past aggressive responses, such as extra attention given to a child who hits classmates or siblings. Assert that children learn from physically abusive parents to be abusive with their own children.
- **Humanistic**. Look for personal values and social conditions that foster self-limiting, aggressive perspectives instead of growth-enhancing, shared experiences.
- **Cognitive**. Explore the hostile thoughts and fantasies people experience while witnessing violent acts, noting both aggressive imagery and intentions to harm others. Study the impact of violence in films and videos, including pornographic violence, on attitudes toward gun control, rape, and war.
- **Biological**. Study the role of specific brain systems in aggression by stimulating different regions and then recording any destructive actions that are elicited. Also analyze the brains of mass murderers for abnormalities; examine female aggression as related to phases of the menstrual cycle.
- **Evolutionary**. Consider what conditions would have rewarded aggression as an adaptive behaviour for early

humans. Identify psychological mechanisms capable of selectively generating aggressive behaviour under those conditions.
- **Sociocultural**. Consider how members of different cultures display and interpret aggression. Identify how cultural forces affect the likelihood of different types of aggressive behaviour.

From this example of aggression, you can see how the different perspectives conspire to provide a full understanding of particular domains of psychological research. In contemporary psychology, most research is informed by multiple perspectives. Throughout *Psychology and Life* you will see how new theories often emerge from combinations of different perspectives. In addition, technological advances have made it easier for researchers to combine perspectives. For example, the innovative brain-imaging techniques you will learn about in Chapter 4 allow researchers to bring a biological perspective to topics as varied as personality differences (Chapter 14) and therapeutic outcomes (Chapter 16). Moreover, developments such as the internet have made it easier for researchers to collaborate across the globe. They can bring a sociocultural perspective to topics as diverse as moral reasoning (Chapter 11) and people's body images (Chapter 12). Psychology's diversity of perspectives helps researchers think creatively about core topics of human experience.

STOP AND REVIEW

❶ What are the central concerns of the structuralist and functionalist approaches?

❷ How do the psychodynamic and behaviourist perspectives conceptualize the forces that shape people's actions?

❸ Which perspective suggests that people are active creatures who strive for positive development?

❹ What is the purpose of cognitive neuroscience?

❺ How do the evolutionary perspective and sociocultural perspective complement each other?

TABLE 1.1 Comparison of Seven Perspectives in Contemporary Psychology		
Perspective	**Focus of Study**	**Primary Research Topic**
Psychodynamic	Unconscious drives Conflicts	Behaviour as overt expression of unconscious motives
Behaviourist	Specific overt responses	Behaviour and its stimuli, causes, and consequences
Humanistic	Human experience and potentials	Life patterns, values, and goals
Cognitive	Mental processes	Mental processes inferred through behavioural indicators
Biological	Brain and nervous system processes	Biochemical basis of behaviour and mental processes
Evolutionary	Evolved psychological adaptations	Mental mechanisms as evolved adaptive functions
Sociocultural	Cross-cultural patterns of attitudes and behaviours	Universal and culture-specific aspects of human experience

Critical Thinking in Your Life

WHY DO FRIENDSHIPS END?

An important goal of *Psychology and Life* is to improve your ability to think critically about the world around you: We want to help you "reach intelligent decisions about what [you] should believe and how [you] should act" (Appleby, 2006, p. 61). Let's consider that aim with respect to a question that has often seemed urgent for the students who enrol in our classes: Why do friendships end?

Try to think back to circumstances in which a valued friendship dissolved. Were you able to understand what went wrong? Psychology can provide theoretical analyses to help you understand what goes on in your life. In fact, researchers have studied the types of events that cause friendships to come to an end (Sheets & Lugar, 2005). People report such incidents as romantic competition ("she slept with my boyfriend"), disrespectful behaviour ("he let his friends destroy my room"), and betrayals of confidence ("he blabbed all my secrets"). If you understand these different categories, you now have a framework to assess any tensions in your own friendships. The research provides even more specific conclusions: In a sample of about 400 American university students, the most common sources of conflicts—the causes of arguments that ended friendships—were romantic competition and disrespectful behaviour. Can you use this information to look more critically at the state of your

friendships? This research illustrates how psychology can help you perceive and apply appropriate distinctions for your life experiences.

But there is another aspect of critical thinking you can engage here: You should try to ask yourself how broadly you should apply the information you learn. For example, we asserted that the results about friendship emerged from American students. In this chapter, we have already identified the sociocultural perspective that prompts contemporary researchers always to be mindful of the impact of culture on research results. To assess the cross-cultural generality of their findings, the researchers collected data from a group of students in Russia. Those students collectively reported that the greatest source of conflict with their friends centred on betrayals of confidence. Why might that be the case? The researchers speculated that Russians are more sensitive to these circumstances because of "Russia's totalitarian history, during which a friend's breach of confidence could threaten one's life" (Sheets & Lugar, 2005, p. 391).

There are a couple of noteworthy implications for this cultural difference between U.S. and Russian university students. First, this result reminds you that an important component of critical thinking is to test a conclusion for its soundness and generality. In Chapter 2, we focus on the scientific method. That discussion will give you

an indication of the standards researchers must meet before we report their research in *Psychology and Life*. In addition, throughout the text we will be mindful of how important it is to consider the ways in which culture can affect basic aspects of human existence. The second implication of this difference between U.S. and Russian students refers to how you might behave toward the people around you. Most people now live and work in settings with cultural diversity. Let your education in psychology make you more sensitive to the domains in which culture does and does not matter. Remember, the goal is to have your psychological knowledge help you make more intelligent decisions with respect to your everyday experiences.

- This *Critical Thinking in Your Life* feature points out that historical and cultural factors tend to influence research findings. Given that information, do you think the findings would be different if the friendship study were conducted in Canada? What factors might influence these results?

- Imagine that you intend to replicate the friendship study using a Canadian sample. Would the results differ if the study were conducted in Vancouver versus Halifax or Montreal? What factors might influence any differences in the results?

What Psychologists Do

You now know enough about psychology to formulate questions that span the full range of psychological inquiry. If you prepared such a list of questions, you would likely touch on the areas of expertise of the great variety of individuals who call themselves psychologists. In **Table 1.2**, we provide our own version of such questions and indicate what sort of psychologist might address each one.

As you examine the table, you will note the great many subdivisions within the profession of psychology. Some of the labels tell you about the major content of a psychologist's expertise. For example, *cognitive psychologists* focus on basic cognitive processes such as memory and language; *social psychologists* focus on the social forces that shape people's attitudes and behaviours. Some of the labels identify the domains in which psychologists apply their expertise. For example, *industrial-organizational psychologists* focus their efforts on improving people's adjustment in the workplace; *school*

TABLE 1.2 The Diversity of Psychological Inquiry

The Question	Who Addresses It?	Focus of Research and Practice
How can people cope better with day-to-day problems?	Clinical psychologists Counselling psychologists Community psychologists Psychiatrists	Study the origins of psychological disorders and evaluate treatment options; provide diagnosis and treatment of psychological disorders and other issues of personal adjustment
How can I cope with the aftereffects of a stroke?	Rehabilitation psychologists	Provide assessment and counselling for people with illnesses or disabilities; offer coping strategies and education to affected individuals, caretakers, employers, and community members
How do memories get stored in the brain?	Biological psychologists Psychopharmacologists	Study the biochemical bases of behaviour, feelings, and mental processes
How can you teach a dog to follow commands?	Experimental psychologists Behaviour analysts	Use laboratory experiments, often with nonhuman participants, to study basic processes of learning, sensation, perception, emotion, and motivation
Why can't I always recall information I'm sure I know?	Cognitive psychologists Cognitive scientists	Study mental processes such as memory, perception, reasoning, problem solving, decision making, and language use
What makes people different from one another?	Personality psychologists Behavioural geneticists	Develop tests and theories to understand differences in personalities and behaviours; study the influence of genetics and environments on those differences
How does peer pressure work?	Social psychologists	Study how people function in social groups as well as the processes by which people select, interpret, and remember social information
What do babies know about the world?	Developmental psychologists	Study the changes that occur in the physical, cognitive, and social functioning of individuals across the life span; study the influence of genetics and environments on those changes
Why does my job make me feel so depressed?	Industrial-organizational psychologists Human factors psychologists	Study the factors that influence performance and morale in the general workplace or on particular tasks; apply those insights in the workplace
How should teachers deal with disruptive students?	Educational psychologists School psychologists	Study how to improve aspects of the learning process; help design school curricula, teaching-training programs, and child-care programs
Why do I get sick before every exam?	Health psychologists	Study how different lifestyles affect physical health; design and evaluate prevention programs to help people change unhealthy behaviours and cope with stress
Was the defendant insane when she committed the crime?	Forensic psychologists	Apply psychological knowledge to human problems in the field of law enforcement
Why do I always choke during important basketball games?	Sports psychologists	Assess the performance of athletes and use motivational, cognitive, and behavioural principles to help them achieve peak performance levels

psychologists focus on students' adjustment in educational settings.

Each type of psychologist achieves a balance between *research*—seeking new insights—and *application*—putting those insights to use in the world. A necessary relationship exists between those two types of activities. For example, we often think of *clinical psychologists* largely as individuals who apply psychological knowledge to better people's lives. However, as we will see in Chapters 15 and 16, clinical psychologists also have important research functions. Contemporary research continues to improve our understanding of the distinctions among psychological disorders and the treatments that best ease patients' distress.

Take another look at Table 1.2. We intended the list of questions to demonstrate why psychology has so many divisions. Did we manage to capture your concerns? If you have the time, make a list of your own questions. Cross off each question as *Psychology and Life* answers it. If, at the end of the course, you still have unanswered questions, please send them to us! (Our email addresses can be found in the preface.)

Have you begun to wonder exactly how many practising psychologists there are in the world? Surveys suggest the number is well over 500 000. **Figure 1.2** gives you an idea of the distribution of settings in which psychologists function. Although the percentage of psychologists in the population is greatest in Western industrialized nations, interest in psychology continues

Developmental psychologists may use puppets or other toys in their study of how children behave, think, or feel. Why might it be easier for a child to express his or her thoughts to a puppet than to an adult?

began to appear at some Canadian universities in the early 1900s, but these courses were usually offered as part of the philosophy curriculum. The first psychology department was established at McGill University in 1924, which was soon followed by the creation of a psychology department at the University of Toronto in 1926. Several other universities followed suit in the 1930s and 40s, such as the University of Western Ontario (in 1931), the University of Manitoba (in 1936), the Université de Montréal (in 1942), the University of Saskatchewan (in 1947), and Dalhousie and Queen's Universities (in 1948). The 1960s and 70s saw the greatest growth in psychology programs as this field of research became somewhat more established within academia (Wright & Myers, 1982).

It probably will not surprise you to learn that, early in its history, research and practice in psychology were dominated by men. Even when women were still few in numbers, however, they made substantial contributions to the field (Russo & Denmark, 1987; Scarborough & Furumoto, 1987). In 1894, Margaret Washburn graduated from Cornell University to become the first woman to receive a PhD in psychology. She went on to write an influential early textbook, *The Animal Mind*. In 1895, Mary Calkins completed all the requirements for a Harvard PhD with an exceptional record. Even so, the Harvard administration refused to grant a PhD to a woman. Despite this insult, Calkins became a successful researcher and the first woman president of the American Psychological Association. Anna Freud, the daughter of Sigmund Freud, brought about important advances in the practice of *psychoanalysis*, a form of therapy based on the psychodynamic perspective. We highlight the work of pioneering women researchers throughout *Psychology and Life*. As psychology continues to contribute to the scientific and human enterprise, more people—women and men, and members of all segments of society—are being drawn to it as a career.

to increase in many countries. The International Union of Psychological Science (IUPsyS) draws together member organizations from 70 countries (Ritchie, 2004). The American Psychological Association (APA), an organization that includes psychologists from all over the world, currently has 148 000 members. A third international organization, the Association for Psychological Science (APS), with more than 20 000 members, focuses more on the scientific aspects of psychology and less on clinical or treatment-related issues. In Canada, many psychologists become members of the Canadian Psychological Association (CPA), which includes more than 6500 members (CPA, 2009a).

Despite the immense popularity of psychology as a major in Canadian universities, the evolution of psychology programs in Canada was fairly slow. For instance, no full psychology curriculum was developed here until the 1920s. Psychology courses

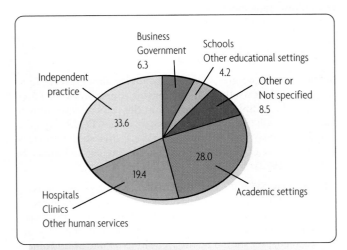

FIGURE 1.2 Work Settings of Psychologists
Shown are percentages of psychologists working in particular settings, according to a survey of American Psychological Association (APA) members holding doctoral degrees in psychology.

In 1894, Margaret Washburn became the first woman to receive a PhD in psychology. She went on to write an influential textbook, *The Animal Mind* (1908). What challenges might she have faced as a pioneer woman researcher?

Brenda Milner is an eminent cognitive scientist at McGill University. She was born in Manchester, England, in 1918 and went on to earn her doctorate in physiological psychology at McGill University in 1952. Her pioneering work enabled a better understanding of how cerebral structures affect memory and cognitive functions.

STOP AND REVIEW

❶ What is the relationship between research and application?

❷ In what two settings are most psychologists employed?

How to Use This Book

You are about to embark with us on an intellectual journey through the many areas of modern psychology. Before we start, we want to share with you some important information that will help guide your adventures. "The journey" is a metaphor used throughout *Psychology and Life*; your instructor serves as the tour director, the text as your tour book, and we, your authors, as your personal tour guides. The goal of this journey is for you to discover what is known about the most incredible phenomena in the entire universe: the brain, the human mind, and the behaviour of all living creatures. Psychology is about understanding the seemingly mysterious processes that give rise to your thoughts, feelings, and actions.

This guide offers general strategies and specific suggestions about how to use this book to get the grade you deserve for your performance and to get the most from your introduction to psychology.

STUDY STRATEGIES

1. **Set aside sufficient time** for your reading assignments and review of class notes. This text contains much new technical information, many principles to learn, and a new glossary of terms to memorize. To master this material, you will need at least three hours of reading time per chapter.

2. **Keep a record of your study time** for this course. Plot the number of hours (in half-hour intervals) that you spend studying at each reading session. Chart your time investment on a cumulative graph. Add each new study time to the previous total on the left-hand axis of the graph and each study session on the baseline axis. The chart will provide visual feedback of your progress and show you when you have not been hitting the books as you should.

3. **Be an active participant**. Optimal learning occurs when you are actively involved with the learning materials. Active involvement requires reading attentively, listening to lectures mindfully, paraphrasing in your own words what you are reading or hearing, and taking good notes. In the text, underline key sections, write notes to yourself in the margins, and summarize points that you think might be included on class tests.

4. **Space out your studying**. Research in psychology tells us that it is more effective to do your studying regularly rather than cramming just before tests. If you let yourself fall behind, you will find it difficult to catch up with all the information included in *Psychology and Life* at last-minute panic time.

5. **Get study-centred**. Find a place with minimal distractions for studying. Reserve that place for studying, reading, and writing course assignments—and do nothing else there. The place will come to be associated with study activities, and you will find it easier to work whenever you are seated at your study centre.

Take the instructor's perspective, anticipating the kinds of questions she or he is likely to ask, and then making sure you can answer them. Find out what kinds of tests you will be given in this course—essay, fill-in-the-blank, multiple-choice, or true/false. That form will affect the extent to which you focus on the big ideas and/or on details. Essays and fill-ins ask for recall-type memory; multiple-choice and true/false tests ask for recognition-type memory.

STUDY TECHNIQUES

In this section, we give you specific advice about a technique you can use to learn the material for this course and your other courses. The technique emerged from the principles of human memory we will discuss in Chapter 8. It is called *PQ4R*, from the initials of the six phases it suggests for effective study: Preview, Questions, Read, Reflect, Recite, and Review (Thomas & Robinson, 1972).

1. **Preview**. Skim through the chapter to get a general sense of the topics to be discussed. Make yourself aware of the organization and major topics. Read the section headings and scan the photos and figures. In fact, your first stop for each chapter should be the section *Recapping Main Points*. There you will find the main ideas of the chapter organized under each of the first-level headings, which will give you a clear sense of what the chapter covers.

2. **Questions**. For each section, make up questions. You should use the section headings and key terms to help you. For example, you might transform the heading "The Goals of Psychology" into the question, "What are the

goals of psychology?" You might use the key term *biological perspective* to generate the question, "What is the major focus of the biological perspective?" These questions will help direct your attention as you read.

3. **Read**. Read the material carefully so that you are able to answer the questions you invented.

4. **Reflect**. As you read the text, reflect on it to relate the material to your prior knowledge about the topics. Think of extra examples to enrich the text. Try to link the ideas together across the subsections.

5. **Recite**. After you have read and reflected on a section, try to demonstrate your recall of the material as concretely as possible. For example, answer the questions you invented earlier by producing the material out loud. For later review, write down the ideas you find difficult to remember.

6. **Review**. After you have read the entire chapter, review the key points. If you are unable to recall important points, or you cannot answer the questions you invented, consult the book and repeat the earlier phases (read, reflect, and recite).

Take a moment now to use PQ4R for one of the earlier sections of this chapter to see how each phase works. It will take you some time to master the flow of PQ4R. Make that investment at the beginning of the semester.

SPECIAL FEATURES

Psychology and Life has several features that will help you acquire psychological knowledge.

1. The *Psychology in Your Life* boxes apply applications of psychological research to your everyday life. Each of these boxes presents an answer to questions that we have been asked in class by our own students and that we imagine you might ask as well.

2. The *Critical Thinking in Your Life* boxes illustrate how you can put your psychological knowledge to use to improve the quality of your thinking. The boxes provide you with tools for evaluating conclusions and seeing where they apply in your day-to-day experiences. We complete each box with questions to help you deepen your understanding.

3. The chapters feature several research studies that help you see the direct link between the experiments researchers conduct and the conclusions they draw. Researchers in psychology seek rigorous answers to questions that are often urgent. We include specific research studies so you have abundant opportunities to experience the concrete details of that type of rigorous research.

4. Each *Stop and Review* list provides questions that refer to the key points you should know before going ahead to the next section. Think of these questions as supplements to those you generated by using PQ4R. Try to answer the questions as you finish your reading of each main section. If any of the questions stumps you, plunge back into the text and reread the appropriate material until you feel you can provide a good answer. Similarly, use these questions as a starting point for your studying before tests. You will find answers to the questions in the Answer Appendix. On some occasions, we will also include more open-ended questions intended to improve your critical thinking with respect to research studies. We leave those questions unanswered to allow you to discuss them with your professor or classmates.

5. Each chapter concludes with a *practice test* with multiple-choice questions based on the material in both the main text and the boxes. In addition, we have provided sample essay questions that allow you to think more broadly about the content of each chapter.

6. *Key terms and major contributors* are highlighted in **boldface type** so they stand out. When you use PQ4R and study for tests, be sure you can define each term and identify each major researcher. Key terms are listed alphabetically at the end of the chapter.

7. The key terms are also gathered together in the *glossary* found at the end of the text. The glossary provides formal definitions of all key terms that appear in the text and the page numbers where they appear. Use it to refresh your memory while studying for tests.

You're on your way. We hope *Psychology and Life* will be a worthwhile journey, full of memorable moments and unexpected pleasures. Let's go!

STOP AND REVIEW

❶ What does it mean to be an active participant in a course?

❷ What is the relationship between the *Questions* and *Read* phases of PQ4R?

❸ What is the purpose of the *Recite* phase of PQ4R?

Recapping Main Points

What Makes Psychology Unique?

- Psychology is the scientific study of the behaviour and the mental processes of individuals.
- The goals of psychology are to describe, explain, predict, and help control behaviour.

Visit **MyPsychLab.com** for more review and practice on the following topics:

✔ **Practice:** What Makes Psychology Unique?

The Evolution of Modern Psychology

- Structuralism emerged from the work of Wundt and Titchener. It attempted to understand the structure of the mind and behaviour by analyzing elemental sensations.
- Functionalism, developed by James and Dewey, emphasized the purpose behind behaviours.
- Taken together, these theories created the agenda for modern psychology.

- Each of the seven contemporary approaches to studying psychology differs in its view of human nature, the determinants of behaviour, the focus of study, and the primary research approach.
- The psychodynamic perspective looks at behaviour as driven by instinctive forces, inner conflicts, and conscious and unconscious motivations.
- The behaviourist perspective views behaviour as determined by external stimulus conditions.
- The humanistic perspective emphasizes an individual's inherent capacity to make rational choices.
- The cognitive perspective stresses mental processes that affect behavioural responses.
- The biological perspective studies relationships between behaviour and brain mechanisms.
- The evolutionary perspective looks at behaviour as having evolved as an adaptation for survival in the environment.
- The sociocultural perspective examines behaviour and its interpretation in cultural context.

Visit **MyPsychLab.com** for more review and practice on the following topics:

 Research: Charles Darwin

What Psychologists Do

- Psychologists work in a variety of settings and draw on expertise from a range of specialty areas. Almost any question that can be generated about real-life experiences is addressed by some member of the psychological profession.
- At the start of the 21st century, the profession of psychology has become more international in scope and more diverse in the composition of its practitioners and researchers.

Visit **MyPsychLab.com** for more review and practice on the following topics:

 Explore: Psychologists at Work

How to Use This Book

- Devise concrete strategies for determining how much study time you need and how to distribute the time most efficiently.
- Take an active approach to your lectures and the text. The PQ4R method provides six phases—Preview, Questions, Read, Reflect, Recite, and Review—for enhanced learning.
- The text includes several special features to help you learn psychological information and apply it to your everyday experiences.

KEY TERMS

behaviour (p. 2)
behavioural data (p. 3)
behavioural neuroscience (p. 10)
behaviourism (p. 9)
behaviourist perspective (p. 9)
biological perspective (p. 10)

cognitive neuroscience (p. 10)
cognitive perspective (p. 10)
evolutionary perspective (p. 10)
functionalism (p. 7)
humanistic perspective (p. 9)
psychodynamic perspective (p. 8)

psychology (p. 2)
scientific method (p. 2)
sociocultural perspective (p. 11)
structuralism (p. 7)

Practice Test

1. The definition of psychology focuses on both _____ and _____.
   a. behaviours; structures
   b. behaviours; mental processes
   c. mental processes; functions
   d. mental processes; structures

2. To what goal of psychology is "level of analysis" most relevant?
   a. explaining what happens
   b. describing what happens
   c. predicting what will happen
   d. controlling what happens

3. If you want to _____ what will happen, you first must be able to _____ what will happen.
   a. describe; explain
   b. describe; control
   c. control; predict
   d. explain; predict

4. Who founded the first laboratory that was devoted to experimental psychology?
   a. William James
   b. Wilhelm Wundt
   c. Max Wertheimer
   d. James Mark Baldwin

5. A researcher tells you that her main goal is to understand mental experiences as the combination of basic components. It is most likely that she finds the historical roots of her research in _____.
   a. functionalism.
   b. the humanistic perspective.
   c. structuralism.
   d. the evolutionary perspective.

6. Two professors at universities in Vancouver and Tokyo are collaborating on a research project to determine how their students in Canada and Japan respond to the same reasoning problems. It is likely that they take a _____ perspective in their research.
   a. humanistic
   b. sociocultural
   c. biological
   d. psychodynamic

7. The _____ perspective draws on the ways in which human mental abilities serve adaptive purposes.
   a. cognitive
   b. humanistic
   c. evolutionary
   d. sociocultural

8. It would not be unusual to see a _____ psychologist testifying at a trial.
   a. health
   b. social
   c. forensic
   d. developmental

9. What type of question would a cognitive psychologist be likely to ask?
   a. Why do children sometimes have imaginary friends?
   b. Why do some students get sick every time they have a major exam?
   c. How can we design a computer keyboard that allows people to type more quickly?
   d. How are bilingual individuals able to switch between their two languages?

10. Which type of psychologist is *least* likely to focus on genetic aspects of human psychology?
    a. industrial-organizational psychologists
    b. developmental psychologists
    c. evolutionary psychologists
    d. biological psychologists

11. Experiences with totalitarian regimes may have made Russian students more sensitive to their friends' _____
    a. betrayals of confidence.
    b. romantic competition.
    c. disrespectful behaviour.
    d. jealousy.

12. Who was the first psychologist to set up a laboratory at a Canadian university?
    a. William James
    b. Brenda Milner
    c. James Mark Baldwin
    d. Wilhelm Wundt

13. Individuals with advanced degrees in psychology are most likely to be working in _____
    a. academic settings.
    b. hospitals and clinics.
    c. business and government.
    d. independent practice.

14. What is the proper order for these phases that are part of PQ4R?
    a. Questions, Recite, Reflect
    b. Read, Reflect, Recite
    c. Preview, Review, Read
    d. Reflect, Review, Recite

15. In what phase of PQ4R should you try to relate the textbook material to your prior knowledge about a topic?
    a. Reflect
    b. Recite
    c. Review
    d. Questions

Essay Questions

1. With respect to the goals of psychology, why is it appropriate to characterize psychologists as "rather optimistic"?

2. Why is it often good to consider the same research question from several of psychology's seven contemporary perspectives?

3. Why does the field of psychology include both research and application?

Discovering Psychology Viewing Guide

Watch the following video by visiting the Media Library at **MyPsychLab.com.** After you have watched the video, answer the following questions.

Program 1: Past, Present, and Promise

PROGRAM REVIEW

1. As scientists, psychologists do which of the following?
   a. develop methods of inquiry that are fundamentally at odds with those of physics and chemistry
   b. test their theories under carefully controlled experimental circumstances
   c. ignore their own observational biases when collecting data
   d. rely completely on introspective techniques

2. What is the main goal of psychological research?
   a. to cure mental illness
   b. to find the biological bases of the behaviour of organisms
   c. to predict and, in some cases, control behaviour
   d. to provide valid legal testimony

3. The reactions of the boys and the girls to the teacher in the Candid Camera episode were essentially similar. Professor Zimbardo attributes this reaction to _____
   a. how easily adolescents become embarrassed.
   b. how an attractive teacher violates expectations.
   c. the way sexual titillation makes people act.
   d. the need people have to hide their real reactions.

4. What do EEGs measure?
   a. heart rate
   b. changes in hormone levels in the body
   c. energy expended in overcoming gravity
   d. brain activity

5. According to Robert Rosenthal's research, you are most likely to detect a liar by
   a. observing eye movements.
   b. listening to tone of voice.
   c. considering sociocultural factors.
   d. looking at body language.

6. Which cluster of topics did William James consider the main concerns of psychology?
   a. reaction times, sensory stimuli, word associations
   b. consciousness, self, emotions
   c. conditioned responses, psychophysics
   d. experimental design, computer models

7. What do we learn from our misreading of the "Paris in the the spring" sign?
   a. We are accustomed to an artist's use of perspective.
   b. Experience disposes us to respond in a particular way.

   c. Unexpected events trigger P-300 waves in the brain.
   d. We laugh at those things that violate our expectations.

8. The amygdala is an area of the brain that processes _____
   a. sound.   c. faces.
   b. social status. d. emotion.

9. Which of the following psychologists was the first to study people's sensory processing, judgment, attention, and word associations?
   a. G. Stanley Hall   c. Wilhelm Wundt
   b. William James   d. Sigmund Freud

10. Most psychologists study human behaviour at which level of analysis?
   a. molecular   c. micro
   b. macro   d. molar

11. Who wrote *Principles of Psychology* and thereby became arguably the most influential psychologist of the last century?
   a. G. Stanley Hall   c. William James
   b. Wilhelm Wundt   d. Sigmund Freud

12. What assumption underlies the use of reaction times to study prejudice indirectly?
   a. People of certain ethnic backgrounds are quicker intellectually than are people of other ethnicities.
   b. Concepts that are associated more strongly in memory are verified more quickly.
   c. Prejudice can't be studied in any other way.
   d. People respond to emotional memories more slowly than emotionless memories.

QUESTIONS TO CONSIDER

1. Although psychologists are involved in many different kinds of research and professional activities, certain fundamental issues form the basic foundation of psychology. What are they?

2. Why would the study of normal behaviour be more important to the science of psychology than an understanding of abnormal behaviour?

3. How do your culture, age, gender, education level, and past experience bias your observations about events, your own actions, and the behaviour of others?

4. Is thinking a behaviour? How can it be studied?

2

Research Methods in Psychology

You may recall that on page 14 of Chapter 1 we asked you to compose a list of questions that you would like to have answered by the end of *Psychology and Life*. Students we have dealt with in the past have responded to this request with a range of interesting concerns. Here are some of their questions:

- Why is eating "hot" food painful?
- Is it bad to spank your children?
- Can memory research help me study for exams?
- Do late-night TV ads really work?

In this chapter, we describe how psychologists generate answers to questions that matter most to students. We focus on the special way in which psychology applies the scientific method to its domain of inquiry. We want you to understand how psychologists design their research: How can solid conclusions ever be drawn from the complex and often fuzzy phenomena that psychologists study—how people think, feel, and behave? Even if you never do any scientific research in your life, mastering the information in this section will be useful. The underlying purpose here is to help improve your *critical thinking* skills by teaching you how to ask the right questions and evaluate the answers about the causes, consequences, and correlates of psychological phenomena. The mass media constantly release stories that begin with, "Research shows that. . . ." By sharpening your intelligent scepticism, we will help you become a more sophisticated consumer of the research-based conclusions that confront you in everyday life.

Scientific theories undergo rigorous testing. Their results must be replicated by independent investigators before the theories are recognized as proven.

theory An organized set of concepts that explains a phenomenon or set of phenomena.

determinism The doctrine that all events—physical, behavioural, and mental—are determined by specific causal factors that are potentially knowable.

hypothesis A tentative and testable explanation of the relationship between two (or more) events or variables; often stated as a prediction that a certain outcome will result from specific conditions.

The Process of Research

The research process in psychology can be divided into several steps that usually occur in sequence (see **Figure 2.1**). The process typically begins with a first step in which observations, beliefs, information, and general knowledge lead someone to come up with a new idea or a different way of thinking about a phenomenon. Where do researchers' questions originate? Some come from direct observations of events, humans, and nonhumans in the environment. Other research addresses traditional parts of the field. Some issues are considered to be "great unanswered questions" that have been passed down from earlier scholars. Researchers often combine old ideas in unique ways that offer an original perspective. The hallmark of the truly creative thinker is the discovery of a new truth that moves science and society in a better direction.

As psychologists accumulate information about phenomena, they create theories that form an important context in which to formulate research questions. A **theory** is an organized set of concepts that *explains* a phenomenon or set of phenomena. At the common core of most psychological theories is the assumption of **determinism**, the idea that all events—physical, mental, and behavioural—are the result of, or are determined by, specific causal factors. These causal factors are limited to those in the individual's environment or within the person. In its most extreme form, determinism suggests that fundamental laws determine all human and nonhuman processes, and that a researcher's role is to discover those laws. For example, a researcher who studies how stress affects behaviours would presume that a combination of a person's genetic factors, along with some specific characteristics of his or her environment, should predict how that person will react to various types of stressors; the task of the researcher is to uncover *which* of these factors affects behaviour, and in what combination. Though not all psychologists hold such extreme views regarding the existence of basic and universal laws, most would agree that a researcher's role is to uncover the factors that cause particular physical and mental activities. Researchers also assume that behaviour and mental processes follow *lawful patterns* of relationships—patterns that can be discovered and revealed through research. Psychological theories are typically claims about the causal forces that underlie such lawful patterns.

When a theory is proposed in psychology, it is generally expected both to account for known facts and, as a second step in the research process, to generate new hypotheses. A **hypothesis** is a tentative and testable statement about the relationship between causes and consequences. Hypotheses are often stated as "if–then" predictions, specifying certain outcomes from specific conditions. We might predict, for example, that *if* children view a lot of violence on television, *then* they will engage in more aggressive acts toward their peers. Research is required to verify the if–then link so we can determine the suitability of the hypothesis. The testability of hypotheses is central to scientific progress, because the accuracy of our predictions can be guaranteed only if we test and retest them to determine their correctness across various conditions. Only then can we become more certain of the accuracy of our if–then causal link.

As a third step, researchers rely on the *scientific method* to put their hypotheses to the test. The scientific method is a general set of procedures for gathering and interpreting evidence in

Step

1 Initial observation or question

People who are succeeding at sports report that the ball looks bigger to them.

Step
2 Form a hypothesis

Softball players who perceive the ball to be bigger will experience better batting performance.

Step

3 Design the study

Players from softball leagues were shown a display with eight black circles and asked to choose the circle they thought represented the size of a softball. The players also provided data that enabled the researchers to compute batting averages.

Step

4 Analyze the data and draw conclusions

The data revealed that the players with higher batting averages tended to choose larger circles as the correct size for the softball.

Step

5 Report the findings

The article appeared in the prestigious journal *Psychological Science*.

Step

6 Consider open questions

The discussion in the article identifies a number of open issues. For example, does the ball appear bigger before or after a player's hitting starts to improve?

Step

7 Act on open questions

These or other researchers can undertake new research to answer the open questions.

FIGURE 2.1 Steps in the Process of Conducting and Reporting Research

To illustrate the steps in the scientific process, we use a project that sought a relationship between softball players' perceptions of the size of the ball and their actual batting averages.

Witt, J. K., & Proffitt, D. R. (2005). See the ball, hit the ball: Apparent ball size is correlated with batting average. *Psychological Science*, 16, 937–938.

ways that limit sources of errors and yield dependable conclusions. Psychology is considered a science to the extent that it follows the rules established by the scientific method. Much of this chapter is devoted to describing this method.

Once researchers have collected their data, they proceed to a fourth step in which they analyze those data and generate conclusions. As a starting point, researchers use descriptive statistics to examine basic information about the data collected, including the nature of the distribution of scores and the extent of variability of the data collected. Thereafter, researchers use inferential statistics to test their hypotheses and determine whether there are legitimate conclusions to be reached on the basis of the study conducted (refer to the Chapter 2 *Statistical Supplement* for more information about the nature and purpose of these analyses). If they believe that those conclusions will have an impact on the field, researchers will take a fifth step and submit the paper for publication in a journal. For publication to be possible, researchers must keep complete records of observations and data analyses in a form that other researchers can understand and evaluate. Secrecy is banned from the research procedure because all data and methods must eventually be open for *public verifiability*—that is, other researchers must have the opportunity to inspect, criticize, replicate, or disprove the data and methods.

At the sixth step of the research process, the scientific community reflects on the research and identifies questions the work leaves unresolved. Most research articles start this process in a *discussion* section in which the researchers lay out the implications and limitations of their work. They might explicitly describe the type of future research they consider desirable. When the data do not fully support a hypothesis, researchers must rethink aspects of their theories. Thus there is continual interaction between theory and research. At a seventh step, the original researchers or their peers might act on open questions and begin the research cycle again.

This research process is centred around appropriate uses of the scientific method. The goal of the scientific method is to allow researchers to draw conclusions with maximum objectivity. Conclusions are *objective* when they are uninfluenced by researchers' emotions or personal biases. Each of the next two sections begins with a *challenge to objectivity* and then describes the *remedy* prescribed by the scientific method.

OBSERVER BIASES AND OPERATIONAL DEFINITIONS

When different people observe the same events, they do not always "see" the same thing. In this section, we describe the problem of *observer bias* and the steps researchers take as remedies.

The Challenge to Objectivity An **observer bias** is an error due to the personal motives and expectations of the viewer. At times, people see and hear what they expect rather than what is. Consider a rather dramatic example of observer bias. Around the beginning of the 20th century, a leading psychologist, **Hugo Munsterberg**, gave a speech on peace to a large

---

observer bias The distortion of evidence because of the personal motives and expectations of the viewer.

audience that included many reporters. He summarized the news accounts of what they heard and saw in this way:

> *The reporters sat immediately in front of the platform. One man wrote that the audience was so surprised by my speech that it received it in complete silence; another wrote that I was constantly interrupted by loud applause and that at the end of my address the applause continued for minutes. The one wrote that during my opponent's speech I was constantly smiling; the other noticed that my face remained grave and without a smile. The one said that I grew purple-red from excitement; and the other found that I grew chalk-white. (1908, pp. 35–36)*

It would be interesting to go back to the original newspapers to see how the reporters' accounts were related to their political views; then we might be able to understand why the reporters supposedly saw what they did.

In a psychology experiment, we would not expect differences between observers to be quite as radical as those reported by Munsterberg. Nonetheless, the example demonstrates how the same evidence can lead different observers to different conclusions. The biases of the observers act as *filters* through which some things are noticed as relevant and significant and others are ignored as irrelevant and not meaningful.

We would like you now to try the demonstration in **Figure 2.2**, to illustrate how easy it is to create an observer bias. This quick demonstration gives an idea of how the experiences you have prior to making an observation can influence how you interpret what you see.

Let's apply this lesson to what happens in psychology experiments. Researchers are often in the business of making observations. Given that every observer brings a different set of prior experiences to making those observations—and often those experiences include a commitment to a particular theory—you can see why observer biases could pose a problem. What can researchers do to ensure that their observations are minimally affected by prior expectations?

The Remedy To minimize observer biases, researchers rely on standardization and operational definitions. **Standardization** means using uniform, consistent procedures in all phases of data collection. All features of the test or experimental situation should be sufficiently standardized so all research participants experience exactly the same experimental conditions. Standardization means asking questions in the same way and scoring responses according to pre-established rules. Having results printed or recorded helps ensure their comparability across different times and places and with different participants and researchers.

---

standardization A set of uniform procedures for treating each participant in a test, interview, or experiment, or for recording data.

operational definition A definition of a variable or condition in terms of the specific operation or procedure used to determine its presence.

variable In an experimental setting, a factor that varies in amount and kind.

independent variable In an experimental setting, a variable that the researcher manipulates with the expectation of having an impact on the value of the dependent variable.

dependent variable In an experimental setting, a variable that the researcher measures to assess the impact of a variation in an independent variable.

Observations themselves must also be standardized: Scientists must solve the problem of how to translate their theories into concepts with consistent meaning. The strategy for standardizing the meaning of concepts is called *operationalization*. An **operational definition** standardizes meaning within an experiment by defining a concept in terms of specific operations or procedures used to measure it or to determine its presence. In other words, operational definitions specify in very precise ways how each variable is measured or manipulated. For example, if you conduct a study that examines whether food intake improves memory, you first have to specify how you will manipulate food intake (e.g., by giving participants a precise number of calories from very specific food sources) and how you will measure memory (e.g., by asking participants to read a list of 50 items that they will be asked to recall after a five-minute delay). All the variables in an experiment must be given operational definitions. A **variable** is any factor that varies in amount or kind.

In experimental settings, researchers most often wish to demonstrate a cause-and-effect relationship between two types of variables. The **independent variable** is the factor that the researcher manipulates; it functions as the causal part of the relationship. The effect part of the relationship is served by the **dependent variable**, which is what the experimenter measures. If the researcher's claims about cause and effect are correct, the value of the dependent variable will *depend* on the value of the independent variable. Imagine, for example, that you wished to test the hypothesis we mentioned earlier: that children who view a lot of violence on television will engage in more aggressive acts toward their peers. You could devise an experiment in which you manipulated the amount of violence each participant viewed (the independent variable) and then assessed how much aggression he or she displayed (the dependent variable).

Take a moment to put these new concepts to use in the context of a real experiment. The research project we will describe begins with a great philosophical question: Do people have free will, or is their behaviour determined by forces of genetics and environment outside their control? The study did not attempt to answer that question. Rather, the researchers argued that the way in which different individuals answer this question—their belief in free will or determinism—has an impact on how they behave (Vohs & Schooler, 2008). The researchers reasoned that people who are guided by a worldview of determinism would feel less personal responsibility for bad behaviour because they would consider it out of their control. To test this hypothesis, the researchers gave students an opportunity to cheat!

Figure 2.2 presents important aspects of the experiment. The researchers recruited roughly 120 university undergraduates to serve as participants. The independent variable for the study was participants' beliefs in free will or determinism. To manipulate this variable, the researchers presented students with a series of 15 statements and asked them to think about each statement for one minute. As you might expect, those statements were different for the free will and determinism conditions. We provide examples in Figure 2.2.

To test their hypothesis, the researchers needed to provide the students with an opportunity to cheat. During the experiment, the students attempted to answer 15 problems from Graduate Record Examination practice tests. They could earn one dollar for each correct answer. Participants scored their own answers in the absence of the experimenter, which provided an

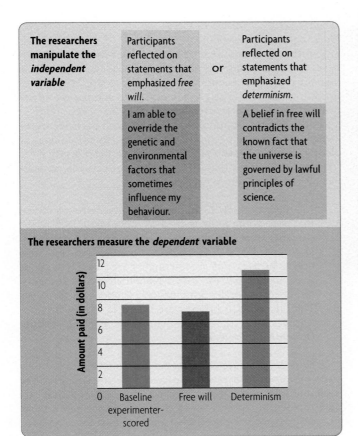

The researchers manipulate the *independent variable*	Participants reflected on statements that emphasized *free will*.	or	Participants reflected on statements that emphasized *determinism*.
	I am able to override the genetic and environmental factors that sometimes influence my behaviour.		A belief in free will contradicts the known fact that the universe is governed by lawful principles of science.

The researchers measure the *dependent* variable

FIGURE 2.2 Elements of an Experiment
To test their hypotheses, researchers create operational definitions for the independent and dependent variables.

From Vohs, K. D., & Schooler, J. W. (2008). The value of believing in free will: Encouraging a belief in determinism increases cheating. *Psychological Science*, 19, pp. 49–54. Reprinted with permission of Wiley-Blackwell.

Participants, as well as spectators and broadcast viewers, are subject to observer bias. How can you determine what really happened?

opportunity for cheating: The experimenter would never know if a participant paid him- or herself more money than was due. However, the researcher could compare the amount of money participants paid themselves and whether there were significant differences in the amount of money participants paid themselves in the free-will versus the determinism condition. Hence, the amount of money participants paid themselves was used as the dependent variable in this study.

Figure 2.2 provides the results of the experiment. To determine how average students would actually score on the 15 GRE questions, the researchers had an extra condition in which they scored participants' performance themselves to see how much money the students would be expected to earn, on average, if they were simply answering the question. The bar labelled "Baseline experimenter-scored" provides that information. As you can see from the other two bars in Figure 2.2, the independent variable had the effect on the dependent variable that the researchers expected. Those students who had been prompted to take the perspective of determinism paid themselves about $4 more than those students who focused on free will. Because of the experimenter-scored baseline—which shows free-will students at the same level as experimenter-scored students—we can infer that the

determinism students were more likely to cheat, which resulted in a higher average level of pay in that condition. Take a moment to think about other ways in which you might operationalize the experimental variables, to test the same hypothesis by other means. You might, for example, want to measure cheating in some other fashion, to show that the results generalize to other life circumstances. These types of concern—including how to design studies in ways that enable a researcher to be confident about the validity of a study and its conclusions—provide a transition to our exploration of experimental methods.

EXPERIMENTAL METHODS: ALTERNATIVE EXPLANATIONS AND THE NEED FOR CONTROLS

You know from day-to-day experience that people can suggest many causes for the same outcome. Psychologists face this same problem when they try to make exact claims about causality. To overcome causal ambiguity, researchers use **experimental methods**: They manipulate an independent variable to look for an effect on a dependent variable. The goal of this method is to make strong causal claims about the impact of one variable on the other. In this section, we describe the problem of *alternative explanations* and some steps that researchers take to counter the problem.

The Challenge to Objectivity When psychologists test a hypothesis, they most often have in mind an explanation for why a change in the independent variable should affect the

---

experimental methods Research methodologies that involve the manipulation of independent variables in order to determine their effects on the dependent variables.

Is violent behaviour caused by viewing violence on television? How could you find out?

dependent variable in a particular way. For example, you might predict, and demonstrate experimentally, that the viewing of television violence leads to high levels of aggression. But how can you be sure that it was precisely the viewing of *violence* that produced aggression? To make the strongest possible case for their hypotheses, psychologists must be very sensitive to the existence of possible *alternative explanations.* The more alternative explanations there might be for a given result, the less confidence there is that the initial hypothesis is accurate. When something other than what an experimenter purposely introduces into a research setting changes a participant's behaviour and adds confusion to the interpretation of the data, it is called a **confounding variable.** When the real cause of some observed behavioural effect is *confounded,* the experimenter's interpretation of the data is put at risk. Suppose, for example, that violent television scenes are louder and involve more movement than do most nonviolent television scenes. In that case, the violent and the superficial aspects of the scenes are confounded.

---

confounding variable A stimulus other than the variable an experimenter explicitly introduces into a research setting that affects a participant's behaviour.

expectancy effects Results that occur when a researcher or observer subtly communicates to participants the kind of behaviour he or she expects to find, thereby creating that expected reaction.

placebo effect A change in behaviour in the absence of an experimental manipulation.

The researcher is unable to specify which factor uniquely produces aggressive behaviour.

Although each different experimental method potentially gives rise to a unique set of alternative explanations, we can identify two types of confounds that apply to almost all experiments, which we will call *expectancy effects* and *placebo effects.* Unintentional **expectancy effects** occur when a researcher or observer subtly communicates to the research participants the behaviours he or she expects to find, thereby producing the desired reaction. Under these circumstances, the experimenter's expectations, rather than the independent variable, actually help trigger the observed reactions.

> In an experiment, 12 students were given groups of rats that were going to be trained to run a maze. Half of the students were told their rats were from a special *maze-bright* breed. The other students were told their rats were bred to be *maze-dull.* As you might have guessed, their rats were actually all the same. Nonetheless, the students' results corresponded with their expectations for their rats. The rats labelled bright were found to be much better learners than those that had been labelled as dull. (Rosenthal & Fode, 1963)

How do you suppose the students communicated their expectations to their rats? Do you see why you should worry even more about expectancy effects when an experiment is carried out within species—with a human experimenter and human participants? Expectation effects distort the content of discovery.

A **placebo effect** occurs when experimental participants change their behaviour in the *absence* of any kind of experimental manipulation. This concept originated in medicine to account for cases in which a patient's health improved after he or she had received medication that was chemically inert or a treatment that was nonspecific. The placebo effect refers to an improvement in health or well-being related to the individual's *belief* that the treatment will be effective. Some treatments with no genuine medical effects have been shown, even so, to produce good or excellent outcomes for 70 percent of the patients on whom they were used (Roberts, Kewman, Mercier, & Hovell, 1993).

In a psychological research setting, a placebo effect has occurred whenever a behavioural response is influenced by a person's expectation of what to do or how to feel, rather than by the specific intervention or procedures employed to produce that response. Recall the experiment relating television viewing to later aggression. Suppose we discovered that experimental participants who had not watched any television at all also showed high levels of aggression. We might conclude that these individuals, by virtue of being put in a situation that allowed them to display aggression, would expect they were *supposed* to behave aggressively and would go on to do so. Experimenters must always be mindful of the possibility that participants change the way they behave simply because they are aware of being observed or tested. For example, participants may feel special about being chosen to take part in a study and thus act differently than they would ordinarily. Such effects can compromise an experiment's results.

The Remedy: Control Procedures Because human and animal behaviours are complex and often have multiple causes, good research design involves anticipating possible confounds and devising strategies for eliminating them. Similar to defensive strategies in sports, good research designs anticipate what the other team might do and then make plans to counteract it. Researchers' strategies are called **control procedures**—methods that attempt to hold constant all variables and conditions other than those related to the hypothesis being tested. In an experiment, instructions, room temperature, tasks, the way the researcher is dressed, time allotted, the way the responses are recorded, and many other details of the situation must be similar for all participants to ensure that their experience is the same. The only differences in participants' experiences should be those introduced by the independent variable. Let's look at remedies for the specific confounding variables of expectancy and placebo effects.

Imagine, for example, that you enriched the aggression experiment to include a treatment group that watched comedy programs. You would want to be careful not to treat your comedy and violence participants in different ways based on your expectations. Thus, in your experiment, we would want the research assistant who greeted the participants and later assessed their aggression to be unaware of whether they had watched a violent program or a comedy. In the best circumstances, bias can be eliminated by keeping *both* experimental assistants and participants unaware of, or *blind* to, which participants get which treatment. This technique is called a **double-blind control**. In our prospective aggression experiment, we couldn't keep participants from knowing whether they had watched comedy or violence. However, we would take great care to ensure that they couldn't guess that our later analyses would focus on their subsequent aggression. To account for placebo effects, researchers generally include an experimental condition in which the treatment is not administered. We call this a **placebo control**. Placebo controls fall into the general category of controls by which experimenters assure themselves they are making appropriate comparisons. Suppose you see a late-night TV commercial that celebrates the herbal supplement ginkgo biloba as an answer to all your memory problems. What might you expect if you buy a supply of ginkgo and take it weekly? One study demonstrated that university students who took ginkgo every morning for six weeks did, in fact, show improvements in their performance on cognitive tasks (Elsabagh, Hartley, Ali, Williamson, & File, 2005). On one task, people were asked to view a series of 20 pictures on a computer screen, name then, and later recall those names. The participants were 14 percent better at this task after six weeks of ginkgo. However, participants who took a placebo—a pill with no active ingredients—also improved by 14 percent. The placebo control suggests that improvement on the task was the result of practice from the initial session. Such data from control conditions provide an important baseline against which the experimental effect is evaluated.

The Remedy: Research Design To implement control conditions, researchers make decisions about what type of research design best suits their goals. In some research designs, which are referred to as **between-subjects designs**, different groups of participants are *randomly assigned*, by chance procedures, to an experimental condition (exposed to one or more experimental treatments) or to a control condition (not exposed to an experimental treatment). **Random assignment** is one of the major steps researchers take to eliminate confounding variables that relate to individual differences among potential research participants. This is the same procedure we had in mind for the aggression experiment. Randomly assigning participants to experimental and control conditions makes it quite likely that the two groups will be similar in important ways at the start of an experiment, because each participant has the same probability of being in a treatment condition as in a control condition. We shouldn't have to worry, for example, that everyone in the **experimental group** loves violent television and everyone in the **control group** hates it. Random assignment will mix both types of people together in each group. If outcome differences are found between conditions, we can be more confident that the differences were caused by a treatment or intervention rather than by pre-existing differences.

Researchers also try to approximate randomness in the way they bring participants into the laboratory, because it is not possible for anyone to study an entire population of interest. For example, imagine that we wanted to study how Canadian undergraduates deal with stress. It simply would not be feasible to recruit all university students across the country. Instead, we would collect data from a **sample**—a group drawn from the population at large—with the goal of generalizing that data to the **population** of interest, the group from which the sample is drawn.

Suppose you would like to test the hypothesis that six-year-old children are more likely to lie than four-year-old children. You can bring only a very small subset of all of the world's four- and six-year-olds into your laboratory. Typically, psychology experiments use from 20 to 100 participants. To generalize beyond your samples, you need to have confidence that your particular four- and six-year-olds are comparable to any other randomly selected groups of children. In other words, you must ensure that your sample is a **representative sample** of a population—a sample that closely matches the overall characteristics of the population from which the participants are selected. For example, researchers must be sure that the sample selected is similar to that of the population of interest with regard to the

---

control procedures Consistent procedures for giving instructions, scoring responses, and holding all other variables constant except those being systematically varied.

double-blind control An experimental technique in which biased expectations of experimenters are eliminated by keeping both participants and experimental assistants unaware of which participants have received which treatment.

placebo control An experimental condition in which treatment is not administered, used in cases where a placebo effect might occur.

between-subjects design A research design in which different groups of participants are randomly assigned to experimental conditions or to control conditions.

random assignment A procedure by which participants have an equal likelihood of being assigned to any condition within an experiment.

experimental group A group in an experiment that is exposed to a treatment or experiences a manipulation of the independent variable.

control group A group in an experiment that is not exposed to a treatment or does not experience a manipulation of the independent variable.

sample A subset of a population selected as participants in an experiment.

population The entire set of individuals about which generalizations will be made based on an experimental sample.

representative sample A subset of a population that closely matches the overall characteristics of the population with respect to the distribution of males and females, racial and ethnic groups, and so on.

distribution of males and females, racial and ethnic groups, age, social class, education, and so on. Imagine that the researchers who are testing the hypothesis that six-year-old children lie more often than four-year-olds selected only boys as participants. No matter the results of the study, their conclusions would not be valid for girls, because that group was not represented in the samples selected. Similarly, the results could not be applied to any other age group; doing so would likely result in incorrect conclusions. Remember that you can generalize from your sample only to the population it adequately represents.

Another type of experimental design—a **within-subjects design**—uses each participant as his or her own control. For example, the behaviour of an experimental participant before getting a particular treatment might be compared with behaviour after. Consider an experiment that assessed whether children display certain observable cues when trying to lie.

People often use eye-gaze information as a cue to social interactions. For instance, it is commonly believed that people will break eye contact and look downward when trying to deceive another person. Is this belief accurate? And, if so, is this a strategy used by adults only, or do children also avoid eye contact when lying? Canadian researchers McCarthy and Lee (2009) designed a set of studies to determine whether children between the ages of 7 and 15 avoid eye contact when lying. In one study, children were asked to answer three types of questions: some that required a truthful answer, others that had to be answered untruthfully, and some that were more complex and required thinking. **Figure 2.3** shows the within-subjects comparison of the average duration of eye contact in each of the three conditions. As the graph shows, although children never maintained eye contact during the entire interaction, they were far more likely to avoid eye contact when trying to lie. In the condition requiring a lie, the children, on average, kept eye contact for only 38 percent of the time in comparison to slightly over 50 percent of the time in the truth and thinking question conditions.

Because the study was within subjects, the experimenters could draw the strong conclusion that the children's likelihood of maintaining eye contact was *changed* by having to tell a lie. Interestingly, the experimenters also compared the pattern of results for the younger versus older children and discovered that the older participants were less likely to avoid eye contact when lying. Thus, as children get older, they begin to understand that eye-gaze cues displayed by a deceiver can be informative about the true state of affairs.

The research methodologies we have described so far all involve the manipulation of an independent variable to look for an effect on a dependent variable. Although this experimental method often allows researchers to make the strongest claims about causal relations among variables, several conditions can make this method less desirable. First, during an experiment, behaviour is frequently studied in an artificial environment,

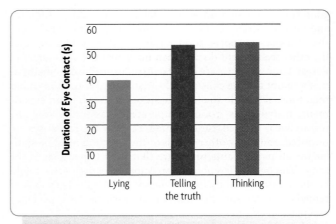

FIGURE 2.3 Children's Average Duration of Eye Contact When Telling Lies, Truths, or When the Question Required More Thinking

Children were asked to answer a series of questions. In one condition, the children were asked to answer the questions untruthfully. In a second condition they were asked to answer the questions truthfully. Finally, in the third condition the questions were slightly more complex and required more thinking. The bar graph plots the average duration of eye contact in seconds in each of the three conditions. As you can see, the children were far less likely to maintain eye contact when lying.

one in which situational factors are controlled so heavily that the environment may itself distort the behaviour from the way it would occur naturally. Critics claim that much of the richness and complexity of natural behaviour patterns is lost in controlled experiments, sacrificed to the simplicity of dealing with only one or a few variables and responses. Second, research participants typically know they are in an experiment and are being tested and measured. They may react to this awareness by trying to please the researcher, attempting to "psych out" the research purpose, or changing their behaviour from what it would be if they were unaware of being monitored. Third, some important research problems are not amenable to ethical experimental treatment. We could not, for example, try to discover whether the tendency toward child abuse is transmitted from generation to generation by creating an experimental group of children who would be abused and a control group of children who would not be. In the next section, we turn to a type of research method that is often used to address these concerns.

CORRELATIONAL METHODS

Is intelligence associated with creativity? Are optimistic people healthier than pessimists? Is there a relationship between experiencing child abuse and later mental illness? These questions involve variables that a psychologist could not easily or ethically manipulate. To answer these questions, as we do in later chapters, requires research based on **correlational methods**. Psychologists use correlational methods when they want to determine to what extent two variables, traits, or attributes are related.

To determine the precise degree of correlation that exists between two variables, psychologists compute a statistical measure known as the **correlation coefficient** (r). This value

---

within-subjects design A research design that uses each participant as his or her own control; for example, the behaviour of an experimental participant before receiving treatment might be compared to his or her behaviour after receiving treatment.

correlational methods Research methodologies that determine to what extent two variables, traits, or attributes are related.

correlation coefficient (r) A statistic that indicates the degree of relationship between two variables.

can vary between +1.0 and −1.0, where +1.0 indicates a perfect positive correlation, −1.0 indicates a perfect negative correlation, and 0.0 indicates no correlation at all. A positive correlation coefficient means that as one set of scores increases, a second set also increases. The reverse is true with negative correlations: the second set of scores goes in the opposite direction to the values of the first scores (see **Figure 2.4**). Correlations that are closer to zero mean that there is a weak relationship or no relationship between scores on two measures. As the correlation coefficient gets stronger, closer to the +1.0 maximum, predictions about one variable based on information about the other variable become increasingly more accurate.

Suppose, for example, researchers were interested in determining the relationship between students' sleep habits and their success in university. They might operationally define *sleep habits* as the average amount of sleep per night. *Success in university* could be defined as cumulative average. The researchers could assess each variable for an appropriate sample of students and compute the correlation coefficient between them. A strongly positive score would mean that the more a student sleeps, the higher his or her average is likely to be. Knowing a student's "hours per night" would then allow

College student in residence

the researchers to make a reasonable prediction about the student's average.

The researchers might want to take the next step and say that the way to improve students' averages would be to force them to sleep more. This intervention is misguided. A strong correlation indicates only that two sets of data are related in a systematic way; the correlation does not ensure that one causes the other. *Correlation does not imply causation.* The correlation could reflect any one of several cause-and-effect possibilities, or none. For example, a positive correlation between sleep and academic average might mean that (1) people who study more efficiently get to bed sooner, (2) people who experience anxiety about schoolwork cannot fall asleep, or (3) people sleep better when they are taking easy courses. You can see from this example that correlations most often require researchers to probe for deeper explanations.

We do not want to leave you with the impression that correlational methods are not valuable research tools. Throughout *Psychology and Life*, we will review many correlational studies that have led to important insights. We will offer just one example here to whet your appetite:

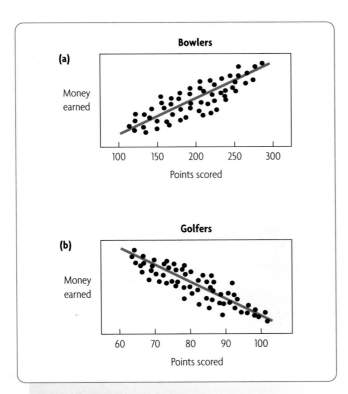

FIGURE 2.4 Positive and Negative Correlations

These imaginary data display the difference between positive and negative correlations. Each point represents a single bowler or golfer. (a) In general, the more points a professional bowler scores, the more money he or she will earn. Thus, there is a positive correlation between the two variables. (b) The correlation for golf is negative, because golfers earn more money when they score fewer points.

Can you tell whether people will be good leaders just by looking at them? To address this question, a pair of researchers gathered photographs of the CEOs of the companies that were listed as the top 25 and bottom 25 on the Fortune 500 website (Rule & Ambady, 2008). The researchers asked 50 students to view the photographs and answer, on a seven-point scale, "How good would this person be at leading a company?" The researchers also collected financial information for each company. The data revealed a positive correlation between participants' judgments and the companies' performance. On the whole, the CEOs who got the highest leadership ratings—again, based only on their photographs—led the most profitable companies. Why might this positive correlation emerge? The researchers were careful to acknowledge that more than one causal pathway is possible: "Of course, we cannot draw any causal inferences as to whether more successful companies choose individuals with a particular appearance to be their CEOs or whether individuals with a particular appearance emerge as more successful in their work as CEOs" (p. 110).

Can you see why a correlational design is appropriate to address this issue? You can't randomly assign people to look like leaders or not, nor can you randomly assign companies to be profitable or not. You must wait to see what differences emerge as leadership unfolds in the real world.

SUBLIMINAL INFLUENCE?

To close this section, we offer one concrete example of how psychological research has been used to assess the vigorous claims of advertisers anxious to make you believe in their products. You almost certainly have been subjected to commercials for products that promise to change your life with messages outside conscious awareness—*subliminal* messages. One CD guarantees a better sex life; another provides a quick cure for low self-esteem; a third promises safe and effective weight loss. How? All you have to do is *listen*—in bed, while jogging, when doing your homework—to the "restful splash of ocean waves breaking on sandy shores."

Subliminal influence has a long history. Although it was almost certainly a hoax, a 1957 study made headlines when the "inventor" of subliminal advertising claimed that flashing the message "Buy Popcorn" on the screen during a movie yielded a 58 percent increase in popcorn sales (Rogers, 1993)! In 1958, the Canadian Broadcasting Corporation (CBC) tested this same idea by subliminally flashing the message "Call Now" 352 times during a popular Sunday-night program. No increase in telephone calls was observed, and no one called the station (Vokey, 2002).

You now have the knowledge to address the critical question: Do subliminal messages really influence mental states and behaviour, as their advocates claim? Our answer comes from an application of the experimental methods we have described (see **Figure 2.5**):

A team of experimenters set out to determine the effectiveness of listening to commercially available audiotapes designed to improve self-esteem or memory. The participants included 237 male and female volunteers, ranging from 18 to 60 years of age. After a pretest session in which their initial self-esteem and memory were measured on standard psychological tests and questionnaires, the participants were randomly assigned to two conditions. Half of them received subliminal memory tapes, and the others received subliminal self-esteem tapes. They listened regularly to the tapes for a five-week period and then returned to the laboratory for a post-test session to evaluate their memories (using four memory tests) and self-esteem (using three self-esteem scales). The researchers were blind to which participants received which treatment (Greenwald, Spangenber, Pratkanis, & Eskenazi, 1991).

Did the tapes boost self-esteem and enhance memory? The results from this controlled experiment indicate no significant improvement on any of the objective measures of either self-esteem or memory. However, one very powerful effect did emerge: the placebo effect of expecting to be helped. Anticipating this placebo effect, the researchers had added another independent variable. Half the participants in each group received memory tapes that were mismarked "self-esteem" and the others received self-esteem tapes that were mismarked "memory." Participants *believed* their self-esteem improved if they received tapes with that label and felt their memory improved if their tapes were labelled "memory"—even when they had been listening to the other tape!

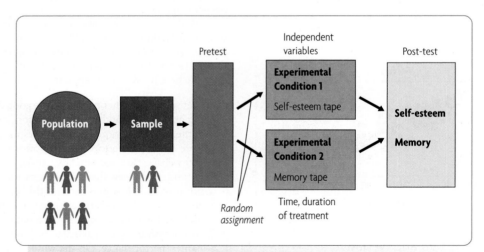

FIGURE 2.5 Experimental Design for Testing Hypotheses about the Effectiveness of Subliminal Messages

In this simplified version of the experiment, a sample of people is drawn from a larger, general population. They are given a series of pretest measures and randomly assigned to receive subliminal tapes with either memory or self-esteem messages. They are then given post-tests that objectively assess any changes in the dependent variables: memory and self-esteem. The study found no significant effects of subliminal persuasion.

Psychology in Your Life

CAN SURVEY RESEARCH AFFECT YOUR ATTITUDES?

Consider this scenario. It's election time. Just when you have finished eating supper, the telephone rings. A friendly voice at the other end asks you if you have a few minutes to answer some questions about the candidates. You say, "Why not?"This is an opportunity for you to be a research participant outside the laboratory. But here is an answer to "Why not?" The questions on the survey can have a strong impact on your attitudes.

Let's look at a laboratory study that illustrates this principle. The study took place in England, so it focused on participants' attitudes toward the prime minister at the time, Tony Blair (Haddock, 2002). Participants filled out a questionnaire that began with the question, "How interested are you in British politics?" After that, the questionnaire continued in one of four ways. One version asked participants to list two positive characteristics for Blair; a second asked participants for five positive characteristics. The remaining two versions of the questionnaires asked for two or five negative characteristics. The next questions on each questionnaire asked the participants to provide favourability ratings toward Blair on seven-point scales, with higher scores reflecting more positive attitudes.

From this description, you can see that one important component of the experiment was the number of characteristics each participant attempted to list. Why might that matter? Suppose you were asked to list negative attributes for a politician, such as Canada's prime minister or the premier of your province. You would probably find it easy to generate two negative attributes, but relatively hard to generate five. After trying to generate five, you might be thinking, "Hey, if I can't think of five things that are bad about this

person, maybe he or she is actually pretty good" (see Schwarz, Bless, Wänke, & Winkielman, 2003). For that reason, if you try to generate more negative characteristics, you might actually come to like the politician better; if you try to generate more positive characteristics, that effort can have a negative impact on your attitudes.

The results presented in the figure support these predictions for the subset of participants who were relatively uninterested in British politics. For example, those participants' ratings of Blair were relatively more positive when they attempted to recall more negative characteristics. For those students who were already interested in British politics—presumably because they had sufficient knowledge and strong attitudes—the ease with which they could retrieve information about Blair did not have a similar impact on their attitudes.

From this pattern of results, here is what you might anticipate when you

get that after-supper call requesting your political opinion: The first thing the caller will likely ask is how interested you are in politics. At that point, the caller will know how easy it might be to alter your attitudes with questions that, on the surface, seem quite reasonable. Would you have anticipated that having people focus at length on Blair's negative characteristics would make them like him more?

So when you answer "research" questions in the real world, be wary of the true purposes of the enterprise. In the laboratory, researchers must provide you with debriefing information (see p. 36) that helps you understand how research participation might have influenced how you think or feel. Those people who catch you after dinner have no similar responsibilities toward full disclosure. Their major hope is that they can change your attitudes in a way that will affect your behaviour when you find yourself in the voting booth.

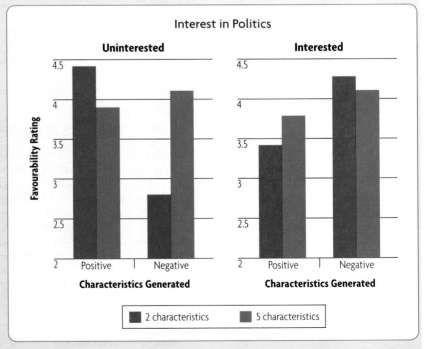

The Process of Research **31**

This rigorous experiment allows for some very concrete advice: Save your money. Subliminal self-help programs offer nothing more than placebo effects. An important goal of *Psychology and Life* is to provide you with such concrete conclusions based on solid experimental methods.

This experiment also gives you a specific example of the types of variables that psychologists measure. In this case, it was participants' beliefs about improvements in self-esteem and memory, as well as objective measures of self-esteem and memory. In the next section, we discuss more generally the way in which psychologists measure important processes and dimensions of experience.

STOP AND REVIEW

❶ What is the relationship between theories and hypotheses?

❷ What steps can researchers take to overcome observer biases?

❸ Why do researchers use double-blind controls?

❹ What is meant by a within-subjects design?

❺ Why does correlation not imply causation?

CRITICAL THINKING Consider the study that tested whether 7- to 15-year-old children avoid eye contact when lying. Why did the researchers decide to test the same children in all three conditions (truthful questions, untruthful questions, or complex questions) instead of using different children for each condition?

Psychological Measurement

Because psychological processes are so varied and complex, they pose major challenges to researchers who want to measure them. Although some actions and processes are easily seen, many—such as anxiety or dreaming—are not. Thus, one task for a psychological researcher is to make the unseen visible, to make internal events and processes external, and to make private experiences public. You have already seen how important it is for researchers to provide operational definitions of the phenomena they wish to study. Those definitions generally provide some procedure for assigning numbers to, or *quantifying*, different levels, sizes, intensities, or amounts of a variable. Many measurement methods are available, each with its particular advantages and disadvantages.

Our review of psychological measurement begins with a discussion of the distinction between two ways of gauging the accuracy of a measure: *reliability* and *validity*. We then review different measurement techniques for data collection. By whatever means psychologists collect their data, they must use appropriate methods to verify their hypotheses; these analyses most often require the use of statistics. A description of how psychologists analyze their data is given in the *Statistical Supplement*, which follows this chapter. Read it in conjunction with this chapter.

ACHIEVING RELIABILITY AND VALIDITY

The goal of psychological measurement is to generate findings that are both reliable and valid. **Reliability** refers to the consistency or dependability of behavioural data resulting from psychological testing or experimental research. A reliable result is one that will be repeated under similar conditions of testing at different times. A reliable measuring instrument yields comparable scores when employed repeatedly (and when the thing being measured does not change). Consider the experiment we just described, which showed that subliminal audiotapes generate only placebo effects. That experiment included 237 participants. The experimenters' claim that the result was "reliable" means that they should be able to repeat the experiment with any new group of participants of comparable size and generate the same pattern of data.

Validity means that the information produced by research or testing accurately measures the psychological variable or quality it is intended to measure. A valid measure of *happiness*, for example, should allow us to predict how happy you are likely to be in particular situations. A valid experiment means that the researcher can generalize to broader circumstances, often from the laboratory to the real world. When we gave you advice based on the audiotapes experiment, we were accepting the researchers' claim that the results are valid. Tests and experiments can be reliable without being valid. We could, for example, use your shoe size as an index of your happiness. This would be reliable (we would always get the same answer), but not valid (we would learn very little about your day-to-day happiness level).

As you now read about different types of measures, try to evaluate them in terms of reliability and validity.

SELF-REPORT MEASURES

Often researchers are interested in obtaining data about experiences they cannot directly observe. Sometimes these experiences are internal psychological states, such as beliefs, attitudes, and feelings. At other times, these experiences are external behaviours—like sexual activities or criminal acts—that are not generally appropriate for psychologists to witness. In these cases, investigations rely on self-reports. **Self-report measures** are verbal answers, either written or spoken, to questions the researcher poses. Researchers devise reliable ways to quantify these self-reports so they can make meaningful comparisons between different individuals' responses.

Self-reports include responses made on questionnaires and during interviews. A *questionnaire* or *survey* is a written set of questions, ranging in content from questions of fact ("Are you a psychology major?"), to questions about past or present behaviour ("How much do you smoke?"), to questions about attitudes and feelings ("How satisfied are you with your present

---

reliability The degree to which a test produces similar scores each time it is used; stability or consistency of the scores produced by an instrument.

validity The extent to which a test measures what it was intended to measure.

self-report measures The behaviours that are identified through a participant's own observations and reports.

job?"). *Open-ended* questions allow respondents to answer freely in their own words. Questions may also have a number of *fixed alternatives* such as *yes, no,* and *undecided.*

An *interview* is a dialogue between a researcher and an individual for the purpose of obtaining detailed information. Instead of being completely standardized, like a questionnaire, an interview is *interactive*. An interviewer may vary the questioning to follow up on something the respondent said. Good interviewers are also sensitive to the process of the social interaction as well as to the information revealed. They are trained to establish *rapport,* a positive social relationship with the respondent that encourages trust and the sharing of personal information.

Although researchers rely on a wide variety of self-report measures, there are limits to their usefulness. Obviously, many forms of self-report cannot be used with preverbal children, illiterate adults, speakers of other languages, some mentally disturbed people, and nonhuman animals. Even when self-reports can be used, they may not be reliable or valid. Participants may misunderstand the questions or not remember clearly what they actually experienced. Furthermore, self-reports may be influenced by social desirability. People may give false or misleading answers to create a favourable (or, sometimes, unfavourable) impression of themselves. They may be embarrassed to report their true experiences or feelings. If respondents are aware of a questionnaire's or interview's purpose, they may lie or alter the truth to get a job, to appear more caring or generous, or to accomplish another goal. An interview situation also allows personal biases and prejudices to affect how the interviewer asks questions and how the respondent answers them.

BEHAVIOURAL MEASURES AND OBSERVATIONS

As a group, psychological researchers are interested in a wide range of behaviours. They may study a rat running a maze, a

By watching from behind a one-way mirror, a researcher can record observations of a child without influencing or interfering with the child's behaviour. Have you ever changed your behaviour when you knew you were being watched?

child drawing a picture, a student memorizing a poem, or a worker repeatedly performing a task. **Behavioural measures** are ways to study overt actions and observable and recordable reactions.

One of the primary ways to study what people do is through *observation*. Researchers use observation in a planned, precise, and systematic manner. Observations focus on either the *process* or the *products* of behaviour. In an experiment on learning, for instance, a researcher might observe how many times a research participant rehearsed a list of words (process) and then how many words the participant remembered on a final test (product). For *direct observations*, the behaviour under investigation must be clearly visible and overt and easily recorded. For example, in a laboratory experiment on emotions, a researcher could observe a participant's facial expressions as the individual looked at emotionally arousing stimuli.

A researcher's direct observations are often augmented by technology. For example, contemporary psychologists often rely on computers to provide very precise measures of the time it takes for research participants to perform various tasks, such as reading a sentence or solving a problem. Although some forms of exact measurement were available before the computer age, computers now provide extraordinary flexibility in collecting and analyzing precise information. In Chapter 4, we will describe the newest types of technologies that allow researchers to produce behavioural measures of a remarkable kind: pictures of the brain at work.

In *naturalistic observations*, some naturally occurring behaviour is viewed by a researcher, who makes no attempt to change or interfere with it. For instance, a researcher behind a one-way mirror might observe the play of children who are not aware of being observed. Some kinds of human behaviour can be studied only through naturalistic observation because it would be unethical or impractical to do otherwise. For example, it would be unethical to experiment with severe deprivation in early life to see its effects on a child's later development.

When studying behaviour in a laboratory setting, a researcher is unable to observe the long-term effects of a subject's natural habitat in shaping complex patterns of behaviour. One of the most valuable examples of naturalistic observation conducted in the field is the work of **Jane Goodall** (1986, 1990; Peterson & Goodall, 1993). Goodall has spent more than 30 years studying patterns of behaviour among chimpanzees in Gombe, on Lake Tanganyika in Africa. Goodall notes that had she ended her research after 10 years—as she originally planned—she would not have drawn the correct conclusions:

> We would have observed many similarities in their behaviour and ours, but we would have been left with the impression that chimpanzees were far more peaceable than humans. Because we were able to continue beyond the first decade, we could document the division of a social group and observe the violent aggression that broke out between newly separated factions. We discovered that in certain circumstances the chimpanzees may kill and even

---

behavioural measures Overt actions and reactions that are observed and recorded, exclusive of self-reported behaviour.

Jane Goodall has spent most of her adult life making naturalistic observations of chimpanzees. What has she discovered that she could not have discovered if the animals were not in their natural habitat?

cannibalize individuals of their own kind. On the other side of the coin, we have learned of the extraordinarily enduring affectionate bonds between family members . . . advanced cognitive abilities, [and the development of] cultural traditions. (Goodall, 1986, pp. 3–4)

In the early stages of an investigation, naturalistic observation is especially useful. It helps researchers discover the extent of a phenomenon or get an idea of what the important variables and relationships might be. The data from naturalistic observation often provide clues for an investigator to use in formulating a specific hypothesis or research plan.

When researchers wish to test hypotheses with behavioural measures, they sometimes turn to *archival data*. Imagine all the types of information you might find in a library or on the web: birth and death records, weather reports, movie attendance figures, voting patterns, and so on. Any of those types of information could become valuable to test the right hypothesis. Consider a study that examined whether men and women differ in their level of *heroism* (Becker & Eagly, 2004). To address this question, the researchers could not create a laboratory test—they could not set a building on fire to see whether more men or women rushed in to help save lives. Instead, they defined behaviours out in the world that were arguably heroic and then looked to archival records to assess the relative contributions of men and women. For example, the researchers examined participation in Doctors of the World, an organization that sends medical personnel to all corners of the globe. Personnel in this program assume a "non-negligible risk [by] delivering health and medical services in environments marked by local violence and unsanitary conditions" (Becker & Eagly, 2004, p. 173). What did the archival data show? More than half of the participants in Doctors of the World (65.8 percent) were women. You can see why archival data are essential to address certain types of questions.

Before we leave the topic of psychological measurement, we must emphasize that many research projects combine both self-report measures and behavioural observations. Researchers may, for example, specifically look for a relationship between how people report they will behave and how they actually behave. In addition, rather than involving large numbers of participants, some research projects will focus all their measures on a single individual or small group in a **case study**. Intensive analyses of particular individuals can sometimes yield important insights into general features of human experience. For example, in Chapter 4 you will learn that careful observations of single patients with brain damage provided the basis for important theories of the localization of language functions in the brain.

We have now described several types of procedures and measures that researchers use. Before we move on, we want to give you an opportunity to see how the same issue can be addressed in different research designs. Consider Shakespeare's question, "What's in a name?" In *Romeo and Juliet*, Juliet asserts, "That which we call a rose by any other name would smell as sweet." But is that correct? Do you think your name has an impact on the way other people treat you? Is it better to have a common, familiar name or a rare, distinctive one? Or does your name not matter at all? In **Table 2.1** we give examples of combinations of measures and methods that researchers might use to answer these questions. As you read through Table 2.1, ask yourself how willing you would be to participate in each type of study. In the next section, we consider the ethical standards that govern psychological research.

STOP AND REVIEW

❶ Why can some measures be reliable but not valid?
❷ Why is it important for interviewers to establish rapport?
❸ Suppose a researcher spends time observing children's behaviour on a playground. What kind of measure would that be?

---

case study Intensive observation of a particular individual or small group of individuals.

TABLE 2.1　What's in a Name? Methods and Measures

Research Goal	Dependent Measure	
	Self-Report	**Observation**
Correlational Methods To assess the correlation between the frequency of people's names and their experience of happiness.	Each participant's assessment of his or her own happiness.	
To assess the correlation between the frequency of children's names and their acceptance by peers.		Children's amount of social interaction on the playground.
Experimental Methods To determine if people judge identical photos differently when different names are assigned to them.	Participants' ratings of baby pictures to which random names have been assigned.	
To determine if people's actual social interactions change because of name-based expectations.		The number of positive facial expressions people produce in conversation with a stranger who has introduced himself as *Mark* or *Marcus*.

Ethical Issues in Human and Animal Research

We noted, in the study that tested the effectiveness of subliminal messages, that the researchers deceived the participants by mislabelling the tapes. They did so to see if the participants' expectations would lead them to believe that the messages were helpful even if objective measures of memory and self-esteem showed no improvement. Deception is always ethically suspect, but in this case, how else could researchers assess the placebo effect of false beliefs held by the participants? How should the *potential gains* of a research project be weighed against the *costs* it incurs to those who are subjected to procedures that are risky, painful, stressful, or deceptive? Psychologists ask themselves these questions all the time (Bersoff, 2008).

Respect for the basic rights of humans and animals is a fundamental obligation of all researchers. Current research practice in Canada is governed by the Tri-Council Policy Statement on research ethics (Interagency Secretariat on Research Ethics, 2005), which guides all Canadian research funded by the Canadian Institute for Health Research, the Natural Sciences and Engineering Research Council, and the Social Sciences and Humanities Research Council. These ethical standards require that researchers respect their participants by treating them with dignity, providing them with information about the study

so they can make a decision about whether or not they want to participate, and protecting their confidentiality and anonymity. By guaranteeing confidentiality, researchers assure participants that their identifying information will not be made available to anyone who is not directly involved in the study. On the other hand, when researchers protect a participant's anonymity, this ensures that that person's identity will remain unknown throughout the study, even to the researchers themselves. Researchers from all disciplines must be especially careful when working with vulnerable people, such as those individuals with psychological disorders. Finally, the guidelines ask researchers to consider the benefits of their research program: Will the knowledge gained from the research be of real value? The guidelines provided by the Tri-Council are designed to guarantee that everyone who takes part in a study is treated with respect and care.

Psychologists, too, are guided by strict codes of conduct, including the *Canadian Code of Ethics for Psychologists* (Canadian Psychological Association [CPA], 2000a) and the ethical guidelines of the Canadian Council on Animal Care (1993). In a manner similar to the Tri-Council guidelines, the *Canadian Code of Ethics* requires that psychologists protect the welfare of their participants, avoid causing harm, explain the study's procedure, and receive participants' consent. These issues are described in detail below.

On the matter of the issue of deception in research, the *Canadian Code of Ethics for Psychologists* states that psychologists must "[n]ot engage in incomplete disclosure, or in temporarily leading research participants to believe that a research project or some aspect of it has a different purpose, if there are alternative procedures available or if the negative effects cannot be predicted or offset" (CPA, 2000a, p. 30). Guidelines of this sort were not always in force. For example, in Chapter 17 we describe classic experiments on *obedience to authority*. In one set of experiments conducted by Stanley Milgram (1965), participants were deceived into believing that they were giving dangerous electric shocks to total strangers. While the participants were never forced to do so, the context of the study and the presence of the experiment were sufficient to impose a strong degree of pressure and, as a result, a high percentage of the participants gave what they thought were high voltage electric shocks to a stranger who was pretending to experience severe pain and the possibility of a heart attack. Evidence from the experiments suggests that the participants were, in fact, experiencing "severe emotional distress." For that reason—although the research conducted by Milgram was quite important to our understanding of human nature—no responsible psychologist could advocate replicating the studies today. In fact, researchers no longer make decisions about issues like the use of deception in isolation. To guarantee that ethical principles are honoured, universities, hospitals, and research institutes each have *research ethics boards* that approve and reject proposals for human and animal research. Let's review some of the factors those boards consider.

INFORMED CONSENT

At the start of nearly all laboratory research with human subjects, participants are given a description of the procedures, potential risks, and expected benefits they will experience. Participants are assured that their privacy is protected: All records of their behaviour are kept strictly confidential; they must approve any public sharing of them. Participants are asked to sign statements indicating that they have been *informed* about these matters and that they *consent* to continue. They are assured in advance that they may leave an experiment any time they wish without penalty, and are given the names and phone numbers of officials to contact if they have any grievances.

RISK/GAIN ASSESSMENT

Most psychology experiments carry little risk to the participants, especially where participants are asked merely to perform routine tasks. However, some experiments that study more personal aspects of human nature—such as emotional reactions, self-images, conformity, stress, or aggression—can be upsetting or psychologically disturbing. Therefore, whenever a researcher conducts such a study, risks must be minimized, participants must be informed of the risks, and suitable precautions must be taken to deal with strong reactions. Where any risk is involved, it is carefully weighed by each institutional review board in terms of its necessity in achieving benefits for the participants of the study, for science, and for society.

---

debriefing A procedure conducted at the end of an experiment in which the researcher provides the participant with as much information about the study as possible and makes sure that no participant leaves feeling confused, upset, or embarrassed.

INTENTIONAL DECEPTION

For some kinds of research, it is not possible to tell the participants the whole story in advance without biasing the results. If you were studying the effects of television violence on aggression, for example, you would not want your participants to know your purpose in advance. But is your hypothesis enough to justify the deception?

We already noted that the *Canadian Code of Ethics for Psychologists* (CPA, 2000a) gives explicit instructions about the use of deception. In addition to the guideline that participants not be misled about the probability of physical or emotional distress, the CPA provides other restrictions: (1) the study must have sufficient scientific and educational importance to warrant deception; (2) researchers must demonstrate that no equally effective procedures excluding deception are available; (3) the deception must be explained to the participants by the conclusion of the research; and (4) participants must have the opportunity to withdraw their data once the deception is explained. In experiments involving deception, a review board may impose constraints, insist on monitoring initial demonstrations of the procedure, or deny approval.

DEBRIEFING

Participation in psychological research should always be a mutual exchange of information between researcher and participant. The researcher may learn something new about a behavioural phenomenon from the participant's responses, and the participant should be informed of the purpose, hypothesis, anticipated results, and expected benefits of the study. At the end of an experiment, each participant must be given a careful **debriefing**, in which the researcher provides as much information about the study as possible and makes sure that no one leaves feeling confused, upset, or embarrassed. As we just mentioned, if it was necessary to mislead the participants during any stage of the research, the experimenter carefully explains the reasons for the deception. Again, participants have the right to withdraw their data if they feel they have been misused or their rights abused in any way.

Researchers who use animal subjects are required to provide a humane environment. Do you think scientific gains justify the use of nonhuman animals in research?

ISSUES IN ANIMAL RESEARCH

Should animals be used in psychological and medical research? This question has often produced polarized responses. On one side are researchers who point to the very important breakthroughs that research with animals has allowed in several areas of science (Carroll & Overmier, 2001). The benefits of animal research have included discovery and testing of drugs that treat anxiety and mental illnesses, as well as important knowledge about drug addiction (N. E. Miller, 1985). Animal research benefits animals as well. For example, psychological researchers have shown how to alleviate the stresses of confinement experienced by zoo animals. Their studies of animal learning and social organization have led to the improved design of enclosures and animal facilities that promote good health (Nicoll, Russel, & Katz, 1988).

For defenders of animal rights "ethical concerns about compromised animal welfare cannot be eased by human benefits alone" (Olsson, Hansen, & Sandøe, 2007, p. 1680). Ethicists encourage researchers to adhere to the 3 Rs: Researchers should devise tests of their hypothesis that enable them to *reduce* the number of animals they require or to *replace* the use of animals altogether, and they should *refine* their procedures to minimize pain and distress (Ryder, 2006). Each animal researcher must judge his or her work with heightened scrutiny. The Canadian Council on Animal Care (1993) provides firm ethical guidelines for researchers who use nonhuman animals in their research.

What are the attitudes of both psychologists and psychology students regarding the use of animals in research? Although no Canadian data are available, we can use U.S.-based surveys to provide an indication of psychologists' attitudes about this important issue. Surveys of 1188 psychology students and 3982 American Psychological Association members on their attitudes toward animal research support a criterion of heightened scrutiny (Plous, 1996a, 1996b):

- Roughly 80 percent of the people surveyed believed that observational studies in naturalistic settings were appropriate. Smaller numbers (30 to 70 percent) supported studies involving caging or confinement, depending in part on the type of animal (e.g., rats, pigeons, dogs, or primates). Both students and their professors disapproved of studies involving physical pain or death.
- A majority of both groups (roughly 60 percent) supported the use of animals in undergraduate psychology courses, but only about a third of each group felt that laboratory work with animals should be a required part of an undergraduate psychology major.

How do your beliefs compare to those of your peers? How would you make decisions about the costs and benefits of animal research?

STOP AND REVIEW

❶ What is the purpose of informed consent?
❷ What is the purpose of debriefing?
❸ What recommendation about research settings do researchers make with respect to the use of nonhuman animals as research participants?

Becoming a Wiser Research Consumer

In the final section of this chapter, we will focus on the kinds of critical thinking skills you need to become a wiser consumer of psychological knowledge. Honing these thinking tools is essential for any responsible person in a dynamic society such as ours—one so filled with claims of truth, with false, supposedly commonsense myths, and with biased conclusions that serve special interests. To be a *critical thinker* is to go beyond the information as given and to delve beneath slick appearances, with the goal of understanding the substance without being seduced by style and image.

Psychological claims are an ever-present aspect of the daily life of any thinking, feeling, and acting person in this psychologically sophisticated society. Unfortunately, much information on psychology does not come from the books, articles, and reports of accredited practitioners. Rather, this information comes from newspaper and magazine articles, TV and radio shows, pop psychology, and self-help books. Let's return to the idea of subliminal mind control. Although it began as a hoax propagated by profit-minded marketing consultant James M. Vicary (Rogers, 1993; Vokey, 2002)—and, as we have seen, has been rigorously discredited in the laboratory—the idea of subliminal influences on overt behaviour continues to exert a pull on people's beliefs and their wallets!

Studying psychology will help you make wiser decisions based on evidence gathered either by you or by others. Always try to apply the insights you derive from your formal study of psychology to the informal psychology that surrounds you: Ask questions about your own behaviour or that of other people, seek answers to these questions using rational psychological theories, and check out the answers against the evidence available to you.

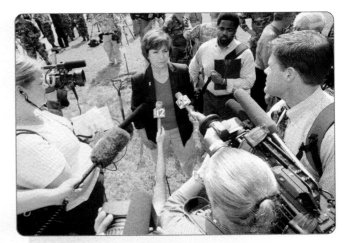

A news interview with an expert may include misleading sound bites taken out of context or oversimplified "nutshell" descriptions of research conclusions. How can you become a wiser consumer of media reports?

Critical Thinking in Your Life

HOW CAN YOU EVALUATE PSYCHOLOGICAL INFORMATION ON THE WEB?

If you access the World Wide Web, you will discover an amazing range of sites devoted to topics in psychology. For example, for the last several years we have been trying the simple experiment of typing the word *schizophrenia* (see Chapter 15) into our preferred search engine. Here are some sample data: Eight years ago, the search turned up 83 760 pages; five years ago the search engine found "about 764 000" pages; this morning, the search retrieved "about 10 900 000" pages. That's some increase! No doubt the numbers will grow even higher during the short interval the publisher needs to turn our paragraphs into your textbook. These three pieces of data make it clear why many people characterize the time in which we live as a time of information explosion. The challenge for all of us is to become wise consumers of all that information. How can you determine which information posted on the web arises from legitimate sources and which does not?

In a physical library, it is much easier to determine the source of information. Most psychological research appears in journals that are published by organizations such as the American or Canadian Psychological Associations or the American Psychological Society. When research manuscripts are submitted to most journals, they undergo a process of peer review. Each manuscript is typically sent to two to five experts in the field. Those experts provide detailed analyses of the manuscript's rationale, methodology, and results. Only when those experts have been sufficiently satisfied do manuscripts become journal articles. This is a rigorous process. For example, in 2005, journals published by the American Psychological Association (APA, 2006) rejected, on average, 69 percent of the manuscripts submitted to them. The process of peer review is not perfect—no doubt some worthy research projects are overlooked and some uneven ones slip through—but, in general, this process ensures that the research you read in the vast majority of journals has met high standards.

In this context, it is easy to identify the problem with much of the information on the web: It is often difficult to tell who, if anyone, has evaluated the advice a webpage offers or the claims it makes. When you accept information from a webpage, you need to assure yourself that the source is legitimate. One good approach is to look for online versions of the journals available in the library. Also, look for the webpages now often maintained by researchers to summarize their projects and list relevant publications. If the information you find on those or any other webpages interests you, try to find the references and publications they list. In general, you should have the greatest confidence in the information provided on a website when the authors of the site are able to point you toward the research sources of that information. You can have confidence in the conclusions we draw throughout *Psychology and Life* because we provide research citations for each of our claims. Make sure to hold webpages to the same standard!

- Why does so much information about psychological topics get posted to the web?

- Why do journals request reviews from more than one expert?

Here are some general rules to keep in mind to be a more sophisticated shopper as you travel through the supermarket of knowledge:

- Avoid the inference that correlation is causation.
- Ask that critical terms and key concepts be defined operationally so that there can be consensus about their meanings.
- Consider first how to disprove a theory, hypothesis, or belief before seeking confirming evidence, which is easy to find when you are looking for a justification.
- Always search for alternative explanations to the obvious ones proposed, especially when the explanations benefit the proposer.
- Recognize how personal biases can distort perceptions of reality.
- Be suspicious of simple answers to complex questions or single causes and cures for complex effects and problems.

- Question any statement about the effectiveness of some treatment, intervention, or product by finding the comparative basis for the effect. Remember to ask, "Compared to what?"
- Be open-minded yet sceptical: Recognize that most conclusions are tentative and not certain. Seek new evidence that decreases your uncertainty while keeping yourself open to change and revision.
- Challenge authority that uses personal opinion in place of evidence for conclusions and is not open to constructive criticism.

We want you to apply open-minded scepticism while you read *Psychology and Life*. We do not want you to view your study of psychology as the acquisition of a list of facts. Instead, we hope you will participate in the joy of observing and discovering and putting ideas to the test.

Recapping Main Points

The Process of Research

- In the initial phase of research, observations, beliefs, information, and general knowledge lead to a new way of thinking about a phenomenon. The researcher formulates a theory and generates hypotheses to be tested.
- To test their ideas, researchers use the scientific method, a set of procedures for gathering and interpreting evidence in ways that limit errors.
- Researchers combat observer biases by standardizing procedures and using operational definitions.
- Experimental research methods determine whether causal relationships exist between variables specified by the hypothesis being tested.
- Researchers rule out alternative explanations by using appropriate control procedures.
- Correlational research methods determine if and how much two variables are related. Correlations do not imply causation.

Visit **MyPsychLab.com** for more review and practice on the following topics:

✳ **Explore:** Correlations Do Not

◂◉ **Simulate:** Show Causation
Media Violence

Psychological Measurement

- Researchers strive to produce measures that are both reliable and valid.
- Psychological measurements include self-reports and behavioural measures.

Visit **MyPsychLab.com** for more review and practice on the following topics:

✔ **Practice:** Psychological Measurement

Ethical Issues in Human and Animal Research

- Respect for the basic rights of human and animal research participants is the obligation of all researchers.
- A variety of safeguards have been enacted to guarantee ethical and humane treatment.

Visit **MyPsychLab.com** for more review and practice on the following topics:

👁 **Watch:** Animal Rights Terrorists

Becoming a Wiser Research Consumer

- Becoming a wiser research consumer involves learning how to think critically and knowing how to evaluate claims about what research shows.

KEY TERMS

behavioural measures (p. 33)
between-subjects designs (p. 27)
case study (p. 34)
confounding variable (p. 26)
control group (p. 27)
control procedures (p. 27)
correlation coefficient (r) (p. 29)
correlational methods (p. 29)
debriefing (p. 36)
dependent variable (p. 24)
determinism (p. 22)

double-blind control (p. 27)
expectancy effects (p. 26)
experimental group (p. 27)
experimental methods (p. 25)
hypothesis (p. 22)
independent variable (p. 24)
observer bias (p. 23)
operational definition (p. 24)
placebo control (p. 27)
placebo effect (p. 26)
population (p. 27)

random assignment (p. 27)
reliability (p. 32)
representative sample (p. 27)
sample (p. 27)
self-report measures (p. 32)
standardization (p. 24)
theory (p. 22)
validity (p. 32)
variable (p. 24)
within-subjects design (p. 28)

Practice Test

1. A(n) _____ is an organized set of concepts that explains a phenomenon or set of phenomena.
   a. theory
   b. hypothesis
   c. operational definition
   d. correlation

2. Professor Peterson is testing the hypothesis that people will co-operate less when a lot of people are in a group. In the experiment he plans, he will vary the number of people in each group. That will be his _____
   a. placebo control.
   b. independent variable.
   c. double-blind control.
   d. dependent variable.

3. Rahul is serving as a research assistant. In the first phase of the experiment, Rahul gives each participant a can of cola or a can of caffeine-free cola. In the second phase of the experiment, Rahul times the participants with a stopwatch while they play a video game. It sounds like this study is lacking a(n) _____
   a. placebo control.
   b. correlational design.
   c. operational definition.
   d. double-blind control.

4. Shirley visits an antique store. The owner explains to her that the rarer an object is, the more he can charge for it. This is an example of a _____
   a. correlation coefficient.
   b. negative correlation.
   c. positive correlation.
   d. placebo effect.

5. Sally is not very interested in movies. Her friend Rob wants her attitude to be more favourable toward his all-time favourite, *Rock 'n' Roll High School*. Rob might be best off asking Sally to generate _____ characteristics for the movie.
   a. two negative
   b. five positive
   c. ten positive
   d. five negative

6. Dr. Paul is developing a new measure of hunger. He says, "I need a measure that will accurately predict how much food people will eat in their next meal." Dr. Paul's statement is about the _____ of the measure.
   a. operational definition
   b. standardization
   c. validity
   d. reliability

7. Giovanna is worried that the results of her experiment may be affected by her participants' desire to provide favourable impressions of themselves. It sounds like she might be using _____ measures.
   a. valid
   b. self-report
   c. reliable
   d. operational

8. Andrew wishes to test the hypothesis that people give more freely to charities when the weather is pleasant. To test this hypothesis, Andrew is likely to make use of _____
   a. double-blind controls.
   b. expectancy effects.
   c. laboratory observation.
   d. archival data.

9. Before you participate in an experiment, the researcher should provide you with information about procedures, potential risks, and expected benefits. This allows you to give _____
   a. a risk/gain assessment.
   b. informed debriefing.
   c. informed consent.
   d. operational definitions.

10. When members of the American Psychological Association were surveyed about the uses of nonhuman animals in research, the majority believed that _____
    a. observational studies in naturalistic settings were appropriate.
    b. nonhuman animals should never be used as replacements for human participants.
    c. intentional deception is unethical for experiments with nonhuman animals.
    d. nonhuman animals should not be used in undergraduate psychology courses.

11. Always search for _____ explanations to the obvious ones proposed.
    a. optimistic
    b. alternative
    c. negative
    d. opposite

12. When articles are submitted to most journals, they are sent out to experts for detailed analyses. This process is known as _____
    a. debriefing.
    b. informed consent.
    c. peer review.
    d. control procedures.

Essay Questions

1. Why is it so important that research procedures be open for public verifiability?

2. Suppose you wanted to measure "happiness." What might you do to assess the validity of your measure?

3. With respect to ethical principles, how are risks and gains defined in the context of psychological research?

Watch the following video by visiting the Media Library at **MyPsychLab.com.** After you have watched the video, answer the following questions:

Program 2: Understanding Research

PROGRAM REVIEW

1. Which of the following describes a field study?
   a. observing a natural, ongoing situation
   b. randomly assigning participants to treatment groups
   c. randomly assigning participants to a control group
   d. distributing a questionnaire to a large group

2. What is the purpose of a double-blind procedure?
   a. to test more than one variable at a time
   b. to repeat the results of previously published work
   c. to define a hypothesis clearly before it is tested
   d. to eliminate experimenter bias

3. According to Jerome Frank, placebos work through _____
   a. emotional arousal.
   b. brainwashing.
   c. chemical alteration of neural transmission.
   d. cognitive reassessment of the illness.

4. A report on children's television watching found that children who watch more TV have lower grades. What cause–effect conclusion are we justified in making on the basis of this study?
   a. TV watching causes low grades.
   b. Poor school performance causes children to watch more TV.
   c. None; cause–effect conclusions can never be based on one study.
   d. None; cause–effect conclusions cannot be based on correlation.

5. What was the major weakness of the Hite Report on women's attitudes toward sex and marriage?
   a. The sample was not representative.
   b. Hypotheses were not clearly stated beforehand.
   c. Experimenter bias arose because the double-blind procedure was not used.
   d. No control group was used.

6. What does the "card trick" in the program demonstrate about good science?
   a. Predictions should be made explicitly before data collection.
   b. Chance must be ruled out as an explanation.
   c. The experimenter's effect on the subject must be ruled out as an explanation.
   d. All of the above.

7. When long-term stress and lack of support on the job lead to chronic deficits in a worker's productivity and health, the worker is likely to be suffering from _____
   a. generalized anxiety disorder.   c. job burnout.
   b. post-traumatic stress.   d. insomnia.

8. How could you improve on Shere Hite's survey techniques?
   a. Redo her study using her methods, but send the survey to 10 times as many recipients.
   b. Hire one subject, pay her for a full day's work, and spend eight hours interviewing her thoroughly.
   c. Redo her study, using her methods, but send the survey to an equal number of men.
   d. Redo her study, but ensure that the percentage of respondents is much higher and much more representative of the population of interest.

9. Because of what it actually does measure, under what circumstances would an innocent person likely fail a polygraph test?
   a. if she is extremely worried about the possibility of being found guilty
   b. if she is drunk
   c. if she is acquainted with the actual guilty party
   d. if she is confident in the validity of the polygraph test

QUESTIONS TO CONSIDER

1. If some people really get healed by faith healers, why condemn the practice of faith healing?

2. What are some of the practical objections to studying mental processes?

3. What is your reaction to the guidelines prohibiting research if it would require deception and if distress is a likely result? Are there studies you think would be valuable to perform but that could not be? Could the same research questions be answered in some other way?

4. Can the results of experiments conducted mostly on college students, who are among the more highly educated members of our society, really be extended to the rest of society? Which sorts of psychological phenomena would be more likely or less likely to generalize to people of other age groups, socioeconomic statuses, and education levels?

Statistical Supplement
Understanding Statistics: Analyzing Data and Forming Conclusions

A s we noted in Chapter 2, psychologists often use statistics to make sense of the data they collect. They also use statistics to provide a quantitative basis for the conclusions they draw. Knowing something about statistics, therefore, can help you appreciate the process by which psychological knowledge is developed. On a more personal level, having a basic understanding of statistics will help you make better decisions when people use data to try to sway your opinions and actions.

Most students perceive statistics as a dry, uninteresting topic. However, statistics have many vital applications in your life. To demonstrate this point, we follow a single project from its real-world inspiration to the statistical arguments that were used to bolster general conclusions. The project began in response to the types of stories that appear on newspaper front pages, about shy individuals who became sudden murderers. Here is an example:

> *Fred Cowan was described by relatives, coworkers, and acquaintances as a "nice, quiet man," a "gentle man who loved children," and a "real pussycat." The principal of the parochial school Cowan had attended as a child reported that his former student had received A grades in courtesy, co-operation, and religion. According to a coworker, Cowan "never talked to anybody and was someone you could push around." Cowan, however, surprised everyone who knew him when, one Valentine's Day, he strolled into work toting a semi-automatic rifle and shot and killed four co-workers, a police officer, and, finally, himself.*

This story has a common plot: A shy, quiet person suddenly becomes violent, shocking everyone who knows him. What did Fred Cowan have in common with other people who are suddenly transformed from gentle and caring into violent and ruthless? What personal attributes might distinguish them from us?

A team of researchers had a hunch that there might be a link between shyness and other personal characteristics and violent behaviour (Lee, Zimbardo, & Bertholf, 1977). They began to collect some data that might reveal such a connection. The researchers reasoned that seemingly nonviolent people who suddenly commit murders are probably typically shy, nonaggressive individuals who keep their passions in check and their impulses under tight control. For most of their lives, they suffer many silent injuries. Seldom, if ever, do they express anger, regardless of how angry they really feel. On the outside, they appear unbothered, but on the inside they may be fighting to control furious rages. They give the impression that they are quiet, passive, responsible people, both as children and as adults. Because they are shy, they probably do not let others get close to them, so no one knows how they really feel. Then, suddenly, something explodes. At the slightest provocation— one more small insult, one more little rejection, one more bit of social pressure—the fuse is lit, and they release the suppressed violence that has been building up for so long. Because they did not learn to deal with interpersonal conflicts through discussion and verbal negotiation, these sudden murderers act out their anger physically.

The researchers' reasoning led them to the hypothesis that shyness would be more characteristic of sudden murderers—people who had engaged in homicide without any prior history of violence or antisocial behaviour—than it would of habitual criminal murderers—those who had committed homicide but had had a previous record of violent criminal behaviour. In addition, sudden murderers should have higher levels of control over their impulses than habitually violent people. Finally, their passivity and dependence would be manifested in more feminine and androgynous (both male and female) characteristics, as measured on a standard sex-role inventory, than those of habitual criminals.

To test their ideas about sudden murderers, the researchers obtained permission to administer psychological questionnaires to a group of inmates serving time for murder in California prisons. Nineteen inmates (all male) agreed to participate in the study. Prior to committing murder, some had committed a series of crimes, whereas the other part of the sample had had no previous criminal record. The researchers collected three kinds of data from these two types of participants: shyness scores, sex-role identification scores, and impulse control scores.

Shyness scores were collected using the Stanford Shyness Survey. The most important item on this questionnaire asked if the individual was shy; the answer could be either yes or no. Other items on the scale tapped degree and kinds of shyness and a variety of dimensions related to origins and triggers of shyness.

The second questionnaire was the Bem Sex-Role Inventory (BSRI), which presented a list of adjectives, such as aggressive and affectionate, and asked how well each adjective described the individual (Bem, 1974, 1981). Some adjectives were typically associated with being "feminine"; the total score of these adjectives was an individual's femininity score. Other adjectives were considered "masculine"; the total score of those adjectives was an individual's masculinity score. The final sex-role score, which reflected the difference between an individual's femininity and masculinity, was calculated by subtracting the masculinity score from the femininity score. A combination of the masculinity and femininity scores was an individual's androgyny score.

The third questionnaire was the Minnesota Multiphasic Personality Inventory (MMPI), which was designed to measure many different aspects of personality (see Chapter 14). The study used only the "ego-overcontrol" scale, which measures the degree to which a person acts out or controls impulses. The higher the individual's score on this scale, the more ego overcontrol the individual exhibits.

The researchers predicted that, compared with murderers with a prior criminal record, sudden murderers would (1) more often describe themselves as shy on the shyness survey, (2) select more feminine traits than masculine ones on the sex-role scale, and (3) score higher in ego overcontrol. What did they discover?

Before you find out, you need to understand some of the basic procedures that were used to analyze these data. The actual sets of data collected by the researchers are used here as the source material to teach you about some of the different types of statistical analyses and also about the kinds of conclusions they make possible.

Analyzing the Data

For most researchers in psychology, analyzing the data is an exciting step. Statistical analysis allows researchers to discover if their predictions are correct. In this section, we work step by

TABLE S.1		Raw Data from the Sudden Murderers Study	
		BSRI	**MMPI**
Inmate	**Shyness**	**Femininity-Masculinity**	**Ego Overcontrol**
Group 1: Sudden Murderers			
1	Yes	+5	17
2	No	−1	17
3	Yes	+4	13
4	Yes	+61	17
5	Yes	+19	13
6	Yes	+41	19
7	No	−29	14
8	Yes	+23	9
9	Yes	−13	11
10	Yes	+5	14
Group 2: Habitual Criminal Murderers			
11	No	−12	15
12	No	−14	11
13	Yes	−33	14
14	No	−8	10
15	No	−7	16
16	No	+3	11
17	No	−17	6
18	No	+6	9
19	No	−10	12

step through an analysis of some of the data from the Sudden Murderers Study. If you have looked ahead, you will have seen numbers and equations. Keep in mind that mathematics is a tool; mathematical symbols are a shorthand for representing ideas and conceptual operations.

The *raw data*—the actual scores or other measures obtained—from the 19 inmates in the Sudden Murderers Study are listed in **Table S.1**. As you can see, there were 10 inmates in the sudden murderers group and 9 in the habitual criminal murderers group. When first glancing at these data, any researcher would feel what you probably feel: confusion. What do all these scores mean? Do the two groups of murderers differ from one another on these various personality measures? It is difficult to know just by examining this disorganized array of numbers.

Psychologists rely on two types of statistics to help make sense of and draw meaningful conclusions from the data they collect: descriptive and inferential. **Descriptive statistics** use

descriptive statistics Statistical procedures that are used to summarize sets of scores with respect to central tendencies, variability, and correlations.

mathematical procedures in an objective, uniform way to describe different aspects of numerical data. If you have ever computed your academic average, you have used descriptive statistics. **Inferential statistics** use probability theory to make sound decisions about which results might have occurred simply through chance variation.

DESCRIPTIVE STATISTICS

Descriptive statistics provide a summary picture of patterns in the data. They are used to describe sets of scores collected from one experimental participant or, more often, from different groups of participants. They are also used to describe relationships among variables. Thus, instead of trying to keep in mind all the scores obtained by each of the participants, researchers get indexes of the scores that are most *typical* for each group. They also get measures of how *variable* the scores are with respect to the typical score—whether the scores are spread out or clustered closely together. Let's see how researchers derive these measures.

Frequency Distributions How would you summarize the data in Table S.1? To present a clear picture of how the various scores are distributed, we can draw up a **frequency distribution**—a summary of how frequently each of the various scores occurs. The shyness data are easy to summarize. Of the 19 scores, there are 9 *yes* and 10 *no* responses; almost all the *yes* responses are in Group 1, and almost all the *no* responses are in Group 2. However, the ego-overcontrol and sex-role scores do not fall into easy *yes* and *no* categories. To see how frequency distributions of numerical responses can allow informative comparisons between groups, we will focus on the sex-role scores.

Consider the sex-role data in Table S.1. The highest score is +61 (most feminine) and the lowest is −33 (most masculine). Of the 19 scores, 9 are positive and 10 negative. This means that 9 of the murderers described themselves as relatively feminine and 10 as relatively masculine. But how are these scores distributed between the groups? The first step in preparing a frequency distribution for a set of numerical data is to *rank order* the scores from highest to lowest. The rank ordering for the sex-role scores is shown in **Table S.2**. The second step is to group these rank-ordered scores into a smaller number of categories called *intervals*. In this study, 10 categories were used, with each category covering 10 possible scores. The third step is to construct a frequency distribution table, listing the intervals from highest to lowest and noting the *frequencies*, the number of scores within each interval. Our frequency distribution shows us that the sex-role scores are largely between −20 and +9 (see **Table S.3**). The majority of the inmates' scores did not deviate much from zero. That is, they were neither strongly positive nor strongly negative.

The data are now arranged in useful categories. The researchers' next step was to display the distributions in graphic form.

inferential statistics Statistical procedures that allow researchers to determine whether the results they obtain support their hypotheses or can be attributed just to chance variation.

frequency distribution A summary of how frequently each score appears in a set of observations.

TABLE S.2	Rank Ordering of Sex-Role Difference Scores	
Highest	+61	−1
	+41	−7
	+23	−8
	+19	−10
	+6	−12
	+5	−13
	+5	−14
	+4	−17
	+3	−29
		−33 Lowest

Note: + scores are more feminine; − scores are more masculine.

Graphs Distributions are often easier to understand when they are displayed in graphs. The simplest type of graph is a *bar graph*. Bar graphs allow you to see patterns in the data. We can use a bar graph to illustrate how many more sudden murderers than habitual criminal murderers described themselves as shy (see **Figure S.1**).

For more complex data, such as the sex-role scores, we can use a *histogram*, which is similar to a bar graph except that the categories are intervals-number categories instead of the name categories used in the bar graph. A histogram gives a visual picture of the number of scores in a distribution that is in each interval. It is easy to see from the sex-role scores shown in the histograms (in **Figure S.2**) that the distributions of scores are different for the two groups of murderers.

TABLE S.3	Frequency Distribution of Sex-Role Difference Scores
Category	**Frequency**
+60 to +69	1
+50 to +59	0
+40 to +49	1
+30 to +39	0
+20 to +29	1
+10 to +19	1
0 to +9	5
−10 to −1	4
−20 to −11	4
−30 to −21	1
−40 to −31	1

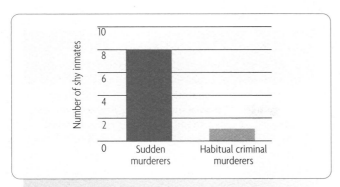

FIGURE S.1 Shyness for Two Groups of Murderers (Bar Graph)

You can see from Figures S.1 and S.2 that the overall distributions of responses conform to two of the researchers' hypotheses. Sudden murderers were more likely to describe themselves as shy and were more likely to use feminine traits to describe themselves than were habitual criminal murderers.

Measures of Central Tendency So far, we have formed a general picture of how the scores are *distributed*. Tables and graphs increase our general understanding of research results, but we want to know more—for example, the one score that is most typical of the group as a whole. This score becomes particularly useful when we compare two or more groups; it is much easier to compare the typical scores of two groups than their entire distributions. A single *representative* score that can be used as an index of the most typical score obtained by a group of participants is called a **measure of central tendency**. (It is located in the centre of the distribution, and other scores tend to cluster around it.) Typically, psychologists use three different measures of central tendency: the *mode*, the *median*, and the *mean*.

The **mode** is the score that occurs more often than any other. For the measure of shyness, the modal response of the sudden murderers was *yes*—8 out of 10 said they were shy. Among habitual criminal murderers, the modal response was *no*. The sex-role scores for the sudden murderers had a mode of +5. Can you figure out what the mode of their ego-overcontrol scores is? The mode is the easiest index of central tendency to determine, but it is often the least useful. You will see one reason for this relative lack of usefulness if you notice that only one overcontrol score lies above the mode of 17, and six lie below it. Although 17 is the score obtained most often, it may not fit your idea of "typical" or "central."

The **median** is more clearly a central score; it separates the upper half of the scores in a distribution from the lower half. The number of scores larger than the median is the same as the number that is smaller. When there are an odd number of scores, the median is the middle score; when there is an even number of scores, researchers most often average the two scores at the middle. For example, if you rank-order the sex-role scores of only the habitual criminal murderers on a separate piece of paper, you will see that the median score is −10, with four scores higher and four scores lower. For the sudden murderers, the median is +5—the average of the fifth and sixth scores, each of which happens to be +5. The median is not affected by extreme scores. For example, even if the sudden murderers' highest sex-role score had been +129 instead of +61, the median value would still have been +5. That score would still separate the upper half of the data from the lower half. The median is quite simply the score in the middle of the distribution.

The **mean** is what most people think of when they hear the word *average*. It is also the statistic most often used to describe a set of data. To calculate the mean, you add up all the scores in a distribution and divide by the total number of scores. The operation is summarized by the following formula:

$$M = (\Sigma X)/N$$

In this formula, M is the mean, X is each individual score, Σ (the Greek letter sigma) is the summation of what immediately follows it, and N is the total number of scores. Because the summation of all the sex-role scores (ΣX) is 115, and the total number of scores (N) is 10, the mean (M) of the sex-role scores of the sudden murderers would be calculated as follows:

$$M = 115/10 = 11.5$$

---

measure of central tendency A statistic, such as a mean, median, or mode, that provides one score as representative of a set of observations.

mode The score appearing most frequently in a set of observations; a measure of central tendency.

median The score in a distribution above and below which lie 50 percent of the other scores; a measure of central tendency.

mean The arithmetic average of a group of scores; the most commonly used measure of central tendency.

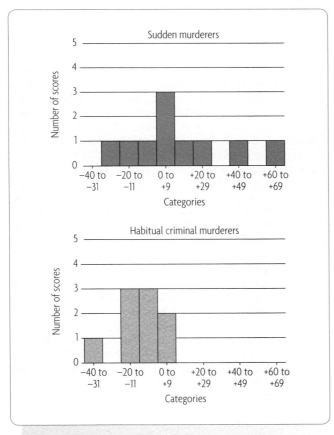

FIGURE S.2 Sex-Role Scores (Histograms)

Try to calculate their mean overcontrol scores yourself. You should come up with a mean of 14.4.

Unlike the median, the mean *is* affected by the specific values of all scores in the distribution, so changing the value of an extreme score changes the value of the mean. For example, if the sex-role score of inmate 4 were +101 instead of +61, the mean for the whole group would increase from 11.5 to 15.5.

Variability In addition to knowing which score is most representative of the distribution as a whole, it is useful to know how representative that measure of central tendency really is. Are most of the other scores fairly close to it or widely spread out? **Measures of variability** are statistics that describe the distribution of scores around some measure of central tendency.

Can you see why measures of variability are important? An example may help. Suppose you are a grade-school teacher. It is the beginning of the school year, and you will be teaching reading to a group of 30 Grade 2 students. Knowing that the average child in the class can now read a Grade 1 book will help you to plan your lessons. You could plan better, however, if you knew how *similar* or how *divergent* the reading abilities of the 30 children were. Are they all at about the same level (low variability)? If so, then you can plan a fairly standard Grade 2 lesson. What if several can read advanced material and others can barely read at all (high variability)? Now the mean level is not so representative of the entire class, and you will have to plan a variety of lessons to meet the children's varied needs.

The simplest measure of variability is the **range**, the difference between the highest and the lowest values in a frequency distribution. For the sudden murderers' sex-role scores, the range is 90: $(+61) - (-29)$. The range of their overcontrol scores is 10: $(+19) - (+9)$. To compute the range, you need to know only two of the scores: the highest and the lowest.

The range is simple to compute, but psychologists often prefer measures of variability that are more sensitive and that take into account *all* the scores in a distribution, not just the extremes. One widely used measure is the **standard deviation (SD)**, a measure of variability that indicates the *average* difference between the scores and their mean. To figure out the standard deviation of a distribution, you need to know the mean of the distribution and the individual scores. The general procedure involves subtracting the value of each individual score from the mean and then determining the average of those mean deviations. Here is the formula:

$$SD = \sqrt{\Sigma(X - M)^2/N}$$

measures of variability A statistic, such as a range or standard deviation, that indicates how tightly the scores in a set of observations cluster together.

range The difference between the highest and the lowest scores in a set of observations; the simplest measure of variability.

standard deviation (SD) The average difference of a set of scores from their mean; a measure of variability.

correlation coefficient (r) A statistic that indicates the degree of relationship between two variables.

TABLE S.4 Calculating the Standard Deviation of Sudden Murderers' Ego-Overcontrol Scores

Score (X)	Deviation (score minus mean) (X − M)	Deviations Squared (score minus mean)^2 (X − M)^2
17	2.6	6.76
17	2.6	6.76
13	−1.4	1.96
17	2.6	6.76
13	1.4	1.96
19	4.6	21.16
14	−.4	.16
9	−5.4	29.16
11	−3.4	11.56
14	−.4	16

$$\text{Standard deviation} = SD = \sqrt{\frac{\Sigma(X - M)^2}{N}} \quad 86.40 = \Sigma(X - M)^2$$

$$\sqrt{\frac{86.40}{10}} = \sqrt{8.64} = 2.94$$

$$SD = 2.94$$

You should recognize most of the symbols from the formula for the mean. The expression $(X - M)$ means "individual score minus the mean" and is commonly called the *deviation score*. The mean is subtracted from each score, and each resulting score is squared (to eliminate negative values). Then the mean of these deviations is calculated by summing them up (Σ) and dividing by the number of observations (N). The symbol $\sqrt{}$ tells you to take the square root of the enclosed value to offset the previous squaring. The standard deviation of the overcontrol scores for the sudden murderers is calculated in **Table S.4.** Recall that the mean of these scores is 14.4. This, then, is the value that must be subtracted from each score to obtain the corresponding deviation scores.

The standard deviation tells us how variable a set of scores is. The larger the standard deviation, the more spread out the scores. The standard deviation of the sex-role scores for the sudden murderers is 24.6, but the standard deviation for the habitual criminals is only 10.7. This shows that there was less variability in the habitual criminals group. Their scores clustered more closely about their mean than did those of the sudden murderers. When the standard deviation is small, the mean is a good representative index of the entire distribution. When the standard deviation is large, the mean is less typical of the whole group.

Correlation Another useful tool in interpreting psychological data is the **correlation coefficient**, a measure of the nature and strength of the relationship between two variables (such as height and weight or sex-role score and ego-overcontrol score). It tells us the extent to which scores on one measure are associated with scores on the other. If people with high scores on one variable tend to have *high* scores on the other variable, then the correlation coefficient will be positive (greater than 0). If, however, most people with high scores on one variable tend to have *low* scores on the other variable, then the correlation coefficient will be negative (less than 0). If there is no consistent relationship between the scores, the correlation will be close to 0 (see also Chapter 2).

Correlation coefficients range from $+1$ (perfect positive correlation) through 0 to -1 (perfect negative correlation). The further a coefficient is from 0 in *either* direction, the more closely related the two variables are, positively or negatively. Higher coefficients permit better predictions of one variable, given knowledge of the other.

In the Sudden Murderers Study, the correlation coefficient (symbolized as r) between the sex-role scores and the overcontrol scores turns out to be $+0.35$. Thus the sex-role scores and the overcontrol scores are positively correlated. In general, individuals seeing themselves as more feminine also tend to be higher in overcontrol. However, the correlation is modest, compared with the highest possible value, $+1$, so we know that there are many exceptions to this relationship. If we had also measured the self-esteem of these inmates and found a correlation of -0.68 between overcontrol scores and self-esteem, it would mean that there was a negative correlation. If this were the case, we could say that the individuals who had high overcontrol scores tended to be lower in self-esteem. It would be a stronger relationship than the relationship between the sex-role scores and the overcontrol scores because -0.68 is farther from 0, the point of no relationship, than is $+0.35$.

INFERENTIAL STATISTICS

We have used a number of descriptive statistics to characterize the data from the Sudden Murderers Study, and now we have an idea of the pattern of results. However, some basic questions remain unanswered. Recall that the research team hypothesized that sudden murderers would be shyer, more overcontrolled, and more feminine than habitual criminal murderers. After we have used descriptive statistics to compare average responses and variability in the two groups, it appears that there are some differences between the groups. But how do we know if the differences are large enough to be meaningful? If we repeated this study with other sudden murderers and other habitual criminal murderers, would we expect to find the same pattern of results, or could these results have been an outcome of chance? If we could somehow measure the entire population of sudden murderers and habitual criminal murderers, would the means and standard deviations be the same as those we found for these small samples?

Inferential statistics are used to answer these kinds of questions. They tell us which inferences we can make from our samples and which conclusions we can legitimately draw from our data. Inferential statistics use probability theory to determine the likelihood that a set of data occurred simply by chance variation.

The Normal Curve To understand how inferential statistics work, we must look first at the special properties of a distribution called the *normal curve*. When data on a variable (for example, height, IQ, or overcontrol) are collected from a large number of individuals, the numbers obtained often fit a curve roughly similar to that shown in **Figure S.3**. Notice that the curve is symmetrical (the left half is a mirror image of the right)

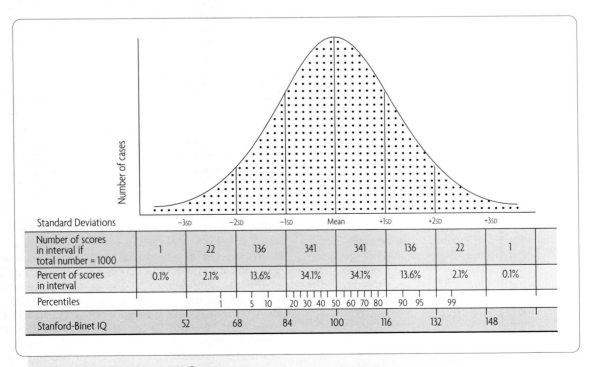

Standard Deviations	−3SD	−2SD	−1SD	Mean	+1SD	+2SD	+3SD	
Number of scores in interval if total number = 1000	1	22	136	341	341	136	22	1
Percent of scores in interval	0.1%	2.1%	13.6%	34.1%	34.1%	13.6%	2.1%	0.1%
Percentiles			1	5 10	20 30 40 50 60 70 80	90 95	99	
Stanford-Binet IQ		52	68	84	100	116	132	148

FIGURE S.3   A Normal Curve

and bell-shaped high in the middle, where most scores are, and lower the further you get from the mean. This type of curve is called a **normal curve**, or *normal distribution*. (A *skewed* distribution is one in which scores cluster toward one end instead of around the middle.)

In a normal curve, the median, mode, and mean values are the same. A specific percentage of the scores can be predicted to fall under different sections of the curve. Figure S.3 shows IQ scores on the Stanford–Binet Intelligence Test. These scores have a mean of 100 and a standard deviation of 16. If you indicate standard deviations as distances from the mean along the baseline, you find that a little over 68 percent of all the scores are between the mean of 100 and one standard deviation above and below—between IQs of 84 and 116. Roughly another 27 percent of the scores are found between the first and second standard deviations below the mean (IQ scores between 68 and 84) and above the mean (IQ scores between 116 and 132). Less than 5 percent of the scores fall beyond the second standard deviation above and below the mean, and very few scores are above the third standard deviation—only about one quarter of 1 percent.

Inferential statistics indicate the probability that the particular sample of scores obtained is actually related to whatever you are attempting to measure or whether it could have occurred by chance. For example, it is more likely that someone would have an IQ of 105 than an IQ of 140, but an IQ of 140 is more probable than one of 35.

A normal curve is also obtained by collecting a series of measurements whose differences are due only to chance. If you flip a coin 10 times in a row and record the number of heads and tails, you will probably get 5 of each—most of the time. If you keep flipping the coin for 100 sets of 10 tosses, you probably will get a few sets with all heads or no heads, more sets where the number is between these extremes, and, most typically, more sets where the number is about half each way. If you made a graph of your 1000 tosses, you would get one that closely fits a normal curve, such as the one in the figure.

Statistical Significance A researcher who finds a difference between the mean scores for two samples must ask if it is a *real* difference or if it occurred simply because of chance. Because chance differences have a normal distribution, a researcher can use the normal curve to answer this question.

A simple example helps illustrate the point. Suppose your psychology professor wants to see if the sex of a person overseeing a test makes a difference in the test scores obtained from male and from female students. For this purpose, the professor randomly assigns half of the students to a male teaching assistant and half to a female assistant. The professor then compares the mean score of each group. The two mean scores would probably be fairly similar; any slight difference would most likely be due to chance. Why? Because if only chance is operating and both groups are from the same population (no difference), then the means of male assistant and female assistant samples should be fairly close most of the time. From the

percentages of scores found in different parts of the normal distribution, you know that less than a third of the scores in the male assistant condition should be greater than one standard deviation above or below the female assistant mean. The chances of getting a male assistant mean score more than three standard deviations above or below most of your female assistant means would be very small. A professor who *did* get a difference that great would feel fairly confident that the difference is a real one and is somehow related to the sex of the assistant who oversaw the test. The next question would be *how* that variable influences test scores.

If male and female students were randomly assigned to each type of assistant, it would be possible to analyze whether an overall difference found between the assistant was consistent across both student groups or was limited to only one sex. Imagine the data show that males grade female students higher than do females, but both grade male students the same. Your professor could use a statistical inference procedure to estimate the probability that an observed difference could have occurred by chance. This computation is based on the size of the difference and the spread of the scores.

By common agreement, psychologists and other scientists accept a difference as "real" when the probability that it might be due to chance is less than 5 in 100 (indicated by the notation $p < .05$). A **significant difference** is one that meets this criterion. However, in some cases, even stricter probability levels are used, such as $p < .01$ (less than 1 in 100) and $p < .001$ (less than 1 in 1000).

With a statistically significant difference, a researcher can draw a conclusion about the behaviour under investigation. There are many different types of tests for estimating the statistical significance of sets of data. The type of test chosen for a particular case depends on the design of the study, the form of the data, and the size of the groups. We mention only one of the most common tests, the *t*-test, which may be used when an investigator wants to know if the difference between the means of two groups is statistically significant.

We can use a *t*-test to see if the mean sex-role score of the sudden murderers is significantly different from that of the habitual criminal murderers. The *t*-test uses a mathematical procedure to confirm the conclusion you may have drawn from Figure S.2: The distributions of sex-role scores for the two groups is sufficiently different to be "real." If we carry out the appropriate calculations—which evaluate the difference between the two means as a function of the variability around those two means—we find that there is a very slim chance, less than 5 in 100 ($p < .05$), of obtaining such a large *t* value if no true difference exists. The difference is, therefore, statistically significant, and we can feel more confident that there is a real difference between the two groups. The sudden murderers *did* rate themselves as more feminine than did the habitual criminal murderers. On the other hand, the difference between the two groups of murderers in overcontrol scores turns out not to be statistically significant ($p < .10$), so we must be more cautious in making claims about this difference. There is a trend in the predicted direction—the difference is one that would occur by chance only 10 times in 100. However, the difference is not within the standard 5-in-100 range. (The difference in shyness, analyzed using another statistical test for frequency of scores, is highly significant.)

So, by using inferential statistics, we are able to answer some of the basic questions with which we began, and we are

---

normal curve The symmetrical curve that represents the distribution of scores on many psychological attributes; allows researchers to make judgments of how unusual an observation or result is.

significant difference A difference between experimental groups or conditions that would have occurred by chance less than an accepted criterion; in psychology, the criterion most often used is a probability of less than 5 times out of 100, or p < .05.

closer to understanding the psychology of people who suddenly change from mild-mannered, shy individuals into murderers. Any conclusion, however, is only a statement of the probable relationship between the events that were investigated; it is never one of certainty. Truth in science is provisional, always open to revision by later data from better studies developed from better hypotheses.

You might take a moment to consider what else you would like to know, to put these data in a richer context. For example, you might want to know how both types of murderers differ from individuals who have never committed murders on measures such as their sex-role scores. If we collected new data we could use descriptive and inferential statistics to answer such questions as whether all murderers are, on such dimensions, different from those who do not commit murders. What might you expect?

Becoming a Wise Consumer of Statistics

Now that we have considered what statistics are, how they are used, and what they mean, we must talk briefly about how they can be misused. Many people accept unsupported so-called facts that are bolstered by the air of authority of a statistic. Others choose to believe or disbelieve what the statistics say without having any idea of how to question the numbers that are presented in support of a product, politician, or proposal. At the end of Chapter 2, we gave you some suggestions about how you can become a wiser research consumer. Based on this brief survey of statistics, we can extend that advice to situations in which people make specific statistical claims.

There are many ways to give a misleading impression using statistics. The decisions made at all stages of research—who the participants are, how the study is designed, what statistics are selected, and how they are used—can have a profound effect on the conclusions that can be drawn from the data.

The group of participants can make a large difference that can easily remain undetected when the results are reported. For example, a survey of views on abortion rights will yield very different results if conducted in a small conservative community rather than at a university in Vancouver, Toronto, or Montreal. Likewise, a pro-life group surveying the opinions of its membership will very likely arrive at conclusions that differ from those obtained by the same survey conducted by a pro-choice group.

Even if the participants are randomly selected and not biased by the methodology, the statistics can produce misleading results if the assumptions of the statistics are violated. For example, suppose 20 people take an IQ test; 19 of them receive scores between 90 and 110, and 1 receives a score of 220. The mean of the group will be strongly elevated by that one outlying high score. With this sort of a data set, it would be much more accurate to present the median or the mode, which would accurately report the group's generally average intelligence, rather than the mean, which would make it look as if the average member of this group had a high IQ. This sort of bias is especially powerful in a small sample. If, however, the number of people in this group were 2000 instead of 20, the one extreme outlier would make virtually no difference, and the mean would be a legitimate summary of the group's intelligence.

One good way to avoid falling for this sort of deception is to check on the size of the sample. Large samples are less likely to be misleading than small ones. Another check is to look at the median or the mode as well as the mean. The results can be interpreted with more confidence if they are similar than if they are different. Always closely examine the methodology and results of the research reported. Check to see if the researchers report their sample size, measures of variability, and significance levels. Try to find out if the methods they used measure accurately and consistently whatever they claim to be investigating.

Statistics are the backbone of psychological research. They are used to understand observations and to determine whether the findings are, in fact, correct. Through the methods we have described, psychologists can prepare a frequency distribution of data and find the central tendencies and variability of the scores. They can use the correlation coefficient to determine the strength and direction of the association between sets of scores. Finally, psychological investigators can then find out how representative the observations are and whether they are significantly different from what would be observed among the general population. Statistics can also be used poorly or deceptively, misleading those who do not understand them. But when statistics are applied correctly and ethically, they allow researchers to expand the body of psychological knowledge.

Visit **MyPsychLab.com** for more review and practice on the following topics:

◀●) **Simulate:** Doing Simple Statistics

KEY TERMS

correlation coefficient (*r*) (p. 46)
descriptive statistics (p. 43)
frequency distribution (p. 44)
inferential statistics (p. 44)
mean (p. 45)
measure of central tendency (p. 45)
measures of variability (p. 46)
median (p. 45)
mode (p. 45)
normal curve (p. 48)
range (p. 46)
significant difference (p. 48)
standard deviation (SD) (p. 46)

3

Evolutionary Psychology

What makes us different from each other, but also so very similar? Next time you are sitting in a classroom, look around you: You will notice that there are many similarities between you and other people in the room—but you will also realize that there are a variety of differences in how each of you speaks, in the skill levels in the class, and even in levels of happiness. Individuals in a population of similar organisms clearly differ in meaningful ways. At home or at a family gathering, you may notice that you share similarities with some family members. Not only do you look similar, but you frequently act similarly as well. People may even mistake you for your mom or dad when you answer the phone. You may have already realized that you share many beliefs with your parents and possibly even your grandparents. Perhaps you share the same moral values, or have similar political orientations, or like the same food. Although we have many unique characteristics and thoughts, there is a historical basis to what we look like and to much of how we think. Understanding the human mind and brain mechanisms over time in living organisms is the goal of **evolutionary psychology**.

Curiosity about the mind is not new. The ancient Greeks studied the mind and wrote volumes on the themes of how the mind works, developing hypotheses about where it was located. More recently, as you have learned, there have been newer theories on how the mind works from Freud, Skinner, and researchers studying the brain. Evolutionary psychologists, unlike many of the other psychologists who have developed theories on the mind, use a unifying theoretical framework that focuses on principles of evolution. Although you are probably aware of the basic assumptions of evolution—that we and other organisms have evolved and changed over time—you may be less aware of how important evolutionary theory is to psychology. The discipline of evolutionary psychology aims to pull together findings from all themes in psychology, including many you have already learned about and will learn about in future chapters, to create a more complete understanding of the human mind.

The goal of this chapter is to introduce the foundations of evolutionary psychology and allow you to understand how some of the basic principles of evolution and evolutionary biology were critical in the emergence of evolutionary psychology. To approach this goal, we will first introduce you to a number of historical figures who developed some of the key ideas that contributed to evolutionary psychology. We then will provide a summary of the more contemporary research in this area. Finally, we will attempt to provide a number of examples of how research in the area of evolutionary psychology is providing insight into human behaviour and mind.

Foundations of Evolutionary Psychology

In Chapter 1, we defined one of the major goals of psychology as being the discovery of the causes underlying the variety of human behaviours. An important dimension of causal explanation within psychology is defined by the end points of *nature* versus *nurture,* or *heredity* versus *environment.* This question of whether we are a product of our genes or our environment has been a fundamental and recurrent debate in psychology. Consider, as we did in Chapter 1, the question of the roots of aggressive behaviour. You might imagine that individuals are aggressive by virtue of some aspect of their biological makeup: They may have inherited a tendency toward violence from one of their parents. Alternatively, you might imagine that all humans are about equally predisposed to aggression and that the degree of aggression that individuals display arises in response to features of the environment in which they are raised. The correct answer to this question has a profound impact on how society treats individuals who are overly aggressive—by focusing resources on changing certain environments or on changing aspects of the people themselves. You need to be able to discriminate the forces of heredity from the forces of environment.

Features of environments can be directly observed, and it is often easy to understand how they affect people's behaviour. You can, for example, actually watch a parent acting aggressively toward a child and wonder what consequences such treatment might have on the child's later tendency toward aggression; you can observe the overcrowded and impoverished settings in which some children grow up and wonder whether these features of the environment lead to aggressive behaviours. The biological forces that shape behaviour, by comparison, are never plainly visible to the naked eye. To make the biology of behaviour more understandable to you, we will begin by describing some of the basic principles that shape a species's potential collection of behaviours—elements of the theory of evolution—and then describe how behavioural variation is passed from generation to generation.

BEFORE DARWIN

One of the first scientists to recognize that the study of life should be a distinct science was **Jean Pierre Antoine de Monet de Lamarck** (1744–1829). Lamarck began to use the word *biologie* to describe this science, and now we routinely use the words *biology* and *biological* to refer to the study of living organisms. In his book published first in 1809, *Philosophie zoologique,* Lamarck indicated his thoughts on two major causes of changes in organisms. First, Lamarck suggested a natural tendency for organisms to progress from one form to a more complex one. Second, he proposed that there was an inheritance of acquired characteristics. Lamarck hypothesized that animals needed to struggle to survive in a difficult world and that the struggle resulted in a release of fluid from nerves that enlarged the organs involved in the struggle. The struggles that Lamarck referred to were not necessarily physical fights between animals, but the more daily struggles all animals faced, such as the struggle to obtain food. Previous authors had indicated that animals outnumbered the resources they needed to survive and reproduce, and Lamarck hypothesized about the impact this shortage of resources would have. As an example of his theories of inheritance, Lamarck pointed to giraffes. He suggested that their long necks—a truly unusual feature in a mammal—were an adaptation that resulted from the animals' attempts to eat leaves higher and higher on the branches of trees. Further, he suggested, the neck changes were passed down from generation to generation of giraffes.

---

evolutionary psychology The study of behaviour and mind using the principles of evolutionary theory.

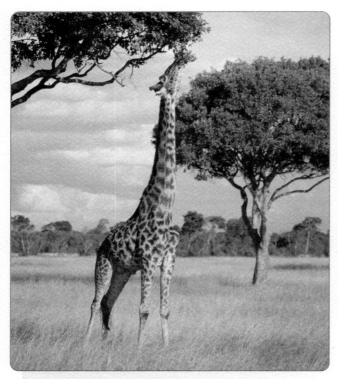

Did the giraffe's long neck evolve so the animal could eat leaves higher in the trees?

What observations ultimately led Charles Darwin to propose the theory of evolution?

Alfred Wallace

EVOLUTION AND NATURAL SELECTION

In 1831, **Charles Darwin**, fresh out of university with a degree in theology, set sail from England on HMS *Beagle*, an ocean research vessel, for a five-year cruise to survey the coast of South America. During the trip, Darwin collected everything that crossed his path: marine animals, birds, insects, plants, fossils, seashells, and rocks. He spent many years thinking about his collection, but was slow to publish his data and theories. In 1858, however, Darwin received a draft manuscript from English naturalist Alfred Russel Wallace, which outlined Wallace's own evolutionary theories. Although they used different terms, Darwin saw that they both defined change over time as a result of selective pressure from the environment. Darwin, concerned that he was going to be second in publishing his own theories on evolution, arranged with influential friends, Joseph Hooker and Charles Lyell, for his writings and those of Wallace to be presented at the Linnaean Society of London in 1858; together they were issued as a joint publication in the proceedings of the society in July of that same year. Although Wallace's writings had theoretically come first, he had not intended his correspondence to Darwin to be published. Darwin was easily given priority among scientific circles for the theory. Darwin then quickly organized his extensive notes and vague speculations about change over time, on which he had been working for the previous 20 years, into an explicit theory in the book *The Origin of Species,* published in 1859. In this work, for which Darwin is most remembered, Darwin set forth what could be claimed to be science's grandest theory: the evolution of life on planet Earth.

It is noteworthy that Charles Lyell, who helped secure Darwin's place in history as the creator of the theory of natural selection, had published his own theories on gradual change over time producing dramatic changes, as a result of his own geological research. Though Darwin was not the first to propose some of these theories on evolution, he caught the attention of many, including highly respected scientists. As such, Darwin's theory had a significant impact on the future of psychology and other scientific disciplines. Darwin's other notes from his HMS

Cartoon of Darwin with an ape's body

Beagle trip became the foundation for his books on topics ranging from geology to emotion to zoology.

Natural Selection Darwin developed his theory of evolution by reflecting on the species of animals he had encountered on his voyage. One of the many places the *Beagle* visited was the Galápagos Islands, a volcanic archipelago off the west coast of South America. These islands are a haven for diverse forms of wildlife, including 13 species of finches, now known as Darwin's finches. Darwin wondered how so many different species of finches could have come to inhabit the islands. He reasoned that they could not have migrated from the mainland because those species did not exist there. He knew about selective breeding, where careful breeding could produce desirable forms and functions in animals. Although this was common in cattle and dogs, Darwin believed the changes found in nature to be under the influence of other mechanisms of change. He suggested, therefore, that the variety of species of finches, and other organisms, reflected the operation of a process he came to call **natural selection**.

Darwin's theory suggests that each species of finch emerged from a common set of ancestors. Originally, a small flock of finches found their way to one of the islands; they mated among themselves and eventually their number multiplied. Over time, some finches migrated to different islands in the archipelago. What happened next was the process of natural selection. Food resources and living conditions—*habitats*—vary considerably from island to island. Some of the islands are lush with berries and seeds, others are covered with cacti, and others have plenty of insects. At first, the populations on different islands were similar—there was *variation* among the groups of finches on each island. However, because food resources on the islands were limited, birds were more likely to survive and reproduce if the shape of their beak was well suited to the food sources available on the island. For example, birds that migrated to islands rich in berries and seeds were more likely to survive and reproduce if they had thick beaks. On those islands, birds with thinner, more pointed beaks, unsuitable for crushing or breaking open seeds, died. The environment of each island determined which among the original population of finches would live and reproduce and which would more likely perish, leaving no offspring. Over time, this led to very different populations on each island and permitted the different species of Darwin's finches to evolve from the original ancestral group.

In general, the theory of natural selection suggests that organisms well adapted to their environment, whatever it happens to be, will produce more offspring than those less well adapted. Over time, organisms possessing traits more favourable for survival will become more numerous than those not possessing these traits. In evolutionary terms, an individual's success is measured by the number of offspring he or she produces.

Contemporary research has shown that natural selection can have dramatic effects, even in the short run. In a series of studies by **Peter and Rosemary Grant** and others (B. R. Grant & P. Grant, 1989; P. R. Grant & B. R. Grant, 2002; J. Weiner, 1994) involving several species of Darwin's finches, records were kept of rainfall, food supply, and the population size of these finches on one of the Galápagos Islands. In 1976, the population numbered well over 1000 birds. The following year brought a murderous drought that wiped out most of the food supply. The smallest seeds were the first to be depleted, leaving only larger and tougher seeds. The year of the drought, the finch population decreased by more than 80 percent; smaller finches with smaller beaks died at a higher frequency than larger finches with thicker beaks. Consequently, as Darwin would have predicted, the larger birds became more numerous in the following years. Why? Only these finches, with their larger bodies and

---

natural selection Darwin's theory that favourable adaptations to features of the environment allow some members of a species to reproduce more successfully than others.

The Havanese was popular among the Cuban elite. The Cuban Revolution of 1959 almost destroyed the breed when the aristocracy fled the country, leaving their dogs behind. In the 1990s, a small number of dogs that were thought to be purebred were found in Cuba. A careful breeding program has resulted in increased numbers of Havanese in a form consistent with those seen before 1959 in Cuba.

A group of finches. Characteristics in these birds developed as a result of natural selection.

thicker beaks, were fit enough to respond to the environmental change caused by the drought. They were the ones most adaptable to deal with the change and to survive! Interestingly, in 1983, rain was plentiful, and seeds, especially the smaller ones, became abundant. As a result, smaller birds survived better than larger birds, probably because their beaks were better suited for pecking the smaller seeds. The Grants' study shows that natural selection can have noticeable effects even over short periods. Researchers continue to document the impact of environments on natural selection in diverse species, including the European fruit fly (Huey, Gilchrist, Carlson, Berrigan, & Serra, 2000) and the stickleback fish (Rundle, Nagel, Boughman, & Schluter, 2000).

Although Darwin provided the foundation for evolutionary theory, researchers continue to study mechanisms of evolutionary change that fell beyond the bounds of Darwin's ideas (Gould, 2002). For example, one important question that Darwin was unable to address fully was how populations with common ancestors evolve so that one species becomes two. As you have already seen in the Grants' research with Darwin's finches, species can change rapidly in response to local environments. One explanation for the appearance of new species is that they emerge when two populations from an original

species become geographically separate—and therefore evolve in response to different environmental events. However, contemporary research on evolution has uncovered many examples of new species that have emerged without that type of geographic isolation (Barton, 2000). Researchers are pursuing a variety of explanations for how species arise under those circumstances. These explanations focus, for example, on how subgroups within a species evolve different cues—such as the chemical signals fruit flies use—to recognize appropriate mates (Higgie, Chenoweth, & Blows, 2000). If, over time, those cues become distinct, separate species may emerge.

Darwin's Theory of Sexual Selection You may have noticed that many animals have characteristics that do not seem to be absolutely essential for survival—and may even put them at risk. The elaborate coloured feathers of the male mallard duck, for example, may make the males more visible to predators than the dull brown plumage of the females. Darwin also noted that there were several characteristics in the animal kingdom that contradicted his theory of natural selection. The vibrant and luminescent plumage of a peacock, for example, seems to have little to do with survival. In response to these contradictions to natural selection, Darwin proposed a second evolutionary theory called the theory of **sexual selection**. There are two means by which sexual selection can operate. The first suggests that there is competition between members of the same sex for mating access to members of the other sex. The most obvious example can be found in horned animals, where males lock horns in combat. The victor gains access to the female, and the loser typically fails to mate. Accordingly, qualities that lead to success in the same-sex contests are passed on, whereas qualities associated with losing fail to be passed on.

The second means by which sexual selection can operate is related to mate choice. When the members of one sex desire a selection of qualities in a member of the opposite sex, the individuals with those qualities will be selected as mates. Evolutionary change, in this case, occurs primarily as a result of desired mate qualities being passed on to future generations. It is interesting to note that Darwin called the latter process *female choice*, because he found that females in the animal kingdom were choosing the males based on their characteristics. Thus, brilliant and luminescent feathers in many avian species

sexual selection Darwin's theory that selecting a mate based on features that are attractive could lead to an increase in those features within a species, whereas unattractive features would decrease.

FIGURE 3.1 Sexual Selection
The feathers of the male duck are much brighter than those of the female, which are often brown. Can you tell which of these ducks are male and which are female?

(see **Figure 3.1**) evolved over time because females preferred to mate with the more colourful males.

A number of theories about mate selection which result from evolutionary theory can be tested experimentally. Evolutionary theory suggests an evolved predisposition for courtship rituals and for seeking a mate. Some of these predispositions are likely to be very specific and context-sensitive. A contextual cue that has been of interest to some researchers is whether mating preferences refer to a brief sexual encounter or a long-term relationship, like marriage. A prediction from evolutionary theory is that males would show an evolved predisposition for younger females for long-term mating, but that age would be less relevant for a brief sexual encounter. The prediction really relies on the idea that a younger mate will have many more years of childbearing ability than an older one. **James Young**, **Joseph Critelli**, and **Kathy Keith** (2005) sought to examine whether male university students in introductory psychology classes would follow this prediction. The male students were given a survey in which they answered a number of questions related to their age preference for females within a number of social scenarios. Since cultural norms impact age preferences, the hypothetical scenarios were constructed to reduce inhibitions that would be likely to bias expressions of age preference. Furthermore, in order to minimize social pressures on preferences, subjects were isolated from each other when they answered the survey to ensure that peer pressure would not affect the age preferences the subjects selected. The males were predominantly between 18 and 19 at the time of the study. Overall, they preferred females with a mean age of 16.87 for marriage; however, 17.76 years was the mean age selected for a brief sexual encounter. Why would young men prefer to have a long-term relationship with a younger female? The preference for a younger female for marriage suggests an evolutionary predisposition for males to select females with the longest remaining reproductive period. Of course, this study did not factor the constraints of female age preference for males or other factors that influence mating. In our culture, evolutionary psychologists assume that age preferences are influenced not only by social and cultural factors in the natural environment, but also by evolved and genetic predispositions that will encourage reproductive success.

STOP AND REVIEW

❶ What theory did Darwin and Wallace propose?
❷ What two things did Darwin propose as a means for selection?
❸ Why did Darwin say that bright feathers resulted from female choice?

Evolution and Behaviour

In Chapter 1 you were introduced to **William James**, who published the first psychology textbook in 1890 and introduced the principles of functionalism. In his text, James argued that complex mental functions had an adaptive significance in the ancestors of the organisms that were currently displaying them. This suggested for the first time that functions like consciousness exist for adaptive reasons, just as physical and physiological characteristics do. James argued that humans had a more complex repertoire of behaviours than other animals and more flexibility in those behaviours because humans had a greater number of instincts. James clearly understood that the complex mental functions of which humans are capable resulted from natural selection. Although this understanding was reflected in highly regarded works in psychology, Darwinian theory lost favour as a means for understanding and explaining complex behaviour. Let's discuss some of the other historical figures who played a role in the decline of the Darwinian theory of evolution.

"SURVIVAL OF THE FITTEST" HURTS DARWIN'S THEORY

In the later part of the 19th century, English philosopher **Herbert Spencer** used the principles of natural selection to justify capitalism, coining the term *survival of the fittest*—although this term is often associated with Darwin. Spencer thought of evolution as a broad concept that resulted in change to the physical world, to organisms as described by Darwin, and to the mind, culture, and human society in general. That evolution

Herbert Spencer

Sir Francis Galton

could come to shape human society and social systems came to be described as *social Darwinism*, and Spencer was a prominent figure in its rise. Comparisons of natural selection with the struggles of the working class were common among social Darwinists, who advocated the idea that competition between individuals, groups, and nations drove social evolution. Although the theory suggests that benefits are available to everyone involved when competition is present, Spencer and many of the wealthy industrialists of the time used the philosophy of social Darwinism to defend the exploitation of the poor working class. To this end, they justified poor working conditions and terrible pay—after all, they were simply following the laws of natural selection and survival of the fittest—despite the horrible outcomes for the poor. Today, of course, we see this type of behaviour as highly unethical.

Sir Francis Galton, a half-cousin to Charles Darwin, attempted to apply Darwinian evolutionary theory to the study of human abilities. He was primarily interested in how and why people differ in their abilities. He wondered, for example, why some people were gifted and successful—like him—whereas many others were not. We will discuss Galton's theories on intelligence and intelligence testing in Chapter 10. Unfortunately, Galton postulated a number of ideas that proved considerably more controversial than simple intelligence testing. He believed, for example, that genius was inherited. In his view, talent, or eminence, ran in families; nurture had only a minimal effect on intelligence. He also believed that intelligence was related to the theory of the survival of the fittest and, somehow, ultimately to one's moral worth. Galton attempted to base public policy on the concept of genetically superior and inferior people. He started the *eugenics* movement, which advocated

---

genetic determinism A theory that genes, and not the environment, contribute to the behaviours exhibited by an individual.

improving the human species by applying evolutionary theory to encouraging biologically superior people to interbreed while discouraging biologically inferior people from having offspring. Galton wrote, "There exists a sentiment, for the most part quite unreasonable, against the gradual extinction of an inferior race" (Galton, 1883/1907, p. 200).

These controversial ideas were later endorsed and extended by many who argued forcefully that the intellectually superior race should propagate at the expense of those with inferior minds. Fascist extremists adopted an even more cruel view of Darwinian theory: Humans must conform to nature's processes, no matter how ruthless. Due to the misuse of evolutionary theory, **genetic determinism** came to be associated with explanations of behaviour. Genetic determinism promotes the principle that genes define one's destiny. According to this view, all the qualities people possess are hardwired in their genetic material. This left no room for the role of environment in behaviour, but it suited the agendas of both industrial social Darwinists and the eugenicists. Eugenics developed into a worldwide movement between 1900 and 1940, proposing to improve the genetic quality of the human species by better breeding. Research programs were developed based on the idea that it was inefficient to allow genetic defects to multiply and then have to deal with the medical costs that resulted (Allen, 1997). Eugenicists argued for the incarceration, sterilization, or euthanasia of genetically defective individuals. Among the proponents of these ideas were American psychologists **Herbert Goddard** and **Lewis Terman**, whose theories we will review later in the book, and, of course, Nazi dictator Adolf Hitler. We will also see later in the chapter on intelligence (Chapter 10) that remnants of these elitist ideas are still being proposed today.

The abuses of Darwinian theory set the stage for another extreme swing in philosophy toward the principles of

environmental determinism. The promoters of environmental determinism inadvertently defined for us an important lesson from the past: Genetic arguments should not be put forward to explain all behaviour and behaviour problems—especially those that are related to social and economic factors. Later we will learn more about the interactions between genes and the environment.

In extreme environmental determinism, humans and all other organisms were seen as the **tabula rasa**, or blank slate, to be sculpted by the environment. In psychology, the environmental determinism perspective was supported by behaviourism. In Chapter 1 you were introduced to the founder of behaviourism, John Watson. Followers of Watson, like B. F. Skinner, provided evidence that complex behaviours were the result of learned associations and reinforcement contingencies. The methodology defined by Skinner has proved to be an extremely successful approach for extinguishing maladaptive behaviours and producing adaptive behaviours. Although the learning principles discovered by behaviourists provided tremendous opportunities for altering behaviour, including training mentally retarded individuals to function at higher levels, it did not offer a broad and useful explanation for human behaviour.

ETHOLOGY

Fortunately for evolutionary theory, the first discipline to form around the study of behaviour from an evolutionary perspective was taking shape in response to extreme environmentalism. **Ethology**, a combination of field and laboratory study of animal behaviour, led to a greater understanding of behavioural processes in animals. The ethology movement was launched in large part by **Konrad Lorenz**, who demonstrated the dramatic phenomenon of **imprinting**. Imprinting is a form of learning where ducklings form an association with the first object they see moving. In most cases, ducklings imprint on their mother, but Lorenz was able to demonstrate that if ducklings first saw a human moving, they would follow that person. Although the mechanisms that underlie imprinting are clearly part of the evolved structures of the duckling brain, the actual process is dependent on an association that is made during a critical period in the ducklings' development. The advantage for a duckling to stay near its mother early in life seems obvious. In 1973, Lorenz and Nikolaas Tinbergen and Karl von Frisch took home the Nobel Prize in physiology and medicine as the founders of ethology.

Each of these researchers had discovered features of behaviour that made the study of behaviour more interesting. Karl von Frisch had demonstrated that honey bees have a flexible and adaptive system of communication. Further work on the honey bees revealed that this communication was genetically encoded in members of the social group. Bees could very precisely relay to other members of the group the location and distance of flowers and sources of pollen, for example. Tinbergen's contributions to the pioneering research on behaviour were mostly conceptual. He proposed a scheme that more fully allowed for thinking about the causes of behaviour. The major divisions in his proposal were between proximate and ultimate behavioural causes. The proximate explanations of behaviour primarily described how behaviour might occur, whereas the ultimate explanations of behaviour concerned the evolution of the behaviour over time. These levels of explanation are not

Konrad Lorenz, the researcher who pioneered the study of imprinting, demonstrated what can happen when young animals become imprinted on someone other than their mother. Why is imprinting important for many animal species?

mutually exclusive; using them together provides the best understanding of a given behaviour. Together, the ideas of proximate and ultimate causes allowed for the understanding of behaviour not only at the level of why the behaviour exists, but also how it came to exist.

ALTRUISM

In virtually all animal species, there are reports of selfless behaviour by one individual toward another. This behaviour has played a very important role in the long-term survival and evolution of all species. A mother bear will protect her young when a human comes near, even though she is potentially putting herself in danger. If you have brothers or sisters, you have likely had the experience of quarrelling with them; but have you also noticed that whenever a sibling is in trouble you feel compelled to come to his or her aid? We often have the perception that

---

environmental determinism A theory that the environment, and not genes, contributes to the behaviours exhibited by an individual.

tabula rasa A theory proposed by philosopher John Locke that when we are born, our brains are like a blank tablet of clay that can be written on. As the theory assumes there is no built-in knowledge, the sensory and general experiences one has are what come to form the overall knowledge base.

ethology The scientific study of animals, often in their natural environment, to understand a behavioural process.

imprinting A primitive form of learning in which some infant animals physically follow and form an attachment to the first moving object they see and/or hear.

damage to a member of the family is like damage to ourselves—so we try to prevent it by coming to the aid of family. It seems less obvious as to why animals or people put themselves in danger for the sake of another individual. For example, we routinely hear news reports of a total stranger rushing to the aid of a person in a car accident or someone trapped in a burning building. This seemingly unselfish behaviour, where one animal puts itself at great risk for the benefit of another, is called **altruism**. Let's talk about why altruism might occur, even when it puts individuals in danger for someone they do not even know.

In the 1960s, **William D. Hamilton** proposed a radical new theory he called **inclusive fitness**, which led to a much greater understanding of altruism. Hamilton noted that the classical evolutionary theories on reproductive success were narrow and could not explain some of the altruistic behaviour that had been observed. He suggested that natural selection encouraged characteristics in all organisms that would promote the passing on of genes, regardless of whether a single organism had offspring. For example, one of the most obvious scenarios for reproductive success is parental care as a means of investing in one's own children and ensuring that one's own genes are passed on; according to Hamilton's theory of inclusive fitness, however, reproductive success can also be promoted by ensuring that one's nieces and nephews are able to survive and reproduce. Hamilton's legacy was acknowledging the fact that all biological relatives have some probability of carrying some representation of one's genes. Thus, inclusive fitness was essentially the sum of one's own reproductive success *in addition to* the reproductive success of one's relatives. The theory of inclusive fitness revolutionized how psychologists thought about family, altruism, the formation of groups, and aggression.

We can see evidence of inclusive fitness across a wide range of "giving" behaviours. Gregory Webster (2004) asked two groups of students to allocate fictional financial lottery winnings to their blood relatives. He found that the students gave direct relatives (parents and grandparents) a bigger reward than more peripheral relatives, including siblings. You might wonder why siblings did not benefit here as much as parents: The genetic argument is that peripheral relatives are those who are genetically related to but are not direct descendants or progenitors of the students participating in the experiment. You share half your genes with your mom, but less than half with a sibling, and even less than that if the sibling is a half-sibling. A study done in British Columbia (Smith, Kish, & Crawford, 1987) examined how individuals divided their estates among relatives. The findings indicated that deceased individuals actually allocated the greatest percentage of their estates to their closest genetic relatives. These patterns are exactly what would be predicted from Hamilton's theory on inclusive fitness.

Favouring individuals with close genetic material seems to occur in a variety of ways in the animal kingdom as well. Ground-dwelling squirrels, or gophers, produce an audible alarm vocalization that warns other gophers of danger. The gophers that hear the call benefit from the detection of predators by the single calling gopher. The callers are able to warn other family members of impending danger, despite the fact that they may put themselves at risk. **James Hare** and his students (Wilson & Hare, 2004) at the University of Manitoba were studying alarm calls in a specific type of gopher, the Richardson ground squirrel. Hare had noticed that occasionally some of the gophers seemed to lose their voices when producing the alarm call: They would open their mouths as if to sound the alarm to others, but only a faint whisper would come out. Yet the gophers clearly had *not* lost their voices, as sometimes the researchers would notice them switch between the loud audible calls they normally seemed to make and the whisper calls. Hare suspected that the gophers were using sounds that were outside the normal human range and attempted to listen in on the gophers using a bat detector. The bat detector works by detecting sounds that are in the ultrasonic range—outside of human hearing. The gophers were clearly signalling in the ultrasonic range. The ultrasonic vocalizations in the gophers seemed to have a clear purpose: to warn other gophers nearby about threats. Hare and his students recorded these ultrasonic calls and, in experimental studies to determine what the calls were for, broadcast them in the natural environment to see what other gophers would do in response to the calls. Gophers nearby noticed the ultrasonic calls and responded as they would to an audible alarm call. Hare and Wilson have suggested that the use of the whisper calls might have a more important purpose. The ultrasonic calls are highly directional, unlike audible sounds, and have a range limitation, which may be favoured by the calling gopher to reduce its chances of being detected by the predator, or to reduce the extent of those that can hear it. Only those nearby could hear the whisper calls, which seemed to reflect a lower level of threat. Perhaps the gophers had evolved an ultrasonic communication strategy to alert nearby kin without alerting predators or even gophers farther away. The next time you take a trip to the zoo, visit the gophers and see if they are calling out your arrival.

Altruism can occur in the absence of any obvious genetic relatedness between individuals. In some sense, some of our greatest heroes have been men and women who have helped strangers. R. L. Trivers (1971) proposed a possible explanation for the altruism between individual members of species where there is no obvious impact on reproductive success. According to this explanation, individuals provide aid to one another with an unspoken understanding that the individual receiving aid will reciprocate such aid. **Reciprocal altruism** requires that members of the group can be identified and that cheaters who will not reciprocate can be removed from the group. For example, one member of a gorilla troop will groom another expecting that the act will be returned to ensure that both are free of lice and parasites. If the behaviour is not returned, the *cheater* may be excluded from future groomings. Of course, humans do not groom each other socially in the way that other primates do, but we do play games and invest in a number of other social interactions that would make us wary of cheaters. If, for example, you went for lunch with a friend who complained that she had forgotten her wallet as the bill arrived, you would probably pay for her—but would you continue to go out for lunch with

---

altruism Prosocial behaviours a person carries out without considering his or her own safety or interests.

inclusive fitness The sum of the overall direct and indirect fitness effects of an individual's behaviours.

reciprocal altruism The idea that people perform altruistic behaviours because they expect that others will perform altruistic behaviours for them in turn.

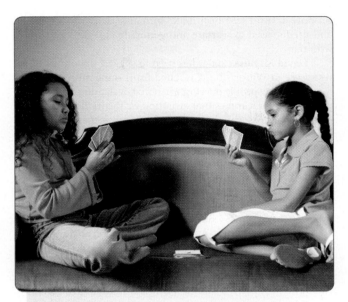

What people do you continue to play games with? Cheaters, or fair players?

her if the favour was not returned? What would you do if you went out for lunch with her again, and again she left her wallet at home?

As no one wants to be influenced by cheaters, there is some suggestion that an evolutionary mechanism is in place to ensure that we can recognize them. **Dan Chiappe** and colleagues (2004) studied a number of students in fictional social situations where cheating was a factor. They found that subjects who had rated someone as a cheater were more likely to categorize that person as important to remember and looked at them longer. People also had a better memory of those individuals who had been categorized as cheaters. This data suggests that some component of the mind evolved in a way that was relevant to social situations and specifically related to the unspoken contract of altruism expected between individuals. A greater understanding of altruism has produced some surprising understandings about conflict. Let's look at one such understanding you are probably familiar with.

You might wonder why there was so much conflict between you and your parents as you grew up. In addition to his writings on theories of reciprocal altruism, Trivers is also well known for his writings on parental investment and parent–offspring conflict. According to Trivers, children try to take more of their parents' resources than the parents are prepared to give. He predicted that the greatest amount of conflict between parents and offspring would occur at about the time the child should be weaned. (In our evolutionary history, children would have been weaned when they reached sexual maturity and could contribute to the community.) Trivers's theories on resources and conflict explain some of the conflict you likely experienced with siblings, who also wanted your parents to bestow resources on them. The greatest amount of conflict would be present when siblings thought that resources had been divided unequally. Did you ever lock your bedroom door or post "stay out" signs to keep your siblings away from your things? Evolutionary theory can explain why you fought with siblings and parents, and

why you had strong feelings about protecting the resources that were yours.

Scott Forbes at the University of Winnipeg believes that conflict between a mother and her child starts even earlier than previously imagined. In fact, he provides evidence for conflict in the womb having an evolutionary history. The conflict that Forbes is particularly interested in is related to the early physiological decision of who decides whether the pregnancy continues—the mother or the fetus. To illustrate his theory, Forbes (2002) asks us to consider an ancestral mother and her offspring. Early in our evolutionary history, the mother would have controlled pregnancy with her levels of luteinizing hormone (LH)—though physiologically and not psychologically, of course. Rather, high levels of stress or adverse pregnancy conditions would have resulted in lower levels of LH and termination of the pregnancy. LH is closely related to human chorionic gonadotropin (hCG), which regulates normal hormone progression during pregnancy. Without normal progesterone production, pregnancy fails. If embryos could somehow develop the ability to manipulate any of the hormones or chemicals involved in pregnancy, they would have great control over the maintenance of pregnancy. As a consequence of having the same complement of genes as the mother and access to her bloodstream, a mutation in the embryo genetic coding could turn on LH production. Embryos with low LH would be aborted, whereas those with high levels of LH would not. Such a mutation would become a selective advantage and fixed in the human genetic code. It appears that this has occurred in primates, horses, and guinea pigs. For human mothers, the normal sequence is that embryos they prefer to abort are accompanied by reduced LH production. However, the embryo, now able to make its own LH, increases production. Mothers retaliate by again reducing LH, but the embryo increases it again—and so on until further escalation becomes too costly for one or the other, leading to natural abortion or the maintenance of the pregnancy. Forbes argues that this escalation has a cost, which we now know as pregnancy sickness. Is it possible that mutations can influence pregnancy and cause pregnancy sickness? Forbes (1997) has noted that embryos with trisomy 21 (Down syndrome) also produce very high levels of hCG and are associated with high levels of nausea and vomiting during pregnancy. Higher levels of hCG are also present when the fetus is female, which means female fetuses are associated with more severe pregnancy sickness (Danzer, Brausein, Rasor, Forsythe, & Wade, 1980). It is interesting to consider how early development plays a role in later behaviour.

You have now seen how many different factors have come to play a role in how we behave, and how the behaviour of all species may change over time. You likely also have a better understanding of why many people are interested in evolution.

STOP AND REVIEW

❶ What overarching ideas did Sir Francis Galton contribute to the study of intelligence?

❷ What did the promoters of environmental determinism seek?

❸ What three researchers shared a Nobel prize, and what did they win it for?

❹ Why do cheaters fail to win in the long run?

Sociobiology

In 1975, **Edward O. Wilson** published a book, *Sociobiology: The New Synthesis*, which was received with a public uproar that was possibly comparable to the one Darwin received in 1859. The text offered a broad synthesis of cellular biology, physiology, ethology, comparative psychology, behavioural ecology, and population biology. Although **sociobiology** relied on theories previously presented by Trivers and Hamilton, Wilson's text synthesized a wide range of scientific fields into a single emerging field. The greatest controversy the book presented was its claim that some of the most complex human behaviour—such as culture, religion, and creativity—could ultimately be explained by the new synthesis. Unfortunately, however, Wilson had little empirical evidence to support his views on human nature. Instead, the evidence he presented was based on observations of nonhuman animals—some of which were phylogenetically far removed from humans. For example, fruit flies and ants, based on evolutionary history, share little of the genetic material of primates. The small chapter on human behaviour helped make sociobiology the target of critics who claimed Wilson was promoting genetic determinism. Wilson's theories

---

sociobiology A field of research that focuses on evolutionary explanations for the social behaviour and social systems of humans and other animal species.

genocide The systematic destruction of one group of people, often an ethnic or racial group, by another.

on how natural selection made humans easily indoctrinated and predisposed to warfare and **genocide** also did not sit well with many.

David M. Buss (2004) has tried to suggest that much of the resistance to Wilson's book resulted from some misunderstandings that many people develop when first evaluating evolutionary psychology. Buss argues that evolutionary theory does not imply that behaviour is genetically predetermined or that behaviour is unchangeable, and it does not imply optimal design. What Buss does advocate is that evolutionary psychology is a way to understand the human mind and complex behaviour from an evolutionary perspective.

Consider the question of happiness: How might an evolutionary perspective explain the human species's general ability to experience happiness? Buss (2000) suggested that some limits are placed on human happiness by the "discrepancies between modern and ancestral environments" (p. 15). For example, although humans evolved in the context of small groups, many people now live in large urban environments in which they are surrounded mostly by large numbers of total strangers. We might no longer have close bonds to the group of individuals who share our space—the types of bonds that could help us weather crises to experience happy lives. What can be done? Although you cannot turn back the tide of cultural evolution that has brought about these changes, you can try to counteract their negative effects by increasing your closeness to your family members and friends (Buss, 2000). This example reveals the contrast between the sociobiological emphasis on the human species in a particular environment versus the behaviour–genetic

---

Critical Thinking in Your Life

THE CINDERELLA EFFECT

The fairy tale *Cinderella* may tell you more about human behaviour than you realize! Martin Daly and Margo Wilson, McMaster University researchers, spent many years investigating human behaviour from a sociobiological perspective. Their research, as well as that of other sociobiologists, is often cited when people think of contemporary evolutionary psychology.

You likely recall the fairy tale of Cinderella from your childhood. In this story, we are introduced to Cinderella, who has been left with a stepmother and two stepsisters. The story revolves around Cinderella's life with the stepfamily, where it is clear that she is not valued except as someone who acts much like a maid to the two stepsisters. One of the questions that Daly and Wilson sought to answer

with some of their research revolved around the issue of whether stepchildren are disproportionately mistreated. In a very striking study (Daly & Wilson, 2005), they reported that fatal beatings of preschoolers in Canada by genetically related fathers was approximately 2.6 per million children per year (each year within a 16-year study period), whereas the rate for stepfathers in the same time period was 321.6 per million children per year. Daly and Wilson (1985) had previously reported that children not living with both biological parents were at a higher risk for suffering child abuse and other behaviours that would put them at risk.

At first glance, some of the behaviours might seem accidental and negligent, but consider for a moment

whether placing a child in a car without a seatbelt would be considered to be an acceptable thing to do. Would failing to put a seatbelt on a stepchild, but enforcing a seatbelt rule for genetically related children, be acceptable? Would this behaviour encourage one's genes to be passed on? Generally, occasionally forgetting to put a seatbelt on one child might seem to be just momentary forgetfulness, but it could, in evolutionary terms, provide a direct benefit for one's own offspring. Daly and Wilson's research seems to be direct confirmation that children living with only one biological parent and a step-parent are at a greater risk for discrimination and for abuse. The term that has come to be associated with this discrimination is the *Cinderella effect*.

emphasis on variation within the general pattern for a species. In the remainder of *Psychology and Life*, we will present several more instances in which the evolutionary perspective sheds light on human experience. These examples range from partner choices in relationships (Chapter 12), to emotional expression (Chapter 13), to patterns of aggression (Chapter 17).

In addition to studying the *Cinderella effect* discussed in the *Critical Thinking in Your Life* box on the opposite page, Martin Daly and Margo Wilson's research has also focused on relationships between men and women. One of their more interesting studies questioned whether pretty women make men discount their future. Generally, evolutionary theory suggests that individuals would discount the future only when the imminent situation seemed very good and when there was some unpredictability about the future. In the experiment (Wilson & Daly, 2004), undergraduate men and women were given a fictional scenario in which they were presented with the opportunity of gaining money from the experimenters. The experiment had three parts. First, participants were seated at a computer and presented with a series of monetary amounts with parameters (e.g., participants were given the choice of a small sum of money now, or a larger amount that would be paid at a later time). Second, they were asked to rate pictures of members of the opposite sex. And third, they were asked to select a monetary amount with parameters again. The faces the participants saw in the pictures were experimentally presented so that some were attractive and some were not. The undergraduate men in this experiment tended to discount the future more when they were presented with attractive faces. That is, the males preferred the payment today, even though it was less money than they would get if they waited for the payout (which was defined as only one day later in the experiment). Although the trend was similar in the undergraduate females, it was more significant among the males, supporting the theory that fitness gains as a result of mating opportunities might be higher in males than females. Wilson and Daly suggest that a "mating opportunity" mindset was producing a more present-oriented response in the young men. Further, they suggest that this discounting is adaptive in the sense that the behaviour was not a result of simply being young or having a simple focus, but was related to mating opportunities.

Daly and Wilson were the target of a variety of criticisms about their evolutionary psychology research, primarily because of the nature of the statements their research makes about human behaviour. The arguments against Wilson, Daly, and other evolutionary psychologists have suggested that evolutionary psychology does not allow the environment to play a role in behaviour, reducing much of human behaviour to the genes we inherit from ancestors. Since evolutionary psychology aims to investigate how evolution could have produced the mind, brain, and behaviour we currently see, there are likely to be behaviours we do not like in the list of those that have evolved with an adaptive function. Although the adaptive function may not be necessary in current times and may not be a desirable behaviour in a developed society, the theory does, however, suggest why we have some difficulty in simply eliminating a selection of unwanted behaviours that are not desirable in our society.

The research Wilson and Daly contributed under the umbrella of evolutionary psychology clearly indicates that men are more likely than women to partake in risky behaviour, they are more likely to engage in intrasexual competition, and they are more likely to commit homicides (reviewed in Daly & Wilson, 2001). They asked undergraduate men and women to choose a job option where pay and pollution were important factors. The women were more likely to consider pollution as an important factor in the decision to take a job, even in the face of significant pay incentives. However, the males clearly indicated a preference that did not put their long-term health into the equation. Sexual selection theory suggests not only that men will men seek risk more than women, but that they will also be more concerned with their status relative to same-sex rivals.

Wilson and Daly have argued that homicidal violence also provides a good window on competitive risk taking. Same-sex, nonrelative homicides are predominantly committed by young males; police reports suggest that the killings are a result of disputes where "saving face" is at stake. Although we tend to hear about violence in communities that have a lower economic status, economics may not play the only role in this type of behaviour. There seems to be considerable evidence that status has quite an impact on a man's "mate value"—the perception of positive characteristics for mating by women. Risk taking can be interpreted as a measure of confidence and competence.

Risk taking can yield prestige and, occasionally, does result in material gains. Think about this for a moment and consider well-known individuals who seem to have benefited from risk taking. You are likely aware of the television show *The Apprentice*, featuring Donald Trump. Trump, with his widely criticized hairstyle, is not very attractive physically, but he is certainly a risk taker when it comes to investing his money. When he divorced his first wife Ivana, she received a rumoured $20 million in the settlement. He has, however, attracted young, beautiful women, including Marla Maples (cousin to Heather Locklear), whom he married and later divorced. Trump then had a child with his third wife, Melania, a former European supermodel who was much younger than he. Trump's most recent son is an uncle to his grandchild. Thinking about our evolutionary history, it is clear that individuals who were risk takers were selected as mates and that this trait has been maintained because it can contribute to gains.

Decline of Behaviourism

A variety of studies in psychology have suggested that simply observing the behaviour of animals and humans does not provide an explanation of human behaviour—and unequivocally demonstrated that the study of behaviour cannot predict behaviour, even if the environment is known. From this context it was clear that understanding behaviour required evaluating what was going on in the mind. With the decline of behaviourism, psychologists were setting the stage for the emergence of evolutionary psychology. Let's look at just a few of the experiments that made psychologists approach the study of behaviour differently.

Harry Harlow (e.g., Harlow & Suomi, 1971) raised a group of monkeys in a laboratory and exposed young monkeys to two types of laboratory mothers. Both mothers were made out of wire mesh, but one had a soft covering. The young monkeys could not obtain food from the soft mothers. Operant conditioning would predict that the young monkeys would prefer the wire mothers because of the reinforcement the young received from them when they were fed. However, Harlow found that the

How did Harlow demonstrate the importance of contact comfort for normal social development?

young monkeys would eat from the wire mothers, but spent their time with the soft-covered mothers. This finding was surprising; clearly there was something other than a response to reinforcement going on. Further, one of the main assumptions of behaviourism was being violated: The main determinant of behaviour in the young monkeys was not reinforcement from the external environment. What was happening was clearly in the monkey's brains and was not directly observable.

The second key set of studies that encouraged the study of the evolution of behaviour came from the cognitive revolution. Generally, cognitive psychologists agree that for an organism to accomplish a task, the organism must solve a series of information-processing problems. For example, though reading this page of your textbook might feel as if it is happening effortlessly, your brain is using a tremendous number of information-processing systems. The actual means by which we do things is very complex, but the cognitive approach is based on a rather simple set of rules: Data are inputted in some way into the system, representations and decisions are made within the system, and then an output is generated. The process is one that is clearly understood, even if the brain machinery that underlies the process is not. For many, the machinery that processes information—the brain—is like a large computer. It is not surprising that psychologists have used computers to try to model human behaviour, because they can input data and look at the output. Of course, the human brain is intrinsically more complex.

By now, you should have a good idea of the philosophical transition from the theories of behaviourism—where humans went from being a blank slate written on by reinforcement contingencies—to theories of cognition, where the mind was a complex computer with software developed through both genes and the environment. The idea that humans were predisposed to process some kinds of information and not others had a key consequence on the study of evolutionary psychology: Problems of survival and reproduction could again be tied to elements that were outside of observable behaviour, but that were in the human mind and shaped by evolution.

STOP AND REVIEW

❶ What was the controversy in sociobiology?
❷ What does Buss suggest may impact our happiness?
❸ What did Harlow's monkeys tell us about reinforcement?
❹ What makes Daly and Wilson's research so controversial?

The Unshakable Foundations of Darwinian Theory

You might be wondering why, if Darwin's theory was so brilliant, it took so long for people to embrace it again—or why it was questioned at all. A major stumbling block was that the theory of natural selection lacked a valid theory of inheritance. When Darwin published *The Origin of Species* he did not know about genes and their mode of action, so he could not adequately explain how characteristics might change over time. Since the prevailing thought was that inheriting characteristics was simply a result of a blending of two parents' characteristics, Darwin's description of the theory of evolution did not have a scientific basis. The earliest systematic research exploring the relationship between parents and their offspring was published in 1866 by **Gregor Mendel** (1822–1884). Mendel's studies were carried out on the humble garden pea. He was able to demonstrate that the physical features of peas that emerged from different seeds—for example, whether the peas appeared *round* or *wrinkled*—could be predicted from the physical features of the plants from which the seeds had been obtained. Based on his observations, Mendel suggested that pairs of "factors"—one inherited from each parent—determined the properties of the offspring (Lander & Weinberg, 2000). Although Mendel's work originally received little attention from other scientists, modern techniques have allowed researchers to visualize and study Mendel's factors, which we now call *genes*.

We now have a greater understanding about the effects of genes and the environment, which brings us again to issues that are related to the debate on nature versus nurture—or genes versus environment. Let's return our focus to the forces that bring about change within an existing species.

GENOTYPES AND PHENOTYPES

The example of the ebb and flow of finch populations demonstrates why Darwin characterized the course of evolution as a

Human chromosomes. At the moment of conception, you inherited 23 from your mother and 23 from your father.

product of reproductive success. Imagine that each environment poses some range of difficulties for each species of living beings. Those members of the species who possess the range of physical and psychological attributes best adapted to the environment are most likely to survive. To the extent that the attributes that foster survival can be passed from one generation to another—and that stresses in the environment endure over time—the species is likely to evolve.

To examine the process of natural selection in more detail, we must introduce some of the vocabulary of evolutionary theory. Let's focus on an individual finch. At conception, that finch inherited a **genotype**, or genetic structure, from its parents. In the context of a particular environment, this genotype determined the finch's development and behaviour. The outward appearance and range of behaviours of the finch are known as its **phenotype**. For our finch, its genotype may have interacted with the environment to yield the phenotype of *large beak* and *ability to crack tougher seeds*.

If seeds of all types were plentiful, this phenotype would have no particular bearing on the finch's survival. Suppose, however, that the environment provided insufficient seeds to feed the whole population of finches. In that case, the individual finches would be in *competition* for resources. When species function in circumstances of competition, phenotypes help determine which individual members are better adapted to ensure survival. Recall our finch with a small beak. If only large, tough seeds were available, our finch would be at a *selective advantage* with respect to finches with small beaks. If only small seeds were available, our finch would be at a disadvantage.

Only finches that survive can reproduce. Only those animals that reproduce can pass on their genotypes. Therefore, if the environment continued to provide only large, tough seeds, over several generations the finches would probably come almost exclusively to have large beaks—with the consequence that they would be almost exclusively capable of eating only large seeds. In this way, forces in the environment can shape a species's pool of possible behaviours. **Figure 3.2** provides a simplified model of the process of natural selection. Let's now apply these ideas to human evolution.

HUMAN EVOLUTION

By looking backward to the circumstances in which the human species evolved, you can begin to understand why certain

---

genotype The genetic structure an organism inherits from its parents.

phenotype The observable characteristics of an organism, resulting from the interaction between the organism's genotype and its environment.

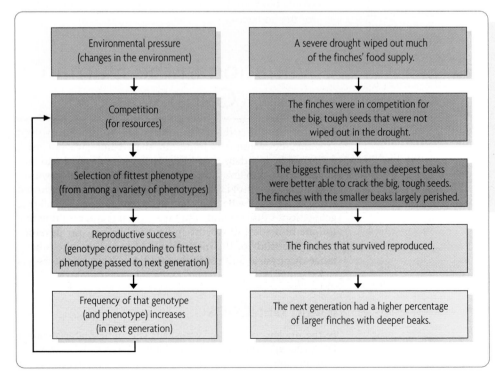

Environmental pressure (changes in the environment)	A severe drought wiped out much of the finches' food supply.
Competition (for resources)	The finches were in competition for the big, tough seeds that were not wiped out in the drought.
Selection of fittest phenotype (from among a variety of phenotypes)	The biggest finches with the deepest beaks were better able to crack the big, tough seeds. The finches with the smaller beaks largely perished.
Reproductive success (genotype corresponding to fittest phenotype passed to next generation)	The finches that survived reproduced.
Frequency of that genotype (and phenotype) increases (in next generation)	The next generation had a higher percentage of larger finches with deeper beaks.

FIGURE 3.2 How Natural Selection Works
Environmental changes create competition for resources among species members. Only those individuals possessing characteristics instrumental in coping with these changes will survive and reproduce. The next generation will have a greater number of individuals possessing these genetically based traits.

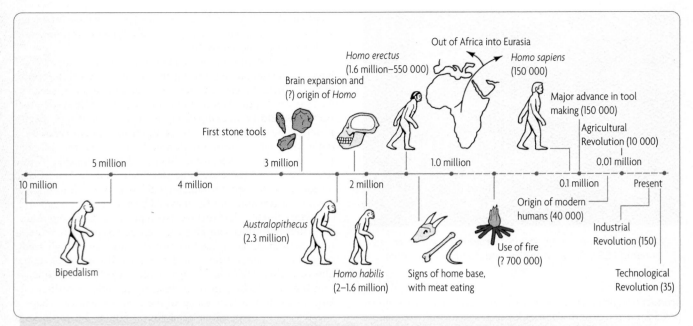

FIGURE 3.3 Approximate Timeline for the Major Events in Human Evolution
Bipedalism freed the hands for grasping and tool use. Encephalization provided the capacity for higher cognitive processes such as abstract thinking and reasoning. These two adaptations probably led to the other major advances in human evolution.
From Robert Lewin, *Human Evolution: An Illustrated Introduction.* Copyright © 1984 by Blackwell Science Ltd. Reprinted by permission.

physical and behavioural features are part of the biological endowment of the entire human species. In the evolution of our species, natural selection favoured two major adaptations—bipedalism and encephalization. Together, they made possible the rise of human civilization. *Bipedalism* refers to the ability to walk upright, and *encephalization* refers to increases in brain size. These two adaptations are responsible for most, if not all, of the other major advances in human evolution, including cultural development (see **Figure 3.3**). As our ancestors evolved the ability to walk upright, they were able to explore new environments and exploit new resources. As brain size increased, our ancestors became more intelligent and developed capacities for complex thinking, reasoning, remembering, and planning. However, the evolution of a bigger brain did not guarantee that humans would become more intelligent—what was important was the kind of tissue that developed and expanded within the brain (Gibbons, 2002). The genotype coding for mobile and intelligent phenotypes slowly squeezed out other, less well-adapted genotypes from the human gene pool, affording only intelligent bipeds the opportunity to reproduce.

---

heredity The biological transmission of traits from parents to offspring.

genetics The study of the inheritance of physical and psychological traits from ancestors.

DNA (deoxyribonucleic acid) The physical basis for the transmission of genetic information.

genes The biological units of heredity; discrete sections of chromosomes responsible for transmission of traits.

Variation in the Human Genotype

You have seen that the conditions in which humans evolved favoured the evolution of important shared biological potential: for example, bipedalism and the capacity for thought and language. There remains, however, considerable variation within that shared potential. Your mother and father have endowed you with a part of what their parents, grandparents, and all past generations of their family lines have given them, resulting in a unique biological blueprint and timetable for your development. The study of the mechanisms of **heredity**—the inheritance of physical and psychological traits from ancestors—is called **genetics.**

BASIC GENETICS

In the nucleus of each of your cells is genetic material called **DNA** (deoxyribonucleic acid; see **Figure 3.4**). DNA is organized into tiny units, called **genes**. Genes contain the instructions for

FIGURE 3.4 Genetic Material

The nucleus of each cell in your body contains a copy of the chromosomes that transmit your genetic inheritance. Each chromosome contains a long strand of DNA arranged in a double helix. Genes are segments of the DNA that contain instructions for the production of the proteins that guide your individual development.

From Lester A. Lefton & Linda Brannon. *Psychology* 8e. Published by Allyn & Bacon, Boston, MA. Copyright © 2003 by Pearson Education. Reprinted by permission of the publisher.

the production of proteins. These proteins regulate the body's physiological processes and the expression of phenotypic traits: body build, physical strength, intelligence, and many behaviour patterns. Although there is not a gene for any particular behaviour, genes are the instructions for the proteins, and the proteins are the molecular bases for changing cells to support behaviour. Alterations at the level of genes can produce changes in behaviour, usually because the way the protein is produced or the way the protein can be used is altered. In Huntington's disease, for example, a mutation in just one gene can result in changes in the amount of the Huntington protein found throughout the brain and body. It is the change in the protein levels that causes abnormal brain function and very pronounced involuntary body movements.

Genes are found on rod-like structures known as *chromosomes*. At the very instant you were conceived, you inherited from your parents 46 chromosomes—23 from your mother and 23 from your father. Each of these chromosomes contains thousands of genes—the union of a sperm and an egg results in only one of many billion possible gene combinations. The **sex chromosomes** are those that contain genes coding for development of male or female physical characteristics. You inherited an X chromosome from your mother and either an X or a Y chromosome from your father. An XX combination codes for development of female characteristics; an XY combination codes for development of male characteristics.

Beginning in 1990, the U.S. government funded an international effort called the Human Genome Project (HGP). The **genome** of an organism is the full sequence of genes found on the chromosomes with the associated DNA. In 2003, the HGP achieved the goal of providing a complete sequencing of the human genome. With that information in hand, researchers have now turned their attention to identifying all 30 000 to 32 000 human genes. The ultimate goal is to provide a complete account of the location and functions of that full set of genes.

GENES AND BEHAVIOUR

We have seen that evolutionary processes have allowed a considerable amount of variation to remain in human genotypes; the interactions of these genotypes with particular environments produce variation in human phenotypes. In other words, over time we have come to believe that we are a product of both our genes and our environment. Researchers in the field of **human behaviour genetics** unite genetics and psychology to explore the causal link between inheritance and behaviour (Plomin, DeFries, Craig, & McGuffin, 2003).

Research in human behaviour genetics often focuses on estimating the **heritability** of particular human traits and

---

sex chromosomes Chromosomes containing the genes that code for the development of male or female characteristics.

genome The genetic information for an organism, stored in the DNA of its chromosomes.

human behaviour genetics The area of study that evaluates the genetic component of individual differences in behaviours and traits.

heritability The relative influence of genetics—versus environment—in determining patterns of behaviour.

WHAT DOES "IT'S GENETIC" MEAN?

The Human Genome Project has put the study of genetics very much into the public domain. The project was started in 1990 and was expected to take 15 years to complete, but the timeframe was reduced to 13 years with many technological advances and multiple groups working on the project. Landmark papers were published in two high-profile journals, *Nature* and *Science*, in 2001 and 2003, respectively. The final project left us with the information that the human genome contained approximately 30 000 genes. The media routinely report on the progress researchers have made in understanding genetic contributions to important aspects of human experience such as obesity, sexuality, and mental illness. We want to give you a framework that should help you evaluate those media reports. We are going to focus our discussion on the behavioural trait of impulsivity.

Would you label this child as impulsive?

Suppose you see a newspaper headline that reads, "Scientists Find Impulsivity Gene." What information should the newspaper article provide? First, it's important to understand exactly what "impulsivity" means in the context of the article. Take a moment to consider how you might define or apply the term: You probably know some people whom you would label as impulsive and others for whom you would not use this label, but what exactly does that mean?

Are your acquaintances impulsive because they never plan ahead? Or are they impulsive because they cannot stop themselves from acting out? Or is it because they take too many risks? If you see the claim "Scientists Find Impulsivity Gene," you need to understand exactly how the researchers are using the term. This level of specificity is important because it is quite possible that the different behaviours associated with the one concept "impulsivity" could have different genetic bases (Congdon & Canli, 2006). If the newspaper article does not offer a careful description of what is meant by "impulsivity," you should be careful about accepting its conclusions.

The next piece of information you need to find is an explanation for why the researchers believe the gene they have identified plays a causal role in producing impulsive behaviour. Sometimes, this information will be given as a statement of fact: "People who have variation A of this gene are impulsive; those who have variation B are not." In contemporary research, however, scientists most often want to provide some sense of the mechanism that allows the gene to influence behaviour. What you will often learn from those accounts is that the gene in question only indirectly has an influence on a trait.

The final piece is why it might be important to know about the gene at all. Researchers have been interested in impulsivity and a gene for it because high levels of impulsivity put people at risk for problems such as drug and alcohol addiction (Sher, Bartholow, & Wood, 2000). Linda Pagani from the Université de Montréal and her colleagues (Pagani, Derevensky, & Japel, 2009) found that high levels of impulsivity in kindergarten children could predict a child's involvement in gambling in the sixth grade. The effect was large, too, with a one-unit increase in impulsivity correlating with a 25 percent increase in gambling behaviour. It is likely that characteristics like impulsivity build up, so a genetic link could lead to changing behaviour with interventions and life trajectory in adolescence and adulthood. Thus, if we do have a gene, or combination of genes, for impulsivity and these can be determined, we might have more insight into behaviour, but also predict impulsivity. Further, if there are consequences that extend beyond the impulsivity alone, we might want to be able to test for it and to curb negative behaviours that result from having such a gene.

For some people, impulsivity means doing activities that are potentially dangerous and unusual.

For some people, impulsivity simply means not being able to control oneself. Does chocolate make you lose control?

FIGURE 3.5 Using Distorted Tunes to Study the Heritability of Pitch Perception
If you heard these two melodies played, could you tell which was correct and which was distorted?

behaviours. Heritability is measured on a scale of 0 to 1. If an estimate is near 0, it suggests that the attribute is largely a product of environmental influences; if an estimate is near 1, it suggests that the attribute is largely a product of genetic influences. To tease apart environment and genes, researchers often use *adoption studies* or *twin studies*. For adoption studies, researchers obtain as much information as possible about the birth parents of children who are raised in adoptive homes. As the children develop, researchers assess the relative similarity of children to their birth families—representing genetics—and their adoptive families—representing environment.

In twin studies, researchers examine the extent to which *monozygotic (MZ)* twins and *dizygotic (DZ)* twins show similarity within pairs on particular traits or behaviours. MZ twins share 100 percent of their genetic material, whereas DZ twins share roughly 50 percent. (DZ twins are no more genetically alike than any other pair of brothers and sisters.) Researchers compute heritability estimates by determining how much more alike MZ twins are than DZ twins on a particular attribute. Consider a twin study that estimated the extent to which people inherit their ability to perceive distortions in simple melodies.

Do your neighbours complain when you sing in the shower? To what extent is your musical ability, or lack thereof, a product of your genetic makeup? Researchers sought to answer this question for one aspect of musical expertise—the ability to perceive distortions in simple tunes (Drayna, Manichaikul, deLange, Snieder, & Spector, 2001). Consider the example in **Figure 3.5**. Even if you cannot read music, you can see that the notes toward the end of the musical phrase have been distorted—but would you *hear* the distortion?

In this experiment, 136 pairs of MZ twins and 148 pairs of DZ twins heard 26 brief tunes and indicated whether each melody was correct or incorrect. The scores of the MZ twins—the number correct out of 26—were more similar, with a correlation of 0.67, than the scores of the DZ twins, with a correlation of 0.44. Based on these data, the researchers obtained a heritability estimate of 0.71. This estimate suggests a large genetic component to pitch perception.

Note that this high heritability estimate does not mean that everyone in a family is going to have the same pitch perception abilities. Just as the same parents will produce some children with blue eyes and some with brown eyes, the same parents will produce some children with exceptional musical ability and some children without. Instead, the high heritability suggests that, with respect to pitch perception, there is relatively little room for life experiences to have an impact on how talented you may or may not become.

This example of the heritability of pitch perception points to some of the ethical issues that have arisen in the wake of the Human Genome Project's successes. Suppose the HGP is able to determine which genes are responsible for the differences in pitch perception. If you were to become a parent, would you choose only to have children who were likely to be superior in musical ability? Although this question might not seem urgent in the context of musicianship, ethicists have already begun to ponder the consequences of genetic knowledge (Bostrom, 2005; Liao, 2005). For example, a variety of techniques already allow prospective parents to choose to have a boy or a girl. Should they be willing and able to make that choice? How about choices with respect to a child's intelligence level, sports ability, or criminal inclinations? As the HGP and related efforts continue to yield new insights, such ethical questions will become increasingly prominent in debates over public policy.

Still, it is important to remember that—except perhaps in cases such as a child's sex—genes are not destiny. Researchers

Psychology in Your Life

PSYCHOLOGY IN MOVIES AND BOOKS

Throughout the history of cinema, science fiction films have attempted to highlight technological advances and have addressed a range of ethical issues associated with the technological revolution. Cinema has focused on both genetics and genetic engineering, with a large number of films using genetic engineering as part of the plot. For example, what would happen if mutated spider venom were injected into a teenage boy? Films also play on society's greatest desires and darkest fears of where genetic engineering might lead. In 2009, James Cameron released *Avatar*, a story that places human beings on Pandora, a moon of the fictional planet Polyphemus, five light years away from Earth, in the future. The moon is like a dreamscape of blue beings and luminescent plant life, but it hosts a hostile environment to humans who wish to reap the rewards of its special ore. The movie has a Darwin-like character in Dr. Grace Augustine, who collects plant life and studies the native inhabitants, but her interest in genetics (and the knowledge she has that Darwin did not) results, in a twist that is both exciting and dangerous. Augustine had genetically grown half-alien/half-human bodies to mimic the Na'vi, a native tribe of 10-foot-tall, blue-skinned individuals.

The Avatars are created from DNA from both human beings and the native species, but look a little like they contain some form of cat DNA, given the movements and tail. Jake, the lead character, merges consciousnesses into an Avatar grown using his twin brother's genes, and is able to learn about Pandora and provide the scientific team with information on the Na'vi and the mining company with information on the Na'vi treasures below the trees. Jake begins to learn the secrets of Pandora from Neytiri, a Na'vi princess, but his consciousness moves between his real-life body and his newly formed Avatar.

Although the movie held a somewhat happy ending for Jake, the ethical questions in the movie, and movies about genetic manipulation, revolve around whether humans have the right to dabble in the manipulations of genes—and, ultimately, whether they have the power to be responsible for the consequences.

Eugenics has been another underlying theme in science fiction cinema for some time. Movies have often focused on how individuals with a certain genetic makeup or special powers could have a much better life than those with bad genes, i.e., without those special powers. Imagine how different young Peter Parker's life would have been if the spider in the laboratory had not bitten him and altered his DNA. Individuals who are concerned about ethics in biology are alarmed about a new eugenics movement that could form as a result of gene technology. Scientists already know some of the genes that are associated with hair colour and skin colour. In the near future, the technology that has allowed us to understand genes may have a very direct impact on our ability to treat genetic disorders—but will there be pressure to remove traits that we deem undesirable as well? The popular media regularly publishes stories that link specific genes with complex human traits; there is already some worry that these stories have led many people to believe that the gene is central to understanding and perhaps even controlling all of human behaviour—and that it is ultimately responsible for our destiny. If more people come to believe in the power of genetic determinism, we will likely see a complex rise in support for a new eugenics. Bioethicists are also concerned that genetic enhancement technologies will be reserved for those who can pay for it.

Books provide another venue for science fiction to be delivered to observers who are taken on a thrill ride alongside an experiment involving genetic engineering. Canadian author Margaret Atwood has published two parallel books in the last decade that explore developments in science and technology, including genetic engineering and the creation of transgenic animals. Atwood, who has close family members with science backgrounds, routinely uses scientific discovery in her fiction. The book *Oryx and Crake* (2003) introduces the reader to a future society that promotes extreme commercialization and commodification of life to the point where facilities, such as Organ Farms Inc., are created to develop transgenic animals such as "pigoons," a cross between a pig and a baboon that would provide harvestable organs for human beings. Crake, one of the main characters, uses his position in a biotechnology company to create engineered humans that are known as Crakers. These beings are nonviolent herbivores that mate at specific times, and have a lemony smell to ward off mosquitoes.

Crake also creates the Blyss-Pluss Pill that is sold as a prophylactic but is a genetic pandemic that destroys virtually every human being on the planet. It is here that the second book starts. *The Year of the Flood* (2009) follows two women who survived and are now living in a world where gene-splice variants are proliferating. Atwood's interpretation of the situation is that the technology is not used to the betterment of mankind, but to its detriment.

How possible is a genetic engineering experiment that uses humans? It seems that with the advances in scientific discovery, we should not be asking *whether* it is possible, but in what cases is it acceptable to do it and who will be the one to control it.

have been documenting important instances in which both genetics and environments play critical roles to determine organisms' behaviours. Consider a study that looked at the nature and nurture of aggression among male rhesus macaques (Newman et al., 2005). Let's start with nature. Within the population of 45 monkeys, there was variation with respect to a gene that affected the levels of neurotransmitters in the brain—some monkeys had the *high-activity* variation of the gene, whereas other monkeys had the *low-activity* variation. With respect to nurture, roughly half of the monkeys were raised with their own or a foster mother; the others were raised without early maternal care. The experimenters measured the monkeys' aggression by observing, for example, how effectively they competed for food. These observations suggested that the monkeys' levels of aggression depended on both genetics and environment: The monkeys who had the low-activity variation of the gene and who also had been raised by mothers showed the most aggressive behaviour. Monkeys with the same gene variation but who had not experienced maternal contact did not show higher levels of aggression. Clearly the monkeys with the low-activity gene that showed the highest levels of aggression were learning something from their mothers about how to behave in their environment. From this example you can see why researchers seek to understand how and why certain environments allow genes to be expressed.

STOP AND REVIEW

❶ What were two evolutionary advances most critical in human evolution?

❷ What is meant by heritability?

CRITICAL THINKING Why should people be concerned with technology associated with DNA?

Evolution of Language and Music

After bipedalism and encephalization, perhaps the most important evolutionary milestone for our species was the advent of language (Bickerton, 1990; Holden, 1998). Think of the tremendous adaptive advantages that language conferred on early humans. Simple instructions for making tools, finding a good hunting or fishing spot, and avoiding danger would save time, effort, and lives. Instead of learning every one of life's lessons firsthand by trial and error, humans could benefit from experiences shared by others. Conversation, even humour, strengthened the social bonds among members of a naturally gregarious species. Most important, the advent of language provided for the transmission of accumulated wisdom, from one generation to future generations. The evolution of music, however, seems to have a less obvious function, but it may be far more important than you might think, and certainly did not show up for us simply to invent iTunes. Music may have evolved as we evolved into social beings, and may now be tied even to how well we remember things.

WHY DID LANGUAGE EVOLVE?

Language is a truly astonishing ability. The simple fact that we can make sounds and that someone else can have representations in their minds of what we mean by those sounds is quite amazing. The process of how this occurs and why it developed in the first place has raised a number of theories and questions. Given that language is so complex, it is not surprising that the study of language has led to much controversy about its nature. Let's talk about two problems that have been an issue for evolutionary psychology: whether language was developed as an adaptation, and what adaptive problems language evolved to solve.

Noam Chomsky (left) and Stephen Jay Gould (right) have argued that language is a side effect resulting from the process of natural selection that caused the brain to increase in size.

Language is the basis for *cultural evolution*, which is the tendency of cultures to respond adaptively, through learning, to environmental change. Cultural evolution has given rise to major advances in tool making, agricultural practices, and the development and refinement of industry and technology. Cultural evolution allows our species to make very rapid adjustments to changes in environmental conditions. Consider, for example, the use of personal computers, an adaptation that has arisen in only the past 20 years. Even so, cultural evolution could not occur without genotype coding for the capacities to learn and to think abstractly. Culture—including art, literature, music, scientific knowledge, and philanthropic activities—is possible only because of the potential of the human genotype.

There has been some debate as to whether language was an adaptation to a specific problem or simply a by-product of human evolution. If language developed as a by-product, it is almost accidental—something that evolution had little control over—and not a direct product of natural selection. On the other hand, if language was an adaptation, it would have been a direct consequence of natural selection. The two key proponents of the by-product theory are **Noam Chomsky** and **Stephen Jay Gould**. These two men believe that the growth of the human brain resulted from a process of natural selection, but they further argue that after the brain reached its current size and complexity, language emerged as a side effect of the process. If language is indeed just a side effect, then we have certainly enjoyed a series of great benefits from this mysterious and spontaneously occurring phenomenon.

The adaptation proponents, including **Steven Pinker** (Pinker & Jackendoff, 2005), of Canadian origin, have argued that language contains too many features to be simply a side effect of a growing brain. The nature of grammar, for example, is quite complex, but it has elements that are universal across all languages: All languages have nouns, verbs, and adjectives. Pinker has pointed at the age at which children become fluent in their native language as evidence for the adaptive concept. Usually children have learned most of the rules of their language by the age of three, without any formal teaching or instruction. Of course, language is also linked to specific regions in the brain in all individuals, suggesting an adaptive function. We have known for some time that damage to two specific brain areas, Wernicke's area or Broca's area, result in very specific types of language impairments. It appears to some extent that language may be an innate function.

We will potentially never know the real answer to the question of how language first developed and whether it really was an adaptation or a by-product. Studies on when language developed have provided various dates, which might provide some insight into why the process may have developed. Some researchers date the process as quite recent, around 40 000 to 50 000 years ago. It is noteworthy that this timing corresponds quite well with what appears to have been a sudden increase in arts, tools, and artifacts, as evidenced in archaeological literature. Others have suggested that language developed much earlier—potentially two million years ago. Likely we will never know when language developed. Let's turn our attention to why it evolved and what purpose it serves.

It seems obvious that language allows for communication. The real question, then, is why evolution provided a process to allow for the exchange of information between individuals.

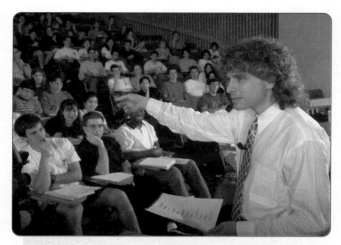

Steven Pinker argues that language evolved over time under the influence of natural selection as an adaptive process, not by accident.

If you spend a moment or two thinking about how you use language, what information you communicate, and what information your ancestors would have needed to communicate, you will likely get a good sense of why language may have developed. The predominant theory of the function of language is that being able to exchange information helps with many of the tasks humans engage in. More recent discussion of why language evolved has turned to theories of language playing a role in the social functioning of humans.

One of the things that you probably already know is that humans like to "gossip." We like a certain amount of information about our network of social relationships: who will make a good friend and alliance, who is not trustworthy, who is in a relationship with whom, who has cheated on whom, and so on. **Robin Dunbar** (1996) wrote an entire book elaborating on his *social gossip hypothesis* for the evolution of language. He argued that language functions as a form of social grooming. Although we tend to think of grooming as a concept related to maintaining hygiene (especially when we see chimpanzees picking lice off one another), grooming is equally important in nonhuman primates for bolstering social bonds. For example, in small groups of nonhuman primates, we see evidence of the physical grooming of allies; larger groups are not amenable to such grooming, regardless of the hygienic or social behaviour it might contribute to. Our earliest ancestors probably lived in small groups, but if social bonding relied on physical grooming, individuals would have spent almost half their time grooming one another even in a group as small as 150 individuals—which would have been almost impossible given other demands. Language, Dunbar argued, evolved to facilitate a social cohesion among groups. You may feel comfortable engaging in a gossip session with some close personal friends, but you likely feel less compelled to gossip among a larger group of people that you know less well.

In the widest sense, we can see that gossip provides a mechanism to allow for the exchange of information about members of our group. Not only does it provide the ability to stay in touch with family and friends, it also facilitates connection with more distant members of the group. Most of us know that occasionally gossip is not truthful, but you might be surprised to learn that there are theories on how and why individuals manipulate information to ensure their own success in the group and reduce the success of others who are more distant members of the group. Have you ever told a tale you knew to be untrue, or that you did not have real evidence for, about someone you know? Or have you agreed with someone telling you a story about someone else even though it seemed to be untrue? If so, think about your purpose at the time: By raising doubt about someone else, you may in fact have been solidifying your connections with members of the group and removing rivals from participating in that group. If potential mates were also members, it would even have conferred a mating advantage, as the rivals would have been denied equal access to the potential mates. Gossip is a very effective means of getting what you want.

Terrance Deacon (1997) proposed the hypothesis that language developed to facilitate clear marriage contracts between mates. The *social contract hypothesis* focuses on problems of long-term mating in situations where one of the mates was required to leave the other—on long hunting trips, for example. Deacon suggests that men and women developed language to publicly announce their mate relationship, signaling to others in the group that mates were off limits to others. This hypothesis presents some difficulties in terms of being a well-rounded theory of language development: It is clearly focused on only one aspect of human social behaviour and does not present arguments for the development of language related to other behaviours,

which also rely on language. Further, it is clear that even with language some mate contracts fail, whereas others that are not dependent on language are long term.

A third theory on the development of language is related to mate selection. The theory suggests that individuals who are able to enchant potential mates with their humour, exotic tales, and use of language have a mating advantage over those who fumble and mumble their words. Language in this case could be used to verbally signal superior fitness to potential mates. Certainly, we all know of cases where a "smooth talker" was able to successfully attract a potential mate.

Each of these adaptive theories may have some basis in fact. Once language developed—for whatever reason it developed—it did not need to be limited to its original function. It was likely in a state of constant evolution, providing a mechanism for social bonding, attracting mates, and other social situations.

WHY DID MUSIC EVOLVE?

Can you imagine the first song humans, or proto-humans, hummed, or sang? When do you think that this first happened? This task is challenging because we really do not know the answer, but what is clear is that music has become a fundamental part of human experience, or maybe even a human obsession. Not a single culture at this point, or known previously, has existed without music. In fact, archaeological artifacts from excavation sites often include musical instruments. It is relatively recently that music produced two classes of individuals, those who performed and those who listened to music; places to listen to music are also relatively recent in our evolutionary past, existing for perhaps 500 years. Our ancestors would all have been actively involved in making and listening to music, and in non-Westernized countries, you will find that almost everyone sings and makes music. Americans spend more money on music than on prescription drugs or other things that make us feel good. Given our interest in music, it may provide a window into normal and abnormal brain function.

In his book *This Is Your Brain on Music* (2006), Canadian neuroscientist **Daniel Levitin** proposes how music and the brain co-evolved. Daniel Levitin is the James McGill Professor of Psychology and Neuroscience at McGill University, but he also holds positions in the School of Computer Science, School of Music, and the Faculty of Education. Levitin's interest in music did not start with his neuroscience professorship; he had been in a number of small bands, and later became a record producer and recording engineer (for many well-known musicians, including Carlos Santana and Blue Oyster Cult). Music led him to psychology to search for more information on music, and here he learned about development, evolution, and the ways in which the brain contributed to music. Although early understanding of the brain suggested that music and art were processed in the right hemisphere and that language and math were localized in the left hemisphere, Levitin's research has suggested that music is actually not so specifically localized, and is represented by neural networks distributed throughout the brain (Levitin & Menon, 2005), which is consistent with how we believe memories are stored.

More recently, Levitin has been touring to promote some of his newer ideas on the evolution of music, found in his book *The World in Six Songs* (2008). In this book, he shows that the "six" songs represent music related to friendship, joy, comfort,

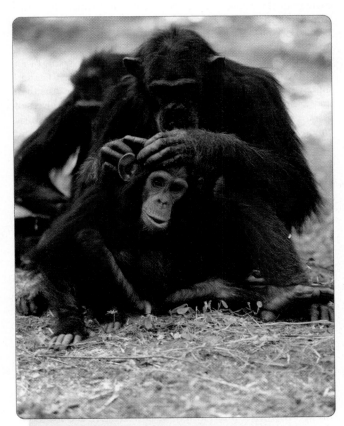

Chimps of similar status are more likely to groom each other if the actions are reciprocated.

Daniel Levitin's research has suggested that music is represented by neural networks distributed throughout the brain.

knowledge, religion, and love. Levitin's evolutionary theory really can be summarized by the idea that music would promote feelings of togetherness and help with memory. Music and dance would be nonviolent ways for individuals to work together and to settle disputes. Music would also serve as a memory aid, providing ways to preserve information and meaningful events in our lives. Consider the fact that Lola Cuddy and Jacalyn Duffin of Queen's University in Kingston, Ontario, have found that patients with Alzheimer's disease who lose memories from much of their life often recall music and lyrics (Cuddy & Duffin, 2005), suggesting that memory for music is not destroyed in some forms of dementia.

How has memory been facilitated by music? You probably have had the experience of listening to a song you have not heard in many years, yet the words come back to you easily. There seems to be something special about music that allows us to remember things later about a song. Do you remember your ABCs? Take a moment to say them—do they come out with a sing-song nature? Song and music have helped with memory formation. Black slaves in the United States were not allowed to read and write, but followed an African tradition of singing to preserve important information. Blues music provided an opportunity for slaves to tell each other the location of safe places and how to arrive there. "Follow the Drinking Gourd" and "Wade in the Water" were songs that many knew, and within each was a set of instructions for an illiterate slave to easily remember and then to follow. "Wade in the Water," for example, told slaves to follow waterways, as dogs could not track them as well in the water. The importance of music is likely far more significant than most people realize.

Amusics are individuals that are unable to process music at all, and are interesting from an evolutionary perspective. There is approximately one amusic in every 100 people; you may have met people who simply have no appreciation for music, or any ability to process what you find enjoyable about music, or any ability to actually produce music, even by repeating a tapping rhythm. We often joke about people being tone deaf, but there is a group of people who are congenital amusics, or people who really cannot easily differentiate tones. This loss cannot be explained by hearing loss, gross brain damage or intellectual difficulties. Canadian researcher **Isabelle Peretz** at the University of Montreal is an expert on amusia. Congenital amusia is hereditary, showing up in 39 percent of first-degree relatives and only

3 percent of controls (Peretz, Cummings, & Dubé, 2007), and is also associated with abnormalities in brain tissue in the auditory and frontal cortex. Peretz and colleagues (Peretz, Brattico, Järvenpää, & Tervaniemi, 2009) suggest that the difficulty is really in having the neural pitch "representation" make contact in the brain with the musical pitch "knowledge" along the auditory-frontal neural pathway. Amusics often can identify specific songs from the lyrics, or the words, but cannot recognize even simple tunes. Expressive amusics, or the people that cannot create music, are thought to have functional deficits in the frontal cortex, although tests such as MRI imaging have not shown any real brain damage. The existence of amusia, which is not normally associated with a cognitive deficit, suggests that music is not a side effect of other brain development, but a true specialization. There is some evidence that the ability to process music may rely on just a few genes; there is a form of hereditary amusia.

What came first, music or language? This question presents a challenge to answer since the fossil record does not provide the answers needed. Levitin would argue that music developed on its own, as something fundamental, but others propose it is something added to our capacities. Steven Pinker, who is most well known for his theories on language development, developed a theory on music that suggests that it evolved after as an aftereffect of developing language in *How the Mind Works* (1997). Pinker writes "Compared with language, vision, social reasoning, and physical know-how, music could vanish from our species and the rest of our lifestyle would be virtually unchanged. Music appears to be a pure pleasure technology, a cocktail of recreational drugs that we ingest through the ear to stimulate a mass of pleasure circuits at once" (p. 528).

To drive home his point, Pinker has referred to music as "auditory cheesecake" (Carroll, 1998). The idea here is that some things, like our love of cheesecake, were the result of an evolutionary need but now are just simple indulgences. Fat and sugar were much less available to our prehistoric ancestors than they are today, but fat and sugar were very beneficial sources of instant energy and therefore a necessity for those prehistoric ancestors. Our ancestors evolved to enjoy the taste of fat and sugar so that they would seek it out, but our current situation—where we can have as much fat and sugar in our diet as we desire—did not produce a rapid change in our physiology. Thus, our liking for cheesecake is an aftereffect of our ancestors' need for energy and the evolution of the response to fat and sugar. Now, cheesecake tastes good because of evolution, but evolution has not caught up. Pinker argues that just like cheesecake tricks the brain, music also tricks the language system into thinking it is something beneficial.

There are critics of Pinker's theories, but there are few other evolutionary theories for how music developed. **Steven Mithen**, a cognitive archaeologist, wrote *The Singing Neanderthals* (2005) to outline his theories on how language and music co-evolved. Mithen claims that Neanderthals would have had the appropriate vocal tract and respiratory control for speech, but that neural circuitry was not present for language. The alternative that is suggested is a musically based communication system that would have allowed for exchange of ideas, but that would have also included gestures, dance, onomatopoeic imitation, and even sound synesthesia. Interestingly, in non-Westernized locations where everyone sings and participates in musical events, dancing is equally important, and song and dance are rarely separated. One of the key points of Mithen's argument is also similar to Levitin's, in that the emotional power of music suggests a lengthy evolutionary history.

Animals do not seem to share human's ability to enjoy or use music. Although researchers would logically look for behaviour like ours in our close relatives, nonhuman primates, musical ability or processing in the nonhuman primates does appear to be a little different. Chimpanzees will beat sticks on logs, gorillas beat on their chests, and macaque monkeys shake branches in the wild or in a cage to communicate dominance. Research has found that macaques process drum sounds in the same regions of the brain that they use for vocal calls, and drumming could attract the attention of the macaques. Interestingly, brain activation was in the frontal cortex, an area associated with generating appropriate social behaviour, and in the amygdala, an area responsible for emotion processing. The authors suggest that—in the same way that humans can add emotional content, such as sadness or anger, to music we hear—macaques can sense things like excitement in drum beats. That, however, is where the similarity ends, as nonhuman primates' musical ability is restricted to hammering out a beat. Another example of an animal having profound musical ability may be surprising. Snowball, a white cockatoo, became a sensation when YouTube videos circulated in early 2009 showing him dancing (as a bird would with head and leg movements) to the Backstreet Boys' hit "Everybody (Backstreet's Back)" and Queen's "Another One Bites the Dust." Snowball's dancing was even featured in a Taco Bell commercial, and Snowball danced to

the Backstreet Boys on the *Late Show with David Letterman*. Snowball could speed up or slow down with the tempo of the music, leading researchers like **Aniruddh Patel** (Patel, Iversen, Bregman, & Schulz, 2009) to suggest that a human nervous system was not necessary for producing movement that matches a musical rhythm. **Adena Schachter** of Harvard analyzed thousands of YouTube videos and found that 14 types of parrots and one type of elephant could keep rhythm. The study suggests that co-ordinated dance may have evolved along with the selection for vocal mimicry, at which parrots are also very efficient. Thus, dancing may be a side effect of being able to imitate sounds.

With the evidence suggesting that music is an early developing feature in human beings and in other animals that can imitate sounds, one is left to ask why music has not continued to be a part of family and community interactions in Westernized countries. Certainly, in a classroom of young children or in a playground, music is still heard. But with the development of two classes of people, those who listen to and those who play music, people have come to believe that, without some special training or noted skill, singing should be done only in the shower or car—when alone.

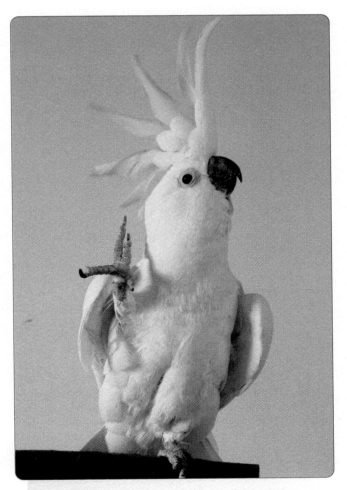

Snowball

WHY DO WE HAVE TO GO TO SCHOOL?

We have learned that there is an innate ability for language, music, and potentially even dancing, but why then is it necessary to go to school to learn about reading, writing, and math? We have amazing abilities to talk, recognize people, remember a tune, and even find our way home using a different path than the one we took to arrive, but other skills require learning. The evolutionary perspective suggests that reading, writing, and math are really novel tasks in our evolutionary past. As such, we have not developed specialized neural pathways and structures that serve these functions. Writing began approximately 8000 years ago and mathematics approximately 5000 years ago. It is no wonder that calculus is difficult for most of us, considering calculus is only about 300 years old. Contrast this with spoken language, which is thought to have begun approximately 100 000 years ago (Pinker, 1994). This long history may explain why two-year-olds have more skill with language than many of us ever master in calculus, even with years of study. Formal training provides the opportunity to master novel tasks and skills that do have advantages.

Reading could be considered an indirect product of evolution as it results from humans that have language. Even with this parallel, many people fail to learn to read, or to read well. Lila Gleitman and Paul Rozin (1973, 1977) outline the differences in the writing of Chinese and Japanese words relative to English words. They argue that we have known some features of reading for approximately three decades, and that the systems are not equal. In Chinese and Japanese, symbols are used for each word or syllable, but in English one to three letters make up a syllable, and words vary in the number of letters used to create them. Children learn the symbol language much more easily than the one with the alphabet, but the benefit does not last long. The range of English words are all made up of the 26 letters of the alphabet, but Japanese and Chinese writing may include many thousands of symbols. Gleitman and Rozin suggested that children who have trouble reading have difficulty because the task of reading becomes increasingly abstract, and that an evolutionary framework for teaching reading would take into consideration what is difficult about reading. Mapping sounds to letters is complicated, but children learn to read much better when the letters are presented in a syllabic format.

If reading is a challenge, math is even harder. Even people who are highly educated will not always also be that good at math. You might even find that your instructors, although knowing a good deal about psychology or other topics, might have difficulty simply adding up your test scores or calculating your grade (computer packages have definitely made final grade calculations much more reliable). Most numerical concepts are relatively new. Infants understand the concepts of more and less, suggesting that this is innate, but counting beyond 4 or 5 and performing complex math is a challenge to brain structures that evolved for a different purpose. Our society and environment require that we use math, and so we send young humans to school to learn about the rules necessary to do math. Those individuals who seem to develop a particular skill for math likely view math and solving math equations a little like others would view solving another, easier type of problem.

The solution to having more people do well with reading and writing should be obvious if you consider an evolutionary perspective. We need to be motivated to complete a task unless the task is to accomplish a goal that we find valuable. You must have some recollection of speeding through a book that you found particularly interesting, but putting more time and effort into one that you did not find interesting. Making material intrinsically interesting results in more motivation. It is partly for this reason that this text tries to relate many of the concepts to events and situations you may encounter. It is the goal of the authors to make your reading easier by connecting the course material with outside material so that you will find the readings intrinsically interesting.

STOP AND REVIEW

❶ Why did language evolve?

❷ How did language help provide a basis for cultural evolution?

❸ Could gossip have evolved?

CRITICAL THINKING What advantages have language skills conferred upon you?

Evolution of Emotion

One of your authors has a very vivid memory of washing floors at her first job. One evening while she was doing it, she felt a small weight drop into her hair. When she brushed the object out of her hair, she found it to be a huge spider. The beast ran when it hit the floor; it was shockingly large, but it disappeared quickly in spite of its size. Though your author does not really have a fear of spiders, the event has stayed with her because of the size of the spider and the fact that it had been in her hair. It

still makes the hairs on the back of her neck stand up. It seems odd that a memory still has the power to do this, especially since she continues to see spiders regularly. Is it possible that some of the emotions you feel are based on your ancestors' evolutionary history? There seems to be some evidence for this when it comes to certain fear responses.

Some individuals have such strong fears about certain stimuli that they cannot enjoy, or function well in, an environment where those stimuli are present. People who have a tremendous fear of spiders, for example, might not go into their basements, and might need someone else do their laundry. Though this sounds extreme, many people with a fear of spiders have taken extreme measures to avoid the eight-legged beasts! Some people who fear heights will not take jobs that require them to take plane trips or work on upper level floors of high-rise buildings. When someone has such a strong fear of a stimulus that it disrupts his or her life, we often call that fear a **phobia**. Phobias may in fact represent once-adaptive predispositions to develop fears to stimuli that were dangerous in ancestral environments. Now, you might instantly question the fear of going up in an elevator or on a plane because our ancestors did not have exposure to them! Of course, modern environments do differ from our ancestral ones. Yet an adaptive predisposition to the fear of falling from high places may still have been passed down from our ancestors—it may simply have expanded to include the fear of flying or being in high-rise buildings. Thus, our ancestors' fears are the basis for ours.

Phobias tend to fall into five categories: (1) animal, (2) natural environment (e.g., fear of heights or water), (3) blood or injury, (4) situational (e.g., elevators or small spaces), and (5) other. **Dominic Murphy** (2005) suggests that the category of "other" covers the phobias related to the features of our modern world—stimuli that were not available to our ancestors. These other phobias, like fear of ice cream, may be related to *conditioning*, where a stimulus is paired with an aversive consequence so that future presentations of that stimulus cause fear. When we are ill, for example, we may eat a food and find that we become nauseated. Later this food may cause nausea even though we are no longer ill. Somehow we have associated the food with feeling ill, so our nervous system acts to prevent us from eating it. The fear of the food does not match with an evolutionary explanation of behaviour. In this case, the behaviour is learned. If you have ever experienced an aversion to some type of food, you can do a simple test to think about whether it was learned or whether it has some evolutionary history. Do either of your parents have the same food aversion? What about your grandparents? Can you think of a specific time when you liked the food and when you stopped liking it? It is likely that the food you now really dislike was one that you ate and had a single aversive reaction to.

As the nervous system does seem specifically designed to address threats, it is interesting to evaluate phobias and our responses to certain stimuli. When a threat presents itself, our nervous system prepares us to fight or flee the threat. The only phobia that is associated with a third response, fainting, is the blood phobia. Evolution can explain this reaction as well: When people see their own blood and faint, the response could very well be adaptive. When we faint, our blood pressure drops—which means we would bleed less if we were cut. Presumably if the bleeding slowed, there would be additional opportunity for the blood to coagulate at the site of the wound and we would have a better opportunity for survival.

---

phobia A persistent and irrational fear (of a specific object, activity, or situation) that is excessive and unreasonable, given the reality of the threat.

Susan Mineka and colleagues (Mineka & Keir, 1983; Mineka, Davidson, Cook, & Keir, 1984; Mineka & Cook, 1986; Cook & Mineka, 1990) did a number of studies to evaluate the possibility of an evolutionary history for phobias. Mineka was interested in finding out if certain stimuli were likely to cause phobias and whether other stimuli could become aversive. When monkeys were shown a video of another monkey recoiling at the sight of a snake, they later responded with a similar recoiling behaviour when they were presented with a snake. Monkeys that were shown a video of a monkey recoiling at the sight of a flower, however, did not show the same response when presented with a flower at a later time. The findings suggest that monkeys—and likely all primates—accept certain stimuli as threatening and not others. The findings also suggest that fear of these stimuli cannot be learned.

Not all emotions can be completely explained by evolutionary theory. It is difficult, for example, to explain depression with evolutionary theory. Let's look at this in a bit more detail.

Depression seems to be related to a reduction in the amount of serotonin in the brain. Interestingly, dominant animals have higher levels of serotonin than more subordinate ones (Raleigh, McGuire, Brammer, & Yuwiler, 1984). Consider what happens to monkeys when they lose their dominance: Their serotonin levels drop, and their behaviour changes. The general consensus is that the monkeys feel "out-competed" and attempt to change their behaviour in order to become more successful again. Here is where an evolutionary explanation of depression does not work. In human beings, if depression is related to a situation where the environment causes individuals to feel out-competed and unable to succeed, it is likely that many more people would be depressed. Although the World Health Organization (2007) has indicated that depression rates are going up, if there were an evolutionary cause to depression, it is also likely that we would see depressives reviewing and changing their behaviour to achieve a better outcome. Depressives do in fact review their behaviour much more than nondepressives, but they do not tend to show a change in behaviour that allows for more success. As such, an evolutionary explanation does not fully explain depression.

SEEING RED

Where does the term *seeing red* come from? Many of you have probably used this expression yourself, and likely know that when people say they are seeing red it means that they are angry. We often associate the colour red with anger and aggression. **Russell Hill** and **Robert Barton** (2005) published a paper in *Nature* indicating that colour may confer a greater advantage than originally thought. They analyzed the colour of shirts worn by contestants in men's combat events from the 2004 Olympics and found there was a significant advantage to those who were wearing red. If you instantly concluded that the more skilled combatants must have been wearing red, you would have been wrong: There was no bias for the more skilled combatants to have been placed in those colours. Hill and Barton suggest that the advantage of wearing red may have been a psychological one over their competitors—an advantage that may result from an evolutionary and cultural association of dominance and aggression with the colour red. Interestingly, the same effect did not hold for females wearing red in the same sports. Despite the appeal of this study, there was a confound in how they evaluated this effect. It turns out that the colour

of shirts worn in events is not random, which would influence the data.

In a second look at this effect as part of research for an upcoming book (*Proofiness: The Dark Arts of Mathematical Deception*), **Charles Seife** looked at the outcomes of 2008 Olympic athletes with the assumption that shirt colour was not random. **Peter Dijkstra** (Dijkstra & Preenen, 2007) also confirmed this effect as a problem with the analysis and the assumption that the shirts were randomly selected. In these studies, there was no advantage to wearing one colour over another, but that does not suggest there might not be an advantage to wearing one colour over another. Norbert Hagemann, Bernd Strauss, and Jan Leissing (2008) used videos of taekwondo or wrestling matches to assess the role of colour scientifically. In the matches, opponents were wearing coloured protective gear over white taekwondo uniforms. Computer software was used to manipulate the protective gear to be blue or red. The videos were shown to experienced referees, who scored the matches. The researchers found that when opponents were wearing red, they were scored higher than when they were wearing blue, even when the performance of the competitors was identical. Thus, the colour effect investigated by Barton and Hill may not be in the performance of the athletes themselves, but in the referees' bias for scoring individuals in red uniforms differently from those in blue. Thus, the perception that colour can influence is possible, but seems to come from a different location—a bias in scoring.

Are there other situations where a change in performance based on seeing red could be directly related to your performance as a student? **Andrew Elliot** and colleagues (Elliot, Maier, Moller, Friedman, & Meinhardt, 2007) investigated volunteers to evaluate the effect of red ink on performance. In a series of studies, the researchers evaluated whether exposure to the colour red prior to an important test impacted test scores. In one experiment, for example, volunteers were given a quiz that had either a red or green number in the corner, and in another experiment volunteers saw red, green, or grey on the cover of an IQ test. Those who saw red got fewer answers correct than did those who saw the other colours. This effect was also outside of the volunteers' conscious awareness; that is, the volunteers did not link seeing the colour red with their performance on the subsequent test. Two other studies by those researchers linked the colour red with avoidance motivation and found that the colour red could be a subtle cue influencing later behaviour. Although many of your instructors will use a red pen to grade assignments out of habit, you may find that some have already learned that red pen is aversive, either from their own experiences or those of students, and will mark in another colour. If you do happen to have an instructor who marks in red pen, be sure to take a quick moment to remember this study, and focus on the marks on the paper rather than the colour they are written in. Further, never take a red pen into your exams to underline important parts of an exam, as you may be inhibiting your own scores without even knowing it.

STOP AND REVIEW

❶ Why is language described as being responsible for cultural evolution?

❷ Why is depression difficult to explain with evolutionary theory?

Applied Evolutionary Psychology

In our previous discussion about depression, we touched on how an evolutionary perspective can be used to look at illness. Today, medicine and psychology are both turning to evolutionary theory and evolutionary biology to attempt to explain certain medical and mental health issues. Consider the issue of fever. For many years it was thought that fever was bad for the body, so parents were advised to immediately give feverish children an antipyretic to reduce it. We now have much evidence that the fever response is in fact a very adaptive one. Medical research has discovered that the fever response has evolved so that the body can fight off infection. As long as the fever is not extreme, living with it can actually help the body fight off the illness. Knowing more about how the body is prepared to tackle illness is a good strategy for defining whether a response is an adaptation or a physical dysfunction that should be addressed by medicine. Let's consider an adaptation that has been a topic of medical intervention: substance abuse.

We may perceive from media and other sources that drug use is a relatively new phenomenon. The fact is that for millions of years humans have had a relationship with many plant substances that are considered drugs of abuse. **R. J. Sullivan** and **E. H. Hagen** (2001) argue that archaeological evidence indicates that people commonly used **psychotropic drugs**, indicating that we have had access to and have used drugs for a very long time. With this in mind, it appears to be no accident that the brain and body of mammals contain receptors for psychotropic drugs. Evolutionary history suggests that human beings may have a natural desire to use plant substances to alter brain function. It also appears that natural selection might be responsible for the fact that many of the chemical structures of psychotropic plant substances closely mimic human neurotransmitters—chemicals found in the human body that are used for cell-to-cell communication.

Though we do not know exactly how drugs of abuse work in the brain to result in addiction, we are closer to understanding more about this phenomenon. **Randolf Nesse** and **Kent Berridge** (1997) have suggested that the brain actually receives a signal from certain psychotropic drugs indicating, in error, that there has been a huge increase in fitness. Drugs today are often used to block negative feelings; in former times, they may have played an equal and adaptive role in reducing negative emotions. The idea that psychotropic drugs and plant chemicals could have an adaptive function and relieve people of negative emotions does not sit well with many people, simply because we have huge social taboos about drug use. We have seen some new drugs emerge that cause more concern, such as heroin from morphine (a chemical that is derived from opium produced by the opium poppy), but most of the drugs that come from plants do not raise many eyebrows. Consider for a moment that the three most regularly used drugs in the world are nicotine, ethanol, and caffeine. Do you consider chocolate to be a psychotropic drug, or is it a food?

Does eating chocolate ever make you feel better?

It is interesting to note that in Western cultures, cigarettes are packaged into neat little bundles, whereas in aboriginal cultures, nicotine was often obtained by chewing leaves or nuts containing nicotine; the aboriginals would routinely use food descriptions for nicotine rather than describing its psychotropic action. For example, they would report that, like all foods, nicotine gave them energy. Perhaps our ancestors had a good reason for drug-seeking behaviour in the sense that drugs provided them with the energy required for their daily activities (Sullivan & Hagen, 2001). However, the benefit to humans of drug seeking may no longer be present. Certainly the social and economic costs of drug use and drug-seeking behaviour suggest that if there had once been an evolutionary advantage to consuming psychotropic chemicals, it is not an advantage in the contemporary world.

In this chapter we have looked at how evolution may have contributed to our behaviour. Though we cannot confirm our theories with all certainty because evolution happened in the past, we can use the prevalent data and the archaeological record to investigate how many of our behaviours may have evolved. By trying to understand how an adaptation may have evolved over time, we may be able to explain the emergence of behaviours. Further, by comparing our society with those of our ancestors, we may be able to more fully realize why some of our nonadaptive or even maladaptive behaviours exist at all.

STOP AND REVIEW

❶ Why would a phobia be adaptive?
❷ Why should you hope to wear the red uniform when you play sports?
❸ Why should fifth-grade teachers not mark with a red pen?

CRITICAL THINKING When does ingestion of a substance change from eating the substance to drug use?

---

psychotropic drugs Substances that are used to alter behaviour, mood, or thought, which have been used for recreational purposes and for treatment of mental illness.

Recapping Main Points

Foundations of Evolutionary Psychology

- The nature versus nurture debate has been a recurrent one in psychology.
- Species originate and change over time because of natural selection.
- Species may change over time due to sexual selection pressures.

Evolution and Behaviour

- *Survival of the fittest* was coined by Herbert Spencer, who was a social Darwinist.
- Sir Francis Galton applied theories of evolution to the discussion of human abilities, such as intelligence.
- Genetic determinism suggests that all behaviour is a result of genes. Environmental determinism suggests that behaviour is influenced by the environment. It is likely that both genes and the environment contribute.
- Ethology was one of the first disciplines to form around evolutionary theory.
- Altruism is more likely when there is some likelihood of reward to the person performing the altruistic act, although it may not always be apparent what the genetic advantage is.

- Sociobiology developed as an area in psychology with the aim of offering a broad explanation of behaviour. It has faced a number of challenges, as much of the theory is based on evidence collected from nonhuman and nonprimate organisms.

The Unshakable Foundations of Darwinian Theory

- The basic unit of heredity is the gene. Genes determine the range of effects that environmental factors can have in influencing the expression of phenotypic traits.
- In the evolution of humans, bipedalism and encephalization were responsible for subsequent advances.
- Language skills provided an added advantage to humans for cultural evolution.

Visit **MyPsychLab.com** for more review and practice on the following topics:

- **Explore:** Building Blocks of Genetics
- **Practice:** Heredity and Behaviour
- **Simulate:** Genetic and Chromosomal Disorders
- **Watch:** Human Cloning: The Ethics

KEY TERMS

altruism (p. 58)
DNA (p. 64)
environmental determinism (p. 57)
ethology (p. 57)
evolutionary psychology (p. 51)
genes (p. 64)
genetic determinism (p. 56)
genetics (p. 64)
genocide (p. 60)

genome (p. 65)
genotype (p. 63)
heredity (p. 64)
heritability (p. 65)
human behaviour genetics (p. 65)
imprinting (p. 57)
inclusive fitness (p. 58)
natural selection (p. 53)
phenotype (p. 63)

phobia (p. 74)
psychotropic drugs (p. 76)
reciprocal altruism (p. 58)
sex chromosomes (p. 65)
sexual selection (p. 54)
sociobiology (p. 60)
tabula rasa (p. 57)

Practice Test

1. When Peter and Rosemary Grant studied several species of Darwin's finches, they discovered that major climate changes affected which populations of finches survived. This is an example of _____
   a. heritability.
   b. the all-or-none law.
   c. natural selection.
   d. nature versus nurture.

2. Sharon is involved in a project in which she observes the behaviours of young children. She is most able to directly observe their _____
   a. genotypes.
   b. phenotypes.
   c. chromosomes.
   d. DNA.

3. Suppose you carried out a study to assess whether there is a genetic component to "sense of humour." To conclude that genetics plays a role, you would want to find that _____
   a. DZ twins are more similar in their sense of humour than MZ twins.
   b. DZ twins always have a better sense of humour than MZ twins.
   c. MZ twins always have a better sense of humour than DZ twins.
   d. MZ twins are more similar in their sense of humour than DZ twins.

4. According to the inclusive fitness theory, if you win the lottery you are most likely to give money to _____
   a. your cousin.
   b. your sister.
   c. your brother.
   d. your father.

5. When would you expect the most amount of conflict between parents and offspring?
   a. about the time of weaning
   b. in the womb
   c. about age seven
   d. never

6. What made sociobiology controversial?
   a. no data
   b. data collected in nonhumans
   c. inconsistent data
   d. plagiarized data

7. What is the Cinderella effect?
   a. when girls believe they are going to meet a prince
   b. when one foot is a different size than the other
   c. when children living with a step-parent are at risk for abuse
   d. when children living with both biological parents are at risk for abuse

8. Why would cognitive psychologists talk about the brain as if it were a computer?
   a. Both contain wires and chips that you do not see.
   b. To do a task, both must solve a series of information-processing problems.
   c. We are really simple organisms.
   d. There have been no other explanations of how organisms do tasks.

9. Is language an adaptation or a by-product?
   a. a by-product
   b. an adaptation
   c. both a by-product and an adaptation
   d. We cannot know because we do not know the true evolutionary history.

10. Suppose you had a phobia. Which of the following is likely *not* to be something you naturally fear?
    a. water
    b. snakes
    c. spiders
    d. heights

Essay Questions

1. What important contrasts exist between research in human behaviour genetics and research in evolutionary psychology?

2. What important differences exist in different cultures with respect to cigarettes or other drugs?

3. What functions does language, and particularly gossip, serve?

The Biological Bases of Behaviour

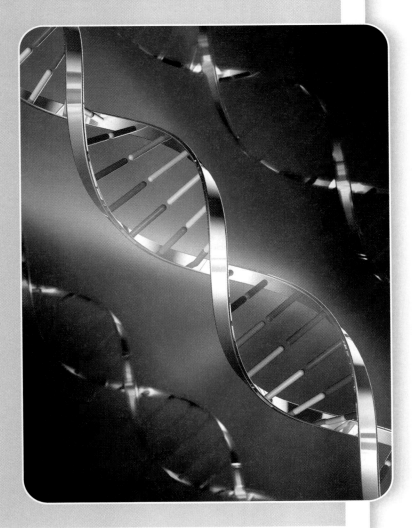

What makes you a unique individual? *Psychology and Life* provides many answers to this question, but in this chapter we will focus on the biological aspects of your individuality. To help you understand what makes you different from the people around you, we already described the role that heredity plays in shaping your life and in forming the brain that controls your experiences. Experiences that you have as an individual can also modify the brain in a short timeframe and make your brain unique. Of course, you can appreciate these differences only against the background of what you have in common with all other people. You might, therefore, think of this as a chapter about biological potential: What possibilities for behaviour define the human species, and how do those possibilities emerge for particular members of that species? How do they emerge for you?

For a number of reasons, this chapter stands as proof of one remarkable aspect of your biological potential: Your brain is sufficiently complex to carry out a systematic examination of its own functions. Why is this so remarkable? The human brain is sometimes likened to a spectacular computer: At only three pounds, your brain contains over 100 billion cells that communicate and store information with astonishing efficiency. Even the world's mightiest computer is incapable of reflecting on the rules that guide its own operation. Thus you are much more than a computer; your consciousness allows you to put your vast computational power to work, trying to determine your species' own rules for operation. The research we describe in this chapter arose from the special human desire for self-understanding.

For many students, this chapter will seem different from the discussion within other chapters in *Psychology and Life*. It requires that you learn some anatomy and many new terms that seem far removed from the information you may have expected to get from an introduction to psychology. Understanding your biological nature, however, will enable you to appreciate more fully the complex interplay among the brain, mind, behaviour, and environment that creates the unique experience of being human.

Our goal for this chapter is to allow you to understand how biology contributes to the creation of unique individuals against a shared background potential. To approach this goal, we will see how laboratory and clinical research provide a view into the workings of the brain, the nervous system, and the endocrine system. Finally, we describe the basic mechanisms of communication among cells in your nervous system that produce the full range of complex human behaviours.

The Nervous System in Action

In Chapter 3 you learned quite a lot about genes. We turn our attention now to the remarkable products of the human genotype: the biological systems that make possible the full range of human thought and performance. Long before Darwin made preparations for his trip aboard the *Beagle*, scientists,

A neuron that affects contractions in the human intestine. What are the roles of the dendrites, soma, and axons in neural transmission?

philosophers, and others debated the role that biological processes play in everyday life. An important figure in the history of brain studies was the French philosopher **René Descartes** (1596–1650). Descartes proposed what at that time was a very new and very radical idea: The human body is an "animal machine" that can be understood scientifically—by discovering natural laws through empirical observation.

Researchers who pursue these natural laws now call themselves *neuroscientists*. Today, **neuroscience** is one of the most rapidly growing areas of research. Important discoveries come with astonishing regularity. We begin with a general description

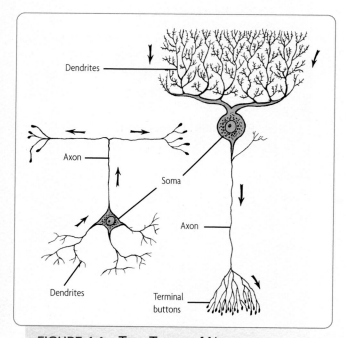

FIGURE 4.1 Two Types of Neurons
Note the differences in shape and dendritic branching. Arrows indicate directions in which information flows. Both cells are types of interneurons.

---

neuroscience The scientific study of the brain and of the links between brain activity and behaviour.

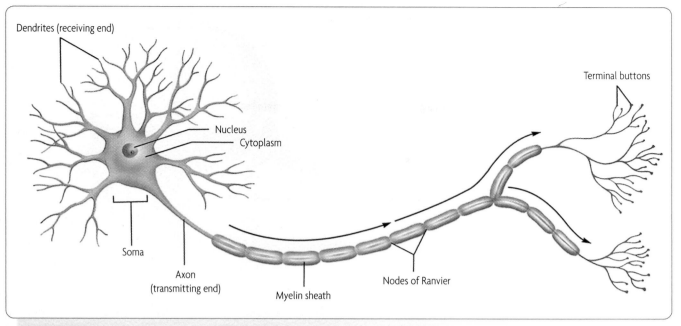

FIGURE 4.2 **The Major Structures of the Neuron**
The neuron receives nerve impulses through its dendrites. It then sends the nerve impulses through its axon to the terminal buttons, where neurotransmitters are released to stimulate other neurons.

of the structure of the nervous system, followed by a more detailed look at the brain itself. We then discuss the activity of the endocrine system, a second biological control system that works in co-operation with your nervous system and brain. Our discussion of neuroscience includes an overview of the techniques researchers use to hasten new discoveries.

One of the major goals of early physiologists was to better understand how the nervous system operates. Modern neuroscientists have made steady progress toward this goal, but they continue to work on solving smaller pieces of the puzzle. Our objective in this section is to analyze and understand how the information available to your senses is ultimately communicated throughout your body and brain by nerve impulses. We begin by discussing the properties of the basic unit of the nervous system, the neuron.

THE NEURON

A **neuron** is a cell specialized to receive, process, and/or transmit information to other cells within the body. Neurons vary in shape, size, chemical composition, and function—over 200 different types have been identified in mammalian brains—but all neurons have the same basic structure (see **Figure 4.1**). There are approximately 100 billion to 1 trillion neurons in your brain.

Neurons typically take in information at one end and send out messages from the other. The part of the cell that receives incoming signals is a set of branched fibres that extend outward from the cell body called **dendrites**. The basic job of the dendrites is to receive stimulation from sense receptors or other neurons. The cell body, or **soma**, contains the nucleus of the cell and the cytoplasm that sustains its life. The soma integrates information about the stimulation received from the dendrites (or in some cases received directly from another neuron) and

passes it on to a single, extended fibre, the **axon**. In turn, the axon conducts this information along its length—which, in the spinal cord, can be more than a metre and, in the brain, less than a millimetre. At the other end of axons are swollen, bulb-like structures called **terminal buttons**, through which the neuron is able to stimulate nearby glands, muscles, or other neurons. Neurons generally transmit information in only one direction: from the dendrites through the soma through the axon to the terminal buttons (see **Figure 4.2**).

There are three major classes of neurons; their names may give you an idea of their functions. **Sensory neurons** carry messages from sense receptor cells *toward* the central nervous system. Receptor cells are highly specialized cells that are sensitive, for example, to light, sound, and body position. **Motor neurons** carry messages *away* from the central nervous system toward the muscles and glands. The bulk of the neurons in the brain are **interneurons**, which relay messages from sensory neurons to other interneurons or to motor neurons. For every motor

---

neuron A cell in the nervous system specialized to receive, process, and/or transmit information from or to other cells.

dendrites The branched fibres of neurons that receive incoming signals.

soma The cell body of a neuron, containing the nucleus and cytoplasm.

axon The extended fibre of a neuron through which nerve impulses travel from the soma to the terminal buttons.

terminal buttons The bulblike structures at the branched endings of axons that contain vesicles filled with neurotransmitters.

sensory neurons The neurons that carry messages from sense receptors toward the central nervous system (CNS).

motor neurons The neurons that carry messages away from the central nervous system (CNS) toward the muscles and glands.

interneurons Brain neurons that relay messages from sensory neurons to other interneurons or to motor neurons.

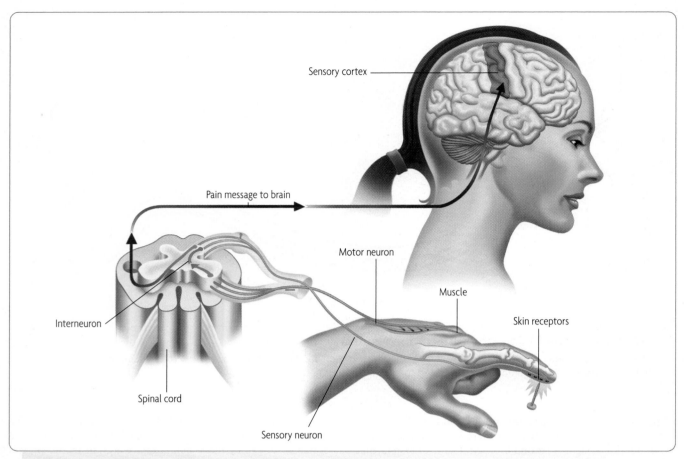

FIGURE 4.3 The Pain Withdrawal Reflex
The pain withdrawal reflex shown here involves only three neurons: a sensory neuron, a motor neuron, and an interneuron. The thumb tack activates sensory receptors in the skin. The sensory neuron makes a connection with an interneuron in the spinal cord, which in turn contacts a motor neuron in the spinal cord that is responsible for sending a signal to muscles to withdraw the hand from the tack. Think about touching something sharp or something hot, and how your hand, without your control and even without the involvement of the brain, moves away.

neuron in the body there are as many as 5000 interneurons in the great intermediate network that forms the computational system of the brain.

As an example of how these three kinds of neurons work together, consider the pain withdrawal reflex (see **Figure 4.3**). When pain receptors near the skin's surface are stimulated by a sharp object, they send messages via sensory neurons to an interneuron in the spinal cord. The interneuron responds by stimulating motor neurons, which, in turn, excite muscles in the appropriate area of the body to pull away from the pain-producing object. It is only *after* this sequence of neuronal events has taken place, and the body has been moved away from the stimulating object, that the brain receives information about the situation. In cases such as this, where survival depends on swift action, your perception of pain often occurs after you have physically responded to the danger. Of course, the information from the incident is then stored in the brain's

memory system so that next time you can avoid the potentially dangerous object altogether, before it can hurt you. **Ron Melzack** (2001, 2005) from McGill University has suggested that chronic pain and pain syndromes actually rely on a more far-ranging neural network than acute pain does. Chronic pain, he suggests, is produced by the output of a widely distributed neural network in the brain, rather than by a direct sensory input evoked by injury, inflammation, or other pathology. This is an interesting approach to looking at pain—one that might suggest why it is so difficult to control pain in chronic pain sufferers.

Interspersed among the brain's vast web of neurons are about 5 to 10 times as many glial cells (**glia**). The word *glia* is derived from the Greek word for *glue*, which gives you a hint of one of the cells' major duties: They hold neurons in place. In vertebrates, glial cells have several other important functions. A first function applies during development. Glial cells help guide newborn neurons to appropriate locations in the brain. A second function is housekeeping. When neurons are damaged and die, glial cells in the area multiply and clean up the cellular junk left behind. Glia can also take up excess neurotransmitters and other substances at the gaps between neurons. A third function is insulation. Glial cells form an insulating cover, called a myelin sheath,

glia The cells that hold neurons together and facilitate neural transmission, remove damaged and dead neurons, and prevent poisonous substances in the blood from reaching the brain.

In a resting state, the fluid surrounding the axon has a different concentration of ions than the fluid inside the axon. For that reason, the fluid within the cell is *polarized* with respect to the exterior fluid, providing the neuron's resting potential.

When a nerve impulse arrives at a segment of the axon, positively charged sodium ions flow into the axon. The inflow of sodium causes the nerve cell to become *depolarized*. The nerve impulse is passed down the axon as each successive segment becomes depolarized.

Once the nerve impulse has been passed along, sodium ions flow back out of the axon to restore the resting potential.

Once the resting potential is restored, the segment of the axon is ready to transmit another impulse.

FIGURE 4.4 The Biochemical Basis of Action Potentials

Action potentials rely on an imbalance of the electrical charge of the ions present inside and outside of axons.

From Lester A. Lefton and Linda Brannon. *Psychology.* 8e. Published by Allyn & Bacon, Boston, MA. Copyright © 2003 by Pearson Education. Reprinted by permission of the publisher.

around some types of axons. This fatty insulation greatly increases the speed of nerve signal conduction. A fourth function of glial cells is to prevent toxic substances in the blood from reaching the delicate cells of the brain. Specialized glial cells, called astrocytes, make up a *blood–brain barrier* that forms a continuous envelope of fatty material around the blood vessels in the brain. Substances that are not soluble in fat do not dissolve through this barrier; therefore, because many poisons and other harmful substances are not fat soluble, they cannot penetrate the barrier to reach the brain. Finally, neuroscientists have come to believe that glia may play an active role in neural communication by affecting the concentrations of ions that allow for the transmission of nerve impulses (Fields & Stevens-Graham, 2002).

ACTION POTENTIALS

So far, we have spoken loosely about neurons "sending messages" or "stimulating" each other. Now let's take a more formal look at the kinds of electrochemical signals used by the nervous system to process and transmit information. These signals are the basis of all you know, feel, desire, and create. It is worth noting that many diseases—including Alzheimer's disease, multiple sclerosis, Lou Gehrig's disease (amyotrophic lateral sclerosis, or ALS), and myasthenia gravis—result from situations where cells do not communicate normally. Obviously, the signals that cells send to one another are very important—not only for our day-to-day functioning, but for our very survival.

Every neuron in your body is concerned with one basic question: Should it or should it not *fire*—produce a response—at

some given time? In loose terms, neurons make this decision by combining all the information arriving at their dendrites and soma (cell body) and determining whether those inputs are predominantly saying "fire" or "don't fire." More formally, each neuron will receive a balance of **excitatory**—fire!—and **inhibitory**—don't fire!—**inputs**. The right pattern of excitatory inputs over time or space will lead to the production of an *action potential*: The neuron fires. If you are having some difficulty imagining how this works, consider when you have a big decision to make, like whether you should vacation during spring break, and you decide you will ask all of your friends to help you make a decision. You decide that if most say you should vacation during the break, then you will go, but if most say you should not, then you will not vacation then. Some of your friends will say "yes" and others will say "no," but the results for how they add up will depend on many factors and how many friends you choose to ask. The neuron decides whether it should fire by using a similar sum of excitatory and inhibitory inputs that come from other cells.

The Biochemical Basis of Action Potentials To explain how an **action potential** works, we need to describe the biochemical environment in which neurons bring together incoming information. All neural communication is produced

---

excitatory inputs Information entering a neuron that signals it to fire.

inhibitory inputs Information entering a neuron that signals it not to fire.

action potential The nerve impulse activated in a neuron that travels down the axon and causes neurotransmitters to be released into a synapse.

by the flow of electrically charged particles, called *ions*, through the neuron's membrane, a thin "skin-like" bilayer of lipids (fatty molecules) separating the cell's internal and external environments. Think of a nerve fibre as a small ball filled with saltwater, floating in a salty soup. The soup and the fluid in the ball both contain ions—atoms of sodium (Na+), chloride (Cl–), calcium (Ca+), and potassium (K+)—that have either positive (+) or negative (–) charges (see **Figure 4.4**). The membrane, or the surface of the ball, plays a critical role in keeping the ingredients of the two fluids in an appropriate balance. When a cell is inactive, or in a *resting state*, there are about 10 times as many potassium ions inside as there are sodium ions outside. The membrane of the ball, like a cell, is not a perfect barrier; it "leaks" a little, allowing some sodium ions to slip in and some potassium ions to slip out. To correct for this, nature has provided transport mechanisms within the membrane of cells that pump out sodium and pump in potassium. The successful operation of these pumps leaves the fluid inside a neuron with a slightly negative voltage (70/1000 of a volt, or 70 millivolts) relative to the fluid outside. This means that the fluid inside the cell is *polarized* with respect to the fluid outside the cell. This slight polarization is called the **resting potential**. It provides the electrochemical context in which a nerve cell can produce an action potential.

The nerve cell begins the transition from a resting potential to an action potential in response to the pattern of inhibitory and excitatory inputs. Each kind of input affects the likelihood that the balance of ions from the inside to the outside of the cell will change. They cause changes in the function of **ion channels**, excitable portions of the cell membrane that selectively permit certain ions to flow in and out. Inhibitory inputs cause the ion channels to work harder to keep the inside of the cell negatively charged, which will keep the cell from firing. Excitatory inputs cause the ion channels to begin to allow sodium ions to flow in, which will allow the cell to fire. Since sodium ions have a positive charge, their influx can begin to change the relative balance of positive and negative charges across the cell membrane. An action potential begins when the excitatory inputs are sufficiently strong with respect to inhibitory inputs to *depolarize* the cell from −70 millivolts to −55 millivolts; sufficient sodium has entered the cell to effect this change.

Once the action potential begins, sodium rushes into the neuron. As a result, the inside of the neuron becomes positive relative to the outside, which means the neuron has become fully depolarized. A domino effect now propels the action potential down the axon. The leading edge of depolarization causes ion channels in the adjacent region of the axon to open and allow sodium to rush in. In this way—through successive depolarization—the signal passes down the axon (see **Figure 4.5**).

How does the neuron return to its original resting state of polarization after it fires? When the inside of the neuron

FIGURE 4.5 Timetable for Electrical Changes in the Neuron during an Action Potential

Sodium ions entering the neuron cause its electrical potential to change from slightly negative during its polarized, or resting, state to slightly positive during depolarization. Once the neuron is depolarized, it enters a brief refractory period during which further stimulation will not produce another action potential. Another action potential can occur only after the ionic balance between the inside and the outside of the cell is restored.

becomes positive, the channels that allow sodium to flow in close and the channels that allow potassium to flow out open. The outflow of potassium ions restores the negative charge of the neuron. Thus, even while the signal is reaching the far end of the axon, the portions of the cell in which the action potential originated are being returned to their resting balance so that they can be ready for their next stimulation.

Properties of the Action Potential The biochemical manner in which the action potential is transmitted leads to several important properties. The action potential obeys the **all-or-none law**: The size of the action potential is unaffected by increases in the intensity of stimulation beyond the threshold level. Once excitatory inputs sum to reach the threshold level, a uniform action potential is generated. If the threshold is not reached, no action potential occurs. An added consequence of the all-or-none property is that the size of the action potential does not diminish along the length of the axon. In this sense, the action potential is said to be *self-propagating*: once started, it needs no outside stimulation to keep itself moving. It is similar to a lit fuse on a firecracker.

After an action potential has passed down a segment of the axon, that region of the neuron enters a **refractory period** (see Figure 4.5). During the *absolute refractory period*, further stimulation, no matter how intense, cannot cause another action potential to be generated; during the *relative refractory period*, the neuron will fire only in response to a stimulus stronger than what is ordinarily necessary. Have you ever tried to flush the toilet while it is filling back up with water? A critical level of water must be present for the toilet to flush again. Similarly, in order for a neuron to be able to generate another action potential, it must "reset" itself and await stimulation beyond its threshold. The refractory period ensures, in part, that the action potential will travel only in one

resting potential The polarization of cellular fluid within a neuron, which provides the capability to produce an action potential.

ion channels The portions of neurons' cell membranes that selectively permit certain ions to flow in and out.

all-or-none law The rule that the size of the action potential is unaffected by increases in the intensity of stimulation beyond the threshold level.

refractory period The period of rest during which a new nerve impulse cannot be activated in a segment of an axon.

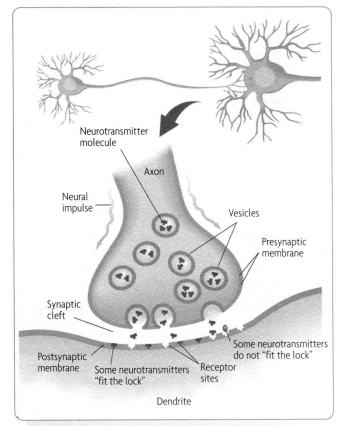

FIGURE 4.6 Synaptic Transmission
The action potential in the presynaptic neuron causes neurotransmitters to be released into the synaptic gap. Once across the gap, they stimulate receptor molecules embedded in the membrane of the postsynaptic neuron. Multiple neurotransmitters can exist within the same nerve cell.

Labels in figure:
Neurotransmitter molecule
Axon
Neural impulse
Vesicles
Presynaptic membrane
Synaptic cleft
Some neurotransmitters do not "fit the lock"
Postsynaptic membrane
Some neurotransmitters "fit the lock"
Receptor sites
Dendrite

direction down the axon: It cannot move backward, because "earlier" parts of the axon are in a refractory state.

Different neurons conduct action potentials along their axons at different speeds: the fastest have signals that move at the rate of 200 metres per second; the slowest plod along at 10 centimetres per second. The axons of the faster neurons are covered with a tightly wrapped myelin sheath—consisting, as we explained earlier, of glial cells—making this part of the neuron resemble short tubes on a string. The tiny breaks between the tubes are called *nodes of Ranvier* (see Figure 4.2). In neurons having myelinated axons, the action potential literally skips along from one node to the next—saving the time and energy required to open and close ion channels at every location on the axon. Damage to the myelin sheath throws off the delicate timing of the action potential and causes serious problems. Multiple sclerosis (MS) is a devastating disorder caused by deterioration of the myelin sheath. It is characterized by double vision, tremors, and eventually paralysis. In MS, specialized cells from the body's immune system actually attack myelinated neurons, exposing the axon and disrupting normal synaptic transmission (Joyce, 1990). Interestingly, researchers from the University of Calgary

(Beck, Metz, Svenson, & Patten, 2005) found that MS is more prevalent in the Prairie and Atlantic provinces than in Ontario, Quebec, and British Columbia, suggesting a regional difference that may be related to environmental causes. Investigating whether there are differences in the environment in some of these areas may uncover unknown factors that contribute to MS risk.

SYNAPTIC TRANSMISSION

When the action potential completes its leapfrog journey down the axon to a terminal button, it must pass its information along to the next neuron. Yet no two neurons ever touch: They are joined at a **synapse**, with a small gap between the *presynaptic membrane* (the terminal button of the sending neuron) and the *postsynaptic membrane* (the surface of a dendrite or soma of a receiving neuron). When the action potential reaches the terminal button, it sets in motion a series of events called **synaptic transmission**, which is the relaying of information from one neuron to another across the synaptic gap (see **Figure 4.6**). Synaptic transmission begins when the arrival of the action potential at the terminal button causes small round packets, called *synaptic vesicles*, to move toward and affix themselves to the interior membrane of the terminal button. Inside each vesicle are **neurotransmitters**, biochemical substances that stimulate other neurons. The action potential also causes ion channels to open that admit calcium ions into the terminal button. The influx of calcium ions causes the rupture of the synaptic vesicles and the release of whatever neurotransmitters they contain. Once the synaptic vesicles rupture, the neurotransmitters are dispersed rapidly across the *synaptic cleft* to the postsynaptic membrane. To complete synaptic transmission, the neurotransmitters attach to *receptor molecules* embedded in the postsynaptic membrane.

The neurotransmitters will bind to the receptor molecules under only two conditions. First, no other neurotransmitters or other chemical substances can be attached to the receptor molecule. Second, the shape of the neurotransmitter must match the shape of the receptor molecule—as precisely as a key fits into a keyhole. If either condition is not met, the neurotransmitter will not attach to the receptor molecule. This means that it will not be able to stimulate the postsynaptic membrane. If the neurotransmitter does become attached to the receptor molecule, then it may provide "fire" or "don't fire" information to this next neuron. Once the neurotransmitter has completed its job, it detaches from the receptor molecule and drifts back into the synaptic gap. There it is either decomposed through the action of enzymes or reabsorbed into the presynaptic terminal button for quick reuse.

Depending on the receptor molecule, a neurotransmitter will have either an excitatory or an inhibitory effect. That is, the same neurotransmitter may be excitatory at one synapse but inhibitory at another. Each neuron integrates the information it obtains at synapses with between 1000 and 10 000 other

synapse The gap between one neuron and another.

synaptic transmission The relaying of information from one neuron to another across the synaptic gap.

neurotransmitters The chemical messengers released from neurons that cross the synapse from one neuron to another, stimulating the postsynaptic neuron.

neurons to decide whether it ought to initiate another action potential. It is the integration of these thousands of inhibitory and excitatory inputs that allows all-or-none action potentials to provide the foundation for all human experience.

You may be wondering why we have taken you so deep into the nervous system. After all, this is a psychology course, and psychology is supposed to be about behaviour and thinking and emotion. In fact, synapses are the biological medium by which all of these activities occur. If you change the normal activity of the synapse, you change how people behave, how they think, and how they feel. Consider, for example, the many mental illnesses caused by a chemical change in brain cells. Understanding the functioning of the synapse has led to tremendous advances in the understanding of learning and memory, emotion, psychological disorders, drug addiction, and, in general, the chemical formula for mental health. You will use the knowledge you have acquired in this chapter throughout *Psychology and Life*.

NEUROTRANSMITTERS AND THEIR FUNCTIONS

Dozens of chemical substances are known or suspected to function as neurotransmitters in the brain. The neurotransmitters that have been studied most intensively meet a set of technical criteria. Each is manufactured in the presynaptic terminal button and is released when an action potential reaches that terminal. The neurotransmitter's presence in the synaptic cleft produces a biological response in the postsynaptic membrane; if its release is prevented, no subsequent responses can occur. To give you a sense of the effects different neurotransmitters have on the regulation of behaviour, we will discuss a set that has been found to play an important role in the daily functioning of the brain. This brief discussion will also enable you to understand many of the ways in which neural transmission can go awry.

Acetylcholine *Acetylcholine* was the first neurotransmitter ever found. Although this transmitter is found all over (in both the central and peripheral nervous systems), one of its most useful roles is setting your skeletal muscles in motion. Memory loss among patients suffering from Alzheimer's disease, a degenerative disease that is increasingly common among older persons, is believed to be caused by the deterioration of neurons that secrete acetylcholine. The McGill Centre for Studies in Aging has been researching the effects of acetylcholine on the disease. In initial studies, patients were administered acetylcholine in the form of pills to relieve their symptoms (Gauthier et al., 1989); more recent studies aim to limit the breakdown of acetylcholine already in the brain and normalize how it moves around between cells.

Acetylcholine is also excitatory at junctions between nerves and muscles, where it causes muscles to contract. A number of toxins affect the synaptic actions of acetylcholine. For example, botulinum toxin, often found in food that has been preserved incorrectly, poisons an individual by preventing release of acetylcholine in the respiratory system. This poisoning, known as *botulism*, can cause death by suffocation. Curare, a poison that indigenous people of the Amazon use on the tips of their blowgun darts, paralyzes lung muscles by occupying critical acetylcholine receptors, preventing the normal activity of the transmitter.

GABA *GABA* (gamma-aminobutyric acid) is the most common inhibitory neurotransmitter in the brain. GABA may be used as a messenger in as many as a third of all brain synapses. Neurons that are sensitive to GABA are particularly concentrated in brain regions involved in sensory communication, in structures that regulate our body, and in the visual system (the thalamus, hypothalamus, and occipital lobes, respectively). GABA appears to play a critical role in some forms of psychopathology by inhibiting neural activity; when levels of this neurotransmitter in the brain become low, people may experience the extra neural activity as feelings of anxiety. Anxiety disorders are often treated with *benzodiazepine* drugs, such as Valium or Xanax, that increase GABA activity (Ballenger, 1999). The benzodiazepine drugs do not attach directly to GABA receptors. Instead, they allow GABA itself to bind more effectively to postsynaptic receptor molecules.

Norepinephrine, Dopamine, and Serotonin The *catecholamines* are a class of chemical substances that include two important neurotransmitters, *norepinephrine and dopamine*. Both have been shown to play prominent roles in psychological disorders, such as mood disturbances and schizophrenia. Norepinephrine appears to be involved in some forms of depression: Drugs that increase brain levels of this neurotransmitter elevate mood and relieve depression. Conversely, higher-than-normal levels of dopamine have been found in persons with schizophrenia. As you might expect, one way to treat people with this disorder is to give them a drug that decreases brain levels of dopamine. In the early days of drug therapy, an interesting but unfortunate problem arose. High doses of the drug used to treat schizophrenia produced symptoms of Parkinson's disease, a progressive and ultimately fatal disorder involving disruption of motor functioning. (Parkinson's disease is caused by the deterioration of neurons that manufacture most of the brain's dopamine.) This finding led to research that improved drug therapy for schizophrenia and to research that focused on drugs that could be used in the treatment of Parkinson's disease.

All the neurons that produce *serotonin* are located in the brain stem, which is involved in the process of arousal and other autonomic processes. The hallucinogenic drug LSD (lysergic acid diethylamide) appears to produce its effects by suppressing

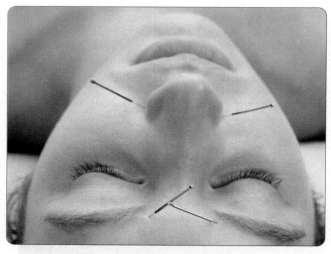

Why do patients experience pain relief from acupuncture?

Psychology in Your Life

HOW DOES YOUR BRAIN DETERMINE TRUST?

Suppose a friend makes you a promise. You worry that the promise is empty, but your friend says, "Trust me!" Should you? In recent years, researchers have begun to understand how your brain responds when you have to make decisions about trust. Much of that research has focused on a hormone called oxytocin.

Oxytocin first became the focus of researchers who were interested in the biological mechanisms that prompt nonhuman animals to form social bonds (Bartz & Hollander, 2006; Lim & Young, 2006). Brain levels of oxytocin affect the likelihood that mother rats will bond with their pups and the likelihood that adult rats will engage in social interaction. Research suggests that oxytocin has an impact because it promotes approach behaviour. Consider again that friend who made you a promise. The decision to trust or not can be boiled down to a choice between approach and avoidance— you decide to continue to interact with this individual or you decide to steer clear. High brain levels of oxytocin tilt the balance toward approach. Oxytocin functions in your brain to make it seem likely that future interactions will continue to be rewarding.

To document the dramatic impact of oxytocin, a team of researchers recruited participants to play a game that focused on trust (Baumgartner, Heinrichs, Vonlanthen, Fischbacher, & Fehr, 2008). The game required two players to distribute a pool of "money units." In each round, the investor had to decide how many money units, out of 12, to invest. The experimenters provided the trustee with returns on those investments. The trustee then had the opportunity to share those returns fairly with the investor or not. In fact, halfway through the game, the investors all got the same feedback:

The experimenters told them that they were only getting their fair share about half the time. The trustees could not be trusted!

What happened in the second half of the game depended on the investors' levels of oxytocin. Before the game started, half the investors received a dose of the hormone through a nasal spray. (Once it is absorbed, the hormone is able to cross into the brain.) The other participants received a placebo. For the first half of the game, it made little difference whether investors had inhaled oxytocin or the placebo. The graph plots the average number of money units participants invested in each round. As you can see, before the feedback oxytocin participants invested nearly the same amount as placebo participants. You might expect that the dramatic feedback— Don't trust this person!—would prompt participants to reduce their investments. That's exactly what the placebo group did. Their investments fell for the second half of the game. However, the oxytocin group didn't reduce their investments. In fact, as you can see in the figure, the trend was in the opposite direction. Apparently, the pre-experimental dose

of oxytocin prevented participants from acting on the information that the other players had violated their trust.

There's one more element to this project: While the investors were making their decisions, they were undergoing fMRI scans. Those brain data enabled the researchers to determine what areas of the brain were affected by the dose of oxytocin. The scans revealed that oxytocin participants showed less brain activity in regions of the brain, such as the amygdala, that are involved in fear responses. The researchers suggested that the oxytocin dampens fear responses and thereby increases participants' ability "to trust in situations characterized by the risk of betrayal" (Baumgartner et al., 2008, p. 645).

After reading about this study, you might wonder about the levels of oxytocin in your own brain: Does your brain chemistry predispose you to trust or distrust your friend? Researchers are starting to consider exactly that question of how individual differences in people's levels of oxytocin may have an important impact on social behaviour (Bartz & Hollander, 2006; Lim & Young, 2006).

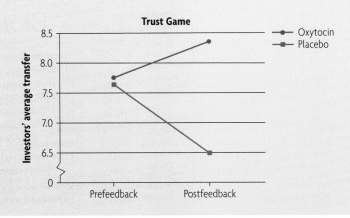

the effects of serotonin neurons. These serotonin neurons normally inhibit other neurons, but the lack of inhibition produced by LSD creates vivid and bizarre sensory experiences, some of which last for hours. Many antidepressant drugs, such as Prozac, enhance the action of serotonin by preventing it from being removed from the synaptic cleft (Barondes, 1994). Antidepressants used for the treatment of seasonal affective disorder, such as fluoxetine, are serotonin uptake inhibitors. Raymond Lam and colleagues (2006) evaluated the effects of light therapy and fluoxetine on seasonal affective disorder in four Canadian treatment centres. Both light therapy and fluoxetine reduced symptoms of depression. The fluoxetine has negative side effects, which may make light treatment a better option for many with seasonal affective disorder.

Endorphins The *endorphins* are a group of chemicals that are usually classified as **neuromodulators**. A neuromodulator is any substance that modifies or modulates the activities of the postsynaptic neuron. Endorphins (short for *endogenous morphines*) play an important role in the control of emotional behaviours (anxiety, fear, tension, pleasure) and pain—drugs like opium and morphine bind to the same receptor sites in the brain. Endorphins have been called the "keys to paradise" because of their pleasure–pain controlling properties. Researchers have examined the possibility that endorphins are at least partially responsible for the pain-reducing effects of acupuncture and placebos (Murray, 1995). Such tests rely on the drug *naloxone*, whose only known effect is to block morphine and endorphins from binding to receptors: Any procedure that reduces pain by stimulating release of endorphins becomes ineffective when naloxone is administered. With the injection of naloxone, acupuncture and placebos do, in fact, lose their power—suggesting that, ordinarily, endorphins help them do their work. A similar drug called *naltrexone*, which also blocks morphine and endorphins, has been used to curb cravings in alcoholics. Like naloxone, naltrexone works by blocking the chemical reactions in your brain that make you "feel" pleasure when you use alcohol and narcotics. The fact that naltrexone reduced cravings suggests that endogenous opioids—peptide hormones that occur naturally in your body and that are similar to drugs like morphine—are also involved in alcohol dependence, at least in some individuals (Romach et al., 2002). Although naloxone and naltrexone are not of themselves cures for addiction, they do appear to reduce users' desire to drink alcohol or use narcotics, making other treatment possibilities more promising.

Other Types of Signals Researchers have also documented that gases like *carbon monoxide* and *nitric oxide* can function as neurotransmitters (Barinaga, 1993). What is most surprising about this new class of neurotransmitters is that they violate many of the normal expectations about synaptic transmission. For example, rather than binding to receptor molecules, as do the other neurotransmitters we have discussed, these gaseous transmitters appear to pass directly through the receptor cell's outer membrane. This surprising discovery should reinforce your impression that the brain possesses many secrets yet to be revealed.

---

neuromodulator Any substance that modifies or modulates the activities of the postsynaptic neuron.

Roughly 100 000 Canadians, including the actor Michael J. Fox, are impaired by Parkinson's disease. Research on the neurotransmitter dopamine has led to advances in understanding this disease. How does basic research in neuroscience allow for improved treatments?

STOP AND REVIEW

❶ What is the pattern of information flow through the major parts of each neuron?

❷ What is meant by the "all-or-none law"?

❸ How do neurotransmitters pass from one neuron to the next?

❹ What chemical substance is the most common inhibitory neurotransmitter in the brain?

Biology and Behaviour

You now have an understanding of the basic mechanisms that allow nerve cells to communicate. The time has come to assemble those neurons into the larger systems that guide your body and mind. We begin this discussion with an overview of the techniques researchers use to hasten new discoveries. We then offer a general description of the structure of the nervous system, followed by a more detailed look at the brain itself. We discuss the activity of the endocrine system, a second biological control system that works in co-operation with your nervous system and brain. Finally, we describe ways in which your life experiences continue to modify your brain.

EAVESDROPPING ON THE BRAIN

Neuroscientists seek to understand how the brain works at a number of different levels—from the operation of large structures visible to the naked eye to the properties and internal

Why do researchers study the brain to understand human psychology?

workings of individual nerve cells visible only under powerful microscopes. The techniques researchers use are suited to their level of analysis. Here, we discuss the techniques that have been used most often to attribute functions and behaviours to particular regions of the brain.

Interventions in the Brain Several research methods in neuroscience involve direct intervention with structures in the brain. These methods find their historical roots in circumstances like the story of railroad foreman Phineas Gage, who, in September of 1848, suffered an accident in which a 3-foot, 7-inch-long pole was blown through his head as the result of an unexpected explosion. Gage's physical impairment was remarkably slight: He lost vision in his left eye, and the left side of his face was partially paralyzed, but his posture, movement, and speech were all unimpaired. Yet, psychologically, he was a changed man, as his doctor's account made clear:

> The equilibrium or balance, so to speak, between his intellectual faculties and animal propensities seems to have been destroyed. He is fitful, irreverent, indulging at times in the grossest profanity (which was not previously his custom), manifesting but little deference for his fellows, impatient of restraint or advice when it conflicts with his desires. . . . Previous to his injury, though untrained in schools, he possessed a well-balanced mind, and was looked upon by those who knew him as a shrewd, smart businessman, very energetic and persistent in executing all his plans of operation. In this regard his mind was radically changed, so decidedly that his friends and acquaintances said he was "no longer Gage." (Harlow, 1868, pp. 339–340)

Gage's injury came at a time when scientists were just beginning to form hypotheses about the links between brain functions and complex behaviour. The behavioural changes following the dramatic piercing of Gage's brain prompted his doctor to hypothesize brain bases for aspects of personality and rational behaviour.

At about the same time that Gage was recovering from his injury, **Paul Broca** was studying the brain's role in language. Broca's first research in this area involved an autopsy of a man whose name was derived from the only word he had been able to

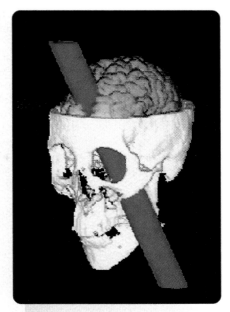

Phineas Gage's skull is preserved in the collections of the Warren Anatomical Museum, Harvard University Medical School. Why were doctors so fascinated by Gage's changes in personality?

speak, "Tan." Broca found that the left front portion of Tan's brain had been severely damaged. This finding led Broca to study the brains of other persons who suffered from language impairments. In each case, Broca's work revealed similar damage to the same area of the brain, a region now known as **Broca's area**. This area is considered the speech area of the brain and is located in the brain's left hemisphere. It is close to and works with the motor cortex to create the movements necessary to speak. You shall see as *Psychology and Life* unfolds that contemporary researchers still attempt to correlate impairment and other patterns of behaviour change with sites of brain damage.

The problem with studying accidentally damaged brains, of course, is that researchers have no control over the location and extent of the damage. To produce a well-founded understanding of the brain and its relationship to behavioural and cognitive functioning, scientists need methods that allow them to specify precisely the brain tissue that has been incapacitated. Researchers have developed a variety of techniques to produce **lesions**, highly localized brain injuries. They may, for example, surgically remove specific brain areas, cut the neural connections to those areas, or destroy those areas through application of intense heat, cold, or electricity. As you would guess, experimental work with permanent lesions is carried out exclusively with nonhuman animals. (Recall from our discussion in Chapter 2 that the ethics of this type of animal research have now come under heightened scrutiny, but some questions cannot be answered using human participants.) Our conception of the brain has been radically changed as researchers have repeatedly

---

Broca's area The region of the brain that translates thoughts into speech or signs.

lesions Injuries to or destruction of brain tissue.

compared and co-ordinated the results of lesioning experiments on animals with the growing body of clinical findings on the effects of brain damage on human behaviour.

On other occasions, neuroscientists learn about the function of brain regions by directly *stimulating* them with small electrical currents. **Wilder Penfield**, a famous neurosurgeon, forged the way in the use of stimulation techniques when he set up the Montreal Neurological Institute (MNI) in the 1930s to help patients with neurological diseases and to unlock the mysteries of the brain. In the 1950s, Penfield had been trying to treat patients with epilepsy. He was aware of the fact that just before a seizure, patients often reported an "aura"—a vivid sensation that preceded the seizure. He hypothesized that if he could evoke the same sensation with an electrical current, he could locate the site of the seizure and remove that tissue from the brain to try to eliminate future episodes. Penfield opened the skulls of anesthetized but fully conscious patients and gently stimulated cortical areas to try to induce the aura. He asked his patients questions about their sensations and feelings. Guided by their answers, Penfield tried to identify the brain area that was the source of the seizures.

Penfield's stimulation technique worked, and many people travelled to the MNI for the "Montreal Procedure." Penfield's technique led him to an even more interesting discovery: He found he was able to reveal functions of the previously unmapped human brain. Penfield discovered that stimulation of the cerebral cortex could bring stimulation-induced responses of a variety of types. He could make people feel that someone had touched them—when in fact this was not the case—and even elicit certain movements. Through this experimental stimulation, Penfield was able to develop a map of the brain, which is often portrayed in textbooks as a miniature human—or the *motor homunculus* (see photo). We will learn

more about this later in this chapter. He also found that only when stimulating the temporal lobes could he elicit responses such as memory. These memories were unusual in that they were much more distinct than general memory, and were often about things human subjects would not remember under ordinary circumstances of recall. Interestingly, when he stimulated the same area again, the exact same memory was recalled. Imagine a simple electric current delivered to a particular brain location repeatedly eliciting the memory of a certain song or the image of a childhood friend every single time. Penfield seemed to have discovered a physical basis for memory.

You can see a re-creation of one of Penfield's stimulation studies here: www.histori.ca/minutes/minute.do?id=10211.

At the same time Penfield was stimulating human brains, similar types of experiments were being performed on animals. In the mid-1950s, **Walter Hess** pioneered the use of electrical stimulation to probe structures deep in the brain when he put electrodes into the brains of freely moving cats. By pressing a button, Hess could then send a small electrical current to the point of the electrode. Hess carefully recorded the behavioural consequences of stimulating 4500 brain sites in nearly 500 cats. He discovered that, depending on the location of the electrode, sleep, sexual arousal, anxiety, or terror could be provoked by the flick of a switch—and turned off just as abruptly. For example, electrical stimulation of certain regions of the brain led the otherwise gentle cats to bristle with rage and hurl themselves upon a nearby object. By going deeper into the brain, Hess was able to identify functions of brain structures that Penfield simply could not access in humans.

In recent years, scientists have developed a procedure called **repetitive transcranial magnetic stimulation (rTMS)**, which uses pulses of magnetic stimulation to create temporary, reversible "lesions" in human participants; without any damage to tissue, brain regions can be briefly inactivated or activated. Imagine having a magnetic pulse to the part of your brain that controls speech and that suddenly stops you from speaking for

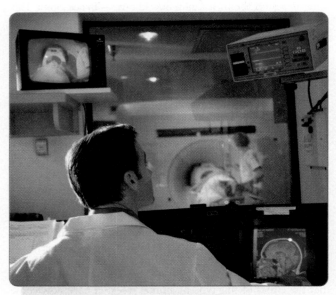

How have new imaging techniques expanded the range of questions researchers can ask?

The homunculus provides a representation of the brain's encoding of body parts. The body parts that are large relative to other body parts have more neurons associated with them.

repetitive transcranial magnetic stimulation (rTMS) A technique for producing temporary inactivation of brain areas using repeated pulses of magnetic stimulation.

just a moment—a momentary reversible lesion—or a magnetic pulse to the part of your brain responsible for arm movement that causes your arm to move—a momentary stimulation. This new technique enables researchers to address a range of questions that would not have been possible with nonhuman experiments. Consider the following application of the rTMS temporary lesion method in studying the brain bases of visual imagery:

> Take a moment to fix your eyes on an object in your environment, perhaps a tree outside the nearest window. Now close your eyes and form a mental image of that same object. What happened in your brain during these two activities? How likely do you think it is that some of the same brain regions are involved in both real acts of perception and in visual imagination? To answer this question, researchers asked participants to memorize displays with four quadrants (see **Figure 4.7**) and then visualize the displays with their eyes closed (Kosslyn et al., 1999). The participants' task was to answer questions about the relative length or width of the stripes in the different quadrants. This task was designed so that participants were obliged to form visual images. The researchers then used rTMS to temporarily "lesion" the parts of the brain people use for ordinary vision (which we will discuss in Chapter 5). Similar to when participants made the quadrant comparisons with their eyes wide open, performance was consistently disrupted in circumstances of visual imagery. This finding strongly suggests that the same brain areas are at work when you look at a tree as when you form a visual image of a tree.

You can see why this experiment would not be possible with nonhuman participants: How could we be certain that a rat had formed a visual image? This study illustrates why an ability to create reversible "lesions" has great potential for improving our understanding of how the brain functions.

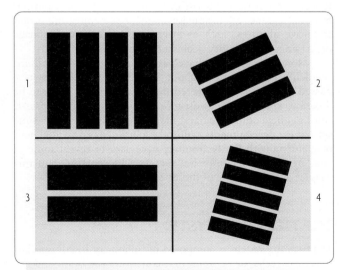

FIGURE 4.7 Test for Visual Imagery
Try to memorize this figure, quadrant by quadrant, until you can form a mental image of all four. Now cover the display with your hand. Answer this question by creating a mental visual image: Are the lines longer in quadrant 1 or quadrant 2? Confirm your answer by looking back at the figure.

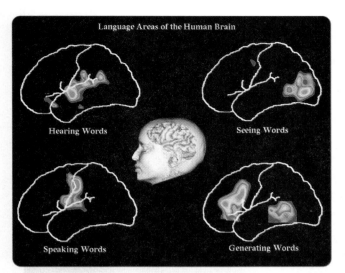

FIGURE 4.8 PET Scans of the Brain at Work
These PET scans show that different tasks stimulate neural activity in distinct regions of the brain.

The **transcranial magnetic stimulation** (TMS) technique has been used to stimulate brain regions with magnetic pulses to evaluate how learning or experience can change the brain. The researchers (Kleim et al., 2006) tested subjects on three fine-motor tasks and used the TMS to evaluate the connection between the cortex and the muscles in the hand. In one experiment, the TMS technique was used to send magnetic pulses to the motor cortex of each subject, which caused a small hand movement. The subject was then asked to press the "1" and "3" keys on a keyboard with the right index finger as fast as possible for 15 seconds, followed by a 15-second break. This was repeated 10 times. The subjects then underwent a second TMS procedure to evaluate whether the keyboard exercise had improved the cortex's ability to send a signal to the hand muscle to move. The TMS pulse was applied to the motor cortex to see if the hand movement was actually bigger following the training. Indeed, the motor-skill learning tasks resulted in a stronger stimulation-induced response of the hand muscle. This is an excellent demonstration of how learning changed the brain, and the method for assessing this was very non-invasive.

Recording and Imaging Brain Activity Contemporary neuroscientists also map brain function by using electrodes to record the electrical activity of the brain in response to environmental stimulation as well as electrical stimulation. The brain's electrical output can be monitored at different levels of precision. At the most specific, researchers can insert ultrasensitive microelectrodes into the brain to record the electrical activity of a single brain cell. Such recordings can illuminate changes in the activity of individual cells in response to stimuli in the environment.

For human subjects, researchers often place a number of electrodes on the surface of the scalp to record larger, integrated patterns of electrical activity. These electrodes provide the data

transcranial magnetic stimulation (TMS) A technique for stimulating brain regions using magnetic pulses.

Magnetic resonance imaging (MRI) produces this colour-enhanced profile of a normal brain. What is the purpose of trying to identify brain regions that underlie particular functions?

for an **electroencephalogram** (**EEG**), or an amplified tracing of the brain activity. EEGs can be used to study the relationship between psychological activities and brain response. For example, in one experiment, participants were asked to view a series of faces and make judgments about whether they thought they would be able to recognize each face in a later memory task. The EEGs revealed a distinctive pattern of brain activity at the time the participants made their judgments that predicted those instances in which the participants were, in fact, later able to recognize the faces (Sommer, Heinz, Leuthold, Matt, & Schweinberger, 1995).

In another experiment, child and adult musicians and non-musicians were tested to evaluate whether their brains respond the same way to musical sounds, and whether their brains actually change when learning musical sounds (Trainor, Shahin, & Roberts, 2003). In this case, subjects were trained by being presented with pure tones, violin tones, and piano tones; they were later tested on frequency discriminations. The EEGs suggested that there was a brain change in EEG patterns with the musical sound training. Interestingly, musicians have a larger amplitude on a key measure than non-musicians, but

---

electroencephalogram (**EEG**) A recording of the electrical activity of the brain.

PET scans Brain images produced by a device that obtains detailed pictures of activity in the living brain by recording the radioactivity emitted by cells during different cognitive or behavioural activities.

magnetic resonance imaging (**MRI**) A technique for brain imaging that scans the brain using magnetic fields and radio waves.

functional MRI (**fMRI**) A brain-imaging technique that combines benefits of both MRI and PET scans by detecting magnetic changes in the flow of blood to cells in the brain.

central nervous system (**CNS**) The part of the nervous system consisting of the brain and spinal cord.

peripheral nervous system (**PNS**) The part of the nervous system composed of the spinal and cranial nerves that connects the body's sensory receptors to the CNS and the CNS to the muscles and glands.

non-musician adults and children can show an increase in amplitude (how big the EEG signal is) with training. The finding suggests that all brains have the ability to undergo change with exposure to musical sounds.

Some of the most exciting technological innovations for studying the brain are machines originally developed to help neurosurgeons detect brain abnormalities, such as damage caused by strokes or diseases. These devices produce images of the living brain without invasive procedures that risk damaging brain tissue.

In research with positron-emission tomography, or **PET scans**, subjects are given different kinds of radioactive (but safe) substances resembling the sugars that the brain normally uses for energy. They eventually travel to the brain, where they are taken up by active brain cells. Recording instruments outside the skull can detect the radioactivity emitted by cells that are active during different cognitive or behavioural activities. This information is then fed into a computer that constructs a dynamic portrait of the brain, showing where different types of psychological activities are actually occurring (see **Figure 4.8**).

Magnetic resonance imaging (**MRI**) uses magnetic fields and radio waves to generate pulses of energy within the brain. As the pulse is tuned to different frequencies, some atoms line up with the magnetic field. When the magnetic pulse is turned off, the atoms vibrate (resonate) as they return to their original positions. Special radio receivers detect this resonance and channel information to a computer, which generates images of the locations of different atoms in areas of the brain. By looking at the image, researchers can link brain structures to psychological processes.

MRI is most useful for providing clear images of anatomical details; PET scans provide better information about function. A newer technique called **functional MRI** (**fMRI**) combines some of the benefits of both techniques by detecting magnetic changes in the flow of blood to cells in the brain; fMRI allows more precise claims about both structure and function. Researchers have begun to use fMRI to discover the distributions of brain regions responsible for many of your most important cognitive abilities, such as attention, perception, language processing, and memory (Cabeza & Nyberg, 2000).

More than 300 years have passed since Descartes sat in his candlelit study and mused about the brain; over 100 years have passed since Broca discovered that brain regions seem to be linked to specific functions; more than 50 years have passed since Penfield stimulated and mapped the cortex. In the time since these developments, cultural evolution has provided neuroscientists with the technology necessary to reveal some of your brain's most important secrets. The remainder of this chapter describes some of those secrets.

THE NERVOUS SYSTEM

The nervous system is composed of billions of highly specialized nerve cells, or *neurons*, that constitute the brain and the nerve fibres found throughout the body. The nervous system is subdivided into two major divisions: the **central nervous system** (**CNS**) and the **peripheral nervous system** (**PNS**). The CNS is composed of all the neurons in the brain and spinal cord; the PNS is made up of all the neurons forming the nerve fibres that connect the CNS to the body. **Figures 4.9** and **4.10** show the relationship of the CNS to the PNS.

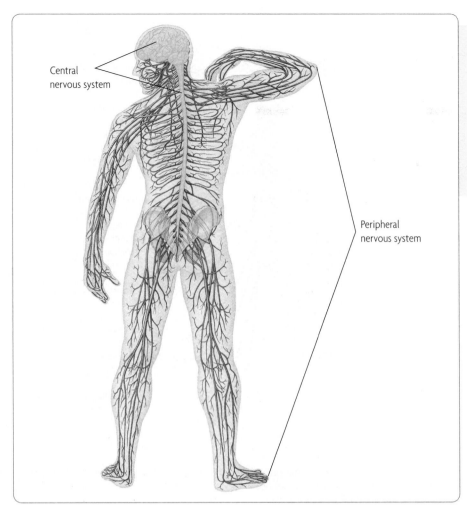

Central
nervous system

Peripheral
nervous system

FIGURE 4.9 Divisions of the Central and Peripheral Nervous Systems

The sensory and motor nerve fibres that constitute the peripheral nervous system are linked to the brain by the spinal cord.

From Richard D. McAnulty and M. Michele Burnette. *Fundamentals of Human Sexuality,* p. 87. Published by Allyn & Bacon, Boston, MA. Copyright © 2003 by Pearson Education. Reprinted by permission of the publisher.

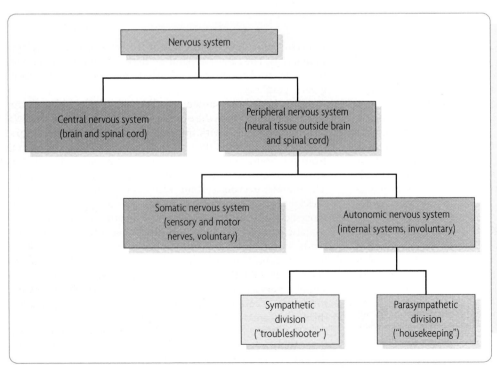

Nervous system

Central nervous system
(brain and spinal cord)

Peripheral nervous system
(neural tissue outside brain and spinal cord)

Somatic nervous system
(sensory and motor nerves, voluntary)

Autonomic nervous system
(internal systems, involuntary)

Sympathetic division
("troubleshooter")

Parasympathetic division
("housekeeping")

FIGURE 4.10 Hierarchical Organization of the Human Nervous System

The central nervous system is composed of the brain and the spinal cord. The peripheral nervous system is divided according to function: The somatic nervous system controls voluntary actions, and the autonomic nervous system regulates internal processes. The autonomic nervous system is subdivided into two systems: The sympathetic nervous system governs behaviour in emergency situations, and the parasympathetic nervous system regulates behaviour and internal processes in routine circumstances.

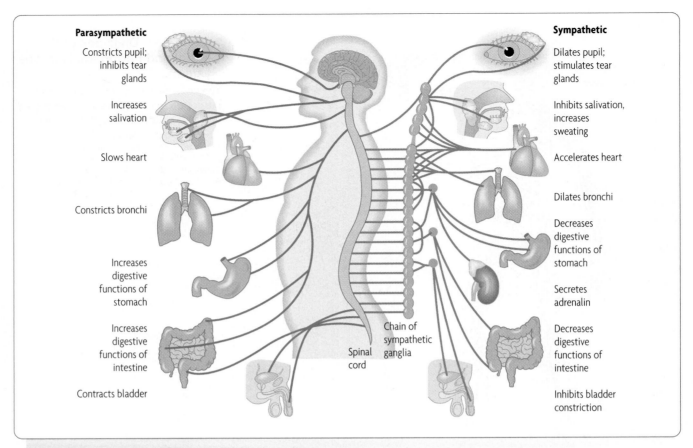

Parasympathetic

Constricts pupil; inhibits tear glands

Increases salivation

Slows heart

Constricts bronchi

Increases digestive functions of stomach

Increases digestive functions of intestine

Contracts bladder

Sympathetic

Dilates pupil; stimulates tear glands

Inhibits salivation, increases sweating

Accelerates heart

Dilates bronchi

Decreases digestive functions of stomach

Secretes adrenalin

Decreases digestive functions of intestine

Inhibits bladder constriction

Chain of sympathetic ganglia

Spinal cord

FIGURE 4.11   The Autonomic Nervous System

The parasympathetic nervous system, which regulates day-to-day internal processes and behaviour, is shown on the left. The sympathetic nervous system, which regulates internal processes and behaviour in stressful situations, is shown on the right. Note that on their way to and from the spinal cord, the nerve fibres of the sympathetic nervous system innervate, or make connections with, ganglia, which are specialized clusters of neuron chains.

The job of the CNS is to integrate and co-ordinate all bodily functions, process all incoming neural messages, and send out commands to different parts of the body. The CNS sends and receives neural messages through the *spinal cord*, a trunk line of neurons that connects the brain to the PNS. The trunk line itself is housed in a hollow portion of the vertebral column, called the spinal column. Spinal nerves branch out from the spinal cord between each pair of vertebrae in the spinal column, eventually connecting with sensory receptors throughout the body and with muscles and glands. The spinal cord co-ordinates the activity of the left and right sides of the body and is responsible for simple, fast-action reflexes that do not involve the brain. For example, an organism whose spinal cord has been severed from its brain can still withdraw its limb from a painful stimulus. Though an intact brain would normally be notified of such action, the organism can complete the action without directions from above. Damage to the nerves of the spinal cord can result in paralysis of the legs or trunk, as seen in paraplegic individuals. The extent of paralysis depends on how high up on the spinal cord the damage occurred; higher damage produces greater paralysis.

Despite its commanding position, the CNS is isolated from any direct contact with the outside world. It is the role of the PNS to provide the CNS with information from sensory receptors, such as those found in the eyes and ears, and to relay commands from the brain to the body's organs and muscles. The PNS is actually composed of two sets of nerve fibres (see Figure 4.10). The **somatic nervous system** regulates the actions of the body's skeletal muscles. For example, imagine you are typing a letter. The movement of your fingers over the keyboard is managed by your somatic nervous system. As you decide what to say, your brain sends commands to your fingers to press certain keys. Simultaneously, the fingers send feedback about their position and movement to the brain. If you strike the wrong key (th**w**), the somatic nervous system informs the brain, which then issues the necessary correction, and, in a fraction of a second, you delete the mistake and hit the right key (th**e**).

The other branch of the PNS is the **autonomic nervous system (ANS)**, which sustains basic life processes. This system is on the job 24 hours a day, regulating bodily functions that you usually do not consciously control, such as respiration, digestion, and

somatic nervous system The subdivision of the peripheral nervous system that connects the central nervous system to the skeletal muscles and skin.

autonomic nervous system (ANS) The subdivision of the peripheral nervous system that controls the body's involuntary motor responses by connecting the sensory receptors to the central nervous system (CNS) and the CNS to the smooth muscle, cardiac muscle, and glands.

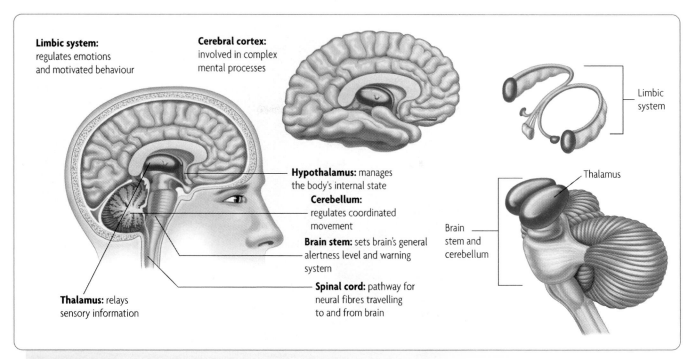

FIGURE 4.12 Brain Structures

The brain contains several major components, including the brain stem, cerebellum, limbic system, and cerebral cortex, all of which fit together in an intricate design.

arousal. The ANS must work even when you are asleep, and it sustains life processes during anesthesia and prolonged coma states.

The autonomic nervous system deals with survival matters of two kinds: those involving threats to the organism and those involving bodily maintenance. To carry out these functions, the autonomic nervous system is further subdivided into the sympathetic and parasympathetic nervous systems (see Figure 4.10). These divisions work in opposition to accomplish their tasks. The **sympathetic division** governs responses to emergency situations, whereas the **parasympathetic division** monitors the routine operation of the body's internal functions. The sympathetic division can be regarded as a troubleshooter; in an emergency or stressful situation, it arouses the brain structures for "fight or flight." Digestion stops, blood flows away from internal organs to the muscles, oxygen transfer increases, and heart rate increases. After the danger is over, the parasympathetic division takes charge, and the individual begins to calm down. Digestion resumes, heartbeat slows, and breathing is relaxed. The parasympathetic division carries out the body's nonemergency housekeeping chores, such as elimination of bodily wastes, protection of the visual system (through tears and pupil constriction), and long-term conservation of body energy. The separate duties of the sympathetic and parasympathetic nervous systems are illustrated in **Figure 4.11**.

BRAIN STRUCTURES AND THEIR FUNCTIONS

The brain is the most important component of your central nervous system. The brains of human beings have three interconnected layers. In the deepest recesses of the brain, in a region called the *brain stem*, are structures involved primarily with

autonomic processes such as heart rate, breathing, swallowing, and digestion. Enveloping this central core is the *limbic system*, which is involved with motivation, emotion, and memory processes. Wrapped around these two regions is the *cerebrum*. The universe of the human mind exists in this region. The cerebrum, and its surface layer, the *cerebral cortex*, integrates sensory information, co-ordinates your movements, and facilitates abstract thinking and reasoning (see **Figure 4.12**). Let's look more closely at the functions of the three major brain regions, beginning with the brain stem, thalamus, and cerebellum.

The Brain Stem, Thalamus, and Cerebellum The **brain stem** is found in all vertebrate species. It contains structures that collectively regulate the internal state of the body (see **Figure 4.13**). The **medulla**, located at the very top of the spinal cord, is the centre for breathing, blood pressure, and the beating of the heart. Since these processes are essential for life, damage to the medulla can be fatal. Nerve fibres ascending from the body and descending from the brain cross over at the medulla, which means that the left side of the body is linked to the right side of the brain and the right side of the body is connected to the left side of the brain.

---

sympathetic division The subdivision of the autonomic nervous system that deals with emergency response and the mobilization of energy.

parasympathetic division The subdivision of the autonomic nervous system that monitors the routine operation of the body's internal functions and conserves and restores body energy.

brain stem The brain structure that regulates the body's basic life processes.

medulla The region of the brain stem that regulates breathing, waking, and heartbeat.

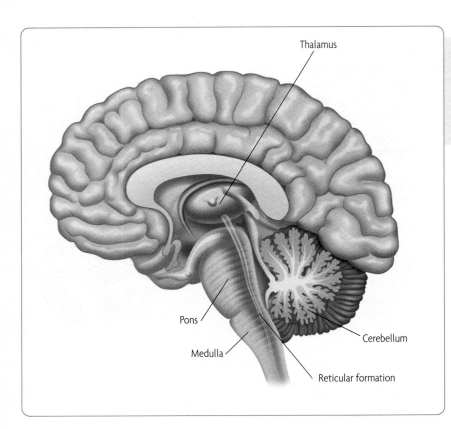

FIGURE 4.13 The Brain Stem, Thalamus, and Cerebellum

These structures are primarily involved in basic life processes: breathing, pulse, arousal, movement, balance, and simple processing of sensory information.

Directly above the medulla is the **pons**, which provides inputs to other structures in the brain stem and to the cerebellum (*pons* is the Latin word for *bridge*). The **reticular formation** is a dense network of nerve cells that serves as the brain's sentinel. It arouses the cerebral cortex to attend to new stimulation and keeps the brain alert even during sleep. Massive damage to this area often results in a coma.

The reticular formation has long tracts of fibres that run to the **thalamus**, which channels incoming sensory information to the appropriate area of the cerebral cortex, where that information is processed. For example, the thalamus relays information from the eyes to cortical areas for vision.

Neuroscientists have long known that the **cerebellum**, attached to the brain stem at the base of the skull, co-ordinates bodily movements, controls posture, and maintains equilibrium. Damage to the cerebellum interrupts the flow of otherwise smooth movement, causing it to appear unco-ordinated

and jerky. More recent research suggests that the cerebellum also plays an important role in the ability to learn and perform sequences of body movements (Hazeltine & Ivry, 2002; Seidler et al., 2002).

The Limbic System The **limbic system** mediates motivated behaviours, emotional states, and memory processes. It also regulates body temperature, blood pressure, and blood-sugar level, and performs other housekeeping activities. The limbic system comprises three structures: the hippocampus, amygdala, and hypothalamus (see **Figure 4.14**).

The **hippocampus**, which is the largest of the limbic system structures, plays an important role in the acquisition of memories. Considerable clinical evidence supports this conclusion, including the notable studies completed at the Montreal Neurological Institute by Brenda Milner and colleagues of a patient, H. M.—perhaps psychology's most famous subject:

> When he was 27, H. M. underwent surgery in an attempt to reduce the frequency and severity of his epileptic seizures. During the operation, parts of his hippocampus were removed. As a result, H. M. could recall only the very distant past; his ability to put new information into long-term memory was gone. W. B. Scoville, who performed the operation, and Milner (Scoville & Milner, 1957) concluded that the hippocampus was responsible for this type of memory. For many years following his surgery, Brenda Milner continued to test H. M.; he still believed he was living in 1953—the year the operation was performed.

There are, however, some types of new memories that can still be formed after damage to the hippocampus. For example, H. M. was able to acquire new skills. This pattern suggests that if

---

pons The region of the brain stem that connects the spinal cord with the brain and links parts of the brain to one another.

reticular formation The region of the brain stem that alerts the cerebral cortex to incoming sensory signals and is responsible for maintaining consciousness and awakening from sleep.

thalamus The brain structure that relays sensory impulses to the cerebral cortex.

cerebellum The region of the brain attached to the brain stem that controls motor co-ordination, posture, and balance, as well as the ability to learn control of body movements.

limbic system The region of the brain that regulates emotional behaviour, basic motivational urges, and memory, as well as major physiological functions.

hippocampus The part of the limbic system involved in the acquisition of explicit memory.

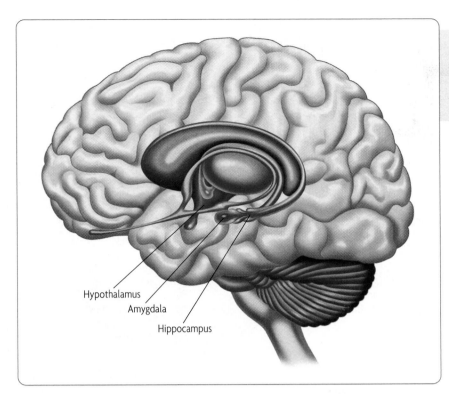

FIGURE 4.14 The Limbic System

The structures of the limbic system, which are present only in mammals, are involved in motivated behaviour, emotional states, and memory processes.

Hypothalamus
Amygdala
Hippocampus

you were in an accident and sustained damage to your hippocampus, you would still be able to learn some new tasks—but you would not be able to remember doing so! As researchers have continued to focus attention on the hippocampus, they have come to a more detailed understanding of how even different types of memories (Zeineh, Engel, Thompson, & Bookheimer, 2003). After H. M.'s death in 2008, his brain was prepared for investigation. It will be some time before his brain is fully evaluated, but in the future we will have an understanding of H. M.'s intact brain function. In Chapter 8, we will return to the functions of the hippocampus for memory acquisition.

The **amygdala** plays a role in emotional control and the formation of emotional memories. Because of this control function, damage to areas of the amygdala may have a calming effect on otherwise mean-spirited individuals. (We discuss *psychosurgery* in Chapter 16.) However, damage to some areas of the amygdala also impairs the ability to recognize the emotional content of facial expressions (Adolphs, Tranel, Damasio, & Damasio, 1994). Those individuals who have suffered amygdala damage are most impaired with respect to negative emotional expressions, especially fear. Researchers speculate that the amygdala may play a special role in people's acquisition and use of knowledge related to threat and danger (Adolphs et al., 1999).

The **hypothalamus** is one of the smallest structures in the brain, yet it plays a vital role in many of your most important daily actions. It is actually composed of several nuclei, small bundles of neurons that regulate physiological processes involved in motivated behaviour (including eating, drinking, temperature regulation, and sexual arousal). The hypothalamus maintains the body's internal equilibrium, or **homeostasis**. When the body's energy reserves are low, the hypothalamus is involved in stimulating the organism to find food and to eat. When body temperature drops, the hypothalamus causes

blood-vessel constriction, or minute involuntary movements you commonly refer to as the "shivers." The hypothalamus also regulates the activities of the endocrine system.

The Cerebrum In humans, the **cerebrum** dwarfs the rest of the brain, occupying two-thirds of its total mass. Its role is to regulate the brain's higher cognitive and emotional functions. The outer surface of the cerebrum, made up of billions of cells in a layer about 2.5 millimetres thick, is called the **cerebral cortex**. The cerebrum is also divided into two almost symmetrical halves, the **cerebral hemispheres** (we discuss the two hemispheres at length in a later section of this chapter). The two hemispheres are connected by a thick mass of nerve fibres, collectively referred to as the **corpus callosum**. This pathway sends messages back and forth between the hemispheres, allowing the two sides to communicate and know what the other is doing.

Neuroscientists have mapped each hemisphere, using two important landmarks as their guides. One groove, called the *central sulcus*, divides each hemisphere vertically, and a second similar groove, called the *lateral fissure*, divides each hemisphere

---

amygdala The part of the limbic system that controls emotion, aggression, and the formation of emotional memory.

hypothalamus The brain structure that regulates motivated behaviour (such as eating and drinking) and homeostasis.

homeostasis Constancy or equilibrium of the internal conditions of the body.

cerebrum The region of the brain that regulates higher cognitive and emotional functions.

cerebral cortex The outer surface of the cerebrum.

cerebral hemispheres The two halves of the cerebrum, connected by the corpus callosum.

corpus callosum The mass of nerve fibres connecting the two hemispheres of the cerebrum.

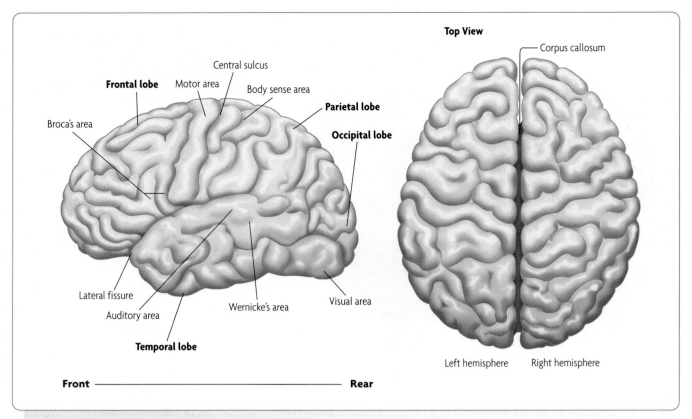

FIGURE 4.15 The Cerebral Cortex

The intact brain has two approximately symmetrical hemispheres. Each of the hemispheres of the cerebral cortex has four lobes. Different sensory and motor functions are associated with specific parts of each lobe.

horizontally (see **Figure 4.15**). These vertical and horizontal divisions help define four areas, or brain lobes, in each hemisphere. The **frontal lobe**, which is involved in motor control and cognitive activities, such as planning, making decisions, and setting goals, is located above the lateral fissure and in front of the central sulcus. Accidents that damage the frontal lobes can have devastating effects on human action and personality. This was the location of the injury that brought about such a dramatic change in Phineas Gage (Damasio, Grabowski, Frank, Galaburda, & Damasio, 1994). The **parietal lobe** is responsible for sensations of touch, pain, and temperature and is located directly behind the central sulcus. The **occipital lobe**, the final destination for visual information, is located at the back of the head. The **temporal lobe**, which is responsible for the processes of hearing, is found below the lateral fissure, on the sides of each cerebral hemisphere.

It would be misleading to say that any lobe alone controls any one specific function. The structures of the brain perform their duties in concert, working smoothly as an integrated unit, similar to a symphony orchestra. Whether you are doing the dishes, solving a calculus problem, or carrying on a conversation with a friend, your brain works as a unified whole, each lobe interacting and co-operating with the others. Nevertheless, neuroscientists can identify areas of the four lobes of the cerebrum that are necessary for specific functions, such as vision, hearing, language, and memory. When a lobe is damaged, its functions are disrupted or lost entirely.

The actions of the body's voluntary muscles, of which there are more than 600, are controlled by the **motor cortex**, located just in front of the central sulcus in the frontal lobes. Recall that commands from one side of the brain are directed to muscles on the opposite side of the body. Also, muscles in the lower part of the body—for example, the toes—are controlled by neurons in the top part of the motor cortex. Muscles in the upper part of the body, such as the throat, are controlled by neurons in the lower part of the motor cortex. As you can see in **Figure 4.16**, the upper parts of the body receive far more detailed motor instructions than the lower parts. In fact, the two largest areas of the motor cortex are devoted to the fingers—especially the thumb—and to the muscles involved in speech. Their greater brain area reflects the importance in human activity of manipulating objects, using tools, eating, and talking.

Bryan Kolb and Ian Whishaw at the Canadian Centre for Behavioural Neuroscience (CCBN) in Lethbridge, Alberta, have completed numerous lesion studies on rodents to determine how the motor cortex influences complex motor skills, especially when lesions occur at different developmental stages

frontal lobe Region of the brain located above the lateral fissure and in front of the central sulcus; involved in motor control and cognitive activities.

parietal lobe Region of the brain behind the frontal lobe and above the lateral fissure; contains somatosensory cortex.

occipital lobe Rearmost region of the brain; contains primary visual cortex.

temporal lobe Region of the brain found below the lateral fissure; contains auditory cortex.

motor cortex The region of the cerebral cortex that controls the action of the body's voluntary muscles.

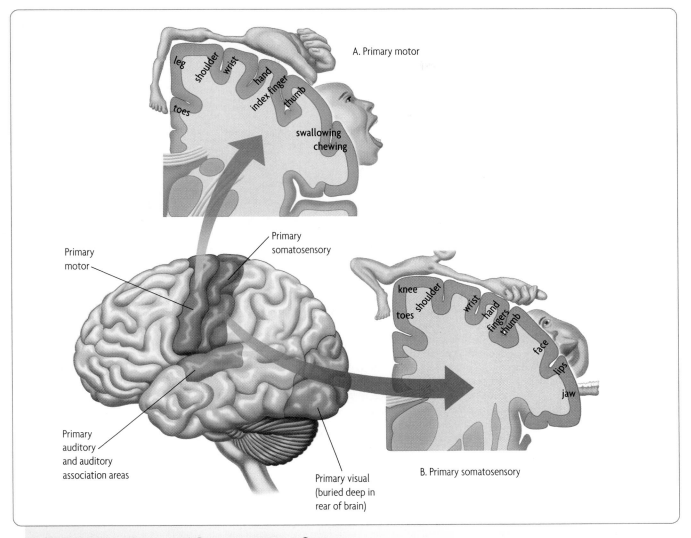

FIGURE 4.16 Motor and Somatosensory Cortex

Neuroscience researchers often refer to the motor homunculus (A) and sensory homunculus (B), shown here. Different parts of the body are more or less sensitive to environmental (and electrical) stimulation and brain control. Sensitivity in a particular region of the body is related to the amount of space in the cerebral cortex devoted to that region. In this figure, the body is drawn so that the size of body parts is relative to the cortical space devoted to them. The larger the body part in the drawing, the greater its sensitivity to environmental stimulation, and the greater the brain's control over its movement. Penfield was able to map the homunculus in his patients.

(Kolb, Cioe, & Whishaw, 2000a, 2000b; Whishaw and Kolb, 1988). During the studies, rats were trained to reach through a slot or series of bars to obtain food pellets. The results show that a completely intact neocortex is not essential for limb use in reaching, for example, but contributes to successful use of the limb. Following lesions early in development, facilitation of movement may be promoted by the other parts of the neocortex. This has many implications for rehabilitation after early childhood and adult head injuries.

The **somatosensory cortex** is located just behind the central sulcus in the left and right parietal lobes. This part of the cortex processes information about temperature, touch, body position, and pain. Similar to the motor cortex, the upper part of the sensory cortex relates to the lower parts of the body, and the lower part to the upper parts of the body. Most of the area of

the sensory cortex is devoted to the lips, tongue, thumb, and index fingers—the parts of the body that provide the most important sensory input (see Figure 4.16). Like the motor cortex, the right half of the somatosensory cortex communicates with the left side of the body, and the left half communicates with the right side of the body.

Auditory information is processed in the **auditory cortex**, which is in the two temporal lobes. The auditory cortex in each hemisphere receives information from *both* ears. One area of the

somatosensory cortex The region of the parietal lobes that processes sensory input from various body areas.

auditory cortex The area of the temporal lobes that receives and processes auditory information.

auditory cortex is involved in the production of language, and a different area is involved in language comprehension. Visual input is processed at the back of the brain in the **visual cortex**, located in the occipital lobes. Here the greatest area is devoted to input from the centre part of the retina, at the back of the eye: the area that transmits the most detailed visual information.

Not all of the cerebral cortex is devoted to processing sensory information and commanding the muscles to action. In fact, the majority of it is involved in *interpreting* and *integrating* information. Processes such as planning and decision making are believed to occur in the **association cortex**. Association areas are distributed to several areas of the cortex—one region is labelled in Figure 4.16. The association cortex allows you to combine information from various sensory modalities to plan appropriate responses to stimuli in the environment.

How do these different areas of the brain work in unison? Consider, as an example, what happens in your brain when you speak a written word (see **Figure 4.17**). Imagine that your psychology instructor hands you a piece of paper with the word *chocolate* written on it and asks you to say the word aloud. The biological processes involved in this action are surprisingly subtle and complex. Neuroscience experiments can break down your verbal behaviour into numerous steps. First, the visual stimulus (the written word *chocolate*) is detected by the nerve cells in the retinas of your eyes, which send nerve impulses to the visual cortex (via the thalamus). The visual cortex then sends nerve impulses to an area in the rear of the temporal lobe (called the angular gyrus), where visual coding for the word is compared with its acoustical coding. Once the proper acoustical code is located, it is relayed to an area of the auditory cortex known as *Wernicke's area*, an area of the brain involved in language comprehension, where it is decoded and interpreted: "Ah! Chocolate! I'd like some now." Once Wernicke's area has interpreted the word, nerve impulses are then sent to Broca's area, which, in turn, sends a message to the motor cortex, stimulating the lips, tongue, and larynx to produce the word *chocolate*.

We have now reviewed the many important structures in your nervous system. When we began to talk about the cerebrum, we noted that each cerebral structure is represented in both hemispheres of your brain. However, the structures in those two hemispheres play somewhat different functions with respect to many types of behaviours. We turn now to those differences between your brain's two hemispheres.

HEMISPHERIC LATERALIZATION

What types of information originally led researchers to suspect that there are differences in the functions of the brain's two hemispheres? Recall that when Paul Broca carried out his autopsy on Tan, he discovered damage in the left hemisphere. As he followed up this original discovery, Broca found that other patients who showed similar disruption of their language abilities—a pattern now known as *Broca's aphasia*—also had damage on the *left* side of their brains. Damage to the same areas on the *right* side of the brain did not have the same effect. What should one conclude?

---

visual cortex The region of the occipital lobes in which visual information is processed.

association cortex The parts of the cerebral cortex in which many high-level brain processes occur.

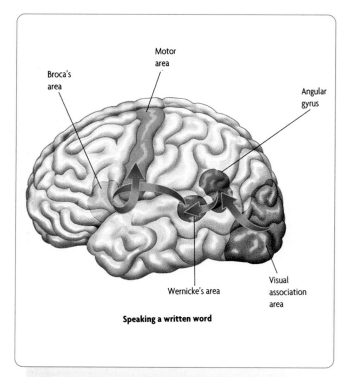

FIGURE 4.17 How a Written Word Is Spoken

Nerve impulses, laden with information about the written word, are sent by the retinas to the visual association area of the cortex via the thalamus. The visual cortex sends the nerve impulses to an area in the rear of the temporal lobe, the angular gyrus, where visual coding for the word (the arrangement of letters and their shapes, etc.) is compared with its acoustical coding (the way it sounds). Once the proper acoustical code is found, it is relayed to an area of the auditory cortex known as Wernicke's area. Here it is encoded and interpreted. Nerve impulses are sent to Broca's area, which sends the message to the motor cortex. The motor cortex allows you to say the word by stimulating the lips, tongue, and larynx to act in synchrony.

That's a lot of mental effort for just one word. Now imagine what you require of your brain every time you read aloud a book or even a billboard. The truly amazing thing is that your brain responds effortlessly and intelligently, translating thousands of marks on paper into a neurological code, informing other brain areas about what's going on, and, finally, speaking those words.

The chance to investigate hemispheric differences first arose in the context of a treatment for severe epilepsy in which surgeons sever the corpus callosum—the bundle of about 200 million nerve fibres that transfers information back and forth between the two hemispheres (see **Figure 4.18**). The goal of this surgery is to prevent the violent electrical activity that accompanies epileptic seizures from crossing between the hemispheres. The operation is usually successful, and a patient's subsequent behaviour in most circumstances appears normal. Patients who undergo this type of surgery are often referred to as *split-brain* patients.

FIGURE 4.18 The Corpus Callosum

The corpus callosum is a massive network of nerve fibres that channels information between the two hemispheres. Severing the corpus callosum impairs this communication process.

Source: Harvard Medical School/Betty G. Martindale.

To test the capabilities of the separated hemispheres of epileptic patients, **Roger Sperry** (1968) and **Michael Gazzaniga** (1970) devised situations that could allow visual information to be presented separately to each hemisphere. Sperry and Gazzaniga's methodology relies on the anatomy of the visual system (see **Figure 4.19**). For each eye, information from the *right visual field* goes to the left hemisphere, and information from the *left visual field* goes to the right hemisphere. Ordinarily, information arriving from both hemispheres is shared very quickly across the corpus callosum. However, because these pathways have been severed in split-brain patients, information presented to the right or left visual field may remain only in the left or right hemisphere (see **Figure 4.20**).

Since for most people speech is controlled by the left hemisphere, the left hemisphere could "talk back" to the researchers, whereas the right hemisphere could not. Communication with the right hemisphere was achieved by confronting it with manual tasks involving identification, matching, or assembly of objects—tasks that did not require the use of words. Consider the following demonstration of a split-brain subject using his left half brain to account for the activity of his left hand, which was being guided by his right half brain:

A snow scene was presented to the right hemisphere and a picture of a chicken claw was simultaneously presented to the left hemisphere. The subject selected, from an array of objects, those that "went with" each of the two scenes. With his right hand, the patient pointed to a chicken head; with his left hand, he pointed to a shovel. The patient reported that the shovel was needed to clean out the chicken shed (rather than to shovel snow). Since the left brain was not privy to what the right brain "saw" because of the severed corpus callosum, it needed to explain why the left hand was pointing at a shovel when the only picture the left hemisphere was aware of seeing was a chicken claw. The left brain's cognitive system provided a theory to make sense of the behaviour of different parts of its body. (Gazzaniga, 1985)

From a variety of research methods in addition to split-brain studies, we now know that, for most people, many language-related functions are *lateralized* to the left hemisphere. A function is considered lateralized when one cerebral hemisphere plays the primary role in accomplishing that function. Speech—the ability to produce coherent spoken language—is perhaps the most highly lateralized of all functions.

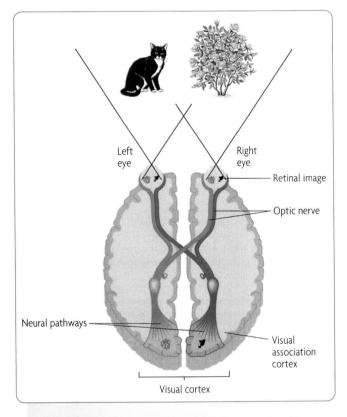

FIGURE 4.19 The Neural Pathways for Visual Information

The neural pathways for visual information coming from the inside portions of each eye cross from one side of the brain to the other at the corpus callosum. The pathways carrying information from the outside portions of each eye do not cross over. Severing the corpus callosum prevents information selectively displayed in the right visual field from entering the right hemisphere, and left visual field information cannot enter the left hemisphere.

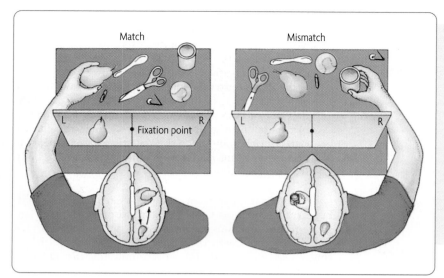

Match   Mismatch

L   Fixation point   R   L   R

FIGURE 4.20 Co-ordination between Eye and Hand

Co-ordination between eye and hand is normal if a split-brain patient uses the left hand to find and match an object that appears in the left visual field, because both are registered in the right hemisphere. However, when asked to use the right hand to match an object seen in the left visual field, the patient cannot do so, because sensory messages from the right hand are going to the left cerebral hemisphere, and there is no longer a connection between the two hemispheres. Here the cup is misperceived as matching the pear.

Neuroscientists have found that only about 5 percent of right-handers and 15 percent of left-handers have speech controlled by the right hemisphere, whereas another 15 percent of left-handers have speech processes occurring in both sides of the brain (Rasmussen & Milner, 1977). For most people, therefore, speech is a left-hemisphere function. As a consequence, damage to the left side of most people's brains can cause speech disorders. What is interesting is that for users of languages like American Sign Language—which use systems of intricate hand positions and movements to convey meaning—left-brain damage is similarly disruptive (Corina & McBurney, 2001; Hickok, Love-Geffen, & Klima, 2002). What is lateralized, therefore, is not speech as such, but, rather, the ability to produce the sequences of gestures—either vocal or manual—that encode communicative meaning. You should not conclude that the left hemisphere is somehow "better" than the right hemisphere. Researchers have suggested that each hemisphere has a different "style" for processing the same information. The left hemisphere

tends to be more *analytical*: It processes information bit by bit. The right hemisphere tends to be more *holistic*: It processes information with respect to global patterns. It is the combined action of the right and left hemispheres—each with its particular processing style—that gives fullness to your experiences. For example, the left hemisphere, with its attention to fine detail, plays a key role in most forms of problem solving. The function of the right hemisphere becomes more apparent, however, when problems require creative solutions or bursts of insight; the right hemisphere helps problem solvers do the broader searches of memory that these types of problems require (Bowden & Beeman, 1998). (If you want to put your right hemisphere to work, you can skip ahead to try some of these types of problems on p. 271 in Chapter 9).

Although researchers can confidently make claims about the way in which functions are lateralized in the "average" brain, there are measurable differences among individuals. For example, the right rather than the left hemisphere (and sometimes both hemispheres) in a small number of left-handers is somewhat more likely to dominate speech. Another distinction that appears to matter greatly with respect to brain lateralization is male versus female: There are general differences in the way male and female brains carry out their functions (Breedlove, 1994; Kimura, 1999). Kimura and Clarke (2002) found that female brains have a distinct advantage with verbal memory for regular words and non-words. Thanks to today's brain-imaging techniques, it has become relatively easy to look for differences in the regions of men's and women's brains that are brought into action for different tasks. For example, one team of researchers used MRI to demonstrate that the brains of men and women become activated in different ways when they make judgments based on language sounds (e.g., Does *sud* rhyme with *wud*?). The brain activity in men was largely localized in the left hemisphere, whereas this task was more likely to engage both left- and right-brain activity for women (Shaywitz et al., 1995). Results like this bring up the issue of *nature* versus *nurture*. Do males and females come into the world with different brains, or do life experiences modify their brains along the way? The techniques of contemporary neuroscience should

How have studies with individuals who use sign language influenced researchers' beliefs about the lateralization of brain function?

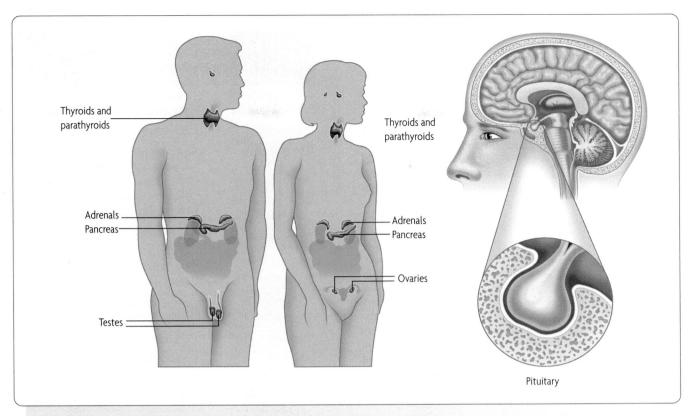

FIGURE 4.21   Endocrine Glands in Males and Females
The pituitary gland is shown at the far right; it is the master gland that regulates the glands shown at the left. The pituitary gland is under the control of the hypothalamus, an important structure in the limbic system.

allow for an interesting answer to this question over the next several years.

Now that we have reviewed the many important structures of your nervous system, let's turn to the endocrine system, a bodily system that functions in close co-operation with the nervous system to regulate bodily functions.

THE ENDOCRINE SYSTEM

The human genotype specifies a second highly complex regulatory system, the **endocrine system**, to supplement the work of the nervous system. The endocrine system is a network of glands that manufacture and secrete chemical messengers called **hormones** into the bloodstream (see **Figure 4.21**). The endocrine system is vital at certain stages of life and in certain situations. Hormones, for example, influence body growth. They initiate, maintain, and stop development of primary and secondary sexual characteristics; influence levels of arousal and awareness; serve as the basis for mood changes; and regulate metabolism, the rate at which the body uses its energy stores. The endocrine system promotes the survival of an *organism* by helping fight infections and disease. It advances the survival of the *species* through regulation of sexual arousal, production of reproductive cells, and production of milk in nursing mothers. You simply could not survive without an effective endocrine system.

Endocrine glands respond to the levels of chemicals in the bloodstream or are stimulated by other hormones or by nerve impulses from the brain. Hormones are then secreted into the blood and travel to distant target cells that have specific receptors; they exert their influence on the body's program of chemical regulation only at the places that are genetically predetermined to respond to them. In influencing diverse but specific target organs or tissue, hormones regulate an enormous range of biochemical processes. This multiple-action communication system allows for control of slow, continuous processes such as maintenance of blood-sugar levels and calcium levels, metabolism of carbohydrates, and general body growth. Yet what happens during crises? The endocrine system also releases the hormone *adrenaline* into the bloodstream; adrenaline energizes your body so that you can respond quickly to challenges.

As mentioned earlier, the brain structure known as the *hypothalamus* serves as a relay station between the endocrine system and the central nervous system. Specialized cells in

---

endocrine system The network of glands that manufacture and secrete hormones into the bloodstream.

hormones The chemical messengers, manufactured and secreted by the endocrine glands, that regulate metabolism and influence body growth, mood, and sexual characteristics.

the hypothalamus receive messages from other brain cells, commanding it to release a number of different hormones to the pituitary gland, where they either stimulate or inhibit the release of other hormones. Hormones are produced in several different regions of the body. These "factories" make a variety of hormones, each of which regulates different bodily processes, as outlined in **Table 4.1.** Let's examine the most significant of these processes.

The **pituitary gland** is often called the "master gland," because it produces about 10 different kinds of hormones that influence the secretions of all the other endocrine glands, as well as a hormone that influences growth. The absence of this growth hormone results in dwarfism; its excess results in gigantic growth. In males, pituitary secretions activate the testes to secrete **testosterone**, which stimulates production of sperm. The pituitary gland is also involved in the development of male secondary sexual characteristics, such as facial hair, voice change, and physical maturation. Testosterone may even increase aggression and sexual desire. In females, a pituitary hormone stimulates production of **estrogen**, which is essential to the hormonal chain reaction that triggers the release of ova from a woman's ovaries, making her fertile. Certain birth-control pills work by blocking the mechanism in the pituitary gland that controls this hormone flow, thus preventing the ova from being released. We will talk a bit more about the role of estrogen in the brain in the next section.

PLASTICITY AND NEUROGENESIS: OUR CHANGING BRAINS

You now have a good basic idea of your nervous system at work: At all times, millions of neurons are communicating to do the essential work of your body and mind. What makes the brain even more interesting, however, is one consequence of all that neural communication: The brain itself changes over time. Do you want to take a moment to change your brain? Go back a few pages and memorize the definition of *action potential*. If you are successful at learning that definition—or any other new information—you will have brought about a modification of your brain. Researchers refer to changes in the brain as **plasticity**. A good deal of research in neuroscience focuses on the physical bases for plasticity. For example, researchers examine how learning arises in association with the formation of new synapses or from changes in communication across existing synapses (Baudry, Davis, & Thompson, 1999).

Since brain plasticity depends on life experiences, you will not be surprised to learn that brains show the impact of different

---

pituitary gland Located in the brain, the gland that secretes growth hormone and influences the secretion of hormones by other endocrine glands.

testosterone The male sex hormone, secreted by the testes, that stimulates production of sperm and is also responsible for the development of male secondary sex characteristics.

estrogen The female sex hormone, produced by the ovaries, that is responsible for the release of eggs from the ovaries as well as for the development and maintenance of female reproductive structures and secondary sex characteristics.

plasticity Changes in the performance of the brain; may involve the creation of new synapses or changes in the function of existing synapses.

neurogenesis The creation of new neurons.

TABLE 4.1	Major Endocrine Glands and the Functions of the Hormones They Produce
These Glands:	**Produce Hormones That Regulate:**
Hypothalamus	Release of pituitary hormones
Anterior pituitary	Testes and ovaries Breast milk production Metabolism Reactions to stress
Posterior pituitary	Water conservation Breast milk excretion Uterus contraction
Thyroid	Metabolism Growth and development
Parathyroid	Calcium levels
Gut	Digestion
Pancreas	Glucose metabolism
Adrenals	Fight-or-flight responses Metabolism Sexual desire in women
Ovaries	Development of female sexual traits Ova production
Testes	Development of male sexual traits Sperm production Sexual desire in men

environments and activities. One line of research was pioneered by **Donald Hebb**, probably one of the most well-known neuroscientists in Canada. Some even suggest he is the father of modern neuroscience due to the impact his research and teaching have had on the field. Hebb was a student of Wilder Penfield at the Montreal Neurological Institute in the late 1930s, where he learned about brain surgery and human brain function. Afterward, Hebb took up a teaching position at Queen's University and, with a colleague, developed a learning task called the Hebb-Williams Maze. This maze, an open field with a number of movable barriers that can produce increasingly more complex mazes, tests how well animals can learn. Hebb is credited with some of the earliest studies on how environmental enrichment can affect learning: When he took rats home to roam around his house, they performed better on the Hebb-Williams Maze and on other learning and memory tasks than rats that were reared in standard laboratory conditions. In 1948, Hebb became the chairman of the Department of Psychology at McGill; the following year, he published one of the most influential books in psychology and neuroscience, called the *Organization of Behavior*. In this book, Hebb developed a theory, which became known as the "Hebbian theory," on how the brain learns and uses information. This method of learning is best expressed by an oft-cited quote from the book:

When an axon of cell A is near enough to excite cell B and repeatedly or persistently takes part in firing it, some growth process or metabolic change takes place in one or both cells such that A's efficiency, as one of the cells firing B, is increased.

This theory is often paraphrased as "Neurons that fire together wire together."

A later series of studies on brain plasticity, carried out by **Mark Rosenzweig** and his colleagues, verified the consequences on the brains of rats being raised in impoverished versus enriched environments (for reviews, see Rosenzweig, 1996, 1999). In the impoverished environments, the rats were kept alone in their cages; in the enriched environments, the rats shared a large cage with several other rats, with playthings that were changed daily. After periods varying from a few days to several months, the experimenters examined the rats' brains.

The results were dramatic. The average cortex of the rats living in the enriched environments was heavier and thicker—positive attributes—than the cortex of their impoverished littermates. Measurable differences emerged even when the rats had been in the enriched environments for only a few days.

With brain-imaging techniques, it is possible to measure very specific brain differences related to people's life experiences as well. Consider musicians who play the violin. They are required to control the fingers of their left hands with an extremely delicate touch. If you refer back to the figure of the homunculus (see Figure 4.16), you will see that a good deal of sensory cortex is devoted to the fingers. Brain scans reveal that the representation of fingers of the left hand is even more enhanced for violin players, as compared to nonplayers (Elbert, Pantev, Wienbruch, Rockstroh, & Taub, 1995). No such increase is found for fingers of the right hand, which do not have as great a sensory role in violin playing. The extra representation of the

Critical Thinking in Your Life

NEW CELLS IN AN OLD BRAIN

In recent years, attention has focused on *stem cells*—unspecialized cells that, under appropriate conditions, can be prompted to function as new neurons (Kintner, 2002; Wilson & Edlund, 2001). Researchers hope that stem cells may ultimately provide a means to replace damaged tissue in the nervous system with new neural growth. Since the most flexible stem cells come from embryos and aborted fetuses, stem cell research has been subject to political controversy and questions about ethics. Still, researchers believe that stem cell research could lead to cures for paralysis and other serious malfunctions in the nervous system. For that reason, the scientific community is highly motivated to discover ways to continue research within accepted societal norms. Fortunately, stem cells are being found in places where they were not expected, including the adult mammalian eye. Though it was not thought to have the ability to regenerate via new cell populations, the rodent eye, Derek Van Der Kooy and colleagues at the University of Toronto (Tropepe et al., 2000) discovered, has stem cells that can turn into the other cells of the eye. Frieda Miller and colleagues at The Hospital for Sick Children in Toronto (McKenzie, Biernaskie, Toma, Midha, & Miller, 2006) have also been investigating stem cells found in the skin of rodents and humans, and have found evidence that they can become cells that myelinate the axons of other cells.

One of the main reasons that stem cells have been of such great interest to the research community is that stem cells have the ability to turn into other cells. Stem cells show remarkable potential to replace cells that die in the brain, which suggests that they may be used for neural transplants in cases of Parkinson's disease. Laurie Doering and colleagues (Meissner, Kirkham, & Doering, 2005) at McMaster University have found that they can implant stem cells into a mouse model of Parkinson's disease to promote recovery, but it will be some time before this procedure could become routine in patients.

Research on brain repair has accelerated in recent years in the face of important new data suggesting that **neurogenesis**—the production of new brain cells from naturally occurring stem cells—occurs in the brains of adult mammals, including humans (E. Gould & Gross, 2002; S. J. Gould, 2002). For nearly 100 years, neuroscientists believed that the adult brains of mammals already had their full supply of neurons, and the widely held theory was the only thing that could happen over the adult years was that neurons could die out. However, the new data have challenged that view. Recall, for example, that we identified the hippocampus as an important structure for the formation of certain types of memories. Now that researchers have documented neurogenesis in the adult hippocampus, they are trying to understand the role newly born neurons play in allowing memories to remain accessible over time (Kempermann, 2002, 2008). Brian Christie and colleagues (Christie & Cameron, 2006) at the University of Victoria have been investigating neurogenesis in the hippocampus in response to experience. There is much interest in the research community as to whether new cells can be formed for specific functional purposes, like helping with learning and memory. The role of other brain functions may be to modulate neurogenesis at different times. Can you think of times where having new cells might be helpful for brain function, or when being able to use stem cells implanted into the brain might be useful?

left fingers was greatest for violinists who took up the instrument before age 12.

One important aspect of research on plasticity concerns circumstances in which humans or animals have sustained injuries to the brain or spinal cord, through strokes, degenerative diseases, or accidents. A good deal of clinical evidence confirms that the brain is sometimes able to "heal itself." For example, patients who suffer from strokes that cause disruptions in language often recover over time. In some instances, the damaged brain areas themselves have enough lingering function that recovery is possible. In other cases, other brain areas take over the functions of those that were damaged.

Bryan Kolb and Ian Whishaw from the University of Lethbridge have been investigating anatomical and behavioural recovery from injury for some time. Strokes often produce impairments in motor function in both humans and rats. These Canadian researchers have found that, following a motor cortex stroke, a number of learned behavioural changes take place, as well as widespread neuronal change (reviewed in Whishaw, Alaverdashvili, & Kolb, 2008). Some of the learning following injury is related to learning how to not use the impaired limb, whereas other learning is simply developing strategies for poor use of the limb. The group has published extensively on the dendritic and dendritic spine changes associated with recovery from brain injury (reviewed in Kolb, 2005). Recently, Kolb (Silasi, Hamilton, & Kolb, 2008) discovered that social interactions that mimic human social instability may negatively influence stroke outcome in rats. This data suggests that social experiences, including stress, may play a role in decreasing spontaneous behavioural recovery following injury. Researchers have also begun to develop techniques to help the brain along in the healing process. Stimulation, for example, may play a role in recovery. This was investigated by Jeffrey Kleim (Kleim et al., 2003) when he was a researcher at the University of Lethbridge. Rats with strokes appear to show greater recovery when the cortex is stimulated with an electrode that sits on the surface of the brain. What the stimulation is doing to help with plasticity remains to be determined, but does suggest some future treatment options. There seems to be a tremendous amount of brain plasticity related to learning and memory. Sometimes we learn about how the brain normally works based on situations when the brain shows less plasticity and is not working correctly, and sometimes what we learn is controversial.

For women who have experienced menopause, estrogen replacement has been an option for reducing some of the age-related cognitive impairment that post-menopausal women report experiencing. There has, however, been controversy in the literature about whether estrogen replacement is ideal, as the risk of cancer increases with estrogen replacement. Clearly, some care is required in prescribing estrogen, but more recent research suggests more positive outcomes of estrogen replacement and modification. Lisa Galea and her lab at the University of British Columbia have reported that estrogen can promote hippocampal brain changes, including the development of new neurons, or hippocampal neurogenesis (Barha, Lieblich, & Galea, 2009). More recently her lab (Barha & Galea, 2009) discovered that previous reproductive experience resulted in the older brain becoming more responsive to the beneficial effects of estrogen. Estrogens caused significant increases in the number of neurons in middle-aged rats that had previously had offspring, but the same was not true for middle-aged virgin rats. Another study from this lab reported that prior sexual experience in rodents was beneficial in that cell numbers increased when rats subsequently experienced a stressful situation (Spritzer, Weinberg, Viau, & Galea, 2009). Rats that did not have the prior sexual experience showed cell loss in response to the stressful situation. These studies reflect the effect of the interaction of hormones and other experience on the ability for cell proliferation.

In this chapter, we have taken a brief peek at the marvellous three-pound universe that is your brain. It is one thing to recognize that the brain controls behaviour and your mental processes, but quite another to understand how the brain serves all those functions. Neuroscientists are engaged in the fascinating quest to understand the interplay among brain, behaviour, and environment. You now have some background that will allow you to appreciate new knowledge as it unfolds.

STOP AND REVIEW

❶ What are the advantages of fMRI over other brain-imaging techniques?

❷ What are the two major divisions of the autonomic nervous system?

❸ What are some of the major functions of the amygdala?

❹ What processing styles are reflected by the two hemispheres of the brain?

❺ Why is the pituitary gland often called the master gland?

❻ What is neurogenesis?

CRITICAL THINKING Consider the study on plasticity in adult rats. Why would the researchers be interested in the effects of hormones?

Recapping Main Points

The Nervous System in Action

- The neuron, the basic unit of the nervous system, receives, processes, and relays information to other cells, glands, and muscles.
- Neurons relay information from the dendrites through the cell body (soma) to the axon to the terminal buttons.
- Sensory neurons receive messages from specialized receptor cells and send them toward the CNS. Motor neurons direct messages from the CNS to muscles and glands. Interneurons relay information from sensory neurons to other interneurons or to motor neurons.
- Once the summation of inputs to a neuron exceeds a specific threshold, an action potential is sent along the axon to the terminal buttons.
- All-or-none action potentials are created when the opening of ion channels allows an exchange of ions across the cell membrane.

- Neurotransmitters are released into the synaptic gap between neurons. Once they diffuse across the gap, they lodge in the receptor molecules of the postsynaptic membrane.
- Whether these neurotransmitters excite or inhibit the membrane depends on the nature of the receptor molecule.
- New cell growth and life experiences reshape the brain after birth.

Visit **MyPsychLab.com** for more review and practice on the following topics:

✳ **Explore:** The Nerve Impulse and Afferent and Efferent Neurons

👁 **Watch:** Studying Squid

Biology and Behaviour

- Neuroscientists use several methods to research the relation between brain and behaviour: studying brain-damaged patients, producing lesions at specific brain sites, electrically stimulating the brain, recording brain activity, and imaging the brain with computerized devices.
- The brain and the spinal cord make up the central nervous system (CNS).
- The peripheral nervous system (PNS) is composed of all neurons connecting the CNS to the body. The PNS consists of the somatic nervous system, which regulates the body's skeletal muscles, and the autonomic nervous system (ANS), which regulates life-support processes.

- The brain consists of three integrated layers: the brain stem, limbic system, and cerebrum.
- The brain stem is responsible for breathing, digestion, and heart rate.
- The limbic system is involved in long-term memory, aggression, eating, drinking, and sexual behaviour.
- The cerebrum controls higher mental functions.
- Some functions are lateralized to one hemisphere of the brain. For example, most individuals have speech localized in the left hemisphere.
- Although the two hemispheres of the brain work smoothly in concert, they typically embody different styles of processing: The left hemisphere is more analytic, while the right hemisphere is more holistic.
- The endocrine system produces and secretes hormones into the bloodstream.
- Hormones help regulate growth, primary and secondary sexual characteristics, metabolism, digestion, arousal, and neurogenesis.

Visit **MyPsychLab.com** for more review and practice on the following topics:

✓ **Practice:** The Nervous System in Action

◆ **Research:** Michael Gazzaniga

◉ **Simulate:** Split-Brain Experiments

KEY TERMS

action potential (p. 83)
all-or-none law (p. 84)
amygdala (p. 97)
association cortex (p. 100)
auditory cortex (p. 99)
autonomic nervous system (ANS) (p. 94)
axon (p. 80)
brain stem (p. 95)
Broca's area (p. 89)
central nervous system (CNS) (p. 92)
cerebellum (p. 96)
cerebral cortex (p. 97)
cerebral hemispheres (p. 97)
cerebrum (p. 97)
corpus callosum (p. 97)
dendrites (p. 80)
electroencephalogram (EEG) (p. 92)
endocrine system (p. 103)
estrogen (p. 104)
excitatory inputs (p. 83)
frontal lobe (p. 98)
functional MRI (fMRI) (p. 92)
glia (p. 82)

hippocampus (p. 96)
homeostasis (p. 97)
hormones (p. 103)
hypothalamus (p. 97)
inhibitory inputs (p. 83)
interneurons (p. 81)
ion channels (p. 84)
lesions (p. 89)
limbic system (p. 96)
magnetic resonance imaging (MRI) (p. 92)
medulla (p. 95)
motor cortex (p. 98)
motor neurons (p. 80)
neurogenesis (p. 104)
neuromodulator (p. 88)
neuron (p. 80)
neuroscience (p. 80)
neurotransmitters (p. 85)
occipital lobe (p. 98)
parasympathetic division (p. 95)
parietal lobe (p. 98)
peripheral nervous system (PNS) (p. 92)
PET scans (p. 92)

pituitary gland (p. 104)
plasticity (p. 104)
pons (p. 96)
refractory period (p. 84)
repetitive transcranial magnetic stimulation (rTMS) (p. 90)
resting potential (p. 84)
reticular formation (p. 96)
sensory neurons (p. 80)
soma (p. 80)
somatic nervous system (p. 94)
somatosensory cortex (p. 99)
sympathetic division (p. 95)
synapse (p. 85)
synaptic transmission (p. 85)
temporal lobe (p. 98)
terminal buttons (p. 80)
testosterone (p. 104)
thalamus (p. 96)
transcranial magnetic stimulation (TMS) (p. 91)
visual cortex (p. 100)

Practice Test

1. One of the jobs of _____ is to receive stimulation from other neurons.
   a. axons
   b. terminal buttons
   c. synapses
   d. dendrites

2. After Jonas withdraws money from the bank, he has to wait two minutes before his card will work again. This sounds a lot like the _____ in neural transmission.
   a. all-or-none law
   b. action potential
   c. refractory period
   d. ion channels

3. Wilma is creating an illustration of neural transmission. She leaves a small gap between a terminal button on one neuron and the dendrite of the next. She should label that gap the _____
   a. ion channel.
   b. glia.
   c. node of Ranvier.
   d. synapse.

4. Bea has decided to undergo an acupuncture treatment to help her with her back pain. You explain that researchers believe that acupuncture leads to the release of _____ in the brain.
   a. GABA
   b. acetylcholine
   c. endorphins
   d. dopamine

5. Suppose you want to understand the genetics of impulsivity. You might concentrate your research on variations in genes that affect the brain's use of _____
   a. glia.
   b. dopamine.
   c. GABA.
   d. ion channels.

6. Which technique allows researchers to create reversible "lesions"?
   a. fMRI
   b. rTMS
   c. PET scans
   d. EEG

7. The _____ nervous system processes incoming neural messages and sends commands to different parts of the body.
   a. central
   b. autonomic
   c. somatic
   d. peripheral

8. After he experienced damage to his _____, H. M. experienced difficulties acquiring new information.
   a. reticular formation
   b. thalamus
   c. hippocampus
   d. Broca's area

9. As you are chatting with Tejus, you notice that she is right-handed. You think it is most likely that her ability to produce speech is controlled by _____
   a. her left hemisphere.
   b. her right hemisphere.
   c. both the left and right hemispheres.
   d. neither the left nor the right hemisphere.

10. Which brain structure serves as a relay station between the brain and the endocrine system?
    a. the hippocampus
    b. the hypothalamus
    c. the pons
    d. the amygdala

11. Brain-imaging techniques reveal that the brain representation of the fingers of the left hand is enhanced for people who play the violin versus nonplayers. This result provides an example of _____
    a. neurogenesis.
    b. heritability.
    c. lateralization.
    d. brain plasticity.

12. When people listen to _____ music, they are likely to experience relatively more activity in the _____ hemisphere of their brains.
    a. happy; left
    b. happy; right
    c. sad; left
    d. upbeat tempo; right

Essay Questions

1. Why does a neuron's behaviour depend on the balance of excitatory and inhibitory inputs it receives?

2. Why are the two hemispheres of the brain often characterized as having distinctive processing styles?

Discovering Psychology Viewing Guide

Watch the following videos by logging on to MyPsychLab (**www.mypsychlab.com**). After you have watched the videos, complete the activities that follow.

Program 3: The Behaving Brain

Program 4: The Responsive Brain

Program 25: Cognitive Neuroscience

PROGRAM REVIEW

Programs 3 & 4

1. E. Roy John cites the example of the staff member responding to a personal question to show how imaging can detect _____
a. abnormal structures in the brain.
b. abnormal personality.
c. abnormal but transient states.
d. pathological states, such as alcoholism.

2. Joseph Martinez taught rats a maze task and then gave them scopolamine. What effect did the drug have on brain functioning?
a. It enhanced the rats' memories.
b. It made the rats forget what they had learned.
c. It enabled the rats to learn a similar task more quickly.
d. It had no effect.

3. What long-term effect did Tiffany Field find massage had on premature infants?
a. Massaged infants had better social relationships.
b. Massaged infants were physically and cognitively more developed.
c. Massaged infants slept and ate better.
d. There were no long-term effects noted.

4. What physical change did Mark Rosenzweig's team note when they studied rats raised in an enriched environment?
a. a thicker cortex
b. more neurons
c. fewer neurotransmitters
d. no physical changes were noted, only functional

5. In Michael Meaney's research on aged rats' performance in a swimming maze, the rats that performed best were those that _____
a. had received doses of glucocorticoid.
b. had been subjected to less stress in their lives.
c. had been handled early in life.
d. could use spatial clues for orientation.

6. In Robert Sapolsky's study of stress physiology among baboons, what is the relationship between high status and "good" physiology?
a. Animals attain high status because they have good physiology.
b. Attaining high status leads to good physiology.
c. Lowering one's status leads to improved physiology.
d. Animals with high status produce high levels of stress hormone, which break down the immune system.

Program 25

7. All of the following areas are specialized for motion, *except* _____
a. V1.
b. the right hemisphere.
c. the left hemisphere.
d. the thalamus.

8. For dyslexics who have trouble processing phonemes, which area of the brain is most likely to be damaged?
a. the thalamus
b. the right hemisphere
c. the parietal lobe
d. the left hemisphere

9. People who show a strong eyeblink response in Banaji's studies also tend to show _____
a. a preference for white faces on the IAT.
b. low activation in the amygdala.
c. a preference for black faces on the IAT.
d. no cultural biases.

QUESTIONS TO CONSIDER

1. Given the advances being made in the imaging of brain activity, will it ever be possible for scientists to "read someone's mind" or to control someone's thoughts?

2. Speculate on why music, having no survival benefit or pharmacological properties, would have the strong effect on people's emotions and brains that it seems to have.

5

Sensation and Perception

ave you ever wondered how your brain—locked in the dark chamber of the skull—experiences the blaze of colour in a van Gogh painting, the driving melodies and rhythms of rock 'n' roll, the refreshing taste of watermelon on a hot day, the soft touch of a child's kiss, or the fragrance of wildflowers in the springtime? Our task in this chapter is to explain how your body and brain make sense of the buzz of stimulation—sights, sounds, and so on—constantly around you. You will see how evolution has equipped you with the capability of detecting many different dimensions of experience.

In this chapter, we will describe how your experience of the world relies on processes of *sensation* and *perception*. We will discover that these processes serve the dual functions of *survival* and *sensuality*. Your sensory and perceptual processes help you survive by sounding alarms of danger, priming you to take swift action to ward off hazards, and directing you toward agreeable experiences. These processes also provide you with sensuality. Sensuality is the quality of being devoted to the gratification of the senses; it entails enjoying the experiences that appeal to your various senses of sight, sound, touch, taste, and smell.

We begin with an overview of sensory and perceptual processes—and some challenges the physical world provides to them.

The term **perception**, in its broad usage, refers to the overall process of apprehending objects and events in the environment—to sense them, understand them, identify and label them, and prepare to react to them. A *percept* is what is perceived—the phenomenological, or experienced, outcome of the process of perception. The process of perception is best understood when we divide it into three stages: sensation, perceptual organization, and identification/recognition of objects.

Sensation is the process by which stimulation of *sensory receptors*—the structures in our eyes, ears, and so on—produces electrical impulses that travel to the brain and represent experiences inside or outside the body. For example, sensation provides the basic facts of the visual field. Nerve cells in your eye pass information along to cells in your brain's cortex, which extract preliminary features from this input.

Perceptual organization refers to the stage in which an internal representation of an object is formed in the brain and a percept of the external stimulus is developed. The representation provides a working description of the perceiver's external environment. With respect to vision, perceptual processes provide estimates of an object's likely size, shape, movement, distance, and orientation. Those estimates are based on mental computations that integrate your past knowledge with the present evidence received from your senses and with the stimulus within its perceptual context. Perception involves *synthesis* (integration and combination) of simple sensory features, such as colours, edges, and lines, into the percept of an object that can be recognized later. These mental activities most often occur swiftly and efficiently, without conscious awareness.

Identification and recognition, the third stage in this sequence, assigns meaning to perceptions. Circular objects "become" baseballs, coins, clocks, oranges, and moons; people may be identified as male or female, friend or foe, relative or rock star. At this stage, the perceptual question "What does the object look like?" changes to a question of identification—"What is this object?"—and to a question of recognition—"What is the object's function?" To identify and recognize what something is, what it is called, and how best to respond to it involves higher-level cognitive processes, which include your theories, memories, values, beliefs, and attitudes concerning the object.

We have briefly introduced the stages of processing that enable you to arrive at a meaningful understanding of the perceptual world around you. In everyday life, perception seems to be entirely effortless. Yet you actually do quite a bit of sophisticated processing—a lot of mental work—to arrive at this "illusion of ease."

What senses are involved in the enjoyment of a slice of watermelon?

Sensory Knowledge of the World

Your experience of external reality must be relatively accurate and error free. If not, you could not survive very long. You need food to sustain you, shelter to protect you, interactions with other people to fulfill social needs, and awareness of danger to keep out of harm's way. To meet these needs, you must get

perception The processes that organize information in the sensory image and interpret it as having been produced by properties of objects or events in the external, three-dimensional world.

sensation The process by which stimulation of a sensory receptor gives rise to neural impulses that result in an experience, or awareness, of conditions inside or outside the body.

perceptual organization The processes that put sensory information together to give the perception of a coherent scene over the whole visual field.

identification and recognition Two ways of attaching meaning to percepts.

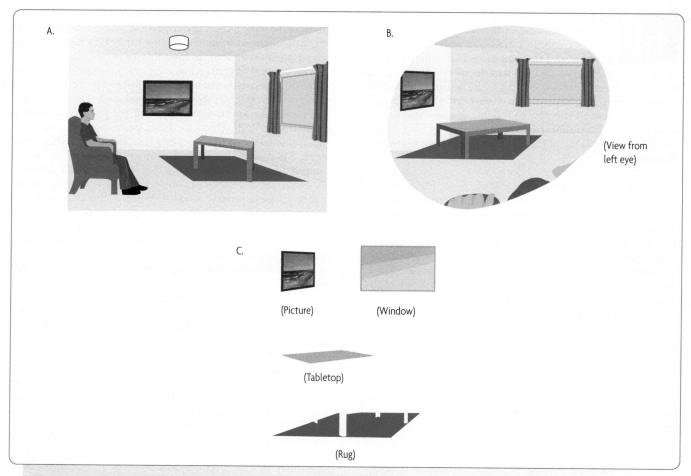

A.

B.

(View from left eye)

C.

(Picture)

(Window)

(Tabletop)

(Rug)

FIGURE 5.1   Interpreting Retinal Images

Suppose you are sitting in an easy chair, looking around a room (A). The light reflected from objects in the room forms images on your retina. Consider the information that arrives at your left eye (B). When you see that information out of context (C), you can appreciate the task that faces your visual system: Your visual perception must interpret or identify the distal stimulus (the actual object in the environment), using the information from the proximal stimulus (the retinal image produced by the object).

reliable information about the world. In this section, we provide an overview of how your sensory processes address these goals.

THE PROXIMAL AND DISTAL STIMULI

Imagine you are the person in **Figure 5.1A**, surveying a room from an easy chair. Some of the light reflected from the objects in the room enters your eyes and forms images on your retinas. **Figure 5.1B** shows what would appear to your left eye as you sit in the room. (The bump on the right is your nose, and the hand and knee at the bottom are your own.) How does this retinal image compare with the environment that produced it?

One very important difference is that the retinal image is *two dimensional*, whereas the environment is *three dimensional*. This difference has many consequences. For instance, compare the shapes of the physical objects in Figure 5.1A with the shapes of their corresponding retinal images (**Figure 5.1C**). The table, rug, window, and picture in the real-world scene are

all rectangular, but only the image of the window actually produces a rectangle in your retinal image. The image of the picture is a trapezoid, the image of the tabletop is an irregular four-sided figure, and the image of the rug is actually three separate regions with more than 20 different sides! Here's our first perceptual puzzle: How do you manage to perceive all of these objects as simple standard rectangles?

The situation, however, is even more complicated. You can also notice that many parts of what you perceive in the room are not actually present in your retinal image. For instance, you perceive the vertical edge between the two walls as going all the way to the floor, but your retinal image of that edge stops at the tabletop. Similarly, in your retinal image, parts of the rug are hidden behind the table, yet this does not keep you from correctly perceiving the rug as a single unbroken rectangle. In fact, when you consider all the differences between the environmental objects and their images on your retina, you may be surprised that you perceive the scene as well as you do.

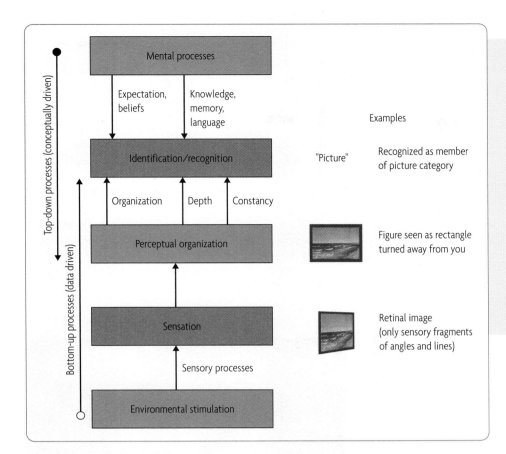

FIGURE 5.2 Sensation, Perceptual Organization, and Identification/ Recognition Stages

The diagram outlines the processes that give rise to the transformation of incoming information at the stages of sensation, perceptual organization, and identification/ recognition. Bottom-up processing occurs when the perceptual representation is derived from the information available in the sensory input. Top-down processing occurs when the perceptual representation is affected by an individual's prior knowledge, motivations, expectations, and other aspects of higher mental functioning.

The differences between a physical object in the world and its optical image on your retina are so profound and important that psychologists distinguish carefully between them as two different stimuli for perception. The physical object in the world is called the **distal stimulus** (distant from the observer) and the optical image on the retina is called the **proximal stimulus** (proximate, or near, to the observer).

The critical point of our discussion can now be restated more concisely: What you wish to *perceive* is the *distal stimulus*—the "real" object in the environment—whereas the stimulus from which you must derive your information is the *proximal stimulus*—the image on the retina. You can think of the major computational task of perception as the process of determining the distal stimulus from information contained in the proximal stimulus. This is true across perceptual domains. For hearing, touch, taste, and so on, perception involves processes that use information in the proximal stimulus to tell you about properties of the distal stimulus.

To show you how the distal stimulus and proximal stimulus fit with the three stages in perceiving, let's examine one of the objects in the scene from Figure 5.1: the picture hanging on the wall. In the sensory stage, this picture corresponds to a two-dimensional trapezoid in your retinal image; the top and bottom sides converge toward the right, and the left and right sides are different in length. This is the proximal stimulus. In the perceptual organization stage, you see this trapezoid as a rectangle turned away from you in three-dimensional space. You perceive the top and bottom sides as parallel but receding into the distance toward the right; you perceive the left and right sides as

equal in length. Your perceptual processes have developed a strong *hypothesis* about the physical properties of the distal stimulus; now it needs an identity. In the recognition stage, you identify this rectangular object as a picture. **Figure 5.2** is a flowchart illustrating this sequence of events. The processes that take information from one stage to the next are shown as arrows between the boxes. By the end of this chapter, we will explain the interactions represented in this figure.

We have defined the task of perception as the identification of the distal stimulus from the proximal stimulus. The earliest researches on sensation, however, recognized that people's experiences of the world have a psychological component. As we will see next, those researchers examined the relationship between events in the environment and people's experience of those events.

PSYCHOPHYSICS

How loud must a fire alarm be in a factory for workers to hear it over the din of the machinery? How bright does a warning light on a pilot's control panel have to be to appear twice as bright as

---

distal stimulus In the processes of perception, the physical object in the world, as contrasted with the proximal stimulus, the optical image on the retina.

proximal stimulus The optical image on the retina; contrasted with the distal stimulus, the physical object in the world.

the other lights? How much sugar do you need to put in a cup of coffee before it begins to taste sweet? To answer these questions, we must be able to measure the *intensity* of sensory experiences. This is the central task of **psychophysics**, the study of the relationship between physical stimuli and the behaviour or mental experiences the stimuli evoke.

The most significant figure in the history of psychophysics was the German physicist **Gustav Fechner** (1801–1887). Fechner coined the term *psychophysics* and provided a set of procedures to relate the intensity of a physical stimulus—measured in physical units—to the magnitude of the sensory experience—measured in psychological units (Fechner, 1860/1966). Fechner's techniques are the same whether the stimuli are for light, sound, taste, odour, or touch: Researchers determine thresholds and construct psychophysical scales relating strength of sensation to strength of stimuli.

Absolute Thresholds and Sensory Adaptation

What is the smallest, weakest stimulus energy an organism can detect? How soft can a tone be, for instance, and still be heard? These questions refer to the concept of **absolute threshold** for stimulation—the minimum amount of physical energy needed to produce a sensory experience. Researchers measure absolute thresholds by asking vigilant observers to perform detection tasks, such as trying to see a dim light in a dark room or trying to hear a soft sound in a quiet room. During a series of many trials the stimulus is presented at varying intensities, and on each trial the observers indicate whether they were aware of it. (If you have ever had your hearing evaluated, you participated in an absolute threshold test.)

The results of an absolute threshold study can be summarized in a **psychometric function**: a graph that shows the percentage of detections (plotted on the vertical axis) at each stimulus intensity (plotted on the horizontal axis). A typical psychometric function is shown in **Figure 5.3**. For very dim lights, detection is at 0 percent; for bright lights, detection is at 100 percent. If there were a single, true absolute threshold, you would expect the transition from 0 to 100 percent detection to be very sharp, occurring right at the point where the intensity reached the threshold. Yet this does not happen, for at least two reasons: Viewers themselves change slightly each time they try to detect a stimulus (because of changes in attention, fatigue, and so on), and sometimes respond even in the absence of a stimulus (a type of false alarm we will discuss shortly, when we describe signal detection theory). Thus, the psychometric curve is usually a smooth S-shaped curve, in which there is a region of transition from no detection to occasional detection to detection all the time.

Since a stimulus does not suddenly become clearly detectable at all times at a specific intensity, the operational definition of

---

psychophysics The study of the correspondence between physical simulation and psychological experience.

absolute threshold The minimum amount of physical energy needed to produce a reliable sensory experience; operationally defined as the stimulus level at which a sensory signal is detected half the time.

psychometric function A graph that plots the percentage of detections of a stimulus (on the vertical axis) for each unit of stimulus intensity (on the horizontal axis).

sensory adaptation A phenomenon in which receptor cells lose their power to respond after a period of unchanged stimulation; allows a more rapid reaction to new sources of information.

FIGURE 5.3 Calculation of Absolute Thresholds
Because a stimulus does not become suddenly detectable at a certain point, absolute threshold is defined as the intensity at which the stimulus is detected half of the time over many trials.

Can you hear the tone? Hearing evaluation is usually done with an absolute threshold test. Why do these tests require multiple trials?

absolute threshold is *the stimulus level at which a sensory signal is detected correctly when it is presented half the time.* Thresholds for different senses can be measured using the same procedure, simply by changing the stimulus dimension. **Table 5.1** shows absolute threshold levels for several familiar natural stimuli.

Although it is possible to identify absolute thresholds for detection, it is also important to note that your sensory systems are more sensitive to *changes* in the sensory environment than to steady states. The systems have evolved so that they favour new environmental inputs over old ones through a process called adaptation. **Sensory adaptation** is the diminishing responsiveness of sensory systems to prolonged stimulus input. You may have noticed, for example, that sunshine seems less blinding after you have been outdoors awhile. People often have their most fortunate experiences of adaptation in the domain of smell: You walk into a room and smell something

TABLE 5.1 Approximate Thresholds of Familiar Events

Sense Modality	Detection Threshold
Light	A candle flame seen at 45 kilometres on a dark, clear night
Sound	The tick of a watch under quiet conditions at 6 metres
Taste	One teaspoon of sugar in 7.5 litres of water
Smell	One drop of perfume diffused into the entire volume of a three-room apartment
Touch	The wing of a bee falling on your cheek from a distance of 1 centimetre

terrible; over time, however, as your smell system adapts, the odour fades out of awareness. Your environment is always full of a great diversity of sensory stimulation. The mechanism of adaptation allows you to notice and react more quickly to the challenges of new sources of information.

Response Bias and Signal Detection Theory In our discussion so far, we have assumed that all observers are created equal. Threshold measurements can also be affected by **response bias**, the systematic tendency for an observer to favour responding in a particular way because of factors unrelated to the sensory features of the stimulus. Suppose, for example, you are in an experiment in which you must detect a weak light. In the first phase of the experiment, the researcher gives you $5 when you are correct in saying, "Yes, a light was there." In the second phase, the researcher gives you $5 when you are correct in saying, "No, there wasn't any light." In each phase, you are penalized $2 any time you are incorrect. Can you see how this reward structure would create a shift in response bias from phase 1 to phase 2? Wouldn't you say yes more often in the first

phase—with the same amount of certainty that the stimulus was present?

Signal detection theory (SDT) is a systematic approach to the problem of response bias (Green & Swets, 1966). Instead of focusing strictly on sensory processes, SDT emphasizes the process of making a *judgment* about the presence or absence of stimulus events. Whereas classical psychophysics conceptualized a single absolute threshold, SDT identifies two distinct processes in sensory detection: (1) an initial *sensory process*, which reflects the observer's sensitivity to the strength of the stimulus; and (2) a subsequent separate *decision process*, which reflects the observer's response biases.

SDT offers a procedure for evaluating both the sensory process and the decision process at once. The basic design is given in **Figure 5.4**. A weak stimulus is presented in half the trials; no stimulus is presented in the other half. In each trial,

If you decline a dinner invitation, will you be avoiding a dull evening (a correct rejection) or sacrificing the chance for a lifetime of love (a miss)?

FIGURE 5.4   The Theory of Signal Detection
The matrix shows the possible outcomes when a subject is asked if a target stimulus occurred on a given trial.

response bias The systematic tendency as a result of nonsensory factors for an observer to favour responding in a particular way.

signal detection theory A systematic approach to the problem of response bias that allows an experimenter to identify and separate the roles of sensory stimuli and the individual's criterion level in producing the final response.

observers respond by saying *yes* if they think the signal was present and *no* if they think it was not. As shown in the figure, each response is scored in one of four ways:

- A response is a *hit* when the signal is present and the observer says "yes."
- A response is a *miss* when the signal is present and the observer says "no."
- A response is a *false alarm* when the signal is absent and the observer says "yes."
- A response is a *correct rejection* when the signal is absent and the observer says "no."

How can we see the impact of the perceivers' decision processes? If Carol is a yea-sayer (she almost always answers yes), she will almost inevitably say yes when the stimulus is present, so she will have a large number of hits. However, she will also have a high number of false alarms because she will also say yes quite often when the stimulus is absent. If Bob is a nay-sayer (he almost always answers no), he will have a lower number of hits, but also a lower number of false alarms.

Working with percentages of hits and false alarms, researchers use mathematical procedures to calculate separate measures of observers' sensitivity and response biases. This procedure makes it possible to find out whether two observers have the same sensitivity despite large differences in response criterion. By providing a way of separating sensory process from response bias, the theory of signal detection allows an experimenter to identify and separate the roles of the sensory stimulus and the individual's criterion level in producing the final response.

Difference Thresholds Imagine you have been employed by a beverage company that wants to produce a cola product that tastes noticeably sweeter than existing colas, but (to save money) the firm wants to put as little extra sugar in the cola as possible. You are being asked to measure a **difference threshold**, the smallest physical difference between two stimuli that can still be recognized as a difference. To measure a difference threshold, you use pairs of stimuli and ask your observers whether they believe the two stimuli to be the same or different.

For the beverage problem, you would give your observers two colas on each trial, one of some standard recipe and one just a bit sweeter. For each pair, the individual would say *same* or *different*. After many such trials, you would plot a psychometric function by graphing the percentage of *different* responses on the vertical axis as a function of the actual differences, plotted on the horizontal axis. The difference threshold is operationally defined as *the point at which the stimuli are recognized as different half of the time*. This difference threshold value is known as a **just noticeable difference**, or **JND**. The JND is a quantitative unit for measuring the magnitude of the psychological difference between any two sensations.

In 1834, **Ernst Weber** pioneered the study of JNDs and discovered the important relationship that we illustrate in **Figure 5.5**. This relationship is summarized as **Weber's law**: *The JND*

---

difference threshold The smallest physical difference between two stimuli that can still be recognized as a difference; operationally defined as the point at which the stimuli are recognized as different half of the time.

just noticeable difference The smallest difference between two sensations that allows them to be discriminated.

Weber's law An assertion that the size of a difference threshold is proportional to the intensity of the standard stimulus.

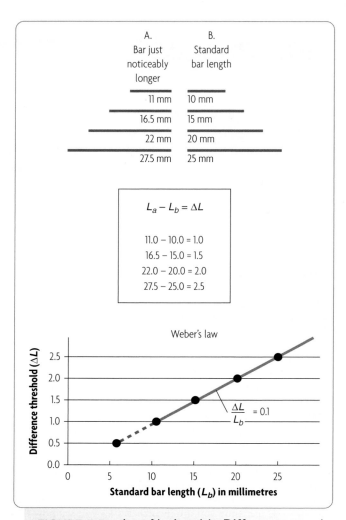

FIGURE 5.5 Just Noticeable Differences and Weber's Law

Suppose you are conducting an experiment in which you challenge participants to detect whether two bars are the same or different in length. The longer the standard bar, the greater the amount you must add ΔL to see a just noticeable difference. The difference threshold is the added length detected on half the trials. When these increments are plotted against standard bars of increasing length, the proportions stay the same; the amount added is always one tenth of the standard length. The relationship is linear, producing a straight line on the graph. We can predict that the ΔL for a bar length of 5 will be 0.5.

between stimuli is a constant fraction of the intensity of the standard stimulus. Thus, the bigger or more intense the standard stimulus, the larger the increment needed to get a just noticeable difference. The formula for Weber's law is $\Delta I/I = k$, where I is the intensity of the standard and ΔI, or delta I, is the size of the increase that produces a JND. Weber found that each stimulus dimension has a characteristic value for this ratio. In this formula, k represents that ratio, or *Weber's constant*, for the particular stimulus dimension. Weber's law provides a good approximation, but not a perfect fit to experimental data, of

TABLE 5.2 Weber's Constant Values for Selected Stimulus Dimensions	
Stimulus Dimension	**Weber's Constant (k)**
Sound frequency	0.003
Light intensity	0.01
Odour concentration	0.07
Pressure intensity	0.14
Sound intensity	0.15
Taste concentration	0.20

Figure from *Introduction to Psychology*, 10th ed., by Atkinson. Copyright © 1989. Reprinted with permission of Wadsworth, a division of Thomson Learning.

how the size of JND increases with intensity (most problems with the law arise when stimulus intensities become extremely high).

You see in **Table 5.2** that Weber's constant (k) has different values for different sensory dimensions—smaller values mean that people can detect smaller differences. So this table tells you that you can differentiate two sound frequencies more precisely than light intensities, which, in turn, are detectable with a smaller JND than odour or taste differences are. Your beverage company would need a relatively large amount of extra sugar to produce a noticeably sweeter cola!

FROM PHYSICAL EVENTS TO MENTAL EVENTS

Our review of psychophysics has addressed the central mystery of sensation: How do physical energies give rise to particular psychological experiences? How, for example, do the various physical wavelengths of light give rise to your experience of a rainbow? Before we consider specific sensory domains, let's begin with an overview of the flow of information from physical events—waves of light and sound, complex chemicals, and so on—to mental events—your experiences of sights, sounds, tastes, and smells.

The conversion of one form of physical energy, such as light, to another form, such as neural impulses, is called **transduction**. As all sensory information is transduced into identical types of neural impulses, your brain differentiates sensory experiences by devoting special areas of cortex to each sensory domain. For each domain, researchers try to discover how the transduction of physical energy into the electrochemical activity of the nervous system gives rise to sensations of different quality (red rather than green) and different quantity (loud rather than soft).

Sensory systems share the same basic flow of information. The trigger for any sensing system is the detection of an environmental event, or *stimulus*. Environmental stimuli are detected by specialized **sensory receptors**. Sensory receptors convert the physical form of the sensory signal into cellular signals that can be processed by the nervous system. These cellular signals contribute information to higher-level neurons that integrate information across different detector units. At this stage, neurons extract information about the basic qualities of the stimulus, such as its size, intensity, shape, and distance. Deeper into the sensory systems, information is combined into even more complex codes that are passed on to specific areas of the sensory cortex and association cortex of the brain.

We move now to specific sensory domains.

STOP AND REVIEW

1 What is the proximal stimulus?
2 What is the subject matter of psychophysics?
3 What is the operational definition of an absolute threshold?
4 In signal detection theory, what two processes contribute to observers' judgments?
5 What is a difference threshold?
6 What is transduction?

The Visual System

Vision is the most complex, highly developed, and important sense for humans and most other mobile creatures. Animals with good vision have an enormous evolutionary advantage, as it helps them detect prey and predators from a distance. Vision enables humans to be aware of changing features in the physical environment and to adapt their behaviour accordingly. Vision is also the most studied of all the senses.

transduction Transformation of one form of energy into another; for example, light is transformed into neural impulses.

sensory receptors Specialized cells that convert physical signals into cellular signals that are processed by the nervous system.

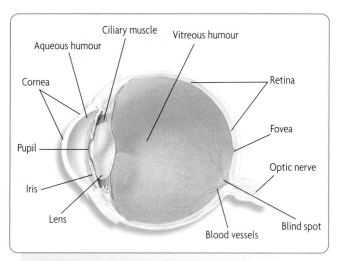

FIGURE 5.6 Structure of the Human Eye

The cornea, pupil, and lens focus light onto the retina. Nerve signals from the retina are carried to the brain by the optic nerve.

THE HUMAN EYE

The eye is the camera for the brain's motion pictures of the world (see **Figure 5.6**). A camera views the world through a lens that gathers and focuses light. The eye also gathers and focuses light. Light enters the *cornea*, a transparent bulge on the front of the eye. Next it passes through the *anterior chamber*, which is filled with a clear liquid called the *aqueous humour*. The light then passes through the *pupil*, an opening in the opaque *iris*. To focus a camera, you move its lens closer to or farther from the object viewed. To focus light in the eye, a bean-shaped crystalline *lens* changes its shape, thinning to focus on distant objects and thickening to focus on near ones. To control the amount of light coming into a camera, you vary the opening of the lens. In the eye, the muscular disk of the iris changes the size of the pupil, the opening through which light passes into the eyeball. At the back of a camera body is the photosensitive film that records the variations in light that have come through the lens. Similarly, in the eye, light travels through the *vitreous humour*, finally striking the *retina*, a thin sheet of cells that lines the rear wall of the eyeball.

As you can see, the features of a camera and the eye are very similar. Now let's examine the components of the vision process in more detail.

THE PUPIL AND THE LENS

The pupil is the opening in the iris through which light passes. The iris makes the pupil dilate or constrict to control the amount of light entering the eyeball. Light passing through the

---

accommodation 1. The process by which the ciliary muscles change the thickness of the lens of the eye to permit variable focusing on near and distant objects. 2. According to Piaget, the process of restructuring or modifying cognitive structures so that new information can fit into them more easily; this process works in tandem with assimilation.

pupil is focused by the lens on the retina; the lens reverses and inverts the light pattern as it does so. The lens is particularly important because of its variable focusing ability for near and far objects. The ciliary muscles can change the thickness of the lens and hence its optical properties in a process called **accommodation**.

People with normal accommodation have a range of focus from about seven centimetres in front of their nose to as far as they can see. However, many people suffer from accommodation problems. For example, people who are nearsighted have their range of accommodation shifted closer to them, with the consequence that they cannot focus well on distant objects; those who are farsighted have their range of accommodation shifted farther away from them, which means they cannot focus normally on nearby objects. Aging also leads to problems in accommodation. The lens starts off as clear, transparent, and convex. As people age, the lens becomes more amber-tinted, opaque, and flattened, and it loses its elasticity. The effect of some of these changes is that the lens cannot become thick enough for close vision. When people age past the 45-year mark, the *near point*—the closest point at which they can focus clearly—gets progressively farther away. The solution for many people is to wear glasses. As they age, those who have never worn glasses may need them for reading and other activities that require close vision; those who already wore glasses to correct their vision may need bifocals. Bifocals allow people to focus on objects that are both far away and close up by simply adjusting their head to see through the correct portion of the lenses of their glasses.

THE RETINA

Though you look with your eyes, you see with your brain. The eye gathers light, focuses it, and starts a neural signal on its way toward the brain. The eye's critical function, therefore, is to convert information about the world from light waves into neural

Visual acuity enables predatory animals to detect potential prey from a distance. What range of functions did evolution provide for the human visual system?

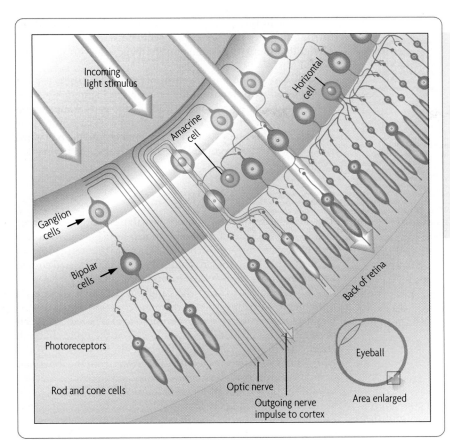

FIGURE 5.7 Retinal Pathways
This is a stylized and greatly simplified diagram showing the pathways that connect three of the layers of nerve cells in the retina. Incoming light passes through all these layers to reach the receptors, at the back of the eyeball, which are pointed away from the source of light. Note that the bipolar cells gather impulses from more than one receptor cell and send the results to ganglion cells. Nerve impulses (blue arrow) from the ganglion cells leave the eye via the optic nerve and travel to the next relay point.

signals. This happens in the **retina**, at the back of the eye. Under the microscope, you can see that the retina has several highly organized layers of different types of neurons.

The basic conversion from light energy to neural responses is performed in your retina by *rods* and *cones*—receptor cells sensitive to light. These **photoreceptors** are uniquely placed in the visual system between the outer world that is ablaze with light and the inner world of neural processing. Since you sometimes operate in near darkness and sometimes in bright light, nature has provided two ways of processing light: rods and cones (see **Figure 5.7**). The 120 million thin **rods** operate best in near darkness. The seven million **cones** are specialized for the bright, colour-filled day.

You experience differences between the functions of your rods and cones each time you turn off the lights to go to sleep at night. You have probably noticed many times that at first it seems as though you cannot see much of anything in the dim light that remains, but over time your visual sensitivity improves again. You are undergoing the process of **dark adaptation**—the gradual improvement of the eyes' sensitivity after a shift in illumination from light to near darkness. Dark adaptation occurs because, as time passes in the dark, your rods become more sensitive than your cones; over time, your rods are able to respond to less light from the environment than your cones are.

Near the centre of the retina is a small region called the **fovea**, which contains nothing but densely packed cones; it is rod free. The fovea is the area of your sharpest vision—both colour and spatial detail are most accurately detected there.

Other cells in your retina are responsible for integrating information across regions of rods and cones. The **bipolar cells** are nerve cells that combine impulses from many receptors and send the results to ganglion cells. Each **ganglion cell** then integrates the impulses from one or more bipolar cells into a single firing rate. The cones in the central fovea send their impulses to the ganglion cells in that region; farther out on the periphery of the retina, rods and cones converge on the same bipolar and ganglion cells. The axons of the ganglion cells make up the optic nerve, which carries this visual information out of the eye and back toward the brain.

---

retina The layer at the back of the eye that contains photoreceptors and converts light energy to neural responses.

photoreceptors Receptor cells in the retina that are sensitive to light.

rods Photoreceptors concentrated in the periphery of the retina that are most active in dim illumination; rods do not produce sensation of colour.

cones Photoreceptors concentrated in the centre of the retina that are responsible for visual experience under normal viewing conditions for all experiences of colour.

dark adaptation The gradual improvement of the eyes' sensitivity after a shift in illumination from light to near darkness.

fovea Area of the retina that contains densely packed cones and forms the point of sharpest vision.

bipolar cells Nerve cells in the visual system that combine impulses from many receptors and transmit the results to ganglion cells.

ganglion cells Cells in the visual system that integrate impulses from many bipolar cells in a single firing rate.

FIGURE 5.8 Find Your Blind Spot
To find your blind spot, hold this book at arm's length, close your right eye, and fixate on the bank figure with your left eye as you bring the book slowly closer. When the dollar sign is in your blind spot, it will disappear, but you will experience no gaping hole in your visual field. Similarly, if you use the same procedure to focus on the plus sign, the line will appear whole when the gap is in your blind spot. In both cases, your visual system fills in the background whiteness of the surrounding area so you "see" the whiteness, which is not there.

Your **horizontal cells** and **amacrine cells** integrate information across the retina. Rather than send signals toward the brain, horizontal cells connect receptors to each other, and amacrine cells link bipolar cells to other bipolar cells and ganglion cells to other ganglion cells.

An interesting curiosity in the anatomical design of the retina exists where the optic nerve leaves each eye. This region, called the optic disk, or *blind spot*, contains no receptor cells at all. You do not experience blindness there, except under very special circumstances, for two reasons: First, the blind spots of the two eyes are positioned so that receptors in each eye register what is missed in the other; second, the brain fills in this region with appropriate sensory information from the surrounding area. This ability has been of interest to psychologists for some time because of the process the brain uses to fill in the sensory information. Though research has not yet provided all the details, the brain must be performing complex actions to allow us to function as though there is no blind spot.

To find your blind spot, you will have to look at **Figure 5.8** under special viewing conditions. Hold this book at arm's length, close your right eye, and fixate on the bank figure with your left eye as you bring the book slowly closer. When the dollar sign is in your blind spot, it will disappear, but you will experience no gaping hole in your visual field. Instead, your visual

horizontal cells The cells that integrate information across the retina; rather than sending signals toward the brain, horizontal cells connect receptors to each other.

amacrine cells Cells that integrate information across the retina; rather than sending signals toward the brain, amacrine cells link bipolar cells to other bipolar cells and ganglion cells to other ganglion cells.

optic nerve The axons of the ganglion cells that carry information from the eye toward the brain.

receptive field The area of the visual field to which a neuron in the visual system responds.

system fills in this area with the background whiteness of the surrounding area so you "see" the whiteness, which is not there. The dollar sign still remains on the page, but you no longer "see" it.

For a second demonstration of your blind spot, use the same procedure to focus on the plus sign in Figure 5.8. As you pull the book closer to you, do you see the gap disappear and the line become whole? How do we do some of our most basic actions with this blind spot? How do you not lose the ball when you play tennis, for example? The answer is that the brain takes over.

PROCESSES IN THE BRAIN

The ultimate destination of much visual information is the part of the occipital lobe of the brain known as primary *visual cortex*. However, most information leaving the retina passes through other brain regions before it arrives at the visual cortex. Let's trace the pathways visual information takes.

The million axons of the ganglion cells that form each **optic nerve** come together in the *optic chiasma*, which resembles the Greek letter χ (*chi*, pronounced *kye*). The axons in each optic nerve are divided into two bundles at the optic chiasma. Half of the fibres from each retina remain on the side of the body from which they originated. The axons from the inner half of each eye cross over the midline as they continue their journey toward the back of the brain (see **Figure 5.9**).

These two bundles of fibres, which now contain axons from both eyes, are renamed *optic tracts*. The optic tracts deliver information to two clusters of cells in the brain. Research supports the theory that visual analysis is separated into pathways for *pattern recognition*—how things look—and *place recognition*—where things are (Pasternak, Bisley, & Calkins, 2003; Rao, Rainer, & Miller, 1997). The division into pattern and place recognition gives you an example of the way in which your visual system consists of several separate subsystems that analyze different aspects of the same retinal image. Although your final perception is of a unified visual scene, your vision of it is accomplished through a host of pathways in your visual system that, under normal conditions, are exquisitely co-ordinated.

Pioneering work on how your visual system pieces together information from the world was done by **David Hubel** and **Torsten Wiesel**, sensory physiologists who won a Nobel Prize in 1981 for their studies of *receptive fields* of cells in the visual cortex. David Hubel was born in Windsor, Ontario, to American parents. After attending medical school at McGill University in Montreal, Hubel moved to the United States in 1954 and was drafted into the army. During this time he was stationed at Walter Reed Army Hospital, a premier medical hospital in Washington, D.C., where he invented microelectrodes and microdrives, the tools necessary for implanting recording electrodes into the brain. These tools were of great value to researchers who followed him. In the late 1950s, Hubel went to Johns Hopkins and began collaborating with Torsten Wiesel on the study of receptive fields. Later, he moved to Harvard University, where he remains today.

The **receptive field** of a cell is the area in the visual field from which it receives stimulation. As shown in **Figure 5.10**, Hubel and Wiesel discovered that cells at different levels of the visual system responded most strongly to different patterns of stimulation. For example, one type of cortical cell, *simple* cells, responded most strongly to bars of light in their "favourite"

Critical Thinking in Your Life

WHAT CAN ANIMAL RESEARCH ON VISION TELL US ABOUT TREATING CHILDHOOD VISION PROBLEMS?

In this section you have learned a little about how information travels from our visual world to our brains. This visual information provides us with a unique perception of the world; imagine for a moment what it might be like if you did not have your visual ability. Let's consider what generally occurs when our visual system is manipulated following an injury.

In the normal visual system, our brain receives input from both eyes, though the visual cortex can be stimulated by a visual scene presented to either eye. A small percentage of children have problems with this distribution of information to the cortex from both eyes. When the brain does not acknowledge information from one of the eyes, that eye is classified as amblyopic. Amblyopia is commonly known as "lazy eye," a condition that generally affects only one eye. Although we do not yet understand all the reasons why a child can have lazy eye, we do know that conditions like crossed eyes can result in amblyopia. We also know that trying to help an eye problem can actually *cause* amblyopia. If, for example, one of the eyes is patched early in life due to injury, the consequence can be that the visual cortex is stimulated only by visual input delivered to the eye that was not patched.

Children who are diagnosed with amblyopia early have a good chance of developing good vision with correct treatments. Depending on the assumed cause, there is a range of treatments available. Children with crossed eyes can have surgery to shorten the muscles around the eyes to correctly align them. If amblyopia is a result of impaired vision in one of the eyes, corrective lenses can be used, or medication can be administered to actually impair vision in the good eye for a short period of time. Impairing vision in a good eye may

seem an odd strategy, but it seems to be very effective. For example, patching the good eye for a short time as well as the injured eye after an injury occurs can greatly reduce the incidence or intensity of amblyopia.

Animal research has revealed some exciting things about how the brain recovers from injury; it has also suggested we use caution with current methods of treating amblyopia. **Kathy Murphy** and **Donald Mitchell** completed a series of studies at Dalhousie University where they patched the eyes of kittens to model the human condition (Murphy & Mitchell, 1986, 1987, 1991). Their research clearly indicated that patching one eye would lead to amblyopia and problems with visual acuity—how well the animals saw items in their environment. What they noted was that a reverse occlusion, a patch on the good eye, would restore some visual acuity to the amblyopic eye, in addition to restoring some of the connections in the brain. A key concern, however, was that there was a reduction of visual acuity in the good eye following the reverse patching. Their studies indicated that there were long-lasting changes in the visual ability of both eyes, and that this change was likely at the level of the brain.

Kathy Murphy, now at McMaster University, and colleagues (Murphy, Duffy, Jones, & Mitchell, 2001; Murphy, Duffy, & Jones, 2004) have continued to investigate how the brain changes following reverse occlusion to help acuity in the amblyopic eye. These studies are likely to help us develop better therapies for amblyopia. Their research has indicated that the early visual experience is essential to the development of normal connections in the brain. Changing visual experience during a critical period of visual development has a large impact on how well the brain receives visual information

from both eyes. The research has led to some interesting data on a very specific type of receptor that may play an important role in visual acuity and in the recovery of the amblyopic eye. This receptor affects how active the cells can be when an axon tries to send a neurotransmitter across the synaptic cleft to signal another cell. If the cells do not communicate efficiently, they cannot make strong connections with each other. (If you recall the discussion in Chapter 4 about the Hebbian theory, strong connections require effective communication between two cells.)

As you might guess, understanding how the animal brain responds to an eye patch is quite important for understanding how a child's brain might respond. Accordingly, animal research is promoting effective strategies in human therapies for amblyopia. Evolving science and technology are providing creative means for both investigating and treating eye problems, especially when they are also brain problems.

- Why could patching an eye result in poor vision?

- In cases of amblyopia, why would patching the other eye be effective?

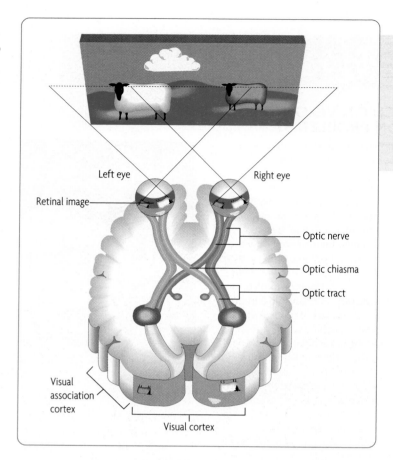

FIGURE 5.9 Pathways in the Human Visual System
The diagram shows the way light from the visual field projects onto the two retinas and the routes by which neural messages from the retina are sent to the two visual centres of each hemisphere.

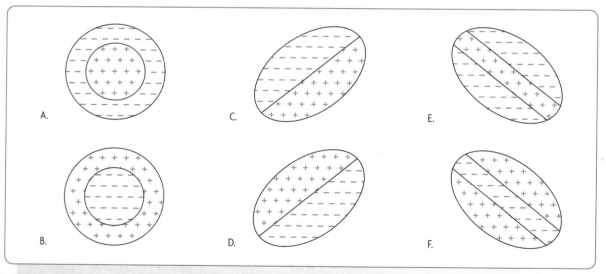

FIGURE 5.10   Receptive Fields of Ganglion and Cortical Cells
The receptive field of a cell in the visual pathway is the area in the visual field from which it receives stimulation. The receptive fields of the ganglion cells in the retina are circular (A, B); those of the simplest cells in the visual cortex are elongated in a particular orientation (C, D, E, F). In both cases, the cell responding to the receptive field is excited by light in the regions marked with plus signs and inhibited by light in the regions marked with minus signs. In addition, the stimulus that most excites the cell is the one in which areas are illuminated where light is excitatory (marked with plus signs), but areas are in darkness where light is inhibitory (marked by minus signs).

orientation (see Figure 5.10). *Complex* cells also each have a "favourite" orientation, but they require as well that the bar be moving. *Hypercomplex* cells require moving bars of a particular length or moving corners or angles. The cells provide types of information to higher visual centres in the brain that ultimately allow the brain to recognize objects in the visual world.

The advances in imaging techniques we described in Chapter 4 have enabled researchers to discover regions of the cortex that are specially responsive to even more complex environmental images.

Take a moment to look at your hand. Now focus on any other object in the room. If a team of researchers is correct, one particular region of your brain just turned on and off as you shifted your focus from your hand—a body part—to an object from a different category (Downing, Jiang, Shuman, & Kanwisher, 2001). To test this hypothesis, the researchers collected functional magnetic resonance imaging (fMRI) data with the range of pictures shown in **Figure 5.11**. The fMRI images of the brain demonstrated that a region of the cortex on the boundary between the occipital and temporal lobes was selectively active to depictions of the human body (A–F). The exceptions to this finding were faces (G) and parts of faces (M). Other brain regions appear to handle the processing of human faces.

Humans are particularly important to other humans, which probably explains why particular brain regions are

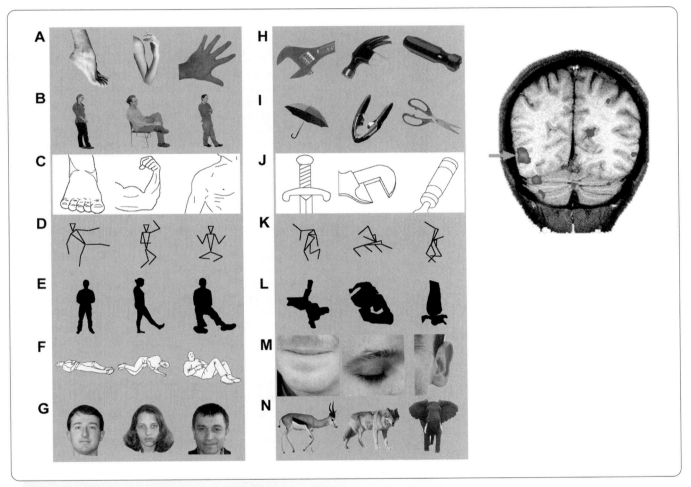

FIGURE 5.11   Cortical Regions for the Visual Processing of the Human Body

Researchers used fMRI to assess participants' brain responses to 19 different types of stimuli. The stimuli represent body parts and visual controls for those body parts. Note, for example, how the tools in panel J echo the body parts in panel C. The brain scan shows the region of the cortex on the boundary between the occipital and temporal lobes that became selectively active in response to all depictions of the human body (A–F). This region was not activated when participants viewed whole faces (G), objects (H–J), or scrambled bodies (K–L). The region became active at an intermediate level in response to face parts (M) and mammals (N).

Reprinted with permission from Downing, P.E., Jiang, Y., Shurman, M. & Kanwisher, N. (2001). A cortical area selective for visual processing of the human body. *Science, 293*, 2470–2473. Copyright © 2001 AAAS.

devoted to the processing of human faces and bodies. Researchers still do not know if these regions of the brain have these special functions at birth, or if the functions are the product of a lifetime of experience.

You have now learned the basics of how visual information is distributed from the eyes to various parts of the brain. Researchers still have more to learn: There are roughly 30 anatomical subdivisions of primate visual cortex, and theories vary about the pattern of communication among those areas (Hilgetag, O'Neill, & Young, 1996). For now, we turn to particular aspects of the visual world. One of the most remarkable features of the human visual system is that your experiences of form, colour, position, and depth are based on processing the same sensory information in different ways. How do the transformations occur that enable you to see these different features of the visual world?

What three dimensions underlie experiences of colour?

SEEING COLOUR

Physical objects seem to have the marvellous property of being painted with colour. You most often have the impression of brightly coloured objects—red valentines, green fir trees, or blue robins' eggs—but your vivid experience of colour relies on the rays of light these objects reflect onto your sensory receptors. Colour is created when your brain processes the information coded in the light source.

Wavelengths and Hues The light you see is just a small portion of a physical dimension called the *electromagnetic spectrum* (see **Figure 5.12**). Your visual system is not equipped to detect other types of waves in this spectrum, such as X-rays, microwaves, and radio waves. The physical property that distinguishes types of electromagnetic energy, including light, is *wavelength*, the distance between the crests of two adjacent waves. Wavelengths of visible light are measured in *nanometres* (billionths of a metre). What you see as light is the range of wavelengths from 400 to about 700 nanometres. Light rays of particular physical wavelengths give rise to experiences of particular colours—for example, violet–blue at the lower end and red–orange at the higher end. Thus, light is described physically in terms of wavelengths, not colours; colours exist only in your sensory system's interpretation of the wavelengths.

All experiences of colour can be described in terms of three basic dimensions: hue, saturation, and brightness. **Hue** is the dimension that captures the qualitative experience of the colour of a light. In pure lights that contain only one wavelength (such as a laser beam), the psychological experience of hue corresponds directly to the physical dimension of the light's wavelength. **Figure 5.13** presents the hues arranged in a colour circle. Those hues perceived to be most similar are in adjacent positions. This order mirrors the order of hues in the spectrum. **Saturation** is the psychological dimension that captures the

purity and vividness of colour sensations. Undiluted colours have the most saturation; muted, muddy, and pastel colours have intermediate amounts of saturation; and greys have zero saturation. **Brightness** is the dimension of colour experience that captures the intensity of light. White has the most brightness; black has the least. When colours are analyzed along these three dimensions, a remarkable finding emerges: Humans are capable of visually discriminating about seven million different colours! Most people can label, or provide names to, only a small number of those colours.

Let's explain some facts about your everyday experience of colour. At some point in your science education, you may have repeated Sir Isaac Newton's discovery that sunlight combines all wavelengths of light: You repeated Newton's proof by using a prism or even the fine mist following a rain shower to separate sunlight into the full rainbow of colours. The prism shows that the right combination of wavelengths yields white light. The combination of wavelengths is called *additive colour mixture*. Take another look at Figure 5.13. Wavelengths that appear directly across from each other on the colour circle—called **complementary colours**—will create the sensation of white light when mixed.

Do you want to prove to yourself the existence of complementary colours? Consider **Figure 5.14** on page 126. The green and black flag should give you the experience of a *negative afterimage* (the afterimage is called "negative" because it is the opposite of the original colour). For reasons that we will explain when we consider theories of colour vision, when you stare at any colour long enough to partially fatigue your photoreceptors, looking at a white surface will allow you to experience the complement of the original colour.

You have probably noticed afterimages from time to time in your everyday exposure to colours. Most of your experience with colours, however, does not come from complementary lights. Instead, you have probably spent your time at play with colours by combining crayons or paints of different hues. The colours you see when you look at a crayon mark, or any other coloured surface, are the wavelengths of light that are not absorbed by the surface. Although yellow crayon looks mostly yellow, it lets some wavelengths escape that give rise to the sensation of green. Similarly, blue crayon lets wavelengths escape that give rise to the sensations of blue and some green.

hue The dimension of colour space that captures the qualitative experience of the colour of light.

saturation The dimension of colour space that captures the purity and vividness of colour sensations.

brightness The dimension of colour space that captures the intensity of light.

complementary colours Colours opposite each other on the colour circle; when additively mixed, they create the sensation of white light.

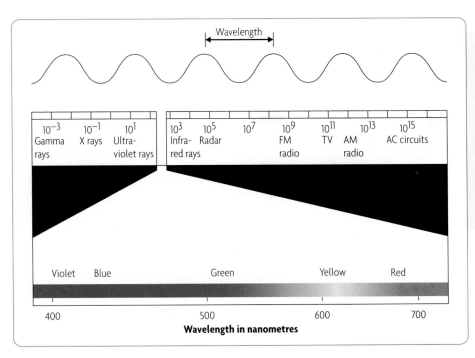

FIGURE 5.12 The Electromagnetic Spectrum

Your visual system can sense only a small range of wavelengths in the electromagnetic spectrum. You experience that range of wavelengths, which is enlarged in the figure, as the colours violet through red.

From "The Electromagnetic Spectrum," *Perception*, 3e, by R. Sekular et al., pp. 27, 221. Copyright © 1994 by the McGraw-Hill Companies. Reprinted by permission of the McGraw-Hill Companies.

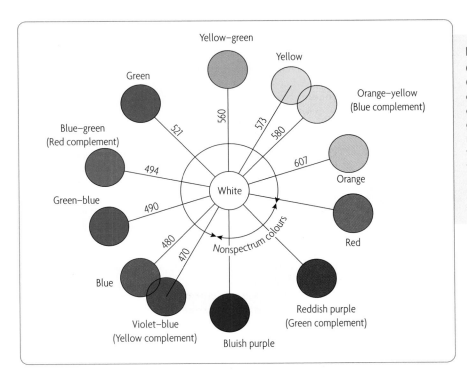

FIGURE 5.13 The Colour Circle

Colours are arranged based on similarity. Complementary colours are placed directly opposite each other. Mixing complementary colours yields a neutral grey or white light at the centre. The numbers next to each hue are the wavelength values for spectral colours—those colours within the regions of visual sensitivity. Nonspectral hues are obtained by mixing short and long spectral wavelengths.

When yellow and blue crayon are combined, yellow absorbs blue and blue absorbs yellow—the only wavelengths that are not absorbed look green! This phenomenon is called *subtractive colour mixture*. The remaining wavelengths that are not absorbed—the wavelengths that are reflected—give the crayon mixture the colour you perceive.

Some of these rules about the experience of colour do not apply to those people born with a colour deficiency. *Colour blindness* is the partial or total inability to distinguish colours. The negative afterimage effect of viewing the green and black Canadian flag will not work if you are colour blind. Colour blindness is usually a sex-linked hereditary defect associated with a gene on the X chromosome. Since males have a single X chromosome, they are more likely than females to show this recessive trait. Females would need to have a defective gene on both X chromosomes to be colour blind. An estimate for colour

FIGURE 5.14 Colour Afterimages
Stare at the dot in the centre of the flag for at least 30 seconds. Then fixate on the centre of a sheet of white paper or a blank wall.

FIGURE 5.15 A Colour-Blindness Test
Individuals who cannot see a number in this display are unable to discriminate red and green.

blindness among white males is about 8 percent, but less than 0.5 percent among females (Coren, Ward, & Enns, 1999).

Most colour blindness involves difficulty distinguishing red from green, especially at weak saturations. It is not that red

looks like green to these individuals; rather, they are unable to distinguish a red apple from a green one or a red traffic light from a green one without the location cues. More rare are people who confuse yellows and blues. Rarest of all are those who are monochromats, who see no colour at all, only variations in brightness. **Figure 5.15** provides an example of the image researchers use to test for colour blindness. Individuals who have appropriate deficiencies in their red–green system will not see the number. Let's see next how scientists have explained facts about colour vision such as complementary colours and colour blindness.

Theories of Colour Vision The first scientific theory of colour vision was proposed by **Sir Thomas Young** around 1800. He suggested that there were three types of colour receptors in the normal human eye that produced psychologically primary sensations: red, green, and blue. All other colours, he believed, were additive or subtractive combinations of these three primaries. Young's theory was later refined and extended by **Hermann von Helmholtz** and came to be known as the Young-Helmholtz **trichromatic theory**.

Trichromatic theory provided a plausible explanation for people's colour sensations and for colour blindness (according to the theory, colour-blind people had only one or two kinds of receptors). Other facts and observations, however, were not as well explained by the theory. Why did adaptation to one colour produce colour afterimages that had the complementary hue? Why did colour-blind people always fail to distinguish pairs of colours: red and green, or blue and yellow?

Answers to these questions became the cornerstones for a second theory of colour vision proposed by **Ewald Hering** in the late 1800s. According to his **opponent-process theory**, all colour experiences arise from three underlying systems, each of which includes two opponent elements: red versus green, blue versus yellow, or black (no colour) versus white (all colours). Hering theorized that colours produced complementary afterimages because one element of the system became fatigued (from overstimulation) and thus increased the relative contribution of its opponent element. According to Hering's theory, types of colour blindness came in pairs because the colour system was actually built from pairs of opposites, not from single primary colours.

For many years, scientists debated the merits of the theories. Eventually, scientists recognized that the theories were not really in conflict; they simply described two different stages of processing that corresponded to successive physiological structures in the visual system (Hurvich & Jameson, 1974). We now know, for example, that there are, indeed, three types of cones. Although the three types each respond to a range of wavelengths, they are each *most* sensitive to light at a particular wavelength. The responses of these cone types confirm Young and Helmholtz's prediction that colour vision relies on three types of colour receptors. People who are colour blind lack one or more of these types of receptor cones.

We also now know that the retinal ganglion cells combine the outputs of these three cone types in accordance with Hering's opponent-process theory (De Valois & Jacobs, 1968). According to the contemporary version of opponent-process theory, as supported by **Leo Hurvich** and **Dorothea Jameson**

---

trichromatic theory The theory that there are three types of colour receptors that produce the primary colour sensations of red, green, and blue.

opponent-process theory The theory that all colour experiences arise from three systems, each of which includes two "opponent" elements (red versus green, blue versus yellow, and black versus white).

(1974), the two members of each colour pair work in opposition (are opponents) by means of neural inhibition. Some ganglion cells receive excitatory input from lights that appear red and inhibitory input from lights that appear green. Other cells in the system have the opposite arrangement of excitation and inhibition. Together, these two types of ganglion cells form the physiological basis of the red/green opponent-process system. Other ganglion cells make up the blue/yellow opponent system. The black/white system contributes to your perception of colour saturation and brightness.

Colour and Other Systems Up to this point we have discussed some of the simple properties of colour and how our visual system allows us to see colour. You may have already noticed that colour can actually impact some of your actions. As you browse the selection of produce at a grocery store, for example, the colours you see guide you in your decision as to which bananas to buy, or whether an avocado is ripe. Interestingly, the colour of an object can reveal more information to our brains than we unconsciously use to code additional characteristics about items in our environment. Consider how you eat a banana. If it is a matte yellow colour, you probably pick it up with a firm grasp to peel it open. If the same banana were to sit on the counter for a week and turn brown, you would likely pick it up with a less firm grasp and hold it more gently as you peel it. A number of individuals have investigated how colour interacts with our other brain systems to create functional and appropriate actions. The data have suggested interconnected vision and action control in the brain, and indicate that we can learn correct actions based on colour cues.

Goodale and colleagues (Haffenden & Goodale, 2000) have used coloured wooden blocks to assess the relationship between colour and action. Subjects in their study were presented with a series of large yellow blocks and small red blocks and were asked to pick each one up and put it down. When these blocks were presented in the same location, the subjects began using the colour to infer how wide apart their fingers needed to be to grasp and pick up the blocks. Later, when medium yellow and red blocks were presented, subjects mistakenly used the colour information to make judgments on how wide apart they needed to hold their fingers to grasp the blocks, rather than the real size information. As such, they either under- or overestimated the grasp needed to pick up and lift the blocks.

Rhode and Marotta (2006) modified the colour-grasping experiment to investigate the specificity of the effect of colour perception on our actions. The assumption was that lighter and darker shades of blocks would also influence grasping. Subjects could easily discriminate size when actually completing a grasp; but, during perceptual estimations, where subjects were asked to simply shape their hand in the grasp that would allow them to pick up the block, both the trained (blocks that had been repeatedly presented) and lighter-shaded untrained (blocks that had been presented less often) colours influenced size judgments. Our perception system uses colour in a very specific way to evaluate characteristics of objects. In yet another experiment, subjects were asked to pick up blocks of varying colours that were assigned differing weights (Dubrowski, Proteau, & Carnahan, 2004). In this case, subjects encoded the association between weight and colour.

Everyday life reveals that we learn from colour information about the nature of objects in order to complete appropriate actions toward them. Think about the objects that you pick up

regularly during your day. You would be quite surprised if you picked up a big, fat grapefruit, and it suddenly collapsed within your fingers as though it were hollow beneath the skin. Similarly, you would be just as surprised if you attempted to pick up a marshmallow and found that it weighed as much as an apple. Although most of us have all the sensory apparatus to detect colour, the perceptions of colour and the features of objects are learned.

We turn now from the world of sight to the world of sound.

STOP AND REVIEW

❶ In the visual system, what is meant by accommodation?

❷ What percentages of rods and cones are found in the fovea?

❸ What patterns of stimulation cause complex cells to respond?

❹ Which theory of colour vision explains why you experience a blue afterimage after staring at a patch of yellow?

CRITICAL THINKING Consider Figure 5.11. Why did the researchers use such a variety of different representations of body parts?

Hearing

Hearing and vision play complementary functions in your experience of the world. You often hear stimuli before you see them, particularly if they take place behind you or on the other side of opaque objects such as walls. Although vision is better than hearing for identifying an object, once it is in the field of view, you often see the object only because you have used your ears to point your eyes in the right direction. To begin our discussion of hearing, we describe the types of physical energy that arrive at your ears.

THE PHYSICS OF SOUND

Clap your hands. Whistle. Tap your pencil on the table. Why do these actions create sounds? The reason is that they cause objects to vibrate. The vibrational energy is transmitted to the surrounding medium—usually air—as the vibrating objects push molecules of the medium back and forth. The resulting slight changes in pressure spread outward from the vibrating objects in the form of a combination of *sine waves* travelling at a rate of about 1100 feet (335 metres) per second (see **Figure 5.16**). Sound cannot be created in a true vacuum (such as outer space) because there are no air molecules in a vacuum for vibrating objects to move.

A sine wave has two basic physical properties that determine how it sounds to you: frequency and amplitude. *Frequency* measures the number of cycles the wave completes in a given amount of time. A cycle, as indicated in Figure 5.16, is the left-to-right distance from the peak in one wave to the

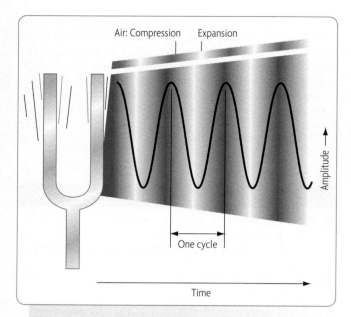

Air: Compression   Expansion

Amplitude →

One cycle

Time

FIGURE 5.16   An Idealized Sine Wave
The two basic properties of sine waves are their
frequency—the number of cycles in a fixed unit of time—
and their *amplitude*—the vertical range of their cycles.

peak in the next wave. Sound frequency is usually expressed in
hertz (Hz), which measures cycles per second. *Amplitude* measures the physical property of strength of the sound wave, as
shown in its peak-to-valley height. Amplitude is defined in
units of sound pressure or energy.

PSYCHOLOGICAL DIMENSIONS OF SOUND

The physical properties of frequency and amplitude give rise to
the three psychological dimensions of sound: pitch, loudness,
and timbre. Let's see how these phenomena work.

Pitch Pitch is the highness or lowness of a sound determined
by the sound's frequency; high frequencies produce high pitch,
and low frequencies produce low pitch. The full range of human
sensitivity to pure tones extends from frequencies as low as 20 Hz
to frequencies as high as 20 000 Hz. (Frequencies below 20 Hz
may be experienced through touch as vibrations rather than as
sound.) You can get a sense of how large this range is by noting
that the 88 keys on a piano cover only the range from about 30
to 4000 Hz.

As you might expect from our earlier discussion of psychophysics, the relationship between frequency (the physical
reality) and pitch (the psychological effect) is not a linear one.

_____

pitch Sound quality of highness or lowness; primarily dependent on the
frequency of the sound wave.

loudness A perceptual dimension of sound influenced by the amplitude
of a sound wave; sound waves in large amplitudes are generally
experienced as loud and those with small amplitudes as soft.

timbre The dimension of auditory sensation that reflects the complexity
of a sound wave.

At the low end of the frequency scale, increasing the frequency
by just a few hertz raises the pitch quite noticeably. At the high
end of frequency, you require a much larger increase in order to
hear the difference in pitch. For example, the two lowest notes
on a piano differ by only 1.6 Hz, whereas the two highest ones
differ by 235 Hz. This is another example of the psychophysics
of just noticeable differences.

Loudness The **loudness** you perceive from a sound is determined by the sound wave amplitude's effect on the structures
within your ear and, ultimately, your brain. Loudness, therefore,
is a psychological property. The amplitude of a sound wave is
something that we can quantify quite accurately, but each individual experiences sound slightly differently. The relationship
between the physical intensity of the sound and the psychological
property is not perfect, but it does move in the same direction.
Generally, sound waves with large amplitudes are experienced as
loud, and those with small amplitudes as soft. Although sound
wave amplitude may change, you may not be able to detect that
the sound is different; it may not seem louder or softer to you
when the changes are very small, or when the changes are close to
the upper and lower ends of the range of intensities. The human
auditory system is sensitive to an enormous range of physical
intensities. At one limit, you can hear the tick of a wristwatch at
20 feet (6.1 metres). This is the system's absolute threshold—if
it were more sensitive, you would hear the blood flowing in
your ears. At the other extreme, a jetliner taking off 100 yards
(91 metres) away is so loud that the sound is painful. In terms of
physical units of sound pressure, the jet produces a sound wave
with more than a billion times the energy of the ticking watch.

Since the range of hearing is so great, physical intensities of
sound are usually expressed in ratios rather than absolute
amounts; sound pressure—the index of amplitude level that
gives rise to the experience of loudness—is measured in units
called decibels (dB). **Figure 5.17** shows the decibel measures of
some representative natural sounds. It also shows the corresponding sound pressures (in dynes/cm^2) for comparison. You
can see that two sounds differing by 20 dB have sound pressures
in a ratio of 10 to 1. Note that sounds louder than about 90 dB
can produce hearing loss, depending on how long a person is
exposed to them.

Timbre The **timbre** of a sound reflects the components of its
complex sound wave. Timbre is what sets apart, for example,
the sound of a piano from the sound of a flute. A few physical
stimuli, such as a tuning fork, produce pure tones consisting of
a single sine wave. A *pure tone* has only one frequency and one
amplitude. Most sounds in the real world are not pure tones.
They are complex waves, containing a combination of frequencies and amplitudes.

The sounds that you call *noise* do not have the clear simple
structures of frequencies. Noise contains many frequencies that
are not systematically related. For instance, the static noise you
hear between radio stations contains energy at all audible frequencies; you perceive it as having no pitch because it has no
fundamental frequency.

THE PHYSIOLOGY OF HEARING

Now that you know something about the physical bases of
your psychological experiences of sound, let's see how those

Decibel level (dB)

Sound pressure level (dynes/cm²)	Decibel level (dB)	
	180	← Rocket launch (from 46 m)
	160	
2000.	140	← Jet plane (takeoff from 24 m)
		← Threshold of pain
200.	120	← Loud thunder; rock band
		← Twin-engine airplane
20.	100	← Inside subway train
		← Hearing loss with prolonged exposure
2.	80	← Inside noisy car
		← Inside quiet car
.2	60	← Normal conversation
		← Normal office
.02	40	← Quiet office
		← Quiet room
.002	20	← Soft whisper (1.5 m)
.0002	0	← Absolute hearing threshold (for 1,000-Hz tone)

FIGURE 5.17 Decibel Levels of Familiar Sounds

This figure shows the range in decibels of the sounds to which you respond from the absolute threshold for hearing to the noise of a rocket launch. Decibels are calculated from sound pressure, which is a measure of a sound wave's amplitude level and generally corresponds to what you experience as loudness.

experiences arise from physiological activity in the auditory system. First, we will look at the way the ear works. Then we will consider some theories about how pitch experiences are coded in the auditory system and how sounds are localized.

The Auditory System You have already learned that sensory processes transform forms of external energy into forms of energy within your brain. For you to hear, as shown in **Figure 5.18**, four basic energy transformations must take place: (1) Airborne sound waves must get translated into *fluid* waves within the *cochlea* of the ear; (2) the fluid waves must then stimulate mechanical vibrations of the *basilar membrane*; (3) these vibrations must be converted into electrical impulses; and (4) the impulses must travel to the *auditory cortex*. Let's examine each of these transformations in detail.

In the first transformation, vibrating air molecules enter the ears (see Figure 5.18). Some sound enters the external canal of the ear directly and some enters after having been reflected off the *external ear*, or *pinna*. The sound wave travels along the canal through the outer ear until it reaches the end of the canal. There it encounters a thin membrane called the eardrum, or *tympanic membrane*. The sound wave's pressure variations set the eardrum into motion. The eardrum transmits the vibrations from the outer ear into the middle ear, a chamber that contains the three smallest bones in the human body: the *hammer*, the

What physical properties of sounds allow you to pick out the timbres of individual instruments from a musical ensemble?

anvil, and the *stirrup*. These bones form a mechanical chain that transmits and concentrates the vibrations from the eardrum to the primary organ of hearing, the *cochlea*, which is located in the *inner ear*.

In the second transformation, which occurs in the cochlea, the airborne sound wave becomes "seaborne." The **cochlea** is a fluid-filled coiled tube that has a membrane, known as the **basilar membrane**, running down its middle along its length. When the stirrup vibrates against the oval window at the base of the cochlea, the fluid in the cochlea causes the basilar membrane to move in a wavelike motion (hence "seaborne"). Researchers speculate that the cochlea's distinctive spiral shape provides greater sensitivity to low-frequency sounds than would be possible without the spiral (Manoussaki, Dimitriadis, & Chadwick, 2006).

In the third transformation, the wavelike motion of the basilar membrane bends the tiny hair cells connected to the membrane. The hair cells are the receptor cells for the auditory system. As the hair cells bend, they stimulate nerve endings, transforming the mechanical vibrations of the basilar membrane into neural activity.

Finally, in the fourth transformation, nerve impulses leave the cochlea in a bundle of fibres called the **auditory nerve**. These fibres meet in the *cochlear nucleus* of the brain stem. Similar to the crossing over of nerves in the visual system, stimulation from one ear goes to both sides of the brain. Auditory signals pass through a series of other nuclei on their way to the *auditory cortex*, in the temporal lobes of the cerebral hemispheres. Higher-order processing of these signals begins in the auditory cortex. (As you will learn shortly, other parts of the ear labelled in Figure 5.18 play roles in your other senses.)

The four transformations occur in fully functioning auditory systems. However, millions of people suffer from some

---

cochlea The primary organ of hearing; a fluid-filled coiled tube located in the inner ear.

basilar membrane A membrane in the cochlea that, when set into motion, stimulates hair cells that produce the neural effects of auditory stimulation.

auditory nerve The nerve that carries impulses from the cochlea to the cochlear nucleus of the brain.

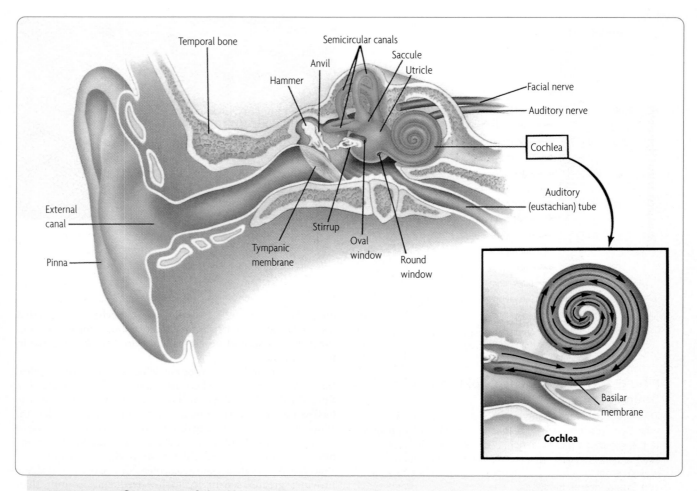

FIGURE 5.18 Structure of the Human Ear

Sound waves are channelled by the external ear, or pinna, through the external canal, causing the tympanic membrane to vibrate. This vibration activates the tiny bones of the inner ear—the hammer, anvil, and stirrup. Their mechanical vibrations are passed along from the oval window to the cochlea, where they set in motion the fluid in its canal. Tiny hair cells lining the coiled basilar membrane within the cochlea bend as the fluid moves, stimulating nerve endings attached to them. The mechanical energy is then transformed into neural energy and sent to the brain via the auditory nerve.

form of hearing impairment. Both general types of hearing impairment are caused by a defect in one or more of the components of the auditory system. The less serious type of impairment is *conduction deafness*, a problem in the conduction of the air vibrations to the cochlea. Often in this type of impairment, the bones in the middle ear are not functioning properly, a problem that may be corrected in microsurgery by insertion of an artificial anvil or stirrup. The more serious type of impairment is *nerve deafness*, a defect in the neural mechanisms that create nerve impulses in the ear or relay them to the auditory cortex. Damage to the auditory cortex can also create nerve deafness.

place theory The theory that different frequency tones produce maximum activation at different locations along the basilar membrane, with the result that pitch can be coded by the place at which activation occurs.

Theories of Pitch Perception To explain how the auditory system converts sound waves into sensations of pitch, researchers have outlined two distinct theories: place theory and frequency theory.

Place theory was initially proposed by Hermann von Helmholtz in the 1800s and was later modified, elaborated, and tested by **Georg von Békésy**, who won a Nobel Prize for this work in 1961. Place theory is based on the fact that the basilar membrane moves when sound waves are conducted through the inner ear. Different frequencies produce their greatest movement at particular locations along the basilar membrane. For high-frequency tones, the wave motion is greatest at the base of the cochlea, where the oval and round windows are located. For low-frequency tones, the greatest wave motion of the basilar membrane is at the opposite end. So place theory suggests that perception of pitch depends on the specific location on the basilar membrane at which the greatest stimulation occurs.

Sustained exposure to loud noise can lead to hearing loss. What can people do to avoid such losses?

operate. Thus, a complex sensory task is divided between two systems that, together, offer greater sensory precision than either system alone could provide. We see next that you also possess two converging neural systems to help you localize sounds in the environment.

Sound Localization Suppose you are walking across campus and you hear someone call your name. In most cases, you can readily locate the spatial location of the speaker. This example suggests how efficiently your auditory system carries out the task of **sound localization**—enabling you to determine the spatial origins of auditory events. You do so through two mechanisms: assessments of the relative timing and assessments of the relative intensity of the sounds that arrive at each ear (Middlebrooks & Green, 1991; Phillips, 1993).

The first mechanism involves neurons that compare the relative times at which incoming sound reaches each ear. A sound occurring off to your right side, for example, reaches your right ear before your left (see point B in **Figure 5.19**). Neurons in your auditory system are specialized to fire most actively for specific time delays between the two ears. Your brain uses this information about disparities in arrival time to make precise estimates for the likely origins of a sound in space.

The second mechanism relies on the principle that a sound has a slightly greater intensity in the first ear at which it arrives—because your head itself casts a *sound shadow* that

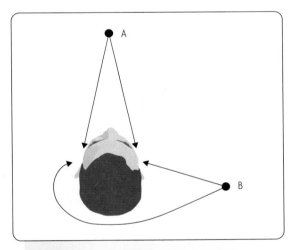

FIGURE 5.19 Time Disparity and Sound Localization

The brain uses differences in the time course with which sounds arrive at the two ears to localize the sounds in space.

The second theory, **frequency theory**, explains pitch by the rate of vibration of the basilar membrane. This theory predicts that a sound wave with a frequency of 100 Hz will set the basilar membrane vibrating 100 times per second. The frequency theory also predicts that the vibrations of the basilar membrane will cause neurons to fire at the same rate, so that rate of firing is the neural code for pitch. One problem with this theory is that individual neurons cannot fire rapidly enough to represent high-pitched sounds because none of them can fire more than 1000 times per second. This limitation makes it impossible for one neuron to distinguish sounds above 1000 Hz—which, of course, your auditory system can do quite well. The limitation might be overcome by the **volley principle**, which explains what might happen at such high frequencies. This principle suggests that several neurons in a combined action, or volley, fire at the frequency that matches a stimulus tone of 2000 Hz, 3000 Hz, and so on (Wever, 1949).

As with the trichromatic and opponent-process theories of colour vision, the place and frequency theories each successfully account for different aspects of your experience of pitch. Frequency theory accounts well for coding frequencies below about 5000 Hz. At higher frequencies, neurons cannot fire quickly and precisely enough to code a signal adequately, even in volley. Place theory accounts for perception of pitch at frequencies above 1000 Hz. Below 1000 Hz, the entire basilar membrane vibrates so broadly that it cannot provide a signal distinctive enough for the neural receptors to use as a means of distinguishing pitch. Between 1000 and 5000 Hz, both mechanisms can

frequency theory The theory that a tone produces a rate of vibration in the basilar membrane equal to its frequency, with the result that pitch can be coded by the frequency of the neural response.

volley principle An extension of frequency theory, which proposes that when peaks in a sound wave come too frequently for a single neuron to fire at each peak, several neurons fire as a group at the frequency of the stimulus tone.

sound localization The auditory processes that allow the spatial origins of environmental sounds.

Why might bats have evolved the ability to use echolocation to navigate through their environment?

Your Other Senses

We have devoted much attention to vision and hearing because scientists have studied them most thoroughly. However, your ability both to survive in and to enjoy the external environment relies on your full repertory of senses. We close our discussion of sensation with brief analyses of several of your other senses.

SMELL

You can probably imagine circumstances in which you would be happy to give up your sense of smell: Did you ever have a family dog who lost a battle with a skunk? Unfortunately, to avoid that skunk experience, you would also have to give up the smells of fresh roses, hot buttered popcorn, and sea breezes. Odours—both good and bad—first make their presence known by interacting with receptor proteins on the membranes of *olfactory cilia* (see **Figure 5.20**). It takes only eight molecules of a substance to initiate one of these nerve impulses, but at least 40 nerve endings must be stimulated before you can smell the substance. Once initiated, these nerve impulses convey odour information to the **olfactory bulb**, located just above the receptors and just below the frontal lobes of the cerebrum. Odour stimuli start the process of smell by stimulating an influx of chemical substances into ion channels in olfactory neurons, an event that, as you may recall from Chapter 4, triggers an action potential.

weakens the signal. These intensity differences depend on the relative size of the wavelength of a tone with respect to your head. Large-wavelength, low-frequency tones show virtually no intensity differences, whereas small-wavelength, high-frequency tones show measurable intensity differences. Your brain, once again, has specialized cells that detect intensity differences in the signals arriving at your two ears.

What happens when a sound creates neither a timing nor an intensity difference? In Figure 5.19, a sound originating at Point A would have this property. With your eyes closed, you cannot tell its exact location. So you must move your head—to reposition your ears—to break the symmetry and provide the necessary information for sound localization.

It is interesting to note that porpoises and bats use their auditory systems rather than their visual systems to locate objects in dark waters or dark caves. These species use *echolocation*—they emit high-pitched sounds that bounce off objects, giving them feedback about the objects' distances, locations, sizes, textures, and movements. In fact, one species of bat is able to use echolocation to differentiate between objects that are just 0.3 millimetres apart (Simmons, Ferragamo, & Moss, 1998).

STOP AND REVIEW

❶ What physical property of a sound produces the perception of pitch?

❷ What role do hair cells play in the auditory system?

❸ Which theory suggests that the perception of pitch depends on the location on the basilar membrane at which the greatest stimulation occurs?

❹ What timing difference would you expect if a sound originated off to your right side?

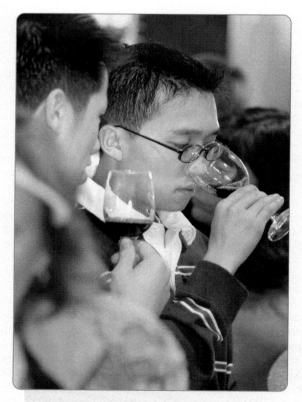

Why would a man with a cold be ill-advised to take up wine tasting?

---

olfactory bulb The centre where odour-sensitive receptors send their signals, located just below the frontal lobes of the cortex.

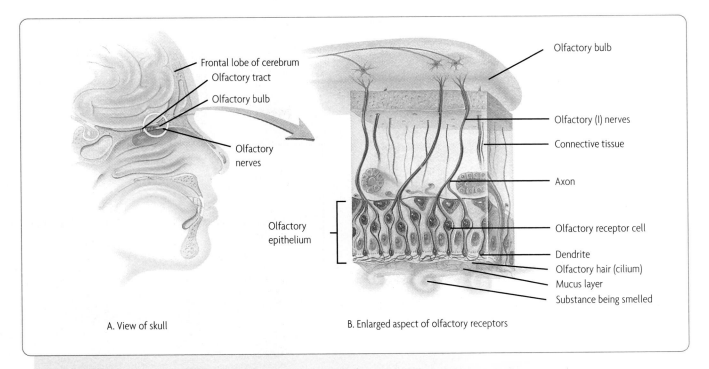

FIGURE 5.20   Receptors for Smell

The olfactory receptor cells in your nasal cavities are stimulated by chemicals in the environment. They send information to the olfactory bulb in your brain.

The significance of the sense of smell varies greatly across species. Smell presumably evolved as a system for detecting and locating food (Moncrieff, 1951). Humans seem to use the sense of smell primarily in conjunction with taste—to seek and sample food. For many species, however, smell is also used to detect potential sources of danger. Dogs, rats, insects, and many other creatures for whom smell is central to survival have a far keener sense of smell than humans do. Accordingly, relatively more of their brain is devoted to smell. Smell serves these species well because organisms do not have to come into direct contact with other organisms in order to smell them.

In addition, smell can be a powerful form of active communication. Members of many species communicate by secreting and detecting chemical signals called **pheromones**, chemical substances used within a given species to signal sexual receptivity, danger, territorial boundaries, and food sources (Luo, Fee, & Katz, 2003). For example, females of various insect species produce sex pheromones to signal that they are available for mating (Carazo, Sanchez, Font, & Desbilis, 2004; De Cock & Matthysen, 2005). Canadian researchers at Agriculture and Agri-Food Canada (e.g., Smith, Wise, & Lamb, 2004) are using knowledge of the sex ratios of insects found wherever wheat is grown to predict when pheromone traps might be used to reduce mating. Although you may not be familiar with it, the wheat midge has destroyed crops in many parts of Canada. To attract male wheat midges looking for mating opportunities, female pheromones are used in traps, like those developed by Phero Tech Inc., a spin-off company from Simon Fraser University in British Columbia. The traps are effective in reducing overall numbers of male wheat midges, curbing mating and the number of offspring. We revisit the topic of pheromones when we discuss both human and nonhuman sexual behaviours in Chapter 12.

TASTE

Although food and wine gourmets are capable of noting remarkably subtle and complex taste distinctions, many of their sensations are really smells, not tastes. Taste and smell work together closely when you eat. In fact, when you have a cold, food seems tasteless because your nasal passages are blocked, which means you cannot smell the food. Demonstrate this principle for yourself: Hold your nose and try to tell the difference between foods of similar texture but different tastes, such as pieces of apple and raw potato. Some students living on campuses with notoriously bad food have reported that wearing nose plugs to meals makes everything taste uniformly bland—which is better than the usual taste!

The surface of your tongue is covered with *papillae*, which give it a bumpy appearance. Many of these papillae contain

---

pheromones Chemical signals released by an organism to communicate with other members of the species; pheromones often serve as long-distance sexual attractors.

Why would riding in the front seat of a roller coaster be less likely to make you nauseated than riding in the rear?

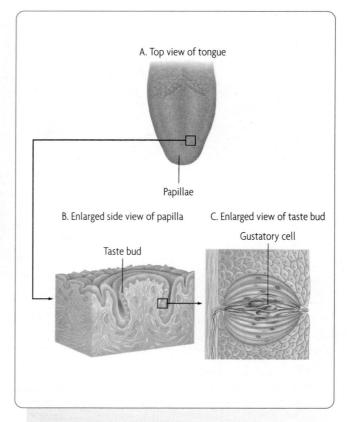

A. Top view of tongue

Papillae

B. Enlarged side view of papilla

Taste bud

C. Enlarged view of taste bud

Gustatory cell

FIGURE 5.21 Receptors for Taste

Part A shows the distribution of the papillae on the upper side of the tongue. Part B shows a single papilla enlarged so that the individual taste buds are visible. Part C shows one of the taste buds enlarged.

clusters of taste receptor cells called the *taste buds* (see **Figure 5.21**). Single-cell recordings of taste receptors show that individual receptor cells respond best to one of the four primary taste qualities: sweet, sour, bitter, and saline (salty) (Frank & Nowlis, 1989). In recent years, researchers have found receptors for a fifth basic taste quality, *umami* (Chaudhari, Landin, & Roper, 2000). Umami is the flavour of monosodium glutamate (MSG), the chemical that is often added to Asian foods and occurs naturally in foods rich in protein, such as meat, seafood, and aged cheese. Although receptor cells for the five qualities may produce small responses to other tastes, the "best" response most directly encodes quality. There appear to be separate transduction systems for each of the basic classes of taste (Bartoshuk & Beauchamp, 1994).

Taste receptors can be damaged by many things you put in your mouth, such as alcohol, cigarette smoke, and acids. Fortunately, your taste receptors get replaced every few days—even more frequently than smell receptors. Indeed, the taste system is the most resistant to damage of all your sensory systems; it is extremely rare for anyone to suffer a total, permanent taste loss (Bartoshuk, 1990).

TOUCH AND SKIN SENSES

The skin is a remarkably versatile organ. In addition to protecting you against surface injury, holding in body fluids, and helping regulate body temperature, it contains nerve endings that produce sensations of pressure, warmth, and cold. These sensations are called the **cutaneous senses** (skin senses).

Consider how you become aware that a stimulus is creating *pressure* on your skin. Since you receive so much sensory information through your skin, different types of receptor cells

---

cutaneous senses The skin senses that register sensations or pressure, warmth, and cold.

operate close to the surface of the body. Each type of receptor responds to somewhat different patterns of contact with the skin (Sekuler & Blake, 2001). As two examples, *Meissner corpuscles* respond best when something rubs against the skin, and *Merkel disks* are most active when a small object exerts steady pressure against the skin.

The skin's sensitivity to pressure varies tremendously over the body. For example, you are 10 times more accurate in sensing the position of stimulation on your fingertips than on your back. The variation in sensitivity of different body regions is shown by the greater density of nerve endings in these regions and also by the greater amount of sensory cortex devoted to them. In Chapter 4 you learned that your sensitivity is greatest where you need it most—on your face, tongue, and hands. Precise sensory feedback from these parts of the body permits effective eating, speaking, and grasping.

Suppose someone rubs an ice cube along your arm. You now have some ideas about how you would feel the pressure of the ice cube. Yet how would you sense that the *temperature* is cold? You may be surprised to learn that you have separate receptors for warmth and coolness. Rather than having one type of receptor that works like a thermometer, your brain integrates separate signals from *cold fibres* and *warm fibres* to monitor changes in environmental temperature.

One aspect of cutaneous sensitivity plays a central role in human relationships: touch. Through touch, you communicate to others your desire to give or receive comfort, support, love, and passion. However, where you get touched or touch someone else makes a difference; those areas of the skin surface that give rise to erotic, or sexual, sensations are called *erogenous zones*. Other touch-sensitive erotic areas vary in their arousal potential for different individuals, depending on learned associations and the concentration of sensory receptors in the areas.

THE VESTIBULAR AND KINESTHETIC SENSES

The next pair of senses we will describe may be entirely new to you, because they do not have receptors you can see directly, like eyes, ears, or noses. Your **vestibular sense** tells you how your body—especially your head—is oriented in the world with respect to gravity. The receptors for this information are tiny hairs in fluid-filled sacs and canals in the inner ear. The hairs bend when the fluid moves and presses on them, which is what happens when you turn your head quickly. The *saccule* and *utricle* (shown in Figure 5.18) tell you about acceleration or deceleration in a straight line. The three canals, called the *semicircular canals*, are at right angles to each other and thus can tell you about motion in any direction. They inform you how your head is moving when you turn, nod, or tilt it.

People who lose their vestibular sense because of accidents or disease are initially quite disoriented and prone to falls and dizziness. However, most of these people eventually compensate by relying more heavily on visual information. *Motion sickness* can occur when the signals from the visual system conflict with those from the vestibular system. People feel nauseated when reading in a moving car because the visual signal is of a stationary object while the vestibular signal is of movement. Drivers rarely get motion sickness because they are both seeing and feeling motion.

Whether you are standing erect, drawing pictures, or making love, your brain needs to have accurate information about the current positions and movement of your body parts relative to one another. The **kinesthetic sense** (also called *kinesthesis*) provides constant sensory feedback about what the body is doing during motor activities. Without it, you would be unable to co-ordinate most voluntary movements.

You have two sources of kinesthetic information: receptors in the joints, and receptors in the muscles and tendons. Receptors that lie in the joints respond to pressures that accompany different positions of the limbs and to pressure changes that accompany movements of the joints. Receptors in the muscles and tendons respond to changes in tension that accompany muscle shortening and lengthening.

The brain often integrates information from your kinesthetic sense with information from touch senses. Your brain, for example, cannot grasp the full meaning of the signals coming from each of your fingers if it does not know exactly where your fingers are in relation to one another. Imagine that you pick up an object with your eyes closed. Your sense of touch may allow

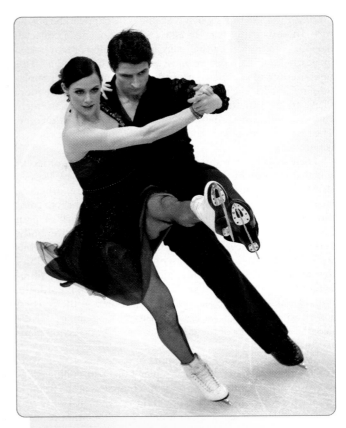

What role does the kinesthetic sense play in the performance of skilled athletes like Tessa Virtue and Scott Moir, Canadians awarded a gold medal for pairs ice dance at the Winter Olympics in 2010?

you to guess that the object is a stone, but your kinesthetic sense will enable you to know how large it is.

PAIN

Pain is the body's response to stimulation from harmful stimuli—those that are intense enough to cause tissue damage or threaten to do so. Are you entirely happy that you have such a well-developed pain sense? Your answer probably should be "yes and no." On the yes side, your pain sense is critical for survival. People born with congenital insensitivity to pain feel no hurt, but their bodies often become scarred and their limbs deformed from injuries that they could have avoided had their brains been able to warn them of danger (Larner, Moss, Rossi, & Anderson, 1994). Their experience shows that pain serves as an essential defence signal—it warns you of potential harm. On the

---

vestibular sense The sense that tells how one's own body is oriented in the world with respect to gravity.

kinesthetic sense The sense concerned with bodily position and movement of the body parts relative to one another.

pain The body's response to noxious stimuli that are intense enough to cause, or threaten to cause, tissue damage.

no side, there are times when you would be happy to be able to turn off your pain sense. In 2001, Statistics Canada collected data on pain indicating that pain and discomfort are reported by nearly 1.5 million people between the ages of 15 and 64. This figure represents 7.5 percent of the total working-age population in Canada. The report also indicates that women are more likely to be afflicted by pain and discomfort than men. Unfortunately, for many individuals, pain means lost income. The resulting cost of care and pain management in this country is significant.

Scientists have begun to identify the specific sets of receptors that respond to pain-producing stimuli. They have learned that some receptors respond only to temperature, others to chemicals, others to mechanical stimuli, and still others to combinations of pain-producing stimuli. This network of pain fibres is a fine meshwork that covers your entire body. Peripheral nerve fibres send pain signals to the central nervous system by two pathways: a fast-conducting set of nerve fibres that are covered with myelin, and slower, smaller nerve fibres without any myelin coating. Starting at the spinal cord, the impulses are relayed to the thalamus and then to the cerebral cortex, where the location and intensity of the pain are identified, the significance of the injury is evaluated, and action plans are formulated.

Within your brain, *endorphins* have an impact on your experience of pain. Recall from Chapter 4 that pain-killing drugs such as morphine bind to the same receptor sites in the brain—the term *endorphin* comes from *endogenous* (self-produced) *morphines*. The release of endorphins within the brain controls your experience of pain. Researchers believe that endorphins are at least partially responsible for the pain-reducing effects of acupuncture and placebos (Benedetti, Mayberg, Wager, Stohler, & Zubieta, 2005; Han, 2004).

Your emotional responses, context factors, and your interpretation of the situation can be as important as actual physical stimuli in determining how much pain you experience (Price, 2000; Turk & Okifuji, 2003). How are pain sensations affected by the psychological context? One theory about the way pain may be modulated is known as the **gate-control theory**, developed by **Ronald Melzack** (1973, 1980) of McGill University. This theory suggests that cells in the spinal cord act as neurological gates, interrupting and blocking some pain signals and letting others get through to the brain. Receptors in the skin and the brain send messages to the spinal cord to open or close those gates. Suppose, for example, you bump your shin on a table while running to answer the telephone. As you rub the skin around the bump, you send inhibitory messages to your spinal cord, closing the gates. Messages descending from the brain can also close the gates. If, for example, a phone call includes urgent news, your brain might close the gates to prevent you from experiencing the distraction of pain.

Melzack (1999) has proposed an updated *neuromatrix theory* of pain that incorporates the reality that people often

Individuals taking part in religious rituals, such as walking on a bed of hot coals, are able to block out pain. What does that tell you about the relationship between the physiology and psychology of pain?

experience pain with little or no physical cause: In these cases, the experience of pain originates wholly in the brain.

Melzack's (2001) theory explains why individuals who are under chronic stress or are depressed feel body pain, despite no physical injury. Melzack points out that pain usually has an adaptive function and that it generally results in actions that may help prevent the spread of disease and further injury. For example, one major consequence of pain is that a person rests while the body attempts to repair itself. There are some forms of pain, however, that seem to serve no purpose, such as **phantom limb pain**. Melzack's analysis of phantom limb pain has suggested that even in the absence of a limb, the brain uses information that arrived before the limb was amputated. Pain is a result of a neural network that continues to be active, despite not obtaining any additional sensory information from the now missing limb. Melzack's neuromatrix theory (2001) relies on a genetic and sensory component, which leads to both the generation of the synaptic architecture of the brain and to the generation of pain. This theory has allowed for the suggestion that some individuals have a genetic predisposition for the development of a neuronal architecture that allows for chronic pain syndrome. It is also consistent with the notion that other normal brain functions, like the response to stress, could interact with this system to result in pain. Further, the perception of pain can be influenced by past experiences (Melzack, Coderre, Katz, & Vaccarino, 2001). These studies are leading to novel treatments for chronic pain and have supported the use of analgesics prior to amputation. Interestingly, Mogil and Chanda (2005) have reported sex differences—differences between males and females—as a result of hormones that relate to pain, pointing to animal studies where pain sensitivity is altered through the rodent estrous cycle.

We have just seen that the way you perceive pain may reveal more about your psychological state than about the intensity of the pain stimulus: What you perceive may be different from, and even independent of, what you sense. This discussion of pain prepares you for the rest of the chapter, in which we discuss the perceptual processes that allow you to organize and label your experiences of the world.

---

gate-control theory A theory about pain modulation that proposes that certain cells in the spinal cord act as gates to interrupt and block some pain signals while sending others to the brain.

phantom limb pain Sensations that appear to originate in a limb that has been amputated.

WHY IS EATING "HOT" FOOD PAINFUL?

Have you ever had this experience? You are eating a very "hot" dish in a Chinese or Mexican restaurant and you accidentally bite directly into a chili pepper. In just moments you go from enjoyment to intense pain. If this has happened, then you know that, in the realm of taste, there is a fine line between what gives pleasure and what gives pain. Let's explore this relationship.

Physiologically, it is easy to explain why hot pepper can cause you pain. On your tongue, your taste buds are associated with pain fibres (Bartoshuk, 1993)—so the very same chemical that can stimulate the receptors in your taste buds can stimulate the closely allied pain fibres as well (Caterina et al., 2000). In the case of hot pepper, this chemical is *capsaicin*. If you want to enjoy a spicy meal, you have to keep the concentration of capsaicin in your meal sufficiently low so that your taste receptors are more active than your pain receptors.

But why, you might wonder, do different people have such obvious differences in their preferences for hot food? People often find it very difficult to understand how their friends can or cannot eat food that is very spicy. Again, we can look to physiology to explain these differences. The figure shows photographs of tongues from two individuals studied by **Linda Bartoshuk** and her colleagues. You can see that one tongue has considerably more taste buds than the other. If there are more taste buds, there will be more pain receptors. Therefore, people with more taste buds are more likely to get a strong pain response from capsaicin. The group of individuals who have more taste buds have been dubbed *supertasters* (Bartoshuk, 1993). In the extremes of their sensory experiences, they form a sharp contrast to *nontasters*. For many taste sensations, these two groups are equivalent; you would not know at most times whether you were a supertaster, a nontaster, or somewhere in between. The differences arise only for certain chemicals, of which capsaicin is an excellent example.

The variations in the density of taste buds on different people's tongues appear to be genetic (Bartoshuk & Beauchamp, 1994). Women are much more likely than men to be supertasters. Supertasters generally have more sensitivity to bitter chemicals—a sensory quality shared by most poisons. You can imagine that if women generally were responsible for nurturing and feeding offspring over the course of evolution, the children of women with greater taste sensitivity would be more likely to survive. Since taster status is genetic, you can find preference differences among children at very young ages (Anliker, Bartoshuk, Ferris, & Hooks, 1991). Five- to seven-year-old supertasters preferred milk to cheddar cheese. This preference was reversed for nontasters. Why? The supertasters may perceive the milk as sweeter and the cheese as more bitter than do the nontasters. Thus, genetic differences may help explain why some young children have such strong (and vocal) taste preferences.

But let's return to the restaurant meal at which you have had your painful accident. What you might have noticed is that the sensation of pain fades over time. In this respect, the pain receptors in your mouth act like other sensory receptors: Over time, you adapt to a constant stimulus. That's good news! You should be glad that your sensory processes offer built-in relief.

(A) The tongue of a supertaster   (B) The tongue of a nontaster

❶ What is an important brain structure involved in the sense of smell?

❷ To what basic taste qualities do your taste buds respond?

❸ How does your skin sense temperature?

❹ What is the purpose of the vestibular sense?

❺ What is the goal of gate-control theory?

Organizational Processes in Perception

Imagine how confusing the world would be if you were unable to put together and organize the information available from the output of your millions of retinal receptors. You would experience a kaleidoscope of disconnected bits of colour moving and swirling before your eyes. The processes that put sensory information together to give you the perception of coherence are referred to collectively as processes of perceptual organization.

We begin our discussion of perceptual organization with a description of the processes of *attention* that prompt you to focus on a subset of stimuli from your kaleidoscope of experience. We then examine the organizational processes first described by *Gestalt* theorists, who argued that what you perceive depends on laws of organization, or simple rules by which you perceive shapes and forms.

ATTENTIONAL PROCESSES

Take a moment now to find 10 things in your environment that had not been, so far, in your immediate awareness. Have you now noticed a spot on the wall? Have you now noticed the ticking of a clock? If you start to examine your surroundings very carefully, you will discover that there are literally thousands of things on which you could focus your **attention**. Generally, the more closely you attend to some object or event in the environment, the more you can perceive and learn about it.

Determining the Focus of Attention What forces determine the objects that become the focus of your attention? The answer to this question has two components, which we will call goal-directed selection and stimulus-driven capture (Yantis, 1993). **Goal-directed selection** reflects the choices that you make about the objects to which you would like to attend, as a function of your own goals. If, for example, you are contemplating a case full of pastries, you might direct your attention only

---

attention A state of focused awareness on a subset of the available perceptual information.

goal-directed selection A determinant of why people select some parts of sensory input for further processing; reflects the choices made as a function of one's own goals.

stimulus-driven capture A determinant of why people select some parts of sensory input for further processing; occurs when features of stimuli—objects in the environment—automatically capture attention, independent of the local goals of a perceiver.

---

to those desserts covered in chocolate. You are probably already comfortable with the idea that you can explicitly choose objects for particular scrutiny. **Stimulus-driven capture** occurs when features of the stimuli themselves—objects in the environment—automatically capture your attention, independent of your local goals as a perceiver. You have experienced stimulus-driven capture, for example, if you have ever been daydreaming at a stop light when out for a drive. The stop light's abrupt change from red to green will often capture your attention even if you were not particularly focused on it.

You might wonder what the relationship is between these two processes: Research suggests that, at least under some circumstances, stimulus-driven capture wins out over goal-directed selection.

Researchers created visual displays that put goal-directed selection and stimulus-driven capture into competition (Theeuwes, Kramer, Hahn, & Irwin, 1998). As shown in Part A of **Figure 5.22**, each trial of an experiment began with a visual display of six grey circles filled with six dim figure eights. After one second, the display changed. In half the trials, as shown in Part B, all but one of the circles changed from grey to red. The participants' task was to shift their eyes to the remaining grey circle and respond whether the character inside was either a forward or a backward letter "c." When they carried out this task, participants were using goal-directed selection: They were purposely shifting their attention to the remaining grey circle.

Now consider Part C of Figure 5.22. In this instance, which represents the remaining half of the trials, a new element is added to the visual array—a new red circle. New objects are the type of visual stimulus that typically engages stimulus-driven capture. Under ordinary circumstances, we would expect participants to shift their eyes to that new object. However, in this particular experiment, the participants did not want their eyes to be pulled to that object: They were asked to report only the contents of the single grey circle. So what happened? Could the participants stop themselves from moving their attention to the new red circle? In fact, on most occasions, the new object automatically drew the participants' attention—even though it was entirely irrelevant to the goal the experimenters had set for them.

You can recognize this phenomenon as stimulus-driven capture because it works in the opposite direction of the perceiver's goals. Since the participants would have performed the task better had they ignored the new red circle, they must have been unable to ignore it (because experimental participants almost always prefer to perform as well as possible on the tasks researchers assign them). The important general conclusion is that your perceptual system is organized so that your attention is automatically drawn to objects that are new to an environment (Yantis & Jonides, 1996).

The Fate of Unattended Information If you have selectively attended to some subset of a perceptual display—by virtue of your own goals or of properties of the stimuli—what is the fate of the information to which you did *not* attend? Imagine listening to a lecture while people on both sides of you are engaged in conversations. How are you able to keep track of the lecture? What do you notice about the conversations? Could

Critical Thinking in Your life

ARE DRIVERS DISTRACTED WHEN THEY USE THEIR CELL PHONES?

In 2001, Canadians were shocked about an accident that seemed to involve a distracted driver on a cell phone. In Pickering, Ontario, a small community east of Toronto, Richard Schewe was driving with his two-year-old daughter Mikaela and was talking to his ex-wife on his cell phone. He did not notice that the level railway crossing he was nearing was marked with red flashing lights and a crossing barrier. Moments later, Schewe and his daughter were killed as the vehicle he was driving was crushed by a train car. Although the accident revived discussion about the use of cell phones when driving, legislation prohibiting cell phone use when driving has been varied and sparse. Depending on where you live, it might already be illegal for you to use some types of cell phones while you drive. You probably also have strong opinions about whether such restrictions are necessary. The goal for researchers has been to provide data that can inform what have often been heated public policy debates on this issue.

A study from the University of Toronto discovered that drivers were four times more likely to be in an accident when driving and talking on their cell phone than when they drove without talking on the their cell phone (Redelmeier & Tibshirani, 1997). More recent research demonstrates similar findings, but much of the more recent research has focused on perceptual consequences of cell phone use. In particular, researchers have evaluated drivers' ability to focus their attention both on their phone calls and on the driving environment (Strayer & Drews, 2007), which would be much more influential in the debate about cell phone use and driving.

Consider a study in which participants drove through a suburban environment in a high-fidelity driving simulator (Strayer et al., 2003). The simulation required participants to display the full range of ordinary driving skills (including accelerating, maintaining speed, and braking). Each participant had two different driving experiences. Half the time, participants performed only the single task of navigating the route. At the other times, participants engaged in a second task: As they drove along, they had hands-free cell phone calls about a variety of ordinary topics. At all times, participants drove routes that included several billboards. At the end of the experiment, they were given a surprise memory test on these billboards. Participants recognized 6.9 (out of 15) billboards from times when they were just driving; they recognized just 3.9 billboards from times when they were also having a cell phone conversation.

Let's try to establish the role that attention plays in this result. There are two reasonable explanations for why participants' memory would not be as good when they were having their conversations: They might never have looked at the billboards at all or they might have looked at the billboards but not have attended to them. To understand this latter hypothesis, look up from your textbook at the room around you. As you gaze in a particular direction, there are many objects you can see, but to acquire detailed information you must focus your attention directly on an object.

In the driving experiment, the researchers obtained measures of participants' eye movements allowing for precise determination of where they looked. In fact, participants were equally likely to look at each billboard with and without the simultaneous conversation—and they even looked for the same amount of time. What seemed to impair participants' memory was that they looked at the billboards without actually focusing attention on them. Researchers have conducted similar experiments with participants driving real cars out on the road (Harbluk, Noy, Trbovich, & Eizenman, 2007). This work has generated the same strong conclusion that cell phone conversations divert drivers' attention from the environment in which they are driving. In addition, this research documented the behavioral consequences of diversions of attention: The most distracted drivers also had to engage in the most "hard braking."

Some people are surprised by these results because they reason that engaging in a conversation and attending to the visual environment are two rather different mental activities. Indeed, different areas of your brain are involved in carrying out these two tasks. Consider, however, an experiment in which participants underwent fMRI scans while they carried out simulated driving (Just, Keller, & Cynkar, 2008). In parallel to the other studies we have described, participants either just drove or they both drove and engaged in language processes. When just driving, participants showed a good deal of activity in regions of their parietal lobes related to spatial processing. However, with the addition of the language task, activity in those parietal regions fell by 37 percent. The language task apparently put sufficient demands on the brain that the spatial task was left with inadequate resources.

- Do these studies convince you that you should discourage people from using even hands-free cell phones while driving? What other data would you want to see?

- Why might the researchers have chosen research designs in which every participant carried out both the single and dual tasks?

- How do ethical considerations constrain the types of studies researchers can carry out on this issue?

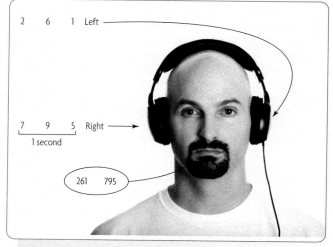

FIGURE 5.22 Processes That Select Attention

At the beginning of each trial of this experiment, participants viewed a display with six grey circles (Part A). When the display changed, the participants' task was to report whether the "c" in the one remaining grey circle was forward or backward. On half of the trials, the displays did not introduce new objects (Part B); on the other half of the trials, they did (Part C). Although the participants' goal was to attend to the single grey circle, the new objects—when they occurred—automatically drew their attention.

anything appear in the content of one or the other conversation to divert your attention from the lecture?

This constellation of questions was first explored by **Donald Broadbent** (1958), who suggested that the mind has only *limited capacity* to carry out complete processing. This limit requires that attention strictly regulate the flow of information from sensory input to consciousness. The *filter theory* of attention asserted that the selection occurs early on in the process, before the input's meaning is accessed.

To test the filter theory, researchers recreated the real-life situation of multiple sources of input in the laboratory with a technique called **dichotic listening**. In this paradigm, a participant wearing earphones listens to two taped messages played at the same time; a different message is played into each ear. The participant is instructed to repeat only one of the two messages to the experimenter while ignoring whatever is presented to the other ear. This procedure is called *shadowing* the attended message (see **Figure 5.23**).

The strongest form of filter theory was challenged when it was discovered that some listeners were recalling things they would not have been able to recall if attention had been totally filtering all ignored material (Cherry, 1953). Consider, for example, your own name. People often report that they hear their name being mentioned in a noisy room, even when they are engaged in their own conversation. This is often called the *cocktail party phenomenon*. Laboratory research has confirmed that people are especially likely to notice their own names among unattended information (Wood & Cowan, 1995a).

Researchers now believe that information in the unattended channel is processed to some extent, but not sufficiently to reach conscious awareness (Wood & Cowan, 1995b). Only if properties of the unattended information are sufficiently distinctive—by virtue, for example, of being a listener's name—will the information become the focus of conscious attention.

FIGURE 5.23 Dichotic Listening Task

A subject hears different digits presented simultaneously to each ear: 2 (left), 7 (right), 6 (left), 9 (right), 1 (left), and 5 (right). He reports hearing the correct sets—261 and 795. However, when instructed to attend only to the right-ear input, the subject reports hearing only 795.

(We will return to the relationship between attention and consciousness in Chapter 6.) The general rule is that unattended information will not make its presence known. You can see, therefore, why it is dangerous to let yourself become distracted from your immediate task or goal. If you fail to pay attention to some body of information—your professor's lecture, perhaps—the material will not just sink in of its own accord!

Let's suppose that you have focused your attention on some stimulus in the environment. It is time for your processes of perceptual organization to go to work.

---

dichotic listening An experimental technique in which a different auditory stimulus is simultaneously presented to each ear.

PRINCIPLES OF PERCEPTUAL GROUPING

Consider the image in **Figure 5.24**. If you are like most people, you will see a vase as the *figure* against a black *ground*. A **figure** is seen as an objectlike region in the forefront, and a **ground** is seen as the backdrop against which the figure(s) stand out. As you can see on the right of Figure 5.24, it is possible to change the relationship between figure and ground—to see two faces rather than one vase. One of the first tasks your perceptual processes carry out is to decide what in a scene counts as figure and what as ground.

How do your perceptual processes determine what should be gathered together into the figure? The principles of perceptual grouping were studied extensively by proponents of **Gestalt psychology**, such as **Kurt Koffka** (1935), **Wolfgang Köhler** (1947), and **Max Wertheimer** (1923). Members of this group maintained that psychological phenomena could be understood only when viewed as organized, structured *wholes* and not when broken down into primitive perceptual elements. The term *gestalt* roughly means "form," "whole," "configuration," or "essence." In their experiments, the Gestalt psychologists studied how perceptual arrays give rise to gestalts: They demonstrated that the whole is often quite different from the sum of its parts. By varying a single factor and observing how it affected the way people perceived the structure of the array, they were able to formulate a set of laws:

1. **The law of proximity**. People group together the nearest (most proximal) elements. That is why you see this display as five columns of objects instead of four rows.

2. **The law of similarity**. People group together the most similar elements. That is why you see a square of O's against a field of X's rather than columns of mixed X's and O's.

    X X X X X
    X O O O X
    X O O O X
    X O O O X
    X X X X X

3. **The law of good continuation**. People experience lines as continuous even when they are interrupted. That is why you interpret this display as an arrow piercing the heart rather than as a design with three separate pieces.

4. **The law of closure**. People tend to fill in small gaps to experience objects as wholes. That is why you fill in the missing piece to perceive a whole circle.

5. **The law of common fate**. People tend to group together objects that appear to be moving in the same direction. That is why you experience this figure as alternating rows moving apart.

SPATIAL AND TEMPORAL INTEGRATION

All the Gestalt laws we have presented to you so far should have convinced you that much of perception consists of putting the pieces of your world together in the "right way." Often, however, you cannot perceive an entire scene in one glance, or *fixation* (recall our discussion of attention). What you perceive at a given time is often a restricted glimpse of a large visual world extending in all directions to unseen areas of the environment. To get a complete idea of what is around you, you must

FIGURE 5.24 Figure and Ground
An initial step in perceptual grouping is for your perceptual processes to interpret part of a scene as a figure standing out against a ground.

---

figure Objectlike regions of the visual field that are distinguished from the background.

ground The backdrop or background areas of the visual field, against which figures stand out.

Gestalt psychology A school of psychology that maintains that psychological phenomena can be understood only when viewed as organized, structured wholes, not when broken down into primitive perceptual elements.

combine information from fixations of different spatial locations—*spatial integration*—at different moments in time—*temporal integration*.

What may surprise you is that your visual system does not work very hard to create a moment-by-moment, integrated picture of the environment. Research suggests that your visual memory for each fixation on the world does not preserve precise details (Simons & Ambinder, 2005). In fact, viewers are sometimes unable to detect when a whole object has changed from one fixation to the next.

In experiments done at the University of Calgary to test drivers (Caird, Edwards, Creaser, & Horrey, 2005), 36 intersection photographs were manipulated so that one object within the scene (pedestrian, vehicle, sign, or traffic-control device) would change within a five- to eight-second window when subjects saw them on a computer screen. Young and middle-aged drivers made significantly more correct decisions about the images and components of the scene than did older drivers. The phenomenon the researchers were testing is called *change blindness*. A similar phenomenon, called *inattention blindness*, can tell us how our brain processes information, especially if it is important. The fact that this phenomenon can be brought into the lab is quite valuable. You have probably had experiences where you were asked "Did you see that?"—but completely missed seeing something in your environment because you were focused on something else. How much attention do we pay to objects in our everyday world?

In another series of experiments (Simons, 1996), participants viewed for two seconds an array showing pictures of five familiar objects. Roughly four seconds later, the participants viewed a second array. In half the trials, the second array was identical to the first. However, as shown in Part A of **Figure 5.25**, on the other half of the trials the second array differed from the first in one of three ways: One of the objects had changed identity (e.g., a *stapler* in the first array might be replaced by a *staple remover* in the second array); two of the objects had switched their spatial position; or the whole set of objects was placed in a new configuration. Participants were challenged to judge whether the arrays were the *same* or *different*. You might imagine, on brief reflection, that this would be an easy task: How could you not notice that a *stapler* had turned into a *staple remover*? However, as shown in Part B of Figure 5.25, performance for *identity* and *switch* changes was well below 100 percent correct. Participants were "blind" to a number of *very* obvious changes!

Many people find this result surprising. How can it be that you have so few processing resources devoted to preserving the details of a scene over time that you would not notice that a stapler has turned into a staple remover? Part of the answer might be that the world itself is generally a stable source of information (O'Regan, 1992). It is simply unnecessary to commit to memory information that remains steadily available in the external environment—so you do not have processes that ordinarily would allow you to do so.

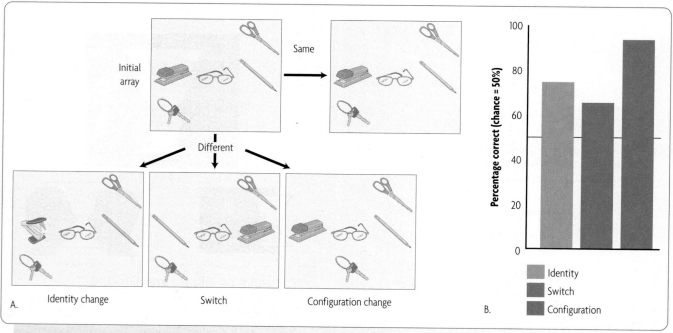

FIGURE 5.25 Change Blindness
(A) Experimental participants were asked to respond whether a second display was the "same as" or "different from" the initial array. (B) When the identity of an object was changed or two objects were switched, participants often were unable to detect the difference. Only when the whole configuration changed were participants nearly always correct.

Reprinted with permission from Roy Lachman and Janet Lachman, *Cognitive Psychology and Information Processing*, p. 189. Copyright © 1979 Lawrence Erlbaum Associates.

MOTION PERCEPTION

One type of perception that does require you to make comparisons across different glimpses of the world is motion perception. Suppose you see a friend across a classroom. If he stands still, the size of his image on your retina will expand as you draw near. The rate at which this image expands gives you a sense of how quickly you are approaching (Gibson, 1979).

As we noted, motion perception requires you to combine information from different glimpses of the world. You can appreciate the consequences of how your perceptual processes combine those glimpses quite strongly when you experience the **phi phenomenon**. This phenomenon occurs when two stationary spots of light in different positions in the visual field are turned on and off alternately at a rate of about four to five times per second. This effect occurs on outdoor advertising signs and in disco light displays. Even at this relatively slow rate of alternation, it appears that a single light is moving back and forth between the two spots. There are multiple ways to conceive of the path that leads from the location of the first dot to the location of the second dot. Yet human observers normally see only the simplest path, a straight line (Cutting & Proffitt, 1982; Shepard, 1984). This straight-line rule is violated, however, when viewers are shown alternating views of a human body in motion. Then the visual system fills in the paths of normal biological motion (Shiffrar, 1994; Stevens, Fonlupt, Shiffrar, & Decety, 2000).

DEPTH PERCEPTION

Until now, we have considered only two-dimensional patterns on flat surfaces. Everyday perceiving, however, involves objects in three-dimensional space. Perceiving all three spatial dimensions is absolutely vital so that you can approach what you want, such as interesting people and good food, and avoid what is dangerous, such as speeding cars and falling pianos. This perception requires accurate information about *depth* (the distance from you to an object) as well as about the *direction* it is moving in in relation to you. Your ears can help in determining direction, but they are not much help in determining depth. Your interpretation of depth relies on many different information sources about distance (often called *depth cues*)—among them binocular cues, motion cues, and pictorial cues.

Binocular and Motion Cues Have you ever wondered why you have two eyes instead of just one? The second eye is more than just a spare—it provides some of the best, most compelling information about depth. The two sources of binocular depth information are *retinal disparity* and *convergence*. Retinal disparity and convergence are extremely useful tools for evaluating objects that are not very far away. Other cues, which we will discuss later in the section, are more effective at longer distances.

Since the eyes are about five to seven centimetres apart horizontally, they receive slightly different views of the world. To convince yourself of this, try the following experiment. First, close your left eye and use the right one to line up your two index fingers with some small object in the distance, holding one finger at arm's length and the other about a foot in front of your face. Now, keeping your fingers stationary, close your right eye and open the left one while continuing to fixate on the distant

What makes you aware that the "protagonist" in this photo is moving—and in what direction is the motion?

object. What happened to the position of your two fingers? The second eye does not see them lined up with the distant object because it gets a slightly different view.

This displacement between the horizontal positions of corresponding images in your two eyes is called **retinal disparity**. It provides depth information because the amount of disparity, or difference, depends on the relative distance of objects from you (see **Figure 5.26**). For instance, when you switched eyes, the closer finger was displaced farther to the side than was the distant finger.

When you look at the world with both eyes open, most objects that you see stimulate different positions on your two retinas. If the disparity between corresponding images in the two retinas is small enough, the visual system is able to fuse them into a perception of a single object in depth. (However, if the images are too far apart, you actually see the double images, as when you cross your eyes.) When you stop to think about it, what your visual system does is pretty amazing: It takes two different retinal

phi phenomenon The simplest form of apparent motion: the movement illusion in which one or more stationary lights going on and off in succession are perceived as a single moving light.

retinal disparity The displacement between the horizontal positions of corresponding images in the two eyes.

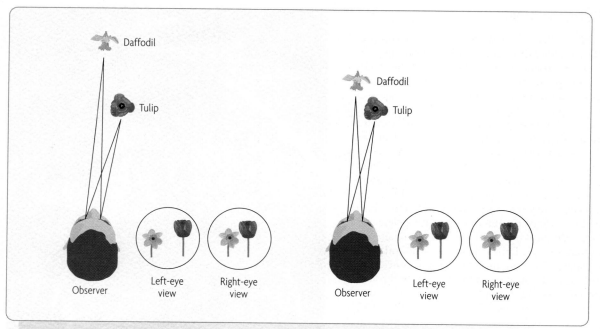

FIGURE 5.26 Retinal Disparity

Retinal disparity increases with the distance in depth between two objects.

images, compares them for horizontal displacement of corresponding parts (binocular disparity), and produces a unitary perception of a single object in depth. In effect, the visual system interprets horizontal displacement between the two images as depth in the three-dimensional world.

Other binocular information about depth comes from **convergence**. The two eyes turn inward to some extent whenever they are fixated on an object (see **Figure 5.27**). When the object is very close—several centimetres in front of your face—the eyes must turn toward each other quite a bit for the same image to fall on both foveae. You can actually see the eyes converge if you watch a friend focus first on a distant object and then on one a half-metre or so away. Your brain uses information from your eye muscles to make judgments about depth. However, convergence information from the eye muscles is useful for depth perception only up to about three metres. At greater distances, the angular differences are too small to detect because the eyes are nearly parallel when you fixate on a distant object.

To see how *motion* is another source for depth information, try the following demonstration. As you did before, close one eye and line up your two index fingers with some distant object. Then move your head to the side while fixating on the distant object and keeping your fingers still. As you move your head, you see both your fingers move, but the close finger seems to move farther and faster than the more distant one. The fixated object does not move at all. This source of information about depth is called **relative motion parallax**. Motion parallax provides information about depth because, as you move, the

---

convergence The degree to which the eyes turn inward to fixate on an object.

relative motion parallax A source of information about depth in which the relative distances of objects from a viewer determine the amount and direction of their relative motion in the retinal image.

FIGURE 5.27 Convergence as a Depth Cue

When an object is close to you, your eyes must converge more than when an object is at a greater distance. Your brain uses information from your eye muscles to use convergence as a cue to depth.

Reprinted with permission from R. Sekular & Blake, *Perception*, 3e, pp. 27, 221. Copyright © 1994 by McGraw-Hill.

relative distances of objects in the world determine the amount and direction of their relative motion in your retinal image of the scene. Next time you are a passenger on a car trip, watch out the window for motion parallax at work. Objects at a distance from the moving car will appear much more stationary than those closer to you.

Pictorial Cues Let's suppose you had vision in only one eye. Would you be unable to perceive depth? In fact, further information about depth is available from just one eye. These sources are called pictorial cues because they include the kinds of depth information found in pictures. Artists who create images in what appear to be three dimensions (on the two dimensions of a piece of paper or canvas) make skilled use of pictorial cues.

Interposition, or *occlusion*, arises when an opaque object blocks out part of a second object (see **Figure 5.28**). Interposition gives you depth information indicating that the occluded object is farther away than the occluding one. Occluding surfaces also block out light, creating shadows that can be used as an additional source of depth information.

Three more sources of pictorial information are all related to the way light projects from a three-dimensional world onto a two-dimensional surface such as the retina: relative size, linear perspective, and texture gradients. *Relative size* involves a basic rule of light projection: Objects of the same size at different distances project images of different sizes on the retina. The closest one projects the largest image and the farthest one the smallest image. This rule is called the *size/distance relation*. As you can see in **Figure 5.29**, if you look at an array with identical objects, you interpret the smaller ones to be farther away.

Linear perspective is a depth cue that also depends on the size/distance relation. When parallel lines (by definition separated along their lengths by the same distance) recede into the distance, they converge toward a point on the horizon in your retinal image. Your visual system's interpretation of converging lines gives rise to the *Ponzo illusion* (see **Figure 5.30**). The upper line looks longer because you interpret the converging sides according to linear perspective as parallel lines receding into the distance. In this context, you interpret the upper line as though it were farther away, so you see it as longer; a farther object

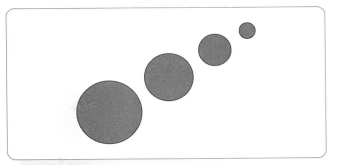

FIGURE 5.29 Relative Size as a Depth Cue
Objects that are closer project larger images on the retina. As a consequence, when you look at an array with identical objects, you interpret the smaller ones to be at a greater distance.

FIGURE 5.30 The Ponzo Illusion
The converging lines add a dimension of depth, and therefore the distance cue makes the top line appear larger than the bottom line, even though they are actually the same length.

would have to be longer than a nearer one for both to produce retinal images of the same size.

Texture gradients provide depth cues because the density of a texture becomes greater as a surface recedes in depth. The wheat field in **Figure 5.31** is an example of the way texture is used as a depth cue. You can think of this as another consequence of the size/distance relation. In this case, the units that make up the texture become smaller as they recede into the distance, and your visual system interprets this increasing density as greater distance in three-dimensional space.

By now, it should be clear that there are many sources of depth information. Under normal viewing conditions, however,

FIGURE 5.28 Interposition as a Depth Cue
What visual cues tell you whether this woman is behind the bars?

FIGURE 5.31 Texture as a Depth Cue
The wheat field is a natural example of the way texture can be used as a depth cue. Notice the way the individual wheat plants slant.

information from these sources comes together in a single, coherent three-dimensional interpretation of the environment. You experience depth, not the different cues to depth that exist in the proximal stimulus. In other words, your visual system uses cues such as differential motion, interposition, and relative size automatically, without your conscious awareness, to make the complex computations that give you a perception of depth in the three-dimensional environment.

PERCEPTUAL CONSTANCIES

To help you discover another important property of visual perception, we are going to ask you to play a bit with your textbook. Put your book down on a table, then move your head closer to it so that it is just a few inches away. Then move your head back to a normal reading distance. Although the book stimulated a much larger part of your retina when it was up close than when it was far away, didn't you perceive the book's size to remain the same? Now set the book upright and try tilting your head clockwise. When you do this, the image of the book rotates counterclockwise on your retina, but didn't you still perceive the book to be upright?

In general, you see the world as *invariant*, *constant*, and *stable* despite changes in the stimulation of your sensory receptors. Psychologists refer to this phenomenon as **perceptual constancy**. Roughly speaking, it means that you perceive the properties of the distal stimuli, which are usually constant, rather than the properties of proximal stimuli, which change every time you move your eyes or head. For survival, it is critical that you perceive constant and stable properties of objects in the

perceptual constancy The ability to retain an unchanging percept of an object despite variations in the retinal image.

size constancy The ability to perceive the true size of an object despite variations in the size of its retinal image.

shape constancy The ability to perceive the true shape of an object despite variations in the shape of the retinal image.

world despite the enormous variations in the properties of the light patterns that stimulate your eyes. The critical task of perception is to discover *invariant* properties of your environment despite the variations in your retinal impressions of them. We see next how this works for size, shape, and orientation.

Size and Shape Constancy What determines your perception of the size of an object? In part, you perceive an object's actual size on the basis of the size of its retinal image. However, the demonstration with your book shows that the size of the retinal image depends on both the actual size of the book and its distance from the eye. As you now know, information about distance is available from a variety of depth cues. Your visual system combines that information with retinal information about image size to yield a perception of an object size that usually corresponds to the actual size of the distal stimulus. **Size constancy** refers to your ability to perceive the true size of an object despite variations in the size of its retinal image.

If the size of an object is perceived by taking distance cues into account, then you should be fooled about size whenever you are fooled about distance. One such illusion occurs in the Ames room shown in **Figure 5.32**. In comparison to the child, the adult looks quite short in the left corner of this room, but he looks enormous in the right corner. The reason for this illusion is that you perceive the room to be rectangular, with the two back corners equally distant from you. Thus you perceive the child's actual size as being consistent with the size of the images on your retina in both cases. In fact, the child is not at the same distance because the Ames room creates a clever illusion. It appears to be a rectangular room, but it is actually made from nonrectangular surfaces at odd angles in depth and height, as you can see in the drawings that accompany the photos. Any person on the right (in location number 2) will make a larger retinal image because he or she is twice as close to the observer. (By the way, to get the illusion you must view the display with a single eye through a peephole—that is the vantage point of the photographs in Figure 5.32. If you could move around while viewing the room, your visual system would acquire information about the unusual structure of the room.)

Another way that the perceptual system can infer objective size is by using prior knowledge about the characteristic size of similarly shaped objects. For instance, once you recognize the shape of a house, a tree, or a dog, you have a good idea of how big each is, even without knowing its distance from you. When past experience does not give you knowledge of what familiar objects look like at extreme distances, size constancy may break down. You have experienced this problem if you have looked down at people from the top of a skyscraper and thought they resembled ants.

Shape constancy is closely related to size constancy. You perceive an object's actual shape correctly even when the object is slanted away from you, making the shape of the retinal image substantially different from that of the object itself. For instance, a rectangle tipped away projects a trapezoidal image onto your retina; a circle tipped away from you projects an elliptical image (see **Figure 5.33**). Yet you usually perceive the shapes accurately as a circle and a rectangle slanted away in space. When there is good depth information available, your visual system can determine an object's true shape simply by taking into account your distance from its different parts.

Lightness Constancy Consider the photograph in **Figure 5.34**. When you look at the brick wall in this picture,

FIGURE 5.32 The Ames Room

The Ames room is designed to be viewed through a peephole with one eye—the vantage point from which these photographs were taken. The Ames room is constructed from nonrectangular surfaces at odd angles in depth and height. However, with only the view from the peephole, your visual system interprets it as an ordinary room and makes some unusual guesses about the relative heights of the occupants.

FIGURE 5.33 Shape Constancy

As a coin is rotated, its image becomes an ellipse that grows narrower and narrower until it becomes a thin rectangle, an ellipse again, and then a circle. At each orientation, however, it is still perceived as a circular coin.

Source: Coin image © 2007 Royal Canadian Mint. All Rights Reserved.

FIGURE 5.34 Lightness Constancy

Lightness constancy helps explain why you perceive all the bricks in the wall to be made of the same material.

you do not perceive some of the bricks to be light red and some of them to be dark red; instead, you perceive this as a wall in which all the bricks are equally light or dark but some of them are in shadow (Goldstein, 1999). This is an example of lightness constancy: **Lightness constancy** is your tendency to perceive the whiteness, greyness, or blackness of objects as constant across changing levels of illumination.

As with the other constancies we have described, you experience lightness constancy quite frequently in everyday life. Suppose, for example, you are wearing a white T-shirt and walk from a dimly lit room outside into a bright sunny day. In bright sunshine, the T-shirt reflects far more light into your eyes than it does in the dim room, yet it looks about equally light to you in both contexts. In fact, lightness constancy works because the *percentage* of light an object reflects remains about the same even as the *absolute* amount of light changes. Your bright white T-shirt is going to reflect 80 to 90 percent of whatever light is available;

lightness constancy The tendency to perceive the whiteness, greyness, or blackness of objects as constant across changing levels of illuminations.

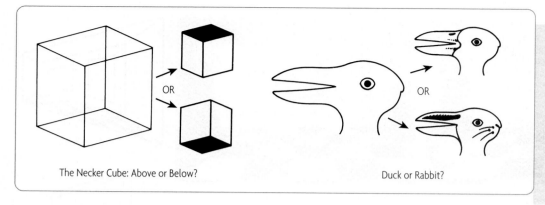

FIGURE 5.35
Perceptual
Ambiguities
Each example allows two
interpretations, but you
cannot experience both at
the same time. Do you
notice your perception
flipping back and forth
between each pair of
possibilities?

The Necker Cube: Above or Below?

Duck or Rabbit?

your black jeans are going to reflect only about 5 percent of the available light. That is why—when you see them in the same context—the T-shirt will always look lighter than the jeans.

In this section, we have described a number of organizational processes in perception. In the final section of the chapter, we consider the identification and recognition processes that give meaning to objects and events in the environment.

STOP AND REVIEW

❶ What is meant by stimulus-driven capture?
❷ What is the law of closure?
❸ What visual information allows you to understand that someone is walking toward you?
❹ How does convergence provide cues to depth?
❺ What is shape constancy?

CRITICAL THINKING   In the experiment of change blindness, why might people perform best when the configuration changes?

REALITY, AMBIGUITY, AND ILLUSIONS

We have defined the task of perception as the identification of the distal stimulus from the proximal stimulus. Before we turn to some of the perceptual mechanisms that make this task successful, let's address some other aspects of stimuli in the environment that make perception complex: *ambiguous* stimuli and perceptual *illusions*.

Ambiguity   A primary goal of perception is to get an accurate "fix" on the world. Survival depends on accurate perceptions of objects and events in your environment—is that motion in the trees a tiger?—that are not always easy to read. **Ambiguity** is an important concept in understanding perception because it shows that a single image at the sensory level can result in *multiple interpretations* at the perceptual and identification levels.

Figure 5.35 shows two examples of ambiguous figures. Each example permits two unambiguous but conflicting interpretations. Look at each image until you can see the two alternative interpretations. Notice that once you have seen both of them, your perception flips back and forth between them as you

---

ambiguity   Property of perceptual object that may have more than one interpretation.

FIGURE 5.36 Ambiguity in Art
This painting by Salvador Dali is called *Slave Market with the Disappearing Bust of Voltaire*. Can you find Voltaire? Dali is one of a large number of modern and contemporary artists who have exploited ambiguity in their work.

look at the ambiguous figure. This perceptual *instability* of ambiguous figures is one of their most important characteristics.

The Necker cube (see Figure 5.35) presents an ambiguity at the perceptual organization stage. You have two different perceptions of the same object in the environment. The Necker cube can be seen as a three-dimensional hollow cube either below you and angled to your left or above you and angled toward your right. The ambiguous alternatives are different physical arrangements of the object in three-dimensional space, both resulting from the same stimulus image.

The duck/rabbit figure (see Figure 5.35) is an example of ambiguity at the recognition stage. It is perceived as the same physical shape in both interpretations. The ambiguity arises in determining the kind of object it represents and in how best to classify it, given the mixed set of information available.

Many prominent artists have used perceptual ambiguity as a central creative device in their works. **Figure 5.36** presents *Slave Market with the Disappearing Bust of Voltaire* by Salvador Dali. This work reveals a complex ambiguity in which a whole section of the picture must be radically reorganized and reinterpreted to allow perception of the "hidden" bust of the French philosopher-writer Voltaire. The white sky under the lower arch is Voltaire's forehead and hair; the white portions of the two ladies' dresses are his cheeks, nose, and chin. (If you have trouble seeing him, try squinting, holding the book at arm's length, or taking off your glasses.) Once you have seen the bust of Voltaire in this picture, however, you will never be able to look at it without knowing where this Frenchman is hiding.

One of the most fundamental properties of normal human perception is the tendency to transform ambiguity and uncertainty about the environment into a clear interpretation that you can act on with confidence. In a world filled with variability and change, your perceptual system must meet the challenges of discovering invariance and stability.

illusion An experience of a stimulus pattern in a manner that is demonstrably incorrect but shared by others in the same perceptual environment.

Illusions Ambiguous stimuli present your perceptual systems with the challenge of recognizing one unique figure out of several possibilities. One or another interpretation of the stimulus is correct or incorrect with respect to a particular context. When your perceptual systems actually deceive you into experiencing a stimulus pattern in a manner that is demonstrably incorrect, you are experiencing an **illusion**. The word *illusion* shares the same root as *ludicrous*—both stem from the Latin *illudere*, which means "to mock." Illusions are shared by most people in the

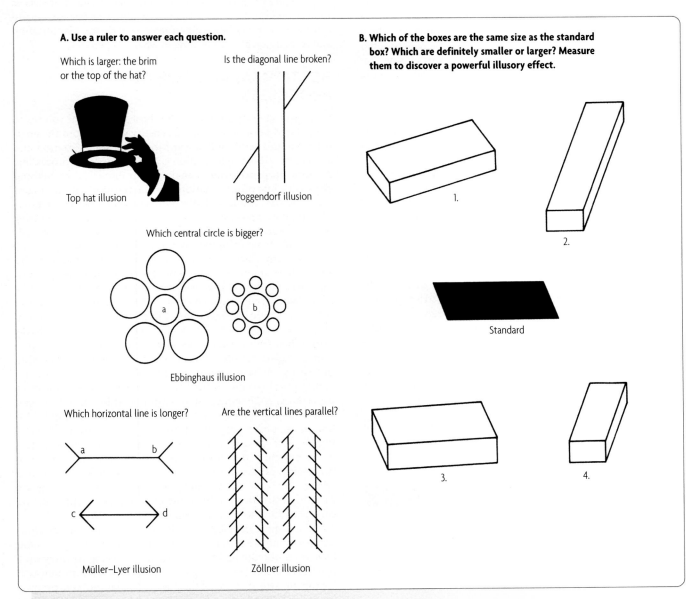

A. Use a ruler to answer each question.

Which is larger: the brim or the top of the hat?

Top hat illusion

Is the diagonal line broken?

Poggendorf illusion

Which central circle is bigger?

a   b

Ebbinghaus illusion

Which horizontal line is longer?

a   b

c   d

Müller–Lyer illusion

Are the vertical lines parallel?

Zöllner illusion

B. Which of the boxes are the same size as the standard box? Which are definitely smaller or larger? Measure them to discover a powerful illusory effect.

1.

2.

Standard

3.

4.

FIGURE 5.37 Five Illusions to Tease Your Brain
Each of these illusions represents circumstances in which perception is demonstrably incorrect. Researchers often use illusions to test their theories about why perceptual systems that generally function quite accurately yield illusions in special circumstances.

same perceptual situation because of shared physiology in sensory systems and overlapping experiences of the world. (As we will explain in Chapter 6, this sets illusions apart from hallucinations. Hallucinations are perceptual distortions that individuals experience as a result of unusual physical or mental states. They are not shared as they are internal to individuals.) Examine the classic illusions in **Figure 5.37**. Although it is most convenient for us to present you with visual illusions, illusions also exist in other sensory modalities, such as hearing (Russo & Thompson, 2005; Sonnadara & Trainor, 2005), taste (Todrank & Bartoshuk, 1991), and touch (Heller, Bracket, Salik, Scroggs, & Green, 2003).

Illusions in Everyday Life Illusions are also a basic part of your everyday life. Consider your day-to-day experience of your home planet, Earth. You have seen the sun "rise" and "set"—even though you know that the sun is sitting out there in the centre of the solar system as stationary as ever. You can appreciate why it was such an extraordinary feat of courage for Christopher Columbus and other voyagers to deny the obvious illusion that Earth was flat and sail off toward one of its apparent edges. Similarly, when a full moon is overhead, it seems to follow you wherever you go even though you know the moon is not chasing you. What you are experiencing is an illusion created by the great distance of the moon from your eye. When they reach Earth, the moon's light rays are essentially parallel and perpendicular to your direction of travel, no matter where you go.

People can control illusions to achieve desired effects. Architects and interior designers use principles of perception to create objects in space that seem larger or smaller than they really are. A small apartment becomes more spacious when it is painted with light colours and sparsely furnished with low, small couches, chairs, and tables in the centre of the room instead of against the walls. Psychologists working with NASA in the U.S. space program have researched the effects of environment on perception in order to design space capsules that have pleasant sensory qualities. Set and lighting directors of movies and theatrical productions purposely create illusions on film and on stage.

Despite all of these illusions—some more useful than others—you generally do pretty well getting around the environment. That is why researchers typically study illusions to help explain how perception ordinarily works so well. The illusions themselves suggest, however, that your perceptual systems cannot perfectly carry out the task of recovering the distal stimulus from the proximal stimulus.

You now have an overview of your sensory and perceptual processes and some awareness of the challenges those processes face. Let's begin to consider those processes in more detail.

STOP AND REVIEW

❶ What are some stages within the overall process of perception?

❷ What makes a stimulus ambiguous?

---

bottom-up processing Perceptual analyses based on the sensory data available in the environment; results of analysis are passed upward toward more abstract representations.

top-down processing Perceptual processes in which information from an individual's past experience, knowledge, expectations, motivations, and background influence the way a perceived object is interpreted and classified.

Identification and Recognition Processes

You can think of all the perceptual processes described so far as providing reasonably accurate knowledge about physical properties of the distal stimulus—the position, size, shape, texture, and colour of objects in a three-dimensional environment. However, you would not know what the objects were or whether you had seen them before. Your experience would resemble a visit to an alien planet where everything was new to you; you would not know what to eat, what to put on your head, what to run away from, or what to date. Your environment appears nonalien because you are able to recognize and identify most objects as things you have seen before and as members of the meaningful categories that you know about from experience. Identification and recognition attach meaning to what you perceive.

BOTTOM-UP AND TOP-DOWN PROCESSES

When you identify an object, you must match what you see to your stored knowledge. Taking sensory data in from the environment and sending it toward the brain for extraction and analysis of relevant information is called bottom-up processing. **Bottom-up processing** is anchored in empirical reality and deals with bits of information and the transformation of concrete, physical features of stimuli into abstract representations. This type of processing is also called *data-driven processing* because your starting point for identification is the sensory evidence you obtain from the environment—the data.

In many cases, however, you can use information you already have about the environment to help you make a perceptual identification. If you visit a zoo, for example, you might be a little more ready to recognize some types of animals than you otherwise would be. You are more likely to hypothesize that you are seeing a tiger there than you would be in your own backyard. When your expectations affect perception, the phenomenon is called top-down processing. **Top-down processing** involves your past experiences, knowledge, motivations, and cultural background in perceiving the world. With top-down processing, higher mental functioning influences how you understand objects and events. Top-down processing is also known as conceptually driven (or hypothesis-driven) processing because the concepts you have stored in memory affect interpretation of the sensory data. The importance of top-down processing can be illustrated by drawings known as *droodles* (Price, 1953/1980). Without the labels, these drawings are meaningless. However, once the drawings are identified, you can easily find meaning in them (see **Figure 5.38**).

For a more detailed example of top-down versus bottom-up processing, we turn to the domain of speech perception. You have undoubtedly had the experience of trying to carry on a conversation at a very loud party. Under those circumstances, it is probably true that not all the physical signal you were producing arrived unambiguously at your acquaintance's ears: Some of what you had to say was almost certainly obscured by coughs, thumping music, or peals of laughter. Even so, people rarely realize that there are gaps in the physical signal they are experiencing. This phenomenon is known as *phonemic restoration* (Warren, 1970). As we explain more fully in Chapter 11, *phonemes* are the minimal meaningful units of sound in a

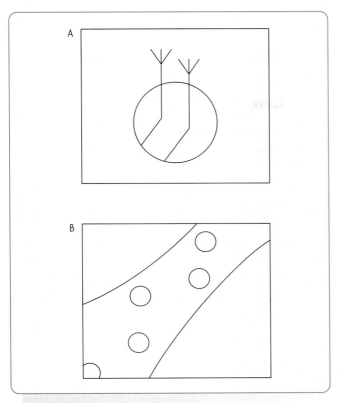

FIGURE 5.38 Droodles

What are these animals? Do you see in (A) an early bird who caught a very strong worm and in (B) a giraffe's neck? Each figure can be seen as representing something familiar to you, although this perceptual recognition usually does not occur until some identifying information is provided.

language; phonemic restoration occurs when people use top-down processes to fill in missing phonemes. Listeners often find it difficult to tell whether they are hearing a word that has a noise replacing part of the original speech signal, or whether they are hearing a word with a noise just superimposed on the intact signal (see part A of **Figure 5.39**) (Samuel, 1981, 1991).

Part B of Figure 5.39 shows how bottom-up and top-down processes could interact to produce phonemic restoration (McClelland & Elman, 1986). Suppose part of what your friend says at a noisy party is obscured so the signal that arrives at your ears is "I have to go home to walk my (noise)og." If noise covers the /d/, you are likely to think that you actually heard the full word *dog*. But why? In Figure 5.39, you see two of the types of information relevant to speech perception. We have the individual sounds that make up words and the words themselves. When the sounds /o/ and /g/ arrive in this system, they provide information—in a bottom-up fashion—to the word level (we have given only a subset of the words in English that end with /og/). This provides you with a range of candidates for what your friend might have said. Now top-down processes go to work—the context helps you select *dog* as the most likely word to appear in this utterance. When all of this happens swiftly enough—bottom-up identification of a set of candidate words and top-down selection of the likely correct candidate—you will never know that the /d/ was missing. Your perceptual processes believe that the word was intact (Samuel, 1997). The next time you are in a noisy environment, you should be glad your perceptual processes fill in sounds so efficiently!

THE INFLUENCE OF CONTEXTS AND EXPECTATIONS

Early in the chapter, we noted that the world often gives you ambiguous information to perceive. Consider **Figure 5.40**. What do you make of it? Suppose we tell you that it is a view into our

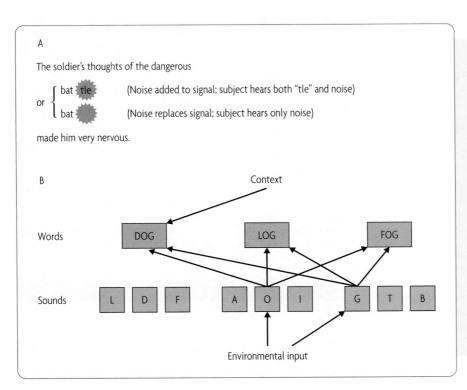

FIGURE 5.39 Phonemic Restoration

(A) Listeners are challenged to say whether noise has been added on top of a syllable or used to replace a syllable. Due to phonemic restoration, they often cannot tell. They "hear" the missing information even when the sound is replaced by noise. (B) In this example, noise obscured the /d/ when your friend said "dog." Based only on the environmental input, your perceptual system can come up with several hypotheses: *dog, log, fog,* and so on. However, top-down information from the context—"I have to go home and walk my . . ."—supports the hypothesis that your friend said "dog."

Reprinted with permission from Irwin Rock, *The Logic of Perception.* Cambridge, MA: The MIT Press. Copyright © 1983.

FIGURE 5.40 An Ambiguous Picture
What do you see in this picture?

neighbour's backyard, showing a tree around which his dalmatian routinely sniffs? Now can you see a dog? (The dog's nose is roughly in the middle of the figure.) This is another top-down aspect of perception: Contexts and expectations can influence your hypotheses about what is out there in the world. Have you ever had the experience of seeing people you knew in places where you did not expect to see them, such as in a different city or a different social group? It takes much longer to recognize them in such situations, and sometimes you are not even sure they are who you think they are. The problem is not that they look any different but that the *context* is wrong; you did not *expect* them to be there. The spatial and temporal contexts in which objects are recognized provide an important source of information: They help you generate expectations about what objects you are and are not likely to see nearby.

Perceptual identification depends on your expectations as well as on the physical properties of the objects you see; object identification is a constructive, interpretive process. Depending on what you already know, where you are, and what else you see around you, your identification may vary. Read the following words:

THE CAT

They say THE CAT, right? Now look again at the middle letter of each word. Physically, these two letters are exactly the same, yet you perceived the first as an H and the second as an A. Why? Clearly, your perception was affected by what you know about words in English. The context provided by T_E makes an H highly likely and an A unlikely, whereas the reverse is true of the context of C_T (Selfridge, 1955).

Researchers have often documented the effects of context and expectation on perception (and response) by studying *set*. Set is a temporary readiness to perceive or react to a stimulus in a particular way. There are three types of set: motor, mental, and perceptual. A *motor set* is a readiness to make a quick, prepared response. A runner trains by perfecting a motor set to come out of the blocks as fast as possible at the sound of the starting gun. A *mental set* is a readiness to deal with a situation, such as a problem-solving task or

a game, in a way determined by learned rules, instructions, expectations, or habitual tendencies. A mental set can actually prevent you from solving a problem when the old rules do not seem to fit the new situation, as we will see when we study problem solving in Chapter 9. A *perceptual set* is a readiness to detect a particular stimulus in a given context. A new mother, for example, is perceptually set to hear the cries of her child.

Often a set leads you to change your interpretation of an ambiguous stimulus. Consider these two series of words:

FOX; OWL; SNAKE; TURKEY; SWAN; D?VE
BOB; RAY; TONY; BILL; HENRY; D?VE

Did you read through the lists? What word came to mind for D?VE in each case? You likely thought DOVE and then DAVE, because each list of words created a set that directed your search of memory in a particular way.

All the effects of context on perception clearly require that your memory be organized in such a fashion that information relevant to particular situations becomes available at the right times. In other words, to generate appropriate (or inappropriate) expectations, you must be able to make use of prior knowledge stored in memory. Sometimes you "see" with your memory as much as you see with your eyes. In Chapter 8, we discuss the properties of memory that make context effects on perception possible.

FINAL LESSONS

To solidify all that you have learned in this chapter, we suggest that you take a look back at Figure 5.2; you now have the knowledge necessary to understand the whole flowchart. Examining Figure 5.2 will also confirm that the important lesson to be learned from the study of perception is that a perceptual experience in response to a stimulus event is a response of the whole person. In addition to the information provided when your sensory receptors are stimulated, your final perception depends on who you are, whom you are with, and what you expect, want, and value. A perceiver often plays two different roles that can be compared to gambling and interior design. As a gambler, a perceiver is willing to bet that the present input can be understood in terms of past knowledge and personal theories. As a compulsive interior decorator, a perceiver is constantly rearranging the stimuli so that they fit better and are more coherent. Incongruity and messy perceptions are rejected in favour of those with clear, clean, consistent lines.

If perceiving were completely bottom-up, you would be bound to the same mundane, concrete reality of the here and now. You could register experience but not profit from it on later occasions, nor would you see the world differently under different circumstances. If perceptual processing were completely top-down, however, you could become lost in your own fantasy world of what you expect and hope to perceive. A proper balance between the two extremes achieves the basic goal of perception: to experience what is out there in a way that optimally serves your needs as a biological and social being, moving about and adapting to your physical and social environments.

STOP AND REVIEW

❶ Why is phonemic restoration an example of top-down processing?

❷ What is the relationship between contexts and expectations?

❸ What is a set?

---

set A temporary readiness to perceive or react to a stimulus in a particular way.

Recapping Main Points

Sensory Knowledge of the World

- Perception is a three-stage process consisting of a sensory stage, a perceptual organization stage, and an identification and recognition stage.
- At the sensory level of processing, physical energy is detected and transformed into neural energy and sensory experience.
- At the organizational level, perceptual processes organize sensations into coherent images and give you perception of objects and patterns.
- At the level of identification and recognition, perceptions of objects are compared with memory representations to be recognized as familiar and meaningful objects.
- The task of perception is to determine what the distal (external) stimulus is from the information contained in the proximal (sensory) stimulus.
- Psychophysics investigates psychological responses to physical stimuli. Researchers measure absolute thresholds and just noticeable differences between stimuli.
- Signal detection allows researchers to separate sensory acuity from response biases.
- Researchers in psychophysics have captured with mathematical functions the relationship between physical intensity and psychological effect.
- Sensation translates the physical energy of stimuli into neural codes via transduction.

Visit **MyPsychLab.com** for more review and practice on the following topics:

✔ **Practice:** Sensory Knowledge of the World

The Visual System

- Photoreceptors in the retina, called rods and cones, convert light energy into neural impulses.
- Ganglion cells in the retina integrate input from receptors and bipolar cells. Their axons form the optic nerves that meet at the optic chiasma.
- Visual information is distributed to several different areas of the brain that process different aspects of the visual environment, such as how things look and where they are.
- The wavelength of light is the stimulus for colour.
- Colour sensations differ in hue, saturation, and brightness.
- Colour vision theory combines the trichromatic theory of three types of colour receptors with the opponent-process theory of colour systems composed of opponent elements.

Visit **MyPsychLab.com** for more review and practice on the following topics:

◆ **Research:** Thomas Young and Hermann von Helmholtz

Hearing

- Hearing is produced by sound waves that vary in frequency, amplitude, and complexity.

- In the cochlea, sound waves are transformed into fluid waves that move the basilar membrane. Hairs on the basilar membrane stimulate neural impulses that are sent to the auditory cortex.
- Place theory best explains the coding of high frequencies, and frequency theory best explains the coding of low frequencies.
- To compute the direction from which the sound is arriving, two types of neural mechanisms compute the relative intensity and timing of sounds coming to each ear.

Your Other Senses

- Smell and taste respond to the chemical properties of substances and work together when people are seeking and sampling food.
- Olfaction is accomplished by odour-sensitive cells deep in the nasal passages.
- Taste receptors are taste buds embedded in papillae, mostly in the tongue.
- The cutaneous (skin) senses give sensations of pressure and temperature.
- The vestibular sense gives information about the direction and rate of body motion.
- The kinesthetic sense gives information about the position of body parts and helps co-ordinate motion.
- Pain is the body's response to potentially harmful stimuli.
- The physiological response to pain involves sensory response at the site of the pain stimulus and nerve impulses moving between the brain and the spinal cord.

Visit **MyPsychLab.com** for more review and practice on the following topics:

 Watch: Brain Pain

Organizational Processes in Perception

- Both your personal goals and the properties of the objects in the world determine where you will focus your attention.
- The Gestalt psychologists provided several laws of perceptual grouping, including proximity, similarity, good continuation, closure, and common fate.
- Perceptual processes integrate over both time and space to provide an interpretation of the environment.
- Binocular, motion, and pictorial cues all contribute to the perception of depth.
- You tend to perceive objects as having stable size, shape, and lightness.
- Ambiguity may arise when the same sensory information can be organized into different percepts.
- Knowledge about perceptual illusions can provide constraints on ordinary perceptual processes.

Visit **MyPsychLab.com** for more review and practice on the following topics:

◆ **Simulate:** Gestalt Laws of Perception

Identification and Recognition Processes

- During the final stage of perceptual processing—identification and recognition of objects—percepts are given meaning through processes that combine bottom-up and top-down influences.
- Context, expectations, and perceptual sets may guide recognition of incomplete or ambiguous data in one direction rather than another equally possible one.

Visit **MyPsychLab.com** for more review and practice on the following topics:

✱ **Explore:** Top-Down Processing

KEY TERMS

absolute threshold (p. 114)
accommodation (p. 118)
amacrine cells (p. 120)
ambiguity (p. 148)
attention (p. 138)
auditory nerve (p. 129)
basilar membrane (p. 129)
bipolar cells (p. 119)
bottom-up processing (p. 149)
brightness (p. 124)
cochlea (p. 129)
complementary colours (p. 124)
cones (p. 119)
convergence (p. 144)
cutaneous senses (p. 134)
dark adaptation (p. 119)
dichotic listening (p. 140)
difference threshold (p. 116)
distal stimulus (p. 113)
figure (p. 141)
fovea (p. 119)
frequency theory (p. 131)
ganglion cells (p. 119)
gate-control theory (p. 136)
Gestalt psychology (p. 141)

goal-directed selection (p. 138)
ground (p. 141)
horizontal cells (p. 120)
hue (p. 124)
identification and recognition (p. 111)
illusion (p. 149)
just noticeable difference (JND) (p. 116)
kinesthetic sense (p. 135)
lightness constancy (p. 147)
loudness (p. 128)
olfactory bulb (p. 132)
opponent-process theory (p. 126)
optic nerve (p. 120)
pain (p. 136)
perception (p. 111)
perceptual constancy (p. 146)
perceptual organization (p. 111)
phantom limb pain (p. 136)
pheromones (p. 133)
phi phenomenon (p. 143)
photoreceptors (p. 119)
pitch (p. 128)
place theory (p. 130)
proximal stimulus (p. 113)
psychometric function (p. 114)

psychophysics (p. 114)
receptive field (p. 120)
relative motion parallax (p. 144)
response bias (p. 115)
retina (p. 119)
retinal disparity (p. 143)
rods (p. 119)
saturation (p. 124)
sensation (p. 111)
sensory adaptation (p. 114)
sensory receptors (p. 117)
set (p. 152)
shape constancy (p. 146)
signal detection theory (SDT) (p. 115)
size constancy (p. 146)
sound localization (p. 131)
stimulus-driven capture (p. 138)
timbre (p. 128)
top-down processing (p. 149)
transduction (p. 117)
trichromatic theory (p. 126)
vestibular sense (p. 135)
volley principle (p. 131)
Weber's law (p. 116)

Practice Test

1. At what stage of perception does meaning get assigned to a percept?
   a. identification and recognition
   b. sensation
   c. perceptual organization
   d. sensory adaptation

2. Suppose you are looking at a globe of the world. Although the _____ is a sphere, you would expect the _____ to be a circle.
   a. distal stimulus; absolute threshold
   b. distal stimulus; proximal stimulus
   c. threshold; distal stimulus
   d. proximal stimulus; distal stimulus

3. In a museum, you are fascinated by a painting. From one angle, you see two faces. From another angle, you see a vase. This is an example of an _____
   a. illusion.
   b. absolute threshold.
   c. opponent process.
   d. ambiguity.

4. When you first walked into a room, you were overwhelmed by the smell of someone's perfume. Over time, you become less aware of the smell. This is an example of _____
   a. a psychometric function.
   b. sensory adaptation.
   c. an illusion.
   d. transduction.

5. You are carrying out an experiment in which you want to find a difference threshold for soft drinks that vary in their sugar concentration. You want to find the point at which the stimuli are recognized as different _____ percent of the time.
   a. 50
   b. 25
   c. 100
   d. 75

6. The conversion of one form of physical energy into another is called _____
   a. sensory adaptation.
   b. transduction.
   c. sensory reception.
   d. photoreception.

7. If you walk into a room that has very low illumination, your _____ are likely to contribute more than your _____ to your visual experience.
   a. rods; amacrine cells
   b. horizontal cells; rods
   c. cones; rods
   d. rods; cones

8. In a lecture on the visual system, Rahul learns about complex cells and hypercomplex cells. The lecture was probably about _____
   a. dark adaptation.
   b. receptive fields.
   c. accommodation.
   d. absolute thresholds.

9. Which of these pairs does not play a role in opponent-process theory?
   a. red versus green
   b. white versus black
   c. yellow versus blue
   d. blue versus green

10. The _____ of a sound is determined by its frequency; the _____ of a sound is determined by its amplitude.
    a. timbre; pitch
    b. loudness; timbre
    c. loudness; pitch
    d. pitch; loudness

11. The airborne sound wave becomes "seaborne" when the auditory information reaches the _____
    a. auditory nerve.
    b. cochlea.
    c. tympanic membrane.
    d. fovea.

12. Teresa is building a robot. She provides the robot with software that allows it to detect when the same sound arrives at slightly different times at its two artificial ears. It appears that Teresa wants the robot to succeed at _____
    a. pitch perception.
    b. timbre detection.
    c. sound localization.
    d. sound discrimination.

13. Which of these is *not* a primary taste quality?
    a. bitter
    b. sweet
    c. tangy
    d. sour

14. Which of these statements is *not* true of the skin senses?
    a. The skin's sensitivity to pressure varies over the body.
    b. The skin senses warmth and coolness with the same receptors.
    c. The skin has several different types of sensory receptors.
    d. Some regions of the skin have more sensory cortex devoted to them.

15. The purpose of _____ theory is to explain some aspects of the relationship between physical and psychological experiences of pain.
    a. gate-control
    b. volley
    c. frequency
    d. place

16. In general, you would predict that people with _____ taste buds would experience _____ pain when they eat spicy food.
    a. fewer; less
    b. fewer; no
    c. more; more
    d. more; less

17. When Shirley walks into a party, she looks around the room to find her husband, Paul. This is an example of _____
    a. goal-driven attention.
    b. stimulus-driven capture.
    c. temporal integration.
    d. sensory adaptation.

18. Tomas owns a ring with a very small gap in it. The law of _____ explains why most people perceive his ring to be intact.
    a. similarity
    b. common fate
    c. good continuation
    d. closure

19. You ask a friend to hold both hands up in the air with one hand about six inches behind the other. You point out to him that the nearer hand covers some parts of the more distant hand. This provides a demonstration of _____ as a cue to depth.
a. relative motion parallax   c. occlusion
b. convergence   d. texture

20. As someone walks toward you, the person's image on your retina expands. However, you do not perceive the person to be actually getting larger. This is an example of _____
a. sensory adaptation.
b. the phi phenomenon.
c. motion constancy.
d. size constancy.

21. When you engage in _____, you begin with sensory data from the environment.
a. bottom-up processing
b. top-down processing
c. pictorial cues
d. hypothesis-driven processing

22. Just as Chris says, "I love you," a truck sounds its horn. Although the horn covered the "l" sound in "love," Pat still perceives "love" as intact. This is an example of _____
a. bottom-up processing.
b. perceptual constancy.
c. top-down processing.
d. good continuation.

23. For a short while after seeing a horror movie, Calvin perceives every shadow as a monster. It sounds like he is experiencing _____
a. a perceptual set.   c. the phi phenomenon.
b. shape constancy.   d. the law of common fate.

Essay Questions

1. How do ambiguous stimuli demonstrate some of the challenges your sensory and perceptual processes face as they help you interpret the world?

2. How do trichromatic theory and opponent-process theory fit together to explain important aspects of colour vision?

3. Why do different contexts give you different expectations of what you might perceive?

Discovering Psychology Viewing Guide

Watch the following video by logging on to MyPsychLab (**www.mypsychlab.com**). After you have watched the video, complete the activities that follow.

Program 7: Sensation and Perception

PROGRAM REVIEW

1. Imagine that a teaspoon of sugar is dissolved in two gallons of water. Rita can detect this level of sweetness at least half the time. This level is called the _____
   a. distal stimulus.
   b. perceptual constant.
   c. response bias.
   d. absolute threshold.

2. What is the job of a receptor?
   a. to transmit a neural impulse
   b. to connect new information with old information
   c. to detect a type of physical energy
   d. to receive an impulse from the brain

3. What is the function of the thalamus in visual processing?
   a. It relays information to the cortex.
   b. It rotates the retinal image.
   c. It converts light energy to a neural impulse.
   d. It makes sense of the proximal stimulus.

4. You want to paint your room yellow, so you get some samples at the paint store. When you hold the sample against your white wall, it looks different from the way it looks against the green curtain. A psychologist would attribute this to _____
   a. perceptual constancy.   c. contrast effects.
   b. visual paradoxes.   d. threshold differences.

5. Which of the following phenomena best illustrates that perception is an active process?
   a. bottom-up processing   c. top-down processing
   b. motion parallax   d. parietal senses

6. How is visual information processed by the brain?
   a. It is processed by the parietal lobe, which relays the information to the temporal lobe.
   b. It is processed entirely within the frontal lobe.
   c. It is processed by the occipital lobe, which projects to the thalamus, which projects to a succession of areas in the cortex.
   d. If the information is abstract, it is processed by the cortex; if it is concrete, it is processed by the thalamus.

7. Which of the following is true about the proximal stimulus in visual perception?
   a. It is identical to the distal stimulus because the retina produces a faithful reproduction of the perceptual world.

   b. It is upside-down, flat, distorted, and obscured by blood vessels.
   c. It is black and white and consists of very sparse information about horizontal and vertical edges.
   d. It contains information about the degree of convergence of the two eyes.

8. Which sensory information is not paired below with the cortical lobe that is primarily responsible for processing it?
   a. visual information, occipital lobe
   b. speech, frontal lobe
   c. body senses, parietal lobe
   d. hearing, central sulcus lobe

9. The researcher David Hubel is best known for _____
   a. mapping visual receptor cells.
   b. discovering subjective contours.
   c. identifying the neural pathways by which body sensations occur.
   d. realizing that hearing and smell originate from the same brain area.

10. The shrinking-square illusion demonstrated by Misha Pavel relies on the processing of which kinds of feature?
    a. edges and corners
    b. colour and texture
    c. torque and angular momentum
    d. density gradients and motion

QUESTIONS TO CONSIDER

1. Choose a familiar context, like a grocery store, and describe how the Gestalt principles of perceptual organization are used to help people perceive objects and group them.

2. Although the neural pathways serving perception are similar in all of us, our internal perceptual experience could theoretically differ. What sorts of differences in our experiences can you imagine as being possible? What sorts of differences would you think would be unlikely?

6

Mind, Consciousness, and Alternate States

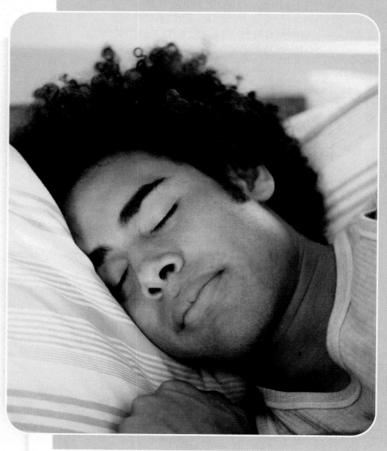

As you begin reading this chapter, take a moment to think about a favourite past event. Now think about what you would like to have happen tomorrow or the next day. Where did these memories of the past and projections into the future *come* from and when did they *arrive*? Although you obviously have a vast body of information stored in your brain, it is very unlikely that the thoughts we asked you to have were "in mind" just as you were sitting down to read your psychology text. Therefore, you might feel comfortable saying that the thoughts arrived in your consciousness—and that they came from some part of your brain that was not then conscious. But how did these particular thoughts come to mind? Did you actually consider several different memories or options for the future? That is, were you consciously aware of making a choice? Or did thoughts somehow just emerge—by virtue of some set of unconscious operations—into your consciousness?

This series of questions provides a preview of the major topics of Chapter 6. In this chapter, we will address a series of questions: What is ordinary conscious awareness? What determines the contents of your consciousness? Why do you need consciousness? Can unconscious mental events really influence your thoughts, emotions, and behaviour? How does consciousness change over the course of a day-and-night cycle, and how can you intentionally alter your state of consciousness? The budding psychologist in you will also want to know how aspects of mind can be studied scientifically. How can you externalize the internal, make public the private, and precisely measure subjective experiences?

Why is self-awareness considered such an important aspect of consciousness?

The Contents of Consciousness

We must start by admitting that the term **consciousness** is ambiguous. We can use the term to refer to a general state of mind *or* to its specific contents: Sometimes you say you were "conscious" in contrast to being "unconscious" (for example, being under anesthesia or asleep); at other times, you say you were conscious—*aware*—of certain information or actions. There is, in fact, a certain consistency here—to be conscious of any particular information, you must be conscious. In this chapter, when we speak of the *contents* of consciousness, we mean the body of information of which you are aware.

AWARENESS AND CONSCIOUSNESS

Some of the earliest research in psychology concerned the contents of consciousness. The nature of consciousness is, in fact, at the root of early theorizing about the nature of the mind and its influence on the body. René Descartes, a 17th-century French philosopher, argued that the experiences of the mind and the body are entirely separate (this concept is known as *Cartesian dualism*), but that mind and body interact in important ways. According to Descartes, not only could the body influence how people perceived events, but the conscious mind could also affect the body—a perspective that has influenced psychological

research over the years. As psychology gradually diverged from philosophy in the 1800s, it became the science of the mind. Wundt and Titchener used introspection to explore the contents of the conscious mind, and William James observed his own stream of consciousness (see Chapter 1). In fact, on the very first page of his classic 1892 text, *Psychology*, James endorsed as a definition of psychology "*the description and explanation of states of consciousness as such.*"

Your ordinary waking consciousness includes your perceptions, thoughts, feelings, images, and desires at a given moment—all the mental activity on which you are focusing your attention. You are conscious of both what you are doing and the fact that you are doing it. At times, you are conscious of the realization that others are observing, evaluating, and reacting to what you are doing. A *sense of self* comes out of the experience of watching yourself from this privileged "insider" position. Taken together, these various mental activities form the contents of consciousness—all the experiences you are consciously aware of at a particular time (Legrand, 2007).

We have defined the general types of information that *might* be conscious at a particular place and time, but what determines what is conscious right now? Were you, for example, aware of your breathing just now? Probably not; its control is part of *nonconscious processes*. Were you thinking about your last vacation or about the author of *Hamlet*? Again, probably not; control of such thoughts is part of *preconscious memories*. Were you aware of background noises, such as the ticking of a clock, the hum of traffic, or the buzzing of a fluorescent light? It would

---

consciousness A state of awareness of internal events and the external environment.

At any given time, thoughts about your job, your parents, or your hungry pet may flow below the level of consciousness until something occurs to focus your attention on one of these topics. Why are these memories considered *preconscious* rather than *unconscious*?

be difficult to be aware of all this and still pay full attention to the meaning of the material in this chapter; these stimuli are part of *unattended information*. Finally, there may be types of information that are *unconscious*—not readily accessible to conscious awareness—such as the set of grammatical rules that enable you to understand this sentence. Let's examine each of these types of awareness.

Nonconscious Processes A range of **nonconscious** bodily activities takes place that rarely, if ever, impinges on consciousness. An example of nonconscious processes at work is the regulation of blood pressure. Your nervous system monitors physiological information to detect and act on changes continually, without your awareness. At certain times, some ordinarily nonconscious activities can be made conscious: You can, for example, choose to exercise conscious control over your pattern of breathing. Even so, your nervous system takes care of many important functions without requiring conscious resources.

Preconscious Memories Memories accessible to consciousness only after something calls your attention to them are known as **preconscious memories**. The storehouse of memory is filled with an incredible amount of information, such as your general knowledge of language, sports, or geography, and recollections of your personally experienced events. Preconscious memories function silently in the background of your mind until a situation arises in which they are consciously necessary (as when we asked you to call to mind a favourite past event). Memory will be discussed in detail in Chapter 8.

---

nonconscious Not typically available to consciousness or memory.

preconscious memories Memories that are not currently conscious but that can easily be called into consciousness when necessary.

Unattended Information At any given time, you are surrounded by a vast amount of stimulation. As we described in Chapter 5, you can focus your attention on only a small part of it. What you focus on, in combination with the memories it evokes, will determine, to a large extent, what is in consciousness. Nevertheless, you sometimes have an unconscious representation of information that is not the focus of your attention. Recall this scenario from Chapter 5: At a noisy party, you try to focus attention on your attractive date and remain seemingly oblivious to a nearby conversation—until you overhear your name mentioned. Suddenly you are aware that you must have been monitoring the conversation—in some unconscious way—to have detected that special signal amid the noise (Wood & Cowan, 1995a).

The Unconscious You typically recognize the existence of *unconscious* information when you cannot explain some behaviour by virtue of forces that were conscious at the time of the behaviour. An initial theory of unconscious forces was developed by Sigmund Freud, who argued that certain life experiences—traumatic memories and taboo desires—are sufficiently threatening that special mental processes permanently banish them from consciousness. (We will describe these processes in Chapter 14.) Freud believed that when the content of unacceptable ideas or motives is *repressed*—put out of consciousness—the strong feelings associated with the thoughts still remain and influence behaviour. Freud's "discovery" of the unconscious contradicted a long tradition of Western thought. From the time the English philosopher John Locke (1690/1975) wrote his classic text on the mind, *An Essay Concerning Human Understanding*, most thinkers firmly believed that rational beings had access to all the activities of their own minds. Freud's initial hypothesis about the existence of unconscious mental processes was considered outrageous by his contemporaries (Dennett, 1987). We will revisit Freud's ideas when we discuss the origin of your unique personality in Chapter 14.

Many psychologists now use the term *unconscious* to refer to information and processes that are more benign than the types of thoughts that Freud suggested needed to be repressed (McGovern & Baars, 2007). For example, many types of ordinary language processing rely on unconscious processes. Consider this sentence (Vu, Kellas, Metcalf, & Herman, 2000):

[She investigated the bark.

How did you interpret this sentence? Did you picture some woman looking after a dog or examining a tree? Because the word *bark* is ambiguous—and the sentence context provides little help—you can only guess at what the writer meant. Now consider the same sentence in a slightly larger context:

[The botanist looked for a fungus. She investigated the bark.

Did you find the sentence easier to understand in this context? If you did, it is because your unconscious understanding of language used the extra context to make a very swift choice between the two meanings of *bark*.

With this example, we demonstrate that processes operating below the level of consciousness often affect your behaviour—in this case, the ease with which you came to a clear understanding of the sentence. We have thus shifted subtly from discussing the contents of consciousness to discussing the functions of consciousness. Before we take up that topic in detail, however, we will briefly describe two ways in which the contents of consciousness can be studied.

STUDYING THE CONTENTS OF CONSCIOUSNESS

To study consciousness, researchers have had to devise methodologies to make deeply private experiences overtly measurable. One method is a new variation on Wundt and Titchener's practice of introspection. Experimental participants are asked to speak aloud as they work through a variety of complex tasks. They report, in as much detail as possible, the sequence of thoughts they experience while they complete the tasks. The participants' reports, called **think-aloud protocols**, are used to document the mental strategies and representations of knowledge the participants employ to do the task. For example, researchers collected think-aloud protocols to understand the different strategies experts and novices bring to their judgments about product designs (Locher, Frens, & Overbeeke, 2008).

In the **experience-sampling method**, participants wear devices that signal to them when they should provide reports about what they are feeling and thinking. For example, in one methodology, participants wear electronic pagers. A radio transmitter activates the pager at various random times each day for a week or more. Whenever the pager signals, participants may be asked to respond to questions such as "How well were you concentrating?" In this way, researchers can keep a running record of participants' thoughts, awareness, and focuses of attention as they go about their everyday lives (Hektner & Csikszentmihalyi, 2002). Consider an experiment that used handheld computers to obtain experience samples:

[The researchers wished to determine how often people's thoughts focus on comparisons between their current reality

TABLE 6.1 Types of Comparisons in People's Thoughts	
Type	**Example**
Social	"I'm a better basketball player than Tom."
Counterfactual	"If I'd left earlier, I could have gotten here on time."
Temporal—past	"I got more sleep when I was in high school."
Temporal—future	"My sister is going to start making new friends."

From A. Summerville & N. J. Roese, Dare to compare: Fact-based versus simulation-based comparison in daily life, *Journal of Experimental Social Psychology, 44*, pp. 664–671, Copyright (2008) with permission from Elsevier.

and other possibilities (Summerville & Roese, 2007). At seven random times daily for two weeks, 34 participants were signaled by handheld computers to report what they were thinking in the moment. If the thoughts centred on comparisons, the participants placed them in the categories indicated in **Table 6.1**. The researchers found that 12 percent of the participants' thoughts were comparisons, which, as they noted, was "a remarkably large proportion given the sheer variety of mental experience" (p. 668). The comparisons were fairly evenly distributed across the four categories in Table 6.1. In addition, when participants' thoughts turned to changing the past (counterfactual comparisons) or contemplating the future (temporal—future comparisons), they were most often thoughts about how circumstances might have been or still could be better.

Have you ever noticed how often these types of comparisons enter into your consciousness? The experience-sampling method allows researchers to provide a nuanced account of what and how people think about their lives.

If you take a quick look around the room right now, you will appreciate once more how many objects in your environment are readily available to, but are not part of, the contents of your consciousness—until you inspect the room. You can carry out the same quick review of your memory to demonstrate how much information you have stored beyond the particular focus of your conscious attention. Techniques such as think-aloud protocols and experience sampling allow researchers to determine—for particular tasks and for particular times—which subset of all available information is present in an individual's consciousness.

---

think-aloud protocols Reports made by experimental participants of the mental processes and strategies they use while working on a task.

experience-sampling method An experimental method that assists researchers in describing the typical contents of consciousness; participants are asked to record what they are feeling and thinking whenever signaled to do so.

❶ What is meant by a preconscious memory?

❷ How did Freud believe information became unconscious?

❸ How do researchers obtain think-aloud protocols?

CRITICAL THINKING Recall the experiment on comparisons. Why is it important that the experience samples be taken at random moments?

The Functions of Consciousness

When we address the question of the *functions* of consciousness, we are trying to understand why we *need* consciousness: What does it add to our human experience? In this section, we describe the importance of consciousness to human survival and social function.

THE USES OF CONSCIOUSNESS

Human consciousness was forged in the crucible of competition with the most hostile force in its evolutionary environment—other humans. The human mind may have evolved as a consequence of the extreme *sociability* of human ancestors, which was perhaps originally a group defence against predators and a means to exploit resources more efficiently. However, close group living then created new demands for co-operative as well as competitive abilities. Natural selection favoured those who could think, plan, and imagine alternative realities that could promote both bonding with kin and victory over adversaries. Those who developed language and tools won the grand prize of survival of the fittest mind—and, fortunately, passed it on to us (Terrace & Metcalfe, 2005).

Because consciousness evolved, you should not be surprised that it provides a range of functions that aid in the survival of the species (Bering & Bjorklund, 2007). Consciousness also plays an important role in allowing for the construction of both personal and culturally shared realities.

Aiding Survival From a biological perspective, consciousness probably evolved because it helped individuals make sense of environmental information and use that information in planning the most appropriate and effective actions. Usually, you are faced with a sensory-information overload. William James described the massive amount of information that strikes the sensory receptors as a "blooming, buzzing confusion" assailing you from all sides. Consciousness helps you adapt to your environment by making sense of this profusion of confusion in three ways.

First, consciousness reduces the flow of stimulus input by restricting what you notice and what you focus on. You might recognize this *restrictive* function of consciousness from the discussion of *attention* in Chapter 5. Consciousness helps you tune out much of the information that is irrelevant to your immediate goals and purposes. Suppose you decide to take a walk to enjoy a spring day. You notice trees blooming, birds singing, and children playing. If, all at once, a snarling dog appears on the scene, you use consciousness to restrict your attention to that dog and assess the level of danger. The restrictive function also applies to information you draw from your internal storehouse of information. When, at the outset of this chapter, we asked you to think about a favourite past event, we were asking you to use your consciousness to restrict your mental attention to a single past memory.

A second function of consciousness is *selective storage*. Even within the category of information to which you consciously attend, not all of it has continuing relevance to your ongoing concerns. After your encounter with the snarling dog, you might stop yourself and think, "I want to remember not to walk down this block." Consciousness allows you to selectively store—commit to memory—information that you want to analyze, interpret, and act on in the future; consciousness allows you to classify events and experiences as relevant or irrelevant to personal needs by selecting some and ignoring others. When we consider memory processes in Chapter 8, we will see that not all the information you add to memory requires conscious processing. Still, conscious memories have different properties—and involve different brain regions—than other types of memories.

A third function of consciousness is to make you stop, think, consider alternatives based on past knowledge, and imagine various consequences. This *planning* function enables you to suppress strong desires when they conflict with moral, ethical, or practical concerns. With this kind of consciousness you can plan a route for your next walk that avoids that snarling dog. Because consciousness gives you a broad time perspective in which to frame potential actions, you can call on knowledge of the past and expectations for the future to influence your current decisions. For all these reasons, consciousness gives you great potential for flexible, appropriate responses to the changing demands in your life.

Personal and Cultural Constructions of Reality No two people interpret a situation in exactly the same way (Higgins & Pittman, 2008). Your personal construction of reality is your unique interpretation of a current situation based on your general knowledge; memories of past experiences; current needs, values, and beliefs; and future goals. Each person attends more to certain features of the stimulus environment than to others precisely because his or her personal construction of reality has been formed from a selection of unique inputs. When your personal construction of reality remains relatively stable, your sense of self has continuity over time.

Individual differences in personal constructions of reality are even greater when people have grown up in different cultures, lived in different environments within a culture, or faced different survival tasks. The opposite is also true; because the people of a given culture share many of the same experiences, they often have similar constructions of reality. *Cultural constructions of reality* are ways of thinking about the world that are shared by most members of a particular group of people. When a member of a society develops a personal construction of reality that fits in with the cultural construction, it is affirmed by the culture; at the same time, it affirms the cultural construction. In Chapter 14, we will describe more fully the relationship between the personal and the cultural sense of self.

STUDYING THE FUNCTIONS OF CONSCIOUSNESS

People's behaviour is most often influenced by both conscious and unconscious processes. Many functions of consciousness include implicit comparisons with what remains unconscious. That is, conscious processes often affect or are affected by unconscious processes. To study the functions of consciousness, researchers often conduct research that demonstrates the different products of conscious and unconscious processes (McGovern & Baars, 2007).

For example, researchers have argued that people may bring either unconscious or conscious processes to bear on the many decisions they face in life (Evans, 2008). Depending on which system of processes they use, people's responses can be quite different. Consider the domain of moral reasoning (to which we will return in Chapter 11). How would you respond to the classic "crying baby" dilemma in which one "must decide whether to smother one's own baby in order to prevent enemy soldiers from finding and killing oneself, one's baby, and several others" (Greene et al., 2008, p. 1147). When people first face this dilemma, their gut response—the product of unconscious processes—is that they could never smother their own child. However, when people face this problem with conscious deliberation, they often conclude that they must make the sacrifice to save the larger number of individuals.

To demonstrate that this shift reflects the use of conscious processes, researchers asked participants to consider dilemmas of this sort in two different circumstances (Greene et al., 2008). In one condition, participants read the dilemmas on a computer screen and indicated a "yes" or "no" judgment to a possible response (e.g., "Is it appropriate for you to smother your child in order to save yourself and the other townspeople?") as swiftly as possible. In the second condition, participants also read and responded to the dilemmas. However, they simultaneously had to monitor a stream of numbers scrolling across the computer screen and press a button every time they saw the number 5. The purpose of this second task is to overload participants'

conscious processes. This simultaneous task should have made it much more difficult for them to use conscious processes to reason about the moral dilemmas. In fact, when participants had this extra load, it took them much longer to give the "yes" responses to the moral dilemmas that represented the use of conscious reasoning. Thus, one way to study the function of consciousness is to demonstrate how people's responses change when conscious processes are not, in fact, allowed to function normally.

Another way to study the functions of consciousness is to determine which of the many tasks you carry out on a day-to-day basis require conscious intervention. To give you an example, we want you to put your book down for a moment and try to find an object in the room that is *red*. Let's assume that there is, in fact, a red object in your room. Under most circumstances, you should have felt as if your eyes were drawn to that object without any conscious effort. Research confirms that people can search for certain basic features of objects such as colour, shape, and size with little or no conscious attention (Wolfe, 2003). Now try to find an object that is both *blue* and *red*. Chances are you had a very different sense of how much conscious effort was involved. Under most circumstances, people have to use conscious attention to find an object that has a combination of two features.

We provide another example of the uses of conscious attention in **Figure 6.1**. In Part A, try to find the yellow and blue item. In Part B, try to find the yellow house with blue windows. Wasn't this second task much easier? Performance is much less affected by all the extra objects in the picture when the two colours are organized into *parts* and *wholes* (Wolfe, Friedman-Hill, & Bilsky, 1994). Could you feel your conscious attention being more engaged when we asked you to find the yellow and blue item? From results of this sort, researchers are assembling a global view of the circumstances in which consciousness functions.

We have seen how the contents and functions of consciousness are defined and studied. We turn now to ordinary and then extraordinary alterations in consciousness.

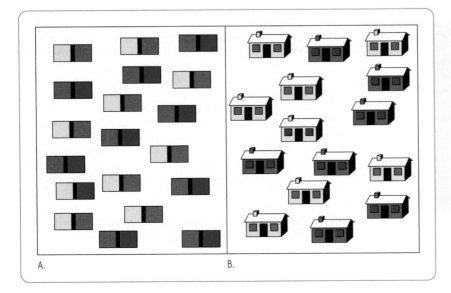

FIGURE 6.1 Search for the Conjunction of Two Colours

(A) Find the yellow and blue item. (B) Find the yellow house with blue windows. (A) Search is very inefficient when the conjunction is between the colours of two parts of a target. (B) However, search is much easier when the conjunction is between the colour of the whole item and the colour of one of its parts.

Adapted with permission from Jerome Kuhl, from "Features and Objects in Visual Processing," by Anne Triesman, *Scientific American*, November 1986, p. 116.

Sleep and Dreams

Almost every day of your life you experience a rather profound change in consciousness: When you decide it is time to end your day, you surrender yourself to sleep—and while you sleep you will undoubtedly dream. A third of your life is spent sleeping, with your muscles in a state of "benign paralysis" and your brain humming with activity. We begin this section by considering the general biological rhythms of wakefulness and sleeping. We then focus more directly on the physiology of sleeping. Finally, we examine the major mental activity that accompanies sleep—dreaming—and explore the role dreams play in human psychology.

CIRCADIAN RHYTHMS

All creatures are influenced by nature's rhythms of day and night. Your body is attuned to a time cycle known as a **circadian rhythm**: Your arousal levels, metabolism, heart rate, body temperature, and hormonal activity ebb and flow according to the ticking of your internal clock. For the most part, these activities reach their peak during the day—usually during the afternoon—and hit their low point at night while you sleep. Research suggests that the clock your body uses is not exactly in synchrony with the clock on the wall: Without the corrective effects of external time cues, the human internal "pacemaker" establishes a cycle that averages 24.18 hours long (Czeisler et al., 1999). The exposure to sunlight you get each day helps you make the small adjustment to a 24-hour cycle. Information about sunlight is gathered through your eyes, but receptors for regulation of circadian rhythms are not the same receptors that allow you to see the world (Vansteensel, Stephan, & Meijer, 2008). For example, animals without rods and cones (see Chapter 5) still sense light in a way that enables them to maintain their circadian rhythms (Van Gelder, 2003).

Life circumstances that bring about a mismatch between your biological clock and your sleep cycle affect how you feel and act (Blatter & Cajochen, 2007). For example, individuals who work night shifts often experience both physical and cognitive difficulties because their circadian rhythms are disrupted (Boivin, Tremblay, & James, 2007). Even after long periods on the night

shift, most people are unable to adjust their circadian rhythms to overcome these negative effects (Folkard, 2008). People also experience disruptions when they engage in long-distance air travel. When people fly across time zones, they may experience jet lag, a condition whose symptoms include fatigue, irresistible sleepiness, and subsequent unusual sleep–wake schedules. Jet lag occurs because the internal circadian rhythm is out of phase with the normal temporal environment (Waterhouse, Reilly, Atkinson, & Edwards, 2007). For example, your body says it's 2 a.m.—and thus is at a low point on many physiological measures—when local time requires you to act as if it is noon.

What variables influence jet lag? The direction of travel and the number of time zones passed through are the most important variables. Travelling eastbound creates greater jet lag than westbound because your biological clock can be more readily extended than shortened, as required on eastbound trips. (In other words, it is easier to stay awake longer than it is to fall asleep sooner.) When healthy volunteers were flown back and forth between Europe and North America, they reached their peak performance on standard tasks within two to four days after westbound flights but nine days after eastbound travel (Klein & Wegmann, 1974).

If you've ever suffered from jet lag, you might have been advised to take a dose of the hormone *melatonin*. Melatonin acts in the brain to help regulate cycles of waking and sleep. People who take melatonin after long flights experience fewer sleep disruptions (Arendt & Skene, 2005). The general advice that emerges from various studies is that travellers should take melatonin at bedtime in their new time zone both on the day of the flight and for four or five subsequent days (Pandi-Perumal, Srinivasan, Spence, & Cardinali, 2007). Melatonin also appears to help night-shift workers adjust their cycles of sleeping and waking (Pandi-Perumal et al., 2007).

Circadian rhythms are also highly affected by exposure to light, and researchers have been exploring the possibilities of helping people adjust their circadian rhythms by exposing them to light. These interventions have often proved successful for night-shift workers (Fahey & Zee, 2006) and air travellers (Paul et al., 2009).

THE SLEEP CYCLE

About a third of your circadian rhythm is devoted to that period of behavioural quiescence called *sleep*. Most of what is known about sleep concerns the electrical activities of the brain. The methodological breakthrough for the study of sleep came in 1937, with the application of a technology that records the brain-wave activity of the sleeper in the form of an electroencephalogram (EEG). The EEG measures the electrical activities of neurons in the brain, which provides an objective, ongoing measure of the way brain activity varies when people are awake or asleep. With the EEG, researchers discovered that brain waves change in form at the onset of sleep and show further systematic, predictable changes during the entire sleep period (Loomis, Harvey, & Hobart, 1937). The next significant discovery in sleep research was that bursts of **rapid eye movements (REM)** occur at periodic intervals during sleep (Aserinsky & Kleitman, 1953). The time when a sleeper is not showing REM is known as **non-REM (NREM) sleep**. We will see in a later section that REM and NREM sleep have significance for one of the night's major activities—dreaming.

---

circadian rhythm A consistent pattern of cyclical body activities, usually lasting 24 to 25 hours and determined by an internal biological clock.

rapid eye movements (REM) A behavioural sign of the phase of sleep during which the sleeper is likely to be experiencing dreamlike mental activity.

non-REM (NREM) sleep The period during which a sleeper does not show rapid eye movement (REM); characterized by less dream activity than during REM sleep.

Let's track your brain waves through the night. As you prepare to go to bed, an EEG records that your brain waves are moving along at a rate of about 14 cycles per second (cps). Once you are comfortably in bed, you begin to relax, and your brain waves slow down to a rate of about 8 to 12 cps. When you fall asleep, you begin a fairly predictable sequence of sleep known as the *sleep cycle*, with each stage showing a distinct EEG pattern. In stage 1 sleep, the EEG shows brain waves of about 3 to 7 cps. During stage 2, the EEG is characterized by *sleep spindles*, minute bursts of electrical activity of 12 to 16 cps. In the next two stages (3 and 4) of sleep, you enter into a very deep state of relaxed sleep. Your brain waves slow to about 1 to 2 cps, and your breathing and heart rate decrease. In a final stage, the electrical activity of your brain increases; your EEG looks very similar to those recorded during stages 1 and 2. It is during this stage that you will experience REM sleep, and you will begin to dream (see **Figure 6.2**). (Because the EEG pattern during REM sleep resembles that of an awake person, REM sleep was originally termed *paradoxical sleep*.)

Cycling through the first four stages of sleep, which are NREM sleep, requires about 90 minutes. REM sleep lasts for about 10 minutes. Over the course of a night's sleep, you pass through this 100-minute cycle four to six times (see **Figure 6.3**).

FIGURE 6.2 EEG Patterns Reflecting the Stages of a Regular Night's Sleep

Each sleep stage is defined by characteristic patterns of brain activity.

With each cycle, the amount of time you spend in deep sleep (stages 3 and 4) decreases, and the amount of time you spend in REM sleep increases. During the last cycle, you may spend as long as an hour in REM sleep. NREM sleep accounts for 75 to 80 percent of total sleep time, and REM sleep makes up 20 to 25 percent of sleep time.

Not all individuals sleep for the same amount of time. Although a genetic sleep need is programmed into the human species, the actual amount of sleep each individual obtains is highly affected by conscious actions. People actively control sleep length in a number of ways, such as by staying up late or using alarm clocks. Sleep duration is also controlled by circadian rhythms; that is, the time one goes to sleep influences sleep duration. Getting adequate amounts of NREM and REM sleep is likely only when you standardize your bedtime and rising time across the entire week, including weekends. In that way, the time you spend in bed is likely to correspond closely to the sleepy phase of your circadian rhythm.

Of further interest is the dramatic change in patterns of sleep that occurs over an individual's lifetime (shown in **Figure 6.4**). You started out in this world sleeping for about 16 hours a day, with nearly half of that time spent in REM sleep. By age 50, you may sleep only 6 hours and spend only about 20 percent of the time in REM sleep. Young adults typically sleep 7 to 8 hours, with about 20 percent REM sleep.

The change in sleep patterns with age does not mean that sleep becomes less important as you grow older. One study followed healthy older adults—those in their 60s through 80s—to see if there was a relationship between their sleep behaviours and how long they remained alive (Dew et al., 2003). The researchers found that people who had higher sleep efficiency—a measure based on the amount of time they were asleep divided by the amount of time they spent in bed—were likely to live longer. This result leads directly to our next question: Why do people need sleep?

WHY SLEEP?

The orderly progression of stages of sleep in humans and other animals suggests that there is an evolutionary basis and a biological need for sleep. People function quite well when they get the time-honoured seven to eight hours of sleep a night (Foster & Wulff, 2005; Hublin, Partinen, Koskenvuo, & Kaprio, 2007). Why do humans sleep so much, and what functions do types of sleep (NREM and REM) serve?

The two most general functions for NREM sleep may be *conservation* and *restoration* (J. M. Siegel, 2005). NREM sleep may have evolved because it enabled animals to conserve energy at times when there was no need to forage for food, search for mates, or work. However, sleep also puts animals at risk for attacks from predators. Researchers speculate that cycles of brain activity across a period of sleep (see Figure 6.2) may have evolved to help animals minimize the risk of predation; some patterns of brain activity might allow animals to retain relatively greater awareness of activity in the environment even while they are asleep (Lesku et al., 2008). Why would animals put themselves at risk by sleeping at all? The answer quite likely lies in the restorative properties of NREM sleep. For example, when brains are hard at work during waking states, oxygen metabolism produces by-products that are ultimately damaging to neurons in areas of the brain such as the brain stem, hippocampus, and hypothalamus (see Chapter 4). NREM sleep provides the brain

FIGURE 6.3 The Stages of Sleep

A typical pattern of the stages of sleep during a single night includes deeper sleep in the early cycles but more time in REM in the later cycles.

From "The March of Sleep Cycles," in *Sleep,* by J. Allan Hobson. Copyright © 1989 by J. Allan Hobson, M.D. Reprinted by permission of Henry Holt and Company, LLC.

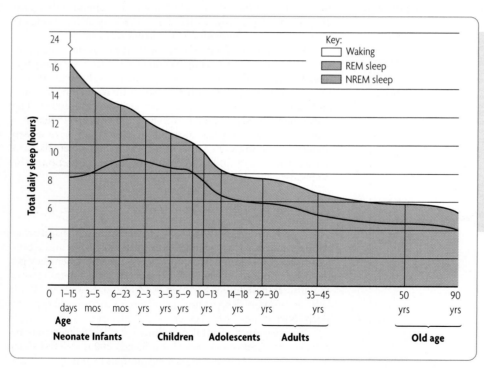

FIGURE 6.4 Patterns of Human Sleep over a Lifetime

The graph shows changes with age in total amounts of daily REM sleep and NREM sleep. Note that the amount of REM sleep decreases considerably over the years, and NREM diminishes less sharply.

Reprinted with permission from Roffwarg et al., "Ontogenetic Development of the Human Sleep-Dream Cycle," *Science, 152,* 604–619, 1966. Copyright © 1966 AAAS.

with an opportunity to interrupt that damage and undertake repairs of brain cells (J. M. Siegel, 2005).

If you were to be deprived of REM sleep for a night, you would have more REM sleep than usual the next night, suggesting that REM sleep also serves some necessary functions. For example, it appears that, during infancy, the brain activity that defines REM sleep is necessary for the development of normal function in the visual system and perhaps other sensory and motor systems (J. M. Siegel, 2005). For adults, research has focused on the role REM sleep plays in learning and memory (Walker & Stickgold, 2006). Consider an experiment conducted at Trent University in which participants were asked to learn a new task:

At the beginning of the experiment, 24 participants spent a night in a sleep lab so that the researchers could obtain a baseline measure for the amount of REM sleep they experienced in a night (Smith, Nixon, & Nader, 2004). The next evening, 6 participants were assigned to a control group. They spent the evening in the lab, but they carried out no special activities. The other 18 participants were asked to learn a new task—a problem-solving task called the Tower of Hanoi. Participants' REM sleep was then assessed for a second time. On this second night, participants in the task-learning group had more intense REM sleep compared to their baseline—they experienced both more rapid eye movements as a percentage of the number of minutes of REM sleep. Members of the control group did not show any comparable changes in their REM sleep. After a week had passed, participants in the training group returned to attempt the Tower of Hanoi once again. The participants generally showed improvement on the task from the initial test to this retest. However, those individuals who showed the greatest intensity of REM sleep after the training session also showed the greatest improvement on the Tower of Hanoi.

This experiment suggests that REM sleep provides a context in which the brain solidifies its attainment of new tasks. It is important to note that NREM sleep also plays a role in the consolidation of learning and memory. Researchers have demonstrated that performance on some tasks is marked by increases in stage 3 and stage 4 sleep early in the night and REM sleep late in the night (Walker & Stickgold, 2006).

After reading about all the important functions that sleep serves, it probably won't surprise you to learn that there are some serious consequences when people get too little sleep. Sleep deprivation has a range of negative effects on cognitive performance, including difficulties with attention and working memory (Banks & Dinges, 2007). Sleep deprivation also impairs people's ability to perform motor skills. For example, drivers who have been sleep deprived are more likely to have car accidents than their well-rested peers. This fact has led some commentators to suggest that engineers should invent a measurement device for excess sleepiness that would parallel the Breathalyzer for excess alcohol (Yegneswaran & Shapiro, 2007).

SLEEP DISORDERS

It would be great if you could always take a good night's sleep for granted. Unfortunately, many people suffer from sleep disorders that pose a serious burden to their personal lives and careers. Disordered sleep can also have societal consequences. Of those individuals whose work schedules include night shifts, more than half nod off at least once a week on the job. This is a worrisome statistic given that nearly 28 percent of employed Canadians work the night shift or engage in other types of shift work (Williams, 2008). Some of the world's most serious industrial accidents have occurred during late evening hours, a time during which key personnel failed to function optimally as a result of insufficient sleep. Even a small change in our sleeping habits can make a significant difference in our alertness. University of British Columbia psychologist **Stanley Coren** demonstrated that even the slight change in our internal clock associated with the one-hour sleep loss we experience when we put our clocks forward in the spring for daylight saving time is associated with a significant increase in traffic accidents and deaths (Coren, 1996). Because sleep disorders affect many students, we will review them here. Their origins involve biological, environmental, and psychological forces. As you read, keep in mind that sleep disorders vary in severity.

Insomnia When people are dissatisfied with their amount or quality of sleep, they are suffering from **insomnia**. This chronic failure to get adequate sleep is characterized by an inability to fall asleep quickly, frequent arousals during sleep, or early-morning awakening. The rates of insomnia in the Canadian population are quite alarming, with more than 3.3 million Canadians (13.4 percent of the population aged 15 or older) dealing with insomnia (Tjepkema, 2005). Insomnia is a complex disorder caused by a variety of psychological, environmental, and biological factors (Drake, Schwartz, & Roth, 2008). However, when insomniacs are studied in sleep laboratories, the objective quantity and quality of their actual sleep vary considerably, from disturbed sleep to normal sleep. Research has revealed that many insomniacs who complain of lack of sleep actually show completely normal physiological patterns of sleep—a condition described as *subjective insomnia*. For example, in one study, 38 percent of the participants who reported that they suffered from insomnia actually had normal sleep (Edinger et al., 2000). Equally interesting, the same study showed detectable sleep disturbances in 43 percent of the participants who had no complaints of insomnia. The discrepancies may result from differences in the cognitions and emotions that surround sleep (Espie, 2002). People who experience insomnia—or those who only think they do—may be less able to banish intrusive thoughts and feelings from consciousness even while they are trying to sleep.

Narcolepsy **Narcolepsy** is a sleep disorder characterized by periodic sleep during the daytime. It is often combined with *cataplexy*, muscle weakness or a loss of muscle control brought on by emotional excitement (such as laughing, anger, fear, surprise, or hunger) that causes the afflicted person to fall down suddenly. When they fall asleep, narcoleptics enter REM sleep almost immediately. This rush to REM causes them to experience—and be consciously aware of—vivid dream images or sometimes terrifying hallucinations. Narcolepsy affects about one of every 2000 individuals. Because narcolepsy runs in families, scientists believe the disease has a genetic basis (Mahowald & Schenck, 2005). Narcolepsy often has a negative social and psychological impact on sufferers because of their desire to avoid the embarrassment caused by sudden bouts of sleep (Ervik, Abdelnoor, Heier, Ramberg, & Strand, 2006).

Nightmares and Sleep Terrors When a dream frightens you by making you feel helpless or out of control, you are having a nightmare. For most people nightmares are relatively infrequent. In one sample of 89 Canadian undergraduates who kept dream logs daily for one month, the average number of nightmares reported in the month was 0.48. That monthly average corresponds to a rate of 5.76 nightmares each year (Zadra & Donderi, 2000). However, some people experience nightmares more frequently, sometimes as often as every night. Children, for example, are more likely than adults to experience nightmares. The peak time for nightmares is between ages 3 and 6, when a majority of children have them at least occasionally (Mason & Pack, 2007). Also, people who have experienced traumatic events, such as rape or war, may have repetitive nightmares that force them to relive some aspects of their trauma (Davis, Byrd, Rhudy, & Wright, 2007). This

---

insomnia The chronic inability to sleep normally; symptoms include difficulty in falling asleep, frequent waking, inability to return to sleep, and early-morning awakening.

narcolepsy A sleep disorder characterized by an irresistible compulsion to sleep during the daytime.

What is the relationship between actual sleep patterns and people's perceptions of insomnia?

general pattern was well documented in research by **Kathryn Belicki** and **Marion Cuddy** of Brock University (1996) who showed that individuals who have been sexually abused are more likely to report frequent nightmares and sleep terrors, and will experience greater disruption of their sleep than will members of non-traumatized groups. Furthermore, their nightmares will frequently involve explicit violence and are more likely to have sexual content.

Sleep terrors (or night terrors) are instances in which sleepers wake up suddenly in a state of extreme arousal, often marked by a panicky scream (DSM-IV-TR, 2000). These episodes typically occur during NREM sleep in the first third of a night's sleep. Most people who have sleep terrors have no memory of the episodes. Sleep terrors are most common during childhood, with the greatest number occurring between ages 5 and 7 (Mason & Pack, 2007). Between the ages of 4 and 12, about 3 percent of children experience sleep terrors. They occur in less than 1 percent of adults. Researchers have begun to document distinctive patterns of brain activity that identify children at particular risk for sleep terrors (Bruni et al., 2008).

Sleep Apnea **Sleep apnea** is an upper-respiratory sleep disorder in which a person stops breathing while asleep. When this happens, the blood's oxygen level drops and emergency hormones are secreted, causing the sleeper to awaken and begin breathing again. Although most people have a few such apnea episodes a night, someone with sleep apnea disorder can have hundreds of such cycles. Sometimes apnea episodes frighten the sleeper, but often they are so brief that the sleeper fails to

attribute accumulating sleepiness to them (Pagel, 2008). Sleep apnea affects roughly 2 percent of adults (Sonnad et al., 2003).

Sleep apnea also occurs frequently among premature infants, who sometimes need physical stimulation to start breathing again. Because of their underdeveloped respiratory system, these infants must remain attached to monitors in intensive care nurseries as long as the problem continues.

Somnambulism Individuals who suffer from **somnambulism**, or *sleepwalking*, leave their beds and wander while still remaining asleep. Sleepwalking is more frequent among children than it is among adults (Mason & Pack, 2007). For example, studies have found that about 7 percent of children sleepwalk (Nevéus, Cnattingius, Olsson, & Hetta, 2001) but only about 2 percent of adults do so (Plazzi, Vertugno, Provini, & Montagna, 2005). Sleepwalking is associated with NREM sleep. When monitored in a sleep laboratory, adult sleepwalkers demonstrated abrupt arousal—involving movement or speech—during stage 3 and stage 4 sleep (see Figures 6.2 and 6.3) in the first third of their night's sleep (Guilleminault, Poyares, Aftab, & Palombini, 2001). Contrary to popular conceptions, it is not particularly dangerous to wake sleepwalkers; they are just likely to be confused by the sudden awakening. Still, sleepwalking in itself can be dangerous because individuals are navigating their environments without conscious awareness.

DREAMS: THEATRE OF THE MIND

During every ordinary night of your life, you enter into the complex world of dreams. Once the province only of prophets, psychics, and psychoanalysts, dreams have become a vital area of study for scientific researchers. Much dream research begins in sleep laboratories, where experimenters can monitor sleepers for REM and NREM sleep. Although individuals report more

---

sleep apnea A sleep disorder of the upper respiratory system that causes the person to stop breathing while asleep.

somnambulism A disorder that causes sleepers to leave their beds and wander while still remaining asleep; also known as sleepwalking.

dreams when they are awakened from REM periods—on about 82 percent of their awakenings—dreaming also takes place during NREM periods—on about 54 percent of awakenings (Foulkes, 1962). Dreaming associated with NREM states is less likely to contain story content that is emotionally involving. It is more akin to daytime thought, with less sensory imagery.

Because dreams have such prominence in people's mental lives, virtually every culture has arrived at the same question: Do dreams have significance? The answer that has almost always emerged is *yes*. That is, most cultures encode the belief that, in one way or another, dreams have important personal and cultural meaning. We now review some of the ways in which cultures attach meaning to dreams.

Freudian Dream Analysis The most prominent dream theory in modern Western culture was originated by Sigmund Freud. Freud called dreams "transient psychoses" and models of "everynight madness." He also called them "the royal road to the unconscious." He made the analysis of dreams the cornerstone of psychoanalysis with his classic book, *The Interpretation of Dreams* (1900/1965). Freud saw dream images as symbolic expressions of powerful, unconscious, repressed wishes. These wishes appear in disguised form because they harbour forbidden desires, such as sexual yearning for the parent of the opposite sex. The two dynamic forces operating in dreams are thus the wish and the censorship, a defence against the wish. The censor transforms the hidden meaning, or **latent content**, of the dream into **manifest content**, which appears to the dreamer after a distortion process that Freud referred to as **dream work**. The manifest content is the acceptable version of the story; the latent content represents the socially or personally unacceptable version—but also the true, "uncut" one.

According to Freud, the interpretation of dreams requires working backward from the manifest content to the latent content. To the psychoanalyst who uses dream analysis to understand and treat a patient's problems, dreams reveal the patient's unconscious wishes, the fears attached to those wishes, and the characteristic defences the patient employs to handle the resulting psychic conflict between the wishes and the fears. Freud believed in both idiosyncratic—special to particular individuals—and universal meanings (many of a sexual nature) for the symbols and metaphors in dreams:

> Boxes, cases, chests, cupboards, and ovens represent the uterus, and also hollow objects, ships, and vessels of all kinds. Rooms in dreams are usually women; if the various ways in and out of them are represented, this interpretation is scarcely open to doubt. . . . A dream of going through a suite of rooms is a brothel or harem dream. . . . It is highly probable that all complicated machinery and apparatus occurring in dreams stand for the genitals (and as a rule male ones). (Freud, 1900/1965, pp. 389–391)

Freud's theory of dream interpretation related dream symbols to his explicit theory of human psychology. Freud's emphasis on the psychological importance of dreams has pointed the way to contemporary examinations of dream content.

Non-Western Approaches to Dream Interpretation Many people in Western societies may never think seriously about their dreams until they become students of psychology or enter therapy. By contrast, in many non-Western cultures, dream sharing and interpretation is part of the very fabric of the culture (Wax, 2004). Consider the daily practice of the Anchuar Indians of Ecuador:

> Like every other morning, the men [of the village] sit together in a small circle. . . . They share their dreams from the night before. This daily ritual of dream-sharing is vital to the life of the Anchuar. It is their belief that each individual dreams, not for themselves, but for the community as a whole. Individual experience serves collective action. (Schlitz, 1997, p. 2)

During these morning gatherings, each dreamer tells his dream story and the others offer their interpretations, hoping to arrive at some consensus understanding of the meaning of the dream. Contrast the belief that individuals dream "for the community as a whole" with the view articulated by Freud, that dreams are the "royal road" to the individual unconscious.

In many cultures, specific groups of individuals are designated as possessing special powers to assist with dream interpretation. Consider the practices of Mayan Indians who live in various parts of Mexico, Guatemala, Belize, and Honduras. In Mayan culture, *shamans* function as dream interpreters. In fact, among some subgroups of Mayans, the shamans are selected for these roles when they have dreams in which they are visited by deities who announce the shaman's calling. Formal instruction about religious rituals is also provided to these newly selected shamans by way of dream revelation. Although the shamans, and other religious figures, have special knowledge relevant to dream interpretation, ordinary individuals also recount and discuss dreams. Dreamers commonly wake their bed partners in the middle of the night to narrate dreams; mothers in some communities ask their children each morning to talk about their dreams. In contemporary times, the Mayan people have been the victims of civil war in their homelands; many people have been killed or forced to flee. One important response, according to anthropologist Barbara Tedlock, has been "an increased emphasis on dreams and visions that enable them to stay in touch with their ancestors and the sacred earth on which they live" (Tedlock, 1992, p. 471).

The cultural practices of many non-Western groups with respect to dreams also reflect a fundamentally different time perspective. Freud's theory had dream interpretation looking backward in time, toward childhood experiences and repressed wishes. In many other cultures, dreams are believed instead to present a vision of the future (Basso, 1987). For example, among the people of the Ingessana Hills, a region along the border of Ethiopia and the Sudan, the timing of festivals is determined by dream visions (Jedrej, 1995). The keepers of religious shrines are visited in their dreams by their fathers and other ancestors who instruct them to "announce the festival." Other groups also have culturally derived connections between dream symbols and meanings. Consider these interpretations from the Kalapalo Indians of central Brazil:

---

latent content In Freudian dream analysis, the hidden meaning of a dream.

manifest content In Freudian dream analysis, the surface content of a dream, which is assumed to mask the dream's actual meaning.

dream work In Freudian dream analysis, the process by which the internal censor transforms the latent content of a dream into manifest content.

When we dream we are burnt by fire, later we will be bitten by a wild thing, by a spider or a stinging ant, for example.

When [we dream] we are making love to women, we will be very successful when we go fishing.

When a boy is in seclusion and he dreams of climbing a tall tree, or another one sees a long path, they will live long. This would also be true if we dreamt of crossing a wide stream in a forest. (Basso, 1987, p. 104)

Note how each interpretation looks to the future. The future orientation of dream interpretation is an important component of a rich cultural tradition.

Contemporary Theories of Dream Content The cornerstone of both Western and non-Western approaches to dream interpretation is that dreams provide information that is of genuine value to the person or community. When researchers first began to consider the biological underpinnings of dreams, they challenged this view. For example, the *activation-synthesis model* suggested that signals emerge from the brain stem that stimulate the forebrain and association areas of the cortex to produce random memories and connections with the dreamer's past experiences (Hobson, 1988; Hobson & McCarley, 1977). According to this view, there are no logical connections, no intrinsic meaning, and no coherent patterns to these random bursts of electrical "signals."

However, contemporary research on dreams contradicts the view that the content emerges from random signals. Brain-imaging studies suggest that the hippocampus—a brain structure critical to the acquisition of certain types of memories (see Chapter 8)—is active during REM sleep (Nielsen &

Psychology in Your Life

DO YOU GET ENOUGH SLEEP?

About 20 years ago, there was very little to do after midnight. When students had finished with their schoolwork, they could pretty much choose between watching late-night television or rolling into bed. By contrast, there are now ample opportunities for you to maintain a 24/7 lifestyle. Consider the World Wide Web and its constant supply of new information. At any time of day or night, you can cruise the web or join a chat room. You can finish your midnight snack in Windsor, Ontario, at the same time you chat with someone eating an early breakfast in Windsor, England.

Easy access to 24/7 stimulation has amplified what we might characterize as many people's love–hate relationship with sleep. People love to sleep because being rested feels good (and being sleepy feels awful). As we have seen in this chapter, your body needs sleep to function effectively. However, people hate to sleep because there are so many enjoyable things to do while they are awake.

From the point of view of many researchers, the 21st century's enticements have only made a bad situation worse. They have been worried for several years that adolescents and university students do not get nearly enough sleep (Carskadon, 2002). Although experts recommend that adolescents and young adults get 8.5 hours of sleep per night (Carskadon, Acebo, & Jenni, 2004), a 2006 Canadian study conducted in Southern Ontario revealed that 70 percent of the students in their sample were mildly to severely sleep deprived (Gibson et al., 2006). Research by Statistics Canada (Williams, 2001) also suggests that 15 percent of Canadians aged 15 and older sleep less than 6.5 hours per night.

These findings are consistent with those from the National Sleep Foundation in the United States (2005), which reports that the average duration of sleep for individuals in this age range is 6.8 hours, with 44 percent reporting that they have missed days of work or events because of lack of sleep. How concerned are you about the amount of sleep you get? Research suggests that university students underestimate the negative consequences of sleep deprivation on their cognitive performance (Pilcher & Walters, 1997). Take a moment to consider the reality that chronic sleep loss is likely to be quite unfortunate for your university performance (Buboltz, Soper, Brown, & Jenkins, 2002). No doubt many university students lose sleep because of the stresses associated with studying for exams and writing papers (Murphy & Archer, 1996). However, 55 percent of poll participants in the 18 to 29 range agreed to the statement that they "often stay up later than they should because they are watching TV or are on the internet" (National Sleep Foundation, 2000). Does this apply to you?

We are not trying to discourage you from leading an exciting and varied life. We are simply offering the observation that progress often seems to bring with it new reasons for people to lose sleep. Sleepiness has many serious consequences: lower grades, work problems, and car accidents are just a few. So far, scientists have been able to invent pills that can stop you from sleeping— but none that can stop you from needing sleep. As you make plans to fill up the whole 24 hours in a day, research strongly suggests that you should still put aside eight hours for sleep.

Stenstrom, 2005). Another brain structure that plays an important role for emotional memories—the amygdala—is also quite active during REM sleep. This deeper understanding of the physiological aspects of dreams supports the assertion that one of the functions of sleep is to draw together "an individual's recent experiences of the past few days along with their goals, desires, and problems" (Paller & Voss, 2004, p. 667). According to this view, the story of the dream reflects the brain's attempt to weave a narrative around the recent fragments of a person's life that become most prominent during REM sleep.

Studies of dream content confirm that content of dreams shows a good deal of continuity with dreamers' waking concerns (Domhoff, 2005). For example, research using experience-sampling methods suggested that girls were more likely than boys to be thinking about friends of both sexes, rather than just friends of their own sex (Richards, Crowe, Larson, & Swarr, 1998). Dream studies with 9- to 15-year-olds demonstrate similar gender differences in dream content about peers (Strauch, 2005; Strauch & Lederbogen, 1999). Similarly, people who spent more waking time engaged in particular activities (such as sports or reading) reported a higher percentage of dreams that included those activities (Schredl & Erlacher, 2008). In addition, across adulthood, the overall content of each individual's dreams stays very much the same over years or even decades (Domhoff, 1999).

You might consider keeping your own dream log—try to write about your dreams as soon as you wake up each morning—to see both how your own dreams relate to daily concerns and how your dream content changes or remains stable over time. Still, we should warn you that some people have more difficulty recalling dreams than other people do (Wolcott & Strapp, 2002). For example, it is easier to recall dreams if you wake up during a REM period or close to one. If you want to recall your dreams, you might consider changing the time you set your alarm. Also, people who have more positive attitudes toward dreaming appear to find it easier to recall their dreams. In that sense, the interest you show in your dreams by undertaking a dream log might help increase your ability to recall them.

We can consider dreams to be at the outer limit of ordinary consciousness. We turn now to circumstances in which individuals deliberately seek to go beyond those everyday experiences.

STOP AND REVIEW

❶ Why do you experience jet lag?

❷ How does the balance of NREM and REM sleep change over the course of a night?

❸ What two functions might NREM sleep serve?

❹ What happens to a person who suffers from sleep apnea?

❺ What did Freud mean by the latent content of a dream?

CRITICAL THINKING Consider the study that documented the impact of new task learning on REM sleep. Why was it important to have the control group?

Altered States of Consciousness

In every culture, some people have been dissatisfied with ordinary transformations of their waking consciousness. They have developed practices that take them beyond familiar forms of consciousness to experiences of altered states of consciousness. Some of these practices are individual, such as meditation. Others, such as certain religious practices, are shared attempts to transcend the normal boundaries of conscious experience. We survey a variety of such practices in which altered states of consciousness are induced by a range of procedures.

LUCID DREAMING

Is it possible to be aware that you are dreaming while you are dreaming? Proponents of the theory of **lucid dreaming** have demonstrated that being consciously aware that one is dreaming is a learnable skill—perfected with regular practice—that enables dreamers to control the direction of their dreams (LaBerge, 2007).

> **Stephen LaBerge** and his colleagues devised a methodology that enabled them to test the reality of reports of lucid dreaming. The demonstration relied on previous research that had shown that some of the eye movements of REM sleep correspond to the reported direction of the dreamer's gaze. The researchers therefore asked experienced lucid dreamers to execute distinctive patterns of *voluntary* eye movements when they realized that they were dreaming. The prearranged eye movement signals appeared on the polygraph records during REM, thus demonstrating that the participants had indeed been lucid during REM sleep (LaBerge, Nagle, Dement, & Zarcone, 1981).

A variety of methods have been used to induce lucid dreaming. For example, in some lucid dreaming research, sleepers wear specially designed goggles that flash a red light when they detect REM sleep. The participants have learned previously that the red light is a cue for becoming consciously aware that they are dreaming (LaBerge & Levitan, 1995). Once aware of dreaming yet still not awake, sleepers move into a state of lucid dreaming in which they can take control of their dreams, directing them according to their personal goals and making the dreams' outcomes fit their current needs. The ability to have lucid dreams reportedly increases when sleepers firmly believe that such dreams are possible and regularly practise the induction techniques (LaBerge & Rheingold, 1990). Researchers such as Stephen LaBerge argue that gaining control over the "uncontrollable" events of dreams is healthy because it enhances self-confidence and generates positive experiences for the individual. However, some therapists who use dream analysis as part of their understanding of a patient's problems oppose such procedures because they feel that they distort the natural process of dreaming.

---

lucid dreaming The theory that conscious awareness of dreaming is a learnable skill that enables dreamers to control the direction and content of their dreams.

Researcher Stephen LaBerge adjusts the special goggles that will alert the sleeping participant that REM sleep is occurring. The individual is trained to enter into a state of lucid dreaming, being aware of the process and content of dream activity. If you had the ability to experience lucid dreaming, in what ways would you shape your dreams?

with changes in perception, memory, motivation, and sense of self-control. In the hypnotic state, participants experience heightened responsiveness to the hypnotist's suggestions—they often feel that their behaviour is performed without intention or any conscious effort.

Researchers have often disagreed about the psychological mechanisms involved in hypnosis (Lynn & Kirsch, 2006). Some early theorists suggested that hypnotized individuals enter into a *trance* state, far different from waking consciousness. Others argued that hypnosis was nothing more than heightened motivation. Still others believed it to be a type of social role playing, a kind of *placebo* (see Chapter 2) response of trying to please the hypnotist. In fact, research has largely ruled out the idea that hypnosis involves a special trancelike change in consciousness. However, even though nonhypnotized individuals can produce some of the same patterns of behaviour as hypnotized individuals, there appear to be some added effects of hypnosis—beyond motivational or placebo processes. After we discuss hypnotic induction and hypnotizability, we describe some of those effects.

Hypnotic Induction and Hypnotizability Hypnosis begins with a hypnotic induction, a preliminary set of activities that minimizes external distractions and encourages participants to concentrate only on suggested stimuli and believe that they are about to enter a special state of consciousness. Induction activities involve suggestions to imagine certain experiences or to visualize events and reactions. When practised repeatedly, the induction procedure functions as a learned signal so that participants can quickly enter the hypnotic state. The typical induction procedure uses suggestions for deep relaxation, but some people can become hypnotized with an active, alert induction—such as imagining that they are jogging or riding a bicycle (Banyai & Hilgard, 1976).

Hypnotizability represents the degree to which an individual is responsive to standardized suggestions to experience hypnotic reactions. There are wide individual differences in susceptibility, varying from a complete lack of responsiveness to total responsiveness. **Figure 6.5** shows the percentage of university-age individuals who presented various levels of hypnotizability

HYPNOSIS

As portrayed in popular culture, hypnotists wield vast power over their witting or unwitting participants. Is this view of hypnotists accurate? What is hypnosis? What are its important features, and what are some of its valid psychological uses? The term **hypnosis** is derived from *Hypnos*, the name of the Greek god of sleep. Sleep, however, plays no part in hypnosis, except that people may in some cases give the *appearance* of being in a deeply relaxed, sleeplike state. (If people were really asleep, they could not respond to hypnosis.) A broad definition of hypnosis is that it is an alternative state of awareness characterized by the special ability some people have of responding to suggestion

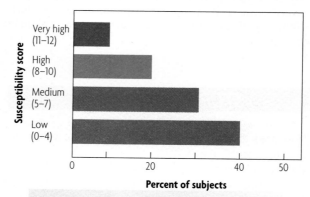

FIGURE 6.5 Level of Hypnosis at First Induction

The graph shows the results for 533 individuals hypnotized for the first time. Hypnotizability was measured on the Stanford Hypnotic Susceptibility Scale, which consists of 12 items.

---

hypnosis An altered state of awareness characterized by deep relaxation, susceptibility to suggestions, and changes in perception, memory, motivation, and self-control.

hypnotizability The degree to which an individual is responsive to standardized hypnotic suggestion.

the first time they were given a hypnotic induction test. What does it mean to have scored "high" or "very high" on this scale? When the test is administered, the hypnotist makes a series of posthypnotic suggestions, dictating the experiences each individual might have. When the hypnotist suggested that their extended arms had turned into bars of iron, highly hypnotizable individuals were likely to find themselves unable to bend their arms. With the appropriate suggestion, they were likely to brush away a nonexistent fly. As a third example, highly hypnotizable individuals probably could not shake their heads "no" when the hypnotist suggested they had lost that ability. Students who scored "low" on the hypnotizability scale experienced few if any of these reactions.

Hypnotizability is a relatively stable attribute. When 50 men and women were retested 25 years after their hypnotizability assessment, the results indicated a remarkably high correlation coefficient of 0.71 (Piccione, Hilgard, & Zimbardo, 1989). Children tend to be more suggestible than adults; hypnotic responsiveness peaks just before adolescence and declines thereafter. Researchers have identified relatively few personality traits that are correlated with hypnotizability (Kihlstrom, 2007). Highly hypnotizable people are not more likely to be gullible or conformist. In fact, the personality trait that has the highest positive correlation with hypnotizability is *absorption*, which is an individual's "predisposition to become highly involved in imaginative or sensory experiences" (Council & Green, 2004, p. 364). If, for example, you often find yourself losing track of the "real" world while you watch a movie, you might also be highly hypnotizable.

Some evidence indicates genetic determinants of hypnotizability. Early research demonstrated that hypnotizability scores of identical twins are more similar than are those of fraternal twins (Morgan, Hilgard, & Davert, 1970). More recently, studies have begun to focus on the particular genes that underlie individual differences. For example, researchers have identified a gene known as *COMT* that influences the brain's use of the neurotransmitter dopamine. Variations in this gene are related to individual differences in hypnotizability (Raz, 2005).

Effects of Hypnosis In describing the way in which hypnotizability is measured, we already mentioned some of the standard effects of hypnosis: While under hypnosis, individuals respond to suggestions about motor abilities (for example, their arms become unbendable) and perceptual experiences (for example, they hallucinate about seeing a fly). How can we be sure, however, that these behaviours arise from special properties of hypnosis and not just a strong willingness on participants' part to please the hypnotist? To address this important question, researchers have often conducted experiments that contrast the effectiveness of suggestions when participants are in waking or hypnotic states.

Researchers created three groups of participants who tested high, medium, and low on hypnotizability, with 12 individuals in each group (De Pascalis, Cacace, & Massicolle, 2008). Before they began the experiment, participants were informed that they were going to receive painful electric stimulation to their fingers. Each participant received the same suggestions about how to lessen the pain both when hypnotized and in a waking state: They were told, for example, to imagine that a glove was covering the finger. In each phase of the experiment, participants provided reports on the amount of pain they were experiencing. For low hypnotizability participants, pain experiences were fairly steady irrespective of their waking or hypnotic state. Medium hypnotizability participants showed some pain relief from hypnosis. High hypnotizability participants provided the clearest evidence that suggestions for pain relief under hypnosis acted more effectively than the same suggestion during the waking state.

The researchers also recorded EEG data (see Chapter 4) to determine whether the participants' brain activity would show the impact of the hypnotic suggestions. In fact, when high hypnotizability participants received hypnotic suggestions for pain reduction, they produced more muted brain responses in sensory areas.

This experiment demonstrates the potential for hypnosis to bring about pain relief (*hypnotic analgesia*). Your mind can amplify pain stimuli through anticipation and fear; you can diminish this psychological effect with hypnosis (Chaves, 1999). Pain control is accomplished through a variety of hypnotic suggestions: imagining the part of the body in pain as nonorganic (made of wood or plastic) or as separate from the rest of the body, thus taking one's mind on a vacation from the body and distorting time in various ways. People can control pain through hypnosis even when they banish all thoughts and images from consciousness (Hargadon, Bowers, & Woody, 1995).

The study also demonstrates that people who are high in hypnotizability are able to obtain greater pain relief through hypnosis. Researchers are trying to understand the brain bases for this difference. For example, a brain-imaging study demonstrated that people who were higher in hypnotizability also had larger regions at the front of the corpus callosum (see Chapter 4) (Horton, Crawford, Harrington, & Downs, 2004). This area of the corpus callosum plays a role in attention and the inhibition of unwanted stimuli, suggesting that people who are highly hypnotizable may have more brain tissue that allows them to use hypnosis to inhibit pain. Studies with EEG measures also demonstrate—in the context of hypnotic pain reduction—differences in the brain responses of low and high hypnotizable individuals (Ray et al., 2002).

One final note on hypnosis: The power of hypnosis does *not* reside in some special ability or skill of the hypnotist, but in the relative hypnotizability of the person or persons being hypnotized. Being hypnotized does not involve giving up one's personal control; instead, the experience of being hypnotized allows an individual to learn new ways to exercise control that the hypnotist—as coach—can train the subject—as performer—to enact. Keep all of this in mind if you watch a stage show in which people perform outlandish acts under hypnosis: Stage hypnotists make a living entertaining audiences by getting highly exhibitionist people to do things in public that most others could never be made to do. As used by researchers and therapists, hypnosis is a technique with the potential to allow you to explore and modify your sense of consciousness.

MEDITATION

Many religions and traditional psychologies of the East work to direct consciousness away from immediate worldly concerns. They seek to achieve an inner focus on the mental and spiritual

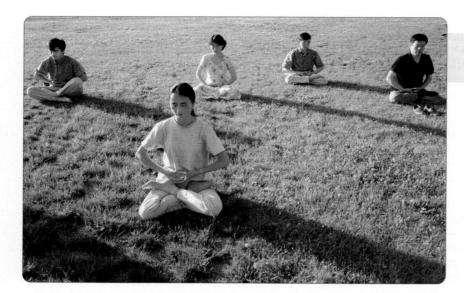

How does meditation create an altered state of consciousness?

self. **Meditation** is a form of consciousness change designed to enhance self-knowledge and well-being by achieving a deep state of tranquility. During *concentrative* meditation, a person may focus on and regulate breathing, assume certain body positions (yogic positions), minimize external stimulation, generate specific mental images, or free the mind of all thought. By contrast, during *mindfulness* meditation, a person learns to let thoughts and memories pass freely through the mind without reacting to them.

Research has often focused on the ability of meditation to relieve the anxiety of those who must function in stress-filled environments (Oman, Hedberg, & Thoresen, 2006; Walach et al., 2007). For example, mindfulness meditation has served as the basis for mindfulness-based stress reduction (Kabat-Zinn, 1990). In one study, women suffering from heart disease were given eight weeks of training on mindfulness meditation; at the end of this intervention, the women reported consistently lower feelings of anxiety than they did before the study (Tacón, McComb, Caldera, & Randolph, 2003). Women in the control group did not experience improvement in their anxiety reports. Because feelings of anxiety play a role in the development of heart disease, this result provides evidence that the mind can help to heal the body. (We will return to this theme when we discuss health psychology in Chapter 13.)

Brain-imaging techniques have begun to reveal the ways in which the practice of meditation affects patterns of brain activity (Cahn & Polich, 2006). In fact, recent evidence suggests that, over time, the practice of meditation might have a positive impact on the brain itself.

The researchers reasoned that the activities associated with meditation—focused attention on internal and external sensations—would bring about positive changes in the brain regions associated with these activities (Lazar et al., 2005). To test this hypothesis, the researchers recruited two groups of participants: 20 individuals with extensive meditation experience and 15 control individuals with no meditation experience. All the participants underwent MRI scans to provide measures of the thickness of relevant areas of cortex. As the researchers had predicted, these scans revealed that the meditation groups had thicker cortex in areas of auditory and somatosensory cortex (see Chapter 4). The two groups did not differ in areas of the cortex that were not directly relevant to meditation. The researchers carried out further analyses that indicated that those individuals who had the most meditation experience also had the greatest extra thickness in relevant areas of cortex.

As people grow older, they typically lose cortical thickness. Based on their findings, the researchers speculated that meditation could help slow this natural loss of neurons. Researchers have begun to confirm that speculation. One study compared 13 individuals with three or more years of experience in Zen meditation with 13 control participants who were matched for age, sex, and education level (Pagnoni & Cekic, 2007). Among the control participants, there was a negative correlation such that the older participants had the least brain volume. The participants who meditated regularly showed no such decline with age.

Practitioners of meditation have suggested that, when practised regularly, some forms of meditation can heighten your consciousness and help you achieve enlightenment by enabling you to see familiar things in new ways. This recent research suggests that meditation might also literally be good for your brain.

In this section, we have reviewed several ways in which people achieve altered states of consciousness in their dreaming and waking lives. We conclude this chapter with a discussion of what might be the most common means people use to affect their consciousness: mind-altering drugs.

STOP AND REVIEW

❶ What is the major goal of lucid dreaming?
❷ What does research suggest about the genetics of hypnotizability?
❸ What are two forms of meditation?

CRITICAL THINKING Consider the study that found differences in cortical thickness for meditators versus nonmeditators. Why was it important to demonstrate that the two groups' brains did not differ in all areas of the cortex?

---

meditation A form of consciousness alteration designed to enhance self-knowledge and well-being through reduced self-awareness.

Mind-Altering Drugs

Since ancient times, people have taken drugs to alter their perception of reality. Archaeological evidence indicates the uninterrupted use of sophora seed (mescal bean) for over 10 000 years in the southwestern United States and Mexico. The ancient Aztecs fermented mescal beans into a beer. From ancient times, individuals in North and South America also ingested *teonanacatl*, the *Psilocybe* mushroom also known as "the flesh of the gods," as parts of rituals. Small doses of these mushrooms produce vivid hallucinations.

In Western cultures, drugs are associated less with sacred communal rituals than with recreation. Individuals throughout the world take various drugs to relax, cope with stress, avoid facing the unpleasantness of current realities, feel comfortable in social situations, or experience an alternate state of consciousness. Over 100 years ago, William James—whom we have cited several times as a founder of psychology in North America—reported on his experiments with a mind-altering drug. After inhaling nitrous oxide, James explained that "the keynote of the experience is the tremendously exciting sense of intense metaphysical illumination. Truth lies open to the view in depth beneath depth of almost blinding evidence. The mind sees all the logical relations of being with an apparent subtlety and instantaneity to which its normal consciousness offers no parallel" (James, 1882, p. 186). Thus James's interest in the study of consciousness extended to the study of self-induced alternate states.

As we will see in Chapter 16, drugs that have an impact on individuals' psychological states are often a critical aspect of the treatment of psychological disorders. In fact, as we indicate in **Table 6.2**, many types of drugs have important medical uses. Still, many individuals use drugs that are not prescribed to enhance physical or psychological health.

The most recent Canadian statistics estimate that 194 000 Canadians, or just under 1 percent of the adult population, had symptoms that suggested dependence on illicit drugs (Statistics Canada, 2004a). These statistics vary significantly by age. About 2.5 percent of 15- to 24-year-olds were dependent on illicit drugs, compared with less than half of 1 percent of people aged 35 or older. The proportion of men who were dependent on illicit drugs was slightly higher at 1.1 percent, compared with 0.5 percent of women. Statistics look quite different if we consider one-time use of illicit drugs. For example, marijuana is probably the most widely used illicit drug in Canada, with 10 million Canadians reporting that they have used this drug at least once in their lifetime (Statistics Canada, 2004a). This number represents just over 41 percent of the population aged 15 or older. These figures support the importance of understanding the physiological and psychological consequences of drug use.

DEPENDENCE AND ADDICTION

Psychoactive drugs are chemicals that affect mental processes and behaviour by temporarily changing conscious awareness. Once in the brain, they attach themselves to synaptic receptors, blocking or stimulating certain reactions. By doing so, they profoundly alter the brain's communication system, affecting perception, memory, mood, and behaviour. However, continued use of a given drug creates **tolerance**—greater dosages are

Drug	Medical Uses
Hallucinogens	
LSD	None
PCP (Phencyclidine)	Veterinary anesthetic
Cannabis (Marijuana)	Nausea associated with chemotherapy
Opiates (Narcotics)	
Morphine	Painkiller
Heroin	None
Depressants	
Barbiturates (e.g., Seconal)	Sedative, sleeping pill, anesthetic, anticonvulsant
Benzodiazepines (e.g., Valium)	Antianxiety, sedative, sleeping pill, anticonvulsant
Rohypnol	Sleeping pill
GHB	Treatment for narcolepsy
Alcohol	Antiseptic
Stimulants	
Amphetamines	Hyperkinesis, narcolepsy, weight control
Methamphetamines	None
MDMA (Ecstasy)	Potential aid to psychotherapy
Cocaine	Local anesthetic
Nicotine	Nicotine gum for cessation of smoking habit
Caffeine	Weight control, stimulant in acute respiratory failure, analgesic

TABLE 6.2 Medical Uses of Psychoactive Drugs

required to achieve the same effect. (We describe some of the psychological roots of tolerance in Chapter 7.) Hand in hand with tolerance is **physiological dependence**, a process in which the body becomes adjusted to and dependent on the substance, in part because neurotransmitters are depleted by the frequent presence of the drug. The tragic outcome of tolerance and dependence is **addiction**. A person who is addicted requires the drug in his or her body, suffering painful withdrawal symptoms (shaking, sweating, nausea, and, in the case of alcohol withdrawal, even death) if the drug is not present.

---

psychoactive drugs Chemicals that affect mental processes and behaviour by temporarily changing conscious awareness of reality.

tolerance A situation that occurs with continued use of a drug in which an individual requires greater dosages to achieve the same effect.

physiological dependence The process by which the body becomes adjusted to or dependent on a drug.

addiction A condition in which the body requires a drug in order to function without physical and psychological reactions to its absence; often the outcome of tolerance and dependence.

When an individual finds the use of a drug so desirable or pleasurable that a *craving* develops, with or without addiction, the condition is known as **psychological dependence**, which can occur with any drug. The result of drug dependence is that a person's lifestyle comes to revolve around drug use so wholly that his or her capacity to function is limited or impaired. Drugs such as hallucinogens and alcohol frequently have physically debilitating effects over time. In addition, the expense involved in maintaining a drug habit of daily—and increasing—amounts often drives an addict to robbery, assault, prostitution, or drug peddling.

VARIETIES OF PSYCHOACTIVE DRUGS

Table 6.2 lists common psychoactive drugs. (In Chapter 16, we discuss other types of psychoactive drugs used to relieve mental illness.) Next, we briefly describe how each class of drugs achieves its physiological and psychological impact. We also note the personal and societal consequences of drug use.

Hallucinogens The most dramatic changes in consciousness are produced by drugs known as *hallucinogens* or *psychedelics*; these drugs alter both perceptions of the external environment and inner awareness. As the name implies, these drugs often create **hallucinations**—vivid perceptions that occur in the absence of objective stimulation. The hallucinations may lead to a loss of boundary between self and nonself. *LSD* and *PCP* are two common hallucinogens that are synthesized in laboratories. Hallucinogenic drugs typically act in the brain by affecting the use of the chemical neurotransmitter serotonin (Beïque et al., 2007). For example, LSD binds very tightly to serotonin receptors so that neurons produce prolonged activation.

Cannabis is a plant with psychoactive effects. Its active ingredient is THC, found in both *hashish* (the solidified resin of the plant) and *marijuana* (the dried leaves and flowers of the plant). The experience derived from inhaling THC depends on its dose—small doses create mild, pleasurable highs, and large doses result in long hallucinogenic reactions. Regular users report euphoria, feelings of well-being, distortions of space and time, and, occasionally, out-of-body experiences. Marijuana has also been used in Canada as an effective treatment for a variety of side effects associated with many medical conditions. For example, it appears to be an effective treatment for AIDS-related symptoms, intra-ocular pressure caused by glaucoma, and chemotherapy-related nausea, as well as muscle spasticity arising from spinal cord injuries, epilepsy, and multiple sclerosis. It is estimated that over 200 000 Canadians currently benefit from marijuana's medical effects. However, depending on the context, the effects of marijuana may be negative—fear, anxiety, and confusion.

Researchers have known for several years that *cannabinoids*, the active chemicals in marijuana, bind to specific receptors in the brain; these cannabinoid receptors are particularly common in the hippocampus, the brain region involved in

How does marijuana have an impact on the brain?

memory (De Oliveira Alvares, Genro, Diehl, & Quillfeldt, 2008). Researchers subsequently discovered substances internal to the brain that bind to the same receptors. The first endocannabinoid (from endogenous cannabinoid) to be discovered was anandamide (named for the Sanskrit word for bliss, *ananda*) (Di Marzo & Cristino, 2008). That discovery led to the insight that cannabinoids achieve their mind-altering effects by binding to brain sites sensitive to naturally occurring substances in the brain. These endocannabinoids function as neuromodulators. For example, they suppress the release of the neurotransmitter GABA (Wilson & Nicoll, 2002). In the *Critical Thinking in Your Life* box, we discuss the important role these substances play in regulating appetite and feeding behaviours.

Opiates *Opiates*, such as *heroin* and *morphine*, suppress physical sensation and response to stimulation. Pain killers such as OxyContin are also opiates and have the same effects. In the last few years, there has been a dramatic increase in the number of people who abuse OxyContin and other prescription opiates (Rawson, Maxwell, & Rutkowski, 2007). In Chapter 4, we noted that the brain contains endorphins (short for *endogenous morphines*) that generate powerful effects on mood, pain, and pleasure. These endogenous opiates play a critical role in the brain's response to both physical and psychological stressors (Ribeiro et al., 2005). Drugs like opium and morphine bind to the same receptor sites in the brain as the endorphins (Trescot, Datta, Lee, & Hansen, 2008). This means that both opiates and, as we described in the previous section, marijuana achieve their effects because they have active components with similar chemical properties to substances that naturally occur in the brain.

The initial effect of an intravenous injection of heroin is a rush of pleasure. Feelings of euphoria supplant all worries and awareness of bodily needs. However, heroin use often leads to addiction. When the neural receptors in the endogenous opiate system are artificially stimulated, the brain loses its subtle balance. People who try to withdraw from opiates often experience harsh physical symptoms (e.g., vomiting, pain, and insomnia) as well as intense craving for the drug. When people undertake medical assistance to help with withdrawal, they often receive treatments that block the opiates' ability to create pleasure responses in the brain (Grüsser et al., 2006).

psychological dependence The psychological need or craving for a drug.

hallucinations False perceptions that occur in the absence of objective stimulation.

Why does heroin use often lead to addiction?

Why does alcohol remain the most popular way in which university students alter their consciousness?

Depressants The *depressants* include *barbiturates* and, most notably, *alcohol*. These substances tend to depress (slow down) the mental and physical activity of the body by inhibiting or decreasing the transmission of nerve impulses in the central nervous system. Depressants achieve this effect, in part, by facilitating neural communication at synapses that use the neurotransmitter GABA (Licata & Rowlett, 2008). GABA often functions to inhibit neural transmission, which explains depressants' inhibiting outcomes. In the past, people were often prescribed barbiturates such as *Nembutol* and *Seconal* to act as sedatives or to treat insomnia. However, because barbiturate use may lead to addiction and overdose, people are now more likely to receive prescriptions for benzodiazepines such as *Valium* or *Xanax*. In Chapter 16, we will see that these drugs are also commonly used to counteract anxiety.

In recent years, two depressants, *Rohypnol* (more commonly known as *roofies*) and *GHB*, have achieved reputations as "date rape drugs." Both substances can be manufactured as colourless liquids so that they can be added to alcohol or other beverages without detection. In that way, victims can be sedated and raped. In addition, *Rohypnol* causes amnesia, so that victims may not remember events that occurred while they were under the drug's influence.

Alcohol was apparently one of the first psychoactive substances used extensively by early humans. Under its influence, some people become silly, boisterous, friendly, and talkative; others become abusive and violent; still others become quietly depressed. Alcohol appears to stimulate the release of dopamine, which enhances feelings of pleasure. Also, as with other depressants, it appears to affect GABA activity (Lobo & Harris, 2008). At small dosages, alcohol can induce relaxation and slightly improve an adult's speed of reaction. However, the body can break down alcohol only at a slow rate, and large amounts consumed in a short period overtax the central nervous system. As the concentration of alcohol increases from 0.05 to 0.10 percent, cognitive, perceptual, and motor processes begin to deteriorate rapidly. When the level of alcohol in the blood reaches 0.15 percent, there are gross negative effects on thinking, memory, and judgment, along with emotional instability and loss of motor co-ordination.

Excess consumption of alcohol is a major social problem in Canada. Alcohol-related automobile accidents are a leading cause of death among people between the ages of 15 and 25. When the amount and frequency of drinking interfere with job performance, impair social and family relationships, and create serious health problems, the diagnosis of *alcoholism* is appropriate. Physical dependence, tolerance, and addiction all develop with prolonged heavy drinking. For some individuals, alcoholism is associated with an inability to abstain from drinking. For others, alcoholism manifests itself as an inability to stop drinking once the person takes a few drinks. In a 2007 U.S. survey, 14.7 percent of 18- to 25-year-olds reported heavy drinking—defined as drinking five or more drinks on the same occasion on each of five or more days in a one-month period (Substance Abuse and Mental Health Services Administration, 2008b). The peak of heavy drinking was age 21, with 17.9 percent of 21-year-olds reporting heavy alcohol use.

According to the most recently collected Canadian statistics, an estimated 641 000 Canadians, or about 2.6 percent of the population aged 15 or older, reported symptoms suggesting that they were dependent on alcohol (Statistics Canada, 2002b).

Driving accidents and fatalities occur six times more often to individuals with 0.10 percent alcohol in their bloodstream than to those with half that amount. Alcohol-related automobile accidents are a leading cause of death among people between the ages of 15 and 25. Given these disturbing statistics, researchers have tried to understand the several ways in which alcohol has a negative impact on driving performance. Part of the answer lies in alcohol's effect on drinkers' ability to inhibit bad impulses.

Suppose you are driving to an important appointment for which you can't be late. As you drive, you might have an

Critical Thinking in Your Life

WHAT CAN WE LEARN FROM "THE MUNCHIES"?

Even if you've never smoked marijuana, you're likely familiar with one of the drug's legendary effects: Marijuana gives people intense cravings for food—cravings often called "the munchies." Observations about marijuana's effects on hunger go back at least to 300 A.D., when texts in India recommended that it be used to stimulate the appetite (Cota et al., 2003). Take a moment to consider how you might turn "the munchies" into a research agenda. What questions might you generate? What hypotheses would you like to test?

The first question you might wish to address would perhaps be "Why?": Why does marijuana affect people's appetite? In the text, we've already told you important parts of that story. Researchers determined that the active chemicals—the cannabinoids—in marijuana bind to specific receptors in the brain.

As research unfolded, researchers also made the breakthrough discovery of the existence of endocannabinoids (endogenous cannabinoids) in the brain. With that discovery in hand, researchers could test the hypothesis that endocannabinoids play an ongoing role in regulating food consumption. This hypothesis was solidly confirmed (Vemuri, Janero, & Makriyannis, 2008). That research even helped to explain observations about the types of food people crave when they have the munchies.

Besides their role in regulating appetite, endocannabinoids also play a role in reward systems in the brain (Cota et al., 2006). For that reason, endocannabinoids have the particular effect of making people seek foods that are tasty or sweet. Thus, it's no coincidence that the munchies are best satisfied with junk food. This range of insights has enabled researchers to develop drug therapies to treat people who are reluctant to eat for psychological or medical reasons (Cota et al., 2003).

Now you know that endocannabinoids increase appetite. Here's the next step your thinking might take: Can researchers devise drugs that will use this same system to suppress appetite? The goal, in this context, is to find drugs that prevent the endocannabinoids from having their ordinary impact. Over the last several years, researchers have begun to have great successes in this quest (Vemuri et al., 2008). One drug that has demonstrated early promise is called *rimonabant*. Rimonabant blocks the brain's cannabinoid receptors from carrying out their normal functions. In one double-blind study testing the impact of rimonabant treatment, 1036 overweight and obese individuals were given either a low or high dose of the drug or a placebo (i.e., an inert substance) (Després, Golay, & Sjöström, 2005). Over the course of the year-long study, participants in the placebo group lost about 5 pounds (2.3 g).

Participants who got the low dose of rimonabant lost about 9 pounds (4.1 g). Participants on the high dose lost about 19 pounds (8.6 g)! Similarly, high-dose participants took considerably more inches off their waists (3.6 in., or 9.1 cm) than did low-dose (1.9 in., or 4.8 cm) or placebo (1.3 in., or 3.3 cm) participants. With results of this sort in hand, researchers have begun the quest for drugs that achieve the same effects as rimonabant with fewer side effects (such as nausea or insomnia) (Vemuri et al., 2008).

From this example, you can see how research progresses from a real-world observation to a productive research agenda. With the goal of understanding why marijuana has an impact on appetite, researchers have generated insights that have led to successful treatments for both people who eat too little and people who eat too much. In fact, the same course of research points to even greater promise for the future: Because the endocannabinoids have an important impact on the brain's reward circuits, researchers believe that drugs targeting the endocannabinoid system may provide successful treatments for both pain and addiction (Fattore et al., 2007; Hosking & Zajicek, 2008).

- Why was it important for the study testing rimonabant to be double-blind?

- Why might there be a link between the brain systems that regulate appetite and reward?

impulse to indulge in bad driving behaviours such as speeding or reckless lane changes. However, those negative impulses are offset by your knowledge that you might get a ticket, have an accident, and so on. A team of researchers tested the hypothesis that people under the influence of alcohol drive particularly badly when they are driving in those sorts of circumstances—in which there's a conflict between good and bad impulses (Fillmore, Blackburn, & Harrison, 2008). The participants in the study engaged in a simulated driving task after consuming either alcohol or a placebo. (You can understand why the researchers couldn't conduct the experiment on real roads.) Participants' driving was considerably worse after alcohol consumption on measures such as failures to stop at red lights and abrupt steering manoeuvres. The impact of alcohol was even greater, however, when the researchers increased the participants' sense of response conflict. The researchers offered the participants cash rewards for reaching their destinations quickly, but they lost money if they drove poorly. When they were in this state of conflict, participants' performance was worst of all: Their bad impulses dramatically won out.

You are no doubt familiar with the claim that people will do things while they're drunk that they would never do if they were sober. In the realm of driving, the lack of impulse control can have deadly consequences.

Stimulants *Stimulants*, such as *amphetamines*, *methamphetamines*, and *cocaine*, have three major effects that users seek: increased self-confidence, greater energy and hyperalertness, and mood alterations approaching euphoria. Heavy users experience frightening hallucinations and develop beliefs that others are out to harm them. These beliefs are known as *paranoid delusions*. Stimulants achieve their effects by increasing the brain levels of neurotransmitters such as norepinephrine, serotonin, and dopamine. For example, stimulants act in the brain to prevent the action of molecules that ordinarily remove dopamine from synapses (Martin-Fardon et al., 2005). The serious addiction that often accompanies stimulant use may arise because of long-term changes in the neurotransmitter systems (Ahmed & Koob, 2004). In recent years, the Canadian Department of Justice has had a "growing concern about the use, production and trafficking of methamphetamine" (Department of Justice, 2007). Rates of use have increased over time, with 6.4 percent of Canadians aged 15 and older having used amphetamines, including methamphetamine, at least once during their lifetime and 0.8 percent of the Canadian population using methamphetamine in the past 10 years. As with other stimulants, methamphetamine has an impact on the brain's use of dopamine. People who take methamphetamine experience feelings of euphoria, decreased anxiety, and intense sexual craving. However, methamphetamine use very quickly has negative consequences: After only days or weeks of continual use, people begin to experience frightening hallucinations and develop paranoid delusions. Methamphetamine is highly addictive. Chronic use causes several types of damage in the brain, including the loss of nerve terminals in the dopamine system (Rose & Grant, 2008). Damage to brain regions involved in decision making and planning may explain why methamphetamine users become overly aggressive and suffer from social isolation (Homer et al., 2008).

MDMA—more commonly known as ecstasy—is a stimulant but also produces hallucinogen-like distortions of time and perception. The stimulant properties of the drug gives users feelings of boundless energy; the hallucinogenic properties makes sounds, colours, and emotions more intense. Ecstasy brings about these effects by altering the functioning of neurotransmitters such as dopamine, serotonin, and norepinephrine. Because ecstasy has a broad impact on these neurotransmitter systems, considerable research has focused on the drug's long-term impact on the brain (Jager et al., 2008). Researchers have been particularly sensitive to ecstasy's status as a party drug. They have attempted to devise studies that accurately reflect human norms of drug use. Researchers recognize, for example, that ecstasy users often ingest the drug at the same time that they have consumed alcohol. This leads to the question of how alcohol and ecstasy jointly affect the brain. Research suggests that the combination of ecstasy and alcohol produces negative effects in rats' brains that would not have occurred with ecstasy alone (Cassel et al., 2005).

A special danger with cocaine use is the contrast between euphoric highs and very depressive lows. This leads users to increase uncontrollably the frequency of drug use and the dosage. *Crack*, a crystallized form of cocaine, increases these dangers. Crack produces a swift high that wears off quickly; craving for the drug is intense.

Two stimulants that you may often overlook as psychoactive drugs are *caffeine* and *nicotine*. As you may know from experience, two cups of strong coffee or tea administer enough caffeine to have a profound effect on heart, blood, and circulatory functions, and make it difficult for you to sleep. Nicotine, a chemical found in tobacco, is a sufficiently strong stimulant to have been used in high concentrations by Native North American shamans to attain mystical states or trances. Unlike some modern users, however, the shamans knew that nicotine is addictive, and they carefully chose when to be under its influence. Like other addictive drugs, nicotine mimics natural chemicals released by the brain. In fact, research has uncovered common regions of brain activation for addiction to nicotine and cocaine (Vezina, McGehee, & Green, 2007). Chemicals in nicotine stimulate receptors that make you feel good whenever you have done something right—a phenomenon that aids survival.

Unfortunately, nicotine teases those same brain receptors into responding as if it were good for you to be smoking. It's not. As you know, smoking is far from good for your health. Approximately 45 000 Canadians die each year from cigarette smoking (Health Canada, 2005b)—roughly five times the number of deaths caused by car accidents, suicides, drug abuse, murder, and AIDS combined. And although the number of Canadians who smoke has steadily declined for the past 40 years, from a high of 50 percent in 1965, 20 percent of Canadians continue to smoke.

We began this chapter by asking you to remember your past and plan for your future. These ordinary activities allowed us to pose some interesting questions about consciousness: Where did your thoughts come from? How did they emerge? When did they arrive? You have now learned some of the theories that apply to these questions and how it has been possible to test those theories. You have seen that consciousness ultimately allows you to have the full range of experiences that define you as human.

We also asked you to consider some increasingly less ordinary uses of consciousness. Why, we asked, do people become dissatisfied with their everyday working minds and seek to alter their consciousness in so many ways? Ordinarily, people primarily focus on meeting the immediate demands of tasks and situations facing them. Sometimes, however, they may feel that these reality-based constraints on consciousness limit the range and depth of their experience and do not allow them to fulfill their potential. This may lead them to reach beyond the confines of ordinary reality to seek the uncertainty of freedom instead of settling for the security of the ordinary.

STOP AND REVIEW

❶ What is the definition of drug tolerance?
❷ How do drugs like heroin work in the brain?
❸ To what category of drugs does nicotine belong?

Recapping Main Points

The Contents of Consciousness

- Consciousness is an awareness of the mind's contents.
- The contents of waking consciousness contrast with nonconscious processes, preconscious memories, unattended information, the unconscious, and conscious awareness.
- Research techniques such as think-aloud protocols and experience sampling are used to study the contents of consciousness.

The Functions of Consciousness

- Consciousness aids your survival and enables you to construct both personal and culturally shared realities.
- Researchers have studied the relationship between conscious and unconscious processes.

Visit **MyPsychLab.com** for more review and practice on the following topics:

✓ **Practice:** The Functions of Consciousness

Sleep and Dreams

- Circadian rhythms reflect the operation of a biological clock.
- Patterns of brain activity change over the course of a night's sleep. REM sleep is signaled by rapid eye movements.
- The amount of sleep and relative proportion of REM to NREM sleep change with age.
- REM and NREM sleep serve different functions, including conservation and restoration.
- Sleep disorders such as insomnia, narcolepsy, night terrors, and sleep apnea have a negative impact on people's ability to function during waking time.
- Freud proposed that the content of dreams is unconscious material slipped by a sleeping censor.
- In other cultures, dreams are interpreted regularly, often by people with special cultural roles.

- Some dream theories have focused on biological explanations for the origins of dreams.

Visit **MyPsychLab.com** for more review and practice on the following topics:

✳ **Explore:** Theories of Dreaming

Altered States of Consciousness

- Lucid dreaming is an awareness that one is dreaming along with the ability to control the dream.
- Hypnosis is an alternate state of consciousness characterized by the ability of hypnotizable people to change perception, motivation, memory, and self-control in response to suggestions.
- Meditation changes conscious functioning by ritual practices that focus attention away from external concerns to inner experience.
- In some cultural groups, people undergo intense religious experiences.

Visit **MyPsychLab.com** for more review and practice on the following topics:

 Watch: Hypnosis

Mind-Altering Drugs

- Psychoactive drugs affect mental processes by temporarily changing consciousness as they modify nervous system activity.
- Among psychoactive drugs that alter consciousness are hallucinogens, opiates, depressants, and stimulants.

Visit **MyPsychLab.com** for more review and practice on the following topics:

◀● **Simulate:** General Model of Drug Addiction

KEY TERMS

addiction (p. 175)
circadian rhythm (p. 164)
consciousness (p. 159)
dream work (p. 169)
experience-sampling method (p. 161)
hallucinations (p. 176)
hypnosis (p. 172)
hypnotizability (p. 172)
insomnia (p. 167)

latent content (p. 169)
lucid dreaming (p. 171)
manifest content (p. 169)
meditation (p. 174)
narcolepsy (p. 167)
nonconscious (p. 160)
non-REM (NREM) sleep (p. 164)
physiological dependence (p. 175)
preconscious memories (p. 160)

psychoactive drugs (p. 175)
psychological dependence (p. 176)
rapid eye movements (REM) (p. 164)
sleep apnea (p. 168)
somnambulism (p. 168)
think-aloud protocols (p. 161)
tolerance (p. 175)

Practice Test

1. The existence of _____ demonstrates that at any given time you are conscious of only a small amount of the information you have available to you.
   a. preconscious memories
   b. nonconscious processes
   c. circadian rhythms
   d. unconscious memories

2. Freud suggested that some memories are sufficiently threatening that they are forced to reside in _____
   a. the unconscious.
   c. consciousness.
   b. the preconscious.
   d. manifest content.

3. You ask a group of men and women to watch the same TV commercial for a new car. If you want to determine what type of information the commercial brings to mind, you could use _____
   a. meditation.
   b. a visual search experiment.
   c. lucid dreaming.
   d. think-aloud protocols.

4. Which of these is an example of the selective storage function of consciousness?
   a. Rob kept his eye on the hoop while he shot the basketball.
   b. Laura decided to get chocolate ice cream instead of vanilla.
   c. Jinder hit the gas pedal as soon as the light turned green.
   d. Salvatore committed to memory the address of his new girlfriend.

5. Because it requires more conscious attention, it is harder to find a _____ object than a _____ object.
   a. red; large and red
   b. green; green and yellow
   c. red and blue; green and yellow
   d. red and blue; red

6. You would probably experience the most jet lag if you traveled from _____ to _____.
   a. Vancouver; Los Angeles
   c. Toronto; Edmonton
   b. Victoria; Montreal
   d. Miami; Halifax

7. You go to sleep at midnight and sleep for eight solid hours. You are likely to experience the most _____ sleep between midnight and 1:00 a.m. and the most _____ sleep between 7:00 a.m. and 8:00 a.m.
   a. delta sleep; NREM
   c. REM; stage 1
   b. NREM; REM
   d. REM; stage 3

8. Both NREM and REM sleep may be important for _____
   a. conservation.
   c. latent and manifest content.
   b. restoration.
   d. learning and memory.

9 Several times a night, Carolyn stops breathing and then wakes up. It sounds like Carolyn suffers from _____
   a. insomnia.
   c. somnambulism.
   b. sleep apnea.
   d. narcolepsy.

10. The activation-synthesis model claimed that _____
    a. dreams arise from random brain activity.
    b. manifest content is synthesized from latent content.
    c. dream content reflects people's day-to-day concerns.
    d. girls and boys have different dream content.

11. Experts recommend that people get _____ hours of sleep.
    a. nine
    c. eight
    b. seven
    d. six

12. To demonstrate that _____ is possible, researchers had participants perform distinctive patterns of voluntary eye movements while they were asleep.
    a. lucid dreaming
    c. meditation
    b. hypnosis
    d. activation and synthesis

13. Which of these individuals would you expect to be most responsive to hypnosis?
    a. 19-year-old Paula
    b. 11-year-old Ralph
    c. 24-year-old Jeannine
    d. 46-year-old George

14. Research suggests that people who practise _____ have thicker areas of cortex than individuals who do not.
    a. hypnosis
    c. somnambulism
    b. lucid dreaming
    d. meditation

15. Craving for a drug in the absence of a physical need is the definition of _____
    a. addiction.
    c. psychological dependence.
    b. drug tolerance.
    d. physiological dependence.

16. Hallucinogens act in the brain by _____ the activation of _____ neurons.
    a. inhibiting; GABA
    c. prolonging; serotonin
    b. prolonging; dopamine
    d. inhibiting; dopamine

17. Endorphins help explain the action of _____ in the brain.
    a. stimulants
    c. hallucinogens
    b. opiates
    d. depressants

18. Heavy use of _____ may lead to paranoid delusions.
    a. stimulants
    c. opiates
    b. depressants
    d. hallucinogens

Essay Questions

1. How has the concept of the unconscious been modified in the time since Freud's theory?

2. What practices of dream interpretation are carried out in non-Western cultures?

3. What physiological mechanisms explain why drug use often leads to addiction?

Discovering Psychology Viewing Guide

Watch the following videos by logging on to MyPsychLab (**www.mypsychlab.com**). After you have watched the videos, complete the activities that follow.

Program 13: The Mind Awake and Asleep

Program 14: The Mind Hidden and Divided

PROGRAM REVIEW

1. Which of the following is an example of a circadian rhythm?
   a. eating three meals a day at approximately the same time
   b. experiencing alternate periods of REM and non-REM sleep
   c. having systematic changes in hormone levels on a 24-hour cycle
   d. having changes in fertility levels during a month

2. Which of the following is an example of the lower-level processing of sensory input that is nonconscious?
   a. recognizing a friend's face
   b. detecting edges
   c. working on an assembly line
   d. noticing something tastes good

3. In Donald Broadbent's research, what happened when people heard two stories but were asked to attend to only one?
   a. They comprehended both stories.
   b. They comprehended only the attended story.
   c. They wove bits of the unattended story into the attended story.
   d. They were not able to follow either story.

4. According to McCarley and Hobson, what is true about REM sleep?
   a. Adults spend more time in REM sleep than infants do.
   b. REM sleep is an unnecessary physiological function.
   c. The random burst of brain activity occurs first, followed by the dreamer's attempt to make sense of it.
   d. The subconscious expresses its deepest desires during REM sleep.

5. In the experiment described in the program, patients under anesthesia were exposed to a positive or negative message. What effect did getting a positive message have?
   a. It meant less anesthesia was needed.
   b. It shortened patients' hospital stays.
   c. It created more positive attitudes toward surgery.
   d. Positive messages had no effect because patients were unaware of them.

6. Which part of the brain is responsible for conscious awareness?
   a. cerebral cortex   c. limbic system
   b. brain stem   d. hypothalamus

7. Michael Gazzaniga has worked with split-brain, or "broken-brain," patients. What has this led him to believe about our individuality?
   a. It comes from an interpreter in the left hemisphere.
   b. It is an illusion based on our emotional needs.
   c. It derives from our unique set of independent mind-modules.
   d. It is located in the corpus callosum.

8. Consciousness performs all of the following functions, except _____
   a. filtering sensory data.
   b. enabling us to respond flexibly.
   c. allowing us to have a sense of our own mortality.
   d. guiding performance of highly routinized actions.

9. One of the most important techniques that psychologists commonly use to confirm the validity of a recovered memory is to _____
   a. have the rememberer recount the memory under hypnosis.
   b. subject the rememberer to a lie-detector test.
   c. count the number of details in the rememberer's story.
   d. collect confirming evidence from other people who knew about the event.

QUESTIONS TO CONSIDER

1. Donald Broadbent conceived of attention as a selective filter that acts like a tuner on a radio, selecting one message from all the others. According to Broadbent, the unattended sensory information is sent to a buffer, where it either receives attention and gets processed or is ignored and lost. How is this buffer similar to the concept of the sensory memory? What role might it play in subliminal perception?

2. Psychoactive drugs are only partially responsible for the changes in the drug taker's consciousness. Mental sets, expectations, and the context in which the drugs are taken can also have significant influences. What are the implications for alcohol and drug education and treatment?

Learning and Behaviour Analysis

Imagine that you are in a movie theatre, watching a horror film. As the hero approaches a closed door, the music on the movie's sound track grows dark and menacing. You suddenly feel the urge to yell, "Don't go through that door!" Meanwhile, you find that your heart is racing. Why? If you think about this question formally, you might realize the answer, "I have learned an association between movie music and movie events—and that is what's making me nervous!" Had you ever thought about this relationship before? Probably not. Somehow, by virtue of watching enough movies, you have learned the association without any particular thought. The main topic of Chapter 7 is the types of associations that you acquire effortlessly in your day-to-day experience.

Psychologists have long been interested in *learning*, the ways in which organisms learn from experiences in the world. In just a moment, we will offer a more precise definition of learning. We then consider two particular types of learning: classical conditioning and operant conditioning. As you will see, each of these types of learning represents a different way in which organisms acquire and use information about the structure of their environments. For each of these types of learning, we will describe both the basic mechanisms that govern its operation in the laboratory and applications to real-life situations.

In this chapter, we also reflect on the way learning is similar and dissimilar across species. You will see that basic processes of conditioning are the same across a wide variety of species. However, we will note that some aspects of learning are constrained by species's particular genetic endowments. In particular, we will see how *cognition*—higher mental processes—affects learning processes in both humans and other species.

The Study of Learning

To begin our exploration of learning, we will first define learning itself, and then offer a brief sketch of the history of psychological research on the topic.

WHAT IS LEARNING?

Learning, a process that results in a relatively consistent change in behaviour or behaviour potential—the likelihood that you will exhibit a new behaviour—is based on experience. Let's look more closely at the three critical parts of this definition.

A Process Based on Experience Learning can take place only through experience, although experience can be very broad. Experience includes taking in information (and evaluating and transforming it) and making responses that affect the environment. Learning consists of a response influenced by the lessons of memory. Learned behaviour does not include

---

learning A process based on experience that results in a relatively permanent change in behaviour or behavioural potential.

learning–performance distinction The difference between what has been learned and what is expressed in overt behaviour.

changes that come about because of physical maturation or brain development as the organism ages, nor those caused by illness or brain damage. Some lasting changes in behaviour require experience following maturational readiness. For example, consider the timetable that determines when an infant is ready to crawl, stand, walk, run, and be toilet trained. No amount of training or practice will produce those behaviours before the child has matured sufficiently to physically be able to do them. Psychologists are especially interested in discovering what aspects of behaviour can be changed through experience and how such changes come about in a variety of organisms, from the most simple to complex organisms like humans.

A Change in Behaviour or Behaviour Potential It is obvious that learning has taken place when you are able to demonstrate the results, such as when you drive a car or use a microwave oven. You cannot directly observe learning itself—you cannot ordinarily see the changes in your brain—but learning is apparent from improvements in your *performance*. Though measurable changes in how well you can do something are indicative of learning, your performance often does not show everything that you have learned. Sometimes you acquire general attitudes, such as an *appreciation* of modern art or an *understanding* of Eastern philosophy, that may not be apparent in your measurable actions. In such instances, you have achieved a potential for behaviour change because you have learned attitudes and values that can influence the kinds of books you read or the way you spend your leisure time. This is an example of the **learning–performance distinction**—the difference between what has been learned and what is expressed, or performed, in overt behaviour.

A Relatively Consistent Change To qualify as learned, a change in behaviour or behaviour potential must be relatively consistent over different occasions. Thus, once you learn to swim, you will probably always be able to do so. Note that consistent changes are not always permanent changes. You may, for

How does consistent form in ballet dancers fit the definition of learning?

example, become quite a consistent dart thrower if you practise every day. If you then give up the sport, however, your skills might deteriorate toward their original level. If, however, you learned once to be a championship dart thrower, it ought to be easier for you to learn a second time. Something has been "saved" from your prior experience to provide this advantage. In that sense, the change may be permanent.

Habituation and Sensitization To help you master the concept of learning, we want to describe two of its most basic forms: habituation and sensitization. Imagine that you are examining a picture of a pleasant scene—an image, for example, of waterskiing or windsurfing. The first time you see it, you might have a fairly strong emotional response. However, if you view the same image repeatedly in short succession, your emotional response will become weaker over time (Leventhal, Martin, Seals, Tapia, & Rehm, 2007). This is an example of **habituation**: You show a decrease in behavioural response when a stimulus is presented repeatedly. Habituation helps keep your focus on novel events in the environment—you do not expend behavioural effort to respond repeatedly to old stimuli.

Think about how habituation fits the definition of learning. There is a change in behaviour (your emotional response is weaker) that is based on experience (you have seen the image repeatedly), and that behaviour change is consistent (you do not return to your original level of emotional response). However, the change in emotional response is unlikely to be permanent. If you see the same picture after sufficient time has passed, you might find it emotionally engaging once again.

When **sensitization** occurs, your response to a stimulus becomes stronger, rather than weaker, when it occurs repeatedly. Suppose, for example, you experience the same painful stimulus several times in short succession. Even if the intensity of the stimulus remained constant, you would report greater pain in response to the final stimulus in the series than you would in response to the first stimulus (Farrell & Gibson, 2007). Once again, sensitization fits the definition of learning because experience in the world (repeated experiences of a painful stimulus) leads to a consistent change in behavioural response (reports that the pain is more intense). You might wonder what determines whether people will experience habituation or sensitization in response to different stimuli. In general, sensitization is more likely to occur when stimuli are intense or irritating.

BEHAVIOURISM AND BEHAVIOUR ANALYSIS

Much of modern psychology's view of learning finds its roots in the work of **John Watson** (1878–1958). Watson founded the school of psychology known as *behaviourism*. For nearly 50 years, American psychology was dominated by the behaviourist tradition expressed in Watson's 1919 book, *Psychology from the Standpoint of a Behaviorist*. Watson argued that **introspection**—people's verbal reports of their own sensations, images, and feelings—was *not* an acceptable means of studying behaviour because it was too subjective. How could scientists verify the accuracy of such private experiences of individuals? Once introspection has been rejected, what should the subject matter of psychology be? Watson's answer was *observable behaviour*. In

Watson's words, "States of consciousness, like the so-called phenomenon of spiritualism, are not objectively verifiable and for that reason can never become data for science" (Watson, 1919, p. 1). Watson also defined the chief goal of psychology as "the prediction and control of behaviour" (Watson, 1913, p. 158).

B. F. Skinner (1904–1990) adopted Watson's cause and expanded his agenda on behaviour. Skinner began the research that would lead him to formulate his position when, after reading Watson's 1924 book, *Behaviorism*, he began his graduate study in psychology at Harvard. Over time, Skinner formulated a position known as *radical behaviourism*. Skinner embraced Watson's complaint against internal states and mental events. However, Skinner focused not so much on their legitimacy as data, but on their legitimacy as *causes of behaviour* (Skinner, 1990). In Skinner's view, mental events, such as thinking and imagining, do not cause behaviour. Rather, they are examples of behaviour that are caused by environmental stimuli. It is from this perspective that behaviour was described as a response to a stimulus.

Suppose that we deprive a pigeon of food for 24 hours, place it in an apparatus where it can obtain food by pecking a small disk, and find that it soon does so. Skinner would argue that the animal's behaviour can be fully explained by environmental events—deprivation and the use of food as reinforcement. The subjective feeling of hunger, which cannot be directly observed or measured, is not a cause of the behaviour, but the result of deprivation. It adds nothing to our account to say that the bird pecked the disk because it was hungry or because it wanted to get the food. To explain what the bird does, you need not understand anything about its inner psychological states—

B. F. Skinner expanded on Watson's ideas and applied them to a wide spectrum of behaviour. Why did Skinner's psychology focus on environmental events rather than internal states?

---

habituation A decrease in a behavioural response when a stimulus is presented repeatedly.

sensitization The behavioural response to stimuli opposite to that seen with habitutation.

introspection People's verbal reports of their own sensations, images, and feelings.

you need only understand the simple principles of learning that allow the bird to acquire the association between behaviour and reward. This is the essence of Skinner's brand of behaviourism (Delprato & Midgley, 1992).

Skinner's brand of behaviourism served as the original philosophical cornerstone of **behaviour analysis**, the area of psychology that focuses on discovering environmental determinants of learning and behaviour (Cooper, Heron, & Heward, 2007). In general, behaviour analysts attempt to discover regularities in learning that are universal, occurring in all types of animal species, including humans, under comparable situations. That is why studies with nonhuman animals have been so critical to progress in this area. Complex forms of learning represent combinations and elaborations of simpler processes and not qualitatively different phenomena. In the sections that follow, we describe classical conditioning and operant conditioning—two simple forms of learning that give rise to quite complex behaviours. It is useful to remember that although your behaviour appears highly complex, it often results from more simple things you have learned and have chained together and used efficiently.

STOP AND REVIEW

❶ What is meant by the learning–performance distinction?
❷ Why did Watson emphasize the study of observable behaviour?
❸ What is a major goal of behaviour analysis?
❹ What is the definition of habituation?

Classical Conditioning: Learning Predictable Signals

Imagine once more that you are watching that horror movie discussed at the beginning of the chapter. Why does your heart race when the sound track signals trouble for the hero? Somehow your body has learned to produce a physiological response (a racing heart) when one environmental event (for example, scary music) is associated with another (scary visual events). This type of learning is known as **classical conditioning**, a basic form of learning in which one stimulus or event predicts the occurrence of another stimulus or event. The organism learns a new *association* between two stimuli—a stimulus that did not previously elicit the response and one that naturally elicited the response. As you shall see, the innate capacity to quickly associate pairs of events in your environment has profound behavioural implications for many organisms.

---

behaviour analysis The area of psychology that focuses on the environmental determinants of learning and behaviour.

classical conditioning A type of learning in which a behaviour (conditioned response) comes to be elicited by a stimulus (conditioned stimulus) that has acquired its power through an association with a biologically significant stimulus (unconditioned stimulus).

PAVLOV'S SURPRISING OBSERVATION

The first rigorous study of classical conditioning was the result of what may well be psychology's most famous accident. The Russian physiologist Ivan Pavlov (1849–1936) did not set out to study classical conditioning or any other psychological phenomenon. He happened on classical conditioning when conducting research on digestion, for which he won a Nobel Prize in 1904.

Pavlov had devised a technique to study digestive processes in dogs by implanting tubes in their glands and digestive organs to divert bodily secretions to containers outside their bodies so that the secretions could be measured and analyzed. To produce at least one of these secretions—saliva—Pavlov's assistants put meat powder into the dogs' mouths. After repeating this procedure a number of times, Pavlov observed an unexpected behaviour in his dogs: They salivated *before* the powder was put in their mouths! They would start salivating at the mere sight of the food and, later, at the sight of the assistant who brought the food or even at the sound of the assistant's footsteps. Indeed, any stimulus that regularly preceded the presentation of food came to elicit salivation. Quite by accident, Pavlov had observed that learning may result from two stimuli becoming associated with each other.

Fortunately, Pavlov had the scientific skills and curiosity to begin a rigorous study on this surprising phenomenon. He ignored the advice of the great physiologist of the time, Sir Charles Sherrington, that he should give up his foolish investigation of "psychic" secretions. Instead, Pavlov abandoned his work on digestion and, in so doing, changed the course of psychology forever (Pavlov, 1928). For the remainder of Pavlov's life, he continued to search for the variables that influence classically conditioned behaviour. Classical conditioning is also called *Pavlovian conditioning* because of Pavlov's discovery of the major phenomena of conditioning and his dedication to tracking down the variables that influence it.

Pavlov's considerable research experience allowed him to follow a simple and elegant strategy to discover the conditions necessary for his dogs to be conditioned to salivate. As

Physiologist Ivan Pavlov (shown here with his research team) observed classical conditioning while conducting research on digestion. What were some of Pavlov's major contributions to the study of this form of learning?

FIGURE 7.1 Pavlov's Original Procedure
In his original experiments, Pavlov used a variety of stimuli such as tones, bells, lights, and metronomes to serve as neutral stimuli. The experimenter presented one of these neutral stimuli and then the food powder. The dog's saliva was collected through a tube.

shown in **Figure 7.1**, dogs in his experiments were first placed in a restraining harness. At regular intervals, a stimulus such as a tone was presented, and a dog was given a bit of food. Importantly, the tone had no prior meaning for the dog with respect to food or salivation. As you might imagine, the dog's first reaction to the tone was only an *orienting response*—the dog pricked its ears and moved its head to locate the source of the sound. However, with *repeated pairings* of the tone and the food, the orienting response stopped and salivation began. What Pavlov had observed in his earlier research was no accident: The phenomenon could be replicated under controlled conditions. Pavlov demonstrated the generality of this effect by using a variety of other stimuli ordinarily neutral with respect to salivation, such as lights and ticking metronomes.

The main features of Pavlov's classical conditioning procedure are illustrated in **Figure 7.2**. At the core of classical conditioning are *reflex* responses such as salivation, pupil contraction, knee jerks, or eye blinking. A **reflex** is a response that is naturally triggered—*elicited*—by specific stimuli that are biologically relevant for the organism. Any stimulus, such as the food powder used in Pavlov's experiments, that naturally elicits a reflexive behaviour is called an **unconditioned stimulus (UCS)**, because learning is not a necessary condition for the stimulus to control the behaviour. The behaviour elicited by the unconditioned stimulus is called the **unconditioned response (UCR)**.

In Pavlov's experiments, the stimuli such as lights and tones did not originally trigger the reflex response of salivation. Over time, however, each neutral stimulus was repeatedly paired with the unconditioned stimulus. This neutral stimulus is called the **conditioned stimulus (CS)**: Its power to elicit behaviour is *conditioned* on its association with the UCS. After several trials, the CS will produce a response called the **conditioned response (CR)**. The conditioned response is whatever response the conditioned stimulus elicits as a product of learning. We will provide several examples as this section unfolds.

Let's review. Nature provides the UCS–UCR connections, but the learning produced by classical conditioning creates the CS–CR connection. The conditioned stimulus acquires some of the power to influence behaviour that was originally limited to the unconditioned stimulus. Let's now look in more detail at the basic processes of classical conditioning.

PROCESSES OF CONDITIONING

Pavlov's original experiments inspired extensive study of how classically conditioned responses appear and disappear. In this section, we describe several important conclusions made by researchers about the basic processes of classical conditioning. These conclusions have emerged from hundreds of different studies across a wide range of animal species.

Acquisition and Extinction **Figure 7.3** displays a hypothetical classical conditioning experiment. The first panel displays **acquisition**, the process by which the CR is first elicited and gradually increases in frequency over repeated trials. In general, the CS and UCS must be paired several times before the CS reliably elicits a CR. With systematic CS–UCS pairings, the CR is elicited with increasing frequency, and the organism may be said to have acquired a conditioned response.

---

reflex An unlearned response elicited by specific stimuli that have biological relevance for an organism.

unconditioned stimulus (UCS) In classical conditioning, the stimulus that elicits an unconditioned response.

unconditioned response (UCR) In classical conditioning, the response elicited by an unconditioned stimulus without prior training or learning.

conditioned stimulus (CS) In classical conditioning, a previously neutral stimulus that comes to elicit a conditioned response.

conditioned response (CR) In classical conditioning, a response elicited by some previously neutral stimulus that occurs as a result of pairing the neutral stimulus with an unconditioned stimulus.

acquisition The stage in a classical conditioning experiment during which the conditioned response is first elicited by the conditioned stimulus.

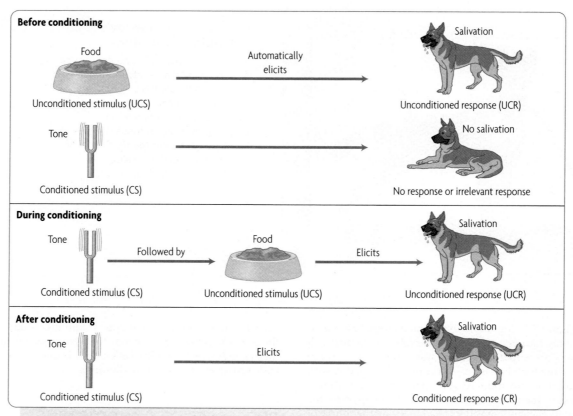

FIGURE 7.2   Basic Features of Classical Conditioning
Before conditioning, the unconditioned stimulus (UCS) naturally elicits the unconditioned response (UCR). A neutral stimulus, such as a tone, has no eliciting effect. During conditioning, the neutral stimulus is paired with the UCS. Through its association with the UCS, the neutral stimulus becomes a conditioned stimulus (CS) and elicits a conditioned response (CR) that is similar to the UCR.

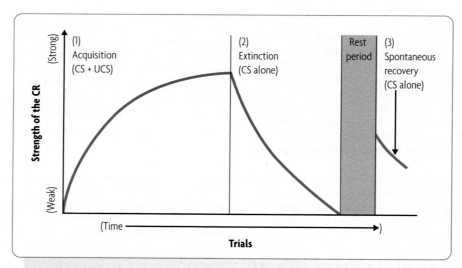

FIGURE 7.3   Acquisition, Extinction, and Spontaneous Recovery in Classical Conditioning
During acquisition (CS + UCS), the strength of the CR increases rapidly. During extinction, when the UCS no longer follows the CS, the strength of the CR drops to zero. The CR may reappear after a brief rest period, even when the UCS is still not presented. The reappearance of the CR is called spontaneous recovery.

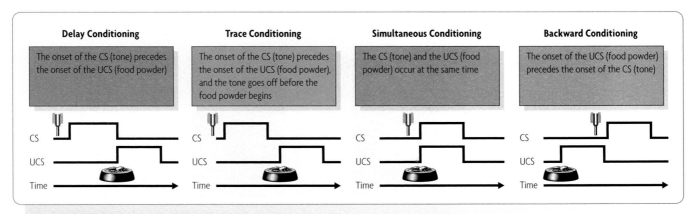

FIGURE 7.4 Four Variations of the CS–UCS Temporal Arrangement in Classical Conditioning

Researchers have explored the four possible timing arrangements between the CS and UCS. Conditioning is generally most effective in a delay conditioning paradigm with a short interval between the onsets of the CS and UCS.

From Robert A. Baron, *Psychology*, 5/e, p. 172. Published by Allyn & Bacon, Boston, MA. Copyright © 2001 by Pearson Education. Reprinted by permission of the publisher.

In classical conditioning, as in telling a good joke, *timing* is critical. The CS and UCS must be presented closely enough in time to be perceived by the organism as being related. (We will describe an exception to this rule in a later section on *taste-aversion learning*.) Researchers have studied four temporal patterns between the two stimuli, as shown in **Figure 7.4** (Hearst, 1988). The most widely used type of conditioning is called *delay conditioning*, in which the CS comes on prior to and stays on at least until the presenting of the UCS. In *trace conditioning*, the CS is discontinued or turned off before the UCS is presented. *Trace* refers to the memory that the organism is assumed to have of the CS, which is no longer present when the UCS appears. In *simultaneous conditioning*, both the CS and UCS are presented at the same time. Finally, in the case of *backward conditioning*, the CS is presented after the UCS.

Conditioning is usually most effective in a delayed conditioning paradigm, with a short interval between the onsets of the CS and UCS. However, the exact time interval between the CS and the UCS that will produce optimal conditioning depends on several factors, including the intensity of the CS and the response being conditioned. (The timing also depends on the organism, as less complex organisms often do not have the cognitive ability to remember associations as long as more complex organisms do.) Let's focus on the response being conditioned. For muscular responses, such as eye blinks, a short interval of a second or less is best. For visceral responses, such as heart rate and salivation, however, longer intervals of 5 to 15 seconds work best.

Conditioning is generally poor with a simultaneous procedure and very poor with a backward procedure. Evidence of backward conditioning may appear after a few pairings of the UCS and CS but disappear with extended training as the animal learns that the CS is followed by a period free of the UCS. In both cases, conditioning is weak because the CS does not actually predict the onset of the UCS. (We will return to the importance of predictability, or *contingency*, in the next section.)

What happens when the CS (for example, the tone) no longer predicts the UCS (the food powder)? Under those circumstances, the CR (salivation) becomes weaker over time and eventually stops occurring. When the CR no longer appears in the presence of the CS (and the absence of the UCS), the process of **extinction** is said to have occurred (see Figure 7.3, panel 2). Conditioned responses, then, are not necessarily a permanent aspect of the organism's behavioural repertoire. However, the CR will reappear in a weak form when the CS is presented alone again after extinction (see Figure 7.3, panel 3). Pavlov referred to this sudden reappearance of the CR after a rest period, or time-out, without further exposure to the UCS, as **spontaneous recovery** after extinction.

When the original pairing is renewed, postextinction, the CR becomes rapidly stronger. This more rapid relearning is an instance of *savings*: Less time is necessary to reacquire the response than to acquire it originally. Thus, some of the original conditioning must be retained by the organism even after experimental extinction appears to have eliminated the CR. In other words, extinction has only weakened performance, not eliminated the residues of the original learning. This is why we made a distinction between learning and performance in our original definition of learning.

Stimulus Generalization Suppose we have taught a dog that presentation of a tone of a certain frequency predicts food powder. Is the dog's response specific to only that stimulus? If you think about this question for a moment, you will probably not be surprised that the answer is "no." In general, once a CR has been conditioned to a particular CS, similar stimuli may also elicit the response. For example, if conditioning was to a high-frequency tone, a slightly lower tone could also elicit the response. A child bitten by a big dog is likely to respond with fear even to smaller dogs. This automatic extension of

---

extinction In conditioning, the weakening of a conditioned association in the absence of a reinforcer or unconditioned stimulus.

spontaneous recovery The reappearance of an extinguished conditioned response after a rest period.

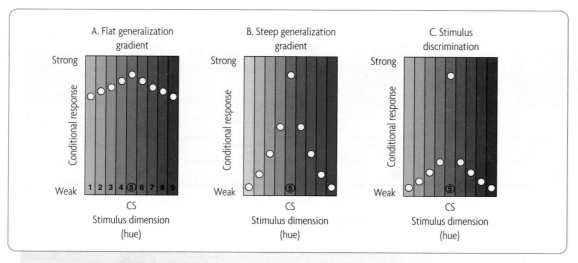

FIGURE 7.5 Stimulus Generalization Gradients

After conditioning to a medium green stimulus, the subject responds almost as strongly to stimuli of similar hues, as shown by the flat generalization gradient in panel A. When the subject is exposed to a broader range of coloured stimuli, responses grow weaker as the colour becomes increasingly dissimilar to the training stimulus. The generalization gradient becomes very steep, as shown in panel B. The experimenter could change the generalization gradient shown in panel A to resemble the one in panel C by giving the subject discrimination training. In this case, the medium green stimulus would be continually paired with the UCS, but stimuli of all other hues would not.

From *Principles and Methods of Psychology* by Robert B. Lawson, Stephen G. Goldstein, & Richard E. Musty. Copyright © 1975 by Oxford University Press, Inc. Used by permission of Oxford University Press, Inc.

Why might a child who has been frightened by one dog develop a fear response to all dogs? Or learn that dogs do not represent a threat?

responding to stimuli that have never been paired with the original UCS is called **stimulus generalization**. The more similar the new stimulus is to the original CS, the stronger the response will be. When response strength is measured for each of a series of increasingly dissimilar stimuli along a given dimension, as shown in **Figure 7.5**, a *generalization gradient* is found.

The existence of generalization gradients should suggest to you the way classical conditioning serves its function in everyday experience. As important stimuli rarely occur in exactly the same form every time in nature, stimulus generalization builds in a similarity safety factor by extending the range of learning beyond the original specific experience. With this feature, new but comparable events can be recognized as having the same meaning, or behavioural significance, despite apparent differences. For example, even when a predator makes a slightly different sound or is seen from a different angle, its prey can still recognize and respond to it quickly.

Stimulus Discrimination In some circumstances, however, it is important that a response be made to only a very small range of stimuli. An organism should not, for example, exhaust itself by fleeing too often from animals that are only superficially similar to its natural predators. **Stimulus discrimination** is the process by which an organism learns to respond differently to stimuli that are distinct from the CS on some dimension (for example, differences in hue or in pitch). An organism's discrimination among similar stimuli (tones of 1000, 1200, and 1500 Hz, for example) is sharpened with discrimination training in which only one of them (1200 Hz, for example) predicts the UCS and in which the others are repeatedly presented without it. Early in

stimulus generalization The automatic extension of a conditioned response to similar stimuli that have never been paired with the unconditioned stimulus.

stimulus discrimination A conditioning process in which an organism learns to respond differently to stimuli that differ from the conditioned stimulus on some dimension.

conditioning, stimuli similar to the CS will elicit a similar response, although not quite as strong. As discrimination training proceeds, the responses to the similar stimuli weaken: The organism gradually learns which signal predicts the onset of the UCS and which signals do not.

For an organism to perform optimally in an environment, the processes of generalization and discrimination must strike a balance. You do not want to be overselective, as it can be quite costly to miss the presence of a predator. You also do not want to be overresponsive, because if you are fearful of every shadow, you will waste time and energy to dispel your worry. Classical conditioning provides a mechanism that allows creatures to react efficiently to the structure of their environments (Garcia, 1990).

FOCUS ON ACQUISITION

In this section, we will examine more closely the conditions that are necessary for classical conditioning to take place. So far, we have *described* the acquisition of classically conditioned responses, but we have not yet *explained* it. Pavlov believed that classical conditioning resulted from the mere pairing of the CS and the UCS. In his view, if a response is to be classically conditioned, the CS and the UCS must occur close together in time—that is, they must be *temporally contiguous*. As we will see next, however, contemporary research has modified that view.

Pavlov's theory dominated classical conditioning until the mid-1960s, when **Robert Rescorla** (1966) conducted a very telling experiment using dogs as subjects. Rescorla designed an experiment using a tone (the CS) and a shock (the UCS). For one group of animals the CS and UCS were merely contiguous—which, if Pavlov were correct, would be sufficient to produce classical conditioning. For the other group of animals, the tone reliably predicted the presence of the shock.

In the first phase of the experiment, Rescorla trained dogs to jump a barrier from one side of a shuttlebox to the other to avoid an electric shock delivered through the grid floor

FIGURE 7.6   A Shuttlebox
Robert Rescorla used the frequency with which dogs jumped over a barrier as a measure of fear conditioning.

(see **Figure 7.6**). If the dogs did not jump, they received a shock; if they did jump, the shock was postponed. Rescorla used the frequency with which dogs jumped the barrier as a measure of fear conditioning.

When the dogs were jumping across the barrier regularly, Rescorla divided his subjects into two groups and subjected them to another training procedure. To the random group, the UCS (the shock) was delivered randomly and independently of the CS (the tone) (see **Figure 7.7**). Although the CS and the UCS often occurred close together in time—they were, by chance, temporally contiguous—the UCS was as likely to be delivered in the absence of the CS as it was in its presence. Thus, the CS had no predictive value. For the contingency group, however, the UCS always followed the CS. Thus, for this group, the sounding of the tone was a reliable predictor of the delivery of the shock.

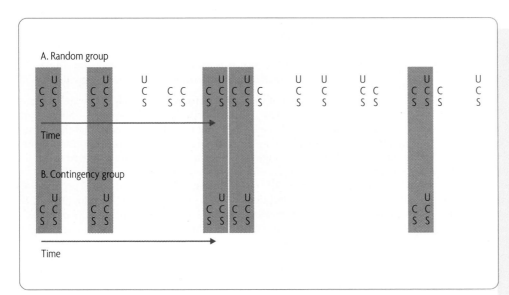

FIGURE 7.7   Rescorla's Procedure for Demonstrating the Importance of Contingency

For the random group, 5-second tones (the CS) and 5-second shocks (the UCS) were distributed randomly through the experimental period. For the contingency group, the dogs experienced only the subset of tones and shocks that occurred in a predictive relationship (the onset of the CS preceded the onset of the UCS by 30 seconds or less). Only the dogs in the contingency group learned to associate the CS with the UCS.

FIGURE 7.8 The Role of Contingency in Classical Conditioning
Rescorla demonstrated that dogs trained under the contingent CS–UCS relation showed more jumping (and thus conditioned fear) than did dogs trained under the contiguous but noncontingent CS–UCS relation. The arrows indicate the onset and offset of the CS tone.

Once this training was complete, the dogs were put back into the shuttlebox, but this time with a twist. Now the tone used in the second training procedure occasionally sounded, signaling shock. What happened? **Figure 7.8** indicates that dogs exposed to the *contingent* (predictable) CS–UCS relation jumped more frequently in the presence of the tone than did dogs exposed only to the *contiguous* (associated) CS–UCS relation. Contingency was critical for the signal to serve as a successful cue for the shock.

Thus, in addition to the CS being contiguous—occurring close in time—with the UCS, the CS must also *reliably predict* the occurrence of the UCS in order for classical conditioning to occur (Rescorla, 1988). This finding makes considerable sense. After all, in natural situations, where learning enables organisms to adapt to changes in their environment, stimuli come in clusters and not in neat, simple units, as they do in laboratory experiments.

There is one last requirement for a stimulus to serve as a basis for classical conditioning: It must be *informative* in the environment. Consider an experimental situation in which rats have learned that a tone predicts a shock. Now, a light is added into the situation so that both the light and tone precede the shock. However, when the light is subsequently presented alone, the rats do not appear to have learned that the light predicts the shock (Kamin, 1969). For these rats, the previous conditioning to the tone in the first phase of the experiment *blocked* any subsequent conditioning that could occur to the light. From the rat's point of view, the light may as well not have existed; it provided no additional information beyond that already given by the tone.

The requirement for the stimulus to be informative explains why conditioning occurs most rapidly when the CS stands out against the many other stimuli that may also be present in an environment. A stimulus is more readily noticed the more *intense* it is and the more it *contrasts* with other stimuli. To generate good conditioning, you must present either a strong, novel stimulus in an unfamiliar situation or a strong, familiar stimulus in a novel context.

You can see that classical conditioning is more complex than even Pavlov originally realized. A neutral stimulus will become an effective CS only if it is both appropriately contingent and informative. Let's now shift your attention a bit. We want to identify real-life situations in which classical conditioning plays a role—situations you probably have experience with.

APPLICATIONS OF CLASSICAL CONDITIONING

Your knowledge of classical conditioning can help you understand significant everyday behaviour. In this section, we help you recognize some real-world instances of emotions and preferences as the products of this form of learning. We also explore the role classical conditioning plays in the unfolding of drug addiction.

Emotions and Preferences Earlier we asked you to think about your experience at a horror movie. In that case, you (unconsciously) learned an association between scary music (the CS) and certain likely events (the UCS—the kinds of things that happen in horror movies that cause reflexive revulsion). If you pay careful attention to events in your life, you will discover that there are many circumstances in which you cannot quite explain why you are having such a strong emotional reaction or why you have such a strong preference about something. You might take a step back and ask yourself, "Is this the product of classical conditioning?"

Consider these situations (Rozin & Fallon, 1987; Rozin, Millman, & Nemeroff, 1986):

- Do you think you would be willing to eat fudge that had been formed into the shape of dog feces?
- Do you think you would be willing to drink a sugar-water solution if the sugar was drawn from a container that you knew was incorrectly labelled poison?
- Do you think you would be willing to drink apple juice into which a sterilized cockroach had been dipped?

If each of these situations makes you say "No way!" you are not alone. The classically conditioned response—feelings of disgust or danger—wins out over the knowledge that the stimulus is really okay. Since classically conditioned responses are not built up through conscious thought, they are also hard to eliminate through conscious reasoning!

One of the most extensively studied real-world products of classical conditioning is *fear conditioning* (Delgado, Olsson, & Phelps, 2006; Kim & Jung, 2006). In the earliest days of behaviourism, John Watson and his colleague Rosalie Rayner sought to prove that many fear responses could be understood as the pairing of a neutral stimulus with something naturally fear provoking. To test their idea, they experimented on an infant who came to be called Little Albert.

How did John Watson and Rosalie Rayner condition Little Albert to fear small, furry objects?

One of the challenges in conditioning is understanding why some events cause us to have strong physical, emotional, and cognitive reactions, and how some of these disappear. Psychologist Karim Nader of McGill University has been investigating fear conditioning with colleagues and has questioned the role of extinction in changing the behavioural response to a fear-inducing stimulus. To test this, Nader presented rats with a small shock in a particular type of environment, which causes them to jump and then freeze for a few moments. This shock would be akin to your getting a good shock from static electricity, which hurts and is surprising, but does not cause any tissue damage. Then the rats were placed in the environment without shocks. As expected, they saw extinction when the shocks stopped, but the response did return as strongly as before if the shocks returned. What Nader's group has discovered is that the memory of the stimulus is not erased at the level of the brain during extinction, but inhibited (Archbold, Bouton, & Nader, 2010). These findings explain why the response returns so quickly after extinction when the stimulus returns. Previous work done by Nader also suggests that there are changes at the cellular level, including RNA and protein changes that underlie fear conditioning (Duvarci, Nader, & LeDoux, 2008). Interestingly, these changes are found in the amygdala, a structure highly involved in emotion.

We do not want to leave you with the impression that only negative responses such as the response to a shock are classically conditioned. In fact, we suspect that you will also be able to interpret responses of happiness or excitement as instances of classical conditioning. Certainly people in the advertising industry hope that classical conditioning works as a positive

Watson and Rayner (1920) trained Albert to fear a white rat he had initially liked, by pairing its appearance with an aversive UCS—a loud noise just behind him created by striking a large steel bar with a hammer. The unconditioned startle response and the emotional distress to the noxious noise formed the basis of Albert's learning to react with fear to the appearance of the white rat. His fear was developed in just seven conditioning trials. The emotional conditioning was then extended to behavioural conditioning when Albert learned to escape from the feared stimulus. The infant's learned fear then generalized to other furry objects, such as a rabbit, a dog, and even a Santa Claus mask! (Albert's mother, a wet nurse at the hospital where the study was conducted, took him away before the researchers could try to treat the experimentally conditioned fear. So we do not know whatever happened to Little Albert [Harris, 1979].)

As you will recall from Chapter 2, researchers in psychology are guided by important ethical principles. Those principles make them look back at Watson and Rayner's experiment with grave discomfort: No ethical researcher would ever replicate an experiment of this type. Concerns about this work are increased by the knowledge that conditioned fear is highly resistant to extinction. A single traumatic event can condition you to respond with strong physical, emotional, and cognitive reactions—perhaps for a lifetime. We will see in Chapter 16 that therapists have designed treatments for these types of fears that are intended to counter the effects of classical conditioning.

How do advertisers exploit classical conditioning to make you feel "passion" toward their products?

force. They strive, for example, to create associations in your mind between their products (for example, jeans, sports cars, and soft drinks) and passion. They expect that elements of their advertisements—"sexy" individuals or situations—will serve as the UCS to bring about the UCR—feelings of sexual arousal. The hope then is that the product itself will be the CS, so that the feelings of arousal will become associated with it. You can evaluate this for yourself the next time you watch commercials on television for products. To find more examples of the classical conditioning of positive emotions, you should monitor your life for circumstances in which you have a rush of good feelings when you return, for instance, to a familiar location.

Learning to Be a Drug Addict Consider this scenario. A man's body lies in a Toronto alley, a half-empty syringe dangling from his arm. Cause of death? The coroner called it an overdose. What is surprising is that the man had ordinarily shot up far greater doses than the one that had supposedly killed him. This inconsistency baffled investigators. How could an addict with high drug tolerance die of an overdose when he did not even get a full hit?

Some time ago, Pavlov (1927) and later his colleague Bykov (1957) pointed out that tolerance to opiates can develop when an individual anticipates the pharmacological action of a drug, which means preparing to take the drug has an impact, as well as actually taking it. McMaster University psychologist **Shepard Siegel** refined these ideas. Siegel suggested that the setting in which drug use occurs acts as a conditioned stimulus for a situation in which the body learns to protect itself by preventing the drug from having its usual effect. When people take drugs, the drug (UCS) brings about certain physiological responses to which the body responds with countermeasures intended to re-establish homeostasis (see Chapter 4). The body's countermeasures to the drug are the unconditioned response (UCR). Over time, this *compensatory response* also becomes the conditioned response. That is, in settings ordinarily associated with drug use (the CS), the body physiologically prepares itself (the CR) for the drug's expected effects. Tolerance arises because, in that setting, the individual must consume an amount of the drug that overcomes the compensatory response before starting to get any "positive" effect. Increasingly larger doses are needed as the conditioned compensatory response itself grows.

Siegel tested these ideas in his laboratory by creating tolerance to heroin in laboratory rats.

In one study, Siegel and his colleagues classically conditioned rats to expect heroin injections (UCS) in one setting (CS_1) and dextrose (sweet sugar) solution injections in a different setting (CS_2) (Siegel, Hinson, Krank, & McCully, 1982). In the first phase of training, all rats developed heroin tolerance. On the test day, all animals received a larger-than-usual dose of heroin—nearly twice the previous amount. Half of them received it in the setting where heroin had previously been administered; the other half received it in the setting where dextrose solutions had been given during conditioning. Twice as many rats died in the dextrose-solution setting as in the usual heroin setting: 64 percent versus 32 percent!

Presumably, those receiving heroin in the usual setting were more prepared for this potentially dangerous situation because the context (CS_1) brought about a physiological response (CR) that countered the drug's typical effects (Poulos & Cappell, 1991).

To find out if a similar process might operate in humans, Siegel and a colleague interviewed heroin addicts who had come close to death from supposed overdoses. In 7 out of 10 cases, the addicts had been shooting up in a new and unfamiliar setting (Siegel, 1984). Although this natural experiment provides no conclusive data, it suggests that a dose for which an addict has developed tolerance in one setting may become an overdose in an unfamiliar setting. This analysis of how our bodies respond to drugs allows us to suggest that the addict we introduced at the beginning of this section died because he had never shot up before in that alley in Toronto.

Siegel has also spent a number of years as a professor and researcher at McMaster University trying to apply his research findings to the issue of treating addictions. The classical conditioning explanation suggests that if people learn about drug-taking behaviours, they may also do things to unlearn them. Think about someone you know who has been trying to quit smoking. She would probably report that it is most difficult not to smoke at social events where others are smoking. Some treatment options to help people quit smoking include the use of items that allow people to enjoy the benefits of the situation, but not those of nicotine. For example, cigarette-shaped items that allow the person to be in the environment and participate in the social exchange but not actually smoke cigarettes have been helpful in some cases. Siegel (reviewed in Siegel & Ramos, 2002) has also investigated the role of drug-onset cues (DOCs)—internal responses to the drug—to discover potential explanations for relapse behaviour. Results from these experiments suggest why some "cue-exposure" treatments for addiction have not worked very well. These treatments, which include exposing people to cues they would have experienced during drug taking, do not wipe out early drug-onset cues. Many of these cues are internal and are not related to the environment, but rather to the drug taking itself. The findings help explain why relapse is more likely when someone is exposed to even a small dose following the development of an addiction. For example, recovering alcoholics can be extremely vulnerable to just one drink because they have been classically conditioned to respond to the learned drug-onset cue with full-blown cravings, which contribute to more drinking.

STOP AND REVIEW

❶ What is the role of reflexive behaviours in classical conditioning?

❷ What is the difference between the UCS and the CS?

❸ What is meant by stimulus discrimination?

❹ Why is contingency so important in classical conditioning?

❺ What is the conditioned response when classical conditioning plays a role in drug addiction?

CRITICAL THINKING Consider the experiment that demonstrated conditioned heroin tolerance in rats. Why were the rats given twice the normal dose of heroin on the test day?

Operant Conditioning: Learning About Consequences

Let's return to the movie theatre. The horror film is now over, and you peel yourself off your seat. Your companion asks you if you are hoping that a sequel will be made. You respond, "I have learned that I should not go to horror films." You are probably right, but what kind of learning is this? Once again our answer begins around the turn of the 20th century.

THE LAW OF EFFECT

At about the same time that Pavlov was using classical conditioning to induce Russian dogs to salivate to the sound of a bell, **Edward L. Thorndike** (1898) was watching American cats trying to escape from puzzle boxes (see **Figure 7.9**). Thorndike reported his observations and inferences about the kind of learning he believed was taking place in his subjects. The cats at first only struggled against their confinement, but once some "impulsive" action allowed them to open the door, "all the other unsuccessful impulses [were] stamped out and the particular impulse leading to the successful act [was] stamped in by the resulting pleasure" (Thorndike, 1898, p. 13).

What had Thorndike's cats learned? According to Thorndike's analysis, learning was an association between stimuli in the situation and a response that an animal learned to make: a *stimulus–response (S–R) connection*. Thus the cats had learned to produce an appropriate response (for example, clawing at a button or loop) that in these stimulus circumstances (confinement in the puzzle box) led to a desired outcome (momentary freedom). Note that the learning of these S–R connections occurred gradually and automatically in a mechanistic way as the animal experienced the consequences of its actions

through blind *trial and error*. Gradually, the behaviours that had satisfying consequences increased in frequency; they eventually became the dominant response when the animal was placed in the puzzle box. Thorndike referred to this relationship between behaviour and its consequences as the **law of effect**: A response that is followed by satisfying consequences becomes more probable, and a response that is followed by dissatisfying consequences becomes less probable.

EXPERIMENTAL ANALYSIS OF BEHAVIOUR

B. F. Skinner embraced Thorndike's view that environmental consequences exert a powerful effect on behaviour. Skinner outlined a program of research whose purpose was to discover, by systematic variation of stimulus conditions, the ways that various environmental conditions affect the likelihood that a given response will occur:

> A natural datum in a science of behaviour is the probability that a given bit of behaviour will occur at a given time. An experimental analysis deals with that probability in terms of frequency or rate of responding. . . . The task of an experimental analysis is to discover all the variables of which probability of response is a function. (Skinner, 1966, pp. 213–214)

Skinner's analysis was experimental rather than theoretical; theorists are guided by derivations and predictions about behaviour from their theories, but empiricists, such as Skinner, advocate the bottom-up approach. They start with the collection and evaluation of data within the context of an experiment and are not theory-driven.

To analyze behaviour experimentally, Skinner developed **operant conditioning** procedures, in which he manipulated the *consequences* of an organism's behaviour in order to see what effect the consequences had on subsequent behaviour. An **operant** is any behaviour that is *emitted* by an organism and can be characterized in terms of the observable effects it has on the environment. Literally, *operant* means *affecting the environment*, or operating on it (Skinner, 1938). Operants are *not elicited* by specific stimuli as classically conditioned behaviours are. Pigeons peck, rats search for food, babies cry and coo, some people gesture while talking, and others stutter. The probability of these behaviours occurring in the future can be increased or decreased by manipulating the effects they have on the environment. If, for example, a baby's coo prompts desirable parental contact, the baby will coo more in the future. Operant conditioning, then, modifies the probability of different types of operant behaviour as a function of the environmental consequences they produce.

To carry out his new experimental analysis, Skinner invented an apparatus that allowed him to manipulate the

FIGURE 7.9 A Thorndike Puzzle Box
To get out of the puzzle box and obtain food, Edward Thorndike's cat had to manipulate a mechanism to release a weight that would then pull the door open.

law of effect A basic law of learning that states that the power of a stimulus to evoke a response is strengthened when the response is followed by a reward and weakened when it is not followed by a reward.

operant conditioning Learning in which the probability of a response is changed by a change in its consequences.

operant Behaviour emitted by an organism that can be characterized in terms of the observable effects it has on the environment.

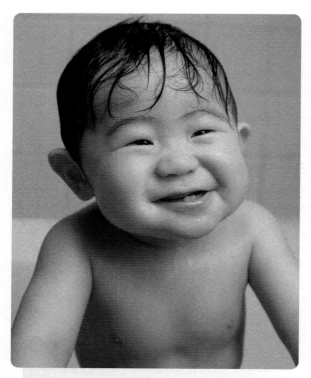

What environmental contingencies might cause babies to smile more often?

FIGURE 7.10 Operant Chamber
In this specially designed apparatus, typical of those used with rats, a press on the lever may be followed by delivery of a food pellet.

consequences of behaviour, the *operant chamber*. **Figure 7.10** shows how the operant chamber works. When, after having produced an appropriate behaviour defined by the experimenter, a rat presses a lever, the mechanism delivers a food pellet. This device allows experimenters to study the variables that allow rats to learn—or not learn—the behaviours they define. For example, if a lever press produces a food pellet only after a rat has turned a circle in the chamber, the rat will swiftly learn (through a process called *shaping*, which we will consider shortly) to turn a circle before pressing the lever.

In many operant experiments, the measure of interest is how much of a particular behaviour an animal carries out in a period of time. Researchers record the pattern and total amount of behaviour emitted in the course of an experiment. This methodology allowed Skinner to study the effect of reinforcement contingencies on animals' behaviour.

REINFORCEMENT CONTINGENCIES

A **reinforcement contingency** is a consistent relationship between a response and the changes in the environment that it produces. Imagine, for example, an experiment in which a pigeon's pecking a disk (the response) is generally followed by the presentation of grain (the corresponding change in the

environment). This consistent relationship, or reinforcement contingency, will usually be accompanied by an increase in the rate of pecking. For delivery of grain to increase *only* the probability of pecking, it must be contingent *only* on the pecking response—the delivery must occur regularly after that response but not after other responses, such as turning or bowing. Based on Skinner's work, modern behaviour analysts seek to understand behaviour in terms of reinforcement contingencies. Let's take a closer look at what has been discovered about these contingencies.

Positive and Negative Reinforcers Suppose you are now captivated by the idea of getting your pet rat to turn a circle in its cage. To increase the probability of circle-turning behaviour, you would want to use a **reinforcer**, any stimulus that—when made contingent on a behaviour—increases the probability of that behaviour over time. *Reinforcement* is the delivery of a reinforcer following a response.

Reinforcers are always defined empirically, in terms of their effects on changing the probability of a response. If you look out at the world, you can probably find three classes of stimuli: those toward which you are neutral, those that you find *appetitive* (you have an "appetite" for them), and those that you find *aversive* (you seek to avoid them). The compositions of these classes of stimuli clearly are not the same for all individuals: What is appetitive or aversive is defined by the behaviour of the individual organism. Consider the strawberry. Although many people find strawberries quite delicious, one of your authors finds strawberries virtually inedible. If you intend to use strawberries to change that author's behaviour, it is important to know that—for him—they are aversive rather than appetitive.

---

reinforcement contingency A consistent relationship between a response and the changes in the environment that it produces.

reinforcer Any stimulus that, when made contingent upon a response, increases the probability of that response.

Psychology in Your Life

HOW DOES CLASSICAL CONDITIONING AFFECT CANCER TREATMENT?

Medical researchers have made great strides in developing more effective treatments to combat cancers. Many of those treatments involve chemotherapy, drug treatments that kill or greatly weaken cancer cells. People who undergo chemotherapy often experience negative consequences such as fatigue and nausea. You might assume that those side effects would arise from the direct action of the chemotherapy drugs. Although that is partially the case, research suggests that processes of classical conditioning contribute greatly to the persistence of those side effects over time.

Consider a study that looked at cancer patients' experiences of fatigue. Patients undergoing chemotherapy often report experiencing fatigue and note that the fatigue prevents them from continuing a "normal life" (Curt et al., 2000). To explain the origins of some of those feelings of fatigue, researchers tested a model based on classical conditioning (Bovbjerg, Montgomery, & Raptis, 2005). The 82 women in the study repeatedly visited the same outpatient clinic to undergo treatment for breast cancer. In each session, the women received infusions of chemotherapy.

Let's evaluate this situation in terms of classical conditioning. The chemotherapy drugs serve as the unconditioned stimulus (UCS) producing post-treatment fatigue as an unconditioned response (UCR). Then, the researchers suggested that the clinic environment served as a conditioned

stimulus (CS). Over the visits to the clinic—as the CS became paired with the UCS—this model suggests that the women would begin to experience anticipatory fatigue as a conditioned response (CR) as soon as they arrived at the clinic.

To test this idea, the researchers measured how the women's fatigue changed over time. They measured both how the women felt before each session of chemotherapy—their level of preinfusion anticipatory fatigue—and how they felt after each session—their level of post-infusion fatigue. The data showed a clear pattern: Over visits to the clinic, the women experienced increasing levels of anticipatory fatigue. You might think that the fatigue was getting worse because of the cumulative effect of chemotherapy. However, the women did not report higher levels of post-infusion fatigue. Consistent with the model based on classical conditioning, the greater levels of anticipatory fatigue seemed to have as one important source the conditioned associations with the clinic environment. In fact, researchers have produced evidence to support a classical conditioning analysis of other aspects of chemotherapy. Many patients, for example, begin to experience nausea before the chemotherapy sessions; in other words, the clinic settings in which they receive treatment begin to function as a conditioned stimulus (Tomoyasu, Bovbjerg, & Jacobsen, 1996).

This classical conditioning model might help explain why some of the

aftereffects of chemotherapy endure well after the end of treatment. Researchers surveyed a group of 273 Hodgkin's disease survivors from 1 to 20 years beyond treatment (Cameron et al., 2001). The participants were asked to reflect on the past six months to indicate whether they "had noticed any smell or odour (anything [they had] seen/places [they had] gone to; any foods or drinks)" that had reminded them of treatment and made them "feel good or bad emotionally or physically" (p. 72). More than half of the participants—55 percent—reported lingering bad responses that were triggered by stimuli associated with their chemotherapy. The researchers suggest that these persistent responses were the result of classically conditioned associations between various aspects of the chemotherapy experience (the CS) and the drug infusions (the UCS).

These studies provide strong evidence for the role of classical conditioning in amplifying the negative effects of chemotherapy. The studies also give researchers a context in which they can begin to design treatments. For example, researchers could devise ways to change contextual cues to decrease the likelihood that a clinic environment would become a conditioned stimulus. Interventions of that sort could not eliminate negative effects of chemotherapy, but they could help stop those negative effects from enduring over time.

When a behaviour is followed by the delivery of an appetitive stimulus, the event is called **positive reinforcement**. Your pet rat will turn circles if a consequence of circle turning is the delivery of desirable food. Humans will tell jokes, if a consequence of their joke telling is a type of laughter they find pleasurable.

When a specific behaviour is followed by the removal of an aversive stimulus, the event is called **negative reinforcement**.

Your author, for example, would be more likely to perform a specific behaviour if it would allow him to cease eating strawberries.

positive reinforcement A behaviour is followed by the presentation of an appetitive stimulus, increasing the probability of that behaviour.

negative reinforcement A behaviour is followed by the removal of an aversive stimulus, increasing the probability of that behaviour.

There are two general types of learning circumstances in which negative reinforcement applies. In *escape conditioning*, animals learn that a response will allow them to escape from an aversive stimulus. Raising an umbrella during a rainstorm is a common example of escape conditioning. You learn to use an umbrella to escape the aversive stimulus of getting wet. In *avoidance conditioning*, animals learn responses that allow them to avoid aversive stimuli before they begin. Suppose your car has a buzzer that sounds when you fail to buckle your seat belt. You will learn to buckle up to avoid the aversive noise.

To distinguish clearly between positive and negative reinforcement, remember the following: Both positive reinforcement and negative reinforcement *increase* the probability of the response that precedes them. Positive reinforcement increases response probability by the presentation of an appetitive stimulus following a response; negative reinforcement does the same in reverse, through the removal, reduction, or prevention of an aversive stimulus following a response.

Recall that for classical conditioning, when the unconditioned stimulus is no longer delivered, the conditioned response suffers extinction. The same rule holds for operant conditioning—if reinforcement is withheld, **operant extinction** occurs. Thus, if a behaviour no longer produces predictable consequences, it returns to its level before operant conditioning—it is extinguished. You can probably catch your own behaviours being reinforced and then *extinguished*. Have you ever had the experience of dropping a few coins into a soda machine and getting nothing in return? If you kicked the machine one time and your soda came out, the act of kicking would be reinforced. However, if the next few times your kicking produced no soda, kicking would quickly be extinguished.

As with classical conditioning, *spontaneous recovery* is also a feature of operant conditioning. Suppose you had reinforced a pigeon by providing food pellets when it pecked a key in the presence of a green light. If you discontinued the reinforcement, the pecking behaviour would extinguish. However, the next time you put the pigeon back in the apparatus with the green light on, the pigeon would likely spontaneously peck again. That's spontaneous recovery. In human terms, you might kick the soda machine again with a time lag after your initial extinction experiences.

Positive and Negative Punishment You are probably familiar with another technique for decreasing the probability of a response—punishment. A **punisher** is any stimulus that—when it is made contingent on a response—decreases the probability of that response over time. Punishment is the delivery of a punisher following a response. Just as we could identify positive and negative reinforcement, we can identify positive punishment and negative punishment. When a behaviour is followed by the delivery of an aversive stimulus, the event is called **positive punishment** (you can remember positive because something is added to the situation). Touching a hot stove, for example, produces pain that punishes the preceding response so that you are less likely next time to touch the stove. When a behaviour is followed by the removal of an appetitive stimulus, the event is referred to as **negative punishment** (you can remember negative because something is subtracted from the situation). Thus when a parent withdraws a child's allowance after she hits her baby brother, the child learns not to hit her brother in the future. Which kind of punishment explains why you might stay away from horror movies?

Although punishment and reinforcement are closely related operations, they differ in important ways. A good way to differentiate them is to think of each in terms of its effects on behaviour. Punishment, by definition, always *reduces* the probability of a response occurring again; reinforcement, by definition, always *increases* the probability of a response recurring. For example, some people get severe headaches after drinking caffeinated beverages. The headache is the stimulus that positively punishes and reduces the behaviour of drinking coffee. However, once the headache is present, people often take aspirin or another pain reliever to eliminate the headache. The aspirin's analgesic effect is the stimulus that negatively reinforces the behaviour of ingesting aspirin.

Discriminative Stimuli and Generalization You are unlikely to want to change the probability of a certain behaviour at all times. Rather, you may want to change the probability of the behaviour in a particular context. For example, you often want to increase the probability that a child will sit quietly in class without changing the probability that he or she will be noisy and active during recess. Through their associations with reinforcement or punishment, certain stimuli that precede a particular response—**discriminative stimuli**—come to set the context for that behaviour. Organisms learn that, in the presence of some stimuli but not of others, their behaviour is likely to have a particular effect on the environment. For example, in the presence of a green street light, the act of crossing an intersection in a motor vehicle is reinforced. When the light is red, however, such behaviour may be punished—it may result in a traffic ticket or an accident. Skinner referred to the sequence of discriminative stimulus–behaviour–consequence as the **three-term contingency** and believed that it could explain almost all human action (Skinner, 1953). **Table 7.1** describes how the three-term contingency might explain several different kinds of human behaviour.

In the laboratory, manipulating the consequences of behaviour in the presence of discriminative stimuli can exert powerful control over that behaviour. For example, a pigeon might be given grain after pecking a disk in the presence of a green light but not a red light. The green light is a discriminative stimulus that sets the occasion for pecking; the red is a discriminative stimulus that sets the occasion for not pecking. Organisms learn quickly to discriminate between these conditions, responding regularly in the presence of one stimulus and not responding in the presence of the other. By manipulating the components of the three-term contingency, you can constrain a specific behaviour to a particular context. Organisms also generalize responses to other stimuli that resemble the discriminative stimulus. Once a response has been reinforced in the presence of one discriminative stimulus, a similar

---

operant extinction When a behaviour no longer produces predictable consequences, its return to the level of occurrence it had before operant conditioning.

punisher Any stimulus that, when made contingent upon a response, decreases the probability of that response.

positive punishment A behaviour is followed by the presentation of an aversive stimulus, decreasing the probability of that behaviour.

negative punishment A behaviour is followed by the removal of an appetitive stimulus, decreasing the probability of that behaviour.

discriminative stimuli Stimuli that act as predictors of reinforcement, signaling when particular behaviours will result in positive reinforcement.

three-term contingency The means by which organisms learn that, in the presence of some stimuli but not others, their behaviour is likely to have a particular effect on the environment.

TABLE 7.1 The Three-Term Contingency: Relationships among Discriminative Stimuli, Behaviour, and Consequences

	Discriminative Stimulus	Emitted Response	Stimulus Consequence
1. Positive reinforcement: A response in the presence of an effective signal produces the desired consequence. This response increases.	Soft-drink machine	Put coin in slot	Get drink
2. Negative reinforcement (escape): An aversive situation is escaped by an operant response. This escape response increases.	Heat	Fan oneself	Escape from heat
3. Positive punishment: A response is followed by an aversive stimulus. The response is eliminated or suppressed.	Attractive matchbox	Play with matches	Get burned or get caught and be grounded
4. Negative punishment: A response is followed by the removal of an appetitive stimulus. The response is eliminated or suppressed.	Brussels sprouts	Refusal to eat them	No dessert

stimulus can become a discriminative stimulus for that same response. For example, pigeons trained to peck a disk in the presence of a green light will also peck the disk in the presence of lights that are lighter or darker shades of green than the original discriminative stimulus. Similarly, you generalize to different shades of green on stop lights as a discriminative stimulus for your "resume driving" behaviour.

Using Reinforcement Contingencies Are you ready to put your new knowledge of reinforcement contingencies to work? Here are some considerations you might have:

- *How can you define the behaviour that you would like to reinforce or eliminate?* You must always carefully target the specific behaviour whose probability you would like to change. Reinforcement should be contingent on exactly that behaviour. When reinforcers are presented noncontingently, their presence has little effect on behaviour. For example, if a parent praises bad work as well as good efforts, a child will not learn to work harder in school—but because of the positive reinforcement, other behaviours are likely to increase. (What might those be?)
- *How can you define the contexts in which a behaviour is appropriate or inappropriate?* Remember that you rarely want to allow or disallow every instance of a behaviour. We suggested earlier, for example, that you might want to increase the probability that a child will sit quietly in class without changing the probability that he or she will be noisy and active during recess. You must define the discriminative stimuli and investigate how broadly the desired response will be generalized to similar stimuli. If, for example, the child learned to sit quietly in class, would that behaviour generalize to other "serious" settings?

- *Have you unknowingly been reinforcing some behaviours?* Suppose you want to eliminate a behaviour. Before you turn to punishment as a way of reducing its probability (more on that in the *Critical Thinking in Your Life* box), try to determine whether you can identify reinforcers for that behaviour. If so, you can try to extinguish the behaviour by eliminating those reinforcers. Imagine, for example, that a young boy throws a large number of tantrums. You might ask yourself, "Have I been reinforcing those tantrums by paying the boy extra attention when he screams?" If so, you can try to eliminate the tantrums by eliminating the reinforcement. Even better, you can combine extinction with positive reinforcement of more socially approved behaviours.

It is important to be aware that the reinforcers parents produce can make children's conduct problems, such as tantrums, more likely. In fact, parenting research has identified unknowing reinforcement as one cause of serious behaviour problems in children. For example, Gerald Patterson and his colleagues (Granic & Patterson, 2006) have outlined a *coercion model* for antisocial behaviour. Family observations suggest that children are put at risk when their parents issue threats in response to small misbehaviours (e.g., whining, teasing, or yelling) without following through. At some moments, however, these parents would issue harsh or explosive discipline toward the same behaviours. The children appear to learn the lesson that relatively large acts of aggressive and coercive behaviour are appropriate and necessary for achieving goals—leading to a cycle of increase in the severity of the children's antisocial behaviour.

Behaviour analysts assume that any behaviour that persists does so because it results in reinforcement. Any behaviour, they argue—even irrational or bizarre behaviour—can be understood by discovering what the reinforcement or payoff is. For example, symptoms of mental or physical disorders are sometimes maintained because the person gets attention and sympathy and is excused from normal responsibilities. These *secondary gains* reinforce irrational and sometimes self-destructive behaviour. Can you see how shy behaviours can be maintained through reinforcement, even though the shy person would prefer not to be shy? Of course, it is not always possible to know what reinforcers are at work in an environment. However, as a specific behaviour becomes more or less probable, you might try to carry out a bit of behaviour analysis.

One final thought: It is often the case that real-life situations will involve intricate combinations of reinforcement and punishment. Suppose, for example, parents use negative punishment by grounding a teenager for two weeks when he stays out past curfew. To soften up his parents, the teen helps more than usual around the house. Assuming his helping behaviour appeals to the parents, the teen is trying to reinforce his parents' "reducing the sentence" behaviour. If this strategy succeeds in changing the punishment to only one week, the teen's helping behaviour will have been negatively reinforced—because helping led to the removal of the aversive stimulus of being grounded. Whenever the teen is grounded again (a discriminative stimulus), his helping behaviour to reduce the term should be more likely. Do you see how all the contingencies fit together to change both the teen's and the parents' behaviours?

Let's now take a look at the ways in which various objects and activities may come to function as reinforcers.

PROPERTIES OF REINFORCERS

Reinforcers are the power brokers of operant conditioning: They change or maintain behaviour. Reinforcers have a number of interesting and complex properties. They can be learned through experience rather than biologically determined and can be activities rather than objects. In some situations, even ordinarily powerful reinforcers may not be enough to change a dominant behaviour pattern (in this case, we would say that the consequences were not actually reinforcers).

Conditioned Reinforcers When you came into the world, there were a handful of **primary reinforcers**, such as food and water, whose reinforcing properties were biologically determined. Over time, however, otherwise neutral stimuli have become associated with primary reinforcers and now function as **conditioned reinforcers** for operant responses. Conditioned reinforcers can come to serve as ends in themselves. In fact, a great deal of human behaviour is influenced less by biologically significant primary reinforcers than by a wide variety of conditioned reinforcers. Money, grades, smiles of approval, gold stars, and various kinds of status symbols are among the many potent conditioned reinforcers that influence much of your behaviour.

Virtually any stimulus can become a conditioned reinforcer by being paired with a primary reinforcer. In one experiment, simple tokens were used with animal learners.

How can parents use reinforcement contingencies to affect their children's behaviour?

> With raisins as primary reinforcers, chimps were trained to solve problems. Then tokens were delivered along with the raisins. When only the tokens were presented, the chimps continued working for their "money" because they could later deposit the hard-earned tokens in a "chimp-o-mat" designed to exchange tokens for the raisins. (Cowles, 1937)

Teachers and experimenters often find conditioned reinforcers more effective and easier to use than primary reinforcers because (1) few primary reinforcers are available in the classroom, whereas almost any stimulus event that is under control of a teacher can be used as a conditioned reinforcer; (2) they can be dispensed rapidly; (3) they are portable; and (4) their reinforcing effect may be more immediate because it depends only on the perception of receiving them and not on biological processing, as in the case of primary reinforcers.

In some institutions, such as psychiatric hospitals or drug treatment programs, *token economies* are set up based on these principles. Desired behaviours (grooming or taking medication, for example) are explicitly defined, and token payoffs are given by the staff when the behaviours are performed. These tokens can later be exchanged by the patients for a wide array of rewards and privileges (Kazdin, 1994; Martin & Pear, 1999). These systems of reinforcement are especially effective in modifying patients' behaviours regarding self-care, upkeep of their environment, and, most important, frequency of their positive social interactions.

Response Deprivation and Positive Reinforcers
Suppose you need to get a child to do something. You do not want to pay her or give her a gold star, so instead you strike this bargain: "When you finish your homework, you can play with your video game." Why might this tactic work? According to *response deprivation theory*, behaviours become preferred and

primary reinforcers Biologically determined reinforcers such as food and water.

conditioned reinforcers In classical conditioning, formerly neutral stimuli that have become reinforcers.

Inedible tokens can be used as conditioned reinforcers. In one study, chimps deposited tokens in a "chimp-o-mat" in exchange for raisins. What types of conditioned reinforcers function in your life?

that one weekend he was secluded in his laboratory with not enough of a food-reward supply for his hardworking rats. He economized by giving the rats pellets only after a certain interval of time—no matter how many times they pressed in between, they could not get any more pellets. Even so, the rats responded as much with this *partial reinforcement schedule* as they had with continuous reinforcement. And what do you predict happened when these animals underwent extinction training and their responses were followed by no pellets at all? The rats whose lever pressing had been partially reinforced continued to respond longer and more vigorously than did the rats who had gotten payoffs after every response. Skinner was on to something important about training behaviour!

The discovery of the effectiveness of partial reinforcement led to extensive study of the effects of different **schedules of reinforcement** on behaviour (see **Figure 7.11**). You have experienced different schedules of reinforcement in your daily life. When you raise your hand in class, the teacher

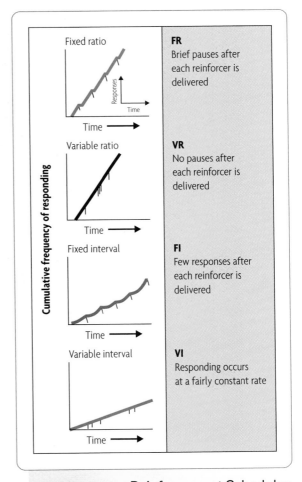

FIGURE 7.11   Reinforcement Schedules
These different patterns of behaviour are produced by four simple schedules of reinforcement. The hash marks indicate when reinforcement is delivered.

therefore reinforcing when an animal is prevented from engaging in them (Timberlake & Allison, 1974). For example, water-deprived rats learned to increase their running in an exercise wheel when their running was followed by an opportunity to drink. Conversely, exercise-deprived rats learned to increase their drinking when that response was followed by a chance to run (Premack, 1965). Can you see how the promise of video games after homework follows this same pattern? For a period of time, the child is video-game-deprived—the rate at which the child would ordinarily play the video game is restricted below normal. To overcome that deprivation, she will learn to work on her homework.

This analysis suggests two important lessons. First, these examples remind you why you should not assume that the same activity will function as a reinforcer for an animal at all times. You need to know, for example, whether the animal is food-deprived before you attempt to use food as a reinforcer. Second, these examples suggest why virtually any activity can come to serve as a reinforcer. You can experience deprivation along any number of dimensions. In fact, if you did not allow a child to do homework for a period of time, she would learn other behaviours to overcome homework-doing deprivation.

SCHEDULES OF REINFORCEMENT

What happens when you cannot or do not want to reinforce your pet on every occasion when it performs a special behaviour? Consider a story about the young B. F. Skinner. It seems

schedules of reinforcement In operant conditioning, the patterns of delivering and withholding reinforcement.

Critical Thinking in Your Life

TO SPANK OR NOT TO SPANK?

If you plan to become a parent (or if you already are one), you have almost certainly considered the question "To spank or not to spank?" In fact, most parents make the choice "to spank." In one sample of 991 parents, 35 percent reported using some form of corporal punishment (e.g., spanking, slapping) on their one- to two-year-olds, and 94 percent had used corporal punishment on their three- to four-year-olds (Straus & Stewart, 1999). Spanking is quite common—but what are the consequences for children who are spanked?

Why is that a difficult question to answer? First, no researchers could ethically conduct an experiment in which they expose children to physical punishment. For that reason, all research on punishment relies on correlational analyses (discussed in Chapter 2): Researchers try to assess whether a relationship exists between the amount of physical punishment children have experienced and negative aspects of their behaviour.

This leads to a second problem with research on spanking. Parents may be unwilling or unable to give accurate indications of how often they spank their children. Researchers can ask the children, but they might also misremember or misrepresent the past. A third problem is getting accurate data on the child behaviours that led parents to spank them: How "bad" were the children before they were spanked? A final problem with research on spanking is understanding its impact as an

element of a larger environment (Kazdin & Benjet, 2003). The households in which parents spank their children the most also tend, for example, to be households with more marital discord. Perhaps it is other factors of that sort that lead children whose parents spanked them to have problems later in life. The spanking itself might have played no causal role.

Despite all these obstacles, researchers have been able to reach important conclusions. For example, we know that physical punishment beyond spanking leads to negative child outcomes (Gershkhoff & Bitensky, 2007). For example, one study involving over 1000 children examined the relationship between the amount of physical punishment the children received as 15-month-olds and the behaviour problems they displayed as 36-month-olds and as first graders (Mulvaney & Mebert, 2007). To account for the fact that some children are more difficult than others—and, therefore, might be more likely to elicit punishment—the analyses focused on changes in each child's behaviour.

The study demonstrated that, for both "easy" and "difficult" children (as reported by their parents), the more the children had been spanked early in life the more likely they were to show increases in, for example, aggressive behaviours as they grew older. Other research has demonstrated a reduction in children's behaviour problems after their parents

underwent an intervention program that trained them to forgo spanking and other harsh forms of discipline (Beauchaine, Webster-Stratton, & Reid, 2005).

In light of these findings, people need to give careful consideration of the question of "To spank or not to spank" with respect to their goals as parents (Benjet & Kazdin, 2003). Parents usually turn to physical punishment to stop children from performing unwanted behaviours. However, experts suggest that parents instead use positive reinforcement: "Many undesirable behaviors can be completely suppressed by positive reinforcement of alternative and incompatible behaviors" (p. 215). For example, you can praise a child for sitting quietly rather than spanking him for running around. Thus, reinforcing children for behaving well is often a better long-term strategy than punishing them for behaving poorly.

As a parent, you presumably want to avoid putting your children at risk. To meet that goal, consider using other strategies besides physical punishment to modify your children's behaviour.

- Why would parents be "unwilling or unable" to provide accurate information about their spanking practices?

- Why was it important for the study looking at change over time to consider both "easy" and "difficult" children?

---

sometimes calls on you and sometimes does not; some slot machine players continue to put coins in the one-armed bandits even though the reinforcers are delivered only rarely. In

real life or in the laboratory, reinforcers can be delivered according to either a *ratio schedule*, after a certain number of responses, or an *interval schedule*, after the first response following a specified interval of time. In each case, there can be either a constant, or *fixed*, pattern of reinforcement or an irregular, or *variable*, pattern of reinforcement, making four major types of schedules in all. So far you have learned about the **partial reinforcement effect**: Responses acquired under

---

partial reinforcement effect The behavioural principle that states that responses acquired under intermittent reinforcement are more difficult to extinguish than those acquired with continuous reinforcement.

schedules of partial reinforcement are more resistant to extinction than those acquired with continuous reinforcement. Let's see what else researchers have discovered about different schedules of reinforcement.

Fixed-Ratio Schedules In **fixed-ratio (FR) schedules**, the reinforcer comes after the organism has emitted a fixed number of responses. When reinforcement follows one response, the schedule is called an FR-1 schedule (this is the original continuous reinforcement schedule). When reinforcement follows only every 25th response, the schedule is an FR-25 schedule. FR schedules generate high rates of responding because there is a direct correlation between responding and reinforcement. A pigeon can get as much food as it wants in a period of time if it pecks often enough. Figure 7.11 shows that FR schedules produce a pause after each reinforcer. The higher the ratio, the longer the pause after each reinforcement. Stretching the ratio too thin by requiring a great many responses for reinforcement without first training the animal to emit that many responses may lead to extinction. Many salespeople are on FR schedules: They must sell a certain number of units before they can get paid.

Variable-Ratio Schedules In a **variable-ratio (VR) schedule**, the average number of responses between reinforcers is predetermined. A VR-10 schedule means that, on average, reinforcement follows every 10th response, but it might come after only one response or after 20 responses. Variable-ratio schedules generate the highest rate of responding and the greatest resistance to extinction, especially when the VR value is large. Suppose you start a pigeon with a low VR value (for example, VR-5) and then move it toward a higher value. A pigeon on a VR-110 schedule will respond with up to 12 000 pecks per hour and will continue responding for hours even with no reinforcement. Gambling would seem to be under the control of VR schedules. The response of dropping coins in slot machines is maintained at a high, steady level by the payoff, which is delivered only after an unknown, variable number of coins has been deposited. VR schedules leave you guessing when the reward will come—you gamble that it will be after the next response, not many responses later (Rachlin, 1990).

Fixed-Interval Schedules On a **fixed-interval (FI) schedule**, a reinforcer is delivered for the first response made after a fixed period of time. On an FI-10 schedule, the subject, after receiving reinforcement, has to wait 10 seconds before another response can be reinforced irrespective of the number of responses. Response rates under FI schedules show a scalloped pattern. Immediately after each reinforced response, the animal makes few if any responses. As the payoff time approaches, the animal responds more and more. You experience an FI schedule when you reheat a slice of pizza. Suppose you set the oven's timer for two minutes. You probably will not check very much for the first 90 seconds, but in the last 30 seconds, you will peek in more often.

Variable-Interval Schedules For **variable-interval (VI) schedules**, the average interval is predetermined. For example, on a VI-20 schedule, reinforcers are delivered at an average rate of one every 20 seconds. This schedule generates a moderate but very stable response rate. Extinction under VI schedules is gradual and much slower than under fixed-interval schedules. In one case, a pigeon pecked 18 000 times during the first four hours after reinforcement stopped and required 168 hours before its responding extinguished completely (Ferster & Skinner, 1957). You have experienced a VI schedule if you have taken a course with a professor who gave occasional, irregularly scheduled pop quizzes. Did you study your notes each day before class?

SHAPING

When describing parts of experiments, we have spoken of rats pressing levers to get food. However, even lever pressing is a learned behaviour. When a rat is introduced to an operant chamber, it is quite unlikely to ever press the lever spontaneously; the rat has learned to use its paws in many ways, but it probably has never pressed a lever before. How should you go about training the rat to perform a behaviour that it would rarely, if ever, produce on its own? You have settled on a reinforcer, food, and a schedule of reinforcement, FR-1—now what? To train new or complex behaviours, you will want to use a method called **shaping by successive approximations**—in which you reinforce any responses that successively approximate and ultimately match the desired response.

Here's how you would do it. First, you deprive the rat of food for a day. (Without deprivation, food is not likely to serve as a reinforcer.) Then you systematically make food pellets available in the food hopper in an operant chamber so that the rat learns to look there for food. Now you can begin the actual shaping process by making delivery of food contingent on specific aspects of the rat's behaviour, such as orienting itself toward the lever. Next, food is delivered only as the rat moves closer and closer to the lever. Soon the requirement for reinforcement is actually to touch the lever. Finally, the rat must depress the lever for food to be delivered. In small increments, the rat has learned that a lever press will produce food. Thus, for *shaping* to work, you must define what constitutes progress toward the target behaviour and use *differential reinforcement* to refine each step along the way.

Let's look at another example, in which shaping was used to improve the performance of a Canadian pole vaulter who was an international competitor.

A 21-year-old university pole vaulter sought a research team's assistance to help him correct a technical problem with his vaulting technique (Scott, Scott, & Goldwater, 1997). The vaulter's particular problem was that he did not

---

fixed-ratio (FR) schedule A schedule of reinforcement in which a reinforcer is delivered for the first response made after a fixed number of responses.

variable-ratio (VR) schedule A schedule of reinforcement in which a reinforcer is delivered for the first response made after a variable number of responses whose average is predetermined.

fixed-interval (FI) schedule A schedule of reinforcement in which a reinforcer is delivered for the first response made after a fixed period of time.

variable-interval (VI) schedule A schedule of reinforcement in which a reinforcer is delivered for the first response made after a variable period of time whose average is predetermined.

shaping by successive approximations A behavioural method that reinforces responses that successively approximate and ultimately match the desired response.

sufficiently extend his arms (holding the pole) above his head before he planted the pole to lift himself off. At the beginning of the intervention, the vaulter's average hand-height at takeoff was calculated as 2.25 metres. The goal was set to use a shaping procedure to help him achieve his physical potential of 2.54 metres. A photoelectric beam was set up so that, when the vaulter achieved a desired extension, the beam was broken and equipment produced a beep. The beep served as a conditioned positive reinforcer. At first, the beam was set at 2.30 metres, but once the vaulter was able to reach that height with 90 percent success, the beam was moved to 2.35 metres. Further success brought further increments of 2.40, 2.45, 2.50, and 2.52 metres. In that way, the vaulter's behaviour was successfully shaped toward the desired goal.

You can imagine how difficult it would have been for the vaulter to show spontaneous improvement of 0.27 metres. (That's about 10 inches.) The shaping procedure allowed him to achieve that gain through successive approximations to the desired behaviour.

Let's return to your rat. Recall that we suggested you might wish to teach it to turn circles in its cage. Can you devise a plan, using shaping, to bring about this behaviour? Think about what each successive approximation would be. At the beginning, for example, you might reinforce the rat if it just turned its head in a particular direction. Next, you would let the rat obtain a food pellet only if it turned its whole body in the right direction. What might you do after that?

The two forms of learning we have examined so far—classical conditioning and operant conditioning—have most often been studied with the assumption that processes of learning are consistent across all animals. In fact, we have cited examples from dogs, cats, rats, mice, pigeons, and humans to show exactly such consistency. However, researchers have come to understand that learning is modified in many situations by the particular biological and cognitive capabilities of individual species. We turn now to the processes that limit the generality of the laws of learning.

STOP AND REVIEW

❶ What is the law of effect?

❷ How do reinforcement and punishment affect the probability of behaviours?

❸ What is the role of discriminative stimuli in operant conditioning?

❹ What is the difference between fixed-ratio and fixed-interval schedules of reinforcement?

❺ What is meant by shaping?

CRITICAL THINKING In the experiment with chimps, why did the researcher start the training with raisins before moving to tokens?

---

biological constraints on learning Any limitations on an organism's capacity to learn that are caused by the inherited sensory, response, or cognitive capabilities of members of a given species.

instinctual drift The tendency for learned behaviour to drift toward instinctual behaviour over time.

Biology and Learning

The contemporary view that a single, general account of the associationist principles of learning is common to humans and all animals was first proposed by English philosopher **David Hume** in 1748. Hume reasoned that "any theory by which we explain the operations of the understanding, or the origin and connexion of the passions in man, will acquire additional authority, if we find that the same theory is requisite to explain the same phenomena in all other animals" (Hume, 1748/1951, p. 104).

The appealing simplicity of such a view has come under scrutiny since the 1960s as psychologists have discovered certain constraints, or limitations, on the generality of the findings regarding conditioning (Domjan, 2005; Griffin, 2008). In Chapter 3, we suggested that animals have evolved in response to the need for survival: We can explain many of the differences among species as adaptations to the demands of their particular environmental niches. The same evolutionary perspective applies to a species's capacity for learning (Leger, 1992). **Biological constraints on learning** are any limitations on learning imposed by a species's genetic endowment. These constraints can apply to the animal's sensory, behavioural, and cognitive capacities. We will examine two areas of research that show how behaviour–environment relations can be biased by an organism's genotype: instinctual drift and taste-aversion learning.

INSTINCTUAL DRIFT

You have no doubt seen animals performing tricks on television or in the circus. Some animals play baseball or Ping-Pong, and others drive tiny race cars. For years, **Keller Breland** and **Marion Breland** used operant conditioning techniques to train thousands of animals from many different species to perform a remarkable array of behaviours. The Brelands believed that general principles derived from laboratory research using virtually any type of response or reward could be directly applied to the control of animal behaviour outside the laboratory.

At some point after training, though, some of the animals began to "misbehave." For example, a raccoon was trained to pick up a coin, put it into a toy bank, and collect an edible reinforcer. The raccoon, however, would not immediately deposit the coin. Even worse, when there were two coins to be deposited, conditioning broke down completely—the raccoon would not give up the coins at all. Instead, it would rub the coins together, dip them into the bank, and then pull them back out. But is this really so strange? Raccoons often engage in rubbing and washing behaviours as they remove the outer shells of a favourite food, crayfish. Similarly, when pigs were given the task of putting their hard-earned tokens into a large piggy bank, they instead would drop the coins onto the floor, root (poke at) them with their snouts, and toss them into the air. Again, should you consider this strange? Pigs root and shake their food as a natural part of their inherited food-gathering repertory.

These experiences convinced the Brelands that, even when animals have learned to make operant responses perfectly, the "learned behaviour drifts toward instinctual behaviour" over time. They called this tendency **instinctual drift** (Breland & Breland, 1951, 1961). The behaviour of their animals is not

How could you use operant conditioning techniques to teach an animal friend to waterski?

case, we became violently ill after eating one of these foods. Although it is unlikely that it was the food itself that made us sick—and we have tried valiantly, particularly for the popcorn, to convince ourselves of that fact—we nonetheless have this queasy response. We can look to nonhuman animals for a clue to why this is so.

Suppose we asked you to devise a strategy for tasting a variety of unfamiliar substances. If you had the genetic endowment of rats, you would be very cautious in doing so. When presented with a new food or flavour, rats take only a very small sample. Only if it fails to make them sick will they go back for more. To flip that around, suppose we include a substance with the new flavour that does make the rats ill—they will never consume that flavour again. This phenomenon is known as **taste-aversion learning**. You can see why having this genetic capacity to sample and learn which foods are safe and which are toxic could have great survival value.

Taste-aversion learning is an enormously powerful mechanism. Unlike most other instances of classical conditioning, taste aversion is learned with only one pairing of a CS (the novel flavour) and its consequences (the result of the underlying UCS—the element that actually brings about the illness). This is true even with a long interval, 12 hours or more, between the time the rat consumes the substance and the time it becomes ill. Finally, unlike many classically conditioned associations that are quite fragile, this one is permanent after one experience. Again, to understand these violations of the norms of classical conditioning, consider how dramatically this mechanism aids survival.

John Garcia, the psychologist who first documented taste-aversion learning in the laboratory, and his colleague Robert Koelling used this phenomenon to demonstrate that, in general, animals are biologically prepared to learn certain associations. The researchers discovered that some CS–UCS combinations can be classically conditioned in particular species of animals, but others cannot.

explainable by ordinary operant principles, but it is understandable if you consider the species-specific tendencies imposed by an inherited genotype. These tendencies override the changes in behaviour brought about by operant conditioning.

The bulk of traditional research on animal learning focused on arbitrarily chosen responses to conveniently available stimuli. The Brelands' theory and demonstration of instinctual drift make it evident that not all aspects of learning are under the control of the experimenters' reinforcers. Behaviours will be more or less easy to change as a function of an animal's normal, genetically programmed responses in its environment. Conditioning will be particularly efficient when you can frame a target response as biologically relevant. For example, what change might you make to get the pigs to place their tokens in a bank? If the token was paired with a water reward for a thirsty pig, it would then not be rooted as food but would be deposited in the bank as a valuable commodity—dare we say a liquid asset?

TASTE-AVERSION LEARNING

Two of your authors have a pair of confessions to make: One of us still gets a bit queasy at the thought of eating pork and beans; the other has the same response, alas, to popcorn. Why? In each

How does instinctual drift affect the behaviours that raccoons can learn to perform?

---

taste-aversion learning A biological constraint on learning in which an organism learns in one trial to avoid a food whose ingestion is followed by illness.

In phase 1 of Garcia and Koelling's experiment, thirsty rats were first familiarized with the experimental situation in which licking a tube produced three CSs: saccharin-flavoured water, noise, and bright light. In phase 2, when the rats licked the tube, half of them received only the sweet water and half received only the noise, light, and plain water. Each of these two groups was again divided: Half of each group was given electric shocks that produced pain, and half was given X-ray radiation that produced nausea and illness.

The amount of water drunk by the rats in phase 1 was compared with the amount drunk in phase 2, when pain and illness were involved (see **Figure 7.12**). Big reductions in drinking occurred when flavour was associated with illness (taste aversion) and when noise and light were associated with pain. However, there was little change in behaviour under the other two conditions—when flavour predicted pain or when the "bright-noisy water" predicted illness.

The pattern of results suggests that rats have an inborn bias to associate particular stimuli with particular consequences (Garcia & Koelling, 1966). Some instances of conditioning, then, depend not only on the relationship between stimuli and behaviour, but also on the way an organism is genetically predisposed toward stimuli in its environment (Barker, Best, & Domjan, 1978). Animals appear to have encoded, within their genetic inheritance, the types of sensory cues—taste, smell, or appearance—that are most likely to signal dimensions of reward or danger. Taste-aversion learning is an example of what researchers call *biological preparedness*: A particular species has evolved so that the members of the species require less learning experience than normal to acquire a conditioned response. Experimenters who try arbitrarily to break these genetic links will look forward to little success. (In Chapter 15, we will see that researchers believe humans are biologically prepared to

acquire intense fears—known as *phobias*—to stimuli such as snakes and spiders that provided dangers over the course of human evolution.)

Researchers have put knowledge of the mechanisms of taste-aversion learning to practical use. To stop coyotes from killing sheep (and sheep ranchers from shooting coyotes), John Garcia and colleagues have put toxic lamb burgers wrapped in sheep fur on the outskirts of fenced-in areas of sheep ranches. The coyotes who eat these lamb burgers get sick, vomit, and develop an instant distaste for lamb meat. Their subsequent disgust at the mere sight of sheep makes them back away from the animals instead of attacking.

The effects of taste-aversion learning may have long-lasting and widespread effects for farmers who use this strategy. Researchers at McMaster University (Galef, 1992; Galef, Whiskin & Bielavska, 1997) found that rats exposed to a particular flavour paired with sickness not only avoided the flavour that made them sick, but somehow communicated this information to rat cagemates. As such, cagemates that had not been sick or exposed to the flavour were more likely to avoid it if one of their rat cagemates had eaten food with the flavour added and then become sick. The research conducted by Galef and colleagues (Galef & Whiskin, 1995) suggests that young rats may learn about nutrition and what foods to avoid from other rats. It is likely that all mammals learn about food choices from watching their parents and friends; certainly humans do.

In this chapter's *Psychology in Your Life* box, we described for you the role that classical conditioning plays in people's experiences of chemotherapy. Classical conditioning also explains why cancer patients become unable to tolerate normal foods in their diets. Their aversions are, in part, a consequence of their chemotherapy treatments, which often follow meals and produce nausea.

A group of 22 women undergoing treatments for breast cancer provided reports on their food preferences over the course of eight sessions of chemotherapy, each separated by three weeks. The women reported everything they had eaten in the 24-hour periods before and after chemotherapy. They rated each type of food and beverage on a scale from one (dislike very much) to nine (like very much). The researchers considered an aversion to have formed if a participant's rating dropped by four points over the course of chemotherapy. Overall, 46 percent of the women developed an aversion to at least one food. However, those aversions formed in the first two sessions of therapy were short-lived. The researchers speculated that, unlike rats and other animals that acquire taste aversions, these women were able to reason that "the chemotherapy caused nausea, not the food." If they tried the food again, the women provided themselves with extinction trials that extinguished the conditioned aversion (Jacobsen et al., 1993).

By showing that aversions are acquired through the mechanisms of classical conditioning, researchers can devise means to counteract them (Bernstein, 1991). Researchers have arranged, for example, for children with cancer not to be given meals just before chemotherapy. They have also created "scapegoat" aversions. The children are given candies or ice cream of unusual flavours to eat before the treatments so the taste aversion becomes conditioned only to those special flavours and not to the flavours they generally like.

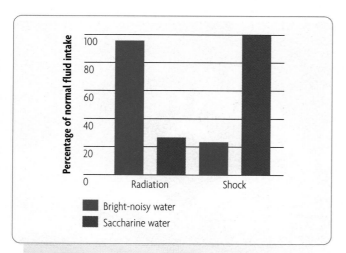

FIGURE 7.12 Inborn Bias

Results from Garcia and Koelling's study (1966) showed that rats possess an inborn bias to associate certain cues with certain outcomes. Rats avoided saccharin-flavoured water when it predicted illness but not when it predicted shock. Conversely, rats avoided the "bright-noisy water" when it predicted shock but not when it predicted illness.

How have researchers used taste-aversion conditioning to prevent coyotes from killing sheep?

You have now seen why modern behaviour analysts must be attentive to the types of responses each species is best suited to learn (Todd & Morris, 1992). If you want to teach an old dog new tricks, you are best off adapting the tricks to the dog's genetic behavioural repertoire! Our survey of learning is not complete, however, because we have not yet dealt with types of learning that might require more complex cognitive processes. We turn now to those types of learning.

STOP AND REVIEW

❶ What is instinctual drift?
❷ What makes taste-aversion learning unusual as a conditioned response?

CRITICAL THINKING Recall the study of taste aversions in cancer patients. What data might the researchers have collected to test their speculation about extinction?

Cognitive Influences on Learning

Our reviews of classical and operant conditioning have demonstrated that a wide variety of behaviours can be understood as the products of simple learning processes. You might wonder, however, if certain classes of learning require more complex, more cognitive types of processes. *Cognition* is any mental activity involved in the representation and processing of knowledge, such as thinking, remembering, perceiving, and language use. In this section, we look at forms of learning in animals and humans that cannot be explained only by principles of classical or operant conditioning. We suggest, therefore, that the behaviours are partially the product of cognitive processes.

COMPARATIVE COGNITION

In this chapter, we have emphasized that—species-specific constraints aside—rules of learning acquired from research on rats and pigeons apply as well to dogs, monkeys, and humans. Researchers who study **comparative cognition** have demonstrated that it is not only classical and operant conditioning that generalize across species (Wasserman & Zentall, 2006). In his original formulation of the theory of evolution, Charles Darwin suggested that cognitive abilities evolved along with the physical forms of animals. In this section, we will describe two impressive types of animal performance that indicate further continuity in the cognitive capabilities of nonhuman and human animals.

Cognitive Maps **Edward C. Tolman** (1886–1959) pioneered the study of cognitive processes in learning by inventing experimental circumstances in which mechanical one-to-one associations between specific stimuli and responses could not explain animals' observed behaviour. Consider the maze shown in **Figure 7.13**. Tolman and his students demonstrated that, when an original goal path is blocked in a maze, a rat with prior experience in the maze will take the shortest detour around the barrier, even though that particular response was never previously reinforced (Tolman & Honzik, 1930). The rats, therefore, behaved as if they were responding to an internal **cognitive map**—a representation of the overall layout of the maze—rather than blindly exploring different parts of the maze through trial and error (Tolman, 1948). Tolman's results showed that conditioning involves more than the simple formation of associations between sets of stimuli or between responses and reinforcers. It includes learning and representing other facets of the total behavioural context.

Research in Tolman's tradition has consistently demonstrated an impressive capacity for spatial memory in birds, bees,

---

comparative cognition The comparative study of the mechanisms and origins of cognition in various species; researchers trace the development of cognitive capabilities across species and the continuity of capabilities from nonhuman to human animals.

cognitive map A mental representation of physical space.

food. What is less clear is how these maps come to be formed. Debbie Kelly at the University of Manitoba has studied how Clark's nutcrackers orient, which may provide them with the skill they need to be such good food-caching birds. In her experiments, birds were assessed on their ability to orient in the right direction of food based on distance from the target and landmark cues in the environment. She found that the nutcrackers relied on cues in the environment, but also used other types of information (e.g., inertia of their own bodies). More importantly, the study determined that the nutcrackers' search strategy was not a simple one, but one that was very flexible in nature (Kelly, Kamil, & Cheng, 2010). In another study, Kelly trained nutcrackers to find food among four food containers arranged in a rectangle. What was unique about this work was that when birds are trained to locate food containers that are marked by nearby objects they can learn the geometry of the array of food containers to more easily find food (Kelly, 2010). Thus, the birds seem to be able to locate their favourite eating places with relative information. This may be very similar to your knowing that your two favourite restaurants are separated by two blocks and a left-hand turn, even though the cars (some of your cues) parked out front are different each time you go there.

Conceptual Behaviour We have seen that cognitive maps, in part, help animals preserve details of the spatial locations of objects in their environments. What other cognitive processes can animals use to find structure, or categories of experiences, in the diverse stimuli they encounter in their environments? In Chapter 11, we will suggest that one of the challenges of language acquisition is for children to form generalizations about new *concepts* and *categories* they are learning, like the words *dog* and *tree*. Human children, however, are not the only animals capable of facing this challenge. Researchers have demonstrated that pigeons also have the cognitive ability to make use of *conceptual* distinctions.

rats, humans, and other animals (Benhamou & Poucet, 1996; Olton, 1992). To understand the efficiency of spatial cognitive maps, consider the functions they serve (Poucet, 1993):

- Animals use spatial memory to recognize and identify features of their environments.
- Animals use spatial memory to find important goal objects in their environments.
- Animals use spatial memory to plan their route through an environment.

You can see these different functions of cognitive maps at work in the many species of birds that store food over a dispersed area but are able to recover that food with great accuracy when they need it:

> *Clark's nutcracker is the champion among food storers that have been studied. In the late summer, these birds bury up to 6000 caches of pine seeds on mountainsides in the American Southwest. They recover the seeds as late as the next spring, when the cached food supports exceptionally early breeding. (Shettleworth, 1993, p. 180)*

The birds are not just roaming their environment and coming upon the seeds through good fortune. They return, with up to 84 percent accuracy, to the thousands of locations in which they buried their seeds (Kamil & Balda, 1990). They are also able to discriminate sites that still have seeds from those that have been emptied (Kamil, Balda, Olson, & Good, 1993). What seems clear is that cognitive maps are created that are used much later to obtain

"This GPS eliminates all the guesswork."

We have seen that cognitive maps, in part, help animals preserve details of the spatial locations of objects in their environments. What other cognitive processes can animals use to find structure, or categories of experiences, in the diverse stimuli they encounter in their environments? In Chapter 8, we will describe some of the ways in which humans carve up the world. For example, people can think about objects like *chairs* and *cars* both as their own basic categories but also understand that both chairs and cars belong to the higher-order category of artificial, human-made stimuli, whereas *flowers* and *people* belong to the higher-order category of natural stimuli.

Pigeons viewed colour photographs of people, flowers, cars, and chairs. For each photograph, the pigeons need to make one of two types of correct responses to obtain food. On half of the trials, the pigeons pecked one of four keys that represented the four basic categories of people, flowers, cars, and chairs. On the other half of the trials, the pigeons pecked one of two keys that represented the higher-order categories of natural stimuli (people and flowers) versus artificial stimuli (cars and chairs). The two types of trials were randomly intermingled: The pigeons could see the same photo and have to categorize it as a "flower" and then as a "natural stimulus" in back-to-back trials. In fact, the pigeons were readily able to learn to respond correctly for both types of category judgments. At the end of the experiment, the researchers tested the pigeons with new photographs—photographs from the same categories that had not been part of the original training set. The pigeons were able to provide correct responses to these new photographs at a level well above chance. The test with novel photographs strongly suggests that the pigeons had learned general categories rather than individual responses to particular stimuli. (Lazareva, Freiburger, & Wasserman, 2004)

We will devote Chapter 9 to an analysis of cognitive processes in humans. However, this experiment that demonstrates flexible categorization in pigeons should convince you that humans are not the only species with impressive and useful cognitive capabilities. Before we conclude this chapter, let's move to another type of learning that requires cognitive processes.

OBSERVATIONAL LEARNING

To introduce this further type of learning, we would like you to return for a moment to the comparison of rats' and humans' approaches to sampling new foods. The rats are almost certainly more cautious than you are, but that's largely because they are missing an invaluable source of information—input from other rats. When you try a new food, it is almost always in a context in which you have good reason to believe that other people have eaten and enjoyed the same food. The probability of your "food-eating behaviour" is thus influenced by your knowledge of patterns of reinforcement for other individuals. This example illustrates your capacity to learn via *vicarious reinforcement* and *vicarious punishment*. You can use your cognitive capacities for memory and reasoning to change your own behaviours in light of the experience of others.

In fact, much *social learning* occurs in situations where learning would not be predicted by traditional conditioning

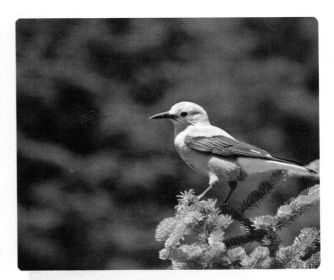

Clark's nutcrackers encode the geometry of an array of food dishes, not just the features of cues in the nearby environment.

theory because a learner has made no active response and has received no tangible reinforcer. The individual, after simply watching another person exhibiting behaviour that was reinforced or punished, later behaves in much the same way, or refrains from doing so. This is known as **observational learning**. Cognition often enters into observational learning in the form of expectations. In essence, after observing a model, you may think, "If I do exactly what she does, I will get the same reinforcer or avoid the same punisher." A younger child may be better behaved than his older sister because he has learned from his sister's mistakes.

This capacity to learn from watching as well as from doing is extremely useful. It enables you to acquire large integrated patterns of behaviour without going through the tedious trial-and-error process of gradually eliminating wrong responses and acquiring the right ones. You can profit immediately from the mistakes and successes of others. Researchers have demonstrated that observational learning is not special to humans. Among other species, mice (Carlier & Jamon, 2006), ravens (Schwab, Bugnyar, & Kotrschal, 2008), and chorus frog tadpoles (Ferrari & Chivers, 2008) are capable of changing their behaviour after observing the performance of another member of their species.

A classic demonstration of human observational learning occurred in the laboratory of **Albert Bandura**. After watching adult models punching, hitting, and kicking a large plastic bobo doll, the children in the experiment later showed a greater frequency of the same behaviours than did children in control conditions who had not observed the aggressive models (Bandura, Ross, & Ross, 1963). Subsequent studies showed that children imitated such behaviours just from watching filmed sequences of models, even when the models were cartoon characters.

---

observational learning The process of learning new responses by watching the behaviour of another.

There is little question now that we learn much—both prosocial (helping) and antisocial (hurting) behaviours—through observation of models, but there are many possible models in the world. What variables are important in determining which models will be most likely to influence you? Research has yielded the following general conclusions (Baldwin & Baldwin, 1973; Bandura, 1977). A model's observed behaviour will be most influential when:

- it is seen as having reinforcing consequences
- it is perceived positively, liked, and respected
- there are perceived similarities between features and traits of the model and the observer
- the observer is rewarded for paying attention to the model's behaviour
- the model's behaviour is visible and salient—it stands out as a clear figure against the background of competing models
- it is within the observer's range of competence to imitate the behaviour

To understand this list of findings, imagine yourself in modelling situations and see how each item in the list would apply. Imagine, for example, you are watching someone who is learning how to parachute jump. Or consider how someone might learn to be a "good" gang member by observing his or her friends.

Since people learn so efficiently from models, you can understand why a good deal of psychological research has been directed at the behavioural impact of television: Are viewers affected by what they see being rewarded and punished on TV? Attention has focused on the link between televised acts of violence—murder, rape, assault, robbery, terrorism, and suicide—and children's and adolescents' subsequent behaviour. Does exposure to acts of violence foster imitation? The conclusion from psychological research is yes—it does for some people, and particularly in the United States (Comstock & Scharrer, 1999). The impact of this research to Canadians is significant, as much of our social behaviour and culture is related to trends that occur in the United States.

The project began in 1977 when a team of researchers measured two years of television viewing for 557 children starting in either Grade 1 or 2. In particular, the researchers obtained measures of the extent to which the children watched TV shows with violent content. Fifteen years later, the researchers were able to conduct interviews with 329 of those children, who were now 20 to 22 years old (Huesmann, Moise-Titus, Podolski, & Eron, 2003). The researchers sought to determine whether there would be a relationship between the amount of television violence the individuals viewed in childhood and their level of aggression as young adults. Their adult level of aggression was measured both through their own self-reports and through the reports of others, such as spouses. As shown in **Figure 7.14**, the men and women who had watched the most violent TV as children also displayed the highest adult levels of aggression. These data suggest that early TV viewing of violence causes later aggression. You might wonder, however, if the causality works in the opposite direction: Could it be that the children destined to be aggressive were already more interested in violent content as children? Fortunately, the researchers collected data that allowed them to argue against this possibility. For example, the data found only a small relationship between childhood aggression and the individuals' viewing of TV violence as adults.

This study argues strongly that children who watch violent TV are at risk to become overly aggressive as adults.

Several decades of research have demonstrated three ways in which television violence has a negative impact on viewers' lives (Smith & Donnerstein, 1998). First, as we have just seen, the viewing of television violence brings about, through the mechanisms of observational learning, increases in aggressive behaviour. This causal association has particularly important implications for children: Aggressive habits born of heavy television viewing early in life may serve as the basis for antisocial behaviour later in life. Second, the viewing of television violence leads viewers to overestimate the occurrences of violence in the everyday world. Television viewers may be unduly afraid of becoming victims of real-world violence. Third, the viewing of television violence may bring about *desensitization*, a reduction in both emotional arousal and distress at viewing violent behaviour.

Note that research has also shown that children can learn prosocial, helping behaviours when they watch television programs that provide prosocial behavioural models (Rosenkoetter, 1999; Singer & Singer, 1990). You should take seriously the idea that children learn from the television they watch. As a parent or caretaker, you may want to help children select appropriate televised models.

An analysis of observational learning acknowledges both that principles of reinforcement influence behaviour and that humans have the capacity to use their cognitive processes to

From left to right: Adult models aggression; boy imitates aggression; girl imitates aggression. What does this experiment demonstrate about the role models play in learning?

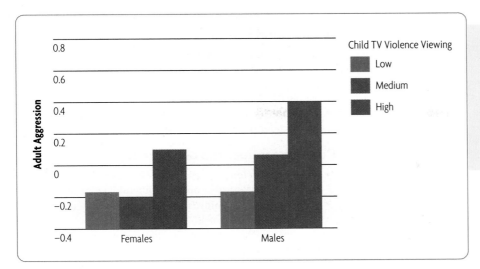

FIGURE 7.14 TV Violence and Aggression
For both men and women, individuals who had viewed the most violent TV as children also displayed the most aggression as adults. The measure of aggression is a composite score that reflects the individuals' self-ratings and ratings by others. Higher scores indicate higher levels of aggression.

change behaviours with vicarious rewards and punishment. This approach to the understanding of human behaviour has proven very powerful. In Chapter 16, we will look at successful programs of therapy that have emerged from the cognitive modification of maladaptive patterns of behaviour.

Let's close this chapter by calling back to mind a visit to a horror movie. How can behaviour analysis explain your experiences? If you went to the movie because of a friend's recommendation, you succumbed to vicarious reinforcement. If you found your way to the theatre despite having to forgo your normal route, you showed evidence of a cognitive map. If the sound of scary music made you fear for the hero's well-being, you felt the effects of classical conditioning. If your failure to enjoy the film made you vow never to see a horror movie again, you discovered the effect a punisher has on your subsequent behaviour.

Are you ready to return to the theatre?

STOP AND REVIEW

❶ What conclusions did Tolman draw from his pioneering work?

❷ What evidence suggests that pigeons are able to categorize stimuli with some flexibility?

❸ What evidence suggests that Clark's nutcrackers encode space using geometry?

❹ What is meant by vicarious reinforcement?

❺ Why is it important to evaluate children's TV viewing in the context of observational learning?

CRITICAL THINKING Consider the TV viewing study. What steps did the researchers take to ensure that they had given the right causal explanation for the correlation revealed in their data?

Recapping Main Points

The Study of Learning

- Learning entails a relatively consistent change in behaviour or behaviour potential based on experience.
- Behaviourists believe that much behaviour can be explained by simple learning processes.
- They also believe that many of the same principles of learning apply to all organisms.

Visit **MyPsychLab.com** for more review and practice on the following topics:

✓ **Practice:** The Study of Learning

Classical Conditioning: Learning Predictable Signals

- In classical conditioning, first investigated by Pavlov, an unconditioned stimulus (UCS) elicits an unconditioned response (UCR). A neutral stimulus paired with the UCS becomes a conditioned stimulus (CS), which elicits a response called the conditioned response (CR).
- Extinction occurs when the UCS no longer follows the CS.
- Stimulus generalization is the phenomenon whereby stimuli similar to the CS elicit the CR.
- Discrimination learning narrows the range of CS's to which an organism responds.
- For classical conditioning to occur, a contingent and informative relationship must exist between the CS and UCS.
- Classical conditioning explains many emotional responses and drug tolerance.

Visit **MyPsychLab.com** for more review and practice on the following topics:

◀◉ **Simulate:** Classical Conditioning

Operant Conditioning: Learning About Consequences

- Thorndike demonstrated that behaviours that bring about satisfying outcomes tend to be repeated.
- Skinner's behaviour analytic approach centres on manipulating contingencies of reinforcement and observing the effects on behaviour.
- Behaviours are made more likely by positive and negative reinforcement. They are made less likely by positive and negative punishment.
- Contextually appropriate behaviour is explained by the three-term contingency of discriminative stimulus–behaviour–consequence.
- Primary reinforcers are stimuli that function as reinforcers even when an organism has not had previous experience with them. Conditioned reinforcers are acquired by association with primary reinforcers.
- Probable activities function as positive reinforcers.
- Behaviour is affected by schedules of reinforcement that may be varied or fixed and delivered in intervals or in ratios.
- Complex responses may be learned through shaping.

Visit **MyPsychLab.com** for more review and practice on the following topics:

※ **Explore:** Dolphins at Sea World

Biology and Learning

- Research suggests that learning may be constrained by the species-specific repertoires of different organisms.
- Instinctual drift may overwhelm some response–reinforcement learning.
- Taste-aversion learning suggests that species are genetically prepared for some forms of associations.

Cognitive Influences on Learning

- Some forms of learning reflect more complex processes than those of classical or operant conditioning.
- Animals develop cognitive maps to enable them to function in a complex environment.
- Conceptual behaviour allows animals to form generalizations about the structure of the environment.
- Behaviours can be vicariously reinforced or punished. Humans and other animals can learn through observation.

Visit **MyPsychLab.com** for more review and practice on the following topics:

 Research: Albert Bandura

 Watch: Television Violence

KEY TERMS

acquisition (p. 187)
behaviour analysis (p. 186)
biological constraints on learning (p. 204)
classical conditioning (p. 186)
cognitive map (p. 207)
comparative cognition (p. 207)
conditioned reinforcers (p. 200)
conditioned response (CR) (p. 187)
conditioned stimulus (CS) (p. 187)
discriminative stimuli (p. 198)
extinction (p. 189)
fixed-interval (FI) schedule (p. 203)
fixed-ratio (FR) schedule (p. 203)
habituation (p. 185)
instinctual drift (p. 204)
introspection (p. 185)

law of effect (p. 195)
learning (p. 184)
learning–performance distinction (p. 184)
negative punishment (p. 198)
negative reinforcement (p. 197)
observational learning (p. 209)
operant (p. 195)
operant conditioning (p. 195)
operant extinction (p. 198)
partial reinforcement effect (p. 202)
positive punishment (p. 198)
positive reinforcement (p. 197)
primary reinforcers (p. 200)
punisher (p. 198)
reflex (p. 187)
reinforcer (p. 196)

reinforcement contingency (p. 196)
schedules of reinforcement (p. 201)
sensitization (p. 185)
shaping by successive approximations (p. 203)
spontaneous recovery (p. 189)
stimulus discrimination (p. 190)
stimulus generalization (p. 190)
taste-aversion learning (p. 205)
three-term contingency (p. 198)
unconditioned response (UCR) (p. 187)
unconditioned stimulus (UCS) (p. 187)
variable-interval (VI) schedule (p. 203)
variable-ratio (VR) schedule (p. 203)

Practice Test

1. You are watching the Olympics and see a young skater fall down several times during a practice session on a jump that is usually easy for her. This provides a good example of _____
   a. classical conditioning.
   b. negative reinforcement.
   c. the law of effect.
   d. the learning-performance distinction.

2. When Joan first moved to the city six months ago, she could not sleep at night because of the traffic noise. Now she hardly hears the traffic at all. This is an example of _____
   a. sensitization.   c. consistency.
   b. habituation.   d. classical conditioning.

3. If a researcher told you he was a close adherent to Skinner's ideas, you would *not* expect his research to focus on _____
   a. internal states as causes of behaviour.
   b. forms of learning conserved across species.
   c. associations between behaviours and rewards.
   d. the environmental stimuli that cause behaviours.

4. In Pavlov's experiments, _____ served as the unconditioned stimulus.
   a. salivation   c. the sight of the assistant
   b. food powder   d. tones

5. A dog has undergone a classical conditioning procedure so that on day 1 it salivates when it hears a tone. On day 3, the dog no longer salivates to the tone. You might guess that on day 2 the dog went through the process of _____
   a. acquisition.   c. extinction.
   b. habituation.   d. sensitization.

6. Six-year-old Pavel has a neighbour with a small dog who barks at him every time he walks by the house. Over time, Pavel has become frightened of all the dogs he sees. This is an example of _____
   a. stimulus discrimination.   c. spontaneous recovery.
   b. backward conditioning.   d. stimulus generalization.

7. Peter wishes to use classical conditioning in which a light will be the CS and an electric shock will be the UCS. You tell him that the light must _____ the shock.
   a. be temporally contiguous with
   b. reliably predict
   c. be in a blocking relationship with
   d. occur after

8. When classical conditioning contributes to drug tolerance, the conditioned stimulus is _____
   a. the setting in which individuals take the drugs.
   b. the body's compensatory reaction to the drug.
   c. the high the drugs give when individuals take them.
   d. the individual's fear of an overdose.

9. For people undergoing chemotherapy, an unconditioned response would be _____
   a. anticipatory fatigue.
   b. the setting in which the individual receives the treatment.
   c. their body's reaction to the drugs.
   d. the infusion of drugs into their bodies.

10. Before you start an operant conditioning experiment, you buy some very expensive chocolate. When people perform a desired behaviour, you will ask them to eat some of the chocolate. You think it is likely that the chocolate will be a _____ of the people.
    a. reinforcer for all   c. punisher for all
    b. reinforcer for none   d. reinforcer for some

11. Which of these concepts is not an element of the three-term contingency?
    a. discriminative stimulus   c. emitted response
    b. operant extinction   d. stimulus consequence

12. Carlotta's parents have not allowed her to watch television for three days. At dinner, she eats her Brussels sprouts on the promise that she will be allowed to watch TV that night. It sounds like Carlotta's parents might be familiar with _____
    a. operant extinction.
    b. conditioned reinforcement theory.
    c. token economies.
    d. response deprivation theory.

13. Which statement is best supported by current research?
    a. Researchers have demonstrated that mild spanking leads to negative outcomes.
    b. Researchers have demonstrated that mild spanking leads to positive outcomes.
    c. Researchers do not know how mild spanking affects children.
    d. Researchers cannot assess the intensity of physical punishment.

14. In your new job, you get paid $2 every time you finish polishing 20 apples. This situation puts you on a _____ schedule.
    a. variable-interval   c. variable-ratio
    b. fixed-interval   d. fixed-ratio

15. In one experiment, raccoons began to rub two coins together rather than learning the target behaviour, which was to deposit the coins into a toy bank. This is an example of _____
    a. operant extinction.
    b. conditioned reinforcers.
    c. instinctual drift.
    d. shaping by successive approximations.

16. In taste-aversion learning, a novel flavour often serves as the _____
    a. UCS.   c. CR.
    b. CS.   d. UCR.

17. One night after eating a hot dog you get very sick. Now you shudder at the idea of eating a hot dog. You want to overcome this aversion to hot dogs. A friend suggests that you allow yourself to experience some extinction trials. This means that you should _____
    a. associate hot dogs with foods you like.
    b. eat some more hot dogs.
    c. make yourself sick eating something else.
    d. use hot dogs as a reward.

18. Birds like Clark's nutcrackers are very successful at finding the seeds they have buried. This provides evidence for species-specific _____
    a. conditioning processes.
    b. applications of classical conditioning.
    c. spatial memory.
    d. shaping processes.

19. Suppose you showed a pigeon a photograph of a car. As a human, you can categorize the photograph as both a *car* and an *artificial stimulus*. You believe that you can train a pigeon to categorize the photograph _____

a. as both a *car* and an *artificial stimulus*.
b. only as a *car*.
c. only as an *artificial stimulus*.
d. as neither a *car* nor an *artificial stimulus*.

20. Zoe watches her older sister slip on ice and bruise her arm. After that, Zoe is very careful when she walks on ice. This is an example of _____
    a. observational learning.   c. operant extinction.
    b. classical conditioning.   d. sensitization.

Essay Questions

1. Given what you have learned about classical conditioning, what information might you share with someone who is about to undergo chemotherapy?

2. Why might you choose one schedule of reinforcement (e.g., fixed-interval versus variable-interval) over another?

3. What mechanisms explain why viewing TV violence might be a cause of aggressive behaviour?

Discovering Psychology Viewing Guide

Program 8: Learning

PROGRAM REVIEW

1. Which of the following is an example of a fixed-action pattern?
  a. a fish leaping at bait that looks like a fly
  b. a flock of birds migrating in winter
  c. a person blinking when something gets in her eye
  d. a chimpanzee solving a problem using insight

2. What is learned in classical conditioning?
  a. a relationship between an action and its consequence
  b. a relationship between two stimulus events
  c. a relationship between two response events
  d. classical conditioning does not involve learning

3. What point is Professor Zimbardo making when he says, "Relax," while firing a pistol?
  a. There are fixed reactions to verbal stimuli.
  b. The acquisition process is reversed during extinction.
  c. Any stimulus can come to elicit any reaction.
  d. Unconditioned stimuli are frequently negative.

4. What is Thorndike's law of effect?
  a. Learning is controlled by its consequences.
  b. Every action has an equal and opposite reaction.
  c. Effects are more easily changed than causes.
  d. A conditioned stimulus comes to have the same effect as an unconditioned stimulus.

5. In Watson's work with Little Albert, why was Albert afraid of the Santa Claus mask?
  a. He had been classically conditioned with the mask.
  b. The mask was an unconditioned stimulus creating fear.
  c. He generalized his learned fear of the rat.
  d. Instrumental conditioning created a fear of strangers.

6. Skinner found that the rate at which a pigeon pecked at a target varied directly with _____
  a. the conditioned stimulus.
  b. the conditioned response.
  c. the operant antecedents.
  d. the reinforcing consequences.

7. Imagine a behaviour therapist is treating a person who fears going out into public places. What would the therapist be likely to focus on?
  a. the conditioning experience that created the fear
  b. the deeper problems that the fear is a symptom of

  c. providing positive consequences for going out
  d. reinforcing the patient's desire to overcome the fear

8. Which psychologist has argued that in order to understand and control behaviour, one has to consider both the reinforcements acting on the selected behaviour and the reinforcements acting on the alternatives?
  a. E. Thorndike   c. B. F. Skinner
  b. J. Watson   d. H. Rachlin

9. In order to produce extinction of a classically conditioned behaviour, an experimenter would _____
  a. reward the behaviour.
  b. pair the behaviour with negative reinforcement.
  c. present the conditioned stimulus in the absence of the unconditioned stimulus.
  d. model the behaviour for the organism.

10. In Pavlov's early work, bell is to food as _____
  a. unconditioned response is to conditioned response.
  b. conditioned stimulus is to unconditioned stimulus.
  c. unconditioned response is to conditioned stimulus.
  d. conditioned stimulus is to conditioned response.

11. Howard Rachlin has discovered that animals can be taught self-control through _____
  a. reinforcement.
  b. operant conditioning.
  c. instrumental conditioning.
  d. all of the above.

QUESTIONS TO CONSIDER

1. You are a school principal, and you are trying to get your students to help clean up the school. Given what you now know about the control of behaviour, what sorts of techniques would you use in order to get students to comply?

2. Is it possible that children learn their native language through operant conditioning? When parents and young children interact, do the parents reinforce the use of some grammatical conventions and punish others? Are some aspects of language, such as the rules of politeness, more likely to be taught through conditioning than other aspects?

8

Memory

A s you begin this chapter on memory processes, we would like you to take a moment to recover your own earliest memory. How long ago did the memory originate? How vivid a scene do you recall? Has your memory been influenced by other people's recollections of the same event?

Now, here is a slightly different exercise. We would like you to imagine what it would be like if you suddenly had no memory of your past—of the people you have known or of events that have happened to you. You would not remember your mother's face, or your 10th birthday, or your high-school graduation. Without such time anchors, how would you maintain a sense of who you are—of your self-identity? Or suppose you lost the ability to form any new memories. What would happen to your most recent experiences? Could you follow a conversation or untangle the plot of a TV show? Everything would vanish, as if events had never existed, as if you had never had any thoughts in mind. Is there any activity you can think of that is not influenced by memory?

If you have never given much thought to your memory, it is probably because it tends to do its job reasonably well—you take it for granted as you do other bodily processes, like digestion or breathing. And as with stomachaches or allergies, the times you notice your memory are likely the times when something goes wrong: You forget your car keys, an important date, lines in a play, or the answer to an examination question that you know you "really knew." You will probably find these occasions irritating, but you should also reflect for a moment on the estimate that the average human brain can store 100 trillion bits of information.

The task of managing such a vast array of information is a formidable one. Perhaps you should not be too surprised when an answer is sometimes not available when you need it!

Our goal in this chapter is to explain how you usually remember so much and why you forget some of what you have known. We will explore how you get your everyday experiences into and out of memory. You will learn what psychology has discovered about different types of memories and about how those memories work. We hope that in the course of learning the many facts of memory, you will gain an appreciation for how wonderful memory is. We also encourage you to take a quick look back into Chapter 4 and remember the discussion of the most famous memory patient, H. M., who was studied by Brenda Milner at the Montreal Neurological Institute.

One last thing: Since this is a chapter on memory, we are going to put your memory immediately to work. We would like you to remember the number 46. Do whatever you need to do to remember 46. And yes, there will be a test!

What Is Memory?

To begin, we will define **memory** as the capacity to store and retrieve information. In this chapter, we will describe memory as a type of *information processing*. The bulk of our attention, therefore, will be trained on the flow of information in and out of your memory systems. Our examination of the processes that guide the acquisition and retrieval of information will enable you to refine your sense of what *memory* means.

FUNCTIONS OF MEMORIES

When you think about memory, what is most likely to come to mind at first are situations in which you use your memory to recall (or try to recall) specific events or information: your favourite movie, the dates of World War II, or your student ID number. In fact, one of the important functions of memory is to allow you to have conscious access to the personal and collective past. But memory does much more for you than that. It also enables you to have effortless continuity of experience from one day to the next. When you drive in a car, for example, it is this second function of memory that makes the buildings along the roadside seem familiar. In defining types of memories, we will make plain to you how hard your memory works to fulfill these functions, often outside of conscious awareness.

Implicit and Explicit Memory Consider **Figure 8.1**. What's wrong with this picture? It probably strikes you as unusual that there is a rabbit in the kitchen, but where does this feeling come from? You probably did not go through the objects in the picture one by one and ask yourself, "Does the refrigerator belong?" "Do the cabinets belong?" Rather, the rabbit jumps out at you as being out of place.

This simple example allows you to understand the difference between **explicit** and **implicit uses of memory**. Your discovery of

How are actors and actresses able to remember all the different aspects—movements, expressions, and words—of their performances?

memory The mental capacity to encode, store, and retrieve information.

explicit uses of memory Conscious effort to encode or recover information through memory processes.

implicit uses of memory Availability of information through memory processes without conscious effort to encode or recover information.

the rabbit is implicit because your memory processes brought your past knowledge of kitchens to bear on your interpretation of the picture without any particular effort on your part. Suppose now we asked you, "What's missing from the picture?" To answer this second question, you probably have to put explicit memory to work. What appears in the typical kitchen? What is missing? (Did you think of the sink or the stove?) Thus, when it comes to using knowledge stored in memory, sometimes the use will be implicit—the information becomes available without any conscious effort—and sometimes it will be explicit—you make a conscious effort to recover the information.

We can make the same distinction when it comes to the initial acquisition of memories. How do you know what should appear in a kitchen? Did you ever memorize a list of what appears there and what the appropriate configuration should be? Probably not. Rather, it is likely that you acquired most of this knowledge without conscious effort. By contrast, you probably learned the names of many of the objects in the room explicitly when you were quite young. As we shall see, to learn the association between words and experiences, your younger self needed to engage in explicit memory processes. You learned the word *refrigerator* because someone called your explicit attention to the name of that object.

The distinction between implicit and explicit memory greatly expands the range of questions researchers must address about memory processes (Bowers & Marsolek, 2003; Buchner & Wippich, 2000). Most early memory research concerned the explicit acquisition of information, like the number of words in a list that could be remembered. Experimenters most frequently provided participants with new information to retain, and theories of memory were directed to explaining what participants could and could not remember under those

circumstances. However, as you will see in this chapter, researchers have now devised methods for studying implicit memory as well. Thus, we can give you a more complete account of the variety of uses to which you put your memory. We can acknowledge that most circumstances in which you encode or retrieve information represent a mix of implicit and explicit uses of memory. Let's turn now to a second dimension along which memories are distributed.

Declarative and Procedural Memory Can you whistle? Go ahead and try. Or, if you cannot whistle, try snapping your fingers. What kind of memory allows you to do these sorts of things? You probably remember having to learn these skills, but now they seem effortless. The examples we gave before of both implicit and explicit memories all involved the recollection of *facts* and *events*, which is called **declarative memory**. Now we see that you also have memories for *how to do things*, which is called **procedural memory**. Since the bulk of this chapter will be focused on how you acquire and use facts, let's take a moment now to consider how you acquire the ability to do things.

Procedural memory refers to the way you remember how things get done. It is used to acquire, retain, and employ perceptual, cognitive, and motor skills. Think about learning to ride a bike: You do not necessarily have all the skills to tell someone exactly how to do it, but once you have learned how to ride a bike, you can hop on virtually any bike and make it move forward. Theories of procedural memory most often concern themselves with the time course of learning (J. R. Anderson, 1996; V. L. Anderson, Levinson, Barker, & Kiewra, 1999): How do you go from a conscious list of declarative facts about some activity to unconscious, automatic performance of that same activity? And why is it that after learning a skill, you often find it difficult to go back and talk about the component declarative facts?

We can see these phenomena at work in even the very simple activity of dialling a phone number that, over time, has become highly familiar. At first, you probably had to think your

---

declarative memory Memory for information such as facts and events.

procedural memory Memory for how things get done; the way perceptual, cognitive, and motor skills are acquired, retained, and used.

Why does pretending to dial a number help you to remember it?

way through each digit, one at a time. You had to work through a list of declarative facts:

First, I must dial 2,

Next, I must dial 0,

Then I dial 7,

and so on.

When you began to dial the number, especially after doing it often enough, you could start to produce it as one unit—a swift sequence of actions on the touch-tone pad. The process at work is called *knowledge compilation* (J. R. Anderson, 1987). As a consequence of practice, you are able to carry out longer sequences of the activity without conscious intervention. But you also do not have conscious access to the content of these compiled units: Once you are at the telephone, you may not actually remember the phone number without pretending to dial it. In general, knowledge compilation makes it hard to share your procedural knowledge with others. You may have noticed this if your parents tried to teach you to drive. Although they may be good drivers themselves, they may not have been very good at communicating the content of compiled good-driving procedures.

You may also have noticed that knowledge compilation can lead to errors. If you are a skilled typist, you have probably suffered from the *the* problem: As soon as you hit the *t* and the *h* keys, your finger may fly to the *e*, even if you are really trying to type *throne* or *thistle*. Once you have sufficiently committed the execution of *the* to procedural memory, you can do little else but finish the sequence. Although this occasionally leads to errors, this procedural memory does much to explain why skilled typists are so adept at executing their task and why even older typists seem to have the ability to maintain great skill. There are many examples in your daily life where you use procedural memory fluidly. Without procedural memory, life would

be extremely laborious—you would be doomed to go step by step through every activity. However, each time you mistakenly type *the*, you can reflect on the trade-off between efficiency and potential error. Let's continue now to an overview of the basic processes that apply to all these different types of memory.

AN OVERVIEW OF MEMORY PROCESSES

No matter what the category of memory, being able to use knowledge at some later time requires the operation of three mental processes: encoding, storage, and retrieval. Memory problems can occur at any of these stages, but the problem may be difficult to determine without a better understanding of each particular stage. **Encoding** is the initial processing of information that leads to a representation in memory. **Storage** is the retention over time of encoded material. **Retrieval** is the recovery at a later time of the stored information. Simply put, encoding gets information in, storage holds it until you need it, and retrieval gets it out. Let's now expand on these ideas.

Encoding requires that you form *mental representations* of information from the external world. You can understand the idea of mental representations if we draw an analogy to representations outside your head. Imagine we wanted to know something about the best gift you got at your last birthday party. (Let's suppose you don't have the gift with you.) What could you do to inform us about the gift? You might describe the properties of the object. Or you might draw us a picture. Or you might pretend that you are using the object. In each case, these are representations of the original object. Although none of the representations is likely to be quite as good as having the real thing present, they should allow us to acquire knowledge of the most important aspects of the gift. Mental representations work much the same way. They preserve important features of past experiences in a way that enables you to *represent* those experiences to yourself.

If information is properly encoded, it will be retained in *storage* over some period of time. The timeframe often depends on how important the information is, and whether injury or illness is playing a role. It is beneficial to you, for example, to remember your mother's name. That said, Alzheimer's disease, which we will learn more about later, can cause individuals to forget the names of their children. Storage requires both short- and long-term changes in the structures of your brain. At the end of the chapter, we will see how researchers are attempting to locate the brain structures that are responsible for storing new and old memories. We will also see what happens in cases of extreme amnesia, where individuals become incapable of storing new memories.

Retrieval is the payoff for all your earlier effort. When it works, it enables you to gain access—often in a split second—to information you stored earlier. Can you remember what comes before storage: decoding or encoding? The answer is simple to retrieve now, but will you still be able to retrieve the concept of encoding as swiftly and with as much confidence when you are tested on this chapter's contents days or weeks

---

encoding The process by which a mental representation is formed in memory.

storage The retention of encoded material over time.

retrieval The recovery of stored information from memory.

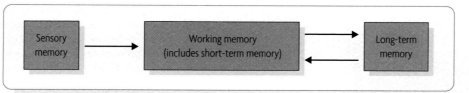

FIGURE 8.2 The Flow of Information Into and Out of Long-Term Memory

Memory theories describe the flow of information to and from long-term memory. The theories address initial encodings of information in sensory and working memory, the transfer of information into long-term memory for storage, and the transfer of information from long-term memory to working memory for retrieval.

from now? Discovering how you are able to retrieve one specific bit of information from the vast quantity of information in your memory storehouse is a challenge facing psychologists who want to know how memory works and how it can be improved.

Although it is easy to define encoding, storage, and retrieval as separate memory processes, the interaction among the three processes is quite complex. For example, to be able to encode the information that you have seen a tiger, you must first retrieve from memory information about the concept *tiger*. Similarly, to commit to memory the meaning of a sentence such as "He's as great as Wayne Gretzky," you must retrieve the meanings of each individual word, retrieve the rules of grammar that specify how word meanings should be combined in English, and retrieve cultural information that specifies exactly how great Wayne Gretzky—a famous Canadian hockey player—was.

We are now ready to look in more detail at the encoding, storage, and retrieval of information. Our discussion will start with short-lived types of memories, beginning with **sensory memory**, and then move to the more permanent forms of long-term memory (see **Figure 8.2**). We will give you an account of how you remember and why you forget. Our plan is to make you forever self-conscious about all the ways in which you use your capacity for memory. We hope this will even allow you to improve some aspects of your memory skills.

STOP AND REVIEW

❶ What is the difference between explicit and implicit uses of memory?

❷ Suppose you are a skilled juggler. Does your skill rely more on declarative or procedural memory?

❸ You suddenly cannot remember the password for your email account. Which memory process is most likely to be causing the difficulty?

---

sensory memory The initial memory processes involved in the momentary preservation of fleeting impressions of sensory stimuli.

iconic memory Memory system in the visual domain that allows large amounts of information to be stored for very brief durations.

Memory Use for the Short Term

Let's begin with a demonstration of the impermanence of some memories. In **Figure 8.3** we have provided you with a reasonably busy visual scene. We would like you to take a quick look at it—about 10 seconds—and then cover it up. Suppose we now ask you a series of questions about the scene:

1. What tool is the little boy at the bottom holding?
2. What is the middle man at the top doing?
3. In the lower right-hand corner, does the woman's umbrella handle hook to the left or to the right?

To answer these questions, wouldn't you be more comfortable if you could go back and have an extra peek at the picture?

This quick demonstration reminds you that much of the information you experience never lodges itself securely in your memory. Instead, you possess and use the information only for the short term. In this section, we examine properties of three less-permanent uses of memory: *iconic memory*, *short-term memory*, and *working memory*.

ICONIC MEMORY

When you first covered up Figure 8.3, did you have the impression that you could briefly still "see" the whole picture in your mind? This extra peek at the picture is provided by your **iconic memory**—a memory system in the visual domain that allows large amounts of information to be stored for very brief durations (Neisser, 1967). A visual memory, or icon, lasts about half a second. Iconic memory was first revealed in experiments that required participants to retrieve information from visual displays that were exposed for only one-twentieth of a second. People were amazingly good at this, suggesting that the image stayed in their mind for extra time.

George Sperling (1960, 1963) presented participants with arrays of three rows of letters and numbers.

8	1	V	F
X	L	5	3
B	4	W	8

Participants were asked to perform two different tasks. In a *whole-report procedure*, they tried to recall as many of the

FIGURE 8.3 How Much Can You Remember from This Scene?

After viewing this scene for about 10 seconds, cover it up and try to answer the questions in the text. Under ordinary circumstances, iconic memory preserves a glimpse of the visual world for a brief time after the scene has been removed.

items in the display as possible. Typically, they could report only about four items. Other participants underwent a *partial-report procedure*, which required them to report only one row rather than the whole pattern. A signal of a high, medium, or low tone was sounded immediately after the presentation to indicate which row the participants were to report. Sperling found that regardless of which row he asked for, the participants' recall was quite high.

Since participants could accurately report any of the three rows in response to a tone, Sperling concluded that all of the information in the display must have gotten into iconic memory. That is evidence for its large capacity. At the same time, the difference between the whole- and partial-report procedures suggests that the information fades rapidly: The participants in the whole-report procedure were unable to recall all the information present in the icon. This second point was reinforced by experiments in which the identification signal was slightly delayed. **Figure 8.4** shows that as the delay interval increases from zero seconds to one second, the number of items accurately reported declines steadily. Researchers have measured quite accurately the time course with which information must be transferred from the fading icon (Becker, Pashler, & Anstis, 2000; Tijus & Reeves, 2004). To take advantage of the "extra peek" at the visual world, your memory processes must very quickly transfer information to more durable stores.

Note that iconic memory is not the same as the "photographic memory" that some people claim to have. The scientific term for "photographic memory" is *eidetic imagery*: People who experience eidetic imagery are able to recall the details of a picture for periods of time considerably longer than iconic memory, as if they were still looking at a photograph. "People" in this case really means children: Researchers have estimated that roughly 8 percent of preadolescent children are eidetikers, but virtually no adults (Neath & Surprenant, 2003). No satisfactory theory has been proposed for why eidetic imagery fades over time (Crowder, 1992). However, if you are reading this book as a high-school, college, or university student, you almost certainly have iconic memory but not eidetic images. We also have a similar type of memory for sounds. Clap your hands and see if you can keep the sound in mind. The term for this is **echoic memory**, which follows many of the same principles as iconic memory.

---

echoic memory Sensory memory that allows auditory information to be stored for brief durations.

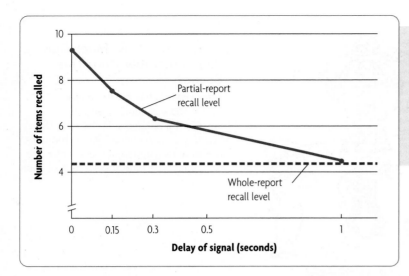

FIGURE 8.4 Recall by the Partial-Report Method

The solid line shows the average number of items recalled using the partial-report method, both immediately after presentation and at three later times. For comparison, the dotted line shows the number of items recalled by the whole-report method.

(Adapted from Sperling, 1960.)

Just like iconic memory, echoic memory briefly preserves more information than participants can report before it fades away (Crowder & Morton, 1969). Echoic memories, however, last longer than iconic memories, perhaps as much as 5 to 10 seconds longer. The longer duration of echoic memories may be related to the way in which sounds unfold over time. For example, when you are trying to understand a spoken sentence, increments of sound arrive at your ear one after the other. Echoic memory may help you to gather those increments into coherent wholes to understand language.

SHORT-TERM MEMORY

Before you began to read this chapter, you may not have been aware that you had iconic memory. It is very likely, however, that you were aware that there are some memories that you possess only for the short term. Consider the common occurrence of consulting a telephone book to find a friend's number and then remembering the number just long enough to dial it. If the line is busy, you often have to go right back to the phone book. When you consider this experience, it is easy to understand why researchers have hypothesized a special type of memory called **short-term memory (STM).**

You should not think of short-term memory as a particular place that memories go to, but rather as a built-in mechanism for focusing cognitive resources on some small set of mental representations (Shiffrin, 2003). The resources of STM are fickle; the memories stored here may not last long. As even your experience with phone numbers shows, you have to take some special care to ensure that memories become encoded into more permanent forms.

The Capacity Limitations of STM In Chapter 5 we described how your attentional resources are devoted to

---

short-term memory (STM) Memory processes associated with preservation of recent experiences and with retrieval of information from long-term memory; short-term memory is of limited capacity and stores information for only a short length of time without rehearsal.

selecting the objects and events in the external world on which you will expend your mental resources. Just as there are limits on your capacity to attend to more than a small sample of the available information, there are limits on your ability to keep more than a small sample of information active in STM. The limited capacity of STM enforces a sharp focus of mental attention.

To estimate the capacity of STM, researchers at first turned to tests of *memory span*. At some point in your life, you have probably been asked to carry out a task like this one:

Read the following list of random numbers once, cover them, and write down as many as you can in the order they appear.

8   1   7   3   4   9   4   2   8   5

How many did you get correct?

Now read the next list of random letters and perform the same memory test.

J   M   R   S   O   F   L   P   T   Z   B

How many did you get correct?

If you are like most individuals, you probably could recall somewhere in the range of five to nine items. **George Miller** (1956) suggested that seven (plus or minus two) was the "magic number" that characterized people's memory performance on random lists of letters, words, numbers, or almost any kind of meaningful, familiar item. It's a good thing that telephone numbers are only seven digits long—but the fact that seven items is at the upper limit of what most people can remember also helps explain why some people have difficulty with them.

Tests of memory span, however, overestimate the true capacity of STM because participants are able to use other sources of information to carry out the task. When other sources of memory are factored out, researchers have estimated the pure contribution of STM to your seven- (or so) item memory span to be only between three and five items (N. Cowan, 2001). If that is all the capacity you have to begin the acquisition of new memories, why don't you notice your limitations more often? Despite the capacity limitations of STM, you function efficiently for at least two reasons. As we will see in the next two sections, the encoding of information in STM can be enhanced through *rehearsal* and *chunking*.

Rehearsal You probably know that a good way to keep your friend's telephone number in mind is to keep repeating the digits in a cycle in your head. This memorization technique is called *maintenance rehearsal*. The fate of unrehearsed information was demonstrated in an ingenious experiment.

> Participants heard three consonants, such as F, C, and V. They had to recall those consonants when given a signal after a variable interval of time, ranging from 3 to 18 seconds. To prevent rehearsal, a *distractor task* was put between the stimulus input and the recall signal; the participants were given a three-digit number and told to count backward from it by 3's until the recall signal was presented. Many different consonant sets were given, and several short delays were used over a series of trials with a number of participants.
>
> As shown in **Figure 8.5**, recall became increasingly poorer as the time required to retain the information became longer. After even 3 seconds, there was considerable memory loss, and by 18 seconds, loss was nearly total. In the absence of an opportunity to rehearse the information, short-term recall was impaired with the passage of time. (Peterson & Peterson, 1959)

What role does short-term memory play when you punch in your ATM password?

Performance suffered because information could not be rehearsed. It also suffered because of *interference* from the competing information of the distractor task. (We will discuss interference as a cause of forgetting later in this chapter.) You may have noticed that a new acquaintance may say his or her name—and still you immediately forget it. One of the most common reasons for this is that you are distracted from performing the type of rehearsal you need to carry out to acquire a new memory. As a remedy, try to encode and rehearse a new name carefully before you continue with a conversation, or use the name directly in asking the person questions.

Our conclusion so far is that rehearsal will help you to keep information from fading out of STM. Yet suppose the information you wish to acquire is, at least at first, too cumbersome to be rehearsed? You might turn to the strategy of chunking.

Chunking A *chunk* is a meaningful unit of information (J. R. Anderson, 1996). A chunk can be a single letter or number, a group of letters or other items, or even a group of words or an entire sentence. For example, the sequence 1–9–8–4 consists of four digits that could exhaust your STM capacity. However, if you see the digits as a year or the title of George Orwell's book *1984*, they constitute only one chunk, leaving you much more capacity for other chunks of information. **Chunking** is the process of reconfiguring items by grouping them on the basis of similarity or some other organizing principle, or by combining them into larger patterns based on information stored in long-term memory (Chen & Cowan, 2005).

See how many chunks you find in this sequence of 20 numbers: 16091939191418121759. You can answer "20" if you see

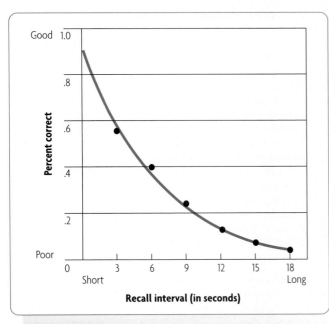

FIGURE 8.5   Short-Term Memory Recall Without Rehearsal

When the interval between stimulus presentation and recall was filled with a distracting task, recall became poorer as the interval grew longer.

---

chunking The process of taking single items of information and recoding them on the basis of similarity or some other organizing principle.

How can you put chunking to good use while listening to a lecture?

the sequence as a list of unrelated digits, or "5" if you are a bit of a history expert and break down the sequence into the dates of major wars in Canadian history. If you do the latter, it is easy for you to recall all the digits in proper sequence after one quick glance. It would be impossible for you to remember them all from a short exposure if you saw them as 20 unrelated items.

Your memory span can always be greatly increased if you can discover ways to organize an available body of information into smaller chunks. A famous subject, S. F., was able to memorize 84 digits by grouping them as racing times (S. F. was an avid runner):

> S. F.'s memory protocols provided the key to his mental wizardry. Since he was a long-distance runner, S. F. noticed that many of the random numbers could be grouped into running times for different distances. For instance, he would recode the sequence 3, 4, 9, 2, 5, 6, 1, 4, 9, 3, 5 as 3:49.2, near record mile; 56:14, 10-mile time; 9:35, slow 2 miles. Later, S. F. also used ages, years of memorable events, and special numerical patterns to chunk the random digits. In this way, he was able to use his long-term memory to convert long strings of random input into manageable and meaningful chunks. S. F.'s memory for letters was still about average, however, because he had not developed any chunking strategies to recall alphabet strings. (Chase & Ericsson, 1981; Ericsson & Chase, 1982)

Like S. F., you can structure incoming information according to its personal meaning to you (linking it to the ages of friends and relatives, for example); or you can match new stimuli with various codes that have been stored in your long-term memory. Even if you cannot link new stimuli to rules, meanings, or codes in your long-term memory, you can still use chunking. You can simply group the items in a rhythmical pattern or temporal group (181379256460 could become 181, pause, 379, pause, 256, pause, 460). You know from everyday experience that this grouping principle works well for remembering telephone numbers.

---

working memory A memory resource that is used to accomplish tasks such as reasoning and language comprehension; consists of the phonological loop, visuospatial sketchpad, and central executive.

WORKING MEMORY

Our focus so far has been on short-term memory, and specifically the role that STM plays in the explicit acquisition of new memories. However, you need more memory resources on a moment-by-moment basis than those that allow you to acquire facts. For example, you also need to be able to retrieve pre-existing memories. At the start of this chapter, we asked you to commit a number to memory. Can you remember now what it was? If you can remember (if not, peek), you have made your mental representation of that memory active once more—that is another memory function. If we ask you to do something more complicated—suppose we ask you to toss a ball from hand to hand while you count backward by 3's from 132—you will put even more demands on your memory resources.

Based on an analysis of the memory functions you require to navigate through life, researchers have articulated theories of **working memory**—the memory resource that you use to accomplish tasks such as reasoning and language comprehension. Suppose you are trying to remember a phone number while you search for a pencil and pad to write it down. Whereas your short-term memory processes allow you to keep the number in mind, your more general working memory resource allows you to execute the mental operations to accomplish an efficient search. Working memory provides a foundation for the moment-by-moment fluidity of thought and action.

Theories of working memory often have as one component the "classic" short-term memory. **Alan Baddeley** (2002, 2003) has provided evidence for three components of working memory:

- A *phonological loop*. This resource holds and manipulates speech-based information. The phonological loop overlaps most with short-term memory, as we have described it in the earlier sections. When you rehearse a telephone number by "listening" to it as you run it through your head, you are making use of the phonological loop.
- A *visuospatial sketchpad*. This resource performs the same types of functions as the phonological loop for visual and spatial information. If, for example, someone asked you how many desks there are in your psychology classroom, you might use the resources of the visuospatial sketchpad to form a mental picture of the classroom and then estimate the number of desks from that picture.
- The *central executive*. This resource is responsible for controlling attention and co-ordinating information from the phonological loop and the visuospatial sketchpad. Any time you carry out a task that requires a combination of mental processes—imagine, for example, you are asked to describe a picture from memory—you rely on the central executive function to apportion your mental resources to different aspects of the task. (We return to this idea in Chapter 9.)

The incorporation of short-term memory into the broader context of working memory should help reinforce the idea that STM is not a place but a process. To do the work of cognition—to carry out cognitive activities like language processing or problem solving—you must bring a lot of different elements together in quick succession. You can think of working memory as a short-term special focus on the necessary elements. If you wish to get a better look at a physical object, you can shine a brighter light on it; working memory shines a brighter mental light on your mental objects—your memory representations.

In what ways is retrieval from STM analogous to retrieval from a vast research library?

Working memory also co-ordinates the activities required to take action with respect to those objects.

Researchers have demonstrated that working memory capacity differs among individuals. They have devised several procedures to measure those differences (Conway et al., 2005). We will give you an example of one of those measures, which is called *working memory span*. To determine working memory span, researchers may ask participants to read aloud a series of sentences and then recall the final words. We have given you some sentences to try in **Table 8.1**. It's really not so easy! People are usually considered to be *high span* if they can recall 4 or more words and *low span* if they recall 2.5 or fewer—these are averages across several trials and sets of sentences, so you will not have gotten much information about yourself just by trying Table 8.1.

Since working memory span is a measure of the resources individuals have available to carry out short-term cognitive processes, researchers can use it to predict performance on a variety of tasks. For example, working memory allows individuals to bring together pieces of information and combine them into more complex memory representations. In general, the greater the working memory capacity, the more information individuals should be able to integrate.

To demonstrate the relationship between working memory capacity and mind wandering, a team of researchers recruited 124 college undergraduates for a study using experience sampling (Kane et al., 2007). At the start of the experiment, participants all completed measures of working memory capacity similar to the operations span task. In the experiment's next phase, participants carried handheld computers for a week. The computers signaled them eight times each day, between noon and midnight, to fill out a questionnaire. The questionnaires gathered information about the tasks in which the participants had been engaged when the beeps sounded. Participants indicated, for example, how challenging they had found the task at hand. The questionnaires also asked participants to report the extent to which their minds had wandered from each task. For nonchallenging tasks, participants' working memory capacity had no impact on the amount of mind wandering. However, when participants were engaged with challenging tasks, people with higher working memory capacity reported much less mind wandering than people with lower working memory capacity.

Recall that one component of working memory is the central executive. This experiment suggests that people with higher working memory capacity are better able to use that central executive resource: They can keep their attention tightly focused on the challenging tasks for which they need it most.

A final note on working memory: Working memory helps maintain your psychological present. It is what sets a context for new events and links separate episodes together into a continuing story. It enables you to maintain and continually update your representation of a changing situation and to keep track of topics during a conversation. All of this is true because working memory serves as a conduit for information coming from and going to long-term memory. Let's turn our attention now to the types of memories that can last a lifetime.

TABLE 8.1 A Test for Working Memory Span

Read these sentences aloud, and then (without looking back) try to recall the final words of each sentence.

He had patronized her when she was a schoolgirl and teased her when she was a student.

He had an elongated skull that sat on his shoulders like a pear on a dish.

The products of digital electronics will play an important role in your future.

The taxi turned up Michigan Avenue where they had a clear view of the lake.

When at last his eyes opened, there was no gleam of triumph, no shade of anger.

Source: Daneman & Carpenter, 1980.

STOP AND REVIEW

❶ Why do researchers believe that the capacity of iconic memory is large?
❷ What is the contemporary estimate of the capacity of short-term memory?
❸ What does it mean to *chunk* a group of items?
❹ What are the components of working memory?

CRITICAL THINKING Recall the study that demonstrated the importance of rehearsal to maintain information in short-term memory. In that study, why were participants asked to count backward by 3's (e.g., 167, 164, 161, . . .) rather than by 1's (e.g., 167, 166, 165, . . .)?

Long-Term Memory: Encoding and Retrieval

How long can memories last? At the chapter's outset, we asked you to recall your own earliest memory. How old is that memory? Fifteen years? Twenty years? Longer? When psychologists speak of *long-term memory*, it is with the knowledge that memories often last a lifetime. Therefore, whatever theory explains how memories are acquired for the long term must also explain how they can remain accessible over the life course. **Long-term memory (LTM)** is the storehouse of all the experiences, events, information, emotions, skills, words, categories, rules, and judgments that have been acquired from sensory and short-term memories. LTM constitutes each person's total knowledge of the world and of the self.

Psychologists know that it is often easier to acquire new long-term information when an important conclusion is stated in advance. With that conclusion in place, you have a framework for understanding the incoming information. For memory, the conclusion we will reach is this: Your ability to remember will be greatest when there is a good match between the circumstances in which you encoded information and the circumstances in which you attempt to retrieve it. We will see over the next several sections what it means to have a "good match."

RETRIEVAL CUES

To begin our exploration between encoding and retrieval, let's consider this general question: How do you "find" a memory? The basic answer is that you use retrieval cues. **Retrieval cues** are the stimuli available as you search for a particular memory. These cues may be provided externally, such as questions on a quiz ("What memory principles do you associate with the research of Sternberg and Sperling?"), or generated internally ("Where have I met her before?"). Each time you attempt to retrieve an explicit memory, you do so for some purpose, and that purpose often supplies the retrieval cue. It won't surprise you that memories can be easier or harder to retrieve depending on the quality of the retrieval cue. If a friend asks you, "Who is the one Roman emperor I can't remember?" you are likely to be involved in a guessing game. If she asks instead, "Who was the emperor after Claudius?" you can immediately respond "Nero."

To give you a full sense of the importance of retrieval cues, we will attempt to replicate classic memory experiments by asking you to learn some word pairs. Keep working at it until you can go through the six pairs three times in a row without an error.

Apple–Boat

Hat–Bone

Bicycle–Clock

Mouse–Tree

Ball–House

Ear–Blanket

Now that you have committed the pairs to memory, we want to make the test more interesting. We need to do something to give you a *retention interval*—a period of time over which you must keep the information in memory. Let's spend a moment, therefore, discussing some of the procedures we might use to test your memory. You might assume that you either know something or you do not, and that any method of testing what you know will give the same results. Not so. Let's consider two tests for explicit memory: recall and recognition.

Recall and Recognition When you **recall**, you reproduce the information to which you were previously exposed. "What is the serial position effect?" is a recall question. **Recognition** refers to the realization that a certain stimulus event is one you have seen or heard before. "Which is the term for a visual sensory memory: (1) echo; (2) engram; (3) icon; or (4) abstract code?" is a recognition question. You can relate recall and recognition to your day-to-day experiences of explicit memory. When trying to identify a criminal, the police would be using a recall method if they asked the victim to describe, from memory, some of the perpetrator's distinguishing features: "Did you notice anything unusual about the attacker?" They would be using the recognition method if they showed the victim photos, one at a time, from a file of criminal suspects or if they asked the victim to identify the perpetrator in a police lineup.

Let's now use these two procedures to test you on the word pairs you learned a few moments ago. What words finished the pairs?

Hat–?   Bicycle–?   Ear–?

Can you select the correct pair from these possibilities?

Apple–Baby	Mouse–Tree	Ball–House
Apple–Boat	Mouse–Tongue	Ball–Hill
Apple–Bottle	Mouse–Tent	Ball–Horn

Was the recognition test (the second one) easier than the recall test? It should be. Let's try to explain this result with respect to retrieval cues.

Both recall and recognition require a search using cues. The cues for recognition, however, are much more useful. For recall, you have to hope that the cue alone will help you locate the information. For recognition, part of the work has been done for you. When you look at the pair *Mouse–Tree*, you only have to answer yes or no to "Did I have this experience?" rather than, in response to *Mouse—?* "What was the experience I had?" In this light, you can see that we made the recognition test reasonably easy for you. Suppose we had given you, instead, recombinations of the original pairs. Which of these are correct?

Hat–Clock   Ear–Boat

Hat–Bone   Ear–Blanket

Now you must recognize not just that you saw the word before, but that you saw it in a particular context. (We will return to the idea of context shortly.) If you are a veteran of difficult multiple-choice exams, you have come to learn how tough even recognition situations can be. However, in most cases, your

---

long-term memory (LTM) Memory processes associated with the preservation of information for retrieval at any later time.

retrieval cues Internally or externally generated stimuli available to help with the retrieval of a memory.

recall A method of retrieval in which an individual is required to reproduce the information previously presented.

recognition A method of retrieval in which an individual is required to identify stimuli as having been experienced before.

recognition performance will be better than your recall because retrieval cues are more straightforward for recognition. Let's look at some other aspects of retrieval cues.

Episodic and Semantic Memories We have already made a pair of distinctions about types of memories. You have implicit and explicit memories as well as declarative and procedural memories. We can define another dimension along which declarative memories differ with respect to the cues that are necessary to retrieve them from memory. Canadian psychologist **Endel Tulving** (1972) first proposed the distinction between *episodic* and *semantic* types of declarative memories.

Episodic memories preserve, individually, the specific events that you have personally experienced. For example, memories of your happiest birthday or of your first kiss are stored in episodic memory. To recover such memories, you need retrieval cues that specify something about the time at which the event occurred and something about the content of the events. Depending on how the information has been encoded, you may or may not be able to produce a specific memory representation for an event. For example, do you have any specific memories to differentiate brushing your teeth 10 times ago from 11 times ago?

Everything you know you began to acquire in some particular context. However, there are large classes of information that, over time, you encounter in many different contexts. These classes of information come to be available for retrieval without reference to their multiple times and places of experience. These **semantic memories** are generic, categorical memories, such as the meanings of words and concepts. For most people, facts like the formula $E = MC^2$ and the capital city of France do not require retrieval cues that make reference to the episodes—the original learning contexts—in which the memory was acquired.

Events of personal importance, like seeing a good friend for the first time after a year's separation, are retained in *episodic* memory. What types of information from *semantic* memory might contribute to a reunion?

Of course, this does not mean that your recall of semantic memories is foolproof. You know perfectly well that you can forget many facts that have become dissociated from the contexts in which you learned them. A good strategy when you cannot recover a semantic memory is to treat it like an episodic memory again. By thinking to yourself, "I know I learned the names of the Roman emperors in my Western civilization course," you may be able to provide the extra retrieval cues that will shake loose a memory.

CONTEXT AND ENCODING

To continue our exploration of encoding and retrieval, we want you to consider a phenomenon that you might call "context shock." You see someone across a crowded room, and you know that you know the person but you just can't place her. Finally, after staring for longer than is absolutely polite, you remember who it is—and you realize that the difficulty is that the person is entirely in the wrong context. What is the woman who delivers your mail doing at your best friend's party? Whenever you have this type of experience, you have rediscovered the principle of **encoding specificity**: Memories emerge most efficiently when the context of retrieval matches the context of encoding. Let's see how researchers have demonstrated that principle.

Encoding Specificity What are the consequences of learning information in a particular context? Endel Tulving and Donald Thomson (1973) first demonstrated the power of encoding specificity by reversing the usual performance relationship between recall and recognition.

> Participants were asked to learn pairs of words like *train–black*, but they were told that they would be responsible for remembering only the second word of the pair. In a subsequent phase of the experiment, participants were asked to generate four free associates to words like *white*. Those words were chosen so that it was likely that the original to-be-remembered words (like *black*) would be among the associates. The participants were then asked to check off any words on their associates lists that they recognized as to-be-remembered words from the first phase of the experiment. They were able to do so 54 percent of the time. However, when the participants were later given the first words of the pair, like *train*, and asked to recall the associate, they were 61 percent accurate.

Why was recall better than recognition? Tulving and Thomson suggested that what mattered was the change in context. After the participants had studied the word *black* in the context of *train*, it was hard to recover the memory representation when the context was changed to *white*. Given the significant effect of even these minimal contexts, you can anticipate that richly organized real-life contexts would have an even greater effect on your memory.

---

episodic memories Long-term memories for autobiographical events and the contexts in which they occurred.

semantic memories Generic, categorical memories, such as the meanings of words and concepts.

encoding specificity The principle that subsequent retrieval of information is enhanced if cues received at the time of recall are consistent with those present at the time of encoding.

After receiving a traffic warning from this man, why might you not recognize him if you ran into him at a party?

Researchers have provided several remarkable demonstrations of context-dependent memory. In one experiment, scuba divers learned lists of words either on a beach or under water. They were then tested for retention of those words, again in one of those two contexts. Performance was nearly 50 percent better when the context at encoding and recall matched—even though the material had nothing at all to do with water or diving (Godden & Baddeley, 1975). Similarly, piano students performed a brief composition more accurately when they played it on the same piano on which they had first learned it (Mishra & Backlin, 2007). In another study, memory performance was improved over the span of four weeks when the same odour—either lemon or lavender—was present at both encoding and recall (Parker, Ngu, & Cassaday, 2001).

In each of the examples we have provided so far, memories are encoded with respect to a context in the external environment—for example, the type of piano or an odour in the air. However, encoding specificity also occurs based on people's internal states. For example, in one study participants drank either alcohol or a placebo before the study and test sessions for a free recall task (Weissenborn & Duka, 2000). In general, alcohol impaired memory performance. However, participants who drank alcohol at both study and test were able to retrieve information that eluded participants who drank alcohol at only study or test alone. When internal states provide the basis for encoding specificity, those effects are called *state-dependent memory*. Researchers have demonstrated that state-dependent memory occurs for other drugs such as marijuana and amphetamine. Also, if you take antihistamines for allergies, you might be interested to learn that they lead to state-dependent memory

(Carter & Cassaday, 1998). How might you use that information when allergy season roles around? Researchers have also examined ways in which emotional states provide an internal context for the encoding and retrieval of memories.

As a final example of encoding specificity, we want you to consider the experience of individuals who are bilingual and thus acquire information in more than one language. Research suggests that memory performance can be strongly language-dependent: People find it easier to recall information when the language at encoding matches the language at retrieval.

> Twenty Mandarin–English bilinguals agreed to participate in a study that tested their general world knowledge (Marian & Kaushanskaya, 2007). For one task, the experimenter asked each participant to name four examples from categories such as "tourist attractions" and "famous actors." The questions were posed in either Mandarin or English. Participants' responses demonstrated language dependence: Although they could name, for example, tourist attractions in both China and the United States, they were more likely to provide answers that matched the language in which the experimenter had posed the question. In a second task, participants received questions that each had two possible answers. Consider the question, "In a famous love story, what were the names of two lovers who died because of family disapproval?" The answer can be either Romeo and Juliet or Liang Shanbo and Zhu Yingtai. Again, the participants' responses showed the impact of the language in which the question was posed: They provided more answers that matched the language of the question.

As you consider these results, recall that all the information is stored in the same brains! What makes the information more or less accessible is the entry point provided by each language. That same conclusion holds true for all these varieties of encoding specificity. It's easiest to find your way back to information when you can reinstate the original context in which you encoded it.

The Serial Position Effect We can also use changes in context to explain one of the classic effects in memory research: the **serial position effect**. Suppose we required you to learn a list of unrelated words. If we asked you to recall those words in order, your data would almost certainly conform to the pattern shown in **Figure 8.6**. You would do very well on the first few words (the **primacy effect**) and very well on the last few words (the **recency effect**) but rather poorly on the middle part of the list. Figure 8.6 shows the generality of this pattern when students are asked to try to remember word lists of varying lengths (6, 10, and 15 words) using either *serial recall* ("Recite the words in the order you heard them") or *free recall* ("Recite as many words as you can") (Jahnke, 1965). Researchers have found primacy and recency in a wide variety of test situations (Neath & Surprenant, 2003). What day is it today? Do you believe that you would be almost a second faster to answer this question at the beginning or end of the week than in the middle (Koriat & Fischoff, 1974)?

The role context plays in producing the shape of the serial position curve has to do with the **contextual distinctiveness** of different items on a list, different experiences in your life, and so on (Neath, Brown, McCormack, Chater, & Freeman, 2006).

---

serial position effect A characteristic of memory retrieval in which the recall of beginning and end items on a list is often better than recall of items appearing in the middle.

primacy effect Improved memory for items at the start of a list.

recency effect Improved memory for items at the end of a list.

contextual distinctiveness The assumption that the serial position effect can be altered by the context and the distinctiveness of the experience being recalled.

FIGURE 8.6 The Serial Position Effect

This figure shows the generality of the serial position effect. Students were asked to try to remember word lists of varying lengths (6, 10, and 15 words) using either serial recall ("Recite the words in the order you heard them") or free recall ("Recite as many words as you can"). Each curve shows better memory for both the beginning (the primacy effect) and end (the recency effect) of the list.

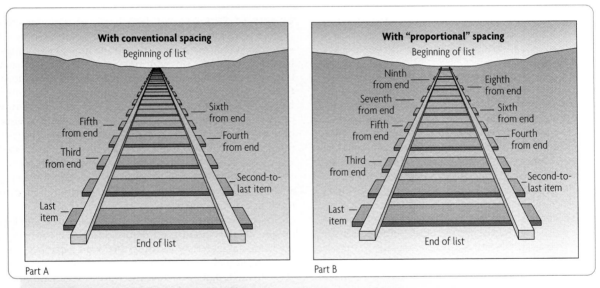

FIGURE 8.7 Contextual Distinctiveness

You can think of items you put into memory as train tracks. In part A, you can imagine that memories further back in time become blurred together, just like train tracks in the distance. In part B, you see that one way to combat this effect is to make the earlier tracks physically farther apart, so the distances look proportional. Similarly, you can make early memories more distinctive by moving them apart psychologically.

To understand contextual distinctiveness, you can ask the question, "How different were the contexts in which I learned this information from the context in which I will try to recall it?" Let's focus on recency. **Figure 8.7** is a visual representation of distinctiveness.

Imagine, in part A, that you are looking at train tracks. What you can see is that they look as if they clump together at the horizon—even though they are equally spaced apart. We could say that the nearest tracks stand out most—are most distinctive—from your

Peanuts: © 2010 Peanuts Worldwide LLC., dist by UFS, Inc.

context. Imagine now that you are trying to remember the last 10 movies you have seen. The movies are like the train tracks. Under most circumstances, you should remember the last movie best because you share the most overlapping context with the experience—it is "closest" to the context of your current experiences. This logic suggests that "middle" information will become more memorable if it is made more distinctive. The idea with respect to our analogy, as shown in part B of Figure 8.7, is to make the train tracks seem equally far apart.

> To make the train tracks seem evenly spaced, engineers would have to make the more distant ones actually be farther apart. Researchers have used the same logic for a memory test, by exploiting the analogy between space and time. They had participants try to learn lists of letters, but they manipulated how far apart in time the letters were made to seem. This manipulation was accomplished by asking participants to read out some number of random digits that appeared on a computer screen between the letters. In the *conventional* condition (like part A of Figure 8.7), each pair of letters was separated by two digits. In the *proportional* condition (like part B), the first pair had four digits and the last pair had zero digits; this should have had the effect of making the early digits more distinctive, just like moving distant train tracks farther apart. Participants, in fact, showed better memory for early items on the list when those items had been made more separate. (Neath & Crowder, 1990)

This experiment suggests that the standard recency effect arises because the last few items are almost automatically distinctive. The same principle may explain primacy: Each time you begin something new, your activity establishes a new context. In that new context, the first few experiences are particularly distinctive. Thus you can think of primacy and recency as two views of the same set of train tracks—one from each end!

_____

levels-of-processing theory A theory suggesting that the deeper the level at which information was processed, the more likely it is to be retained in memory.

THE PROCESSES OF ENCODING AND RETRIEVAL

We have seen so far that a match between the context of encoding and of retrieval is beneficial to good memory performance. We will now refine this conclusion somewhat by considering the actual processes that are used to get information to and from long-term memory. We will see that memory functions best when encoding and retrieval processes make a good match as well.

Levels of Processing Let's begin with the idea that the type of processing you perform on information—the type of attention you pay to information at the time of encoding—will have an influence on your memory for the information. Canadians have been prominent in research on memory. **Gus Craik**, a senior scientist at the Rotman Research Institute at the University of Toronto, has made significant contributions to our understanding of how attention at the time of encoding influences memory. **Levels-of-processing theory** suggests that the deeper the level at which information was processed, the more likely it is to be committed to memory (Craik & Lockhart, 1972; Lockhart & Craik, 1990). If processing involves more analysis, interpretation, comparison, and elaboration, it should result in better memory.

The depth of processing is often defined by the types of judgments participants are required to make with respect to experimental materials. Consider the word *grape*. We could ask you to make a physical judgment—is the word in capital letters? Or a rhyme judgment—does the word rhyme with *tape*? Or a meaning judgment—does the word represent a type of fruit? Do you see how each of these questions requires you to think a little bit more deeply about *grape*? In fact, the deeper the original processing participants carry out, the more words they remember (Lockhart & Craik, 1990).

A difficulty of the levels-of-processing theory, however, is that researchers have not always been able to specify exactly what makes certain processes "shallow" or "deep." Even so, results of this sort confirm that the way in which information is committed to memory—the mental processes that you use to encode information—has an effect on whether you can retrieve that information later. However, so far we have discussed only explicit memory. We will now see that the match between processes at encoding and retrieval is particularly critical for implicit memory.

Processes and Implicit Memory Earlier, we defined the explicit versus implicit dimension for memories as a distinction that applies both at encoding and at retrieval (Bowers & Marsolek, 2003). Under many circumstances, for example, you will retrieve implicitly memories that you originally encoded explicitly. This is true when you greet your best friend by name without having to expend any particular mental effort. Even so, implicit memories are often most robust when there is a strong match between the processes at implicit encoding and the processes at implicit retrieval. This perspective is called **transfer-appropriate processing**: Memory is best when the type of processing carried out at encoding *transfers* to the processes required at retrieval (Roediger, Gallo, & Geraci, 2002). To support this perspective, we will first describe some of the methodologies that are used to demonstrate implicit memories. Then we will show how the match between encoding and retrieval processes matters.

Let's consider a typical experiment in which implicit memory is assessed. The researchers presented students with lists of concrete nouns (suppose that a word on one list was *unicorn*) and asked them to judge the pleasantness of each word on a 1 (least pleasant) to 5 (most pleasant) scale (Rajaram & Roediger, 1993). The pleasantness ratings required participants to think about the meaning of a word without explicitly committing it to memory. After this study phase, participants' memory was assessed using one of four implicit memory tasks:

- *Word fragment completion.* The participant is given fragments of a word, like___*ni*___*or*___, and asked to complete the fragments with the first word that comes to mind.
- *Word stem completion.* The participant is asked to complete a stem, like *uni*_____, with the first word that comes to mind.
- *Word identification.* Words are flashed on a computer screen in such a fashion that participants cannot see them clearly. They must try to guess each word that is flashed. In this case, one of the words would be *unicorn*.
- *Anagrams.* Participants are given a scrambled word, like *corunni*, and asked to give the first unscrambled word that comes to mind.

Just like our example with *unicorn*, correct responses to each of the tasks can be provided by words from the earlier lists. What is critical, however, is that the experimenters have not called attention to the relationship between the words on the earlier list and appropriate responses on these new tasks—that is why the use of memory is implicit.

To assess the degree of implicit memory, the researchers compared the performance of participants who had seen a particular word, like *unicorn*, on the pleasantness lists with those who had not. **Figure 8.8** plots the improvement brought about by implicit memory for a word—percentage correct when the word had appeared on the participant's list minus percentage correct when it had not. (Different participants experienced different word lists.) You can see that for each task there was an advantage to having seen a word before, even though participants had been asked only to say whether the word had a pleasant meaning. This advantage is known as **priming** because the first experience of the word *primes* memory for later experiences. For some memory

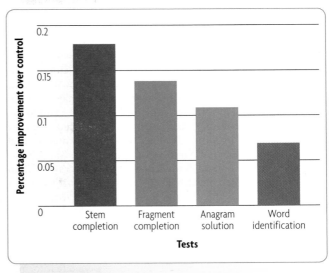

FIGURE 8.8 Priming on Implicit Memory Tests

Priming indicates improvement on the various tasks over performance on control words. Some implicit memory tests demonstrate that priming can last a week or more.

Adapted with permission from Table 1 in "Direct Comparison of Four Implicit Memory Tests," by Suparna Rajaram & H.L. Roediger III, 1993.

tasks, like word fragment completion, researchers have found priming effects lasting a week and beyond (Sloman, Hayman, Ohta, Law, & Tulving, 1988).

Let's turn now to the nature of the match between encoding and retrieval. The four implicit memory tests we have mentioned so far all rely on a *physical* match between the original stimulus and the information given at test. In a sense, whatever processes allow you to encode *unicorn* also make that word available when you are asked to complete the stem *uni*_____, and so on. We can, however, introduce another test, *general knowledge*, that relies on *meaning* or *concepts* instead of on a physical match. Imagine we gave you the question, "What mythological creature had a single horn?" You might very well say unicorn. However, if you became more likely to say unicorn because you had seen the word on an earlier list, in a different context, that would be evidence of implicit memory.

Using two different types of implicit memory tests based on priming—by physical features or by meaning—we can look for a relationship between encoding and retrieval.

Memory researchers designed a levels-of-processing experiment to demonstrate that different implicit memories rely on different types of processes. Participants were asked to respond to each word on a list. For *deep* judgments, they responded to the words' meanings—for example, "Can you buy this?" For *shallow* judgments, they responded to the

---

transfer-appropriate processing The perspective that suggests memory is best when the type of processing carried out at encoding matches the processes carried out at retrieval.

priming In the assessment of implicit memory, the advantage conferred by prior exposure to a word or situation.

words' physical features—for example, "Does this word contain a 'c'?" The researchers assessed implicit memory by using general knowledge questions and word fragment completion. Let's examine the tasks with an eye to transfer-appropriate processing. The deep judgments engage conceptual processes at encoding, but the shallow judgments do not. The general knowledge questions engage conceptual processes at retrieval, but word fragment completion does not. Accordingly, the researchers predicted that they should find a priming advantage for deep judgments when processes at encoding and retrieval matched (deep judgments with general knowledge questions) rather than when they mismatched (deep judgments with fragment completion). The results confirmed the prediction. (Hamilton & Rajaram, 2001)

This type of research supports the idea of transfer-appropriate processing: If you use a certain type of processing—for example, physical or meaning analysis—to encode information, you will retrieve that information most efficiently when the processing uses the same type of analysis.

Earlier we made this assertion: Your ability to remember will be greatest when there is a good match between the circumstances in which you encode information and the circumstances in which you attempt to retrieve it. This section provided the research evidence for this assertion. Note that this analysis defines both when your memory processes will function relatively well (i.e., when circumstances of encoding and retrieval match) and when those processes will function relatively less well (i.e., when there is a mismatch). In that sense, we have already provided you with some initial ideas about why you might not be capable of retrieving memories when you need them. Let's now look more generally at circumstances in which your memory processes fall short.

WHY WE FORGET

Much of the time, your memory works just fine. You see a new acquaintance walking toward you, and you retrieve her name from memory without hesitation. Unfortunately, every once in a while, you end up greeting her in awkward silence—with that awful realization that you cannot remember her name. How does that happen? Sometimes the answer will reside with the forces we have already discussed. It could be the case, for example, that you are trying to recall the name in a context that is very different from the one in which you learned it. However, researchers have studied other explanations for forgetting. In fact, the earliest formal body of research on memory, published in 1885, focused directly on that topic. Let's begin with that work.

Ebbinghaus Quantifies Forgetting See if this statement rings true: "Facts crammed at examination time soon vanish, if they were not sufficiently grounded by other study and later subjected to a sufficient review." In other words, if you cram for a test, you are not likely to remember very much a few days later. This astute, and very contemporary, observation was made in 1885 by the German psychologist **Hermann Ebbinghaus**, who outlined a series of such phenomena to motivate his new science of memory. Ebbinghaus's observations added up to a convincing argument in favour of an empirical investigation of memory. What was needed was a methodology,

and Ebbinghaus invented a brilliant one. Ebbinghaus used nonsense syllables—meaningless three-letter units consisting of a vowel between two consonants, such as CEG or DAX. He used nonsense syllables rather than meaningful words, like DOG, because he hoped to obtain a "pure" measure of memory—one uncontaminated by previous learning or associations that a person might bring to the experimental memory task. Not only was Ebbinghaus the researcher, he was also his own subject. He performed the research tasks himself and measured his own performance. The task he assigned himself was memorization of lists of varying length. Ebbinghaus chose to use *rote learning*, memorization by mechanical repetition, to perform the task.

Ebbinghaus started his studies by reading through the items one at a time until he finished the list. Then he read through the list again in the same order, and again, until he could recite all the items in the correct order—the *criterion performance*. Then he distracted himself from rehearsing the original list by forcing himself to learn many other lists. After this interval, Ebbinghaus measured his memory by seeing how many trials it took him to *relearn* the original list. If he needed fewer trials to relearn it than he had needed to learn it initially, information had been *saved* from his original study. (This concept should be familiar from Chapter 7. Recall that there is often a savings when animals relearn a conditioned response.)

For example, if Ebbinghaus took 12 trials to learn a list and 9 trials to relearn it several days later, his savings score for that elapsed time would be 25 percent (12 trials – 9 trials = 3 trials; 3 trials ÷ 12 trials = 0.25, or 25 percent). Using savings as his measure, Ebbinghaus recorded the degree of memory retained after different time intervals. The curve he obtained is shown in **Figure 8.9**. As you can see, he found a rapid initial loss of memory, followed by a gradually declining rate of loss.

You have experienced the pattern revealed in Ebbinghaus's forgetting curve countless times in your life. Consider, for example, how reluctant you would be to take an exam a week after you studied for it. You know from experience that much of what you learned will no longer be accessible. Similarly, you

FIGURE 8.9 Ebbinghaus's Forgetting Curve
The curve shows how many nonsense syllables are remembered by individuals using the savings method when tested over a 30-day period. The curve decreases rapidly and then reaches a plateau of little change.

might find it easy to recall a name right after you have learned it, but if a week goes by when you do not use it, you might find yourself thinking, "I know I knew her name!"

Interference   Why else might you forget a name that you knew a week ago? One important answer is that you did not learn that name in isolation. Before you learned it, you had lots of other names in your head; after you learned it, you probably acquired a few more new ones. All those other names can have a negative impact on your ability to retrieve the one name you need in the moment. To make this point more formally, we want you to try to learn some new word pairs. Once again, keep working on these word pairs until you can repeat them three times in a row without an error.

> Apple–Robe
>
> Hat–Circle
>
> Bicycle–Roof
>
> Mouse–Magazine
>
> Ball–Baby
>
> Ear–Penny

How did it go? Examine the list. You can see what we have done—each old prompt is paired with a new response. Was it harder for you to learn these new pairs? Do you think it would now be harder for you to recall the old ones? (Go ahead and try.) The answer in both cases is typically "yes." This brief exercise should give you a sense of how memories can compete—or provide *interference*—with each other.

We have already given you a real-life example of the problem of interference when we asked you to try to differentiate your recollections of your episodes of toothbrushing. All of the specific memories interfere with each other. **Proactive interference** (*proactive* means "forward acting") refers to circumstances in which information you have acquired in the past makes it more difficult to acquire new information (see **Figure 8.10**). **Retroactive interference** (*retroactive* means "backward acting") occurs when the acquisition of new information makes it harder for you to remember older information. The word lists we have provided demonstrate both of these types of interference. You have also experienced both proactive and retroactive interference if you have ever moved and had to change your phone number. At first, you probably found it hard to remember the new number—the old one kept popping out (proactive interference). However, after finally being able to reliably reproduce the new one, you may have found yourself unable to remember the old number—even if you had used it for years (retroactive interference).

As with many other memory phenomena, Hermann Ebbinghaus was the first researcher to document interference rigorously through experiments. Ebbinghaus, after learning dozens of lists of nonsense syllables, found himself forgetting about 65 percent of the new ones he was learning. Fifty years later, students at Northwestern University who studied Ebbinghaus's lists had the same experience; after many trials with many lists, what the students had learned earlier interfered proactively with their recall of current lists (Underwood, 1948, 1949).

In this section, we have suggested reasons why you might forget information. It seems fitting that we move now to research that gives advice on how to make memory function better.

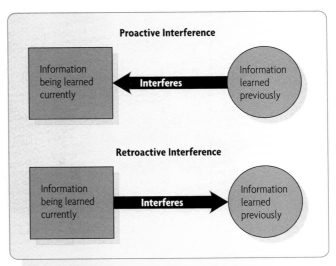

FIGURE 8.10   Proactive and Retroactive Interference

Proactive and retroactive interference help explain why it can be difficult to encode and retrieve memories. What you have learned in the past can make it more difficult for you to encode new information (proactive interference). And what you are learning now can make it more difficult for you to retrieve old information (retroactive interference).

From Robert A. Baron, *Psychology*, 5e, p. 225. Published by Allyn & Bacon, Boston, MA. Copyright © 2001 by Pearson Education. Reprinted by permission of the publisher.

IMPROVING MEMORY FOR UNSTRUCTURED INFORMATION

After reading this whole section, you should have some concrete ideas about how you could improve your everyday memory performance—how you can remember more and forget less. (The *Critical Thinking in Your Life* box, later in the chapter, will help you solidify those ideas with respect to school work.) You know, especially, that you are best off trying to recover a piece of information in the same context, or by performing the same types of mental tasks, as when you first acquired it. Yet there is a slightly different problem with which we still must give you some help. It has to do with encoding unstructured or arbitrary collections of information.

For example, imagine that you are working as a clerk in a store. You must try to commit to memory the several items that each customer wants: "The woman in the green blouse wants hedge clippers and a garden hose. The man in the blue shirt wants a pair of pliers, six quarter-inch screws, and a paint scraper." This scenario, in fact, comes very close to the types of experiments in which researchers ask you to memorize paired associates. How did you go about learning the word pairs we presented earlier? The task probably was somewhat of a chore because the pairs were not particularly meaningful for you—and

---

proactive interference   Circumstances in which past memories make it more difficult to encode and retrieve new information.

retroactive interference   Circumstances in which the formation of new memories makes it more difficult to recover older memories.

How might a waiter or waitress use elaborative rehearsal or mnemonics to get the right meals to the right customers?

Mnemonics Another memory-enhancing option is to draw on special mental strategies called *mnemonics* (from the Greek word meaning "to remember"). **Mnemonics** are devices that encode a long series of facts by associating them with familiar and previously encoded information. Many mnemonics work by giving you ready-made retrieval cues that help organize otherwise arbitrary information.

Consider the *method of loci*, first practised by ancient Greek orators. The singular of *loci* is *locus*, and it means "place." The method of loci is a means of remembering the order of a list of names or objects—or, for the orators, the individual sections of a long speech—by associating them with some sequence of places with which you are familiar. To remember a grocery list, you might mentally put each item sequentially along the route you take to get from home to school. To remember the list later, you mentally go through your route and find the item associated with each spot (see **Figure 8.11**).

The *peg-word method* is similar to the method of loci, except that you associate the items on a list with a series of cues rather than with familiar locations. Typically, the cues for the peg-word method are a series of rhymes that associate numbers with words. For example, you might memorize "one is a *bun*," "two is a *shoe*," "three is a *tree*," and so on. Then you would associate each item on your list interacting with the

information that is not meaningful is hard to remember. To find a way to get the right items to the right customer, you need to make associations seem less arbitrary. Let's explore *elaborative rehearsal* and *mnemonics*.

Elaborative Rehearsal A general strategy for improving encoding is called **elaborative rehearsal**. The basic idea of this technique is that while you are rehearsing information—while you are first committing it to memory—you elaborate on the material to enrich the encoding. One way to do this is to invent a relationship that makes an association seem less arbitrary. For example, if you wanted to remember the pair *Mouse–Tree*, you might conjure up an image of a mouse scurrying up a tree to look for cheese. Recall is enhanced when you encode separate bits of information into this type of miniature story line. Can you imagine, in the clerk situation, swiftly making up a story to link each customer with the appropriate items? (It will work with practice.) You may have already guessed that it is also often helpful to supplement your story line with a mental picture—a visual image—of the scene you are trying to remember. Visual imagery can enhance your recall because it gives you codes for both verbal and visual memories simultaneously (Paivio, 2006).

Elaborative rehearsal can also help save you from what has been called the *next-in-line effect*: When, for example, people are next in line to speak, they often cannot remember what the person directly before them said. If you have ever had a circle of people each give his or her name, you are probably well acquainted with this effect. What was the name of the person directly in front of you? The origin of this effect appears to be a shift in attention toward preparing to make your own remarks or to say your own name (Bond, Pitre, & van Leeuwen, 1991). To counter this shift, you should use elaborative rehearsal. Keep your attention focused on the person in front of you and enrich your encoding of his or her name: "*Erin*—I can't help st-erin at her."

---

elaborative rehearsal A technique for improving memory by enriching the encoding of information.

mnemonics Strategies or devices that use familiar information during the encoding of new information to enhance subsequent access to the information in memory.

Bread

Orange juice

Ice cream

Bananas

FIGURE 8.11   The Method of Loci

In the method of loci, you associate the items you wish to remember (such as the items on a grocery list) with locations along a familiar path (such as your route to and from school).

HOW CAN MEMORY RESEARCH HELP YOU PREPARE FOR EXAMS?

One important use of critical thinking is to apply new knowledge to your life's important tasks. As you read about memory, you should ask yourself questions of this sort: "How can I put the information to immediate use? How will this research help me prepare for my next exam?" Let's see what advice can be generated from this type of critical thinking:

- *Encoding specificity.* As you will recall, the principle of encoding specificity suggests that the context of retrieval should match the context of encoding. In school settings, "context" often will mean "the context of other information." If you always study material in the same context, you may find it difficult to retrieve it in a different context—so, if a professor's questions approach a topic in a slightly unusual way, you might be entirely at a loss. As a remedy, you should change contexts even while you study. Rearrange the order of your notes. Ask yourself questions that mix different topics together. Try to make your own novel combinations. If you get stuck when you are taking an exam, try to generate as many retrieval cues as you can that reinstate the original context: "Let's see. We heard about this in the same lecture we learned about short-term memory. . . ."

- *Serial position.* You know from the serial position curve that, under very broad circumstances, information presented in the "middle" is least well remembered. In fact, college students fail more exam items on material from the middle of a lecture than on material from the start or end of the lecture (Holen & Oaster, 1976; Jensen, 1962). When you are listening to a lecture, you should remind yourself to pay special attention in the middle of the session. When it comes time to study, you should devote some extra time and effort to that material—and make sure not to study the material in the same order each time. You might also note that the chapter you are reading now is about at the middle of *Psychology and Life*. If you have a final examination that covers all the course material, you are going to want to make an especially careful review of this chapter.

- *Elaborative rehearsal and mnemonics.* Sometimes when you study for exams, you will feel as if you are trying to acquire "unstructured information." You might, for example, be asked to memorize the functions of different parts of the brain. Under these circumstances, you need to find ways to provide the structure yourself. Try to form visual images or make up sentences or stories that use the concepts in creative ways. One of your authors still uses his mnemonic from introductory psychology to remember the function of the *ventromedial hypothalamus*, which is often abbreviated VMH: Very Much Hungry (however, as you will learn in Chapter 12, research in the 30 intervening years has made that mnemonic less accurate). Elaborative rehearsal allows you to use what you know already to make new material more memorable.

- *Metamemory.* Research on metamemory suggests that people generally have good intuitions about what they know and what they do not know. If you are in an exam situation in which there is time pressure, you should allow those intuitions to guide how you allocate your time. You might, for example, read the whole test over quickly and see which questions give you the strongest feelings-of-knowing. If you are taking an exam on which you lose points for giving wrong answers (which happens, for example, on SAT and some GRE exams), you should be particularly attentive to your metamemory intuitions, so you can avoid answering those questions on which you "sense" you are most likely to be incorrect.

As you read the basic facts from memory research, you might not have immediately seen how to put the information to use. We have given you these concrete ideas so you can see how critical thinking will allow you to apply psychological knowledge directly to your life.

- Why might it be a good idea to shuffle your notes before you study for an exam?
- What could a professor do to help students overcome the impact of serial position on lecture material?

---

appropriate cue. Suppose a history professor asked you to memorize, in order, the rulers of the Roman empire. You might have Augustus eating a platter of buns, Tiberius wearing oversized shoes, Caligula sitting in a tree, and so on. You can see that the key to learning arbitrary information is to encode the information in such a fashion that you provide yourself with efficient retrieval cues.

METAMEMORY

Suppose you are in a situation in which you would really like to remember something. You are doing your best to use retrieval cues that reflect the circumstances of encoding, but you just cannot get the bit of information to emerge. Part of the reason you are expending so much effort is that you are sure that you are in possession of the information. But are you correct to be so confident about the contents of your memory? Questions like this one—about how your memory works or how you know what information you possess—are questions of **metamemory**. One major question on metamemory has been when and why *feelings-of-knowing*—the subjective sensations that you do have information stored in memory—are accurate.

Research on feelings-of-knowing was pioneered by **J. T. Hart** (1965), who began his studies by asking students a series of general knowledge questions. Suppose, for example, we asked you, "What planet is the largest in our solar system?" Do you know the answer? If you don't, how would you respond to this question: "Even though I don't remember the answer now, do I know the answer to the extent that I could pick the correct answer from among several wrong answers?" This was the question Hart put to his participants. He allowed them to give ratings from 1, to say they were quite sure they wouldn't choose correctly on the multiple choice, to 6, to say they were quite sure they would choose correctly. What would your rating be? Now here are your alternatives:

a. Pluto
b. Venus
c. Earth
d. Jupiter

If you made an accurate feeling-of-knowing judgment, you should have been less likely to get the correct answer, d, if you gave a 1 rating than if you gave a 6. (Of course, to have a fair test, we would want to give you a long series of questions.) Hart found that when participants gave 1 ratings, they answered the questions correctly only 30 percent of the time, whereas 6 ratings predicted 75 percent success. That is pretty impressive evidence that feelings-of-knowing can be accurate.

Research on metamemory focuses on both the processes that give rise to feelings-of-knowing and on how their accuracy is ensured (Benjamin, 2005; Koriat & Levy-Sadot, 2001; Metcalfe, 2000):

- The *cue familiarity hypothesis* suggests that people base their feelings-of-knowing on their familiarity with the retrieval cue. Suppose you were asked, "What is the name of the singer of the song 'Waving Flag'?" If you have prior familiarity with the song "Waving Flag," you might think that you probably would be able to recognize the correct alternative when given the multiple choice.
- The *accessibility hypothesis* suggests that people base their judgments on the accessibility, or availability, of partial information from memory. Thus, if the question "What is the name of the singer of the song 'Waving Flag'?" calls quite easily to mind information you believe to be related to the correct answer, you are likely to think that you will be able to recognize the correct answer as well.

Both of these theories have obtained empirical support—and both suggest that you can generally trust your instincts when you believe that you know something. (Later in the chapter, we will describe research on eyewitness testimony, which provides some exceptions to this general rule.)

---

metamemory Implicit or explicit knowledge about memory abilities and effective memory strategies; cognition about memory.

You have now learned quite a bit about how you get information into and out of memory. You know what we mean by a "good match" between the circumstances of encoding and of retrieval. In the next section, we will shift our focus from your memory processes to the content of your memories.

STOP AND REVIEW

❶ Do circumstances of recall or recognition generally provide more retrieval cues?

❷ At a party, why might you have the best recall of the first person to whom you spoke?

❸ What does the perspective known as transfer-appropriate processing suggest?

❹ For your English class, you memorize "The Raven." When you are done, you can no longer recite last week's assignment. Is this an example of proactive or retroactive interference?

❺ How could you use the method of loci to remember the order of elements in the periodic table?

❻ What two types of information contribute to feelings of knowing?

CRITICAL THINKING Recall the experiment in which odours served as memory cues. How could the experimenter know which odours were novel, appropriate, and inappropriate?

Structures in Long-Term Memory

In most of our examples so far, we have asked you to try to acquire and retrieve isolated or unrelated bits of information. What you mostly have represented in memory, however, are large bodies of *organized knowledge*. Recall, for example, that we asked you to consider whether *grape* is a fruit. You could say *yes* very quickly. How about *porcupine*? Is it a fruit? How about *tomato*? In this section, we will examine how the difficulty of these types of judgments relates to the way information is structured in memory. We will also discuss how memory organization allows you to make a best guess at the content of experiences you can't remember exactly.

MEMORY STRUCTURES

An essential function of memory is to draw together similar experiences, to enable you to discover patterns in your interactions with the environment. (Recall a similar description in Chapter 5 on the functions of perception.) You live in a world filled with countless individual events, from which you must continually extract information to combine them into a smaller, simpler set that you can manage mentally. Apparently you do not need to expend any particular conscious effort to find structure in the world. Just as we suggested when we defined the implicit acquisition of memories, it is unlikely that you ever formally thought to yourself something like, "Here's what belongs in a kitchen." It is through ordinary experience in the world that you have acquired mental structures to mirror environmental structures. Let's look at the types of memory structures you have formed in your moment-by-moment experience of the world.

Categories and Concepts We will begin by previewing one of the topics we will discuss in Chapter 11—the mental effort a child must go through to acquire the meaning of a word, such as *doggie*. For this word to have meaning, the child must be able to store each instance in which the word *doggie* is used, as well as information about the context. In this way, the child finds out what common core experience—a furry creature with four legs—is meant by *doggie*. The child must acquire the knowledge that *doggie* applies not just to one particular animal, but to a whole category of creatures. This ability to categorize individual experiences—to take the same action toward them or give them the same label—is one of the most basic abilities of thinking organisms (G. L. Murphy, 2002).

The mental representations that you form of the categories are called **concepts**. The concept *doggie*, for example, names the set of mental representations of experiences of dogs that a young child has gathered together in memory. (As we will see in Chapter 11, if the child has not yet refined his or her meaning for *doggie*, the concept might also include features that adults would not consider to be appropriate.) You have acquired a vast array of concepts. You have categories for *objects* and *activities*, such as *barns* and *baseball*. Concepts may also represent *properties*, such as *red* or *large*; *abstract ideas*, such as *truth* or *love*; and *relations*, such as *smarter than* or *sister of*. Each concept represents a summary unit for your experience of the world.

As you consider the many categories you experience in the world, you will recognize that some category members are more or less typical. You can develop this intuition if you think about a category like *bird*. You would probably agree that a robin is a typical bird, whereas an ostrich or a penguin is atypical. The degree of typicality of a category member has real-life consequences. Classic research has shown, for example, that people respond more quickly to typical members of a category than to its more unusual ones. Your reaction time to determine that a robin is a bird would be quicker than your reaction time to determine that an ostrich is a bird (Rosch et al., 1976). But what makes people consider a robin to be a typical bird, rather than an ostrich? Answers to this question have often focused on *family resemblance*—typical category members have attributes that overlap with many other members of the category (Rosch & Mervis, 1975). Robins have most of the attributes you associate with birds—they are about the right size, they fly, and so on. Ostriches, by contrast, are unusually large and they do not fly. These examples suggest that family resemblance plays a role in judgments of typicality. However, recent research suggests that the most typical category members are also the *ideal* category members.

A team of researchers recruited individuals from two communities who had several decades of fishing experience: One group was Native American Menominee Indians from northern central Wisconsin; the second group was European Americans from roughly the same geographical location (Burnett, Medin, Ross, & Blok, 2005). The experiment used these two groups because they differ with

How does the formation of categories—such as what constitutes a healthy head of lettuce, a sweet melon, or a flavourful tomato—help you make daily decisions like what to buy for dinner?

respect to the species of fish they consider to be most desirable or ideal. For example, the Menominee people consider sturgeon to be sacred. The researchers presented the participants with a group of 44 cards printed with the names of local fish. Participants sorted these cards into groups—the researchers used the participants' verbal justifications (e.g., "good eating") for which fish they grouped together as an index of desirability. Also, the participants rated the extent to which each species was a good example of the "fish" category. The researchers found a 0.80 correlation between desirability and typicality. (Recall from Chapter 2 that correlations range from −1.0 to +1.0.) That is impressive evidence that the participants' notions of the "ideal" fish played a role in their judgments of typicality. In addition, the ratings were influenced by cultural differences in desirability. For example, the Menominee group rated sturgeon as even more typical than did the European American group.

If you do not have a lot of fishing experience, you might have less of a sense than these participants did about which fish are desirable. However, you can think about categories with which you have a lot of experience to see how your notions of what is ideal inform your judgments about what is typical.

Basic Levels and Hierarchies Concepts, and their prototypes, do not exist in isolation. As shown in **Figure 8.12**, concepts can often be arranged into meaningful organizations. A broad category like *animal* has several subcategories, such as *bird* and *fish*, which in turn contain exemplars such as *canary*, *ostrich*, *shark*, and *salmon*. The animal category is itself a subcategory of the still larger category of *living beings*. Concepts are also linked to other types of information: You store the knowledge that some birds are *edible*, some are *endangered*, some are *national symbols*.

There seems to be a level in such hierarchies at which people best categorize and think about objects. This has been called

---

concepts Mental representations of kinds or categories of items and ideas.

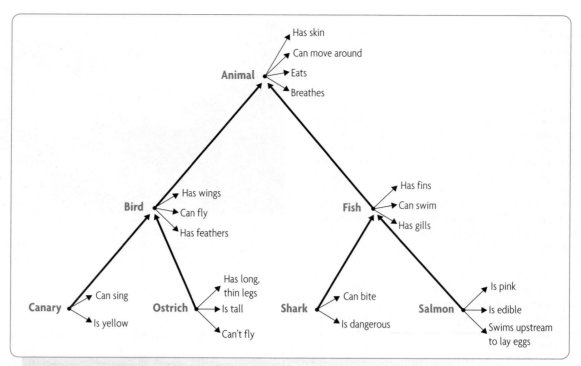

FIGURE 8.12 Hierarchically Organized Structure of Concepts

The category *animal* can be divided into subcategories such as *bird* and *fish*; similarly, each subcategory can be further divided. Some information (such as *has skin*) applies to all concepts in the hierarchy; other information (such as *can sing*) applies only to concepts at lower levels (for example, a canary).

the **basic level** (Rosch, 1973, 1978). For example, when you buy an apple at the grocery store, you could think of it as a *piece of fruit*—but that seems imprecise—or a *Golden Delicious*—but that seems too specific or narrow. The basic level is just *apple*. If you were shown a picture of such an object, that is what you would be likely to call it. You would also take less time to say that it was an apple than that it was a piece of fruit (Rosch, 1978). The basic level emerges through your experience of the world. You are more likely to encounter the term *apple* than its more or less specific alternatives. If you became an apple grower, however, you might find yourself having daily conversations about *Cortlands* or *Granny Smiths*. With those experiences, your basic level would probably shift lower in the hierarchy.

Schemas We have seen that concepts are the building blocks of memory hierarchies. They also serve as building blocks for more complex mental structures. Recall Figure 8.1. Why did you instantly know that the rabbit didn't belong in the kitchen? We suggested earlier that this judgment relied on implicit memory—but we did not say what type of memory structure you were using. Clearly, what you need is some representation in memory

that combines the individual concepts of a kitchen—your knowledge about ovens, sinks, and refrigerators—into a larger unit. We call that larger unit a schema. **Schemas** are conceptual frameworks, or clusters of knowledge, regarding objects, people, and situations. Schemas are "knowledge packages" that encode complex generalizations about your experience of the structure of the environment. You have schemas for kitchens and bedrooms, race car drivers and professors, surprise parties and graduations. In later chapters, we will provide more illustrations of the types of schemas that shape your day-to-day experiences. For example, in Chapter 11 we will see that the attachment relationships children form with their parents provide schemas for later social interactions. In Chapter 14, we will see that you possess a *self-schema*—a memory structure that allows you to organize information about yourself.

One thing you may have guessed is that your schemas do not include all the individual details of all your varied experiences. A schema represents your average experience of situations in the environment. Thus your schemas are not permanent but shift with your changing life events. Your schemas also include only those details in the world to which you have devoted sufficient attention. For example, when asked to draw the information on the head sides of U.S. coins, college students virtually never filled in the word *Liberty*, although it appears on every coin (Rubin & Kontis, 1983). Thus your schemas provide an accurate reflection of what you have *noticed* about the world. Let's now look at all the ways in which you use your concepts and schemas.

---

basic level The level of categorization that can be retrieved from memory most quickly and used most efficiently.

schemas General conceptual frameworks, or clusters of knowledge, regarding objects, people, and situations; knowledge packages that encode generalizations about the structure of the environment.

FIGURE 8.13 Theories of Categorization
A. What is this unusual object? B. One theory suggests that you categorize this object as a chair by comparing it to a single prototype stored in memory. C. An alternative theory suggests that you categorize this object by comparing it to the many exemplars you have in memory.

FIGURE 8.14 Recognition Illusion
Duck or rabbit?

Using Memory Structures Let's consider some instances of memory structures in action. To begin, consider the picture in part A of **Figure 8.13**. What is it? Although we purposefully chose an unusual member of the category, you probably reached the conclusion "It's a chair" with reasonable ease. However, to do so, you needed to draw on your memory representations of members of that category. You can say "It's a chair" because the object in the figure calls to mind your past experiences of chairs.

Researchers have provided two theories of how people use concepts in memory to categorize the objects they encounter in the world. One theory suggests that, for each concept in memory, you encode a **prototype**—a representation of the most central or average member of a category (Rosch, 1978). On this view, you recognize objects by comparing them to prototypes in memory. Because the picture in part A of Figure 8.13 matches many of the important attributes of the prototype in part B, you can recognize the picture as a chair.

An alternative theory suggests that people retain memories of the many different **exemplars** they experience for each category. In part C of Figure 8.13, we give you a subset of the exemplars of chairs you might have seen. On the exemplar view, you recognize an object by comparing it to the exemplars you have stored in memory. You recognize the picture as a chair because it is similar to several of those exemplars. Researchers have conducted a large number of studies to contrast prototype and exemplar accounts of categorization. The data largely support the exemplar view: People appear to categorize the objects they encounter by comparing them to multiple representations in memory (Nosofsky & Stanton, 2005; Voorspoels, Vanpaemel, & Storms, 2008).

We intended the picture in Figure 8.13 to be an unusual chair but clearly a chair nonetheless. However, as we saw in Chapter 5, sometimes the world provides ambiguous stimuli—and you use prior knowledge to help interpret those stimuli.

---

prototype The most representative example of a category.

exemplars Members of categories that people have encountered.

Do you remember Figure 5.35, which is presented here as **Figure 8.14**? Do you see a duck or a rabbit? Let's suppose we give you the expectation that you are going to see a duck. If you match the features of the picture against the features of a duck that are present in exemplars in memory, you are likely to be reasonably content. The same thing would happen if we told you to expect a rabbit. You use information from memory to generate—and confirm—expectations.

As we have previously noted, memory representations also allow you to understand when something is unusual in the world. That is why you could quickly notice the anomalous bunny in the centre of Figure 8.1. In fact, because the bunny jumps out as inconsistent with your kitchen schema, you would also be particularly likely to remember seeing it in the picture. In one study, researchers illustrated that schema-inconsistent information is more memorable by filling a graduate student office with both typical objects (e.g., notebook, pencil) and atypical objects (e.g., harmonica, toothbrush) (Lampinen, Copeland, & Neuschatz, 2001). Participants spent one minute in the room. In a later phase of the experiment, participants indicated which items on a list had been present in the room.

Their memory was consistently more accurate for the atypical items than for the typical items. In addition, the participants were likely to have more specific memories of having seen the atypical items, whereas their memories for the typical items were based more on a general sense of familiarity. This study illustrates how memory structures direct your attention to unusual aspects of a scene.

Taken together, these examples demonstrate that the availability of memory structures can influence the way you think about the world. Your past experiences colour your present experiences and provide expectations for the future. You will see shortly that, for much the same reasons, concepts and schemas can sometimes work against accurate memory.

REMEMBERING AS A RECONSTRUCTIVE PROCESS

Let's turn now to another important way in which you use memory structures. In many cases, when you are asked to remember a piece of information, you cannot remember the information directly. Instead, you *reconstruct* the information based on more general types of stored knowledge. To experience **reconstructive memory**, consider this trio of questions:

- Did Chapter 3 have the word *the* in it?
- Did 1991 contain the day July 7?
- Did you breathe yesterday between 2:05 and 2:10 p.m.?

You probably were willing to answer "Yes!" to each of these questions without much hesitation, but you almost certainly do not have specific, episodic memories to help you (unless, of course, something happened to fix these events in memory—perhaps July 7 is your birthday or you crossed out all the *the*'s in Chapter 3 to curb your boredom). To answer these questions, you must use more general memories to reconstruct what is likely to have happened. Let's examine this process of reconstruction in a bit more detail.

The Accuracy of Reconstructive Memory If people reconstruct some memories, rather than recovering a specific memory representation for what happened, then you might expect that you could find occasions on which the reconstructed memory differed from the real occurrence—distortions. One of the most impressive demonstrations of memory distortions is also the oldest. In his classic book *Remembering: A Study in Experimental and Social Psychology* (1932), **Sir Frederic Bartlett** undertook a program of research to demonstrate how individuals' prior knowledge influenced the way they remembered new information. Bartlett studied the way British undergraduates remembered stories whose themes and wording were taken from another culture. His most famous story was "The War of the Ghosts," an American Indian tale.

Bartlett found that his readers' reproductions of the story were often greatly altered from the original. The distortions Bartlett found involved three kinds of reconstructive processes:

- *Levelling*—simplifying the story.
- *Sharpening*—highlighting and overemphasizing certain details.

- *Assimilating*—changing the details to better fit the participant's own background or knowledge.

Thus readers reproduced the story with words familiar in their culture taking the place of those unfamiliar: *Boat* might replace *canoe* and *go fishing* might replace *hunt seals*. Bartlett's participants also often changed the story's plot to eliminate references to supernatural forces that were unfamiliar in their culture.

Following Bartlett's lead, contemporary researchers have demonstrated a variety of memory distortions that occur when people use constructive processes to reproduce memories (Bergman & Roediger, 1999). How, for example, do you remember what you did as a child? Participants in one experiment were asked to indicate whether, before the age of 10, they had "Met and shook hands with a favourite TV character at a theme resort" (Braun, Ellis, & Loftus, 2002, p. 7). After answering that question—as part of a larger life-experiences inventory—some of the participants read an advertisement for Disneyland that evoked the idea of a family visit: "Go back to your childhood . . . and remember the characters of your youth, Mickey, Goofy, and Daffy Duck." Later the ad described circumstances in which the visitor was able to shake hands with a childhood hero: "Bugs Bunny, the character you've idolized on TV, is only several feet away. . . . You [reach up] to grab his hand" (p. 6). After reading this type of ad, participants were now more likely to indicate—though they hadn't before—that they shook a character's hand. Moreover, they were more likely to report a specific memory that they had shaken Bugs Bunny's hand at Disneyland: 16 percent of the participants in this advertisement group remembered having done so versus 7 percent of the participants in a group that had not read the autobiographical ad. Of course, none of these memories can be accurate: Bugs Bunny is not a Disney character!

This study suggests how even memories for your own life events are reconstructed from various sources. The study also illustrates the fact that people are not always accurate at recalling the original sources for various components of their memories (Mitchell & Johnson, 2000). In fact, researchers have

Suppose, while you were at this party, someone told you the man on your left was a millionaire. How would this affect your memories of his actions at the party? What if you had been told he only had delusions of being a millionaire?

---

reconstructive memory The process of putting information together based on general types of stored knowledge in the absence of a specific memory representation.

demonstrated that individuals will sometimes come to believe that they actually carried out actions that they, in fact, only accomplished in their imaginations.

> A group of 40 college students participated in an experiment that had three sessions. In session 1, the students joined an experimenter for a one-hour walk around campus. The group stopped 48 times during the walk. At each stop, the experimenter read an action statement such as "Check the Pepsi machine for change." After hearing each statement, the students did one of four things: They performed the actions themselves, they watched the experimenter perform the actions, they imagined that they were performing the actions, or they imagined that the experimenter was performing them. In addition, half the actions were bizarre. For example, rather than "Check the Pepsi machine for change," half the students got "Get down on one knee and propose marriage to the machine." The experimenter and the participants took a second walk during session 2, which took place 24 hours later. On the second walk, the students imagined themselves or the experimenter performing some new and some old actions (both ordinary and bizarre) at locations that were also divided between new and old. In session 3, which took place two weeks after session 2, the students were asked to think back to the first session. They tried to recall whether each action had been performed or imagined. For both ordinary and bizarre actions, the same finding held true: Students often recalled that the actions they had only been asked to imagine had actually been performed by them or the experimenter. Thus, some participants agreed that they had actually proposed marriage to a Pepsi machine or patted a dictionary to ask how it was doing when they had only imagined doing so. (Seamon, Philbin, & Harrison, 2006)

Can you find applications of this result in your own life? Suppose you keep reminding yourself to set your alarm clock before you go to bed. Each time you remind yourself, you form a picture in your head of the steps you must go through. If you imagine setting the clock often enough, you might mistakenly come to believe that you actually did so!

It is important to keep in mind, however, that, just as in Chapter 5, when we discussed perceptual illusions, psychologists often infer the normal operation of processes by demonstrating circumstances in which the processes lead to errors. You can think of these memory distortions as the consequences of processes that usually work pretty well. In fact, a lot of the time, you do not need to remember the exact details of a particular episode. Reconstructing the gist of events will serve just fine.

Flashbulb Memories For most of your past life experiences, you would probably agree that you need to reconstruct the memories. For example, if we asked you to tell us how you celebrated your birthday three years ago, you'd likely count backward and try to reconstruct the context. However, there are some circumstances in which people believe that their memories remain completely faithful to the original events. These types of memories—which are called **flashbulb memories**—arise when people experience emotionally charged events: People's memories are so vivid that they seem almost to be photographs of the original incident. The first research on flashbulb memories focused on people's recollections of public events (Brown & Kulik, 1977). For example, the researchers asked participants if they had specific memories of how they first learned about the assassination of President John F. Kennedy. All but one of the 80 participants reported vivid recollections.

The concept of flashbulb memory applies to both private and public events. People might have vivid memories, for example, of an accident they experienced or how they learned about the September 11 attacks. However, research on flashbulb memories has largely focused on public events. To conduct these studies, researchers recruit participants and ask them to share their memories of emotionally resonant events. For different age groups, such events might be the Challenger explosion, the death of Princess Diana, or the attack on Pearl Harbor. The content of flashbulb memories reflects how people learned about the events. For example, people who acquired their information from the media tend to include more event facts in their memory reports than do people who acquired information from another individual (Bohannon, Gratz, & Cross, 2007). U.S. citizens had more specific recollections of the September 11 attacks than did citizens of other countries such as Italy, the Netherlands, and Japan (Curci & Luminet, 2006).

Research on these public events confirms that people acquire flashbulb memories. The question remains, however, whether these memories are as accurate as people believe them to be. To address the question of accuracy, researchers recruit participants directly after the events and then assess their memories at one or more points later in time. One such study began on September 12, 2001.

> The day after the September 11 attacks, students provided answers to a series of questions, including "Where were you when you first heard the news?" and "Were there others with you and, if so, who?" (Talarico & Rubin, 2003). For purposes of comparison, the students also reported memories for an everyday event (such as a party or sporting event) that occurred in the few days before the attack. The students answered the same types of questions for those everyday memories (for example, "Where were you physically?" and "Were there others present and, if so, who?"). The researchers called the students back to the laboratory 1, 6, or 32 weeks after the initial memory test. At each delay, the students answered the same series of memory questions they had answered on September 12. The researchers determined which details were consistent with the original reports and which were inconsistent. As you can see in **Figure 8.15**, there were no differences between September 11 memories and everyday memories. The students recalled consistent details and introduced inconsistent details at nearly the same rate for both types of memories.

The researchers extended their project by inviting the original participants for another memory test after a full year had passed (Talarico & Rubin, 2007). The conclusions remained the same: In a pattern that was quite similar for both types of memories, the participants' ability to provide correct details decreased, whereas their tendency to introduce incorrect details increased. There was, however, one feature that set flashbulb

---

flashbulb memory People's vivid and richly detailed memory in response to personal or public events that have great emotional significance.

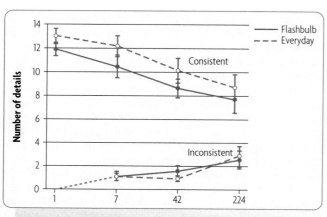

FIGURE 8.15 Students' Recall of Flashbulb and Everyday Memories

On September 12, 2001, students reported details of their memories of the September 11 attack as well as an everyday memory that occurred in the few days preceding that event. When they were tested for the memories 1, 6, or 32 weeks later, the students' performance was highly similar for both types of memories. Over time, they reported fewer details consistent with their first reports and more details that were inconsistent.

From J. M. Talarico & D. C. Rubin. (2003). Confidence, not consistency, characterizes flashbulb memories. *Psychological Science, 14,* pp. 445–461. Reprinted with permission of Wiley-Blackwell.

memories apart from everyday memories: For their flashbulb memories, participants were considerably more confident that they were providing accurate memories.

That final result indicates why it is often difficult for people to accept the results of research on flashbulb memories. How could memories that feel so vivid and true actually be inaccurate (or, at least, be no more accurate than other less vivid memories)? The same processes of reconstruction we discussed earlier apply to flashbulb memories. However, people's desire to hold tight to their memories for particularly emotional events makes it quite difficult for them to consider the possibility that those memories might not be accurate.

We turn now to a domain in which people's overconfidence in their memories can have negative real-world consequences. In the domain of eyewitness testimony, people are always held responsible for reporting exactly what happened.

Eyewitness Memory A witness in a courtroom swears "to tell the truth and nothing but the truth." Throughout this chapter, however, we have seen that whether a memory is accurate or inaccurate depends on the care with which it was encoded and the match between the circumstances of encoding and retrieval. Consider the cartoon of a crowd scene we asked you to examine earlier in the chapter. Without looking back, try to write down or think through as much as you can about the scene. Now turn back to page 221. How did you do? Was everything you recalled accurate? Since researchers understand that people may not be able to report "the truth," even when they genuinely wish to do so, they have focused a good deal of attention on the topic of *eyewitness memory*. The goal is to help the legal system discover the best methods for ensuring the accuracy of witnesses' memories.

Influential studies on eyewitness memory were carried out by **Elizabeth Loftus** (1979; Wells & Loftus, 2003) and her colleagues. The general conclusion from their research was that eyewitnesses' memories for what they had seen were quite vulnerable to distortion from *post-event information*. For example, participants in one study were shown a film of an automobile accident and were asked to estimate the speeds of the cars involved (Loftus & Palmer, 1974). However, some participants were asked, "How fast were the cars going when they smashed into each other?" whereas others were asked, "How fast were the cars going when they contacted each other?" *Smash* participants estimated the cars' speed to have been over 40 miles per hour; *contact* participants estimated the speed at 30 miles per hour. About a week later, all the eyewitnesses were asked, "Did you see any broken glass?" In fact, no broken glass had appeared in the film. However, about a third of the *smash* participants reported that there had been glass, whereas only 14 percent of the *contact* eyewitnesses did so. Thus, post-event information had a substantial effect on what eyewitnesses reported they had experienced.

This experiment represents what is probably the real-life experience of most eyewitnesses: After the events, they have many opportunities to acquire new information that can interact with their original memories. In fact, Loftus and her colleagues demonstrated that participants often succumb to a *misinformation effect* (Loftus, 2005). For example, in one study participants watched a slide show of a traffic accident. They were then asked a series of questions. For half of the participants, one question was "Did another car pass the red Mazda while it was stopped at the stop sign?" For the other half, the question read, "Did another car pass the red Mazda while it was stopped at the yield sign?" The original slide show displayed a stop sign. Still, when participants were asked to recognize the original slide between options with a stop sign or a yield sign, those who had been asked about the stop sign were 75 percent correct, whereas those who had been asked about a yield sign were only 41 percent correct (Loftus, Miller, & Burns, 1978). That is a large impact of misinformation.

In one experiment, participants viewed a slide show of an office theft. The slide show was accompanied by a tape recording of a woman's voice describing the sequence of events. Immediately after the slide show, the participants heard the woman describe the events again. However, this post-event narrative contained misinformation. For example, for participants who had seen *Glamour* magazine, the tape mentioned *Vogue* instead. Forty-eight hours later, the researcher tested his participants' memory for the information pictured in the slides, but he explicitly informed them that there was no question on the memory test for which the correct answer was mentioned in the post-event narrative. Thus, if participants were able to make a clear distinction in memory between the original events and the post-event information, they should have remained unaffected by that post-event information. That was not the case. Even with fair warning, participants often recalled post-event misinformation rather than real memories. (Lindsay, 1990)

The participants had been unable to discriminate between the original sources—event or post-event—of the memory representations. Researchers continue to refine their understanding of circumstances that lead eyewitnesses astray. They have

Why might the different words eyewitnesses use to describe an accident affect their later recall?

demonstrated, for example, that misinformation has a greater impact when the source seems similar to the source of the original events—when sources are dissimilar, people can keep better track of what information emerged from each source (Lindsay, Allen, Chan, & Dahl, 2004). This type of result puts a limit on the extent to which eyewitness memories might be contaminated by other information.

We have now considered several important features of the encoding, storage, and retrieval of information. In the final section of the chapter, we discuss the brain bases of these memory functions.

STOP AND REVIEW

❶ What is the relationship between categories and concepts?

❷ What claim is made by the exemplar theory of categorization?

❸ According to Frederic Bartlett, what three processes create distortions in reconstructive memory?

❹ How did Elizabeth Loftus and her colleagues demonstrate misinformation effects?

CRITICAL THINKING Recall the study that investigated the typicality of fish. Why might the researchers have used two groups from the same geographical region?

Biological Aspects of Memory

The time has come, once again, for us to ask you to recall the number you committed to memory at the beginning of the chapter. Can you still remember it? What was the point of this exercise? Think for a minute about biological aspects of your ability to look at an arbitrary piece of information and commit it instantly to memory. How can you do that? To encode a memory requires that you instantly change something inside your brain. If you wish to retain that memory for at least the length of a chapter, the change must have the potential to become permanent.

Have you ever wondered how this is possible? Our reason for having you recall an arbitrary number was so that we could ask you to reflect on how remarkable the biology of memory really is. Let's take a closer look inside the brain.

SEARCHING FOR THE ENGRAM

Let's consider your memory for the number 46 or, more specifically, your memory that the number 46 was the number we asked you to remember. How could we determine where in your brain that memory resides? **Karl Lashley** (1929, 1950), who performed pioneering work on the anatomy of memory, referred to this question as the search for the **engram**, the physical memory representation. Lashley trained rats to learn mazes, removed varying-sized portions of their cortices (plural of cortex), and then retested their memories for the mazes. Lashley found that memory impairment from brain lesioning was proportional to the amount of tissue removed. The impairment grew worse as more of the cortex was damaged. However, memory was not affected by *where* in the cortex the tissue was removed. Lashley concluded that the elusive engram did not exist in any localized regions but was widely distributed throughout the entire cortex.

Perhaps Lashley could not localize the engram partly because of the variety of types of memories that are called into play even in an apparently simple situation. Maze learning, in fact, involves complex interactions of spatial, visual, and olfactory signals. Neuroscientists now believe that memory for complex sets of information is distributed across many neural systems, even though discrete types of knowledge are separately processed and localized in limited regions of the brain (Markowitsch, 2000; McDonald & White, 1993; Rolls, 2000; White & McDonald, 2002).

Four major brain structures are involved in memory:

- The *cerebellum*, essential for procedural memory, memories acquired by repetition, and classically conditioned responses.
- The *striatum*, a complex of structures in the forebrain; the likely basis for habit formation and for stimulus–response connections.
- The *cerebral cortex*, responsible for sensory memories and associations between sensations.
- The *amygdala* and *hippocampus*, largely responsible for declarative memory of facts, dates, and names and also for memories of emotional significance.

Other parts of the brain, such as the thalamus, the basal forebrain, and the prefrontal cortex, are involved also as way stations for the formation of particular types of memories (see **Figure 8.16**).

In Chapter 4, we focused directly on brain anatomy. Here, let's take a look at the methods that neuroscientists use to draw conclusions about the role of specific brain structures for memory. We will examine two types of research. First, we consider the insights generated by "experiments of nature"—circumstances in which individuals who have suffered brain damage volunteer to further memory research. Second, we describe the ways in which researchers are applying new brain-imaging techniques to improve their understanding of memory processes in the brain.

---

engram The physical memory trace for information in the brain.

WHY DOES ALZHEIMER'S DISEASE AFFECT MEMORY?

In recent years, researchers have acquired a deeper understanding of how memories are formed in the brain. This knowledge has allowed for focused attention on *Alzheimer's disease*—a biological condition in which memory function gradually breaks down. This disease afflicts about 5 percent of Americans aged 65 to 74. Beyond age 65, the risk of the disease doubles every 5 years—it affects nearly 50 percent of individuals over 85 (National Institute on Aging, 2008). Alzheimer's disease onset is deceptively mild—in early stages the only observable symptom may be memory impairment. However, its course is one of steady deterioration. Individuals with Alzheimer's disease may show gradual personality changes, such as apathy, lack of spontaneity, and withdrawal from social interactions. In advanced stages, people with Alzheimer's disease may become completely mute and inattentive, even forgetting the names of their spouse and children.

The symptoms of Alzheimer's disease were first described in 1906 by the German psychiatrist Alois Alzheimer. In those earliest investigations, Alzheimer noted that the brains of individuals who had died from the disease contained unusual tangles of neural tissue and sticky deposits called plaques. Still, Alzheimer could not determine whether those brain changes were the cause of the disease or its products. (As you might recall from Chapter 2, correlation does not necessarily imply causation.) Only in the past 10 to 15 years have researchers been able to assemble the evidence that the plaques themselves cause the brain to deteriorate (Hardy & Selkoe, 2002). The plaques are formed from a substance called *amyloid ß-peptide* (*Aß*). Ordinary processes in the human brain that aid in the growth and maintenance of neurons create *Aß* as a by-product. Normally, *Aß* dissolves in the fluid surrounding neurons, without any consequences. However, in Alzheimer's disease, *Aß* becomes deadly to neurons: *Aß* forms plaques and causes brain cells to self-destruct (Li, Chen, Lee, Yu, & Zhang, 2007).

This understanding of the role of *Aß* in the progress of Alzheimer's disease has led to important recent breakthroughs. For example, researchers are beginning to improve their ability to diagnose the disease. As we will see in Chapter 11, human aging is accompanied by some ordinary changes in memory function. To make a timely diagnosis of Alzheimer's disease, doctors need a way to determine whether older adults' memory impairments are something more than ordinary change. For most of the past 100 years, that was a difficult task. Alzheimer's disease could be definitively diagnosed only when doctors could see the patients' brains—something that was not possible while the patients were living. However, researchers have begun to develop applications of PET scans (see Chapter 3) that enable them to detect the presence of *Aß* in the living brain (Nordberg, 2008). The key advance was manufacturing a radioactive marker that attaches itself to the *Aß* plaques. This radioactive marker becomes visible through PET scans—providing a mechanism for early diagnosis of ominous patterns of *Aß* in the brain.

Early diagnosis would allow early treatment, with the goal of minimizing the negative impact of the disease. Although scientists are pursuing a number of preventive measures and treatments, several lines of research once again focus on *Aß* (Salloway, Mintzer, Weiner, & Cummings, 2008). For example, researchers are seeking methods to interrupt the biochemical processes that produce *Aß* in the first place. They are also exploring techniques to destroy the *Aß* plaques once they have begun to form. Taken together, these approaches hold out great hope that Alzheimer's disease will be less devastating for future generations.

MEMORY DISORDERS

You have already learned about patient H. M., but other patients have also provided information on where memories are stored, particularly when they suffer from damage that impairs their ability to remember. In 1960, Nick A., a young Air Force radar technician, experienced a freak injury that permanently changed his life. Nick had been sitting at his desk while his roommate played with a miniature fencing foil. Then, suddenly, Nick stood up and turned around—just as his buddy happened to lunge with the sword. The foil pierced Nick's right nostril and continued to cut into the left side of his brain. The accident left Nick seriously disoriented. His worst problem was **amnesia**, the failure of memory over a prolonged period. As a result of Nick's amnesia, he forgets many events immediately after they happen. After he reads a few paragraphs of writing, the first sentences slip from his memory. He cannot remember the plot of a television show unless, during commercials, he actively thinks about and rehearses what he was just watching.

---

amnesia A failure of memory caused by physical injury, disease, drug use, or psychological trauma.

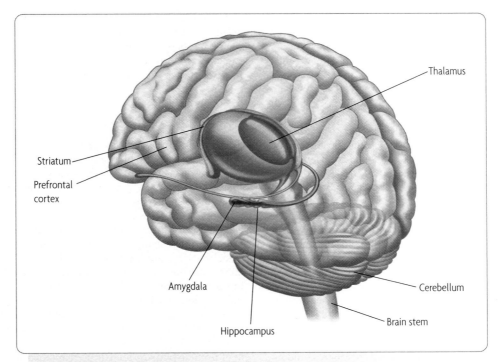

FIGURE 8.16 Brain Structures Involved in Memory
This simplified diagram shows some of the main structures of the brain that are involved in the formation, storage, and retrieval of memories.

The particular type of amnesia from which Nick suffers is called *anterograde* amnesia. This means that Nick can no longer form explicit memories for events that occur after the time at which he suffered physical damage. Other patients suffer from *retrograde* amnesia. In those cases, brain damage prevents access to memories that preceded the moment of injury. If you have ever had the misfortune of receiving a sharp blow to the head (during, for example, a car crash), you are likely to have experienced retrograde amnesia for the events leading up to the accident.

Researchers are grateful to patients like Nick for allowing themselves to be studied as "experiments of nature." By relating the locus of brain injuries like Nick's to patterns of performance deficit, researchers have begun to understand the mapping between regions of the brain and the types of memories we have introduced you to in this chapter (O'Connor & Lafleche, 2005). Nick still remembers how to do things: His procedural knowledge appears to be intact even in the absence of declarative knowledge. So, for example, he remembers how to mix, stir, and bake the ingredients in a recipe, but he forgets what the ingredients are.

The selective impairment of explicit memory of the sort demonstrated by Nick is one of the major facts of the biology of memory: There is abundant evidence to support the conclusion that different brain regions underlie explicit and implicit uses of memory (Voss & Paller, 2008). However, researchers continue to explore exactly what types of implicit memory processes are left intact when people acquire anterograde amnesia. Is it possible, for example, for people with amnesia to learn new associations between words?

Twenty people with amnesia and 21 control individuals participated in a study that assessed their explicit and implicit memory ability (Verfaellie, Martin, Page, Parks, & Keane, 2006). In the experiment, participants read aloud word pairs such as *moss–newspaper* and also read statements that provided a relation between the words, such as "Adding moss to compost helps decompose newspaper." Later, the participants performed explicit and implicit memory tasks. For the explicit task, participants were presented with the first word in each pair and asked to recall the second. By comparison to the control individuals, the people with amnesia performed quite poorly on this explicit task. For the implicit memory task, participants were given the first word from a pair (for example, moss or banana) and then asked to generate four words from a category (such as "reading material"). Both the control individuals and the people with amnesia were more likely to generate words as examples of categories if they had seen the word earlier in the experiment. This result illustrates that the people with amnesia were able to acquire new information. However, the responses of the people with amnesia didn't show evidence that they learned any new associations. For example, if participants had encoded a new association between moss and newspaper, we would expect that they would be even more likely to generate "newspaper" among their four examples of "reading material" than they would have been without that association. In fact, the control individuals generated newspaper more often in the context of moss—but the people with amnesia did not.

This experiment demonstrates some of the subtle differences between the implicit memory processes that are spared and disrupted when people experience anterograde amnesia. People with amnesia are able to learn information about single items (so that, for example, "newspaper" is more accessible when they provide examples of "reading material"). However, implicit memory processes do not generally allow people with amnesia to learn new associations.

The cases in which people lose the ability to recall past information or acquire new information are the most dramatic forms of memory disorders. However, people experience less extensive memory disruptions as a result of injury or disease. For example, the *Psychology in Your Life* box describes the progressive course of Alzheimer's disease. Four researchers from the University of Toronto, Drs. Kelly Murphy, Angela Troyer, Brian Levine, and Morris Moscovitch, study individuals who are at high risk for Alzheimer's disease to understand the biological basis for successive changes in memory function (Murphy, Troyer, Levine, & Moscovitch, 2008). The four are leaders in a newly emerging group of researchers called Cogniciti, from the University of Toronto, Baycrest Hospital, and the Rotman Institute in Toronto. Cogniciti has become connected with philanthropists and other investors to create products such as Memory@Work, which targets aging brains in the workplace. The idea for this product was that there could be a strengthening and a better maintenance of cognitive abilities for aging individuals. It is kind of like a treadmill for the brain! Cogniciti's researchers hope to bring out more products to help exercise the aging brain, create plasticity in aging individuals, and promote better aging.

Researchers often seek out people with damage in particular brain regions to test specific theories about the biology of memory processes. Recall, for example, our discussion of metamemory which revealed that people's feeling-of-knowing judgments are often reasonably accurate. Researchers suggested that regions of the prefrontal cortex (PFC) (see **Figure 8.17**) provide the brain basis for those judgments (Modirrousta & Fellows, 2008). To test that claim, the researchers identified five individuals who had damage in those PFC regions. These individuals with PFC damage and matched controls all tried to learn new associations between faces and names. Even when the two participant groups performed equally well on a recognition test, the individuals with PFC damage were consistently less accurate on their feeling-of-knowing judgments. This experiment supports the claim that prefrontal cortex plays a role in metamemory. It also provides an example of the value of research that examines more subtle forms of memory disorder.

BRAIN IMAGING

Psychologists have gained a great deal of knowledge about the relationship between anatomy and memory from the amnesic patients who generously serve as participants in these experiments. However, the advent of brain-imaging techniques has enabled researchers to study memory processes in individuals without brain damage (Nyberg & Cabeza, 2000). (You may want to review the section on imaging techniques in Chapter 4.) For example, using positron-emission tomography (PET), Endel Tulving and his colleagues (Habib, Nyberg, & Tulving, 2003) have identified a difference in activation between the two brain hemispheres in the encoding and retrieval of episodic information. Their studies parallel standard memory studies, except that the participants' cerebral blood flow is monitored through PET scans during encoding or retrieval. As you can see in Figure 8.17, these researchers discovered disproportionately high brain activity in the left prefrontal cortex for encoding of episodic information and in the right prefrontal cortex for retrieval of episodic information. Thus, the processes show some anatomical distinctions in addition to the conceptual distinctions made by cognitive psychologists.

Research with functional magnetic resonance imaging (fMRI) has also provided remarkable detail about the way that memory operations are distributed in the brain. For example, studies with fMRI have begun to identify the specific brain regions that are activated when new memories are formed. Consider a study in which participants underwent fMRI scans while watching an episode of the sitcom "Curb Your Enthusiasm" that was new to them (Hasson, Furman, Clark, Dudai, & Davachi, 2008). Over the course of 27 minutes, the main character engaged in a series of events such as attending a dinner party and arguing with friends. Three weeks later, the participants returned to the laboratory to take a 77-question memory test on the episode. Each participant remembered some details but not others. The

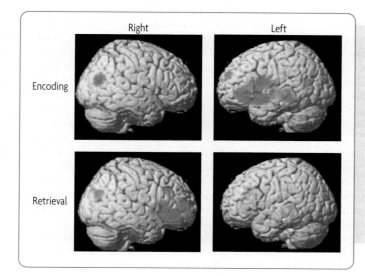

Right   Left

Encoding

Retrieval

FIGURE 8.17 Brain Activity for Encoding and Retrieval

The figure displays the regions of the brain that were most highly activated for encoding versus retrieval. The PET scans display disproportionately high brain activity in the left prefrontal cortex for the encoding of episodic information and in the right prefrontal cortex for the retrieval of episodic information.

Reprinted from *Trends in Cognitive Sciences,* 7(6). Reza Habib, Lars Nyberg, and Endel Tulving, "Brain activity for encoding versus retrieval," p. 241, Copyright © 2003, with permission from Elsevier.

FIGURE 8.18 Brain Regions That Predict Successful Memory

When this set of brain regions was particularly active at time of encoding, people were more likely to remember details from their viewing of a sitcom. The areas are the right temporal pole (TP), superior temporal gyrus (STG), anterior parahippocampal cortex (aPHG), posterior parahippocampal gyrus (pPHG), and temporal parietal junction (TPJ). RH and LH refer to the right and left hemispheres.

researchers analyzed the fMRI data to identify those brain regions that were particularly active when information was successfully encoded. As shown in **Figure 8.18**, several brain regions emerged from that analysis. Unless you pursue studies in cognitive neuroscience, you needn't worry why activity in exactly this set of structures predicts later recall. Figure 8.18 should suggest to you that researchers are making progress toward the goal of witnessing the birth and consolidation of new memories.

Brain scans also provide information about how memory processes unfold in time. If you try to recall the capital of France, the answer might present itself to you (or not) rather quickly. However, if you try to recall what happened the first time you met someone from France, you'll likely need more time to retrieve and elaborate that memory. For those sorts of rich autobiographical memories, the role of different regions of the brain changes over time.

A team of researchers asked participants to retrieve autobiographical memories while undergoing fMRI scans (Daselaar et al., 2008). Participants heard a cue word, such as *tree*, and attempted to bring a specific event to mind that was associated with the word. Participants pushed a button on a response box to indicate when they had retrieved a memory. Because this process unfolded over several seconds, the researchers were able to determine how different brain areas became involved in different aspects of autobiographical memory. For example, early on, structures like the hippocampus were active as participants searched their episodic memories. As participants elaborated their memories, activity in other areas became more prominent. For example, participants' visual cortex became more active as they enriched their memories with visual images. When the visual cortex was particularly active, participants reported the strongest sense that they were actually reliving the memory.

Take a moment to retrieve your own memory in response to *tree*. Do you feel your recollection of the event becoming more elaborate over time? The fMRI scans provide a moment-by-moment account of where and how that elaboration occurs in your brain.

The results from imaging studies illustrate why researchers from different disciplines must work closely together in the quest for a full understanding of memory processes. Psychologists provide the data on human performance that become fuel for neurophysiologists' detection of specialized brain structures. At the same time, the realities of physiology constrain psychologists' theories of the mechanisms of encoding, storage, and retrieval. Through shared effort, scientists in these fields of research provide great insight into the operation of memory processes.

STOP AND REVIEW

❶ What did Karl Lashley conclude about the location of the engram?

❷ What has been learned about the impairment of implicit memory for individuals with amnesia?

❸ What have PET studies indicated about the brain bases of encoding and retrieval of episodic information?

CRITICAL THINKING What structures seem to be involved in memory? Why would visual cortex be involved?

Recapping Main Points

What Is Memory?

- Cognitive psychologists study memory as a type of information processing.
- Memories involving conscious effort are explicit. Unconscious memories are implicit.
- Declarative memory is memory for facts; procedural memory is memory for how to perform skills.
- Memory is often viewed as a three-stage process of encoding, storage, and retrieval.

Visit **MyPsychLab.com** for more review and practice on the following topics:

✳ **Explore:** Encoding, Storage, and Retrieval in Memory

Memory Use for the Short Term

- Iconic memory has a large capacity but very short duration.
- Short-term memory (STM) has a limited capacity and lasts only briefly without rehearsal.
- Maintenance rehearsal can extend the presence of material in STM indefinitely.
- STM capacity can be increased by chunking unrelated items into meaningful groups.
- The broader concept of working memory includes STM.
- The three components of working memory provide the resources for moment-by-moment experiences of the world.

Visit **MyPsychLab.com** for more review and practice on the following topics:

◀◉ **Simulate:** How Good is Your Memory for Stories?

Long-Term Memory: Encoding and Retrieval

- Long-term memory (LTM) constitutes your total knowledge of the world and of yourself. It is nearly unlimited in capacity.
- Your ability to remember information relies on the match between circumstances of encoding and retrieval.
- Retrieval cues allow you to access information in LTM.
- Episodic memory is concerned with memory for events that have been personally experienced. Semantic memory is memory for the basic meaning of words and concepts.
- Similarity in context between learning and retrieval aids retrieval.
- The serial position curve is explained by distinctiveness in context.
- Information processed more deeply is typically remembered better.

- For implicit memories, it is important that the processes of encoding and retrieval be similar.
- Ebbinghaus studied the time course of forgetting. Interference occurs when retrieval cues do not lead uniquely to specific memories.
- Memory performance can be improved through elaborative rehearsal and mnemonics.
- In general, feelings-of-knowing accurately predict the availability of information in memory.

Visit **MyPsychLab.com** for more review and practice on the following topics:

◆◉ **Research:** Hermann Ebbinghaus

Structures in Long-Term Memory

- Concepts are the memory building blocks of thinking. They are formed when memory processes gather together categories of objects or ideas with common properties.
- Concepts are often organized in hierarchies, ranging from general, to basic level, to specific.
- Schemas are more complex cognitive clusters.
- All these memory structures are used to provide expectations and a context for interpreting new information.
- Remembering is not simply recording but is a constructive process.
- Past experiences affect what you remember.
- New information can bias recall, making eyewitness memory unreliable when contaminated by post-event input.

Visit **MyPsychLab.com** for more review and practice on the following topics:

✓ **Practice:** Structures in Long-Term Memory

Biological Aspects of Memory

- Different brain structures (including the hippocampus, the amygdala, the cerebellum, and the cerebral cortex) have been shown to be involved in different types of memories.
- Experiments with individuals with amnesia have helped investigators understand how different types of memories are acquired and represented in the brain.
- Brain-imaging techniques have extended knowledge about the brain bases of memory encoding and retrieval.

Visit **MyPsychLab.com** for more review and practice on the following topics:

◉ **Watch:** Alzheimers and Dementia

KEY TERMS

amnesia (p. 244)
basic level (p. 238)
chunking (p. 223)
concepts (p. 237)
contextual distinctiveness (p. 228)
declarative memory (p. 218)
echoic memory (p. 221)
elaborative rehearsal (p. 234)
encoding (p. 219)
encoding specificity (p. 227)
engram (p. 243)
episodic memories (p. 227)
exemplars (p. 239)
explicit uses of memory (p. 217)

flashbulb memory (p. 241)
iconic memory (p. 220)
implicit uses of memory (p. 217)
levels-of-processing theory (p. 230)
long-term memory (LTM) (p. 226)
memory (p. 217)
metamemory (p. 236)
mnemonics (p. 234)
primacy effect (p. 228)
priming (p. 231)
proactive interference (p. 233)
procedural memory (p. 218)
prototype (p. 239)
recall (p. 226)

recency effect (p. 228)
recognition (p. 226)
reconstructive memory (p. 241)
retrieval (p. 219)
retrieval cues (p. 226)
retroactive interference (p. 233)
schemas (p. 238)
semantic memories (p. 227)
sensory memory (p. 220)
serial position effect (p. 228)
short-term memory (STM) (p. 222)
storage (p. 219)
transfer-appropriate processing (p. 231)
working memory (p. 224)

Practice Test

1. Early in the day, Toby passes a man selling oranges. Later, his mother asks him what he would like to have as a snack. He says, "I'd like an orange." She asks him, "Why an orange?" Toby replies, "It's just what came to mind." It sounds like this is a(n) _____ use of memory.
   a. explicit
   b. implicit
   c. procedural
   d. iconic

2. At her school's talent show, Noa answers questions about politics while spinning basketballs on her fingers. Answering the questions mostly requires _____ memory, whereas spinning the ball mostly requires _____ memory.
   a. implicit; procedural
   b. declarative; procedural
   c. procedural; declarative
   d. implicit; declarative

3. Which is the correct order of these processes?
   a. retrieval, encoding, storage
   b. encoding, retrieval, storage
   c. encoding, storage, retrieval
   d. storage, encoding, retrieval

4. To demonstrate the capacity of iconic memory, George Sperling showed that participants performed better with the _____ procedure.
   a. whole-report
   b. procedural memory
   c. partial-report
   d. implicit memory

5. Mark looks a number up in a phone book but he forgets it before he has a chance to make the call. It sounds as if Mark should have spent more effort on _____.
   a. rehearsal.
   b. chunking.
   c. memory span.
   d. iconic memory.

6. Which of these is *not* a component of working memory?
   a. the iconic memory buffer
   b. the phonological loop
   c. the central executive
   d. the visuospatial sketchpad

7. Because of the usefulness of the retrieval cues, _____ is usually easier than _____.
   a. recall; episodic memory
   b. recognition; recall
   c. semantic memory; recognition
   d. recall; recognition

8. After Meghan meets a group of people, she can remember the name of only the last person she met. This is an example of a(n) _____ effect.
   a. primacy
   b. contextual distinctiveness
   c. encoding specificity
   d. recency

9. Consider the word *Mississippi*. Which of these questions asks you to process that word at the deepest level of processing?
   a. How many times does the letter "s" appear in the word?
   b. Is this word the name of a river?
   c. How many syllables does the word have?
   d. What is the word's first letter?

10. You have just memorized a list of nonsense words. You are going to try to recall the words every day for the next 30 days (without looking back at the list). You would expect to show the most forgetting between _____
    a. day 1 and day 2.
    b. day 3 and day 5.
    c. day 5 and day 10.
    d. day 10 and day 30.

11. Pavel needs to learn the order of the planets with respect to their distance from the sun. To begin, he imagines Mercury as a giant bun and Venus shaped like a shoe. It sounds like Pavel is using _____
    a. the method of loci.
    b. the peg-word method.
    c. metamemory.
    d. iconic memory.

12. At the start of each exam, Sarah reads over the full set of questions to determine which ones she feels pretty sure she will get right. To make these judgments, Sarah is using _____
    a. encoding specificity.
    b. mnemonics.
    c. elaborative rehearsal.
    d. metamemory.

13. Which of these is a term at the basic level of the category?
    a. animal
    b. shark
    c. fish
    d. canary

14. At the petting zoo, Tabitha sees a lamb and a bear cub. When she gets home, Tabitha will probably find it easier to remember the _____ because the schema was _____.
    a. bear cub; inconsistent
    b. lamb; inconsistent
    c. bear cub; consistent
    d. lamb; inconsistent

15. Which of these is *not* one of the reconstructive processes Sir Frederic Bartlett identified?
    a. sharpening
    b. assimilating
    c. levelling
    d. localizing

16. In an experiment, participants watch a movie of a teenager driving through a yellow light and swerving into a parked car. Which of these questions might the researcher use to demonstrate a misinformation effect?
    a. How fast was the car going when it went through the yellow light?

b. How fast was the car going when it hit the parked car?

c. How fast was the car going when it went through the green light?

d. How fast was the car going when it swerved into the parked car?

17. Karl Lashley carried out his search for the engram by training rats on mazes and then removing different amounts of the _____
   a. cortex.   c. striatum.
   b. cerebellum.   d. amygdala.

18. Constantine suffers from amnesia. You would expect to find that his ability to acquire _____ memories is more impaired than his ability to acquire _____ memories.
   a. declarative; explicit   c. implicit; procedural
   b. explicit; implicit   d. implicit; declarative

19. If you were asked to identify the brain bases of the encoding and retrieval of episodic memories, you should point to _____
   a. the striatum.   c. the prefrontal cortex.
   b. the cerebellum.   d. the amygdala.

20. Alois Alzheimer was able to demonstrate that _____
   a. plaques in the brain caused Alzheimer's disease.
   b. amyloid ß-peptide caused Alzheimer's disease.
   c. plaques in the brain could be used to prevent Alzheimer's disease.
   d. people who died of Alzheimer's disease had plaques in their brains.

Essay Questions

1. What are the relationships among encoding, storage, and retrieval?

2. What are the primary functions of working memory?

3. In what ways have brain-imaging techniques helped confirm some of the theoretical distinctions made by memory researchers?

Watch the following video by logging on to MyPsychLab (**www.mypsychlab.com**). After you have watched the video, complete the activities that follow.

Program 9: Remembering and Forgetting

PROGRAM REVIEW

1. The way psychologists thought about and studied memory was changed by the invention of _____
   a. television.
   b. electroconvulsive shock therapy.
   c. the computer.
   d. the electron microscope.

2. What do we mean when we say that memories must be encoded?
   a. They must be taken from storage to be used.
   b. They must be put in a form the brain can register.
   c. They must be transferred from one network to another.
   d. They must be put in a passive storehouse.

3. About how many items can be held in short-term memory?
   a. three
   b. seven
   c. eleven
   d. an unlimited number

4. According to Gordon Bower, what is an important feature of good mnemonic systems?
   a. There is a dovetailing between storage and retrieval.
   b. The acoustic element is more important than the visual.
   c. The learner is strongly motivated to remember.
   d. Short-term memory is bypassed in favour of long-term memory.

5. According to Freud, what is the purpose of repression?
   a. to protect the memory from encoding too much material
   b. to preserve the individual's self-esteem
   c. to activate networks of associations
   d. to fit new information into existing schemas

6. What was Karl Lashley's goal in teaching rats mazes and then removing part of their cortices?
   a. finding out how much tissue was necessary for learning to occur
   b. determining whether memory was localized in one area of the brain
   c. discovering how much tissue loss led to memory loss
   d. finding out whether conditioned responses could be eradicated

7. What is the chief cause of functional amnesia?
   a. Alzheimer's disease
   b. substance abuse
   c. traumatic injury to the brain
   d. severe anxiety

8. Long-term memory is organized as _____
   a. a complex network of associations.
   b. a serial list.
   c. a set of visual images.
   d. a jumble of individual memories with no clear organizational scheme.

9. What did Karl Lashley conclude about the engram?
   a. It is localized in the brain stem.
   b. It is localized in the right hemisphere only.
   c. It is localized in the left hemisphere only.
   d. Complex memories cannot be pinpointed within the brain.

10. Drawing on Richard Thompson's work, Diana Woodruff-Pak suggests that eye-blink conditioning may be a _____
    a. precursor to early-onset dementia
    b. predictor of musical genius
    c. mechanism for growing brain cells in intact animals
    d. tool for training long-term visual memories

QUESTIONS TO CONSIDER

1. What is your earliest memory? How accurate do you think it is? Can you recall an experience that happened before you could talk? If not, why not? How does language influence what we remember? How do photographs and other mementoes aid memory?

2. As a member of a jury, you are aware of the tendency to reconstruct memories. How much weight do you give to eyewitness testimony? Is it possible ever to get "the whole truth and nothing but the truth" from an eyewitness? Do you think memory distortions (for details of what was said during a trial) occur in jurors as well?

9

Cognitive Processes

I t is midnight. There is a knock on your door. When you answer, no one is there, but you see an envelope on the floor. Inside the envelope is a single sheet of paper with a handwritten message: "The cat is on the mat." What do you make of this?

You must now begin to engage a variety of cognitive processes. You will need language processes to put together some basic meanings for the words, but what then? Can you find any episode in memory to which these words are relevant? (Recall that in Chapter 8 we discussed memory as a type of cognitive processing.) If you cannot, you will have to give other types of thought to the matter. Is the message a code? What kind of code? Whom do you know who might encode a message? Does the fate of something important rest in your hands?

Perhaps we are getting a bit carried away, but we want to make plain to you what kinds of activities count as **cognitive processes** and why they might interest you. The capacity to use language and to think in abstract ways has often been cited as the essence of the human experience. You tend to take cognition for granted because it is an activity you do continually during your waking hours. Even so, when a carefully crafted speech wins your vote or when you read a detective story in which the sleuth combines a few scraps of apparently trivial clues into a brilliant solution to a crime, you are forced to acknowledge the intellectual triumph of cognitive processes.

Cognition is a general term for all forms of knowing: As shown in **Figure 9.1**, the study of cognition is the study of your mental life. (Note that Chapter 5 already discussed some of the topics shown in Figure 9.1.) Cognition includes both contents and processes. The *contents* of cognition are *what* you know—concepts, facts, propositions, rules, and memories: "A dog is a mammal." "A red light means stop." "I first left home at age 18."

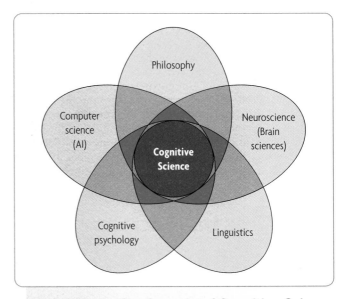

FIGURE 9.2   The Domain of Cognitive Science

The domain of cognitive science occupies the intersection of philosophy, neuroscience, linguistics, cognitive psychology, and computer science (artificial intelligence).

Cognitive *processes* are *how* you manipulate these mental contents—in ways that enable you to interpret the world around you and to find creative solutions to your life's dilemmas.

Within psychology, the study of cognition is carried out by researchers in the field of **cognitive psychology**. Over the past three decades, the field of cognitive psychology has been supplemented by the interdisciplinary field of **cognitive science** (see **Figure 9.2**). Cognitive science focuses the collected knowledge of several academic specialties on the same theoretical issues. It benefits the practitioners of each of these fields to share their data and insights. You saw this cognitive science philosophy at work in Chapter 8, when we described how studies of the biology of memory can be used to constrain—limit and refine—theories of memory processes. Many of the theories we will describe in this chapter have similarly been shaped through the interactions of researchers from a number of disciplinary perspectives.

We will begin our study of cognition with a brief description of the ways in which researchers try to measure the inner, private processes involved in cognitive functioning. Then we will examine, at some length, topics in cognitive psychology that generate much basic research and practical application: language use, visual cognition, problem solving, reasoning, and judging and decision making.

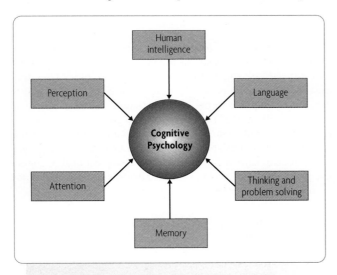

FIGURE 9.1   The Domain of Cognitive Psychology

Cognitive psychologists study higher mental functions with particular emphasis on the ways in which people acquire knowledge and use it to shape and understand their experiences in the world.

From Solso, Robert L., *Cognitive Psychology*, 3e, pp. 7, 289, 290. Copyright © 1991. Published by Allyn & Bacon, Boston, MA. Copyright © 2003 by Pearson Education. Reprinted by permission of the publisher.

cognitive processes Higher mental processes, such as perception, memory, language, problem solving, and abstract thinking.

cognition Processes of knowing, including attending, remembering, and reasoning; also the content of the processes, such as concepts and memories.

cognitive psychology The study of higher mental processes such as attention, language use, memory, perception, problem solving, and thinking.

cognitive science The interdisciplinary field of study of the approach systems and processes that manipulate information.

Studying Cognition

How can you study cognition? The challenge, of course, is that it goes on inside the head. You can see the input—for example, a note that says, "Call me"—and experience the output—you make a phone call—but how can you determine the series of mental steps that connected the note to your response? How, that is, can you reveal what happened in the middle—the cognitive processes and the mental representations on which your action relies? In this section, we describe the types of logical analyses that have made possible the scientific study of cognitive psychology.

DISCOVERING THE PROCESSES OF MIND

One of the fundamental methodologies for studying mental processes was devised, in 1868, by the Dutch physiologist F. C. Donders. To study the "speed of mental processes," Donders invented a series of experimental tasks that he believed were differentiated by the mental steps involved for successful performance (R. Lachman, J. L. Lachman, & Butterfield, 1979). **Table 9.1** provides a paper-and-pencil experiment that follows Donders's logic. Before reading on, please take a moment to complete each task.

How long did you take to do task 1? Suppose you wanted to give a list of the steps you carried out to perform the task. It might look something like this:

a. Determine whether a character is a capital letter or a small letter.

b. If it is a capital letter, draw a C on top.

How long did you take for task 2? When we have used this exercise, students have often taken an additional half minute or more. You can understand why, once we spell out the necessary steps:

a. Determine whether a character is a capital letter or a small letter.

b. Determine whether each capital letter is a vowel or a consonant.

c. If it is a consonant, draw a C on top. If it is a vowel, draw a V.

Thus, going from task 1 to task 2, we add two mental steps, which we can call *stimulus categorization* (vowel or consonant?) and *response selection* (draw a C or draw a V). Task 1 requires one stimulus categorization step. Task 2 requires two such categorizations. Task 2 also requires selecting between two responses. Since task 2 requires you to do everything you did for task 1 and more, it takes you more time. That was Donders's fundamental insight: Extra mental steps will often result in more time to perform a task.

You may be wondering why we included task 3. This is a necessary procedural control for the experiment. We have to ensure that the time difference between tasks 1 and 2 does not

---

serial processes Two or more mental processes that are carried out in order, one after the other.

parallel processes Two or more mental processes that are carried out simultaneously.

TABLE 9.1 Donders's Analysis of Mental Processes

Note how long (in seconds) it takes you to complete each of these three tasks. Try to complete each task accurately, but as quickly as possible.

Task 1: Draw a C on top of all the capitalized letters:

TO Be, oR noT To BE: tHAT Is thE qUestioN:
WhETher 'Tis noBlEr In tHE MINd tO SuFfER
tHe SLings AnD ARroWS Of OUtrAgeOUs forTUNe,
or To TAke ARmS agaINST a sEa Of tROUBleS,
AnD by oPPOsinG END theM.   TIME: _____

Task 2: Draw a V on top of the capitalized vowels and a C on top of the capitalized consonants:

TO Be, oR noT To BE: tHAT Is thE qUestioN:
WhETher 'Tis noBlEr In tHE MINd tO SuFfER
tHe SLings AnD ARroWS Of OUtrAgeOUs forTUNe,
or To TAke ARmS agaINST a sEa Of tROUBleS,
AnD by oPPOsinG END theM.   TIME: _____

Task 3: Draw a V on top of all the capitalized letters:

TO Be, oR noT To BE: tHAT Is thE qUestioN:
WhETher 'Tis noBlEr In tHE MINd tO SuFfER
tHe SLings AnD ARroWS Of OUtrAgeOUs forTUNe,
or To TAke ARmS agaINST a sEa Of tROUBleS,
AnD by oPPOsinG END theM.   TIME: _____

---

stem from the fact that it takes much longer to draw V's than to draw C's. Task 3 should still be much swifter than task 2. Was it?

Researchers still follow Donders's basic logic. They frequently use *reaction time*—the amount of time it takes experimental participants to perform particular tasks—as a way of testing specific accounts of how some cognitive process is carried out. Computers now make the calculation of reaction time very simple. Donders's basic premise that extra mental steps will result in extra time is still fundamental to a great deal of cognitive psychological research. Let's see how this successful idea has been developed over the past 135 years.

MENTAL PROCESSES AND MENTAL RESOURCES

When cognitive psychologists break down high-level activities, like language use or problem solving, into their component processes, they often act as if they are playing a game with blocks. Each block represents a different component that must be carried out. The goal is to determine the shape and size of each block and to see how the blocks fit together to form the whole activity. For the Donders tasks, you saw that the blocks can be laid out in a row (see **Figure 9.3**, part A). Each step comes directly after another. The block metaphor allows you to see that we could also stack the blocks so more than one process occurs simultaneously (part B). These two pictures illustrate the distinction between **serial** and **parallel processes**. Processes are

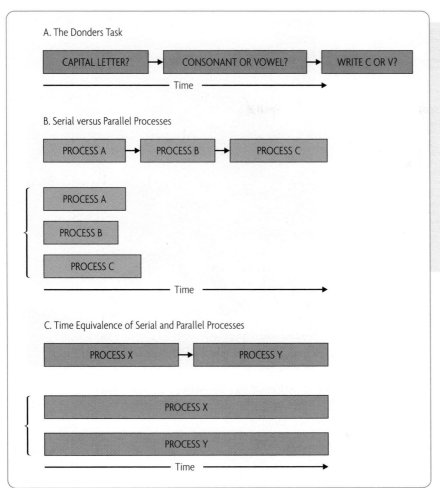

A. The Donders Task

| CAPITAL LETTER? | → | CONSONANT OR VOWEL? | → | WRITE C OR V? |

Time →

B. Serial versus Parallel Processes

| PROCESS A | → | PROCESS B | → | PROCESS C |

PROCESS A

PROCESS B

PROCESS C

Time →

C. Time Equivalence of Serial and Parallel Processes

| PROCESS X | → | PROCESS Y |

PROCESS X

PROCESS Y

Time →

FIGURE 9.3 Breaking Down High-Level Cognitive Activities

Cognitive psychologists attempt to determine the identity and organization of the mental processes that are the building blocks of high-level cognitive activities. (A) Our version of the Donders task requires that at least three processes be carried out one after the other. (B) Some processes are carried out serially, in sequence; others are carried out in parallel, all at the same time. (C) The time taken to perform a task does not always allow researchers to conclude whether serial or parallel processes were used.

serial when they take place one after the other. Suppose you are in a restaurant and you need to decide what to order. You focus on entries one at a time and then judge whether they qualify as "yes," "no," or "maybe." For each entry, your judgment processes follow your reading processes. Processes are *parallel* when they overlap in time. When it comes time to place your order, the language processes that enable you to understand the waiter's question (e.g., "What can I get for you?") are likely to operate at the same time as the processes that allow you to formulate your reply (e.g., "I'd like the osso buco"). That is why you are ready to respond as soon as the waiter finishes his question.

Cognitive psychologists often use reaction times to determine whether processes are carried out in parallel or serially. However, the examples in part C of Figure 9.3 should convince you that this is a tricky business. Imagine that we have a task that we believe can be broken down into two processes, *X* and *Y*. If the only information we have is the total time needed to complete the process, we can never be sure if processes *X* and *Y* happen side by side or one after the other. Much of the challenge of research in cognitive psychology is to invent task circumstances that allow the experimenter to determine which of many possible configurations of blocks is correct. In task 2 of the exercise you just did, we could be reasonably certain that the processes were serial because some activities logically required others. For

example, you could not execute your response (prepare to draw a C or a V) until you had determined what the response might be.

In many cases, theorists try to determine if processes are serial or parallel by assessing the extent to which the processes place demands on *mental resources*. Suppose, for example, you are walking to class with a friend. Ordinarily, it should be easy for you to walk a straight path at the same time you carry on a conversation—your navigation processes and your language processes can go on in parallel. What would happen, however, if you suddenly get to a patch of sidewalk that is dotted with puddles? As you pick your way among the puddles, you may have to stop talking. Now your navigation processes require extra resources for planning, and your language processes are momentarily squeezed out.

A key assumption in this example is that you have *limited* processing resources that must be spread over different mental tasks (Logan, 2002). Your *attentional processes* are responsible for distributing these resources. In Chapter 5 we discussed attention as the set of processes that allow you to select, for particular scrutiny, some small subset of available perceptual information. Our use of *attention* here preserves the idea of selectivity. The decision now, however, concerns which mental processes will be selected as the recipients of processing resources.

TABLE 9.2   Size Judgments
Your task is to circle the number that is *physically* larger in each pair. Try to judge which list is harder.

List A

61 —67   22 —28   25 —29   47 —41

68 —64   27 —23   43 —49   44 —48

List B

47 —41   61 —67   27 —23   25 —29

22 —28   68 —64   43 —49   44 —48

Why is it difficult to carry on a conversation while you are trying to avoid puddles?

We have one more complication to add: Not all processes put the same demands on resources. We can, in fact, define a dimension that goes from processes that are *controlled* to those that are *automatic* (Shiffrin & Schneider, 1977). **Controlled processes** require attention; **automatic processes** generally do not. It is often difficult to carry out more than one controlled process at a time because they require more resources; automatic processes can often be performed alongside other tasks without interference.

We want to give you an example of an automatic process. To get started, take a moment to carry out the task in **Table 9.2**. Did you find list A somewhat harder than list B?

Experimental participants were asked to make the types of judgments illustrated in Table 9.2. If you look closely at the table, you'll see that the items on List A present a mismatch between physical size and the magnitude of each number (i.e., 61 is physically larger but it's a number of smaller magnitude than 67). On List B, there is a match between the physical size and the magnitude of the numbers. If you worked your way through Table 9.2, you won't be surprised to learn that participants took longer to make size judgments when there was a mismatch (List A) than when there was a match (List B) (Ganor-Stern, Tzelgov, & Ellenbogen, 2007). But why should the magnitude of the numbers matter for a judgment of physical size? The researchers suggested that when you look at 61 or 67 you can't help but think of the quantity it represents—even when the quantity, in this case, impairs performance on the task you've been asked to carry out. That is, you automatically access the meaning of a number, even when you don't need (or want) to do so.

This number task illustrates that automatic processes rely heavily on the efficient use of memory (Barrett, Tugade, & Engle, 2004). When you see 61, 67, and so on, your memory processes swiftly provide information about quantity.

The number task also illustrates the way in which tasks that first involved controlled processes can become automatic with sufficient practice. You probably remember, as a small child, having to learn how numbers work. Now, the association between numbers and the quantities they represent has become so automatic you cannot shut off the association. You can probably think of other instances in which you have practised enough to make tasks automatic. Did you learn to play an instrument? Can you type without looking at the keyboard?

Let's apply this knowledge of controlled and automatic processes back to the situation of walking and talking. When you are walking a straight route, you feel little interference between the two activities, suggesting that maintaining your path and planning your utterances are each relatively automatic activities. The situation changes, however, when the puddles force you to choose between a greater number of options for your path. Now you must select where to go and what to say. Université de Montréal professor and Canada Research Chair Pierre Jolicoeur suggests that since you cannot make both choices simultaneously, you have come up against the limits of your processing resources (Tombu & Jolicoeur, 2005). This example shows why controlled and automatic processes are defined along a dimension, rather than constituting strict categories. When circumstances become challenging, what previously seemed automatic now requires controlled attention. Thus, processes may require more or less attention, depending on the context. Jolicoeur is now investigating how

controlled processes Processes that require attention; it is often difficult to carry out more than one controlled process at a time.

automatic processes Processes that do not require attention; they can often be performed along with other tasks without interference.

this psychological problem might have real-world implications, such as when you are driving and talking on your cell phone. How many times have you been cut off by a driver who is talking on a cell phone and has clearly not been keeping track of the demands of both actions? Although many people believe the demands of driving and talking on a cell phone are too challenging, real research on the topic is necessary to know whether we have the capability to do both simultaneously (see the *Critical Thinking in Your Life* box in Chapter 5). Jolicoeur is using techniques such as measuring brain activity to evaluate our ability for multitasking (Brisson & Jolicoeur, 2007).

You now know a lot about the logic of mental processes. To explain how complex mental tasks are carried out, theorists propose models that combine serial and parallel as well as controlled and automatic processes. The goal of much cognitive psychological research is to invent experiments that confirm each of the components of such models. Now that you understand some of the logic behind cognitive psychological research into mental processes, it is time to move to more specific domains in which you put cognitive processes to work. We begin with language use.

STOP AND REVIEW

❶ What was Donders's goal when he asked participants to carry out different experimental tasks?

❷ What is the distinction between serial and parallel processes?

❸ What types of processes do not generally require attentional resources?

CRITICAL THINKING How might a controlled process become an automatic one over time?

Language Use

Let's return to the message you received at midnight, "The cat is on the mat." What could we do to change the situation so that this message immediately made sense to you? The easiest step we could take would be to introduce appropriate background knowledge. Suppose you are a secret agent who always gets instructions in this curious fashion. You might know "the cat" is your contact and "on the mat" means in the wrestling arena. Off you go.

You do not really have to be a spy for "The cat is on the mat" to take on a variety of meanings:

- Suppose your cat waits on a mat by the door when she wants to be let out. When you say to your roommate, "The cat is on the mat," you use those words to communicate, "Could you get up and let the cat out?"
- Suppose your friend is worried about pulling the car out of the driveway because she is uncertain where the cat is. When you say, "The cat is on the mat," you use those words to communicate, "It's safe to pull out of the driveway."
- Suppose your friend wants to have a race between your cat and his dog. When you say, "The cat is on the mat," you use those words to communicate, "My cat will not race!"

These examples illustrate the difference between *sentence meaning*—the generally simple meaning of the combined words of a sentence—and *speaker's meaning*—the unlimited number of meanings a speaker can communicate by putting a sentence to good use (Grice, 1968). When psychologists study language use, they want to comprehend both the *production* and the *understanding* of speakers' meanings:

- How do speakers produce the right words to communicate the meaning they intend?
- How do listeners recover the messages the speakers wished to communicate?

We will examine each of these questions in turn. We also consider the evolutionary and cultural context of language use.

LANGUAGE PRODUCTION

Look at **Figure 9.4**. Try to formulate a few sentences about this picture. What did you think to say? Suppose now we asked you to describe the person in the photo for someone who was blind. How would your description change? Does this second description seem to require more mental effort? The study of **language production** concerns both what people say—what they choose to say at a given time—and the processes they go through to

FIGURE 9.4   Language Production
How would you describe this person to a friend? How might your description change if your friend were blind?

---

language production What people say, sign, and write, as well as the processes they go through to produce these messages.

TABLE 9.3 Grice's Maxims in Language Production

1. *Quantity:* Make your contribution as informative as is required (for the current purposes of the exchange). Do not make your contribution more informative than is required.

   The consequence for the speaker: You must try to judge how much information your audience really needs. Often this judgment will require you to assess what your listener is likely to know already.

2. *Quality:* Try to make your contribution one that is true. Do not say what you believe to be false. Do not say that for which you lack adequate evidence.

   The consequence for the speaker: When you speak, listeners will assume that you can back up your assertions with appropriate evidence. As you plan each utterance, you must have in mind the evidence on which it is based.

3. *Relation:* Be relevant.

   The consequence for the speaker: You must make sure that your listeners will see how what you are saying is relevant to what has come before. If you wish to shift the topic of conversation—so that your utterance is not directly relevant—you must make that clear.

4. *Manner:* Be perspicacious*. Avoid obscurity of expression. Avoid ambiguity. Be brief. Be orderly.

   The consequence for the speaker: It is your responsibility to speak in as clear a manner as possible. Although you will inevitably make errors, as a co-operative speaker you must ensure that your listeners can understand your message.

   In this conversation, can you see how Chris follows (or violates) Grice's maxims?

What Is Said	What Chris Might Be Thinking
Pat: *Have you ever been to New York City?* Chris: *I was there once in 2002.*	I don't know why Pat is asking me this question, so I probably should say a little more than just "yes."
Pat: *I'm supposed to visit, but I'm worried about being mugged.* Chris: *I think a lot of areas are safe.*	I can't say that he shouldn't worry because he won't believe me. What can I say that will sound true but make him feel okay?
Pat: *How was your hotel?* Chris: *We didn't stay overnight.*	If I say, "We didn't stay in a hotel," that might suggest we stayed somewhere else. I need to say something relevant that will make clear why I can't answer the question.
Pat: *Would you like to go to New York with me?* Chris: *I'd have to find a way to see if it would be possible for me to leave without it being too impossible.*	I don't want to go, but I don't want to seem rude. Will Pat notice that I'm being evasive in my response?
Pat: *Huh?* Chris: *Well . . .*	Trapped.

*Perspicacious = having keen judgment or understanding

produce the message. Note that language users need not produce language out loud. Language production also includes both signing and writing. Also, it is worth noting that language producers cannot always be defined as those who understand language. Imagine going to another country where you do not speak the language. The natives in that country are not poor language producers; rather, you would be considered a poor understander of that language. For convenience, we will call language producers *speakers* and language understanders *listeners*. For effective *communication*, you need to have speakers and listeners.

Audience Design We asked you to imagine the different descriptions you would give of Figure 9.4 to a sighted and a blind person as a way of getting you to think about **audience**

audience design The process of shaping a message depending on the audience for which it is intended.

design in language production. Each time you produce an utterance, you must have in mind the audience you will be addressing, as well as what knowledge you share with members of that audience (H. H. Clark, 1996; H. H. Clark & Van Der Wege, 2002). For example, it will not do you the least bit of good to say, "The cat is on the mat" if your listener does not know that the cat sits on the mat only when she wishes to be let out. An overarching rule of audience design, the *co-operative principle*, was first proposed by the philosopher **H. Paul Grice** (1975). Grice phrased the co-operative principle as an instruction to speakers that they should produce utterances appropriate to the setting and meaning of the ongoing conversation. To expand on this instruction, Grice defined four maxims that co-operative speakers live by. In **Table 9.3**, we present each of those maxims, as well as an invented conversation that illustrates the effect the maxims have on moment-by-moment choices in language production.

As you can see from **Table 9.3**, being a co-operative speaker depends, in large part, on having accurate expectations about what your listener is likely to know and understand. Thus, you certainly would not tell a friend "I'm having lunch with Alex" if you did not have good reason to believe that your friend knew who Alex was. You also must assure yourself that, of all the Alexes your friend might know and knows that you know, only one would come to mind as the specific Alex you would mention in these circumstances. More formally, we can say that there must be some Alex who is prominent in the *common ground*—common knowledge—you share with your friend.

Herbert Clark (1996) suggested that language users have different bases for their judgments of common ground:

- *Community membership.* Language producers often make strong assumptions about what is likely to be mutually known based on shared membership in communities of various sizes.
- *Co-presence for actions.* Language producers often assume that the actions and events they have shared with other conversationalists become part of common ground. This includes information discussed in earlier parts of a conversation (or in past conversations).
- *Perceptual co-presence.* Perceptual co-presence exists when a speaker and a listener share the same perceptual events (sights, sounds, and so on).

Thus, your use of "Alex" in "I'm having lunch with Alex" might succeed because your friend and you are part of a small community (for example, roommates) that includes only one Alex (community membership). Or it might succeed because you have introduced the existence of Alex earlier in the conversation (co-presence for actions). Or Alex might be standing right there in the room (perceptual co-presence). You can see from this example why judgments of common ground often rely on the ability of your memory processes to provide information about individuals and communities (Horton & Gerrig, 2005a, 2005b). For you to say "I'm having lunch with Alex," you must be reasonably certain that "Alex" will be sufficiently memorable for your particular listener.

Let's focus a bit more on community membership. Take a moment to think about this question: What information would you expect the community members of your college or university to know? What information would you expect students to know—but not the professors? Researchers have examined the extent to which people's estimates of community knowledge are accurate and useful.

In a first experiment, undergraduates in Hong Kong viewed a series of slides of 30 landmarks from Hong Kong, Macau, and New York City (Lau, Chiu, & Hong, 2001). The participants were asked whether they recognized each landmark and whether they could name it. In addition, the participants tried to estimate what percentage of their classmates would recognize each landmark. The results from this experiment indicated that the students were pretty accurate at guessing what members of their own communities were likely to know: Their estimates were reasonably close to the actual percentages of students who got the landmarks correct. However, the students also tended to err in the direction of believing other people knew the same things they did: They gave higher estimates for those landmarks they themselves knew. In a second experiment, a new group of participants were asked to provide descriptions of each of the 30 landmarks. Their goal was to provide a description that would allow one of their classmates to choose correctly each landmark from among the 30 pictures. The researchers demonstrated that the length of the descriptions was related to community knowledge: Participants generally used more words to describe the landmarks that the first experiment showed to be the least recognizable.

You can think about these results with respect to your own day-to-day experiences. If you are talking to a classmate, you can probably say something like "Meet me at the Union for lunch." If you are expecting a visit from a friend for whom the campus is new, you would probably add something like "It's the red building on the left, about 100 metres beyond the fountain." The comparative lengths of your descriptions suggest that you are using community membership to plan your utterances.

Our discussion so far has focused on language production at the level of the message: How you shape what you wish to say will depend on the audience to whom you are speaking. Let's turn now to a discussion of the mental processes that allow you to produce these messages.

Speech Execution and Speech Errors Would you like to be famous for tripping over your tongue? Consider the Reverend W. A. Spooner of Oxford University, who lent his name to the term *spoonerism*: an exchange of the initial sounds of two or more words in a phrase or sentence. Reverend Spooner came by this honour honestly. When, for example, he was tongue-lashing a lazy student for wasting the term, Reverend Spooner said, "You have tasted the whole worm!" A spoonerism is one of the limited types of speech errors that language producers make. These errors give researchers insight into the planning that goes on as speakers produce utterances. As you can see in **Table 9.4**, you need to engage in several types of planning, and speech errors give evidence for each type (Dell, 2004). What should impress you about all these examples of errors is that they are not just random—they make sense given the structure of spoken English. Thus, a speaker might exchange initial consonants—"tips of the slung" for "slips of the tongue"—but would never say, "tlips of the sung," which would violate the rule of English that "tl" does not occur as an initial sound (Fromkin, 1980).

Among ichthyologists (scientists who study fish), this is a *Choerodon fasciatus*. What would you call it if you were talking or writing about it to a friend?

TABLE 9.4 Errors in Planning Speech Production

Types of planning:

- Speakers must choose the content words that best fit their ideas.

  If the speaker has two words in mind, such as *grizzly* and *ghastly*, a blend like *grastly* might result.

- Speakers must put the chosen words in the right places in the utterance.

  Because speakers plan whole units of their utterances while they produce them, content words will sometimes become misplaced.

  a tank of gas → a gas of tank

  wine is being served at dinner → dinner is being served at wine

- Speakers must fill in the sounds that make up the words they wish to utter.

  Once again, because speakers plan ahead, sounds will sometimes get misplaced.

  left hemisphere → heft lemisphere

  pass out → pat ous

why speakers find it easier to produce some sounds than others in ongoing speech (Goldrick & Larson, 2008). The analyses focus on such factors as the relative frequency of certain sounds in particular positions (for example, an *s* sound is more likely than a *z* sound to occur at the beginning of an English word). Other projects examine the time course with which people produce the particular words of an utterance. Researchers have demonstrated, for example, that people find it harder to produce a word (such as *cow*) when they have recently spoken another word with which it is associated (such as *milk*). Such results are explained as a consequence of different memory representations competing to be included in an utterance (Rahman & Melinger, 2007).

For structures, researchers often examine the factors that lead speakers to choose one or another way of expressing the same idea. Consider **Figure 9.5**. If you described this scene, you might either say "The girl was frightened by the jack-in-the-box" or "The jack-in-the-box frightened the girl." To understand why speakers choose a particular structure, researchers point to such factors as the recent language that the speaker has heard and understood (Bock, Dell, Chang, & Onishi, 2007). If, for example, you have recently heard a sentence such as "The embassy staff isn't being evacuated by the government," you would be more likely to produce an utterance that has the same global structure (such as "The girl was frightened by the jack-in-the-box").

We have now looked at some of the forces that lead speakers to produce particular utterances and at some of the processes that allow them to do so. We turn next to the listeners, who are responsible for understanding what speakers intend to communicate.

Given the importance of speech errors to developing theoretical models of speech production, researchers have not always been content just to wait around for errors to happen naturally. Instead, researchers have explored a number of ways to produce artificial errors in controlled experimental settings (e.g., Hartsuiker, Schriefers, & Kikstra, 2003; Warker & Dell, 2006). One classic technique is called SLIP (for "spoonerisms of laboratory-induced predisposition"; Baars, 1992). In this procedure, participants are asked to read silently lists of word pairs that provide models for the sound structure of a target spoonerism: *ball doze, bash door, bean deck, bell dark*. They then are required to pronounce out loud a word pair like *darn bore*, but under the influence of the earlier pairs it will sometimes come out *barn door*.

With this technique, researchers can study the factors that affect the likelihood that speakers will produce errors. For example, a spoonerism is more likely when the error will still result in real words (Baars, Motley, & MacKay, 1975). Thus an error on *darn bore* (to produce *barn door*) is more likely than an error on *dart board* (to produce *bart doard*). Findings like this suggest that while you are producing utterances, some of your cognitive processes are devoted to detecting and editing potential errors (Nooteboom & Quené, 2008). Those processes are reluctant to let you pronounce sounds like *doard*, which are not real English words.

Contemporary theories of speech production attempt to predict how people's utterances unfold in time for sounds, words, and structures. For example, researchers might study

FIGURE 9.5 Selecting a Sentence Structure

How would you describe this scene?

Reprinted from *Cognition, 104*, Bock, K., Dell, G. S., Chang, F., & Onishi, K. H., Persistent Structural Priming from Language Comprehension to Language Production, 437–458. Copyright (2007) with permission from Elsevier.

LANGUAGE UNDERSTANDING

Suppose a speaker has produced the utterance "The cat is on the mat." You already know that, depending on the context, this utterance can be used to communicate any number of different meanings. How, as a listener, do you settle on just one meaning? We will begin this discussion of language understanding by considering more fully the problem of the ambiguity of meaning.

Resolving Ambiguity What does the word *bank* mean? You can probably think of at least two meanings, one having to do with rivers and the other having to do with money. Suppose you hear the utterance "He came from the bank." How do you know which meaning is intended? You need to be able to resolve the *lexical ambiguity* between the two meanings. (Lexical is related to *lexicon*, a synonym for *dictionary*.) If you think about this problem, you will realize that you have some cognitive processes that allow you to use surrounding context to eliminate the ambiguity—to *disambiguate*—the word. Have you been talking about rivers or about money? That broader context should enable you to choose between the two meanings. But how?

Before we answer that question, we would like to introduce another type of ambiguity. What does this sentence mean: "The mother of the boy and the girl will arrive soon?" You may detect only one meaning right off, but there is a *structural*

ambiguity here (Akmajian, Demers, Farmer, & Harnish, 1990). Take a look at **Figure 9.6**. Linguists often represent the structure of sentences with tree diagrams to show how the various words are gathered together into grammatical units. In part A, we have shown you an analysis of "The cat is on the mat." The structure is pretty simple: a noun phrase made up of an article and a noun, plus a verb phrase made up of a verb and a prepositional phrase. In the other two parts, you see the more complex structures for the two different meanings of the sentence starting "The mother. . . ." In part B, the analysis shows that the whole phrase "of the boy and the girl" applies to the mother. One person—the mother of two children—will arrive soon. In part C, the analysis shows that there are two noun phrases, "the mother of the boy" and "the girl." There are two people, both of whom will arrive soon. Which understanding of the sentence did you come to when you first read it? Now that you can see that two meanings are possible, we arrive at the same question we did for lexical ambiguity: How does prior context enable you to settle on one meaning when more than one is possible?

Let's return to lexical ambiguity (an ambiguity of word meaning). Consider this sentence (from Mason & Just, 2007):

> To their surprise, the bark was unusual because it sounded high-pitched and hoarse.

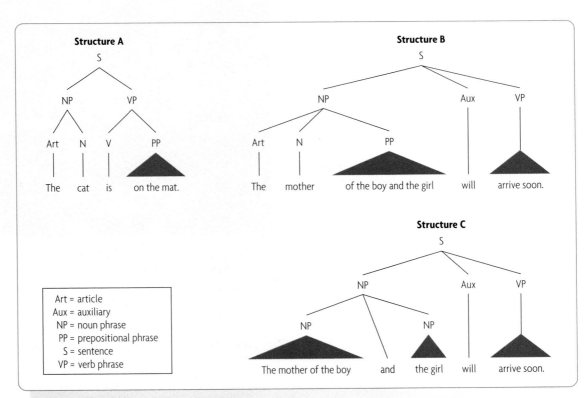

FIGURE 9.6 Sentence Structures

Linguists use tree diagrams to display the grammatical structure of sentences. Part A shows the structure of "The cat is on the mat." Parts B and C show that the sentence "The mother of the boy and the girl will arrive soon" can be represented by two different structural analyses. Who will arrive soon, one person (structure B) or two (structure C)?

Now that you are looking at a picture of a dancing couple, what comes to mind when you think of the word *ball*?

When you read this sentence, how do you interpret the word *bark*? If you imagine that you have a dictionary in your head, your entry for bark might look something like this:

Definition 1. The exterior covering of a tree.
Definition 2. The sound a dog makes.

Research suggests that both definitions become accessible in memory when you first encounter such an ambiguous word, but you swiftly use contextual information to determine which definition is appropriate. The word bark is called a balanced ambiguity because people use its two meanings with roughly equal frequency. Now consider this sentence:

Last year the pen was abandoned because it was too dirty for the animals to live in.

Did that sentence give you any trouble? Pen also has two definitions:

Definition 1. An implement for writing with ink.
Definition 2. An enclosure for animals.

Pen is called a biased ambiguity because people use one meaning (that is, Definition 1) much more often than the other. You may have experienced some momentary trouble understanding this sentence because your initial bias toward understanding pen to mean "an implement for writing with ink" was proved wrong by the context that followed its use. Research suggests that your brain responds differently to these two types of ambiguity.

Twelve participants read sentences while undergoing fMRI scans. The sentences included balanced or biased ambiguities or were matched control sentences (Mason & Just, 2007). For example, in the sentence "To their surprise, the bark was unusual because it sounded high-pitched and hoarse," *howl* replaced *bark* (that is, "the howl was unusual . . .") to provide an unambiguous sentence. The researchers predicted that, because participants need to select between meanings, ambiguous sentences would produce different patterns of brain activity than control sentences. As seen in **Figure 9.7**, that prediction was confirmed. The researchers also predicted that, because participants need to recover from their biased interpretations, the biased ambiguities would produce different brain activity than balanced ambiguities. Again, the brain scans shown in Figure 9.7 confirm that prediction.

This experiment identifies brain regions that help you understand an ambiguous word: You put contextual information to swift and efficient use to arrive at a single meaning. Context wields a similar influence on structural ambiguities (Farmer, Anderson, & Spivey, 2007; Grodner, Gibson, & Watson, 2005). Contextual information speeds decisions when you must choose among different possible grammatical structures.

The overall conclusion you can draw is that your language processes use context powerfully and efficiently to resolve ambiguities. In a way, this shows that there is a good match between production and understanding. When we discussed language production, we emphasized audience design—the

FIGURE 9.7 The Brain Bases of Ambiguity Resolution

Participants underwent fMRI scans while understanding low and high ambiguity sentences. The brain regions indicated in blue are those areas that were more active during the low ambiguity sentences than during the control noise condition. The regions in yellow were more active (with respect to the control) for both types of ambiguous sentences. The regions in red were more active for high ambiguity sentences than for low ambiguity sentences.

From J. M. Rodd, M. H. Davis, & I. S. Johnsrude, "The neural mechanisms of speech comprehension: fMRI studies of semantic ambiguity," *Cerebral Cortex, 15,* 1261–1269, 2005. By permission of Oxford University Press.

processes by which speakers try to make their utterances appropriate in the current context. Our analysis of understanding suggests that listeners expect speakers to have done their jobs well. Under those circumstances, it makes sense for listeners to let context guide their expectations about what speakers will have meant.

The Products of Understanding Our discussion of ambiguity resolution focused on the *processes* of understanding. In this section, we shift our attention to the products of understanding. The question now is: What *representations* result in memory when listeners understand utterances or texts? What, for example, would be stored in memory when you hear our old standby, "The cat is on the mat"? Research has suggested that meaning representation begins with basic units called *propositions* (Clark & Clark, 1977; Kintsch, 1974). Propositions are the main ideas of utterances. For "The cat is on the mat," the main idea is that something is on something else. When you read the utterance, you will extract the proposition on and understand the relationship that it expresses between *the cat* and *the mat*. Often propositions are written like this: *ON (cat, mat)*. Many utterances contain more than one proposition. Consider "The cat watched the mouse run under the sofa." We have as the first component proposition *UNDER (mouse, sofa)*. From that, we build up *RUN (mouse, UNDER (mouse, sofa))*. Finally, we get to *WATCH (cat, RUN (mouse, UNDER (mouse, sofa)))*.

How can we test whether your mental representations of meaning really work this way? Some of the earliest experiments in the psychology of language were devoted to showing the importance of propositional representations in understanding (Kintsch, 1974). Research has shown that if two words in an utterance belong to the same proposition, they will be represented together in memory even if they are not close together in the actual sentence.

> Consider the sentence "The mausoleum that enshrined the tzar overlooked the square." Although *mausoleum* and *square* are far apart in the sentence, a propositional analysis suggests that they should be gathered together in memory in the proposition *OVERLOOKED (mausoleum, square)*. To test this analysis, researchers asked participants to read lists of words and say whether each had appeared in the sentence. Some participants saw *mausoleum* directly after *square* on the list. Other participants saw *mausoleum* after a word from another proposition. The response "Yes, I saw *mausoleum*" was swifter when *mausoleum* came directly after *square* than when its predecessor came from another proposition. This finding suggests that the concepts *mausoleum* and *square* had been represented together in memory. (Ratcliff & McKoon, 1978)

Have you ever noticed how hard it is to remember *exactly* what someone said? You might, for example, have tried to remember a line from a movie word-for-word, but you realized when you got home that you could only remember the general sense of what was said. This experiment indicates why word-for-word memory is not so good: Since one of the main operations your language processes carry out is the extraction of propositions, the exact form with which those propositions were rendered gets lost pretty quickly (for example, "The cat chased the mouse" versus "The mouse was chased by the cat").

Not all the propositions listeners store in memory are made up of information directly stated by the speaker. Often listeners fill gaps with **inferences**—logical assumptions made possible by information in memory. Consider this pair of utterances:

> I'm heading to the deli to meet Donna.
> She promised to buy me a sandwich for lunch.

To understand how these sentences go together, you must draw at least two important inferences. You must figure out both who *she* is in the second sentence and how going to a deli is related to a promise to buy a sandwich. Note that a friend who actually uttered this pair of sentences would be confident you could figure these things out. You would never expect to hear this:

> I'm heading to the deli to meet Donna. She—and by *she* I mean Donna—promised to buy me a sandwich—and a *deli* is a place where you can buy a sandwich—for lunch.

Speakers count on listeners to draw inferences of this sort.

A great deal of research has been directed toward determining what types of inferences listeners draw on a regular basis (Gerrig & O'Brien, 2005). The number of potential inferences after any utterance is unlimited. For example, because you know that Donna is likely to be a human, you could infer that she has a heart, a liver, a pair of lungs, and so on (and on), but it is unlikely that you would feel compelled to call any of those (perfectly valid) inferences to mind when you heard "I'm heading to the deli to meet Donna."

Research suggests, in fact, that the models readers develop for the whole situation of a text affect which inferences they encode. For example, read the text in part 1 of **Table 9.5**. At the end of this text, did you encode the inference that Carol is likely to dump the spaghetti on the customer? Research suggests that readers consistently draw that inference (Guéraud, Tapiero, & O'Brien, 2008). Now read the text numbered 2. In this latter case, readers now infer that Carol will experience pain because it will hurt her to do something which she has told her kids not to do and which goes against her beliefs.

Our discussion of language use has demonstrated how much work a speaker does to produce the right sentence at the right time and how much work a listener does to figure out exactly what the speaker meant. You usually are not aware of all this work! Does this give you a greater appreciation for the elegant efficiency of your cognitive processes?

LANGUAGE AND EVOLUTION

We just concluded you have a range of processes working diligently in the background to help you produce and understand language. A question that has long fascinated researchers is whether any other species possesses the same range of processes. We know of no other species that uses a language as complex as any human language. That observation raises an interesting question: What processes did humans evolve that make human language possible? To answer that question, researchers have largely turned to research with other species:

---

inferences Missing information filled in on the basis of a sample of evidence or on the basis of prior beliefs and theories.

TABLE 9.5 Text Situations and Inferences

1. Carol was a single mother with two young children. She had to work two jobs to make ends meet. She worked full-time as a teacher and part-time as a waitress. She hated not having much free time. Carol was known for her short temper and her tendency to act without thinking. She never thought about the consequences of her actions, so she often suffered negative repercussions. She refused to let people walk all over her. In fact, she had just gotten a ticket for road rage. She decided she would never put up with anyone who was not nice to her. One particular night, Carol had an extremely rude customer. He complained about the spaghetti, and he yelled at Carol as if it were her fault. Carol lifted the spaghetti above his head.

2. Carol was a single mother with two young children. She had to work two jobs to make ends meet. She worked full-time as a teacher and part-time as a waitress. She hated not having much free time. Carol was known for her ability to peacefully settle any confrontation. She would never even think to solve her problems with physical violence. She taught her students and her own children how to solve problems through conversation. She believed this was an effective way to stop the increasing violence in the schools. Carol also helped other parents learn to deal with their anger. One particular night, Carol had an extremely rude customer. He complained about the spaghetti, and he yelled at Carol as if it were her fault. Carol lifted the spaghetti above his head.

They attempt to define what makes humans and human languages special. We will focus on *language structure* and *audience design*.

One property that makes human language special is that people can produce an unlimited number of messages with a limited number of words: You follow the grammatical rules of your language—of the types represented by the structures in Figure 9.6—to produce as many sentences as you will ever need from the set of words you know. Researchers have suggested that humans are the only species that can apply rules of the complexity found in human languages (Fitch & Hauser, 2004; Hauser, Chomsky, & Fitch, 2002). This conclusion was reached after several decades of research in which people tried to teach nonhuman species languages with humanlike structure.

Beginning as early as the 1920s, psychologists tried to address this question by attempting to teach language to chimpanzees. Chimps do not have the appropriate vocal apparatus to produce spoken language, so researchers had to devise other methods of communication. For example, a chimp named Washoe was taught a highly simplified version of American Sign Language (Gardner & Gardner, 1969); a chimp named Sarah was taught to manipulate symbols (which stood for concepts like *apple* and *give*) on a magnetic board (Premack, 1971). The results of these experiments inspired great controversy (Seidenberg & Petitto, 1979). Sceptics asked whether the chimps' occasional combinations of gestures or symbols (for example, *Washoe sorry*, *You more drink*) constituted any meaningful kind of language use. They also wondered whether most of the meaning attributed to the chimps' utterances was arising in the heads of the humans rather than in the heads of the chimps.

Sue Savage-Rumbaugh and her colleagues (Savage-Rumbaugh, Shanker, & Taylor, 1998) have conducted research that has provided more solid insights into the language capabilities of chimps. Savage-Rumbaugh works primarily with *bonobos*, a species of great ape that is evolutionarily more similar to humans even than common chimpanzees. Rather remarkably, two of the bonobos in her studies, Kanzi and Mulika, acquired the meanings of plastic symbols *spontaneously*: They received no explicit training; rather, they acquired the symbols by observing others (humans and bonobos) using them to communicate. Moreover, Kanzi and Mulika were able to understand some *spoken* English. For example, when Kanzi heard a spoken word, he was able to locate either the symbol for the word or a photograph of the object. Kanzi was also able to follow simple commands such as "Take off Sue's shoe." Kanzi's performance strongly suggests that some aspects of human language performance can be found in other species. However, Kanzi still falls short of human abilities: He was not able to acquire the type of rule system that would allow him to produce an unlimited number of utterances. Other cross-species research reinforces the conclusion that humans alone evolved the processes to produce and understand appropriately complex grammatical structures (Fitch & Hauser, 2004).

Another focus of cross-species comparison has been on what we earlier called *audience design*. When you are successful at audience design, you take into account what your listener does and does not know. Are nonhuman animals able to modify their messages based on what members of their audience know? Researchers have set out to answer this question. For example, **Dorothy Cheney** and **Robert Seyfarth** (1990) have done extensive research on the communicative capabilities of *vervet monkeys*. Vervet monkeys make distinct *calls* to signal the presence of different dangers, such as leopards, eagles, and snakes. These monkeys are able to modify their calls depending on their audience: Female monkeys gave alarms at much higher rates when they were with their own offspring than when they were with monkeys unrelated to them. However, the vervets do not modify their calls based on what their audience knows: In an experimental setting, mother vervets produced the same calls irrespective of whether their offspring had also witnessed the events that evoked the calls.

Researchers continue to try to understand exactly what sets humans apart from other species with respect to their ability to engage in audience design (Hare, 2007). For example, one study examined the extent to which members of other species are able to understand the relationship between where people focus their attention and what they can see (Okamoto-Barth, Call, & Tomasello, 2007). In the study, experimenters directed their gaze toward a barrier that was either solid or had a window.

Some bonobos have learned the meanings of words without explicit training. What other abilities must these animals demonstrate before it can be said that they have genuinely acquired a human language?

The Dani people of Papua New Guinea speak a language with only two basic colour terms—they make a distinction between black and white (or light and dark). English, by comparison, has 11 basic colour terms. Could this language difference affect the way people experience the world?

Imagine yourself in that situation. You would quickly infer that the experimenter's gaze could only indicate the presence of an object on the far side of the barrier when the barrier had a window. Bonobos, chimpanzees, and gorillas constructed the same inference, but orangutans did not. When confronted with the solid barrier, bonobos and chimpanzees were more sophisticated in their visual search than were gorillas. These data illustrate some steps in the evolution of human's ability to take the perspective of others.

An evolutionary perspective on language examines the critical processes humans evolved to make language possible. However, that general set of processes allows a wide variety of languages to emerge. In the next section, we discuss some potential consequences of the differences among languages.

LANGUAGE, THOUGHT, AND CULTURE

Have you had the opportunity to learn more than one language? If so, do you believe that you *think* differently in the two languages? Does language affect thought? This question is one that researchers have addressed in a variety of ways. Let's give you a cross-linguistic example to make this question more concrete. Imagine a scene in which a child has watched her father throw a ball. If the child were an English speaker, she might utter the sentence, "Daddy threw the ball." If, by contrast, the child were a Turkish speaker, she would say, "Topu babam atti." Is this just a different collection of words for the same idea? Not entirely: the *-ti* suffix at the end of the Turkish sentence indicates that the event was witnessed by the speaker; if the event had not been witnessed by the speaker, a different suffix (*mi̇s*) would be added to *at* (which is the equivalent of *threw*) to form *atmi̇s*. As an English speaker, you are not required to divide the world into events you witnessed yourself versus those you learned about through other sources; as a Turkish speaker, you would be (Slobin, 1982; Slobin & Aksu, 1982). Could it be that the different grammatical requirements of these two languages would affect, in very basic ways, the manner in which people

think about the world? No one knows the answer to this specific question about English and Turkish—would you like to carry out appropriate research?—but this distinction provides a good example of why people have so often been intrigued by the question of language's potential influence on thought.

Scholarly work on this question was originated by **Edward Sapir** and his student **Benjamin Lee Whorf**, whose cross-linguistic explorations led them to the somewhat radical conclusion that differences in language would create differences in thought. Here is how Sapir put it:

> We see and hear and otherwise experience very largely as we do because the language habits of our community predispose certain choices of interpretation. (Sapir, 1941/1964, p. 69)

For Sapir and Whorf, this conclusion emerged directly from relationships they believed to exist in their own data. From the hypotheses that Sapir and Whorf proposed, the one that has received the most attention is called *linguistic relativity* (Brown, 1976). According to this hypothesis, the structure of the language an individual speaks has an impact on the way in which that individual thinks about the world. Contemporary researchers in psychology, linguistics, and anthropology have attempted to create rigorous tests of these ideas (Gentner & Goldin-Meadow, 2003). Let's look at a particular domain in which researchers have demonstrated an impact of language on thought.

You may be surprised to learn that languages of the world differ with respect to the number of basic colour terms they use. As determined by linguistic analysis, English has 11 (*black, white, red, yellow, green, blue, brown, purple, pink, orange,* and *grey*); some languages of the world, such as the language spoken by the Dani people of Papua New Guinea, have only two, a simple distinction between *black* and *white* (or *light* and *dark*) (Berlin & Kay, 1969). Researchers speculate that the category structure implied by colour terms might influence the ways in which speakers of different languages are able to think about colours. As Whorf suggested, language users "dissect

Psychology in Your Life

WHY AND HOW DO PEOPLE LIE?

In this section on language use, we have emphasized that people aspire to be co-operative conversationalists. For example, we suggested that people follow the principle, "Try to make your contribution one that is true." However, we know that people often fall away from this standard. When people were asked to keep diaries of the lies they told, most averaged one or two a day (DePaulo et al., 2003).

Why do people lie? When the lies are relatively mild, more people lie for psychological reasons (e.g., they wish to spare themselves embarrassment) than for personal advantage (e.g., they wish to avoid an unpleasant chore). However, when lies become more serious, the motives for lying shift in the direction of personal advantage.

In one study, participants were asked to reveal the most serious lie they had ever told (DePaulo, Ansfield, Kirkendol, & Boden, 2004). People quite frequently committed serious lies to conceal affairs or other forbidden forms of social contact. People felt that they were entitled to cheat on their partners and lied in service to that sense of entitlement. Thus, the lies worked for personal advantage.

Let's focus on the mental processes that people use to lie. Should it be easier or harder to tell a lie than to tell the truth? The answer is: It depends (DePaulo et al., 2003).

Suppose you are asked, "What did you do last night?" If you choose to lie spontaneously, it might be harder for you to formulate a lie than to tell the truth. However, if you have prepared your lie in advance—because you anticipate the awkward question—you might produce your lie with great fluidity. Still, lies and truths differ from each other in some consistent ways. A study that reviewed the literature on the content of lies reported that liars provide fewer details in their accounts than do people who are telling the truth (DePaulo et al., 2003). In addition, liars' accounts were consistently less plausible and less fluent than truthful accounts.

These results suggest that speakers may engage different mental processes to produce their lies. To test this hypothesis, researchers have begun to analyze patterns of brain activity that underlie truth-telling and lying. In one study, participants were asked to lie or tell the truth about their participation in an incident in which a gun was fired in a hospital (Mohamed et al., 2006). To make the experience of lying as real as possible, participants in the *guilty* condition actually fired a starter pistol (loaded with blanks) in the testing room. Participants in both the *guilty* and *not-guilty* conditions answered a series of questions while undergoing fMRI

scans. Participants in the guilty condition received instructions to lie about their role in the incident. The fMRI scans revealed that several areas of the brain were more active for lying than for truth-telling. For example, brain regions responsible for planning and emotion were harder at work when participants prepared their lies.

Another study looked into the brains of people who qualify as *pathological liars*—these are individuals who lie with sufficient regularity that the behaviour is considered abnormal (by the types of *DSM-IV* criteria we describe in Chapter 15). The overall structure of brains of the pathological liars were compared using MRI to the brains of matched controls (Yang et al., 2005). Those brain comparisons revealed consistent differences in the prefrontal cortex. The pathological liars, for example, had more of the type of brain tissue that allows neurons to communicate with each other. Prefrontal cortex is a region of the brain that plays an important role in planning—suggesting that the pathological liars are particularly well equipped to plan their lies. These results, however, leave open the question of cause and effect: Did pathological liars start life with brains of this type (which, perhaps, caused or allowed them to lie frequently), or did frequent lying change their brains?

---

nature along the lines laid down by [their] native languages" (1956, p. 213).

Researchers asked 12 speakers of Himba from northern Namibia to examine triads of colour chips all taken from the blue–green continuum. The participants' task was to indicate "which of these three colours look most like each other, in the way that brothers look like each other?" (Roberson, Davidoff, Davies, & Shapiro, 2005, p. 395) Unlike English, the Himba language does not make a lexical distinction between *blue* and *green*. Instead, Himba speakers use the term *borou*, which covers most green and blue

hues. The researchers looked for evidence of *categorical perception*: They assessed the extent to which Himba speakers perceived hues to be more similar within the categories marked by the language than between categories. Indeed, the Himba participants' similarity judgments showed a clear impact of the categorical structure of their language.

The results provide support for the claim of linguistic relativity—that language may, in some circumstances, have an impact on thought.

As a second example of research on linguistic relativity, let's consider the contrast between English and Italian. To assess the impact of grammatical gender, researchers asked English monolinguals, Italian monolinguals, and English–Italian bilinguals to perform a task in which they tried to name the animals in pictures flashed for, on average, less than a second (Kousta, Vinson, & Vigliocco, 2008). Because the task was difficult, participants sometimes made errors by giving the wrong animal name. However, English and Italian monolinguals produced different patterns of errors: Italian speakers were more likely to produce incorrect names that had the same grammatical gender as the correct name. The bilinguals made English-type errors when they performed the task in English and Italian-type errors when they performed the task in Italian!

There are thousands of languages in the world, which provide many interesting distinctions. As researchers have examined a broader range of those distinctions, they find the hypothesis of linguistic relativity is better supported in some domains than in others (see January & Kako, 2007; Papafragou, Li, Choi, & Han, 2007). Still, interesting hypotheses about the link between language and thought have yet to be tested. As we describe cultural differences throughout *Psychology and Life*, it is worth keeping an open mind about linguistic relativity. Given the many situations in which members of different cultures speak very different languages, we can wonder to what extent language plays a causal role in bringing about cultural differences.

Let's turn now from circumstances in which meaning is communicated through words to those in which meaning relies also on pictures.

STOP AND REVIEW

❶ What is the relationship between the co-operative principle and audience design?

❷ Suppose you are trying to pronounce "big pet" and "bird pen." Why would you be more likely to commit the speech error "pig bet" than "pird ben"?

❸ How would you detect inferences in people's representations?

❹ What are two language abilities that researchers suggest might set humans apart from other species?

❺ What does the linguistic relativity hypothesis suggest?

CRITICAL THINKING Recall the study on community membership. Why might the researchers have used landmarks from three different cities?

Visual Cognition

In **Figure 9.8**, we give you two choices for visual representations of the sentence "The cat is on the mat." Which one seems right? If you think in terms of language-based propositions, each alternative captures the right meaning—the cat *is* on the mat. Even so, you are probably happy only with option A because it matches the scene you likely called to mind when you first read the sentence (Searle, 1979b). How about option B? It probably makes you somewhat nervous because it seems as if the cat is going to tip over. This anxious feeling must arise because you

FIGURE 9.8   Visual Representations
Are both of these cats on the mat?

can think with pictures. In a sense, you can *see* exactly what is going to happen. In this section, we will explore some of the ways in which visual images and visual processes contribute to the way you think.

USING VISUAL REPRESENTATIONS

History is full of examples of famous discoveries apparently made on the basis of mental imagery (Shepard, 1978). Frederick Kekulé, the discoverer of the chemical structure of benzene, often conjured up mental images of dancing atoms that fastened themselves into chains of molecules. His discovery of the benzene ring occurred in a dream in which a snakelike molecule chain suddenly grabbed its own tail, thus forming a ring. Michael Faraday, who discovered many properties of magnetism, knew little about mathematics, but he had vivid mental images of the properties of magnetic fields. Albert Einstein claimed to have thought entirely in terms of visual images, translating his findings into mathematical symbols and words only after the work of visually based discovery was finished.

We have given you these examples to encourage you to try to indulge in visual thinking. Even without trying, you regularly use your capabilities for manipulating visual images. Consider a

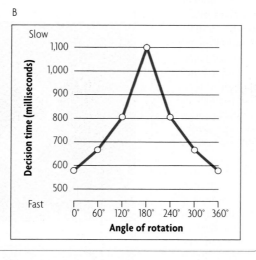

FIGURE 9.9 Rotated *R* Used to Assess Mental Imagery

Participants presented with these figures in random order were asked to say, as quickly as possible, whether each figure was a normal *R* or a mirror image. The more the figure was rotated from upright, the longer the reaction time was.

classic experiment in which participants were asked to transform images in their heads.

> Researchers presented students with examples of the letter *R* and its mirror image that had been rotated various amounts, from 0 to 180 degrees (see **Figure 9.9**). As the letter appeared, the student had to identify it as either the normal *R* or its mirror image. The reaction time taken to make that decision was longer in direct proportion to the amount the figure had been rotated. This finding indicated that a subject was imagining the figure in his or her "mind's eye" and rotating the image into an upright position at some fixed rate before deciding whether the figure was an *R* or a mirror image. The consistency of the rate of rotation suggested that the process of mental rotation was very similar to the process of physical rotation (Shepard & Cooper, 1982).

You put this ability for mental rotation to very good use. You often see objects in the environment from unfamiliar points of view. Mental rotation allows you to transform the image to one that matches representations stored in memory (Lloyd-Jones & Luckhurst, 2002). For example, in Figure 9.8, you almost certainly had to rotate the image (or did you just tilt your head?) to recognize the object as a cat on a mat.

Doreen Kimura, at Simon Fraser University, investigated the ability of men and women to do mental rotations. Kimura's work is highly indicative of a strong sex difference in the ability of men and women to do mental rotation of objects, whether they are three-dimensional or more like two-dimensional line drawings (Collins & Kimura, 1997). Males have a significant advantage over women in this type of task. **Deborah Saucier**, at the University of Lethbridge, has investigated the nature of these and other sex differences. She and her colleagues found that the ability to do the mental rotation task was correlated with the ability to use Euclidian properties in a spatial navigation task, but not landmark information (Saucier et al., 2002). The finding suggests that people who were good at doing the mental rotation task were more likely to give or understand directions that were presented as "take this highway four kilometres, take a right turn, and travel another four kilometres,"

rather than "take this highway to the big red church, take a right, and drive until you see the house with the big horse sign." How do you provide directions to the stranger that stops to ask?

You can also use visual images to answer certain types of questions about the world. Suppose, for example, we asked you whether a golf ball is bigger than a Ping-Pong ball. If you cannot retrieve that fact directly from memory, you might find it convenient to form a visual image of them side by side. This use of an image, once again, has much in common with the properties of real visual perception.

There are, of course, limits to the use of your visual imagination. Consider this problem:

> *Imagine that you have a very large piece of blank paper. In your mind, fold it in half (making two layers), fold it in half again (four layers), and continue folding it over 50 times. About how thick is the paper when you are done? (Adams, 1986)*

The actual answer is about 80 million kilometres ($2^{50} \times 0.7112$ mm, the thickness of a piece of paper)—approximately half the distance between Earth and the sun. Your estimate was probably considerably lower. Your mind's eye was overwhelmed by the information you asked it to represent.

We want you to try one last exercise using visual imagery. Find any object in your environment and examine it for a few seconds. Now, close your eyes and try to create a visual image of the same object. Consider this question: How much overlap was there in the brain regions that were active when you engaged in visual perception versus visual imagery? To answer this question, researchers had participants learn a series of line drawings of common objects such as a tree (Ganis, Thompson, & Kosslyn, 2004). In the next phase of the experiment, participants underwent fMRI scans while they either inspected the same drawings on a computer screen or generated visual images of the drawings. For each drawing, they answered a simple question, such as whether the object contained circular parts. **Figure 9.10** presents the results of the fMRI scans from different regions of the brain. The left and middle columns show the regions of the brain that differed for each task from the baseline condition (i.e., when participants were not engaged in a task). The right column shows the brain regions that were particular

FIGURE 9.10 The Brain Bases of Visual Imagery

The figure shows the results of fMRI scans when participants were engaged in either a perception task or an imagery task. The left and middle columns show brain activity for each task: Regions marked with red, orange, and yellow were more active with respect to a no-task baseline; regions marked in blues were less active. The right column shows the brain regions that were affected by the perception task but not the imagery task. These fMRI scans demonstrate that much the same brain regions are used for perception and imagery.

Reprinted from *Cognitive Brain Research, 20*, G. Ganis et al., "Brain areas underlying visual mental imagery and visual perception: An fMRI study," pp. 226–241, copyright © 2004, with permission from Elsevier.

to the perception task. These data support two important conclusions. First, there was substantial overlap between brain processes for perception and imagery. Second, brain regions for imagery were a subset of those for perception; participants did not use any special regions to create a visual image. With respect to brain activity, you use much the same resources to encode the visual world as to recreate a visual representation.

COMBINING VERBAL AND VISUAL REPRESENTATIONS

Our discussion so far has largely focused on the types of visual representations that you form by committing to memory—or, in the case of imagery, retrieving from memory—visual stimuli from the environment. However, you often form visual images based on verbal descriptions. You can, for example, create a mental picture of a cat with three tails, although you have almost certainly never seen one. The verbal description enables you to form a visual representation. Your ability to produce a mental image of a verbal scene is particularly useful when you read works of fiction that involve spatial details. Consider this passage from the James Bond short story "From a View to a Kill":

> The clearing was about as big as two tennis courts and floored in thick grass and moss. There was one large patch of lilies of the valley and, under the bordering trees, a scattering of bluebells. To one side there was a low mound . . . completely surrounded and covered with brambles and briar roses now thickly in bloom. Bond walked round this and gazed in among the roots, but there was nothing to see except the earthy shape of the mound. (Fleming, 1959, pp. 19–20)

Did you try to imagine the scene—and help Bond search for danger? (He will find it.) When you read, you can form a *spatial mental model* to keep track of the whereabouts of characters (Zwaan & Radvansky, 1998). Researchers have often focused on the ways in which spatial mental models capture properties of real spatial experiences (Rinck, Hähnel, Bower, & Glowalla, 1997).

Suppose, for example, you read a passage of a text that places you in the middle of an interesting environment.

> You are hob-nobbing at the opera. You came tonight to meet and chat with interesting members of the upper class. At the moment, you are standing next to the railing of a wide, elegant balcony overlooking the first floor. Directly behind you, at your eye level, is an ornate lamp

attached to the balcony wall. The base of the lamp, which is attached to the wall, is gilded in gold. (Franklin & Tversky, 1990, p. 65)

In a series of experiments, readers studied descriptions of this sort that vividly described the layout of objects around the viewer (Franklin & Tversky, 1990). The researchers wished to show that readers were faster or slower to access information about the scene, depending on where the objects were in the mental space around them. Readers, for example, were quicker to say what object was in front of them in the scene than what object was behind them, even though all objects were introduced equally carefully in the stories (see **Figure 9.11**). It is easiest to understand this result if you believe that the representation you form when reading actually places you, in some sense, in the scene. You are able to transform a verbal experience into a visual, spatial experience.

You also regularly combine verbal and visual representations when you attempt to find your way to a new destination. Suppose you want to drive from your hometown to Vegreville, Alberta, site of the world's largest Easter egg. Nowadays, you'd probably go to a website like MapQuest or GoogleMaps to get your directions. However, research suggests that some types of directions immediately yield more flexible spatial mental models than do others.

Participants learned descriptions for a pair of neighbourhoods (adapted from areas of Pittsburgh, PA, and Detroit, MI) (Brunyé, Rapp, & Taylor, 2008). The descriptions had two different formats. The survey descriptions provided a "bird's-eye view," as if the person providing the information were hovering above the neighbourhood: "From Moore Field Playground, Pioneer Avenue runs south. Portions of Pioneer Avenue have been blocked off due to repair. Capital Avenue heads east from Pioneer Avenue." The route descriptions moved readers through the neighbourhoods on mental tours: "Turn left from Moore Field Playground to Pioneer Avenue heading south. Portions of Pioneer Avenue have been blocked off due to repair. Head left on Capital Avenue driving from Pioneer Avenue." After learning the descriptions, participants responded to a series of questions that tested their knowledge of the neighbourhoods. Participants' performance was affected by the type of description they had learned: They were more flexible in their ability to answer questions when they had formed spatial mental models based on survey information.

The researchers suggested that survey descriptions allow readers to get a better sense of how the various parts of a neighbourhood fit together. By contrast, route descriptions focus attention on a single path through the neighbourhood. If you've ever downloaded directions that mistakenly led you to a dead end, you'll know how inflexible your mental models based on route descriptions can be: It's hard to find your own path around the obstacle!

In this section, we have seen that you have visual processes and representations to complement your verbal abilities. These two types of access to information give you extra help in dealing with the demands and tasks of your life. We turn now to domains in which you put both visual and verbal representations to use in coping with your life's complexities: problem solving and reasoning.

FIGURE 9.11 Spatial Mental Models
You can use imagination to project yourself into the middle of a scene. Just as if you were really standing in the room, you would take less time to say what is in front of you (the lamp) than what is behind you (the bust).

STOP AND REVIEW

❶ How similar are the processes of physical rotation and mental rotation?

❷ What has research shown about the brain bases of visual images?

❸ If you are imagining yourself in a scene, does it matter how you place yourself in the room?

CRITICAL THINKING Consider the idea of a mirror image discussed earlier. How often do you think you must deal with exactly this kind of mental rotation and in what tasks?

Problem Solving and Reasoning

Let's return for a minute to your mysterious message, "The cat is on the mat." If you have come to understand the message, what do you do next? For those of you whose lives are less filled with mystery, consider a more common situation: You have accidentally locked yourself out of your home, room, or car. Again, what do you do next? For both situations, reflect on the types of mental steps you might take to overcome your difficulty. Those mental

FIGURE 9.12 Can You Solve It? (Part I)

Try to solve each of these problems (the answers are given in **Figure 9.13** on page 272, but do not look until you try to solve them all).

(A) Can you connect all the dots in the pattern by drawing 4 straight, connected lines without lifting your pen from the paper?

(B) A prankster has put 3 Ping-Pong balls into a 2-metre-long pipe that is standing vertically in the corner of the physics lab, fastened to the floor. How would you get the Ping-Pong balls out?

(C) The checkerboard shown has had 2 corner pieces cut out, leaving 62 squares. You have 31 dominoes, each of which covers exactly 2 checkerboard squares. Can you use them to cover the whole checkerboard?

(D) You are in the situation depicted and given the task of tying the 2 strings together. If you hold one string, the other is out of reach. Can you do it?

(E) You are given the objects shown (a candle, tacks, matches in a matchbox). The task is to mount a lighted candle on a door. Can you do it?

(F) You are given 3 "water-jar" problems. Using only the 3 containers (water supply is unlimited), can you obtain the exact amount specified in each case?

steps will almost certainly include the cognitive processes that make up **problem solving** and **reasoning**. Both of these activities require you to combine current information with information stored in memory to work toward some particular goal: a conclusion or a solution. We will look at aspects of problem solving and at two types of reasoning: deductive and inductive.

PROBLEM SOLVING

What goes on four legs in the morning, on two legs at noon, and on, three legs in the twilight? According to Greek mythology, this was the riddle posed by the Sphinx, an evil creature who threatened to hold the people of Thebes in tyranny until someone could solve the riddle. To break the code, Oedipus had to recognize elements of the riddle as metaphors. Morning, noon, and twilight represented different periods in a human life. A baby crawls and so (effectively) has four legs, an adult walks on two legs, and an older person walks on two legs but uses a cane, making a total of three legs. Oedipus's solution to the riddle was *humans*.

Although your daily problems may not seem as monumental as the one faced by young Oedipus, problem-solving activity

is a basic part of your everyday existence. You continually come up against problems that require solutions: how to manage work and tasks within a limited timeframe, how to succeed at a job interview, how to break off a relationship, and so on. Many problems involve discrepancies between what you know and what you need to know. When you solve a problem, you reduce that discrepancy by finding a way to get the missing information. To get into the spirit of problem solving, try the problems in **Figure 9.12**. After you are done, we will see how psychological research can shed light on your performance—and, perhaps, provide some suggestions about how to improve it.

Problem Spaces and Processes How do you define a problem in real-life circumstances? You usually perceive the difference between your current state and a desired goal: For

---

problem solving Thinking that is directed toward solving specific problems and that moves from an initial state to a goal state by means of a set of mental operations.

reasoning The process of thinking in which conclusions are drawn from a set of facts; thinking directed toward a given goal or objective.

FIGURE 9.13   Can You Solve It? (Part II)

Here are the solutions to the problems. How did you do? As the section on problem solving and reasoning unfolds, we will talk about what makes these problems hard.

Reprinted with permission from *How to Solve Problems*, by Wayne A. Wickelgran, p. 31. Copyright © 1974 by W. H. Freeman and Company.

example, you are broke, and you would like to have some money. You are also usually aware of some of the steps you would be able (or willing) to take to bridge the gap: You will try to get a part-time job, but you will not become a pickpocket. The formal definition of a *problem* captures these three elements (Newell & Simon, 1972). A problem is defined by: (1) an *initial state*—the incomplete information or unsatisfactory conditions you start with; (2) a *goal state*—the information or state of the world you hope to obtain; and (3) a *set of operations*—the steps you may take to move from an initial state to a goal state. Together, these three parts define the **problem space**. You can think of solving a problem as walking through a maze (the problem space) from where you are (the initial state) to where you want to be (the goal state), making a series of turns (the allowable operations).

Much of the initial difficulty in solving a problem will arise if any of these elements are not well defined (Simon, 1973). A *well-defined problem* is similar to a textbook problem in which the initial state, the goal state, and the operations are all clearly

specified. Your task is to discover how to use allowable, known operations to get the answer. By contrast, an *ill-defined problem* is similar to designing a home, writing a novel, or finding a cure for AIDS. The initial state, the goal state, and/or the operations may be unclear and vaguely specified. In such cases, the problem solver's first task is to work out, as much as possible, exactly what the problem is—to make explicit a beginning, an ideal solution, and the possible means to achieve it.

As you know from your own experience, even when the initial and goal states are well defined, it can still be difficult to find the right set of operations to get from the beginning to the end. If you think back to your experience in math classes, you know that this is true. Your teacher gave you a formula like $x^2 + x - 12 = 0$ and asked you to solve for possible values of x. What do you do next? To solve this algebra problem, you can use an **algorithm**: a step-by-step procedure that always provides the right answer for a particular type of problem. If you apply the rules of algebra correctly, you are guaranteed to obtain the correct values of x (i.e., 3 and -4). If you have ever forgotten the combination to a lock, you may also have engaged in behaviour guided by an algorithm. If you try solutions systematically (e.g., 1, 2, 3; 1, 2, 4) you will definitely arrive at the right combination—though you may be at it for a good long time! Since well-defined problems have clear initial states and goal states, algorithms are more likely to be available for them than for ill-defined problems. When algorithms are unavailable, problem solvers often rely on **heuristics**, which are strategies or "rules of

problem space The elements that make up a problem: the initial state (the incomplete information or unsatisfactory conditions the person starts with); the goal state (the set of information or state the person wishes to achieve); and the set of operations (the steps the person takes to move from the initial state to the goal state).

algorithm A step-by-step procedure that always provides the right answer for a particular type of problem.

heuristics Cognitive strategies, or "rules of thumb," often used as shortcuts in solving a complex inferential task.

thumb," to solve the problem. Suppose, for example, you are reading a mystery and you would like to solve the problem of who murdered an e-commerce tycoon. You might rule out the possibility that "the butler did it" because you use the heuristic that authors would not use such a trite plot line. As we shall see shortly, heuristics are also a critical aspect of *judgment* and *decision making*.

Researchers at McGill University asked 63 undergraduates to complete an assessment used to evaluate pathological gambling and were asked about their gambling behaviour (Hardoon, Baboushkin, Derevensky, & Gupta, 2001). Sixteen Lotto 6/49 tickets were given to the students. These tickets were of four types: completely random; containing long sequences of consecutive numbers (23, 24, 25, 26, 27, 28); patterns of numbers (5, 10, 15, 20, 25, 30); or unbalanced (containing six numbers between 1 and 24 and six between 25 and 49). Subjects were asked the following question: "If you were to buy a lottery ticket, which one would you select, and why?" The students ranked the 16 tickets in order of preference until all but four tickets had been selected. At this point, they were told they could exchange tickets to change their ranking. The largest percentage of tickets selected in the first four picks were tickets that were perceived as random selections. Further, individuals who had played the lottery previously relied on past experiences to help them select tickets. The participants failed to recognize that each number in the Lotto 6/49 draws is independent of any other number drawn; as such, no ticket had a better chance of winning than any other.

At the beginning of the study, the researchers had also collected data on the potential to engage in pathological gambling. They found that those who scored highest on the pathological gambling scale were also most likely to engage in the use of heuristics to select tickets, including sense of control, selection of pattern, and significant numbers (e.g., my birthday). It is interesting that using heuristics (believing they can control events that are random or that pattern exists in random situations) helps problem gamblers develop a false set of beliefs about gambling—one that perpetuates their desire to gamble. Findings like those of Hardoon et al. (2001) are being used to develop intervention programs for problem gamblers and to educate all gamblers. The Manitoba Gaming Commission, for example, has endorsed television advertisements illustrating the nature of randomness in slot machines: There is simply no pattern, and no guarantee of a payout—even if you sit in front of a machine all day.

Although heuristics can help us manage during our day without having to devote a lot of energy to thinking about things, there are times when using them is not a good idea. Let's talk more about the nature of decision making and the use of heuristics.

Researchers have been interested in understanding the way people apply both algorithms and heuristics as they make their way through a problem space. To study the steps problem solvers take, researchers have often turned to think-aloud protocols. In this procedure, participants are asked to verbalize their ongoing thoughts (Ericsson & Simon, 1993). For example, a pair of researchers was interested in capturing the mental processes that enable participants to solve the mutilated checkerboard problem that is part C of Figure 9.12 (Kaplan &

How do scientists approach the ill-defined problem of curing AIDS?

Simon, 1990). Here is the think-aloud of one of the participants while having the crucial breakthrough that the problem could not be solved with only horizontal and vertical placement of pieces (the checkerboard was pink and black):

> So you're leaving . . . it's short—how many, you're leaving uhhhh . . . there's more pinks than black, and in order to complete it you'd have to connect two pinks but you can't because they are diagonally . . . is that getting close? (Kaplan & Simon, 1990, p. 388)

The solver has just realized that the goal cannot be accomplished if the dominoes can be placed only horizontally or vertically. Researchers have often used participants' own accounts of their thinking as the starting point for more formal models of problem solving (Simon, 1979, 1989).

Improving Your Problem Solving What makes problem solving hard? If you reflect on your day-to-day experience, you might come up with the answer "There are too many things to consider all at once." Research on problem solving has led to much the same conclusion. What often makes a problem difficult to solve is that the mental requirements for solving a particular problem overwhelm processing resources (Kotovsky & Simon, 1990; MacGregor, Ormerod, & Chronicle, 2001). To solve a problem, you need to plan the series of operations you will take. If that series becomes too complex, or if each operation itself is too complex, you may be unable to see your way through from the initial state to the goal state. How might you overcome this potential limitation?

An important step in improving problem solving is to find a way to represent a problem so that each operation is possible, given your processing resources. If you must habitually solve similar problems, a useful procedure is to practise each of the components of the solution so that, over time, those components require fewer resources (Kotovsky, Hayes, & Simon, 1985). Suppose, for example, you were a cab driver in Montreal and were faced with daily traffic jams. You might mentally practise your responses to jams at various points in the city, so that you would have ready solutions to components of the overall problem of getting your fare from a pickup spot to a destination. By practising these component solutions, you could keep more of your attention on the road!

Sometimes, finding a useful representation means finding a whole new way to think about the problem. (Novick & Bassok, 2005). Read the puzzle given in **Table 9.6**. How would you go about offering this proof? Think about it for a few minutes before you read on. How well did you do? If the word *proof* suggested to you something mathematical, you probably did not make much progress. A better way to think about the problem is to imagine two monks, one starting at the top and another starting at the bottom (Adams, 1986). As one climbs and one descends, it is clear that they will pass at some point along the mountain, right? (See **Figure 9.14**.) Now replace the pair of monks with just the one—conceptually it is the same—and there is your proof. What makes this problem suddenly very easy is using the right sort of representation: visual rather than verbal or mathematical.

If you go back to the problems in Figure 9.12, you have other good examples of the importance of an appropriate representation of the problem space. To get the Ping-Pong balls out of the pipe, you had to realize that the solution did not involve reaching into the pipe. To connect the two strings, you had to see one of the tools on the floor as a weight. To mount the candle on the door, you had to alter your usual perspective and perceive the matchbox as a platform instead of as a container, and you had to perceive the candle as a tool as well as the object to be mounted on the door. The last two problems show a phenomenon called functional fixedness (Duncker, 1945; Maier, 1931). **Functional fixedness** is a mental block that adversely

---

functional fixedness An inability to perceive a new use for an object previously associated with some other purpose; adversely affects problem solving and creativity.

TABLE 9.6 The Monk Puzzle

One morning, exactly at sunrise, a Buddhist monk began to climb a tall mountain. A narrow path, no more than a foot or two wide, spiralled around the mountain to a glittering temple at the summit. The monk ascended at varying rates of speed, stopping many times along the way to rest and eat dried fruit he carried with him. He reached the temple shortly before sunset. After several days of fasting and meditation, he began his journey back along the same path, starting at sunrise and again walking at variable speeds with many pauses along the way. His average speed descending was, of course, greater than his average climbing speed. Prove that there is a spot along the path that the monk will occupy on both trips at precisely the same time of day.

See a "proof" for the Monk Puzzle in Figure 9.14.

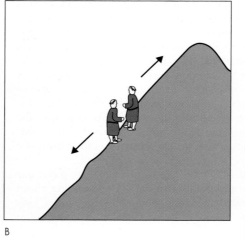

FIGURE 9.14   A "Proof" for the Monk Puzzle (shown in Table 9.6)
Panel A shows two monks, one who starts at the bottom of the mountain and one who starts at the top. Panel B shows that they must meet at some time during the day. Now replace the two monks with the single monk from the puzzle going both ways, and you have your proof!

affects problem solving by inhibiting the perception of a new function for an object that was previously associated with some other purpose. Whenever you are stuck on a problem, you should ask yourself, "How am I representing the problem? Are there different or better ways that I can think about the problem or components of its solution?" If words do not work, try drawing a picture. Or try examining your assumptions, and see what "rules" you can break by making novel combinations.

Often, when you try to solve problems, you engage in special forms of thinking that are called reasoning. Let's turn now to a first type of reasoning you use to solve problems: deductive reasoning.

DEDUCTIVE REASONING

Suppose you are on your way to a restaurant and you want to pay for your meal with your only credit card, MasterCard. You call the restaurant and ask, "Do you accept MasterCard?" The restaurant's hostess replies, "We accept all major credit cards." You can now safely conclude that they accept MasterCard. To see why, we can reformulate your interchange to fit the structure of the *syllogism*, introduced by the Greek philosopher Aristotle over 2000 years ago:

> *Premise 1.* The restaurant accepts all major credit cards.
> *Premise 2.* MasterCard is a major credit card.
> *Conclusion.* The restaurant accepts MasterCard.

Aristotle was concerned with defining the logical relationships between statements that would lead to *valid* conclusions. **Deductive reasoning** involves the correct application of such logical rules. We gave the credit-card example to show that you are quite capable of drawing conclusions that have the form of logical, deductive proofs. Even so, psychological research has focused on the question of whether you actually have the formal rules of deductive reasoning represented in your mind (Evans, 2008; Goel, 2007). This body of research suggests that you may have some general, abstract sense of formal logic, but your real-world deductive reasoning is affected both by the specific knowledge you possess about the world and the representational resources you can bring to bear on a particular reasoning problem. Let's expand on these conclusions.

How does knowledge influence deductive reasoning? Consider this syllogism:

> *Premise 1.* All things that have a motor need oil.
> *Premise 2.* Automobiles need oil.
> *Conclusion.* Automobiles have motors.

Is this a valid conclusion? According to the rules of logic, it is *not*—because premise 1 leaves open the possibility that some things that do not have motors will also need oil. The difficulty is that what is invalid in a logic problem is not necessarily untrue in real life. That is, if you take premises 1 and 2 to be all the information in your possession—as you should if you accept this simply as an exercise in formal logic—the conclusion is not valid. Even so, when participants judge whether the conclusion "follows logically from the premises," they are much more inclined to say yes when the conclusion considers *automobiles* than they are when the nonsense term *oppobines* is substituted (Markovitz & Nantel, 1989).

This result illustrates a general **belief-bias effect**: People tend to judge as valid those conclusions that they find believable

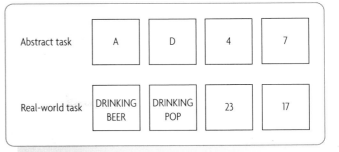

FIGURE 9.15 Abstract versus Real-World Reasoning

In the top row, you are required to say which cards you must turn over to test the rule "If a card has a vowel on one side, then it has an even number on the other side." In the bottom row, you must say which cards you need to turn over to test the rule "If a customer is to drink an alcoholic beverage, then she must be at least 18." People typically do better on the second task, which allows them to use real-world strategies.

and judge as invalid those conclusions they find unbelievable (Janis & Frick, 1943). Research suggests that belief bias represents a conflict between two types of mental processes you apply when you engage in deductive reasoning (Evans, 2008). One set of processes uses past experiences to provide rapid, automatic responses to the problems. (These are the heuristic processes we'll explore at greater length when we discuss judgment and decision making.) The other set of processes allows for slower, conscious applications of formal logic. Suppose you judge "Automobiles have motors" to be a valid conclusion. That suggests that the processes that bring past experience to bear on the judgment are winning the conflict with the processes responsible for logical analysis. Researchers have confirmed this account of belief bias by, for example, forcing experimental participants to respond to syllogisms within 10 seconds (Evans & Curtis-Holmes, 2005). Under time pressure, people showed more belief bias. That result supports the idea that people require conscious effort to apply the rules of formal logic.

In some cases, your ability to apply real-world knowledge helps you to perform better on reasoning tasks. Imagine that you are given the array of four cards pictured in **Figure 9.15**. On one side is printed *A*, *D*, *4*, and *7*. Your task is to determine which cards you must turn over to test the rule "If a card has a vowel on one side, then it has an even number on the other side" (Johnson-Laird & Wason, 1977). What would you do? Most people say that they would turn over the *A*, which is correct, and the *4*—which is incorrect. No matter what character appears on the flip side of the *4*, the rule will not be invalidated. (Can you see why that is true?) Instead, you must flip the *7*. If you were to find a vowel there, you would have invalidated the rule.

---

deductive reasoning A form of thinking in which one draws a conclusion that is intended to follow logically from two or more statements or premises.

belief-bias effect A situation that occurs when a person's prior knowledge, attitudes, or values distort the reasoning process by influencing the person to accept invalid arguments.

Copyright © Sidney Harris/ScienceCartoonsPlus.com

The original research on this task, which is often called the Wason selection task, prompted doubts about people's ability to reason effectively. However, deductive reasoning is improved when participants are able to apply their real-world knowledge to the Wason task. (Holyoak & Spellman, 1993). Suppose you were asked to perform what is a logically comparable task, on the lower set of cards in Figure 9.15. In this case, however, you are asked to evaluate the rule "If a customer is to drink an alcoholic beverage, then she *must* be at least 18" (Cheng & Holyoak, 1985). Now you can probably see immediately which are the correct cards to turn over: *17* and *drinking beer*. If you look at Figure 9.15, you will see that *7* and *17* have the same logical function. You need to turn *17* over for the same reasons of logic you need to turn *7* over. However, your real-world experience helps you appreciate why turning *17* over is logically necessary.

This example of age and alcohol comes from the more general category of permission situations. You probably have a good deal of experience with these sorts of situations; recall all the times you were given conditions like, "You can't watch television unless you do your homework." Likely you never recognized that deductive inference was involved in such circumstances! Some researchers suggest that people encode a *pragmatic reasoning schema* based on early life experiences with permission situations (Chao & Cheng, 2000). This schema allows individuals to reason effectively in the types of permissions situations that have occurred in their environments. The real-life situation linking age to drinking calls to mind this schema; the arbitrary situation linking even numbers and

vowels does not. As a consequence, the arbitrary reasoning task underestimates your ability to make correct deductions.

Note that researchers who take an evolutionary perspective on human cognition have proposed an alternative to the view that people *acquire* a schema with respect to permissions. In a version of the card-turning task adapted for children, participants as young as three years old could reason successfully about what was and was not permitted by a rule. This result suggests that reasoning about permission situations may be innate (Cummins, 1996). That is, the ability to determine when actions do not follow social norms may be part of the genetic package you inherited as a member of the highly social human species (Cummins, 1999).

To begin this section on deductive reasoning, we described a situation in which you drew a valid deductive inference about your ability to use your MasterCard card to buy a meal. Unfortunately, life provides many occasions on which you cannot be so certain that you have drawn valid inferences from valid premises. We turn now to a version of the restaurant scenario that requires you to use a different form of reasoning.

INDUCTIVE REASONING

Let's suppose that you have arrived outside the restaurant and only then think to check to see if you have enough cash. Once again you find that you will want to use your MasterCard, but there is no helpful sign on the outside of the restaurant indicating whether it will be accepted. You peek through the restaurant's windows and see well-dressed clientele. You look at the expensive prices on the menu. You consider the upscale quality of the neighbourhood. All these observations lead you to believe that the restaurant is likely to take your credit card. This is not deductive reasoning, because your conclusion is based on probabilities rather than logical certainties. Instead, this is **inductive reasoning**—a form of reasoning that uses available evidence to generate likely, but not certain, conclusions.

Although the name might be new, we have already described to you several examples of inductive reasoning. We saw repeatedly in Chapters 5 and 8 that people use past information stored as schemas to generate expectations about the present and future. You are using inductive reasoning, for example, if you decide that a certain odour in the air indicates that someone is making popcorn; you are using inductive reasoning if you agree that the words on this page are unlikely to suddenly become invisible (and that, if you study, your knowledge of this material will not become invisible on test day). Finally, earlier in this chapter, we discussed the types of inferences people draw when they use language. Your belief that *she* must be *Donna* in the sequence of utterances we gave you relies on inductive inference.

In real-life circumstances, much of your problem-solving ability relies on inductive reasoning. Return to our opening example: You have accidentally locked yourself out of your home, room, or car. What should you do? A good first step is to call up from memory solutions that worked in the past. This process is called *analogical problem solving*: You establish an analogy between the features of the current situation and the features of previous situations (Christensen & Schunn, 2007; Lee & Holyoak, 2008). In this case, your past experiences of "being locked out" may have allowed you to form the *generalization* "find other people with keys." With that generalization

---

inductive reasoning A form of reasoning in which a conclusion is made about the probability of some state of affairs, based on the available evidence and past experience.

Deductive reasoning:	Inductive reasoning:
Either he likes country music or he listens to opera.	If he is either an accountant or a librarian he listens to opera.
He does not like country music.	He listens to opera.
He listens to opera.	He is an accountant.
Is the conclusion valid?	**Is the conclusion more likely to be true than false?**

FIGURE 9.16 Reasoning in the Brain

When students were asked to carry out deductive reasoning, brain structures on the right sides of their brain were relatively more active. (Those areas are shown in green.) When students were asked to carry out inductive reasoning, brain structures on the left sides of their brain were relatively more active. (Those areas are shown in yellow.)

in hand, you can start to figure out who those individuals might be and how to find them. This task might require you to retrieve the method you developed for tracking down your roommates at their afternoon classes. If this problem seems easy to you, it is—because you have grown accustomed to letting your past inform your present. Inductive reasoning allows you to access tried-and-true methods that speed current problem solving.

We have one caution to add about inductive reasoning. Often a solution that has worked in the past can be reused for a successful solution. However, sometimes you must recognize that relying on the past can hamper your problem-solving ability when there is a critical difference between the old and current situations. The water-jar problem given in Figure 9.12 is a classic example of circumstances in which relying on the past may cause you to miss a solution to a problem (Luchins, 1942). If you had discovered, in the first two problems in part F, the conceptual rule that $B - A - 2(C) = answer$, you probably tried the same formula for the third problem and found it did not work. Actually, simply filling jar A and pouring off enough to fill jar C would have left you with the right amount. If you were using your initial formula, you probably did not notice this simpler possibility; your previous success with the other rule would have given you a mental set. A **mental set** is a pre-existing state of mind, habit, or attitude that can enhance the quality and speed of perceiving and problem solving under some conditions. However, the same set may inhibit or distort the quality of your mental activities at times when old ways of thinking and acting are nonproductive in new situations. When you find yourself frustrated in a problem-solving situation, you might take a step back and ask yourself, "Am I allowing past successes to narrow my focus too much?" Try to make your problem

solving more creative by considering a broader spectrum of past situations and past solutions.

Before we leave this discussion of reasoning, we are going to turn once more to your brain. In this section, we have made a rather strong distinction between deductive and inductive reasoning. Research suggests that separation also exists in the way your brain accomplishes the two types of reasoning.

Participants carried out two types of reasoning tasks while their brains were undergoing PET scans. As shown in the top portion of **Figure 9.16**, one type of problem required deduction. Participants viewed classic syllogisms and assessed whether the conclusions were valid or not. A second type of problem provided premises that left conclusions uncertain. For that reason, the problems required participants to engage in inductive reasoning. Participants indicated whether the arguments were more likely to be true than false. As shown in the bottom portion of Figure 9.16, the two types of reasoning brought about different patterns of activation. The data are easy to summarize: Deductive reasoning produced greater activation in the right hemisphere; inductive reasoning produced greater activation in the left hemisphere. (Parsons & Osherson, 2001)

To make sense of this result, think back to Chapter 4. Recall that your left hemisphere plays a large role in language processing, whereas your right hemisphere does not. The results of this study on reasoning suggest that deductive reasoning involves a

---

mental set The tendency to respond to a new problem in the manner used to respond to a previous problem.

type of logical analysis that is relatively independent of language. Inductive reasoning calls upon the language-based comprehension and inferencing processes we described earlier in the chapter.

In this section, we have examined a range of types of problem solving and reasoning—and have suggested, in each case, concrete steps you can take to improve your performance in real-world circumstances. We follow the same strategy in the final section of the chapter. We describe some major research findings on the processes of *judgment* and *decision making* and then suggest how you can apply those findings to important situations in your life.

STOP AND REVIEW

❶ With respect to problem solving, what is an algorithm?

❷ What does it mean to overcome functional fixedness?

❸ What happens when people succumb to the belief-bias effect?

❹ What role does memory play in inductive reasoning?

CRITICAL THINKING Consider the experiment on the brain bases of reasoning processes. For the inductive reasoning problems, why did participants judge likely rather than absolute truth or falsehood?

Judgment and Decision Making

For a final time, we are back to "The cat is on the mat." Let's engage the processes of *judgment* and *decision making*. How likely is it that the message was just a prank? How likely is it that the message has some real importance that has eluded you? Should you just give up and go to sleep?

This series of questions illustrates one of the great truths of your day-to-day experience: You live in a world filled with *uncertainty*. Here are some more questions, of a sort that will be entirely familiar. Should you spend $10 on a movie you may or may not enjoy? Before an exam, would you be better off studying your notes or rereading the chapter? Are you ready to commit yourself to a long-term relationship? Since you can only guess at the future, and because you almost never have full knowledge of the past, very rarely can you be completely certain that you have made a correct judgment or decision. Thus, the processes of judgment and decision making must operate in a way that allows you to deal efficiently with uncertainty. As **Herbert Simon**, one of the founding figures of cognitive psychology, put it: because "human thinking powers are very modest when compared with the complexities of the environments in which human beings live" they must be content "to find 'good enough' solutions to their problems and 'good enough' courses

---

judgment The process by which people form opinions, reach conclusions, and make critical evaluations of events and people based on available material; also, the product of the mental activity.

decision making The process of choosing between alternatives; selecting or rejecting available options.

---

of action" (1979, p. 3). In this light, Simon suggested that thought processes are guided by *bounded rationality*. Your judgments or decisions might not be as good—as "rational"—as they always could be, but you should be able to see how they result from your applying limited resources to situations that require swift action.

Before we move to a closer analysis of the products of bounded rationality, let's quickly distinguish between the two processes of judgment and decision making. **Judgment** is the process by which you form opinions, reach conclusions, and make critical evaluations of events and people. You often make judgments spontaneously, without prompting. **Decision making** is the process of choosing between alternatives, selecting and rejecting available options. Judgment and decision making are interrelated processes. For example, you might meet someone at a party and, after a brief discussion and a dance together, *judge* the person to be intelligent, interesting, honest, and sincere. You might then *decide* to spend most of your party time with that person and to arrange a date for the next weekend; decision making is more closely linked to behavioural actions. Let's turn now to research on these two types of thinking.

HEURISTICS AND JUDGMENT

What is the best way to make a judgment? Suppose, for example, you are asked whether you enjoyed a movie. To answer this question, you could fill out a chart with two columns, "What I liked about the movie" and "What I did not like about the movie," and see which column was longer. To be a bit more accurate, perhaps you would weight the entries in each list according to their importance (thus, you might weight "the actors' performances" as more important on the plus side than "the blaring sound track" on the minus side). If you went through this whole procedure, you would probably be pretty confident of your judgment—but you know already that this is an exercise you rarely undertake. In real-life circumstances, you have to make judgments frequently and rapidly. You do not have the time—and often you do not have sufficient information—to use such a formal procedure.

What do you do instead? An answer to this question was pioneered by **Amos Tversky** and **Daniel Kahneman**, who argued that people's judgments often rely on heuristics rather than on formal methods of analysis. As we noted in our discussion of problem solving, heuristics are informal rules of thumb that provide shortcuts, reducing the complexity of making judgments. Following the lead of Tversky and Kahneman, researchers have suggested that humans evolved an adaptive toolbox: A repertory of "fast and frugal" heuristics that yield judgments that are most often likely to be correct (Gigerenzer, 2008; Todd & Gigerenzer, 2007). The important claim is that the ability to make correct judgments quickly (fast) and with limited resources (frugal) is adaptive—the ability has survival value. Researchers have defined a number of fast and frugal heuristics and demonstrated that they often lead to correct judgments (Hertwig, Herzog, Schooler, & Reimer, 2008).

Even so, research on heuristics has typically focused on circumstances in which they lead to incorrect judgments. There are two explanations for this focus. To begin, the research follows a logic that might sound familiar from earlier chapters: Just as you can understand perception by studying perceptual illusion and memory by studying memory failures, you can

If you were in a happy mood, would you be more likely to remember good times from your younger days?

understand judgment processes by studying judgment errors. In addition, there's value in being able to recognize circumstances in which heuristics might lead to errors. That gives people the opportunity to engage other mental properties to make better judgments.

Availability Heuristic We will begin by asking you to make a rather trivial judgment. If we were to give you a brief excerpt from a novel, do you believe more words in the excerpt would begin with the letter *k* (for example, *kangaroo*) or have *k* in third position (for example, *duke*)? If you are like the participants in a study by Tversky and Kahneman (1973), then you probably judged that *k* is found more often at the beginning of words. In fact, *k* appears about twice as often in the third position.

Why do most people believe that *k* is more likely to appear in first position? The answer has to do with the *availability* of information from memory. It is much easier to think of words that begin with *k* than to think of those in which *k* comes third. Your judgment, thus, arises from use of the **availability heuristic**: You base your judgment on information that is readily available in memory. This heuristic makes sense because much of the time what is available from memory will lead to accurate judgments. If, for example, you judge bowling to be a less dangerous sport than hang gliding, availability is serving you well. Trouble only arises when either (1) memory processes give rise to a biased sample of information, or (2) the information you have stored in memory is not accurate. Let's look at an example of each of these potential problems.

Recall from Chapter 8 the discussion of how retrieval cues function to give you access to memories. We concluded that the same retrieval cues will be more or less effective, depending on the context in which you put them to use. Suppose, before we asked you the *k* question, we started you out with some examples of *k* in the third position (such as *bike, cake, poke,* and *take*). By changing the context of retrieval, we could possibly change your judgment. In that way, the fluency of information—the ease with which you can retrieve information from memory—will vary from context to context. Consider a study in which participants provided typicality ratings for exemplars from categories (Oppenheimer & Frank, 2008). In some cases, the exemplars appeared in easy-to-read fonts:

hummingbird

In other cases, the exemplars were hard to read:

hummingbird

Participants gave higher typicality ratings to the same exemplars when they appeared in the easy-to-read fonts! An explanation for this result is that participants' assessments of fluency—the difficulty they experienced making their way from the printed word to their representations in memory—contributed to their judgments of typicality. This study illustrates how judgments you make based on fluency may depend on context. Different contexts may yield different judgments (as with the change in font). When you are making important judgments, ask yourself, "How might this context affect the ease with which I can retrieve particular information?"

A second difficulty with availability as a judgment heuristic arises when the information you have stored in memory has a bias to it. Consider people's judgments of the populations of various countries (Brown & Siegler, 1992). See if you can order these four countries from smallest to largest population:

a. Sweden
b. Indonesia
c. Israel
d. Nigeria

Researchers demonstrated that, in general, the more participants knew about a country, the higher their population estimates. Furthermore, there was a sizeable correlation between participants' rated knowledge about a country and the number of times it had been mentioned in *New York Times* articles in a given year. (The right answer, by the way, is Israel, Sweden, Nigeria, Indonesia. Did availability lead you astray?)

You might not be terribly concerned that your estimates of population size are affected by a flawed database. We will offer a second example that should strike you as more urgent: Many students show a bias in the way they commit information to memory that has a negative impact on test performance. Suppose you are taking a multiple-choice exam. You answer a question, but then, after giving it some additional thought, you decide to change your answer. Are you more likely to change from wrong to right or right to wrong? If you are like most students, you probably believe that you should stick with your first answer—it probably makes you nervous to change your answer. Should you do it?

Researchers inspected the multiple-choice exams of a group of 1561 students to determine the consequences of answer changes (Kruger, Wirtz, & Miller, 2005). Of the 3291 answers those students changed, 23 percent were from one wrong answer to another wrong answer. Of the remaining changes, 51 percent made a wrong answer right; 25 percent made a right answer wrong. This pattern suggests that you should not be reluctant to consider changing an answer. However, when a subset of this group were asked about the wisdom of changing answers, 75 percent indicated that it is a better idea to stick with one's original answer. The researchers argued that students' prejudice against changing answers comes from a memory bias: They

availability heuristic A judgment based on the information readily available in memory.

suggested that students find more memorable instances in which changed answers led to negative outcomes than when they led to positive outcomes. How many times have you complained to yourself, "I had that one right!" Now, how many times have you complained, "I had that one wrong!" To test the hypothesis that students are more likely to commit negative outcomes to memory, the researchers carried out a second experiment. In this case, the researchers gave students feedback on correct and incorrect answers shortly after they completed a multiple-choice exam. Four to six weeks later, the researchers asked the participants to try to recall the instances in which they had considered changing their answers, what they had decided, and the consequences of those decisions. A student might, for example, have reported that she had deliberated on three problems and always stuck with her original answer. The memory data showed a consistent bias: Participants *overestimated* how often they switched an answer and then got the question wrong; they *underestimated* how often they switched an answer and then got the question right.

Put yourself in a classroom when you are taking a test. You get to a moment at which you are trying to decide whether to change an answer. These data suggest that you make this judgment with respect to a biased database: You have committed more negative outcomes to memory than positive outcomes—those are the outcomes that are available. This analysis certainly does not mean that you should *always* change your answers. However, you should be aware now of why your feelings of distress arise when you contemplate a change.

Representativeness Heuristic When you make judgments based on the **representativeness heuristic**, you assume that if something has the characteristics considered typical of members of a category, it is, in fact, a member of that category. This heuristic will seem familiar to you because it captures the idea that people use past information to make judgments about similar circumstances in the present. That is the essence of inductive reasoning. Under most circumstances—as long as you have unbiased ideas about the features and categories that go together—making judgments along the lines of similarity will be quite reasonable. Thus, if you are deciding whether to begin a new activity like hang gliding, it makes sense to determine how representative that sport is of the category of activities you have previously enjoyed.

Representativeness will lead you astray, however, when it causes you to ignore other types of relevant information, as you will now see (Kahneman & Frederick, 2002; Kahneman & Tversky, 1973). Consider, for example, the description of a successful attorney, given in **Figure 9.17**.

In one experiment, researchers provided their participants with a list of options, including those in Figure 9.17, and gave them the chance to win $45—real money—by ranking the correct option as number 1. Which option seems correct to you? If you are like a majority of the original participants, you will lose the $45 because you will say *tennis* rather than *a ball game*. The lower part of Figure 9.17

---

representativeness heuristic A cognitive strategy that assigns an object to a category on the basis of a few characteristics regarded as representative of that category.

A successful Jerusalem attorney. Colleagues say his whims prevent him from being a team worker, attributing his success to competitiveness and drive. Slim and not tall, he watches his body and is vain. Spends several hours a week on his favourite sport. What sport is that?

a. Fast walking
b. A ball game
c. Tennis
d. A track and field sport

The more inclusive category <u>must</u> be more probable.

FIGURE 9.17   Using the Representativeness Heuristic
When asked to choose the attorney's favourite sport, the representativeness heuristic leads most people to choose "tennis." However, as shown in the bottom part of the figure, the more probable answer is "a ball game," because that includes within it "tennis."

shows why *tennis* could never be as good a bet: it is included within the category *a ball game*. Participants judge *tennis* to be a better answer because it seems to have all the features of the sport the attorney is likely to play. However, this judgment by representativeness causes participants to neglect another sort of information—category structure. In this case, the measurable cost is $45 (Bar-Hillel & Neter, 1993).

The implication for your day-to-day life is that you should not be fooled into grabbing at a representative alternative before you consider the structure of all the alternatives.

Let's look at another use of representativeness. Consider the last time you went to hear live music. Suppose we ask you, "How much did you enjoy the concert?" How do you answer such a question? Most live performances unfold over a period of time; they have some good moments and some not-so-good moments. To answer the global question (that is, "How much . . . ?"), you need to provide a value that is representative of all those various moments. Research suggests that representative values often reflect an average of an event's moment of peak intensity and the intensity at the event's end (Kahneman & Frederick, 2002). For example, in one study participants experienced two trials in which they immersed their hands in painfully cold water (Kahneman, Fredrickson, Schreiber, & Redelmeier, 1993). In the short trial, they kept their hand in 14°C water for 60 seconds. In the long trial, after that first 60 seconds, they kept their hand immersed for 30 seconds more as the water gradually warmed to 15°C. (Participants were able to notice the 1° change.) When asked whether they would prefer to repeat the short or the long trial, a majority of participants chose the longer trial! Are you surprised that participants preferred 90 seconds of pain to 60 seconds of pain?

The researchers explained that the peak-end average is lower for the short trial (for which the peak equals the end so that 14° and 14° are averaged) than for the long trial (for which 15° and 14° are averaged). The higher value that represents the long trial makes that trial seem less painful in retrospect. The same pattern applies to positive experiences (Do, Rupert, & Wolford, 2008). In one study, people were happier when they received less candy if the single piece of "peak" candy was better than the average of the "peak" candy and the "end" candy. Can you see how you might apply this peak-end rule to your own life? To influence people's evaluation of an event, you should think about how to arrange the components of the event so that people encode the desired representative value.

Anchors Aweigh! To introduce you to a third heuristic, we need you to try a thought experiment. First take five seconds to estimate the following mathematical product and write down your answer:

$$1 \times 2 \times 3 \times 4 \times 5 \times 6 \times 7 \times 8 = \_\_\_\_\_$$

In five seconds, you can probably make only a couple of calculations. You get a partial answer, perhaps 24, and then adjust up from there. Now try this series of numbers:

$$8 \times 7 \times 6 \times 5 \times 4 \times 3 \times 2 \times 1 = \_\_\_\_\_$$

Even if you notice that this is the same list in reverse, you can see how the experience of carrying out the multiplication would feel quite different. You would start with 8×7, which is 56, and then attempt 56×6, which already feels quite large. Once again, you can only make a partial guess and then adjust upward. When Tversky and Kahneman (1973) gave these two arrangements of the identical problem to experimental participants, the 1 to 8 order produced median estimates of 512, and the 8 to 1 group produced estimates of 2250 (*the real answer is 40 320*). Apparently, when participants adjusted up from their five-second estimates, the higher partial solutions led to higher estimates.

Performance on this simple multiplication task provides evidence for the **anchoring heuristic**: People's judgments of the probable value of some event or outcome represent insufficient adjustments—either up or down—from an original starting value. In other words, your judgment is "anchored" too firmly to an original guess. People show a strong tendency to be influenced by an anchor, even when the information is clearly of little or no use. For example, in one study students were given an arbitrary identification number (in the range 1928 to 1935) that they were instructed to copy onto their questionnaires. Subsequently, the students estimated the number of physicians listed in the local Yellow Pages. Students in the control group—who had not received an ID anchor—produced an average estimate of 219 physicians. Students with the ID anchors produced an estimate of 539—even though they had been specifically warned that the ID number might affect their judgments (Wilson, Houston, Etling, & Brekke, 1996). You can see how hard it is not to let an anchor have an impact.

Why do people make insufficient adjustments from anchors? Researchers have begun to address this question in real-life circumstances—in which people produce their own anchors before beginning the adjustment process. Consider this question: What is the duration of Mars's orbit around the sun?

How might you answer that question? Research suggests that you start with the duration of Earth's orbit of 365 days as an anchor. What next? You might use the knowledge that Mars is farther from the sun than Earth is to adjust away from the 365-day anchor toward a larger value. In fact, participants in an experiment estimated Mars's orbit to be about 492 days (Epley & Gilovich, 2006). This estimate is still short of the actual value, which is 869 days. What people appeared to do in the experiment was to start with a reasonable anchor (i.e., 365 days) and keep adjusting until they reached a value that seemed *plausible*. When you find yourself in situations of anchoring and adjustment, put this result to use: You should expend some extra effort to confirm that a plausible value is, in fact, the right answer.

You employ judgmental heuristics like availability, representativeness, and anchoring because, in most situations, they allow you to make efficient, acceptable judgments. In a sense, you are doing the best you can, given the uncertainties of situations and constraints on your processing resources. We have shown you, however, that heuristics can lead to errors. Try to use this knowledge to examine your own thought processes when the time comes to make important judgments.

Whittlesea and Leboe (2000) found that when people are trying to classify information, they use three different heuristics. For example, if you are looking at a novel object, there are a few obvious ways that you can think about it to put it into a category with other things you are familiar with. First, you might have an easy time remembering it because you have seen it a lot, which researchers often call *fluency*. Second, perhaps you can identify some facts or details about the object that allow you to put it into a category, which is the *generation* heuristic. Third, you may realize that the object looks a little like something you have seen before, so you use the *resemblance* heuristic to put it into a particular category. Interestingly, researchers can manipulate how you categorize objects and information by providing extra experience with certain types of information—but researchers are not the only ones who do this kind of thing. Think about this question: "Who makes fast-food burgers?" It was probably easy to come up with a list of names, even if you do not eat at those fast-food restaurants. Did you, however, think about the smaller, less well-known burger joints? One reason why you likely did not do so is that companies that advertise—usually the bigger chains that can afford it—have given you much experience with their products and names. So, when you were asked about burgers, the fluency heuristic came into play. The example suggests that you should be especially critical when you feel others might be trying to bias your judgments by giving you extra experience with their products. Let's move now to the decisions you make, often on the basis of those judgments.

THE PSYCHOLOGY OF DECISION MAKING

Let's begin with a powerful example of the way that psychological factors affect the decisions people make. Consider the problem given in part 1 of **Table 9.7**. Read the instructions, and then

---

anchoring heuristic An insufficient adjustment up or down from an original starting value when judging the probable value of some event or outcome.

TABLE 9.7   The Effect of Psychological Factors on Decision Making

Part 1: Prefer Version

1. Imagine that you are planning a week's vacation in a warm spot over spring break. You currently have two options that are reasonably priced. The travel brochure gives only a limited amount of information about the two options. Given the information available, which vacation spot would you prefer?

Part 2: Cancel Version

2. Imagine that you are planning a week's vacation in a warm spot over spring break. You currently have two options that are reasonably priced, but you can no longer retain your reservation for both. The travel brochure gives only a limited amount of information about the two options. Given the information available, which reservation do you decide to cancel?

Part 1		Part 2	
Spot A	average weather	Spot A	average weather
	average beaches		average beaches
	medium-quality hotel		medium-quality hotel
	medium-temperature water		medium-temperature water
	average nightlife		average nightlife
Spot B	lots of sunshine	Spot B	lots of sunshine
	gorgeous beaches and coral reefs		gorgeous beaches and coral reefs
	ultramodern hotel		ultramodern hotel
	very cold water		very cold water
	very strong winds		very strong winds
	no nightlife		no nightlife

make your choice between spot A and spot B. Now read the version of the problem given in part 2. Would you like to change your choice?

In an experiment, students read one version of this problem (Shafir, 1993). When they were asked in part 1 which option they preferred, 67 percent of the students opted for spot B. However, when students were asked in part 2 to cancel an option, this figure fell to 52 percent (that is, 48 percent said they would cancel spot B). Why is this change odd? If you take a close look at the "prefer" and "cancel" versions of the problem, you will see that there is no difference in the information available in the two cases. On first pass, you might expect that the same information would lead to the same decision, but that is not what people do. It seems that the "prefer" question focuses people's attention on positive features of options—you are gathering evidence in favour of something—whereas the "cancel" question focuses attention on negative features of options—you are gathering evidence against something. Your decision may shift.

This straightforward example demonstrates that the way in which a question is phrased can have great consequences for the

decision you will make (Slovic, 1995). This is why you need to understand the psychological aspects of decision making: You need to be able to test your own decisions to see whether they hold up under careful analysis. In this case, you might ask yourself, "How would my choice change if I were asked to reject an option rather than to choose one?" If you find that your top preference is also your top candidate for rejection, you will have learned that the option has both many positive and many negative features. Now ask, "Is that acceptable?" This is a key step in developing your critical thinking skills.

The Framing of Decisions One of the most natural ways to make a decision is to judge which option will bring about the biggest gain or which option will bring about the smallest loss. Thus, if we offer you $5 or $10, you will feel very little uncertainty that the better option is $10. What makes the situation a bit more complicated, however, is that the perception of a gain or a loss often depends on the way in which a decision is *framed*. A **frame** is a particular description of a choice. Suppose, for example, you were asked how happy you would be to get a $1000 raise in your job. If you were expecting no raise at all, this would seem like a great gain, and you would probably be quite happy. Yet suppose you had been told several times to expect a raise of $10 000. Now how do you feel? Suddenly, you may feel as if you have lost money because the $1000 is less than what you had expected. You are not happy at all! In either case, you

---

frame A particular description of a choice; the perspective from which a choice is described or framed affects how a decision is made and which option is ultimately exercised.

would be getting $1000 more a year—objectively, you would be in exactly the same position—but the psychological effect is very different. That is why *reference points* are important in decision making (Kahneman, 1992). What seems like a gain or a loss will be determined in part by the expectations—a $0 raise or a $10 000 raise—to which a decision maker refers. (The decision, in this case, might be whether to stay in the job.)

Let's now take a look at a slightly more complex example in which framing has a sizeable impact on the decisions people make. In **Table 9.8**, you are asked to imagine making a choice between surgery and radiation for treatment of lung cancer. First, read the *survival* frame for the problem and choose your preferred treatment; then read the *mortality* frame and see if you feel like changing your preference. Note that the data are objectively the same in the two frames. The only difference is whether statistical information about the consequences of each treatment are presented in terms of survival rates or of mortality rates. When this decision was presented to participants, the focus on relative gains and losses had a marked effect on choice of treatment. Radiation therapy was chosen by only 18 percent of the participants who were given the survival frame, but by 44 percent of those given the mortality frame. This framing effect held equally for a group of clinic patients, statistically sophisticated business students, and experienced physicians (McNeil, Pauker, Sox, & Tversky, 1982).

Now that you know about frames, you should start to look for them in your everyday life. You're especially likely to find them when people are trying to get you to buy their products. Consider a study that looked at people's judgments about the choices they would make between two butchers.

> The participants in an experiment read a brief scenario that described two neighbourhood butchers (Keren, 2007). Butcher A advertised his meat as 25 percent fat; Butcher B advertised his meat as 75 percent lean. Participants imagined that they were preparing for a large dinner party and had to buy their meat from one of the two butchers. Which would they choose? The majority of the participants (82 percent) went with Butcher B. You can probably see why: The meat that's 75 percent lean sounds much healthier. Of course, the two butchers are actually offering the same product (because meat that is 75 percent lean would have 25 percent fat). Despite that math, the frame has a large impact. Now consider a judgment made by a second group of participants: They indicated which of the two butchers they would trust more. For trust judgments, participants' preferences were reversed: A majority (73 percent) said they trusted more the butcher who told them how much fat the meat had!

This experiment illustrates that the same frame can have an opposite impact on different judgments. Do you suppose the butchers would be happier to be trusted by their customers or to sell their products? As you think about frames in the real world, you should consider what judgments people are trying to affect.

These results we've shared with you should encourage you to think about important decisions from the perspective of different frames. Suppose, for example, you are going to buy a new car. The salesperson will be inclined to frame everything as a gain: "Seventy-eight percent of the Xenons require no repairs in the first year!" You can reframe that to "Twenty-two percent

TABLE 9.8 The Effect of Framing

Survival frame

Surgery. Of 100 people having surgery, 90 live through the post-operative period, 68 are alive at the end of the first year, and 34 are alive at the end of five years.

Radiation therapy. Of 100 people having radiation therapy, all live through the treatment, 77 are alive at the end of one year, and 22 are alive at the end of five years.

What do you choose: surgery or radiation?

Mortality frame

Surgery. Of 100 people having surgery, 10 die during surgery or the postoperative period, 32 die by the end of one year, and 66 die by the end of five years.

Radiation therapy. Of 100 people having radiation therapy, none dies during treatment, 23 die by the end of one year, and 78 die by the end of five years.

What do you choose: surgery or radiation?

require some repairs in the first year!" Would the new frame change how you feel about the situation? It's an exercise worth trying in real life.

The car salesperson is a good example of a situation in which someone is trying to frame information in a fashion that will have a desired effect on your decision. This, of course, is a regular part of your life. For example, as each election approaches, the opposing candidates compete to have their framings of themselves and of the issues prevail among the voters. One candidate might say, "I believe in sticking with policies that have been successful." His opponent might counter, "He is afraid of new ideas." One candidate might say, "That policy will

In what ways can salespeople frame their products to get prospective customers to consider them in a positive light?

bring about economic growth." Her opponent might counter, "That policy will bring about environmental destruction." Often both claims are true—the same policy often will bring about both economic good and environmental harm. In this light, whichever frame seems more compelling may be largely a matter of personal history. Thus your knowledge of framing effects can help you understand how people can come to such radically different decisions when they are faced with exactly the same evidence. If you want to understand other people's actions, try to think about how those individuals have framed a decision.

Consequences of Decision Making What happens when you make a decision? In the best of all possible worlds, everything goes well—and you never look back. However, as you likely know, not all decisions yield the best of all possible worlds. When decisions turn out badly, you will likely experience regret. Studies suggest that the categories in which people express the greatest regret is their decisions with respect to their education and careers (Roese & Summerville, 2005). To explain this finding, researchers point to the fact that these two domains provide a particularly wide range of opportunities: There are many ways to pursue an education and many careers to which someone might aspire. That range of opportunities makes it quite easy for people to wonder, "Did I make the right decision?"

People also experience more regret when they are clear on the costs associated with particular decisions (van Dijk & Zeelenberg, 2005). Consider a moment on a game show when a contestant must choose between *Box A* and *Box B*. If the contestant chooses the box with $10 instead of $10 000, it is easy to understand why he would experience regret. Some decisions in life are like the game show. You have the apple pie. Your friend has the pecan pie. After you each take one bite, you know that you made the wrong decision. You experience regret because you have a clear grasp on what you gave up. In other cases, you have a much vaguer grasp on the consequences of your decision. If you choose a poodle as a pet, you will never know exactly how different your life would have been had you chosen a bulldog. In that type of situation, it is less likely that you will experience regret.

When people anticipate regret, they are likely to be more deliberate in the way they face decisions—they will take more time and gather more information (Reb, 2008). In fact, under some circumstances, people will try hard to avoid making any decision at all (known as **decision aversion**). In **Table 9.9**, we provide an example of circumstances that can bring about an increasing unwillingness to make a decision. Consider the scenario in part A. Which would you choose? Researchers found that only 34 percent of their participants said they would wait for more information (Tversky & Shafir, 1992). Now consider the slightly altered scenario given in part B. Do you want to change your choice? In fact, 46 percent of the participants who read this version said they would wait for new information. How could this be? Ordinarily, you would expect that adding an option would decrease the share of the other options. If, for example, a third candidate enters a political race, you would expect that candidate to pull votes away from the original pair. Here, however, the addition of a third possibility increases the share of one of the original choices by 12 percent. What's going on?

decision aversion The tendency to avoid decision making; the tougher the decision, the greater the likelihood of decision aversion.

TABLE 9.9 Decision Aversion

A. Suppose you are considering buying a CD player and have not yet decided what model to buy. You pass by a store that is having a one-day clearance sale. They offer a popular Sony player for just $99, well below the list price. Do you

  1. buy the Sony player
  2. wait until you learn more about the various models

B. Suppose you are considering buying a CD player and have not yet decided what model to buy. You pass by a store that is having a one-day clearance sale. They offer a popular Sony player for just $99, and a top-of-the-line Aiwa player for just $159, both well below the list price. Do you

  1. buy the Aiwa player
  2. buy the Sony player
  3. wait until you learn more about the various models

Reprinted with permission from "Decision Aversion," *Psychological Science*, 3(6). Copyright © 1992 by Blackwell Publishing.

The key to obtaining this effect is to make the decision difficult. When the researchers tested participants on a version of the problem that provided a low-quality CD player as an extra option, only 24 percent said they would wait for more information—a decrease rather than an increase—which reflects the ease of choosing the Sony. The decision between the less-expensive Sony model and the top-quality Aiwa, however, is difficult. It is convenient to put the difficult decision off, to wait for more information.

One final observation: Not all decision makers are created equal. Suppose you go to a video store to choose a DVD for a Saturday night rental. If you are a *satisficer*, you would likely browse the DVDs until you got to one that struck you as interesting enough. If you are a *maximizer*, you would likely browse all the DVDs until you had convinced yourself that you had found exactly the best one. Researchers have demonstrated that there are both satisficers and maximizers in the world—and that the style of decision making has important consequences (Schwartz et al., 2002).

One study followed a group of 548 students from 11 colleges and universities as they entered the job market (Iyengar, Wells, & Schwartz, 2006). The students completed a questionnaire that revealed the extent to which they were satisficers or maximizers: They indicated their agreement with statements such as "When shopping, I have a hard time finding clothes that I really love." The researchers contacted the students three months and six months after they completed the initial questionnaire; at those points in time, the students were interviewing and then accepting jobs. The researchers collected a variety of data to determine how the students experienced the process. Those data showed a clear pattern: The maximizers had accepted jobs that, on average, provided 20 percent higher salaries—yet they were miserable. As the researchers put it, "Despite their relative success, maximizers [were] less satisfied with

Critical Thinking in Your Life

CAN POLITICAL EXPERTS PREDICT THE FUTURE?

Here is an exercise you might try: Spend about 15 minutes out on the web gathering experts' predictions about what lies in the political future: Will one party gain a new majority in the next election? Will the Middle East become more democratic? You are likely to find a diversity of opinions on every issue. Whom should you believe? According to a long-term study conducted by psychologist Philip Tetlock (2005), the safest answer is that you should not believe anyone—or, more exactly, you cannot know whom to believe. Let's see why.

To study the collective wisdom of experts, Tetlock recruited a sample of 284 individuals who had strong credentials for making political predictions with respect to certain countries or regions of the world. (Tetlock assured his participants anonymity, so he was unable to reveal exactly who any of his experts were.) He asked individuals to make predictions of this sort: "How likely is it that, after the next election, the party that currently has the most representatives in the legislative branch of government will *retain this status* . . . , *will lose this status*, or *will strengthen this position*?" (p. 46) The questions were made concrete for different countries and regions. The participants were officially experts for some of the questions, whereas for other questions they had to rely on more general knowledge. For example, one participant might be an expert on questions about Russia but not for questions

about Italy. The participants were asked to rate each of the three options (e.g., retain this status, lose this status, strengthen this position) on a scale from a likelihood of 0 percent ("impossible") to a likelihood of 100 percent ("certainty"). Tetlock examined the accuracy of 27 451 political forecasts by waiting long enough to see, in each case, what actually happened.

Since there were three options for each question, participants should have been right one third of the time just by chance. If they had true expertise, they should have been right much more often than that, but they were not. In fact, in some comparisons experts did worse than chance. Moreover, the participants overall did no better in their official areas of expertise than when they just used their general knowledge to answer questions. That is, in general, experts on Russia did just about as well answering questions on Italy—and vice versa. You might wonder if fame played a role. Did better known experts outperform their lesser known peers? The answer is decidedly no. As Tetlock put it, "experts in demand were more overconfident than their colleagues who eked out existences far from the limelight" (p. 63).

If experts fare so poorly in their predictions, why does anyone still listen to them? An important reason is that experts are not generally held accountable for their predictions: The media rarely tracks down the expert who made the confident prediction

that Smith would win, to ask her why Jones is now president. Tetlock, however, *did* ask his experts to explain why they had been wrong. The experts provided explanations in categories that will likely be familiar to you from your own life. They explained, for example, why they were "almost right" or why they were "wrong for the right reasons." They identified "out of the blue" forces that no one could have foreseen in advance of the outcome they had predicted.

Here is a safe conclusion from Tetlock's research: With respect to politics, no one can routinely predict the future. Some people do a bit better than others, but you cannot use their confidence or fame to know who those people are. Still, it is important to note that this research is about a particular type of expert and a particular type of prediction. You should not discount all experts. For example, when you consult medical doctors, they should be able to make their predictions—"Here's the likely impact of treatment"—based on years of education and prior experience. Also, they are regularly held accountable for the accuracy of those predictions!

- Why might Tetlock have given the participants three explicit options for each prediction?

- Why might overconfidence help people become or stay famous, even if their predictions are incorrect?

---

the outcomes of the job search, and more pessimistic, stressed, tired, anxious, worried, overwhelmed, and depressed throughout the process" (Iyengar et al., 2006, p. 147). Apparently, the quest for an elusive "best" outcome provided the maximizers with a substantial psychological burden.

We imagine that most people would like to have a good job without making themselves miserable. As you undertake your own job searches, you might think back to this distinction between maximizers and satisficers—to consider how you might achieve a decision that affords your life a sense of balance.

Throughout this chapter, we have asked you to imagine the mysterious midnight message, "The cat is on the mat." Our goal has been to get you to consider your many types of cognitive processing—language use, visual cognition, problem solving, reasoning, judging, and deciding. Now that this chapter has come to an end, we hope that the example will stick with you—so that you will never take your cognitive processes for granted. Every chance you get, give some thought to your thought, reason about your reasoning, and so on. You will be reflecting on the essence of the human experience.

STOP AND REVIEW

❶ Why do people rely on heuristics when they are making judgments?

❷ What heuristic might you use to answer the question, "What is the age of the oldest living human being?"

❸ Why do frames play such a large role in the psychology of decision making?

❹ What is the distinction between satisficers and maximizers?

CRITICAL THINKING Recall the study on representativeness. Why did the researchers offer participants $45 if they got the right answer?

Recapping Main Points

Studying Cognition

- Cognitive psychologists study the mental processes and structures that enable you to perceive, use language, reason, solve problems, and make judgments and decisions.
- Researchers use reaction time measures to break up complex tasks into underlying mental processes.

Visit **MyPsychLab.com** for more review and practice on the following topics:

◀─◉ **Simulate:** Explore Your Mental Space

Language Use

- Language users both produce and understand language.
- Speakers design their utterances to suit particular audiences.
- Speech errors reveal many of the processes that go into speech planning.
- Much of language understanding consists of using context to resolve ambiguities.
- Memory representations of meaning begin with propositions supplemented with inferences.
- Studies of language evolution have focused on grammatical structure and audience design.
- The language individuals speak may play a role in determining how they think.

Visual Cognition

- Visual representations can be used to supplement propositional representations.
- Visual representations allow you to think about visual aspects of your environment.
- People form visual representations that combine verbal and visual information.

Visit **MyPsychLab.com** for more review and practice on the following topics:

✔ **Practice:** Visual Cognition

Problem Solving and Reasoning

- Problem solvers must define initial state, goal state, and the operations that get them from the initial to the goal state.
- Deductive reasoning involves drawing conclusions from premises based on rules of logic.
- Inductive reasoning involves inferring a conclusion from evidence based on its likelihood or probability.

Visit **MyPsychLab.com** for more review and practice on the following topics:

✳ **Explore:** The Two-String Problem

Judgment and Decision Making

- Much of judgment and decision making is guided by heuristics—mental shortcuts that can help individuals reach solutions quickly.
- Availability, representativeness, and anchoring can all lead to errors when they are misapplied.
- Decision making is affected by the way in which different options are framed.
- The possibility of regret makes some decisions hard, particularly for individuals who are maximizers rather than satisficers.

Visit **MyPsychLab.com** for more review and practice on the following topics:

 Watch: Artificial Intelligence

KEY TERMS

algorithm (p. 272)
anchoring heuristic (p. 281)
audience design (p. 258)
automatic processes (p. 256)
availability heuristic (p. 279)
belief-bias effect (p. 275)
cognition (p. 253)
cognitive processes (p. 253)
cognitive psychology (p. 253)
cognitive science (p. 253)

controlled processes (p. 256)
decision aversion (p. 284)
decision making (p. 278)
deductive reasoning (p. 275)
frame (p. 282)
functional fixedness (p. 274)
heuristics (p. 272)
inductive reasoning (p. 276)
inferences (p. 263)
judgment (p. 278)

language production (p. 257)
mental set (p. 277)
parallel processes (p. 254)
problem solving (p. 271)
problem space (p. 272)
reasoning (p. 271)
representativeness heuristic (p. 280)
serial processes (p. 254)

Practice Test

1. According to the logic of Donders's analysis, _____
   a. categorization is among the hardest mental processes.
   b. it should always take longer to draw a capital C than a capital V.
   c. extra mental steps often result in more time to complete a task.
   d. reaction time is useful for understanding the order of mental processes.

2. When Jerry goes with friends to a fast-food restaurant, they each wait in a different line to see who gets to the counter first. That is a good example of _____ processing.
   a. serial
   b. automatic
   c. parallel
   d. ambiguity

3. Lauren can juggle and talk at the same time. Warren cannot. It sounds like juggling is more of a(n) _____ process for Lauren than for Warren.
   a. controlled
   b. automatic
   c. parallel
   d. serial

4. A friend walks up to you and says, "Remember what I said yesterday? Well, forget about it." If you understand all of this, it is because your friend has made an appropriate assessment of common ground based on _____
   a. co-presence for actions.
   b. perceptual co-presence.
   c. community membership.
   d. linguistic membership.

5. Which of these sentences would likely produce a different pattern of brain activity than the other three?
   a. There was sugar in Tom's coffee.
   b. Melissa was hoping to discover the name and address of the criminal.
   c. Lisa was making many enemies.
   d. As Aileen walked into the bank, she pulled a muscle in her calf.

6. Research has demonstrated that _____ can learn the meanings of plastic symbols without any explicit training.
   a. vervet monkeys
   b. pileated gibbons
   c. chimpanzees
   d. bonobos

7. The hypothesis of linguistic relativity suggests that _____
   a. languages can carve up the colour spectrum in any way they choose.
   b. the languages individuals speak affect the way they think about the world.
   c. people have evolved to use languages with greater complexity than other species.
   d. some languages do not allow people to engage in audience design.

8. People's motive for telling mild lies is more likely to be _____, whereas for serious lies the motive is more likely to be _____
   a. selfishness; psychological reasons
   b. personal advantage; vanity
   c. psychological reasons; personal advantage
   d. personal advantage; selfishness

9. You are lying on your side when a friend walks up to say hello. To recognize your friend, you might have to use _____
   a. mental rotation.
   b. mental scanning.
   c. a spatial mental model.
   d. a problem space.

10. Take a moment to form a visual image of the Statue of Liberty. Focus on Lady Liberty's face. If you use the visual image to form your responses, which of these questions should take the longest for you to answer?
    a. What is Lady Liberty holding in her right hand?
    b. What is Lady Liberty holding in her left hand?
    c. What is Lady Liberty wearing on her feet?
    d. What is Lady Liberty wearing on her head?

11. Suppose you study a text that inserts you into the middle of a room with objects around you. It should take you the least time to verify an object that is _____
    a. in front of you.
    b. behind you.
    c. on your left side.
    d. on your right side.

12. A(n) _____ is *not* one component of the definition of a problem space.
    a. algorithm
    b. set of operations
    c. goal state
    d. initial state

13. You are asked to test the rule, "If a card has a vowel on one side, it has an even number on the other side." Which of these cards should you turn over to see if the rule has been violated?
    a. F
    b. H
    c. 9
    d. 16

14. When you are engaging in _____ reasoning, you should be wary of a(n) _____
    a. inductive reasoning; algorithm
    b. inductive reasoning; mental set
    c. deductive reasoning; premise
    d. deductive reasoning; think-aloud protocol

15. Suppose you are asked to estimate whether Hollywood releases more comedies or horror flicks each year. To answer this question, you are most likely to use the _____ heuristic.
    a. anchoring
    b. adjustment
    c. representativeness
    d. availability

16. You ask a friend whether you should stick with your current romantic partner. The friend suggests that you focus on the ways in which the partner improves

your life. Your friend is trying to use ———— to influence your decision making.

a. reference points
c. an algorithm
b. decision aversion
d. a frame

17. Since Paul is a satisficer, you would expect him to ————
   a. watch the first TV channel that catches his interest.
   b. be unhappy even though he recently obtained a high-paying job.
   c. test drive dozens of new cars before making a purchase.
   d. try every flavour of coffee at the new corner market.

18. Suppose you asked an expert on Canada and an expert on Mexico to make predictions about an upcoming election in Mexico. According to Philip Tetlock's research, you would expect that ————
   a. their predictions would be about equally accurate.
   b. the predictions of the Canada expert would be better.
   c. the predictions of the Mexico expert would be better.
   d. only one of them would be correct.

Essay Questions

1. Why is ambiguity an important problem for language comprehension?

2. What factors affect your ability to engage in accurate deductive reasoning?

3. Under what circumstances are decisions most likely to cause people regret?

Watch the following videos by logging on to MyPsychLab (**www.mypsychlab.com**). After you have watched the videos, complete the activities that follow.

Program 10: Cognitive Processes

Program 11: Judgment and Decision Making

PROGRAM REVIEW

1. Michael Posner's work on brain imaging showed _____
   a. major differences between the brains of young and old adults, with cognitive processes more localized in brains of the elderly.
   b. that blood flow decreases in the brain as thinking becomes more efficient.
   c. that electrical stimulation of the brain can enhance performance on logic puzzles reliably.
   d. that patterns of brain activity differ in predictable ways when people see words, versus read them aloud, versus name the function of the objects to which they refer.

2. What analytic tool did Donald Broadbent use to model the process by which information is perceived and stored in memory?
   a. statistical analysis on a computer
   b. a flow chart
   c. a set of categories
   d. an analogy to a steam engine

3. When we distinguish between groups of letters on the basis of the kinds of lines that form them, we are performing the mental process of _____
   a. relating.
   b. categorizing.
   c. creating prototypes.
   d. activating schema.

4. According to the program, why do we assume that Montreal is farther north than Seattle?
   a. because we have learned it
   b. because we are less familiar with Montreal than with Seattle
   c. because Canada is north of the United States in our mental maps
   d. because we are not good at making such judgments

5. How did Freud explain the fact that human beings sometimes make irrational decisions?
   a. They are driven by primitive needs.
   b. They are influenced by the emotions of the crowd.
   c. They are basing their decisions on availability.
   d. They are using standard human mental processes.

6. A *heuristic* is a kind of _____
   a. mistake.
   b. meaning.
   c. mathematical model.
   d. shortcut.

7. When people were confronted with a choice of a sure loss of $85 or an 85 percent chance of losing $100, how did most people react?
   a. They chose the loss.
   b. They chose the chance.
   c. They pointed out the statistical equivalence of the alternatives.
   d. They revised to make the choice.

8. According to Max Bazerman, all of the following are mistakes commonly made during negotiation, except _____
   a. being willing to compromise on points of lesser importance.
   b. failure to consider the judgments made by one's counterpart.
   c. limiting one's thinking to the specific points of conflict.
   d. assuming that whenever one side wins, the other must lose.

9. Al's parents are paying for his college tuition. Joe is working two jobs to put himself through college. Both are taking a fairly dry chemistry course together. Who is more likely to say he likes the course, and why?
   a. Al, because of cognitive dissonance
   b. Joe, because of cognitive dissonance
   c. Al, because of the availability heuristic
   d. Joe, because of the availability heuristic

QUESTIONS TO CONSIDER

1. Think of all the ways you can categorize people (for example, by their sex, their age, their ethnicity, their intelligence, their taste in music). Do you have different schemas for people who belong to these various groups? How does your schema influence your behaviour toward people?

2. Knowing about problem-solving strategies and using them are two different things. Based on the information in the program and in your text, what are some of the pitfalls you need to avoid in both day-to-day problem solving and decision making about major life changes? How optimistic are you that you can really learn to consistently avoid these pitfalls?

10

Intelligence and Intelligence Assessment

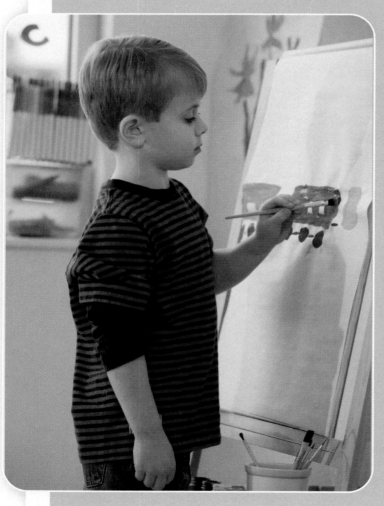

uppbose you were asked to define the word *intelligence*. What types of behaviours would you include in your definition? Think back on your own experiences. What was it like when you first started school? What was it like when you laboured at your first job? It is very likely that you heard your behaviours labelled as intelligent or unintelligent—smart or not so smart—in those and other situations. When those labels are applied in casual conversation, they have relatively few consequences. However, in many settings it matters whether your behaviours are considered intelligent or not. For example, if you grew up in North America, it is likely that your "potential" was measured at an early age. In most school districts, teachers and administrators attempt, very early in your life, to measure your *intelligence*. The goal, most often, is to match students with classroom work that makes appropriate demands. However, as you have almost certainly observed, people's lives often seem to be affected by intelligence testing in areas well outside the classroom.

In this chapter, we will examine the foundations and uses of intelligence assessment. We will review the contributions psychologists have made to understanding individual differences in the areas of intelligence. We will also discuss the types of controversies that almost inevitably arise when people begin to interpret these differences. Our focus will be on how intelligence tests work, what makes any test useful, and why they do not always do the job they are intended to do. Finally, we will conclude on a personal note, by considering the role of psychological assessment in society.

We begin now with a brief overview of the general practice of psychological assessment.

What Is Assessment?

Psychological assessment is the use of specified testing procedures to evaluate the abilities, behaviours, and personal qualities of people. Psychological assessment is often referred to as the measurement of *individual differences* because the majority of assessments specify how an individual is different from or similar to other people on a given dimension. Before we examine in detail the basic features of psychological testing, let's outline the history of assessment. This historical overview will help you to understand both the uses and limitations of assessment, as well as prepare you to appreciate some current controversies.

HISTORY OF ASSESSMENT

The development of formal tests and procedures for assessment is a relatively new enterprise in Western psychology, coming into wide use only in the early 1900s. However, long before Western psychology began to devise tests to evaluate people, assessment techniques were commonplace in ancient China. In fact, China employed a sophisticated program of civil service testing over 4000 years ago: Officials were required to demonstrate their competence every third year at an oral examination. Two thousand years later, during the Han Dynasty, written civil service tests were used to measure competence in the areas of law, the military, agriculture, and geography. During the Ming Dynasty (A.D. 1368–1644), public officials were chosen on the

What important ideas about the assessment of intelligence are credited to Sir Francis Galton (1822–1911)?

basis of their performance at three stages of an objective selection procedure. During the first stage, examinations were given at the local level. The 4 percent who passed these tests had to endure the second stage: nine days and nights of essay examinations on the classics. The 5 percent who passed the essay exams were allowed to complete a final stage of tests conducted at the nation's capital.

China's selection procedures were observed and described by British diplomats and missionaries in the early 1800s. Modified versions of China's system were soon adopted by the British and later by the Americans for the selection of civil service personnel (Wiggins, 1973).

The key figure in the development of Western intelligence testing was an upper-class Englishman, **Sir Francis Galton**, to whom you were introduced in Chapter 3. His book *Hereditary Genius*, published in 1869, greatly influenced subsequent thinking on the methods, theories, and practices of intelligence testing. Galton was the first to postulate four important ideas about the assessment of intelligence. First, differences in intelligence were *quantifiable* in terms of degrees of intelligence. In other words, numerical values could be assigned to distinguish among different people's levels of intelligence. Second, differences among people formed a *bell-shaped curve*, or *normal distribution*. On a bell-shaped curve, most people's scores cluster in the middle, and fewer are found toward the two extremes of genius and mental deficiency (we return to the bell-shaped curve later in the chapter). Third, intelligence, or mental ability, could be measured by objective tests—tests on which each question had only one "right" answer. And fourth, the precise extent to which two sets of test scores were related could be determined by a statistical procedure he called *co-relations*, now known as *correlations*. Sir Francis Galton's work created a context for contemporary intelligence assessment. Let's now see what features define circumstances of formal assessment.

---

psychological assessment The use of specified procedures to evaluate the abilities, behaviours, and personal qualities of people.

BASIC FEATURES OF FORMAL ASSESSMENT

To be useful for classifying individuals or for selecting those with particular qualities, a **formal assessment** procedure should meet three requirements. The assessment instrument should be (1) reliable, (2) valid, and (3) standardized. If it fails to meet these requirements, we cannot be sure whether the conclusions of the assessment can be trusted. Although this chapter focuses on intelligence assessment, formal assessment procedures apply to all types of psychological testing. To ensure that you will understand the broad application of these principles, we will draw on examples from both intelligence testing and other domains of psychological assessment.

Reliability As you will recall from Chapter 2, *reliability* is the extent to which an assessment instrument can be trusted to give consistent scores. If you stepped on your bathroom scale three times in the same morning and it gave you a different reading each time, the scale would not be doing its job. You would call it *unreliable* because you could not count on it to give consistent results. Of course, if you ate a big meal in between two weighings, you would not expect the scale to produce the same result. That is, a measurement device can be considered reliable or unreliable only to the extent that the underlying concept it is measuring remains unchanged.

One straightforward way to find out if a test is reliable is to calculate its **test–retest reliability**—a measure of the correlation between the scores of the same people, on the same test, given on two different occasions. A perfectly reliable test will yield a correlation coefficient of +1.00. This means that the identical pattern of scores emerges both times. The same people who got the highest and lowest scores the first time do so again. A totally unreliable test results in a 0.00 correlation coefficient. That means there is no relationship between the first set of scores and the second set. Someone who initially got the top score gets a completely different score the second time. As the correlation coefficient moves higher (toward the ideal of +1.00), the test is increasingly reliable.

There are two other ways to assess reliability. One is to administer **parallel forms** of a test instead of giving the same test twice. Using parallel forms reduces the effects of direct practice of the test questions, memory of the test questions, and the desire of an individual to appear consistent from one test to the next. Reliable tests yield comparable scores on parallel forms of the test. The other measure of reliability is the **internal consistency** of responses on a single test. For example, we can compare a person's score on the odd-numbered items of a test with the score on the even-numbered items. A reliable test yields the same score for each of its halves. It is then said to have high internal consistency on this measure of **split-half reliability**.

In most circumstances, not only should the measurement device itself be reliable, but so should the method for using the device. Suppose researchers wished to observe children in a classroom in order to assess different levels of aggressive play. The researchers might develop a *coding scheme* that would allow them to make appropriate distinctions. The scheme would be reliable to the extent that all the people who viewed the same behaviour would give highly similar ratings to the same children. This is one of the reasons that quite a bit of training is required before individuals can carry out accurate psychological assessment. They must learn to apply systems of distinctions in a reliable fashion.

The researchers who develop and administer assessment devices work hard to ensure reliability. You have probably seen television shows and movies where U.S. high-school students write the SAT, a formal exam, to get into college or university. This is a very important exam, as it is often the most important tool a college uses to determine admission. Yet one section of questions does not affect students' scores. The questions on this unscored section are most likely being considered for future exams. The researchers who develop the exam can compare performance on the scored questions to performance on the unscored questions to ensure that people's scores on future exams are comparable to the scores on the exam they have already written. For that reason, if you have taken the SAT I, you provided some of the information that helps to make the test reliable.

Validity Recall from Chapter 2 that the *validity* of a test is the degree to which it measures what an assessor intends it to measure. A valid test of intelligence measures that trait and predicts performance in situations where intelligence is important. Scores on a valid measure of creativity reflect actual creativity, not drawing ability or moods. In general, then, validity reflects a

---

formal assessment The systematic procedures and measurement instruments used by trained professionals to assess an individual's functioning, aptitudes, abilities, or mental states.

test–retest reliability A measure of the correlation between the scores of the same people on the same test given on two different occasions.

parallel forms Different versions of a test used to assess test reliability; the change of forms reduces effects of direct practice, memory, or the desire of an individual to appear consistent on the same items.

internal consistency A measure of reliability; the degree to which a test yields similar scores across its different parts, such as odd versus even items.

split-half reliability A measure of the correlation between test takers' performance on different halves (e.g., odd- and even-numbered items) of a test.

The wrong way to measure split-half reliability.

test's ability to make accurate predictions about behaviours or outcomes related to the purpose or design of the test. Three important types of validity are *face validity*, *criterion validity*, and *construct validity*.

The first type of validity is based on the surface *content* of a test. When test items appear to be directly related to the attribute of interest, the test has **face validity**. Face-valid tests are very straightforward—they simply ask what the test maker needs to know: How anxious do you feel? Are you creative? The person taking the test is expected to answer accurately and honestly. Unfortunately, face validity is often not sufficient to ensure accurate measurement. First, people's perceptions of themselves may not be accurate, or they may not know how they should rate themselves in comparison to other people. Second, a test that too obviously measures some attribute may allow test takers to manipulate the impression they make. Consider the classic case of institutionalized mental patients who did not want to be released from their familiar, structured environment.

These long-term patients with schizophrenia were interviewed by the staff about how disturbed they were. When they were given a *transfer* interview to assess if they were well enough to be moved to an open ward, these patients gave generally positive self-references. However, when the purpose of the interview was to assess their suitability for *discharge*, the patients gave more negative self-references because they did not want to be discharged. Psychiatrists who rated the interview data, without awareness of this experimental variation in the purpose of the interview, judged those who gave more negative self-references as more severely disturbed and recommended against their discharge. So the patients achieved the assessment outcome they wanted. The psychiatrists' assessment may also have been influenced by their perspective that anyone who wanted to stay in a mental hospital must be very disturbed. (Braginsky & Braginsky, 1967)

This example makes it particularly clear that test givers cannot rely only on measures that have face validity. Let's consider other types of validity that overcome some of these limitations.

To assess the **criterion validity** (also known as **predictive validity**) of a test, psychologists compare a person's score on the test with his or her score on some other standard, or *criterion*, associated with what the test measures. For example, if a test is designed to predict success in university, then university grades would be an appropriate criterion. If the test scores correlate highly with university grades, then the test has criterion validity. A major task of test developers is to find appropriate, measurable criteria. Once criterion validity has been demonstrated for an assessment device, researchers feel confident using the device to make future predictions. Let's consider a study that evaluated intelligence testing between two Canadian cultures that suggests we must be careful in selecting tests in order to make predictions.

When it comes to intelligence testing of children who come from different cultures, it has been proposed that many populations might benefit from testing that does not rely solely on verbal meanings, or on symbols specific to one language. A trio of researchers (Kowal, Watson, & Madak, 1990) in Winnipeg evaluated non-indigenous suburban children and Native children on a general IQ test that is widely used and on a test of nonverbal intelligence that is used less frequently. All children were assessed using the common intelligence test that evaluates general intelligence and transforms scores into Verbal IQ, Performance IQ, and a Full Scale IQ. They were also tested on the nonverbal test that relies on problem solving and identifying relationships between abstract figures. The authors discovered that the Native children and non-indigenous group had similar Performance IQs, Full Scale IQs, and nonverbal intelligence scores. The real difference between them was that the Native children had a lower performance on the Verbal IQ portion of the testing. The study suggested that the Native children were much better visual learners than the general population. The data have some implications for how we might test minorities and ethnic groups who may not have English as their first language, or who have early learning experiences that are not language based.

For many personal qualities of interest to psychologists, no ideal criterion exists. No single behaviour or objective measure of performance can indicate, for example, how anxious, depressed, or aggressive a person is overall. Psychologists have theories, or *constructs*, about these abstract qualities—what causes them, how they affect behaviour, and how they relate to other variables. The **construct validity** of a test is the degree to which it adequately measures the underlying construct. For example, a new measure of depression has construct validity if the scores it produces correlate highly with valid measures of the features that define the construct of depression. In addition, the new measure should not show relationships with features that fall outside the construct of depression.

The conditions under which a test is valid may be very specific, so it is always important to ask about a test, "For what purpose is it valid?" Knowing which other measures a test does and does not correlate with may reveal something new about the measures, the construct, or the complexity of human behaviour. For example, suppose you design a test to measure the ability of medical students to cope with stress. You then find that scores on that test correlate well with students' ability to cope with classroom stress. You presume your test will also correlate with students' ability to deal with stressful hospital emergencies, but you discover it does not. Since you have demonstrated some validity, you have learned something both about your test—the circumstances in which it is valid—and about your construct—different categories of stressors have different consequences. You would then modify your test to take account of the kinds of special stressors found in hospital emergencies.

Consider for a moment the relationship between validity and reliability. Whereas reliability is measured by the degree to which a test correlates with itself (administered at different times or using different items), validity is measured by the degree to which the test correlates with something external to it

---

face validity The degree to which test items appear to be directly related to the attribute the researcher wishes to measure.

criterion validity The degree to which test scores indicate a result on a specific measure that is consistent with some other criterion of the characteristic being assessed; also known as predictive validity.

predictive validity See criterion validity.

construct validity The degree to which a test adequately measures an underlying construct.

(another test, a behavioural criterion, or judges' ratings). Usually, a test that is not reliable is also not valid because a test that cannot predict itself will be unable to predict anything else. For example, if your class took a test of aggressiveness today and scores were uncorrelated with scores from a parallel form of the test tomorrow (demonstrating unreliability), it is unlikely that the scores from either day would predict which students had fought or argued most frequently over a week's time: After all, the two sets of test scores would not even make the same prediction! Conversely, it is quite possible for a test to be highly reliable without being valid. Suppose, for example, we decided to use your adult height as a measure of intelligence. Do you see why that would be reliable, but not valid?

Norms and Standardization So we have a reliable and valid test, but we still need *norms* to provide a context for interpreting different test scores. Suppose, for example, you get a score of 18 on a test designed to reveal how depressed you are. What does that mean? Are you a little depressed, not at all depressed, or about averagely depressed? To find out what your score means, you would want to compare your individual score with typical scores, or statistical **norms**, of other students. You would check the test norms to see what the usual range of scores is and what the average is for students of your age and sex. That would provide you with a context for interpreting your depression score.

You probably encountered test norms when you received your scores on aptitude tests, or potentially on the provincial exams you wrote in your last year of high school. The norms told you how your scores compared with those of other students and helped you interpret how well you had done relative to that *normative population*. Group norms are most useful for interpreting individual scores when the comparison group shares important qualities with the individuals tested, such as age, social class, culture, and experience.

For norms to be meaningful, everyone must take the same test under standardized circumstances. **Standardization** is the administration of a testing device to all persons in the same way and under the same conditions. The need for standardization seems obvious, but it does not always occur in practice. Some people may be allowed more time than others, be given clearer or more detailed instructions, be permitted to ask questions, or be motivated by a tester to perform better. Consider the experience of one of your authors:

> As a graduate student at Yale, I administered a scale to assess children's degree of test anxiety in grade-school classes. Before starting, one teacher told her class, "We're going to have some fun with this new kind of question game this nice man will play with you." A teacher in another classroom prepared her class for the same assessment by cautioning, "This psychologist from Yale University is going to give you a test to see what you are thinking; I hope you will do well and show how good our class is!" (Zimbardo, personal communication, 1958)

How would you feel if someone used your adult height to assess intelligence? The measure would be reliable, but would it be valid?

Could you directly compare the scores of the children in these two classes on this "same" test? The answer is "no," because the test was not administered in a standardized way. In this case, the children in the second class scored higher on test anxiety. (You are probably not surprised!) When procedures do not include explicit instructions about the way to administer the test or the way to score the results, it is difficult to interpret what a given test score means or how it relates to any comparison group.

We have now reviewed some of the concerns researchers have when they construct a test and find out whether it is indeed testing what they wish to test. They must assure themselves that the test is reliable and valid. They must also specify the standard conditions under which it should be administered, so that resulting norms have meaning. Therefore, you should evaluate any test score you get in terms of the test's reliability and validity, the norms of performance, and the degree of standardization of the circumstances in which you took the test.

We are now ready to turn to the measurement of intelligence.

STOP AND REVIEW

❶ What is meant by split-half reliability?
❷ How would a researcher determine whether a measure has predictive validity?
❸ Why is it important to have norms for measures?

CRITICAL THINKING Recall the study that looked at psychiatrists' assessments of patients. What might the psychiatrists do to mask the purpose of the assessment?

---

norms Standards based on measurements of a large group of people; used for comparing the scores of an individual with those of others within a well-defined group.

standardization A set of uniform procedures for treating each participant in a test, interview, or experiment, or for recording data.

intelligence The global capacity to profit from experience and to go beyond given information about the environment.

Intelligence Assessment

How intelligent are you or your friends? To answer this question, you must begin by defining **intelligence**. Doing so is not an easy task, but a group of 52 intelligence researchers concurred on this general definition: "Intelligence is a very general mental capability that, among other things, involves the ability to reason, plan, solve problems, think abstractly, comprehend complex ideas, learn quickly and learn from experience" (Gottfredson, 1997, p. 13). Given this range of capabilities, it should be clear immediately why controversy has almost always surrounded how intelligence is measured. The way in which theorists conceptualize intelligence and higher mental functioning greatly influences the way they try to assess it (Sternberg, 1994). Some psychologists believe that human intelligence can be quantified and reduced to a single score. Others argue that intelligence has many components that should be separately assessed. Still others say that there are actually several distinct kinds of intelligence, across different domains of experience.

In this section, we will describe how tests of intelligence mesh with these different conceptions of intelligence. Let's begin by considering the context in which interest in intelligence and more contemporary intelligence testing first arose.

THE ORIGINS OF INTELLIGENCE TESTING

The year 1905 marked the first published account of a workable intelligence test. **Alfred Binet** had responded to the call of the French minister of public instruction for the creation of more effective teaching methods for developmentally disabled children. Binet and his colleague **Théophile Simon** believed that measuring a child's intellectual ability was necessary for planning an instructional program. Binet attempted to devise an objective test of intellectual performance that could be used to classify and separate developmentally disabled from normal schoolchildren. He hoped that such a test would reduce the school's reliance on the more subjective, and perhaps biased, evaluations of teachers.

To *quantify*—measure—intellectual performance, Binet designed age-appropriate problems or test items on which many children's responses could be compared. The problems on the test were chosen so that they could be scored objectively as correct or incorrect, could vary in content, were not heavily influenced by differences in children's environments, and assessed judgment and reasoning rather than rote memory (Binet, 1911).

Children of various ages were tested, and the average score for normal children at each age was computed. Then each individual child's performance was compared with the average for other children of his or her age. Test results were expressed in terms of the average age at which normal children achieved a particular score. This measure was called the **mental age**. For instance, when a child's score equaled the average score of a group of five-year-olds, the child was said to have a *mental age* of five, regardless of his or her actual **chronological age**, or the number of years since birth.

Binet's successful development of an intelligence test had great impact in the United States. A unique combination of historical events and social-political forces had prepared the United States for an explosion of interest in assessing mental ability. At the beginning of the 20th century, the United States was a nation in turmoil. As a result of global economic, social, and political conditions, millions of immigrants entered the country. New universal education laws flooded schools with students. Some form of assessment was needed to identify, document, and classify immigrant adults and schoolchildren (Chapman, 1988). When World War I began, millions of volunteers marched into recruiting stations. Recruiters needed to determine who of these many people had the ability to learn quickly and benefit from special leadership training. New nonverbal, group-administered tests of mental ability were used to evaluate over 1.7 million recruits. A group of prominent psychologists, including Lewis Terman, Edward Thorndike, and Robert Yerkes, responded to the wartime emergency and designed these tests in only one month's time (Lennon, 1985).

One consequence of this large-scale testing program was that the American public came to accept the idea that intelligence tests could differentiate people in terms of leadership ability and other socially important characteristics. This acceptance led to the widespread use of tests in schools and industry. Assessment was seen as a way to inject order into a chaotic society and as an inexpensive, democratic way to separate those who could benefit from education or military leadership training from those who could not. To facilitate the wide-scale use of intelligence testing, researchers strove for more broadly applicable testing procedures. It was not long before other countries, including Canada, started to consider the value in intelligence testing.

IQ TESTS

Although Binet began the standardized assessment of intellectual ability in France, U.S. psychologists soon took the lead. They also developed the IQ, or intelligence quotient. The IQ was a numerical, standardized measure of intelligence. Two families of individually administered IQ tests are used widely today: the Stanford–Binet scales and the Wechsler scales.

The Stanford–Binet Intelligence Scale Stanford University's **Lewis Terman**, a former public school administrator, appreciated the importance of Binet's method for assessing intelligence. He adapted Binet's test questions for U.S. schoolchildren, standardized the administration of the test, and developed age-level norms by giving the test to thousands of children. In 1916, he published the Stanford Revision of the Binet Tests, commonly referred to as the *Stanford–Binet Intelligence Scale* (Terman, 1916). If you have taken a pen-and-paper intelligence test as a Canadian student, it is likely that you took a version of this test.

With his new test, Terman provided a base for the concept of the **intelligence quotient**, or IQ (a term coined by William Stern in 1914). The IQ was the ratio of mental age to chronological age multiplied by 100 to eliminate decimals:

$$\text{IQ} = \text{mental age} \div \text{chronological age} \times 100$$

---

mental age In Binet's measure of intelligence, the age at which a child is performing intellectually, expressed in terms of the average age at which normal children achieve a particular score.

chronological age The number of months or years since an individual's birth.

intelligence quotient (IQ) An index derived from standardized tests of intelligence; originally obtained by dividing an individual's mental age by chronological age and then multiplying by 100; now directly computed as an IQ test score.

TABLE 10.1   Questions and Problems Similar to Those on the WAIS-IV

Verbal Comprehension Scale	
Similarities	In what ways are airplanes and submarines alike?
Vocabulary	What does *emulate* mean?
Perceptual Reasoning Scale	
Block Design	The test taker uses patterned blocks to reproduce designs provided by the examiner.
Picture Completion	The test taker examines a picture and says what is missing (for example, a horse does not have a mane).
Working Memory Scale	
Digit Span	Repeat the following numbers: 3 2 7 5 9.
Arithmetic	If you paid $8.50 for a movie ticket and $2.75 for popcorn, how much change would you have left from a $20 bill?
Processing Speed Scale	
Symbol Search	The test taker tries to determine whether one of two abstract symbols (such as Θ, ∀) appears on a longer list of symbols.
Cancellation	The test taker looks at visual displays and carries out the examiner's instructions (for example, "Draw a line through each blue square and green triangle").

A child with a chronological age of 8 whose test scores revealed a mental age of 10 had an IQ of 125 ($10 \div 8 \times 100 = 125$), whereas a child of that same chronological age who performed at the level of a 6-year-old had an IQ of 75 ($6 \div 8 \times 100 = 75$). Individuals who performed at the mental age equivalent to their chronological age had IQs of 100. Thus, the score of 100 was considered to be the average IQ.

The new Stanford–Binet test soon became a standard instrument in clinical psychology, psychiatry, and educational counselling. The Stanford–Binet contains a series of subtests, each tailored for a particular mental age. Since it was first introduced, the Stanford–Binet has undergone a series of revisions (Terman & Merrill, 1937, 1960, 1972; Thorndike, Hagen, & Sattler, 1986). Through those revisions, the range of the test has been extended to measure the IQ of very young children and very intelligent adults. In addition, the revisions have provided updated norms for age-appropriate average scores. The most recent, fifth edition of the Stanford–Binet test provides IQ estimates for individuals in the normal range of performance as well as for those individuals who are either mentally impaired or mentally gifted (Roid, 2003).

The Wechsler Intelligence Scales David Wechsler of Bellevue Hospital in New York set out to correct the dependence on verbal items in the assessment of adult intelligence. In 1939, he published the Wechsler–Bellevue Intelligence Scale, which combined verbal subtests with nonverbal, or performance, subtests. Thus, in addition to an overall IQ score, people were given separate estimates of verbal IQ and nonverbal IQ. After a few changes, the test was retitled the *Wechsler Adult Intelligence Scale*—the WAIS—in 1955. Today, you would take the WAIS-IV.

The WAIS-IV has 14 subtests that span *verbal* and *performance* aspects of IQ. **Table 10.1** provides examples of the types of questions you would find on the test. The verbal subtests cover areas such as vocabulary and comprehension. The performance subtests involve manipulation of materials and have little or no verbal content. If you were to take the WAIS-IV, you would perform the full range of subtests and receive three scores: a Verbal IQ, a Performance IQ, and a Full Scale or overall, IQ.

The WAIS-IV is designed for people age 16 years and older, but similar tests have been developed for children (see **Figure 10.1**). The Wechsler Intelligence Scale for Children—Fourth Edition (WISC-IV; Wechsler, 2003) is suited for children ages 6 to 16, and the Wechsler Preschool and Primary Scale of

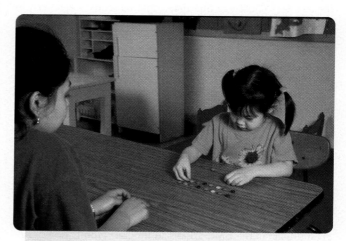

FIGURE 10.1   Intelligence Testing

A psychologist administers an intelligence test to a four-year-old child. The performance part of the test includes sorting an array of coloured candy. Why is performance an important component of an IQ assessment?

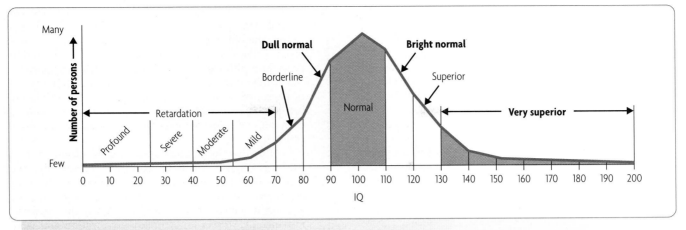

FIGURE 10.2 **Distribution of IQ Scores among a Large Sample**

IQ scores are normed so that a score of 100 is the population average (which means that just as many people score below 100 as score above 100). Scores between 90 and 110 are labelled normal. Scores above 120 are considered to be superior or very superior; scores below 70 represent increasing levels of mental disability.

From *Wechsler's Measurement and Appraisal of Adult Intelligence,* 5e by Joseph D. Matarazzo, copyright © 1978 by Oxford University Press, Inc. Used by permission of Oxford University Press, Inc.

Intelligence—Third Edition (WPPSI-III; Wechsler, 2002) is for children ages 2½ to 7¼ years. The recent revisions of both of these tests have made the materials more colourful, more contemporary, and more enjoyable for children.

The WAIS-IV, the WISC-IV, and the WPPSI-III form a family of intelligence tests that yield a Verbal IQ, a Performance IQ, and a Full Scale IQ at all age levels. In addition, they provide comparable subtest scores that allow researchers to track the development over time of more specific intellectual abilities. For this reason, the Wechsler scales are particularly valuable when the same individual is to be tested at different ages—for example, when a child's progress in response to different educational programs is monitored.

EXTREMES OF INTELLIGENCE

IQ scores are no longer derived by dividing mental age by chronological age. If you took the test today, your score would be added up and directly compared with the scores of other people your age; computers and large databases make this a much easier task than it would have been in the past. An IQ of 100 is "average" and would indicate that 50 percent of people your age had earned lower scores. As you can see in **Figure 10.2**, scores between 90 and 110 are labelled "normal." In this section, we consider controversial debates in psychology over differences in intelligence and the individuals whose IQ scores fall on either side of this range.

Intellectual Disabilities and Learning Disorders

When individuals below the age of 18 obtain valid IQ scores of 70 to 75 or below, they meet one criterion for a classification of **mental retardation**. However, as shown in **Table 10.2**, to be considered mentally retarded, individuals must also demonstrate limitations in their ability to bring adaptive skills to bear on life tasks (American Association on Mental Retardation [AAMR], 1992). In earlier times, the term mental retardation

TABLE 10.2	Diagnosis of Intellectual Disability
Intellectual disability is diagnosed if:	
• The individual's IQ is approximately two standard deviations below the mean on an intelligence test.	
• The individual demonstrates limitations in adaptive behaviour, such as	
Conceptual	
Language use	
Reading and writing	
Money concepts	
Social	
Responsibility for actions	
Gullibility	
Avoiding victimization	
Practical	
Meal preparation and eating	
Dressing	
Occupational skills	
• The age of onset is below 18.	

Source: Excerpted from American Association on Mental Retardation, 2002, p. 42.

mental retardation Condition in which individuals have IQ scores of 70 to 75 or below and also demonstrate limitations in their ability to bring adaptive skills to bear on life tasks.

was used to refer to people with IQs 70 to 75 and below. However, because of the expanded definition that includes consideration of adaptive behaviour, intellectual disability has become the more appropriate term (Schalock et al., 2007). When clinicians diagnose individuals with intellectual disability, they attempt to understand as much as possible what limitations each individual has with adaptive skills. Rather than categorizing people just on IQ, the contemporary goal is to provide environmental and social supports that are closely matched to each individual's needs.

Intellectual disability can be brought about by a number of genetic and environmental factors. For example, individuals with *Down syndrome*—a disorder caused by extra genetic material on the 21st chromosome—often have low IQs. Another genetic disorder, known as *phenylketonuria* (PKU), also has a potential negative impact on IQ (Gassio et al., 2005). However, through strict adherence to a special diet, people can control the negative effects of PKU if the disorder is diagnosed in infancy. Family studies suggest that genetic inheritance likely plays a role only in the range of what historically would have been called mild retardation (see Figure 10.2) (Plomin & Spinath, 2004). The more severe forms of retardation appear to be caused by the occurrence of spontaneous genetic abnormalities in an individual's development that are not heritable. The environment that is most often critical for intellectual disability is the prenatal environment. Pregnant women who suffer diseases such as rubella and syphilis are at risk for having children with intellectual disability. In addition, pregnant women who consume alcohol or other drugs, particularly during the early weeks of pregnancy, also increase the likelihood of having children with cognitive deficits (Bennet, Bendersky, & Lewis, 2008; Huizink & Mulder, 2006).

Historically, individuals with intellectual disability were educated—to the extent that they *were* educated—almost entirely in separate facilities. However, because evidence accumulated that these separate programs were not effective, the North American governments passed legislation requiring that students with disabilities be educated to the greatest extent possible in general classrooms (P. Williamson, McLeskey, Hoppey, & Rentz, 2006). The law recognizes that some levels of impairment still require students to receive separate instruction. However, about 45 percent of students diagnosed with intellectual disability spend some or much of each school day in classrooms with their peers.

In Canada, legislation has been put in place to protect those with intellectual disabilities. Unfortunately, however, this was not always the case. For example, in 1928 Alberta passed the Sexual Sterilization Act (Germany followed suit five years later). Then, in 1929, the province established a Eugenics Board to provide orders for the sterilization of individuals with reduced mental capacity. Some of the people who were considered to be unfit to bear children included new immigrants, alcoholics, epileptics, the poor, and Native people. Between 1929 and 1972, close to 3000 sterilization procedures took place in Alberta (for review see Wahlsten, 1997). Leilani Muir was admitted to the Provincial Training School (PTS) for Mental Defectives at age 11. As she had little formal education, she did not do well on the single IQ test she was given. Leilani subsequently underwent the sterilization procedure, although she was told only that her appendix was being removed. Later, when Leilani was in her twenties and had been trying unsuccessfully to have children, her physician discovered that her fallopian tubes had been cut and informed her as to why she could not have children.

After two failed marriages and the discovery that she was unable to have children, Leilani became depressed and attempted to enter a mental health program. She was required to take an IQ test—and did quite well on it. Leilani made headlines when she sued the Province of Alberta for wrongful sterilization and won. The 1996 settlement set a precedent for future settlements awarded to other sexual sterilization victims. The trial also revealed that the Eugenics Board, which made recommendations to the PTS, had acted outside of the law: The children in the PTS were routinely used in experiments, and there was cavalier disregard for their rights. Today there are many more laws that protect the rights of individuals with mental disabilities. There is also more interest in developing tests that accurately assess IQ in all populations.

IQ scores give general information about how well people are able to perform—with respect to age-appropriate norms—on a variety of verbal and nonverbal tasks. In some instances, there is cause for concern when IQ scores and performance fail to match up. People who present a sufficiently large discrepancy between their achievement and their measured IQ might be diagnosed with a **learning disorder**. Before clinicians diagnose a learning disorder, they need to rule out other factors that can lead to poor performance, such as low motivation, mediocre teaching, or physical problems (e.g., visual deficits). Many schools provide special assistance to students who have been diagnosed with learning disorders.

Giftedness Individuals are most likely to be labelled as *gifted* if they have an IQ score above 130. However, as with the definition of intellectual disability, researchers have suggested that the conception of giftedness is not adequately captured by IQ alone. For example, **Joseph Renzulli** (2005) has argued in favour of a "three-ring" conception of giftedness that characterizes giftedness along the dimensions of ability, creativity, and task commitment. In this view, individuals can be considered gifted with IQs that are above average but not necessarily superior. In addition, they need to show high levels of creativity and exert high levels of commitment to particular problems or domains of performance. This expanded definition of giftedness explains why people often are not gifted across the academic spectrum (Winner, 2000). Abilities, creativity, and task commitment may all differ, for example, between verbal and mathematical domains.

What qualities do gifted children generally possess? The formal study of gifted children began in 1921 when Lewis Terman (1925) began a long-term study of a group of over 1500 boys and girls who tested in the top 1 percent of their school populations. This group of individuals was followed all

---

learning disorder A disorder defined by a large discrepancy between individuals' measured IQ and their actual performance.

the way into their 80s (Holahan & Sears, 1995). Terman and his successors wanted to see how these children fared as they made their way through life. The questions Terman asked continue to shape the research agenda. For example, Terman explored the myth that gifted children have problems with social and emotional adjustment. Terman concluded just the opposite: He found his sample to be better adjusted than their less-gifted peers. However, more contemporary studies support the conclusion that gifted children are more introverted—more internally oriented (see Chapter 14)—than their peers (Sak, 2004). That orientation toward their own inner lives supports, in part, the task commitment that helps define giftedness. Still, gifted students report a reasonable level of participation in school activities. For example, a sample of 230 students attending a summer gifted program reported sports as their most frequent extracurricular or out-of-school activity (Olszewski-Kubilius & Lee, 2004). They were also involved in many academic clubs and competitions, many of which focused on mathematics.

Terman also documented that the children were largely successful in life. This is not surprising: As we will note again later in the chapter, IQ is a good predictor of occupational status and income. Thus, the concern about gifted individuals is not that they are not doing well. The concern, instead, is that they do not receive sufficient educational support to allow them to develop their gifts fully (Sternberg & Grigorenko, 2003; Winner, 2000). When giftedness is recognized as a multidimensional construct, gifted education must also have the flexibility to address individual students' particular talents. Smaller schools and school districts may have difficulty providing gifted education to a small population of students, in the same way that they may have difficulty providing additional support to a small population of students with learning disabilities.

STOP AND REVIEW

❶ What measures were originally used to compute the intelligence quotient?

❷ What two types of subtests appear on the latest version of the Wechsler Adult Intelligence Scale?

❸ How has the diagnosis of intellectual disability changed over the last 20 years?

❹ What dimensions define giftedness in the "three-ring" conception?

Theories of Intelligence

So far, we have seen some of the ways in which intelligence has been measured. You are now in a position to ask yourself: Do these tests capture everything that is meant by the word *intelligence*? Do these tests capture all abilities you believe constitute your own intelligence? To help you to think about those questions, we now review theories of intelligence. As you read about each theory, ask yourself whether its proponents would be comfortable using IQ as a measure of intelligence.

PSYCHOMETRIC THEORIES OF INTELLIGENCE

Psychometric theories of intelligence originated in much the same philosophical atmosphere that gave rise to IQ tests. **Psychometrics** is the field of psychology that specializes in mental testing in any of its facets, including personality assessment, intelligence evaluation, and aptitude measurement. Thus, psychometric approaches are intimately related to methods of testing. These theories examine the *statistical relationships* between different measures of ability, such as the 14 subtests of the WAIS-IV, and then make inferences about the nature of human intelligence on the basis of those relationships. The technique used most frequently is called *factor analysis*, a statistical procedure that detects a smaller number of dimensions, clusters, or factors within a larger set of independent variables. The goal of factor analysis is to identify the basic psychological dimensions of the concept being investigated. Of course, a statistical procedure only identifies statistical regularities; it is up to psychologists to suggest and defend interpretations of those regularities.

Charles Spearman carried out an early and influential application of factor analysis in the domain of intelligence. Spearman discovered that the performance of individuals on each of a variety of intelligence tests was highly correlated. From this pattern he concluded that there is a factor of *general intelligence*, or **g**, underlying all intelligent performance (Spearman, 1927). Each individual domain also has associated with it specific skills that Spearman called *s*. For example, a person's performance on tests of vocabulary or arithmetic depends both on his or her general intelligence and on domain-specific abilities. Researchers have used MRI scans to identify the basis for *g* in the brain. **Figure 10.3** displays some of the regions of the brain in which people who were relatively high on general intelligence had more brain tissue than people who were lower on general intelligence (Haier, Jung, Yeo, Head, & Alkire, 2004).

FIGURE 10.3 The Brain Bases of General Intelligence

After completing the WAIS to measure general intelligence, individuals underwent MRI scans to reveal the structure of their brains. The coloured regions are areas in which individuals with relatively higher general intelligence had more brain tissue.

Reprinted from *NeuroImage, 23*, R. J. Haier et al., "Structural brain variation and general intelligence," pp. 425–433, copyright © 2004, with permission of Elsevier.

psychometrics The field of psychology that specializes in mental testing.

g According to Spearman, the factor of general intelligence underlying all intelligent performance.

CAN YOU TRUST ASSESSMENT ON THE WEB?

After reading a chapter on intelligence, students often wonder how they would do if they took an IQ test. Nowadays, it is pretty easy for you to visit one of several websites to click through a test and get an IQ score. Do the numbers you get mean much of anything? We will answer that question by reviewing some of the concepts we have introduced in this chapter.

To give our analysis, we needed some data—so we asked a friend, whom we will call Poindexter, to take some online IQ tests for us. The first site he visited had four different tests, which gave us the opportunity to assess reliability. Recall that reliability is about consistency: Does each test, which claims to be measuring the same thing, yield very nearly the same score? In fact, Poindexter's four scores were 116, 117, 129, and 130. If you refer back to Figure 10.2, you will see that all these scores indicate that Poindexter is above average (how nice for Poindexter!), but two place him in "bright normal" and two place him right at the border of "superior"

and "very superior." These supposed IQ tests are not particularly reliable.

If the tests are not reliable, they cannot be valid. For the moment, let's suppose they were reliable. Let's consider why, in any case, we would be concerned about their validity: To what extent do the tests measure what they are supposed to measure? The IQ scores at the site Poindexter visited were calculated by comparing his performance (the number he got right out of 20 questions) to the performance of those individuals who had preceded him to the site. By assuming a bell-shaped distribution like the one shown in Figure 10.2, the site estimates IQ. Can you see the problems here? First, we have no reason to believe that, for the people who visit this site, the average IQ (measured by a traditional, reliable offline test) would be, as it should be, 100. Does it not seem likely that there would be self-selection among the people who would take IQ tests on the web? Second, we have no reason to believe that everyone took the tests under the same standard

circumstances. For example, the tests rely somewhat on vocabulary questions. How can we be sure that people did not pull out a handy dictionary (or access one online) to enhance their scores? ("Look, Ma, I always told you I was a genius!")

The World Wide Web provides a vast number of opportunities for you to assess IQ as well as other performance and personality constructs. Use the knowledge you have gained in this chapter to do your own careful assessment of the reliability and validity of any scores you obtain on the web.

Meanwhile, Poindexter has become something of an online IQ addict. His best score so far is a 159 on a "European IQ test." Poindexter is convinced that 159 is a valid measure of his IQ. Are you convinced too?

- Besides comparing overall scores, how might you assess the reliability of different IQ tests on the web?

- What could you do to standardize conditions for test taking on the web?

Raymond Cattell (1963), using more advanced factor analytic techniques, determined that general intelligence can be broken down into two relatively independent components, which he called crystallized and fluid intelligence. **Crystallized intelligence** involves the knowledge a person has already acquired and the ability to access that knowledge; it is measured by tests of vocabulary, arithmetic, and general information. **Fluid intelligence** is the ability to see complex relationships and solve problems; it is measured by tests of block designs and spatial visualization in which the background information needed to solve a problem is included or readily apparent. Crystallized intelligence allows you to cope well with your life's recurring, concrete challenges; fluid intelligence helps you attack novel, abstract problems.

As shown in **Figure 10.4**, there are five kinds of *content* in this model—visual, auditory, symbolic, semantic, and behavioural; six kinds of *products*—units, classes, relations, systems, transformations, and implications; and five kinds of *operations*—evaluation, convergent production, divergent production, memory, and cognition. Each task performed by the intellect can be identified according to the particular types of content, products, and operations involved. Further, Guilford believes that each content-product-operation combination (each small cube in the model) represents a distinct mental ability. For example, as Figure 10.4 shows, a test of vocabulary would assess your ability for *cognition* of *units* with *semantic content*. Learning a dance routine, in contrast, requires *memory* for *behavioural systems*.

This theoretical model is analogous to a chemist's periodic table of elements. By means of such a systematic framework, intellectual factors, like chemical elements, may be postulated before they are discovered. In 1961, when Guilford proposed his model, nearly 40 intellectual abilities had been identified. Researchers have since accounted for over 100, which shows the predictive value of Guilford's conception of intelligence (Guilford, 1985).

---

crystallized intelligence The facet of intelligence involving the knowledge a person has already acquired and the ability to access that knowledge; measured by vocabulary, arithmetic, and general information tests.

fluid intelligence The aspect of intelligence that involves the ability to see complex relationships and solve problems.

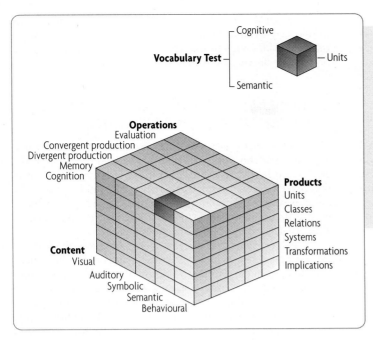

Vocabulary Test — Cognitive / Semantic — Units

Operations
Evaluation
Convergent production
Divergent production
Memory
Cognition

Products
Units
Classes
Relations
Systems
Transformations
Implications

Content
Visual
Auditory
Symbolic
Semantic
Behavioural

FIGURE 10.4 The Structure of Intellect

In his structure of intellect model, J. P. Guilford specified three features of intellectual tasks: the content, or type of information; the product, or form in which information is represented; and the operation, or type of mental activity performed. Each task performed by the intellect can be identified according to the particular types of content, products, and operations involved. For example, a test of vocabulary would assess your ability for *cognition* of *units* with *semantic content.*

Reprinted with permission from J. P. Guilford, "The Structure of the Intellect" from *Way Beyond the IQ,* 1977, p. 161. Copyright © 1977 Creative Education Foundation.

Since Guilford, many psychologists have broadened their conceptions of intelligence to include much more than performance on traditional IQ tests. We now examine two types of theories that go beyond IQ.

STERNBERG'S TRIARCHIC THEORY OF INTELLIGENCE

Robert Sternberg (1999) also stresses the importance of cognitive processes in problem solving as part of his more general theory of intelligence. Sternberg outlines a triarchic—three-part—theory. His three types of intelligence—analytical, creative, and practical—all represent different ways of characterizing effective performance.

Analytical intelligence provides the basic information-processing skills that people apply to life's many familiar tasks. This type of intelligence is defined by the components, or mental processes, that underlie thinking and problem solving. Sternberg identifies three types of components that are central to information processing: (1) knowledge acquisition components, for learning new facts; (2) performance components, for problem-solving strategies and techniques; and (3) metacognitive components, for selecting strategies and monitoring progress toward success. To put some of your analytical intelligence to work, we would like you now to try the exercise in **Table 10.3**.

How did you do on the anagrams? To solve these anagrams, you mostly needed to use performance components and metacognitive components. The performance components are what allowed you to manipulate the letters in your head; the metacognitive components are what allowed you to have strategies for finding solutions. Consider T-R-H-O-S. How did you mentally transform that into SHORT? A good strategy to get started is to try consonant clusters that are probable in English—such as S-H and T-H. Selecting strategies requires metacognitive components; carrying them out requires

performance components. Note that a good strategy will sometimes fail. Consider T-N-K-H-G-I. What makes this anagram hard for many people is that K-N is not a very likely combination to start a word, whereas T-H is. Did you stare at this anagram for a while, trying to turn it into a word beginning with T-H? If you have not figured it out yet, think about kings and horses.

By breaking down various tasks into their components, researchers can pinpoint the processes that differentiate the

TABLE 10.3   Using Analytical Intelligence

The following is a list of *anagrams*—scrambled words. As quickly as possible, try to find a solution for each anagram (Sternberg, 1986b).

1. H-U-L-A-G _____
2. P-T-T-M-E _____
3. T-R-H-O-S _____
4. T-N-K-H-G-I _____
5. T-E-W-I-R _____
6. L-L-A-O-W _____
7. R-I-D-E-V _____
8. O-C-C-H-U _____
9. T-E-N-R-E _____
10. C-I-B-A-S _____

Turn to page 315 for the solutions.

performance outcomes of individuals with different IQs. For example, researchers might discover that the metacognitive components of high-IQ students prompt them to select different strategies to solve a particular type of problem than do their lower-IQ peers. The difference in strategy selection accounts for the high-IQ students' greater problem-solving success. Did you come up with the word KNIGHT for the anagram in Table 10.3?

Creative intelligence captures people's ability to deal with two extremes: novel versus very routine problems. Suppose, for example, a group of individuals found themselves stranded after an accident. You would credit with intelligence the person in the group who could most quickly help the group find its way home. In other circumstances, you would recognize as intelligent the behaviour of someone who was able to perform routine tasks automatically. If, for example, a group of people carried out the same tasks day after day, you would be most impressed by the individual who could complete the tasks successfully with the least amount of "new" thought.

Practical intelligence is reflected in the management of day-to-day affairs. It involves your ability to *adapt* to new and different contexts, *select* appropriate contexts, and effectively *shape* your environment to suit your needs. Practical intelligence is bound to particular contexts. To measure practical intelligence, researchers must immerse themselves in those contexts.

> A team of researchers set the goal of measuring practical intelligence among adolescents from the Yup'ik Eskimo group in Alaska (Grigorenko et al., 2004). Although the Yup'ik people live in modern houses with electricity, oil, and telephones, many communities can be reached only by airplane during the long, harsh winters. For that reason, the measure of practical intelligence focused on the types of knowledge that remain relevant to survival in Yup'ik communities. Consider this question:
>
> Uncle Markus knows a lot about hunting wolverines. He is most likely to catch a wolverine when he sets his trap:
>
> **a.** on a slanted tree.
> **b.** in the hollow of a dead tree.
> **c.** far from any water.
> **d.** near a frozen river.
>
> Did you choose (a) as the correct answer? The practical intelligence test consisted of 36 items of this sort. The adolescent students in the sample completed this test. In addition, the researchers gathered evaluations from other members of the group, including adults and elders, about which adolescents they thought could be best described as, for example, *umyuartuli*—"a good thinker, one who comes up with novel solutions to problems and uses the mind to survive" (p. 191). The Yup'ik adolescents produced a range of scores on the measure of practical intelligence. In general, those who lived in urban environments had less practical intelligence than those who lived in rural environments. In addition, the adolescents who had the highest levels of practical intelligence also earned the most positive evaluation for traits such as *umyuartuli*.

---

emotional intelligence (EI) Type of intelligence defined as the abilities to perceive, appraise, and express emotions accurately and appropriately, to use emotions to facilitate thinking, to understand and analyze emotions, to use emotional knowledge effectively, and to regulate one's emotions to promote both emotional and intellectual growth.

You can see from this example why the concept of practical intelligence has different meanings in different contexts. However, the general idea remains the same: People can bring more or less practical intelligence to bear on their day-to-day tasks.

GARDNER'S MULTIPLE INTELLIGENCES AND EMOTIONAL INTELLIGENCE

Howard Gardner (1983, 1999) has also proposed a theory that expands the definition of intelligence beyond those skills covered on an IQ test. Gardner identifies numerous intelligences that cover a range of human experience. The value of any of the abilities differs across human societies, according to what is needed by, useful to, and prized by a given society. As shown in **Table 10.4**, Gardner identified eight intelligences.

Gardner argues that Western society promotes the first two intelligences, whereas non-Western societies often value others. For example, in the Caroline Islands of Micronesia, sailors must be able to navigate long distances without maps, using only their spatial intelligence and bodily kinesthetic intelligence. Such abilities count more in that society than the ability to write a term paper. In Bali, where artistic performance is part of everyday life, musical intelligence and talents involved in co-ordinating intricate dance steps are highly valued. Interpersonal intelligence is more central to collectivist societies such as Japan, where co-operative action and communal life are emphasized, than it is in individualistic societies such as the United States (Triandis, 1990) and Canada.

Assessing these kinds of intelligence demands more than paper-and-pencil tests and simple quantified measures. Gardner's theory of intelligence requires that the individual be observed and assessed in a variety of life situations as well as in the small slices of life depicted in traditional intelligence tests.

In recent years, researchers have begun to explore a type of intelligence—*emotional intelligence*—that is related to Gardner's concepts of *interpersonal* and *intrapersonal* intelligence (see Table 10.4). **Emotional intelligence (EI)** is defined as having four major components (Mayer, Roberts, & Barsade, 2008a; Mayer, Salovey, & Caruso, 2008b):

- The ability to perceive, appraise, and express emotions accurately and appropriately
- The ability to use emotions to facilitate thinking
- The ability to understand and analyze emotions and to use emotional knowledge effectively
- The ability to regulate one's emotions to promote both emotional and intellectual growth

This definition reflects a new view of the positive role of emotion as it relates to intellectual functioning: Emotions can make thinking more intelligent, and people can think intelligently about their emotions and those of others.

Researchers have begun to demonstrate that emotional intelligence has important consequences for everyday life. Consider the emotional experiences students have in school settings. Suppose Poindexter does poorly on an exam. If he can prevent himself from being overwhelmed by negative emotions, he's likely to fare better in the future. In general, higher emotional intelligence should allow students to deal more successfully with emotional aspects of academic performance. Let's see how researchers have tested that hypothesis.

A team of researchers had a group of 378 students complete a measure of emotional intelligence (EI) (Rode et al., 2007). The measure required the students, for example, to view colour photographs of faces and indicate which emotions the faces portrayed. As a measure of academic performance, the researchers obtained the cumulative GPA of each student. In addition, the researchers videotaped the students giving three-minute speeches during group discussions. Judges viewed the videotapes to determine features such as the quality of each student's arguments. When the researchers assessed the relationship between EI and performance, they discovered that high-EI students were more effective public speakers. For other academic measures, the students' relative motivation affected the importance of EI. For example, only those high-EI students who reported themselves to be thorough and careful had higher GPAs than their peers.

These results confirm the importance of emotional intelligence. Our review of intelligence testing and theories of intelligence sets the stage for a discussion of the societal circumstances that make the topic of intelligence so controversial.

STOP AND REVIEW

❶ Why did Spearman come to believe in *g*, general intelligence?

❷ What are the three types of intelligence in Sternberg's triarchic theory?

❸ In Gardner's theory, what kind of intelligence might determine whether someone could be a successful sculptor?

CRITICAL THINKING Consider the study relating emotional intelligence to performance. Why is it important to obtain measures of the participants' success from their GPAs?

The Politics of Intelligence

We have seen that contemporary conceptions of intelligence reject the narrow linking of a score on an IQ test with a person's intelligence. Even so, IQ tests remain the most frequent measure of "intelligence" in Western society. Due to the prevalence of IQ testing and the availability of IQ scores, it becomes easy to compare different groups according to their "average" IQ. In many countries, such ethnic and racial group comparisons have often been used as evidence for the innate genetic inferiority of members of minority groups. We will briefly examine the history of this practice of using IQ test scores to index the alleged mental inferiority of certain groups. We will then briefly review one of the main controversial issues in intelligence research: that of racial differences in IQ. Finally, we will look at current evidence on the nature and nurture of intelligence and IQ test performance. You will see that this is one of the most politically volatile issues in psychology because public policies about immigration

Why were IQ tests given to immigrants as they arrived at Ellis Island? How were these tests used to draw conclusions about genetic inferiority?

good–bad in Greek.) Martin Kallikak was a Revolutionary War soldier who had an illegitimate son with a woman described as developmentally disabled. Their union eventually produced 480 descendants. Goddard classified 143 of them as "defective" and only 46 as normal. He found crime, alcoholism, mental disorders, and illegitimacy common among the rest of the family members. By contrast, when Martin Kallikak later married a "good woman," their union produced 496 descendants, only three of whom were classified as "defective." Goddard also found that many offspring from this high-quality union had become "eminent" (Goddard, 1914). Goddard came to believe that heredity determined intelligence, genius, and eminence on the positive side. On the negative side, he arrayed delinquency, alcoholism, sexual immorality, developmental disability, and maybe even poverty (McPherson, 1985).

Goddard's genetic inferiority argument was further reinforced by the fact that, on the World War I Army Intelligence tests, African-Americans and other racial minorities scored lower than the white majority. Louis Terman, who promoted IQ testing in the United States, commented in this unscientific manner on the data he had helped collect on U.S. racial minorities:

> Their dullness seems to be racial. . . . There seems no possibility at present of convincing society that they should not be allowed to reproduce, although from a eugenics point of view, they constitute a grave problem because of their unusually prolific breeding. (Terman, 1916, pp. 91–92)

The names have changed, but the problem remains the same. In the United States today, African-Americans and Latinos score, on average, lower than Asian-Americans and whites on standardized intelligence tests. Of course, there are individuals in all groups who score at the highest (and the lowest) extremes of the IQ scale. Some Canadian studies have also shown similar patterns of results between white, Asian and black (Rushton, 1992, 1995; Rushton & Jensen, 2005), and the findings have resulted in much controversy.

Controversy regarding Race and Intelligence

J. Philippe Rushton, a professor of psychology at the University of Western Ontario in London, Ontario, and a Fellow of the American, British, and Canadian Psychological Associations, has been involved in one of the most highly contentious debates in psychology related to the existence of differences in intelligence between ethnic groups. Since the early 1990s, Rushton reported on a number of measures including intelligence, brain size, and social variables. In these reports (Rushton, 1991, 1992, 1995, 1999; Rushton & Jensen, 2005), Rushton indicated that a clear pattern existed: Individuals of black (African and Negroid) descent scored lowest on measures of intelligence and brain size; individuals of Oriental (East Asian and Mongoloid) descent scored highest on intelligence tests and had the largest brains; and whites (Europeans and Caucasoids) scored somewhere in the middle on intelligence and brain size. The findings were met with an immediate accusation of racism. Many people in Ontario and around Canada argued that Rushton should be fired for his racist thoughts. He was even investigated by the Ontario Provincial Police and the Ontario Human Rights Commission for "infecting the learning environment with academic racism" (Rushton, 1998). These charges were dismissed. Although the university was forced to cancel his classes for fear for his safety, Rushton was not fired.

quotas, educational resources, and more may be based on how group IQ data are interpreted.

THE HISTORY OF GROUP COMPARISONS

In the early 1900s, psychologist Henry Goddard advocated mental testing of all immigrants and the *selective exclusion* of those who were found to be "mentally defective." Such views may have contributed to a hostile national climate against admission of certain immigrant groups (Zenderland, 1998). Indeed, the United States Congress passed the 1924 Immigration Restriction Act, which made it national policy to administer intelligence tests to immigrants as they arrived at Ellis Island in New York Harbor. Vast numbers of Jewish, Italian, and Russian immigrants, as well as immigrants of other nationalities, were classified as "morons" on the basis of standard IQ tests. Some psychologists interpreted these statistical findings as evidence that immigrants from southern and eastern Europe were genetically inferior to those from the hardy northern and western European stock (see Ruch, 1937). However, as you may have already suspected, these "inferior" groups were also least familiar with the dominant language and culture embedded in the IQ tests because they had immigrated most recently. Within a few decades, these group differences completely disappeared from IQ tests, but the theory of racially inherited differences in intelligence persisted.

Goddard (1917) and others then went beyond merely associating low IQ with hereditary racial and ethnic origins. They added moral worthlessness, mental deficiency, and immoral social behaviour to the mix of negatives related to low IQ. Evidence for their view came from case studies of infamous families. Consider the *Kallikak* family, a family with one "good seed" side and one "bad seed" side to its family tree. (In his study, Goddard renamed the family Kallikak, which means

Since Rushton first reported on his findings, there have been both supporters and critics of his work. Some have argued that his work has the scientific rigour required for serious scholarly work (Gottfredson, 2005; Lynn, 2005; Jensen, 1995), whereas others have challenged this argument and have questioned the methodology of the research, the accuracy of the measurements, and whether the studies actually test intelligence (e.g., Lieberman, 2001; Nisbett, 2005; Peters, 1995a; 1995b). The controversy lives on in the media and online about whether his research was discriminatory.

A similar controversy emerged when *The Bell Curve* (Herrnstein & Murray, 1994), a best-selling book, highlighted British psychologist Richard Lynn's two-decades-long survey of global patterns of intelligence. Lynn found East Asian descendants of peoples populating the Pacific Rim to have IQs in the range of 101 to 111, caucasians in Europe to have IQs of approximately 100, and blacks in Africa to have IQs of approximately 70. Interestingly, the students of mixed race in South Africa had an IQ of approximately 85, which is similar to that found in the blacks in the United States, Britain, and the Caribbean. The data, of course, do not mean that all blacks have IQ scores lower than all whites and Asians; in each group, there are individuals who score at the highest and lowest levels.

Is it reasonable to compare the IQ scores of members of different races? Many would argue that it is very important to consider. Some research suggests that IQ tests can predict school (Lynn, Misenberg, Mikk, & Williams, 2007) and job performance for individuals from all groups. Some, like Rushton (1995, 1999), argue that IQ can predict things such as crime, delinquency, health, and other socially relevant behaviours. Perhaps not surprisingly, many scholars propose a different interpretation of these findings by suggesting that the definition of IQ and its measurement have been somewhat biased (Valencia & Suzuki, 2001), or that it is difficult to tease out the "pure" contribution of heredity versus environment when these two factors interact (Suzuki & Aronson, 2005).

Whether people question the validity of the findings, or even their intent, we are left with the results of many studies that document differences in IQ scores. The controversy we just reviewed pits one research tradition or interpretation against another. One tradition has been to attribute these differences to genetic inferiority (nature). After we discuss the evidence for genetic differences in IQ, we will consider a second possibility—that differences in environments (nurture) exert a significant impact on IQ. The validity of either explanation, or some combination of them, has important social, economic, and political consequences.

HEREDITY AND IQ

How can researchers assess the extent to which intelligence is genetically determined? Any answer to this question requires that the researcher choose some measure as an index of intelligence. Thus the question becomes not whether "intelligence," in the abstract, is influenced by heredity but, in most cases, whether IQs are similar within family trees. To answer this more limited question, researchers need to tease apart the effects of shared genes and shared environment. One method is to compare functioning in identical twins (monozygotic), fraternal twins (dizygotic), and relatives with other degrees of genetic overlap. **Figure 10.5** presents correlations between IQ scores of individuals on the basis of their degree of genetic relationship (Plomin & Petrill, 1997). As you can see, the greater the genetic similarity, the greater the IQ similarity. (Note in these data that the impact of environment is also revealed in the greater IQ similarities among those who have been reared together.)

Researchers use results of this sort to try to estimate the *heritability* of IQ. A **heritability estimate** of a particular trait, such as intelligence, is based on the proportion of the variability in test scores on that trait that can be traced to genetic factors. The estimate is found by computing the variation in all the test scores for a given population (university students or psychiatric patients, for example) and then identifying what portion of the total variance is due to genetic or inherited factors. This is done by comparing individuals who have different degrees of genetic overlap. Researchers who have reviewed the variety of studies on heritability of IQ conclude that about 50 percent of the variance in IQ scores is due to genetic makeup (Grigorenko, 2000).

What is perhaps even more interesting, however, is that heritability *increases* across the life span: To document this increase, researchers have often assessed twins' IQ repeatedly over several years. Let's consider a study that took 13 years to complete.

> A team of researchers began their study by recruiting 209 pairs of 5-year-old twins (Hoekstra, Bartels, & Boomsma, 2007). At age 5, the children completed an IQ test that provided estimates for both verbal and nonverbal IQ. The researchers measured the twins' IQs again at ages 7, 10, 12, and 18 years. Given the duration of the study, you won't be surprised that some twins dropped out over time. However, the researchers were able to obtain IQs for 115 pairs at all five ages. The data analyses showed that the twins' IQs were reasonably stable over time. Across all the twin pairs, the correlations between scores at age 5 and scores at age 18 were 0.51 for verbal IQ and 0.47 for nonverbal IQ. To estimate heritability, the researchers compared the correlations between MZ and DZ twins at each age. For verbal IQ, the heritability estimate was 46 percent at age 5 and increased to 84 percent at age 18. For nonverbal IQ, the heritability estimate was 64 percent at age 5 and increased to 74 percent at age 18.

Many people are surprised by this sort of result, because it seems that environments should have more, not less, of an effect as people get older. Here's how researchers explain such counterintuitive findings: "It is possible that genetic dispositions nudge us toward environments that accentuate our genetic propensities, thus leading to increased heritability throughout the life span" (Plomin & Petrill, 1997, p. 61).

Let's return now to the point at which genetic analysis becomes controversial: test score differences between African-Americans and white Americans. Several decades ago, the gap between the scores of whites and blacks was roughly 15 IQ points. However, researchers estimated that the gap closed by 4 to 7 points in the 30 years from 1972 to 2002 (Dickens & Flynn, 2006). The closing of the gap suggests environmental influences, but the lingering difference has prompted many people to suggest that there are unbridgeable genetic differences

---

heritability estimate A statistical estimate of the degree of inheritance of a given trait or behaviour, assessed by the degree of similarity between individuals who vary in their extent of genetic similarity.

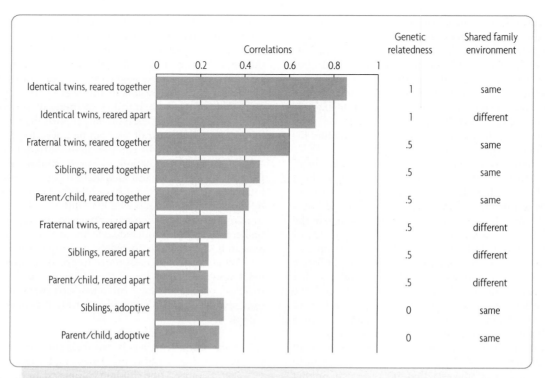

FIGURE 10.5 IQ and Genetic Relationship

This figure presents the correlations between the IQ scores of identical (monozygotic) and fraternal (dizygotic) twins reared together (in the same home environments) or reared apart (in different home environments). For comparison, it also includes data for siblings (brothers and sisters) and parents and children, both biological and adoptive. The data demonstrate the importance of both genetic factors (the numbers under "genetic relatedness" specify the overlap of genetic material) and environmental factors. For example, identical twins show higher correlations between their IQs than do fraternal twins—a genetic influence. However, both types of twins show higher correlations when raised together—an environmental influence.

Reprinted from *Intelligence, 24,* R. Plomin & S. A. Petrill, "Genetics and Intelligence: What's New?" pp. 53–77, copyright © 1997, with permission from Elsevier.

between the races (Hernnstein & Murray, 1994). However, even if IQ is highly heritable, does this difference reflect genetic inferiority of individuals in the lower-scoring group? The answer is no. Heritability is based on an estimate *within* one given group. It cannot be used to interpret differences *between* groups, no matter how large those differences are on an objective test.

Heritability estimates pertain only to the average in a given population of individuals. We know, for instance, that the heritability estimate for height is quite high—in the range of 0.93 to 0.96 (Silventoinen et al., 2006). Still, you cannot determine how much of your height is due to genetic influences. The same argument is true for IQ; despite high heritability estimates, we cannot determine the specific genetic contribution to any individual's IQ or to mean IQ scores among groups. The fact that on an IQ test one racial or ethnic group scores lower than another group does not mean that the difference between these groups is genetic in origin, even if the heritability estimate for IQ scores is high as assessed within a group (Hunt & Carlson, 2007).

Another point of controversy is the concept of race itself. When people assert that an IQ gap is caused by genetics, they make the strong assumption that genetic analysis permits clear distinctions among races. Researchers on IQ generally

acknowledge that race is both a biological and a social construct. For example, the social convention in the United States is typically to call people who have any African ancestry *black*. Consider the remarkable golfer Tiger Woods, who has often been labelled—and discriminated against—as African-American even though his actual heritage is much more complex (his ancestors were white, black, Thai, Chinese, and Native American). Woods provides an excellent example of circumstances in which social judgments do not follow biological reality. Even so, some intelligence researchers argue that genetic differences are sufficient among races for meaningful comparisons to be made (Hunt & Carlson, 2007). Other researchers argue just as strenuously that the concept of race is so driven by social circumstances that group comparisons are useless (Sternberg & Grigorenko, 2007; Sternberg, Grigorenko, & Kidd, 2005).

Surely genetics plays a sizeable role in influencing individuals' scores on IQ tests, as it does on many other traits and abilities. We have argued, however, that heredity does not constitute an adequate explanation for IQ differences between racial and ethnic groups. It has a necessary, but not sufficient, role in our understanding of such performance effects. Let's turn now to the role the environment may play in creating the IQ gap.

This photo shows Nobel-Prize-winning chemist Marie Curie with her daughters Irene (on the left) and Eve (on the right). Irene also won a Nobel Prize in chemistry and Eve became a famous author. Why do families like this one encourage researchers to attempt to understand the impact of heredity and environment on IQ?

ENVIRONMENTS AND IQ

Since heritability estimates are less than 1.0, we know that genetic inheritance is not solely responsible for anyone's IQ.

Environments must also affect IQ, but how can we assess what aspects of the environment are important influences on IQ? What features of your environment affect your potential to score well on an IQ test (Beiser & Gotowiec, 2000; Ceci, 1999; Rowe, 1997; Suzuki & Valencia, 1997)? Environments are complex stimulus packages that vary on many dimensions, both physical and social, and may be experienced in different ways by those within them. Even children in the same family setting do not necessarily share the same critical psychological environment. Think back to growing up in your family. If you had siblings, did they all get the same attention from parents, did conditions of stress change over the course of time, did the family's financial resources change, did your parents' marital status change? It is obvious that environments are made up of many components that are in a dynamic relationship and that change over time. So it becomes difficult for psychologists to say what kinds of environmental conditions—attention, stress, poverty, health, war, and so on—actually have an impact on IQ.

Researchers have most often focused on more global measures of environment, such as the socioeconomic status of the family. For example, in a large-scale longitudinal study of more than 26 000 children, the best predictors of a child's IQ at age four were the family's socioeconomic status and the level of the mother's education. This was equally true for African-American and white children (Broman, Nichols, & Kennedy, 1975). Similarly, **Figure 10.6** shows an overall impact of social class on IQ.

Why does social class affect IQ? Wealth versus poverty can affect intellectual functioning in many ways, health and educational resources being two of the most obvious. Poor health during pregnancy and low birth weight are solid predictors of a child's lowered mental ability. Children born into impoverished families often suffer from poor nutrition; many go to school hungry and are thus less able to concentrate on learning tasks. Furthermore, impoverished homes may suffer from a lack of

The personal attention children receive can affect their intelligence. In the "separate but equal" schoolroom of 1940s Tennessee (at left), African-American children received little attention. In contrast, this parent (at right) is deeply involved in her child's education. How do these types of environmental differences affect IQ?

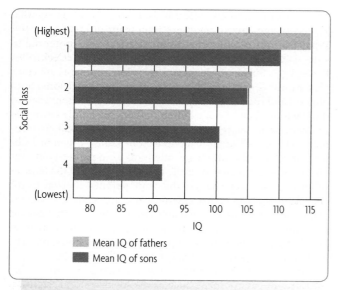

FIGURE 10.6 The Relationship Among Heredity, Environment, and IQ

This chart shows evidence for the contribution of heredity and environment to IQ scores. There are similar IQs for fathers and sons (influence of heredity), but the IQs of both fathers and sons are related to social class (influence of environment).

books, written media, computers, and other materials that add to one's mental stimulation. The "survival orientation" of poor parents, especially in single-parent families, which leaves parents little time or energy to play with and intellectually stimulate their children, is detrimental to performance on tasks such as those on standard IQ tests.

Researchers have spent the past 40 years developing programs intended to counteract the effects of impoverished environments. The Head Start program was first funded by the U.S. federal government in 1965 to address the "physical health, developmental, social, educational, and emotional needs of low-income children and to increase the capacity of the families

to care for their children, through empowerment and supportive services" (Kassebaum, 1994, p. 123). The idea of Head Start and similar programs was not to move children into privileged environments, but to improve the environments into which they were born. Children are exposed to special preschool education, they receive decent daily meals, and their parents are given advice on health and other aspects of child rearing.

Consider a program started in 1962 at the High/Scope Perry preschool in Ypsilanti, Michigan (Schweinhart, 2004). The program focused on a group of three- and four-year-old low-income African-American children who had been evaluated as being at risk for school failure. The High/Scope Perry program provided the children with a classroom environment that focused on *participatory education*: Children were encouraged to initiate and plan their own activities and activities for the classroom group. In addition, the program involved parents in the children's educations through home visits and parent group meetings. The researchers followed the students who participated in the program for the next 40 years. **Figure 10.7** compares the outcomes of participants to a group of students from the same population who did not participate. As you can see, High/Scope Perry students had higher IQs at age five than their peers outside the program. They were also considerably more likely to graduate from a regular high school and have higher paying jobs at age 40.

Similar data have emerged from an early intervention program in Chicago: Fifteen years after participating in a preschool program, students saw many of the same advantages as the High/Scope Perry group, including much higher rates of high-school graduation (Reynolds, Temple, Robertson, & Mann, 2001). These studies provide strong evidence for the importance of the environment for intellectual development. They also provide concrete models for programs that can change the lives of children who are at risk.

CULTURE AND THE VALIDITY OF IQ TESTS

People would probably care much less about IQ scores if they did not allow for such useful predictions: Extensive research

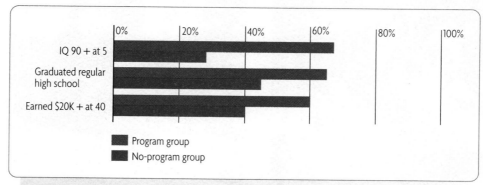

FIGURE 10.7 The Impact of a Preschool Intervention

Students who participated in the High/Scope Perry preschool program had better outcomes than students who were not participants.

From Lawrence J. Schweinhart, "The High/Scope Perry Preschool Study Through Age 40."

shows that IQ scores are valid predictors of school grades from elementary school through college or university, of occupational status, and of performance in many jobs (Gottfredson, 2002; Nettlebeck & Wilson, 2005). These patterns of results suggest that IQ tests validly measure intellectual abilities that are very basic and important for the types of success that are valued in Western cultures: Intelligence, as measured by IQ, directly affects success. IQ distinctions can also affect academic and job performance indirectly by changing one's motives and beliefs. Those with higher IQ scores are likely to have had more success experiences in school, to have become more motivated to study, to have developed an achievement orientation, and to have become optimistic about their chances of doing well. Also, children scoring low on IQ tests may get "tracked" into schools, classes, or programs that are inferior and may even be stigmatizing to the students' sense of self-competence. In this way, IQ can be affected by environment and, in turn, can create new environments for the child—some better, some worse. IQ assessment may thus become destiny—whatever the child's underlying genetic endowment for intelligence.

To make meaningful comparisons, researchers must use tests that have been validated for each separate group (Hunt & Carlson, 2007). However, critics have often argued that there are systematic biases in IQ tests that make them invalid across cultures. For example, questions on IQ tests that assess verbal comprehension presuppose that certain types of knowledge will have been accessible to all test takers (see Table 10.1). In reality, people from different cultures often have quite different background knowledge that affects the difficulty of those questions (Fagan & Holland, 2007). In addition, forms of tests and testing may not match cultural notions of intelligence or appropriate behaviour (Sternberg, 2007). Consider one case of negative evaluations in the classroom:

> When children of Latino immigrant parents go to school, the emphasis on understanding rather than speaking, on respecting the teacher's authority rather than expressing one's own opinions leads to negative academic assessment in the new school. . . . Hence, a valued mode of communication in one culture—respectful listening— becomes the basis for a rather sweeping negative evaluation in the school setting where self-assertive speaking is the valued mode of communication. (Greenfield, 1997, p. 1120)

These immigrant children must learn how they must behave in the new classrooms to make their teachers understand the extent of their intelligence.

One of the standard concerns about IQ tests is that they are biased toward or against members of different cultures: Critics have argued that group differences in IQ scores are caused by systematic bias in the test questions, making them invalid and unfair for minorities. Even when tests are made more "culture-fair," there remains a racial gap (Neisser et al., 1996). In fact, the issue may be more a problem of the *context* of the test rather than the *content* of the test. **Claude Steele** (1997; Steele & Aronson, 1995, 1998) has argued that people's performance on ability tests is influenced by **stereotype threat** (also known as *stereotype vulnerability*)—the threat of being at risk for confirming a negative stereotype of one's group. Research suggests that a person's belief that a negative stereotype is relevant in a situation can function to bring about the poor performance encoded in the stereotype. Let's consider an example of stereotype threat at work.

The study focused on first- and second-generation immigrants from the West Indies (Deaux et al., 2007). The researchers hypothesized that first-generation immigrants, who were born in the West Indies, would not generally have had enough U.S. cultural experience to acquire the negative stereotypes about their intellectual abilities. By contrast, the researchers expected that second-generation immigrants, who had been born in the United States, would possess these stereotypes. That prediction was upheld when groups of students who were first- and second-generation immigrants completed scales that assessed their knowledge of the stereotypes. To demonstrate the consequences of this distribution of knowledge, the researchers had both types of immigrants complete a series of questions from the verbal portion of a GRE practice test. The researchers led half the students to believe that their performance was diagnostic of their verbal abilities. The researchers told the other half that they were only answering the questions to assist with test development. As you can see in **Figure 10.8**, for the second-generation immigrants who possessed the negative stereotype, performance was impaired in the diagnostic condition: When the situation made the stereotype relevant, stereotype threat had a negative impact. However, because the first-generation immigrants didn't possess the stereotype, they didn't suffer the effects of stereotype threat.

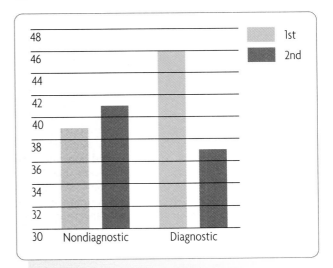

FIGURE 10.8 Stereotype Threat
The study contrasted second-generation immigrants— who possessed a negative stereotype about their group's intellectual ability—with first-generation immigrants—who did not possess that stereotype. Because the second-generation immigrants possessed the stereotype, their performance was impaired when they believed a test was diagnostic of their intellectual ability.

From Deaux, L., Bikmen, N., Gilkes, A., Venuneac, A., Joseph, Y., Payne, Y. A., & Steele, C. A. (2007). Becoming American: Stereotype threat effects in Afro-Caribbean immigrant groups. *Social Psychological Quarterly, 70,* 384–404. Copyright © 2007 by the American Sociological Association. Reprinted with permission.

stereotype threat The threat associated with being at risk for confirming a negative stereotype of one's group.

We want to emphasize again that what affected the performance of the second-generation immigrants was how they defined the situation. Only when people believe the situation is relevant to the stereotype—because, for example, they believe that the test measures their intelligence—does knowledge of the stereotype impair performance. Given results of this type, do you think it would be possible to measure IQ without invoking stereotype threat?

Why does stereotype threat have a negative impact? Researchers have identified three mechanisms that disrupt performance (Schmader, Johns, & Forbes, 2008). First, stereotype threat produces a physiological stress response (of the type we will describe in Chapter 13) that has a negative impact on people's ability to focus their attention. Second, stereotype threat leads people to monitor their performance more closely in ways that can lead, for example, to more cautious and less creative responses. Third, when people experience stereotype threat they have to expend mental resources to suppress negative thoughts and feelings. Recall our discussion of working memory in Chapter 8. The net effect of stereotype threat is to overwhelm test takers' working memory resources—leaving them less able to succeed on the problems at hand.

One final thought on intelligence and culture. Taken as a whole, the United States demonstrates a cultural bias toward genetic explanations of individual differences. **Harold Stevenson** and his colleagues (Stevenson, Chen, & Lee, 1993) spent several years tracking the mathematics achievement of Chinese, Japanese, and U.S. children. In 1980, Asian children on the average vastly outperformed their U.S. peers. In 1990, the gap remained: "Only 4.1% of the Chinese children and 10.3% of the Japanese children . . . had scores as low as those of the average American child" (p. 54). Are Asian children genetically superior? In fact, people in the United States are more likely to answer yes. When Stevenson and his colleagues asked Asian and U.S. students, teachers, and parents to contrast the importance of "studying hard" versus "innate intelligence," Asian respondents emphasized hard work. U.S. respondents emphasized innate ability. Do you see how this perspective could lead to the conclusion by North Americans that Asians must be genetically superior in mathematics? Since such beliefs have public policy implications—how much money should be expended on teaching mathematics if Americans cannot learn math anyway?—it is important to examine rigorous research to sort out what can and cannot be changed with respect to intellectual performance.

STOP AND REVIEW

❶ Under what circumstances did Goddard and others begin to make IQ comparisons among groups?

❷ Why is it inappropriate to use heritability estimates to make claims about racial differences in IQ?

❸ What aspects of people's lives are affected by preschool interventions?

❹ What did Harold Stevenson's research reveal about cross-cultural views of academic achievements?

CRITICAL THINKING Consider the study on stereotype threat. In what ways do real-life circumstances of testing make stereotypes seem relevant?

Creativity

Before we leave the area of intelligence and its assessment, we turn to the topic of creativity. **Creativity** is an individual's ability to generate ideas or products that are both *novel* and *appropriate* to the circumstances in which they were generated (Sternberg & Lubart, 1999). Consider the invention of the wheel. The device was novel because no one before its unknown inventor had seen the application of rolling objects. It was appropriate because the uses of the novel object were very clear. Without appropriateness, new ideas or objects are often considered strange or irrelevant.

Our discussion of creativity falls within a chapter on intelligence because many people believe that there is a strong relationship between intelligence and creativity. To determine if this is the case, we need to be able first to test creativity and then to determine the relationship between creativity and intelligence. Thus, we first discuss methods for judging ideas or products to be creative and then look at the link to intelligence. Next, we look at situations of exceptional creativity and evaluate the relationship between creativity and madness. We will see what lessons can be learned from people who are possessed of exceptional creative abilities.

ASSESSING CREATIVITY AND THE LINK TO INTELLIGENCE

How might you go about rating individuals as (relatively) creative or uncreative? Researchers have used tasks that measure both divergent and convergent thinking (Nielsen, Pickett, & Simonton, 2008; Runco, 2007). Many approaches focus on **divergent thinking**, which is defined as the ability to generate a variety of unusual solutions to a problem. Questions that test divergent thinking give the test taker the opportunity to demonstrate fluid (swift) and flexible thinking (Torrance, 1974; Wallach & Kogan, 1965):

- Name all the things you can think of that are square.
- List as many white edible things as you can in 3 minutes.
- List all the uses that you can think of for a brick.

Responses are scored along such dimensions as fluency, the overall number of distinct ideas; uniqueness, the number of ideas that were given by no other person in an appropriate sample; and unusualness, the number of ideas that were given by, for example, less than 5 percent of a sample (Runco, 1991).

Convergent thinking is defined as the ability to gather together different sources of information to solve a problem. We credit people as being creative if they can put information together in a way that produces novel solutions. One test researchers use to study convergent thinking is called the

---

creativity The ability to generate ideas or products that are both novel and appropriate to the circumstances.

divergent thinking An aspect of creativity characterized by an ability to produce unusual but appropriate responses to problems.

convergent thinking Often considered the opposite of divergent thinking; a single answer is required, generally requiring little creativity to get a correct answer, e.g., most types of multiple-choice questions in a school setting.

(A)

(B)

FIGURE 10.9 Making Judgments About Creativity

Hypothetical photography class assignment: Take the best picture you can.
(A) A noncreative response. (B) A creative response.

remote associates test. Test takers are challenged to find the term that provides a link for other words (Bowden & Beeman, 2003):

- *What* word are all three of these words related to? *Cottage, Swiss, cake*
- What word are all three of these words related to? *Fish, mine, rush*
- What word are all three of these words related to? *Flower, friend, scout*

(We'll give you the answers at the end of this section.) Other measures of convergent thinking focus on insight, which is defined as circumstances in which solutions suddenly come to mind. A different approach to judging some individuals as creative or uncreative is to ask them specifically to generate a creative product—a drawing, a poem, or a short story. Judges then rate the creativity of each of the products. Consider the two photographs shown in **Figure 10.9**. Which do you think is more creative? Could you explain why you think so? Do you think your friends would agree? Research has shown that agreement is quite high when judges rank products for creativity (Amabile, 1983). People can be reliably identified across judges as being high or low in creativity. In fact, people are also pretty accurate at judging whether their own efforts are creative.

In one study, 226 students completed a test of divergent thinking (Slivia, 2008b). For example, the students tried to generate unusual uses for a knife. After completing each task, the participants read their responses and chose the two they thought showed the most creativity. The participants' responses were also evaluated by a group of three judges. On the whole, the participants and the judges showed good agreement about which responses counted as the most creative. Still, some students were better than others at judging their own products. In particular, those students who judged themselves as being particularly creative and open to new experiences were also best at identifying their most creative responses. The researcher concluded that "creative people are doubly skilled: they are better at generating creative ideas and at discerning which ones are the best" (p. 145).

You might be happy to know that others are likely to agree with your judgments when you believe you have been creative.

Researchers have often tried to assess the relationship between creativity and intelligence. For example, one study obtained measures of IQ and divergent thinking for German school children who ranged in age from 12 to 16 (Preckel, Hollin, & Wiese, 2006). In that sample, the correlation between IQ and divergent thinking was 0.54, suggesting that students with higher IQ also generally showed greater divergent thinking. Similar results have been found with U.S. college students (Slivia, 2008a). These studies measure creativity with divergent thinking tasks which, as we have noted, only represent one way of assessing creativity (Runco, 2008). We know less about the relationship of IQ to other measures of creativity. On balance, as one researcher suggested, "intelligence appears to enable creativity to some extent but not to promote it" (Perkins, 1988, p. 319). In other words, a certain level of intelligence gives a person the opportunity to be creative, but the person may not avail himself or herself of that opportunity. In the *Psychology in Your Life* box, we review research on how you might increase your creativity.

How did you do on the convergent thinking problems? The answers were *cheese, gold,* and *girl.*

EXTREMES OF CREATIVITY

There are some exceptional individuals who would emerge from assessments of creativity as almost off the scale. Whom do you think of when you are asked to name someone who is exceptionally creative? Your answer is likely to depend partly on your own areas of expertise and your own preferences. Psychologists might nominate Sigmund Freud. Those people interested in fine art, music, or dance might mention Pablo Picasso, Igor Stravinsky, or Martha Graham. Is it possible to detect the commonalities in the personalities or backgrounds of such individuals that could be predictive of exceptional creativity? Howard Gardner (1993) chose a selection of individuals whose extraordinary abilities were relevant to the eight types of intelligence we described earlier, including Freud, Picasso, Stravinsky, and Graham. Gardner's analysis allows him to yield

HOW CAN YOU BECOME MORE CREATIVE?

When researchers measure creativity, some people always display more creativity than others (Runco, 2007). That doesn't mean, however, that any individual can't become more creative. In fact, researchers have begun to demonstrate how contexts greatly influence the quality of people's creative products. We're going to describe three manipulations that researchers have invented that make people more creative. As you read about each project, think how you might apply the insights in your own everyday life.

In the first study, researchers demonstrated the positive impact of multicultural experience on students' creativity (Leung, Maddux, Galinsky, & Chin, 2008). The researchers reasoned that exposure to another culture gives people experience, for example, in recruiting "ideas from unfamiliar sources and places" and synthesizing "seemingly incompatible ideas from diverse cultures" (p. 173). However, to demonstrate the impact of culture, the researchers did not send their experimental participants overseas. Instead, they had participants watch different versions of a 45-minute slide show. One version focused only on Chinese culture (which was unfamiliar to the participants). The other version juxtaposed Chinese and American cultures. After each slideshow, the participants attempted to write a creative version of the Cinderella story. Those participants who watched the slideshow juxtaposing the two cultures were consistently more creative in their stories. The key to increased creativity was that the students experienced the two cultures side-by-side.

A second method to increase creativity comes from a study that contrasted people's thoughts about the near and distant future (Förster, Friedman, & Liberman, 2004). Suppose we asked you how you might plan a party either for tomorrow or for a year from now. When you consider the near future, you're likely to focus on concrete details; when you consider the far future, your thoughts are likely to be more abstract. When you thought about planning a party, did you experience that shift from concrete to abstract? The researchers predicted that they could get participants to be more creative if they could get them thinking in that more abstract fashion. To test that prediction, the researchers began by prompting participants to adopt a near or distant future time perspective. They asked participants to spend two minutes imagining their lives either "tomorrow" or "one year from now." After a brief interval, participants responded to this scenario: "Ms. Miller likes her plants. Please help her to find as many creative ways as you can regarding how she can further improve her room" (p. 184). Participants who had imagined what their lives would be like in a year consistently provided more creative responses to the scenario.

A third method to increase creativity focuses on how people ponder what might have been (Markman Lindberg, Kray, & Galinsky, 2007). When people think back on their lives, they often contemplate counterfactual thoughts (for example, "If I had left a few minutes earlier, I wouldn't have gotten in that traffic jam"). Some of these counterfactuals are additive because they encode a broader range of possible actions with respect to a negative outcome (such as, "If I had done . . . , the outcome would have been better"). Some of the counterfactuals are subtractive because they encode a narrower range of actions (such as, "If I had not done . . . , the outcome would have been better"). The researchers asked some participants to construct additive counterfactuals with respect to a negative outcome in their lives. The researchers reasoned that "additive counterfactuals—those that add new . . . elements to reconstruct reality—evoke an expansive processing style that facilitates creative generation" (p. 322). In fact, participants who constructed additive counterfactuals produced more short-term creative behaviour (for example, they were able to generate more creative novel uses for a brick) than participants who generated subtractive counterfactuals.

Can you see how you might apply each of these projects to improve your everyday creativity?

a portrait of the life experiences of the *exemplary creator*, whom he dubs E. C.:

> *E. C. discovers a problem area or realm of special interest, one that promises to [lead] into uncharted waters. This is a highly charged moment. At this point E.C. becomes isolated from her peers and must work mostly on her own. She senses that she is on the verge of a breakthrough that is as yet little understood, even by her. Surprisingly, at this crucial moment, E. C. craves both cognitive and affective support so that she can retain her bearings. Without such support, she might well experience some kind of breakdown. (Gardner, 1993, p. 361)*

What lessons are there for you in tales of exceptional creativity that would allow you to be more creative? You can emulate a pattern of *risk taking*. Highly creative individuals are willing to go into "uncharted waters" (Gardner, 1993; Sternberg & Lubart, 1996). There is a pattern of *preparation*. Highly creative individuals typically have spent years acquiring expertise

Art historians have often speculated that Vincent van Gogh's creativity as an artist was influenced by mental illness. What, in general, have researchers discovered about the link between creativity and madness?

in the domains in which they will excel (Weisberg, 1986). There is a pattern of *intrinsic motivation*. Highly creative individuals pursue their tasks because of the enjoyment and satisfaction they take in the products they generate (Collins & Amabile, 1999). If you can bring all these factors together in your own life, you should be able to increase your personal level of creative performance.

Before we leave the topic of creativity, we want to consider one of the most common stereotypes of exemplary creators: Their life experiences border on—or include the experience of—madness. The idea that great creativity is intimately related to madness has a history that has been traced as far back as Plato (Kessel, 1989). In more modern times, Kraepelin (1921) argued that the manic phases of individuals who suffer from "manic-depressive insanity," or bipolar disorder, provide a context of free-flowing thought processes that facilitate great creativity. Mania, as we will see in Chapter 15, is characterized by periods of enduring excitedness; the person generally acts and feels elated and expansive. There is little doubt that many great figures in the arts and humanities have suffered from such mood disorders (Keiger, 1993). However, to establish a link between creativity and mental illness, researchers have attempted to go beyond those anecdotal reports. A review of the literature suggests that there is at least a weak association between some forms of mental illness—such as bipolar disorder—and creativity (Lauronen et al., 2004). However, as always, a correlation does not indicate whether there is a causal relationship. It could be that some forms of mental illness allow people to be more creative; it could be that the effort to be highly creative increases the likelihood that people will experience mental illness. There could also be some features of people's brains that make them highly creative and also more prone

to mental illness—with no causal link between the two phenomena (Dietrich, 2004).

You have now learned some of the ways in which psychologists assess and interpret individual differences in intelligence and creativity. You have a good understanding of how researchers have tried to measure and understand these difficult concepts. In this chapter's final section, we consider why psychological assessment can sometimes generate controversy.

STOP AND REVIEW

❶ How is creativity measured?
❷ What is the relationship between IQ and creativity?
❸ What three factors appear to play a role in exceptional creativity?

Assessment and Society

The primary goal of psychological assessment is to make accurate assessments of people that are as free as possible of errors of assessors' judgments. This goal is achieved by replacing subjective judgments of teachers, employers, and other evaluators with more objective measures that have been carefully constructed and are open to critical evaluation. This is the goal that motivated Alfred Binet in his pioneering work. Binet and others hoped that testing would help democratize society and minimize decisions based on arbitrary criteria of sex, race, nationality, privilege, or physical appearance. However, despite these lofty goals, there is no area of psychology more controversial than assessment. Three ethical concerns that are central to the controversy are the fairness of test-based decisions, the utility of tests for evaluating education, and the implications of using test scores as labels to categorize individuals.

Critics concerned with the fairness of testing practices argue that the costs or negative consequences may be higher for some test takers than for others (Bond, 1995). The costs are quite high, for example, when tests on which minority groups receive low scores are used to keep them out of certain jobs. In some cities, applicants for civil service janitor jobs must pass a verbal test, rather than a more appropriate test of manual skills. According to researcher William Banks, this is a strategy that unions use to keep minorities from accessing jobs (1990). Sometimes, minority group members test poorly because their scores are evaluated relative to inappropriate norms. In addition, arbitrary cutoff scores that favour applicants from one group may be used to make selection decisions, when, in reality, a lower cutoff score that is fairer would produce just as many correct hiring decisions. In addition, over-reliance on testing may make personnel selection an automatic attempt to fit people into available jobs. Instead, sometimes society might benefit more by changing job descriptions to fit the needs and abilities of people.

A second ethical concern is that testing not only helps evaluate students but may also play a role in the shaping of education. The quality of school systems and the effectiveness of teachers are frequently judged on the basis of how well their students score on standardized achievement tests. In many parts of the United States, local support of the schools through tax levies, and even individual teacher salaries, may ride on test scores. The high stakes associated with test scores have led to cheating scandals

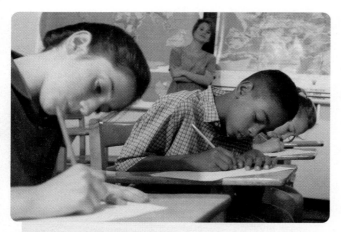

When schools are rewarded for high scores on standardized tests, are teachers likely to place more emphasis on test-taking skills than on broader learning goals?

to their parents that they had been asked or allowed to cheat: They wondered why the adults at the school had insisted that they do so. These circumstances illustrate how damaging it can be when test scores are taken to matter more than education.

A third ethical concern is that test outcomes can take on the status of unchangeable labels. People too often think of themselves as being an IQ of 110 or a B student, as if the scores were labels stamped on their foreheads. Such labels may become barriers to advancement and real learning as people come to believe that their mental and personal qualities are fixed and unchangeable—that they cannot improve their lot in life. For those who are negatively assessed, the scores can become self-imposed motivational limits that lower their sense of self-efficacy and restrict the challenges they are willing to tackle. That is another insidious consequence of pronouncements about group deficiencies in IQ. Those stigmatized publicly in this way come to believe what the "experts" are saying about them and do not identify with schools and education as means to improve their lives.

in several school districts (Kantrowitz & McGinn, 2000). For example, in Potomac, Maryland, an elementary school principal resigned when strong evidence suggested that fifth-graders at her school had been given several types of assistance, including extra time and second chances, to improve their test scores (Thomas & Wingert, 2000). The evidence against the school had come from the students themselves. The 10-year-olds reported

STOP AND REVIEW

❶ Why might assessment have negative consequences for particular groups of individuals?
❷ Why might assessment play a role in shaping education?
❸ Why might test scores become labels that have broad consequences?

Recapping Main Points

What Is Assessment?

- Psychological assessment has a long history, beginning in ancient China. Many important contributions were made by Sir Francis Galton.
- A useful assessment tool must be reliable, valid, and standardized. A reliable measure gives consistent results. A valid measure assesses the attributes for which the test was designed.
- A standardized test is always administered and scored in the same way; norms allow a person's score to be compared with the averages of others of the same age, sex, and culture.

Intelligence Assessment

- Binet began the tradition of objective intelligence testing in France in the early 1900s. Scores were given in terms of mental ages and were meant to represent children's current level of functioning.
- In the United States, Terman created the Stanford–Binet Intelligence Scale and popularized the concept of IQ.
- Wechsler designed special intelligence tests for adults, children, and preschoolers.
- The definitions of mental retardation and giftedness focus both on IQ scores and day-to-day performance.

Visit **MyPsychLab.com** for more review and practice on the following topics:

 Research: Lewis Terman

Theories of Intelligence

- Psychometric analyses of IQ suggest that several basic abilities, such as fluid and crystallized aspects of intelligence, contribute to IQ scores.
- Contemporary theories conceive of and measure intelligence very broadly by considering the skills and insights people use to solve the types of problems they encounter.
- Sternberg differentiates analytical, creative, and practical aspects of intelligence.
- Gardner identifies eight types of intelligence that both include and go beyond the types of intelligence assessed by standard IQ measures. Recent research has focused on emotional intelligence.

Visit **MyPsychLab.com** for more review and practice on the following topics:

◀◉ **Simulate:** Gardner's Theory of Intelligence

The Politics of Intelligence

- Almost from the outset, intelligence tests have been used to make negative claims about ethnic and racial groups.
- Because of the reasonably high heritability of IQ, some researchers have attributed the lower scores of some racial and cultural groups to innate inferiority.
- Environmental disadvantages and stereotype threat appear to explain the lower scores of certain groups. Research

shows that group differences can be affected through environmental interventions.

Visit **MyPsychLab.com** for more review and practice on the following topics:

✱ **Explore:** Correlations Between IQ Scores of Persons of Varying Relationships

Creativity

- Creativity is often assessed using tests of divergent thinking.
- Exceptionally creative people take risks, prepare, and are highly motivated.
- Although there is an association between creativity and some forms of mental illness, a causal link has not been established.

Visit **MyPsychLab.com** for more review and practice on the following topics:

✓ **Practice:** Creativity

Assessment and Society

- Though often useful for prediction and as an indication of current performance, test results should not be used to limit an individual's opportunities for development and change.
- When the results of an assessment will affect an individual's life, the techniques used must be reliable and valid for that individual and for the purpose in question.

Visit **MyPsychLab.com** for more review and practice on the following topics:

👁 **Watch:** School Gets an F

KEY TERMS

chronological age (p. 295)
creativity (p. 310)
construct validity (p. 293)
convergent thinking (p. 310)
criterion validity (p. 293)
crystallized intelligence (p. 300)
divergent thinking (p. 310)
emotional intelligence (EI) (p. 302)
face validity (p. 293)
fluid intelligence (p. 300)

formal assessment (p. 292)
g (p. 299)
heritability estimate (p. 305)
intelligence (p. 294)
intelligence quotient (IQ) (p. 295)
internal consistency (p. 292)
learning disorders (p. 298)
mental age (p. 295)
mental retardation (p. 297)
norms (p. 294)

parallel forms (p. 292)
predictive validity (p. 293)
psychological assessment (p. 291)
psychometrics (p. 299)
split-half reliability (p. 292)
standardization (p. 294)
stereotype threat (p. 309)
test–retest reliability (p. 292)

SOLUTIONS TO THE ANAGRAMS IN TABLE 10.3 (p. 301)

1. laugh
2. tempt
3. short
4. knight
5. write

6. allow
7. drive
8. couch
9. enter
10. basic

Practice Test

1. Which of these was *not* one of the ideas Sir Francis Galton formulated about intelligence assessment?
   (a. Differences in intelligence are quantifiable.
   b. Intelligence can be measured by objective tests.
   c. Intelligence scores follow a bell-shaped curve.
   d. Intelligence scores change over the lifespan.

2. To measure the _____ of his Latin exam, Caligula compared his score on even-numbered items with his score on odd-numbered items.
   a. test–retest reliability   c. internal consistency
   b. face validity   d. criterion validity

3. Martin filled out a test to measure his happiness. He got a score of 72. To interpret that score, Martin needs to consult the _____ the test.
   a. norms for   c. standardization of
   b. split-half reliability for   d. predictive validity of

4. Deborah is 10 years old, but she has a mental age of 12. Using the original method for calculating IQ, you conclude that Deborah has an IQ of _____
   a. 90.   c. 150.
   b. 120.   d. 100.

5. Which cause of mental retardation is easiest to treat?
   a. Down syndrome
   b. the mother's prenatal consumption of alcohol
   c. the mother's prenatal consumption of cocaine
   d. PKU

6. Which of these qualities is *not* part of the "three-ring" conception of giftedness?
   a. creativity   c. task commitment
   b. mathematical genius   d. high ability

7. When Poindexter took IQ tests on the web, he took four tests at the same site and obtained scores of 116, 117, 129, and 130. Given these scores, you conclude that the IQ tests are _____
   a. both reliable and valid.   c. reliable but not valid.
   b. neither reliable nor valid. d. valid but not reliable.

8. _____ intelligence is defined as the knowledge a person has already acquired.
   a. Fluid   c. Crystallized
   b. Analytical   d. Creative

9. Felix is applying for chef school. He takes an entrance exam that poses a series of questions on food preparation. This sounds most like a test of _____ intelligence.
   a. practical   c. fluid
   b. analytic   d. creative

10. Julian is rarely aware when the people around him are upset. You suspect that Julian is not very high on _____ intelligence.
    a. naturalist   c. emotional
    b. spatial   d. bodily kinesthetic

11. Which of these abilities is *not* part of practical intelligence?
    a. understanding complex mathematical problems
    b. adapting to new and different contexts
    c. selecting appropriate contexts
    d. shaping your environment to suit your needs

12. Goneril and Regan are sisters. You would expect them to have the most similar IQs if they _____
    a. are fraternal twins.
    b. are identical twins.
    c. grew up in the same home.
    d. were adopted before age two.

13. Studies of the impact of socioeconomic status (SES) on IQ suggests that _____
    a. individuals with higher SES generally have higher IQs.
    b. SES has an impact on IQ scores only for specific racial groups.
    c. SES has no overall impact on IQ scores.
    d. individuals with lower SES do not benefit from preschool programs.

14. Stereotype threat has an impact on people's test performance when they believe that _____
    a. the testing situation is relevant to the stereotype.
    b. the stereotype is widespread in a culture.
    c. the testing situation is unfair to certain ethnic groups.
    d. stereotypes change over time.

15. A test of _____ might include a question like, "Name all the things you can think of that are round."
    a. analytic intelligence
    b. crystallized intelligence
    c. convergent thinking
    d. divergent thinking

16. If you want to understand the origins of exceptional creativity, you *do not* need to focus on _____
    a. preparation.   c. IQ.
    b. intrinsic motivation.   d. risk taking.

17. Which of these statements best captures the relationship between mental illness and creativity?
    a. Researchers have demonstrated that the hard work of being creative causes people to become mentally ill.
    b. Researchers have demonstrated that people who are mentally ill are more creative.
    c. Researchers have demonstrated that people who are highly creative experience less mental illness than other individuals.
    d. Researchers have not demonstrated that there is a causal relationship between mental illness and creativity.

18. The goal of psychological assessment is often to replace _____ with _____.
   a. objective measures; verifiable labels
   b. reliable measures; valid measures
   c. valid measures; subjective impressions
   d. subjective impressions; objective measures

19. Children at a Maryland school reported to their parents that they had been allowed to cheat on standardized exams. To what societal concern about assessment does that incident relate?
   a. The consequences of assessment may be worse for some groups than for others.
   b. Assessment can yield outcomes that become unchangeable labels.
   c. Assessment plays a role in the shaping of educational practices.
   d. People may have to work harder to overcome negative assessments.

20. When Cyrus was 12, he was told he was a genius. As an adult, he never feels as if he is living up to his potential. This is a good example of circumstances in which assessment has _____
   a. generated an incorrect outcome.
   b. yielded a label that has personal implications.
   c. shaped the educational experiences of an individual.
   d. had negative consequences for Cyrus's group.

Essay Questions

1. What is the goal of Howard Gardner's theory of multiple intelligences?

2. How have Head Start and other early intervention programs demonstrated the impact of environments on IQ?

3. Why is it difficult to establish a causal link between mental illness and creativity?

Watch the following video by logging on to MyPsychLab (**www.mypsychlab.com**). After you have watched the video, complete the activities that follow.

Program 16: Testing and Intelligence

PROGRAM REVIEW

1. What is the goal of psychological assessment?
   a. to derive a theory of human cognition
   b. to see how people vary in ability, behaviour, and personality
   c. to measure the stages of growth in intellectual abilities
   d. to diagnose psychological problems

2. You are taking a test in which you are asked to agree or disagree with statements such as "I give up too easily when discussing things with others." Which test would this be?
   a. the Scholastic Aptitude Test
   b. the Rorschach test
   c. the Strong Interest Inventory
   d. the Minnesota Multiphasic Personality Inventory

3. What was Binet's aim in developing a measure of intelligence?
   a. to identify children in need of special help
   b. to show that intelligence is innate
   c. to weed out inferior children
   d. to provide an empirical basis for a theory of intelligence

4. What formula did Terman create to express intelligence?
   a. MA/CA = IQ   c. CA/MA × 100 = IQ
   b. MA × CA = IQ   d. MA/CA × 100 = IQ

5. Cultural biases in tests can lead to the overvaluing of some attributes and the undervaluing of others. Which of the following is likely to be overvalued in the United States?
   a. common sense   c. creativity
   b. motivation   d. verbal ability

6. Imagine that anyone who wants a job as a hospital orderly has to take a test. The test is valid for its norm group, white men. Imagine a black woman is taking the test. Which statement about the woman's score is most likely to be accurate?
   a. It will accurately predict her job performance.
   b. It will be lower than that of white men.
   c. It may indicate she is not capable when she in fact is capable.
   d. It cannot indicate anything about her because there were no black people or women in the norm group.

7. What new perspective did Howard Gardner introduce to the study of intelligence?
   a. He redefined intelligence as "practical intelligence."
   b. He expanded intelligence to include other types.
   c. He argued for a biological basis for describing intelligence in terms of brain waves.
   d. He argued that the term intelligence should be abolished.

8. Robert Sternberg has devised a test for managers. How does its prediction of success compare with predictions from a standard IQ test?
   a. They predict equally well and are not correlated.
   b. They predict equally well, probably because they are measuring the same thing.
   c. Sternberg's test predicts twice as well as IQ and is not correlated with IQ.
   d. Sternberg's test predicts twice as well as IQ and is moderately correlated with IQ.

9. The growing practice of "teaching for tests" creates the possibility of _____
   a. lessened ecological validity.
   b. eliminating stereotype threat.
   c. lowered reliability.
   d. eliminating genetic influences on intelligence.

10. Which of the following is an innovation in intelligence assessment that David Wechsler introduced?
   a. displaying physical co-ordination
   b. demonstrating social sensitivity
   c. producing appropriate verbal metaphors
   d. putting pictures in a logical sequence

QUESTIONS TO CONSIDER

1. Does evidence of a genetic basis for intelligence mean that intelligence is unchangeable?

2. What would happen if everyone knew everyone else's IQ scores? How might it affect decisions about whom to marry or hire?

3. What are some of the ethical questions related to intelligence testing and psychological assessment?

Human Development Across the Life Span

I magine you are holding a newborn baby. How might you predict what this child will be like as a one-year-old? At 5 years? At 15? At 50? At 70? At 90? Your predictions would almost certainly consist of a mixture of the general and the specific—the child is extremely likely to learn a language, but might or might not be a gifted author. Your predictions would also rely on considerations of heredity and of environment. For example, if both the child's parents were gifted authors, you might be willing to guess that the child would also show literary talent, but if the child were educated in an enriched environment, you might predict that the child's accomplishments would exceed those of the parents. In this chapter, we describe the theories of developmental psychology that enable us to think systematically about the types of predictions we can make for the life course of a newborn child.

Developmental psychology is the area of psychology that is concerned with changes in physical and psychological functioning, which occur from conception across the entire life span. The task of developmental psychologists is to find out how and why organisms change over time—to document and explain development. Investigators study the time periods in which different abilities and functions first appear and observe how those abilities are modified. The basic premise is that mental functioning, social relationships, and other vital aspects of human nature develop and change throughout the entire life cycle. **Table 11.1** presents a rough guide to the major periods of the life span.

In this chapter we will provide a general account of how researchers document development and the theories they use to explain patterns of change over time. We will then divide your life experiences into different domains and trace development in each domain. Early in the chapter, we focus on physical, cognitive, and language development. We then shift our attention to the changing nature of social relationships over the life span as well as the specific tasks individuals face at different moments in their lives. Some of what we have learned about human development has actually been discovered by studying animals. Part of this is because animals generally have shorter life spans, but show many similar patterns in development to humans. Let's begin now with the question of what it means to study development.

Studying Development

Suppose we ask you to make a list of all the ways in which you believe you have changed in the last year. What sorts of things would you put on the list? Have you undertaken a new physical

TABLE 11.1	Stages in Life Span Development
Stage	**Age Period**
Prenatal	Conception to birth
Infancy	Birth at full term to about 18 months
Early childhood	About 18 months to about 6 years
Middle childhood	About 6 years to about 11 years
Adolescence	About 11 years to about 20 years
Early adulthood	About 20 years to about 40 years
Middle adulthood	About 40 years to about 65 years
Late adulthood	About 65 years and older

fitness program? Or have you let an injury heal? Have you developed a range of new hobbies? Or have you decided to focus on just one interest? Have you developed a new circle of friends? Or have you become particularly close to one individual? When we describe development, we will conceptualize it in terms of *change*. We have asked you to perform this exercise of thinking about your own changes to make the point that change almost always involves trade-offs.

Often people conceptualize the life span as mostly *gains*—changes for the better—in childhood and mostly *losses*—changes for the worse—over the course of adulthood. However, the perspective on development we will take here emphasizes that *options*, and therefore gains and losses, are features of all development (Dixon, 2003; Lachman, 2004). When, for example, people choose a lifetime companion, they give up variety but gain security. When people retire, they give up status but gain leisure time.

It is also important that you not think of development as a *passive* process. You will see that many developmental changes require an individual's *active* engagement with his or her environment (Bronfenbrenner, 2004).

To document change, a good first step is to determine what an average person is like—in physical appearance, cognitive abilities, and so on—at a particular age. **Normative investigations** seek to describe a characteristic of a specific age or developmental stage. This type of information is important as general baseline data on what would be age appropriate. By systematically testing individuals of different ages, researchers can determine developmental landmarks or milestones. These data provide *norms*, standard patterns of development or achievement, based on observing many people.

Normative standards allow psychologists to make a distinction between **chronological age**—the number of months or years since a person's birth—and **developmental age**—the chronological age at which most people show the particular level of physical or mental development demonstrated by that child. A three-year-old child who has verbal skills typical of most five-year-olds is said to have a developmental age of five for verbal skills. Norms provide a standard basis for comparison both between individuals and between groups.

---

developmental psychology The branch of psychology concerned with interaction between physical and psychological processes and with stages of growth from conception throughout the entire life span.

normative investigations Research efforts designed to describe what is characteristic of a specific age or developmental stage.

chronological age The number of months or years since an individual's birth.

developmental age The chronological age at which most children show a particular level of physical or mental development.

In a longitudinal design, observations are made of the same individual at different ages, often for many years. This well-known woman might be part of a longitudinal study of British children born in 1926. How might she be similar to and different from other children in that cohort?

Developmental psychologists use several types of research designs to understand possible mechanisms of change. In a **longitudinal design**, the same individuals are repeatedly observed and tested over time, often for many years (see **Figure 11.1**). Recall the study on the effectiveness of the High/Scope Perry preschool program described in Chapter 10. The researchers first collected data on a group of children when they were 3 and 4 years old (Schweinhart, 2004). To assess the long-term impact of the preschool program, the researchers studied the children every year until age 11, and then again at ages 14, 15, 19, 27, and 40. This longitudinal data collection allowed the researchers to draw strong conclusions about the program's lifelong benefits. The studies suggested that children living in low-income housing who had access to preschool programs similar to the High/Scope Perry program were less likely to break the law and were more likely to hold down well-paying jobs. These types of studies have a large impact on policy statements. Researchers also often use longitudinal designs to study *individual differences*. To understand the life outcomes of different people, researchers may assess a range of potential causal factors early in life and see how those factors influence each individual's life course.

A general advantage of longitudinal research is that because the participants have lived through the same socioeconomic period, age-related changes cannot be confused with variations in differing societal circumstances. A disadvantage, however, is that some types of generalizations can be made only to the same *cohort*, the group of individuals born in the same time period as the research participants. Also, longitudinal studies are costly because it is difficult to keep track of the participants over extended time, and data are easily lost because participants quit or cannot be tracked by the researcher (they may have moved, married and changed names, etc.).

Much research on development uses a **cross-sectional design**, in which groups of participants of different chronological ages are observed and compared at one and the same time. A researcher can then draw conclusions about behavioural differences that may be related to age changes. For example, Statistics

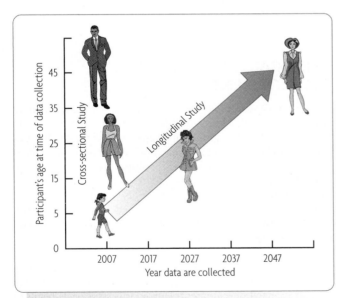

FIGURE 11.1 Longitudinal and Cross-Sectional Research

In longitudinal studies, researchers follow the same group of individuals over days, months, or years. In cross-sectional studies, researchers test individuals of different ages at the same moment in time.

longitudinal design A research design in which the same participants are observed repeatedly, sometimes over many years.

cross-sectional design A research method in which groups of participants of different chronological ages are observed and compared at a given time.

A drawback of cross-sectional research is the cohort effect. What differences might exist between these two groups of women as a result of the eras in which they lived?

Canada has possibly collected data from you or your parents at some time on your habits and compared this data with that collected from other Canadians during their census. In 2008, Statistics Canada reported on social behaviour and living conditions using a cross-sectional design with Canadians of all ages in their census. In the psychology lab, researchers who wanted to determine how children learn to walk without falling down tested children of ages 15, 21, 27, 33, and 39 months on the same laboratory task (Joh & Adolph, 2006). A disadvantage of cross-sectional designs comes from comparing individuals who differ by year of birth as well as by chronological age. Age-related changes are confounded by differences in the social or political conditions experienced by different birth cohorts. Thus a study comparing samples of 10- and 18-year-olds now might find that the participants differ from 10- and 18-year-olds who grew up in the 1970s, in ways related to their different eras as well as to their developmental stages.

Each methodology gives researchers the opportunity to document change from one age to another. Researchers use these methodologies to study development in each of several domains. As we now consider some of those domains—physical, cognitive, and social development—you will come to appreciate and understand some of the vast changes you have already experienced.

STOP AND REVIEW

❶ What is developmental age?
❷ Why are longitudinal designs often used to study individual differences?
❸ What is the relevance of birth cohorts to cross-sectional designs?

---

physical development The bodily changes, maturation, and growth that occur in an organism starting with conception and continuing across the life span.

zygote The single cell that results when a sperm fertilizes an egg.

Physical Development Across the Life Span

Many of the types of development we describe in this chapter require some special knowledge to detect. For example, you might not notice landmarks in social development until you read about them here. We will begin, however, with a realm of development in which changes are often plainly visible to the untrained eye: **physical development**. You have undergone enormous physical change since you were born. Such changes will continue until the end of your life. Since physical changes are so numerous, we will focus on the types that have an impact on psychological development.

PRENATAL AND CHILDHOOD DEVELOPMENT

You began life with unique genetic potential: At the moment of conception a male's sperm cell fertilized a female's egg cell to form the single-cell **zygote**; you received half of the 46 chromosomes found in all normal human body cells from your mother and half from your father. In this section, we outline physical development in the *prenatal period*, from the moment of conception until the moment of birth. We also describe some of the sensory abilities children have obtained even before birth. Finally, we describe the important physical changes that you experienced during childhood.

Physical Development in the Womb The first two weeks after formation of the zygote are known as the *germinal stage* of prenatal development. During this stage, cells begin to divide rapidly and after about one week a mass of microscopic cells attaches itself to the mother's uterine wall. The third through eighth week of prenatal development is called the *embryonic stage*. During this stage, rapid cell division continues, but the cells begin to become specialized to form different organs. As these organs develop, the first heartbeat occurs.

As the brain grows in the developing fetus, it generates 250 000 new neurons per minute. What must the brain be prepared to do, as soon as the child enters the world?

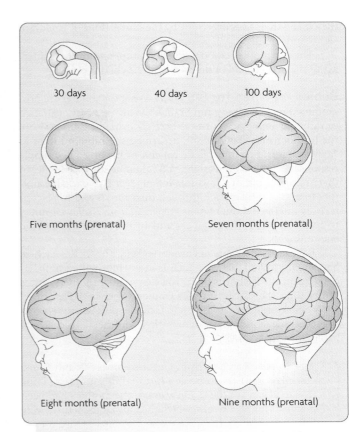

30 days   40 days   100 days

Five months (prenatal)   Seven months (prenatal)

Eight months (prenatal)   Nine months (prenatal)

FIGURE 11.2 The Development of the Human Brain

During the nine months before birth, the brain reaches its complement of over 100 billion neurons.

Adapted from *The Brain* by W. M. Cowan. Copyright © 1979 W. M. Cowan.

Responses to stimulation have been observed as early as the sixth week when the embryo is only a few centimetres in length. Spontaneous movements are observed by the eighth week (Kisilevsky & Low, 1998).

After the eighth week, the developing embryo is called a *fetus*. The mother feels fetal movements in about the 16th week after conception. At this point, the fetus is about 20 centimetres long (the average length at birth is almost half a metre). As the brain grows in utero, it generates new neurons at the rate of 250 000 per minute, reaching a full complement of over 100 billion neurons by birth (Cowan, 1979). In humans and many other mammals, most of this cell proliferation and migration of neurons to their correct locations take place prenatally; the development of the branching processes of axons and dendrites, which allows cells to communicate with each other, largely occurs after birth (Kolb, 1989, 1995). The sequence of brain development, from 30 days to 9 months, is shown in **Figure 11.2**.

Over the course of pregnancy, environmental factors such as infection, radiation, or drugs can prevent the normal formation of organs and body structures. Any environmental factor that causes structural abnormalities in the fetus is often called a *teratogen*. For example, when mothers are infected with rubella (German measles) two to four weeks after conception, the probability is roughly 50 percent that the child will suffer negative consequences such as mental retardation, eye damage, deafness, or heart defects. When the infection occurs in the first six weeks after conception, the probability of birth defects may be as high as 100 percent (De Santis et al., 2006). If exposure occurs later, the probability of adverse effects is much lower (e.g., 22 percent in the second month; 8 percent in the third month) (Murata, McGlynn, Siu, & Brook, 1992). Similarly, mothers who consume certain substances, such as alcohol, during sensitive periods put their unborn children at risk for brain damage and other impairments (Bailey & Sokol, 2008). Children with fetal alcohol syndrome often have small heads and bodies and facial abnormalities. Disruptions of the central nervous system cause cognitive and behavioural impairments (Niccols, 2007).

Pregnant women who smoke also put their children at risk, particularly in the second half of pregnancy. Smoking during pregnancy increases the risk of miscarriage, premature births, and low-birth-weight babies (Salihu & Wilson, 2007). In fact, women who are exposed to secondhand smoke during pregnancy are also more likely to have babies with low birth weights (Dejin-Karlsson, Hsonson, Oestergren, Sjoeberg, & Karel, 1998).

Some substances may bring about damage at virtually any time during pregnancy. Cocaine, for example, travels through the placenta and can affect fetal development directly. In adults, cocaine causes blood vessels to constrict, but in pregnant women, cocaine restricts placental blood flow and oxygen supply to the fetus. Researchers investigating cocaine use and births in Toronto found that infants exposed to cocaine are more likely to have low birth weight and shorter body length (Forman et al, 1993). Babies exposed to cocaine are also more likely to need medical attention at birth. If severe oxygen deprivation results, blood vessels in the fetus's brain may burst, leading to lifelong mental handicaps (Bennett, Bendersky, & Lewis, 2008; Singer et al., 2002). Research suggests that the brain systems most damaged by cocaine are those responsible for controlling attention: Children exposed to cocaine in the womb may spend their lives overcome by the distractions of irrelevant sights and sounds.

These examples emphasize that nature and nurture interact to shape body and brain even before a child is born.

Babies Prewired for Survival What capabilities are programmed into this body and brain at birth? We are accustomed to thinking about newborns as entirely helpless. John Watson, the founder of behaviourism, described the human infant as "a lively, squirming bit of flesh, capable of making a few simple responses." If that sounds right, you might be surprised to learn that, moments out of the womb, infants reveal remarkable abilities to obtain information through their senses and to react to it. They might be thought of as *prewired for survival*, well suited to respond to adult caregivers and to influence their social environments.

For example, infants can hear even before birth. Researchers have demonstrated that what infants hear while in the womb has consequences. Newborns prefer to listen to their mothers' voices rather than the voices of other women (Spence & DeCasper, 1987; Spence & Freeman, 1996). In fact, the most recent research suggests that children recognize their mothers' voices even before they are born.

A team of researchers from Queen's University and China recruited mothers-to-be at a hospital in southeast China (Kisilevsky et al., 2003). On average, the mothers had been pregnant for 38.4 weeks, which meant that the fetuses were full term. The mothers were asked to tape-record a two-minute poem. The recordings of the poem were played to the fetuses through a loudspeaker that was poised about four inches above the mothers' abdomens. Half the fetuses were played the poem read in their own mothers' voice; the other half heard the poem read by someone else's mother. The researchers monitored fetal heart rate. The results were quite dramatic: Fetal heart rate increased in response to the mother's voice and decreased in response to the strangers' voices! Barbara Kisilevsky points to the brain's ability to be hardwired for language with this research!

Given these strong results favouring mothers, you might wonder whether children also respond more to their fathers' voices. Unfortunately, research so far indicates that children do not seem to have enough auditory experience with their dads. Newborns show no preference for their fathers' voices (DeCasper & Prescott, 1984). Even at age four months, infants still do not prefer their father's voice to a stranger's voice (Ward & Cooper, 1999).

Infants also put their visual systems to work almost immediately: A few minutes after birth, a newborn's eyes are alert, turning in the direction of a voice and searching inquisitively for the source of certain sounds. Even so, vision is less well developed than the other senses at birth. The visual acuity of adults is roughly 40 times better than the visual acuity of newborns (Sireteanu, 1999). Visual acuity improves rapidly over the first six months of a baby's life. Newborns also are ill equipped to experience the world in three dimensions: It is only at about four months of age that children are able to combine information from their two eyes to perceive depth. Although the eyes and the optic nerve to the brain provide some hardwired capability for vision, the ability to have good vision depends on experience. Good vision—sensitivity to contrast, visual acuity, and colour discrimination—requires that a great many photoreceptor cells function in the centre of the eye's receptive area and that the optics of the eye develop appropriately (see Chapter 4). Many of these components have yet to mature in the infant's visual system. McMaster University researchers suggest that good vision also requires that numerous connections between neurons in the brain's visual cortex be made in response to visual experience (Maurer, Lewis, Brent, & Levin, 1999). At birth, not enough of these connections are laid down. Individuals examining how the visual cortex grows postnatally across different mammals found that the visual cortex of macaque monkeys increased

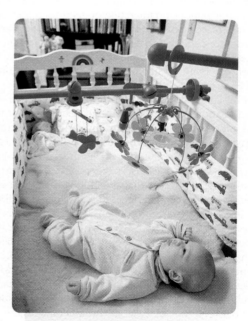

Early on, infants can perceive large objects that display a great deal of contrast. What visual experiences do newborns find particularly appealing?

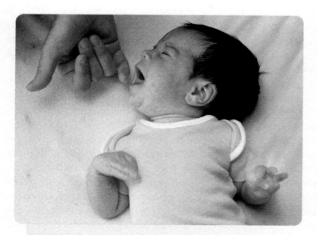

When something touches a newborn's cheek, the rooting reflex prompts the baby to seek something to suck. In what other ways are children prewired for survival?

FIGURE 11.3 The Visual Cliff

Once children have gained experience crawling around their environment, they show fear of the deep side of the visual cliff.

approximately 18 percent after birth, whereas the visual cortex increased by more than 100 percent in cats (Duffy, Murphy, & Jones, 1998). Kevin Duffy at Dalhousie University has also found that visual deprivation causes the cat brain to develop differently (Duffy and Slusar, 2009). Humans do not often suffer deprivation of visual input, but occasionally eye injuries or unusual development can cause visual deprivation that probably affects brain growth as well.

Even without perfect vision, however, children have visual preferences. Pioneering researcher **Robert Fantz** (1963) observed that babies as young as four months old preferred looking at objects with complex features over those that were more plain. More recent research suggests that—by the age of three days—infants have a preference for *top*-heavy patterns (Macchi Cassia, Turati, & Simion, 2004). To experience a top-heavy pattern, take a look at your face in a mirror: your eyes, eyebrows, and so on, take up much more space than your lips. The fact that faces are top heavy might explain why infants prefer to look at human faces versus other types of visual displays.

Once children start to move around in their environment, they quickly acquire other perceptual capabilities. For example, classic research by **Eleanor Gibson** and **Richard Walk** (1960) examined how children respond to depth information. This research used an apparatus called a *visual cliff*. The visual cliff had a board running across the middle of a solid glass surface. As shown in **Figure 11.3**, checkerboard cloth was used to create a deep end and a shallow end. In their original research, Gibson and Walk demonstrated that children would readily leave the centre board to crawl across the shallow end, but they were reluctant to crawl across the deep end. Subsequent research has demonstrated that fear of the deep end depends on crawling experience: Children who have begun to crawl experience fear of the deep end, whereas their noncrawling same-age peers do not (Campos, Bertenthal, & Kermoian, 1992). Thus, wariness of heights is not quite "prewired," but it develops quickly as children begin to explore the world under their own power.

Growth and Maturation in Childhood Newborn infants change at an astonishing rate but, as shown in **Figure 11.4**, physical growth is not equal across all physical structures. At birth, a baby's head, for example, is already about 60 percent of its adult size and measures a quarter of the whole body length (Bayley, 1956). An infant's body weight doubles in the first six months and triples by the first birthday; by the age of two, a child's trunk is about half of its adult length. Genital tissue shows little change until the teenage years and then develops rapidly to adult proportions.

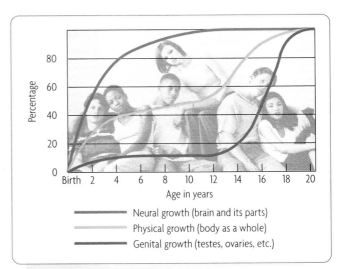

FIGURE 11.4 Growth Patterns Across the First Two Decades of Life

Neural growth occurs very rapidly in the first year of life. It is much faster than overall physical growth. By contrast, genital maturation does not occur until adolescence.

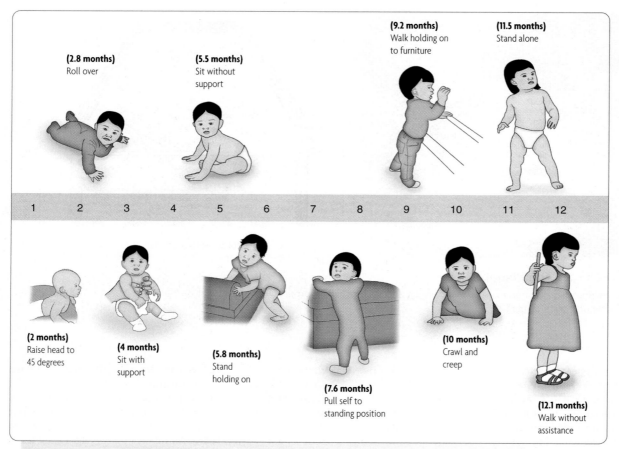

(2.8 months)
Roll over

(5.5 months)
Sit without
support

(9.2 months)
Walk holding on
to furniture

(11.5 months)
Stand alone

1 2 3 4 5 6 7 8 9 10 11 12

(2 months)
Raise head to
45 degrees

(4 months)
Sit with
support

(5.8 months)
Stand
holding on

(7.6 months)
Pull self to
standing position

(10 months)
Crawl and
creep

(12.1 months)
Walk without
assistance

FIGURE 11.5 Maturational Timetable for Locomotion
The development of walking requires no special teaching. It follows a fixed time-ordered
sequence that is typical of all physically capable members of our species.

For most children, physical growth is accompanied by the maturation of motor ability. **Maturation** refers to the process of growth typical of all members of a species who are reared in the species's usual habitat. The characteristic maturational sequences newborns experience are determined by the interaction of inherited biological boundaries and environmental inputs. For example, in the sequence for locomotion, as shown in **Figure 11.5**, a child learns to walk without special training. This sequence applies to the great majority of babies. Even so, in cultures in which there is less physical stimulation, children begin to walk later. The Native American practice of carrying babies in tightly bound back cradles retards walking, but, once released, the child goes through the same sequence. Therefore, you can think of all unimpaired newborn children as possessing the same potential for physical maturation.

PHYSICAL DEVELOPMENT IN ADOLESCENCE

The first concrete indicator of the end of childhood is the *pubescent growth spurt*. At around age 10 for girls and age 12 for boys, growth hormones flow into the bloodstream. For several years, the adolescent may grow three to six inches a year and gain weight rapidly as well. The adolescent's body does not

reach adult proportions all at once. Hands and feet grow to full adult size first. The arms and legs come next, with the torso developing most slowly. Thus, an individual's overall shape changes several times over the teenage years.

What effect does a cradleboard have on an infant's ability
to learn to walk?

___
maturation The continuing influence of heredity throughout development; the age-related physical and behavioural changes characteristic of a species.

Another important process that occurs during adolescence is **puberty**, which brings about sexual maturity. (The Latin word *pubertas* means "covered with hair" and signifies the growth of hair on the arms and legs, under the arms, and in the genital area.) Puberty for males brings about the production of live sperm; for girls it leads to **menarche**, the onset of menstruation. In much of North America, the average time for menarche is between the ages of 12 and 13, although the normal range extends from 11 to 15. For boys, the production of live sperm first occurs, on average, between the ages of 12 and 14, but again there is considerable variation in this timing. These physical changes often bring about an awareness of sexual feelings. In Chapter 12, we will discuss the onset of sexual motivation.

Some other important physical changes happen inside adolescents' brains. Researchers once thought that most brain growth was over within the first few years of life. However, recent studies using brain-imaging techniques have demonstrated continuing development within the adolescent brain (Paus, 2005). The areas of the brain that undergo the greatest change from puberty into young adulthood are the *frontal lobes*—the areas responsible for planning and regulation of emotions. New connections form between the frontal lobes and the limbic system, which plays a role in memory. The frontal lobes reach maturity as people move from adolescence into adulthood (Steinberg, 2008). The new growth beginning around ages 10 to 12 is followed by pruning of unused connections through about age 20. This pruning process leaves individuals with efficient and well-organized adult brains. Those new connections also enable individuals to exercise more cognitive control over the emotional impulses that are often seen during adolescence.

With the passing of adolescence, your body once again reaches a period of the life span in which biological change is comparatively minimal. You may affect your body in a variety of ways—by diet and exercise, for example—but the next striking set of changes that are consistent consequences of aging occurs in middle and late adulthood.

PHYSICAL CHANGES IN ADULTHOOD

Some of the most obvious changes that occur with age relate to your physical appearance and abilities. As you grow older, you can expect your skin to wrinkle, your hair to thin and grey, and your height to decrease an inch or two. You can also expect some of your senses to become less acute. These changes do not appear suddenly at age 65. They occur gradually, beginning as soon as early adulthood. However, before we describe some common age-related changes, we want to make a more general point: Many physical changes arise not from aging but from *disuse*; research supports a general belief in the maxim "Use it or lose it." Older adults who maintain (or renew) a program of physical fitness may experience fewer of the difficulties that are often thought to be inevitable consequences of aging. (Note that we will reach exactly the same conclusion when we discuss cognitive and social aspects of middle and late adulthood.) Let's now look, however, at some changes that are largely unavoidable and frequently have an impact on the way adults think about their lives.

Vision The vast majority of people over 65 experience some loss of visual function (Carter, 1982; Pitts, 1982). With age, the lenses of people's eyes become yellowed and less flexible. The yellowing

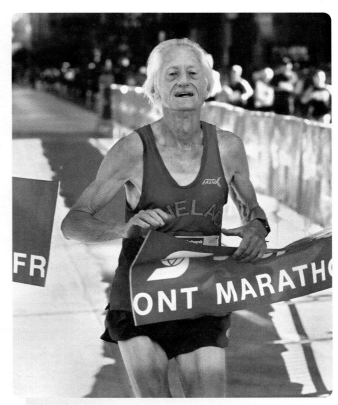

Why do researchers give the advice "Use it or lose it"?

of the lens is thought to be responsible for diminished colour vision experienced by some older people. Colours of lower wavelengths—violets, blues, and greens—are particularly hard for some older adults to discriminate. The rigidity of the lens can make seeing objects at close range difficult. Lens rigidity also affects dark adaptation, making night vision a problem for older people. Many normal visual changes can be aided with corrective lenses.

Hearing Hearing loss is common among those 60 and older. The average older adult has difficulty hearing high-frequency sounds (Corso, 1977). This impairment is usually greater for men than for women. Older adults can have a hard time understanding speech—particularly that spoken by high-pitched voices. (Oddly enough, with age, people's speaking voices increase in pitch due to stiffening of the vocal cords.) Deficits in hearing can be gradual and difficult for an individual to notice until they are extreme. In addition, even when individuals become aware of hearing loss, they may deny it because it is perceived as an undesirable sign of aging. Some of the physiological aspects of hearing loss can be overcome with the help of hearing aids. You should also be aware, as you grow older or interact with older adults, that it helps to speak in low tones, enunciate clearly, and reduce background noise, but it is usually not necessary to increase volume.

---

puberty The process through which sexual maturity is attained.

menarche The onset of menstruation.

Older adults can and do enjoy the many benefits of intimacy and sexual relationships. Why does this image clash with stereotypes of late adulthood?

Cognitive Development Across the Life Span

How does an individual's understanding of physical and social reality change across the life span? **Cognitive development** is the study of the processes and products of the mind as they emerge and change over time. As researchers have been particularly fascinated by the earliest emergence of cognitive capabilities, we will focus much of our attention on the earliest stages of cognitive development. However, we will also describe some of the discoveries researchers have made about cognitive development across the adult years.

As we begin this discussion of cognitive development, we want to remind you of a distinction we introduced in Chapter 4—*nature versus nurture*. The question is how best to account for the profound differences between a newborn and, for example, a 10-year-old: To what extent is such development determined by heredity (nature), and to what extent is it a product of learned experiences (nurture)? The debate concerning nature and nurture has a long history among philosophers, psychologists, and educators. On one side of this debate are those who believe that the human infant is born without knowledge or skills and that experience, in the form of human learning, etches messages on the blank tablet (in Latin, the *tabula rasa*) of the infant's unformed mind. This view, originally proposed by British philosopher **John Locke**, is known as *empiricism*. It credits human development to experience. Empiricists believe that what directs human development is the stimulation people receive as they are *nurtured*. Among the scholars opposing empiricism was French philosopher **Jean-Jacques Rousseau**. He argued the *nativist* view that *nature*, or the evolutionary legacy that each child brings into the world, is the mould that shapes development. Our discussion of cognitive development should lead you to see that there is truth to both sides of the debate. Children have innate preparation to learn from their experiences in the world.

We begin our discussion of cognitive development with the pioneering work of the late Swiss psychologist Jean Piaget.

PIAGET'S INSIGHTS INTO MENTAL DEVELOPMENT

For nearly 50 years, **Jean Piaget** (1929, 1954, 1977) developed theories about the ways that children think, reason, and solve problems. Perhaps Piaget's interest in cognitive development grew out of his own intellectually active youth: Piaget published his first article at age 10 and was offered a post as a museum curator at age 14 (Brainerd, 1996). Piaget used simple demonstrations and sensitive interviews with his own children and with other children to generate complex theories about early mental development. His interest was not in the amount of information children possessed, but in the ways their thinking and inner representations of physical reality changed at different stages in their development.

Reproductive and Sexual Functioning We saw that puberty marks the onset of reproductive functioning. In middle and late adulthood, reproductive capacity diminishes. Around age 50, most women experience *menopause*, the cessation of menstruation and ovulation. For men, changes are less abrupt, but the quantity of viable sperm falls off after age 40, and the volume of seminal fluid declines after age 60. Of course, these changes are relevant primarily to reproduction. Increasing age and physical change do not necessarily impair other aspects of sexual experience (DeLamater & Sill, 2005; Lindau et al., 2007). Indeed, sex is one of life's healthy pleasures that can enhance successful aging because it is arousing, provides aerobic exercise, stimulates fantasy, and is a vital form of social interaction.

You have had a brief review of the landmarks of physical development. Against that background, let's turn now to the ways in which you developed an understanding of the world around you.

STOP AND REVIEW

❶ How does experience with crawling influence children's performance on the visual cliff?

❷ What have recent studies demonstrated with respect to brain development in adolescence?

❸ Why does increasing age often have an effect on colour vision?

CRITICAL THINKING Consider the study on prenatal voice recognition. Why did the researchers have mothers tape-record the poems rather than having them read them "live"?

Building Blocks of Developmental Change Piaget gave the name **schemes** to the mental structures that enable individuals to interpret the world. Schemes are the building blocks of developmental change. Piaget characterized the

cognitive development The development of processes of knowing, including imagining, perceiving, reasoning, and problem solving.

schemes Piaget's term for cognitive structures that develop as infants and young children learn to interpret the world and adapt to their environment.

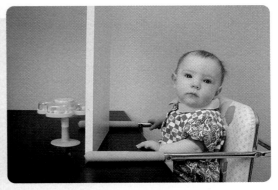

Piaget observed that the typical six-month-old will attend to an attractive toy (left) but will quickly lose interest if a screen blocks the toy from view (right). What understanding about objects will the child achieve by age two?

infant's initial schemes as *sensorimotor intelligence*—mental structures or programs that guide sensorimotor sequences, such as sucking, looking, grasping, and pushing. With practice, elementary schemes are combined, integrated, and differentiated into ever more complex, diverse action patterns, as when a child pushes away undesired objects to seize a desired one behind him or her. According to Piaget, two basic processes work in tandem to achieve cognitive growth—assimilation and accommodation. **Assimilation** modifies new environmental information to fit into what is already known; the child accesses existing schemes to structure incoming sensory data. **Accommodation** restructures or modifies the child's existing schemes so that new information is accounted for more completely.

Consider the transitions a baby must make from sucking at a mother's breast, to sucking the nipple of a bottle, to sipping through a straw, and then to drinking from a cup. The initial sucking response is a reflex action present at birth, but it must be modified somewhat so that the child's mouth fits the shape and size of the mother's nipple. In adapting to a bottle, an infant still uses many parts of the sequence unchanged (assimilation), but must grasp and draw on the rubber nipple somewhat differently from before and learn to hold the bottle at an appropriate angle (accommodation). The steps from bottle to straw to cup require more accommodation but continue to rely on earlier skills. Piaget saw cognitive development as the result of exactly this sort of interweaving of assimilation and accommodation. The balanced application of assimilation and accommodation permits children's behaviour and knowledge to become less dependent on concrete external reality, relying more on abstract thought.

TABLE 11.2 Piaget's Stages of Cognitive Development

Stage/Ages	Characteristics and Major Accomplishments
Sensorimotor (0–2)	Child begins life with small number of sensorimotor sequences. Child develops object permanence and the beginnings of symbolic thought.
Preoperational (2–7)	Child's thought is marked by egocentrism and centration. Child has improved ability to use symbolic thought.
Concrete operations (7–11)	Child achieves understanding of conservation. Child can reason with respect to concrete, physical objects.
Formal operations (11→)	Child develops capacity for abstract reasoning and hypothetical thinking.

Stages in Cognitive Development Piaget believed that children's cognitive development could be divided into a series of four ordered, discontinuous stages (see **Table 11.2**). All children are assumed to progress through these stages in the same sequence, although one child may take longer than another to pass through a given stage.

Sensorimotor Stage The sensorimotor stage extends roughly from birth to age two. In the early months, much of an infant's behaviour is based on a limited array of inborn schemes, like sucking, looking, grasping, and pushing. During the first year, sensorimotor sequences are improved, combined, co-ordinated, and integrated (sucking and grasping, looking and manipulating, for example). They become more varied as infants discover that their actions have an effect on external events.

assimilation According to Piaget, the process whereby new cognitive elements are fitted in with old elements or modified to fit more easily; this process works in tandem with accommodation.

accommodation According to Piaget, the process of restructuring or modifying cognitive structures so that new information can fit into them more easily; this process works in tandem with assimilation.

The most important cognitive acquisition of the infancy period is the ability to form mental representations of absent objects—those with which the child is not in direct sensorimotor contact. In the first months of life, children follow objects with their eyes, but, when the objects disappear from view, they turn away as if the objects had also disappeared from their minds. At around 3 months of age, however, they keep looking at the place where the objects had disappeared. Between 8 and 12 months, children begin to search for those disappearing objects. By age 2 years, children have no remaining uncertainty that "out of sight" objects continue to exist (Flavell, 1985). **Object permanence** refers to children's understanding that objects exist and behave independently of the child's own actions or awareness.

Preoperational Stage The preoperational stage extends roughly from two to seven years of age. The big cognitive advance in this developmental stage is an improved ability to represent mentally objects that are not physically present. In this case, children must have some type of stored representation of objects that they can use when the objects are not present. A child can, for example, tell you about her dog when she is in the grocery store, even though the dog is not around. Except for this development, Piaget characterizes the preoperational stage according to what the child *cannot* do. For example, Piaget believed that young children's preoperational thought is marked by **egocentrism**, the child's inability to take the perspective of another person. You have probably noticed egocentrism if you have heard a two-year-old's conversations with other children. Children at this age often seem to be talking to themselves rather than interacting.

Preoperational children also experience **centration**—the tendency to have their attention captured by the more perceptually striking features of objects. Centration is illustrated by Piaget's classic demonstration of a child's inability to understand that the amount of a liquid does not change as a function of the size or shape of its container.

> When an equal amount of lemonade is poured into two identical glasses, children of ages five and seven report that the glasses contain the same amount. When, however, the lemonade from one glass is poured into a tall, thin glass, their opinions diverge. The five-year-olds know that the lemonade in the tall glass is the same lemonade, but they report that it now is *more*. The seven-year-olds correctly assert that there is no difference between the amounts.

In Piaget's demonstration, the younger children centre on a single, perceptually salient dimension—the height of the lemonade in the glass. The older children take into account

both height and width and correctly infer that appearance is not reality.

Concrete Operations Stage The concrete operations stage goes roughly from 7 to 11 years of age. At this stage, the child has become capable of *mental operations*, actions performed in the mind that give rise to logical thinking. The preoperational and concrete operations stages are often put in contrast because children in the concrete operations stage are now capable of what they failed at earlier on. Concrete operations allow children to replace physical action with mental action. For example, if a child sees that Adam is taller than Zara and, later, that Zara is taller than Tanya, the child can reason that Adam is the tallest of the three—without physically manipulating the three individuals. However, the child still cannot draw the appropriate inference ("Adam is tallest") if the problem is just stated with a verbal description. This inability to determine relative heights (and solve similar problems) without direct physical observation suggests that abstract thought is still in the offing during the period of concrete operations.

The lemonade study illustrates another hallmark of the concrete operations period. The seven-year-olds have mastered what Piaget called **conservation**: They know that the physical properties of objects do not change when nothing is added or taken away, even though the objects' appearance changes. **Figure 11.6** presents examples of Piaget's tests of conservation for different dimensions. One of the newly acquired operations children can bring to bear on conservation tasks is reversibility. *Reversibility* is the child's understanding that both physical actions and mental operations can be reversed: The child can reason that the amount of lemonade *cannot* have changed because when the physical action is reversed—when the lemonade is poured back into the original glass—the two volumes will once again look identical.

Formal Operations Stage The formal operations stage covers a span roughly from age 11 on. In this final stage of cognitive growth, thinking becomes abstract. Adolescents can see how their particular reality is only one of several imaginable realities, and they begin to ponder deep questions of truth, justice, and existence. They seek answers to problems in a systematic fashion: Once they achieve formal operations, children can start to play the role of scientist, trying each of a series of possibilities in careful order. Adolescents also begin to be able to use the types of advanced deductive logic we described in Chapter 9. Unlike their younger siblings, adolescents have the ability to reason from abstract premises ("If A, then B" and "not B") to their logical conclusions ("not A").

CONTEMPORARY PERSPECTIVES ON EARLY COGNITIVE DEVELOPMENT

Piaget's theory remains the classic reference point for the understanding of cognitive development (Flavell, 1996; Lourenço & Machado, 1996; Scholnick, Nelson, Gelman, & Miller, 1999). However, contemporary researchers have come up with more flexible ways of studying the development of the child's cognitive abilities.

Infant Cognition We have already detailed some of the tasks Piaget used to draw conclusions about cognitive development. However, contemporary researchers have developed innovative techniques that have allowed them to re-evaluate some of Piaget's

---

object permanence The recognition that objects exist independently of an individual's action or awareness; an important cognitive acquisition in infancy.

egocentrism In cognitive development, the inability of a young child at the preoperational stage to take the perspective of another person.

centration A thought pattern common during the beginning of the preoperational stage of cognitive development; characterized by the child's inability to take more than one perceptual factor into account at the same time.

conservation According to Piaget, the understanding that physical properties do not change when nothing is added or taken away, even though appearances may change.

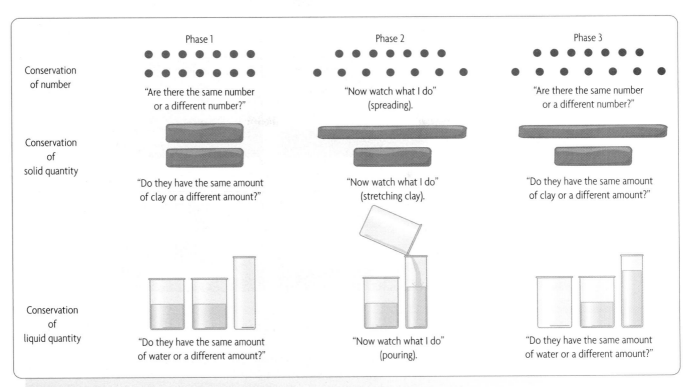

Phase 1 | Phase 2 | Phase 3

Conservation of number

"Are there the same number or a different number?"

"Now watch what I do" (spreading).

"Are there the same number or a different number?"

Conservation of solid quantity

"Do they have the same amount of clay or a different amount?"

"Now watch what I do" (stretching clay).

"Do they have the same amount of clay or a different amount?"

Conservation of liquid quantity

"Do they have the same amount of water or a different amount?"

"Now watch what I do" (pouring).

"Do they have the same amount of water or a different amount?"

FIGURE 11.6 Tests of Conservation

conclusions. Consider object permanence, which Piaget suggested was the major accomplishment of the two-year-old child. Contemporary research techniques suggest that infants as young as three months old have already developed aspects of this concept. This important finding has been shown with different tasks devised by researcher **Renée Baillargeon** and her colleagues.

In one study, four-month-old infants watched while an experimenter lowered a wide rectangular object (see **Figure 11.7**) (Wang, Baillargeon, & Brueckner, 2004). In one condition, the path of the rectangular object would put it behind a *wide occluder*—a second object wide enough to hide the rectangular object completely. In the other condition, the rectangular object was destined to pass behind a *narrow occluder*—an object too narrow to occlude the object fully. As this event unfolded, a screen appeared that hid the final moment in which the rectangular object was lowered. When the screen disappeared, the rectangular object was fully hidden. How did the infants respond in the two conditions? If they did not have object permanence, we would expect them to be equally unbothered in both cases; once the rectangular object was gone, we would expect them to have no recollection that it had ever existed. Suppose they did have some recollection of

This five-year-old girl is aware that the two containers have the same amount of coloured liquid. However, when the liquid from one is poured into a taller container, she indicates that there is more liquid in the taller one. She has not yet grasped the concept of conservation, which she will understand by age six or seven. Why would the five-year-old child not understand the concept, even if she were told the right answer?

Wide-Occluder Event

Narrow-Occluder Event

FIGURE 11.7 Four-month-olds and Object Permanence

Four-month-olds watched an experimenter lower a rectangular object (shown in brown) behind a wide occluder or a narrow occluder (each shown in patterned green). As the event unfolded, a screen appeared to mask the moment at which the object passed behind the occluder. When the screen disappeared, the experimenter's hand was empty. The infants who saw the narrow-occluder event spent more time looking at the display, suggesting they were surprised that a wide object could be hidden behind a narrow occluder. The infants' surprise suggests they have attained some aspects of object permanence: The rectangular object was out of sight but not out of mind.

From *Cognition, 93*, Su-hua Wang et al., "Young infants' reasoning about hidden objects: Evidence from violation-of-expectation tasks with test trials only," pp. 167–198. Copyright © 2004, with permission from Elsevier.

the object. In that case, we would expect that they—like adults who watched the events—would be rather surprised that a wide object could be hidden by a narrow occluder. To assess the infants' degree of surprise, the researchers recorded how long infants looked at the displays after the screen disappeared. The infants who saw the large rectangular object disappear behind the narrow occluder event looked at the display for about 16 seconds longer than their peers who saw the wide occluder event.

We cannot take the infants' surprise as evidence that they have acquired the full concept of object permanence—they may only know that something is wrong without knowing exactly what that something is (Lourenço & Machado, 1996). Even so, the research by Baillargeon and her colleagues suggests that even very young children have acquired important knowledge of the physical world.

The innovative methods researchers have developed to penetrate infants' minds continue to transform our understanding of what infants know and how they know it. Consider the relationship between actions and goals. As an adult, you are accustomed to inferring people's goals when you watch them perform actions. For example, if you see someone pull out a set of keys, you easily infer that he or she needs to unlock something. When did you start to understand how actions relate to goals? Research suggests that three-month-olds have begun to understand these relationships—but only when they have

appropriate experience of their own (Sommerville, Woodward, & Needham, 2005). To support that claim, researchers outfitted one group of three-month-olds with special Velcro mittens that allowed them to pick up toys. (Children of this age do not have difficulty grasping objects without this extra assistance.) A second group of children did not have that novel experience of picking up toys. Both groups of children watched an experimenter perform a series of events that also involved grasping toys. An adult watching those events would infer that the experimenter had the particular goal, for example, of picking up a teddy bear. The group of children with grasping experience appeared to make that inference, but their inexperienced peers did not. This result brings us full circle to Piaget. Piaget suggested that children's knowledge is built up from active experience in the environment. What you may have noticed about this study was that the children were watching the behaviour of someone and learned from this. When do we learn to do this about more complex behaviours, like using language? University of British Columbia's Susan Birch found that three- and four-year-olds are able to use the behaviour of others to learn new words and functions of objects (Birch, Vauthier, & Bloom, 2008). These studies confirm that active experience helps children learn how actions and goals fit together.

Children's Foundational Theories Piaget's theory is built around stages in which landmark changes take place in children's ways of thinking. More recently, researchers have

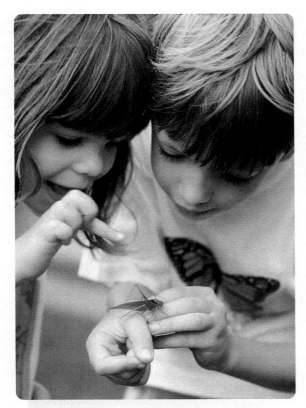

How do children begin to form generalizations about the world based on what they have experienced and observed?

Many prominent figures, such as Nelson Mandela, continue to make important professional contributions through their 70s and beyond. How can some aspects of intellectual performance be kept from declining through late adulthood?

explored the idea that changes occur separately, in each of several major domains, as children develop **foundational theories**—frameworks for initial understanding—to explain their experiences of the world (Gelman & Raman, 2002; Wellman & Inagaki, 1997). For example, children accumulate their experiences of the properties of mental states into a *theory of mind*, or naive psychology. By doing so, they are better able to understand the thought processes of themselves and others. This understanding, although requiring experience of the world, occurs at similar ages across the world and in different cultures (Callaghan et al., 2005). At approximately five years of age children will, for example, understand that if you put marbles in a box made for crayons, another person would assume there are crayons in the box. Before this age, children assume that the observer has the same knowledge they do and would indicate that the box contained marbles. The ability to do this seems to be impaired in children with autism and may indicate not that they do not understand the world, but that they do not understand the thoughts others would have.

Researchers have formally studied the development of scientific concepts, such as the way in which children project biological properties from one species to another. When asked which of a series of animals sleep or have bones, four-year-old children were inclined to make their judgments based on their perceptions of the similarity of the animal to humans (Carey, 1985). For example, more four-year-olds attributed these properties (i.e., "sleep" and "have bones") to dogs than they did to fish, and attributions to fish were, in turn, greater than those to

flies. Over time, children must replace a theory based on similarity to humans with one that acknowledges more structure in the animal kingdom; for example, they must acquire the formal distinction between *vertebrates* and *invertebrates*, which defines the types of animals that have bones. Similarly, three- and four-year-old children understand that what is inside an object affects its functions—although they have no clear idea what those insides are (Gelman, 2003; Gelman & Wellman, 1991). Thus although three- and four-year-olds are not entirely sure what kinds of things are inside dogs, they are quite certain that a dog would cease to be a dog if you removed whatever is inside. In each domain, you see that children begin to develop a general theory and then use a range of new experiences to provide successive refinements.

Social and Cultural Influences on Cognitive Development Another focus of contemporary research is on the role of social interactions in cognitive development. Much of this research has its origins in the theories of Russian psychologist **Lev Vygotsky**. Vygotsky argued that children develop through a process of **internalization**: They absorb knowledge from their social context that has a major impact on how cognition unfolds over time.

The social theory Vygotsky pioneered has found support in cross-cultural studies of development. As Piaget's theory initially seized the attention of developmental researchers, many of them sought to use his tasks to study the cognitive achievements of children in diverse cultures (Rogoff, 2003; Rogoff & Chavajay, 1995). These studies began to call into question the

---

foundational theories Frameworks for initial understanding formulated by children to explain their experiences of the world.

internalization According to Vygotsky, the process through which children absorb knowledge from the social context.

universality of Piaget's claims because, for example, people in many cultures failed to show evidence that they had acquired formal operations, as defined by Piaget. Late in his life, Piaget himself began to speculate that the specific achievements he characterized as formal operations may rely more on the particular type of science education children obtain rather than on an unfolding of biologically predetermined stages of cognitive development (Lourenço & Machado, 1996).

Vygotsky's concept of internalization helps explain the effect culture has on cognitive development. Children's cognition develops to perform culturally valued functions (Serpell, 2000; Serpell & Boykin, 1994). Piaget, for example, invented tasks that reflected his own preconceptions about appropriate and valuable cognitive activities. Other cultures prefer their children to excel in other ways. If Piaget's children had been evaluated with respect to their understanding of the cognitive complexities of weaving, they probably would have appeared to be retarded in their development relative to Mayan children in Guatemala (Rogoff, 1990). Cross-cultural studies of cognitive development have quite often demonstrated that type of schooling plays a large role in determining children's achievement on Piagetian tasks (Rogoff & Chavajay, 1995). Psychologists must use these types of findings to sort out the nature and nurture of cognitive development.

The developmental changes we have documented so far are very dramatic. It is easy to tell that a 12-year-old has all sorts of cognitive capabilities unknown to a 1-year-old. We now shift to the more subtle changes that take place throughout adulthood.

COGNITIVE DEVELOPMENT IN ADULTHOOD

As we have traced cognitive development across childhood into adolescence, "change" has usually meant "change for the better." When we arrive at the period of late adulthood, though, cultural stereotypes suggest that "change" means "change for the worse" (Parr & Siegert, 1993). However, even when people believe that the course of adulthood brings with it general decline, they still anticipate certain types of gains very late into life (Dixon & de Frias, 2004).

The Canadian Study of Health and Aging (CSHA) began in 1991 and has continued with multiple follow-ups on over 10 000 participants across Canada. The provinces have developed similar kinds of studies on smaller cohorts. The Aging in Manitoba studies have yielded a tremendous amount of data that researchers have used to assess healthy aging and differences in aging with respect to memory and health. Verena Menec, the director for the Centre on Aging at the University of Manitoba, and colleagues (Menec, Shooshtari, & Lambert, 2007) found that eastern Europeans were more likely to rate their health as bad than were individuals with Canadian or British backgrounds. The data are informative since many tests of functioning are done by asking participants to self-report on their ability to function as they age. The study suggests that cultural factors may impact how participants report. Other researchers (Bailis & Chipperfield, 2002) used the data to assess how individuals who felt they had control over their lives reported health. The data suggest that perceived control and high levels of self-esteem are predictive of better health outcomes as individuals age.

Let's now turn to intelligence and memory to further explore the interplay of losses and gains as people age.

Intelligence There is little evidence to support the notion that general cognitive abilities decline among the healthy elderly. Only about 5 percent of the population experiences major losses in cognitive functioning. When age-related decline in cognitive functioning occurs, it is usually limited to only some abilities. When intelligence is separated into the components that make up your verbal abilities (*crystallized intelligence*) and those that are part of your ability to learn quickly and thoroughly (*fluid intelligence*), fluid intelligence shows the greater decline with age (Baltes & Staudinger, 1993; Singer, Verhaegen, Ghisletta, Lindenberger, & Baltes, 2003). Much of the decrease in fluidity has been attributed to a general slowing down of processing speed: Older adults' performance on intellectual tasks that require many mental processes to occur in small amounts of time is greatly impaired (Sheppard & Vernon, 2008).

Researchers who study cognitive performance have been quite interested in determining what older adults might do to minimize declines with age. Much research attention has considered the maxim "use it or lose it." One study, for example, focused on a group of older adults whose average age was 69 (Bielak et al., 2007). The adults whose everyday lives had the highest levels of social, physical, and intellectual activities also showed the fastest processing speed on cognitive tasks. These results seem to support the "use it or lose it" philosophy. We do have to consider these results with the caveat that correlation is not causation: Although the results could indicate that high levels of activity cause cognitive processing to remain relatively high, there is also the possibility that smaller declines in processing speed allow some older adults to remain more active.

Even if it is difficult to prove that "using it" prevents "losing it," researchers have provided evidence that "using it more" can bring about better intellectual functioning. They have devised training programs that are able to reverse older adults' decline in some cognitive processing abilities (Schaie, 2005).

Not all change is in the direction of poorer functioning. Research indicates that older adults who pursue high levels of environmental stimulation tend to maintain high levels of cognitive abilities.

> A group of 22 senior professors, ages 60 to 71, from the University of California, Berkeley, were compared in their intellectual functioning to their younger colleagues (ages 30 to 59) and to a control group of older adults in the same age range. The professors performed a variety of tests that tapped different aspects of cognitive functioning. On some of the tests the senior professors showed typical patterns of age-related impairment. However, on other measures, the senior professors kept pace with their younger colleagues. For example, they were equally able to listen to tape recordings of brief stories and recall information from those stories. The control group of older adults showed typical age-related impairment on this task. How can we explain preserved function for the professors? The researchers suggest that the professors' occupation, which requires them to maintain a high level of mental activity, may protect them from some typical losses of aging (Shimamura, Berry, Mangels, Rusting, & Jurica, 1995).

Does this finding make you want to become a university professor? Other studies suggest that you need not go to that extreme. Research using fMRI scans has suggested, for example, that older adults with more education are better able to

Psychology in Your Life

WILL YOUR BRAIN WORK DIFFERENTLY AS YOU AGE?

If you have spent time with older adults, you have probably heard them make casual claims like, "My brain just doesn't work as well as it used to work." Researchers have believed for a long time that older brains function differently from younger brains. However, as brain-imaging techniques have become more available as research tools, an understanding of those changes has grown. Images of the brain at work reveal consistent differences in patterns of brain activity over the adult years.

Let's consider brain activity related to two tasks that should be roughly familiar from earlier chapters. One task assessed participants' ability to use working memory: They attempted to commit four words to working memory and then indicated whether a subsequent probe word had been among that original group. A second task assessed participants' ability to engage visual attention: They monitored a video display of the letter B to determine whether it had briefly disappeared one time, or two times, or not at all, over the course of a trial. The participants for the two tasks were younger adults (with an average age of 22.6 years) and older adults (with an average age of 70.3 years). The two groups were equally accurate on the two tasks, although the younger adults were faster. The figure reveals the results of fMRI scans that participants underwent as they performed each task (Cabeza et al., 2004). The coloured areas are the regions that were most active for each task. What you can see, as indicated by the arrows, is that the older adults showed a pattern of brain activity in which both hemispheres of the brain were more active.

To understand these results, recall from Chapter 4 the finding that the brain's two hemispheres typically carry out different types of processes. The fMRI scans in the figure indicate that the brains of older adults become more symmetrical with respect to the functions in which they play a role (Cabeza, 2002). Researchers have offered two general explanations for this developmental change in the way that processes are distributed to the brain's two hemispheres. Some researchers have argued that when older brains recruit areas different from those used by younger brains, that activity represents *compensations* for other aging-related changes in the brain. Other researchers have argued that brain activation unique to older adults reflects *distraction*—an inability to inhibit unnecessary brain activity.

In fact, researchers have found evidence suggesting that both compensation and distraction are at work in the aging brain. To provide evidence for compensation, a study using PET scans examined the relationship between individual differences in brain activity and recognition memory performance (Grady, McIntosh, & Craik, 2005). As in earlier studies, older adults were likely to show activity in brain areas that were mostly not active for younger adults. Moreover, there was a positive correlation such that the *more* active those areas were, the *better* the older adults performed on recognition memory. That result supports the idea that the use of these brain areas yields an advantage for older adults. However, researchers have also carried out fMRI studies spanning several memory tasks to demonstrate that there are certain areas that older brains appear unable to turn off (Grady, Springer, Hongwanishkul, McIntosh, & Winocur, 2006). The consistent appearance of brain activity that is not task-relevant provides evidence that some age-related differences in brain function result in distraction from the task at hand.

This body of research supports the conclusion that your brain will, in fact, work differently as you age. The changes in function reflect compensation and distraction with respect to day-to-day cognitive tasks.

From R. Cabeza et al., "Task-independent and task-specific age effects in brain activity during working memory, visual attention, and episodic retrieval," *Cerebral Cortex, 14, 372,* 2004, by permission of Oxford University Press, Inc.

compensate for natural decline in their aging brains than are their less educated peers (Springer, McIntosh, Wincour, & Grady, 2005). There is another good reason to continue your education. Animal research, particularly that of Greenough and colleagues (Black, Greenough, Anderson, & Isaacs, 1987; Black, Polinsky, & Greenough, 1989; Studenski et al., 2006), suggests that maintaining novelty in your life and environment as you age also has significant benefits to healthy aging.

The general conclusion is that you should keep your mind at work. It appears that disuse, rather than decay, may be responsible for the deficits in intellectual performance that are not related to processing speed (Hultsch, Hertzog, Small, & Dixon, 1999). As promised, we have again arrived at the conclusion that "Use it or lose it (or seek training to get it back)" is an appropriate motto for the wise older adult.

How can older adults cope successfully with whatever changes inevitably accompany increasing age? Successful aging might consist of making the most of gains while minimizing the impact of the normal losses that accompany aging. This strategy for successful aging, proposed by psychologists **Paul Baltes** and **Margaret Baltes**, is called **selective optimization with compensation** (Baltes, Smith, & Staudinger, 1992; Freund & Baltes, 1998). *Selective* means that people scale down the number and extent of their goals for themselves. *Optimization* refers to people exercising or training themselves in areas that are of highest priority to them. *Compensation* means that people use alternative ways to deal with losses—for example, choosing age-friendly environments. Let's consider an example:

> When the concert pianist [Arthur] Rubinstein was asked, in a television interview, how he managed to remain such a successful pianist in his old age, he mentioned three strategies: (1) In old age he performed fewer pieces, (2) he now practiced each piece more frequently, and (3) he produced more ritardandos [slowings of the tempo] in his playing before fast segments, so that the playing speed sounded faster than it was in reality. These are examples of selection (fewer pieces), optimization (more practice), and compensation (increased use of contrast in speed). (Baltes, 1993, p. 590)

Memory A common complaint among the elderly is the feeling that their ability to remember things is not as good as it used to be. On a number of tests of memory, adults over 60 *do* perform worse than young adults in their 20s (Hess, 2005). People experience memory deficits with advancing age, even when they have been highly educated and otherwise have good intellectual skills (Zelinski, Gilewski, & Schaie, 1993). Aging does *not* seem to diminish elderly individuals' ability to access their general knowledge store and personal information about events that occurred long ago. In a study of name and face recognition, middle-aged adults could identify 90 percent of their high-school classmates in yearbooks 35 years after graduation; older adults were still able to recognize 70 to 80 percent of their classmates some 50 years later (Bahrick, Bahrick, & Wittlinger, 1975). However, aging affects the processes that allow new

information to be effectively organized, stored, and retrieved (Craik, 1994; Giambra & Arenberg, 1993; Grady & Craik, 2000).

Other memory disadvantages may be influenced by aging as well. Researchers in Toronto at the Baycrest Centre for Geriatric Care and the Rotman Institute collaborated to look at how young and older individuals recalled list of words. On each test day, the participants learned a different list of 15 words over four trials. Younger adults did much better on recall, delayed recall, and recognition tasks than the older participants did. Older adults also showed a greater frequency of false memory, where lists learned previously influenced what was recalled. In addition, their memories did not allow them to recall exactly when the lists had been presented.

As yet, researchers have been unable to develop a wholly adequate description of the mechanisms that underlie memory impairment in older adults, perhaps because the impairment has multiple sources (Hess, 2005). Some theories focus on differences between older and younger people in their efforts to organize and process information. Other theories point to elderly people's reduced ability to pay attention to information. Another type of theory looks to neurobiological changes in the brain systems that produce the physical memory traces. We explore these ideas in the *Psychology in Your Life* box. Note that these brain changes are not the same as the abnormal tangles of neural tissue and plaques that cause the memory loss of Alzheimer's disease (see Chapter 8). Researchers also believe that older adults' performance may be impaired by their very belief that their memory will be poor (Hertzog, Dixon, & Hultsch, 1990; Levy & Langer, 1994). Researchers continue to evaluate the relative contributions of each of these factors.

Let's now narrow our focus from general cognitive development to the more specific topic of the acquisition of language.

STOP AND REVIEW

❶ In Piaget's theory, what is the relationship between assimilation and accommodation?

❷ What does it mean when a child is able to overcome centration?

❸ How has contemporary research modified conclusions about object permanence?

❹ What was the major emphasis of Lev Vygotsky's theory?

❺ What is meant by selective optimization with compensation?

CRITICAL THINKING Recall the experiment that looked at the performance of older professors. Why was it important to use younger professors as the comparison group of younger adults?

Acquiring Language

Here is a remarkable fact: By the time they are six years old, children can analyze language into its units of sound and meaning, use the rules they have discovered to combine sounds into words and words into meaningful sentences, and take an active part in coherent conversations. Children's remarkable language

---

selective optimization with compensation A strategy for successful aging in which one makes the most gains while minimizing the impact of losses that accompany normal aging.

TABLE 11.3 The Structure of Language

Grammar is the field of study that seeks to describe the way language is structured and used. It includes several domains:

Phonology—the study of the sounds that are put together to form words.

A **phoneme** is the smallest unit of speech that distinguishes between any two utterances. For example, *b* and *p* distinguish *bin* from *pin*.

Phonetics is the study and classification of speech sounds.

Syntax—the way in which words are strung together to form sentences. For example, subject *(I)* + verb *(like)* + object *(you)* is standard English word order.

A **morpheme** is the minimum distinctive unit of grammar that cannot be divided without losing its meaning. The word *bins* has two morphemes, *bin* and *s*, indicating the plural.

Semantics—the study of the meanings of words and their changes over time.

Lexical meaning is the dictionary meaning of a word. Meaning is sometimes conveyed by the *context* of a word in a sentence ("Run *fast*" versus "Make the knot *fast*") or the *inflection* with which it is spoken (try emphasizing different words in *white house cat*).

Pragmatics—rules for participation in conversations; social conventions for communicating, sequencing sentences, and responding appropriately to others.

accomplishments have prompted most researchers to agree that the ability to learn language is biologically based—that you are born with an innate language capacity (Pinker, 1994). Even so, depending on where a child happens to be born, he or she may end up as a native speaker of any one of the world's 4000 different languages. In addition, children are prepared to learn both spoken languages and gestural languages, like American Sign Language. This means that the innate predisposition to learn language must be both quite strong and quite flexible (Meier, 1991).

To explain how it is that infants are such expert language learners, we will describe the evidence that supports the claim of an innate language capacity. We will also discuss the role that the environment plays; after all, children learn the particular languages that are being used in the world around them. **Table 11.3** outlines the various types of knowledge children must acquire for their particular signed or spoken language. You might review the language use section of Chapter 9 (pages 257 to 267) to remind yourself how adults put all these types of knowledge to use in fluent conversation.

PERCEIVING SPEECH AND PERCEIVING WORDS

Imagine you are a newborn child, hearing a buzz of noise all around you. How do you start to understand that some of those sounds are relevant to communicating with other people? A child's first step in acquiring a particular language is to take note

of the sound contrasts that are used meaningfully in that language. (For signed languages, the child must attend to contrasts in hand positions, for example.) Each spoken language samples from the set of possible distinctions that can be produced by the human vocal tract; no language uses all of the speech–sound contrasts that can be made. The minimal meaningful units in a language are known as **phonemes**. There are about 45 distinct phonemes in English. Imagine you heard someone speak the words *right* and *light*. If you are a native speaker of English, you would have no trouble hearing the difference—/r/ and /l/ are different phonemes in English. If your only language experience was with Japanese, however, you would not be able to hear the difference between these two words because /r/ and /l/ are not distinct phonemes in Japanese. Do English speakers acquire the ability to make this distinction, or do Japanese speakers lose it?

To answer this type of question, researchers needed to develop methods to obtain linguistic information from prelinguistic children.

Using principles of operant conditioning we described in Chapter 7, researchers condition infants to turn their head toward a sound source when they detect a change from one speech sound to another. The reward that reinforces this behaviour is an illuminated box that contains a clapping and drumming toy animal. The procedure ensures that, if the children detect changes, they are very likely to turn toward the sound source. To measure the children's ability to perceive a distinction, researchers monitor how frequently the children turn their heads when a change is present.

Janet Werker and her colleagues (Werker, 1991; Werker & Lalond, 1988) have used this technique to examine the innate basis of speech perception abilities, a version of the /r/–/l/ question we posed earlier. Werker's earlier studies investigated sound distinctions that are used in Hindi, but not in English—distinctions that make it difficult for adult English speakers to learn Hindi. Werker and her colleagues measured the ability of infants learning English or Hindi, as well as adults who spoke English or Hindi, to hear the differences between the Hindi phonemes. She found that all the infants, regardless of which language they were learning, could hear the differences until the age of eight months. However, among the infants older than eight months as well as the adults, only the Hindi speakers or speakers-to-be could hear the Hindi contrasts.

In more recent studies, Werker has shown that even really young infants are more predisposed to listening to speech than to nonsense syllables that are similar to speech (Vouloumanos & Werker, 2007). A variety of research of this type strongly suggests that you started out with an innate ability to perceive sound contrasts that are important for spoken languages. However, you swiftly lose the ability to perceive some of the contrasts that are not present in the language you begin to acquire (Vouloumanos & Werker, 2007; Werker & Tees, 1999).

---

phonemes Minimal units of speech in any given language that make a meaningful difference in speech production and reception; /r/ and /l/ are two distinct phonemes in English but variations of one in Japanese.

Along with this biological head start for speech perception, many children also get an environmental head start. When adults in many cultures speak to infants and young children, they use a special form of language that differs from adult speech: an exaggerated, high-pitched intonation known as **child-directed speech**, or less formally as *motherese* or *parentese*. The features that define child-directed speech appear in many but not all cultures (Fernald & Morikawa, 1993; Kitamura, Thanavishuth, Burnham, & Luksaneeyanawin, 2002). Child-directed speech may help infants acquire language by keeping them interested in and attentive to the things that their parents say to them. The sound patterns of child-directed speech also emphasize emotional content, which might help forge an emotional bond between infants and their caregivers (Trainor, Austin, & Desjardins, 2000).

At what age are children able to perceive the repetition of patterns of sounds—words—within the stream of speech directed to them? This is the first big step toward acquiring language: You cannot learn that *doggie* has something to do with the shaggy thing in the corner until you recognize that the sound pattern *doggie* seems to recur in that shaggy thing's presence. Infants, on average, appear to gain the insight that repeated sounds have significance somewhere between ages six and seven months (Jusczyk, 2003; Jusczyk & Aslin, 1995). For one special word, however, the breakthrough comes a couple of months early: Children at age four months already show a recognition preference for their own names (Mandel, Jusczyk, & Pisoni, 1995)!

LEARNING WORD MEANINGS

Once you could detect the co-occurrence of sounds and experiences, you were prepared to start learning word meanings. There is no denying that children are excellent word learners. At around 18 months, children's word learning often takes off at an amazing rate. Researchers have called this phase the *naming explosion* because children begin to acquire new words, especially names for objects, at a rapidly increasing rate (see **Figure 11.8**). By the age of 6, the average child is estimated to understand 14 000 words (Templin, 1957). Assuming that most of these words are learned between the ages of 18 months and 6 years, this works out to about nine new words a day or almost one word per waking hour (Carey, 1978). How is this possible?

Imagine a straightforward situation in which a child and her father are walking through a park and the father points and says, "That's a doggie." The child must decide to which piece of the world *doggie* applies. This is no easy feat (Quine, 1960). Perhaps *doggie* means "any creature with four legs" or "the animal's fur" or "the animal's bark" or any of the other large set of meanings that will be true each time someone points toward a dog. Given all the possibilities, how are children able to fix the meanings of individual words?

Researchers suggest that children act like scientists—developing *hypotheses* about what each new word might mean. You can, for example, see children's scientific minds actively at work when they *overextend* words, using them incorrectly to cover a wide range of objects. They may use the word *doggie* to

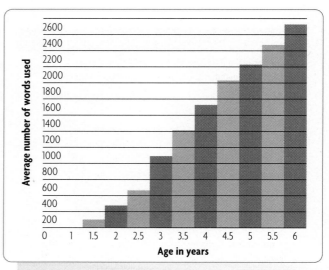

FIGURE 11.8 Children's Growth in Vocabulary

The number of words a child can use increases rapidly between the ages of 18 months and 6 years. This study shows children's average vocabularies at intervals of 6 months.

Source: B. A. Moskowitz, 1978. The acquisition of language. *Scientific American*, Inc. All rights reserved. Reprinted by permission.

refer to all animals, or the word *moon* to refer to all round objects, including clocks and coins. Other times, children might *underextend* a word—believing, for example, that *doggie* refers only to their own family dog.

The view that children form hypotheses, however, does not explain how children acquire particular meanings in particular contexts. Researchers have suggested that children's hypotheses are guided by expectations such as the *principle of contrast*. This principle suggests that differences in *forms* signal differences in *meaning*: When children hear new words, they should look for meanings that contrast with those for the words they already know (Clark, 2003). Suppose, for example, a father and daughter are watching a TV scene in which a kangaroo is jumping. The child knows the word *jump* but not the word *kangaroo*. Suppose the parent says, "Kangaroo!" What might happen next? Since the child already knows *jump*, she supposes that her parent would just say *jump* if *kangaroo* just meant "jump"—different forms should signal contrasts in meaning. The child can now hypothesize that *kangaroo* must label the object rather than the action. She is on her way to acquiring a meaning for *kangaroo*. If you have spent time around small children, you have probably noticed the principle of contrast at work. For example, a child will often become upset if his mother calls his fire *engine* a fire *truck*!

ACQUIRING GRAMMAR

To explain how children acquire meanings, we characterized children as scientists whose hypotheses are constrained by innate principles. We can use the same analogy to describe how children acquire the rules by which units of meaning are combined into larger units—in other words, grammar. The challenge for the child is that different languages follow different rules. For example, in English the typical ordering of units in a

---

child-directed speech A special form of speech with an exaggerated and high-pitched intonation that adults use to speak to infants and young children.

sentence is subject-verb-object, but in Japanese the ordering is subject-object-verb. Children must discover what order is present in the language being used around them. How do they do that?

Most researchers now believe that a large part of the answer resides in the human genome. Linguist **Noam Chomsky** (1965, 1975), for example, argued that children are born with mental structures that facilitate the comprehension and production of language. Some of the best evidence for such a biological basis for grammar comes from children who acquire complete grammatical structure in the absence of well-formed input. For example, researchers have studied deaf children whose hearing loss was sufficiently severe that they could not acquire spoken language but whose parents did not expose them to full-fledged signed languages such as American Sign Language (Goldin-Meadow, 2003). These children began to invent signing systems of their own and—despite the lack of environmental support for these invented languages—the gestural systems came to have regular, grammatical structure: "With or without an established language as a guide, children appear to be 'ready' to seek structure at least at word and sentence levels when developing systems for communication" (Goldin-Meadow & Mylander, 1990, p. 351). It turns out this is true whether children sign one language or multiple languages, as is the case in children in Quebec (Petitto et al., 2001).

How can researchers go about specifying exactly what knowledge is innately given? The most productive approach to this question is to study language acquisition across many languages—*cross-linguistically*. By examining what is hard and what is easy for children to acquire across the world's many languages, researchers can determine what aspects of grammar are most likely to be supported by innate predispositions.

Here we arrive back at the child as scientist. Children bring innate constraints to the task of learning a particular language. **Dan Slobin** has defined these guidelines as a set of *operating principles* that together constitute the child's **language-making capacity**. According to Slobin's (1985) theory, the operating principles take the form of directives to the child. Here, for

example, is an operating principle that helps children discover the words that go together to form a grammatical unit: "store together ordered sequences of word classes and functor classes that co-occur in the expression of a particular proposition type, along with a designation of the proposition type" (p. 1252). In simpler language, this operating principle suggests that children must keep track of the relationship between the order in which words appear and the meanings they express. Slobin derived the operating principles by summarizing across the data provided by a large number of other researchers, who examined a variety of different languages. We will use English examples to demonstrate the principles at work.

Consider what English-speaking children can do when they begin, at about age two, to use combinations of words—the *two-word stage*. Children's speech at this point has been characterized as *telegraphic* because it is filled with short, simple sequences using mostly nouns and verbs. Telegraphic speech lacks function words, such as *the*, *and*, and *of*, which help express the relationships between words and ideas. For example, "All gone milk" is a telegraphic message.

For adults to understand two-word utterances, they must know the context in which the words are spoken. "Tanya ball," for example, could mean, among other things, "Tanya wants the ball" or "Tanya throws the ball." Even so, children at the two-word stage show evidence that they have already acquired some knowledge of the grammar of English. Operating principles allow them to discover that word order is important in English and that the three critical elements are actor-action-object (subject-verb-object), arranged in that order. Evidence for this "discovery" comes when children misinterpret a sentence such as "Mary was followed by her little lamb to school" as *Mary* (actor) *followed* (action) *her lamb* (object) (see **Figure 11.9**). Over time, children must apply other operating principles to discover that there are exceptions to the actor-action-object rule.

Consider now an operating principle that Slobin calls *extension*, which requires children to try to use the same unit of meaning, or *morpheme*, to mark the same concept. Examples of such concepts are possession, past tense, and continuing action. In English, each of these concepts is expressed by adding a grammatical morpheme to a content word, such as -'s (e.g., Maria*'s*), -*ed* (e.g., call*ed*), and -*ing* (e.g., laugh*ing*). Note how the addition of each of these sounds to a noun or verb changes its meaning.

Children use operating principles like extension to form hypotheses about how these morphemes work. As this principle requires that the child try to mark all cases in the same way, however, the error of **over-regularization** often results. For example, once children learn the past-tense rule (adding -*ed* to the verb), they add -*ed* to all verbs, forming words such as *doed* and *breaked*. As children learn the rule for plurals (adding the sound -*s* or -*z* to the end of a word), they again overextend the rule, creating words such as *foots* and *mouses*. Over-regularization is an especially interesting error because it usually appears *after* children have learned and used the correct forms of verbs and nouns. The children first use the correct verb forms (for example, *came* and *went*), apparently because they learned them as

Children develop linguistic fluency by listening to the speech patterns of those around them. What are the roles of nature and nurture in the acquisition of grammar?

language-making capacity The innate guidelines or operating principles that children bring to the task of learning a language.

over-regularization A grammatical error, usually appearing during early language development, in which the rules of a language are applied too widely, resulting in incorrect linguistic forms.

FIGURE 11.9 Acquiring Grammar
Many toddlers would interpret "Mary was followed by the lamb" and "Mary followed the lamb" to have identical meanings.

separate vocabulary items; but when they learn the general rule for the past tense, they extend it even to verbs that are exceptions to the rule—words that they previously used correctly. Over time, children use other operating principles to overcome this temporary over-application.

Children's acquisition of language has a major impact on their ability to participate in social interactions. Keep that in mind as we shift our focus now to social development across the life span.

STOP AND REVIEW

❶ What are important functions of child-directed speech?
❷ Why do children overextend word meanings?
❸ How does research with deaf children support the idea that aspects of grammar are innate?
❹ How would you notice when a child is over-regularizing English past-tense constructions?

CRITICAL THINKING Consider the study on children's ability to perceive sound distinctions. Why was it important to compare English-speaking adults with infants who are English speakers-to-be?

Social Development Across the Life Span

We have seen so far how radically you change as a physical and cognitive being from birth to older adulthood. In this section of the chapter we explore **social development**: how individuals' social interactions and expectations change across the life span.

_____

social development The ways in which individuals' social interactions and expectations change across the life span.

We will see that social and cultural environment interacts with biological aging to provide each period of the life span with its own special challenges and rewards.

As we discuss social development, it is particularly important for you to consider the way in which culture and environment affect certain aspects of our lives. For example, people who live in circumstances of economic hardship undergo types of stresses that are absent from the "normal" course of development (Crockett & Silbereisen, 2000; Leventhal & Brooks-Gunn, 2000). Current trends in countries throughout the world make it imperative for developmental psychologists to consider the difficult circumstances in which many children, adolescents, and adults are forced to live—circumstances that continually put their sanity, safety, and survival at risk (Huston, 2005). As it is often difficult to travel to these countries to do research, much of the information comes from assessments of youth and young adults in North America, particularly of the differences between different ethnic groups in an area. North American culture also enforces different outcomes for men and for women and for individuals who belong to minority groups. For example, elderly women are more often economically disadvantaged than elderly men; elderly African-American women are worse off even than elderly white women (Carstensen & Pasupathi, 1993). In Canada, individuals from ethnic minorities often live in regions that have been defined as "stressed." Individuals from these areas are more likely to suffer from depression than the general population (Matheson et al., 2006). These differences are direct products of structural inequities in contemporary North America.

When we draw conclusions about the "average" life course, keep in mind that culture dictates that some individuals will depart from this average; as we describe the psychological challenges facing the "ordinary" individual, bear in mind that many individuals face extraordinary challenges. It is the role of researchers to document the impact of contemporary problems—and to design interventions to alleviate their harshest consequences. Major reforms are clearly needed to institute and co-ordinate better health care, welfare programs, and social policy. Psychologists will play a role in helping define what is in the best interest of families and their children (Scarr & Eisenberg, 1993). As we discuss social development, we will have several opportunities to revisit the impact of culture.

As you read the remainder of this chapter, keep in mind how the tasks of life are jointly determined by a biological accumulation of years and a social accumulation of cultural experiences. To begin our discussion of social development, we describe Erik Erikson's life span theory, which makes explicit the challenges and rewards in each of life's major periods.

ERIKSON'S PSYCHOSOCIAL STAGES

Erik Erikson (1963), who was trained by Sigmund Freud's daughter, Anna Freud, proposed that every individual must successfully navigate a series of **psychosocial stages**, each of which presents a particular conflict or crisis. Erikson identified eight stages in the life cycle. At each stage, a particular crisis comes into focus, as shown in **Table 11.4**. Although each conflict never completely disappears, it needs to be sufficiently resolved at a given stage if an individual is to cope successfully with the conflicts of later stages.

In Erikson's first stage, an infant needs to develop a basic sense of *trust* in the environment through interaction with caregivers. Trust is a natural accompaniment to a strong attachment relationship with a parent who provides food, warmth, and the comfort of physical closeness. A child whose basic needs are not met, and who experiences inconsistent handling, lack of physical closeness and warmth, and the frequent absence of a caring adult, may develop a pervasive sense of mistrust, insecurity, and anxiety.

With the development of walking and the beginnings of language, there is an expansion of a child's exploration and manipulation of objects (and sometimes people). With these

Erik Erikson's psychosocial stage model is a widely used tool for understanding human development over the life span. What crisis did Erikson suggest dominates individuals of your age?

psychosocial stages Proposed by Erik Erikson, successive developmental stages that focus on an individual's orientation toward the self and others; these stages incorporate both the sexual and social aspects of a person's development and the social conflicts that arise from the interaction between the individual and the social environment.

TABLE 11.4	Erikson's Psychosocial Stages		
Approximate Age	**Crisis**	**Adequate Resolution**	**Inadequate Resolution**
0–1½	Trust vs. mistrust	Basic sense of safety	Insecurity, anxiety
1½–3	Autonomy vs. self-doubt	Perception of self as agent capable of controlling own body and making things happen	Feelings of inadequacy to control events
3–6	Initiative vs. guilt	Confidence in oneself as initiator, creator	Feelings of lack of self-worth
6–puberty	Competence vs. inferiority	Adequacy in basic social and intellectual skills	Lack of self-confidence, feelings of failure
Adolescent	Identity vs. role confusion	Comfortable sense of self as a person	Sense of self as fragmented; shifting, unclear sense of self
Early adult	Intimacy vs. isolation	Capacity for closeness and commitment to another	Feeling of aloneness, separation; denial of need for closeness
Middle adult	Generativity vs. stagnation	Focus of concern beyond oneself to family, society, future orientation	Self-indulgent concerns; lack of future generations
Later adult	Ego integrity vs. despair	Sense of wholeness, basic satisfaction with life	Feelings of futility, disappointment

Childhood and Society by Erik H. Erikson. Copyright © 1950, 1963 by W.W. Norton & Company, Inc. renewed © 1978, 1991 by Erik H. Erikson. Used with permission of W.W. Norton & Company, Inc.

activities should come a comfortable sense of *autonomy* and of being a capable and worthy person. Excessive restriction or criticism at this second stage may lead instead to self-doubts, whereas demands beyond the child's ability, as in too-early or too-severe toilet training, can discourage the child's efforts to persevere in mastering new tasks.

Toward the end of the preschool period, a child who has developed a basic sense of trust, first in the immediate environment and then in himself or herself, can now *initiate* both intellectual and motor activities. The ways that parents respond to the child's self-initiated activities either encourage the sense of freedom and self-confidence needed for the next stage or produce guilt and feelings of being an inept intruder in an adult world.

During the elementary school years, the child who has successfully resolved the crises of the earlier stages is ready to go beyond random exploring and testing to the systematic development of *competencies*. School and sports offer arenas for learning intellectual and motor skills, and interaction with peers offers an arena for developing social skills. Successful efforts in these pursuits lead to feelings of competence. Some youngsters, however, become spectators rather than performers or experience enough failure to give them a sense of inferiority, leaving them unable to meet the demands of the next life stages.

Erikson believed that the essential crisis of adolescence is discovering one's true *identity* amid the confusion created by playing many different roles for the different audiences in an expanding social world. Resolving this crisis helps the individual develop a sense of a coherent self; failing to do so adequately may result in a self-image that lacks a central, stable core.

The essential crisis for the young adult is to resolve the conflict between *intimacy* and *isolation*—to develop the capacity to make full emotional, moral, and sexual commitments to other people. Making that kind of commitment requires that the individual compromise some personal preferences, accept some responsibilities, and yield some degree of privacy and independence. Failure to resolve this crisis adequately leads to isolation and the inability to connect to others in psychologically meaningful ways.

The next major opportunity for growth, which occurs during adult midlife, is known as *generativity*. People in their 30s and 40s move beyond a focus on self and partner to broaden their commitments to family, work, society, and future generations. Those people who have not resolved earlier developmental tasks are still self-indulgent, question past decisions and goals, and pursue freedom at the expense of security.

The crisis in later adulthood is the conflict between *ego integrity* and *despair*. Resolving the crises at each of the earlier stages prepares the older adult to look back without regrets and to enjoy a sense of wholeness. When previous crises are left unresolved, aspirations remain unfulfilled, and the individual experiences futility, despair, and self-depreciation.

You will see that Erikson's framework is very useful for tracking individuals' progress across the life span. We begin with childhood.

---

socialization The lifelong process whereby an individual's behavioural patterns, values, standards, skills, attitudes, and motives are shaped to conform to those regarded as desirable in a particular society.

temperament A child's biologically based level of emotional and behavioural response to environmental events.

SOCIAL DEVELOPMENT IN CHILDHOOD

Children's basic survival depends on forming meaningful, effective relationships with other people. **Socialization** is the lifelong process through which an individual's behaviour patterns, values, standards, skills, attitudes, and motives are shaped to conform to those regarded as desirable in a particular society. This process involves many people—relatives, friends, teachers—and institutions—schools, houses of worship—that exert pressure on the individual to adopt socially approved values and standards of conduct. The family, however, is the most influential shaper and regulator of socialization. The concept of family itself is being transformed to recognize that many children grow up in circumstances that include either less (a single parent) or more (an extended household) than a mother, father, and siblings. Whatever the configuration, though, the family helps the individual form basic patterns of responsiveness to others—and these patterns, in turn, become the basis of the individual's lifelong style of relating to other people.

Temperament Even as infants begin the process of socialization, they do not all start at the same place. Children begin life with differences in **temperament**—biologically based levels of emotional and behavioural response to the environment (Thomas & Chess, 1977). Researcher **Jerome Kagan** and his colleagues have demonstrated that some infants are "born shy" and other are "born bold" (Kagan & Snidman, 2004). These groups of children differ in sensitivity to physical and social stimulation: The shy or *inhibited* babies are consistently "cautious and emotionally reserved when they confront unfamiliar persons or contexts"; the bold or *uninhibited* babies are consistently "sociable, affectively spontaneous, and minimally fearful in the same unfamiliar situations" (Kagan & Snidman, 1991, p. 40). In one sample, about 10 percent of the infants were inhibited and about 25 percent were uninhibited; the rest of the infants fell between those endpoints (Kagan & Snidman, 1991). Researchers have demonstrated that differences in temperament can be detected even while babies are still in the womb: High levels of fetal activity are associated with increased difficulty with social interactions once the children are born (DiPietro, Hodgson, Costigan, & Johnson, 1996).

Longitudinal studies have demonstrated the long-term impact of early temperament. Children who, at age four months, displayed inhibited and uninhibited temperaments continue to behave differently as they get older (Kagan & Snidman, 2004). At age two, the inhibited children generally showed the most fear—and the uninhibited children the least fear—when they were faced with unfamiliar events. At age four, the uninhibited children were considerably more likely to be sociable when interacting with unfamiliar children. However, not all children who start out at the extreme ends of the dimension of inhibited versus uninhibited remain at those extremes; some children become less shy or more bold as they age (Pfeifer, Goldsmith, Davidson, & Rickman, 2002). Yet even when children's responses become less extreme, they very rarely shift from one category to the other. For example, a child who started out life as inhibited might become less shy over time, but he or she would rarely switch over to being a bold child.

Infant temperament sets the stage for later aspects of social development. Next, we consider the *attachment* bonds children form as their social relationships.

Attachment Social development begins with the establishment of a close emotional relationship between a child and a mother, father, or other regular caregiver. This intense, enduring, social–emotional relationship is called **attachment**. Since children are incapable of feeding or protecting themselves, the earliest function of attachment is to ensure survival. In some species, the infant automatically becomes *imprinted* on the first moving object it sees or hears (Johnson & Gottlieb, 1981). **Imprinting** occurs rapidly during a critical period of development and cannot easily be modified. The automaticity of imprinting can sometimes be problematic. In Chapter 3 we discussed that ethologist **Konrad Lorenz** demonstrated that young geese raised by a human will imprint on the human instead of on one of their own kind. In nature, fortunately, young geese mostly see other geese first.

You will not find human infants imprinting on their parents, and this difference suggests that something occurs differently in humans than it does in geese. Even so, **John Bowlby**, an influential theorist on human attachment, suggested that infants and adults are biologically predisposed to form attachments. That attachment relationship has broad consequences. Beginning with Bowlby (1973), theorists have suggested that the experiences that give rise to an attachment relationship provide individuals with a lifelong schema for social relationships called an *internal working model* (Bretherton, 1996). An internal working model is a memory structure that gathers together a child's history of interactions with his or her caretakers—the interactions that yielded a particular pattern of attachment. The internal working model provides a template that an individual uses to generate expectations about future social interactions.

One of the most widely used research procedures for assessing attachment is the *Strange Situation Test*, developed by **Mary Ainsworth** and her colleagues (Ainsworth, Blehar, Waters, & Wall, 1978). In the first of several standard episodes, the child is brought into an unfamiliar room filled with toys. With the

mother present, the child is encouraged to explore the room and to play. After several minutes, a stranger comes in, talks to the mother, and approaches the child. Next, the mother exits the room. After this brief separation, the mother returns, there is a reunion with her child, and the stranger leaves. The researchers record the child's behaviours at separation and reunion. Researchers have found that children's responses on this test fall into three general categories (Ainsworth et al., 1978):

- *Securely attached* children show some distress when the parent leaves the room; seek proximity, comfort and contact upon reunion; and then gradually return to play.
- *Insecurely attached–avoidant* children seem aloof and may actively avoid and ignore the parent upon her return.
- *Insecurely attached–ambivalent/resistant* children become quite upset and anxious when the parent leaves; at reunion, they cannot be comforted, and they show anger and resistance to the parent but, at the same time, express a desire for contact.

In middle-class U.S. samples, about 70 percent of babies are classified as securely attached; among the insecurely attached children, about 20 percent are classified as avoidant and 10 percent as resistant. Cross-cultural research on attachment relationships—in countries as diverse as Sweden, Israel, Japan, and China—reveals reasonable consistency in the prevalence of types of attachments (van Ijzendoorn & Kroonenberg, 1988). In every country, the majority of children are securely attached; most of the cultural differences occur with respect to the prevalence of different types of insecure attachments. Researchers also find a high rate of agreement between attachment classifications made in the Strange Situation and those based on naturalistic observation of children and mothers in their homes (Pederson & Moran, 1996).

Categorizations based on the Strange Situation Test have proven to be highly predictive of a child's later behaviour in a wider variety of settings, particularly the overall division between children who are securely and insecurely attached. For example, longitudinal research revealed that children who showed secure or insecure behaviour in the Strange Situation at 15 months differed widely in their school behaviour at ages 8 to 9 years (Bohlin, Hagekull, & Rydell, 2000). Those children who had been securely attached at 15 months were more popular and less socially anxious than their peers who had been insecurely attached. Similar continuity from the quality of attachment to later years has been demonstrated in 10-year-olds (Urban, Carlson, Egeland, & Stroufe, 1991) and adolescents (Weinfield, Ogawa, & Sroufe, 1997). This suggests that the quality of attachment, as revealed in the Strange Situation, really does have long-term importance (Stams, Juffer, & van Ijzendoorn, 2002). We will see in Chapter 17 that researchers also use attachment measures to predict the quality of adults' loving relationships.

Attachment relationships are quite important in young lives. Secure attachment to adults who offer dependable social support enables the child to learn a variety of prosocial behaviours, to take risks, to venture into novel situations, and to seek and accept intimacy in personal relationships.

Why is it important for a child to develop a secure attachment to a parent or other caregiver?

attachment Emotional relationship between a child and the parent or regular caregiver.

imprinting A primitive form of learning in which some infant animals physically follow and form an attachment to the first moving object they see and/or hear.

Parent's responsiveness

	Accepting Responsive Child-centred	Rejecting Unresponsive Parent-centred
Demanding *Controlling*	Authoritative- reciprocal High in bidirectional communication	Authoritarian Power assertive
Undemanding *Low in control attempts*	Indulgent	Neglecting Ignoring Indifferent Uninvolved

Parent's demandingness

FIGURE 11.10   A Classification of Parenting Styles

Parenting styles can be classified with respect to the two dimensions of demandingness—the parent's willingness to act as a socializing agent—and responsiveness—the parent's recognition of the child's individuality. The authoritative style is most likely to produce an effective parent–child bond.

Parenting Styles and Parenting Practices As we noted earlier, children bring individual temperaments to their interactions with their parents. Children's temperaments may cause parents' best (or worst) efforts at parenting to have unexpected consequences. Researchers recognize that children's temperaments and parents' behaviours each influence the other to yield developmental outcomes such as the quality of attachment relationships: As much as parents change their children, children change their parents (Collins, Maccoby, Steinberg, Hetherington, & Bornstein, 2000).

Even so, researchers have located a **parenting style** that is generally most beneficial. This style resides at the intersection of the two dimensions of *demandingness* and *responsiveness* (Maccoby & Martin, 1983): "Demandingness refers to the parent's willingness to act as a socializing agent, whereas responsiveness refers to the parent's recognition of the child's individuality" (Darling & Steinberg, 1993, p. 492). As shown in **Figure 11.10,** *authoritative* parents make appropriate demands on their children—they demand that their children conform to appropriate rules of behaviour—but are also responsive to their children. They keep channels of communication open to foster their children's ability to regulate themselves (Gray & Steinberg,

1999). This authoritative style is most likely to produce an effective parent–child bond. The contrast, as seen in Figure 11.10, is to parenting styles that are *authoritarian*—parents apply discipline with little attention to the child's autonomy—or *indulgent*—parents are responsive, but they fail to help children learn about the structure of social rules in which they must live—or *neglecting*—parents neither apply discipline nor are they responsive to their children's individuality.

Even parents with the same overall styles put different priorities on the *socialization goals* they consider important for the children. **Parenting practices** arise in response to particular goals (Darling & Steinberg, 1993). Thus authoritative parents who wish their children to do well in school may create a home environment in which the children come to understand why their parents value that as a goal—and may strive to do well in school because they are effectively socialized toward that goal (Noack, 2004). However, because not all authoritative parents value school success, you could not predict children's school performance based only on their parents' style (Steinberg, Lamborn, Dornbusch, & Darling, 1992). Parents' general attitudes and specific behaviours are both important for charting their children's life course.

A close interactive relationship with loving adults is a child's first step toward healthy physical growth and normal socialization. As the original attachment to the primary caregiver extends to other family members, they too become models for new ways of thinking and behaving. From these early attachments, children develop the ability to respond to their own needs and to the needs of others.

---

parenting style The manner in which parents rear their children; an authoritative parenting style, which balances demandingness and responsiveness, is seen as the most effective.

parenting practices Specific parenting behaviours that arise in response to particular parental goals.

Critical Thinking in Your Life

HOW DOES DAYCARE AFFECT CHILDREN'S DEVELOPMENT?

If you plan to have both children and a career, you are likely to face a difficult question: Is it wise to put your children in daycare? This is an issue that receives a lot of attention—with highly polarized views—in the popular press. To make this important judgment, you need to get beyond the false dichotomy of "daycare is good" versus "daycare is bad." Rather, you should formulate the more specific questions that allow you to put the decision in perspective. Let us suggest two of those questions: In what ways is daycare better or worse for the developing child? What is the optimal form of daycare?

We have already provided the context in which you can interpret the first question: If the attachments between children and mothers are so critical, is anything that disrupts the formation of those attachments—such as daycare—necessarily bad for the children? The answer to this question is, "On balance, *no*" (Scarr, 1998). To arrive at this answer, researchers typically made comparisons between children who stayed at home and those who were placed in daycare on measures of both intellectual and social development. Researchers have found that children placed in daycare are often at an *advantage* with respect to these measures, primarily because daycare provides more opportunities for social interaction and environmental experiences (Burchinal et al., 2000; Clarke-

Stewart, 1991, 1993). Intellectual development can benefit from a greater range of educational and play activities; social development can benefit from a wider variety of social interactions than would be available in the home.

There are two reasons, however, that the answer "no" must be qualified by "on balance." One is that there are individual differences in the way children respond to care outside the home. The second is that daycare takes many forms. Researchers, therefore, have turned their attention away from the "better or worse" question toward the issue of what constitutes quality care for particular children (Sagi, Koren-Karie, Gini, Ziv, & Joels, 2002; Zaslow, 1991).

Alison Clarke-Stewart (1993), an expert on daycare, has summarized the research literature to provide a series of guidelines for quality daycare. Some of her recommendations relate to the physical comfort of the children:

- The daycare centre should be physically comfortable and safe.

- There should be at least one caretaker for every six or seven children (more for children under age three).

Other recommendations cover educational and psychological aspects of the daycare curriculum:

- Children should have a free choice of activities intermixed with explicit lessons.

- Children should be taught social problem-solving skills.

Clarke-Stewart has also suggested that daycare providers should share the qualities of good parents:

- Caregivers should be responsive to the children's needs and actively involved in their activities.

- Caregivers should not put undue restrictions on the children.

- Caregivers should have sufficient flexibility to recognize differences among the needs of individual children.

If these guidelines are followed, quality daycare can be provided to all children whose parents work outside the home. As psychologists spread the message that daycare does not harm and may even enhance children's development, parents should feel less distress about the necessity for a dual-career family. Such a reduction in stress could only improve the child's overall psychological environment.

- If you are trying to compare outcomes for children who do and do not participate in daycare, on what dimensions should you try to match the children?

- How might you assess whether daycare providers interact with children in appropriate ways?

Contact Comfort and Social Experience What do children obtain from the attachment bond? Sigmund Freud and other psychologists argued that babies become attached to their parents because the parents provide them with food—their most basic physical need. This view is called the *cupboard theory* of attachment. If the cupboard theory were correct, children should thrive as long as they are adequately fed. Does this seem right?

Harry Harlow (1965) did not believe that the cupboard theory explained the importance of attachment. He set out to

test the cupboard theory against his own hypothesis that infants might also attach to those who provide **contact comfort** (Harlow & Zimmerman, 1958). In Chapter 3 you learned that Harlow separated macaque monkeys from their mothers at birth and placed them in cages where they had access to two

---

contact comfort Comfort derived from an infant's physical contact with the mother or caregiver.

artificial "mothers": a wire one and a terry cloth one. Harlow found that the baby monkeys nestled close to the terry cloth mother and spent little time on the wire one. They did this even when only the wire mother gave milk! Further studies by Harlow and his colleagues found that the monkeys' formation of a strong attachment to the mother substitute was not sufficient for healthy social development. At first, the experimenters thought the young monkeys with terry cloth mothers were developing normally, but a very different picture emerged when it was time for the female monkeys who had been raised in this way to become mothers. Monkeys who had been deprived of chances to interact with other responsive monkeys in their early lives had trouble forming normal social and sexual relationships in adulthood. The studies clearly demonstrated that normal interactions early in development are necessary for normal social development.

Primate researcher **Stephen Suomi** (1999; Champoux, Boyce, & Suomi, 1995) has shown that putting emotionally vulnerable infant monkeys in the foster care of supportive mothers virtually turns their lives around. Suomi notes that male monkeys put in the care of mothers known to be particularly loving and attentive are transformed from marginal members of the monkey troop into bold, outgoing young males who are among the first to leave the troop at puberty to work their way into a new troop. This *cross-fostering* gives the young monkeys coping skills and information essential for recruiting support from other monkeys and for maintaining a high social status in the group. Let's see now what lessons this research with monkeys holds for human deprivation.

Human Deprivation

Tragically, human societies have sometimes created circumstances in which children are deprived of contact comfort. Many studies have shown that a lack of close, loving relationships in infancy affects physical growth and even survival. In 1915, a doctor at Johns Hopkins Hospital reported that, despite adequate physical care, 90 percent of the infants admitted to orphanages in Baltimore died within the first year. Studies of hospitalized infants over the next 30 years found that, despite adequate nutrition, the children often developed respiratory infections and fevers of unknown origin, failed to gain weight, and showed general signs of physiological deterioration (Bowlby, 1969; Spitz & Wolf, 1946).

Contemporary studies continue to demonstrate patterns of disruption. For example, one study compared attachment outcomes for children raised at home to those for children largely (90 percent of their lives) raised in institutions (Zeanah, Smyke, Koga, & Carlson, 2005). The researchers found that 74 percent of the home-reared children had secure attachments; for institutionally reared children, only 20 percent had secure attachments. Moreover, a lack of normal social contact may have a long-lasting effect on children's brain development. One study compared a group of children who had spent their first year or so in orphanages to those who had been raised by their biological parents (Wismer Fries, Ziegler, Kurian, Jacoris, & Pollak, 2005). At age four, the two groups of children interacted with a stranger. The children who spent their earliest days in orphanages failed to show a normal pattern of brain response—as indicated by brain hormone levels—to the interaction with the stranger.

In this section, you have seen how experiences during childhood have an impact on later social development. We now shift our focus to later periods of life, beginning with adolescence.

SOCIAL DEVELOPMENT IN ADOLESCENCE

Earlier in the chapter, we defined adolescence by physical and cognitive changes. In this section, those changes will serve as background to social experiences. Since the individual has reached a certain level of physical and mental maturity, new social and personal challenges present themselves. We will first consider the general experience of adolescence and then turn to the individual's changing social world.

The Experience of Adolescence The traditional view of adolescence predicts a uniquely tumultuous period of life, characterized by extreme mood swings and unpredictable, difficult behaviour: "storm and stress." This view can be traced back to romantic writers of the late 18th and early 19th centuries, such as Goethe. The storm-and-stress conception of adolescence was strongly propounded by **G. Stanley Hall**, the first psychologist of the modern era to write at length about adolescent development (1904). Following Hall, the major proponents of this view have been psychoanalytic theorists working within the Freudian tradition (for example, Blos, 1965; Freud, 1946, 1958). Some of them have argued that not only is extreme turmoil a normal part of adolescence, but that failure to exhibit such turmoil is a sign of arrested development. **Anna Freud** wrote that "to be normal during the adolescent period is by itself abnormal" (1958, p. 275).

Two early pioneers in cultural anthropology, **Margaret Mead** (1928) and **Ruth Benedict** (1938), argued that the storm-and-stress theory is not applicable to many non-Western cultures. They described cultures in which children gradually take on more and more adult responsibilities without any sudden stressful transition or period of indecision and turmoil. Contemporary research has confirmed that the experience of adolescence differs across cultures (Arnett, 1999). Those cross-cultural differences argue against strictly biological theories of adolescent experience. Instead, researchers focus on the transitions children are expected to make in different cultures.

Recall that in Erikson's description of the life span, the essential task of adolescence is to discover one's true identity. For cultures like the majority culture in Canada, one consequence is that children attempt to achieve *independence* from their parents. Parents and their adolescent children must weather a transition in their relationship from one in which a parent has unquestioned authority to one in which the adolescent is granted reasonable independence to make important decisions (Allen & Land, 1999; Holmbeck & O'Donnell, 1991). Consider the results of a study that followed 1330 adolescents from age 11 to age 14 (McGue, Elkins, Walden, & Iacono, 2005). As 14-year-olds, these adolescents reported greater conflict with their parents than they had at age 11. At age 14, the adolescents' parents were less involved in their lives; the adolescents had less positive regard for their parents, and they believed that their parents had less positive regard for them. These data illustrate some of the relationship costs that arise when children strive for independence. We do not want to paint an overly negative picture: Most adolescents at most times still are able to use their parents as ready sources of practical and emotional support (Smetana, Campione-Barr, & Metzger, 2006). However, against that background, the striving for identity and independence explains why individuals might experience a certain amount of "storm and stress."

Now that we have considered the general adolescent experience, let's turn to the increasing importance of peers in adolescents' social experience.

Peer Relationships Much of the study of social development in adolescence focuses on the changing roles of family (or adult caretakers) and friends (Smetana et al., 2006). We have already seen that attachments to adults form soon after birth. Children also begin to have friends at very young ages. Adolescence, however, marks the first period in which peers appear to compete with parents to shape a person's attitudes and behaviours. Adolescents participate in peer relations at the three levels of friendships, cliques, and crowds (Brown & Klute, 2003). Over the course of these years, adolescents come to count increasingly on their one-on-one *friendships* to provide them with help and support (Furman & Buhrmester, 1992). *Cliques* are groups that most often consist of 6 to 12 individuals. Membership in these groups may change over time, but they tend to be drawn along lines of, for example, age and race (Smetana et al., 2006). Finally, *crowds* are the larger groups such as "jocks" or "nerds" that exist more loosely among individuals of this age. Through interaction with peers at these three levels, adolescents gradually define the social component of their developing identities, determining the kinds of people they choose to be and the kinds of relationships they choose to pursue (Berndt, 1992; Hartup, 1996).

The peer relationships that adolescents form are quite important to social development. They give individuals opportunities to learn how to function in what can often be demanding social circumstances. In that sense, peer relationships play a positive role in preparing adolescents for their futures. At the same time, parents often worry—with reasonable cause—about negative aspects of peer influence. For example, research supports the conclusion that adolescents are more likely to engage in risky behaviours when they are under the influence of their peers.

To study developmental changes in peer influence, researchers recruited three groups of participants: adolescents (ages 13 to 16), young adults (ages 18 to 22), and adults (ages 24 and older) (Gardner & Steinberg, 2005). Participants in each age range played a video game called *Chicken*. In this game, players act as drivers. They must decide how soon to stop their car when a light changes from green to yellow. Their goal is to achieve as much distance as they can before the light turns red and a wall pops up. If they do not stop in time, they will crash into the wall. About half of the participants played the game alone. The other half played in groups of three: Each participant played in turn while the other two watched. **Figure 11.11** presents the results of the experiment. As you can see, adolescents were far more likely to engage in risky driving (within the context of the video game) when in the presence of their peers.

This study confirms a general tendency for peer influence to prompt adolescents to engage in riskier behaviours.

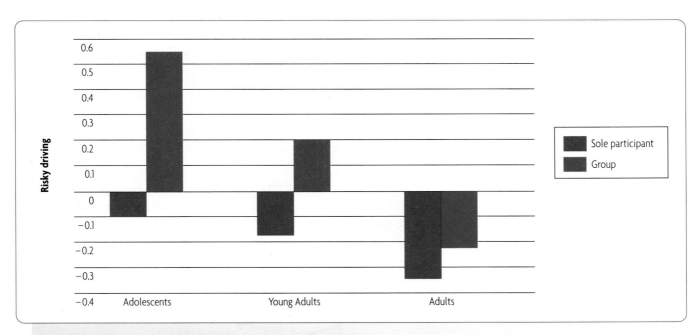

FIGURE 11.11 Peer Influence on Risky Behaviour

Adolescents, young adults, and adults played a video game called *Chicken* by themselves or in a group setting. The video game allowed participants to take risks while driving. The y-axis plots a measure of risky driving: Larger positive scores indicate higher risk. Adolescents showed the largest impact of the presence of peers.

From Margo Gardner and Laurence Steinberg, "Peer Influence on Risk Taking, Risk Preference, and Risky Decision Making in Adolescence and Adulthood: An Experimental Study," *Developmental Psychology, 41*(4), 625–635. Copyright © 1997 by the American Psychological Association. Reprinted with permission.

However, some adolescents are more susceptible to peer influence than others—and that susceptibility has consequences. In a longitudinal study, students who were more susceptible to their close friends' influence at the study's outset were more likely to have problems with drugs and alcohol one year later (Allen, Porter, & McFarland, 2006). We note, once again, that adolescence need not be a time of storm and stress. However, research of this type indicates the patterns of behaviour that indicate some adolescents are at risk.

SOCIAL DEVELOPMENT IN ADULTHOOD

Erikson defined two tasks of adulthood as intimacy and generativity. Freud identified the needs of adulthood as *Lieben und Arbeiten*, or love and work. Abraham Maslow (1968, 1970) described the needs of this period of life as love and belonging, which, when satisfied, develop into the needs for success and esteem. Other theorists label these needs as affiliation, or social acceptance and achievement, or competence needs. The shared core of these theories is that adulthood is a time in which both social relationships and personal accomplishments take on special priority. In this section, we track these themes across the breadth of adulthood.

Intimacy Erikson described **intimacy** as the capacity to make a full commitment—sexual, emotional, and moral—to another person. Intimacy, which can occur in both friendships and romantic relationships, requires openness, courage, ethical strength, and usually some compromise of one's personal preferences. Research has consistently confirmed Erikson's supposition that social intimacy is a prerequisite for a sense of psychological well-being across the adult life stages (Fernandez-Ballesteros, 2002; Ishii-Kuntz, 1990). **Figure 11.12** demonstrates

intimacy The capacity to make a full commitment—sexual, emotional, and moral—to another person.

that interactions with family and friends trade off over this long span of years to provide a fairly constant level in people's reports of their own well-being. The changes in these sources of support reflect, in part, the life events that are typically correlated with each age. Let's examine these correlations.

Young adulthood is the period in which many people enter into marriage or other stable relationships. The group that counts as family thus will ordinarily grow larger. Historically, most research on relationships and families across adulthood focused on the so-called standard configurations of a mother, father, and a house full of children. However, as the realities of people's families have changed, researchers have tried to document and understand the consequences of those changes (Mason, Skolnick, & Sugarman, 1998). For example, studies now focus on the ways in which homosexual couples enter into and sustain long-term relationships (James & Murphy, 1998). Research suggests that the strategies heterosexuals and homosexuals use to maintain relationships over time have much in common: Both types of couples try to remain close by, for example, sharing tasks and activities together (Haas, 2003; Haas & Stafford, 1998). However, to combat a lack of social acceptance for gay and lesbian relationships, homosexual couples also need to take special measures to maintain relationships, such as being publicly "out" as a couple. Some heterosexual couples also must persevere in the face of continuing barriers to social acceptance; research suggests that interracial couples also face types of prejudices that have a negative impact on the ability of relationships to endure (Chan & Wethington, 1998; Gaines & Agnew, 2003).

Each of these types of relationships increases the role of family in adults' social lives. Families also grow when individuals decide to include children in their lives. What may surprise you, however, is that the birth of children can often pose a threat to the overall happiness of a couple. Why might that be? Researchers have focused on differences in the way that men and women make the transition to parenthood in heterosexual relationships (Cowan & Cowan, 1998, 2000). In contemporary Western society, marriages are more often founded on notions

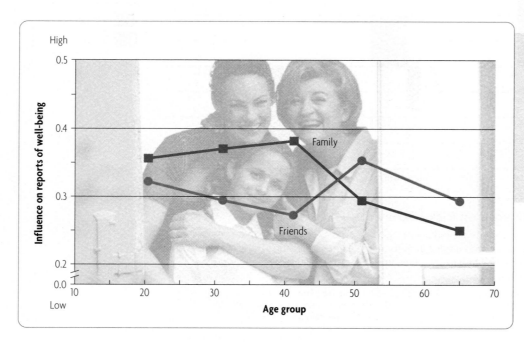

FIGURE 11.12 The Effects of Social Interaction on Well-Being

Across the life span, social interactions with family and friends trade off to provide a fairly constant level of individuals' reports of well-being.

of equality between men and women than was true in the past. However, children's births can have the effect of pushing husbands and wives in the direction of more traditional gender roles. The wife may feel too much of the burden of child care; the husband may feel too much pressure to support a family. The net effect may be that, following the birth of a child, the marriage changes in ways that both spouses find to be negative (Cowan et al., 1985). Although research on gay male and lesbian couples raising children is far more limited, that research suggests that, as you might expect, concerns about gender roles with respect to parenting have less of a negative impact on homosexual relationships (Patterson, 2002).

For many heterosexual couples, satisfaction with the marriage continues to decline because of conflicts as the child or children pass through their adolescent years. Contrary to the cultural stereotype, many parents look forward to the time when their youngest child leaves home and leaves them with an "empty nest" (White & Edwards, 1990). Parents may enjoy their children most when they are no longer under the same roof (Levenson, Carstensen, & Gottman, 1993). Have we discouraged you from having children? We certainly hope not! Our goal, as always, is to make you aware of research that can help you anticipate and interpret the patterns in your own life.

If marriages are, on the whole, happier when the spouses reach late adulthood, should everyone try to stay married late into life? In the United States, about half of all first marriages end in divorce (Bramlett & Mosher, 2001). Researchers would like to be able to determine which couples are fundamentally mismatched—with respect, for example, to their patterns of interactions—and which couples could avoid divorce (Orbuch, Veroff, Hassan, & Horrocks, 2002; Story & Bradbury, 2004).

In 1983, researchers began a longitudinal study of married couples. After following the couples for 14 years, the researchers were able to form some generalizations about why some of the couples remained married while others divorced (Gottman & Levenson, 2000). During the initial data collection in 1983, the couples visited the laboratory to have conversations on a neutral topic (events of the day) and a conflictual topic (each couple's area of continuing disagreement). Trained research assistants viewed tapes of these conversations and evaluated the extent of positive and negative affect—emotional content—the spouses expressed toward each other. Some couples discussed difficult topics with a sense of humour, whereas other couples discussed similar topics with put-downs and complaints. The affective content of their discussions was highly predictive of the couples' fates. From the sample of 79 couples, 11 percent got divorced relatively early—after, on average, 7.4 years of marriage. On the whole, those couples had shown high levels of *negative* affect in their discussions of conflictual topics. Sixteen percent of the couples divorced relatively late—after, on average, 13.9 years. On the whole, these couples had shown low levels of *positive* affect toward each other.

Why did this pattern emerge? The researchers suggested that "intense marital conflict likely makes it difficult to stay in the marriage for long, but its absence makes marriage somewhat more acceptable. Nonetheless, the absence of positive affect takes its toll" (Gottman & Levenson, 2000, p. 743). You can probably find both types of relationships around you: those in which couples fight constantly and those in which couples are calm but do not respond positively to each other.

Statistically speaking, which spouse is likely to outlive the other? What effect might the quality of the marriage have on this outcome?

When individuals stay together late into life, one member of the couple must cope with the death of a spouse. When we contemplate the death of a spouse or partner, we have come back to one reason that the balance of social interactions shifts somewhat from family to friends late in life (see Figure 11.12). A stereotype about late adulthood is that individuals become more socially isolated. Although it is true that older individuals may interact socially with fewer people, the nature of those interactions changes so that intimacy needs continue to be met. This trade-off is captured by the **selective social interaction theory**. This view suggests that, as people age, they become more selective in choosing social partners who satisfy their emotional needs. According to **Laura Carstensen** (1991, 1998), selective interaction may be a practical means by which people can regulate their emotional experiences and conserve their physical energy. Older adults remain vitally involved with some people—particularly family members and longtime friends.

Let's conclude this section where we began, with the idea that social intimacy is a prerequisite for psychological well-being. What matters most is not the quantity of social interaction, but the quality (particularly for women). As you grow into older adulthood, you will begin to protect your need for intimacy by selecting those individuals who provide the most direct emotional support.

Let's turn now to a second aspect of adult development: *generativity*.

Generativity Those people who have established an appropriate foundation of intimate relationships are most often able to turn their focus to issues of **generativity**. This is a commitment beyond oneself to family, work, society, or future generations—typically a crucial step in development in one's 30s and 40s

---

selective social interaction theory The theory that, as people age, they become more selective in choosing social partners who satisfy their emotional needs.

generativity A commitment beyond one's self and one's partner to family, work, society, and future generations; typically, a crucial state in development in one's 30s and 40s.

TABLE 11.5 Differences between Best- and Worst-Outcome Subjects on Factors related to Psychosocial Maturity

	Best Outcomes (30 Men)	Worst Outcomes (30 Men)
Personality integration rated in bottom fifth percentile during college	0%	33%
Dominated by mother in adult life	0%	40%
Bleak friendship patterns at 50	0%	57%
Failure to marry by 30	3%	37%
Pessimism, self-doubt, passivity, and fear of sex at 50	3%	50%
Childhood environment poor	17%	47%
Current job has little supervisory responsibility	20%	93%
Subjects whose career choice reflected identification with father	60%	27%
Children's outcome described as good or excellent	66%	23%

(McAdams & de St. Aubin, 1998). An orientation toward the greater good allows adults to establish a sense of psychological well-being that offsets any longing for youth.

George Vaillant studied the personality development of 95 highly intelligent men through interviews and observations over a 30-year period following their graduation from university in the mid-1930s. Many of the men showed great changes over time, and their later behaviour was often quite different from their behaviour in university. The interviews covered the topics of physical health, social relationships, and career achievement. At the end of the 30-year period, the 30 men with the best outcomes and the 30 with the worst outcomes were identified and compared (see **Table 11.5**). By middle life, the best-outcome men were carrying out generativity tasks, assuming responsibility for others, and contributing in some way to the world. Their maturity even seemed to be associated with the adjustment of their children; the more mature fathers were better able to give children the help they needed in adjusting to the world (Vaillant, 1977).

This study illustrates the prerequisites for generativity: For the best-outcome men, other aspects of their lives were sufficiently stable to allow them to direct their resources outward, toward generations to come. When asked what it means to be well adjusted, middle-aged adults (average age 52) and older adults (average age 74) gave the same response. Both groups suggested that adjustment relies on being "others oriented"— on being a caring, compassionate person and having good relationships (Ryff, 1989). This is the essence of generativity.

Let us also note that most older adults looking back on their lives do so with a degree of well-being that is unchanged from earlier years of adulthood (Carstensen & Freund, 1994). As we have seen with respect to social relationships, late adulthood is a time when goals are shifted; priorities change when the future does not apparently flow as freely. Across that change in priorities, however, older adults preserve their sense of the value of their lives. Erikson defined the last crisis of adulthood

to be the conflict between ego integrity and despair. The data suggest that few adults look back over their lives with despair. Most older adults review their lives—and look to the future—with a sense of wholeness and satisfaction.

We have worked our way through the life span by considering social and personal aspects of childhood, adolescence, and adulthood. To close out the chapter, we will trace two particular domains in which experience changes over time: the domains of sex and gender differences and of moral development.

STOP AND REVIEW

❶ At what life stage did Erik Erikson suggest people navigate the crisis of intimacy versus isolation?
❷ What long-term consequences have been demonstrated for children's early attachment quality?
❸ What dimensions define parenting styles?
❹ In what levels of peer relationships do adolescents engage?
❺ What is meant by selective social interaction?

CRITICAL THINKING Recall the longitudinal study that looked at the precursors to divorce. At the study's outset, why were the couples asked to discuss conflictual topics?

Sex and Gender Differences

One type of information most children begin to acquire in the first few months in life is that there are two categories of people in their social world: males and females. Over time, children learn that there are many respects in which the psychological experiences of males and females are quite similar. However, when differences do, in fact, occur, children acquire an understanding that some of those differences arise from biology and others arise from cultural expectations. Biologically based characteristics that distinguish males and females are referred to as **sex differences**. These characteristics include different reproductive functions and differences in hormones and anatomy. However, the first differences children perceive are entirely social: They begin to sense differences between males and females well before they understand anything about anatomy. In contrast to biological sex, **gender** is a psychological phenomenon referring to learned sex-related behaviours and attitudes. Cultures vary in how strongly gender is linked to daily activities and in the amount of tolerance for what is perceived as cross-gender behaviour. In this section, we consider both sex differences and gender development: the nature and nurture of children's sense of maleness and of femaleness.

SEX DIFFERENCES

Starting at about six weeks after conception, male fetuses being to diverge from female fetuses when the male testes develop and begin to produce the hormone *testosterone*. The presence or absence of testosterone plays a critical role in determining whether a child will be born with male or female anatomy. Testosterone also has an impact on brain development: Experiments with nonhuman animals have demonstrated that sex differences in neural structure are largely brought about by this hormone (Morris, Jordan, & Breedlove, 2004).

The exact role of testosterone is less clear for the development of the human brain. However, brain scans have revealed consistent structural differences between men's and women's brains (Goldstein et al., 2001). Men typically have bigger brains than women; appropriate comparisons across the sexes adjust for that overall variation, as men usually also have bigger bodies than women. The differences that remain after those adjustments are intriguing with respect to behavioural dissimilarities between men and women. For example, MRI scans reveal that the regions of the frontal lobe that play an important role in regulating social behaviour and emotional functioning are relatively bigger in women than in men (Gur, Gunning-Dixon, Bilker, & Gur, 2002). To confirm that sex differences of this type are biological—rather than the product of a lifetime of experience as men or women in particular cultural roles—researchers have undertaken similar studies with children and adolescents (de Bellis et al., 2001; Suzuki et al., 2005). Those studies confirm that sex differences emerge in the brain as a part of ordinary biological development.

Other analyses of sex differences focus on the distinct ways in which men's and women's brains accomplish cognitive and emotional tasks (Kimura, 1999). Consider the brain processes engaged when the two sexes view emotionally charged pictures.

Twelve men and 12 women underwent fMRI scans while viewing 96 pictures that ranged from neutral (e.g., a book or a fork) to negative (e.g., an autopsy or a gravestone) (Canli, Desmond, Zhao, & Gabrieli, 2002). As the participants viewed the pictures, they provided ratings of the intensity of their emotional experience on a scale ranging from 0 ("not emotionally intense at all") to 3 ("extremely emotionally intense"). Three weeks after this initial experience, the participants completed a test of recognition memory for the pictures; they had not been warned when they first viewed the pictures that this test was forthcoming. The

researchers assessed the relationship between brain activity at the time of encoding and subsequent memory performance. They found distinct patterns of activity for men and for women. For example, greater activity in the left amygdala (see Chapter 4) preceded recognition success for women; greater activity in the right amygdala preceded success for men.

Further studies of the brain at work confirm sex differences in the encoding and recognition of emotionally arousing stimuli (Cahill et al., 2004). These studies suggest that some of the behavioural differences that set men and women apart can be traced to biological differences rather than to cultural roles.

Most research on the biology of sex differences with human subjects focuses on global differences between men and women. However, researchers have recently begun to look at the biological origins of more fine-grained differences among individuals. These studies turn once again to the impact of the hormone testosterone on later development. In this case, the researchers determined the level of testosterone in the amniotic fluid of each individual participant. The researchers correlated those fetal testosterone levels with, for example, the quality of each boy's or girl's social relationships when they were four years old (Knickmeyer, Baron-Cohen, Raggatt, & Taylor, 2005). In general, boys had higher levels of fetal testosterone than girls. Against that background, individuals' higher levels of fetal testosterone were associated with poorer social relationships for both boys and girls. These results suggest that the extent to which individuals conform to expectations for male and female behaviour may depend, in part, on their prenatal hormonal environment (Morris et al., 2004).

GENDER IDENTITY AND GENDER ROLES

You have just seen that important aspects of men's and women's behaviour are shaped by biological differences. However, cultural expectations also have an important impact on **gender identity**—an individual's sense of maleness or femaleness. Gender identity includes awareness and acceptance of one's sex. This awareness develops at quite a young age: 10- to 14-month-old children already demonstrate a preference for a video showing the abstract movements of a child of the same sex (Kujawski & Bower, 1993). **Gender roles** are patterns of behaviour regarded as appropriate for males and females in a particular society. They provide the basic definitions of masculinity and femininity.

Much of what people consider masculine or feminine is shaped by culture (Leaper, 2000). Many researchers have suggested that gender-role socialization begins at birth. In one study, parents described their newborn daughters using

---

sex differences Biologically based characteristics that distinguish males from females.

gender A psychological phenomenon that refers to learned sex-related behaviours and attitudes of males and females.

gender identity One's sense of maleness or femaleness; usually includes awareness and acceptance of one's biological sex.

gender roles Sets of behaviours and attitudes associated by society as being male or female and expressed publicly by the individual.

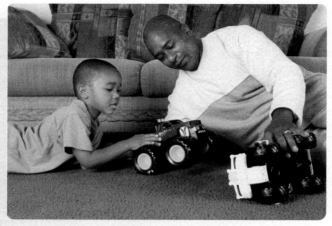

How do parents and peers influence children's acquisition of gender roles?

words such as *little*, *delicate*, *beautiful*, and *weak*. By contrast, parents described their newborn sons as *firm*, *alert*, *strong*, and *co-ordinated*. The babies actually showed no differences in height, weight, or health (Rubin, Provenzano, & Luria, 1974). Parents dress their sons and daughters differently, give them different kinds of toys to play with, and communicate with them differently. For children as young as 18 months, parents tend to respond more positively when their children play with sex-appropriate toys. For example, in one experiment fathers gave fewer positive reactions to boys engaging in play with toys typical for girls (Fagot & Hagan, 1991). In general, children receive encouragement from their parents to engage in sex-typed activities (Lytton & Romney, 1991; Witt, 1997).

Parents are not the only socializers of gender roles. **Eleanor Maccoby** (1998) argues, for example, that parents do not merely stamp in gender roles. She has found evidence that play styles and toy preferences are not, in fact, highly correlated with parental preferences or roles. Young children are segregationists—they seek out peers of the same sex even when adults are not supervising them or in spite of adult encouragement for mixed-group play. Maccoby believes that many of the differences in gender behaviour among children are the results of peer relationships.

In fact, boys and girls show consistent differences in their patterns of social interaction. Some differences relate to the structure of those interactions. For example, at least by the age of six, boys prefer to interact in groups, whereas girls prefer one-on-one interactions (Benenson, Apostoleris, & Parnass, 1997; Benenson & Heath, 2006). Other differences between boys and girls relate to the content of their play (Rose & Rudolph, 2006). Girls are more likely than boys to engage in social conversations and disclose information about themselves. Boys are more likely than girls to engage in rough-and-tumble play. These differences become more prominent as children grow older, providing evidence for the development of gender roles.

Interactions with their parents and peers provide children with an abundance of opportunities to acquire gender roles. Even so, young children themselves appear to believe that biology is destiny.

Groups of children ages 4, 5, 8, 9, and 10 were asked to make predictions about a 10-year-old character named Chris or Pat. The children all believed that the character had been brought up on a beautiful island. However, some of the children were told that Chris or Pat was raised on that isolated island entirely by members of the same sex (e.g., Chris was a boy and all of his caretakers were also male) or entirely by members of the opposite sex (e.g., Chris was a boy and all of his caretakers were female). How did the environment affect the 4- to 10-year-olds' predictions about Chris or Pat's sex-stereotyped behaviour? Until age 9, children believed that sex-stereotyped behaviour would emerge regardless of the social context. For example, the younger children thought it was equally likely that boy Chris would want to be a firefighter and girl Chris would want to be a nurse, no matter who raised him or her. The older children's judgments were, by contrast, sensitive to the context in which the child was raised: Now Chris's career choice was influenced by his or her caretakers' sex as well as his or her own (Taylor, 1996).

These results suggest that younger children underestimate the effects environments have on the ways in which boys and girls become different. They are also consistent with the finding that children between the ages of two and six seem to have more extreme and inflexible perceptions of gender than adults do (Stern & Karraker, 1989). When shown infants dressed in neutral clothing, children of this age are much more consistently affected in their judgments about the infant by an arbitrary label of "male" or "female" than adults are. Younger children's extreme reactions may be linked to the fact that they are at an age when they are trying to establish their own gender identity.

They appear, on the whole, to be much more attuned to the "scripts" for gender-appropriate behaviour than are their older siblings (Levy & Fivush, 1993).

We have briefly considered how and why it is that boys and girls experience social development in different fashions. In the next section you will see that some researchers believe that gender also has an impact on moral development.

STOP AND REVIEW

❶ What is the distinction between sex differences and gender differences?

❷ What does research suggest about differences between men and women for the processing of emotional stimuli?

❸ In what ways are young children "segregationists"?

CRITICAL THINKING Recall the experiment that examined children's understanding of sex differences. Why might the researchers have identified Chris or Pat specifically as a 10-year-old?

Moral Development

So far we have seen, across the life span, how important it is to develop close social relationships. Let's now consider another aspect of what it means to live as part of a social group: On many occasions you must judge your behaviour according to the needs of society, rather than just according to your own needs. This is the basis of *moral behaviour*. **Morality** is a system of beliefs, values, and underlying judgments about the rightness or wrongness of human acts. Society needs children to become adults who accept a moral value system and whose behaviour is guided by moral principles (Killen & Hart, 1999). As you know, however, what constitutes moral and immoral behaviour in particular situations can become a matter of heated public debate. Perhaps it is no coincidence, therefore, that the study of moral development has also proved to be controversial. The controversy begins with the foundational research of Lawrence Kohlberg.

KOHLBERG'S STAGES OF MORAL REASONING

Lawrence Kohlberg (1964, 1981) founded his theory of moral development by studying *moral reasoning*—the judgments people make about what courses of action are correct or incorrect in particular situations. Kohlberg's theory was shaped by the earlier insights of Jean Piaget (1965), who sought to tie the development of moral judgment to a child's general cognitive development. In Piaget's view, as the child progresses through the stages of cognitive growth, he or she assigns differing relative weights to the *consequences* of an act and to the actor's *intentions*. For example, to the preoperational child, someone who breaks 10 cups accidentally is "naughtier" than someone who breaks 1 cup intentionally. As the child gets older, the actor's intentions weigh more heavily in the judgment of morality.

Children aged three, four, and five years old were asked to make moral judgments about people's behaviour that varied along three dimensions: actions, outcomes, and intentions. The *actions* were defined as either positive or negative within a particular scenario (e.g., petting vs. hitting an animal) as were the *outcomes* (e.g., the animal either cried or smiled). To vary *intentions*, the experimenters described some behaviours as intentional and others as accidental (e.g., the actor hit the pet either on purpose or by mistake). The children were asked to rate the *acceptability* of the behaviour by choosing one of a series of five faces that represented values from "really, really bad" to "really, really good." The younger children based their acceptability ratings almost entirely on the outcome; only the five-year-olds took intention into account. However, when children were asked whether the actor should be *punished*, more younger children than older children took the actor's intention into account (Zelazo, Helwig, & Lau, 1996).

These results suggest that as children become more sophisticated cognitively, they are able to shift their focus from just outcomes to consideration of both outcomes and intentions together. However, the difference between acceptability judgments and punishment judgments suggests that some types of moral judgments allow children to consider more factors at an earlier age. As we saw earlier in the chapter, what children are specifically asked to do determines, in part, how "mature" they seem.

Kohlberg expanded Piaget's view to define stages of moral development. Each stage is characterized by a different basis for making moral judgments (see **Table 11.6**). The lowest level of moral reasoning is based on self-interest; higher levels centre on social good, regardless of personal gain. To document these stages, Kohlberg used a series of dilemmas that pit different moral principles against one another:

> In one dilemma, a man named Heinz is trying to help his wife obtain a certain drug needed to treat her cancer. An unscrupulous druggist will only sell it to Heinz for 10 times more than what the druggist paid. This is much more money than Heinz has and more than he can raise. Heinz becomes desperate, breaks into the druggist's store, and steals the drug for his wife. Should Heinz have done that? Why? An interviewer probes the participant for the reasons for the decision and then scores the answers.

The scoring is based on the *reasons* the person gives for the decision, not on the decision itself. For example, someone who says that the man should steal the drug because of his obligation to his dying wife or that he should not steal the drug because of his obligation to uphold the law (despite his personal feelings) is expressing concern about meeting established obligations and is scored at Stage 4 (see Table 11.6).

Four principles govern Kohlberg's stage model: (1) an individual can be at only one stage at a given time; (2) everyone goes through the stages in a fixed order; (3) each stage is more comprehensive and complex than the preceding; and (4) the same

---

morality A system of beliefs and values that ensures that individuals will keep their obligations to others in society and will behave in ways that do not interfere with the rights and interests of others.

TABLE 11.6 Kohlberg's Stages of Moral Reasoning

Levels and Stages	Reasons for Moral Behaviour
I Preconventional morality	
Stage 1 Pleasure/pain orientation	To avoid pain or not to get caught
Stage 2 Cost–benefit orientation; reciprocity—an eye for an eye	To get rewards
II Conventional morality	
Stage 3 Good-child orientation	To gain acceptance and avoid disapproval
Stage 4 Law and order orientation	To follow rules and avoid censure by authorities
III Principled morality	
Stage 5 Social contract orientation	To promote the society's welfare
Stage 6 Ethical principle orientation	To achieve justice and avoid self-condemnation
Stage 7 Cosmic orientation	To be true to universal principles and feel oneself part of a cosmic direction that transcends social norms

stages occur in every culture. Kohlberg inherited much of this stage philosophy from Piaget, and, in fact, the progression from Stages 1 to 3 appears to match the course of normal cognitive development. The stages proceed in order, and each can be seen to be more cognitively sophisticated than the preceding. Almost all children reach Stage 3 by the age of 13.

Much of the controversy with Kohlberg's theory occurs beyond Stage 3. In Kohlberg's original view, people would continue their moral development in a steady progression beyond Stage 3. However, not all people attain Stages 4 to 7. In fact, many adults never reach Stage 5, and only a few go beyond it. The content of Kohlberg's later stages appears to be subjective, and it is hard to understand each successive stage as more comprehensive and sophisticated than the preceding. For example, "avoiding self-condemnation," the basis for moral judgments at Stage 6, does not seem obviously more sophisticated than "promoting society's welfare," the basis for Stage 5. Furthermore, the higher stages are not found in all cultures (Eckensberger & Zimba, 1997). We turn now to extended contemporary critiques of Kohlberg's theory that arise from considerations of gender and culture.

GENDER AND CULTURAL PERSPECTIVES ON MORAL REASONING

Most critiques of Kohlberg's theory take issue with his claims of universality: Kohlberg's later stages have been criticized because they fail to recognize that adult moral judgments may reflect different, but equally moral, principles. In a well-known critique, **Carol Gilligan** (1982) pointed out that Kohlberg's original work was developed from observations only of boys. She argued that this research approach overlooked potential differences between the habitual moral judgments of men and

women. Gilligan proposed that women's moral development is based on a standard of *caring for others* and progresses to a stage of self-realization, whereas men base their reasoning on a standard of *justice*. Thus Gilligan's theory broadens Kohlberg's ideas about the range of considerations that may be relevant to moral judgments beyond childhood. Although we can value this contribution, research has suggested that she is incorrect to identify unique styles of moral reasoning for men and women. Let's examine the evidence.

Some studies have indicated that women mould their moral decisions to maintain harmony in their social relationships, whereas men refer more to fairness (Lyons, 1983). Even so, researchers continue to dispute whether gender differences in moral reasoning really exist at all (Jaffee & Hyde, 2000). Although men and women may arrive at their adult levels of moral development through different processes, the actual judgments they make as adults are highly similar (Boldizar, Wilson, & Deemer, 1989). One possibility is that the gender differences are really consequences of the different types of social situations that arise in the lives of men and women. When asked to reason about the same moral dilemmas, men and women gave highly similar patterns of care and justice responses (Clopton & Sorell, 1993).

We can thus characterize adult reasoning about moral dilemmas as a mix between considerations of justice and considerations of caring. This mix will remain in place over most of the life span. However, as you might expect, moral judgments are affected by general changes in adult cognition. One relevant change of late adulthood is that individuals shift the grounds for their judgments away from the details of specific situations toward the use of general principles. Consequently, moral judgments come to be based more on general societal concerns—for example, "What is the law?"—than on particular dilemmas—for example, "Should an exception be made in this case?" (Pratt, Golding, Hunter, & Norris, 1988).

Note that debates about gender differences in moral reasoning have still mostly been carried out with respect to moral reasoning in Western cultures. Cross-cultural research has provided an important critique of this whole body of research: Comparisons between cultures suggest that it is not even possible to make universal claims about the set of situations in which moral judgments are relevant. Consider this situation: You see a stranger at the side of the road with a flat tire. Should you stop to help? Suppose you say no. Is that immoral? If you have grown up in North America you probably think helping, under these circumstances, is a matter of personal choice, so it is not immoral. If, however, you had grown up as a Hindu in India, a culture that puts considerably more emphasis on interdependence and mutual assistance, you probably *would* view a failure to help as immoral (Miller, Bersoff, & Harwood, 1990).

Let's consider a study that made cross-cultural comparisons of moral reasoning.

Participants for a study on moral judgments were recruited from two locations: New Haven, Connecticut, and Mysore, in southern India. These representatives of Western and Hindu cultures were asked to respond to scenarios that made a contrast between *justice* and *interpersonal responsibility*. Suppose, for example, the only way you could deliver the wedding rings to your best friend's wedding was to steal money for a train ticket. The principle of *justice* suggests that you should not steal; the principle of *interpersonal responsibility* suggests that you should honour your interpersonal commitment. If you grew up in a Western culture, you probably do not think of interpersonal responsibility in moral terms: It would be unfortunate, but not immoral, to fail to deliver the wedding rings. However, we just noted that members of the Hindu culture in India do generally consider interpersonal commitments to have a moral character. As a consequence, the researchers predicted that Indian respondents would be more likely to favour interpersonal responsibility than would U.S. respondents. As shown in **Figure 11.13**, at three different ages Indian respondents were more likely to choose the options that favoured interpersonal responsibility (Miller & Bersoff, 1992).

You can see from this example the role that culture plays in defining what is moral or immoral. If you have grown up in North America you are probably surprised how strongly individuals from India believe that the commitment to the friend must be honoured—it is better to steal than to fail to deliver the rings. Note that this difference in cultural norms most likely applies beyond the two countries of the United States and India.

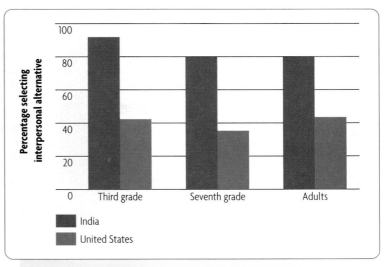

FIGURE 11.13 Cross-Cultural Responses to Moral Dilemmas
Schoolchildren and adults in India and the United States were asked to choose which courses of action they thought characters should take to resolve moral dilemmas. The participants from India were much more likely to favour interpersonal responsibility options over justice options.

❸ What cultural difference explains why some moral judgments differ for groups in the United States and India?

CRITICAL THINKING Consider the study that examined the effects of actions, outcomes, and intentions on children's moral reasoning. Why might children have been more sensitive to intentions when judging punishment versus acceptability?

Learning to Age Successfully

Let us now review some of the themes of this chapter, to form a prescription for successful aging. Early in the chapter, we encouraged you to think of development as a type of change that always brings with it gains and losses. In this light, the trick to prospering across the life span is to solidify one's gains and minimize one's losses. We saw that the rule "use it or lose it" applies in both physical and cognitive domains of life. Many of the changes that are stereotypically associated with aging are functions of disuse rather than decay. Our first line of advice is straightforward: Keep at it!

We also suggested that part of successful aging means to employ *selective optimization with compensation* (Baltes et al., 1992; Freund & Baltes, 1998). As you may recall, *selective* means that people choose the most appropriate goals for themselves. *Optimization* refers to people's exercising or training themselves

STOP AND REVIEW

❶ What are the three major levels of moral reasoning in Kohlberg's theory?

❷ What distinction did Carol Gilligan believe separates the moral reasoning of men and women?

How do friends contribute to successful aging?

in areas that are of highest priority to them. *Compensation* refers to the alternative ways that people use to deal with losses. In this chapter, we saw another good example of this process when we considered the ways in which social relationships change during adulthood. Older adults select the goal of having friends who provide optimal levels of emotional support; the choice of friends must change over time to compensate for deaths or other disruptions (Carstensen, 1998; Lang & Carstensen, 1994). Although the selective optimization perspective originated in research on the aging process, it is a good way to characterize the choices you must make throughout your life span. You should always try to select the goals most important to you, optimize your performance with respect to those goals, and compensate when progress toward those goals is blocked. That is our final bit of advice about life span development. We hope you will age wisely and well.

Recapping Main Points

Studying Development

- Researchers collect normative, longitudinal, and cross-sectional data to document change.

Physical Development Across the Life Span

- Environmental factors can affect physical development while a child is still in the womb.
- Newborns and infants possess a remarkable range of capabilities: They are prewired for survival.
- Through puberty, adolescents achieve sexual maturity.
- Some physical changes in late adulthood are consequences of disuse, not inevitable deterioration.

Visit **MyPsychLab.com** for more review and practice on the following topics:

 Simulate: Aging and Changes in Physical Appearance

Cognitive Development Across the Life Span

- Piaget's key ideas about cognitive development include the development of schemes, assimilation, accommodation, and the four-stage theory of discontinuous development. The four stages are sensorimotor, preoperational, concrete operational, and formal operational.
- Many of Piaget's theories are now being altered by ingenious research paradigms that reveal infants and young children to be more competent than Piaget had thought.
- Researchers suggest that children develop foundational theories, which change over time, in different psychological and physical domains.
- Cross-cultural research has questioned the universality of cognitive developmental theories.

- Age-related declines in cognitive functioning are typically evident in only some abilities. Research suggests that some cognitive deficits are caused by disuse rather than inevitable decay.
- Successful cognitive aging can be defined as people optimizing their functioning in select domains that are of highest priority to them and compensating for losses by using substitute behaviours.

Visit **MyPsychLab.com** for more review and practice on the following topics:

Research: Jean Piaget

Acquiring Language

- Many researchers believe that humans have an inborn language-making capacity. Even so, interactions with adult speakers is an essential part of the language acquisition process.
- Like scientists, children develop hypotheses about the meanings and grammar of their language. These hypotheses are often constrained by innate principles.

Social Development Across the Life Span

- Social development takes place in a particular cultural context.
- Erik Erikson conceptualized the life span as a series of crises with which individuals must cope.
- Children begin the process of social development with different temperaments.
- Socialization begins with an infant's attachment to a caregiver.

- Failure to make this attachment leads to numerous physical and psychological problems.
- Lack of nurturing relationships in childhood can impair social development.
- Adolescents must develop a personal identity by forming comfortable social relationships with parents and peers.
- The central concerns of adulthood are organized around the needs of intimacy and generativity.
- People become less socially active as they grow older because they selectively maintain only those relationships that matter most to them emotionally.
- People assess their lives, in part, by their ability to contribute positively to the lives of others.

Visit **MyPsychLab.com** for more review and practice on the following topics:

👁 **Watch:** Being a Single Parent

Sex and Gender Differences

- Research has revealed biologically based sex differences between the brains of men and women.

- Beginning at birth, parents and peers help bring about the socialization of gender roles.

Visit **MyPsychLab.com** for more review and practice on the following topics:

 Explore: Different Gender Stereotypes

Moral Development

- Kohlberg defined stages of moral development.
- Subsequent research has evaluated gender and cultural differences in moral reasoning.
- Different cultures have different standards for what types of situations and behaviours count as moral or immoral.

Visit **MyPsychLab.com** for more review and practice on the following topics:

✓ **Practice:** Moral Development and Learning to Age Successfully

KEY TERMS

accommodation (p. 329)
assimilation (p. 329)
attachment (p. 343)
centration (p. 330)
child-directed speech (p. 338)
chronological age (p. 320)
cognitive development (p. 328)
conservation (p. 330)
contact comfort (p. 346)
cross-sectional design (p. 321)
developmental age (p. 320)
developmental psychology (p. 320)
egocentrism (p. 330)
foundational theories (p. 333)
gender (p. 351)

gender identity (p. 351)
gender roles (p. 351)
generativity (p. 349)
imprinting (p. 343)
internalization (p. 333)
intimacy (p. 348)
language-making capacity (p. 339)
longitudinal design (p. 321)
maturation (p. 326)
menarche (p. 327)
morality (p. 353)
normative investigations (p. 320)
object permanence (p. 330)
over-regularization (p. 339)
parenting practices (p. 344)

parenting style (p. 344)
physical development (p. 322)
phonemes (p. 337)
psychosocial stages (p. 341)
puberty (p. 327)
schemes (p. 328)
selective optimization with
    compensation (p. 336)
selective social interaction
    theory (p. 349)
sex differences (p. 351)
social development (p. 340)
socialization (p. 342)
temperament (p. 342)
zygote (p. 322)

Practice Test

1. Rachel just had her fourth birthday. She has the language ability of a six-year-old. With respect to language ability, Rachel's _____ age is greater than her _____ age.
   a. chronological; normative
   b. developmental; cross-sectional
   c. developmental; chronological
   d. chronological; developmental

2. Professor Bale wishes to determine the impact of early-life TV viewing on university grades. To address this question, Professor Bale will most likely use a _____ research design.
   a. cross-sectional
   b. longitudinal
   c. chronological
   d. normative

3. You want to determine how many "close friends" people of different ages say they have. For your project, you interview 10-, 30-, and 50-year-olds. This is a _____ research design.
   a. chronological
   b. longitudinal
   c. cross-sectional
   d. maturational

4. Your friend Pat says, "I'm sure Caroline recognized my voice as soon as she was born." If Pat is Caroline's _____, Pat's claim is probably correct.
   a. mother
   b. father
   c. mother or father
   d. sister

5. Jack and Jill are twins. Under most circumstances, you would expect that Jack would begin his pubescent growth spurt _____ Jill.
   a. at the same time as
   b. earlier than
   c. a year before
   d. later than

6. Thomas is beginning to have difficulty hearing high-pitched voices. If Thomas has followed an ordinary course of life-span development, you would guess that he is about _____.
   a. 85.
   b. 25.
   c. 60.
   d. 40.

7. Tamara is a child whose thought is marked by egocentrism and centration. With respect to Piaget's theory, you infer that Tamara is in the _____ stage.
   a. sensorimotor
   b. preoperational
   c. concrete operations
   d. formal operations

8. As a four-year-old, Jasnit has begun to understand certain aspects of the biological world. His initial framework for understanding is called a(n) _____.
   a. foundational theory.
   b. formal operation.
   c. concrete operation.
   d. internalization.

9. Paul and Margaret Baltes have identified a strategy for successful aging. Which of these concepts is *not* a component of that strategy?
   a. optimization
   b. selective
   c. compensation
   d. centration

10. You are looking at fMRI scans from an experiment on working memory. Compared to his 38-year-old son Max, you would expect to see_____for 68-year-old Tony.
    a. more symmetry in activations across brain hemispheres
    b. less activation of brain areas irrelevant to the task
    c. more activation in the left hemisphere
    d. less symmetry in activations across hemispheres

11. You are examining data from an experiment on speech perception. Participant 27 was able to hear a sound distinction that is used in Hindi but not in English. You conclude the Participant 27 is *least* likely to be an _____
    a. infant in a Hindi language environment.
    b. adult who is a Hindi speaker.
    c. infant in an English language environment.
    d. adult who is an English speaker.

12. If Silvia believes that "mommy" applies to all women, that is a(n) _____. If she believes that "mommy" applies only to her own mother, that is a(n) _____.
    a. contrast; overextension
    b. underextension; hypothesis
    c. overextension; underextension
    d. hypothesis; contrast

13. "Extension," which requires children to use the same morpheme to mark the same concept, is an example of _____
    a. an overextension.
    b. an operating principle.
    c. the principle of contrast.
    d. a pragmatic principle.

14. According to Erik Erikson, the major crisis of age six to puberty is _____
    a. autonomy versus self-doubt.
    b. identity versus role confusion.
    c. generativity versus stagnation.
    d. initiative versus guilt.

15. You observe Keith in the Strange Situation Test. He seems aloof and appears to ignore his mother when she returns to the room. Based on this evidence, you suspect that Keith is _____
    a. securely attached.
    b. insecurely attached–avoidant.
    c. insecurely attached–ambivalent.
    d. insecurely attached–resistant.

16. As a mother, Lisbeth is high on the dimension of demandingness and low on the dimension of responsiveness. This combination would be described as a(n) _____ style of parenting.
    a. indulgent
    b. authoritative
    c. neglecting
    d. authoritarian

17. You have just made an arrangement to conduct a longitudinal study on Matthew from birth to age 40. You expect to find that Matthew will be most

susceptible to peer influence at the age of
_____ years.

a. 14   c. 19
b. 9   d. 24

18. As people become older adults, you would generally expect them to have _____

a. social interactions with more people.
b. social interactions with fewer people.
c. lower quality social interactions with friends.
d. lower quality social interactions with family members.

19. Which of these statements was *not* mentioned as a recommendation for quality daycare?

a. Children should be taught social problem-solving skills.
b. Children should have similar levels of intellectual development.
c. Caregivers should not put undue restrictions on the children.
d. Children should have a free choice of activities intermixed with explicit lessons.

20. Whereas _____ differences are affected by culture, _____ differences are affected by biology.

a. gender; sex   c. sex; identity
b. generativity; gender   d. sex; gender

21. Professor Clark wishes to study sex differences in the rate at which children learn to count from 1 to 10. He might be most interested in the _____

a. way in which testosterone influences the developing brain.
b. rate at which fathers praise their daughters when they count correctly.
c. number of opportunities boys and girls are given to count in school.
d. errors that boys and girls make before they learn the adult counting system.

22. You are asked to guess whether six-year-old Chris is a girl or boy. Which observation would most lead you to believe that Chris is a girl?

a. Chris enjoys rough-and-tumble play.
b. Chris does not like to engage in social conversations.
c. Chris most enjoys one-on-one relationships.
d. Chris prefers to have social interactions in groups.

23. When it comes to moral behaviour, Gracie is most concerned about following rules and avoiding the censure of authorities. She is at the stage of _____ morality.

a. principled   c. preconventional
b. cultural   d. conventional

24. Carol Gilligan criticized Kohlberg's theory by arguing that women are more focused on the standard of_____, whereas men are more focused on the standard of _____.

a. caring for others; avoiding pain
b. caring for others; justice
c. justice; caring for others
d. avoiding self-condemnation; justice

25. Cross-cultural analyses of moral reasoning suggest that _____

a. people in some cultures never achieve preconventional morality.
b. moral judgments within cultures are rarely consistent.
c. different features of situations have moral relevance in different cultures.
d. people's moral judgments across cultures are almost always the same.

Essay Questions

1. Why do researchers believe that some aspects of cognitive development occur within specific domains of knowledge?

2. Why do deprivation and abuse have consequences for social development?

3. Why is it sometimes difficult to discriminate between sex differences and gender differences?

Watch the following videos by logging on to MyPsychLab (**www.mypsychlab.com**). After you have watched the videos, complete the activities that follow.

Program 5: The Developing Child

Program 18: Maturing and Aging

Program 6: Language Development

PROGRAM REVIEW

Program 5

1. A toy company wants to use Robert Fantz's research to design a new mobile for babies to look at in their cribs. The research suggests that the mobile should _____
   a. be as simple as possible.
   b. use soft colours such as pink.
   c. be made of a shiny material.
   d. have a complex design.

2. Renée Baillargeon and other researchers have investigated object permanence in babies. How do their results compare with Piaget's views?
   a. They show Piaget's age estimates for achieving object permanence were too high.
   b. They contradict Piaget's concept of what object permanence consists of.
   c. They support Piaget's timetable.
   d. They indicate that babies show more variation than Piaget found.

3. How does Steven Suomi modify shyness reactions in young monkeys?
   a. by putting them in an enriched environment
   b. by providing highly supportive foster mothers
   c. by placing a shy monkey with other shy monkeys
   d. by administering drugs that reduce the level of social anxiety

Program 6

4. Before Chomsky's work, what assumption was generally made about language acquisition?
   a. Babies have an innate capacity for extracting meaning.
   b. There is a built-in language acquisition device.
   c. Language development varies widely, depending on culture.
   d. Language is a skill learned by imitating parents.

5. When Anne Fernald says "the melody is the message," she means that _____
   a. babies take meaning from pitch contours.
   b. mothers need to sing to their babies.
   c. babies need to learn the intonation patterns of their native language.
   d. mothers speak slowly and clearly to their babies.

6. What mental ability must a child have developed in order to use words as symbols?
   a. storing and retrieving memory codes
   b. recognizing the letters of the alphabet
   c. composing questions
   d. recognizing the spatial relationships between objects

Program 18

7. According to Erikson, the young adult faces a conflict between _____
   a. isolation and intimacy.
   b. heterosexuality and homosexuality.
   c. autonomy and shame.
   d. wholeness and futility.

8. There is a(n) _____ in paranoid disorders with age largely because _____.
   a. decrease; people have become more at peace with their lives
   b. decrease; life becomes more sheltered and more predictable during retirement
   c. increase; life becomes more chaotic during retirement
   d. increase; hearing and vision losses make the world harder to process

9. The elderly are particularly adept at processing information with _____
   a. emotional content.　　c. mathematical content.
   b. spatial content.　　　 d. folkloric content.

QUESTIONS TO CONSIDER

1. As people age and restructure their lives based on gains and losses in what they are capable of doing, do you think their values change to fit their capabilities? For example, do you think they come to value physical activity less as they become physically more restricted?

2. Is language unique to humans? Although chimps and gorillas lack the vocal apparatus for spoken language, they can use symbols and signs for communication. Consider your textbook's definition of language. Why is there so much resistance to the idea that animals use language?

Motivation

Your alarm clock went off this morning. You would have loved to hit the snooze button to get a few extra minutes of sleep, but you dragged yourself right out of bed. Why? Were you desperately hungry? Did you have to complete some important assignment? Had you made a date with someone who has captured your heart? When you consider the question "Why did I get out of bed this morning?" you have arrived directly at the core question of *motivation*: What makes you act as you do? What makes you persistently try to attain some goals despite the high effort, pain, and financial costs involved? Why, conversely, do you sometimes procrastinate too long before attempting to achieve other goals or give in and quit too soon?

It is the task of psychological researchers to bring theoretical rigour to such questions of motivation. How might motivational states affect the outcome of a sports competition or an exam? Why do some people become overweight and others starve themselves to death? Are our sexual behaviours determined by our genetic heritage? In this chapter, you will learn that human actions are motivated by a variety of needs—from fundamental physiological needs like hunger and thirst to psychological needs like personal achievement. But you will see that physiology and psychology often are not easy to separate. Even a seemingly biological drive such as hunger competes with an individual's need for personal control and social acceptance to determine patterns of eating.

We begin the chapter by providing you with a framework to understand general issues about the nature and study of motivation. In the second part of the chapter, we will look in depth at three types of motivation, each important in a different way and each varying in the extent to which biological and psychological factors operate. These three are hunger, sex, and personal achievement.

What different motivational questions might be asked about this individual's behaviour?

Understanding Motivation

Motivation is the general term for all the processes involved in starting, directing, and maintaining physical and psychological activities. The word *motivation* comes from the Latin *movere*, which means "to move." All organisms move toward some stimuli and activities and away from others, as dictated by their appetites and aversions. Theories of motivation explain both the general patterns of "movement" of each animal species, including humans, and the personal preferences and performances of the individual members of each species. We begin our analysis of motivation by considering the different ways in which motivation has been used to explain and predict species and individual behaviour.

FUNCTIONS OF MOTIVATIONAL CONCEPTS

Psychologists have used the concept of motivation for five basic purposes:

Motivation The process of starting, directing, and maintaining physical and psychological activities; includes mechanisms involved in preferences for one activity over another and the vigour and persistence of responses.

- *To relate biology to behaviour.* As a biological organism, you have complex internal mechanisms that regulate your bodily functioning and help you survive. Why did you get out of bed this morning? You may have been hungry, thirsty, or cold. In each case, internal states of deprivation trigger bodily responses that motivate you to take action to restore your body's balance.
- *To account for behavioural variability.* Why might you do well on a task one day and poorly on the same task another day? Why does one child do much better at a competitive task than another child with roughly the same ability and knowledge? Psychologists use motivational explanations when the variations in people's performance in a constant situation cannot be traced to differences in ability, skill, practice, or chance. If you were willing to get up early this morning to get in some extra studying but your friend was not, we would be comfortable describing you as in a different motivational state from your friend.
- *To infer private states from public acts.* You see someone sitting on a park bench, chuckling. How can you explain this behaviour? Psychologists and laypersons are alike in typically moving from observing some behaviour to inferring some internal cause for it. People are continually interpreting behaviour in terms of likely reasons for why it occurred as it did. The same rule applies to your own behaviours. You often seek to discover whether your own actions are best understood as internally or externally motivated.
- *To assign responsibility for actions.* The concept of personal responsibility is basic in law, religion, and ethics. Personal responsibility presupposes inner motivation and the ability to control your actions. People are judged less responsible for their actions when (1) they did not intend negative consequences to occur, (2) external forces were powerful enough to provoke the behaviours, or (3) the

actions were influenced by drugs, alcohol, or intense emotion. Thus a theory of motivation must be able to discriminate among the different potential causes of behaviour.

- *To explain perseverance despite adversity.* A final reason psychologists study motivation is to explain why organisms perform behaviours when it might be easier not to perform them. Motivation gets you to work or class on time even when you are exhausted. Motivation helps you persist in playing the game to the best of your ability even when you are losing and realize that you cannot possibly win.

You now have a general sense of the circumstances in which psychologists might invoke the concept of motivation to explain and predict behaviour. Before we turn to specific domains of experience, let's consider general sources of motivation.

SOURCES OF MOTIVATION

In 1999, cyclist Lance Armstrong won the Tour de France—completing one of the most remarkable comebacks in sports history. In 1996, Armstrong had been diagnosed with testicular cancer that had spread to his lungs and brain. After enduring aggressive chemotherapy, Armstrong chose to go back into training. Within three years, he was victorious in his sport's most prestigious event. In 2005, Armstrong won the Tour de France for the seventh time in a row. Detractors had claimed that the field he beat in 1999 was weak; his six additional victories proved that he could repeatedly beat the world's best cyclists.

Could you do what Lance Armstrong did? Could you come back from a serious illness to challenge your body again? Do you think that whatever motivated his behaviour was something *internal* to him? Would it take a special set of life experiences for someone to persevere in this manner? Or was it something *external*—something about the situation—that enabled him to rise above his illness and excel as an athlete? Would many or most people behave in this way if they were put in the same situation? Or does his behaviour represent an *interaction* of aspects of the person and features of the situation? To help you think about the sources of motivation, we will explore this distinction between internal and external forces. Let's begin with theories that explain certain types of behaviour as arising from internal biological drives.

Drives and Incentives Some forms of motivation seem very basic: If you feel hungry, you eat; if you feel thirsty, you drink. The theory that much important behaviour was motivated by internal drives was most fully developed by theorist **Clark Hull** (1943, 1952). In Hull's view, **drives** are internal states that arise in response to an animal's physiological needs. Organisms seek to maintain a state of equilibrium, or **homeostasis**, with respect to biological conditions such as the body's temperature and energy supply (see Chapter 4). Drives are aroused when deprivation creates disequilibrium or *tension*. These drives activate the organism toward *tension reduction*; when the drives are satisfied or reduced—when homeostasis is restored—the organism ceases to act. Thus, according to Hull, when an animal has been deprived of food for many hours, a state of hunger is aroused that motivates food-seeking and eating behaviours. The animal's responses that have led to the food goal will be reinforced because they are associated with the tension reduction that eating produces.

What combination of internal and external motivational forces may have helped cyclist Lance Armstrong to overcome cancer and win the Tour de France?

Can tension reduction explain all motivated behaviour? Apparently not. Let's consider an experiment that demonstrated that hunger and thirst do not always explain rats' most important motivation.

> Groups of either food- or water-deprived rats were placed in a square maze that consisted of nine equally sized units with doorways that allowed passage between the units (Zimbardo & Montgomery, 1957). Each unit of the maze had a sunken bowl that could contain either water or food. Drive theory would predict that the rats experiencing deprivation would eat or drink at their first opportunity. However, rather than immediately reducing that tension, the rats often chose to explore the maze instead. For example, rats that had been deprived of food for 48 or 72 hours spent 80 percent of their first two minutes in the maze exploring the maze; they spent only 20 percent of their time eating.

In this experiment, it appeared that the rats began to satisfy their hunger or thirst only once they had first satisfied their curiosity. Researchers have provided several similar examples of instances in which other motivational forces prevail over drive reduction (Berlyne, 1960; Fowler, 1965).

---

drives Internal states that arise in response to a disequilibrium in an animal's physiological needs.

homeostasis Constancy or equilibrium of the internal conditions of the body.

These experiments demonstrate that behaviour is not only motivated by internal drives: Behaviour is also motivated by **incentives**—external stimuli or rewards that do not relate directly to biological needs. When the rats or monkeys were attuned to objects in the environment rather than to their own internal states, they demonstrated that their behaviour was controlled by incentives. Human behaviour is also controlled by a variety of incentives. Why do you stay up late at night browsing the web instead of getting a good night's sleep? Why do you watch a movie that you know will make you feel anxious or frightened? Why do you eat junk food at a party even when you are already feeling full? In each case, elements of the environment serve as incentives to motivate your behaviour.

You can see already that behaviours find their origins in a mixture of internal and external sources of motivation. Even though rats might feel biological pressure to eat or drink, they also indulge an impulse to explore a new environment. We turn now to a different tradition of research on motivation, one that focuses on species-specific instinctual behaviours.

Instinctual Behaviours and Learning Why do organisms behave the way they do? Part of the answer is that some aspects of a species's behaviour are governed by **instincts**—preprogrammed tendencies that are essential for the survival of their species. Instincts provide repertoires of behaviour that are part of each animal's genetic inheritance. Salmon swim thousands of kilometres back to the exact stream where they were spawned, leaping up waterfalls until they come to the right spot, where the surviving males and females engage in ritualized courtship and mating. Fertilized eggs are deposited, the parents die, and, in time, their young swim downstream to live in the ocean until, a few years later, it is time for them to return to complete their part in this continuing drama. Similarly remarkable activities can be reported for most species of animals. Bees communicate the location of food to other bees, army ants go on highly synchronized hunting expeditions, birds build nests, and spiders spin complex webs—exactly as their parents and ancestors did.

Early theories of human function tended to overestimate the importance of instincts for humans. William James, writing in 1890 (James, 1890/1950), stated his belief that humans rely even more on instinctual behaviours than other animals (although human instincts were generally not carried out with fixed-action patterns). In addition to the biological instincts humans share with animals, a host of social instincts, such as sympathy, modesty, sociability, and love, come into play. For James, both human and animal instincts were *purposive*—they served important purposes, or functions, in the organism's adaptation to its environment.

Sigmund Freud (1915) proposed that humans experience drive states arising from life instincts (including sexuality) and death instincts (including aggression). He believed that instinctive urges direct *psychic energy* to satisfy bodily needs. Tension results when this energy cannot be discharged; this tension drives people toward activities or objects that will reduce the tension. By the 1920s, psychologists had compiled lists of over

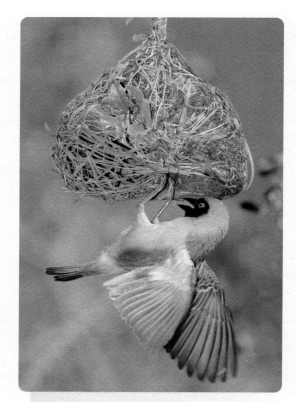

Instinctive behaviours, like the nest-building practices of the African masked weaver, are motivated by genetic inheritance. What instincts have theorists attributed to human practice?

10 000 human instincts (Bernard, 1924). At this same time, however, the notion of instincts as universal explanations for human behaviour was beginning to stagger under the weight of critical attacks. Cross-cultural anthropologists, such as Ruth Benedict (1959) and Margaret Mead (1939), found enormous behavioural variation between cultures. Their observations contradicted theories that considered only the universals of inborn instincts.

Within psychology, behaviourists objected to the circular reasoning that often gave rise to claims about human instincts: People are sympathetic because they have an instinct to be sympathetic; sympathetic behaviour confirms the existence of the instinct. We read in Chapter 7 that human and nonhuman animals alike are highly sensitive to the ways in which stimuli and responses are associated in the environment. If you want to explain why one animal performs a behaviour and another does not, you may need to know nothing more than that one animal's behaviour was reinforced and the other's was not. Under those circumstances, you do not need a separate account of motivation at all (that is, it would be a mistake to say that one animal is "motivated" and the other is not).

Recall, however, that in Chapter 7 we also saw that the types of behaviours animals will most readily learn are determined, in part, by species-specific instincts. That is, each animal displays a combination of learned and instinctive behaviours.

In Chapter 7, we also noted that cognitively oriented researchers have challenged the belief that instincts and reinforcement history are sufficient to explain all the details of an

---

incentives External stimuli or rewards that motivate behaviour although they do not relate directly to biological needs.

instincts Preprogrammed tendencies that are essential to a species's survival.

animal's behaviour. We now turn our attention to the role of expectations and cognition in motivation.

Expectations and Cognitive Approaches to Motivation Consider *The Wizard of Oz* as a psychological study of motivation. Dorothy and her three friends work hard to get to the Emerald City, overcoming barriers and persisting against all adversaries. They do so because they expect the Wizard to give them what they are missing. Instead, the wonderful (and wise) Wizard makes them aware that they, not he, always had the power to fulfill their own wishes. For Dorothy, *home* is not a place but a feeling of security, of comfort with people she loves; it is wherever her heart is. The courage the Lion wants, the intelligence the Scarecrow longs for, and the emotions the Tin Man dreams of are attributes they already possess. They need to think about these attributes not as internal conditions but as positive ways in which they are already relating to others. After all, have they not already demonstrated those qualities on the journey to Oz, a journey motivated by little more than an *expectation*, an idea about the future likelihood of getting something they wanted? The Wizard of Oz himself was clearly among the first cognitive psychologists because he recognized the importance of people's thought processes in determining their goals and the behaviours needed to reach those goals.

Contemporary psychologists use cognitive analyses to explore the forces that motivate a variety of personal and social behaviours. These psychologists share the Wizard's point of view that significant human motivation comes not from objective realities in the external world but from subjective interpretations of reality. The reinforcing effect of a reward is lost if you do not perceive that your actions obtained it. What you do now is often controlled by what you think was responsible for your past successes and failures, by what you believe is possible for you to do, and by what you anticipate the outcome of an action to be. Cognitive approaches explain why human beings are often motivated by expectations of future events.

The importance of *expectations* in motivating behaviour was developed by **Julian Rotter** (1954) in his **social-learning theory** (we touched on social learning in our discussion of observational learning in Chapter 7). For Rotter, the probability that you will engage in a given behaviour (studying for an exam instead of partying) is determined by your *expectation* of attaining a goal (getting a good grade) that follows the activity and by the *personal value* of that goal. A *discrepancy* between expectations and reality can motivate an individual to perform corrective behaviours (Festinger, 1957; Lewin, 1936). Suppose you find that your own behaviours do not match the standards or values of a group to which you belong—you might be motivated to change your behaviours to achieve a better fit with the group. For example, you might be motivated to change your style of dress or the type of music to which you listen so that you can reduce the discrepancy between expectations and reality.

How do expectations relate to internal and external forces of motivation? **Fritz Heider** (1958) postulated that the outcome of your behaviour (a poor grade, for example) can be attributed to *dispositional forces*, such as lack of effort or insufficient intelligence, or to *situational forces*, such as an unfair test or a biased teacher. These attributions influence the way you will behave. You are likely to try harder next time if you see your poor grade as a result of your lack of effort, but you may give up if you see it as resulting from injustice or lack of ability (Dweck, 1975).

Thus the identification of a source of motivation as internal or external may depend, in part, on your own subjective interpretation of reality.

Let's review the various sources of motivation. We began with the observation that researchers can differentiate internal and external factors that bring about behaviours. Drives, instincts, and histories of learning are all internal sources of motivation that affect behaviours in the presence of appropriate external stimuli. Once organisms begin to think about their behaviours—something humans are particularly prone to do—expectations about what should or should not happen also begin to provide motivation. Thinking animals can choose to attribute some motivations to themselves and others to the outside world.

A HIERARCHY OF NEEDS

We have now reviewed several sources of motivation. As a preview for the rest of the chapter, we want to return to a more global account of the domains in which motivational concepts apply. Our intent is to give you a general sense of the forces that could guide your life.

Humanist psychologist **Abraham Maslow** (1970) formulated the theory that basic motives form a **hierarchy of needs**, as illustrated in **Figure 12.1**. In Maslow's view, the needs at each level of the hierarchy must be satisfied before the next level can be achieved (the needs are arranged in a sequence from primitive to advanced). At the bottom of this hierarchy are the basic *biological needs*, such as hunger and thirst. They must be met before any other needs can begin to operate. When biological needs are pressing, other needs are put on hold and are unlikely to influence your actions. When they are reasonably well satisfied, the needs at the next level—*safety needs*—motivate you. When you are no longer concerned about danger, you become motivated by *attachment needs*—needs to belong, to affiliate with others, to love, and to be loved. If you are well fed and safe and if you feel a sense of social belonging, you move up to *esteem needs*—needs to like oneself, to see oneself as competent and effective, and to do what is necessary to earn the esteem of others.

At the top of the hierarchy are people who are nourished, safe, loved and loving, secure, thinking, and creating. These people have moved beyond basic human needs in the quest for the fullest development of their potentials, or *self-actualization*. A self-actualizing person is self-aware, self-accepting, socially responsive, creative, spontaneous, and open to novelty and challenge, among other positive attributes.

Maslow's theory is a particularly upbeat view of human motivation. At the core of the theory is the need for each individual to grow and actualize his or her highest potential. However, you know from your own experience that Maslow's strict hierarchy breaks down. You may have skipped a meal so that you could help out a friend. You may have endured the danger of a wilderness trek to boost your self-esteem. Even so,

---

social-learning theory The learning theory that stresses the role of observation and the imitation of behaviours observed in others.

hierarchy of needs Maslow's view that basic human motives form a hierarchy and that the needs at each level of the hierarchy must be satisfied before the next level can be achieved; these needs progress from basic biological needs to the need for self-actualization.

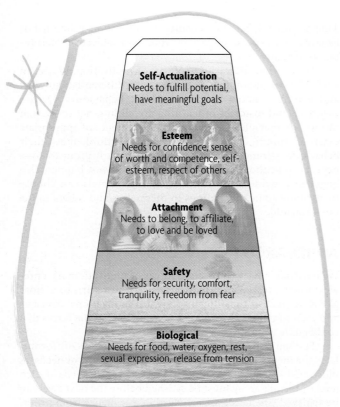

FIGURE 12.1 Maslow's Hierarchy of Needs
According to Maslow, needs at the lower level of the hierarchy dominate an individual's motivation as long as they are unsatisfied. Once these needs are adequately met, the higher needs occupy the individual's attention.

Self-Actualization
Needs to fulfill potential, have meaningful goals

Esteem
Needs for confidence, sense of worth and competence, self-esteem, respect of others

Attachment
Needs to belong, to affiliate, to love and be loved

Safety
Needs for security, comfort, tranquility, freedom from fear

Biological
Needs for food, water, oxygen, rest, sexual expression, release from tension

Where does the need to belong, to form attachments, and to experience love fit in Maslow's hierarchy?

we hope Maslow's scheme will enable you to bring some order to different aspects of your motivational experiences.

We have now given you a general framework for understanding motivation. In the remainder of the chapter, we will take a closer look at three different types of behaviours that are influenced by interactions of motives: eating, sexual performance, and personal achievement.

STOP AND REVIEW

❶ As you are sitting on a bench, you see another student run by. Which function of motivational concepts applies to how you interpret the situation?

❷ What does it mean for an organism to achieve homeostasis?

❸ Why did cross-cultural research cast doubt on claims about human instincts?

❹ What distinction did Fritz Heider make with respect to explanations for outcomes?

❺ What did Abraham Maslow mean by *attachment needs*?

CRITICAL THINKING Recall the experiment on food- or water-deprived rats. Why was it important that each unit of the maze could contain food or water?

Eating

We would like to ask you to make a prediction. We are about to offer a slice of pizza to a student enrolled in an introductory psychology course. How likely do you think it is that the student will eat the slice of pizza? Are you willing to make a guess? Your response should probably be, "I need more information." In the last section, we gave you a way of organizing the extra information you need to acquire before making such a prediction. You would want to know about *internal* information. How much has the student eaten already? Is the student trying to diet? You would also want to know about *external* information. Does the pizza look tasty? Are friends there to share the pizza and conversation? You can see already that we have to consider many factors to explain the types of forces that might influence even a simple outcome, such as whether someone is going to eat a slice of pizza. Let's begin with some of the physiological processes that evolution has provided to regulate eating.

THE PHYSIOLOGY OF EATING

When does your body tell you it is time to eat? You have been provided with a variety of mechanisms that contribute to your physical sense of hunger or satiety (Logue, 1991). To regulate food intake effectively, organisms must be equipped with mechanisms that accomplish four tasks: (1) detect internal food need, (2) initiate and organize eating behaviour, (3) monitor the quantity and quality of food eaten, and (4) detect when enough food has been consumed and stop eating. Researchers have tried to understand these processes by relating them either to *peripheral* mechanisms in different parts of the body, such as stomach contractions, or to *central* brain mechanisms, such as the functioning of the hypothalamus. Let's look at these processes in more detail.

Peripheral Responses Where do sensations of hunger come from? Does your stomach send out distress signals to indicate that it is empty? A pioneering physiologist, **Walter Cannon** (1934), believed that gastric activity in an empty stomach was the sole basis for hunger. To test this hypothesis,

Why do people tend to eat more food when a variety of tastes is available?

Cannon's intrepid student A. L. Washburn trained himself to swallow an uninflated balloon attached to a rubber tube. The other end of the tube was attached to a device that recorded changes in air pressure. Cannon then inflated the balloon in Washburn's stomach. As the student's stomach contracted, air was expelled from the balloon and activated the recording device. Reports of Washburn's hunger pangs were correlated with periods when the record showed his stomach was severely contracted but not when the record showed his stomach was distended. Cannon thought he had proved that stomach cramps were responsible for hunger (Cannon & Washburn, 1912).

Although Cannon and Washburn's procedure was ingenious, later research showed that stomach contractions are not even a necessary condition for hunger. Injections of sugar into the bloodstream will stop the stomach contractions but not the hunger of an animal with an empty stomach. Human patients whose stomachs have been entirely removed still experience hunger pangs (Janowitz & Grossman, 1950), and rats without stomachs still learn mazes when rewarded with food (Penick, Smith, Wienske, & Hinkle, 1963). These studies suggest that although sensations originating in the stomach may play a role in the way people usually experience hunger, they do not fully explain how the body detects its need for food and is motivated to eat.

An empty stomach may not be necessary to feel hungry, but does a "full" stomach terminate eating? Research has shown that gastric distension caused by food—but not by an inflated balloon—will cause an individual to end a meal (Logue, 1991). Thus the body is sensitive to the source of pressure in the stomach. The oral experience of food also provides a peripheral source of *satiety* cues—cues relevant to feelings of satiation or fullness. You may have noticed that you become less enthusiastic about the tastes of even your favourite foods over the course of a meal, a phenomenon called *sensory-specific satiety* (Raynor & Epstein, 2001). This reduction in interest for foods as you eat them may be one way in which your body regulates intake. However, the "specific" in sensory-specific satiety means that the satiety applies to specific flavours and not to the food itself. In one experiment, participants had reached satiety for particular foods, such as pineapple or cucumber. However, when the flavours of the food were slightly altered—by the addition of vanilla-flavoured whipped cream or salt and pepper—people showed renewed interest in the foods (Romer et al., 2006). This body of research suggests that variety in food tastes—as is common in many multicourse meals—might counteract other bodily indications that you've already had enough to eat.

We now turn our attention to the brain mechanisms involved in eating behaviours, where information from peripheral sources is gathered together.

Central Responses As is often the case, simple theories about the brain centres for the initiation and cessation of eating have given way to more complex theories. The earliest theories of the brain control of eating were built around observations of the *lateral hypothalamus (LH)* and the *ventromedial hypothalamus (VMH)*. (The location of the hypothalamus is shown in Figure 4.14 on page 97.) Research showed that if the VMH was lesioned (or the LH stimulated), the animal consumed more food. If the procedure was reversed so that the LH was lesioned (or the VMH stimulated), the animal consumed less food. These observations gave rise to the *dual-centre model*, in which the LH was thought to be the "hunger centre" and the VMH the "satiety centre."

Over time, however, researchers provided additional data to suggest that this simple theory was incomplete (Gao & Horvath, 2007). Sugar (in the form of glucose in the blood) and fat are the energy sources for metabolism. The two basic signals that initiate eating come from receptors that monitor the levels of sugar and fat in the blood. When stored glucose is low or unavailable for metabolism, signals from liver cell receptors are sent to the LH, where neurons acting as glucose detectors change their activity to initiate eating behaviour. Other hypothalamic neurons gather information that indicates high blood levels of glucose or fatty acids and use that information to terminate eating behaviour. The hypothalamic circuits also monitor more long-term aspects of the body's state of satiety. For example, fat cells release substances that provide signals to the arcuate nucleus (usually called the *ARC*), an area in the brain's hypothalamus that controls satiety, to decrease eating. Of course, other parts of our brain and body also play a role in the control of food intake. For instance, researchers at the University of Calgary have a long-standing research program that examines how neural messages and hormonal signals emanating in the gastrointestinal tract affect signals to the brain that regulate eating. Much of that research examines the role of chemicals found naturally in the human body that mimic those in marijuana. These researchers have shown that blocking these cannabinoid (CB1) receptors reduces appetite and food intake (Chambers, Koopmans, Pittman, & Sharkey, 2006; Chambers, Sharkey, & Koopmans, 2007).

We have seen so far that you have body systems dedicated to getting you to start and to stop eating. You almost certainly know, however, from an enormous amount of personal experience, that your need for food depends on more than just the cues generated by your body. Let's look now at psychological factors that motivate you to eat more or less food.

THE PSYCHOLOGY OF EATING

You know now that your body is equipped with a variety of mechanisms that regulate the amount of food you eat. But do you eat only in response to hunger? You are likely to respond, "Of course not!" If you think back over the last couple of days, you can probably recall several occasions on which when and what you ate had little to do with hunger. In this section on the psychology of eating, we begin by reviewing the impact of culture on what and how much you eat. Next, we focus on ways in which people attempt to control their eating to affect body shape and size by exploring some of the roots and consequences of obesity and dieting. We then describe how eating disorders may arise as an extreme response to concerns about body image and weight.

Cultural Impact on Eating How do you decide when and what you should eat? To answer this question, first think about the impact of culture. For example, people in Canada typically eat three daily meals at set times; the timing of those meals relies more on social norms than on body cues. Moreover, people often choose what to eat based on social or cultural norms. Would you say yes if you were offered a free lobster dinner? Your answer might depend on whether, for example, you are an observant Jew (in which case you would say no) or a vegetarian (in which case your answer would still depend on whether you are a strict vegetarian or vegan, or whether you are mostly vegetarian and sometimes eat seafood). These examples suggest immediately why culture, in its various forms, can trump your body's cues.

Let's look more closely at the culture of eating in Canada. One important source of information about food consumption is the Canadian government. The government regulates what counts as a "serving size," as described on food packages, and what types of nutritional information food manufacturers must provide to their customers. The government also provides periodic advice on the components of a healthy diet. For example, since 1942, the Canadian government has provided the public with the *Canada Food Guide* (Health Canada, 2005a). This guide provides specific recommendations about nutritional requirements, portion sizes, and how to maintain a healthy diet. The government also publishes *Canada's Guide to Healthy Eating and Physical Activities* (Health Canada, 2007), which promotes the combined benefits of healthy eating and an active lifestyle. These guides are revised regularly to reflect the current state of scientific knowledge: Recommendations change over time as research advances. You can be quite certain that the dietary guidelines will change again in your lifetime. As with any other type of research-based advice, it is important for you to understand how data support the recommendations as they evolve.

Unfortunately, and despite the government's efforts to promote a healthy lifestyle, other aspects of Canadian life and culture work against recommendations for healthy eating. For example, unhealthy food is relatively inexpensive compared to healthy food. People with limited amounts of money might find a healthy diet relatively unaffordable. This observation has led to the suggestion that people's nutrition would improve if the price differential between healthy and unhealthy food changed (Epstein et al., 2006). Consider the findings from the Canadian Community Health Survey, which demonstrated that Canadian adults and adolescents in low income groups, who inevitably have little money for food, often select foods that lack in nutrients (Kirkpatrick & Tarasuk, 2008). This study reinforces findings from past studies which showed that Canadians have limited access to high-quality foods such as milk products, fruits, and vegetables because of the high cost of these more nutritious foods (Kirkpatrick & Tarasuk, 2003). In a related U.S. study, researchers worked with an Alabama deli to decrease prices on healthy foods (Horgen & Brownell, 2002). When the healthy food cost less, people ate more of it. This type of research supports the conclusion that some barriers to healthy eating are the product of economic constraints.

Obesity and Dieting Psychologists have spent a good deal of time considering circumstances that have given rise to what has often been labelled an "epidemic" of obesity. To determine who is overweight and who is obese, researchers often turn to a measure called *body mass index (BMI)*. To calculate BMI, one divides an individual's weight in kilograms by the square of height in metres. For example, a person who weighs 70 kilograms and is 1.70 metres tall would have a BMI of 24.2 (70/$(1.70)^2 = 24.2$). (You can also use your internet search engine to find a BMI calculator on the web.) In most instances, individuals who have BMIs between 25 to 29.9 are considered overweight. Those individuals with BMIs 30 and above are considered obese. By those standards, roughly 36.1 percent of the Canadian adult population (or 8.6 million people) is overweight, and 15.2 percent is obese (Statistics Canada, 2005a). Among children and adolescents, 26 percent are overweight and 8 percent are categorized as obese (Shields, 2006).

These figures suggest why there is a certain urgency to answer the question, "Why do people become overweight?" It probably will not surprise you that the answer lies partly in nature and partly in nurture—as you have seen throughout *Psychology and Life*. Some people have a genetic predisposition toward obesity. Researchers have provided ample evidence that people are born with innate tendencies to be lighter or heavier. For example, studies of monozygotic (identical) twins reveal higher correlations for BMI and other measures of body size than those of dizygotic (fraternal) twins (Schousboe et al., 2004; Silventoinen et al., 2007). That consistent pattern provides strong evidence for a genetic influence on people's weight.

Researchers have begun to discover some of the genetic mechanisms that may predispose some individuals to obesity (Farooqi & O'Rahilly, 2007). For example, a gene has been isolated that appears to control the signals to the brain that indicate enough fat has been stored in the body in the course of a meal—so the individual should stop eating (Dahlman & Arner, 2007). The gene influences the production of a hormone called leptin. Recall from Chapter 6 that cannabinoids in your brain play a role in stimulating appetite (Kirkham, 2005). Leptin works in opposition to those cannabinoids to keep appetite under control (Jo, Chen, Chua, Talmage, & Role, 2005). If leptin is not available to balance these cannabinoids, it is likely that individuals will continue to eat. Thus the gene that controls leptin appears to have a critical influence on weight regulation and the potential for obesity. Research continues to reveal additional genes that influence the likelihood of obesity (Boutin & Frougel, 2005).

However, even a biological predisposition may not be enough to "cause" a particular person to become overweight. What matters, in addition, is the way in which an individual *thinks* about food as well as that person's eating behaviours.

Psychology in Your Life

HOW DOES THE PRESENCE OF OTHERS INFLUENCE YOUR EATING?

We'd like you to think back to the last meal you shared with other people. Do you think you ate more than, less than, or about the same amount as you would have eaten if you'd been eating alone? In the chapter so far, we hope we've convinced you that the amount people eat is only partially determined by internal hunger cues. Research suggests that the social context—the presence of others—is an important external cue that affects people's eating. In fact, when you eat with others your most important motive may be to produce a positive impression (Herman, Roth, & Polivy, 2003). Let's see what impact that motive has.

Consider a study by Canadian researcher Sarah-Jeanne Salvy and her colleagues (2007) in which college students had 10-minute conversations with their romantic partners, friends, or strangers. To make the conversations more "convivial," the researchers provided bowls of cookies and crackers. At the end of each conversation, the researchers determined how much food each participant had consumed. The amounts differed substantially across the different pairings: Males chatting with male friends ate the most; females chatting with male strangers ate the least. Can you see how those results might emerge if the participants were motivated to make a positive impression? The women, for example, might not have wanted to cast themselves in a negative light by appearing gluttonous in front of male strangers.

In a similar study (Salvy, Kieffer, & Epstein, 2008), Salvy examined the impact of social context on food consumption for overweight and normal-weight children. The 10- to 12-year-old participants visited the laboratory for two sessions. In one session, the children played and ate snacks on their own. In the other session, the children played and ate snacks in a peer's company. The normal-weight children ate about the same amount of food in both sessions. However, the overweight children consistently ate less while they were with a peer. The researchers provided two explanations for this pattern. First, they suggested that the overweight children might have eaten less "to avoid incurring the stigmas attributed to overweight individuals" (p. 195). Second, they suggested that the children might have eaten less to match the consumption of the normal-weight children. Both these explanations support the general conclusion that the overweight children controlled their eating to make a positive impression.

The researchers also discussed their results in the context of changes that have taken place in family's eating patterns over the last decades—the "trend away from family meals towards grazing and eating alone" (p. 195). They suggested that, historically, children may have learned to limit food consumption in the context of meals with parents and siblings.

The absence of that social context could explain some aspects of the increase in childhood obesity. The researchers suggest that social interventions—returning to circumstances in which children eat in the presence of others—could help overweight children eat less.

A final thought on the social context of eating: People tend to greatly underestimate its influence. In one study, pairs of students ate pizza while watching a video together. Within the pairs, the correlation for pizza consumption was 0.64. Even so, when asked why they had eaten the amount they had, only 3 out of the 122 participants mentioned being influenced by their companion's consumption (Vartanian, Herman, & Wansink, 2008). The participants were much more likely to mention other factors such as how hungry they felt, the time since the last meal, or how good the food tasted. However, a second study found that those factors were not actually correlated with the amount that students ate in social circumstances!

Let's return to the question with which we began: The last time you ate with other people, do you think you ate more than, less than, or about the same amount as you would have eaten if you'd been eating alone? To provide the right answer, you must really address a different question: How might you have adjusted your eating to provide a particular impression?

Early research on psychological aspects of eating focused on the extent to which overweight individuals are attentive to their bodies' internal hunger cues versus food in the external environment (Schachter, 1971a). The suggestion was that, when food is available and prominent, overweight individuals ignore the cues their bodies give them. This theory proved to be insufficient, however, because weight itself does not always predict eating patterns. That is, not all people who are overweight have the same psychological makeup with respect to eating behaviours. Let's see why.

University of Toronto psychologists **Janet Polivy** and **Peter Herman** have proposed that the critical dimension that underlies the psychology of eating behaviours is *restrained* versus *unrestrained* eating (Polivy & Herman, 1999). *Restrained* eaters put constant limits on the amount of food they will let themselves eat: They are chronically on diets; they constantly worry about food. Although obese people may be more likely to report these kinds of thoughts and behaviours, individuals can be restrained eaters whatever their body size. How do people gain weight if they are constantly on a diet? Research suggests that when restrained eaters become *disinhibited*—when life circumstances cause them to let down their restraints—they tend to indulge in high-calorie binges. Unfortunately, many types of life circumstances appear to lead restrained eaters to become disinhibited. Disinhibition will occur, for example, when restrained eaters are made to feel stress about their capabilities and self-esteem (Tanofsky-Kraff, Wilfley, & Spurrell, 2000; Wallis & Hetherington, 2004). In fact, one type of stress is the *anticipation* of being on a strict diet.

> Based on self-evaluations of their behaviours and thoughts with respect to food and dieting, female students at the University of Toronto were classified as either restrained (17 women) or unrestrained (24 women) eaters. The students were told they were taking part in a study "investigating the effects of food deprivation on taste perception" (Urbszat, Herman, & Polivy, 2002, p. 398). When they arrived for the experiment, half of the students were asked to undertake a low-calorie diet—approved by "the Canadian Government and the University of Toronto"—for one week. Participants in both the *diet* and *no-diet* conditions were then asked to perform taste tests on three plates of cookies. The participants believed that these taste tests were the baseline data for the study of taste perception. In fact, the researchers were measuring the total grams of cookies each participant consumed. The results of the study are shown in **Figure 12.2**. For unrestrained eaters, it made no difference whether they were anticipating a strict diet. However, for the restrained eaters, anticipation of the diet led them to eat more than twice as many cookies.

This result suggests why diets are often unsuccessful for restrained eaters. As the researchers note, their diets can be broken even "by the prospect of not being able to eat forbidden food" (Urbszat et al., 2002, p. 399).

You see now why it might be difficult for people to lose weight once they have become overweight. Many overweight people report themselves as constantly on diets, and as such are often restrained eaters. If stressful life events occur that cause these eaters to become disinhibited, binge eating can easily lead to weight gain. Thus the psychological consequences of being constantly on a diet can, paradoxically, create circumstances that are more likely to lead to weight gain than to weight loss. Perhaps this is why the latest movement in Canada is to change the eating habits of children through school programs and reduced availability of junk food in schools so that children are less likely to begin the endless pattern of restrained eating and constant dieting. In the next section, we will see how the same psychological forces that result in constant concerns over weight regulation can lead to health- and life-threatening eating disorders.

anorexia nervosa An eating disorder in which an individual weighs less than 85 percent of her or his expected weight but still expresses intense fear of becoming fat.

bulimia nervosa An eating disorder characterized by binge eating followed by measures to purge the body of excess calories.

binge eating disorder An eating disorder characterized by out-of-control binge eating without subsequent purges.

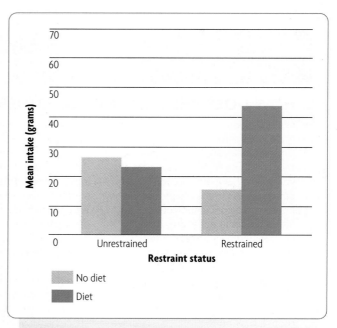

FIGURE 12.2   The Effects of Anticipated Diets
Restrained and unrestrained eaters sampled cookies to rate their taste. Half of the women in each group had agreed to undertake a reduced-calorie diet for one week. For unrestrained eaters, the amount of cookies (in grams) they ate while making the taste ratings was unaffected by the anticipation of a diet. However, those restrained eaters who anticipated dieting ate more than twice as much as their no-diet peers.

Eating Disorders and Body Image We have already seen that people's internal cues—the hunger they experience—only partially determines how much they eat. For people with eating disorders, the mismatch between their body's internal signals and their eating behaviour becomes particularly dramatic. **Anorexia nervosa** is diagnosed when an individual weighs less than 85 percent of her or his expected weight but still expresses an intense fear of becoming fat (*DSM-IV-TR*, 2000). The behaviour of people diagnosed with **bulimia nervosa** is characterized by binges—periods of intense, out-of-control eating—followed by measures to purge the body of the excess calories—self-induced vomiting, misuse of laxatives, fasting, and so on (*DSM-IV-TR*, 2000). Sufferers from anorexia nervosa may also binge and then purge as a way of minimizing calories absorbed. Both of these syndromes can have serious medical consequences. In the worst cases, sufferers may even starve to death.

Binge eating disorder (BED) is diagnosed when people engage in regular episodes of binge eating without the purges that accompany bulimia nervosa. People who suffer from this disorder feel, during their binges, that they have lost control; the binges cause them great distress. Compared to anorexia and bulimia, binge eating disorder is a relatively new diagnostic category.

In **Table 12.1**, we present the prevalence for each eating disorder. These data are drawn from a large-scale face-to-face interview study of 9282 men and women in the United States, ages 18 and over (Hudson, Hiripi, Pope, & Kessler, 2007) and the numbers reported are similar to those reported recently in

TABLE 12.1	Prevalence of Eating Disorders	
	Women (%)	Men (%)
Anorexia nervosa	0.9	0.3
Bulimia nervosa	1.5	0.5
Binge eating disorder	3.5	2.0

Note: Each figure is the percent of the sample of 9282 U.S. adults who had experienced the disorder in his or her lifetime.

Canadian research (Government of Canada, 2006). Table 12.1 shows that women suffer from these disorders more than men do. However, the difference in prevalence has become smaller in the last few years. Earlier estimates suggested that women suffered from anorexia and bulimia at approximately 10 times the rate of men (*DSM-IV-TR*, 2000). However, the data in Table 12.1 show only a three-to-one ratio between women and men. As we describe the causes of eating disorders, we will consider why the gap might be closing.

Research on the causes of eating disorders has confirmed the importance of genetic factors. There is evidence that a predilection toward eating disorders may be genetically transmitted (Kortegaard, Hoerder, Joergensen, Gillberg, & Kyvik, 2001). One study followed pairs of female twins longitudinally from ages 11 to 18 (Klump, Burt, McGue, & Iacono, 2007). The researchers made comparisons between monozygotic (MZ) and dizygotic (DZ) twins of the sort you have encountered several times before. The data revealed that genetics plays a larger role as the twins get older: Over the seven-year period, MZ twins tended to remain similar, whereas, by mid- to late adolescence, greater differences emerged within the pairs of DZ twins. This pattern suggests that genetic risk mattered more as the young girls passed through puberty. Researchers have also conducted twin studies to explore personality variables that may put people at risk for eating disorders. For example, female twins who had high levels of perfectionism (such as concerns over mistakes or doubts about actions) were also more likely to be diagnosed with anorexia (Wade et al., 2008). If this general drive for perfection leads people to seek a "perfect" body, eating disorders may be a consequence.

In fact, high levels of body dissatisfaction—discomfort with weight, body shape, and appearance—put people at risk for eating disorders (Lynch, Heil, Wagner, & Havens, 2008). For many people with eating disorders, body dissatisfaction is not related to their actual bodies but to their own inaccurate perceptions of their bodies. People with anorexia who are perceived by others as dangerously thin often look in the mirror and still perceive themselves as overweight. Consider a study that looks at the brain bases of these misperceptions.

Ten women with anorexia and ten control women (without the disorder) underwent fMRI scans while they viewed a series of digital images (Sachdev, Mondraty, Wen, & Gulliford, 2008). Each participant had a personalized set of

What do these photographs of Nicole Richie and Marilyn Monroe suggest about changes over time in how thin women must be for the media to promote them as sexy?

images: Half of the images showed each woman herself; the other half showed another woman matched for age and body mass index. The women were all photographed wearing the same outfit that made the body's contour easy to detect.

Finally, so that participants would pay most attention to the bodies, the faces in the images were obscured. As they viewed each image, participants were told whether it was a self-image or an other-image. For women in the control group, the fMRI scans revealed the same patterns of brain activity when they studied both types of images. However, for the women with anorexia, the patterns for self-images and other-images were quite distinct. For example, when viewing self-images, women with anorexia showed less activity in brain regions that allow people to obtain accurate information from the external world.

An important aspect of this result is that the women with anorexia showed entirely normal patterns of brain activity when looking at the bodies of other women. Only the self-images yielded unusual patterns of brain activity.

Research on body dissatisfaction has yielded consistent group differences in judgments about body size (Roberts, Cash, Feingold, & Johnson, 2006). For example, in one study, white university students revealed themselves to be less satisfied with their bodies than did their black peers. In addition, when asked to choose a drawing to represent their preferred size, white students chose smaller figures than black students did (Aruguete, DeBord, Yates, & Edman, 2005). Similarly, when black and white women who attend university rated photographs of thin, average, and large models, only the white women rated the large models lower (compared to the thin and average models) on dimensions such as attractiveness, intelligence, and popularity (Hebl & Heatherton, 1998). To explain these differences between black and white women, researchers often call attention to the role cultural norms and media plays in shaping white women's expectations for their ideal weight and ideal bodies (Durkin & Paxton, 2002; Striegel-Moore & Bulik, 2007). For example, women who make negative comparisons between their own bodies and those of their favourite celebrities are at risk for eating disorders (Shorter, Brown, Quinton, & Hinton, 2008). Perhaps because the media provides relatively more images of thin white women, those media images have a greater impact on body dissatisfaction for white women than for their black peers.

Against this background, you will probably not be surprised to learn that white females are also more likely to suffer from eating disorders than are black females. One study involved 985 white women and 1061 black women who were all about 21 years of age (Striegel-Moore et al., 2003). In those groups, 1.5 percent of the white women had suffered from anorexia nervosa at some point in their lives; no black women had experienced that disorder. Bulimia nervosa had affected 2.3 percent of the white women but only 0.4 percent of the black women. Fewer studies have examined other racial and ethnic groups, but evidence to date suggests that eating disturbances are also less frequent in Asian-Americans than whites, but equally as common among hispanic females as among whites. For each of these findings, researchers try to draw a link between cultural values about body size and dieting behaviours.

To close out this section, let's return to the decreasing gap in the prevalence of eating disorders for women and for men.

Researchers have begun to study the impact of media images on men's body dissatisfaction. That research interest has emerged because, in the last decade, the number of media images of thin, muscular men has grown considerably. In general, men who view images of ideal male bodies experience increases in body dissatisfaction (Blond, 2008). Other studies conducted in Canada (Johnson, McCreary, & Mills, 2007; McCreary et al., 2007) and abroad, including a meta-analysis of 25 studies (Barlett, Vowels, & Saucier, 2008) have shown a link between media exposure and men's body image. While this relationship exists, a causal link must still be demonstrated to support the speculation that media representations of men's bodies have led to the increasing prevalence of male eating disorders.

STOP AND REVIEW

❶ What is sensory-specific satiety?
❷ What evidence suggests that the VMH plays a different role in eating from that suggested by the dual-centre model?
❸ What pattern of eating do restrained eaters generally follow?
❹ What are the symptoms of bulimia nervosa?

CRITICAL THINKING Recall the study that demonstrated the impact of anticipated diets on food consumption. Why did the researchers lead the students to believe that the study was focused on taste perception?

Sexual Behaviours

Your body physiology makes it essential that you think about food every day. But what about sex? It is easy to define the biological function of sex—reproduction—but does that explain the frequency with which you think about sexual behaviours? When asked how often they think about sex, 54 percent of adult men and 19 percent of adult women report they think about sex at least once every day (Michael, Gagnon, Laumann, & Kolata, 1994). When a similar question was asked of a sample of Canadian university students, 84 percent of participants reported having sexually intrusive thoughts, with men reporting more frequent and diverse types of intrusive thoughts (Byers, Purdon, & Clark, 1998). How can we explain the frequency with which people think about sex? How do thoughts about sex relate to sexual behaviours?

The question of motivation, once again, is the question of why people carry out certain ranges of behaviour. As we already acknowledged, sexual behaviours are biologically necessary only for reproduction. Thus, although eating is essential to individual survival, sex is not. Some animals and humans remain celibate for a lifetime without apparent detriment to their daily functioning. But reproduction is crucial to the survival of the species as a whole. To ensure that effort will be expended toward reproduction, nature has made sexual stimulation intensely pleasurable. An orgasm serves as the ultimate reinforcer for the energy expended in mating.

This potential for pleasure gives to sexual behaviours motivating power well beyond the need for reproduction.

Individuals will perform a great variety of behaviours to achieve sexual gratification. But some sources of sexual motivation are external. Cultures establish norms or standards for what is acceptable or expected sexual behaviour. Whereas most people may be motivated to perform behaviours that accord with those norms, some people achieve their sexual satisfaction primarily by violating them.

In this section, we will first consider some of what is known about the sex drive and mating behaviour in nonhuman animals. Then we shift our attention to selected issues in human sexuality.

NONHUMAN SEXUAL BEHAVIOURS

The primary motivation for sexual behaviours in nonhuman animals is reproduction. For species that use sex as a means of reproduction, evolution has generally provided two sexual types, males and females. The female produces relatively large eggs (which contain the energy store for the embryo to begin its growth), and the male produces sperm that are specialized for motility (to move into the eggs). The two sexes must synchronize their activity so that sperm and egg meet under the appropriate conditions, resulting in conception.

Sexual arousal is determined primarily by physiological processes. Animals become receptive to mating largely in response to the flow of hormones controlled by the pituitary gland and secreted from the *gonads*, the sex organs. In males, these hormones are known as *androgens*, and they are continuously present in sufficient supply so that males are hormonally ready for mating at almost any time. In the females of many species, however, the sex hormone *estrogen* is released according to regular time cycles of days or months, or according to seasonal changes. Therefore, the female is not always hormonally receptive to mating.

These hormones act on both the brain and genital tissue and often lead to a pattern of predictable *stereotyped sexual behaviour* for all members of a species. If, for example, you've seen one pair of rats in their mating sequence, you've seen them all. The receptive female rat darts about the male until she gets

What factors determine the sexual behaviours of most species?

his attention. Then he chases her as she runs away. She stops suddenly and raises her rear, and he enters her briefly, thrusts, and pulls out. She briefly escapes him and the chase resumes—interrupted by 10 to 20 intromissions before he ejaculates, rests awhile, and starts the sex chase again. Apes also copulate only briefly (for about 15 seconds). For sables (a species of marten), copulation is slow and long, lasting for as long as eight hours. Predators, such as lions, can afford to indulge in long, slow copulatory rituals—as much as every 30 minutes over four consecutive days. Their prey, however, such as antelope, copulate for only a few seconds, often on the run (Ford & Beach, 1951).

Sexual arousal is often initiated by stimuli in the external environment. In many species, the sight and sound of ritualized display patterns by potential partners is a necessary condition for sexual response. Furthermore, in species as diverse as sheep, bulls, and rats, the novelty of the female partner affects a male animal's behaviour. A male that has reached sexual satiation with one female partner may renew sexual activity when a new female is introduced (Dewsbury, 1981). Touch, taste, and smell can also serve as external stimulants for sexual arousal. As we described in Chapter 5, some species secrete chemical signals, called *pheromones*, that attract suitors, sometimes from great distances (Carazo et al., 2004; De Cock & Matthysen 2005). In many species, the female emits pheromones when her fertility is optimal (and hormone level and sexual interest are peaking). These secretions are unconditioned stimuli for arousal and attraction in the males of the species, who have inherited the tendency to be aroused by the stimuli. When captive male rhesus monkeys smell the odour of a sexually receptive female in an adjacent cage, they respond with a variety of sex-related physiological changes, including an increase in the size of their testes (Hopson, 1979).

Although sexual response in nonhuman animals is largely determined by innate biological forces, this still leaves room for "cultural" aspects to affect choices of mate. Consider the sailfin molly.

Under most circumstances, the female sailfin mollies from the Comal River in Texas show a mating preference for larger males. However, what happens when a female sailfin molly observes another female showing a preference for a smaller male? To answer this question, researchers arranged a set of tanks so that female sailfin mollies swam in a large tank that had two smaller tanks at each end (Witte & Noltemeier, 2002). In the initial phase of the experiment, a large and a small male fish were put into small tanks at either end. As seen in **Figure 12.3**, the females spent considerably more time swimming in proximity to the larger male. In the second phase of the experiment, a second female was placed in another small tank so that she appeared to be swimming near the smaller of the two males. The original female had 20 minutes to observe the second female fraternizing with the smaller male. In the final phase of the experiment, the researchers removed the second female and again observed the original females' preferences. As seen in Figure 12.3, in the second preference test the pattern had largely reversed. The female sailfin mollies were now spending most of their time swimming near the smaller males.

Are you surprised to learn that innocent fish swimming in aquariums are paying attention to which other fish have been

FIGURE 12.3 Female Sailfin Mollies' Mate Selection

Researchers calculated how long female sailfin mollies swam in proximity to larger versus smaller male fish. In the first preference test, the females spent much more time swimming near the larger fish. Next, the original females observed a second female swim close to the smaller male for 20 minutes. In the second preference test, which took place after those 20 minutes, the original females reversed their original pattern to spend more time close to the smaller males.

judged desirable and undesirable? This experiment sets the stage for our discussion of human sexuality. We will soon see that researchers believe that human sexual response is also shaped by both our evolutionary history and the preferences of those around us.

HUMAN SEXUAL AROUSAL AND RESPONSE

Hormonal activity, so important in regulating sexual behaviour among other animal species, has relatively little effect on sexual receptiveness or gratification in the majority of men and women. Individual differences in hormone levels, within normal limits, are not predictive of the frequency or quality of sexual activity. However, when hormone levels fall below normal levels because of illness or aging, there is often a negative impact on sexual desire. This is particularly true for the hormone testosterone. Both men and women experience restored sexual desire when they undergo treatments that supplement low testosterone levels (Abdallah & Simon, 2007; Allan, Forbes, Strauss, & McLachlan, 2008). Still, men who have undergone surgical castration (and, therefore, no longer produce testosterone) often continue to experience some level of sexual desire, illustrating that human sexuality is motivated by more than hormones (Weinberger, Sreenivasan, Garrick, & Osran, 2005).

sexual arousal The motivational state of excitement and tension brought about by physiological and cognitive reactions to erotic stimuli.

How did William Masters and Virginia Johnson legitimize the study of human sexuality?

Sexual arousal in humans is the motivational state of excitement and tension brought about by physiological and cognitive reactions to erotic stimuli. *Erotic stimuli*, which may be physical or psychological, give rise to sexual excitement or feelings of passion. Sexual arousal induced by erotic stimuli is reduced by sexual activities that are perceived by the individual as satisfying, especially by achieving orgasm.

Researchers have studied sexual practices and sexual responses in nonhuman animals for several decades, but for many years studies of similar behaviours in humans were off limits. **William Masters** and **Virginia Johnson** (1966, 1970, 1979) broke down this traditional taboo. They legitimized the study of human sexuality by directly observing and recording, under laboratory conditions, the physiological patterns involved in ongoing human sexual performance. By doing so, they explored not what people said about sex, but how individuals actually reacted or performed sexually.

For their direct investigation of the human response to sexual stimulation, Masters and Johnson conducted controlled laboratory observations of thousands of volunteer males and females during tens of thousands of sexual response cycles of intercourse and masturbation. Following are four of the most significant conclusions drawn from this research: (1) men and women have similar patterns of sexual response; (2) although the sequence of phases of the sexual response cycle is similar in the two sexes, women are more variable, tending to respond more slowly but often remaining aroused longer; (3) many women can have multiple orgasms, whereas men rarely do in a comparable time period; and (4) penis size is generally unrelated to any aspect of sexual performance (except in the male's attitude toward having a large penis).

Four phases were found in the human sexual response cycle: excitement, plateau, orgasm, and resolution (see **Figure 12.4**).

- In the excitement phase (lasting from a few minutes to more than an hour), there are vascular (blood vessel) changes in the pelvic region. The penis becomes erect and the clitoris swells; blood and other fluids become congested in the testicles and vagina; a reddening of the body, or sex flush, occurs.
- During the plateau phase, a maximum (though varying) level of arousal is reached. There are rapidly increased

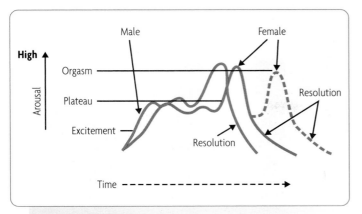

FIGURE 12.4　Phases of Human Sexual Response
The phases of human sexual response in males and females have similar patterns. The primary differences are in the time it takes for males and females to reach each phase, and in the greater likelihood that females will achieve multiple orgasms.

heartbeat, respiration, and blood pressure; increased glandular secretions; and both voluntary and involuntary muscle tension throughout the body. Vaginal lubrication increases, and the breasts swell.

- During the orgasm phase, males and females experience a very intense, pleasurable sense of release from the sexual tension that has been building. Orgasm is characterized by rhythmic contractions that occur approximately every eight-tenths of a second in the genital areas. Respiration and blood pressure reach very high levels in both men and women, and heart rate may double. In men, throbbing contractions lead to ejaculation, an "explosion" of semen.

- During the resolution phase, the body gradually returns to its normal pre-excitement state, with both blood pressure and heartbeat slowing down. After one orgasm, most men enter a refractory period, lasting anywhere from a few minutes to several hours, during which no further orgasm is possible. With sustained arousal, some women are capable of multiple orgasms in fairly rapid succession.

Although Masters and Johnson's research focused on the physiology of sexual response, perhaps their most important discovery was the central significance of *psychological* processes in both arousal and satisfaction. They demonstrated that problems in sexual response often have psychological rather than physiological origins and can be modified or overcome through therapy. Of particular concern is the inability to complete the response cycle and achieve gratification. Often the source of the inability is a preoccupation with personal problems, fear of the consequences of sexual activity, anxiety about a partner's evaluation of one's sexual performance, or unconscious guilt or negative thoughts. However, poor nutrition, fatigue, stress, and excessive use of alcohol or drugs can also diminish sexual drive and performance.

We have now reviewed some physiological aspects of human sexuality and sexual arousal. But we have not yet considered the forces that give rise to *differences* in sexual expression. We begin with the idea that the goal of reproduction ensures different patterns of sexual behaviour for men and for women.

THE EVOLUTION OF SEXUAL BEHAVIOURS

For nonhuman animals, we have already seen that the pattern of sexual behaviours was largely fixed by evolution. The main goal is reproduction—preservation of the species—and sexual behaviours are highly ritualized and stereotyped. Can the same claim be made for general patterns of human sexual behaviours?

Evolutionary psychologists have explored the idea that men and women have evolved to have different *strategies* that underlie sexual behaviour (Buss, 2008). To describe these strategies, we have to remind you of some of the realities of human reproduction. Human males could reproduce hundreds of times a year if they could find enough willing mates. To produce a child, all they need to invest is a teaspoon of sperm and a few minutes of intercourse. Women can reproduce at most about once a year, and each child then requires a huge investment of time and energy. (Incidentally, the world record for the number of times a woman has given birth falls short of 50, but men have fathered many more children. A Moroccan despot, King Ismail the Blood-Thirsty, is said to have had over 700 children, and the first emperor of China is said to have fathered over 3000; both had large harems.)

Thus, when reproduction is a goal, eggs are the limited resource and males compete for opportunities to fertilize them. The basic problem facing a male animal is to maximize the number of offspring he produces by mating with the largest number of females possible. But the basic problem facing a female animal is to find a high-quality male to ensure the best, healthiest offspring from her limited store of eggs. Furthermore, human offspring take so long to mature and are so helpless while growing that substantial **parental investment** is required (Bell, 2001; Sear & Mace, 2008). Mothers and fathers must spend time and energy raising the children—unlike fish or spiders, which simply lay eggs and depart. Females thus have the problem of selecting not just the biggest, strongest, smartest, highest-status, most thrilling mate, but also the most loyal, committed partner to help raise their children.

One evolutionary psychologist, **David Buss** (2008), has suggested that men and women evolved different strategies, emotions, and motivations for short-term mating versus long-term mating. The male strategy of seducing and abandoning as many women as possible—showing signs of loyalty and commitment and then leaving—is a short-term strategy. The male strategy of staying committed to the female and investing in the offspring is a long-term strategy. The female strategy of attracting a loyal male who will stay to help raise her children is a long-term strategy. The female strategy of acquiring resources or obtaining men of high status is a short-term strategy. Because these claims about men's and women's differing strategies are based on evolutionary analyses, researchers have sought cross-cultural data to support them. For example, one study involved over 16 000 participants from 52 nations (Schmitt, 2003). The men and women in the study provided information about their interest in short-term sexual relationships. Across the whole sample, men consistently reported greater desire for sexual variety than did women. This result supports the evolutionary claim that men's and women's different reproductive roles have an impact on sexual behaviour.

---

parental investment　The time and energy parents must spend raising their offspring.

Researchers have provided a variety of types of evidence to support predictions of evolutionary theory. Consider how men's and women's mating strategies could give rise to different experiences of jealousy. According to evolutionary theory, a woman should experience jealousy when she suspects that her partner might no longer feel committed to providing resources to raise her children—these concerns focus on *emotional involvement*. By contrast, a man should experience jealousy when he suspects that he is being burdened by children with whom he has no genetic relationship—these concerns focus on *sexual infidelity*.

To test evolutionary theory's predictions about men's and women's experiences of jealousy, a researcher asked male and female participants to recall or imagine a committed heterosexual relationship (Schützwohl, 2006). The participants were then asked to consider this scenario, with sex-appropriate terms: "Imagine that of late your partner is frequently tardy in coming home. At your insistence, s/he admits meeting another man/woman." Participants then generated a list of questions; under these circumstances, what would they ask their partners? The participants' questions fell into several categories. **Table 12.2** presents the categories relevant to evolutionary theory: emotional involvement questions and sexual infidelity questions. **Figure 12.5** shows the percentage of men and women who wished to ask each type of question. As you can see, women were much more likely to devise questions based on emotional involvement; men were much more likely to devise questions based on sexual infidelity.

Does this pattern seem familiar from your own experiences of jealousy? Lorne Campbell at the University of Western Ontario and his colleague Bruce Ellis from the University of Canterbury in Arizona (2005) have argued that, in addition to jealousy, other emotions—from love to hate—play an important evolutionary role in long-term relationship maintenance. This research illustrates how important aspects of human lives may be guided by our evolutionary history.

Although research supports many of the predictions of the evolutionary account of human sexual behaviours, other theorists believe that the account greatly underestimates the role of culture (Baumeister & Twenge, 2002; Eastwick et al., 2006). For example, women demonstrate greater *erotic plasticity* than men: Women show greater variation in sexual responses and sexual behaviours than men do (Baumeister, 2000). These variations appear, in large part, to be a consequence of cultural constraints (Hyde & Durik, 2000). Consider the "sexual revolution" of the 1960s: Changes in sexual behaviour were brought about by women's increased willingness to

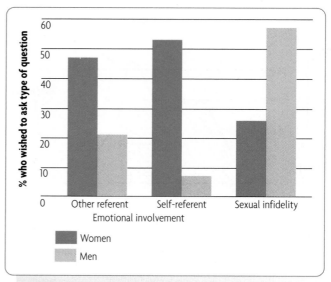

FIGURE 12.5 Sex Differences in Jealousy

Heterosexual men and women wrote questions they imagined asking if they learned their partners had been unfaithful. Women devised more questions that focused on emotional involvement. Men devised more questions that focused on sexual infidelity.

Adapted from a study by Achim Schützwohl, "Sex differences in jealousy: Information search and cognitive preoccupation," *Personality and Individual Differences*, Science Direct online.

TABLE 12.2	Questions for an Unfaithful Partner	
Emotional involvement questions		
Other referent	Do you love him?	
	Have you fallen in love with her?	
Self-referent	Do you still love me?	
	Don't you love me anymore?	
Sexual infidelity questions		
	Did you have sex?	
	Have you slept with him?	

Adapted from a study by Achim Schützwohl, "Sex differences in jealousy: Information search and cognitive preoccupation," *Personality and Individual Differences*, Science Direct online.

Although sex fulfills the biological function of reproduction, most humans engage in sex many more times than they reproduce. Even so, how does the evolutionary perspective explain contemporary sexual strategies?

engage in casual sexual relations. What had changed was not, of course, women's evolutionary history but, rather, cultural attitudes toward the expression of sexuality.

Although the evolutionary approach explains some aspects of human sexual behaviour, the critique calls attention to variability imposed by culture. Norms of sexual behaviour are highly sensitive to time and place. We turn now to sexual norms and how they influence our sexual behaviour.

SEXUAL NORMS

What is an average sex life like? Scientific investigation of human sexual behaviour was given the first important impetus by the work of **Alfred Kinsey** and his colleagues beginning in the 1940s (1948, 1953). They interviewed some 17 000 Americans about their sexual behaviour and revealed—to a generally shocked public—that certain behaviours, previously considered rare and even abnormal, were actually quite widespread—or at least were reported to be. The norms for sexual behaviour have changed over the years, in part because of scientific advances. For example, the availability of birth control pills in the early 1960s allowed women more sexual freedom because it reduced the likelihood of pregnancy. The arrival of Viagra in 1998 allowed men to prolong their years of sexual activity. Alongside the impact of science, there has been a general trend in many cultures toward more open discourse about sexual issues. **Table 12.3** provides data from a study that surveyed members of the classes of 1950, 1975, and 2000 from the same high school in the northeastern United States with respect to their sexual experiences in high school (Caron & Moskey, 2002). You can see that there have been general trends for

people to talk more openly with their families about sexual issues at the same time that actual sexual experiences have increased. This pattern would be very similar if the study had been conducted in Canada, as cultural norms about sex have been quite similar.

Sexual norms are part of what you acquire as a member of a culture. We already suggested that some general "male" and "female" aspects of sexual behaviour may be products of the evolution of the human species. Even so, different cultures define ranges of behaviour that are considered to be appropriate for expressing sexual impulses. **Sexual scripts** are socially learned programs of sexual responsiveness that include prescriptions, usually unspoken, of what to do; when, where, and how to do it; with whom or with what to do it; and why it should be done (Krahé, Bieneck, & Scheinberger-Olwig, 2007; Seal et al., 2008). Different aspects of these scripts are assembled through social interaction over your lifetime. The attitudes and values embodied in your sexual script are an external source of sexual motivation: The script suggests the types of behaviours you might or should undertake.

Let us focus more specifically on the sexual practices of university students. Researchers have often been interested in understanding the decisions students make about their sexual activities—and how students feel about those decisions. For example, in one sample of 152 sexually active university women, 77 percent expressed at least "a few" regrets about their sexual decisions (Eshbaugh & Gute, 2008). Two particular behaviours prompted the most intense regret. First, "engaging in intercourse with someone once and only once" (p. 83), something

---

sexual scripts Socially learned programs of sexual responsiveness.

TABLE 12.3 Sexual Experiences of the Classes of 1950, 1975, and 2000	1950	1975	2000	χ^2
In high school, how much did you discuss sexual intercourse, birth control, sexually transmitted diseases, or pregnancy with your parents/family?				52.32*
We never talked about sex issues.	65%	50%	15%	
We talked about sex occasionally/a few times.	25%	41%	45%	
We talked about sex many times/regularly.	10%	9%	40%	
Which statement *best* describes your sexual experience while in high school?				88.24*
I did not think about sex.	25%	2%	6%	
I had kissed someone.	41%	9%	3%	
I had "made out" with someone.	10%	24%	22%	
I had sex 1–3 times.	8%	13%	11%	
I had sex more than 3 times.	16%	52%	58%	

*p < 001

Adapted from Sandra L. Caron and Eilean G. Moskey, "Changes over time in teenage sexual relationships: Comparing the high school class of 1950, 1975, and 2000." University of Maine, 2002.

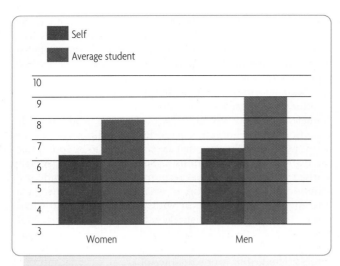

FIGURE 12.6   Judgments About Hooking Up

College students provided ratings on a scale of 1 (not at all comfortable) to 11 (very comfortable) to two questions about "hooking up." For the self ratings, they indicated how comfortable they personally were with the amount of hooking up that went on at their school. For the average student ratings, they indicated how comfortable they believed the average student was with the amount of hooking up.

From *Journal of Sex Research* by Lambert, T. A., Kahn, A. S., & Apple, K. J. Copyright 2003 by Taylor and Francis Informa UK Ltd–Journals. Reproduced with permission of Taylor & Francis Informa UK Ltd–Journals in the format Textbook via Copyright Clearance Center.

How might instances of sexual harassment arise from conflicting sexual scripts?

36 percent of the women reported having done. Second, "engaging in intercourse with someone known for less than 24 [hours]" (p. 83), something 29 percent of the women said they had done. You may recognize those behaviours as part of the definition of "hooking up" (Bogle, 2008). In another study of 327 university undergraduates, "hooking up" was defined as "a sexual encounter between two people who may or may not know each other well, but who usually are not seriously dating" (Lambert, Kahn, & Apple, 2003, p. 131). Given that definition, 78 percent of the women and 84 percent of the men reported that they had hooked up. The researchers also asked the students who had hooked up to make two judgments: The students rated how comfortable they personally were with the amount of hooking up that went on at their school; they also rated how comfortable the average student was with the amount of hooking up. As you can see in **Figure 12.6**, men reported themselves more comfortable with hooking up than did women. However, what you also see is that people's self-ratings were consistently lower than their guesses about others' comfort levels. Thus, the true norm for comfort level (which is the average of people's self-reports) was lower than what the students perceived the norm to be! How might this perception affect people's behaviours?

Research into the sexual experience of university students has revealed another area in which male and female sexual scripts come into devastating conflict: rape. In one study, researchers asked 4446 women enrolled at universities to provide information about their experiences of sexual aggression in seven months of a school year (Fisher, Cullen, & Turner, 2000). In that reference period, 1.1 percent of the women had experienced attempted rape and 1.7 percent had experienced completed rape. The researchers extended those numbers to estimate the likelihood that a woman would experience an attempted or completed rape during her university career: They concluded that the number of victimized women might climb to 20 to 25 percent. The researchers also examined a particular type of rape: **date rape**. Date rape applies to circumstances in which someone is coerced into sexual activity by a social acquaintance. For this sample of women, 12.8 percent of rapes and 35.0 percent of attempted rapes occurred on dates. Researchers have documented that men and women have different date rape scripts. In one study, college men and women read the same account of a scenario in which a woman had resisted having sex (Clark & Carroll, 2008). Male participants were less likely than female participants to label the incident as a rape. Male participants were also more likely to place responsibility on the victim.

Throughout most of our discussion of sexual motivation, we have been ignoring a major category of sexual experience: homosexuality. We conclude this section on sexual motivation with a discussion of lesbians and gay men. This discussion will give us another opportunity to see how sexual behaviour is controlled by the interplay of internal and external motivational forces.

HOMOSEXUALITY

Our discussion so far has focused on the motivations that cause people to perform a certain range of sexual behaviours. In this same context we can discuss the existence of homosexuality. That is, rather than presenting homosexuality as a set of behaviours that is "caused" by a deviation from heterosexuality, our discussion of sexual motivation should allow you to see that all sexual behaviour is "caused." In this view, homosexuality and

---

date rape Unwanted sexual violation by a social acquaintance in the context of a consensual dating situation.

heterosexuality result from similar motivational forces. Neither of them represents a motivated departure from the other.

Most surveys of sexual behaviour have tried to obtain an accurate estimate of the incidence of homosexuality. In his early research, Alfred Kinsey found that 37 percent of men in his sample had had at least some homosexual experience and that about 4 percent were exclusively homosexual (percentages for women were somewhat smaller). One major project found that about 4 percent of women in their sample were sexually attracted to individuals of the same sex, but only 2 percent of the sample had actually had sex with another woman in the past year. Similarly, 6 percent of the men in their survey were sexually attracted to other men, but again only 2 percent of the sample had actually had sex with another man in the past year (Michael, Gagnon, Laumann, & Kolata, 1994). In a recent survey of over 2000 adults in the United States, 3.2 percent of the men and 2.5 percent of the women reported same-sex activity in the previous year (Turner et al., 2005); these figures would be relatively similar in Canada. In your view, are these figures correct? As long as there is societal hostility directed toward acting on homosexual desires, it may be impossible to get entirely accurate estimates of the incidence of homosexuality because of people's reluctance to confide in researchers.

In this section we consider the origins of homosexuality and heterosexuality. We also review research on societal and personal attitudes toward homosexual behaviour.

The Nature and Nurture of Homosexuality After our discussion of evolution and sexual behaviours, it should not surprise you to learn that research evidence suggests that sexual preference has a genetic component. As is often the case, researchers have made this assertion based on studies that compare concordance rates of monozygotic (MZ) twins (those who are genetically identical) and dizygotic (DZ) twins (those who, like siblings, share only half their genes). When both members of a pair of twins have the same orientation—homosexual or heterosexual—they are concordant. If one twin is homosexual and the other is heterosexual, they are discordant. Studies of both gay men and lesbians have demonstrated considerably higher concordance rates for MZ than for DZ twins (Rahman & Wilson, 2003). For example, in one sample of roughly 750 pairs of twins, 32 percent of the MZ twins were concordant for non-heterosexual orientations versus 8 percent of DZ twins (Kendler, Thornton, Gilman, & Kessler, 2000). Although MZ twins may also be reared in more similar environments than DZ twins—they may be treated more similarly by their parents—this pattern strongly suggests that sexuality may, in part, be genetically determined.

Researchers have also begun to document brain differences between homosexuals and heterosexuals. For example, one study used MRI and PET scans to compare brain shapes and volumes (Savic & Lindström, 2008). The brain images revealed that heterosexual men had asymmetric brains, with slightly larger right cerebral hemispheres—as did homosexual women. Both the heterosexual women and the homosexual men had symmetrical cerebral hemispheres. The study also identified patterns of connections between the amygdala (which, as you might recall, plays an important role in emotional control and memories) and other brain regions. Once again, the patterns of connections in the homosexual participants' brains were more similar to those in the opposite-sex heterosexual participants.

What evidence suggests that sexual orientation has a genetic component?

Further research may strengthen or weaken the case for such broad brain differences. Still, it seems clear that some aspects of homosexuality and heterosexuality emerge in response to purely biological forces.

Social psychologist **Daryl Bem** (1996, 2000) has suggested that biology does not affect sexual preference directly, but rather has an indirect impact by influencing the temperaments and activities of young children. Recall from Chapter 11 that researchers have suggested that boys and girls engage in different activities—boys' play, for example, tends to be more rough-and-tumble. According to Bem's theory, depending on whether they engage in sex-typical or sex-atypical play, children come to feel dissimilar to either their same-sex or opposite-sex peers. In Bem's theory, "exotic becomes erotic": Feelings of dissimilarity lead to emotional arousal; over time this arousal is transformed into erotic attraction. For example, if a young girl feels dissimilar from other girls because she does not wish to engage in girl-typical activities, over time her emotional arousal will be transformed into homosexual feelings. Note that Bem's theory supports the assertion that homosexuality and heterosexuality arise from the same causal forces: In both cases, the sex the child perceives as dissimilar becomes, over time, eroticized.

Society and Homosexuality Suppose Bem is correct to argue that childhood experiences matter enormously. Does everyone act on the urgings set down in childhood? Perhaps what most sets homosexuality apart from heterosexuality is the continuing hostility toward homosexual behaviours in many corners of society. One Canadian study of 3636 high-school students clearly exemplifies this point. In that study, gay, lesbian, bisexual, and questioning adolescents were more likely than heterosexual youth to be victims of bullying, peer sexual harassment, and peer or dating-partner physical abuse (Williams, Connolly, Pepler, & Craig, 2003). Similarly,

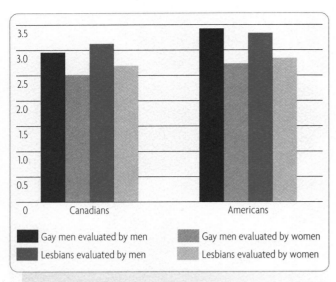

FIGURE 12.7 Attitudes Toward Homosexuality in Canada versus the United States

Male and female students from Canada and the United States were asked to complete a measure that assesses their attitudes toward gays and lesbians on a 5-point scale. As the figure indicates, Canadians' attitudes toward both groups were significantly less negative. Also, women, in general, tend to have more positive views of both gays and lesbians.

From Melanie A. Morrison, Todd G. Morrison, and Randall Franklin, "Modern and old-fashioned homonegativity among samples of Canadian and American university students," *Journal of Cross-Cultural Psychology, 40(4)*, 523–542. Copyright © 2009, Sage Publications. Reprinted by Permission of SAGE Publications.

in a survey conducted in the United States, a sample of 1335 heterosexual men and women were asked how uncomfortable they would feel being around "a man who is homosexual" or "a woman who is a lesbian" (Herek, 2002). Both men and women anticipated more discomfort being around homosexuals who match their own sex. But attitudes toward homosexuals tend to differ from one country to the next. For instance, **Figure 12.7** presents the results of a recent study (Morrison, Morrison, & Franklin, 2009) which assesses attitudes toward gays and lesbians in samples of Canadian and American university students. As the data show, women in the two countries generally have less negative attitudes toward gays and lesbians, but most notable is the difference between the perceptions of Canadians and Americans of both sexes, with Canadians, on average, showing significantly less negative attitudes toward gays and lesbians than Americans. Researchers have labelled highly negative attitudes toward gay people *homophobia* and, as this study suggests, these attitudes vary depending on the general norms of the culture in which one lives.

Most homosexuals come to the realization that they are motivated toward same-sex relationships in the hostile context of societal homophobia. Even so, research suggests that many individuals begin to recognize those feelings at fairly young ages. For example, researchers asked students attending a conference for gay, lesbian, bisexual, and transgendered youth to indicate the age at which they became aware of their sexual orientation (Maguen, Floyd, Bakeman, & Armistead, 2002). Among the gay men, the mean age was 9.6 years; among the lesbians the mean age was 10.9 years. The men reported having same-sex sexual contact at 14.9 years and the women reported same-sex contact at 16.7 years. These data suggest that many people become aware of their homosexual orientation at a time when they must still function in school environments that are often quite hostile to homosexuality (Espelage, Aragon, Birkett, & Koenig, 2008). In addition, homosexual youths must often make the difficult decision of whether to disclose their sexual orientation to their parents (Heatherington & Lavner, 2008). Most adolescents rely on their parents for both emotional and financial support; to disclose their homosexuality puts them at risk to lose both types of sustenance. In fact, parental rejection is related to increases in suicide attempts (D'Augelli, Hershberger, & Pilkington, 2001).

These findings for adolescents reinforce the point that most gay and lesbian individuals find homophobia more psychologically burdensome than homosexuality itself. In 1973, the American Psychiatric Association voted to remove homosexuality from the list of psychological disorders; the American Psychological Association, an organization whose directives guide both American and Canadian psychologists, followed in 1975 (Morin & Rothblum, 1991). Spurring this action were research reports suggesting that, in fact, most gay men and lesbians are happy and productive. Contemporary research suggests that much of the stress associated with homosexuality arises not from the sexual motivation itself—gay people are happy with their orientations—but from the way in which people respond to the revelation of that sexual motivation. Much of lesbians' and gay men's anxiety about homosexuality arises not from being homosexual, but from an ongoing need either to reveal their sexual identity ("come out") to or conceal it ("stay in the closet") from family, friends, and coworkers (D'Augelli, Grossman, & Starks, 2005). More generally, homosexuals experience distress because they cannot speak openly about their lives (Lewis et al., 2006). As you might expect, gay men and lesbians also spend time worrying about establishing and maintaining loving relationships, just as heterosexuals do.

The willingness of lesbians and gay men to "come out" may serve as a first step toward decreasing societal hostility. Research has shown that people's attitudes toward gay men and lesbians are much less negative when they actually *know* individuals in these groups; in fact, on average, the more gay men and lesbians a person knows, the more favourable is his or her attitude (Liang & Alimo, 2005; Vonofakou, Hewstone, & Voci, 2007). (When we turn to the topic of prejudice in Chapter 17, we will see again how experiences with members of minority groups can lead to more positive attitudes.) This brief review of homosexuality allows us to reinforce our main conclusions about human sexual motivation. Some of the impetus for sexual behaviours is internal—genetic endowment and species evolution provide internal models for both heterosexual and homosexual behaviours. But the external environment also gives rise to sexual motivation. You learn to find some stimuli particularly alluring and some behaviours culturally acceptable. In the case of homosexuality, external societal norms may work against the internal dictates of nature.

Let's move now to our third example of important motivation: the forces that set an individual's course for relative success or failure.

❶ What is meant by stereotyped sexual behaviour?

❷ What four phases did Masters and Johnson identify for human sexual response?

❸ According to evolutionary theories, why do men desire more sexual variety than do women?

❹ What are sexual scripts?

❺ What does twin research suggest about the genetics of homosexuality?

CRITICAL THINKING Recall the study that looked at jealousy in men and women. Why was it important to break the emotional involvement category of questions into smaller categories that referred to the self and to the other?

These men are participating in the International Games for the Disabled. How can motivation explain variability among individuals—the fact, for example, that some people do better in competition than others?

Motivation for Personal Achievement

Why do some people succeed, whereas other people, relatively speaking, fail? Why, for example, are some people able to swim the English Channel, whereas other people just wave woefully from the shore? You are likely to attribute some of the difference to genetic factors like body type, and you are correct to do so. But you also know that some people are simply much more interested in swimming the English Channel than are others. So we are back at one of our core reasons for studying motivation. We want, in this case, to understand the motivational forces that lead different people to seek different levels of personal achievement. Let's begin with a construct that is actually called the *need for achievement*.

NEED FOR ACHIEVEMENT

As early as 1938, **Henry Murray** had postulated a need to achieve that varied in strength in different people and influenced their tendency to approach success and evaluate their own performances. **David McClelland** and his colleagues (1953) devised a way to measure the strength of this need and then looked for relationships between strength of achievement motivation in different societies, conditions that had fostered the motivation, and the results of this motivation in the work world. To gauge the strength of the need for achievement, McClelland used his participants' fantasies. On what is called the **Thematic Apperception Test (TAT)**, participants were asked to generate stories in response to a series of ambiguous drawings. Participants shown TAT pictures were asked to make up stories about them—to say what was happening in the picture and describe probable outcomes. Presumably, they projected onto the scene reflections of their own values, interests, and motives. According to McClelland, "If you want to find out what's on a person's mind, don't ask him, because he can't always tell you accurately. Study his fantasies and dreams. If you do this over a period of time, you will discover the themes to which his mind returns again and again. And these themes can be used to explain his actions" (McClelland, 1971, p. 5).

From participant responses to a series of TAT pictures, McClelland worked out measures of several human needs, including needs for power, affiliation, and achievement. The **need for achievement** was designated as *n Ach*. It reflected individual differences in the importance of planning and working toward attaining one's goals. **Figure 12.8** shows an example of how a high–*n Ach* individual and a low–*n Ach* individual might interpret a TAT picture. Studies in both laboratory and real-life settings have validated the usefulness of this measure.

For example, high-scoring *n Ach* people were found to be more upwardly mobile than those with low scores; sons who had high *n Ach* scores were more likely than sons with low *n Ach* scores to advance above their father's occupational status (McClelland, Atkinson, Clark, & Lowell, 1976). Men and women who measured high on *n Ach* at age 31 tended to have higher salaries than their low–*n Ach* peers by age 41 (McClelland & Franz, 1992). Do these findings indicate that high–*n Ach* individuals are always willing to work harder? Not really. In the face of a task that they are led to believe will be difficult, high–*n Ach* individuals quit early on (Feather, 1961). What, in fact, seems to typify high–*n Ach* individuals is a need for *efficiency*—a need to get the same result for less effort. If they outearn their peers, it might be because they also value concrete feedback on how well they are doing. As a measure of progress, salary is very concrete (McClelland, 1961; McClelland & Franz, 1992).

How does a high need for achievement arise? Researchers have considered whether parenting practices can bring about a high or low need for achievement. The following data

---

Thematic Apperception Test (TAT) A projective test in which pictures of ambiguous scenes are presented to an individual, who is encouraged to generate stories about them.

need for achievement (n Ach) An assumed basic human need to strive for achievement of goals that motivates a wide range of behaviour and thinking.

FIGURE 12.8 Alternative Interpretations of a TAT Picture

Story Showing High n Ach

This boy has just finished his violin lesson. He is happy at the progress he is making and is beginning to believe that all his progress is making the sacrifices worthwhile. To become a concert violinist, he will have to give up much of his social life to practise for many hours each day. Although he knows he could make more money by going into his father's business, he is more interested in being a great violinist and giving people joy with his music. He renews his personal commitment to do whatever it takes to make it.

Story Showing Low n Ach

This boy is holding his brother's violin and wishes he could play it. But he knows it is not worth the time, energy, and money for lessons. He feels sorry for his brother; he has given up all the enjoyable things in life to practise, practise, practise. It would be great to wake up one day and be a top-notch musician, but it does not work that way. The reality is boring practice, no fun, and the strong possibility of becoming just another guy playing a musical instrument in a small-town band.

come from a longitudinal analysis of a group of Boston-area children.

> David McClelland and Carol Franz (1992) compared measures of parenting practice, collected in 1951 when the children were about five years old, with measures of *n Ach* and earnings, collected in 1987–1988, when the children were 41. In 1951, the parents were asked to indicate their practices with respect to feeding and toilet training the child. McClelland and Franz considered children to have experienced a high degree of *achievement pressure* when their parents had fed and toilet trained them by strict rules. Overall, there was a positive correlation between early parental achievement pressure and subsequent adult *n Ach*. Furthermore, children who had experienced a high degree of achievement pressure were earning about $10 000 more annually than their peers who had experienced little such pressure.

These data suggest that the degree to which you experience a need to achieve may have been established in the first few years of your life.

ATTRIBUTIONS FOR SUCCESS AND FAILURE

Need for achievement is not the only variable that affects motivation toward personal success. To see why, consider a hypothetical example. Suppose you have two friends who are taking the same class. On the first midterm, each gets a C. Do you think they would be equally motivated to study hard for the second midterm? Part of the answer will depend on the **attributions** they made to explain the C to themselves. (We will develop attribution theory at length in Chapter 17.) Attributions can have an important impact on motivation. Let's see why.

Suppose that one friend attributed her performance to construction noise during the exam, whereas the other attributed his performance to poor memory. These attributions provide an answer to the question, "To what extent does a causal factor reside within an individual, or is it a general factor in the environment?" In this example, one friend made an external attribution (construction noise) whereas the other made an internal attribution (poor memory). These attributions would often have an effect on motivation. If your friend attributes her performance to construction noise, she is likely to study hard for the next midterm. If your other friend thinks the fault lies in his poor memory, he's more likely to give up.

The internal–external dimension is one of three dimensions along which attributions can vary. We can also ask: "To what extent is a causal factor likely to be stable and consistent over time, or unstable and varying?" The answer gives us the dimension of stability versus instability. Or we can ask: "To what extent is a causal factor highly specific, limited to a particular task or situation, or global, applying widely across a variety of settings?" This gives us the dimension of *global* versus *specific*.

An example of how two of these dimensions can interact is given in **Figure 12.9**. Let's stay with the example of attributions about exam grades. Students can interpret their grades as the result of internal factors, such as ability (a stable personality characteristic) or effort (a varying personal quality). Or they may view the grades as caused primarily by external factors such as the difficulty of the task, the actions of others (a stable situational problem), or luck (an unstable external feature). Depending on the nature of the attribution they make for this success or failure, they are likely to experience one of the emotional responses depicted in **Table 12.4**. What is important here is that the type of interpretation will influence both their emotions and subsequent attribution.

Let's return to your two friends. We suggested that one friend made an external attribution (construction noise) whereas the other made an internal attribution (poor memory). Researchers have shown that the way people explain events in their lives—from winning at cards to being turned down for a date—can become lifelong, habitual *attributional styles* (Cole et al., 2008). The way people account for their successes and failures along the three dimensions we've identified can influence motivation, mood, and even ability to perform appropriately. Attributional style affects people's activity and passivity, whether they persist or give up easily, take risks, or play it safe (Seligman, 1991).

---

attributions Judgments about the causes of outcomes.

FIGURE 12.9 Attributions regarding Causes for Behavioural Outcomes

Locus of Control

	Internal	External
Stable	Ability	Task difficulty
Unstable	Effort	Luck

(Stability on vertical axis)

Four possible outcomes are generated with just two sources of attributions about behaviour: the locus of control (internal or external) and the stability of the situation in which the behaviour occurs (stable or unstable). *Ability* attributions are made for the internal–stable combination, *effort* for the internal but unstable combination, *a difficult task* (test) when external–stable forces are assumed to be operating, and *luck* for the unstable–external combination.

TABLE 12.4 Attribution-Dependent Emotional Responses

Your feelings in response to success and failure depend on the kinds of attributions you make regarding the cause of those outcomes. For example, you take pride in success when you attribute it to your ability but are depressed when you perceive lack of ability to cause failure. Or you feel gratitude when you attribute your success to the actions of others but anger when they are seen as contributing to your failure.

Attribution	Emotional Responses	
	Success	**Failure**
Ability	Competence	Incompetence
	Confidence	Resignation
	Pride	Depression
Effort	Relief	Guilt
	Contentment	Shame
	Relaxation	Fear
Action of others	Gratitude	Anger
	Thankfulness	Fury
Luck	Surprise	Surprise
	Guilt	Astonishment

In Chapter 15, we will discuss the research evidence that an internal–global–stable explanatory style ("I never do anything right") puts individuals at risk for depression (and one of the symptoms of depression is impaired motivation). For now, however, we will focus on the way in which explanatory style might lead one of your friends to have earned an A and the other an F by the end of the semester. Seligman's research team has worked on the problem of explaining one person's ability and another's inability to resist failure. The secret ingredient has turned out to be familiar and seemingly simple: *optimism* versus *pessimism*. These two divergent ways of looking at the world influence motivation, mood, and behaviour.

The *pessimistic attributional style* focuses on the causes of failure as internally generated. Furthermore, the bad situation and the individual's role in causing it are seen as stable and global—"It won't ever change and it will affect everything." The *optimistic attributional style* sees failure as the result of external causes—"The test was unfair"—and of events that are unstable or modifiable and specific—"If I put in more effort next time, I'll do better, and this one setback won't affect how I perform any other task that is important to me."

These causal explanations are reversed when it comes to the question of success. Optimists take full, personal internal–stable–global credit for success. However, pessimists attribute their success to external–unstable–global or specific factors. Because they believe themselves to be doomed to fail, pessimists perform worse than others would expect, given objective measures of their talent. A body of research supports these generalizations about optimists and pessimists. For example, one study measured the explanatory styles of 130 male salespeople in a leading United Kingdom insurance company (Corr & Gray, 1996). In the study, salespeople with more positive attributional styles were also likely to have higher sales. In everyday life, interpretations of events affect both optimists' and pessimists' levels of motivation for future performance.

To close this section, consider a research example of the powerful impact of causal attributions in an academic setting.

When students from minority groups attend university, they often report that they do not feel socially comfortable in their new environment. Those feelings of social displacement can undermine students' achievement motivation. A pair of researchers predicted that they could improve black students' academic performance if they changed the students' attributions about their lack of social belonging (Walton & Cohen, 2007). Participants in the study read survey material about university experiences. For the experimental group, some of that material provided a new way to make attributions about difficulties with social belonging: The survey asserted, for example, that "quantitative statistics indicated that most upperclassmen had 'worried [as first-year students] whether other students would accept them,' but that now most are sure 'that other students accept them'" (p. 88). The control group did not read this type of information. To test the impact of this brief intervention, the researchers obtained participants' grades for the following semester. They calculated whether each student's grades were higher or lower than would be expected based on earlier semesters. Participants in the experimental group obtained grades that were better than expected; participants in the control group did worse than expected.

Because of the way in which attributions affected motivation, a small amount of information about feelings of social belonging had a lasting effect on students' performance.

We believe that there is much value to you in this line of psychological research. You can work at developing an optimistic explanatory style for your successes and failures. You can avoid making negative, stable, dispositional attributions for your failures by examining possible causal forces in the situation. Finally, do not let your motivation be undermined by momentary setbacks. You can apply this research-based advice to better your life—a recurring theme of *Psychology and Life*.

WORK AND ORGANIZATIONAL PSYCHOLOGY

Now suppose your positive philosophy has helped you to get a job in a big corporation. Can we predict exactly how motivated you will be just by knowing about you, as an individual—your *n Ach* score or your explanatory style? Your individual level of motivation will depend, in part, on the overall context of people and rules in which you work. Recognizing that work settings are complex social systems, **organizational psychologists** study various aspects of human relations, such as communication among employees, socialization or enculturation of workers, leadership, attitudes and commitment toward a job and/or an organization, job satisfaction, stress and burnout, and overall quality of life at work (Blustein, 2008; Hodgkinson & Healey, 2008). As consultants to businesses, organizational psychologists may assist in recruitment, selection, and training of employees. They also make recommendations about job redesign—tailoring a job to fit the person. Organizational psychologists apply theories of management, decision making, and development to improve work settings.

We now review two influential theories organizational psychologists have developed to understand motivation in the workplace. *Equity theory* and *expectancy theory* attempt to explain and predict how people will respond under different working conditions. These theories assume that workers engage in certain cognitive activities, such as assessing fairness through processes of social comparison with other workers or estimating expected rewards associated with their performance. Although both equity theory and expectancy theory originated over 40 years ago, researchers continue to use these perspectives to understand workplace motivation (for example, Bolino & Turnley, 2008; Grant, 2008; Siegel, Schraeder, & Morrison, 2008).

Equity theory proposes that workers are motivated to maintain fair or equitable relationships with other relevant persons (Adams, 1965). Workers take note of their inputs (investments or contributions they make to their jobs) and their

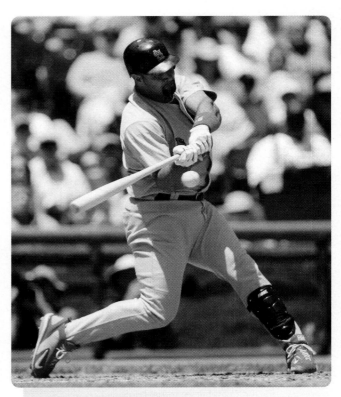

How does expectancy theory explain some players' choice to favour hitting home runs over achieving a higher batting average?

outcomes (what they receive from their jobs), and then they compare these with the inputs and outcomes of other workers. When the ratio of outcomes to inputs for Worker A is equal to the ratio for Worker B (outcome A ÷ input A = outcome B ÷ input B), then Worker A will feel satisfied. Dissatisfaction will result when these ratios are not equal. Because feeling this inequity is aversive, workers will be motivated to restore equity by changing the relevant inputs and outcomes. These changes could be behavioural (for example, reducing input by working less, increasing outcome by asking for a raise), or they could be psychological (for example, reinterpreting the value of the inputs—"My work isn't really that good"—or the value of the outcome—"I'm lucky to have a weekly paycheque I can count on").

Have you noticed the consequences of equity or inequity in your own work situations? Consider a situation in which a coworker leaves for a better job. How does that make you feel? Equity theory suggests that you may feel like you have been unfairly left behind in an undesirable job. In fact, when coworkers leave in circumstances in which they have expressed dissatisfaction, the people remaining tend to become less productive in their jobs—they decrease productivity to restore their sense of equity (Sheehan, 1993). If you end up in a management position, you should try to prevent this pattern by addressing the psychological needs of your employees with respect to equity. For example, keep in mind the benefit of adequate explanations for changes in the relationship of inputs to outcomes.

Expectancy theory proposes that workers are motivated when they expect that their effort and performance on the job

---

organizational psychologists Psychologists who study various aspects of the human work environment, such as communication among employees, socialization or enculturation of workers, leadership, job satisfaction, stress and burnout, and overall quality of life.

equity theory A cognitive theory of work motivation that proposes that workers are motivated to maintain fair and equitable relationships with other relevant persons; also, a model that postulates that equitable relationships are those in which the participants' outcomes are proportional to their inputs.

expectancy theory A cognitive theory of work motivation proposing that workers are motivated when they expect their efforts and job performance to result in desired outcomes.

will result in desired outcomes (Harder, 1991; Porter & Lawler, 1968; Vroom, 1964). In other words, people will engage in work they find attractive (leading to favourable consequences) and achievable. Expectancy theory emphasizes three components: expectancy, instrumentality, and valence. *Expectancy* refers to the perceived likelihood that a worker's efforts will result in a certain level of performance. *Instrumentality* refers to the perception that performance will lead to certain outcomes, such as

rewards. *Valence* refers to the perceived attractiveness of particular outcomes. With respect to a particular work situation, you can imagine different probabilities for these three components. You might, for example, have a job in which there is a high likelihood of reward if performance is successful (high instrumentality) but a low likelihood that performance will be successful (low expectancy), or a low likelihood that the reward will be worthwhile (low valence). According to expectancy theory,

Critical Thinking in Your Life

HOW DOES MOTIVATION AFFECT ACADEMIC ACHIEVEMENT?

Suppose you have signed up for your introductory psychology course with two friends, Angela and Blake. On the first day of class, Angela says, "I want to get the top grade in the class." Blake replies, "I'll just be happy if I don't get an F." Can you see how Angela's and Blake's goals would motivate them to engage in very different behaviours? One of them is likely to spend much more time reading this text! We can develop the contrast between Angela and Blake to examine, more generally, what researchers have learned about how students' goals affect their motivation and classroom performance. The purpose of this review is to allow you to think critically about your own goals and motivation.

Analyses of students' performance have identified three general types of achievement goals (Meece, Anderman, & Anderman, 2006). Angela is representative of a student who has *performance-approach goals*. She focuses on appearing more competent than others. Blake is representative of a student who has *performance-avoidance goals*. He focuses on avoiding being judged as less competent than others. The third type of goal is *mastery goals*. Students who are motivated by mastery goals focus on mastering new skills: "Success is evaluated in term of self-improvement, and students derive satisfaction from the inherent qualities of the task, such as its interest and challenge" (Meece et al., 2006, p. 490). Researchers measure

students' goal orientation by asking them to agree with statements such as "I desire to completely master the material presented in this class," and "I just want to avoid doing poorly in this class" (McGregor & Elliot, 2002, p. 381).

In general, students with mastery goals are most highly motivated to engage in the behaviours that help ensure academic achievement. One study assessed students' behaviours two weeks before an introductory psychology exam and then immediately before the exam (McGregor & Elliott, 2002). Those students with performance-avoidance goals avoided studying: Two weeks before the exam, they admitted they had not yet done much to prepare; immediately before the exam they admitted they did not feel ready. Students with mastery goals and performance-approach goals all started preparing for the exam well in advance. However, students with mastery goals were distinguished by the calm with which they anticipated the exam: From two weeks before the exam to immediately before the exam, they became less concerned about avoiding it.

As you examine the goals that underlie your own academic achievement, also think back to your classroom experiences: Teachers differ with respect to the goals they instill (Meece et al., 2006). Teachers can emphasize mastery goals by acknowledging students' effort and enjoyment when acquiring new abilities; they can emphasize performance goals by

identifying students whose test scores are highest or ignoring poor students. In general, students' goals tend to mirror their teachers' goals. Students may not always have had opportunities to develop mastery goals.

In addition, teachers observe students' behaviour to make attributions about their motivation. Suppose you do poorly on an exam. As we noted in the text, you can explain your performance with respect to dimensions such as stability and controllability. Teachers use the same dimensions to respond to their students (Reyna & Weiner, 2001; Weiner, 2006). Consider controllability. Suppose a professor believes that Blake failed an exam because he never works, whereas Angela failed an exam because she transferred late into the class. The professor is likely to be considerably more sympathetic toward Angela than toward Blake. It will be to Blake's advantage to change his professor's attributions!

When students do poorly in our classes, we encourage them to examine the goals they bring to the course and how those goals motivate their behaviour. We hope you can see the importance of undertaking this exercise.

- Why might students with mastery goals grow increasingly calm as an exam approaches?
- What could students do to change professor's attributions about their performance?

workers assess the probabilities of these three components and combine them by multiplying their individual values. Highest levels of motivation, therefore, result when all three components have high probabilities, whereas lowest levels result when any single component is zero.

Can you see how an expectancy theory analysis might help you if you were in a management position? You should be able to think more clearly about expectancy, instrumentality, and valence. You should be able to determine if one piece of the picture is out of kilter. Suppose, for example, your employees came to believe that there was not enough of a relationship between their efforts and how much they are rewarded. What could you do to change the workplace to restore high values for instrumentality?

As a conclusion to this section, we offer a cautionary note on achievement and motivation in work settings. When you make a personal choice about how hard you can work at a career, keep a careful watch on other aspects of your life. As we will see in the next chapter, aggressive striving for success may, in some respects, work counter to the goal of having a long and healthy life.

We have come a long way since we asked you to consider why you got out of bed this morning. We have described the biology and psychology of hunger and eating, and the evolutionary and social dimensions of human sexuality. We have explored individual differences in people's need to achieve and explain personal success. Throughout this discussion, you have seen the intricate interplay of nature and nurture, at the level of both the species and the individual. So, with all this information in hand, why *did* you get out of bed this morning?

STOP AND REVIEW

❶ What is *need for achievement (n Ach)*?
❷ Along what dimensions do people make attributions?
❸ How does expectancy theory explain motivation in the workplace?

CRITICAL THINKING Consider the study that demonstrated the impact of attributions on academic performance of students from minority groups. How might your own university apply the study's findings to improve the odds of success of minority students?

Recapping Main Points

Understanding Motivation

- Motivation is a dynamic concept used to describe the processes directing behaviour.
- Motivational analysis helps explain how biological and behavioural processes are related and why people pursue goals despite obstacles and adversity.
- Drive theory conceptualizes motivation as tension reduction.
- People are also motivated by incentives—external stimuli that are not related to physiological needs.
- Instinct theory suggests that motivation often relies on innate stereotypical responses.
- Social and cognitive psychologists emphasize the individual's perception of, interpretation of, and reaction to a situation.
- Abraham Maslow suggested that human needs can be organized hierarchically.
- Although real human motivation is more complex, Maslow's theory provides a useful framework for summarizing motivational forces.

Visit **MyPsychLab.com** for more review and practice on the following topics:

✱ **Explore:** Maslow's Hierarchy of Needs

Eating

- The body has a number of mechanisms to regulate the initiation and cessation of eating.
- Cultural norms have an impact on what and how much people eat.

- If individuals become restrained eaters, their diets may result in weight gain rather than weight loss.
- Eating disorders are life-threatening illnesses that may arise from cultural pressure and misperceptions of body image.

Visit **MyPsychLab.com** for more review and practice on the following topics:

👁 **Watch:** Urban Sprawl and Obesity

Sexual Behaviours

- From an evolutionary perspective, sex is the mechanism for producing offspring.
- In animals, the sex drive is largely controlled by hormones.
- The work of Masters and Johnson provided the first hard data on the sexual response cycles of men and women.
- Evolutionary psychologists suggest that much of human sexual behaviour reflects different mating strategies for men and women.
- Sexual scripts define culturally appropriate forms of sexual behaviours.
- Homosexuality and heterosexuality are determined both by genetics and by personal and social environments.

Visit **MyPsychLab.com** for more review and practice on the following topics:

◆ **Research:** Alfred Kinsey

Motivation for Personal Achievement

- People have varying needs for achievement. Motivation for achievement is influenced by how people interpret success and failure.
- Two attributional styles, optimism and pessimism, lead to different attitudes toward achievement and influence motivation.

- Organizational psychologists study human motivation in work settings.

Visit **MyPsychLab.com** for more review and practice on the following topics:

 Practice: Motivation For Personal Achievement

KEY TERMS

anorexia nervosa (p. 370)

attributions (p. 382)

binge eating disorder (BED) (p. 370)

bulimia nervosa (p. 370)

date rape (p. 378)

drives (p. 363)

equity theory (p. 384)

expectancy theory (p. 384)

hierarchy of needs (p. 365)

homeostasis (p. 363)

incentives (p. 364)

instincts (p. 364)

motivation (p. 362)

need for achievement (p. 381)

organizational psychologists (p. 384)

parental investment (p. 375)

sexual arousal (p. 374)

sexual scripts (p. 377)

social-learning theory (p. 365)

Thematic Apperception Test (TAT) (p. 381)

Practice Test

1. You are watching your friend Carlos who is playing tennis with little success. At the end of the match, he comes over and says, "I just couldn't get motivated today." How is Carlos using the concept of motivation?
   a. to infer private states from public acts
   b. to relate biology to behaviour
   c. to account for behavioural variability
   d. to explain perseverance despite adversity

2. A(n) _____ is a preprogrammed tendency that is essential for the survival of a species.
   a. incentive
   b. drive
   c. behaviour
   d. instinct

3. According to Maslow, you should always try to satisfy your _____ needs before you satisfy your _____ needs.
   a. attachment; biological
   b. esteem; attachment
   c. safety; esteem
   d. self-actualization; esteem

4. At every meal, Jonah eats only food with one flavour. Because of _____, this should generally _____ the amount of food Jonah eats.
   a. stomach contractions; increase
   b. lateral hypothalamus stimulation; decrease
   c. sensory-specific satiety; increase
   d. sensory-specific satiety; decrease

5. When restrained eaters become disinhibited, they tend to _____
   a. engage in high-calorie binges.
   b. reduce their food consumption further.
   c. go off their diets permanently.
   d. behave more like unrestrained eaters.

6. Which of these statements is *not* true?
   a. Anorexia is diagnosed when people weigh less than 85 percent of their expected body weight.
   b. Men and women suffer from anorexia at the same rate.
   c. Bulimia is characterized by bingeing and purging.
   d. Bulimia occurs more often than anorexia.

7. Barney and Wilma have just watched a movie together while eating popcorn. Suppose you asked Barney why he ate the amount of popcorn he ate. It's least likely that he would mention _____
   a. how hungry he had been.
   b. being influenced by the amount that Wilma ate.
   c. how long it had been since he had eaten a meal.
   d. the taste of the popcorn.

8. Because of the action of _____, you would expect _____ of many species not always to be receptive to mating.
   a. androgens; females
   b. estrogen; males
   c. androgens; males
   d. estrogen; females

9. According to Masters and Johnson's research on human sexual arousal, the _____ phase precedes the _____ phase.
   a. resolution; plateau
   b. plateau; excitement
   c. plateau; orgasm
   d. resolution; orgasm

10. You have a friend who focuses a lot of energy on having brief sexual relationships. This sounds like a _____ mating strategy for a _____.
    a. long-term; female
    b. short-term; male
    c. long-term; male
    d. short-term; female

11. According to research, which pair of siblings should be most likely to share the same sexual orientation?
    a. Larry and John, DZ twins
    b. Deborah and Patty, MZ twins
    c. Rose and Leo, DZ twins
    d. Anne and Charlotte, DZ twins

12. Which of these statements is *not* true for individuals high in need for achievement?
    a. They always complete their tasks.
    b. They like work to go efficiently.
    c. They like to attain their goals.
    d. They spend time on planning.

13. Every day, Victor gets a perfect score on his local newspaper's trivia quiz. Victor thinks this is possible because the trivia questions are really easy. This is an _____ attribution for his performance.
    a. internal–stable
    b. external–unstable
    c. external–stable
    d. external–unstable

14. During a lecture, your professor talks a lot about "valence" and "instrumentality." The lecture most likely concerns _____
    a. attributions.
    b. equity theory.
    c. need for achievement.
    d. expectancy theory.

15. On the way in to an exam, you overhear Saba say, "I'm going to get a perfect score on this exam." You suspect that Saba is motivated by _____ goals.
    a. performance-approach
    b. mastery
    c. performance-avoidance
    d. equity

Essay Questions

1. How does culture affect the development of eating disorders?

2. What is the origin of sexual scripts?

3. What impact do optimistic versus pessimistic attributional styles have on people's lives?

Discovering Psychology Viewing Guide

Watch the following video by logging on to MyPsychLab (**www. mypsychlab. com**). After you have watched the video, complete the activities that follow.

Program 12: Motivation and Emotion

PROGRAM REVIEW

1. What is the general term for all the physical and psychological processes that start behaviour, maintain it, and stop it?
   a. explanatory style
   b. repression
   c. addiction
   d. motivation

2. Phoebe has a phobia regarding cats. What is her motivation?
   a. environmental arousal
   b. overwhelming fear
   c. repressed sexual satisfaction
   d. a need for attachment to others

3. Which activity most clearly involves a "reframing" of the tension between desire and restraint?
   a. eating before you feel hungry
   b. seeking pleasurable physical contact with others
   c. working long hours for an eventual goal
   d. getting angry at someone who interferes with your plans

4. Compared with Freud's view of human motivation, that of Abraham Maslow could be characterized as being more _____
   a. negative.
   b. hormonally based.
   c. optimistic.
   d. pathologically based.

5. Behaviours such as male peacocks displaying their feathers or male rams fighting are related to which part of sexual reproduction?
   a. providing a safe place for mating
   b. focusing the male's attention on mating
   c. selecting a partner with good genes
   d. mating at the correct time of year

6. According to Norman Adler's research on mating behaviour in rats, what is the function of the 10 or so mountings?
   a. to trigger hormone production
   b. to prepare the male for ejaculation
   c. to cause fertilization
   d. to impress the female

7. Pictures of happy and sad U.S. workers are shown to North American college students and to Italian workers.

Based on your knowledge of Paul Ekman's research, what would you predict about how well the groups would identify the emotions?
   a. Both groups will identify the emotions correctly.
   b. Only the North Americans will identify the emotions correctly.
   c. Only the Italians will identify the emotions correctly.
   d. Neither group will identify the emotions correctly.

8. Which of the following is *not* a possible origin of a pessimistic explanatory style?
   a. assessments by important adults in our lives
   b. the reality of our first major negative life event
   c. our mother's pessimism level
   d. our level of introversion/extraversion

9. Which theorist is best known for positing a hierarchy of needs that humans strive to meet?
   a. Freud
   b. Rogers
   c. Maslow
   d. Seligman

10. Although motivation can lead to unpleasant states (e.g., hunger, frustration), it seems to have evolved because of its benefits to:
   a. survival.
   b. propagation of the species.
   c. health.
   d. all of the above.

QUESTIONS TO CONSIDER

1. Human sexual motivation expresses itself in sexual scripts that include attitudes, values, social norms, and expectations about patterns of behaviour. Consider how males and females might develop different sexual scripts. How might lack of synchronization affect a couple? How might sexual scripts change as the bad news about sexually transmitted infections and AIDS increases?

2. If degree of self-restraint and stress determines how likely it is that people will "cheat" on their diets, what sorts of psychological supports would you build into a diet plan?

3. Consider how eating disorders, such as anorexia and bulimia, contradict the pleasure–pain principle.

13

Emotion, Stress, and Health

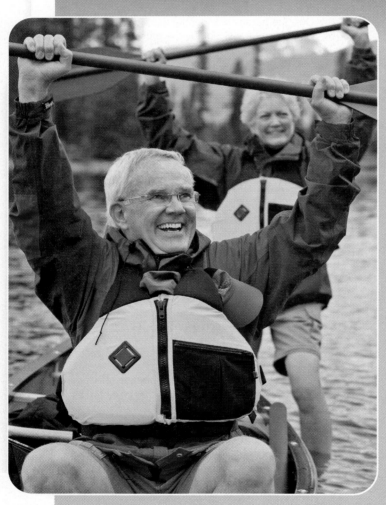

S uppose we asked you right now, "How are you feeling?" How would you answer that question? There are at least three different types of information you might provide. First, you might reveal to us the mood you are in—the *emotions* you are feeling. Are you happy because you know you can finish reading this chapter in time to go to a party? Are you angry because your boss just yelled at you over the telephone? Second, you might tell us something more general about the amount of *stress* you are experiencing. Do you feel as if you can cope with all the tasks you have to get done? Or are you feeling a bit overwhelmed? Third, you might report on your psychological or physical *health*. Do you feel some illness coming on? Or do you feel an overall sense of wellness?

This chapter will explore interactions among these three ways in which you might answer the question "How are you feeling?"—in relation to your emotions, stress, and health. *Emotions* are the touchstones of human experience. They give richness to your interactions with people and nature and significance to your memories. In this chapter, we will discuss the experience and functions of emotions. But what happens if the emotional demands on your biological and psychological functioning are too great? You may become overwhelmed and unable to deal with the stressors in your life. This chapter will also examine how *stress* affects you and how you can combat it. Finally, we will broaden our focus to consider psychology's contributions to the study of health and illness. *Health psychologists* investigate the ways in which environmental, social, and psychological processes contribute to the development of disease. Health psychologists also use psychological processes and principles to help treat and prevent illness while also developing strategies to enhance personal wellness.

We begin now by looking at the content and meaning of emotions.

Emotions

Just imagine what your life would be like if you could think and act but not feel. Would you be willing to give up the capacity to experience fear if you would also lose the passion of a lover's kiss? Would you give up sadness at the expense of joy? Surely these would be bad bargains, promptly regretted. We will soon see that emotions serve a number of important functions. Let's begin, however, by offering a definition of emotion and by describing the roots of your emotional experiences.

Although you might be tempted to think of emotion as only a feeling—"I feel happy" or "I feel angry"—we need a more inclusive definition of this important concept that involves both the body and the mind. Contemporary psychologists define **emotion** as a complex pattern of bodily and mental changes that includes physiological arousal, feelings, cognitive processes, visible expressions (including face and posture), and specific behavioural reactions made in response to a situation perceived as personally significant. To see why all of these components are necessary, imagine a situation in which you would feel a surge of happiness. Your physiological arousal might include a gently beating heart. Your feeling would be positive. The associated cognitive processes include interpretations, memories, and expectations that allow you to label the situation as happy. Your overt behavioural reactions might be expressive (smiling) and/ or action-oriented (embracing a loved one).

Charles Darwin was one of the first to use photographs in the study of emotion. These plates are from *The Expression of Emotions in Man and Animals* (1872/1965). Why did Darwin believe that emotions were the product of evolution?

Before we provide an account that unites arousal, feelings, thoughts, and actions, we need to make a distinction between emotions and moods. We have defined emotions as specific responses to specific events; in that sense, emotions are typically relatively short-lived and relatively intense. By contrast, moods are often less intense and may last several days. There is often a weaker connection between moods and triggering events. You might be in a good or bad mood without knowing exactly why. Keep this distinction between emotions and moods in mind as we describe the theories that explain them.

BASIC EMOTIONS AND CULTURE

Suppose you could gather together in one room representatives from a great diversity of human cultures. What would be common in their experiences of emotion? For an initial answer, you might look to Charles Darwin's book *The Expression of Emotions in Man and Animals* (1872/1965). Darwin believed that emotions evolve alongside other important aspects of human and nonhuman structures and functions. He was interested in the *adaptive* functions of emotions, which he thought of not as vague, unpredictable, personal states, but as highly specific, co-ordinated modes of operation of the human brain. Darwin viewed emotions as inherited, specialized mental states designed to deal with a certain class of *recurring situations* in the world. Over the history of our species, humans have been attacked by predators, fallen in love, given birth to children, fought each other, confronted their mates' sexual infidelity, and witnessed the death of loved ones—innumerable times. We might expect, therefore, that certain types of emotional responses would emerge in all members of the human species. Researchers have tested this claim of the *universality of emotions*

---

emotion A complex pattern of changes, including physiological arousal, feelings, cognitive processes, and behavioural reactions, made in response to a situation perceived to be personally significant.

by looking at the emotional responses of newborn children as well as the consistency of facial expressions across cultures.

Are Some Emotional Responses Innate?

If the evolutionary perspective is correct, we would expect to find much the same patterns of emotional responses in children all over the world (Izard, 1994). **Silvan Tomkins** (1911–1991) was one of the first psychologists to emphasize the pervasive role of immediate, unlearned affective (emotional) reactions. Tomkins (1962, 1981) pointed out that, without prior learning, infants respond to loud sounds with fear or with difficulties in breathing. They seem "prewired" to respond to certain stimuli with an emotional response general enough to fit a wide range of circumstances.

Cross-cultural research has confirmed the expectation that some emotional responses are quite similar in children from very different cultures.

> A team of researchers wished to determine how 11-month-old infants from the United States, Japan, and China display anger and fear (Camras et al., 2007). To elicit anger responses, the researchers grasped each infant's wrists and held them against a tray table so that the infants could not move their arms. To elicit fear responses, the researchers presented each infant with "a disembodied toy gorilla head that could be remotely activated to emit loud unpleasant growling noises while its eyes lit up and its lips moved" (p. 136). The infants produced different behavioural responses to the two procedures. For example, they were more likely to increase their breathing rate as an indication of fear versus anger. Those behavioural responses were similar across cultures. In addition, the infants' facial expressions were similar across the cultures. However, those facial expressions were not consistently different for fear and anger. Apparently, children's ability to display distinct facial expressions for negative emotions emerges after the first year of life.

Although this study demonstrates important cross-cultural consistency, there were also subtle differences among the facial expressions for the infants from the three countries. For example, U.S. children were more likely to produce facial expressions that combined *lowered eyebrows* and a *cry mouth* than were their Chinese peers. Such results suggest that culture acts very early in life to have an impact on emotional responses (Camras et al., 1998).

Note that infants also seem to have an innate ability to interpret the facial expressions of others. In one experiment, 5-month-old infants habituated—they showed decreasing interest—to repeated presentations of an adult face showing smiles of different intensities (Bornstein & Arterberry, 2003). The infants were subsequently shown two new photographs: One photograph showed the same adult with a novel smile (that is, a smile with a different intensity); the second photograph showed the same adult with a fearful expression. The infants consistently spent more time looking at the fearful expression—suggesting both that they experienced the fearful expression as something new and also that they sorted the different smiles into the same category. Other research has demonstrated that patterns of brain activity for 7-month-old infants are different in response to angry and fearful expressions (Kobiella, Grossmann, Reid, & Striano, 2008). Thus, infants have distinctive responses to facial expressions that, as we just saw for 11-month-olds, they are not yet able to produce.

Are Emotional Expressions Universal?

We have seen that infants produce and perceive standard emotional expressions. If that is so, we might also expect to find adult members of even vastly different cultures showing reasonable agreement in the way they believe emotion is communicated by facial expressions.

According to **Paul Ekman**, the leading researcher on the nature of facial expressions, all people share an overlap in "facial language" (Ekman, 1984, 1994). Ekman and his associates have demonstrated what Darwin first proposed—that a set of emotional expressions is universal to the human species, presumably because they are innate components of our evolutionary heritage. Before you read on, take a look at **Figure 13.1** to see how well you can identify these seven universally recognized expressions of emotion (Ekman & Friesen, 1986).

There is considerable evidence that these seven expressions in Figure 13.1 are recognized and produced worldwide in response to the emotions of happiness, surprise, anger, disgust, fear, sadness, and contempt. Cross-cultural researchers have asked people from a variety of cultures to identify the emotions associated with expressions in standardized photographs. Individuals are generally able to identify the expressions associated with the seven emotions.

> In one study, members of a preliterate culture in New Guinea (the Fore culture), who had had almost no exposure to Westerners or to Western culture prior to this experiment, accurately identified the emotions expressed in the white faces shown in Figure 13.1. They did so by referring to situations in which they had experienced the same emotion. For example, photo 5 (fear) suggested being chased by a wild boar when you did not have your spear, and photo 6 (sadness) suggested your child had died. Their only confusion came in distinguishing surprise, photo 2, from fear, perhaps because these people are most fearful when taken by surprise.

Next, researchers asked other members of the culture (who had not participated in the first study) to model the expressions that they used to communicate six of the emotions (excluding contempt). When U.S. college students

Why do researchers believe that some emotional responses are innate?

FIGURE 13.1 Judgments of Emotional Expressions
Match these seven emotion terms with the faces shown at left: fear, disgust, happiness, surprise, contempt, anger, and sadness. The answers are given at the end of the chapter.

viewed videotapes of the facial expressions of the Fore people, they were able to identify their emotions accurately—with one exception. Not surprisingly, the Americans had difficulty distinguishing between the Fore poses of fear and surprise, the same emotions that the Fore had confused in the Western poses (Ekman & Friesen, 1971).

More recent research has compared judgments of facial expressions across individuals in Hungary, Japan, Poland, Sumatra, the United States, and Vietnam; high agreement was found across these diverse populations (Biehl et al., 1997). The general conclusion is that people all over the world, regardless of cultural differences, race, sex, or education, express basic emotions in much the same way and are able to identify the emotions others are experiencing by reading their facial expressions. This finding was also supported in a recent Canadian study (Beaupré & Hess, 2005) that investigated whether sub-Saharan African, Chinese, and French-Canadian individuals living in Canada differ in their perceptions of emotions (i.e., happiness, anger, sadness, fear, disgust, and shame) when these expressions were displayed by members of the same or other ethnic groups. No in-group advantage was shown for any of these emotional expressions.

Note that the claim of universality is focused on the basic set of seven emotions. Ekman and his colleagues make no claim that all facial expressions are universal or that cultures express all emotions in the same way (Ekman, 1994). In fact, Ekman (1972) called his position on universality the *neuro-cultural* theory, to reflect the joint contributions of the brain (the product of evolution) and culture in emotional expression. The brain specifies which facial muscles move to produce a particular expression when a particular emotion is aroused. Different cultures, however, impose their own constraints beyond universal

biology. For instance, in the Canadian study that compared participants from three ethnic groups, French-Canadians were more accurate in decoding expressions of shame and sadness, whereas fear expressions were best recognized by sub-Saharan Africans.

Why might these differences arise? Let's now look directly at cultural influences on emotionality.

How Does Culture Constrain Emotional Expression?

We have just seen that some aspects of emotional expression are universal. Even so, different cultures have different standards for how emotion should be managed. Some forms of emotional response, even facial expressions, are unique to each culture. Cultures establish social rules for when people may show certain emotions and for the social appropriateness of certain types of emotional displays by given types of people in particular settings (Mesquita & Leu, 2007). Consider the three following examples of cultures that express emotions in manners different from the Western norm.

The Wolof people of Senegal live in a society where status and power differences among people are rigidly defined. High-caste members of this culture are expected to show great restraint in their expressions of emotionality; low-caste individuals, particularly a caste called the *griots*, are expected to be more volatile. The griots, in fact, are often called upon to express the "undignified" emotions of the nobility.

> One afternoon, a group of women (some five nobles and two griots) were gathered near a well on the edge of town when another woman strode over to the well and threw herself down it. All the women were shocked at the apparent suicide attempt, but the noblewomen were shocked in silence. Only the griot women screamed, on behalf of all. (Irvine, 1990, p. 146)

Can you imagine how you would respond in this situation? It might be easier to put yourself in the place of the griots rather than in the place of the noblewomen: How could you do anything but scream? The answer, of course, is that these noblewomen have acquired cultural norms for emotional expression that require them not to show any overt response.

A second example of cultural variation in emotional expression arose in the life of one of your authors. At the funeral of an American friend of Syrian descent, he was surprised to see and hear a group of women shrieking and wailing when a visitor entered the funeral parlour. They then stopped just as suddenly until the next visitor arrived, when once again they started their group wailing. What is the explanation for this behaviour? Because it is difficult for the family members of the deceased to sustain a high emotional pitch over the three days and nights of such wakes, they hire these professional criers to display, on their behalf, appropriately strong emotions to each newcomer. This is an expected practice among a number of Mediterranean and Near Eastern cultures.

For our third example, we turn to a cross-cultural difference in norms for emotional displays related to pain. Recall from Chapter 5 that psychological context has a major impact on the extent to which people experience pain. Similarly, the cultural context has an impact on the extent to which it is considered appropriate for people to perform behaviours that reveal they are experiencing pain (Rollman, 2004). For example, one study demonstrated a contrast between what people in North America and Japan consider proper behavioural displays for pain (Hobara, 2005). Participants in both cultures completed the Appropriate Pain Behavior Questionnaire (APBQ), which includes such items as "Women should be able to tolerate pain in most circumstances," and "It is acceptable for men to cry when in pain." In general, Japanese participants provided lower scores on the APBQ: They indicated less approval for open emotional expressions of pain. In addition, both cultural groups suggested more approval for women's emotional displays than for men's. The researcher attributed the cultural difference to the "traditional stocisim . . . of many Asian cultures" (Hobara, 2005, p. 392).

When you think about the types of emotional patterns that may have evolved over the course of human experience, always bear in mind that culture may have the last word. Western notions of what is necessary or inevitable in emotional expression are as bound to Canadian or American culture as are those of any other societies. Can you see how different standards for emotional expression could cause misunderstandings between people of different cultural origins?

We have seen so far that some physiological responses to emotional situations—such as smiles and grimaces—may be innate. Let's turn now to theories that consider the link between other physiological responses and their psychological interpretations.

THEORIES OF EMOTION

Theories of emotion generally attempt to explain the relationship between physiological and psychological aspects of the experience of emotion. We will begin this section by discussing the responses your body gives in emotionally relevant situations. We will then review theories that explore the way these physiological responses contribute to your psychological experience of emotion.

Physiology of Emotion What happens when you experience a strong emotion? Your heart races, respiration goes up, your mouth dries, your muscles tense, and maybe you even shake. In addition to these noticeable changes, many others occur beneath the surface. All these responses are designed to mobilize your body for action to deal with the source of the emotion. Let's look at their origins.

The *autonomic nervous system* (ANS) prepares the body for emotional responses through the action of both its sympathetic and parasympathetic divisions (see Chapter 4). The balance between the divisions depends on the quality and intensity of the arousing stimulation. With mild, *unpleasant* stimulation, the *sympathetic* division is more active; with mild, *pleasant* stimulation, the *parasympathetic* division is more active. With more intense stimulation of either kind, both divisions are increasingly involved. Physiologically, strong emotions such as fear or anger activate the body's *emergency reaction system*, which swiftly and silently prepares the body for potential danger. The sympathetic nervous system takes charge by directing the release of hormones (epinephrine and norepinephrine) from the adrenal glands, which in turn causes the internal organs to release blood sugar, raise blood pressure, and increase sweating and salivation. To calm you after the emergency has passed, the parasympathetic nervous system inhibits the release of the activating hormones. You may remain aroused for a while after an experience of strong emotional activation because some of the hormones continue to circulate in your bloodstream.

As we will see when we describe specific theories of emotion, researchers have debated the question, "Do particular emotional experiences give rise to distinct patterns of activity in the autonomic nervous system?" Cross-cultural research suggests that the answer to the question is yes. A team of researchers measured autonomic responses such as heart rate and skin temperature while men and women from the United States and Minangkabau men from West Sumatra generated emotions and emotional expressions. Given that members of the Minangkabau culture are socialized not to display negative emotions, would they show the same underlying autonomic patterns for negative emotions as did the American participants? The data revealed a high level of similarity across the two cultures, leading the researchers to suggest that patterns of autonomic activity are "an important part of our common evolved biological heritage" (Levenson, Ekman, Heider, & Friesen, 1992, p. 986).

In addition to the autonomic nervous system, we must also consider the role of the central nervous system. Integration of both the hormonal and the neural aspects of arousal is controlled by the *hypothalamus* and the *limbic system*, control systems for emotions and for patterns of attack, defence, and flight. Neuroanatomy research has particularly focused on the *amygdala* as a part of the limbic system that acts as a gateway for emotion and as a filter for memory. The amygdala does this by attaching significance to the information it receives from the senses. It plays an especially strong role in attaching meaning to negative experiences. For example, when people view pictures of fearful facial expressions, the left amygdala (each side of your brain has a separate amygdala) shows increasing activity as the intensity of the expression increases; by contrast, happy facial expressions produce less activity in the same structure the more intensely happy the face becomes (Morris et al., 1996).

In Chapter 11, we described research demonstrating that the left and right amygdalas assume different processing roles

In what ways do cultures constrain emotional expressions in situations like funerals?

when men and women encounter and remember emotionally charged pictures (Cahill et al., 2004; Canli et al., 2002). Recent evidence from PET scans suggests that men's and women's brains are organized differently for emotions even when they are not actively engaged with a task (Kilpatrick, Zald, Pardo, & Cahill, 2006). Paralleling the results for emotional memories, men show greater resting activity in the right amygdala, whereas women show more activity in the left amygdala. However, men and women also differ with respect to patterns of connections to other brain regions. For men, the right amygdala communicates extensively with brain regions such as areas of the motor and visual cortex that are oriented toward the external environment. For women, the left amygdala communicates extensively with regions such as the hypothalamus that are oriented toward the body's inner environment. These data suggest that men and women may be biologically predisposed to respond differently to emotional events.

The *cortex* is involved in emotional experiences through its internal neural networks and its connections with other parts of the body. The cortex provides the associations, memories, and meanings that integrate psychological experience and biological responses. Research using brain-scanning techniques has begun to map particular responses for different emotions. For example, positive and negative emotions are not just opposite responses in the same portions of the cortex. Rather, opposite emotions lead to activity in quite different parts of the brain. Consider a study in which participants underwent fMRI scans while viewing positive pictures (e.g., puppies, brownies, and sunsets) and negative pictures (angry people, spiders, and guns). The scans showed greater activity in the brain's left hemisphere for positive pictures and in the right hemisphere for negative pictures (Canli et al., 1998). In fact, researchers have suggested that there are two distinct systems in the brain that handle *approach-related* and *withdrawal-related* emotional responses (Davidson, Jackson, & Kalin, 2000; Maxwell & Davidson, 2007). Consider puppies and spiders. It is likely that most people would want to approach the puppies but withdraw from the spiders. Research suggests that different brain circuits—apportioned to the different hemispheres of the brain—underlie those responses.

We have seen so far that your body provides many responses to situations in which emotions are relevant. But how do you know which feeling goes with which physiological response? We now review three theories that attempt an answer to this question.

James–Lange Theory of Body Reaction

You might think, at first, that everyone would agree that emotions precede responses: For example, you yell at someone (response) because you feel angry (emotion). However, over 100 years ago, William James argued, as Aristotle had much earlier, that the sequence was reversed—you feel *after* your body reacts. As James put it, "We feel sorry because we cry, angry because we strike, afraid because we tremble" (James, 1890/1950, p. 450). This view that emotion stems from *bodily feedback* became known as the **James–Lange theory of emotion** (Carl Lange was a Danish scientist who presented similar ideas the same year as James). According to this theory, perceiving a stimulus causes autonomic arousal and other bodily actions that lead to the experience of a specific emotion (see **Figure 13.2**). The James–Lange theory is considered a *peripheralist* theory because it assigns the most prominent role in the emotion chain to visceral reactions—the actions of the autonomic nervous system that are peripheral to the central nervous system.

Cannon–Bard Theory of Central Neural Processes

Physiologist **Walter Cannon** (1927, 1929) rejected the peripheralist theory in favour of a *centralist* focus on the action of the central nervous system. Cannon (and other critics) raised a number of objections to the James–Lange theory (Leventhal, 1980). They noted, for example, that visceral activity is irrelevant for emotional experience—experimental animals continue to respond emotionally even after their viscera are separated surgically from the CNS. They also argued that ANS responses are typically too slow to be the source of split-second elicited emotions. According to Cannon, emotion requires that the brain intercede between the input stimulation and the output response. Signals from the thalamus get routed to one area of the cortex to produce emotional feeling and to another for emotional expressiveness.

James–Lange theory of emotion A peripheral-feedback theory of emotion stating that an eliciting stimulus triggers a behavioural response that sends different sensory and motor feedback to the brain and creates the feeling of a specific emotion.

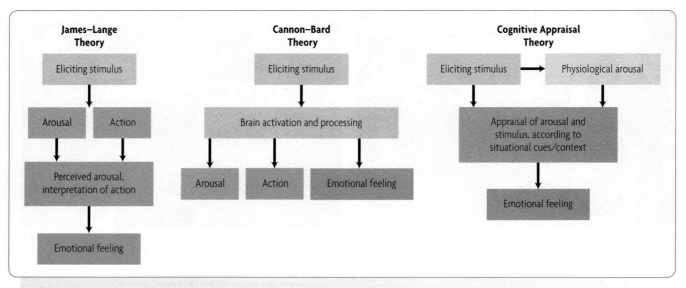

FIGURE 13.2 Comparing Three Theories of Emotion

These classic theories of emotion propose different components of emotion. They also propose different process sequences by which a stimulus event results in the experience of emotion. In the James–Lange theory, events trigger both autonomic arousal and behavioural action, which are perceived and then result in a specific emotional experience. In the Cannon–Bard theory, events are first processed at various centres in the brain, which then direct the simultaneous reactions of arousal, behavioural action, and emotional experience. In the cognitive appraisal theory, both stimulus events and physiological arousal are cognitively appraised at the same time according to situational cues and context factors, with the emotional experience resulting from the interaction of the level of arousal and the nature of appraisal.

Figure from Spencer A. Rathus, *Psychology,* 3/e. Copyright © 1987. Reprinted with permission of Wadsworth, a division of Thomson Learning.

Another physiologist, **Philip Bard**, also concluded that visceral reactions were not primary in the emotion sequence. Instead, an emotion-arousing stimulus has two simultaneous effects, causing both bodily arousal via the sympathetic nervous system and the subjective experience of emotion via the cortex. The views of these physiologists were combined in the **Cannon–Bard theory of emotion**. This theory states that an emotion stimulus produces two concurrent reactions—arousal and experience of emotion—that do not cause each other (see Figure 13.2). If something makes you angry, your heartbeat increases at the same time as you think "I'm ticked off!"—but neither your body nor your mind dictates the way the other responds.

The Cannon–Bard theory predicts independence between bodily and psychological responses. We will see next that contemporary theories of emotion reject the claim that these responses are necessarily independent.

Cognitive Appraisal Theories of Emotion Because arousal symptoms and internal states are similar for many different emotions, it is possible to confuse them at times when they are experienced in ambiguous or novel situations. **Stanley Schachter**

(1922–1997) originated the **two-factor theory of emotion** to explain how people deal with such uncertainty. According to Schachter (1971b), the experience of emotion is the joint effect of physiological arousal and cognitive appraisal, with both parts necessary for an emotion to occur. According to this view, all arousal is assumed to be general and undifferentiated, and arousal is the first step in the emotion sequence. You appraise your physiological arousal in an effort to discover what you are feeling, what emotional label best fits, and what your reaction means in the particular setting in which it is being experienced.

How does the brain respond differently to experiences of puppies and spiders?

Cannon–Bard theory of emotion A theory stating that an emotional stimulus produces two co-occurring reactions—arousal and experience of emotion—that do not cause each other.

two-factor theory of emotion The theory that emotional experiences arise from autonomic arousal and cognitive appraisal.

Richard Lazarus (1922–2002) was another leading proponent of the importance of cognitive appraisal. Lazarus (1991, 1995; Lazarus & Lazarus, 1994) maintained that "emotional experience cannot be understood solely in terms of what happens in the person or in the brain, but grows out of ongoing transactions with the environment that are evaluated" (Lazarus, 1984a, p. 124). Lazarus also emphasizes that appraisal often occurs without conscious thought. When you have past experiences that link emotions to situations—for example, when you once again encounter a bully with whom you have clashed before—you need not explicitly search the environment for an interpretation of your arousal. This position has become known as the **cognitive appraisal theory of emotion** (see Figure 13.2).

To test this theory, experimenters have sometimes created situations in which environmental cues were available to provide a label for an individual's arousal.

> A female researcher interviewed male participants who had just crossed one of two bridges in Vancouver. One bridge was a safe, sturdy bridge; the other was a wobbly, precarious bridge. The researcher pretended to be interested in the effects of scenery on creativity and asked the men to write brief stories about an ambiguous picture that included a woman. She also invited them to call her if they wanted more information about the research. Those men who had just crossed the dangerous bridge wrote stories with more sexual imagery, and four times as many of those men called the female researcher than did those who had crossed the safe bridge. To show that arousal was the independent variable influencing the emotional misinterpretation, the research team also arranged for another group of men to be interviewed 10 minutes or more after crossing the dangerous bridge, enough time for their physical arousal symptoms to be reduced. These nonaroused men did not show the signs of sexual response that the aroused men did. (Dutton & Aron, 1974)

In this situation, the male participants came to an emotional judgment ("I am interested in this woman") based on a *misattribution* of the source of arousal (the woman rather than the danger of the bridge). In a similar experiment conducted at the University of Alberta, students who performed two minutes of aerobic exercise reported less extreme emotions just after the exercise—when they could easily attribute their arousal to the exercise rather than to an emotional state—by comparison to the emotions they reported after a brief delay that made the exercise seem less relevant to their continuing arousal (Sinclair et al., 1994).

Some of the specific aspects of the cognitive appraisal theory have been challenged. For example, you learned earlier that arousal states—the activity of the autonomic nervous system—accompanying different emotions are not identical (Levenson et al., 1992). Therefore, interpretations of at least some emotional experiences may not require appraisal. Furthermore, experiencing strong arousal without any obvious cause does not lead to a neutral, undifferentiated state, as the theory assumes. Stop for a moment and imagine that, right now, your heart suddenly starts beating quickly, your breathing becomes fast and shallow, your chest muscles tighten, and your palms become drenched with sweat. What interpretation would you put on these symptoms? Are you surprised to learn that people generally interpret *unexplained* physical arousal as *negative*, a sign that something is wrong? In addition, people's search for an explanation tends to be biased toward finding stimuli that will explain or justify this negative interpretation (Marshall & Zimbardo, 1979; Maslach, 1979).

Another critique of the cognitive appraisal theory of emotion comes from researcher **Robert Zajonc** (pronounced Zy-Onts). Zajonc demonstrated conditions under which people have preferences—emotional responses to stimuli—without knowing why (Zajonc, 2000, 2001). In an extensive series of experiments on the *mere exposure effect*, participants were presented with a variety of stimuli, such as foreign words, Chinese characters, sets of numbers, and strange faces. These stimuli were flashed so briefly that participants could not consciously recognize the items. Later on, participants were asked how much they liked particular stimuli, some of which were old (i.e., those stimuli had been flashed below the threshold of consciousness) and some of which were new. The participants tended to give higher ratings to the old items. Because participants experienced these positive emotions without conscious awareness of their origins, the emotional response could not emerge from an appraisal process.

It is probably safest to conclude that cognitive appraisal is an important process of emotional experience, but not the only one (Izard, 1993). Under some circumstances, you will, in fact, look to the environment (at least unconsciously) to try to interpret why you feel the way you do. Under other circumstances, your emotional experiences may be under the control of the innate links provided by evolution. The physiological response will not require any interpretation. These different routes to emotional experiences suggest that emotions may have a variety of impacts on your day-to-day experiences. We will now consider some of those consequences.

What emotions would you be likely to feel if people all around you were wildly cheering your favourite team?

---

cognitive appraisal theory of emotion A theory stating that the experience of emotion is the joint effect of physiological arousal and cognitive appraisal, which serves to determine how an ambiguous inner state of arousal will be labelled.

THE IMPACT OF MOOD AND EMOTIONS

Let's begin this section by considering the impact of mood and emotion on social interactions. As a positive social glue, they bind you to some people; as a negative social repellent, they distance you from others. You back off when someone is bristling with anger, and you approach when another person signals receptivity with a smile, dilated pupils, and a "come hither" glance. You might suppress strong negative emotions out of respect for another person's status or power. Consider D. R., a woman who lost the function of her amygdala—and with it the ability to perceive anger and fear (Scott et al., 1997). Imagine what life would be like if you couldn't understand when people were trying to communicate negative emotions. For example, what would it be like not to be able to learn from others that a situation was dangerous? Or that your actions had given rise to an angry response? When D. R. lost function in her amygdala, she also lost her ability to function fully in her social world.

The moods you experience have a strong impact on how you function in social settings. Researchers have demonstrated that positive or negative moods affect the way in which people process information (Clore & Huntsinger, 2007; Forgas, 2008). In particular, people in negative moods tend to process information in a more detailed and effortful fashion than their peers in positive moods. Consider the consequences of people's positive or negative moods on the ways they made judgments of guilt or innocence.

Participants in an experiment watched short films that put them in happy, neutral, or sad moods (Forgas & East, 2008). Once the mood was established, participants watched four videotapes of people denying that they had stolen a movie ticket. In fact, two people were being truthful (that is, they hadn't stolen the ticket) and two were not (that is, they had stolen the ticket)—but participants did not have that information. After watching each videotape, the participants judged each person's guilt or innocence. In general, participants in sad moods were more likely to believe that people were being dishonest. In addition, mood had a major impact on participants' ability to make correct judgments of guilt: Participants in sad moods performed better than chance whereas participants in neutral and happy moods did not.

In discussing their results, the researchers suggest that negative moods may make people less gullible. Think about your own life: Are you more sceptical when you are in a sad mood? And do you think that a positive or negative mood may also affect how people make decisions? Here is a Canadian study that investigated whether mood affects our sense of fairness.

In that study (Inness et al., 2005), participants' mood was manipulated in a manner similar to the study described above, resulting in an equal number of men in a positive, neutral, or negative mood. Participants were then asked to take part in a task with a partner; after completing the task, they were asked to divide a monetary reward of $8.00 between themselves and their collaborator. No matter what mood they were in, participants allocated the reward equally between themselves and their partner when they were told that the partner had contributed more to the

task. However, when participants were told that they had contributed more to the final product, they tended to take significantly more money for themselves (an average of $4.87) when they were in a negative mood compared to when they were in a neutral ($4.01) or positive ($4.05) mood. Interestingly, when male participants worked with a female collaborator, they were not as self-serving and tended to allocate rewards equally. The same study also considered women's division of rewards, but no mood differences were found; women tended to allocate the reward equally no matter the sex of the partner or the mood condition they were in.

In light of this study, do you think you would act differently if you were in a positive or negative mood? For example, when you work on a school project with a friend, do you think your contribution to the project is greater than your friend's? Does mood play a role in this assessment?

We have just illustrated how the global mood you are in may have an impact on the judgments you make. In addition, researchers have explored ways in which thoughts and feelings interact to yield behavioural responses (Storbeck & Clore, 2007). Consider the two reasoning problems given in **Table 13.1**. How would you answer the question at the end of each problem? If you analyze the situations carefully—trying to stick only to the outcomes—you'll see that in each case one person dies so that five others might live. However, most people respond differently to the scenarios: They believe it is appropriate to flip the switch, but they find it difficult to agree that they would actually push a stranger onto trolley tracks. One hypothesis for this difference is that the first type of problem engages emotional processing. It's hard to be unemotional about the idea of actually pushing someone onto the tracks. Evidence in favour of this hypothesis comes directly from the brain. In one study, researchers asked participants to consider moral reasoning problems while undergoing fMRI scans (Greene, Sommerville, Nystrom, Darley, & Cohen, 2001). As in example 1 in Table 13.1, some of the problems were personal—they asked participants to consider actions that required direct personal involvement. The contrasting problems, as in example 2, were relatively impersonal. The two types of problems led to quite different responses in the brain. In particular, for the personal problems, the fMRI scans showed considerably more activity in those brain regions that had been associated, in prior research, with emotional processing. This study provides strong evidence that the content of the problems you face in life determines the way in which cognition and emotion interact to yield solutions.

One final note about the relationship between mood and cognition: Researchers have consistently demonstrated that people in positive moods produce more efficient and more creative thinking and problem solving than do people in more neutral moods (Baas, De Creu, & Nijstad, 2008). Consider a study in which physicians were asked to solve problems that required a certain level of creativity. Those who had been placed in a mildly pleasant mood (the experimenters gave the doctors a small gift of candy) performed reliably better on the creativity test than did those doctors in the control group (who got no prior gift) (Estrada, Isen, & Young, 1994). You can see an immediate application of these types of findings: You are likely to carry out your schoolwork more efficiently and creatively if you can maintain a happy mood. You might be thinking, "How am I

TABLE 13.1 Moral Reasoning Problems

1. A runaway trolley is heading down the tracks toward five workmen who will be killed if the trolley proceeds on its present course. You are on a footbridge over the tracks, between the approaching trolley and the five workmen. Next to you on this footbridge is a stranger who happens to be very large.

   The only way to save the lives of the five workmen is to push this stranger off the bridge and onto the tracks below where his large body will stop the trolley. The stranger will die if you do this, but the five workmen will be saved.

   Is it appropriate for you to push the stranger onto the tracks in order to save the five workmen?

2. You are at the wheel of a runaway trolley quickly approaching a fork in the tracks. On the tracks extending to the left is a group of five railway workmen. On the tracks extending to the right is a single railway workman.

   If you do nothing, the trolley will proceed to the left, causing the deaths of the five workmen. The only way to avoid the deaths of these workmen is to hit a switch on your dashboard that will cause the trolley to proceed to the right, causing the death of the single workman.

   Is it appropriate for you to hit the switch in order to avoid the deaths of the five workmen?

supposed to stay happy with all the work I have to do?" We will now consider research that addresses individual differences in people's long-term feelings of happiness.

SUBJECTIVE WELL-BEING

At the outset of the chapter, we asked you to consider the question, "How are you feeling?" So far, our focus has been on the present moment: What mood or emotion are you experiencing now? However, we can also extend the question over time, to ask "How are you feeling about your life in general?" This question addresses subjective well-being—individuals' overall evaluation of life satisfaction and happiness. In recent years, psychologists have paid considerable research attention to the factors that contribute to people's judgments about their own subjective well-being (Kesebir & Diener, 2008). This research focus reflects, in part, the emergence of positive psychology as an important movement within the profession of psychology. The goal of **positive psychology** is to provide people with the knowledge and skills that allow them to experience fulfilling lives. Positive psychology asks this question: "Can psychologists take what they have learned about the science and practice of treating mental illness and use it to create a practice of making people lastingly happier?" (Seligman, Steen, Park, & Peterson, 2005, p. 410). Much of the research on subjective well-being focuses on trying to determine why some people are happier than others. As is true in most psychological domains, researchers have tried to assess the impact of genetics and environment.

To understand the impact of genetics, researchers have conducted studies using the classic methodology of behaviour genetics: They have examined the extent to which monozygotic (MZ) twins and dizygotic (DZ) twins show similar reports of subjective well-being. For example, in one study, researchers obtained measures of subjective well-being from 4322 Norwegian twins (Nes et al., 2006). Comparisons between MZ and DZ twins revealed that genetic factors accounted for 51 percent of the variance in subjective well-being for men and 49 percent of the variance for women. The researchers also gathered subjective well-being judgments at two points in time, six years apart. Genetic factors accounted for 85 percent of the correlation across time for men and 78 percent of that correlation for women. Research with a sample of 973 twin pairs from the United States also indicated a large impact of genetics on subjective well-being (Weiss, Bates, & Luciano, 2008). However, those data also suggested that personality plays an important role in these genetic effects. In Chapter 14, we will discuss the evidence that personality traits are highly heritable. Results from the U.S. twin sample suggest that differences in subjective well-being are consequences of the personality traits people inherit at birth. For example, people who are high in emotional stability and social engagement are also more likely to report high subjective well-being.

We have just seen that genetics has an important impact on individual differences in subjective well-being. Still, life experiences also matter. An important component of people's judgments of subjective well-being is the balance of positive and negative emotions in their lives.

A team of researchers obtained data from 8557 participants across 46 countries (Kuppens, Realo, & Diener, 2008). Participants provided ratings of their life satisfaction by responding to statements such as "In most ways, my life is close to my ideal" (p. 71) on a 7-point scale that ranged from "strongly disagree" to "strongly agree." They used a 9-point scale—ranging from "not at all" to "all the time"—to indicate how often they had felt positive emotions (such as pride, gratitude, and love) and negative emotions (such as guilt, shame, and jealousy) in the last week. The researchers' analyses disclosed consistent relationships among these measures. In general, participants reported higher levels of life satisfaction when they had more positive emotional experiences and fewer negative emotional experiences. However, positive emotions had about twice as much impact on life satisfaction judgments as did negative emotions. The analyses also revealed somewhat different patterns across cultures. For example, cultures differ with respect to the amount of effort people need to expend to ensure their day-to-day survival. For cultures in which survival is an issue, judgments of life satisfaction depended less on positive emotional experiences.

You can probably relate these results to your own feelings of subjective well-being: As you cast your thoughts over the last week, what types of emotional experiences come readily to mind? You might also think about the features of your life that gave rise to that particular assortment of emotional experiences.

---

positive psychology A movement within psychology that applies research to provide people with the knowledge and skills that allow them to experience fulfilling lives.

Psychology in Your Life

CAN YOU ACCURATELY PREDICT YOUR FUTURE EMOTIONS?

Suppose you're about to submit an assignment. A researcher stops you and asks you to look into the future. First, he asks you to predict what grade you think you'll get. Next, he asks you to predict how you imagine you will feel—on the dimensions of rejoicing and regret—if your actual grade were higher or lower than that prediction or pretty much accurate. Take a minute to consider how you might respond.

When researchers conducted this experiment, their goal was to compare students' predictions about their emotional responses to their actual responses (Sevdalis & Harvey, 2007). After the students received their grades, the researchers asked them how the outcomes made them feel. On average, the students did somewhat better on their assignments than they had predicted. However, those better-than-expected outcomes didn't make them nearly as happy as they thought they would: The students experienced much less rejoicing than they predicted they would.

Before we consider why people's predictions about their future emotions might be inaccurate, let's consider a second example. Here's a situation that will be familiar to many city dwellers: You dash down a stairway just in time to watch the doors

close on your subway car. How would you feel? Suppose you missed the train by a wider margin of time. Now how would you feel? A team of researchers conducted exactly that study (Gilbert, Morewedge, Risen, & Wilson, 2004). They approached people on a subway platform and offered them $1 to fill out a brief questionnaire. One group of participants were Experiencers. The researchers provided them with accurate information that they had missed a train by either a narrow margin (one minute) or a wide margin (five minutes). The participants indicated how regretful they felt about missing the train by providing a rating on a scale ranging from "not at all" to "extremely." Participants cast in the role of Forecasters used the same scale to predict how regretful they imagined they would feel had they missed the train by a narrow or wide margin (that is, each forecaster answered the question for just one margin).

Earlier, we cast you in the role of forecasters by asking you "How would you feel?" If your responses were similar to those of the experimental participants, you likely had the same expectations as the Forecasters: They predicted that people would experience more regret for the narrow margin than for the wide margin.

However, the Experiencers actually reported nearly the same regret for the narrow margin and the wide margin. Once again, we see that people's predictions about their future feelings aren't very accurate.

Why do people have difficulty predicting how they might respond to particular outcomes? In large part, it seems that people are better than they anticipate at putting outcomes into a broader perspective (Kermer et al., 2006). When people actually miss a subway train, they are able to take that outcome in stride by putting it in the larger context of their unfolding day. They don't dwell on the isolated event in a way that makes them continue to feel negative emotions. By contrast, when people predict how they're going to feel, they aren't able to interpret the outcome in the fuller context. The same is true for positive emotions. You might not rejoice as much as you predict to a better-than-expected grade because that outcome occurs as part of your whole ongoing life.

You often make important decisions based on how you anticipate particular outcomes will make you feel. As you make your decisions, try to be aware why your predictions of future feelings may not be accurate.

Researchers have tested a variety of hypotheses about life events that may affect subjective well-being. For example, major negative life events, such as the loss of a job or the death of a spouse often have a damaging impact on subjective well-being (Lucas, 2007). Researchers have also looked at ongoing differences in the circumstances of people's lives. For example, researchers have suggested that "the single most important source of happiness" is good social relationships (Kesebir & Diener, 2008, p. 122). That conclusion should be familiar from earlier sections of *Psychology and Life*; later in this chapter, we'll emphasize social support as an important resource for coping with stress.

Researchers have also tried to understand the relationship between wealth and subjective well-being. When people

struggle to meet their basic needs, they often report low levels of life satisfaction and happiness (Howell & Howell, 2008). However, once people pass the threshold at which those basic needs are secure, the correlation between wealth and subjective well-being is quite modest. If you must make a choice between more money and more friends, the results of positive psychology suggest that you should most often opt for more friends.

We have now explored important short- and long-term consequences of moods and emotions. In the next section, we turn to the topic of stress and how to cope with it. You will learn how to take cognitive control over how you are "feeling."

Why might you worry that a positive mood could make you more gullible?

STOP AND REVIEW

❶ What has cross-cultural research revealed about the recognition of facial expressions?

❷ What role does the autonomic nervous system play in experiences of emotion?

❸ What is the main claim of the Cannon–Bard theory of emotion?

❹ What is the general impact of mood on information processing?

❺ What might be the single most important source of happiness?

CRITICAL THINKING Recall the study that examined mood effects on judgments of guilt. Why was it important that the videotapes showed people that were genuinely innocent and guilty?

Stress of Living

Suppose we asked you to keep track of how you are "feeling" over the course of a day. You might report that for brief periods you felt happiness, sadness, anger, astonishment, and so on. There is one feeling, however, that people often report as a kind of background noise for much of their day-to-day experience, and that is stress (Sapolsky, 1994). Modern industrialized society sets a rapid, hectic pace for living. People often have too many demands placed on their time, are worried about uncertain futures, and have little time for family and fun. But would you be better off without stress? A stress-free life would offer no challenge—no difficulties to surmount, no new fields to conquer, and no reasons to sharpen your wits or improve your abilities. Every organism faces challenges from its external environment and from its personal needs. The organism must solve these problems to survive and thrive.

Stress is the pattern of responses an organism makes to stimulus events that disturb its equilibrium and tax or exceed its ability to cope. The stimulus events include a large variety of external and internal conditions that collectively are called stressors. A **stressor** is a stimulus event that places a demand on an organism for some kind of adaptive response: a bicyclist swerves in front of your car, your professor moves up the due date of your term paper, you are asked to run for class president. An individual's response to the need for change is made up of a diverse combination of reactions taking place on several levels, including physiological, behavioural, emotional, and cognitive. People typically associate stress with *distress*—and assume that all stress is bad. However, you also experience *eustress*. ("Eu" is an ancient Greek prefix meaning "good.") As you'll see by the end of this section, in many circumstances stress can bring about positive changes in your life.

Figure 13.3 diagrams the elements of the stress process. Our goal for this section is to give you a clear understanding of all the features represented in this figure. We will begin by considering general physiological responses to stressors. We then describe the particular effects of different categories of stressors. Finally, we explore different methods you can use to cope with the stress in your life.

PHYSIOLOGICAL STRESS REACTIONS

How would you respond if you arrived at a class and discovered that you were about to have a pop quiz? You would probably agree this would cause you some stress, but what does that mean for your body's reactions? Many of the physiological responses we described for emotional situations are also relevant to day-to-day instances of stress. Such transient states of arousal, with typically clear onset and offset patterns, are examples of **acute stress**. **Chronic stress**, in contrast, is a state of enduring arousal, continuing over time, in which demands are perceived as greater than the inner and outer resources available for dealing with them. An example of chronic stress might be a continuous frustration with your inability to find time to do all the things you want to do. We will now consider how your body responds to these different types of stresses.

Emergency Reactions to Acute Threats In the 1920s, Walter Cannon outlined the first scientific description of the way animals and humans respond to danger. He found that a sequence of activity is triggered in the nerves and glands to prepare the body either to defend itself and struggle or to run away to safety. Cannon called this dual stress response the **fight-or-flight response**. At the centre of this stress response is the *hypothalamus*, which is involved

---

stress The pattern of specific and nonspecific responses an organism makes to stimulus events that disturb its equilibrium and tax or exceed its ability to cope.

stressor An internal or external event or stimulus that induces stress.

acute stress A transient state of arousal with typically clear onset and offset patterns.

chronic stress A continuous state of arousal in which an individual perceives demands as greater than the inner and outer resources available for dealing with them.

fight-or-flight response A sequence of internal activities triggered when an organism is faced with a threat; prepares the body for combat and struggle or for running away to safety; recent evidence suggests that the response is characteristic only of males.

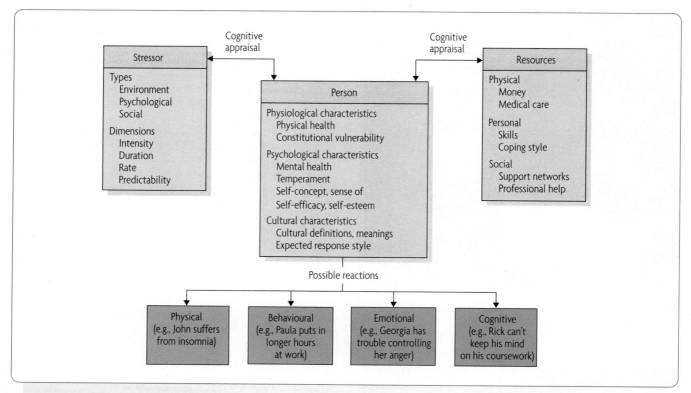

FIGURE 13.3   A Model of Stress
Cognitive appraisal of the stress situation interacts with the stressor and the physical, social, and personal resources available for dealing with the stressor. Individuals respond to threats on various levels: physical, behavioural, emotional, and cognitive. Some responses are adaptive, and others are maladaptive or even lethal.

in a variety of emotional responses. The hypothalamus has sometimes been referred to as the stress centre because of its twin functions in emergencies: (1) It controls the autonomic nervous system (ANS), and (2) it activates the pituitary gland.

The ANS regulates the activities of the body's organs. In stressful conditions, breathing becomes faster and deeper, heart rate increases, blood vessels constrict, and blood pressure rises. In addition to these internal changes, muscles open the passages of the throat and nose to allow more air into the lungs while also producing facial expressions of strong emotion. Messages go to smooth muscles to stop certain bodily functions, such as digestion, that are irrelevant to preparing for the emergency at hand.

Another function of the ANS during stress is to get adrenaline flowing. It signals the inner part of the adrenal glands, the *adrenal medulla*, to release two hormones, *epinephrine* and *norepinephrine*, which, in turn, signal a number of other organs to perform their specialized functions. The spleen releases more red blood corpuscles (to aid in clotting if there is an injury), and the bone marrow is stimulated to make more white corpuscles (to combat possible infection). The liver is stimulated to produce more sugar, building up body energy.

The *pituitary gland* responds to signals from the hypothalamus by secreting two hormones vital to the stress reaction. The *thyrotropic hormone* (TTH) stimulates the *thyroid gland*, which makes more energy available to the body. The *adrenocorticotropic hormone* (ACTH), known as the "stress hormone," stimulates the outer part of the adrenal glands, the *adrenal cortex*, resulting in the release of hormones that control metabolic processes and the release of sugar from the liver into the blood. ACTH also signals various organs to release about 30 other hormones, each of which plays a role in the body's adjustment to this call to arms. A summary of this physiological stress response is shown in **Figure 13.4**.

An analysis by health psychologist **Shelley Taylor** and her colleagues (2000; Taylor, 2006) suggests that these physiological responses to stress may have different consequences for females than for males. Taylor et al. suggest that females do not experience "fight or flight." Rather, these researchers argue that stressors lead females to experience a **tend-and-befriend response**: In times of stress, females ensure the safety of their offspring by tending to their needs; females befriend other members of their social group with the same goal of reducing the vulnerability of their offspring. You can see how this analysis of sex differences in stress responses fits with our earlier discussions of evolutionary perspectives on human behaviour. For example, when we discussed human sexual behaviours in Chapter 12, we noted that men's and women's *mating strategies* differ, in part, because of the relative roles men and women have played—over the course of evolution—in child rearing. The idea here is very much the same: Because of men's and women's different evolutionary niches with respect to nurturing offspring, the same

---

tend-and-befriend response A response to stressors that is hypothesized to be typical for females; stressors prompt females to protect their offspring and join social groups to reduce vulnerability.

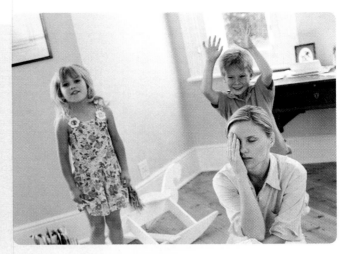

Whether at work or play, individuals in contemporary society are likely to encounter a stressful environment. What situations in your life do you find most stressful?

initial physiological responses to stress ultimately produce quite different behaviours.

Unfortunately, neither the fight-or-flight nor the tend-and-befriend response is entirely useful for contemporary lives. Many of the stressors both men and women experience on a day-to-day basis make the physiological stress responses fairly maladaptive. Suppose, for example, you are taking a difficult exam and the clock is swiftly ticking away. Although you might value the heightened attentiveness brought about by your stress response, the rest of the physiological changes do you no good: There is no one to fight or to tend, and so on. The responses that developed in the species as adaptive preparations for dealing with external dangers are counterproductive for dealing with many contemporary types of psychological stressors. This

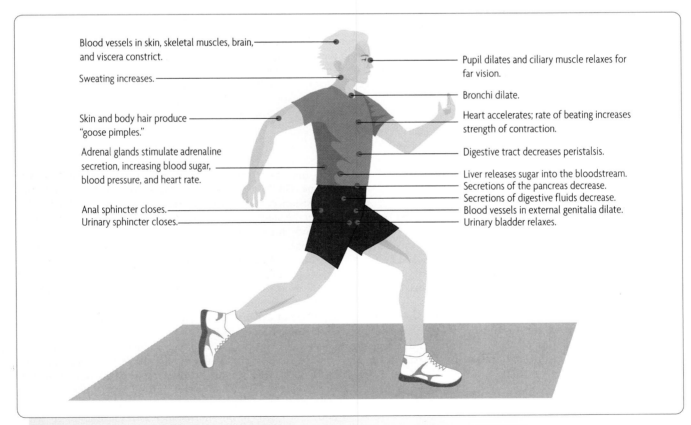

Blood vessels in skin, skeletal muscles, brain, and viscera constrict.

Sweating increases.

Skin and body hair produce "goose pimples."

Adrenal glands stimulate adrenaline secretion, increasing blood sugar, blood pressure, and heart rate.

Anal sphincter closes.
Urinary sphincter closes.

Pupil dilates and ciliary muscle relaxes for far vision.

Bronchi dilate.

Heart accelerates; rate of beating increases strength of contraction.

Digestive tract decreases peristalsis.

Liver releases sugar into the bloodstream.
Secretions of the pancreas decrease.
Secretions of digestive fluids decrease.
Blood vessels in external genitalia dilate.
Urinary bladder relaxes.

FIGURE 13.4 The Body's Reaction to Stress
Stress produces a wide range of physiological changes in your body.

Stage I: Alarm reaction (continually repeated throughout life)	Stage II: Resistance (continually repeated throughout life)	Stage III: Exhaustion
• Enlargement of adrenal cortex • Enlargement of lymphatic system • Increase in hormone levels • Response to specific stressor • Epinephrine release associated with high levels of physiological arousal and negative affect • Greater susceptibility to increased intensity of stressor • Heightened susceptibility to illness (If prolonged, the slower components of the GAS are set into motion, beginning with Stage II.)	• Shrinkage of adrenal cortex • Return of lymph nodes to normal size • Sustaining of hormone levels • High physiological arousal • Counteraction of parasympathetic branch of ANS • Enduring of stressor; resistance to further debilitating effects • Heightened sensitivity to stress (If stress continues at intense levels, hormonal reserves are depleted, fatigue sets in, and individual enters Stage III.)	• Enlargement/dysfunction of lymphatic structures • Increase in hormone levels • Depletion of adaptive hormones • Decreased ability to resist either original or extraneous stressors • Affective experience—often depression • Illness • Death

Time →

Level of normal resistance

Successful resistance

Illness/Death

Alarm reaction

Resistance

Exhaustion

FIGURE 13.5   The General Adaptation Syndrome (GAS)
Following exposure to a stressor, the body's resistance is diminished until the physiological changes of the corresponding alarm reaction bring it back up to the normal level. If the stressor continues, the bodily signs characteristic of the alarm reaction virtually disappear; resistance to the particular stressor rises above normal but drops for other stressors. This adaptive resistance returns the body to its normal level of functioning. Following prolonged exposure to the stressor, adaptation breaks down: signs of alarm reaction reappear, the stressor effects are irreversible, and the individual becomes ill and may die.

is particularly true because, as we will see next, many people live their lives under circumstances of chronic stress.

The General Adaptation Syndrome (GAS) and Chronic Stress The first modern researcher to investigate the effects of continued severe stress on the body was **Hans Selye,** a Canadian endocrinologist. Beginning in the late 1930s, Selye reported on the complex response of laboratory animals to damaging agents such as bacterial infections, toxins, trauma, forced restraint, heat, cold, and so on. According to Selye's theory of stress, many kinds of stressors can trigger the same reaction or general bodily response. All stressors call for *adaptation*: An organism must maintain or regain its integrity and well-being by restoring equilibrium, or homeostasis. The response to

general adaptation syndrome (GAS) The pattern of nonspecific adaptational physiological mechanisms that occurs in response to continuing threat by almost any serious stressor.

psychosomatic disorders Physical disorders aggravated by or primarily attributable to prolonged emotional stress or other psychological causes.

stressors was described by Selye as the **general adaptation syndrome (GAS)**. It includes three stages: an alarm reaction, a stage of resistance, and a stage of exhaustion (Selye, 1976a, 1976b). *Alarm reactions* are brief periods of bodily arousal that prepare the body for vigorous activity. If a stressor is prolonged, the body enters a stage of *resistance*—a state of moderate arousal. During the stage of resistance, the organism can endure and *resist* further debilitating effects of prolonged stressors. However, if the stressor is sufficiently long-lasting or intense, the body's resources become depleted and the organism enters the stage of *exhaustion*. The three stages are diagrammed and explained in **Figure 13.5.**

Selye identified some of the dangers associated with the stage of exhaustion. Recall, for example, that ACTH plays a role in the short-term response to stress. In the long term, however, its action reduces the ability of natural killer cells to destroy cancer cells and other life-threatening infections. When the body is stressed chronically, the increased production of "stress hormones" compromises the integrity of the immune system. This application of the general adaptation syndrome has proven valuable to explain **psychosomatic disorders**—illnesses that could not be wholly explained by physical causes—that had baffled physicians who had never considered stress as a cause for illness and disease. What serves the body well in adapting to acute stress impairs the body's response to chronic stress.

Selye's research makes disease seem an inevitable response to stress. We will see, however, that your psychological interpretation of what is stressful and what is not stressful—the way in which you appraise potentially stressful events—has an impact on your body's physiological response. To give a full account of the effect of stress on your body, we will have to combine Selye's foundational physiological theory with later research on psychological factors.

PSYCHOLOGICAL STRESS REACTIONS

Your physiological stress reactions are automatic, predictable, built-in responses over which you normally have no conscious control. However, many psychological reactions are learned. They depend on perceptions and interpretations of the world. In this section, we discuss psychological responses to different categories of stressors, such as major life changes and traumatic events.

Major Life Events The influence of life events on subsequent mental and physical health has been a target of considerable research. It started in the 1960s with the development of the Social Readjustment Rating Scale (SRRS), a simple measure for rating the degree of adjustment required by the various life changes, both pleasant and unpleasant, that many people experience. The scale was developed from the responses of adults, from all walks of life, who were asked to identify from a list those life changes that applied to them. These adults rated the amount of readjustment required for each change by comparing each to marriage, which was arbitrarily assigned a value of 50 life-change units. Researchers then calculated the total number of

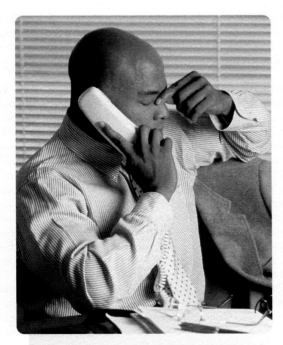

What are the physiological consequences of chronic stress?

TABLE 13.2 Student Stress Scale

The Student Stress Scale represents an adaptation of Holmes and Rahe's Social Readjustment Rating Scale. Each event is given a score that represents the amount of readjustment a person has to make in life as a result of the change. People with scores of 300 and higher have a high health risk. People scoring between 150 and 300 points have about a 50–50 chance of serious health change within two years. People scoring below 150 have a one-in-three chance of serious health change. Calculate your total life-change units (LCUs) three times during the semester and then correlate those scores with any changes in your health status.

Event	Life-Change Units
Death of a close family member	100
Death of a close friend	73
Divorce between parents	65
Jail term	63
Major personal injury or illness	63
Marriage	58
Being fired from a job	50
Failing an important course	47
Change in health of a family member	45
Pregnancy	45
Sex problems	44
Serious argument with a close friend	40
Change in financial status	39
Change of major	39
Trouble with parents	39
New girl- or boyfriend	38
Increased workload at school	37
Outstanding personal achievement	36
First quarter/semester in university	35
Change in living conditions	31
Serious argument with instructor	30
Lower grades than expected	29
Change in sleeping habits	29
Change in social activities	29
Change in eating habits	28
Chronic car trouble	26
Change in number of family get-togethers	26
Too many missed classes	25
Change of university	24
Dropping of more than one class	23
Minor traffic violations	20

My 1st total	[ ]	(date: _____)
My 2nd total	[ ]	(date: _____)
My 3rd total	[ ]	(date: _____)

life-change units (LCUs) an individual had undergone, using the units as a measure of the amount of stress the individual had experienced (Holmes & Rahe, 1967).

The SRRS was updated in the 1990s (see **Table 13.2**). The researchers used the same procedure of asking participants to rate the stress of life events as compared to marriage (Miller & Rahe, 1997). In this update, the LCU estimates went up 45 percent over the original values—that is, participants in the 1990s reported that they were experiencing overall much higher levels of stress than their peers had in the 1960s. Women in the 1990s also reported experiencing more stress in their lives than did men. Researchers continue to relate reports on the SRRS to mental and physical health outcomes. Consider a study in which 268 people completed the scale (Lynch, McGrady, Alvarez, & Forman, 2005). There was a positive correlation between SRRS scores and participants' total number of medical visits in the following six months: In general, the participants who had the highest SRRS scores also visited their doctors most often.

Researchers have found a variety of ways to examine the relationship between life events and health outcomes. In one study, participants volunteered to be exposed to viruses that cause the common cold. Those participants who reported a rate of negative life events above the group's average were about 10 percent more likely to actually come down with a cold (Cohen, Tyrrell, & Smith, 1993). Consider another study that should have immediate relevance to the choices you make about how to organize your schoolwork.

When a professor gives you an assignment—a stressful life event in every student's life—do you try to take care of it as soon as possible or do you put it off to the very last minute? Psychologists have developed a measurement device called the General Procrastination Scale (Lay, 1986) to differentiate those individuals who habitually put things off—*procrastinators*—from those who do not—*nonprocrastinators*. A pair of researchers administered this scale to students in a health psychology course who had a paper due late in the semester. The students were also asked to report, early and late in the semester, how many symptoms of physical illness they had experienced. Not surprisingly, procrastinators, on average, turned their papers in later than did nonprocrastinators; procrastinators also, on average, obtained lower grades on those papers. **Figure 13.6** displays the effect of procrastination on physical health. As you can see, early in the semester, procrastinators reported fewer symptoms, but by late in the semester, they were reporting more symptoms than their nonprocrastinating peers (Tice & Baumeister, 1997).

You see in this study why not all life events have the same impact on all people. The nonprocrastinators got to work right away and so experienced stress and symptoms early in the semester. However, the consequences for the procrastinators of avoiding the early semester stress was a great increase in physi-

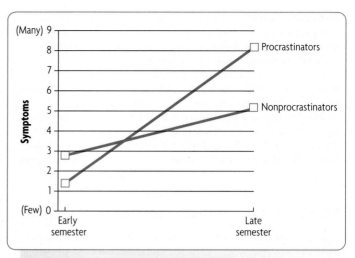

FIGURE 13.6   The Health Costs of Procrastination
Researchers identified students who were, generally, procrastinators and nonprocrastinators. The students were asked to report, early and late in the semester, how many symptoms of physical illness they had experienced. By late in the semester all students showed increases in symptoms. However—as all their work came due—procrastinators were reporting even more symptoms than their nonprocrastinating peers.

cal illness toward the end of the semester. Therefore, they were likely to be feeling ill just at the point in the semester when they needed to be in good health to complete all the work they had put off! Since a recent review of research clearly points out the negative consequences of procrastination (Steel, 2007), we believe it may be wise for you to think about these results as you develop your own plan for navigating each semester. If you believe that you habitually procrastinate, consider consulting with a psychologist or school counsellor to modify your behaviour. Your grades and health are at stake!

Traumatic Events An event that is negative but also uncontrollable, unpredictable, or ambiguous is particularly stressful. These conditions hold especially true in the case of *traumatic events*. Some traumatic events, such as rape and other personal traumas, affect individuals in very negative ways. Others, such as earthquakes and tornadoes, have a broader impact since they affect a large group of people at once. In recent years, no traumatic event has had as widespread consequences as the events of September 11, 2001. On that day, attacks on the World Trade Center and the Pentagon with commercial aircraft led to the deaths of almost 3000 people. With the goal of providing appropriate mental health care, researchers moved swiftly to assess the psychological aftermath of the attacks.

One particular focus was on the prevalence of **posttraumatic stress disorder (PTSD)**. PTSD is a stress reaction in which individuals suffer from persistent re-experiences of the traumatic event in the form, for example, of flashbacks or nightmares (*DSM-IV*, 1994). Sufferers experience an emotional numbing in relation to everyday events and feelings of alienation from other people. Finally, the emotional pain of this

---

life-change units (LCUs) In stress research, the measure of the stress levels of different types of change experienced during a given period.

post-traumatic stress disorder (PTSD) An anxiety disorder characterized by the persistent re-experience of traumatic events through distressing recollections, dreams, hallucinations, or dissociative flashbacks; develops in response to rape, life-threatening events, severe injury, and natural disasters.

reaction can result in an increase in various symptoms, such as sleep problems, guilt about surviving, difficulty in concentrating, and an exaggerated startle response.

In October and November 2001, a team of researchers conducted a web-based survey of 2273 adults across the United States (Schlenger et al., 2002). The survey assessed both the participants' exposure to the incidents and their mental health symptoms. As seen in **Table 13.3,** greater exposure made it more likely that people would experience PTSD. The ones most affected were those who lived in the New York City metropolitan area. Those individuals were most likely to have been personally involved in the tragedy. As seen in Table 13.3, the events did not have extra impact on people in the Washington, DC, area. The researchers suggested that the difference between New York and Washington might reflect the difference between attacks on a civilian target (the World Trade Center) and a military target (the Pentagon). Table 13.3 also shows that individuals who watched the most television coverage of the events also reported higher levels of symptoms of PTSD. Researchers have also tried to evaluate the impact of the September 11 attacks on residents of other countries, including places as diverse as the United Kingdom, Australia, Belgium, Argentina, Israel, Turkey, and Canada (Meldrum, 2002); results suggest there were some increases in traumatic stress reactions immediately following the attack. One Canadian study demonstrated that greater perceived threat and greater initial distress reactions following the September 11 attack significantly predicted the extent to which people reported positive changes in their lives (e.g., becoming closer to family, refocusing priorities) (Davis & MacDonald, 2004). Researchers will continue to assess the mental health consequences of September 11: They attempt to form generalizations from people's responses to catastrophes so that they can alleviate the worst consequences when new circumstances present themselves.

As we noted earlier, people also suffer from individual traumatic events with a negative impact on their psychological health. For example, rape victims often show many of the signs

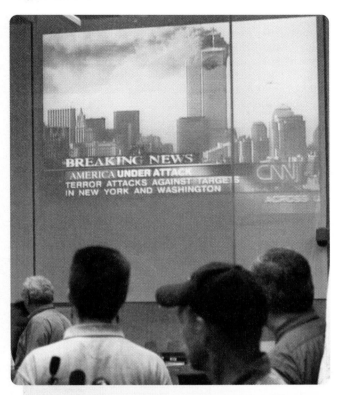

Why might TV viewing have an impact on people's experiences of PTSD?

of post-traumatic stress (Ullman, Filipas, Townsend, & Starzynski, 2007). In assessments two weeks after being assaulted, 94 percent of rape victims were diagnosed with PTSD; 13 weeks after the assault, 51 percent of the victims still met diagnostic criteria (Foa & Riggs, 1995). These data illustrate that the emotional responses of post-traumatic stress can occur in an acute form immediately following a disaster and can subside over a period of several months. We will return to the topic of PTSD when we discuss anxiety disorders in Chapter 15.

Chronic Stressors In our discussion of physiological responses to stress, we made a distinction between stressors that are acute, with clear onsets and offsets, versus those that are chronic—that is, endure over time. With psychological stressors, it is not always easy to draw a sharp distinction. Suppose, for example, your bicycle is stolen. Originally, this is an acute source of stress. However, if you begin to worry constantly that your new bike will also be stolen, the stress associated with this event can become chronic. Researchers have found this pattern in people who suffer from serious illnesses like cancer (Kangas, Henry, & Bryant, 2005; Stanton, Revenson, & Tennen, 2007). The chronic stress of coping with the anxiety of a cancer diagnosis and treatment may impair health more rapidly than the disease alone would.

For many people, chronic stress arises from conditions in society and the environment. What cumulative effects do overpopulation, crime, economic conditions, pollution, AIDS, and the threat of terrorism have on you? How do these and other environmental stressors affect your mental well-being? Some groups of people suffer chronic stress by virtue of their socioeconomic status or racial identity, with stark consequences for

TABLE 13.3	The Psychological Impact of Exposure to the Events of September 11, 2001
	Probable PTSD
Proximity to Crash Sites	
New York City metropolitan area	11.2
District of Columbia metropolitan area	2.7
Other major metropolitan area	3.6
Remainder of the United States	4.0
Television Viewing Per Day (In Hours)	
Less than 4	0.8
4 to 7	3.9
8 to 11	4.2
12 or more	10.1

overall well-being (Gallo & Matthews, 2003; Mays, Cochran, & Barnes, 2007). Consider a study that measured economic hardships for more than a thousand participants over three decades (Lynch, Kaplan, & Shema, 1997). Economic hardship was defined as household income of less than 200 percent of the poverty level criteria established by the federal government. As assessed in 1994, the more periods of economic hardship adults experienced between 1965 and 1983, the more difficulties they had with physical functioning related to basic activities of daily living, such as cooking, shopping, and bathing. Similar effects were found for psychological and cognitive functioning. Compared to those with no period of economic hardship, people with three episodes of poverty were three times more likely to have experienced symptoms of clinical depression; they were more than five times more likely to be assessed as cynically hostile and lacking optimism; and they were more than four times more likely to report difficulties with cognitive functioning. To confirm that these results were caused by economic hardship and not by initial poor health, the researchers demonstrated comparable patterns of disability among those participants whose health at the initial measurement in 1965 had been good or excellent.

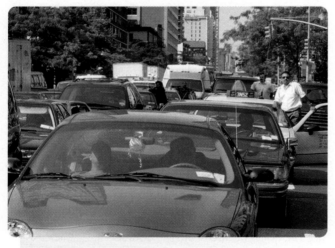

These residents live through their daily experience of chronic stress as they travel from home to work each morning. What are some of the likely consequences of this stress for their physical and mental health?

Daily Hassles You may agree that the end of a relationship, an earthquake, or prejudice might cause stress, but what about the smaller stressors you experience on a day-to-day basis? What happened to you yesterday? You probably did not get a divorce or survive a plane crash. However, it is quite possible that you lost your notes or textbook, were late for an important appointment, got a parking ticket, or had your sleep ruined by a noisy neighbour. These are the types of recurring day-to-day stressors that confront most people most of the time.

In a diary study, a group of white middle-class middle-aged men and women kept track of their daily hassles over a one-year period (along with a record of major life changes and physical symptoms). A clear relationship emerged between hassles and health problems: The more frequent and intense the hassles people reported, the poorer was their health, both physical and mental (Lazarus, 1981, 1984b). Consider a study that demonstrated the impact of daily hassles in the workplace.

Participants in the study worked full-time in university administration, with their effort largely focused on the quality of student life (Luong & Rogelberg, 2005). For a period of five days, participants kept records of the number of meetings they attended. An interaction counted as a meeting if it involved two or more people and was more than a brief chat or five-minute phone call. Participants also provided daily accounts of well-being: They recorded their levels of *fatigue* (e.g., the extent to which they were worn out at the present moment) and their levels of *subjective workload* (e.g., the extent to which they felt busy or rushed). The results demonstrated positive correlations between the number of meetings and both of these measures: More meetings were associated with greater fatigue and higher subjective workload.

If you have ever worked in an office, these results probably have a familiar ring: The more often you are interrupted for meetings, the less you feel like you are making progress on your work. But the impact of daily hassles is even felt by people whose work is generally perceived to be very stressful. For instance, a recent study of police officers conducted at the University of Ottawa (Otis & Pelletier, 2005) showed that daily hassles affect police officers' physical symptoms of stress.

We have been focusing largely on day-to-day hassles. It is worth noting, however, that for many people daily hassles may be balanced out by daily positive experiences (Lazarus & Lazarus,

1994). For example, one study asked 132 men and women to report the frequency and intensity of the hassles (that is, irritating events) and uplifts (that is, happy events) in their lives (Jain et al., 2007). The researchers also measured the participants' blood levels of substances (such as inflammatory factors) that are indicators of risk for cardiovascular disease. Higher levels of reported hassles were associated with higher levels of these risk indicators; higher levels of reported uplifts were associated with lower levels. Therefore, if we want to predict your life course based on daily hassles, we also need to know something about the daily pleasures your life provides (Lyubomirsky, King, & Diener, 2005).

We have just reviewed many sources of stress in people's lives. Psychologists have recognized for quite a long time that the impact of these different types of stressors depends in large part on how effectively people can cope with them. Let's now consider how people cope successfully and unsuccessfully with stress.

COPING WITH STRESS

If living is inevitably stressful, and if chronic stress can disrupt your life and even kill you, you need to learn how to manage stress. **Coping** refers to the process of dealing with internal or external demands that are perceived as straining or exceeding an individual's resources (Lazarus & Folkman, 1984). Coping may consist of behavioural, emotional, or motivational responses and thoughts. We begin this section by describing how cognitive appraisal affects what you experience as stressful. We then consider types of coping responses; we describe both general principles of coping and specific interventions. Finally, we consider some individual differences in individuals' ability to cope with stress.

Appraisal of Stress When you cope with stressful situations, your first step is to define in what ways they are, in fact, stressful. *Cognitive appraisal* is the cognitive interpretation and evaluation of a stressor. Cognitive appraisal plays a central role in defining the situation—what the demand is, how big a threat it is, and what resources you have for meeting it (Lazarus, 1993; Lazarus & Lazarus, 1994). Some stressors, such as undergoing bodily injury or finding one's house on fire, are experienced as threats by almost everyone. However, many other stressors can be defined in various ways, depending on your personal life situation, the relation of a particular demand to your central goals, your competence in dealing with the demand, and your self-assessment of that competence. The situation that causes acute distress for another person may be all in a day's work for you. Try to notice, and understand, the life events that are different for you and your friends and family: Some situations cause stress to you but not your friends and family; other events cause stress to them but not you. Why?

Richard Lazarus, whose general theory of appraisal we addressed in our discussion of emotions, has distinguished two stages in the cognitive appraisal of demands. *Primary appraisal* describes the initial evaluation of the seriousness of a demand. This evaluation starts with the questions "What's happening?" and "Is this thing good for me, stressful, or irrelevant?" If the answer to the second question is "stressful," you appraise the potential impact of the stressor by determining whether harm has occurred or is likely to and whether action is required (see **Table 13.4**). Once you decide something must be done,

TABLE 13.4	Stages in Stable Decision Making/Cognitive Appraisal
Stage	**Key Questions**
1. Appraising the challenge	Are the risks serious if I don't change?
2. Surveying alternatives	Is this alternative an acceptable means for dealing with the challenge?
	Have I sufficiently surveyed the available alternatives?
3. Weighing alternatives	Which alternative is best?
	Could the best alternative meet the essential requirements?
4. Deliberating about commitment	Will I implement the best alternative and allow others to know?
5. Adhering despite negative feedback	Are the risks serious if I *don't* change?
	Are the risks serious if I *do* change?

secondary appraisal begins. You evaluate the personal and social resources that are available to deal with the stressful circumstance and consider the action options that are needed. Appraisal continues as coping responses are tried; if the first ones do not work and the stress persists, new responses are initiated, and their effectiveness is evaluated.

Cognitive appraisal is an example of a stress moderator variable. **Stress moderator variables** are those variables that change the impact of a stressor on a given type of stress reaction. Moderator variables filter or modify the usual effects of stressors on the individual's reactions. For example, your level of fatigue and general health status are moderator variables influencing your reaction to a given psychological or physical stressor. When people are in good shape, they can deal with a stressor better than when they are not. You can see how cognitive appraisal also fits the definition of a moderator variable. The way in which you appraise a stressor will determine the types of coping responses you need to bring to it. We now consider the general types of coping responses.

Types of Coping Responses Suppose you have a big exam coming up. You have thought about it—you have appraised the situation—and you are quite sure that this is a stressful situation. What can you do? It is important to note that coping can precede a potentially stressful event in the form of

---

coping The process of dealing with internal or external demands that are perceived to be threatening or overwhelming.

stress moderator variables Variables that change the impact of a stressor on a given type of stress reaction.

TABLE 13.5 Taxonomy of Coping Strategies

Type of Coping Strategy	Example
Problem-Directed Coping	
Change stressor or one's relationship to it through direct actions and/or problem-solving activities	Fight (destroy, remove, or weaken the threat)
	Flight (distance oneself from the threat)
	Seek alternatives to fight or flight (negotiating, bargaining, compromising)
	Prevent future stress (act to increase one's resistance or decrease strength of anticipated stress)
Emotion-Focused Coping	
Change self through activities that make one feel better but do not change the stressor	Somatically focused activities (use of antianxiety medication, relaxation, biofeedback)
	Cognitively focused activities (planned distractions, fantasies, thoughts about oneself)
	Therapy to adjust conscious or unconscious processes that lead to additional anxiety

anticipatory coping (Folkman, 1984). How do you deal with the stress of the upcoming exam? How do you tell your parents that you are dropping out of school or tell your lover that you are no longer in love? Anticipating a stressful situation leads to many thoughts and feelings that may be stress inducing, as in the cases of interviews, speeches, or blind dates. You need to know how to cope.

The two main ways of coping are defined by whether the goal is to confront the problem directly—*problem-directed coping*—or to lessen the discomfort associated with the stress—*emotion-focused coping* (Billings & Moos, 1982; Lazarus & Folkman, 1984). Several subcategories of these two basic approaches are shown in **Table 13.5**.

Let's begin with problem-directed coping. "Taking the bull by the horns" is how we usually characterize the strategy of facing up to a problem situation. This approach includes all strategies designed to deal *directly* with the stressor, whether through overt action or through realistic problem-solving activities. You face up to a bully or run away; you try to win him or her over with bribes or other incentives. Your focus is on the problem to be dealt with and on the agent that has induced the stress. You acknowledge the call to action, you appraise the situation and your resources for dealing with it, and you undertake a response that is appropriate for removing or lessening the threat. Such problem-solving efforts are useful for managing *controllable stressors*—those stressors that you can change or eliminate through your actions, such as overbearing bosses or underwhelming grades.

The emotion-focused approach is useful for managing the impact of more *uncontrollable stressors*. Suppose you are responsible for the care of a parent with Alzheimer's. In that

situation, there is no "bully" you can eliminate from the environment; you cannot make the disease go away. Even in this situation, some forms of problem-directed coping would be useful. For example, you could modify your work schedule to make it easier to provide care. However, because you cannot eliminate the source of stress, you also can try to change your feelings and thoughts about the disease. For example, you might take part in a support group for Alzheimer's caregivers or learn relaxation techniques. These approaches still constitute a coping strategy because you are acknowledging that there is a threat to your well-being and you are taking steps to modify that threat.

You will be better off if you have multiple strategies to help you cope in stressful situations (Fresco, Williams, & Nugent, 2006; Tennen, Affleck, Armeli, & Carney, 2000). If coping is to be successful, your resources need to match the perceived demand. Thus the availability of multiple coping strategies is adaptive because you are more likely to achieve a match and manage the stressful event. Consider a study that examined the ways in which women cope with the stress of undergoing surgery for breast cancer (Roussi et al., 2007). The women reported their distress levels and coping strategies (such as problem-directed and/or emotion-focused strategies) a day before the surgeries, three days after the procedure, and again three months later. The women who reported that they were using multiple coping strategies in the days after their surgeries reported less distress three months later.

Researchers who study coping have discovered that some individuals meet stressors with a particular degree of resilience—they are able to achieve positive outcomes despite serious threats to their well-being (Bonanno & Mancini, 2008). Research has focused on the types of coping skills that resilient individuals have acquired and how they have acquired them. An important part of the answer is that children who become resilient have been raised by supportive parents with good parenting skills (Matheson et al., 2005; see also Chapter 11). In addition, resilient children appear to have developed coping

---

anticipatory coping Efforts made in advance of a potentially stressful event to overcome, reduce, or tolerate the imbalance between perceived demands and available resources.

Why are multiple coping strategies beneficial for individuals such as Alzheimer's caregivers?

behaviour therapist **Donald Meichenbaum** (1977, 1985, 1993), a long-standing faculty member at the University of Waterloo, has proposed a three-phase process that allows for such *stress inoculation*. In phase 1, people work to develop a greater awareness of their actual behaviour, what instigates it, and what its results are. One of the best ways of doing this is to keep daily logs. By helping people redefine their problems in terms of their causes and results, these records can increase their feelings of control. You may discover, for example, that your grades are low (a stressor) because you always leave too little time to do a good job on your class assignments. In phase 2, people begin to identify new behaviours that negate the maladaptive, self-defeating behaviours. Perhaps you might create a fixed "study time" or limit your phone calls to 10 minutes each night. In phase 3, after adaptive behaviours are being performed, individuals appraise the consequences of their new behaviours, avoiding the former internal dialogue of put-downs. Instead of telling themselves, "I was lucky the professor called on me when I happened to have read the text," they say, "I'm glad I was prepared for the professor's question. It feels great to be able to respond intelligently in that class."

This three-phase approach means initiating responses and self-statements that are incompatible with previous defeatist cognitions. Once started on this path, people realize that they are changing—and can take full credit for the change, which promotes further successes. **Table 13.6** gives examples of the new kinds of self-statements that help in dealing with stressful situations. *Stress inoculation training* has been used successfully in a wide variety of domains. Here's a study that applied this method in a law school setting.

skills that relate to their ability to regulate their own behaviour (Buckner, Mezzacappa, & Beardslee, 2003). They can stay focused on tasks (which allows for problem-directed coping) and control their emotional responses (which allows for emotion-focused coping) in ways that better their life outcomes.

Up to now, we have been discussing general approaches to coping with stressors. Now we review specific cognitive and social approaches to successful coping.

Modifying Cognitive Strategies A powerful way to adapt to stress is to change your evaluations of stressors and your self-defeating cognitions about the way you are dealing with them. You need to find a different way to think about a given situation, your role in it, and the causal attributions you make to explain the undesirable outcome. Two ways of mentally coping with stress are *reappraising* the nature of the stressors themselves and *restructuring* your cognitions about your stress reactions.

We have already described the idea that people control the experience of stress in their lives in part by the way they appraise life events (Lazarus & Lazarus, 1994). Learning to think differently about certain stressors, to relabel them, or to imagine them in a less threatening (perhaps even humorous) context is a form of cognitive reappraisal that can reduce stress. Worried about giving a speech to a large, forbidding audience? One stressor reappraisal technique is to imagine your potential critics sitting there in the nude—this surely takes away a great deal of their fearsome power. Anxious about being shy at a party you must attend? Think about finding someone who is shier than you and reducing his or her social anxiety by initiating a conversation.

You can also manage stress by changing what you tell yourself about it and by changing your handling of it. Cognitive

TABLE 13.6	Examples of Coping Self-Statements
Preparation	
I can develop a plan to deal with it.	
Just think about what I can do about it. That's better than getting anxious.	
No negative self-statements, just think rationally.	
Confrontation	
One step at a time; I can handle this situation.	
This anxiety is what the doctor said I would feel; it's a reminder to use my coping exercises.	
Relax; I'm in control. Take a slow, deep breath.	
Coping	
When fear comes, just pause.	
Keep focused on the present; what is it I have to do?	
Don't try to eliminate fear totally; just keep it manageable.	
It's not the worst thing that can happen.	
Just think about something else.	
Self-reinforcement	
It worked; I was able to do it.	
It wasn't as bad as I expected.	
I'm really pleased with the progress I'm making.	

This study involved 22 students who were beginning their first year of law school (Sheehy & Horan, 2004). The students received stress inoculation training that was specifically geared to the types of stressors that arise in law school. For example, the training focused on the anxiety students experience when they interact with professors and compete with peers. In addition, the students learned cognitive restructuring techniques to combat negative self-statements and irrational beliefs. Although all of the students ultimately received the training, roughly half began training immediately at the start of the study, whereas the other half waited several weeks to begin. That research design gave the researchers the opportunity to demonstrate the benefits of the stress inoculation training (by comparing the immediate group to the delayed group) without denying some students those benefits. In fact, participants who completed immediate training reported lower levels of stress at the end of the delay period than their classmates whose training was delayed. In addition, several of the students who completed the training outperformed expectations (based on their LSAT scores) when the semester's grades were posted.

The whole law school class of 158 students had the opportunity to participate in the stress inoculation training. Only this small subset was wise enough to reap the benefits.

York University psychologist **Norm Endler** and his colleagues identified another main component of successful coping. In several studies they showed that establishing **perceived control** over the stressor, a belief that you can make a difference in the course or the consequences of some event or experience, greatly improves your ability to cope (Endler et al., 2000; Roussi, 2002). If you believe that you can affect the course of an illness or the daily symptoms of a disease, you are probably adjusting well to the disorder. However, if you believe that the source of the stress is another person whose behaviour you cannot influence or a situation that you cannot change, chances increase for a poor psychological adjustment to your chronic condition. Consider a study of women who had undergone surgery for breast cancer (Bárez et al., 2007). The women who reported higher levels of perceived control experienced the least physical and psychological distress over the whole year following surgery.

While you file away these control strategies for future use, we will turn to a final aspect of coping with stress—the social dimension.

Social Support as a Coping Resource

Social support refers to the resources others provide, giving the message that one is loved, cared for, esteemed, and connected to other people in a network of communication and mutual obligation. In addition to these forms of *emotional support*, other people may provide *tangible support* (money, transportation, housing) and *informational support* (advice, personal feedback, information). Anyone with whom you have a significant social relationship—

such as family members, friends, coworkers, and neighbours—can be part of your social support network in time of need.

Much research points to the power of social support in moderating the vulnerability to stress (Kim, Sherman, & Taylor, 2008). When people have other people to whom they can turn, they are better able to handle job stressors, unemployment, marital disruption, and serious illness, as well as their everyday problems of living. Consider individuals who serve as peacekeepers in the world's many troubled regions. The traumas associated with life in battle zones often leads to post-traumatic stress disorder. However, a study of Dutch peacekeepers who served in Lebanon demonstrated that those individuals who experienced higher levels of positive social interactions had fewer symptoms of PTSD (Dirkzwager, Bramsen, & van der Ploeg, 2003).

Researchers are trying to identify which types of social supports provide the most benefit for specific life events. One study examined the impact of informational support and emotional support for men and women who were undergoing facial surgery (Krohne & Slangen, 2005). Overall, people who had more social support anticipated their surgery with less anxiety, required less anesthesia during surgery, and had briefer hospital stays. However, the more specific results differed for men and women. Although patients of both sexes obtained an advantage from greater informational support, only women were much affected by the level of emotional support. More generally, what appears to matter is the match between the type of support an individual needs and what that individual gets. People are best off when there is a match between what they want and what they get. As shown in **Figure 13.7**, there are four different possibilities for how desires and reality can be related (Reynolds & Perrin, 2004). For a sample of women with breast cancer, they had the worst psychological outcomes when they received support they did not want ("support commission") (Reynolds & Perrin, 2004). This pattern might have emerged because the unwanted assistance made it difficult for women to obtain the emotional support they really needed.

Researchers are also trying to determine how social support changes the way people's bodies and brains respond to stressors. Let's consider a study that demonstrated consistent

Support is	wanted	not wanted
received	positive congruent support	support commission
not received	support omission	null support

FIGURE 13.7 Matches and Mismatches for Social Support

When people need to cope with difficult situations, there can be matches or mismatches between the social support they want or need and the social support they receive.

From Julie S. Reynolds and Nancy Perrin, "Matches and Mismatches for Social Support and Psychosocial Adjustment to Breast Cancer," *Health Psychology, 23*(4), 425–430. Copyright © 2004 by the American Psychological Association. Reprinted with permission.

---

perceived control The belief that one has the ability to make a difference in the course or the consequences of some event or experience; often helpful in dealing with stressors.

social support Resources, including material aid, socioemotional support, and informational aid, provided by others to help a person cope with stress.

changes in brain response resulting from simple acts of hand holding.

Sixteen married women underwent fMRI scans while under threat to receive electric shocks: Whenever a red X appeared on a screen in front of them, there was a 20 percent chance of a shock to their ankle; all the women received some shocks as the study unfolded (Coan, Schaefer, & Davidson, 2006). Each woman completed three blocks of trials. For one block, she held her husband's hand. For a second block, she held a male stranger's hand. The third control block did not have any hand holding. When the women were holding their husbands' hands, their brains showed greatly reduced activity in brain regions that typically register and respond to threat (as compared to brain activity in the control block). This reduction in threat response was greater for women who reported themselves as being in better relationships. Holding a stranger's hand also reduced the women's brain responses to threat, but not as much as holding their husband's hand.

In this study, the very literal social support of holding their spouse's hand (or even a stranger's hand) had the impact of making the women's brains respond as if a threat were less threatening. In this case, social support directly influenced how the women's brains perceived a stressor.

Being part of an effective social support network means that you believe others will be there for you if you need them—even if you do not actually ask for their help when you

Why are some forms of social support more welcome than others?

experience stress. One of the most important take-home messages from *Psychology and Life* is that you should always work at being part of a social support network and never let yourself become socially isolated.

POSITIVE EFFECTS OF STRESS

In this section, we have focused largely on the potential for stress to bring about negative life outcomes. This focus reflects the great effort researchers have expended to help people prevent and overcome those negative outcomes. However, in recent years, psychologists have turned more attention to the potential for stress to have positive effects in people's lives. This new focus is another outcome of the positive psychology movement that we introduced when we discussed subjective well-being. Let's consider stress and coping from a positive psychology perspective.

When we first defined stress, we made a distinction between *distress* and *eustress*. It is probably easy for you to generate circumstances in which you experienced distress—but what about eustress? Consider the last time you watched any kind of running race. Did you enjoy the experience of seeing who would win? Did you feel your heart race as the runners approached the finish line? Researchers have demonstrated that eustress—the experience of excitement and anxiety—is often an important motivation for people to watch, for example, sporting events (Cohen & Avrahami, 2005; Wann et al., 2002). If a team or competitor you favour ultimately loses, you may experience some distress. However, along the way, you probably have a more positive emotional experience when competitions stimulate eustress. Search your life for other circumstances in which the experience of stressful events gives you pleasure. We will offer one more example: Why do some people feel happy while they are riding a roller coaster?

For some types of stressful events, it might be hard to anticipate how any positive effects could emerge. However, research has demonstrated that people can experience positive outcomes and personal growth from deeply negative events. One type of research focuses on *benefit finding*—people's ability to identify positive aspects of negative life events (Helgeson, Reynolds, & Tomich, 2006; Littlewood, Venable, Carey, & Blair, 2008). Consider a study of women with early-stage breast cancer.

Researchers recruited a group of women who had been diagnosed with breast cancer, on average, about a half-year earlier. The women were asked, "Have there been any benefits that have resulted from your experience with breast cancer?" (Sears, Stanton, & Danoff-Burg, 2003, p. 491) Of the 92 women in the study, 83 percent were able to report benefits. The women provided responses such as "My husband and I have gotten a lot closer since this happened" and "When you come close to death, life becomes more real to you." The researchers followed the women over the course of a year to determine how their mental and physical health evolved. In general, the women who were doing the best were the ones who were able to use perceived benefits to engage in *positive reappraisal coping*. That is, some women were able to cope with the consequences of their illness by attempting to reappraise the situation in terms of its positive impact.

We noted earlier that reappraisal is an important tool for coping with stress. In this case, people's ability to perceive benefits of negative events aids in that process of reappraisal.

People also may experience *post-traumatic growth*—positive psychological change—in response to serious illnesses, accidents, natural disasters, and other traumatic events. Post-traumatic growth occurs in five domains (Cryder, Kilmer, Tedeschi, & Calhoun, 2006; Tedeschi & Calhoun, 2004):

- New possibilities: "I have new things that I like to do."
- Relating to others: "I feel closer to other people than I did before."
- Personal strength: "I learned I can count on myself."
- Appreciation of life: "I learned that life is important."
- Spiritual change: "I understand religious ideas more."

Not everyone who experiences trauma will experience post-traumatic growth. For example, one study focused on a group of 6- to 15-year-old children who had survived Hurricane Floyd in North Carolina (Cryder et al., 2006). The children who experienced the most post-traumatic growth were the ones who perceived themselves to have the best array of strategies (of the sort we have described in this section) to cope with problems. More generally, people seem likely to experience post-traumatic growth when they frequently turn their thoughts back to the original traumatic events, to help themselves understand and make sense of those events.

At many points in this discussion of stress, we have noted the effect of stress on physical or psychological well-being. We will now turn directly to the ways in which psychologists apply their research knowledge to issues of illness and health.

STOP AND REVIEW

❶ What are the three stages of the general adaptation syndrome?

❷ How did life-change unit estimates change from the 1960s to the 1990s?

❸ How do daily hassles and daily pleasures affect well-being?

❹ What does it mean to engage in emotion-focused coping?

❺ Why is perceived control important in the context of coping?

❻ What is meant by benefit finding?

CRITICAL THINKING Recall the study that demonstrated the value of stress inoculation training. Why are law students a particularly good participant population in which to demonstrate the effects of this type of training?

---

health psychology The field of psychology devoted to understanding the ways people stay healthy, the reasons they become ill, and the ways they respond when they become ill.

health A general condition of soundness and vigour of body and mind; not simply the absence of illness or injury.

hozho A Navajo concept referring to harmony, peace of mind, goodness, ideal family relationships, beauty in arts and crafts, and health of body and spirit.

Health Psychology

How much do your psychological processes contribute to your experiences of illness and wellness? We have already given you reason to believe that the right answer may be "quite a bit." This acknowledgment of the importance of psychological and social factors in health has spurred the growth of a new field: health psychology. **Health psychology** is the branch of psychology that is devoted to understanding the way people stay healthy, the reasons they become ill, and the way they respond when they do get ill. **Health** refers to the general condition of the body and mind in terms of soundness and vigour. It is not simply the absence of illness or injury; it is more a matter of how well all the body's component parts are working together. We will begin our discussion of health psychology by describing how the field's underlying philosophy departs from a traditional Western medical model of illness. We then consider the contributions of health psychology to the prevention and treatment of illness and dysfunction.

THE BIOPSYCHOSOCIAL MODEL OF HEALTH

Health psychology is guided by a *biopsychosocial model* of health. We can find the roots of this perspective in many non-Western cultures. To arrive at a definition of the biopsychosocial model, we will start with a description of some of these non-Western traditions.

Traditional Health Practices Psychological principles have been applied in the treatment of illness and the pursuit of health for all of recorded time. Many cultures understand the importance of communal health and relaxation rituals in the enhancement of the quality of life. Among the Navajo, for example, disease, illness, and well-being have been attributed to social harmony and mind–body interactions. The Navajo concept of **hozho** (pronounced whoa-zo) means harmony, peace of mind, goodness, ideal family relationships, beauty in arts and crafts, and health of body and spirit. Illness is seen as the outcome of any *disharmony* caused by evil introduced

The Navajo, like people in many other cultures around the world, place a high value on aesthetics, family harmony, and physical health. What do the Navajo people consider to be the origins of illness?

TABLE 13.7	Leading Causes of Death in Canada		
Rank	**Percentage of Deaths**	**Cause of Death**	**Contributors to Cause of Death***
1	29.3	Cancer	D, S
2	22.4	Heart disease	D, S
3	6.1	Stroke	D, S
4	4.6	Respiratory diseases	S
5	4.1	All accidents	A/DA
6	3.4	Diabetes	D
7	2.5	Influenza and pneumonia	S
8	2.5	Degenerative diseases (e.g., Alzheimer's)	
9	1.6	Intentional self-harm (suicide)	A/DA
10	1.6	Kidney diseases	D

*D = diet, S = smoking, A/DA = alcohol/drug abuse

Source: Statistics Canada, 2009.

through violation of taboos, witchcraft, overindulgence, or bad dreams. Traditional healing ceremonies seek to banish illness and restore health, not only through the medicine of the shaman but also through the combined efforts of all family members, who work together with the ill person to reachieve a state of hozho. The illness of any member of a tribe is seen not as his or her individual responsibility (and fault) but rather as a sign of broader disharmony that must be repaired by communal healing ceremonies. This cultural orientation guarantees that a powerful social support network will automatically come to the aid of the sufferer.

Toward a Biopsychosocial Model We have just seen that healing practices in non-Western cultures often assume a link between the body and the mind. By contrast, modern Western scientific thinking has relied almost exclusively on a *biomedical model* that has a dualistic conception of body and mind. According to this model, medicine treats the physical body as separate from the psyche; the mind is important only for emotions and beliefs and has little to do with the reality of the body. Over time, however, researchers have begun to document types of interactions that make the strict biomedical model unworkable. You have already seen some of the evidence: Good and bad life events can affect immune function; people are more or less resilient with respect to the negative consequences of stress; adequate social support can decrease the probability of death. These realizations yield the three components of the **biopsychosocial model**. The *bio* acknowledges the reality of biological illness. The *psycho* and the *social* acknowledge the psychological and social components of health.

The biopsychosocial model links your physical health to your state of mind and the world around you. Health psychologists view health as a dynamic, multidimensional experience. Optimal health, or **wellness**, incorporates physical, intellectual, emotional, spiritual, social, and environmental aspects of your life. When you undertake an activity for the purpose of

preventing disease or detecting it in the asymptomatic stage, you are exhibiting health behaviour. The general goal of health psychology is to use psychological knowledge to promote wellness and positive health behaviours. Let's now consider theory and research relevant to this goal.

HEALTH PROMOTION

Health promotion means developing general strategies and specific tactics to eliminate or reduce the risk that people will get sick. The prevention of illness in the 21st century poses a much different challenge than it did at the beginning of the 20th century. In 1900, the primary cause of death was infectious disease. Health practitioners at that time launched the first revolution in public health. Over time, through the use of research, public education, the development of vaccines, and changes in public health standards (such as waste control and sewage), they were able to reduce substantially the deaths associated with such diseases as influenza, tuberculosis, polio, measles, and smallpox.

If researchers wish to contribute to the trend toward improved quality of life, they must attempt to decrease those deaths associated with lifestyle factors (see **Table 13.7**). Smoking, being overweight, eating foods high in fat and cholesterol, drinking too much alcohol, driving without seat belts, and leading stressful lives all play a role in heart disease, cancer, strokes, accidents, and suicide. Changing the behaviours

---

biopsychosocial model A model of health and illness that suggests links among the nervous system, the immune system, behavioural styles, cognitive processing, and environmental domains of health.

wellness Optimal health, the ability to function fully and actively; incorporates the physical, intellectual, emotional, spiritual, social, and environmental domains of health.

health promotion The development and implementation of general strategies and specific tactics to eliminate or reduce the risk that people will become ill.

TABLE 13.8	Ten Steps to Personal Wellness
1.	Exercise regularly.
2.	Eat nutritious, balanced meals (high in vegetables, fruits, and grains; low in fat and cholesterol).
3.	Maintain proper weight.
4.	Sleep seven to eight hours nightly; rest/relax daily.
5.	Wear seat belts and bike helmets.
6.	Do not smoke or use drugs.
7.	Use alcohol in moderation, if at all.
8.	Engage only in protected, safe sex.
9.	Get regular medical/dental checkups; adhere to medical regimens.
10.	Develop an optimistic perspective and friendships.

associated with these diseases of civilization will prevent much illness and premature death.

Based on this knowledge, it is easy to make some recommendations. You are more likely to stay well if you practise good health habits, such as those listed in **Table 13.8**. Many of these suggestions probably are familiar to you already. However, health psychologists would like to use psychological principles to increase the probability that you will actually do the things you know are good for you. To show you how that works, we now consider a pair of concrete domains: smoking and AIDS.

Smoking It would be impossible to imagine that anyone reading this book would be unaware that smoking is extremely dangerous. Roughly 45 000 Canadians die each year from smoking-related illnesses—roughly five times the number of deaths caused by car accidents, suicides, drug abuse, murder, and AIDS combined (Health Canada, 2005b). Even so, 20 percent of the Canadian population still smokes cigarettes (Health Canada, 2005b), although it is important to note that this number has decreased steadily for the past 40 years, from a high of 50 percent in 1965. Health psychologists would like to understand both why people begin to smoke—so that the psychologists can help prevent it—and how to assist people in quitting—so those people can reap the substantial benefits of becoming ex-smokers.

Analyses of why some people start smoking have focused on interactions of nature and nurture. Studies comparing monozygotic (MZ) and dizygotic (DZ) twins for the similarity of their tobacco use consistently find heritability estimates of 0.50 or higher (Munafò & Johnstone, 2008). Consider one study that examined the smoking behaviour of 1198 pairs of adolescent siblings (that is, identical twins, fraternal twins, and non-twin pairs) (Boardman et al., 2008). The researchers reported heritability estimates of 0.51 for whether individuals began to smoke and 0.58 for how much they smoked each day. The study also documented an impact of the environment. For example, when the adolescents attended schools in which the popular students were also smokers, genes mattered more: Apparently, in that social context, students could realize their "genetic potential."

To understand the link between genes and smoking, researchers have often focused on personality differences that predict which people will start smoking. One personality type that has been associated with the initiation of smoking is called *sensation seeking* (Zuckerman, 2007). Individuals characterized as sensation seeking are more likely to engage in risky activities. One study compared personality assessments of men and women in the mid-1960s (1964–1967) with their smoking or nonsmoking behaviour in the late 1980s and early 1990s (1987–1991). Both men and women who had revealed themselves to be sensation seeking in the 1960s were more likely to be smoking 20 to 25 years later (Lipkus, Barefoot, Williams, & Siegler, 1994). Health psychologists understand that successful interventions to prevent the initiation of smoking must address the aspects of individuals' personalities that make smoking attractive to them.

The best approach to smoking is never to start at all. But for those of you who have begun to smoke, what has research revealed about quitting? Although many Canadians who try to quit have relapses, almost half of current smokers have tried to quit at least once in the past year (Leatherdale & Shields, 2009) and many of them eventually succeed. Ninety percent have done so on their own, without professional treatment programs. Researchers have identified stages people pass through that represent increasing readiness to quit (Norman, Velicer, Fava, & Prochaska, 1998, 2000):

- *Precontemplation*. The smoker is not yet thinking about quitting.
- *Contemplation*. The smoker is thinking about quitting but has not yet undertaken any behavioural changes.
- *Preparation*. The smoker is getting ready to quit.
- *Action*. The smoker takes action toward quitting by setting behavioural goals.
- *Maintenance*. The smoker is now a nonsmoker and is trying to stay that way.

This analysis suggests that not all smokers are psychologically equivalent in terms of readiness to quit. Interventions can be designed that nudge smokers up the scale of readiness until, finally, they are psychologically prepared to take healthy action (Velicer, Redding, Sun, & Prochaska, 2007).

Of course, several normative factors also affect people's attitudes about smoking and influence smoking-cessation. This point was clearly demonstrated in a series of studies conducted at the University of Waterloo by **David Hammond** and his colleagues (Hammond, Costello, Fong, & Topham, 2006; Hammond, Fong, Zanna, Thrasher, & Borland, 2006). In a large-scale longitudinal study of over 18 000 people from four countries where smoking restrictions differ significantly (Canada, the United Kingdom, the United States, and Australia; Hammond, Fong, et al., 2006), the degree of local social disapproval for smoking was associated with greater smoking-cessation in the population. Have you ever wondered whether those revolting warning labels displayed on cigarette packages actually have any effect? Hammond and his colleagues (2004) showed that smokers report negative emotional responses to the warnings, including fear (44 percent) and disgust (58 percent), and that those who report greater negative emotion are more likely to have quit, attempted to quit, or reduced their smoking three months later.

In addition to social norms that reinforce the negative impact of smoking and the use of graphic warnings about the negative outcomes of smoking, successful smoking-cessation treatment also requires that smokers' physiological and psychological needs both be met (Fiore, Jaén, & Baker, 2008). On the physiological side, smokers are best off learning an effective form of *nicotine replacement therapy*, such as nicotine patches or nicotine gum. On the psychological side, smokers must understand that there are huge numbers of ex-smokers and realize that it *is* possible to quit. Furthermore, smokers must learn strategies to cope with the strong temptations that accompany efforts to quit. Treatments often incorporate the types of cognitive coping techniques we described earlier, which allow people to alleviate the effects of a wide range of stressors. For smoking, people are encouraged to find ways to avoid or escape from situations that may bring on a renewed urge to smoke.

AIDS AIDS is an acronym for *acquired immune deficiency syndrome*. Although hundreds of thousands are dying from this virulent disease, many more are now living with HIV infection. **HIV** (*human immunodeficiency virus*) is a virus that attacks the white blood cells (T lymphocytes) in human blood, thus damaging the immune system and weakening the body's ability to fight other diseases. The individual then becomes vulnerable to infection by a host of other viruses and bacteria that can cause such life-threatening illnesses as cancer, meningitis, and pneumonia. The period of time from initial infection with the virus until symptoms occur (incubation period) can be five years or longer. Although most of the estimated millions of those infected with the HIV virus do not have AIDS (a medical diagnosis), they must live with the continual stress that this life-threatening disease might suddenly emerge. Currently, there are treatments that delay the onset of full-blown AIDS, but there is neither a cure for AIDS nor a vaccine to prevent its spread.

The HIV virus is not airborne; it requires direct access to the bloodstream to produce an infection. The HIV virus is generally passed from one person to another in one of two ways: (1) the exchange of semen or blood during sexual contact, and (2) the sharing of intravenous needles and syringes used for injecting drugs. The virus has also been passed through blood transfusions and medical procedures in which infected blood or organs are unwittingly given to healthy people. Many people suffering from hemophilia have contracted AIDS in this way. However, everyone is at risk for AIDS.

The only way to protect oneself from being infected with the AIDS virus is to change those lifestyle habits that put one at risk. This means making permanent changes in patterns of sexual behaviour and use of drug paraphernalia. Health psychologist **Thomas Coates** is part of a multidisciplinary research team that is using an array of psychological principles in a concerted effort to prevent the further spread of AIDS (Coates & Szekeres, 2004). The team is involved in many aspects of applied psychology, such as assessing psychosocial risk factors, developing behavioural interventions, training community leaders to be effective in educating people toward healthier patterns of sexual and drug behaviour, assisting with the design of media advertisements and community information campaigns, and systematically evaluating changes in relevant attitudes, values, and behaviours. Successful AIDS interventions require three components (Starace, Massa, Amico, & Fisher, 2006):

- *Information.* People must be provided with knowledge about how HIV/AIDS is transmitted and how its transmission may be prevented; they should be counselled to practise safer sex (for example, use condoms during sexual contact) and to use sterile needles.

- *Motivation.* People must be motivated to practise HIV/AIDS prevention.
- *Behavioural skills.* People must be taught how to put the knowledge to use.

Why are all three of these components necessary? People might be highly motivated but uninformed, or vice versa. They may have both sufficient knowledge and sufficient motivation but lack requisite skills. In addition, information must be delivered in a fashion that does not undermine people's motivation. For example, people were more likely to participate in HIV-prevention counselling when information was framed so that the participants felt in control of their own behaviour (Albarracín, Durantini, Earl, Gunnoe, & Leeper, 2008).

TREATMENT

Treatment focuses on helping people adjust to their illnesses and recover from them. We will look at three aspects of treatment. First, we consider the role of psychologists in encouraging patients to adhere to the regimens prescribed by health-care practitioners. Next, we look at techniques that allow people to explicitly use psychological techniques to take control over the body's responses. Finally, we examine instances in which the mind can contribute to the body's cure.

Patient Adherence Patients are often given a *treatment regimen*. This might include medications, dietary changes, prescribed periods of bed rest and exercise, and follow-up procedures such as return checkups, rehabilitation training, and chemotherapy. Failing to adhere to treatment regimens is one of the most serious problems in health care (Christensen & Johnson, 2002; Quittner et al., 2008). The rate of patient nonadherence is estimated to be as high as 50 percent for some treatment regimens.

What factors affect the likelihood that patients will adhere to prescribed treatments? One type of research has focused on the relationship between patients' perceptions of the severity of their disease. As you might expect, people who perceive greater threat from a disease also show greater likelihood to adhere to treatments (DiMatteo, Haskard, & Williams, 2007). However, the relationship becomes more complicated when researchers consider patients' objective health (rather, that is, than patients' subjective perceptions). Patients who face serious diseases that leave them in poor physical health show lower levels of adherence than patients who are less debilitated by the same diseases. This lack of adherence may reflect growing pessimism about the likelihood that the treatment will succeed. A second type of research has demonstrated the importance of social support for patient adherence (DiMatteo, 2004). Patients obtain the greatest benefits when they receive practical support that allows them to accomplish their regimens correctly.

Research has shown that health-care professionals can take steps to improve patient adherence. Consider a study that

---

AIDS Acronym for acquired immune deficiency syndrome, a syndrome caused by a virus that damages the immune system and weakens the body's ability to fight infection.

HIV Human immunodeficiency virus, a virus that attacks white blood cells (T lymphocytes) in human blood, thereby weakening the functioning of the immune system; HIV causes AIDS.

Why does relaxation through meditation have health benefits?

demonstrated the importance of a match between patients' and physicians' attitudes.

A team of researchers recruited 146 patients and the 16 physicians who had most recently provided them with medical care (Cvengros, Christensen, Hillis, & Rosenthal, 2007). Both the patients and the physicians completed a questionnaire that assessed their attitudes about the role patients play in their own health outcomes. Patients responded to statements such as "I am in control of my own health" and "When I get sick it is my own behaviour which determines how soon I get well." The physicians responded to a version of the questionnaire that focused on the patients (for example, "Patients are in control of their own health"). The patients also reported their satisfaction with their physician and the extent to which they had adhered to the regimen the physician had provided. The results indicated that patients were both more satisfied and more likely to adhere when their attitudes matched their physicians' attitudes.

To understand this result, imagine what might happen when, for example, a patient who believes she is in control of her own health faces a physician who believes otherwise. That mismatch is likely to undermine the patient's trust in her physician. The researchers suggest that physicians should try to understand their patients' attitudes—and modify their own behaviours to match those attitudes.

Harnessing the Mind to Heal the Body More and more often, the treatments to which patients must adhere

---

relaxation response A condition in which muscle tension, cortical activity, heart rate, and blood pressure decrease and breathing slows.

biofeedback A self-regulatory technique by which an individual acquires voluntary control over nonconscious biological processes.

involve a psychological component. Many investigators now believe that psychological strategies can improve well-being. For example, many people react to stress with tension, resulting in tight muscles and high blood pressure. Fortunately, many tension responses can be controlled by psychological techniques, such as *relaxation* and *biofeedback*.

Relaxation through meditation has ancient roots in many parts of the world. In Eastern cultures, ways to calm the mind and still the body's tensions have been practised for centuries. Today, Zen discipline and yoga exercises from Japan and India are part of daily life for many people both there and increasingly in the West. Growing evidence suggests that complete relaxation is a potent antistress response (Dusek et al., 2008). The **relaxation response** is a condition in which muscle tension, cortical activity, heart rate, and blood pressure all decrease and breathing slows (Benson, 2000). There is reduced electrical activity in the brain, and input to the central nervous system from the outside environment is lowered. In this low level of arousal, recuperation from stress can take place. Four conditions are regarded as necessary to produce the relaxation response: (1) a quiet environment, (2) closed eyes, (3) a comfortable position, and (4) a repetitive mental device such as the chanting of a brief phrase over and over again. The first three conditions lower input to the nervous system, and the fourth lowers its internal stimulation.

Biofeedback is a self-regulatory technique used for a variety of special applications, such as control of blood pressure, relaxation of forehead muscles (involved in tension headaches), and even diminishment of extreme blushing. As pioneered by psychologist **Neal Miller** (1978), biofeedback is a procedure that makes an individual aware of ordinarily weak or internal responses by providing clear external signals. The patient is allowed to "see" his or her own bodily reactions, which are monitored and amplified by equipment that transforms them into light and sound cues of varying intensity. The patient's task is then to control the level of these external cues.

Let's consider one application of biofeedback. Participants who suffered from either high or low blood pressure were brought into a laboratory (Rau, Bührer, & Wietkunat, 2003). Feedback from equipment measuring an index of the participants' blood pressure on each heart cycle was delivered to a computer screen so that growing green bars indicated changes in the right direction and growing red bars indicated changes in the wrong direction. In addition, the researchers provided verbal reinforcement: "You did it the right way!" After three training sessions, the participants were able to raise or lower their blood pressure, as desired. If you ever become concerned about your blood pressure or other physical disorders, results of this sort might encourage you to seek a course of biofeedback to complement a drug regimen.

Psychoneuroimmunology In the early 1980s, researchers made a series of discoveries that confirmed another way in which the mind affects the body: Psychological states can have an impact on immune function. Historically, scientists had assumed that immunological reactions—rapid production of antibodies to counterattack substances that invade and damage the organism—were automatic biological processes that occurred without any involvement of the central nervous system. However, conditioning experiments of the type we described in Chapter 7 proved that assumption to be incorrect.

Critical Thinking in Your Life

CAN HEALTH PSYCHOLOGY HELP YOU GET MORE EXERCISE?

An important goal of health psychology is to increase the likelihood that people will engage in behaviours that are good for their health. High on that list is exercise: There is abundant evidence that people who get enough exercise experience better health. But how much is "enough"? The Public Health Agency of Canada (2003) makes these recommendations:

- "Accumulate 30 to 60 minutes of moderate physical activities most days. Aerobic activity should be performed in episodes of at least 10 minutes, and preferably, it should be spread throughout the week."
- "As you get older, walking, stretching, and keeping your muscles in good condition will help you to maintain your independence."

The activities in these recommendations lead to increased fitness of the heart and respiratory systems, improvement of muscle tone and strength, and many other health benefits. So how can your knowledge of health psychology help you reap these benefits?

Researchers have explored the questions of who exercises regularly and why. They are trying to determine what programs or strategies are most effective in getting people to start and continue exercising (Nigg, Borrelli, Maddock, & Dishman, 2008). In fact, much of the model that we outlined for people's readiness to quit smoking applies to people's readiness to begin exercising (Buckworth et al., 2007). In the precontemplation stage, an individual is still more focused on the barriers to exercise (for example, too little time, no exercise partners) rather than the benefits (for example, helps relaxation, improves appearance). As the individual moves through the contemplation and preparation stages, the emphasis shifts from barriers to benefits. People who have been exercising for less than six months are in the action stage; those who have exercised regularly for over six months are in the maintenance stage.

If you do not exercise regularly now, how can you get beyond precontemplation? Research suggests that individuals can learn strategies that allow them to overcome obstacles to exercise (Scholz et al., 2008). One strategy is to formulate action plans: You should create specific plans about when, where, and how you foresee becoming physically active. Another strategy is to formulate *coping plans*: You should anticipate what obstacles might arise to interfere with your action plans and determine how best to cope with those obstacles. In one study, researchers taught patients with coronary heart disease how to formulate these types of plans (Sniehotta, Scholz, & Schwarzer, 2006). Two months later, patients who combined both types of planning had engaged in considerably more physical activity than patients in the control group (who did not receive the training). Studies of this sort indicate why you can treat exercise like any other situation in which you use cognitive appraisal to cope with stress. When you read that the Public Health Agency of Canada suggests 30 to 60 minutes of moderate-intensity exercise on most days, you might want to cope with this recommendation by avoiding the topic altogether. Don't let yourself be overwhelmed! Instead, use action plans and coping plans to work your way toward your goals for healthy living.

- Why might the same stages apply to undertaking healthy behaviours as apply to overcoming unhealthy behaviours?
- Why is it stressful to contemplate healthy behaviours such as regular exercise?

Groundbreaking researchers **Robert Ader** and **Nicholas Cohen** (1981) taught one group of rats to associate sweet-tasting saccharin with cyclophosphamide (CY), a drug that weakens immune response. A control group received only the saccharin. Later, when both groups of rats were given only saccharin, the animals that had been conditioned to associate saccharin with CY produced significantly fewer antibodies to foreign cells than the rats in the control group. Thus the learned association alone was sufficient to elicit suppression of the immune system, making the experimental rats vulnerable to a range of diseases. The learning effect was so powerful that, later in the study, some of the rats died after drinking only the saccharin solution.

Results like this strongly suggest that immune function can be modified by psychological states. A new field of study, **psychoneuroimmunology**, has emerged to explore these types of results that involve psychology, the nervous system, and the immune system (Ader & Cohen, 1993; Coe, 1999).

Research over the past 25 years has confirmed that stressors—and how people cope with them—have a consistent impact on the ability of the immune system to function effectively (Kiecolt-Glaser, McGuire, Robles, & Glaser, 2002).

---

psychoneuroimmunology The research area that investigates interactions between psychological processes, such as responses to stress, and the functions of the immune system.

Consider one of the immune system's basic functions: to heal small wounds in your skin. In one study, a research team led by **Janet Kiecolt-Glaser** gave 13 caretakers for relatives with Alzheimer's disease (see Chapter 8) and 13 control participants standardized small wounds to their skin. On average, the Alzheimer's caretakers, who experience chronic stress, took nine days longer for their wounds to heal (Kiecolt-Glaser, Marucha, Malarkey, Mercado, & Glaser, 1995)! People can also experience chronic stress as a consequence of their own personalities—with similar implications for immune function. For example, individuals who reported having difficulty controlling their anger generally took more days to heal the same type of standardized wounds than individuals with better anger control (Gouin, Kielcolt-Glaser, Malarkey, & Glaser, 2008). You can see from this finding how small differences in stress level may affect the speed with which a person's body can heal even the smallest scratch or scrape. From that basic insight, you can understand why research suggests that stress responses play an even more profound role with respect to the progression of serious medical conditions such as infectious diseases and cancer. Researchers wish to understand how the mind affects immune function so they can harness that power to slow these serious illnesses.

Psychological Impact on Health Outcomes Let us add one last note on treatment. Have you ever had a secret too shameful to tell anyone? If so, talking about the secret could very well improve your health. That is the conclusion from a large body of research by health psychologist **James Pennebaker** (1990, 1997; Petrie, Booth, & Pennebaker, 1998), who has shown that suppressing thoughts and feelings associated with personal traumas, failures, and guilty or shameful experiences takes a devastating toll on mental and physical health. Such inhibition is psychologically hard work and, over time, undermines the body's defences against illness. The experience of letting go often is followed by improved physical and psychological health weeks and months later. Consider the effects of emotional disclosure on health outcomes for people with HIV infection.

Thirty-seven adults with HIV infection participated in this study. Roughly half of the patients were assigned to an emotional writing group. In four 30-minute sessions on consecutive days, participants wrote about "the most traumatic and emotional experiences of their lives" (Petrie et al., 2004, p. 273). The control group spent the same amount of time on a neutral task, writing accounts, for example, about what they had done in the previous day. To assess the impact of emotional writing, the researchers measured *HIV viral load*—the number of HIV copies in a millilitre of blood. **Figure 13.8** displays the dramatic impact of emotional writing. Those participants who had engaged in emotional writing had consistently lower viral loads two weeks, three months, and six months after the writing sessions.

Type A behaviour pattern A complex pattern of behaviours and emotions that includes excessive emphasis on competition, aggression, impatience, and hostility; hostility increases the risk of coronary heart disease.

Type B behaviour pattern As compared to Type A behaviour pattern, a less competitive, less aggressive, less hostile pattern of behaviour and emotion.

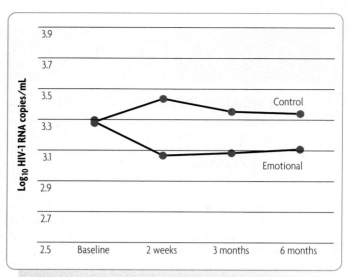

FIGURE 13.8   The Impact of Emotional Writing on HIV Infection

Participants engaged in four sessions of either emotional or neutral writing. Their HIV viral load was assessed two weeks, three months, and six months after the writing sessions. Participants who had engaged in emotional writing had consistently lower viral loads.

From Figure "Viral Load" in "Effect of Written Emotional Expression on Immune Function in Patients with Human Immunodeficiency Virus Infection: A Randomized Trial" by Keith J. Petrie et al., Psychosomatic Medicine, Vol. 66, pp. 272–275, © 2004 by the American Psychosomatic Society. Reprinted with permission of the author.

This result is consistent with other data indicating that individuals' stress level has an impact on the course of HIV infection. Emotional writing helped participants cope with some negative psychological consequences of the infection.

PERSONALITY AND HEALTH

Do you know a person like this: Someone who is driven to succeed, no matter what obstacles; someone whose high-school class voted him or her "Most likely to have a heart attack before age 20"? Are you that person? As you have observed the way in which some people charge through life while others take a more relaxed pace, you may have wondered whether these different personalities affect health. Research in health psychology strongly suggests that the answer is *yes*.

In the 1950s, **Meyer Friedman** and **Ray Rosenman** reported what had been suspected since ancient times: There was a relationship between a constellation of personality traits and the probability of illness, specifically coronary heart disease (Friedman & Rosenman, 1974). These researchers identified two behaviour patterns that they labelled Type A and Type B. The **Type A behaviour pattern** is a complex pattern of behaviour and emotions that includes being excessively competitive, aggressive, impatient, time urgent, and hostile. Type A people are often dissatisfied with some central aspect of their lives, are highly competitive and ambitious, and are often loners. The **Type B behaviour pattern** is everything Type A is not—individuals are less competitive, less hostile, and so on. Importantly, these behaviour patterns have an impact on health. In their original discussion, Friedman and Rosenman reported that people who showed Type A behaviour patterns were stricken with coronary heart disease considerably more often than individuals in the general population.

Because the Type A behaviour pattern has many components, researchers have focused their attention on identifying the specific Type A elements that most often put people at risk. The personality trait that has emerged most forcefully as "toxic" is hostility.

A longitudinal study began in 1986, with 774 men in the sample who were free of any evidence of cardiovascular disease (Niaura et al., 2002). In 1986, each participant's level of hostility was measured (using a set of questions from the Minnesota Multiphasic Personality Inventory, a device we will describe in Chapter 14). Hostility is defined as the consistency with which individuals look at the world and other people in a cynical and negative manner. To display the relationship between hostility and coronary heart disease, the researchers divided the hostility scores into percentile groups. As shown in **Figure 13.9**, those individuals whose hostility scores were in the upper 20 percent had a dramatically larger number of episodes of incident coronary heart disease in the subsequent years. In this sample of men, hostility was a better predictor of future illness than several behavioural risk factors such as smoking and drinking.

Hostility may affect health for both physiological reasons—by leading to chronic overarousal of the body's stress responses—and psychological reasons—by leading hostile people to practise poor health habits and avoid social support (Smith & Ruiz, 2002).

The good news is that researchers have begun to implement behavioural treatments to reduce hostility and other aspects of

the Type A behaviour pattern (Pischke, Scherwitz, Weidner, & Ornish, 2008). For example, one intervention was directed toward high-hostile men who had been diagnosed with coronary heart disease (Gidron, Davidson, & Bata, 1999). As part of the intervention, the men were taught how to use problem-focused coping to reduce anger; they were taught how to use cognitive restructuring to reduce cynicism. After eight weeks, men in the intervention group reported consistently lower levels of hostility than their peers in the control (nonintervention) group. In addition, the men in the intervention group had lower average blood pressure than their control peers. Do you recognize yourself in the definition of hostility? If you do, protect your health by seeking out this type of intervention.

To round out this section on personality and health we want to remind you of the concept of *optimism* we introduced in Chapter 12. We saw there that optimistic individuals attribute failures to external causes and to events that were unstable or modifiable (Seligman, 1991). This style of coping has a strong impact on the optimist's well-being. The particular impact depends on the difficulty of the stressor (Segerstrom, 2005). Because optimists believe they can prevail over stressors, they tend to engage them head on. When the stressor is difficult, this strategy of continued engagement may have negative physiological consequences. Consider a study that assessed the health impact of optimism for students making the transition to law school (Segerstrom, 2006, 2007). For some students this transition was relatively more stressful—because they had social and family demands on top of their academic demands. Each student completed a test that measured optimism. Each student also underwent a procedure to assess immune response. They received an injection of a preparation that tests susceptibility to mumps. In response to the injection, the skin swells. The measure of immune response is the amount of swelling or *induration*. As shown in **Figure 13.10**, those students with the highest optimism showed better immune response in the face of lower demands; they showed worse immune response in the face of higher demands. These data suggest that optimists must recognize that there are some stressors for which the best style of coping is not to engage them directly.

JOB BURNOUT AND THE HEALTH-CARE SYSTEM

One final focus of health psychology is to make recommendations about the design of the health-care system. Researchers, for example, have examined the stress associated with being a health-care provider. Even the most enthusiastic health-care providers run up against the emotional stresses of working intensely with large numbers of people suffering from a variety of personal, physical, and social problems.

The special type of emotional stress experienced by these professional health and welfare practitioners has been termed *burnout* by **Christina Maslach**, a leading researcher on this widespread problem. **Job burnout** is a syndrome of emotional exhaustion, depersonalization, and reduced personal accomplishment that is often experienced by workers in professions that demand high-intensity interpersonal contact with patients,

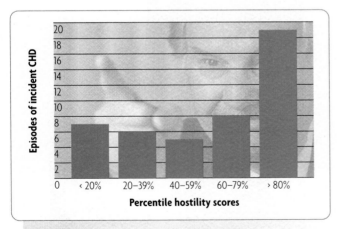

FIGURE 13.9 Hostility Predicts Coronary Heart Disease (CHD)

Study participants were divided into percentile groups based on their self-reports of hostility. Men whose scores placed them in the top 20 percent on the measure (i.e., the group greater than 80 percent) had the highest levels of coronary heart disease.

---

job burnout The syndrome of emotional exhaustion, depersonalization, and reduced personal accomplishment, often experienced by workers in high-stress jobs.

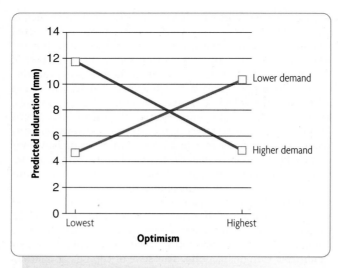

FIGURE 13.10 Optimism and Immune Function

Students with the highest levels of optimism showed better immune response in the face of lower demands. However, they showed worse immune response in the face of higher demands.

From S. C. Segerstrom, "Stress, energy and immunity," *Current Directions in Psychological Science.* Copyright © 2007 by Blackwelll Publishers Ltd. Reprinted with permission.

clients, or the public. Health practitioners begin to lose their caring and concern for patients and may come to treat them in detached and even dehumanized ways. They feel bad about themselves and worry that they are failures. Burnout is correlated with greater absenteeism and turnover, impaired job performance, poor relations with coworkers, family problems, and poor personal health (Maslach & Leiter, 2008).

Job burnout in today's workforce is reaching ever higher levels because of the effects of organizational downsizing, job restructuring, and greater concerns for profits than for employee morale and loyalty. Burnout then is not merely a concern of workers and health caregivers, but it also reveals organizational dysfunction that needs to be corrected by re-examining goals, values, workloads, and reward structures (Leiter & Maslach, 2005).

What recommendations can be made? Several social and situational factors affect the occurrence and level of burnout and, by implication, suggest ways of preventing or minimizing it (Leiter & Maslach, 2005; Prosser et al., 1997). For example, the quality of the patient–practitioner interaction is greatly influenced by the number of patients for whom a practitioner is providing care—the greater the number, the greater the cognitive, sensory, and emotional overload. Another factor in the quality of that interaction is the amount of direct contact with patients. Longer work hours in continuous direct contact with patients are correlated with greater burnout. This is especially true when the nature of the contact is difficult and upsetting, such as contact with patients who are dying (Jackson et al., 2008). The emotional strain of such prolonged contact can be eased by a number of means. For example, practitioners can modify their work schedules in order to withdraw temporarily from such high-stress situations. They can use teams rather than one-on-one contact. They can arrange opportunities to get positive feedback for their efforts.

A TOAST TO YOUR HEALTH

It is time for some final advice. Instead of waiting for stress or illness to come and then reacting to it, set goals and structure your life in ways that are most likely to forge a healthy foundation. The following nine steps to greater happiness and better mental health are presented as guidelines to encourage you to take a more active role in your own life and to create a more positive psychological environment for yourself and others. Think of the steps as *year-round resolutions*.

1. Never say bad things about yourself. Look for the sources of your unhappiness in elements that can be modified by future actions. Give yourself and others only *constructive criticism*—what can be done differently next time to get what you want?
2. Compare your reactions, thoughts, and feelings with those of friends, coworkers, family members, and others so that you can gauge the appropriateness and relevance of your responses against a suitable social norm.
3. Have several close friends with whom you can share feelings, joys, and worries. Work at developing, maintaining, and expanding your social support networks.
4. Develop a sense of *balanced time perspective* in which you can flexibly focus on the demands of the task, the situation, and your needs; be future-oriented when there is work to be done, present-oriented when the goal is achieved and pleasure is at hand, and past-oriented to keep you in touch with your roots.
5. Always take full credit for your successes and happiness (and share your positive feelings with other people). Keep an inventory of all the qualities that make you special and unique—those qualities you can offer others. For example, a shy person can provide a talkative person with the gift of attentive listening. Know your sources of personal strength and available coping resources.

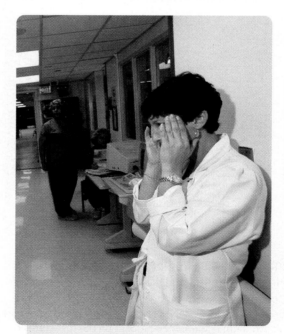

Why are health-care providers particularly prone to job burnout?

6. When you feel you are losing control over your emotions, distance yourself from the situation by physically leaving it, role-playing the position of another person in the situation or conflict, projecting your imagination into the future to gain perspective on what seems an overwhelming problem now, or talking to a sympathetic listener. Allow yourself to feel and express your emotions.

7. Remember that failure and disappointment are sometimes blessings in disguise. They may tell you that your goals are not right for you or may save you from bigger letdowns later on. Learn from every failure. Acknowledge setbacks by saying, "I made a mistake," and move on. Every accident, misfortune, or violation of your expectations is potentially a wonderful opportunity in disguise.

8. If you discover you cannot help yourself or another person in distress, seek the counsel of a trained specialist in your student health department or community. In some cases, a problem that appears to be psychological may really be physical, and vice versa. Check out your student mental health services before you need them, and use them without concern about being stigmatized.

9. Cultivate healthy pleasures. Take time out to relax, to meditate, to get a massage, to fly a kite, and to enjoy hobbies and activities you can do alone and that help you get in touch with and better appreciate yourself.

So how are you feeling? If the stressors in your life have the potential to put you in a bad mood, we hope you will be able to use cognitive reappraisal to minimize their impact. If you are feeling ill, we hope you will be able to use your mind's healing capacity to speed your way back toward health. Never underestimate the power of these different types of "feelings" to exercise control over your life. Harness that power!

STOP AND REVIEW

❶ What has research revealed about the genetics of smoking?
❷ What are the three components of successful AIDS interventions?
❸ What conditions are necessary to produce the relaxation response?
❹ What is the central goal for researchers who study psychoneuroimmunology?
❺ What is the "toxic" aspect of Type A personalities?
❻ How is job burnout defined?

CRITICAL THINKING Consider the study that examined the health impact of emotional disclosure for adults with HIV infection. Why did the researchers ask participants in the control group to write texts?

Recapping Main Points

Emotions

- Emotions are complex patterns of changes made up of physiological arousal, cognitive appraisal, and behavioural and expressive reactions.
- As a product of evolution, all humans may share a basic set of emotional responses.
- Cultures, however, vary in their rules of appropriateness for displaying emotions.
- Classic theories emphasize different parts of emotional response, such as peripheral bodily reactions or central neural processes.
- More contemporary theories emphasize the appraisal of arousal.
- Moods and emotions affect information processing and decision making.
- Subjective well-being is influenced by both genetics and life experiences.

Visit **MyPsychLab.com** for more review and practice on the following topics:

◆●◆ **Research:** Richard Lazarus

◆●◆ **Simulate:** Recognizing Facial Expressions of Emotions

Stress of Living

- Stress can arise from negative or positive events. At the root of most feelings of stress are change and the need to adapt to environmental, biological, physical, and social demands.

- Physiological stress reactions are regulated by the hypothalamus and a complex interaction of the hormonal and nervous systems.
- Depending on the type of stressor and its effect over time, stress can be a mild disruption or can lead to health-threatening reactions.
- Cognitive appraisal is a primary stress moderator variable.
- Coping strategies either focus on problems (direct strategies) or attempt to regulate emotions (indirect or avoidant strategies).
- Cognitive reappraisal and restructuring can be used to cope with stress.
- Social support is also a significant stress moderator, as long as it is appropriate to the circumstances.
- Stress can lead to positive changes, such as post-traumatic growth.

Visit **MyPsychLab.com** for more review and practice on the following topics:

✳ **Explore:** Coping Strategies and Their Effects

Health Psychology

- Health psychology is devoted to the treatment and prevention of illness.
- The biopsychosocial model of health and illness looks at the connections among physical, emotional, and environmental factors in illness.

- Illness prevention in the 21st century focuses on lifestyle factors such as smoking and AIDS-risk behaviours.
- Psychological factors influence immune function.
- Psychosocial treatment of illness adds another dimension to patient treatment.
- Individuals who are characterized by Type A (especially hostile), Type B, and optimistic behaviour patterns will experience different likelihoods of illness.

- Health-care providers are at risk for burnout, which can be minimized by appropriate situational changes in their helping environment.

Visit **MyPsychLab.com** for more review and practice on the following topics:

👁 **Watch:** Nutrition

KEY TERMS

acute stress (p. 401)
AIDS (p. 417)
anticipatory coping (p. 410)
biofeedback (p. 418)
biopsychosocial model (p. 415)
Cannon–Bard theory of emotion (p. 396)
chronic stress (p. 401)
cognitive appraisal theory of emotion (p. 397)
coping (p. 409)
emotion (p. 391)
fight-or-flight response (p. 401)
general adaptation syndrome (GAS) (p. 404)

health (p. 414)
health promotion (p. 415)
health psychology (p. 414)
HIV (p. 417)
hozho (p. 414)
James–Lange theory of emotion (p. 395)
job burnout (p. 421)
life-change units (LCUs) (p. 406)
perceived control (p. 412)
positive psychology (p. 399)
post-traumatic stress disorder (PTSD) (p. 406)
psychoneuroimmunology (p. 419)

psychosomatic disorders (p. 404)
relaxation response (p. 418)
social support (p. 412)
stress (p. 401)
stress moderator variables (p. 409)
stressor (p. 401)
tend-and-befriend response (p. 402)
two-factor theory of emotion (p. 396)
Type A behaviour pattern (p. 420)
Type B behaviour pattern (p. 420)
wellness (p. 415)

ANSWERS FOR FIGURE 13.1 (p. 393)

First row: happiness, surprise, anger, disgust
Second row: fear, sadness, contempt

Practice Test

1. Which statement is true of moods, but not emotions?
   a. They may last several days.
   b. They can be either positive or negative.
   c. They may arise from specific events.
   d. They are relatively intense.

2. Which of these facial expressions is *not* among the seven universally recognized expressions of emotion?
   a. concern
   b. contempt
   c. disgust
   d. happiness

3. The _____ prepares the body for physiological aspects of emotional responses.
   a. hypothalamus
   b. amygdala
   c. autonomic nervous system
   d. hippocampus

4. According to the _____ theory of emotion, you feel after your body reacts.
   a. Cannon–Bard
   b. cognitive appraisal
   c. James–Lange
   d. approach-related

5. Which piece of evidence suggests that not all emotional experiences rely on cognitive appraisal?
   a. Across cultures, facial expressions are highly similar.
   b. The cortex has a separate circuit for withdrawal-related emotional responses.
   c. People in some cultures do not express pain.
   d. People experience the mere exposure effect.

6. Professor Rollins wishes to predict Henrik's level of happiness from Horace's level of happiness. That prediction is likely to be the most accurate if Horace is Henrik's _____
   a. older brother.
   b. DZ twin.
   c. MZ twin.
   d. closest friend.

7. The brain structure that plays an important role in the fight-or-flight response is the _____
   a. pituitary gland.
   b. amygdala.
   c. hypothalamus.
   d. thyroid gland.

8. For people in the 1990s, reports of life-change units were _____ people's reports in the 1960s.
   a. higher than
   b. the same as
   c. lower than
   d. predicted by

9. If you are faced by _____ stressors, the type of coping that is likely to be most useful is _____ coping.
   a. uncontrollable; problem-directed
   b. controllable; emotion-focused
   c. controllable; delay-based
   d. uncontrollable; emotion-focused

10. Which type of coping self-statement is this: "It worked; I was able to do it"?
    a. coping
    b. preparation
    c. confrontation
    d. self-reinforcement

11. When May was diagnosed with skin cancer, Al searched the web to help her learn more about treatment options. This type of social support is _____ support.
    a. tangible
    b. informational
    c. emotional
    d. inoculation

12. A few months after surviving a tornado, Judy says, "I am grateful for every new day." It sounds like Judy experienced post-traumatic growth in which domain?
    a. spiritual change
    b. relating to others
    c. appreciation of life
    d. personal strength

13. Consider the stages people pass through as they attempt to quit smoking. Which of these pairs is in the wrong order?
    a. preparation; contemplation
    b. contemplation; action
    c. action; maintenance
    d. preparation; maintenance

14. Marsea is participating in a laboratory study. Every time her blood pressure goes up, she sees a "sad face" on a computer display. It seems that Marsea is learning how to use _____
    a. the relaxation response.
    b. biofeedback.
    c. anticipatory coping.
    d. stress inoculation.

15. Researchers gave caretakers of Alzheimer's patients and control individuals standardized wounds. What was the result of the study?
    a. The wounds of the Alzheimer's caretakers took longer to heal.
    b. The wounds of the control individuals took longer to heal.
    c. There was no difference in the time it took the wounds to heal.
    d. The wounds of the control individuals were larger.

16. The aspect of the _____ behaviour pattern that has the greatest impact on health is _____.
    a. Type B; hostility
    b. Type A; optimism
    c. Type B; pessimism
    d. Type A; hostility

17. Which of these features is *not* part of the definition of job burnout?
    a. depersonalization
    b. disharmony
    c. emotional exhaustion
    d. reduced personal accomplishment

18. Rhonda takes a 15-minute break every afternoon to take a walk in a park near her office. Rhonda appears to be heeding the advice to ————
a. have a balanced time perspective.
b. cultivate healthy pleasures.
c. distance herself from conflicts.
d. recognize blessings in disguise.

Essay Questions

1. What evidence suggests that some emotional responses are innate while others are not?

2. Why does perceived control have an impact on people's ability to cope with stress?

3. What factors affect the likelihood that patients will adhere to treatment regimens?

Discovering Psychology Viewing Guide

Watch the following video by logging on to MyPsychLab (**www.mypsychlab.com**). After you have watched the video, complete the activities that follow.

Program 23: Health, Mind, and Behaviour

PROGRAM REVIEW

1. How are the biopsychosocial model and the Navaho concept of hozho alike?
   a. Both are dualistic.
   b. Both assume individual responsibility for illness.
   c. Both represent holistic approaches to health.
   d. Both are several centuries old.

2. Dr. Wizanski told Thad that his illness was psychogenic. This means that ──────
   a. Thad is not really sick.
   b. Thad's illness was caused by his psychological state.
   c. Thad has a psychological disorder, not a physical one.
   d. Thad's lifestyle puts him at risk.

3. Headaches, exhaustion, and weakness ──────
   a. are not considered to be in the realm of health psychology.
   b. are considered to be psychological factors that lead to unhealthful behaviours.
   c. are usually unrelated to psychological factors.
   d. are considered to be symptoms of underlying tension and personal problems.

4. What mind–body question is Judith Rodin investigating in her work with infertile couples?
   a. How do psychological factors affect fertility?
   b. Can infertility be cured by psychological counselling?
   c. What effect does infertility have on marital relationships?
   d. Can stress cause rejection of in vitro fertilization?

5. Psychologist Neal Miller uses the example of the blindfolded basketball player to explain ──────
   a. the need for information to improve performance.
   b. how chance variations lead to evolutionary advantage.
   c. the correlation between life-changing events and illness.
   d. how successive approximations can shape behaviour.

6. Imagine a family is moving to a new and larger home in a safer neighbourhood with better schools. Will this situation be a source of stress for the family?
   a. No, because the change is a positive one.
   b. No, because moving is not really stressful.
   c. Yes, because any change requires adjustment.
   d. Yes, because it provokes guilt that the family does not really deserve this good fortune.

7. What important factor in stress did Hans Selye not consider?
   a. the role of hormones in mobilizing the body's defences
   b. the subjective interpretation of a stressor
   c. the length of exposure to a stressor
   d. the body's vulnerability to new stressors during the resistance stage

8. The body's best external defence against illness is the skin, whereas its best internal defence is ──────
   a. the stomach.   c. T-cells.
   b. the heart.   d. the spinal cord.

9. What claim is Richard Lazarus most closely associated with?
   a. The individual's cognitive appraisal of a stressor is critical.
   b. The biopsychosocial model is an oversimplified view.
   c. Peptic ulcers can be healed through biofeedback.
   d. The general adaptation syndrome can account for 80 percent of heart attacks in middle-aged men.

10. How should an advertising campaign ideally be designed in order to get people to use condoms and avoid high-risk sexual activities?
    a. It should be friendly, optimistic, and completely nonthreatening.
    b. It should have enough threat to arouse emotion but not so much that viewers will go into denial.
    c. It should contain a lot of humour.
    d. It should feature an older, white, male doctor and a lot of scientific terminology.

QUESTIONS TO CONSIDER

1. How can you help another person cope with stress?

2. How do defence mechanisms help you deal with stress?

3. What common lifestyle differences might make men or women more susceptible to different kinds of health problems?

14
Understanding Human Personality

Suppose we asked you to compare and contrast your two closest friends. In what ways are they similar? In what ways are they different? It seems likely that your analysis would very quickly come to focus on your friends' *personalities*. You might, for example, assert that one is friendlier than the other, or one has more self-confidence than the other. Assertions of this sort would suggest that you have brought your own personality theory to bear on your relationships—you have your own system for appraising personality. You use your beliefs to determine who in a new class would be friend or foe; you worked out techniques for dealing with your parents or teachers based on the way you read their personalities.

Psychologists define personality in many different ways, but common to all of the ways are two basic concepts: *uniqueness* and *characteristic patterns of behaviour*. We define **personality** as the complex set of psychological qualities that influence an individual's characteristic patterns of behaviour across different situations and over time.

Theories of personality are hypothetical statements about the structure and functioning of individual personalities. They help to achieve two of the major goals of psychology: (1) understanding the structure, origins, and correlates of personality; and (2) predicting behaviour and life events based on what we know about personality. Different theories make different predictions about the way people will respond and adapt to certain conditions.

Before we examine some of the major theoretical approaches, we should ask why there are so many different (often competing) theories. Theorists differ in their approaches to personality by varying their starting points and sources of data and by trying to explain different types of phenomena. Some are interested in the structure of individual personality and others in how that personality developed and will continue to grow. Some are interested in what people do, either in terms of specific behaviours or important life events; others study how people feel about their lives. Finally, some theories try to explain the personalities of people with psychological problems, whereas others focus on healthy individuals. Thus each theory can teach something about personality, and together they can teach much about human nature.

Our goal for this chapter is to provide you with a framework for understanding your everyday experience of personality. However, before we begin, consider this series of questions: If psychologists studied *you*, what portrait of your personality would they draw? What early experiences might they identify as contributing to the way you now act and think? What conditions in your current life exert strong influences on your thoughts and behaviours? What makes you different from other individuals who are functioning in many of the same situations as you? This chapter should help you formulate specific answers to these questions.

Type and Trait Personality Theories

Two of the oldest approaches to describing personality involve classifying people into a limited number of *distinct types* and scaling the degree to which they can be described by *different*

traits. There seems to be a natural tendency for people to place their own and others' behaviour into different categories. Let's examine the formal theories psychologists have developed to capture these differences in types and traits.

CATEGORIZING BY TYPES

We are always categorizing people according to distinguishing features. These include academic major, sex, and race, to name but a few categories. Some personality theorists also group people into distinct, non-overlapping categories that are called **personality types**. Personality types are all-or-none phenomena, not matters of degree: If a person is assigned to one type, he or she could not belong to any other type within that system. Many people like to use personality types in everyday life because they help simplify the complex process of understanding other people.

One of the earliest type theories was originated in the fifth century B.C. by **Hippocrates**, the Greek physician who gave medicine the Hippocratic oath. He theorized that the body contained four basic fluids, or *humours*, each associated with a particular *temperament*, a pattern of emotions and behaviours. In the second century A.D., a later Greek physician, **Galen**, suggested that an individual's personality depended on which humour was predominant in his or her body. Galen paired Hippocrates's body humours with personality temperaments according to the following scheme:

- *Blood.* Sanguine temperament: cheerful and active
- *Phlegm.* Phlegmatic temperament: apathetic and sluggish
- *Black bile.* Melancholy temperament: sad and brooding
- *Yellow bile.* Choleric temperament: irritable and excitable

The theory proposed by Galen was believed for centuries, up through the Middle Ages, although it has not held up to modern scrutiny. (However, we will see a modern echo of these temperaments in Hans Eysenck's trait theory, which we present on page 432.)

In more modern times, **William Sheldon** (1942) originated a type theory that related physique to temperament. He assigned people to three categories based on their body builds: *endomorphic* (fat, soft, round), *mesomorphic* (muscular, rectangular, strong), or *ectomorphic* (thin, long, fragile). Sheldon believed that endomorphs are relaxed, fond of eating, and sociable. Mesomorphs are physical people, filled with energy, courage, and assertive tendencies. Ectomorphs are brainy, artistic, and introverted; they think about life rather than consuming it or acting on it. For a period of time, Sheldon's theory was sufficiently influential that nude "posture" photographs were taken of thousands of students at U.S. colleges like Yale and Wellesley to allow researchers to study the relationships between body type and life factors. However, like Hippocrates's much earlier theory, Sheldon's notion of body types has proven to be of very little value in predicting an individual's behaviour (Tyler, 1965).

---

personality The psychological qualities of an individual that influence a variety of characteristic behaviour patterns across different situations and over time.

personality types Distinct patterns of personality characteristics used to assign people to categories; qualitative differences, rather than differences in degree, used to discriminate among people.

Hippocrates theorized that the body contains four essential fluids, or humours, each associated with a particular temperament. Clockwise: a melancholy patient suffers from an excess of black bile; blood impassions a sanguine lutenist to play; a maiden, dominated by phlegm, is slow to respond to her lover; choler, too much yellow bile, makes an angry master. Do you believe Hippocrates's personality types apply to the people you know?

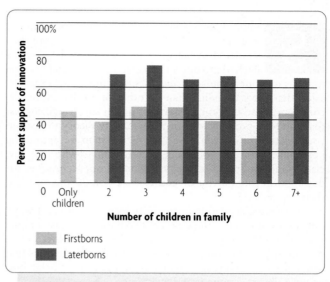

FIGURE 14.1 Birth Position and Support for Scientific Innovation

Frank Sulloway examined 23 innovative scientific theories and determined the birth positions of 1218 scientists who had adopted or rejected those theories. For every family size, laterborns were more likely to adopt the innovative theory than were firstborns.

From *Born to Rebel* by Frank J. Sulloway, Copyright © 1966 by Frank J. Sulloway. Used by permission of Pantheon Books, a division of Random House, Inc.

More recently, **Frank Sulloway** (1996) has proposed a contemporary type theory based on *birth order*. Are you the *firstborn* child (or *only* child) in your family, or are you a *laterborn* child? Because you can take on only one of these birth positions, Sulloway's theory fits the criteria for being a type theory. (For people with unusual family constellations—for example, a very large age gap between two children—Sulloway still provides ways of categorizing individuals.) Sulloway makes birth-order predictions based on Darwin's idea that organisms diversify to find niches in which they will survive. According to Sulloway, firstborns have a ready-made niche: They immediately command their parents' love and attention; they seek to maintain that initial attachment by identifying and complying with their parents. By contrast, laterborn children need to find a different niche—one in which they do not so clearly follow their parents' example. As a consequence, Sulloway characterizes laterborns as "born to rebel": "they seek to excel in those domains where older siblings have not already established superiority. Laterborns typically cultivate openness to experience—a useful strategy for anyone who wishes to find a novel and successful niche in life" (Sulloway, 1996, p. 353). To test the prediction that laterborns embrace innovation whereas firstborns prefer the status quo, Sulloway examined scientific, historical, and cultural revolutions and determined the birth position of large numbers of historical and contemporary figures who had supported or opposed those revolutions. **Figure 14.1** presents data on the extent to which firstborn and laterborn scientists supported 23 innovative theories in science. As you can see, for all of the family sizes, laterborns were more likely to support the innovative theory than were firstborns. Do you have brothers or sisters? Can you find this pattern in your own family?

Studies by Brock University researcher Anthony Bogaert (Bogaert & Purves, 2006; Bogaert, Blanchard, & Crosthwait,

2007) extend the line of research on birth-order effects in a very different direction. In one paper, Bogaert and Purves (2006) examined the reasons for a common research finding that has shown a significant positive correlation between sexual orientation in men and the number of older brothers: The more older brothers a man has, the more likely he is to be gay. What past research had left unclear is whether this effect is due to older brothers having a socializing effect on younger male siblings' sexuality, or whether this effect is due to biological factors. The results suggest that it is the number of older biological brothers the mother carried, and not the presence of older brothers while growing up, that increases the likelihood of some boys growing up to be gay. Bogaert argues that these results support a "prenatal origin to sexual orientation development in men and indicate that the fraternal birth-order effect may be due to a maternal 'memory' for male gestations or births" (p. 10772). However, not all researchers agree with this argument. Recent Australian research by **Nathaniel McConaghy** and his colleagues (2006) concludes that the influence of birth order on homosexual feelings is not due to biological factors but instead to the social process associated with the acquisition of one's own sexuality. What do you think?

DESCRIBING WITH TRAITS

Do you know people whom you would label as particular "types"? Does the "type" include all there is to know about the person? Type theories presume that there are separate, discontinuous categories into which people fit, such as firstborn or laterborn, which we just discussed. However, type theories often

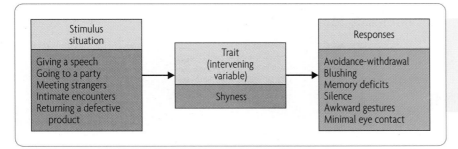

FIGURE 14.2   Shyness as a Trait
Traits may act as intervening variables, relating sets of stimuli and responses that might seem, at first glance, to have little to do with each other.

do not seem to capture more subtle aspects of people's personalities. By contrast, trait theories propose *continuous dimensions*, such as intelligence or friendliness. **Traits** are enduring qualities or attributes that predispose individuals to behave consistently across situations. For example, you may demonstrate honesty on one day by returning a lost wallet and on another day by not cheating on a test. Some trait theorists think of traits as *predispositions* that cause behaviour, but more conservative theorists use traits as *descriptive dimensions* that simply summarize patterns of observed behaviour. Let's examine prominent trait theories.

Allport's Trait Approach Gordon Allport (1937, 1961, 1966) viewed traits as the building blocks of personality and the source of individuality. According to Allport, traits produce coherence in behaviour because they connect and unify a person's reactions to a variety of stimuli. Traits may act as *intervening variables*, relating sets of stimuli and responses that might seem, at first glance, to have little to do with each other (see **Figure 14.2**).

Allport identified three kinds of traits: cardinal traits, central traits, and secondary traits. *Cardinal traits* are traits around which a person organizes his or her life. For Mother Teresa, a cardinal trait might have been self-sacrifice for the good of others. However, not all people develop such overarching cardinal traits. Instead, *central traits* are traits that represent major characteristics of a person, such as honesty or optimism. *Secondary traits* are specific personal features that help predict an individual's behaviour but are less useful for understanding an individual's personality. Food or dress preferences are examples of secondary traits. Allport was interested in discovering the unique combination of these three types of traits that make each person a singular entity, and championed the use of case studies to examine these unique traits.

Allport saw *personality structures*, rather than *environmental conditions*, as the critical determiners of individual behaviour. "The same fire that melts the butter hardens the egg" was a phrase he used to show that the same stimuli can have different effects on different individuals. Many contemporary trait theories have followed in Allport's tradition.

Identifying Universal Trait Dimensions In 1936, a dictionary search by Gordon Allport and his colleague H. S. Odbert

---

traits Enduring personal qualities or attributes that influence behaviour across situations.

In the absence of personality test results, traits can be inferred from observed behaviour. For example, Gandhi (left) would be thought to have the cardinal trait of peacefully resisting injustice; self-confidence would be one of Pierre Elliot Trudeau's central traits (centre); and Pamela Anderson's thirst for attention (right) would be one of her secondary traits.

found over 18 000 adjectives in the English language to describe individual differences. Researchers since that time have attempted to identify the fundamental dimensions that underlie that enormous trait vocabulary. They have tried to determine how many dimensions exist and which ones will allow psychologists to give a useful, universal characterization of all individuals.

Raymond Cattell (1979) used Allport and Odbert's list of adjectives as a starting point in his quest to uncover the appropriate small set of basic trait dimensions. His research led him to propose that 16 factors underlie human personality. Cattell called these 16 factors *source traits* because he believed they provide the underlying source for the surface behaviours we think of as personality. Cattell's 16 factors included important behavioural oppositions such as *reserved* versus *outgoing*, *trusting* versus *suspicious*, and *relaxed* versus *tense*. Even so, contemporary trait theorists argue that even fewer dimensions than 16 capture the most important distinctions among people's personalities.

Hans Eysenck (1973, 1990) derived just two broad dimensions from personality test data: *extraversion* (internally versus externally oriented) and *neuroticism* (emotionally stable versus emotionally unstable). As shown in **Figure 14.3**, Eysenck plotted the two dimensions of extraversion and neuroticism on a circular display. He suggested that each quadrant of the display represents one of the four personality types associated by Galen with Hippocrates's humours. Eysenck's trait theory, however, allows for individual variation within these categories. Individuals can fall anywhere around the circle, ranging from very introverted to very extraverted and from very unstable (neurotic) to very stable. The traits listed around the circle describe people with combinations of these two dimensions. For example, a person who is very extraverted and somewhat unstable is likely to be impulsive.

Five-Factor Model Research evidence supports many aspects of Eysenck's theory. However, in recent years, a consensus has emerged that five factors, which overlap imperfectly with Eysenck's two dimensions, best characterize personality structure. The five dimensions are very broad because each brings into one large category many traits that have unique connotations but a common theme. These five dimensions of personality are now called the **five-factor model**, or, more informally, the *Big Five* (McCrae & Costa, 1999). The five factors are summarized in **Table 14.1**. You will notice again that each dimension has two poles: Terms that are similar in meaning to the name of the dimension describe the high pole, and terms that are opposite in meaning describe the low pole.

The movement toward the *five-factor model* represented attempts to find structure among the large list of traits that Allport and Odbert (1936) had extracted from the dictionary. The traits were boiled down into about 200 synonym clusters that were used to form trait dimensions that have a high pole and a low pole, such as *responsible* versus *irresponsible*. Next, people were asked to rate themselves and others on the bipolar dimensions, and the ratings were subjected to statistical procedures to determine how the synonym clusters were interrelated.

five-factor model A comprehensive descriptive personality system that maps out the relationships among common traits, theoretical concepts, and personality scales; informally called the Big Five.

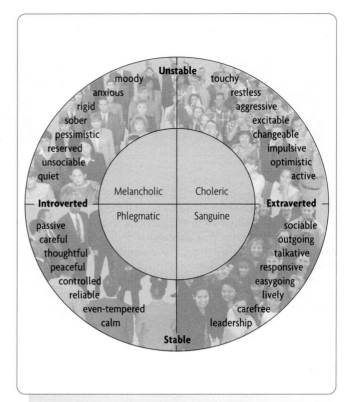

FIGURE 14.3 The Four Quadrants of Eysenck's Personality Circle

The two dimensions of extraversion and neuroticism yield a circular display. Eysenck related each quadrant of the display to one of the four personality types defined by Galen. Eysenck's trait theory, however, allows for individual variation within these categories.

TABLE 14.1 The Five-Factor Model	
Factor	**Endpoints of the Dimension**
Extraversion	Talkative, energetic, and assertive VERSUS quiet, reserved, and shy
Agreeableness	Sympathetic, kind, and affectionate VERSUS cold, quarrelsome, and cruel
Conscientiousness	Organized, responsible, and cautious VERSUS careless, frivolous, and irresponsible
Neuroticism	Stable, calm, and contented VERSUS anxious, unstable, and temperamental
Openness to experience	Creative, intellectual, and open-minded VERSUS simple, shallow, and unintelligent

Using this method, several independent research teams came to the same conclusion: that there are only *five basic dimensions* underlying the traits people use to describe themselves and others (Norman, 1963, 1967; Tupes & Christal, 1961).

Since the 1960s, very similar dimensions have also been found in personality questionnaires, interviewer checklists, and other data (Costa & McCrae, 1992; Digman, 1990; Wiggins & Pincus, 1992). To demonstrate the universality of the five-factor model, researchers have broadened their studies beyond the English language: The five-factor structure has been replicated in a number of languages, including German, Portuguese, Hebrew, Chinese, Korean, and Japanese (McCrae & Costa, 1997). The five factors are not meant to replace the many specific trait terms that carry their own nuances and shades of meaning. Rather, they outline a taxonomy—a classification system—that allows you to describe all the people you know in ways that capture the important dimensions on which they differ.

We have emphasized that the five-factor model originally emerged from statistical analyses of clusters of trait terms, rather than from a theory that said, "These are the factors that must exist" (Ozer & Reise, 1994). However, researchers have started to demonstrate that there are differences in the ways that individuals' brains function that correspond to trait differences in the five-factor model.

Recall from Chapter 13 that a brain structure called the amygdala plays an important role in the processing of emotional stimuli. However, researchers have begun to suspect that not all amygdalas—and, therefore, not all people—respond to stimuli in the same way. To test this idea, a team of researchers recruited 15 participants who differed in their level of extraversion (Canli, Sivers, Whitfield, Gotlib, & Gabrieli, 2002). The researchers predicted that extraversion would have an impact on emotional processing because that trait captures important aspects of people's emotional lives. To look for individual differences, the researchers had the participants view fearful, happy, and neutral faces while they underwent fMRI scans. **Figure 14.4** displays the correlation between participants' self-reports of extraversion and activity in the left and right amygdalas: The areas in red are those areas for which high levels of extraversion were associated with high levels of brain activity. As you can see, extraversion was not correlated with the brains' responses to fearful faces (i.e., there are no areas in red). In fact, fearful faces activated both the left and right amygdalas, but more or less equally across all levels of extraversion. By contrast, for happy faces the highly extraverted individuals showed abundant activity in their left amygdala.

You might recall from Chapter 13 that researchers have characterized emotions as either *approach-related* or *withdrawal-related*. This study suggests that people who are most content to approach other people—which is what makes them extraverted—have more activation in brain regions that support approach-related emotions.

Evolutionary Perspectives on Trait Dimensions

Supporters of the five-factor model have also tried to explain why exactly these five dimensions emerge by looking to evolution: They try to relate the five dimensions to consistent types of interactions that people had with each other and with the external world over the course of human evolution (Buss, 1995; Costa & McCrae, 1992; McCrae et al., 2000). They suggest that because humans are essentially a social species, we can view variation on the five dimensions as answers to fundamental social questions: "who is good company (Extraversion), who is kind and supportive (Agreeableness), who puts in sustained effort (Conscientiousness), who is emotionally undependable (Neuroticism), and who has ideas that pan out (Openness [to experience])" (Bouchard & Loehlin, 2001, p. 250). This evolutionary analysis would help explain the universality of the five factors across diverse cultures (Yamagata et al., 2006).

Researchers who take this evolutionary approach have also considered why there is such great variation along these dimensions (Penke, Denissen, & Miller, 2007). Consider extraversion. As we just noted, humans are a highly social species. For that reason, it might seem maladaptive for an individual to be unsociable and reserved rather than sociable and active. However, we need to factor in differences among environments. People who are highly extraverted are more likely to engage in risky behaviours than those who are not (Nettle, 2006). In particularly dangerous environments, people who were relatively more cautious about social interactions would be more likely to survive. The diversity of environments over human evolution explains why people embody both low and high values on each of the five dimensions. If this explanation is correct, we might also expect that, like other aspects of human experience that have been shaped by evolution, traits can be passed from one generation to the next. We turn now to that claim.

TRAITS AND HERITABILITY

You have probably heard people say things such as "Jim's artistic, like his mother" or "Mary's as stubborn as her grandfather." Or maybe you have felt frustrated because the characteristics that you find irritating in your siblings are those you would like to change in yourself. Consider the evidence that supports the heritability of personality traits.

FIGURE 14.4
Extraversion Affects the Function of the Left Amygdala

Participants viewed fearful and happy faces. The figure displays in red those areas of the brain for which there was a positive correlation between extraversion and amygdala activity. For the fearful faces, there was no correlation. However, for happy faces, the most extraverted participants also showed the highest levels of activity in their left amygdalas.

Recall that *behavioural genetics* is the study of the degree to which personality traits and behaviour patterns are inherited. To determine the effect of genetics on personality, researchers study the personality traits of family members who share different proportions of genes and who have grown up in the same or different households. For example, if a personality characteristic such as *sociability* is passed on genetically, then sociability should correlate more highly between identical, *monozygotic* twins (who share 100 percent of their genes) than between fraternal, *dizygotic* twins or other siblings (who share, on average, 50 percent of their genes).

Heritability studies show that almost all personality traits are influenced by genetic factors (Bouchard, 2004). The findings are the same with many different measurement techniques, whether they measure broad traits, such as extraversion and neuroticism, or specific traits, such as self-control or sociability. Let's consider one sample study.

Recall from Chapter 13 that researchers in the field of positive psychology wish to identify factors that determine positive features of people's lives. To understand the genetic basis of positive personality traits, researchers asked 336 twins to complete an inventory that listed statements related to 24 traits such as bravery, kindness, and fairness (Steger et al., 2007). For each statement (for example, "I am never too busy to help a friend"), the participants responded on a scale ranging from "very much like me" to "very much unlike me." The researchers' analyses showed a strong genetic impact for 21 out of the positive 24 traits. For example, for the trait of bravery, MZ twins yielded a 0.50 correlation between their responses whereas DZ twins yielded a 0.19 correlation.

These data illustrate the general conclusion that genetics have a strong impact on personality. Look back to Table 14.1. Which poles of the five factors seem to apply best to you? Can you find similarities between you and your parents?

DO TRAITS PREDICT BEHAVIOURS?

Suppose we ask you to choose some trait terms that you believe apply particularly well to yourself. You might tell us, for example, that you are *very friendly*. What do we now know? If personality theories allow us to make predictions about behaviours, what can we predict from knowing that you rate yourself as being very friendly? How can we determine the validity of your belief? Let's explore this question.

One idea you might have is that knowing a person can be characterized by a particular trait would enable you to predict his or her behaviour across different *situations*. Thus, we would expect you to produce friendly behaviours in all situations. However, in the 1920s, several researchers who set out to observe trait-related behaviours in different situations were surprised to find little evidence that behaviour was consistent across situations. For example, two behaviours presumably related to the trait of honesty—lying and cheating on a

Research with identical twins demonstrates the heritability of personality traits. What personality traits do you believe run in your family?

test—were only weakly correlated among schoolchildren (Hartshorne & May, 1928). Similar results were found by other researchers who examined the *cross-situational consistency* for other traits such as introversion and punctuality (Dudycha, 1936; Newcomb, 1929).

If trait-related behaviours are not cross-situationally consistent—that is, if people's behaviour changes in different situations—why do you perceive your own and others' personalities to be relatively stable? Even more puzzling, the personality ratings of observers who know an individual from one situation correlate with the ratings of observers who know the individual from another situation. The observation that personality ratings across time and among different observers *are consistent*, whereas behaviour ratings of a person across situations *are not consistent*, came to be called the **consistency paradox** (Mischel, 1968).

The identification of the consistency paradox led to a great deal of research (Mischel, 2004). Over time, the consensus emerged that the appearance of behavioural inconsistency arose, in large part, because situations had been categorized in the wrong way: The paradox fades away once theorists can provide an appropriate account of the *psychological features* of situations (Mischel & Shoda, 1995, 1999). Suppose, for example, you want to try to assess behavioural consistency by determining if a friend acts in much the same way at every party she attends. You are likely to discover that her behaviour varies widely if your level of analysis is just "parties." What you need to determine is what psychologically relevant features separate parties into different categories. Perhaps your friend feels uncomfortable in situations in which she is expected to disclose personal information to strangers. As a consequence, she might seem very unfriendly at some parties (where she is expected to disclose personal information) but quite friendly at others (where she is not). Meanwhile, other situations that require her to be disclosing—such as job interviews—might also bring out negative behaviours. Thus we find consistency in the way that features of situations elicit people's distinctive responses.

---

consistency paradox The observation that personality ratings across time and among different observers are consistent while behaviour ratings across situations are not consistent.

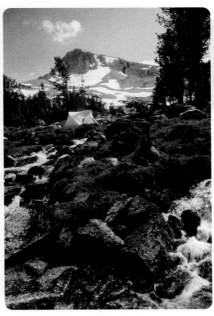

Assuming you could afford either one, which of these vacations would you prefer? What might your choice tell us about the ways in which personality traits interact with features of situations?

Researchers have described the knowledge people have of the relationships between dispositions and situations as *if . . . then . . .* personality signatures: *If* an individual brings a particular disposition to a specific situation, *then* he or she will behave in a particular way (Mischel, 2004). Consider a study that demonstrated the richness of participants' *if . . . then . . .* knowledge.

The researchers asked participants to imagine a university student named Jane (Kammrath et al., 2005). However, different subsets of the participants imagined that Jane was a friendly person, a kiss-up, a flirtatious person, a shy person, or an unfriendly person. After spending a few moments contemplating Jane with that disposition, participants provided judgments of how much warmth they believed Jane would display in six situations: interacting with peers or with professors, with women or with men and with people she was meeting for the first time or with people she has known for a long time. **Figure 14.5** shows participants' warmth predictions for the contrast between new acquaintances (*unfamiliar*) and old acquaintances (*familiar*). You can see that people made very different predictions for different situations. For example, they expected that *if* Jane were shy *then* she would be far less warm with unfamiliar than with familiar individuals.

Take a moment to trace through the rest of the data in Figure 14.5. You should be able to convince yourself that you also possess a good deal of knowledge of the *if . . . then . . .* relationships that explain the interactions of dispositions and situations.

EVALUATION OF TYPE AND TRAIT THEORIES

We have seen that type and trait theories allow researchers to give concise descriptions of different people's personalities.

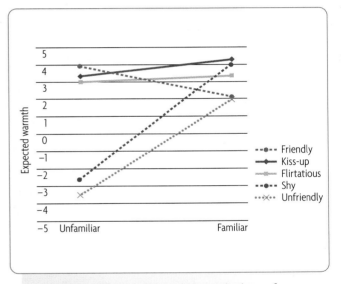

FIGURE 14.5 Students' Knowledge of *If . . . Then . . .* Personality Signatures

Participants imagined a student named Jane as a friendly person, a kiss-up, a flirtatious person, a shy person, or an unfriendly person. They were asked to imagine how warmly Jane would behave on a scale from −5 (Jane feels basically cold and indifferent) to +5 (Jane feels genuine warmth and caring). The participants' predictions for how warmly each version of Jane would behave differed greatly when they imagined her interacting with unfamiliar versus familiar individuals.

Adapted from L. K. Kammrath, R. Mendoza-Denton, and W. Mischel, "Incorporating *If . . . Then . . .* Personality Signatures in Person Perception: Beyond the Person–Situation Dichotomy," *Journal of Personality and Social Psychology, 88*(4), 605–618. Copyright © 2005 by the American Psychological Association. Adapted with permission.

These theories have been criticized, however, because they do not generally explain how behaviour is generated or how personality develops; they only identify and describe characteristics that are correlated with behaviour. Although contemporary trait theorists have begun to address these concerns, trait theories typically portray a *static*, or at least stabilized, view of *personality structure* as it currently exists. By contrast, psychodynamic theories of personality, to which we next turn, emphasize conflicting forces within the individual that lead to change and development.

STOP AND REVIEW

❶ How are personality types defined?

❷ What are the endpoints of the trait dimension of neuroticism?

❸ How have researchers assessed the heritability of traits?

❹ What is the consistency paradox?

CRITICAL THINKING Recall the study that looked at *if . . . then . . .* knowledge. Why was it important for each participant to make predictions for a range of situations?

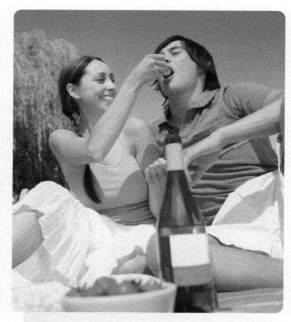

Why did Freud believe that eating is motivated not only by the self-preservation drive to satisfy hunger but also by the "erotic" drive to seek oral gratification?

Psychodynamic Theories

Common to all **psychodynamic personality theories** is the assumption that powerful inner forces shape personality and motivate behaviour. Sigmund Freud, the originator of psychodynamic theories, was characterized by his biographer Ernest Jones as "the Darwin of the mind" (1953). Freud's theory of personality boldly attempts to explain the origins and course of personality development, the nature of mind, aspects of abnormal personality, and the way personality can be changed by therapy. Here we will focus only on normal personality; Freud's views on psychopathology and treatment will be treated in Chapters 15 and 16. After we explore Freud, we will describe some criticisms and reworkings of his theories.

FREUDIAN PSYCHOANALYSIS

According to psychoanalytic theory, at the core of personality are events within a person's mind (*intrapsychic events*) that motivate behaviour. Often, people are aware of these motivations; however, some motivation also operates at an unconscious level. The *psychodynamic* nature of this approach comes from its emphasis on these inner wellsprings of behaviour, as well as the clashes among these internal forces. For Freud, *all behaviour was motivated*. No chance or accidental happenings cause behaviour; all acts are determined by motives. Every

---

psychodynamic personality theories Theories of personality that share the assumption that personality is shaped by, and behaviour is motivated by, inner forces.

libido The psychic energy that drives individuals toward sensual pleasures of all types, especially sexual ones.

human action has a cause and a purpose that can be discovered through analysis of thought associations, dreams, errors, and other behavioural clues to inner passions. The primary data for Freud's hypotheses about personality came from clinical observations and in-depth case studies of individual patients in therapy. He developed a theory of normal personality from his intense study of those with mental disorders. Let's look at some of the most important aspects of Freud's theory.

Drives and Psychosexual Development Freud's medical training as a neurologist led him to postulate a common biological basis for the behavioural patterns he observed in his patients. He ascribed the source of motivation for human actions to *psychic energy* found within each individual. Each person was assumed to have inborn instincts or drives that were *tension systems* created by the organs of the body. These energy sources, when activated, could be expressed in many different ways.

Freud originally postulated two basic drives. One he saw as involved with *self-preservation* (meeting such needs as hunger and thirst). The other he called *Eros*, the driving force related to sexual urges and preservation of the species. Freud greatly expanded the notion of human sexual desires to include not only the urge for sexual union but all other attempts to seek pleasure or to make physical contact with others. He used the term **libido** to identify the source of energy for sexual urges—a psychic energy that drives us toward sensual pleasures of all types. Sexual urges demand immediate satisfaction, whether through direct actions or through indirect means such as fantasies and dreams.

According to Freud, Eros, as a broadly defined sexual drive, does not suddenly appear at puberty but operates from birth. Eros is evident, he argued, in the pleasure infants derive from physical stimulation of the genitals and other sensitive areas, or *erogenous zones*. Freud's five stages of *psychosexual development*

Psychology in Your Life

WHY ARE SOME PEOPLE SHY?

Surveys reveal that more than 50 percent of university students consider themselves to be "currently shy" (Carducci & Zimbardo, 1995). Most of them say that shyness is an undesirable condition that has negative personal and social consequences. Another group of students say that they are "situationally shy." They feel "shy in certain situations that are novel, awkward, or socially pressured," such as blind dates, singles bars, or being put on the spot to perform in public without preparation. Researchers investigating shyness in adults were surprised to discover that it is the "not shy" person who is the rare, unusual breed in North America as well as in every other country surveyed (Zimbardo, 1991).

Shyness may be defined as an individual's discomfort and/or inhibition in interpersonal situations that interferes with pursuing one's interpersonal or professional goals. Shyness can be the mild reticence and social awkwardness many people feel in new situations, but it can escalate into the extreme of a totally inhibiting fear of people (we will discuss this social phobia in Chapter 15). Many shy people are also introverted; they prefer solitary, nonsocial activities. Others are "shy extraverts," publicly outgoing yet privately shy, preferring to engage in social activities, having the social skills to do so effectively, yet doubting that others will really like or respect them (Pilkonis & Zimbardo, 1979). Differences in the outward expression of shyness often results in a discrepancy between people's own perceptions of shyness and those of people who are expected to know them well.

This was the conclusion of a study conducted at the University of Guelph wherein parents and teachers had difficulty identifying a significant minority of children who self-identified as shy (Spooner, Evans, & Santos, 2005).

So why are some people shy and others not?" One explanation may be nature. Research evidence suggests that about 10 percent of infants are "born shy" (Kagan, 1994). From birth, these children are unusually cautious and reserved when they interact with unfamiliar people or situations. A complementary explanation focuses on nurture. As children, some individuals are ridiculed, laughed at, or singled out for public shame; others grow up in families that make "being loved" contingent on competitive success in appearance and performance.

A third explanation focuses on culture. Shyness is highest in some Asian countries, notably Japan and Taiwan, and lowest in Israel, among nine countries studied (Zimbardo, 1991). This difference is attributed in part to cultural emphases on shame for social failure and obedience to authority in these Asian countries versus encouragement for taking risks and externalizing blame in Israel (Pines & Zimbardo, 1978). A fourth explanation accounts, in part, for a recent rise in reported prevalence of shyness in North America: Young people are intensively involved with electronic technology. Spending long hours, typically alone, watching TV, playing video games, surfing the web, and checking email is socially isolating and reduces daily face-to-face contact. Heavy use of the internet has the potential to make people feel lonely, isolated, and more shy (Shaw & Black, 2008).

As shyness gets more extreme, it intrudes on more and more aspects of one's life, minimizing social pleasures and maximizing social discomfort and isolation. There are some simple concepts and tactics we suggest for shy students to think about and try out (Zimbardo, 1991):

- Realize that you are not alone in your shyness; every person you see is more like you than different from you in his or her shyness.

- Shyness can be modified, even when there is a genetic component, but it takes dedication and a resolve to change, as with any long-standing habit you want to break.

- Practise smiling and making eye contact with most people you meet.

- Speak up; talk in a loud, clear voice, especially when giving your name or asking for information.

- Be the first to ask a question or make a comment in a new social situation. Be prepared with something interesting to say, and say it first; everyone appreciates an "ice breaker."

- Never put yourself down. Instead, think about what you can do next time to gain the outcome you want.

- Focus on making others feel comfortable, especially searching out other shy people. Doing so lowers your self-consciousness.

If you are shy, we hope you will adopt these suggestions. Other students who have followed them have been released from the prison of shyness into a life filled with newfound liberties.

---

are shown in **Table 14.2.** Freud believed that the physical source of sexual pleasure changed in this orderly progression. One of the major obstacles of psychosexual development, at least for boys, occurs in the phallic stage. Here, the four- or five-year-old child must overcome the *Oedipus complex.* Freud named this complex after the mythical figure Oedipus, who unwittingly killed his father and married his mother. Freud believed that every young boy has an innate impulse to view his father as a sexual rival for his mother's attentions. Because the young boy

---

shyness An individual's discomfort and/or inhibition in interpersonal situations that interferes with pursuing an interpersonal or professional goal.

TABLE 14.2 Freud's Stages of Psychosexual Development

Stage	Age	Erogenous Zones	Major Developmental Task (Potential Source of Conflict)	Some Adult Characteristics of Children Who Have Been Fixated at This Stage
Oral	0–1	Mouth, lips, tongue	Weaning	Oral behaviour, such as smoking, overeating, passivity, and gullibility
Anal	2–3	Anus	Toilet training	Orderliness, parsimoniousness, obstinacy, or the opposite
Phallic	4–5	Genitals	Oedipus complex	Vanity and recklessness, or the opposite
Latency	6–12	No specific area	Development of defence mechanisms	None: Fixation does not normally occur at this stage
Genital	13–18	Genitals	Mature sexual intimacy	Adults who have successfully integrated earlier stages should emerge with a sincere interest in others and a mature sexuality

cannot displace his father, the Oedipus complex is generally resolved when the boy comes to *identify* with his father's power. (Freud was inconsistent with respect to his theoretical account of the experiences of young girls.)

Freud believed that either too much gratification or too much frustration at one of the early stages of psychosexual development leads to **fixation**, an inability to progress normally to the next stage of development. As shown in Table 14.2, fixation at different stages can produce a variety of adult characteristics. The concept of fixation explains why Freud put such emphasis on early experiences in the continuity of personality. He believed that experiences in the early stages of psychosexual development had a profound impact on personality formation and adult behaviour patterns.

Psychic Determinism The concept of fixation gives us a first look at Freud's belief that early conflicts help *determine* later behaviours. **Psychic determinism** is the assumption that all mental and behavioural reactions (symptoms) are determined by earlier experiences. Freud believed that symptoms were not arbitrary. Rather, symptoms were related in a meaningful way to significant life events.

Freud's belief in psychic determinism led him to emphasize the **unconscious**—the repository of information that is unavailable to conscious awareness (see **Figure 14.6**). Other writers had discussed this construct, but Freud put the concept of the unconscious determinants of human thought, feeling, and action at centre stage in the human drama. According to Freud, behaviour can be motivated by drives of which a person is not aware. You may act without knowing why or without direct access to the true cause of your actions. There is a *manifest* content to your behaviour—what you say, do, and perceive—of which you are fully aware, but there is also a concealed, *latent* content. The meaning of neurotic (anxiety-based) symptoms, dreams, and slips of the pen and tongue is found at the uncon-

FIGURE 14.6 Freud's Conception of the Human Mind

In a famous metaphor, Freud suggested that the human mind is like an iceberg. The tip of the iceberg, which you can see, represents consciousness. The unconscious is the vast bulk of the iceberg, which remains hidden beneath the water.

scious level of thinking and information processing. Many psychologists today consider this concept of the unconscious to be Freud's most important contribution to the science of psychology. Much modern literature and drama also explores the implications of unconscious processes for human behaviour.

According to Freud, impulses within you that you find unacceptable still strive for expression. A *Freudian slip* occurs

---

fixation A state in which a person remains attached to objects or activities more appropriate for an earlier stage of psychosexual development.

psychic determinism The assumption that mental and behavioural reactions are determined by previous experiences.

unconscious The domain of the psyche that stores repressed urges and primitive impulses.

when an unconscious desire is betrayed by your speech or behaviour. For example, one of your authors felt obligated to write a thank-you note to a friend who had hosted him for a weekend, even though he had not much enjoyed the time he had spent at the friend's home. He intended to write, "I'm glad we got to spend a chunk of time together." However, in a somewhat testy phone call, the friend informed him that he had actually written, "I'm glad we got to spend a *junk* of time together." Do you see how the substitution of *junk* for *chunk* could be the expression of an unconscious desire? The concept of unconscious motivation adds a new dimension to personality by allowing for greater complexity of mental functioning.

We have now reviewed some basic aspects of Freud's theory. Let's see how they contribute to the structure of personality.

The Structure of Personality In Freud's theory, personality differences arise from the different ways in which people deal with their fundamental drives. To explain these differences, Freud pictured a continuing battle between two antagonistic parts of the personality—the *id* and the *superego*—moderated by a third aspect of the self, the *ego*. Although we will refer to these three aspects almost as if they are separate creatures, keep in mind that Freud believed them all to be just different mental *processes*. He did not, for example, identify specific brain locations for the id, ego, and superego.

The **id** is the storehouse of the fundamental drives. It operates irrationally, acting on impulse and pushing for expression and immediate gratification without considering whether what is desired is realistically possible, socially desirable, or morally acceptable. The id is governed by the *pleasure principle*, the unregulated search for gratification—especially sexual, physical, and emotional pleasures—to be experienced here and now without concern for consequences.

The **superego** is the storehouse of an individual's values, including moral attitudes learned from society. The superego corresponds roughly to the common notion of *conscience*. It develops as a child comes to accept as his or her own values the prohibitions of parents and other adults against socially undesirable actions. It is the inner voice of *oughts* and *should nots*. The superego also includes the *ego ideal*, an individual's view of the kind of person he or she should strive to become. Thus the superego is often in conflict with the id. The id wants to do what feels good, whereas the superego insists on doing what is right.

The **ego** is the reality-based aspect of the self that arbitrates the conflict between id impulses and superego demands. The ego represents an individual's personal view of physical and social reality—his or her conscious beliefs about the causes and consequences of behaviour. Part of the ego's job is to choose actions that will gratify id impulses without undesirable consequences. The ego is governed by the *reality principle*, which puts reasonable choices before pleasurable demands. Thus the ego would block an impulse to cheat on an exam because of concerns about the consequences of getting caught, and it would substitute the resolution to study harder the next time or solicit the teacher's sympathy. When the id and the superego are in conflict, the ego arranges a compromise that at least partially satisfies both. However, as id and superego pressures intensify, it becomes more difficult for the ego to work out optimal compromises.

Repression and Ego Defence Sometimes this compromise between id and superego involves "putting a lid on the id." Extreme desires are pushed out of conscious awareness into the

Why might a person's enthusiasm for boxing suggest the use of displacement as an ego defence mechanism?

privacy of the unconscious. **Repression** is the psychological process that protects an individual from experiencing extreme anxiety or guilt about impulses, ideas, or memories that are unacceptable and/or dangerous to express. The ego remains unaware of both the mental content that is censored and the process by which repression keeps information out of consciousness. Repression is considered to be the most basic of the various ways in which the ego defends against being overwhelmed by threatening impulses and ideas.

Ego defence mechanisms are mental strategies the ego uses to defend itself in the daily conflict between id impulses that seek expression and the superego's demand to deny them (see **Table 14.3**). In psychoanalytic theory, these mechanisms are considered vital to an individual's psychological coping with powerful inner conflicts. By using them, a person is able to maintain a favourable self-image and to sustain an acceptable social image. For example, if a child has strong feelings of hatred toward his father—which, if acted out, would be dangerous—repression may take over. The hostile impulse is then no longer consciously pressing for satisfaction or even recognized as existing. However, although the impulse is not seen or heard, it is not gone; these feelings continue to play a role in personality functioning. For example, by developing a strong *identification* with his father, the child may increase his sense of self-worth and reduce his unconscious fear of being discovered as a hostile agent.

In Freudian theory, **anxiety** is an intense emotional response triggered when a repressed conflict is about to emerge

---

id The primitive, unconscious part of the personality that acts on impulse without considering society's values, standards, and morals; governed by the pleasure principle.

superego The aspect of personality that represents the internalization of society's values, standards, and morals.

ego The aspect of personality involved in self-preservation activities and in directing instinctual drives and urges into appropriate channels.

repression The basic defence mechanism by which painful or guilt-producing thoughts, feelings, or memories are excluded from conscious awareness.

ego defence mechanisms Mental strategies (conscious or unconscious) used by the ego to defend itself against conflicts experienced in the normal course of life.

anxiety An intense emotional response caused by the preconscious recognition that a repressed conflict is about to emerge into consciousness.

TABLE 14.3	Major Ego Defence Mechanisms
Denial of reality	Protecting self from unpleasant reality by refusing to perceive it
Displacement	Discharging pent-up feelings, usually of hostility, on objects less dangerous than those that initially aroused the emotion
Fantasy	Gratifying frustrated desires in imaginary achievements ("daydreaming" is a common form)
Identification	Increasing feelings of worth by identifying self with another person or institution, often of illustrious standing
Isolation	Cutting off emotional charge from hurtful situations or separating incompatible attitudes into logic-tight compartments (holding conflicting attitudes that are never thought of simultaneously or in relation to each other); also called *compartmentalization*
Projection	Placing blame for one's difficulties on others or attributing one's own "forbidden" desires to others
Rationalization	Attempting to prove that one's behaviour is "rational" and justifiable and thus worthy of the approval of self and others
Reaction formation	Preventing dangerous desires from being expressed by endorsing opposing attitudes and types of behaviour and using them as "barriers"
Regression	Retreating to earlier developmental levels involving more childish responses and usually a lower level of aspiration
Repression	Pushing painful or dangerous thoughts out of consciousness, keeping them unconscious; this is considered to be *the most basic of the defence mechanisms*
Sublimation	Gratifying or working off frustrated sexual desires in substitutive nonsexual activities socially accepted by one's culture

into consciousness. Anxiety is a danger signal: Repression is not working! Red alert! More defences needed! This is the time for a second line of defence, one or more additional ego defence mechanisms that will relieve the anxiety and send the distressing impulses back down into the unconscious. For example, a mother who does not like her son and does not want to care for him might use *reaction formation*, which transforms her unacceptable impulse into its opposite: "I don't hate my child" becomes "I love my child. See how I smother the dear little thing with love?" Such defences serve the critical coping function of alleviating anxiety.

If defence mechanisms defend you against anxiety, why might they still have negative consequences for you? Useful as they are, ego mechanisms of defence are ultimately self-deceptive. When overused, they create more problems than they solve. It is psychologically unhealthy to spend a great deal of time and psychic energy deflecting, disguising, and rechanneling unacceptable urges in order to reduce anxiety. Doing so leaves little energy for productive living or satisfying human relationships. Some forms of mental illness result from excessive reliance on defence mechanisms to cope with anxiety, as we will see in Chapter 15 on mental disorders.

EVALUATION OF FREUDIAN THEORY

We have devoted a great deal of space to outlining the essentials of psychoanalytic theory because Freud's ideas have had an enormous impact on the way many psychologists think about normal and abnormal aspects of personality. However, there probably are more psychologists who criticize Freudian concepts than who support them. What is the basis of some of their criticisms?

First, psychoanalytic concepts are vague and not operationally defined; thus much of the theory is difficult to evaluate scientifically. Because some of its central hypotheses cannot be disproved, even in principle, Freud's theory remains questionable.

How can the concepts of libido, the structure of personality, and repression of infantile sexual impulses be studied in any direct fashion?

A second, related criticism is that Freudian theory is good history but bad science. It does not reliably *predict* what will occur; it is applied *retrospectively*—after events have occurred. Using psychoanalytic theory to understand personality typically involves historical reconstruction, not scientific construction of probable actions and predictable outcomes. In addition, by overemphasizing historical origins of current behaviour, the theory directs attention away from the current stimuli that may be inducing and maintaining the behaviour.

There are three other major criticisms of Freudian theory. First, it is a developmental theory, but it never included observations or studies of children. Second, it minimizes traumatic experiences (such as child abuse) by reinterpreting memories of them as fantasies (based on a child's desire for sexual contact with a parent). Third, it has an *androcentric* (male-centred) bias because it uses a male model as the norm without trying to determine how females might be different.

Some aspects of Freud's theory, however, continue to gain acceptance as they are modified and improved through empirical scrutiny. For example, in Chapter 6, we saw that the concept of the unconscious is being systematically explored by contemporary researchers (McGovern & Baars, 2007). This research reveals that much of your day-to-day experience is shaped by processes outside of your awareness. These results support Freud's general concept but weaken the link between unconscious processes and psychopathology: Little of your unconscious knowledge will cause you anxiety or distress. Similarly, researchers have found evidence for some of the habits of mind Freud characterized as defence mechanisms. We suggested earlier that individuals are most likely to use defence mechanisms when they are experiencing anxiety. Researchers have tested this hypothesis in a variety of ways.

One study focused on a group of 9- to 11-year-old girls (Sandstrom & Cramer, 2003). The researchers carried out interviews with the girls' peers to determine who among the group of 50 girls was relatively popular and who was relatively unpopular. Each of the 50 girls underwent a laboratory experience in which they were rejected by another young girl. The researchers reasoned that—because of their history of negative social interactions—the unpopular girls would experience more anxiety than the popular girls in the face of this rejection. They also suggested that the unpopular girls would show evidence for more frequent use of defence mechanisms as a result of their unconscious efforts to cope with that anxiety. To test this hypothesis, the researchers asked the girls to tell stories based on cards from the *Thematic Apperception Test* (see p. 457). The stories were analyzed for evidence of the defence mechanisms *denial* and *projection* (see Table 14.3). These analyses supported the hypothesis: The unpopular girls used more defence mechanisms than the popular girls after the episode of peer rejection.

Some of the styles for coping with stress that we described in Chapter 13 fall within the general category of defence mechanisms. You might recall, for example, that inhibiting the thoughts and feelings associated with personal traumas or guilty or shameful experiences can take a devastating toll on mental and physical health (Pennebaker, 1997; Petrie et al., 2004). These findings echo Freud's beliefs that repressed psychic material can lead to psychological distress.

Freud's theory is the most complex, comprehensive, and compelling view of normal and abnormal personality functioning—even when its predictions prove wrong. However, like any other theory, Freud's theory is best treated as one that must be confirmed or disconfirmed element by element. Freud retains his influence on contemporary psychology because some of his ideas have been widely accepted. Others have been abandoned. Some of the earliest revisions of Freud's theory arose from within his own original circle of students. Let's see how they sought to amend Freud's views.

EXTENDING PSYCHODYNAMIC THEORIES

Some of those who came after Freud retained his basic representation of personality as a battleground on which unconscious primal urges conflict with social values. However, many of Freud's intellectual descendants made major adjustments in the psychoanalytic view of personality. In general, these post-Freudians have made the following changes:

- They put greater emphasis on ego functions, including ego defences, development of the self, conscious thought processes, and personal mastery.
- They view social variables (culture, family, and peers) as playing a greater role in shaping personality.
- They put less emphasis on the importance of general sexual urges, or libidinal energy.
- They have extended personality development beyond childhood to include the entire life span.

We will now review key features of the theories of Alfred Adler, Karen Horney, and Carl Jung.

Alfred Adler (1929) rejected the significance of Eros and the pleasure principle. Adler believed that as helpless, dependent, small children, all people experience feelings of *inferiority*. He argued that all lives are dominated by the search for ways to overcome those feelings. People compensate to achieve feelings of adequacy or, more often, overcompensate in an attempt to become *superior*. Personality is structured around this underlying striving; people develop lifestyles based on particular ways of overcoming their basic, pervasive feelings of inferiority. Personality conflict arises from incompatibility between external environmental pressures and internal strivings for adequacy, rather than from competing urges within the person.

Karen Horney (1937, 1939) was trained in the psychoanalytic school but broke from orthodox Freudian theory in several ways. She challenged Freud's phallocentric emphasis on the importance of the penis, hypothesizing that male envy of pregnancy, motherhood, breasts, and suckling is a dynamic force in the unconscious of boys and men. This "womb envy" leads men to devalue women and to overcompensate by unconscious impulses toward creative work. Horney also placed greater emphasis on cultural factors and focused on present character structure rather than on infantile sexuality. Because Horney also had influence on the development of humanistic theories, we will return to her ideas in the next section.

Carl Jung (1959) greatly expanded the conception of the unconscious. For him, the unconscious was not limited to an individual's unique life experiences but was filled with fundamental psychological truths shared by the whole human race, a **collective unconscious**. The collective unconscious explains your intuitive understanding of primitive myths, art forms, and symbols, which are the universal archetypes of existence. An **archetype** is a primitive symbolic representation of a particular experience or object. Each archetype is associated with an instinctive tendency to feel and think about it or experience it in a special way. Jung postulated many archetypes that give rise to myths and symbols: the sun god, the hero, the earth mother. *Animus* was the male archetype, *anima* was the female archetype, and all men and women experienced both archetypes to varying degrees. The archetype of the self is the *mandala*, or magic circle; it symbolizes striving for unity and wholeness (Jung, 1973).

Jung saw the healthy, integrated personality as balancing opposing forces, such as masculine aggressiveness and feminine sensitivity. This view of personality as a constellation of compensating internal forces in dynamic balance was called **analytic psychology**. In addition, Jung rejected the primary importance of libido, so central to Freud's own theory. Jung added two equally powerful unconscious instincts: the need to create and the need to become a coherent, whole individual. In the next section on humanistic theories, we will see this second need parallelled in the concept of *self-actualization*.

---

collective unconscious The part of an individual's unconscious that is inherited, evolutionarily developed, and common to all members of the species.

archetype A universal, inherited, primitive, and symbolic representation of a particular experience or object.

analytic psychology A branch of psychology that views the person as a constellation of compensatory internal forces in a dynamic balance.

❶ According to Freud's theory, what behaviours might arise if an individual became fixated at the oral stage of development?

❷ How is the ego guided by the reality principle?

❸ Although Leon is highly aggressive, he always blames others for starting fights. What defensive mechanism might be at work here?

❹ In Alfred Adler's view, what drive motivates much of people's behaviour?

CRITICAL THINKING Recall the study on the use of defence mechanisms. Why might the researchers have specifically used a rejection episode to produce anxiety?

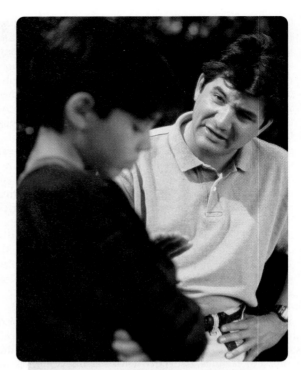

Why did Carl Rogers emphasize parents' unconditional positive regard for their children?

Humanistic Theories

Humanistic approaches to understanding personality are characterized by a concern for the integrity of an individual's personal and conscious experience and growth potential. The key feature of all humanistic theories is an emphasis on the drive toward self-actualization. **Self-actualization** is a constant striving to realize one's inherent potential—to fully develop one's capacities and talents. In this section, you will see how humanistic theorists have developed this concept of self-actualization. You will also learn what additional features set humanistic theories apart from other types of personality theories.

FEATURES OF HUMANISTIC THEORIES

Humanistic personality theorists, such as Carl Rogers, Abraham Maslow, and Karen Horney, believed that the motivation for behaviour comes from a person's unique tendencies, both innate and learned, to develop and change in positive directions toward the goal of self-actualization. Recall from Chapter 12 that Maslow placed self-actualization at the pinnacle of his hierarchy of needs. The striving toward self-fulfillment is a constructive, guiding force that moves each person toward generally positive behaviours and enhancement of the self.

The drive for self-actualization at times comes into conflict with the need for approval from the self and others, especially when the person feels that certain obligations or conditions must be met in order to gain approval. For example, Carl Rogers (1947, 1951, 1977) stressed the importance of **unconditional positive regard** in raising children. By this, he meant that children should feel they will always be loved and approved of, in spite of their mistakes and misbehaviour, and that they do not have to earn their parents' love. He recommended that when a child misbehaves, parents should emphasize that it is the behaviour they disapprove of, not the child.

self-actualization A concept in personality psychology referring to a person's constant striving to realize his or her potential and to develop inherent talents and capabilities.

unconditional positive regard Complete love and acceptance of an individual by another person, such as a parent for a child, with no conditions attached.

Unconditional positive regard is important in adulthood, too, because worrying about seeking approval interferes with self-actualization. As an adult, you need to give unconditional positive regard to and receive it from those to whom you are close. Most important, you need to feel unconditional positive *self-regard*, or acceptance of yourself, in spite of the weaknesses you might be trying to change.

Although not often given due credit, Karen Horney was another major theorist whose ideas created the foundation of humanistic psychology (Frager & Fadiman, 1998). Horney came to believe that people have a "real self" that requires favourable environmental circumstances to be actualized, such as an atmosphere of warmth, the goodwill of others, and parental love for the child as a "particular individual" (Horney, 1945, 1950). In the absence of those favourable nurturing conditions, the child develops a basic anxiety that stifles spontaneity of expression of real feelings and prevents effective relations with others. To cope with their basic anxiety, individuals resort to *interpersonal* or *intrapsychic* defences. Interpersonal defences produce movement toward others (through excessive compliance and self-effacing actions), against others (by aggressive, arrogant, or narcissistic solutions), and away from others (through detachment). Intrapsychic defences operate to develop for some people an unrealistic idealized self-image that generates a "search for glory" to justify it and a pride system that operates on rigid rules of conduct to live up to a grandiose self-concept. Such people often live by the "tyranny of shoulds," self-imposed obligation such as "I should be perfect, generous, attractive, brave," and so forth. Horney believed that the goal of a humanistic therapy was to help the individual achieve the joy of self-realization and promote the inherent constructive forces in human nature that support a striving for self-fulfillment.

An important aspect of each of the theories of Maslow, Rogers, and Horney is the emphasis on self-actualization or progress toward the real self. In addition, humanistic theories have been described as being holistic, dispositional, and phenomenological. Let's see why.

Humanistic theories are *holistic* because they explain people's separate acts in terms of their entire personalities; people are not seen as the sum of discrete traits that each influence behaviour in different ways. Maslow believed that people are intrinsically motivated toward the upper levels of the hierarchy of needs (discussed in Chapter 12), unless deficiencies at the lower levels weigh them down.

Humanistic theories are *dispositional* because they focus on the innate qualities within a person that exert a major influence over the direction behaviour will take. Situational factors are seen as constraints and barriers (like the strings that tie down balloons). Once freed from negative situational conditions, the actualizing tendency should actively guide people to choose life-enhancing situations. However, humanistic theories are not dispositional in the same sense as trait theories or psychodynamic theories. In those views, personal dispositions are recurrent themes played out repeatedly in behaviours throughout one's life. Humanistic dispositions are oriented specifically toward creativity and growth. Each time a humanistic disposition is exercised, the person changes a little, so that the disposition is never expressed in the same way twice. Over time, humanistic dispositions guide the individual toward self-actualization, the purest expression of these motives.

Humanistic theories are *phenomenological* because they emphasize an individual's frame of reference and subjective view of reality—not the objective perspective of an observer or of a therapist. Thus a humanistic psychologist always strives to see each person's unique point of view. This view is also a present-oriented view; past influences are important only to the extent that they have brought the person to the present situation, and the future represents goals to achieve. Unlike psychodynamic theories, humanistic theories do not see people's present behaviours as unconsciously guided by past experiences.

The upbeat humanist view of personality was a welcome treat for many psychologists who had been brought up on a diet of bitter-tasting Freudian medicine. Humanistic approaches focus directly on improvement—on making life more palatable—rather than dredging up painful memories that are sometimes better left repressed. The humanist perspective emphasizes each person's ability to realize his or her fullest potential.

EVALUATION OF HUMANISTIC THEORIES

Freud's theory was often criticized for providing the too-pessimistic view that human nature develops out of conflicts, traumas, and anxieties. Humanistic theories arose to celebrate the healthy personality that strives for happiness and self-actualization. It is difficult to criticize theories that encourage and appreciate people, even for their faults. Even so, critics have complained that humanistic concepts are fuzzy and difficult to explore in research. They ask, "What exactly is self-actualization? Is it an inborn tendency, or is it created by the cultural context?" Humanistic theories also do not traditionally focus on the particular characteristics of individuals. They are more theories about human nature and about qualities all

people share than about the individual personality or the basis of differences among people. Other psychologists note that, by emphasizing the role of the self as a source of experience and action, humanistic psychologists neglect the important environmental variables that also influence behaviour.

Despite these limitations, a type of contemporary research can be traced in part to the humanist tradition that focuses directly on individual *narratives* or *life stories* (McAdams, 2001). The tradition of using psychological theory to understand the details of an individual's life—to produce a *psychobiography*—can be traced back to Freud's analysis of Leonardo da Vinci (Freud, 1910/1957; see Elms, 1988, for a critique of Freud's work). **Psychobiography** is defined as "the systematic use of psychological (especially personality) theory to transform a life into a coherent and illuminating story" (McAdams, 1988, p. 2). Consider the great artist Pablo Picasso. Picasso suffered a series of traumas as a young child, including a serious earthquake and the death of a young sister. A psychobiography might attempt to explain some of Picasso's vast artistic creativity as the lifelong residue of his responses to these early traumas (Gardner, 1993).

When a well-known or historical figure is the subject of a psychobiography, a researcher may turn to published work, diaries, and letters as sources of relevant data. For more ordinary individuals, researchers may directly elicit narratives of life experiences. The request might be, for example, for participants to reflect on key events in their lives: "Why do you think this (was) an important event in your life story? What might this event say about who you are, who you were, who you might be, or how you have developed over time?" (McAdams et al., 2006, p. 1379). The characteristic themes that emerge over series of narrative accounts support the holistic and phenomenological version of personality that was put forth by the early humanists: People construct their identities by weaving life stories out of the strands of narrative. Personal accounts provide a window on people's views of themselves and of their interpersonal relationships.

Humanistic theorists emphasized each individual's drive toward self-actualization. This group recognized, however, that people's progress toward this goal is determined, in part, by the realities of their environments. We turn now to theories that directly examine how individuals' behaviours are shaped by their environments.

STOP AND REVIEW

❶ What is self-actualization?
❷ In what ways are humanistic theories dispositional?
❸ What is a psychobiography?

Social-Learning and Cognitive Theories

Common to all the theories we have reviewed so far is an emphasis on hypothesized inner mechanisms—traits, instincts, impulses, tendencies toward self-actualization—that propel behaviour and form the basis of a functioning personality.

---

psychobiography The use of psychological (especially personality) theory to describe and explain an individual's course through life.

What most of these theories lack, however, is a solid link between personality and particular behaviours. Psychodynamic and humanistic theories, for example, provide accounts of the total personality but do not predict specific actions. Another tradition of personality theory emerged from a more direct focus on individual differences in behaviour. Recall from Chapter 7 that much of a person's behaviour can be predicted from contingencies in the environment. Psychologists with a *learning theory* orientation look to the environmental circumstances that control behaviour. Personality is seen as the sum of the overt and covert responses that are reliably elicited by an individual's *reinforcement history*. Learning theory approaches suggest that people are different because they have had different histories of reinforcement.

The theories we will review have as a shared starting point that behaviour is influenced by environmental contingencies. However, these contemporary social-learning and cognitive theories go one step further to emphasize the importance of cognitive processes as well as behavioural ones. Those who have proposed cognitive theories of personality point out that there are important individual differences in the ways people think about and define any external situation. Like humanistic theories, cognitive theories emphasize that you participate in creating your own personality. For example, you actively choose your own environments to a great extent; you do not just react passively. You weigh alternatives and select the settings in which you act and are acted upon—you choose to enter situations that you expect to be reinforcing and to avoid those that are unsatisfying and uncertain.

Let's look now at more concrete embodiments of these ideas. We examine the theories of Julian Rotter, Walter Mischel, Albert Bandura, and Nancy Cantor.

ROTTER'S EXPECTANCY THEORY

Julian Rotter (1954) focused his theory on **expectancy**, which is the extent to which people believe that their behaviours in particular situations will bring about rewards. Suppose, for example, that you need to decide how much to practise before a presentation in class. You would like to get at least a B. Having a high expectancy means that you think it is very likely that extra practice will lead to a B or better; having a low expectancy means that you are not at all confident that extra practice will help with your grade. Your expectancies arise, in part, because of your own history of reinforcement: If practice has led to rewards in the past, you'll have a stronger expectancy that it will lead to a reward again. Rotter also emphasized reward value—the value that an individual assigns to a particular reward. If you've had a tough semester, a B might have more value to you than it would in a different context. In Rotter's view, you can begin to predict people's behaviour only if you can assess both their expectancy with respect to a reward and the extent to which they value a reward.

Rotter emphasized that people bring specific expectancies to the many situations they face in life. However, Rotter also believed that people develop a more general expectancy about the extent to which they can control the rewards they obtain. Rotter (1966) defined a dimension of locus of control: Some people—known as internals—believe more strongly that the outcomes of their actions are contingent on what they do; other

If your parents complimented you every time you got a new haircut, how might that affect your confidence about your appearance and grooming as an adult? Suppose they were regularly critical. What effect could that have?

TABLE 14.4	Sample Items from Rotter's Internal–External Scale

1. a. In the long run people get the respect they deserve in the world.

   b. Unfortunately, an individual's worth often passes unrecognized no matter how hard he tries.

2. a. Without the right breaks, one cannot be an effective leader.

   b. Capable people who fail to become leaders have not taken advantage of their opportunities.

3. a. Most people don't realize the extent to which their lives are controlled by accidental happenings.

   b. There really is no such thing as "luck."

4. a. What happens to me is my own doing.

   b. Sometimes I feel that I don't have enough control over the direction my life is taking.

Note: 1a, 2b, 3b, and 4a indicate a more internal locus of control orientation.

From J. B. Rotter, Generalized expectancies for internal versus external locus of control of reinforcement, Table 1. *Psychological Monographs, 80* (1):11–12. Copyright © 1966 by the American Psychological Association. Adapted with permission.

---

expectancy The extent to which people believe that their behaviours in particular situations will bring about rewards.

people—known as externals—believe that the outcomes of their actions are contingent on environmental factors. In **Table 14.4**, we've given you sample items from Rotter's Internal–External Scale. To complete the scale, you choose (a) or (b) from each item as the statement you believe to be more accurate. These examples should give you a sense of some differences in the ways that internals and externals generate expectancies about life outcomes. Researchers have consistently demonstrated the importance of people's locus-of-control orientations. For example, one study examined the relationship between people's locus-of-control orientation at age 10 and their mental and physical health at age 30 (Gale, Batty, & Deary, 2008). The 30-year-olds who had been more internally oriented as children were, on the whole, in better health. They were, for example, at lower risk for obesity, high blood pressure, and psychological distress. The researchers suggested that people with external orientations might be in poorer shape because they believe that their health is outside their control—and therefore they take few actions to improve their health.

MISCHEL'S COGNITIVE–AFFECTIVE PERSONALITY THEORY

Walter Mischel developed an influential theory of the cognitive basis of personality. Mischel emphasizes that people actively participate in the cognitive organization of their interactions with the environment. His approach emphasizes the importance of understanding how behaviour arises as a function of interactions between persons and situations (Mischel, 2004). Consider this example:

> John's unique personality may be seen most clearly in that he is always very friendly when meeting someone for the first time, but that he also predictably becomes rather abrupt and unfriendly as he begins to spend more time with that person. Jim, on the other hand, is unique in that he is typically shy and quiet with people who he does not know well but becomes very gregarious once he begins to know someone well. (Shoda, Mischel, & Wright, 1993a, p. 1023)

If we were to average John's and Jim's overall friendliness, we would probably get about the same value on this trait—but

that would fail to capture important differences in their behaviour. According to Mischel (1973, 2004), how you respond to a specific environmental input depends on the variables defined in **Table 14.5**. Do you see how each variable listed would affect the way in which a person would behave in particular situations? We have given you examples for each variable. Try to imagine a situation in which you would produce behaviour different from the characters listed in the table, because you contrast on the particular variable. You may wonder what determines the nature of these variables for a specific individual. Mischel believes that they result from his or her history of observations and interactions with other people and with inanimate aspects of the physical environment (Mischel, 1973).

We want to provide you with a concrete example of how the variables in Mischel's theory explain differences with respect to the particular behaviours people produce in the same situations. Let's consider a study that documented how interactions of competencies and self-regulatory plans (see Table 14.5) interact to predict aggressive behaviour among 10-year-old boys.

The study focused on 59 boys who were attending a summer camp (Ayduk, Rodriguez, Mischel, Shoda, & Wright, 2007). To measure their competencies, the researchers gave each boy a test of verbal intelligence. To measure their self-regulatory abilities, the researchers had each boy engage in a task that measured his capacity to delay his gratification. The boys were brought into a room with a small and large pile of food of a type they particularly enjoyed (for example, M&M candies). To obtain the larger pile, the boys had to wait 25 minutes without ringing a bell to call a researcher back—if they used the bell, they got only the small pile. To endure the 25-minute wait, the boys needed to be able to regulate their own behaviour. In particular, to make the time pass more easily, they needed to be able to divert their attention from the candy and the bell. For that reason, the researchers used the boys' ability to control their attention as a measure of self-regulatory ability. Finally, to measure aggression, the researchers obtained multiple assessments from the camp counsellors about the boys' verbal and physical aggression during group activities. As you can see in

TABLE 14.5 Person Variables in Mischel's Cognitive–Affective Personality Theory		
Variable	**Definition**	**Example**
Encodings	The way you categorize information about yourself, other people, events, and situations.	As soon as Bob meets someone, he tries to figure out how wealthy he or she is.
Expectancies and beliefs	Your beliefs about the social world and likely outcomes for given actions in particular situations; your beliefs about your ability to bring about outcomes.	Greg invites friends to the movies, but he never expects them to say "yes."
Affects	Your feelings and emotions, including physiological responses.	Cindy blushes very easily.
Goals and values	The outcomes and affective states you do and do not value; your goals and life projects.	Peter wants to be president of his college class.
Competencies and self-regulatory plans	The behaviours you can accomplish and plans for generating cognitive and behavioural outcomes.	Jan can speak English, French, Russian, and Japanese and expects to work for the United Nations.

FIGURE 14.7 Boys' Levels of Aggressive Behaviour

Boys' levels of aggressive behaviour at a summer camp reflected an interaction between their verbal intelligence and their ability to control their attention to delay gratification.

Reprinted from O. Ayduk, M. L. Rodriguez, W. Mischel, Y. Shoda, & J. Wright. Verbal intelligence and self-regulatory competencies: Joint predictors of boys' aggression. *Journal of Research in Personality, 41,* 374–388. Copyright © 2007, with permission from Elsevier.

Would you feel comfortable making personality judgments about these boys from this one snapshot? Why might you want to know their patterns of behaviour across different types of situations?

Figure 14.7, to predict the boys' levels of aggressions it is important to know both about competencies and self-regulatory abilities. In particular, boys with high verbal intelligence but low ability to control their attention were substantially more aggressive than their peers who had both high intelligence and high ability to control their attention.

You might expect that more intelligent boys would have knowledge that would allow them to function in social environments without resorting to aggression. This study demonstrates that knowledge alone is not sufficient—the boys also need to have the ability and motivation to perform alternative behaviours. The results allow you to understand why Mischel's personality theory focuses on the interactions among several different types of variables.

BANDURA'S COGNITIVE SOCIAL-LEARNING THEORY

Through his theoretical writing and extensive research with children and adults, Albert Bandura (1986, 1999) has been an eloquent champion of a social-learning approach to understanding personality. (Recall from Chapter 7 his studies of aggressive behaviour in children.) This approach combines principles of learning with an emphasis on human interactions

in social settings. From a social-learning perspective, human beings are not driven by inner forces, nor are they helpless pawns of environmental influence. The social-learning approach stresses the cognitive processes that are involved in acquiring and maintaining patterns of behaviour and, thus, personality.

Bandura's theory points to a complex interaction of individual factors, behaviour, and environmental stimuli. Each can influence or change the others, and the direction of change is rarely one way—it is *reciprocal*. Your behaviour can be influenced by your attitudes, beliefs, or prior history of reinforcement as well as by stimuli available in the environment. What you do can have an effect on the environment, and important aspects of your personality can be affected by the environment or by feedback from your behaviour. This important concept, **reciprocal determinism**, implies that you must examine all components if you want to completely understand human behaviour, personality, and social ecology (Bandura, 1999; see **Figure 14.8**). So, for example, if you do not generally think of yourself as an athlete, you may not choose to be active in track-and-field events, but if you live near a pool, you may nonetheless spend time swimming. If you are outgoing, you will talk to others sitting around the pool and thereby create a more sociable atmosphere, which, in turn, will make it a more enjoyable environment. This is one instance of reciprocal determinism among person, place, and behaviour.

You may recall from Chapter 7 that Bandura's social-learning theory emphasizes observational learning as the process by which a person changes his or her behaviour based on observations of another person's behaviour. Through observational learning, children and adults acquire an enormous range of information about their social environment. Through observation, you learn what is

───────────

reciprocal determinism A concept of Albert Bandura's social-learning theory that refers to the notion that a complex reciprocal interaction exists among the individual, his or her behaviour, and environmental stimuli, and that each of these components affects the others.

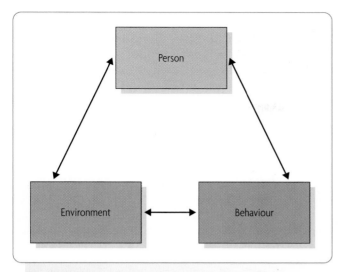

FIGURE 14.8 Reciprocal Determinism

In reciprocal determinism, the individual, the individual's behaviour, and the environment all interact to influence and modify the other components.

appropriate and gets rewarded and what gets punished or ignored. Because you can use memory and think about external events, you can foresee the possible consequences of your actions without having to actually experience them. You may acquire skills, attitudes, and beliefs simply by watching what others do and the consequences that follow.

As his theory developed, Bandura (1997) elaborated self-efficacy as a central construct. **Self-efficacy** is the belief that one can perform adequately in a particular situation. Your sense of self-efficacy influences your perceptions, motivation, and performance in many ways. You do not even try to do things or take chances when you expect to be ineffectual. You avoid situations when you do not feel adequate. Even when you do, in fact, have the ability—and the desire—you may not take the required action or persist to complete the task successfully, if you think you lack what it takes.

Beyond actual accomplishments, there are three other sources of information for *self-efficacy judgments*:

- Vicarious experience—your observations of the performance of others
- Persuasion—others may convince you that you can do something, or you may convince yourself
- Monitoring of your emotional arousal as you think about or approach a task—for example, anxiety suggests low expectations of efficacy; excitement suggests expectations of success

Self-efficacy judgments influence how much effort you expend and how long you persist when faced with difficulty in a wide range of life situations (Bandura, 1997, 2006). For example, how vigorously and persistently you study this chapter may depend more on your sense of self-efficacy than on actual ability (Zimmerman, Bandura, & Martinez-Pons, 1992).

Let's consider the impact of self-efficacy in academic settings.

A group of 202 students participated in a study that examined the impact of self-efficacy beliefs on university performance (Elias & MacDonald, 2007). Each student completed a measure of academic self-efficacy: They used a 10-point scale ranging from "no confidence at all" to "complete confidence" to indicate their sense of the likelihood they would, for example, "Successfully pass all classes enrolled in over the next three semesters" and "Complete a course in biology with a grade of B" (p. 2531). The students also reported their high-school and university GPAs. As you might guess, students' high-school GPAs were good predictors of their university GPAs. High-school GPAs were also good predictors of students' reports of self-efficacy: Students who had been more successful in the past expected to be more successful in the future. However, self-efficacy still mattered over and above past performance. Students who had higher self-efficacy did better than their peers with equal past performance but lower self-efficacy.

Based on this study, you might wonder if it is possible for students to increase their beliefs of self-efficacy—with the potential to improve their grades. As we will see in Chapter 16 (page 512), the answer is "yes, it is possible." Researchers have designed interventions that successfully increase self-efficacy.

Bandura's theory of self-efficacy also acknowledges the importance of the environment. Expectations of failure or success—and corresponding decisions to stop trying or to persevere—may be based on perceptions of the supportiveness or unsupportiveness of the environment, in addition to perceptions of one's own adequacy or inadequacy. Such expectations are called *outcome-based expectancies*. **Figure 14.9** displays how the parts of Bandura's theory fit together. Behavioural outcomes depend both on people's perceptions of their own abilities and their perceptions of the environment.

CANTOR'S SOCIAL INTELLIGENCE THEORY

Building on these earlier cognitive and social theories, **Nancy Cantor** and her colleagues have outlined a *social intelligence* theory of personality (Cantor & Kihlstrom, 1987; Kihlstrom & Cantor, 2000). **Social intelligence** refers to the expertise people bring to their experience of life tasks. The theory defines three types of individual differences:

- *Choice of life goals.* People differ as to which life goals or life tasks are most important to them. People's goals may also change over time.
- *Knowledge relevant to social interactions.* People differ with respect to the expertise they bring to tasks of social and personal problem solving.
- *Strategies for implementing goals.* People have different characteristic problem-solving strategies.

Can you see how these three dimensions interact to give rise to the different patterns of behaviour you would recognize as

self-efficacy The set of beliefs that one can perform adequately in a particular situation.

social intelligence Theory of personality that refers to the expertise people bring to their experience of life tasks.

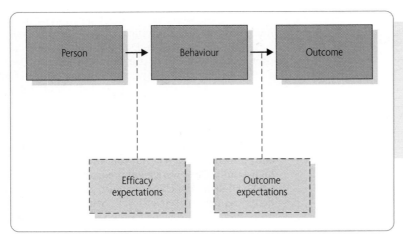

FIGURE 14.9 Bandura's Self-Efficacy Model
This model positions efficacy expectations between the person and his or her behaviour; outcome expectations are positioned between behaviour and its anticipated outcomes.

personality? You might, for example, have two friends—one of whom is more concerned about "getting and keeping friends," whereas the other one gives more weight to "getting good grades." Or suppose two other friends both value getting good grades. Depending on what they know and how they are able to put that knowledge to use, the moment-by-moment decisions they make about how to behave could be very different. One may have been taught explicit strategies for studying, and the other muddles through without special help. The theory of social intelligence gives a new perspective on how personality predicts consistency: For a given period of time, consistency is found in people's goals, knowledge, and strategies.

Let's examine concrete circumstances in which people's disparate goals yield different outcomes. Researchers have demonstrated that *intimacy goals* have an impact on relationship satisfaction.

When people enter into friendships, they differ in the extent to which they have *intimacy* as a goal—some people strongly seek to foster interdependence and engage in self-disclosure, whereas other people do not bring those needs to friendships. One study with 80 participants (40 men and 40 women) examined how the strength of intimacy goals affects the way in which people deal with conflict in their close same-sex friendships (Sanderson, Rahm, & Beigbeder, 2005). The researchers hypothesized that those individuals with strong intimacy goals would have more constructive responses to conflict and, therefore, would be more likely to have their friendships endure. To measure the importance of intimacy as a goal, the researchers asked the participants to respond to statements such as "In my close friendships, I want to share my thoughts and feelings." Participants indicated the ways in which they cope with conflict by responding to statements such as "My friend and I always express our feelings in an open and honest manner that prevents little problems from becoming big ones." In keeping with the researchers' hypothesis, students with strong intimacy goals were most likely to endorse responses to conflicts that helped minimize those conflicts. Because of those constructive responses, students with strong intimacy goals also reported greater satisfaction with their friendships.

Do you see how this pattern could follow from the individuals' goals? People with stronger intimacy goals are highly motivated to behave in ways that will help preserve the friendships. In this case, you recognize personality in the consistent way in which people's goals lead them to behave.

EVALUATION OF SOCIAL-LEARNING AND COGNITIVE THEORIES

One set of criticisms levelled against social-learning and cognitive theories is that they often overlook emotion as an important component of personality. In psychodynamic theories, emotions like anxiety play a central role. In social-learning and cognitive theories, emotions are perceived merely as by-products of thoughts and behaviour or are just included with other types of thoughts rather than being assigned independent importance. For those who feel that emotions are central to the functioning of human personality, this is a serious flaw. Cognitive theories are also attacked for not fully recognizing the impact of unconscious motivation on behaviour and affect.

A second set of criticisms focuses on the vagueness of explanations about the way personal constructs and competencies are created. Cognitive theorists have often had little to say about the developmental origins of adult personality; their focus on the individual's perception of the current behaviour setting obscures the individual's history.

Despite these criticisms, cognitive personality theories have made major contributions to current thinking. Mischel's awareness of situation has brought about a better understanding of the interaction between what a person brings to a behaviour setting and what that setting brings out of the person. Bandura's ideas have led to improvements in the way teachers educate children and help them achieve, as well as to new treatments in the areas of health, business, and sports performance. Finally, Cantor's theory shifts the search for personality consistency to the level of life goals and social strategies.

Do these cognitive personality theories provide you with insights about your own personality and behaviours? You can start to see how you define yourself in part through interactions with the environment. We turn now to theories that can add even further to your definition of self.

❶ In Julian Rotter's theory, what does it mean to have an external locus-of-control orientation?

❷ In Walter Mischel's theory, what five types of variables explain individual differences?

❸ What three components are involved in Albert Bandura's theory of reciprocal determinism?

❹ How is social intelligence defined?

CRITICAL THINKING Recall the study that examined boys' aggression at summer camp. Why was it important that the researchers obtained multiple assessments of the boys' levels of aggression?

Self Theories

Our review of personality theories now turns to those theories that are most immediately personal: They deal directly with how each individual manages his or her sense of *self*. What is your conception of your *self*? Do you think of your *self* reacting consistently to the world? Do you try to present a consistent *self* to your friends and family? What impact do positive and negative experiences have on the way you think about your *self*? We will begin our consideration of these questions with a brief historical review.

The concern for analysis of the self found its strongest early advocate in William James (1892). James identified three components of self-experience: the *material me* (the bodily self, along with surrounding physical objects), the *social me* (your awareness of how others view you), and the *spiritual me* (the self that monitors private thoughts and feelings). James believed that everything that you associate with your identity becomes, in some sense, a part of the self. This explains why people may react defensively when their friends or family members—a part of the self—are attacked. The concept of self was also central to psychodynamic theories. Self-insight was an important part of the psychoanalytic cure in Freud's theory, and Jung stressed that to fully develop the self, one must integrate and accept all aspects of one's conscious and unconscious life.

How has the self been treated in contemporary theory? We will first describe cognitive aspects of the self: self-concepts and possible selves. We then examine the way that people present their selves to the world. Finally, we look at the important topic of how views of the self differ across cultures.

DYNAMIC ASPECTS OF SELF-CONCEPTS

The **self-concept** is a dynamic mental structure that motivates, interprets, organizes, mediates, and regulates intrapersonal and interpersonal behaviours and processes. The self-concept includes many components. Among them are your memories about yourself; beliefs about your traits, motives, values, and abilities; the ideal self that you would most like to become; the possible selves that you contemplate enacting; positive or negative evaluations of yourself (self-esteem); and beliefs about what others think of you (Chen, Boucher, & Tapias, 2006). In Chapter 8, we discussed *schemas* as "knowledge packages" that embody complex generalizations about the structure of the environment. Your self-concept contains schemas about the self—*self-schemas*—that allow you to organize information about yourself, just as other schemas allow you to manage other aspects of your experience. However, self-schemas influence more than just the way you process information about yourself. Research indicates that these schemas, which you frequently use to interpret your own behaviour, influence the way you process information about other people as well (Krueger & Stanke, 2001; Mussweiler & Bodenhausen, 2002). Thus you interpret other people's actions in terms of what you know and believe about yourself.

Another important component of your cognitive sense of self may be the other *possible selves* to which you compare your current self-concept. **Hazel Markus** and her colleagues have defined **possible selves** as "the ideal selves that we would very much like to become. They are also the selves we could become, and the selves we are afraid of becoming" (Markus & Nurius, 1986, p. 954). Possible selves play a role in motivating behaviour—they spur action by allowing you to consider what directions your "self" could take, for better or for worse.

---

self-concept A person's mental model of his or her abilities and attributes.

possible selves The ideal selves that a person would like to become, the selves a person could become, and the selves a person is afraid of becoming; components of the cognitive sense of self.

Imagine for a moment your different "possible selves." What effect might consideration of possible selves have on your behaviour?

Consider the following Canadian study that explored individuals' ideas about whether they were prepared to become parents.

A team of researchers developed an assessment device intended to measure the extent to which young adults could imagine themselves becoming parents (Bloom, Delmore-Ko, Masataka, & Carli, 1999). The 683 college students who participated in the study responded on a scale of *not at all like me* to *very much like me* to statements such as "In the future I see myself as the kind of person who would get married but choose not to have children." To discourage students from guessing the study's purpose, the items relevant to parenting were dispersed into a longer questionnaire. After completing the questionnaire, each student was assigned a *parent possible-self score* (PPS). On average, men and women did not differ on these scores. However, the researchers defined subsets of both men and women who were particularly high and low on the scale. The individuals in those subsets rated their perceptions of videotaped infants whose behaviour ranged from happy to fussy. The high-PPS students gave consistently more favourable ratings to the infants than the low-PPS students did.

Can you think of reasons why a person's ability to envision him- or herself as a parent might have an impact on that person's interpretations of an infant's behaviour?

SELF-ESTEEM

A person's **self-esteem** is a *generalized* evaluation of the self. People differ in their levels of self-esteem. Because we have described the importance of genetics for other aspects of personality, you may not be surprised to learn that individual differences in self-esteem have a genetic component: People inherit a tendency toward high or low self-esteem (Neiss, Sedikides, & Stevenson, 2006). However, environmental factors also have important effects. For example, people's satisfaction or dissatisfaction with their physical appearance has a major impact on their reports of self-esteem (Donnellan, Trzesniewski, Conger, & Conger, 2007). Self-esteem also varies with respect to people's perceptions of their ability to navigate in the social world. People who are high in self-esteem typically feel that they will function well in social relationships; people with low self-esteem have doubts about their social value (Anthony, Holmes, & Wood, 2007).

Self-esteem can strongly influence thoughts, moods, and behaviour (Swann, Chang-Schneider, & McClarty, 2007). In fact, researchers have linked a number of negative outcomes to low levels of self-esteem. For example, among adolescents and university students, low self-esteem was related to aggression and antisocial behaviour (Donnellan et al., 2005). Similarly, people who reported low self-esteem as adolescents had poorer

mental and physical health as well as more financial problems as adults (Orth, Robins, & Roberts, 2008; Trzesniewski et al., 2006). These results suggest that having low self-esteem can undermine people's ability to set goals for positive outcomes and cope with negative life events.

Some people clearly experience low self-esteem. However, evidence suggests that most people go out of their way to maintain self-esteem and to sustain the integrity of their self-concept (Vignoles et al., 2006). To preserve their self-image, people engage in a variety of forms of *self-enhancement*. People take steps to view their own actions and behaviours as consistently positive (Sedikides & Gregg, 2008). For example, when people doubt their ability to perform a task, they may engage in **self-handicapping** behaviour. They deliberately sabotage their performance! The purpose of this strategy is to have a ready-made excuse for failure that does not imply *lack of ability* (McCrae & Hirt, 2001). Thus, a student might party with friends instead of studying for an important exam. That way, if he doesn't succeed, he can blame his failure on low effort rather than low aptitude. Note that our use of "he" in this example is deliberate. Research suggests that men consistently engage in more self-handicapping than do women.

Before taking an intelligence test, male and female psychology students were given the opportunity to work through 18 practice items (McCrae, Hirt, & Milner, 2008). The researchers gave half the students *practice matters* instructions: Those students were told that without appropriate practice their intelligence tests scores would not be valid. The other students received *practice does not matter* instructions: Those students were told that practice would likely have no effect on their test scores. Suppose you were in the practice matters condition. If you wanted to have a ready excuse for your (potentially) low intelligence score, you might choose not to practise very much. As you can see in **Figure 14.10**, that's, on average, what the men chose to do. Women who were told that practice mattered did practise quite a bit. Men who had the same instructions practised least of all. To understand this difference, the researchers asked the participants to complete a scale that had items such as "I try to devote my full effort to every class I take" and "I pride myself in being a hard worker" (p. 309). The women consistently agreed more with such statements than did their male peers.

These results support the researchers' claim that women put too much value on effort to engage in self-handicapping. The effort women expend is an important contributor to their self-esteem.

In this section, we have emphasized that people engage in behaviours such as self-handicapping to maintain a high sense of self-esteem. For that reason, you might not be surprised to learn that high self-esteem is not a good predictor of performance across domains (Baumeister, Campbell, Krueger, & Vohs, 2003). Instead, people's self-views with respect to more specific domains of performance (such as particular academic subjects) provide better predictive information about their likely performance (Swann et al., 2007). Similarly, programs to boost self-esteem are best targeted toward particular domains in which people can learn strategies that actually change performance.

---

self-esteem A generalized evaluative attitude toward the self that influences both moods and behaviour and that exerts a powerful effect on a range of personal and social behaviours.

self-handicapping The process of developing, in anticipation of failure, behavioural reactions and explanations that minimize ability deficits as possible attributions for the failure.

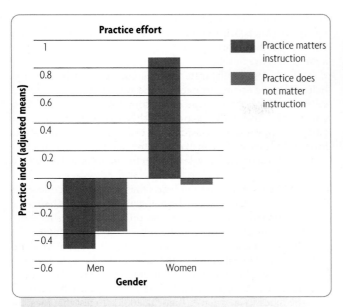

Practice effort

Practice matters instruction

Practice does not matter instruction

FIGURE 14.10 Men's and Women's Self-Handicapping

The *practice index* combined the number of practice items a student completed and the amount of time he or she spent practising into a single measure. Positive scores indicate more than average practice; negative scores indicate less than average practice. When instructions suggested that practice didn't matter, the difference between men's and women's practice was small. However, when students believed their practice did matter, the women practised considerably more than the men.

Reprinted from S. M. McCrae, E. R. Hirt, & B. J. Milner, She works hard for the money: Valuing effort underlies gender differences in behavioral self-handicapping. *Journal of Experimental Social Psychology, 44,* 292–311. Copyright © 2008, with permission from Elsevier.

THE CULTURAL CONSTRUCTION OF SELF

Our discussion so far has focused on constructs relevant to the self, such as self-esteem and possible selves, that apply quite widely across individuals. However, researchers on the self have also begun to study the way in which self-concepts and self-development are affected by differing cultural constraints. If you have grown up in a Western culture, you are likely to be pretty comfortable with the research we have reviewed so far: The theories and constructs match the ways that Western cultures conceptualize the *self.* However, the type of culture from which the Western self emerges—an *individualistic* culture—is in the minority with respect to the world's population, which includes about 70 percent *collectivist* cultures. Individualistic cultures emphasize individuals' needs, whereas collectivist cultures emphasize the needs of the group (Triandis, 1994, 1995). This overarching emphasis has important implications for how each member of these cultures conceptualizes his or her *self.* Hazel Markus and Shinobu Kitayama (1991; Kitayama, Markus, & Lieberman, 1995; Markus, Mullally, & Kitayama, 1997) have argued that each

Self-handicapping behaviour in action: Instead of studying for tomorrow's exam, you fall asleep in the library, thereby enabling yourself to say, "Well, I didn't really study" if you don't ace the test. Are there situations in which you resort to self-handicapping?

culture gives rise to different interpretations of the meaning of self—or different *construals* of self:

- Individualistic cultures encourage **independent construals of self**—"Achieving the cultural goal of independence requires construing oneself as an individual whose behaviour is organized and made meaningful primarily by reference to one's own internal repertoire of thoughts, feelings, and actions, rather than by reference to the thoughts, feelings, and actions of others" (Markus & Kitayama, 1991, p. 226).
- Collectivist cultures encourage **interdependent construals of self**—"Experiencing interdependence entails seeing oneself as part of an encompassing social relationship and recognizing that one's behaviour is determined, contingent on, and, to a large extent organized by what the actor perceives to be the thoughts, feelings, and actions of *others* in the relationship" (Markus & Kitayama, 1991, p. 227).

Researchers have documented the reality and implications of these distinctions in a number of ways.

One type of cross-cultural research on the self has used a measurement device called the *Twenty Statements Test* (TST) (Kuhn & McPartland, 1954). When they take this test, participants are asked to give 20 different answers to the question "Who am I?" Take a moment to reflect on that question. As shown in **Table 14.6**, responses typically fall into six different categories. Culture has an impact on the categories that are most likely for people's responses. For example, one study had roughly 300 students from the United States and India perform the TST procedure (Dhawan et al., 1995). In keeping with their independent sense of self, about 65 percent of the responses of U.S. women and 64 percent of the responses of U.S. men fell into the category of *self-evaluations.* For the Indian students,

---

independent construals of self Conceptualization of the self as an individual whose behaviour is organized primarily by reference to one's own thoughts, feelings, and actions, rather than by reference to the thoughts, feelings, and actions of others.

interdependent construals of self Conceptualization of the self as part of an encompassing social relationship; recognizing that one's behaviour is determined, contingent on, and, to a large extent, organized by what one perceives to be the thoughts, feelings, and actions of others.

TABLE 14.6 Categories of *Twenty Statements Test* Responses

Category	Examples
Social identity	I am a student.
	I am a daughter.
Ideological beliefs	I believe that all human beings are good.
	I believe in God.
Interests	I like playing the piano.
	I enjoy visiting new places.
Ambitions	I want to become a doctor.
	I want to learn more psychology.
Self-evaluations	I am honest and hardworking.
	I am a tall person.
	I worry about the future.
Other	I have noisy friends.
	I own a dog.

33 percent of women's responses and 35 percent of men's responses fell into this category. Thus the Indian students were about half as likely to produce self-evaluations. Note that differences between men and women overall were rather small; culture mattered more.

You might wonder how the export of Western culture affects the self-concepts of members of collectivist cultures. One study compared the TST responses of Kenyans who had virtually no exposure to Western culture—members of pastoral Samburu and Maasai tribes—to those who had moved to the Westernized capital city of Nairobi. Roughly 82 percent of the tribe members' responses on the TST were social responses; workers in Nairobi gave 58 percent social responses; and students at the University of Nairobi gave only 17 percent social responses (Ma & Schoeneman, 1997). This pattern suggests that when a nation imports Western products, they may also import a Western sense of self.

These studies illustrate that the cultures to which people belong have a strong impact on the way they construe their selves. You have already read about some consequences of these construals. You will encounter this distinction again in Chapter 16 when we consider, for example, how ideas about love are influenced by construals of the self. For now, consider a study that has particular relevance to theories about the self.

Earlier we reviewed evidence that people are concerned with *self-enhancement*—bringing about positive changes in self-esteem. However, people in different cultures have different interpretations of the *self* in self-enhancement. For that reason, a team of researchers predicted that students from the United States would be more likely to choose individualistic behaviours for self-enhancement, whereas students from Japan would choose collectivist behaviours (Sedikides, Gaertner, & Toguchi, 2003). To test that idea, the researchers asked each participant from the United States and Japan to spend 10 minutes imagining that he or she was part of a task force responsible for solving business problems. The students were asked to consider a range of issues and write down their ideas on those issues. After performing this exercise, the students made predictions about how likely it was that they would outperform the other (imaginary) task force members on a range of behaviours. Some of those behaviours were individualistic: Would they "disagree with [their] group when [they] believe the group is wrong?" Some of those behaviours were collectivist: Would they "avoid open confrontation with [their] group?" For each behaviour, the students gave responses ranging from 25 ("much less likely than the typical group member") to 15 ("much more likely than the typical group member"). As shown in **Table 14.7**, the students predicted that they would outperform their peers—the more positive numbers indicate more self-enhancement—with respect to those behaviours that were matched with their construals of self.

Over the next few days, you might try to experience both construals of self by trying to attend to how the events that happen around you have an impact both on your self as an individual and your self as a member of a larger social structure.

In what ways is an individual's sense of self different when he or she is a member of a culture with an interdependent construal of self rather than an independent construal of self?

TABLE 14.7 Self-Enhancement Across Cultures

Culture	Behaviours	
	Individualist	Collectivist
American	1.28	−0.45
Japanese	0.06	0.63

From Sedikides, C., Gaertner, L., & Toguchi, Y. (2003). Pancultural self-enhancement. *Journal of Personality and Social Pscyhology, 84,* 60–79.

EVALUATION OF SELF THEORIES

Self theories succeed at capturing people's own concepts of their personalities and the way they wish to be perceived by others. Furthermore, examinations of cross-cultural construals of the self have had great influence on the way psychologists assess the universality of their theories. However, critics of self theory approaches to personality argue against its limitless boundaries. Because so many things are relevant to the self and to the self-concept, it is not always clear which factors are most important for predicting behaviour. In addition, the emphasis on the self as a social construct is not entirely consistent with evidence that some facets of personality may be inherited. As with the other theories we have described, self theories capture some but not all of what you think of as personality.

STOP AND REVIEW

❶ What role do possible selves play in motivation?
❷ What is self-handicapping?
❸ What does it mean to have an interdependent construal of self?

CRITICAL THINKING Consider the study that demonstrated gender differences in self-handicapping. Why was it important that participants completed the worker scale before they had the opportunity to practise?

Comparing Personality Theories

There is no unified theory of personality that a majority of psychologists can endorse. Several differences in basic assumptions have come up repeatedly in our survey of the various theories. It may be helpful to recap five of the most important differences in assumptions about personality and the approaches that advance each assumption.

- *Heredity versus environment.* As you have learned throughout *Psychology and Life*, this difference is also referred to as *nature versus nurture.* What is more important to personality development: genetic and biological factors or environmental influences? Trait theories have been split on this issue; Freudian theory depends heavily on heredity; humanistic, social-learning, cognitive, and self theories all emphasize either environment as a determinant of behaviour or interaction with the environment as a source of personality development and differences.

- *Learning processes versus innate laws of behaviour.* Should emphasis be placed on the view that personalities are modified through learning, or on the view that personality development follows an internal timetable? Again, trait theories have been divided. Freudian theory has favoured the inner determinant view, whereas humanists postulate an optimistic view that experience changes people. Social-learning, cognitive, and self theories clearly support the idea that behaviour and personality change as a result of learned experiences.

- *Emphasis on past, present, or future.* Trait theories emphasize past causes, whether innate or learned; Freudian theory stresses past events in early childhood; social-learning theories focus on past reinforcements and present contingencies; humanistic theories emphasize present reality or future goals; and cognitive and self theories emphasize past and present (and the future if goal setting is involved).

- *Consciousness versus unconsciousness.* Freudian theory emphasizes unconscious processes; humanistic, social-learning, and cognitive theories emphasize conscious processes; trait theories pay little attention to this distinction; and self theories are unclear on this score.

- *Inner disposition versus outer situation.* Social-learning theories emphasize situational factors; traits play up dispositional factors; and the others allow for an interaction between person-based and situation-based variables.

Each type of theory makes different contributions to the understanding of human personality. Trait theories provide a catalogue that describes parts and structures. Psychodynamic theories add a powerful engine and the fuel to get the vehicle moving. Humanistic theories put a person in the driver's seat. Social-learning theories supply the steering wheel, directional signals, and other regulation equipment. Cognitive theories add reminders that the way the trip is planned, organized, and remembered will be affected by the mental map the driver chooses for the journey. Finally, self theories remind the driver to consider the image his or her driving ability is projecting to backseat drivers and pedestrians.

To complete our discussion of personality, we now consider personality assessment. We will describe some of the ways in which psychologists obtain information about the range of personality attributes that make each individual unique.

STOP AND REVIEW

❶ In what ways do personality theories differ on the dimension of heredity versus environment?
❷ Does Freud's theory of personality focus most directly on the past, present, or future?
❸ Which dimension of personality theories refers to people's awareness of the forces that shape their behaviours?

Assessing Personality

Think of all the ways in which you differ from your best friend. Psychologists wonder about the diverse attributes that characterize an individual, set one person apart from others, or distinguish people in one group from those in another (for example, shy people from outgoing or depressed individuals from happy). Two assumptions are basic to these attempts to understand and describe human personality: first, that there are personal characteristics of individuals that give coherence to their

HOW IS PERSONALITY CONVEYED IN CYBERSPACE?

Let's start with a straightforward question: Does your email address allow people to make accurate guesses about your personality? To address that question, a team of researchers used a web-based survey to obtain email addresses and self-reports of personality from 599 individuals (Back, Schmukle, & Egloff, 2008). Next, the researchers asked a different group of 100 students to make personality judgments on the same personality dimensions—based only on the email addresses. Consider the researchers' example, honey.bunny77@hotmail.de. How agreeable and conscientious would you imagine the person with that email address to be?

The researchers found that personality ratings based on just the email addresses were quite consistent among the group of 100 raters. The researchers also found positive correlations between the raters' assessments and the email users' self-reports on most of the personality dimensions. That is, the raters were able to make reasonably valid personality judgments based only on the email addresses! The raters appeared to be using a number of features of the addresses to make their judgments. For example, the raters gave higher conscientiousness ratings to addresses with a larger number of characters; they gave lower conscientiousness ratings to addresses with a larger number of digits.

Of course, if you are like many students, your email address is only one of a very large number of decisions you need to make to determine your exact presence in cyberspace. Suppose, for example, you have a page on a social networking site such as MySpace or Facebook. To manage the impression you make on people who visit your page, you need to make decisions about any number of variables including how many friends you have, how much personal detail you provide, and what types of photos you upload (Krämer & Winter, 2008). These variables contribute to how the people who visit your page perceive you. For example, one study varied the number of friends (102, 302, 502, 702, or 902) on a mock Facebook page (Tong, Van Der Heide, Langwell, & Walther, 2008). Participants rated the social attractiveness of the page's owner. Those ratings were highest for 302 friends: Both too few and too many friends counted against the owner. Why 302? The median number of friends reported by the participants themselves was 300. Perhaps participants gave the highest ratings when they thought the page owner was similar to them.

Another study examined the way in which the photographs on Facebook pages contributed to judgments on the particular personality trait of narcissism (Buffardi & Campbell, 2008). People who are narcissistic have an overly positive self-image. Take a moment to consider how that trait might be expressed through Facebook photos. The researchers found that participants rated page owners as being particularly narcissistic when the main photo on their Facebook pages was attractive and self-promoting (that is, the photo seemed dedicated to "persuading others about [the page owner's] own positive qualities," p. 1307). Raters also gave higher judgments of narcissism to owners whose pages indicated a large amount of social interaction. Finally, there was a positive correlation between raters' judgments and the page owner's self-reports of narcissism: The Facebook pages communicated valid information on this trait!

Do these results make you want to rethink how you present yourself in cyberspace?

- Why might people be comfortable making personality judgments based on Facebook content?

- How might you determine other circumstances in which similarity has an impact on people's judgments of Facebook pages?

---

behaviour, and, second, that those characteristics can be assessed or measured. Personality tests must also meet the standards of reliability and validity (see Chapter 10). In addition, clinicians and researchers receive thorough training to administer and interpret the tests. We will describe *objective* and *projective* personality tests. Psychologists often combine different measures to obtain a full understanding of an individual's personality.

OBJECTIVE TESTS

Objective tests of personality are those in which scoring and administration are relatively simple and follow well-defined rules. Some objective tests are scored, and even interpreted, by computer programs. The final score is usually a single number, scaled along a single dimension (such as *adjustment* versus *maladjustment*), or a set of scores on different traits (such as impulsiveness, dependency, or extraversion) reported in comparison with the scores of a normative sample.

A *self-report inventory* is an objective test in which individuals answer a series of questions about their thoughts, feelings, and actions. One of the first self-report inventories, the *Woodworth Personal Data Sheet* (written in 1917), asked questions such as "Are you often frightened in the middle of the night?" (see DuBois, 1970). Today, a person taking a **personality inventory** reads a series of statements and indicates whether each one is true or typical for himself or herself.

The most frequently used personality inventory is the *Minnesota Multiphasic Personality Inventory*, or MMPI (Dahlstrom, Welsh, & Dahlstrom, 1975). It is used in many clinical settings to aid in the diagnosis of patients and to guide their treatment. After reviewing its features and applications, we will briefly discuss the *NEO Personality Inventory* (NEO-PI), which is used widely with nonpatient populations.

The MMPI The MMPI was developed at the University of Minnesota during the 1930s by psychologist **Starke Hathaway** and psychiatrist **J. R. McKinley** (Hathaway & McKinley, 1940, 1943). Its basic purpose is to diagnose individuals according to a set of psychiatric labels. The first test consisted of 550 items, which individuals determined to be either true or false for themselves or to which they responded, "Cannot say." From that item pool, scales were developed that were relevant to the kinds of problems patients showed in psychiatric settings.

The MMPI scales were unlike other existing personality tests because they were developed using an *empirical* strategy rather than the intuitive, theoretical approach that dominated at the time. Items were included on a scale only if they clearly distinguished between two groups—for example, patients with schizophrenia and a normal comparison group. Each item had to demonstrate its validity by being answered similarly by members within each group but differently between the two groups. Thus the items were not selected on a theoretical basis (what the content seemed to mean to experts) but on an empirical basis (did they distinguish between the two groups?).

The MMPI has 10 *clinical scales*, each constructed to differentiate a special clinical group (such as individuals with schizophrenia) from a normal comparison group. The test also includes *validity scales* that detect suspicious response patterns, such as blatant dishonesty, carelessness, defensiveness, or evasiveness. When an MMPI is interpreted, the tester first checks the validity scales to be sure the test is valid and then looks at the rest of the scores. The pattern of the scores—which are highest, how they differ—forms the "MMPI profile." Individual profiles are compared with those common for particular groups, such as felons and gamblers.

In the mid-1980s, the MMPI underwent a major revision, and it is now called the *MMPI-2* (Butcher et al., 2001). The MMPI-2 has updated language and content to better reflect contemporary concerns, and new populations provided data for norms. The MMPI-2 also adds 15 new *content scales* that were derived using, in part, a theoretical method. For each of 15 clinically relevant topics (such as anxiety or family problems), items were selected on two bases: if they seemed theoretically related to the topic area and if they statistically formed a

homogeneous scale, meaning that each scale measures a single, unified concept. The clinical and content scales of the MMPI-2 are given in **Table 14.8** and **Table 14.9**. You will notice that most of the clinical scales measure several related concepts and that the names of the content scales are simple and self-explanatory.

Because the MMPI-2 plays such a critical role in clinical research and practice, researchers continue to assess the test's reliability and validity to make appropriate clinical judgments. Important aspects of that research were incorporated into the MMPI-2-RF (for "revised form") which appeared in 2008 (Tellegen & Ben-Porath, 2008). The MMPI-2-RF features revised clinical scales that supplement the MMPI-2 clinical scales. The goal of these revised scales is to allow better discrimination among people with different types of psychological disorders. The revised clinical scales have begun to undergo tests of reliability and validity that will allow psychologists to put the MMPI-2-RF to appropriate uses (Hoelzle & Meyer, 2008; Rouse et al., 2008).

The MMPI was designed to assess individuals with clinical problems. In the next section, we will describe devices more suited to assess personality in the general, nonpatient population.

TABLE 14.8   MMPI-2 Clinical Scales

Hypochondriasis (Hs): Abnormal concern with bodily functions

Depression (D): Pessimism; hopelessness; slowing of action and thought

Conversion hysteria (Hy): Unconscious use of mental problems to avoid conflicts or responsibility

Psychopathic deviate (Pd): Disregard for social custom; shallow emotions; inability to profit from experience

Masculinity–femininity (Mf): Differences between men and women

Paranoia (Pa): Suspiciousness; delusions of grandeur or persecution

Psychasthenia (Pt): Obsessions; compulsions; fears; guilt; indecisiveness

Schizophrenia (Sc): Bizarre, unusual thoughts or behaviour; withdrawal; hallucinations; delusions

Hypomania (Ma): Emotional excitement; flight of ideas; overactivity

Social introversion (Si): Shyness; disinterest in others; insecurity

---

personality inventory A self-report questionnaire used for personality assessment that includes a series of items about personal thoughts, feelings, and behaviours.

TABLE 14.9	MMPI-2 Content Scales
Anxiety	Antisocial practices
Fears	Type A (workaholic)
Obsessiveness	Low self-esteem
Depression	Social discomfort
Health concerns	Family problems
Bizarre mentation (thoughts)	Work interference
Anger and cynicism	Negative treatment indicators (negative attitudes about doctors and treatment)

Excerpted from the MMPI-2™ (Minnesota Multiphasic Personality Inventory-2)™ Manual for Administration, Scoring, and Interpretation. Revised Edition). Copyright © 2001 by the Regents of the University of Minnesota. All rights reserved. Used by permission of the University of Minnesota Press. "MMPI-2" and "Minnesota Multiphasic Personality-2" are trademarks owned by the Regents of the University of Minnesota.

The NEO-PI The NEO Personality Inventory (NEO-PI) was designed to assess personality characteristics in nonclinical adult populations. It measures the five-factor model of personality we discussed earlier. If you took the NEO-PI, you would receive a profile sheet that showed your standardized scores relative to a large normative sample on each of the five major dimensions: neuroticism, extraversion, openness, agreeableness, and conscientiousness (Costa & McCrae, 1985). The recent NEO-PI-3 assesses 30 separate traits organized within the five major factors (McCrae, Costa, & Martin, 2005). For example, the neuroticism dimension is broken down into six facet scales: anxiety, angry hostility, depression, self-consciousness, impulsiveness, and vulnerability. Much research has demonstrated that the NEO-PI dimensions are homogeneous, highly reliable, and show good criterion and construct validity (Furnham, Crump, & Whelan, 1997; McCrae et al., 2004). The NEO-PI is being used to study personality stability and change across the life span as well as the relationship of personality characteristics to physical health and various life events, such as career success or early retirement.

PROJECTIVE TESTS

Have you ever looked at a cloud and seen a face or the shape of an animal? If you asked your friends to look, too, they may have seen a reclining nude or a dragon. Psychologists rely on a similar phenomenon in their use of projective tests for personality assessment.

As we just saw, objective tests take one of two forms: Either they provide test takers with a series of statements and ask them

---

projective test A method of personality assessment in which an individual is presented with a standardized set of ambiguous, abstract stimuli and asked to interpret their meanings; the individual's responses are assumed to reveal inner feelings, motives, and conflicts.

---

to give a simple response (such as "true," "false," or "cannot say") or they ask test takers to rate themselves with respect to some dimension (such as "anxious" versus "nonanxious"). Thus the respondent is constrained to choose one of the predetermined responses. *Projective tests*, by contrast, have no predetermined range of responses. In a **projective test**, a person is given a series of stimuli that are purposely ambiguous, such as abstract patterns, incomplete pictures, or drawings that can be interpreted in many ways. The person may be asked to describe the patterns, finish the pictures, or tell stories about the drawings. Projective tests were first used by psychoanalysts, who hoped that such tests would reveal their patients' unconscious personality dynamics. Because the stimuli are ambiguous, responses to them are determined partly by what the person brings to the situation—namely, inner feelings, personal motives, and conflicts from prior life experiences. These personal, idiosyncratic aspects, which are *projected* onto the stimuli, permit the personality assessor to make various interpretations.

Projective tests are among the assessment devices most commonly used by psychological practitioners (Butcher & Rouse, 1996). They have also been used outside North America, such as in the Netherlands, Hong Kong, and Japan, more often than objective tests like the MMPI (Piotrowski, Keller, & Ogawa, 1993). Objective tests often fail to be adequately translated or adequately standardized for non-English-speaking populations. Projective tests are less sensitive to language variation. However, because projective tests are so widespread, critics have often worried that they are used in ways that are not valid. As we examine two of the most common projective tests, the Rorschach test and the Thematic Apperception Test, we will discuss those issues of validity.

The Rorschach In the Rorschach test, developed by Swiss psychiatrist **Hermann Rorschach** in 1921, the ambiguous stimuli are symmetrical inkblots (Rorschach, 1942). Some are black and white and some are coloured (see **Figure 14.11**). During the test, a respondent is shown an inkblot and asked, "What might this be?" Respondents are assured that there are no right or wrong answers (Exner, 1974). Testers record verbatim what people say, how much time they take to respond, the total time they take per inkblot, and the way they handle the inkblot card. Then, in a second phase called an *inquiry*, the respondent is reminded of the previous responses and asked to elaborate on them.

FIGURE 14.11   An Inkblot Similar to Those Used in the Rorschach Test
What do you see? Does your interpretation of this inkblot reveal anything about your personality?

The responses are scored on three major features: (1) the *location*, or part of the card, mentioned in the response—whether the respondent refers to the whole stimulus or to part of it and the size of the details mentioned; (2) the *content* of the response—the nature of the object and activities seen; and (3) the *determinants*—which aspects of the card (such as its colour or shading) prompted the response. Scorers may also note whether responses are original and unique or popular and conforming.

You might think that ambiguous inkblots would give rise to an uninterpretable diversity of responses. In fact, researchers have devised a comprehensive scoring system for Rorschach responses that allows for meaningful comparisons among different test takers (Exner, 2003; Exner & Weiner, 1994). For example, the scoring system specifies content categories that frequently appear in people's responses. Those categories include *whole human* (the response mentions or implies a whole human form) and *blood* (the response mentions blood, either human or animal). Researchers have developed training procedures to ensure that clinicians can learn to use the comprehensive scoring system reliably (Hilsenroth, Charnas, Zodan, & Streiner, 2007). In addition, the Rorschach has proven to be valid for diagnosing specific psychological disorders such as abnormal patterns of thought (Dean, Viglione, Perry, & Meyer, 2007). However, practitioners also make diagnoses based on people's Rorschach responses without any formal evidence that supports the validity of the practitioners' inferences. For that reason, the Rorschach test remains controversial (Garb, Wood, Lilienfeld, & Nezworski, 2005).

The TAT In the Thematic Apperception Test (TAT), developed by **Henry Murray** in 1938, respondents are shown pictures of ambiguous scenes and asked to generate stories about them, describing what the people in the scenes are doing and thinking, what led up to each event, and how each situation will end (see **Figure 14.12**). The person administering the TAT evaluates the structure and content of the stories as well as the behaviour of the individual telling them, in an attempt to discover some of the respondent's major concerns, motivations, and personality characteristics. For example, an examiner might evaluate a person as conscientious if his or her stories concerned people who lived up to their obligations and if the stories were told in a serious, orderly way. As with the Rorschach test, critics have suggested that the TAT is often used for purposes for which its validity remains uncertain (Lilienfeld, Wood, & Garb, 2001). In Chapter 12, we noted one use of the TAT that has received research support: The TAT has often been used to reveal individual differences in dominant needs, such as needs for power, affiliation, and achievement (McClelland, 1961). Over several decades of research, the TAT has proven to be a valid measure of the need for achievement (Spangler, 1992).

Let us offer some concluding remarks on the subject of personality assessment. Did you see the relationship between these personality assessment devices and the theories of personality we reviewed earlier? The conclusion we reached was that each of the types of theories best illuminated different aspects of human experience. We can reach much the same conclusions for personality tests: Each has the potential to provide unique insights into an individual's personality. Clinicians most often use a combination of tests when they carry out a personality assessment. Under many circumstances, the profiles that arise from objective, even computer-based analyses may allow accurate predictions to be made for specific outcomes. Under other circumstances, clinical expertise and skilled intuition must supplement objective norms. In practice, the best predictions are made when the strengths of each approach are combined.

To close the chapter, we want you to consider a series of questions in light of what you have just learned: If psychologists studied you, what portrait of your personality would they draw? What early experiences might they identify as contributing to how you now act and think? What conditions in your current life exert strong influences on your thoughts and behaviours? What makes you different from other individuals who are functioning in many of the same situations as you? You now can see that each type of personality theory provides a framework against which you can begin to form your answers to these questions. Suppose the time has really come to paint your psychological portrait. Where would you begin?

FIGURE 14.12 A Sample Card from the TAT Test

What story do you want to tell? What does your story reveal about your personality?

Reprinted by permission of the publishers from Henry A. Murray, *Thematic Apperception Test,* Plate 12 F, Cambridge, Mass.: Harvard University Press, Copyright © 1943 by the President and Fellows of Harvard College. © by Henry A. Murray.

STOP AND REVIEW

❶ What is the purpose of the MMPI's 10 clinical scales?

❷ What is the purpose of the NEO Personality Inventory (NEO-PI)?

❸ What three major features do clinicians use to interpret Rorschach responses?

Recapping Main Points

Type and Trait Personality Theories

- Some theorists categorize people by all-or-none types, assumed to be related to particular characteristic behaviours.
- Other theorists view traits—attributes along continuous dimensions—as the building blocks of personality.
- The five-factor model is a personality system that maps out the relationships among common trait words, theoretical concepts, and personality scales.
- Twin and adoption studies reveal that personality traits are partially inherited.
- People display behavioural consistency when situations are defined with respect to relevant psychological features.

Visit **MyPsychLab.com** for more review and practice on the following topics:

✔ **Practice:** Type and Trait Personality Theories

Psychodynamic Theories

- Freud's psychodynamic theory emphasizes instinctive biological energies as sources of human motivation.
- Basic concepts of Freudian theory include psychic energy as powering and directing behaviour, early experiences as key determinants of lifelong personality, psychic determinism, and powerful unconscious processes.
- Personality structure consists of the id, the superego, and the reconciling ego.
- Unacceptable impulses are repressed and ego defence mechanisms are developed to lessen anxiety and bolster self-esteem.
- Post-Freudians like Adler, Horney, and Jung put greater emphasis on ego functioning and social variables and less on sexual urges. They saw personality development as a lifelong process.

Visit **MyPsychLab.com** for more review and practice on the following topics:

 Explore: Freud's Five Psychosexual Stages of Personality Development

Humanistic Theories

- Humanistic theories focus on self-actualization—the growth potential of the individual.
- These theories are holistic, dispositional, and phenomenological.
- Contemporary theories in the humanist tradition focus on individuals' life stories.

Social-Learning and Cognitive Theories

- Social-learning theorists focus on understanding individual differences in behaviour and personality as a consequence of different histories of reinforcement.
- Cognitive theorists emphasize individual differences in perception and subjective interpretation of the environment.
- Julian Rotter emphasized people's expectancies about rewards, including general internal or external locus-of-control orientations.
- Walter Mischel explored the origins of behaviours as interactions of persons and situations.
- Albert Bandura described the reciprocal determinism among people, environments, and behaviours.
- Nancy Cantor's theory emphasized the impact of goals, knowledge, and strategies on people's behaviour.

Visit **MyPsychLab.com** for more review and practice on the following topics:

◆ **Research:** Walter Mischel

Self Theories

- Self theories focus on the importance of the self-concept for a full understanding of human personality.
- People engage in behaviours such as self-handicapping to maintain self-esteem.
- Cross-cultural research suggests that individualistic cultures give rise to independent construals of self, whereas collectivist cultures give rise to interdependent construals of self.

Comparing Personality Theories

- Personality theories can be contrasted with respect to the emphasis they put on heredity versus environment; learning processes versus innate laws of behaviour; the past, present, or future; consciousness versus unconsciousness; and inner dispositions versus outer situations.
- Each theory makes different contributions to the understanding of human personality.

Assessing Personality

- Personality characteristics are assessed by both objective and projective tests.
- The most common objective test, the MMPI-2, is used to diagnose clinical problems.
- The NEO-PI is an objective personality test that measures five major dimensions of personality.
- Projective tests of personality ask people to respond to ambiguous stimuli.
- Two important projective tests are the Rorschach test and the TAT.

Visit **MyPsychLab.com** for more review and practice on the following topics:

👁 **Watch:** Set In Your Ways

KEY TERMS

analytic psychology (p. 441)

anxiety (p. 439)

archetype (p. 441)

collective unconscious (p. 441)

consistency paradox (p. 434)

ego (p. 439)

ego defence mechanisms (p. 439)

expectancy (p. 444)

five-factor model (p. 432)

fixation (p. 438)

id (p. 439)

independent construals of self (p. 451)

interdependent construals of self (p. 451)

libido (p. 436)

personality (p. 429)

personality inventory (p. 455)

personality types (p. 429)

possible selves (p. 449)

projective test (p. 456)

psychic determinism (p. 438)

psychobiography (p. 443)

psychodynamic personality theories (p. 436)

reciprocal determinism (p. 446)

repression (p. 439)

self-actualization (p. 442)

self-concept (p. 449)

self-efficacy (p. 447)

self-esteem (p. 450)

self-handicapping (p. 450)

shyness (p. 437)

social intelligence (p. 447)

superego (p. 439)

traits (p. 431)

unconditional positive regard (p. 442)

unconscious (p. 438)

Practice Test

1. William Sheldon predicted that _____ would be brainy, artistic, and introverted.
   - a. endomorphs
   - b. ectomorphs
   - c. mesomorphs
   - d. polymorphs

2. Which of these factors is *not* a trait dimension in the five-factor model?
   - a. creativeness
   - b. neuroticism
   - c. agreeableness
   - d. extraversion

3. Which of these is a *nature* explanation for why people are shy?
   - a. Many of the activities people carry out on the internet are socially isolating.
   - b. Some cultures put a greater emphasis on obedience to authority.
   - c. Some children are more reserved with unfamiliar people from birth.
   - d. Parents may withhold love if children are not successful.

4. According to Freud, at ages four to five children are in the _____ stage of development.
   - a. genital
   - b. oral
   - c. phallic
   - d. anal

5. You attend a lecture that is focusing on archetypes in the collective unconscious. The lecture seems to be about the ideas of _____
   - a. Carl Jung.
   - b. Sigmund Freud.
   - c. Karen Horney.
   - d. Alfred Adler.

6. One of the most important claims of humanistic theories of personality is that people strive for _____
   - a. superiority.
   - b. erogenous zones.
   - c. self-preservation.
   - d. self-actualization.

7. Humanistic theories are _____ because they emphasize an individual's subjective view of reality.
   - a. holistic
   - b. deterministic
   - c. phenomenological
   - d. dispositional

8. With respect to Walter Mischel's personality theory, which of these statements relates to the variable of goals and values?
   - a. Bart wants to graduate from college before he turns 30.
   - b. Reese thinks she can persuade her brother to lend her his car.
   - c. Piper sweats a lot before she takes an exam.
   - d. Vito can do multiplication without a calculator.

9. Jody's best friend Buffy is trying to convince him that he can get a new job. If Buffy is successful, that could have an impact on Jody's sense of _____
   - a. self-efficacy.
   - b. self-regulation.
   - c. libido.
   - d. reciprocal determinism.

10. Brian spends the whole night before he is going to compete in a triathalon reviewing the notes for his philosophy class. This might be an example of _____
    - a. self-efficacy.
    - b. psychic determinism.
    - c. self-handicapping.
    - d. neuroticism.

11. Because Miriam lives in a _____ culture, she is likely to have a(n) _____ construal of self.
    - a. collectivist; dependent
    - b. collectivist; interdependent
    - c. individualistic; interdependent
    - d. collectivist; independent

12. Which features of Facebook pages were *not* related to judgments of narcissism?
    - a. the number of funny quotations
    - b. the attractiveness of the main photograph
    - c. the self-promotion of the main photograph
    - d. the owner's amount of social interaction

13. Chad and Jeremy are both personality theorists. Chad believes that personalities are largely determined before birth. Jeremy believes that personalities arise from life experiences. The dimension on which they disagree is _____
    - a. learning processes versus innate laws of behaviour.
    - b. consciousness versus unconsciousness.
    - c. inner disposition versus outer situation.
    - d. heredity versus environment.

14. The personality test that most directly assesses the dimensions of the five-factor model is the _____
    - a. Rorschach.
    - b. NEO-PI.
    - c. TAT.
    - d. MMPI-2.

15. If you wanted to measure need for achievement, your first choice might be the _____
    - a. Rorschach.
    - b. TAT.
    - c. MMPI-2.
    - d. NEO-PI.

Essay Questions

1. How do traits and situations interact to affect predictions of behaviours?

2. How do humanistic theories give rise to a focus on life stories and psychobiography?

3. What theoretical ideas led to the development of projective personality tests?

Discovering Psychology Viewing Guide

Watch the following video by logging on to MyPsychLab (**www.mypsychlab.com**). After you have watched the video, complete the activities that follow.

Program 15: The Self

PROGRAM REVIEW

1. What name did William James give to the part of the self that focuses on the images we create in the mind of others?
- a. the material self
- b. the spiritual self
- c. the social self
- d. the outer self

2. In Freudian theory, the part of the person that acts as a police officer restraining drives and passions is called the _____
- a. superego.
- b. ego.
- c. id.
- d. libido.

3. When we characterize self-image as a schema, we mean that _____
- a. we use it to organize information about ourselves.
- b. other people see us in terms of the image we project.
- c. it is a good predictor of performance in specific situations.
- d. we rationalize our behaviour to fit into an image.

4. In Albert Bandura's research, people were given the task of improving production at a model furniture factory. They performed best when they believed that performance _____
- a. depended on their intelligence.
- b. related mainly to how confident they felt.
- c. would be given a material reward.
- d. was based on learning an acquirable skill.

5. Which of the following behaviours signals low status in a status transaction?
- a. maintaining eye contact
- b. using complete sentences
- c. moving in slow, smooth way
- d. touching one's face or hair

6. According to the principles of behavioural confirmation, what reaction do people generally have to a person who is depressed?
- a. People sympathetically offer help to the person.
- b. People regard the person as inadequate.
- c People act falsely cheerful to make the person happy.
- d. People treat a depressed person the same as anybody else.

7. What was referred to in the film as a type of psychological genocide?
- a. drugs
- b. decreasing emphasis on education
- c. prejudice
- d. immigration

8. In Teresa Amabile's work on creativity, how did being in a competitive situation affect creativity?
- a. It reduced creativity.
- b. It increased creativity.
- c. Its effects varied depending on the person's innate creativity.
- d. There was no effect.

9. The phrase *mutual constitution* refers to which two components, according to Hazel Markus?
- a. parent and child
- b. art and scholarship
- c. religion and society
- d. self and culture

10. Teresa Amabile is to creativity as _____ is to behavioural confirmation.
- a. Alfred Adler
- b. Patricia Ryan
- c. Mark Snyder
- d. Albert Bandura

QUESTIONS TO CONSIDER

1. Different kinds of standardized tests have been criticized over the years because they may not apply equally well to people of different genders, socioeconomic statuses, or cultural backgrounds. Speculate on what sorts of problems might arise when standardized personality tests (such as the MMPI-2) are used. Think about what sorts of items might lead to problems, and think about what sorts of consequences might arise from the use of a biased instrument.

2. Do you have higher self-esteem in some situations than in others? How do different environments and conditions affect you? Do you think that self-esteem is constant or variable?

3. Compare the social skills of your friends and yourself to people who did not grow up with computers and the internet playing a central role in their lives. Do you see systematic differences in sociability, shyness, and apparent self-concept?

15

Psychological Disorders

onsider these words, written by a 30-year-old woman who was receiving treatment for schizophrenia:

I want to let you know what it is like to be a functional person with schizophrenia in these days and times and what someone with my mental illness faces. . . . I live pretty normal and no one can tell [I'm] mentally ill unless I tell them. . . . The delusions before I got my medicine picked any story line it chose, and changed it at will. As time went by before help, I felt it was taking over my whole brain, and I'd cry wanting my mind and life back.

What are your reactions as you read this young woman's words, an excerpt from a letter to your authors?

If your reactions are similar to ours, you feel a mixture of sadness at her plight, of delight in her willingness to do all she can to cope with the many problems her mental illness creates, of anger toward those who stigmatize her because she may act differently at times, and of hope that, with medication and therapy, her condition may improve. These are but a few of the emotions that clinical and research psychologists and psychiatrists feel as they try to understand and treat mental disorders.

This chapter focuses on the nature and causes of psychological disorders: what they are, why they develop, and how we can explain their causes. The next chapter builds on this knowledge to describe the strategies used to treat and prevent mental illness. Research indicates that 46.4 percent of individuals over age 18 in the United States have suffered from a psychological disorder at some point in their lives (Kessler et al., 2005a). By contrast, the most recent Canadian data estimate that 20 percent of Canadians will experience a mental illness during their lifetime (Public Health Agency of Canada, 2002a). Why is there such a substantial difference between the Canadian and U.S. estimates? This difference is mainly due to the methodology used in the two national studies. While Canadian data were collected from hospitalization rates, the U.S. estimates were drawn from a random sample of 9282 U.S. adults (Kessler et al., 2005a). The method used in the Canadian study is likely to underestimate the prevalence of psychological disorders, so it is quite possible that Canadian rates are higher than those reported. Whatever the actual numbers, in some way or another psychological disorders affect us all. Thus, many of you who read this text are likely to benefit directly from knowledge about psychopathology. Facts alone, however, will not convey the serious impact psychological disorders have on the everyday lives of individuals and families. For instance, the Public Health Agency of Canada (2002a) estimates that 80 percent of us will be affected by the illness of a family member, friend, or colleague. Throughout this chapter, as we discuss categories of psychological disorders, try to envision the real people who live with such a disorder every day. We will share with you their words and lives, as we did at the start of the chapter. We now begin with a discussion of the concept of abnormality.

suicide? Used alcohol or drugs to escape a problem? Almost everyone will answer *yes* to at least one of these questions, which means that almost everyone has experienced the symptoms of a psychological disorder. This chapter looks at the range of psychological functioning that is considered unhealthy or abnormal, often referred to as *psychopathology* or *psychological disorder*. **Psychopathological functioning** involves disruptions in emotional, behavioural, or thought processes that lead to personal distress or that block one's ability to achieve important goals. The field of **abnormal psychology** is the area of psychological investigation most directly concerned with understanding the nature of individual pathologies of mind, mood, and behaviour.

We begin this section by exploring a more precise definition of abnormality and then look at problems of objectivity. We then examine how this definition evolved over hundreds of years of human history.

DECIDING WHAT IS ABNORMAL

What does it mean to say someone is *abnormal* or *suffering from a psychological disorder*? How do psychologists and other clinical practitioners decide what is abnormal? Is it always clear when behaviour moves from the normal to the abnormal category? The judgment that someone has a mental disorder is typically based on the evaluation of the individual's *behavioural* functioning by people with some special authority or power. The terms used to describe these phenomena—*mental disorder*, *mental illness*, or *abnormality*—depend on the particular perspective, training, and cultural background of the evaluator, the situation, and the status of the person being judged.

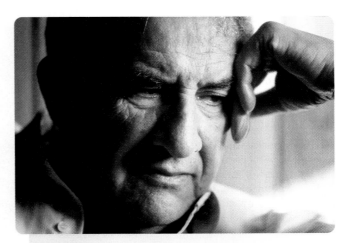

What do you imagine the lives of people with mental illnesses are like?

The Nature of Psychological Disorders

Have you ever worried excessively? Felt depressed or anxious without really knowing why? Been fearful of something you rationally knew could not harm you? Had thoughts about

---

psychopathological functioning Disruptions in emotional, behavioural, or thought processes that lead to personal distress or block one's ability to achieve important goals.

abnormal psychology The area of psychological investigation concerned with understanding the nature of individual pathologies of mind, mood, and behaviour.

Consider the following seven criteria that are used to label behaviour as "abnormal" (Butcher, Mineka, & Hooley, 2008):

1. *Distress or disability.* An individual experiences personal distress or disabled functioning, which produces a risk of physical or psychological deterioration or loss of freedom of action. For example, a man who cannot leave his home without weeping would be unable to pursue ordinary life goals.

2. *Maladaptiveness.* An individual acts in ways that hinder goals, do not contribute to personal well-being, or interfere strongly with the goals of others and the needs of society. Someone who is drinking so heavily that she cannot hold down a job or who is endangering others through her intoxication is displaying maladaptive behaviour.

3. *Irrationality.* An individual acts or talks in ways that are irrational or incomprehensible to others. A man who responds to voices that do not exist in objective reality is behaving irrationally.

4. *Unpredictability.* An individual behaves unpredictably or erratically from situation to situation, as if experiencing a loss of control. A child who smashes his fist through a window for no apparent reason displays unpredictability.

5. *Unconventionality and statistical rarity.* An individual behaves in ways that are statistically rare and that violate social standards of what is acceptable or desirable. Just being statistically unusual, however, does not lead to a psychological judgment of abnormality. For example, possessing genius-level intelligence is extremely rare, but it is also considered desirable. Conversely, having extremely low intelligence is also rare but is considered undesirable; thus it has often been labelled abnormal.

6. *Observer discomfort.* An individual creates discomfort in others by making them feel threatened or distressed in some way. A woman walking down the middle of the sidewalk having a loud conversation with herself creates observer discomfort in other pedestrians trying to avoid her.

7. *Violation of moral and ideal standards.* An individual violates expectations for how one ought to behave with respect to societal norms. Thus, if people generally think it is important to provide care to one's offspring, parents who abandon their children might be considered abnormal.

Can you see why most of these indicators of abnormality may not be immediately apparent to all observers? Consider just the last criterion. Are you mentally ill if you do not wish to work, even if that is abnormal with respect to the norms of society? Or consider a more serious symptom: It is "bad" to have hallucinations in our culture because they are taken as signs of mental disturbance, but it is "good" in cultures in which hallucinations are interpreted as mystical visions from spirit forces. Whose judgment is correct? At the end of this chapter, we will consider some negative consequences and dangers associated with such socially regulated judgments and the decisions based on them.

We are more confident in labelling behaviour as "abnormal" when more than just one of the indicators is present and valid. The more extreme and prevalent the indicators are, the more confident we can be that they point to an abnormal condition. None of these criteria is a *necessary* condition shared by all cases of abnormality. For example, during his murder trial, a Stanford University graduate student who had killed his math professor with a hammer, and then taped a note to the professor's office door that read "No office hours today," reported feeling neither guilt nor remorse. Despite the absence of personal suffering, we would not hesitate to label his overall behaviour as abnormal. It is also true that no single criterion, by itself, is a *sufficient* condition that distinguishes all cases of abnormal behaviour from normal variations in behaviour. The distinction between normal and abnormal is not so much a difference between two independent types of behaviours as it is a matter of the degree to which a person's actions resemble a set of agreed-upon criteria of abnormality. Mental disorder is best thought of as a *continuum* that varies between *mental health* and *mental illness*.

How comfortable do you feel with these ideas about abnormality? Although the criteria seem fairly clear-cut, psychologists still worry about the problem of objectivity.

THE PROBLEM OF OBJECTIVITY

The decision to declare someone psychologically disordered or abnormal is always a *judgment* about behaviour: The goal for many researchers is to make these judgments *objectively*, without any type of bias. For some psychological disorders, like depression or schizophrenia, diagnosis often easily meets the standards of objectivity. Other cases are more problematic. As we have seen throughout our study of psychology, the meaning of behaviour is jointly determined by its *content* and by its *context*. The same act in different settings conveys very different meanings. For example, if a man kisses another man, it may signify a gay relationship in Canada, a ritual greeting in France, or a Mafia "kiss of death" in Sicily. The meaning of a behaviour always depends on context.

Why is objectivity such an important or complex issue? After all, isn't an objective criterion undeniably accurate? History is full of examples of situations in which judgments of abnormality were made by individuals to preserve their moral or political power. This was certainly true of European settlers to Canada who brought with them the attitudes and perceptions of colonizers. For them, everything European was considered superior: European values and tastes were "normal" and civilized whereas Canadian Aboriginals were seen as dangerous savages. In his 1992 book entitled *Contact and Conflict: Indian–European Relations in British Columbia, 1774–1890*, historian Robin Fisher documents the negative views of British colonizers. He quotes one writer, J. R. Anderson, who described the Aboriginal character as "treacherous, vindictive, revengeful and murderous" (Fisher, 1992, p. 73); another, Capt. W. C. Grant, noted that "the red man is savage and perverse. He prefers war to peace, noise to quiet, dirt to cleanliness, and jugglery to religion" (Fisher, 1992, p. 90). Because British colonists accepted these racist views of the "abnormal" character of Native Canadians as accurate and irrefutable, their consequences were often horrific. Theories of Aboriginal inferiority handily rationalized colonialism, persecution, and maltreatment: "The imagined 'savagery' of Natives justified the use of violence as a natural and inevitable process in the expansion of 'civilized' European societies" (Furniss, 1997–1998, p. 24).

Once an individual has obtained an "abnormal" label, people are inclined to interpret later behaviour to confirm that judgment. **David Rosenhan** (1973, 1975) and his colleagues demonstrated that it may be impossible to be judged "sane" in an "insane place."

> Rosenhan and seven other sane people gained admission to different psychiatric hospitals by pretending to have a single symptom: hallucinations. All eight of these pseudo-patients were diagnosed on admission as having either paranoid schizophrenia or bipolar disorder. Once admitted, they behaved normally in every way. Rosenhan observed, however, that when a sane person is in an insane place, he or she is likely to be judged insane, and any behaviour is likely to be reinterpreted to fit the context. If the pseudo-patients discussed their situation in a rational way with the staff, they were reported to be using "intellectualization" defences, while their taking notes of their observations was evidence of "writing behaviour." The pseudo-patients remained on the wards for almost three weeks, on average, and not one was identified by the staff as sane. When they were finally released—only with the help of spouses or colleagues—their discharge diagnosis was still "schizophrenia" but "in remission." That is, their symptoms were no longer active.

Rosenhan's research demonstrates how judgments of abnormality rely on factors beyond behaviour itself.

In the view of psychiatrist **Thomas Szasz**, mental illness does not even exist—it is a "myth" (1974, 2004). Szasz argues that the symptoms used as evidence of mental illness are merely medical labels that sanction professional intervention into what are social problems—deviant people violating social norms. Once labelled, these people can be treated either benignly or harshly for their problem "of being different," with no threat of disturbing the existing status quo.

Few clinicians would go this far, in large part because the focus of much research and treatment is on understanding and alleviating personal distress. For most of the disorders we will describe in this chapter, individuals experience their own behaviour as abnormal, or poorly adapted to the environment. Even so, this discussion suggests that there can be no altogether objective assessments of abnormality. As we describe each type of psychological disorder, try to understand why clinicians believe the cluster of symptoms represents behaviour patterns that are more serious for the individual than mere violations of social norms.

CLASSIFYING PSYCHOLOGICAL DISORDERS

Why is it helpful to have a classification system for psychological disorders? What advantages are gained by moving beyond a global assessment that abnormality exists to distinguish among different types of abnormalities? A **psychological diagnosis** is the label given to an abnormality by classifying and categorizing the observed behaviour pattern into an approved diagnostic system. Such a diagnosis is in many ways more difficult to make than a medical diagnosis. In the medical context, a doctor can rely on physical evidence, such as X-rays, blood tests, and biopsies, to inform a diagnostic decision. In the case of psychological disorders, the evidence for diagnosis comes from interpretations of a person's actions and thoughts. To create greater consistency among clinicians and coherence in their diagnostic evaluations, psychologists have helped to develop a system of diagnosis and classification that provides

precise descriptions of symptoms, as well as other criteria to help practitioners decide whether a person's behaviour is evidence of a particular disorder.

To be most useful, a diagnostic system should provide the following three benefits:

- *Common shorthand language.* To facilitate a quick and clear understanding among clinicians or researchers working in the field of psychopathology, practitioners seek a common set of terms with agreed-upon meanings. A diagnostic category, such as *depression*, summarizes a large and complex collection of information, including characteristic symptoms and the typical course of the disorder. In clinical settings, such as clinics and hospitals, a diagnostic system allows mental health professionals to communicate more effectively about the people they are helping. Researchers studying different aspects of psychopathology or evaluating treatment programs must agree on the disorder they are observing.
- *Understanding of causality.* Ideally, a diagnosis of a specific disorder should make clear the causes of the symptoms. As is the case for physical illness, the same symptoms may arise for more than one disorder. A goal of a classification system is to indicate why practitioners should interpret particular patterns of symptoms as evidence for specific underlying disorders.
- *Treatment plan.* A diagnosis should also suggest what types of treatments to consider for particular disorders. Researchers and clinicians have found that certain treatments or therapies work most effectively for specific kinds of psychological disorders. For example, drugs that are quite effective in treating schizophrenia do not help and may even hurt people with depression. Further advances in knowledge about the effectiveness and specificity of treatments will make fast and reliable diagnosis even more important.

Historical Perspectives on Classification Throughout history, humans have feared psychological disorders, often associating them with evil. Because of this fear, people have reacted aggressively and decisively to any behaviours they perceived as bizarre or abnormal. People who have exhibited such behaviours have been imprisoned and subjected to radical medical treatments. Until the end of the 18th century, the mentally ill in Western societies were perceived as mindless beasts who could be controlled only with chains and physical discipline.

In the latter part of the 18th century, a new perspective about the origins of abnormal behaviour emerged: People began to perceive those with psychological problems as *sick*, suffering from illness, rather than as *possessed* or *immoral*. As a result, a number of reforms were gradually implemented in the facilities for the insane. French physician **Philippe Pinel** (1745–1826) was one of the first clinicians to use these ideas to attempt to develop a classification system for psychological difficulties based on the idea that disorders of thought, mood, and behaviour are similar in many ways to physical, organic illnesses. According to such a system, each disorder has a group of characteristic symptoms that distinguishes it from other disorders and from healthy functioning. Disorders are classified

---

psychological diagnosis The label given to a psychological abnormality by classifying and categorizing the observed behaviour pattern into an approved diagnostic system.

according to the patterns of observed symptoms, the circumstances surrounding the onset of the disturbance, the natural course of the disorder, and its response to treatment. Such classification systems are modelled after the biological classification systems naturalists use and are intended to help clinicians identify common disorders more easily.

In 1896, **Emil Kraepelin** (1855–1926), a German psychiatrist, was responsible for creating the first truly comprehensive *classification system* of psychological disorders. Strongly motivated by a belief that there was a physical basis to psychological problems, he gave the process of psychological diagnosis and classification the flavour of medical diagnosis. That flavour remains today in the diagnostic system we now review.

DSM-IV-TR In Canada and the United States, the most widely accepted classification scheme is one developed by the American Psychiatric Association. It is called the *Diagnostic and Statistical Manual of Mental Disorders*. The most recent version, published in 2000 as a revision of the fourth edition, is known by clinicians and researchers as **DSM-IV-TR**. It classifies, defines, and describes over 200 mental disorders.

To reduce the diagnostic difficulties caused by variability in approaches to psychological disorders, *DSM-IV-TR* emphasizes the *description* of patterns of symptoms and courses of disorders rather than etiological theories or treatment strategies. The purely descriptive terms allow clinicians and researchers to use a common language to describe problems while leaving room for disagreement and continued research about which theoretical models best *explain* the problems.

The first version of the *DSM*, which appeared in 1952 (*DSM-I*), listed several dozen mental illnesses. *DSM-II*, introduced in 1968, revised the diagnostic system to make it more compatible with another popular system, the World Health Organization's *International Classification of Diseases (ICD)*. The fourth edition of the *DSM* (*DSM-IV*, 1994) emerged after several years of intense work by committees of scholars. To make their changes (from the *DSM-III-Revised*, which appeared in 1987), these committees carefully scrutinized large bodies of research on psychopathology and also tested proposed changes for workability in actual clinical settings. *DSM-IV* is also fully compatible with the 10th edition of the *ICD*. *DSM-IV-TR* (2000) incorporated a review of the research literature that had accumulated since *DSM-IV*. Because the changes largely affected the supporting text, rather than the system of classification, the revision was termed a "text revision" which yielded the name *DSM-IV-TR*. After this brief history of the *DSM*, you probably won't be surprised to learn that committees are meeting to bring the newest research to bear on *DSM-V*, which is scheduled to appear in 2012. In the *Critical Thinking in Your Life* box, we give you a sense of the process that could lead to the inclusion of new disorders in *DSM-V*.

To encourage clinicians to consider the psychological, social, and physical factors that may be associated with a psychological disorder, *DSM-IV-TR* uses dimensions, or *axes*, that portray information about all these factors (see **Table 15.1**). Most of the principal clinical disorders are contained on Axis I. Included here are all disorders that emerge in childhood, except for mental retardation. Axis II lists mental retardation as well as personality disorders. These problems may accompany Axis I disorders. Axis III incorporates information about general medical conditions, such as diabetes, that may be relevant to understanding or treating an Axis I or II disorder. Axes IV and V provide supplemental information that can be useful when planning an individual's treatment or assessing the *prognosis* (predictions of future change). Axis IV assesses psychosocial and environmental problems that may explain patients' stress responses or their resources for coping with stress. On Axis V, a clinician evaluates the global level of an individual's functioning. A full diagnosis in the *DSM-IV-TR* system would involve consideration of each of the axes.

Throughout this chapter, we will provide estimates of the frequency with which individuals experience particular psychological disorders. These estimates arise from research projects in which mental health histories are obtained from large samples of the population. Most of the Canadian figures are available for the prevalence of different disorders over a one-year period, with some occasional evidence of prevalence over a lifetime (Public Health Agency of Canada, 2002a). The figures we will generally cite come from *A Report on Mental Illnesses in Canada*, which was based on national and provincial hospitalizations and mortality data. It is important to emphasize that often the same individuals have experienced more than one disorder simultaneously at some point in their life span, a phenomenon known as **comorbidity**. (*Morbidity* refers to the occurrence of disease. *Comorbidity* refers to the co-occurrence of diseases.) A recent U.S. study found that 45 percent of the people who had experienced one disorder in a 12-month period had actually experienced two or more; although there are no comparable Canadian data, there is no reason to believe that comorbidity rates would be any different in Canada. Researchers have begun to study intensively the patterns of comorbidity of different psychological disorders (Kessler, Chiu, Demler, & Walters, 2005b).

In the United States, the Salem witchcraft trials were an outgrowth of a desperate attempt to affix blame for frighteningly bizarre behaviour among the Puritan colonists. What general attitudes were common toward the mentally ill in those times?

DSM-IV-TR The current diagnostic and statistical manual of the American Psychological Association that classifies, defines, and describes mental disorders.

comorbidity The experience of more than one disorder at the same time.

TABLE 15.1 The Five Axes of *DSM-IV-TR*

Axis	Classes of Information	Description
Axis I	Clinical disorders	These mental disorders present symptoms or patterns of behavioural or psychological problems that typically are painful or impair an area of functioning. Included are disorders that emerge in infancy, childhood, or adolescence.
Axis II	(a) Personality disorders (b) Mental retardation	These are dysfunctional patterns of perceiving and responding to the world.
Axis III	General medical conditions	This axis codes physical problems relevant to understanding or treating an individual's psychological disorders on Axes I and II.
Axis IV	Psychosocial and environmental problems	This axis codes psychosocial and environmental stressors that may affect the diagnosis and treatment of an individual's disorder and the likelihood of recovery.
Axis V	Global assessment of functioning	This axis codes the individual's overall level of current functioning in the psychological, social, and occupational domains.

Evolution of Diagnostic Categories The diagnostic categories and the methods used to organize and present them have shifted with each revision of the *DSM*. These shifts reflect changes in the opinions of a majority of mental health experts about exactly what constitutes a psychological disorder and where the lines between different types of disorders should be drawn. They also reflect changing perspectives among the public about what constitutes *abnormality*.

In the revision process of each *DSM*, some diagnostic categories were dropped and others added. For example, with the introduction of *DSM-III*, in 1980, the traditional distinction between *neurotic* and *psychotic* disorders was eliminated. **Neurotic disorders**, or *neuroses*, were originally conceived of as relatively common psychological problems in which a person did not have signs of brain abnormalities, did not display grossly irrational thinking, and did not violate basic norms, but he or she did experience subjective distress or a pattern of self-defeating or inadequate coping strategies. **Psychotic disorders**, or *psychoses*, were thought to differ in both quality and severity from neurotic problems. It was believed that psychotic behaviour deviated significantly from social norms and was accompanied by a profound disturbance in rational thinking and general emotional and thought processes. The *DSM-III* advisory committees felt that the terms *neurotic disorders* and *psychotic disorders* had become too general in their meaning to have much usefulness as diagnostic categories. (However, they continue to be used by many psychiatrists and psychologists to characterize the general level of disturbance in a person.)

We want to note a final aspect of classification that has evolved over time. Historically, people with mental illnesses were often labelled with the name of their disorder. For example, clinicians referred to people as "schizophrenics" or "phobics." That didn't happen for physical illnesses—people with cancer were never known as "cancerics." Clinicians and researchers now take care to separate the person from the diagnosis. People have schizophrenic disorders or phobias, just as they have cancer or the flu. The hope is that appropriate treatments can alleviate each condition so it no longer applies to the person.

The Concept of Insanity Before we turn to the causes of mental illness, we want to turn our attention briefly to the concept of insanity. **Insanity** is not defined in *DSM-IV-TR*; there is no accepted clinical definition of insanity. Rather, insanity is a concept that belongs to popular culture and to the legal system. The treatment of insanity in the law dates back to England in 1843, when Daniel M'Naghten was found not guilty of murder by reason of insanity. M'Naghten's intended victim was the British prime minister—M'Naghten believed that God had instructed him to commit the murder. (He accidentally killed the prime minister's secretary instead.) Because of M'Naghten's delusions, he was sent to a mental hospital rather than to prison.

The anger surrounding this verdict—even Queen Victoria was infuriated—prompted the House of Lords to articulate a guideline, known as the M'Naghten rule, to limit claims of insanity. This rule specifies that a criminal must not "know the nature and quality of the act he was doing; or, if he did know it, that he did not know he was doing what was wrong." Does the M'Naghten rule seem like a fair test of guilt or innocence? With advances in the understanding of mental illness, researchers became more aware of circumstances in which a criminal might know right from wrong—a criminal might understand that what he or she was doing was illegal or immoral—but still might not be able to suppress the actions.

"Not guilty due to mental disorder" is a legal phrase used by the Canadian courts to declare people not legally responsible for their acts. And despite the great attention that this plea receives in the media—and thus the public's great awareness of it—very few people in Canada use this plea and even fewer

---

neurotic disorders Mental disorders in which a person does not have signs of brain abnormalities and does not display grossly irrational thinking or violate basic norms but does experience subjective distress; a category dropped from *DSM-III*.

psychotic disorders Severe mental disorders in which a person experiences impairments in reality testing manifested through thought, emotional, or perceptual difficulties; no longer used as diagnostic category after *DSM-III*.

insanity The legal (not clinical) designation for the state of an individual judged to be legally irresponsible or incompetent.

of these cases relate to murder or even attempted murder (Hart & Roesch, 2007). One study estimated that about 0.2 percent of all cases that come to court consider this option (Hylton, 1995) and, of them, fewer than 10 percent relate to murder or attempted murder (Roesch et al., 1997).

THE ETIOLOGY OF PSYCHOPATHOLOGY

Etiology refers to the factors that cause or contribute to the development of psychological and medical problems. Knowing why the disorder occurs, what its origins are, and how it affects thought and emotional and behavioural processes may lead to new ways of treating and, ideally, preventing it. An analysis of causality will be an important part of our discussion of each individual disorder. Here we introduce two general categories of causal factors: biological and psychological.

Biological Approaches Building on the heritage of the medical model, modern biological approaches assume that psychological disturbances are directly attributable to underlying biological factors. Biological researchers and clinicians most often investigate structural abnormalities in the brain, biochemical processes, and genetic influences.

The brain is a complex organ whose interrelated elements are held in delicate balance. Subtle alterations in its chemical messengers—the neurotransmitters—or in its tissue can have significant effects. Genetic factors, brain injury, and infection are a few of the causes of these alterations. We have seen in earlier chapters that technological advances in brain-imaging techniques allow mental health professionals to view the structure of the brain and specific biochemical processes in living individuals without surgery. Using these techniques, biologically oriented researchers are discovering new links between psychological disorders and specific abnormalities in the brain. In addition, continuing advances in the field of behavioural genetics have improved researchers' abilities to identify the links between specific genes and the presence of psychological disorders. We will look to these different types of biological explanations throughout the chapter as we try to understand the nature of various forms of abnormality.

Psychological Approaches Psychological approaches focus on the causal role of psychological or social factors in the development of psychopathology. These approaches perceive personal experiences, traumas, conflicts, and environmental factors as the roots of psychological disorders. We will outline four dominant psychological models of abnormality: the psychodynamic, the behavioural, the cognitive, and the sociocultural.

Psychodynamic. Like the biological approach, the psychodynamic model holds that the causes of psychopathology are located inside the person. However, according to **Sigmund Freud**, who developed this model, the internal causal factors are psychological rather than biological. As we noted in earlier chapters, Freud believed that many psychological disorders were simply an extension of "normal" processes of psychic conflict and ego defence that all people experience. In the psychodynamic model, early childhood experiences shape both normal and abnormal behaviour.

In psychodynamic theory, behaviour is motivated by drives and wishes of which people are often unaware. Symptoms of psychopathology have their roots in *unconscious conflict* and thoughts. If the unconscious is conflicted and tension-filled, a person will be plagued by anxiety and other disorders. Much of this psychic conflict arises from struggles between the irrational, pleasure-seeking impulses of the *id* and the internalized social constraints imposed by the *superego*. The *ego* is normally the arbiter of this struggle; however, its ability to perform its function can be weakened by abnormal development in childhood (see Chapter 14). Individuals attempt to avoid the pain caused by conflicting motives and anxiety with *defence mechanisms*, such as repression or denial. Defences can become overused, distorting reality or leading to self-defeating behaviours. The individual may then expend so much psychic energy in defences against anxiety and conflict that there is little energy left to contribute to a productive and satisfying life.

Behavioural. Because of their emphasis on observable responses, behavioural theorists have little use for hypothetical psychodynamic processes. These theorists argue that abnormal behaviours are acquired in the same fashion as healthy behaviours—through learning and reinforcement. They do not focus on internal psychological phenomena or early childhood experiences. Instead, they focus on the *current* behaviour and the *current* conditions or reinforcements that sustain the behaviour. The symptoms of psychological disorders arise because an individual has learned self-defeating or ineffective ways of behaving. By discovering the environmental contingencies that maintain any undesirable, abnormal behaviour, an investigator or clinician can then recommend treatment to change those contingencies and extinguish the unwanted behaviour. Behaviourists rely on both classical and operant conditioning models (recall Chapter 7) to understand the processes that can result in maladaptive behaviour.

Cognitive. Cognitive perspectives on psychopathology are often used to supplement behavioural views. The cognitive perspective suggests that the origins of psychological disorders cannot always be found in the objective reality of stimulus environments, reinforcers, and overt responses. What matters as well is the way people perceive or think about themselves and about their relations with other people and the environment. Among the cognitive variables that can guide—or misguide—adaptive responses are a person's perceived degree of control over important reinforcers, a person's beliefs in his or her ability to cope with threatening events, and interpretations of events in terms of situational or personal factors. The cognitive approach suggests that psychological problems are the result of distortions in perceptions of the reality of a situation, faulty reasoning, or poor problem solving.

Sociocultural. The sociocultural perspective on psychopathology emphasizes the role culture plays in both the diagnosis and etiology of abnormal behaviour. We already gave you a taste of the impact of culture on diagnosis when we described the problem of objectivity. We suggested that behaviours are interpreted in different ways in different cultures: The threshold at which a certain type of behaviour will cause problems in adjustment for an individual will depend, in part, on how that behaviour is viewed in its cultural context. With respect to etiology, the particular cultural circumstances in which people live may define an environment that helps bring about distinctive types or subtypes of psychopathology.

---

etiology The causes of, or factors related to, the development of a disorder.

We have now given you a general sense of the types of explanations researchers give for the emergence of mental illness. It is worth noting that contemporary researchers increasingly take an *interactionist* perspective on psychopathology, seeing it as the product of a complex interaction between a number of biological and psychological factors. For example, genetic predispositions may make a person vulnerable to a psychological disorder by affecting neurotransmitter levels or hormone levels, but psychological or social stresses or certain learned behaviours may be required for the disorder to develop fully.

Now that we have given you a basic framework for thinking about abnormality, we get to the core information that you will want to know: the causes and consequences of major psychological disorders, such as anxiety, depression, and schizophrenia. For each category, we will begin by describing what sufferers experience and how they appear to observers. Then we will consider how each of the major biological and psychological approaches to etiology explains the development of these disorders.

There are many other categories of psychopathology that we will not have time to examine. However, what follows is a capsule summary of some of the most important we must omit:

- *Substance-use disorders* include both dependence on and abuse of alcohol and drugs. We discussed many issues of substance abuse in the broader context of states of consciousness (see Chapter 6).
- *Sexual disorders* involve problems with sexual inhibition or dysfunction and deviant sexual practices.
- *Eating disorders*, such as anorexia and bulimia, were discussed in Chapter 12.

As you read about the symptoms and experiences that are typical of the various psychological disturbances, you may begin to feel that some of the characteristics seem to apply to you—at least part of the time—or to someone you know. Some of the disorders that we will consider are not uncommon, so it would be surprising if they sounded completely alien. Many people have human frailties that appear on the list of criteria for a particular psychological disorder. Recognition of this familiarity can further your understanding of abnormal psychology, but remember that a diagnosis for any disorder depends on a number of criteria and requires the judgment of a trained mental health professional. Please resist the temptation to use this new knowledge to diagnose friends and family members as pathological. However, if the chapter leaves you uneasy about mental health issues, please note that most colleges and universities have counselling centres for students with such concerns.

STOP AND REVIEW

❶ Jerry has such an overwhelming fear of spiders that he will not enter a room until someone he trusts assures him the room has no spiders in it. By what criteria might we decide that Jerry's behaviour is abnormal?

❷ What are three important benefits provided by the classification of mental disorders?

❸ Why does culture play a role in the diagnosis of psychopathology?

CRITICAL THINKING Consider the study in which David Rosenhan and seven other people were admitted to psychiatric hospitals. Why might they have chosen "hallucinations" as their pretend symptom?

Anxiety Disorders

Everyone experiences anxiety or fear in certain life situations. For some people, however, anxiety becomes problematic enough to interfere with their ability to function effectively or enjoy everyday life. It has been estimated that 12.6 percent of the Canadian adult population has experienced symptoms characteristic of the various **anxiety disorders** within a single year (Public Health Agency of Canada, 2002b). Although anxiety plays a key role in each of these disorders, they differ in the extent to which anxiety is experienced, the severity of the anxiety, and the situations that trigger the anxiety. We will review five major categories: generalized anxiety disorder, panic disorder, phobic disorder, obsessive-compulsive disorder, and post-traumatic stress disorder. We then consider the causes of these disorders.

GENERALIZED ANXIETY DISORDER

When a person feels anxious or worried most of the time for at least six months when not threatened by any specific danger, clinicians diagnose **generalized anxiety disorder**. The anxiety is often focused on specific life circumstances, such as unrealistic concerns about finances or the well-being of a loved one. The way the anxiety is expressed—the specific symptoms—varies from person to person, but for a diagnosis of generalized anxiety disorder to be made, the patient must also suffer from at least three other symptoms, such as muscle tension, fatigue, restlessness, poor concentration, irritability, or sleep difficulties. Among Canadian adults, 1.1 percent have experienced generalized anxiety disorder in a one-year period (Public Health Agency of Canada, 2002b).

Generalized anxiety disorder leads to impaired functioning because the person's worries cannot be controlled or put aside. With the focus of attention on the sources of anxiety, the individual cannot attend sufficiently to social or job obligations. These difficulties are compounded by the physical symptoms associated with the disorder.

PANIC DISORDER

In contrast to the chronic presence of anxiety in generalized anxiety disorder, sufferers of **panic disorder** experience unexpected, severe *panic attacks* that may last only minutes. These attacks begin with a feeling of intense apprehension, fear, or terror. Accompanying these feelings are physical symptoms of anxiety, including autonomic hyperactivity (such as rapid heart rate), dizziness, faintness, or sensations of choking or smothering. The attacks are unexpected in the sense that they are not brought about by something concrete in the situation. A panic disorder is diagnosed when an individual has recurrent unexpected panic attacks and also begins to have persistent concerns about the possibility of having more attacks. Research suggests

anxiety disorders Mental disorders marked by psychological arousal, feeling of tension, and intense apprehension without apparent reason.

generalized anxiety disorder An anxiety disorder in which an individual feels anxious and worried most of the time for at least six months when not threatened by any specific danger or object.

panic disorder An anxiety disorder in which sufferers experience unexpected, severe panic attacks that begin with a feeling of intense apprehension, fear, or terror.

HOW DO DISORDERS ENTER THE DSM?

As this chapter unfolds, you will read several descriptions of psychological disorders that are outlined in *DSM-IV-TR* (2000). Before you consider these disorders, we'd like you to reflect on the process through which clinicians achieve consensus that a particular disorder belongs in the *DSM*. For each disorder, this process begins with close observation: Therapists and researchers pay careful attention to people's symptoms and how those symptoms cluster together. Even for diagnostic categories that are well established—such as the mood disorders that we discuss later in the chapter—researchers continue to collect new data with the goal of improving the reliability and validity of the system of classification (Klein, 2008).

Although *DSM-IV-TR* is a formidable volume, clinical observations continue to lead to proposals for new disorders. An appendix in *DSM-IV* (1994) briefly described about 20 disorders that had been proposed but required "further study": The authors of *DSM-IV* asserted that, given the state of research knowledge, insufficient evidence supported the inclusion of those disorders at that moment in time.

To provide you with a concrete example of how researchers build the case for a new disorder, we will explore one disorder from that list: *binge eating disorder*.

You already had a brief encounter with binge eating disorder (BED) in Chapter 12. There, we defined BED partially in contrast to another eating disorder: We suggested that BED is diagnosed when people engage in regular episodes of binge eating without the purges that accompany bulimia nervosa. In addition, we suggested that people who suffer from BED experience a loss of control during these binges and that the binges cause them great distress.

Note two important features of this definition (Striegel-Moore & Franko, 2008). First, the definition suggests how BED is different from other eating disorders, despite the overlap in some symptoms (that is, bingeing). When clinicians propose a new diagnostic category, they must firmly establish that the new disorder is distinct from well-established disorders. Second, the definition of BED mentions a cluster of symptoms. When clinicians propose a new diagnostic category, they are making a strong assertion that a particular set of experiences regularly co-occur.

The definition of a disorder serves, in a sense, as a hypothesis: The clinicians who propose the disorder are predicting that data will confirm that people experience this distinctive constellation of symptoms. For BED, this has proven to be the case. In one study, researchers engaged in face-to-face interviews with 9282 adults in the United States (Hudson et al., 2007). To determine whether people suffered from BED, they used the major criteria from *DSM-IV*. In their sample, 3.5 percent of the women and 2.0 percent of the men met those criteria. Data of this type support the hypothesis that BED exists as a disorder with a unique set of symptoms and consequences.

Still, some data on BED has encouraged researchers to re-examine features of the diagnosis (Striegel-Moore & Franko, 2008). For example, the definitions of other eating disorders include the diagnostic feature "undue influence of body weight or shape on self-evaluation" (*DSM-IV*, 1994, p. 545). Researchers have begun to consider whether this feature should also be included for BED (Grilo et al., 2008). Studies suggest that people who meet the criteria for BED and who also show "undue influence," experience greater distress than people who do not show this influence. However, researchers have yet to reach consensus on how the inclusion of this feature would affect diagnoses of BED.

The goal of research on BED—as well as on other disorders, old and new—is to provide the most valid possible diagnoses. Researchers labour so that the *DSM* will provide valid diagnoses that allow for the provision of appropriate treatments—and, ultimately, for a minimization of people's distress.

- Why do the definitions of disorders include clusters of symptoms?

- Why does improved diagnosis often allow improved treatment?

---

that 0.7 percent of Canadian adults experienced panic disorder in a single year (Public Health Agency of Canada, 2002b).

In *DSM-IV-TR*, panic disorder must be diagnosed as occurring with or without the simultaneous presence of agoraphobia. **Agoraphobia** is an extreme fear of being in public places or open spaces from which escape may be difficult or embarrassing. Individuals with agoraphobia usually fear such places as crowded rooms, malls, buses, and freeways. They are often afraid that if they experience some kind of difficulty outside the home, such as a loss of bladder control or panic attack symptoms, help might not be available or the situation will be embarrassing to them. These fears deprive individuals of their freedom, and, in extreme cases, they become prisoners in their own homes.

---

agoraphobia An extreme fear of being in public places or open spaces from which escape may be difficult or embarrassing.

Why might agoraphobia cause people to become "prisoners" in their own homes?

TABLE 15.2 Common Phobias
Social phobias (fear of being observed doing something humiliating)
Specific phobias
Animal type
Cats (ailurophobia)
Dogs (cynophobia)
Insects (insectophobia)
Spiders (arachnophobia)
Snakes (ophidiophobia)
Rodents (rodentophobia)
Natural environment type
Storms (brontophobia)
Heights (acrophobia)
Blood–injection–injury type
Blood (hemophobia)
Needles (belonephobia)
Situational type
Closed spaces (claustrophobia)
Railways (siderodromophobia)

Can you see why agoraphobia is related to panic disorder? For some (but not all) people who suffer from panic attacks, the dread of the next attack—the helpless feelings it engenders—can be enough to imprison them. The person suffering from agoraphobia may leave the safety of home but almost always with extreme anxiety.

PHOBIAS

Fear is a rational reaction to an objectively identified external danger (such as a fire in one's home or a mugging attack) that may induce a person to flee or to attack in self-defence. In contrast, a person with a **phobia** suffers from a persistent and irrational fear of a specific object, activity, or situation that is excessive and unreasonable given the reality of the threat.

Many people feel uneasy about spiders or snakes (or even multiple-choice tests). These mild fears do not prevent people from carrying out their everyday activities. Phobias, however, interfere with adjustment, cause significant distress, and inhibit necessary action toward goals. Even a very specific, apparently limited phobia can have a great impact on one's whole life. *DSM-IV-TR* defines two categories of phobias: *social phobias* and *specific phobias* (see **Table 15.2**).

Social phobia is a persistent, irrational fear that arises in anticipation of a public situation in which an individual can be observed by others. A person with a social phobia fears that he or she will act in ways that could be embarrassing. The person recognizes that the fear is excessive and unreasonable yet feels compelled by the fear to avoid situations in which public scrutiny is possible. Social phobia often involves a self-fulfilling prophecy. A person may be so fearful of the scrutiny and rejection of others that enough anxiety is created to actually impair performance. Even positive social exchanges cause anxiety for people with social phobias: They worry that they have set standards that they will not be able to meet in the future (Weeks, Heimberg, Rodebaugh, & Norton, 2008). Among Canadian adults, one-year prevalence estimates are that 6.7 percent experience a social phobia (Public Health Agency of Canada, 2002b).

Specific phobias occur in response to several different types of objects or situations. As shown in Table 15.2, specific phobias are further categorized into several subtypes. For exam-

ple, an individual suffering from an *animal-type specific phobia* might have a phobic response to spiders. In each case, the phobic response is produced either in the presence of or in anticipation of the feared specific object or situation. Research suggests that between 6.2 and 8 percent of adults in Canada experience a specific phobia during a single year (Public Health Agency of Canada, 2002b).

OBSESSIVE-COMPULSIVE DISORDER

Some people with anxiety disorders get locked into specific patterns of thought and behaviour. Consider the following case:

> Only a year or so ago, 17-year-old Jim seemed to be a normal adolescent with many talents and interests. Then, almost overnight, he was transformed into a lonely outsider, excluded from social life by his psychological disabilities. Specifically, he developed an obsession with washing.

fear A rational reaction to an objectively identified external danger that may induce a person to flee or attack in self-defence.

phobia A persistent and irrational fear (of a specific object, activity, or situation) that is excessive and unreasonable, given the reality of the threat.

social phobia A persistent, irrational fear that arises in anticipation of a public situation in which an individual can be observed by others.

specific phobias Phobias that occur in response to specific types of objects or situations.

Haunted by the notion that he was dirty—in spite of what his senses told him—he began to spend more of his time cleansing himself of imaginary dirt. At first, his ritual washings were confined to weekends and evenings, but soon they began to consume all his time, forcing him to drop out of school. (Rapoport, 1989)

Jim is suffering from a condition known as **obsessive-compulsive disorder (OCD)**, which has been estimated to affect 1.8 percent of Canadian adults each year (Public Health Agency of Canada, 2002b). *Obsessions* are thoughts, images, or impulses (such as Jim's belief that he is unclean) that recur or persist despite a person's efforts to suppress them. Obsessions are experienced as an unwanted invasion of consciousness; they seem to be senseless or repugnant; and they are unacceptable to the person experiencing them. You probably have had some sort of mild obsessional experience, such as the intrusion of petty worries—"Did I really lock the door?" or "Did I turn off the oven?" The obsessive thoughts of people with obsessive-compulsive disorder are much more compelling, cause much more distress, and may interfere with their social or occupational functioning.

Compulsions are repetitive and purposeful *acts* (such as Jim's washing) performed according to certain rules or in a ritualized manner in response to an obsession. Compulsive behaviour is performed to reduce or prevent the discomfort associated with some dreaded situation, but it is either unreasonable or clearly excessive. Typical compulsions include irresistible urges to clean, to check that lights or appliances have been turned off, and to count objects or possessions.

At least initially, people with obsessive-compulsive disorder resist carrying out their compulsions. When they are calm, they view their compulsion as senseless. When anxiety rises, however, the power of the ritual compulsive behaviour to relieve tension seems irresistible. Part of the pain experienced by people with this mental problem is created by their frustration at recognizing the irrationality or excessive nature of their obsessions without being able to eliminate them.

POST-TRAUMATIC STRESS DISORDER

In Chapter 13, we described one psychological consequence of traumatic events: People experience post-traumatic stress disorder (PTSD), an anxiety disorder that is characterized by the persistent re-experience of traumatic events through distressing recollections, dreams, hallucinations, or flashbacks (see also Chapter 13). Individuals may develop PTSD in response to rape, life-threatening events, severe injury, or natural disasters. People can develop PTSD when they themselves have been the victims of the trauma or when they have witnessed others

Why do people with obsessive-compulsive disorder engage in behaviours such as repetitive hand-washing?

being victimized. People who suffer from PTSD are also likely to suffer simultaneously from other psychopathologies, such as major depression, substance-abuse problems, and sexual dysfunction (Kilpatrick et al., 2003).

It is difficult to provide an accurate estimate of the percentage of Canadians who experience PTSD during their lifetime because research to date provides inconsistent information. However, the most reliable data suggest that PTSD affects between 2 and 5 percent of Canadians (Centre for Addiction and Mental Health, 2004). Studies consistently reveal that most adults have experienced an event that could be defined as traumatic, such as a serious accident, a tragic death, or physical or sexual abuse (Widom, Dutton, Czaja, & DuMont, 2005). One study with 1824 Swedish adults found that 80.8 percent had experienced at least one traumatic event (Frans, Rimmö, Åberg, & Fredrikson, 2005). In this sample, men had experienced more traumatic events than women, but women were twice as likely to develop PTSD. The researchers suggested that women's greater distress in response to traumatic events helped explain this difference.

Much attention has focused on the prevalence of PTSD in the wake of traumas with widespread impact. The issue caught the attention of Canadian media following Major General Roméo Dallaire's personal battle with this disorder following his return from the Rwandan civil war of 1994 in which he unsuccessfully tried to convince Western governments to help stop the genocide (see Fisher, 1998). Thereafter, the Canadian military ombudsman conducted an investigation of PTSD among members of the Canadian armed forces and estimated that the number of military personnel suffering from PTSD could be as high as 10 to 20 percent (Marin, 2001). In the United States, one study evaluated Pentagon employees for symptoms of PTSD two years after the terrorist attack (Grieger et al., 2005). Among the employees in the sample, 14 percent reported symptoms of PTSD. Perhaps not surprisingly, individuals who had actually been injured or who had witnessed dead bodies were the most affected.

Post-traumatic stress disorder severely disrupts sufferers' lives. How do researchers go about the complex task of exploring the origins of PTSD and other anxiety disorders? Understanding the origins gives hope for eliminating the psychological distress.

---

obsessive-compulsive disorder (OCD) A mental disorder characterized by obsessions—recurrent thoughts, images, or impulses that recur or persist despite efforts to suppress them—and compulsions—repetitive, purposeful acts performed according to certain rules or in a ritualized manner.

post-traumatic stress disorder (PTSD) An anxiety disorder characterized by the persistent re-experience of traumatic events through distressing recollections, dreams, hallucinations, or dissociative flashbacks; develops in response to rape, life-threatening events, severe injury, and natural disasters.

CAUSES OF ANXIETY DISORDERS

How do psychologists explain the development of anxiety disorders? Each of the four etiological approaches we have outlined (biological, psychodynamic, behavioural, and cognitive) emphasizes different factors. Let's analyze how each adds something unique to the understanding of anxiety disorders.

Biological Various investigators have suggested that anxiety disorders have biological origins. One theory attempts to explain why certain phobias, such as those for spiders or heights, are more common than fears of other dangers, such as electricity. Because many fears are shared across cultures, it has been proposed that, at one time in the evolutionary past, certain fears enhanced our ancestors' chances of survival. Perhaps humans are born with a predisposition to fear whatever is related to sources of serious danger in the evolutionary past. This *preparedness hypothesis* suggests that we carry around an evolutionary tendency to respond quickly and "thoughtlessly" to once-feared stimuli (LoBue & DeLoache, 2008; Öhman & Mineka, 2001). However, this hypothesis does not explain types of phobias that develop in response to objects or situations that would not have had survival meaning over evolutionary history, like fear of needles, driving, or elevators.

The ability of certain drugs to relieve and of others to produce symptoms of anxiety offers evidence of a biological role in anxiety disorders (Hoffman & Mathew, 2008; Kalueff & Nutt, 2007). For example, recall from Chapter 4 that when the level of the neurotransmitter GABA in the brain becomes low, people often experience feelings of anxiety. As we will see in Chapter 16, drugs that affect GABA levels are used as successful treatments for some types of anxiety disorders.

Researchers are also using imaging techniques to examine the brain bases of these disorders. Consider a study of post-traumatic stress disorder conducted at the University of Western Ontario.

Some people who suffer traumatic events develop PTSD, whereas others do not. A team of researchers used fMRI scans to explore differences in patterns of brain activity for individuals in those two categories (Lanius et al., 2003). The study focused on the brain activity that arose when the individuals recalled memories of sad, anxious, and traumatic events. As shown in **Figure 15.1**, those individuals who had experienced a trauma but not developed PTSD showed more activity in areas of the brain (the thalamus and the anterior cingulate) that play a role in emotional processing compared to individuals whose traumatic experiences led to PTSD. These differences in brain activity applied for all three types of memories (i.e., sad, anxious, and traumatic). The generality of the finding suggests that the traumatic experiences for the individuals who developed PTSD led to a broad disruption of the way in which their brains respond to emotional events.

This study illustrates why brain-imaging techniques can help deepen the understanding of the biological bases of anxiety disorders. Similar results have emerged for other disorders. For example, PET scans have revealed a difference in the function of serotonin receptors between the brains of individuals who suffer from panic disorder and those of control individuals (Nash et al., 2008). These differences may help explain the onset of panic disorder. MRI techniques have revealed widespread abnormalities in the brains of patients with OCD. For example, patients with OCD have greater cortical thickness in areas of the brain that normally allow people to inhibit some behaviours (Narayan et al., 2008). This brain abnormality, which potentially hinders communication among neurons, may partially explain why people with OCD have difficulty controlling their behavioural compulsions.

Finally, family and twin studies suggest that there is a genetic basis for the predisposition to experience anxiety disorders (Hettema et al., 2005). For example, the probability that a pair of male identical twins both suffered from a social or specific phobia was consistently greater than the probability that both male fraternal twins were sufferers (Kendler, Myers, Prescott, & Neale, 2001). Still, it is important to remember that nature and nurture always interact. For example, recall from Chapter 14 that many aspects of personality are heritable. Research suggests that part of the influence of genes on PTSD arises because people with different personality traits make life choices that decrease or increase the probability that they will experience traumas (Stein et al., 2002).

Psychodynamic The psychodynamic model begins with the assumption that the symptoms of anxiety disorders come from underlying psychic conflicts or fears. The symptoms are attempts to protect the individual from psychological pain. Thus panic attacks are the result of unconscious conflicts bursting into consciousness. Suppose, for example, a child represses conflicting thoughts about his or her wish to escape a difficult home environment. In later life, a phobia may be activated by an object or situation that symbolizes the conflict. A bridge, for example, might come to symbolize the path that the person must traverse from the world of home and family to the outside

FIGURE 15.1 Brain Activity and Emotional Memories
The study compared individuals who developed PTSD in response to traumatic experiences with those who did not. Members from each group recalled emotional memories while undergoing fMRI scans. This figure shows the brain activity of the group of individuals without PTSD across memories of traumatic, sad, and angry events.

world. The sight of a bridge would then force the unconscious conflict into awareness, bringing with it the fear and anxiety common to phobias. Avoiding bridges would be a symbolic attempt to stay clear of anxiety about the childhood experiences at home.

In obsessive-compulsive disorders, the obsessive behaviour is seen as an attempt to displace anxiety created by a related but far more feared desire or conflict. By substituting an obsession that symbolically captures the forbidden impulse, a person gains some relief. For example, the obsessive fears of dirt experienced by Jim, the adolescent we described earlier, may have their roots in the conflict between his desire to become sexually active and his fear of "dirtying" his reputation. Compulsive preoccupation with carrying out a minor ritualistic task also allows the individual to avoid the original issue that is creating unconscious conflict.

Behavioural Behavioural explanations of anxiety focus on the way symptoms of anxiety disorders are reinforced or conditioned. Investigators do not search for underlying unconscious conflicts or early childhood experiences, because these phenomena cannot be observed directly. As we saw in Chapter 7, behavioural theories are often used to explain the development of phobias, which are seen as classically conditioned fears: Recall Little Albert, in whom John Watson and Rosalie Rayner instilled a fear of a white rat (see page 193). The behavioural account suggests that a previously neutral object or situation becomes a stimulus for a phobia by being paired with a frightening experience. For example, a child whose mother yells a warning when he or she approaches a snake may develop a phobia about snakes. After this experience, even thinking about snakes may produce a wave of fear. Phobias continue to be maintained by the reduction in anxiety that occurs when a person withdraws from the feared situation.

A behavioural analysis of obsessive-compulsive disorders suggests that compulsive behaviours tend to reduce the anxiety associated with obsessive thoughts—thus reinforcing the compulsive behaviour. For example, if a woman fears contamination by touching garbage, then washing her hands reduces the anxiety and is therefore reinforcing. In parallel to phobias, obsessive-compulsive disorders continue to be maintained by the reduction in anxiety that follows from the compulsive behaviours.

Cognitive Cognitive perspectives on anxiety concentrate on the perceptual processes or attitudes that may distort a person's estimate of the danger that he or she is facing. A person may either overestimate the nature or reality of a threat or underestimate his or her ability to cope with the threat effectively. For example, before delivering a speech to a large group, a person with a social phobia may feed his or her anxiety:

> *What if I forget what I was going to say? I'll look foolish in front of all these people. Then I'll get even more nervous and start to perspire, and my voice will shake, and I'll look even sillier. Whenever people see me from now on, they'll remember me as the foolish person who tried to give a speech.*

People who suffer from anxiety disorders may often interpret their own distress as a sign of impending disaster. Their reaction may set off a vicious cycle in which the person fears disaster, which leads to an increase in anxiety, which in turn worsens the anxiety sensations and confirms the person's fears (Beck & Emery, 1985).

Psychologists have tested this cognitive account by measuring *anxiety sensitivity*: individuals' beliefs that bodily symptoms—such as shortness of breath or heart palpitations—may have harmful consequences. People high in anxiety sensitivity are likely to agree with statements such as "When I notice that my heart is beating rapidly, I worry that I might have a heart attack." In one study, researchers assessed the anxiety sensitivity of a group of 68 children, ages 10 to 17, all of whom had been exposed to traumatic events (for example, they had witnessed people being killed) (Leen-Feldner et al., 2008). The researchers found a positive correlation between anxiety sensitivity and the children's symptoms of post-traumatic stress disorder. The children who reported the highest levels of anxiety sensitivity were also most likely to report PTSD symptoms. The researchers suggested that high levels of anxiety sensitivity would make re-experience of traumatic events (such as flashbacks) even more frightening.

Research has also found that anxious patients contribute to the *maintenance* of their anxiety by employing cognitive biases that highlight the threatening stimuli. For example, one study examined people's ability to name either body-related words (e.g., *dizzy*, *fainting*, and *breathless*) versus control words (e.g., *delicate*, *slow*, and *friendly*) when they were presented on a computer screen for only 1/100th of a second. Individuals who suffered from panic disorder showed much greater ability to recognize the body-related words than the healthy control words (Pauli et al., 1997). Similarly, patients whose symptoms of obsessive-compulsive disorder focused on issues of cleanliness watched a researcher touch a series of objects with a "clean and unused" tissue or a "dirty and already used" tissue. In a later memory test, these OCD patients showed greater ability to recall which objects were "dirty" than which were "clean" (Ceschi et al., 2003). Studies of this type confirm that people suffering from anxiety disorders focus their attention on aspects of the world that may help to sustain their anxiety.

Each of the major approaches to anxiety disorders may explain part of the etiological puzzle. Continued research of each approach will clarify causes and, therefore, potential avenues for treatment. Now that you have this basic knowledge about anxiety disorders, we would like you to consider the next of the three major categories of abnormality we are covering in some detail—*mood disorders*.

STOP AND REVIEW

❶ What is the relationship between fear and phobias?

❷ What is the difference between an obsession and a compulsion?

❸ With respect to phobias, what is the preparedness hypothesis?

❹ What is the impact of anxiety sensitivity?

CRITICAL THINKING Recall the study in which participants were asked to retrieve memories while undergoing fMRI. Why might the researchers have chosen the three categories of sad, anxious, and traumatic memories?

Mood Disorders

There have almost certainly been times in your life when you would have described yourself as terribly depressed or incredibly happy. For some people, however, extremes in mood come to disrupt normal life experiences. A **mood disorder** is an emotional disturbance, such as severe depression or depression alternating with mania. Canadian research estimates that up to 16 percent of adults have suffered from mood disorders (Public Health Agency of Canada, 2002c). We will describe two major categories: major depressive disorder and bipolar disorder.

MAJOR DEPRESSIVE DISORDER

Depression has been characterized as the "common cold of psychopathology," both because it occurs so frequently and because almost everyone has experienced elements of the full-scale disorder at some time in his or her life. Everyone has, at one time or another, experienced grief after the loss of a loved one or felt sad or upset when failing to achieve a desired goal. These sad feelings are only one symptom experienced by people suffering from a **major depressive disorder** (see **Table 15.3**). Consider one individual's description of his struggle to carry out normal daily tasks while in the depths of depression:

> It seemed to take the most colossal effort to do simple things. I remember bursting into tears because I had used up the cake of soap that was in the shower. I cried because one of the keys stuck for a second on my computer. I found everything excruciatingly difficult, and so, for example, the prospect of lifting the telephone receiver seemed to me like bench-pressing four hundred pounds. The reality that I had to put on not just one but two socks and then two shoes so overwhelmed me that I wanted to go back to bed. (Solomon, 2001, pp. 85–86)

What are some differences between the occasional feelings of unhappiness that most people feel and the symptoms of major depressive disorder?

This excerpt illustrates some vivid consequences of major depressive disorder.

People diagnosed with depression differ in terms of the severity and duration of their symptoms. Many individuals struggle with clinical depression for only several weeks at one point in their lives, whereas others experience depression episodically or chronically for many years. Estimates of the prevalence of major depression are at about 8 percent for the Canadian population. However, data reveal that women are twice as likely to be diagnosed with a major depression at some time in their lives (Public Health Agency of Canada, 2002c).

Depression takes an enormous toll on those afflicted, on their families, and on society. A study undertaken on behalf of the World Health Organization estimated the loss of healthy life years that could be attributed to physical and mental illnesses (World Health Organization, 2008). In this analysis, major depressive disorder ranked third (behind lower respiratory infections and diarrheal diseases) in terms of the burden it

TABLE 15.3	Characteristics of Major Depressive Disorder
Characteristics	**Example**
Dysphoric mood	Sad, blue, hopeless; loss of interest or pleasure in almost all usual activities
Appetite	Significant weight loss (while not dieting) or weight gain
Sleep	Insomnia or hypersomnia (sleeping too much)
Motor activity	Markedly slowed down (motor retardation) or agitated
Guilt	Feelings of worthlessness; self-reproach
Concentration	Diminished ability to think or concentrate; forgetfulness
Suicide	Recurrent thoughts of death; suicidal ideas or attempts

mood disorder A mood disturbance such as severe depression or depression alternating with mania.

major depressive disorder A mood disorder characterized by intense feelings of depression over an extended time, without the manic high phase of bipolar depression.

places on people's lives around the world. For middle- and high-income countries, major depressive disorder ranked first. In Canada, depression accounts for the majority of all mental hospital admissions, but it is still believed to be underdiagnosed and undertreated. U.S. data from the National Comorbidity Study found that only 37.4 percent of individuals sought treatment in the first year after a major depressive episode (Wang et al., 2005); a recent joint Canada–U.S. study reveals that treatment-seeking rates for depression are similar in the two countries (Mojtabai & Olfson, 2006). The median period people wait between experiencing a major depressive episode and seeking treatment is eight years (Wang et al., 2005).

BIPOLAR DISORDER

Bipolar disorder is characterized by periods of severe depression alternating with manic episodes. A person experiencing a **manic episode** generally acts and feels unusually elated and expansive. However, sometimes the individual's predominant mood is irritability rather than elation, especially if the person feels thwarted in some way. During a manic episode, a person often experiences an inflated sense of self-esteem or an unrealistic belief that he or she possesses special abilities or powers. The person may feel a dramatically decreased need to sleep and may engage excessively in work or in social or other pleasurable activities.

Caught up in a manic mood, the person shows unwarranted optimism, takes unnecessary risks, promises anything, and may give everything away. Consider this first-person account:

> Manic depression is about buying a dozen bottles of Heinz ketchup and all eight bottles of Windex in stock at the Food Emporium on Broadway at 4:00 a.m., flying from Zurich to the Bahamas and back to Zurich in three days to balance the hot and cold weather, [and] carrying $20 000 in $100 bills in your shoes into the country on your way back from Tokyo. . . . It's about blips and burps of madness, moments of absolute delusion, bliss, and irrational and dangerous choices made in order to heighten pleasure and excitement and to ensure a sense of control. (Behrman, 2002)

When the mania begins to diminish, people are left trying to deal with the damage and predicaments they created during their period of frenzy. Thus manic episodes almost always give way to periods of severe depression.

The duration and frequency of the mood disturbances in bipolar disorder vary from person to person. Some people experience long periods of normal functioning punctuated by occasional short manic or depressive episodes. A small percentage of unfortunate individuals go right from manic episodes to clinical depression and back again in continuous, unending cycles that are devastating to them, their families, their friends, and their coworkers. While manic, they may gamble away life savings or give lavish gifts to strangers, acts that later add to

___

bipolar disorder A mood disorder characterized by alternating periods of depression and mania.

manic episode A component of bipolar disorder characterized by extreme elation, unbounded euphoria without sufficient reason, and grandiose thoughts or feelings about personal abilities.

guilt feelings when they are in the depressed phase. Bipolar disorder is much rarer than major depressive disorder. Some data suggest that 1 percent of Canadian adults are suffering from this disorder (Public Health Agency of Canada, 2002c), whereas other evidence estimates that 444 000, or 2.6 percent of Canadians aged 25 to 64, had bipolar disorder in their lifetime (Statistics Canada, 2004b).

CAUSES OF MOOD DISORDERS

What factors are involved in the development of mood disorders? We will address this question from the biological, psychodynamic, behavioural, and cognitive perspectives. Note that, because of its prevalence, major depressive disorder has been studied more extensively than bipolar disorder. Our review will reflect that distribution of research.

Biological Several types of research provide clues to the contribution of biology to mood disorders. For example, the ability of different drugs to relieve manic and depressive symptoms provides evidence that different brain states underlie the two extremes of bipolar disorder (Thase & Denko, 2008). Reduced levels of two chemical messengers in the brain, serotonin and norepinephrine, have been linked to depression; increased levels of these neurotransmitters are associated with mania.

Researchers are using brain-imaging techniques to understand the causes and consequences of mood disorders (Gotlib & Hamilton, 2008). For example, researchers have used fMRI to demonstrate that the brains of people who suffer from bipolar disorder respond differently when they are in depressed versus manic states (Blumberg et al., 2003). **Figure 15.2** reports the data from 36 individuals with bipolar disorder. At the time of the study, 11 were in elevated moods, 10 were in depressed moods, and 15 were in *euthymic* (or balanced) emotional states.

FIGURE 15.2 Brain Activity and Bipolar Disorder

Individuals with bipolar disorder underwent fMRI scans while performing a cognitive task. The brain response was different in an area known as the *caudal ventral prefrontal cortex* (cVPFC) depending on whether the individuals were experiencing elevated, depressed, or balanced moods. As shown in A, individuals in depressed moods showed increased left cVPFC activity by comparison to those in balanced moods. As shown in B, individuals in elevated moods showed reduced right cVPFC activity by comparison to those in balanced moods.

All of the individuals performed the same cognitive task—naming the colours in which words were printed—while undergoing fMRI scans. Figure 15.2 indicates that particular regions of cortex were more active or less active depending on each individual's particular phase of bipolar disorder.

The contribution of biology to the etiology of mood disorders is also confirmed by evidence that the incidence of mood disorder is influenced by genetic factors (Edvardsen et al., 2008; Kendler, Gatz, Gardner, & Pedersen, 2006). For example, one twin study assessed the likelihood that both twins were diagnosed with bipolar disorder. The correlation was 0.82 for monozygotic twins but only 0.07 for dizygotic twins. These data led to a heritability estimate of 0.77 (Edvardsen et al., 2008). You will see in the *Psychology in Your Life* box that researchers have begun to make progress identifying the actual genes that have an impact on individuals' predispositions to experience mood disorders.

Let's see now what the three major psychological approaches can add to your understanding of the onset of mood disorders.

Psychodynamic In the psychodynamic approach, unconscious conflicts and hostile feelings that originate in early childhood are seen to play key roles in the development of depression. Freud was struck by the degree of self-criticism and guilt that depressed people displayed. He believed that the source of this self-reproach was anger, originally directed at someone else, that had been turned inward against the self. The anger was believed to be tied to an especially intense and dependent childhood relationship, such as a parent–child relationship, in which the person's needs or expectations were not met. Losses, real or symbolic, in adulthood reactivate hostile feelings, now directed toward the person's own ego, creating the self-reproach that is characteristic of depression.

Behavioural Rather than searching for the roots of depression in the unconscious, the behavioural approach focuses on the effects of the amount of positive reinforcement and punishments a person receives (Lewinsohn, 1975; Lewinsohn, Hoberman, Teri, & Hautzinger, 1985). In this view, depressed feelings result when an individual receives insufficient positive reinforcements and experiences many punishments in the environment following a loss or other major life changes. Without sufficient positive reinforcement, a person begins to feel sad and withdraws. This state of sadness is initially reinforced by increased attention and sympathy from others (Biglan, 1991). Typically, however, friends who at first respond with support grow tired of the depressed person's negative moods and attitudes and begin to avoid him or her. This reaction eliminates another source of positive reinforcement, plunging the person further into depression. Research also shows that depressed people tend to underestimate positive feedback and overestimate negative feedback (Kennedy & Craighead, 1988; Nelson & Craighead, 1977).

Cognitive At the centre of the cognitive approach to depression are two theories. One theory suggests that negative *cognitive sets*—"set" patterns of perceiving the world—lead people to take a negative view of events in their lives for which they feel responsible. The second theory, the *explanatory style* model, proposes that depression arises from the belief that one has little or no personal control over significant life events. Each of these models explains some aspects of the experience of depression. Let's see how.

Aaron Beck (1983, 1985, 1988), a leading researcher on depression, has developed the theory of cognitive sets. Beck has argued that depressed people have three types of negative cognitions, which he calls the *cognitive triad* of depression: negative views of themselves, negative views of ongoing experiences, and negative views of the future. Depressed people tend to view themselves as inadequate or defective in some way, to interpret ongoing experiences in a negative way, and to believe that the future will continue to bring suffering and difficulties. This pattern of negative thinking clouds all experiences and produces the other characteristic signs of depression. An individual who always anticipates a negative outcome is not likely to be motivated to pursue any goal, leading to the *paralysis of will* that is prominent in depression.

In the explanatory style view, pioneered by **Martin Seligman**, individuals believe, correctly or not, that they cannot control future outcomes that are important to them. Seligman's theory evolved from research that demonstrated depression-like symptoms in dogs (and later in other species). Seligman and Maier (1967) subjected dogs to painful, unavoidable shocks: No matter what the dogs did, there was no way to escape the shocks. The dogs developed what Seligman and Maier called **learned helplessness**. Learned helplessness is marked by three types of deficits: *motivational deficits*—the dogs were slow to initiate known actions; *emotional deficits*—they appeared rigid, listless, frightened, and distressed; and *cognitive deficits*—they demonstrated poor learning in new situations. Even when put in a situation in which they could, in fact, avoid shock, they did not learn to do so (Maier & Seligman, 1976).

Seligman believed that depressed people are also in a state of learned helplessness: They have an expectancy that nothing they can do matters (Abramson, Seligman, & Teasdale, 1978; Peterson & Seligman, 1984; Seligman, 1975). However, the emergence of this state depends, to a large extent, on how individuals explain their life events. As we discussed in Chapter 12, there are three dimensions of explanatory style: *internal–external*, *global–specific*, and *stable–unstable*. Suppose that you have just received a poor grade on a psychology exam. You attribute the negative outcome on the exam to an internal factor ("I'm stupid"), which makes you feel sad, rather than to an external one ("The exam was really hard"), which would have made you angry. You could have chosen a less stable internal quality than intelligence to explain your performance ("I was tired that day"). Rather than attributing your performance to an internal, stable factor that has global or far-reaching influence (stupidity), you could even have limited your explanation to the psychology exam or course ("I'm not good at psychology courses"). Explanatory style theory suggests that individuals who attribute failure to internal, stable, and global causes are vulnerable to depression. This prediction has been confirmed repeatedly (Lau & Eley, 2008; Peterson & Vaidya, 2001).

Once people begin to experience the negative moods associated with major depressive disorder, ordinary cognitive processes make it more difficult for them to escape those moods. Consider a study that demonstrated that depression

---

learned helplessness A general pattern of nonresponding in the presence of noxious stimuli that often follows after an organism has previously experienced noncontingent, inescapable aversive stimuli.

FIGURE 15.3 Attentional Biases in Major Depressive Disorder
Depressed participants and control participants viewed displays with sad, threat, positive, and neutral photographs. Compared to control participants, depressed participants spent more time looking at sad photographs and less time looking at positive photographs. The figure shows eye movement data from a depressed participant. The larger circles indicate that the participant spent more time looking at a particular location.

From Kellough, J. L., Beevers, C. G., Ellis, A. J., & Wells, T. T. (2008). Time-course of selective attention in clinically depressed young adults: An eye tracking study. *Behaviour Research and Therapy, 46,* 1238–1243.

changes the way in which people attend to information in the world.

> Researchers recruited a group of 15 depressed participants and 45 control participants (who had never experienced depression) (Kellough, Beevers, Ellis, & Wells, 2008). The participants wore a device that allowed the researchers to monitor eye movements while they viewed visual displays. As you can see in **Figure 15.3**, each display had four photographs that represented the emotion categories sad, threat, positive, and neutral. The participants were told that they were wearing the eye-tracking device so that the researchers could determine the relationship between pupil dilation and emotional images. In fact, the researchers wished to test the hypothesis that depressed individuals would spend more time than control individuals looking at the sad photos and less time looking at the positive photos. The data supported that prediction. The information superimposed on the photographs in Figure 15.3 shows the eye movements of one of the depressed participants. Note that this individual spent most of the trial looking at the crying boy.

This research demonstrates that people with major depressive disorder find it difficult to remember anything happy about their lives. You can understand how this memory bias could help make depression feel inescapable.

In Chapter 16, we will see that insights generated from cognitive theories of depression have given rise to successful forms of therapy. For now, there are two other important aspects of the study of depression that we will review: the large differences between the prevalence of depression in men and women and the link between depression and suicide.

GENDER DIFFERENCES IN DEPRESSION

One of the central questions of research on depression is why women are afflicted twice as often as men (Hyde, Mezulis, & Abramson, 2008). We noted in an earlier section that the prevalence of mood disorders in Canada is roughly twice as high for women as it is for men (Public Health Agency of Canada, 2002c). Data from U.S. studies are also consistent with this evidence, with about 21 percent of females and 13 percent of males who suffer from a major depression at some time in their lives (Kessler et al., 1994). This gender difference emerges in adolescence, by about ages 13 to 15. One factor that contributes to this difference is, unfortunately, quite straightforward: On average, women experience more negative events and life stressors than men do (Kendler, Kuhn, & Prescott, 2004; Shih, Eberhart, Hammen, & Brennan, 2006). For example, women have a greater likelihood of experiencing physical or sexual abuse, and they are more likely to live in poverty while being the primary caregiver for children and elderly parents. Thus, women's lives provide more of the types of experiences that lay the groundwork for serious depression.

Research on gender differences has focused on a number of factors that might make women more vulnerable to depression (Hyde et al., 2008). Some of those factors are biological. For example, there might be hormonal differences that start at puberty that put adolescent girls more at risk for depression than their male peers. Researchers have also looked intensively at cognitive factors that set men and women apart. Research by **Susan Nolen-Hoeksema** (2002; Nolen-Hoeksema, Larson, & Grayson, 1999) contrasts the response styles of men and women once they begin to experience negative moods. According to this view, when women experience sadness, they tend to think about the possible causes and implications of their feelings. In

What factors help explain why more women than men experience depression?

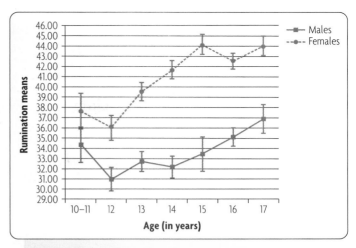

FIGURE 15.4 Gender Differences in Rumination
Across the adolescent years, the gap grows between girls' and boys' reports of rumination.

From Jose, P. E. & Brown, I. (2008). When does the gender difference in rumination begins? Gender and age differences in the use of rumination by adolescents. *Journal of Youth and Adolescence, 37,* 180–192. With kind permission of Springer Science + Business Media.

contrast, men attempt actively to distract themselves from depressed feelings, either by focusing on something else or by engaging in a physical activity that will take their minds off their current mood state.

This model suggests that it is the more thoughtful, *ruminative* response style of women, the tendency to focus obsessively on their problems, that increases women's vulnerability to depression. Consider a study that examined rumination among a large sample of adolescents.

A group of 1218 students between the ages of 10 and 17 completed a questionnaire that assessed their responses to life events (Jose & Brown, 2008). The questionnaire included statements like "I sit at home and think about how I feel" and "I think no one will want to be around me if I don't snap out of this mood." The students responded to each statement on a five-point scale that ranged from "never" to "always." As you can see in **Figure 15.4**, at the youngest ages there was a modest difference between males and females. However, over the adolescent years the gap grew, with girls engaging in considerably more rumination. The students in the study also completed a measure of depression. For both boys and girls, the students who ruminated the most were also most likely to report the most symptoms of depression. However, the relationship between rumination and depression was even stronger for the girls.

This study supports the hypothesis that rumination is a risk factor for depression: Paying attention to negative moods can increase thoughts of negative events, which eventually increases the quantity and/or the intensity of negative feelings. The study also confirms that men who ruminate are also at risk for depression. The gender difference for depression emerges, in part, because more women ruminate.

SUICIDE

"The will to survive and succeed had been crushed and defeated. . . . There comes a time when all things cease to shine, when the rays of hope are lost" (Shneidman, 1987, p. 57). This sad statement by a suicidal young man reflects the most extreme consequence of any psychological disorder—*suicide*. Although most depressed people do not commit suicide, analyses suggest that many suicides are attempted by those who are suffering from depression (Bolton, Belik, Enns, Cox, & Sareen, 2008). In Canada, the number of deaths officially designated as suicide has varied between roughly 3500 to 4000 per year since 2000 (Statistics Canada, 2010); however, because many suicides are attributed to accidents or other causes, the actual rate is probably much higher. Because depression occurs more frequently in women, it is not surprising that women *attempt* suicide about three times more often than men do; attempts by men, however, are more often successful (Nock et al., 2008). This difference occurs largely because men use guns more often, and women tend to use less lethal means, such as sleeping pills.

One of the most alarming social problems in recent decades is the rise in youth suicide. Although suicide is currently the ninth leading cause of death in Canada across all age groups (Statistics Canada, 2009), it is even more common for people ages 15 to 24: It accounts for 24 percent of all deaths of young people. For every completed suicide, there may be as many as 8 to 20 suicide attempts. To assess the risk of youth suicide, a team of researchers reviewed 128 studies that involved about 500 000 individuals between the ages of 12 and 20 (Evans,

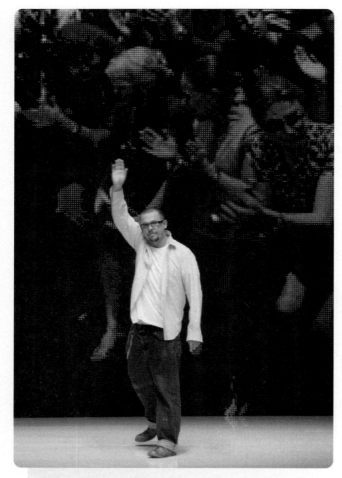

Highly successful individuals, like internationally acclaimed designer Alexander McQueen, are not immune to the feelings of despair that can trigger suicide. McQueen committed suicide in February 2010. What has research revealed about the relationship between depression and suicide?

and outer distress. The majority of young suicide victims have talked to others about their intentions or have written about them. Thus, talk of suicide should always be taken seriously (Rudd et al., 2006). As is the case for adults, adolescents are very likely to attempt suicide when they are experiencing depression (Gutierrez, Watkins, & Collura, 2004; Nrugham, Larsson, & Sund, 2008). Feelings of hopelessness and isolation, as well as negative self-concepts, are also associated with suicide risk (Rutter & Behrendt, 2004). Furthermore, gay and lesbian youths are at even higher risk for suicide than are other adolescents (D'Augelli et al., 2005). These higher suicide rates undoubtedly reflect the relative lack of social support for homosexual orientation. Suicide is an extreme reaction that occurs especially when adolescents feel unable to cry out to others for help. Being sensitive to signs of suicidal intentions and caring enough to intervene are essential for saving the lives of both youthful and mature people who have come to see no exit for their troubles except total self-destruction.

STOP AND REVIEW

❶ What experiences characterize bipolar disorder?
❷ In Aaron Beck's theory, what types of negative cognitions make up the cognitive triad?
❸ How does the ruminative response style help explain gender differences in depression?
❹ What are some suicide risk factors for adolescents?

CRITICAL THINKING Recall the study that demonstrated attentional biases in major depressive disorder. Why might participants have been led to believe the study was about pupil dilation?

Personality Disorders

A **personality disorder** is a long-standing (chronic), inflexible, maladaptive pattern of perceiving, thinking, or behaving. These patterns can seriously impair an individual's ability to function in social or work settings and can cause significant distress. They are usually recognizable by the time a person reaches adolescence or early adulthood. Personality disorders are coded on Axis II of *DSM-IV-TR*. As shown in **Table 15.4**, *DSM-IV-TR* organizes 10 types of personality disorders into three clusters.

Diagnoses of personality disorders have sometimes been controversial because of the overlap among the disorders: Some of the same behaviours contribute to diagnoses of different disorders. In addition, researchers have tried to understand the relationship between normal and abnormal personalities: At what point does an extreme on a particular dimension of personality indicate a disorder (Livesley & Jang, 2005)? For example, most people are somewhat dependent on other people. When does dependence become sufficiently extreme to signal dependent personality disorder? As with other types of psychological disorders, clinicians must understand when and how personality traits become maladaptive—when and how those traits cause either the person or society to suffer. To illustrate that conclusion, we focus on *borderline personality disorder* and *antisocial personality disorder*.

Hawton, Rodham, & Deeks, 2005). Across that broad sample, 29.9 percent of the adolescents had thought about suicide at some point in their lives, and 9.7 percent had actually attempted suicide. Adolescent girls were roughly twice as likely as adolescent boys to have made a suicide attempt.

Teen suicide rates are not the same across various regions of Canada. The Yukon, the Northwest Territories, and Nunavut have suicide rates that are 4 to 5 times higher than those in the southern provinces (World Health Organization, 2002). But these regional differences should be interpreted with caution, as they simply reflect a troubling Canadian reality whereby suicide rates across all age groups of Aboriginal people are on average about three times higher than in the non-Aboriginal population (Miller Chenier, 1995). These rates may be even higher for Aboriginal teens.

Youth suicide is not a spur-of-the-moment, impulsive act; typically, it occurs as the final stage of a period of inner turmoil

---

personality disorder A chronic, inflexible, maladaptive pattern of perceiving, thinking, and behaving that seriously impairs an individual's ability to function in social or other settings.

Psychology in Your Life

HOW CAN WE PINPOINT INTERACTIONS OF NATURE AND NURTURE?

Throughout this chapter, we have asserted that major types of mental illnesses have a genetic component. The majority of those claims have been based on methods that should be quite familiar to you by this point in *Psychology and Life*. Researchers, for example, compare the rate at which monozygotic and dizygotic twins share the same psychopathology to offer estimates of the heritability of each type of disorder (Coolidge, Thede, & Jang, 2001; Hettema, Neale, & Kendler, 2001). However, in recent years, researchers have begun to move beyond calculations of heritability to pinpoint the actual differences in genetic material that predispose some individuals to experience mental illness. Let's consider a study that establishes an important relationship between genetic variation and life experiences in the etiology of depression.

When we discussed mood disorders, we noted that disruptions in the function of the neurotransmitter serotonin play a role in depression. For that reason, researchers have focused attention on a gene that has an impact on the serotonin system (Caspi et al., 2003). The gene comes in short (s) and long (l) forms. For 847 individuals in a longitudinal study in New Zealand, researchers determined their status for this gene. In the sample, 17 percent had two short versions of the gene (s/s), 51 percent had one short and one

long (s/l), and 31 percent had two long versions (l/l). The participants themselves provided information about the stressors they had weathered in their lives. For ages 21 to 26, they indicated whether they had experienced such events as employment or financial crises, health problems, or relationship issues. Across the genotypes (i.e., s/s, s/l, l/l), no one group experienced more life stressors than another. That is an important result: It suggests that any group differences in the prevalence of depression cannot be attributed to easier or harder lives. Instead, we learned that people's genotypes predispose them to respond differently to similar experiences.

The researchers' final step was to determine which participants in the study had suffered from major depressive disorder. As seen in the figure, the pattern that emerged was

quite dramatic. In general, people who had experienced more stressful life events were more likely to experience an episode of major depression. However, as the figure shows, genotype had an important impact as well. For participants in possession of one or—even more so—two copies of the short version of the gene, the impact of negative life events was amplified.

This study makes many of the ideas we have discussed about nature and nurture quite concrete. The researchers have demonstrated that a known genetic difference in combination with negative life events greatly increases the likelihood that people will experience depression. Breakthroughs in the understanding of the human genome allow researchers to determine exactly how nature and nurture interact.

BORDERLINE PERSONALITY DISORDER

Individuals with **borderline personality disorder** experience great instability and intensity in personal relationships. These difficulties arise in part from difficulties controlling anger. The disorder leads people to have frequent fights and temper tantrums. In addition, people with this disorder display great impulsivity in their behaviours—particularly with respect to behaviours that can relate to self-harm, such as substance abuse or suicide attempts. No study has been conducted to assess the

prevalence of borderline personality disorder in Canada. The best estimates to date suggest that the rate is slightly less than 2 percent (Public Health Agency of Canada, 2002d), which is similar to recent estimates from the United States (Lenzenweger, Lane, Loranger, & Kessler, 2007).

---

borderline personality disorder A disorder defined by instability and intensity in personal relationships as well as turbulent emotions and impulsive behaviours.

TABLE 15.4 Personality Disorders

Disorder	Characteristics
Cluster A: People's behaviour appears odd or eccentric	
Paranoid	Distrust and suspiciousness about the motives of the individuals with whom they interact
Schizoid	Lack of desire to have social relationships; lack of emotionality in social situations
Schizotypal	Cognitive or perceptual distortions as well as discomfort in social relationships
Cluster B: People's behaviour appears dramatic or erratic	
Antisocial	Inability to respect the rights of others; irresponsible or unlawful behaviour that violates social norms
Borderline	Instability and intensity in personal relationships; impulsivity, particularly with respect to behaviours that include self-harm
Histrionic	Excessive emotionality and attention seeking; inappropriate sexual or seductive behaviour
Narcissistic	Grandiose sense of self-importance and a need for constant admiration; lack of empathy for others
Cluster C: People's behaviour appears anxious or fearful	
Avoidant	Avoidance of interpersonal contact because of risk of rejection; fear of criticism and feelings of inadequacy in social situations
Dependent	Need for others to take responsibility for major areas of life; feelings of discomfort or helplessness without support from other people
Obsessive-Compulsive	Preoccupation with rules and lists; perfectionism interferes with ability to complete tasks

One important component of borderline personality disorder is an intense fear of abandonment (Lieb et al., 2004). People engage in frantic behaviours to prevent abandonment, such as frequent phone calls and physical clinging. However, because of their difficulty with emotional control, people are likely to engage in behaviours—angry outbursts and bouts of self-harm—that make it quite difficult to maintain relationships with them. One study that followed people with borderline personality disorder over the course of two years found impaired social functioning across the whole period (Skodol et al., 2005). This research suggests that borderline personality disorder remains stable over time.

Causes of Borderline Personality Disorder As with other disorders, researchers have focused on both the nature and nurture of borderline personality disorder. Twin studies provide strong evidence in favour of a genetic contribution. For example, one study compared the rate of concordance for monozygotic versus dizygotic twins (Torgersen et al., 2000). When one MZ twin had borderline personality disorder, 35.3 percent of the siblings also had the disorder; for DZ twins, only 6.7 percent of the siblings also had the disorder. If you recall the discussion in Chapter 14 about the strong heritability of personality traits, you might not be surprised that disorders of those traits are also heritable.

Still, research suggests that environmental factors make a strong contribution in the etiology of borderline personality disorder (Cohen et al., 2008; Lieb et al., 2004). One study compared the incidence of early traumatic events for 66 patients with the disorder to 109 healthy controls (Bandelow et al.,

2005). The patients had considerably different lives. For example, 73.9 percent of the patients with borderline personality disorder reported childhood sexual abuse; only 5.5 percent of the controls did so. The patients reported, on average, that the abuse started at age six and lasted for three and a half years. That early trauma likely contributed to the incidence of the disorder. However, not all people who endure childhood sexual abuse develop borderline personality disorder—witness the 5.5 percent of control participants in this study who survived childhood sexual abuse but did not develop the disorder. It is likely that a combination of genetic risk and traumatic events explains the etiology of the disorder.

ANTISOCIAL PERSONALITY DISORDER

Antisocial personality disorder is marked by a long-standing pattern of irresponsible or unlawful behaviour that violates social norms. Lying, stealing, and fighting are common behaviours. People with antisocial personality disorder often do not experience shame or remorse for their hurtful actions. Violations of social norms begin early in their lives—disrupting class, getting into fights, and running away from home. Their actions are marked by indifference to the rights of others. The most recent U.S. data suggest a prevalence rate of about 1.0 percent among adults (Lenzenweger et al., 2007). Canadian data on the prevalence of all personality disorders are lacking (Public Health Agency of Canada, 2002d), but the most recent Ontario study estimated the one-year prevalence rate to be 1.7 percent (Offord et al., 1996).

Antisocial personality disorder is often comorbid with other pathologies. For example, in one study of adults with histories of alcohol or drug abuse, the prevalence of antisocial personality disorder was 18.3 percent for men and 14.1 percent for

---

antisocial personality disorder A disorder characterized by stable patterns of irresponsible or unlawful behaviour that violates social norms.

women—considerably higher than the 1.0 percent prevalence for the general population (Goldstein et al., 2007). In addition, antisocial personality disorder also puts people at risk for suicide, even in the absence of major depressive disorder (Hills, Cox, McWilliams, & Sareen, 2005). This suicide risk is likely to be a product of the impulsivity and disregard for safety that characterizes the disorder.

Causes of Antisocial Personality Disorder Researchers have used twin studies to examine genetic components of specific behaviours associated with antisocial personality disorder. For example, one study examined the concordance in behaviours for 3687 pairs of twins (Viding, Blair, Moffitt, & Plomin, 2005). Teachers responded to statements about each twin to indicate the presence of callous–unemotional traits (e.g., "Does not show feelings or emotions") and antisocial behaviour (e.g., "Often fights with other children or bullies them"). The comparisons of MZ and DZ twins suggested that the tendency to display callous–unemotional traits had a strong genetic component. In addition, for twins who displayed high levels of those callous–unemotional traits, genetics also made a strong contribution to antisocial behaviour.

Research has also focused on the environmental circumstances that give rise to personality disorders (Paris, 2003). Consider this study of the relationship between parenting practices and antisocial personality traits.

A team of researchers assessed 742 men and women for personality traits that met *DSM-IV* criteria for antisocial personality disorder (Reti et al., 2002). The participants reported on their parents' behaviours toward them during childhood by completing the *Parental Bonding Instrument* (PBI). The PBI posed a range of questions to which participants responded on a four-point scale. Some of the questions measured the extent to which parents showed caring for the child (e.g., "Could make me feel better when I was upset"). Other questions measured the extent to which parents restricted the child's behaviour (e.g., "Let me dress in any way I pleased"). A third type of question measured the extent to which parents allowed the child psychological freedom (e.g., "Tried to control everything I did"). The researchers looked for relationships between the participants' responses on the PBI and the extent to which they showed antisocial personality traits. They found that the people who reported low levels of parental care had high levels of antisocial personality traits. Also, those individuals who believed that their mothers had been particularly overprotective also had high levels of antisocial personality traits.

The researchers were quick to assert that correlation is not causation. It is possible that parenting behaviours brought about antisocial personality traits, but it is also possible that children whose behaviour was influenced by antisocial traits negatively affected the way their parents behaved toward them. Still, the results suggest that researchers could observe family patterns to determine what children might be at risk to develop adult forms of antisocial personality disorder.

STOP AND REVIEW

❶ What intense fear do people with borderline personality disorder have with respect to interpersonal relationships?

❷ How do the early lives of people with borderline personality disorder compare to those of healthy controls?

❸ Why are people with antisocial personality disorder at risk for suicide?

CRITICAL THINKING Consider the study that assessed the impact of parenting on antisocial personality traits. Why might the researchers have assessed the three different dimensions of parenting?

Somatoform and Dissociative Disorders

As we have reviewed various types of psychological disorders, you have seen how certain everyday experiences can, when pushed to the limit, lead to disability or maladaptive behaviours. For example, everyone experiences anxiety, but for some people those experiences become so severe that they develop an anxiety disorder. Similarly, many people experience symptoms for physical illnesses that do not have any obvious causes; many people have days when they just "don't feel like themselves." However, when those types of experiences impair an individual's day-to-day life, they may indicate *somatoform disorders* or *dissociative disorders*. We review the symptoms and etiology of each type of disorder.

SOMATOFORM DISORDERS

A person suffering from a **somatoform disorder** has physical illnesses or complaints that cannot be fully explained by actual

Why do people with antisocial personality disorder often have legal difficulties?

---

somatoform disorder A disorder in which people have physical illnesses or complaints that cannot be fully explained by actual medical conditions.

medical conditions. To be diagnosed with one of these disorders, people must experience the illnesses or complaints to an extent that they cause sufficient distress to interfere with their everyday functioning. We will focus on *hypochondriasis*, *somatization disorder*, and *conversion disorder*.

Individuals with **hypochondriasis** believe they have physical illnesses despite assurance from medical practitioners that they do not. Even when they are currently healthy, they may be constantly fearful that they will contract physical illnesses. In addition, this preoccupation with being or getting ill causes sufficient distress so that individuals are impaired in their day-to-day lives. To assess the prevalence of hypochondriasis and other somatoform disorders, researchers often focus on people who present themselves for medical treatment. In that context, the question becomes what proportion of people have physical complaints that do not allow medical explanations. The Canadian Psychological Association (2009b) suggests that 3 to 10 percent of the Canadian population suffers from intense concern about illness, and that as much as 30 percent of the population experiences intermittent or milder fears about disease.

Individuals with **somatization disorder** present a long history of physical complaints over many years. Those complaints—which remain medically unexplained—must span several medical categories. To meet *DSM-IV-TR* criteria for the diagnosis, individuals must have experienced four pain symptoms (e.g., headaches or stomach aches), two gastrointestinal symptoms (e.g., nausea or diarrhea), one sexual symptom (e.g., erectile dysfunction or excessive menstrual bleeding), and one neurological symptom (e.g., paralysis or double vision). Among adults seeking medical treatment, 1.5 percent meet criteria for somatization disorder (Fink, Hansen, & Oxhøj, 2004).

Both hypochondriasis and somatization disorder are defined by people's complaints about physical symptoms. However, people with hypochondriasis worry about having a specific underlying disease whereas those with somatization disorder focus more on the symptoms themselves. In addition, as you've just seen, to be diagnosed with somatization disorder people must have reported a wide variety of unexplained physical complaints.

Conversion disorder is characterized by a loss of motor or sensory function that cannot be explained by damage to the nervous system or other physical damage. For example, individuals may experience paralysis or blindness without a medical cause. In addition, the onset of the physical symptoms must be preceded by psychological factors such as interpersonal conflict or emotional stressors. Historically, conversion disorder was called *hysteria*—and was believed to represent, in some eras, possession by the devil. Sigmund Freud helped bring about the contemporary understanding of conversion disorder. One of his most enduring insights was that psychological trauma could yield physical symptoms. No Canadian data are currently available on the rates of conversion disorder, but U.S. research

indicates that 1.5 percent of adults seek medical treatment for this disorder (Fink et al., 2004).

Causes of Somatoform Disorders The defining characteristic of somatoform disorders is that individuals experience physical ailments that have no adequate medical explanation. Researchers have attempted to understand how that could be possible: How, for example, could individuals whose motor systems are intact experience paralysis? Studies have used neuroimaging techniques to discover the brain bases of conversion disorder (Black, Seritan, Taber, & Hurley, 2004). Consider a study that demonstrated that individuals with conversion symptoms show different patterns of brain activity than individuals who are only pretending to have the symptoms.

> The study focused on four patients who had weakness in one of their ankles that was not the result of any neurological disorder (Stone et al., 2007). The patients underwent fMRI scans while they attempted to flex both the affected ankles and their normal ankles. The researchers also recruited four healthy individuals to serve as controls. The researchers instructed the controls to simulate the conversion symptoms by imagining that one ankle was "too weak and heavy to move" (p. 963). The patterns of brain activity for the patients and controls showed intriguing differences. In particular, the patients' fMRI scans suggested that they were expending greater mental effort than the controls when they tried to flex their weak ankles.

To understand these results, you might take a moment to see what it feels like to simulate an ankle that you cannot flex. It takes some mental effort not to let the ankle bend. However, the study suggests that people with conversion symptoms focus even more effort in their unsuccessful attempts to overcome the weakness.

Researchers have also focused on cognitive processes that contribute to somatoform disorders (R. J. Brown, 2004). For example, an important aspect of hypochondriasis is an attentional bias in the way that individuals respond to bodily sensations. Suppose you wake up one morning with a scratchy throat. If you have an attentional bias that makes it difficult to divert your thoughts from that scratchy throat, you might come to believe that you are seriously ill. In fact, one study demonstrated that people who experience a high level of anxiety about their health find it difficult to disengage their attention even from words such as *cancer*, *tumour*, and *stroke* (Owens, Asmundson, Hadjistavropoulos, & Owens, 2004). The tight focus on symptoms and illness contributes to a vicious cycle: Stress and anxiety have physical consequences (e.g., increased sweating and elevated heart rate) that can feel like the symptoms of illness—providing further proof that the health anxiety is appropriate. Someone who attributes all physical symptoms to illness may perceive a perilous pattern in the co-occurrence of a scratchy throat, excessive sweating, and a swiftly beating heart. Thus the cognitive biases associated with somatoform disorders serve to exaggerate minor bodily sensations.

DISSOCIATIVE DISORDERS

A **dissociative disorder** is a disturbance in the integration of identity, memory, or consciousness. It is important for people

---

hypochondriasis A disorder in which individuals are preoccupied with having or getting physical ailments despite reassurances that they are healthy.

somatization disorder A disorder characterized by unexplained physical complaints in several categories over many years.

conversion disorder A disorder in which psychological conflict or stress brings about loss of motor or sensory function.

dissociative disorder A personality disorder marked by a disturbance in the integration of identity, memory, or consciousness.

After walking into a Toronto hospital in November 1999, this man lapsed into a coma and woke up unable to recall any part of his identity. An ID in his wallet identified him as Philip Saufen. Now living in Vancouver, depressed, stateless, afraid of outsiders, he describes his life as senseless. What types of traumas may lead to dissociative disorders?

to see themselves as being in control of their behaviour, including emotions, thoughts, and actions. Essential to this perception of self-control is the sense of selfhood—the consistency of different aspects of the self and the continuity of identity over time and place. Psychologists believe that in dissociated states, individuals escape from their conflicts by giving up this precious consistency and continuity—in a sense, disowning part of themselves. The forgetting of important personal experiences, a process caused by psychological factors in the absence of any organic dysfunction, called **dissociative amnesia**, is one example of dissociation. For some people, the loss of ability to recall their past is accompanied by an actual flight from their home or place of work. This disorder is called **dissociative fugue**. People may remain in a fugue state for hours, days, or months; they may even live with a new identity in a new location.

Dissociative identity disorder (DID), formerly known as *multiple personality disorder,* is a dissociative mental disorder in which two or more distinct personalities exist within the same individual. At any particular time, one of these personalities is dominant in directing the individual's behaviour. Dissociative identity disorder is popularly known as *split personality,* and sometimes mistakenly called *schizophrenia,* a disorder, as we will see in the next section, in which personality often is impaired but is not split into multiple versions. In DID, each of the emerging personalities contrasts in some significant way with the original self—it might be outgoing if the person is shy, tough if the original personality is weak, and sexually assertive if the other is fearful and sexually naive. Each personality has a unique identity, name, and behaviour pattern. In some cases, dozens of different characters emerge to help the person deal with a difficult life situation. Here is an excerpt from a first-person account of a woman who experiences DID:

> Just as waves turn the ocean inside out and rearrange the water, different ones of us cycle in and out in an ebb

and flow that is sometimes gentle, sometimes turbulent. A child colours with Crayola markers. She moves aside to make way for the administrator, who reconciles the bank statement. A moment later, the dead baby takes over and lies paralyzed on the floor. She remains that way for a while, but no one gets upset—it's her turn. The live baby stops in her crawl, engrossed by a speck of dust. The cooker prepares meals for three days and packages each separately—we all have different likes and dislikes. A terrified one screams aloud, a wounded one moans, a grieving one wails. (Mason, 1997, p. 44)

Can you put yourself in this woman's place, and imagine what it would be like to have this range of "individuals"—the child, the dead baby, the live baby, the cooker, and so on—inside your one head?

Causes of Dissociative Disorders Psychologists who take a psychodynamic perspective have suggested that dissociation serves a vital survival function. They suggest that people who have experienced traumatic stress will sometimes use defence mechanisms to push the traumatic events out of conscious awareness. Consider a study that focused on the life experiences of 891 11- to 17-year-old adolescents in Puerto Rico (Martinez-Taboas et al., 2006). The children completed questionnaires that assessed the presence of victimization experiences and dissociative symptoms in their lives. As you can see in **Figure 15.5**, relatively few of the children in the sample had experienced high levels of victimization. For example, 74 percent of the adolescents had not experienced any emotional abuse. However Figure 15.5 also reveals that increasing levels of emotional, physical, and sexual abuse were accompanied by higher levels of dissociative symptoms.

Although these data—and personal accounts of the type we quoted earlier—seem compelling, many psychologists remain sceptical about the link between trauma and dissociation (Kihlstrom, 2005). The scepticism has been particularly focused on dissociative identity disorder. No solid data exist about the prevalence of this disorder (*DSM-IV-TR,* 2000). In fact, some critics have suggested that diagnoses of DID have increased because of the media attention paid to individuals who claim to have large numbers of distinct personalities (Lilienfeld & Lynn, 2003). Sceptics have often suggested that therapists who "believe" in DID may create DID—these therapists question their patients, often under hypnosis, in a way that encourages multiple personalities to "emerge." Researchers have tried to find rigorous methods to test the claims people with DID make about the separation between different identities. For example, studies have examined inter-identity amnesia by assessing the extent to which information acquired by one identity is known to another. Research results fail to support the claim that amnesia occurs between identities (Kong, Allen, & Glisky, 2008).

---

dissociative amnesia The inability to remember important personal experiences, caused by psychological factors in the absence of any organic dysfunction.

dissociative fugue A disorder characterized by a flight from home or work accompanied by a loss of ability to recall the personal past.

dissociative identity disorder (DID) A dissociative mental disorder in which two or more distinct personalities exist within the same individual; formerly known as multiple personality disorder.

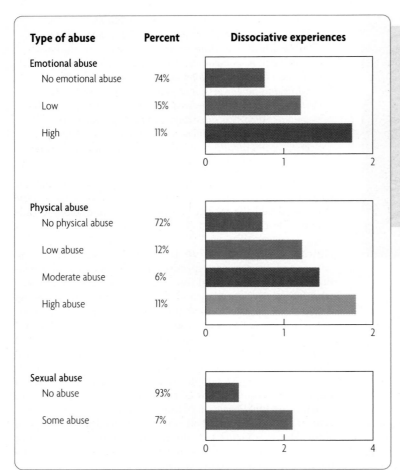

Type of abuse	Percent	Dissociative experiences
Emotional abuse		
No emotional abuse	74%	
Low	15%	
High	11%	
Physical abuse		
No physical abuse	72%	
Low abuse	12%	
Moderate abuse	6%	
High abuse	11%	
Sexual abuse		
No abuse	93%	
Some abuse	7%	

FIGURE 15.5 Victimization and Dissociative Symptoms

Adolescents provided information about their experiences of victimization and their dissociative symptoms. As indicated by the percent figures, the majority of the children had not experienced any abuse. The children who had been abused reported more dissociative symptoms.

Data from Martínez-Taboas, A., Canino, G., Wang, M. Q., Garcías, P., & Bravo, M. (2006). Prevalence of victimization correlates of pathological dissociation in a community sample of youths. *Journal of Traumatic Stress, 19*, 439–448. Reprinted with permission of John Wiley & Sons.

Researchers who study DID generally acknowledge that not all diagnoses are appropriate. However, many psychologists believe that sufficient evidence has accumulated in favour of the DID diagnosis to indicate that it is not always the product of zealous therapists (Gleaves, May, & Cardeña, 2001). The safest conclusion may be that, of the group of people diagnosed with DID, some cases are genuine, whereas other cases emerge in response to therapists' demands.

STOP AND REVIEW

❶ Howard believes that his headaches prove he has a brain tumour, despite his doctor's assurances that he is fine. From which somatoform disorder might Howard suffer?

❷ How is dissociative amnesia defined?

❸ What does research suggest about the life experiences that play a role in the etiology of dissociative identity disorder?

CRITICAL THINKING Recall the study that examined the brain bases of conversion symptoms. Why was it important for the control patients to simulate the conversion symptoms?

---

schizophrenic disorder Severe form of psychopathology characterized by the breakdown of integrated personality functioning, withdrawal from reality, emotional distortions, and disturbed thought processes.

Schizophrenic Disorders

Everyone knows what it is like to feel depressed or anxious, even though most of us never experience these feelings to the degree of severity that constitutes a disorder. Schizophrenia, however, is a disorder that represents a qualitatively different experience from normal functioning. A **schizophrenic disorder** is a severe form of psychopathology in which personality seems to disintegrate, thought and perception are distorted, and emotions are blunted. The person with a schizophrenic disorder is the one you most often conjure up when you think about madness or insanity. Although schizophrenia is relatively rare—estimates vary depending on the measures used—it is generally believed to affect approximately 1 percent of the Canadian adult population (Public Health Agency of Canada, 2002e). This figure translates to around 320 000 Canadians affected by this most mysterious and tragic mental disorder.

Mark Vonnegut, son of novelist Kurt Vonnegut, was in his early 20s when he began to experience symptoms of schizophrenia. In *The Eden Express* (1975), he tells the story of his break with reality and his eventual recovery. Once, while pruning some fruit trees, his reality became distorted:

> *I began to wonder if I was hurting the trees and found myself apologizing. Each tree began to take on personality. I began to wonder if any of them liked me. I became completely absorbed in looking at each tree and*

began to notice that they were ever so slightly lumines-cent, shining with a soft inner light that played around the branches. And from out of nowhere came an incredi-bly wrinkled, iridescent face. Starting as a small point infinitely distant, it rushed forward, becoming infinitely huge. I could see nothing else. My heart had stopped. The moment stretched forever. I tried to make the face go away but it mocked me. . . . I tried to look the face in the eyes and realized I had left all familiar ground. (1975, p. 96)

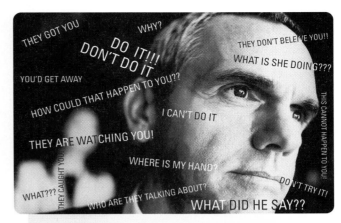

What patterns of thoughts may indicate that a person is experiencing schizophrenia?

Vonnegut's description gives you a glimpse at the symptoms of schizophrenia.

In the world of schizophrenia, *thinking* becomes illogical; associations among ideas are remote or without apparent pat-tern. *Hallucinations* often occur, involving imagined sensory perception—sights, smells, or, most commonly, sounds (usu-ally voices)—that patients assume to be real. A person may hear a voice that provides a running commentary on his or her behaviour or may hear several voices in conversation. **Delusions** are also common; these are false or irrational beliefs maintained in spite of clear contrary evidence. *Language* may become incoherent—a "word salad" of unrelated or made-up words—or an individual may become mute. *Emotions* may be flat, with no visible expression, or they may be inappropriate to the situation. *Psychomotor behaviour* may be disorganized (gri-maces, strange mannerisms), or posture may become rigid. Even when only some of these symptoms are present, deterio-rated functioning in work and interpersonal relationships is likely as the patient withdraws socially or becomes emotionally detached.

Psychologists divide the symptoms between a positive cate-gory and a negative category. During *acute* or *active* phases of schizophrenia, the positive symptoms—hallucinations, delu-sions, incoherence, and disorganized behaviour—are promi-nent. At other times, the negative symptoms—social withdrawal and flattened emotions—become more apparent. Some individ-uals, such as Mark Vonnegut, experience only one or a couple of acute phases of schizophrenia and recover to live normal lives. Others, often described as chronic sufferers, experience either repeated acute phases with short periods of negative symptoms or occasional acute phases with extended periods of negative symptoms. Even the most seriously disturbed are not acutely delusional all the time.

MAJOR TYPES OF SCHIZOPHRENIA

Because of the wide variety of symptoms that can characterize schizophrenia, investigators consider it not a single disorder but rather a constellation of separate types. The five most com-monly recognized subtypes are outlined in **Table 15.5**.

Disorganized Type In this subtype of schizophrenia, a person displays incoherent patterns of thinking and grossly bizarre and disorganized behaviour. Emotions are flattened or inappropriate to the situation. Often, a person acts in a silly or childish manner, such as giggling for no apparent reason. Language can become so incoherent, full of unusual words and incomplete sentences, that communication with others breaks down. If delusions or hallucinations occur, they are not organ-ized around a coherent theme.

Mr. F. B. was a hospitalized patient in his late twen-ties. When asked his name, he said he was trying to forget it because it made him cry whenever he heard it. He then proceeded to cry vigorously for several minutes. Then, when asked about something serious and sad, Mr. F. B. giggled or laughed. When asked the meaning of the proverb "When the cat's away, the mice will play," Mr. F. B. replied, "Takes less place. Cat didn't know what mouse did and mouse didn't know what cat did. Cat represented more on the suspicious side than the mouse. Dumbo was a good guy. He saw what the cat did, put himself with the cat so people wouldn't look at them as comedians." (Zimbardo, personal communication, 1957)

TABLE 15.5	Types of Schizophrenic Disorders
Types of Schizophrenia	**Major Symptoms**
Disorganized	Inappropriate behaviour and emotions; incoherent language
Catatonic	Frozen, rigid, or excitable motor behaviour
Paranoid	Delusions of persecution or grandeur
Undifferentiated	Mixed set of symptoms with thought disorders and features from other types
Residual	Free from major symptoms but evidence from minor symptoms of continuation of the disorder

delusions False or irrational beliefs maintained despite clear evidence to the contrary.

Mr. F. B.'s mannerisms, depersonalized, incoherent speech, and delusions are the hallmarks of the disorganized type of schizophrenia.

Catatonic Type The major feature of the catatonic type of schizophrenia is a disruption in motor activity. Sometimes people with this disorder seem frozen in a stupor. For long periods of time, the individual can remain motionless, often in a bizarre position, showing little or no reaction to anything in the environment. At other times, these patients show excessive motor activity, apparently without purpose and not influenced by external stimuli. The catatonic type is also characterized by extreme *negativism*, an apparently unmotivated resistance to all instructions.

Paranoid Type Individuals suffering from this form of schizophrenia experience complex and systematized delusions focused around specific themes:

- *Delusions of persecution.* Individuals feel that they are being constantly spied on and plotted against and that they are in mortal danger.
- *Delusions of grandeur.* Individuals believe that they are important or exalted beings—millionaires, great inventors, or religious figures such as Jesus Christ. Delusions of persecution may accompany delusions of grandeur—an individual is a great person but is continually opposed by evil forces.
- *Delusional jealousy.* Individuals become convinced—without due cause—that their mates are unfaithful. They contrive data to fit the theory and "prove" the truth of the delusion.

Individuals with paranoid schizophrenia rarely display obviously disorganized behaviour. Instead, their behaviour is likely to be intense and quite formal.

Undifferentiated Type This is the grab-bag category of schizophrenia, describing a person who exhibits prominent delusions, hallucinations, incoherent speech, or grossly disorganized behaviour that fits the criteria of more than one type or of no clear type. The hodgepodge of symptoms experienced by these individuals does not clearly differentiate among various schizophrenic reactions.

Residual Type Individuals diagnosed as residual types have usually suffered from a major past episode of schizophrenia but are currently free of major positive symptoms such as hallucinations or delusions. The ongoing presence of the disorder is signaled by minor positive symptoms or negative symptoms like flat emotion. A diagnosis of residual type may indicate that the person's disease is entering *remission*, or becoming dormant.

CAUSES OF SCHIZOPHRENIA

Different etiological models point to very different initial causes of schizophrenia, different pathways along which it develops, and different avenues for treatment. Let's look at the contributions several of these models can make to an understanding of the way a person may develop a schizophrenic disorder.

Genetic Approaches It has long been known that schizophrenia tends to run in families (Bleuler, 1978; Kallmann, 1946). Three independent lines of research—family studies, twin studies, and adoption studies—point to a common conclusion: Persons related genetically to someone who has had schizophrenia are more likely to become affected than those who are not (Owen & O'Donovan, 2003). A summary of the risks of being affected with schizophrenia through various kinds of relatives is shown in **Figure 15.6**. Schizophrenia researcher **Irving Gottesman** (1991) pooled these data from about 40 reliable studies conducted in Western Europe between 1920 and 1987; he dropped the poorest data sets. As you can see, the data are arranged according to degree of genetic relatedness, which correlates highly with the degree of risk. For example, when both parents have suffered from schizophrenia, the risk for their offspring is 46 percent, as compared with 1 percent in the general population. When only one parent has had schizophrenia, the risk for the offspring drops sharply, to 13 percent. Note also that the probability that identical twins will both have schizophrenia is roughly three times greater than the probability for fraternal twins.

Because the heritability of schizophrenia is so firmly established, researchers have turned their attention toward discovering the specific genes that may put people at risk for the disorder. As you've seen, there are several major types of schizophrenia with a variety of different symptoms. For that reason, researchers believe that a number of genes will have an impact on when and how people will be affected: Research evidence has emerged that associates several candidate genes with the disorder (Shi, Gershon, & Liu, 2008). Different people's experience of schizophrenia—with respect, for example, to the severity of their symptoms—may depend on the precise combination of genes they inherit.

Brain Function Another biological approach to the study of schizophrenia is to look for abnormalities in the brains of individuals suffering from the disorder. Much of this research now relies on brain-imaging techniques that allow direct comparisons to be made between the structure and functioning of the brains of individuals with schizophrenia and normal control individuals (Keshavan, Tandon, Boutros, & Nasrallah, 2008). For example, as shown in **Figure 15.7**, magnetic resonance imaging (MRI) has shown that the ventricles—the brain structures through which cerebrospinal fluid flows—are often enlarged in individuals with schizophrenia (Barkataki et al., 2006). MRI studies also demonstrate that individuals with schizophrenia have measurably thinner regions in frontal and temporal lobes of cerebral cortex; the loss of neural tissue presumably relates to the disorder's behavioural abnormalities (Kuperberg et al., 2003).

Researchers have also begun to document that some brain abnormalities are related to the progress of the disease (Brans et al., 2008). For example, **Figure 15.8** presents the data from a longitudinal study of 12 individuals who began to experience symptoms of schizophrenia by age 12 (Thompson et al., 2001). The study focused on changes in grey matter (largely the cell bodies and dendrites of nerve cells in the cortex) over a five-year period. The 12 patients underwent repeated MRI scans, as did an age-matched group of healthy control participants. You may recall from Chapter 11 that adolescent brains are still undergoing processes of change. That's why even the normal adolescents experience some loss of grey matter. However, as

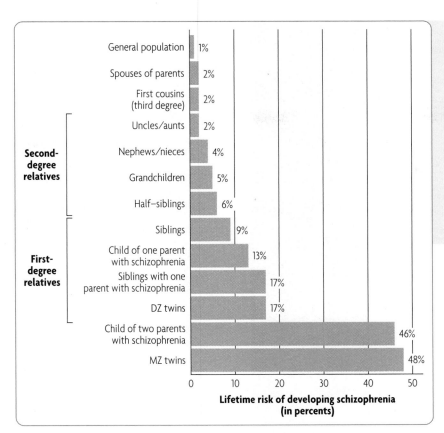

FIGURE 15.6 Genetic Risk of Developing Schizophrenia

FIGURE 15.6 Genetic Risk of
Developing Schizophrenia

The graph shows average risks for developing schizophrenia. Data were compiled from family and twin studies conducted in European populations between 1920 and 1987; the degree of risk correlates highly with the degree of genetic relatedness. Except when the label indicates otherwise, the data reflect the relationship between an individual and someone who has been diagnosed with schizophrenia. For example, the DZ twin of someone diagnosed with schizophrenia has a 17 percent chance of sharing the diagnosis.

you can see in Figure 15.8, the loss of grey matter for the adolescents with schizophrenia was quite dramatic. By monitoring for such changes in people at genetic risk for schizophrenia, clinicians may be able to offer diagnosis and treatment earlier in the disorder (Wood et al., 2008).

Given the wide range of symptoms of schizophrenia, you are probably not surprised by the comparably wide range of biological abnormalities that may be either causes or consequences of the disorder. What are the ways in which features of the environment may prompt people who are at risk to develop the disease?

Environmental Stressors We have been focusing on genetic and biological aspects of schizophrenia. However, as you can see in Figure 15.6, even in the groups with the greatest genetic similarity, the risk factor is less than 50 percent. This indicates that, although genes play a role, environmental conditions may also be necessary to give rise to the disorder. A widely accepted hypothesis for the cause of schizophrenia is the **diathesis-stress hypothesis**. According to the diathesis-stress hypothesis, genetic factors place the individual at risk, but environmental stress factors must impinge for the potential risk to be manifested as a schizophrenic disorder. Let's consider some of those factors.

For example, research has demonstrated that people who live in urban settings, people who experience greater economic difficulties, and people who have migrated from one country to another all experience higher rates of schizophrenia (Tandon, Keshavan, & Nasrallah, 2008). Explanations for these relationships

FIGURE 15.7 Schizophrenia and
Ventricle Size

Male identical twins underwent MRI scans. The scan of the twin with schizophrenia (on the right) reveals enlarged ventricles compared to the scan of the twin without the disorder (on the left).

Photo courtesy of Drs. E. Fuller Torrey and Daniel Weinberger.

diathesis-stress hypothesis A hypothesis about the cause of certain disorders, such as schizophrenia, that suggests that genetic factors predispose an individual to a certain disorder, but that environmental stress factors must impinge in order for the potential risk to manifest itself.

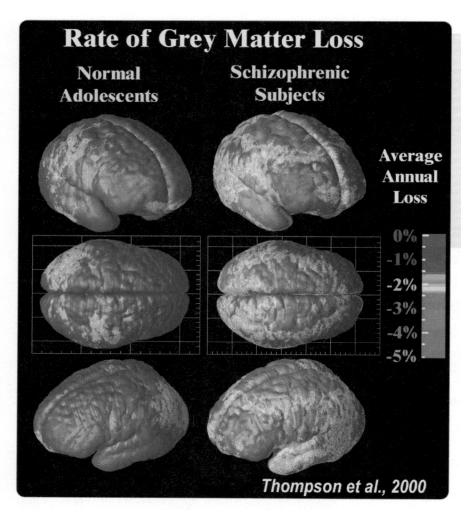

Rate of Grey Matter Loss

Normal Adolescents

Schizophrenic Subjects

Average Annual Loss

0%
-1%
-2%
-3%
-4%
-5%

Thompson et al., 2000

FIGURE 15.8 Grey Matter Loss in Adolescents with Schizophrenia

Researchers carried out MRI scans on 12 adolescents with schizophrenia and 12 age-matched healthy controls. Over a five-year period, the adolescents with schizophrenia showed substantial loss of grey matter in several areas of their brains.

Thompson, P. M., Vidal, C., Giedd, J. N., Gochman, P., Blumenthal, J., Nicolson, R., Toga, A. W., & Rapoport, J. L. (2001). Mapping adolescent brain change reveals dynamic wave of accelerated gray matter loss in very early-onset schizophrenia. *PNAS*, *98*, 11650–11655.

often focus on social stressors and social adversity. Research also suggests that people who experience traumatic life events are at higher risk for schizophrenia. One study examined large samples of individuals in both the United States and Great Britain: The more people had experienced traumas such as physical or sexual abuse, the more likely they were to suffer from a schizophrenic disorder (Shevlin, Houston, Dorahy, & Adamson, 2008).

Researchers have also examined how life events affect changes in people's symptoms once they have been diagnosed with a schizophrenic disorder. Consider a study that demonstrated a relationship between patients' responses to life events and changes in their symptoms.

Researchers assessed the symptoms of patients with a schizophrenic disorder at the beginning and end of a nine-month period (Docherty, St-Hilaire, Aakre, & Seghers, 2008). At the study's outset, the researchers also measured each patient's emotional reactivity—the intensity of an individual's emotional responses to life events. The patients, for example, responded to statements such as "I have big ups and downs in mood" and "I experience very intense emotions" on a scale ranging from "never, or almost never" to "always, or almost always." Nine months later, the patients gave an account of life events from the preceding month. Based on their reports, the researchers sorted them into categories of people who had experienced moderate or severe life events in the past month and those who hadn't. The researchers predicted that negative life events would lead to greater symptoms of schizophrenia—but only for patients who regularly had intense emotional responses to those events. As you can see in **Figure 15.9**, the data supported the prediction. Only patients who had both negative life events and high emotional reactivity showed increases in symptoms (that is, delusions and hallucinations).

We saw earlier that differences in people's responses to life events affect the likelihood that they will experience, for example, major depressive disorder. This study demonstrated a similar pattern for symptoms of schizophrenia.

Research has also looked at family stressors that may affect both the likelihood that people will develop schizophrenic disorders and the likelihood that they will relapse if the symptoms go into remission (Miklowitz & Tompson, 2003). For example, several studies have focused on the concept of expressed emotion. Families are high on expressed emotion if they make a lot of critical comments about the patient, if they are emotionally overinvolved with the patient (that is, if they are overprotective and intrusive), and if they have a generally hostile attitude

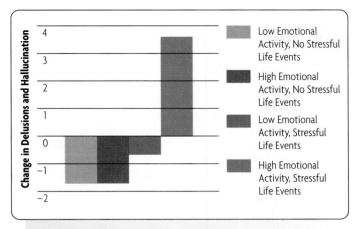

FIGURE 15.9 Changes in Symptoms of Schizophrenic Disorders

Researchers measured patients' emotional reactivity and symptom change over a nine-month period. Only patients who had both negative life events and high emotional reactivity showed increases in symptoms (that is, delusions and hallucinations).

From Docherty, N. M., St-Hillaire, A., Aakre, J. M., & Seghers, J. P. (2008). Life events and high-trait reactivity together predict psychotic symptom increases in schizophrenia. *Schizophrenia Bulletin.*

toward the patient. When patients in remission leave hospitals and return to high-expressed-emotion homes, the risk of relapse is more than twice as high as when they return to low-expressed-emotion homes (Hooley, 2007). If parents are able to reduce their criticism, hostility, and intrusiveness toward offspring with schizophrenia, the recurrence of acute symptoms and the need for re-hospitalization are also reduced (Wearden et al., 2000). The implication is that treatment should be for the entire family as a system, to change the operating style toward the disturbed child.

The number of explanations of schizophrenia that we have reviewed—and the questions that remain despite significant research—suggests how much there is to learn about this powerful psychological disorder. Complicating understanding is the likelihood that the phenomenon called schizophrenia is probably better thought of as a group of disorders, each with potentially distinct causes. Genetic predispositions, brain processes, and family interactions have all been identified as participants in at least some cases. Researchers must still determine the exact ways in which these elements may combine to bring about schizophrenia.

STOP AND REVIEW

❶ Are social withdrawal and flattened emotions positive or negative symptoms of schizophrenia?

❷ For what type of schizophrenic disorder would delusions of persecution or grandeur be symptoms?

❸ What impact does a family's level of expressed emotion have on relapse for schizophrenic disorders?

CRITICAL THINKING Recall the study that looked at the impact of life events on symptoms of schizophrenia. Why was emotional reactivity measured at the beginning of the nine-month period?

Psychological Disorders of Childhood

Our discussion so far has largely focused on adults who suffer from psychopathology. It is important to note, however, that many individuals begin to experience symptoms of mental illness in childhood and adolescence. Researchers have recently intensified their study of the types of stressors that increase the risk of psychopathology in young lives (Zahn-Waxler, Shirtcliff, & Marceau, 2008). Researchers often try to identify behaviour patterns that allow for early diagnosis and treatment. For example, problems with social functioning may provide clues that children and adolescents are at risk for schizophrenia (Tarbox & Pogue-Geile, 2008).

DSM-IV-TR also identifies a range of disorders that are "usually first diagnosed in infancy, childhood, or adolescence." We discussed one of these disorders, *mental retardation*, in Chapter 10. Here, we focus on *attention-deficit hyperactivity disorder* and *autistic disorder*.

ATTENTION-DEFICIT HYPERACTIVITY DISORDER

The definition of **attention-deficit hyperactivity disorder (ADHD)** refers to two clusters of symptoms (*DSM-IV-TR*, 2000). First, children must show a degree of *inattention* that is not consistent with their level of development. They might, for example, have difficulty paying attention in school or often lose items such as toys or school assignments. Second, children must show signs of *hyperactivity–impulsivity* that, once again, are not consistent with their developmental level. Hyperactive behaviours include squirming, fidgeting, and excessive talking; impulsive behaviours include blurting out answers and interrupting. A diagnosis of ADHD requires that children have shown these patterns of behaviour for at least six months before age seven.

Researchers' estimates of the prevalence of ADHD in Canada varies greatly on the basis of the measures used, but they tend to be between 5 and 12 percent of school-age children and 2 to 4 percent of adults (Canadian ADHD Resource Alliance, 2007). Many studies suggest that more boys than girls experience ADHD. However, research also suggests that cultural biases (for example, expectations of gender differences) lead to fewer diagnoses of ADHD among girls than are justified—making it difficult to provide an exact estimate of the gender difference. However, in one large-scale study of adults, 3.2 percent of women and 5.4 percent of men met diagnostic criteria for ADHD (Kessler et al., 2006). These figures may accurately reflect gender differences across the lifespan.

---

attention-deficit hyperactivity disorder (ADHD) A disorder of childhood characterized by inattention and hyperactivity–impulsivity.

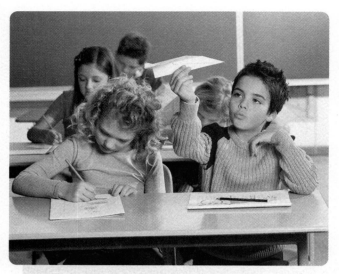

What psychological disorders of childhood might lead to classroom disruptions?

The diagnosis of ADHD is complicated by the fact that many children are prone to episodes of inattention, hyperactivity, or impulsiveness. For that reason, the diagnosis has sometimes been controversial: People have worried that children's normal disorderliness was being labelled as abnormal. However, there is now a large consensus among clinicians that some children's behaviour reaches a level at which it is maladaptive—the children are unable to control their behaviour or to complete tasks. Although there has often been a popular perception that ADHD is overdiagnosed, research evidence contradicts that perception (Sciutto & Eisenberg, 2007). In fact, as we noted earlier, ADHD might actually be underdiagnosed for girls.

As with the other disorders we have described, researchers have considered both the nature and nurture of ADHD. Twin and adoption studies have provided strong evidence for the heritability of the disorder (Biederman & Faraone, 2005). Researchers have started to document relationships between specific genes that affect the brain's neurotransmitter function and the symptoms of ADHD (Smoller et al., 2006). Important environmental variables are also associated with ADHD. For example, children who come from families with economic disadvantages or families with high levels of conflict are more likely to experience the disorder (Biederman, Faraone, & Monteaux, 2002). Some environmental variables have a greater impact on children in different birth positions. For example, the eldest children in families that lack cohesion—families in which members are not committed to providing support to each other—are more at risk for ADHD than are younger siblings in such families (Pressman et al., 2006). Results of this sort suggest that parenting experience has an impact on the incidence of ADHD.

---

autistic disorder A developmental disorder characterized by severe disruption of children's ability to form social bonds and use language.

AUTISTIC DISORDER

Children with **autistic disorder** present severe disruption in their ability to form social bonds. They are likely to have greatly delayed and very limited development of spoken language as well as very narrow interests in the world. Consider a report on a child who was diagnosed with this disorder:

> [Audrey] seemed frightened by nearly any changes in her customary routine, including the presence of strange people. She either shrank from contact with other children or avoided them altogether, seemingly content to engage in nonfunctional play by herself for hours at a time. When she was with other children, she seldom engaged in reciprocal play or even copied any of their motor movements. (Meyer, 2003, p. 244)

Many children with autistic disorder also engage in repetitive and ritualistic behaviours: They might, for example, place objects in lines or symmetrical patterns (Greaves, Prince, Evans, & Charman, 2006).

The number of Canadians with autistic disorder (and related disorders) is estimated to be 1 in 450, or approximately 69 000 (Norris, Paré, & Starky, 2006). A recent U.S. study estimated the prevalence of autistic disorder (and related disorders) in children to be about 1 out of 150 (Centers for Disease Control and Prevention, 2007). Because many of the symptoms of autistic disorder relate to language and social interaction, it has often been difficult to diagnose the disorder until parents notice that their children are failing to use language or interact, starting in their second year. However, recent research has begun to document behaviours in the first year of life that predict later diagnoses of autistic disorder (Zwaigenbaum et al., 2005). For example, children at risk for autistic disorder are less likely to smile in response to social smiles and less likely to respond to their names than are other children.

Causes of Autistic Disorder As with ADHD, autistic disorder has a large genetic component. In fact, researchers have begun to identify the variations in the human genome that may predispose individuals to experience the disorder (Bartlett et al., 2005; Liu et al., 2008). Researchers have also discovered brain markers of the disorder. For example, individuals with autistic disorder experience more rapid brain growth than do their peers (Amaral, Schumann, & Nordahl, 2008). The ongoing question is how such brain abnormalities bring about the symptoms of the disorder.

Researchers have suggested that individuals who suffer from autistic disorder have an inability to develop an understanding of other people's mental states (Baron-Cohen, 2008). Under ordinary circumstances, children develop what has been called a *theory of mind*. At first, they interpret the world only from their own perspective. However, with rapid progress between ages three and four, children develop an understanding that other people have different knowledge, beliefs, and intentions than they do. Research suggests that individuals with autistic disorder lack the ability to develop this understanding. Without a theory of mind, it is quite difficult for people to establish social relationships. Individuals with autistic disorder find it virtually impossible to understand and predict other people's behaviour, making everyday life seem mysterious and hostile.

❶ What types of behaviours characterize ADHD?
❷ Why has it been difficult to diagnose autistic disorder before age two or three?
❸ Why is theory of mind relevant to autistic disorder?

The Stigma of Mental Illness

One of our most important goals for this chapter has been to demystify mental illness—to help you understand how, in some ways, abnormal behaviour is really ordinary. People with psychological disorders are often labelled as *deviant*. However, the deviant label is not true to prevailing realities: When over 20 percent of adults in Canada are hospitalized each year after experiencing some form of psychiatric disorder (Public Health Agency of Canada, 2002a), and other North American studies report that as many as 46.4 percent of adults experience some psychiatric disorder in their lifetime (Kessler et al., 2005a), psychopathology is, at least statistically, relatively normal.

Even given the frequency with which psychopathology touches "normal lives," people who are psychologically disordered are often stigmatized in ways that most physically ill people are not. A **stigma** is a mark or brand of disgrace; in the psychological context, it is a set of negative attitudes about a person that places him or her apart as unacceptable (Hinshaw & Stier, 2008). The woman with schizophrenia we quoted at the beginning of the chapter had this to say: "The patient and public, in my [opinion], needs to be educated about mental illness because people ridicule and mistreat, even misunderstand, us at crucial times." Another recovered patient wrote, "For me, the stigma of mental illness was as devastating as the experience of hospitalization itself. Repeated rejections, the awkwardness of others around me, and my own discomfort and self-consciousness propelled me into solitary confinement" (Houghton, 1980, pp. 7–8). Negative attitudes toward the psychologically disturbed come from many sources: The mass media portray psychiatric patients as prone to violent crime; jokes about the mentally ill are acceptable; families deny the mental distress of one of their members; legal terminology stresses mental incompetence. People also stigmatize themselves by hiding current psychological distress or a history of mental health care.

Researchers have documented a number of ways in which the stigma of mental illness has a negative impact on people's lives (Hinshaw & Stier, 2008). In one sample of 84 men who had been hospitalized for mental illness, 6 percent reported having lost a job because of their hospitalization; 10 percent reported having been denied an apartment or room; 37 percent reported being avoided by others; and 45 percent reported that others had used their history of mental illness to hurt their feelings. Only 6 percent of the men reported no incidents of rejection (Link et al., 1997). This group of men went through a year-long course of treatment that resulted in considerable improvement in their mental health. Even so, at the end of that year, there were no changes in their perception of stigma: Despite their improvements in functioning, the patients did not expect to be treated any more kindly by the world. This type of research shows the great duality of many people's experience with mental disorders: Seeking help—allowing one's problems to be labelled—generally brings both relief *and* stigma; treatment improves quality of life at the same time that stigma degrades it (Rosenfield, 1997).

An added difficulty is that people with mental illness often internalize expectations of rejections that may, in turn, bring about negative interactions (Pachankis, 2007). Consider this classic experiment.

> Twenty-nine men who had formerly been hospitalized for mental illness volunteered to participate in this study. They believed that the research concerned the difficulties ex-psychiatric patients have with finding jobs. The participants were informed that they would interact with a personnel trainee recruited from a business establishment. Half of the participants were told that the trainee knew of their status as ex-psychiatric patients; the other half were told that the trainee had been led to believe they had been medical or surgical patients at the hospital. In fact, the "trainee" was a confederate of the experimenter who did not have any prior information about the participants' beliefs about his knowledge. That is, he did not know which participants thought that *he* knew that they were ex-patients. Therefore, any differences in the interactions during the time the participants and confederate spent together can be attributed to the participants' *expectations*. In fact, the participants who believed themselves to have been labelled as ex-psychiatric patients talked less during the session and performed less well on a co-operative task. Furthermore, the confederate rated members of this group as more "tense and anxious" without, again, knowing which group each participant was in. (Farina et al., 1971)

The important conclusion here is that people who believe that others have attached the "mental illness" label to them may change their interactions in a way that brings about genuine discomfort: The expectation of rejection can create rejection; mental illness can be another of life's unfortunate self-fulfilling prophecies.

A final note on stigma: Research suggests that people who have had prior contact with individuals with mental illnesses hold attitudes that are less affected by stigma (Couture & Penn, 2003). For example, students who read a vignette about a man named Jim who had recovered from schizophrenia were more optimistic about Jim's future prospects when the students had had prior contact with someone who suffered from a mental illness (Penn et al., 1994). Similarly, students' ratings of the dangerousness of patients with schizophrenia were lower when they had had prior contact with people affected by schizophrenia (Penn, Kommana, Mansfield, & Link, 1999). We hope that one consequence of reading this chapter and the next will be to help modify your beliefs about what it means to be mentally ill and what it means to be "cured"—and to increase your tolerance and compassion for mentally ill individuals.

---

stigma The negative reaction of people to an individual or group because of some assumed inferiority or source of difference that is considered unacceptable.

In making sense of psychopathology, you are forced to come to grips with basic conceptions of normality, reality, and social values. In discovering how to understand, treat, and, ideally, prevent psychological disorders, researchers not only help those who are suffering and losing out on the joys of living, but also expand the basic understanding of human nature. How do psychologists and psychiatrists intervene to right minds gone wrong and to modify behaviour that does not work? We will see in the next chapter on therapies.

STOP AND REVIEW

❶ In the context of mental illness, how does stigma function?

❷ Why does treatment for mental illness often bring about both relief and stigma?

❸ What types of experience reduce stigma?

CRITICAL THINKING Consider the study on ex-psychiatric patients' expectations of rejections. Why was it important that the confederate not know which patients were in which group?

Recapping Main Points

The Nature of Psychological Disorders

- Abnormality is judged by the degree to which a person's actions resemble a set of indicators that include distress, maladaptiveness, irrationality, unpredictability, unconventionality, observer discomfort, and violation of standards or societal norms.
- Objectivity is an important problem for discussions of mental illness.
- Classification systems for psychological disorders should provide a common shorthand for communicating about general types of psychopathologies and specific cases.
- The most widely accepted diagnostic and classification system is *DSM-IV-TR*.
- The biological approach to the etiology of mental illness concentrates on abnormalities in the brain, biochemical processes, and genetic influences.
- Psychological approaches include psychodynamic, behavioural, cognitive, and sociocultural models.

Visit **MyPsychLab.com** for more review and practice on the following topics:

✓ **Practice:** The Nature of Psychological Disorders

Anxiety Disorders

- The five major types of anxiety disorders are generalized, panic, phobic, obsessive-compulsive, and post-traumatic stress.
- Research has confirmed genetic and brain bases for anxiety disorders as well as behavioural and cognitive components of causality.

Visit **MyPsychLab.com** for more review and practice on the following topics:

👁 **Watch:** Fear of Flying

Mood Disorders

- Major depressive disorder is the most common mood disorder; bipolar disorder is much rarer.

- People have genetic predispositions toward mood disorders.
- Mood disorders change the way people respond to life experiences.
- Women's higher level of major depressive disorder may reflect differences in negative life experiences as well as cognitive responses to those experiences.
- Suicides are most frequent among people suffering from depression.

Visit **MyPsychLab.com** for more review and practice on the following topics:

✱ **Explore:** Learned Helplessness: An Experimental Procedure

Personality Disorders

- Personality disorders are patterns of perception, thought, or behaviour that are long-standing and inflexible and that impair an individual's functioning.
- Both borderline personality disorder and antisocial personality disorder arise because of genetic and environmental factors.

Somatoform and Dissociative Disorders

- Somatoform disorders such as hypochondriasis, somatization disorder, and conversion disorder are characterized by circumstances in which physical illnesses or complaints cannot be fully explained by actual medical conditions.
- Dissociative disorders involve a disruption of the integrated functioning of memory, consciousness, or personal identity.

Schizophrenic Disorders

- Schizophrenia is a severe form of psychopathology characterized by extreme distortions in perception, thinking, emotion, behaviour, and language.
- The five subtypes of schizophrenia are disorganized, catatonic, paranoid, undifferentiated, and residual.

- Evidence for the causes of schizophrenia has been found in a variety of factors, including genetics, brain abnormalities, and family processes.

Visit **MyPsychLab.com** for more review and practice on the following topics:

⏴⦿ **Simulate:** Schizophrenia

Psychological Disorders of Childhood

- Children with ADHD display inattention and hyperactivity–impulsivity.

- Autistic disorder is characterized by severe disruption of children's ability to form social bonds and use language.

The Stigma of Mental Illness

- Those with psychological disorders are often stigmatized in ways that most physically ill people are not.
- Although treatment for psychological disorders brings about positive changes, the stigma associated with mental illness has a negative impact on quality of life.

KEY TERMS

abnormal psychology (p. 463)
agoraphobia (p. 470)
antisocial personality disorder (p. 482)
anxiety disorders (p. 469)
attention-deficit hyperactivity
    disorder (p. 491)
autistic disorder (p. 492)
bipolar disorder (p. 476)
borderline personality disorder (p. 481)
comorbidity (p. 466)
conversion disorder (p. 484)
delusions (p. 487)
diathesis-stress hypothesis (p. 489)
dissociative amnesia (p. 485)
dissociative disorder (p. 484)

dissociative fugue (p. 485)
dissociative identity disorder (DID) (p. 485)
DSM-IV-TR (p. 466)
etiology (p. 468)
fear (p. 471)
generalized anxiety disorder (p. 469)
hypochondriasis (p. 484)
insanity (p. 467)
learned helplessness (p. 477)
major depressive disorder (p. 475)
manic episode (p. 476)
mood disorder (p. 475)
neurotic disorders (p. 467)
obsessive-compulsive disorder (OCD)
    (p. 472)

panic disorder (p. 469)
personality disorder (p. 480)
phobia (p. 471)
post-traumatic stress disorder (PTSD)
    (p. 472)
psychological diagnosis (p. 465)
psychopathological functioning (p. 463)
psychotic disorders (p. 467)
schizophrenic disorder (p. 486)
social phobia (p. 471)
somatization disorder (p. 484)
somatoform disorder (p. 483)
specific phobias (p. 471)
stigma (p. 493)

Practice Test

1. Comorbidity refers to circumstances in which an individual _____
   a. cannot be accurately diagnosed using *DSM-IV-TR*.
   b. has a neurotic disorder that cannot be easily cured.
   c. has a psychotic disorder that includes a fear of death.
   d. experiences more than one psychological disorder at the same time.

2. Professor Hexter believes that unconscious conflicts often cause psychological disorders. Which approach to psychopathology does Professor Hexter use?
   a. psychodynamic   c. cognitive
   b. sociocultural   d. behavioural

3. Analyses of legal records suggest that the use of the insanity defence is quite _____ and the probability of its succeeding is quite _____
   a. rare; low   c. common; low
   b. rare; high   d. common; high

4. For binge eating disorder, which criterion is still being researched as a potential part of the diagnosis?
   a. regular episodes of binge eating without purges
   b. a loss of control during binges
   c. binges causing great distress
   d. undue influence of body weight or shape on self-evaluation

5. For over a year, Jane has felt anxious or worried throughout the day. It sounds like Jane is suffering from _____
   a. panic disorder.
   b. generalized anxiety disorder.
   c. obsessive-compulsive disorder.
   d. agoraphobia.

6. What attribution style puts people at risk for depression?
   a. internal–specific–stable
   b. external–specific–unstable
   c. internal–global–stable
   d. external–global–unstable

7. When something bad happens, Chris spends a lot of time ruminating about the problem. Based on this behaviour, you think it is _____
   a. more likely that Chris is a man.
   b. equally likely that Chris is a man or a woman.
   c. likely that Chris will develop a specific phobia.
   d. more likely that Chris is a woman.

8. You are trying to assess the probability that Paula will develop major depressive disorder. You would be most concerned if she had the _____ form of the serotonin gene as well as _____ stressful life events.
   a. s/l; two   c. l/l; four
   b. s/s; three   d. s/l; three

9. Nadine alternates between yelling at Tricia and begging her to remain friends. Tricia is convinced that Nadine suffers from _____ personality disorder.
   a. schizotypal   c. borderline
   b. narcissistic   d. obsessive-compulsive

10. To diagnose conversion disorder, you would try to find _____ that preceded the appearance of symptoms.
    a. a serious physical illness
    b. psychological conflict or stress
    c. a visit to a medical doctor
    d. both pain and gastrointestinal complaints

11. Although Eve does not have any organic dysfunction, she often forgets important personal experiences. This could be an instance of _____
    a. dissociative amnesia.   c. somatization disorder.
    b. hypochondriasis.   d. dependent personality disorder.

12. Which of these is a negative symptom of schizophrenia?
    a. hallucinations   c. delusions
    b. incoherent language   d. social withdrawal

13. Which of these behaviours would *not* generally support a diagnosis of attention-deficit hyperactivity disorder?
    a. Manfred blurts out answers during class activities.
    b. Manfred loses his toys and school assignments.
    c. Manfred squirms and fidgets in the classroom.
    d. Manfred cries when other children tease him.

14. Professor Wyatt believes that one-year-old Brian is at risk for autistic disorder. The professor might observe Brian to determine whether he _____
    a. fails to respond to his name.
    b. can walk without assistance.
    c. responds appropriately to loud noises.
    d. shows smooth pursuit with his eyes.

15. As part of an introductory psychology class, a professor has her students interview people who have recovered from psychological disorders. This exercise should _____
    a. prompt the students to be more affected by the stigma of mental illness.
    b. have no impact on the students' experience of stigma.
    c. prompt the students to be less affected by the stigma of mental illness.
    d. decrease the probability that students would seek treatment for mental illness.

Essay Questions

1. Why is it not always possible to be objective about diagnoses of mental illness?

2. What are some benefits of a useful classification system for psychological disorders?

3. What life circumstances lead some people to contemplate suicide?

Discovering Psychology Viewing Guide

Watch the following video by logging on to MyPsychLab (**www.mypsychlab.com**). After you have watched the video, complete the activities that follow.

Program 21: Psychopathology

PROGRAM REVIEW

1. Psychopathology is defined as the study of _____
   a. organic brain disease.
   b. perceptual and cognitive illusions.
   c. clinical measures of abnormal functioning.
   d. mental disorders.

2. What happened after David Rosenhan and his colleagues were admitted to mental hospitals by pretending to have hallucinations and then behaved normally?
   a. Their sanity was quickly observed by the staff.
   b. It took several days for their deception to be realized.
   c. In most cases, the staff disagreed with each other about these "patients."
   d. Nobody ever detected their sanity.

3. Agoraphobia is one of the most common phobias. What does a person with this condition fear?
   a. being at the top of a tall building
   b. going out in public
   c. being violently attacked
   d. experiences in general

4. When Freud studied patients with anxiety, he determined that their symptoms were caused by _____
   a. actual childhood abuse, both physical and sexual.
   b. imbalances in body chemistry.
   c. childhood conflicts that had been repressed.
   d. cognitive errors in the way patients viewed the world.

5. What happens to most people who are suffering from serious clinical depression?
   a. They commit suicide.
   b. They are hospitalized.
   c. They receive treatment outside a hospital.
   d. They receive no treatment at all.

6. People lose touch with reality in cases of _____
   a. neurosis but not psychosis.
   b. psychosis but not neurosis.
   c. both psychosis and neurosis.
   d. all psychoses and some neuroses.

7. Irving Gottesman and Fuller Torrey have been studying twins to learn more about schizophrenia. If the brain of a twin with schizophrenia is compared with the brain of a normal twin, the former has _____
   a. less cerebrospinal fluid.
   b. larger ventricles.
   c. a larger left hemisphere.
   d. exactly the same configuration as the latter.

8. Which of the following people would argue that psychopathology is a myth?
   a. Philippe Pinel   c. Teresa LaFromboise
   b. Thomas Szasz   d. Sigmund Freud

9. What might a severe viral infection do to a woman who has a genetic predisposition toward schizophrenia?
   a. make her schizophrenic
   b. destroy the genetic marker and make her mentally more stable
   c. redirect the predisposition toward a different class of mental illness
   d. kill her with greater likelihood than if she did not have a predisposition toward mental illness

10. All of the following are typically true about schizophrenia, except that _____
    a. fewer than one-third improve with treatment.
    b. the people who have it are aware that they are mentally ill.
    c. about 1 percent of the world's total population is schizophrenic.
    d. it is associated with impaired thinking, emotion, and perception.

11. Who is credited as being the first to introduce the idea that insane people are ill?
    a. Sigmund Freud   c. Emil Kraepelin
    b. Jean Charcot   d. Philippe Pinel

12. Which of the following is characterized by boundless energy, optimism, and risk-taking behaviour?
    a. a manic episode   c. anxiety disorders
    b. paranoid schizophrenia   d. depression

QUESTIONS TO CONSIDER

1. If a person is mentally ill and has violated the law, under what circumstances should he or she be considered responsible for the criminal actions? Under what circumstances should we consider the person able to be rehabilitated?

2. Why has the *DSM* been criticized?

3. Are standards for psychological health the same for men and women? Why are most patients women?

4. How can you tell whether your own behaviour, anxieties, and moods are within normal limits or whether they signal mental illness?

16
Therapies for Psychological Disorders

As you read Chapter 15, you might at some points have felt overwhelmed by all the ways in which individuals can experience mental illness. Fortunately, psychologists and other providers of mental health care have worked intently to create therapies that address the full range of psychopathology. We will see in this chapter that researchers continue to generate innovations in therapeutic techniques. The more researchers learn about the causes and consequences of psychopathology—the research we described in Chapter 15—the better they are able to fine-tune their repertory of therapies.

In this chapter, we will examine the types of therapies that can help restore personal control to individuals with a range of disorders. We address a number of formidable questions: How has the treatment of psychological disorders been influenced by historical, cultural, and social forces? How do theory, research, and practice interact as researchers develop and test treatment methods? What can be done to influence a mind ungoverned by ordinary reason, to modify uncontrolled behaviour, to alter unchecked emotions, and to correct abnormalities of the brain?

This chapter surveys the major types of treatments currently used by health-care providers: psychoanalysis, behaviour modification, cognitive alteration, humanistic therapies, and drug therapies. We will examine the way these treatments work. We will also evaluate the validity of claims about the success of each therapy.

The Therapeutic Context

There are different types of therapies for mental disorders, and there are many reasons some people seek help (and others who need it do not). The purposes or goals of therapy, the settings in which therapy occurs, and the kinds of therapeutic helpers also vary. Despite any differences between therapies, however, all are *interventions* into a person's life, designed to change the person's functioning in some way.

GOALS AND MAJOR THERAPIES

The therapeutic process can involve four primary tasks or goals:

1. Reaching a *diagnosis* about what is wrong, possibly determining an appropriate psychiatric (*DSM-IV-TR*) label for the presenting problem, and classifying the disorder.
2. Proposing a probable *etiology* (cause of the problem)— that is, identifying the probable origins of the disorder and the functions being served by the symptoms.
3. Making a *prognosis*, or estimate, of the course the problem will take with and without any treatment.
4. Prescribing and carrying out some form of *treatment*, a therapy designed to minimize or eliminate the troublesome symptoms and, perhaps, their sources.

Biomedical therapies focus on changing the mechanisms that run the central nervous system. Practised largely by psychiatrists and physicians, these therapies try to alter brain functioning with chemical or physical interventions, including surgery, electric shock, and drugs that act directly on the brain–body connection.

Psychological therapies, which are collectively called **psychotherapy**, focus on changing the faulty behaviours people have learned: the words, thoughts, interpretations, and feedback that direct daily strategies for living. These therapies are practised by clinical psychologists as well as by psychiatrists. There are four major types of psychotherapies: psychodynamic, behavioural, cognitive, and existential-humanistic.

The *psychodynamic* approach views neurotic suffering as the outer symptom of inner, unresolved traumas and conflicts. Psychodynamic therapists treat mental disorders with a "talking cure," in which a therapist helps a person develop insights about the relation between the overt symptoms and the unresolved hidden conflicts that presumably caused them.

Behaviour therapy treats the behaviours themselves as disturbances that must be modified. Disorders are viewed as learned behaviour patterns rather than as the symptoms of mental disease. Behaviours are transformed in many ways, including changing reinforcement contingencies for desirable and undesirable responding, extinguishing conditioned responses, and providing models of effective problem solving.

Cognitive therapy tries to restructure the way a person thinks by altering the often distorted self-statements a person makes about the causes of a problem. Restructuring cognitions changes the way a person defines and explains difficulties, often enabling the person to cope with the problems.

Therapies that have emerged from the *existential humanistic tradition* emphasize the patients' values. They are directed toward self-actualization, psychological growth, the development of more meaningful interpersonal relationships, and the enhancement of freedom of choice. They tend to focus more on improving the functioning of essentially healthy people than on correcting the symptoms of seriously disturbed individuals.

Although we have introduced each type of psychotherapy separately, it is important to note that many psychotherapists take an *integrative* approach to practice: They integrate different theoretical approaches to provide maximum benefit to their patients or clients. In many cases, psychotherapists begin their careers adhering to a particular theoretical orientation. However, as their careers unfold, they begin to mix together the most effective elements of different therapies (Norcross, Karpiak, & Lister, 2005). Psychotherapists integrate across virtually every pair of orientations (e.g., cognitive and humanistic; behavioural and psychodynamic). However, the most prominent integrative therapies combine aspects of the cognitive and behavioural approaches (Goldfried, 2003; Norcross et al., 2005). Later in the chapter, we describe integrative cognitive behavioural therapies.

THERAPISTS AND THERAPEUTIC SETTINGS

When psychological problems arise, most people initially seek out informal counsellors who operate in familiar settings. Many people turn to family members, close friends, personal physicians, lawyers, or favourite teachers for support, guidance, and

---

biomedical therapies Treatments for psychological disorders that alter brain functioning with chemical or physical interventions such as drug therapy, surgery, or electroconvulsive therapy.

psychotherapy Any of a group of therapies used to treat psychological disorders that focuses on changing faulty behaviours, thoughts, perceptions, and emotions that may be associated with specific disorders.

counsel. Those with religious affiliations may seek help from a clergy member. Others get advice and a chance to talk by opening up to bartenders, salesclerks, cabdrivers, or other people willing to listen. In our society, these informal therapists carry the bulk of the daily burden of relieving frustration and conflict. When problems are limited in scope, informal therapists can often help.

Although more people seek out therapy now than in the past, people usually turn to trained mental health professionals only when their psychological problems become severe or persist for extended periods of time. When they do, they can turn to several types of therapists.

A **clinical social worker** is a mental health professional whose specialized training in a school of social work prepares him or her to work in collaboration with psychiatrists and clinical psychologists. Unlike many psychiatrists and psychologists, these counsellors are trained to consider the social contexts of people's problems, so they may also involve other family members in the therapy or at least become acquainted with clients' homes or work settings.

A **pastoral counsellor** is a member of a religious group who specializes in the treatment of psychological disorders. Often, these counsellors combine spirituality with practical problem solving.

A **clinical psychologist** is required to have concentrated his or her graduate school training in the assessment and treatment of psychological problems, completed a year-long supervised internship in a clinical setting, carried out an independent line of research, and earned a PhD. These psychologists tend to have a broader background in psychology, assessment, and research than do psychiatrists.

A **counselling psychologist** also typically has obtained a PhD. He or she usually provides guidance in areas such as vocation selection, school problems, drug abuse, and marital conflict. Often, these counsellors work in community settings related to the problem areas—within a business, a school, a prison, the military service, or a neighbourhood clinic—and

use interviews, tests, guidance, and advising to help individuals solve specific problems and make decisions about future options.

A **psychiatrist** must have completed all medical school training for an MD degree and also have undergone some postdoctoral specialty training in mental and emotional disorders. Psychiatrists are trained more in the biomedical basis of psychological problems, and they are currently the only therapists who can prescribe medical or drug-based interventions.

A **psychoanalyst** is a therapist with either an MD or a PhD degree who has completed specialized postgraduate training in the Freudian approach to understanding and treating mental disorders.

These different types of therapists practise in many settings: hospitals, clinics, schools, and private offices. Some humanistic therapists prefer to conduct group sessions in their homes in order to work in a more natural environment. Community-based therapies, which take the treatment to the client, may operate out of local storefronts or houses of worship. Finally, some therapists work with clients in the life setting that is associated with their problem. For example, they work in airplanes with clients who suffer from flying phobias or in shopping malls with people who have social phobias.

Psychotherapists have also begun to provide mental health care using email or the internet (King & Moreggi, 1998; Rochlen, Zack, & Speyer, 2004; Taylor & Luce, 2003). In this type of computer-assisted therapy, individuals often interact with their therapists through exchanges of email. Researchers have been quick to point out both potential dangers and benefits of therapy on the internet. One danger is that researchers worry patients may be misdiagnosed if they present limited or distorted information without the extra scrutiny that is possible face to face (Bhuvaneswar & Gutheil, 2008; King & Moreggi, 1998). Furthermore, consumers rarely are able to verify the credentials of online therapists; in cyberspace anyone can claim to be an expert. Despite these dangers, email therapy may also provide unique opportunities for therapists and their clients. For example, some therapists believe that the relative anonymity of this form of therapy allows clients to reveal their most pressing problems and concerns more quickly and with less embarrassment; individuals may be more honest when they do not have to worry about their therapist's overt reactions to their difficult confessions (Grohol, 1998).

People who enter therapy are usually referred to as either patients or clients. The term **patient** is used by professionals who take a biomedical approach to the treatment of psychological problems. The term **client** is used by professionals who think of psychological disorders as "problems in living" and not as mental illnesses. We will use the preferred term for each approach: *patient* for biomedical and psychoanalytic therapies and *client* for other therapies.

Whatever the form of the treatment, it is important that the individual seeking help enter into an effective therapeutic alliance. A *therapeutic alliance* is a mutual relationship that a client or patient establishes with a therapist: The individual and the therapist collaborate to bring about relief. Research suggests that the quality of the therapeutic alliance has an impact on psychotherapy's ability to bring about improved mental health (Goldfried & Davila, 2005; Joyce, Ogrodniczuk, Piper, & McCallum, 2003). When you enter into therapy, you should believe that you can establish a strong therapeutic alliance with your therapist.

---

clinical social worker A mental health professional whose specialized training prepares him or her to consider the social context of people's problems.

pastoral counsellor A member of a religious order who specializes in the treatment of psychological disorders, often combining spirituality with practical problem solving.

clinical psychologist An individual who has earned a doctorate in psychology and whose training is in the assessment and treatment of psychological problems.

counselling psychologist Psychologist who specializes in providing guidance in areas such as vocational selections, school problems, drug abuse, and marital conflict.

psychiatrist An individual who has obtained an MD degree and also has completed postdoctoral specialty training in mental and emotional disorders; a psychiatrist is authorized to prescribe medications for the treatment of psychological disorders.

psychoanalyst An individual who has earned either a PhD or an MD degree and has completed postgraduate training in the Freudian approach to understanding and treating mental disorders.

patient The term used by those who take a biomedical approach to the treatment of psychological problems to describe the person being treated.

client The term used by clinicians who think of psychological disorders as problems in living, and not as mental illnesses, to describe those being treated.

DIVERSITY ISSUES IN PSYCHOTHERAPY

An important goal for clinicians is to provide relief to all people who suffer from psychological disorders. However, that goal is complicated by cultural and gender diversity. To begin, not all cultural groups are equally likely to undergo treatment (Wang et al., 2005). For example, in North America, Caucasians are more likely to seek treatment than are members of racialized or minority groups. An important part of that difference is unequal access to both physical and mental health care. However, cultural norms also affect the extent to which people seek psychological care (Snowden & Yamada, 2005).

Another diversity issue arises once people actually seek therapy: The important question becomes whether particular therapies are equally effective across all cultural groups. Although there are large bodies of research that address the effectiveness of various forms of psychotherapy, only a very small part of the research literature assesses effectiveness in minority groups (Miranda et al., 2005). Fortunately, the limited number of studies that do exist are largely optimistic with respect to the broad applicability of standard therapies. For example, one review found that cognitive behavioural therapies (which we review later in the chapter) are mostly effective for adult clients from minority cultures (Voss Horrell, 2008). More research is required to confirm these early results.

Similarly, more research is needed to assess the extent to which men and women benefit from the same therapies (Sigmon et al., 2007). In earlier chapters, we reviewed gender differences in the prevalence of psychological disorders. Recall, for example, that women experience more eating disorders than men do. For that reason, most psychotherapies for eating disorders have been developed for girls and young women (Greenberg & Schoen, 2008). Researchers must determine to what extent the same approaches are effective for men. Similarly, researchers must determine whether therapies that clinicians originated to treat men must be modified to bring relief to women.

A final diversity issue arises with respect to the training of psychotherapists: Therapists must be prepared to provide treatments that are sensitive to cultural differences. Researchers have suggested, in particular, that therapists must have cultural competence (Whaley & Davis, 2007). Cultural competence has been defined as having three components (Sue, 2006, p. 238):

- "Cultural awareness and beliefs: Provider's sensitivity to her or his personal values and biases and how these may influence perceptions of the client, client's problem, and the counselling relationship."
- "Cultural knowledge: Counsellor's knowledge of the client's culture, worldview, and expectations for the counselling relationship."
- "Cultural skills: Counsellor's ability to intervene in a manner that is culturally sensitive and relevant."

Research suggests that therapists with greater cultural competence also have better therapeutic outcomes with patients and clients from diverse groups (Worthington, Soth-McNett, & Moreno, 2008).

Before looking at contemporary therapies and therapists in more detail, we will first consider the historical contexts in which treatment of the mentally ill was developed.

HISTORICAL PERSPECTIVES ON INSTITUTIONAL TREATMENT

What kind of treatment might you have received in past centuries if you were suffering from psychological problems? For much of history, chances are the treatment would not have helped—and could even have been harmful. We will trace the institutional treatment of psychological disorders to the 21st century, in which *deinstitutionalization*—the practice of moving people from psychiatric hospitals to other venues for treatment—has become an important issue.

History of Treatment Increases in population and migration to big cities in 14th-century Western Europe created unemployment and social alienation. These conditions led to poverty, crime, and psychological problems. Special institutions were soon created to warehouse society's three emerging categories of so-called misfits: the poor, criminals, and the mentally disturbed.

In 1403, a London hospital—St. Mary of Bethlehem—admitted its first patient with psychological problems. For the next 300 years, mental patients of the hospital were chained, tortured, and exhibited to an admission-paying public. Over time, a mispronunciation of Bethlehem—*bedlam*—came to mean chaos because of the horrible confusion reigning in the hospital and the dehumanized treatment of patients there (Foucault, 1975).

Treatment of mental disorders in the 18th century focused on banishing "ill humours" from the body. Shown here is the "tranquilizing chair" advocated by Philadelphia physician Benjamin Rush. Why did attitudes toward the treatment of the mentally ill change?

It was not until the late 18th century that the perception of psychological problems as mental illness emerged in Europe. In 1792, the French physician Philippe Pinel received permission from the government installed after the French Revolution to remove the chains from some of the inmates in mental hospitals. In North America, psychologically disturbed individuals were confined for their own protection and for the safety of the community, but they were given no treatment. However, by the mid-1800s, when psychology as a field of study was gaining some credibility and respectability, "a cult of curability" emerged. Spurred on by her firsthand experience working in prison settings, **Dorothea Dix** laboured continuously between 1841 and 1881 to improve the physical treatment of the mentally ill in the United States and Canada.

In the late 19th and early 20th centuries, many people argued that mental illness arose from the environmental stresses brought on by the turmoil of newly developing cities. To ease those stresses, the disturbed were confined to asylums in rural areas, far from the stress of the city, not only for protection but also for treatment (Rothman, 1971). Unfortunately, many of the asylums that were built became overcrowded. The humane goal of alleviating mental illness was replaced with the pragmatic goal of containing strange people in remote places. These large, understaffed state mental hospitals became little more than human warehouses for disturbed individuals (Scull, 1993). Beginning in the 1960s, reformers began to agitate against these warehouses in favour of the deinstitutionalization of at least those mental patients who could thrive with outpatient treatment and appropriate community supports. Unfortunately, as we will see next, many deinstitutionalized patients do not obtain adequate assistance in their communities.

Deinstitutionalization and Homelessness In the late 1940s and early 1950s, about 66 000 people in Canada were residents in mental hospitals (Rae-Grant, 2001). This number remained relatively constant until the mid-1960s, but declined sharply thereafter, with the number of psychiatric hospital beds available decreasing by more than 62 percent between 1975 and 1980 (from 53 801 to 20 301); that number decreased by an additional 41 percent between 1985 and 1999 (Sealy & Whitehead, 2004). This substantial reduction in the number of hospitalized psychiatric patients in Canada has been parallelled in other countries around the world (Fakhoury & Priebe, 2002). As you read in Chapter 15, it is not the case that the number of people affected by psychological disorders has fallen. Rather, the change reflects a process of **deinstitutionalization**, which means that many people with disorders are now treated outside of hospital settings. Deinstitutionalization arose from both social forces (i.e., the movement against the warehousing of people with mental illness) and genuine advances in treatment. For example, later in this chapter we will describe drug treatments that allowed people with schizophrenia to live outside of institutions.

Many people have been deinstitutionalized with the assumption that they will receive mental health care in some other setting. Unfortunately, that has not always proven to be the case. In fact, many people who leave psychiatric hospitals are not able to cope with their psychological disorders once

they are in the community. One consequence is that people who leave institutions become homeless. This point was well-illustrated in a 2004 study that Riordan conducted in Toronto, which estimated that approximately 66 percent of homeless people in that city had a lifetime diagnosis of mental illness, roughly two to three times the rate of the general population. In addition, 66 percent had a substance abuse problem, and many had both. In total, 86 percent had either a mental illness or an addiction. The most recent comprehensive study of homelessness in Canada (CIHI, 2007) estimates that, on any given night, roughly 10 000 people do not have a roof over their head. This shocking estimate may in fact underestimate the extent of homelessness in Canada since recent figures from British Columbia suggest that 11 750 people are chronically homeless in that province alone (Patterson et al., 2008). This problem is not unique to Canada. For instance, in the United States, among people who were admitted to a major state mental hospital in 1980, 15.3 percent were homeless. By 1996, that figure had risen to 20.2 percent, and by 2003 to 29.2 percent (Appleby, Luchins, & Freels, 2006).

Even when deinstitutionalized people are not homeless, ongoing mental health issues can cause substantial problems. For example, a report from the Correctional Service of Canada revealed that in 1998 just over 7 percent of the federal penitentiary inmates had some mental illness; that number rose to about 12 percent by 2004 (The Correctional Investigator, 2004–2005). Those who suffer from mental illness are also significantly more likely to be the victims of violent crime. In a recent U.S. study (Teplin, McClelland, Abram, & Weiner, 2005) of 936 men and women with mental illness, 25.3 percent had experienced a violent crime—a rate 11 times higher than for individuals in the general population. The researchers suggested that the individuals' mental illnesses may prevent them from recognizing risk or appropriately protecting themselves.

Another consequence of deinstitutionalization is what has sometimes been called the "revolving door": People leave institutions for only brief periods of time before needing help once again. For example, one large-scale study looked at 29 373 patients with schizophrenia who had been released from hospitals. The researchers found that 42.5 percent of the patients were readmitted within 30 days of their initial release (Lin et al., 2006). More generally, approximately 40 to 50 percent of psychiatric patients are readmitted within one year after their initial discharge (Bridge & Barbe, 2004). In many of these cases, individuals left institutional care with the symptoms of their psychological disorders at a level that could have allowed them to function in the outside world. Unfortunately, people often do not have appropriate community or personal resources to adhere to treatment outside the structure provided by an institution. In that sense, the problem is not so much with deinstitutionalization as it is with the lack of community resources outside the institutions.

STOP AND REVIEW

❶ What are the primary goals of the therapeutic process?
❷ What special training does a psychoanalyst have?
❸ Why is cultural competence important for therapists?
❹ With respect to deinstitutionalization, what is meant by the "revolving door"?

---

deinstitutionalization The movement to treat people with psychological disorders in the community rather than in psychiatric hospitals.

Psychodynamic Therapies

Psychodynamic therapies assume that a patient's problems have been caused by the psychological tension between unconscious impulses and the constraints of his or her life situation. These therapies locate the core of the disorder inside the disturbed person. We will review the origins of this approach in the work of Sigmund Freud and his followers. We will then describe how contemporary clinicians use psychodynamic therapies.

FREUDIAN PSYCHOANALYSIS

Psychoanalysis, as developed by Sigmund Freud, is an intensive and prolonged technique for exploring unconscious motivations and conflicts in neurotic, anxiety-ridden individuals. As we saw in earlier chapters, Freudian theory views anxiety disorders as inabilities to resolve adequately the inner conflicts between the unconscious, irrational impulses of the *id* and the internalized social constraints imposed by the *superego*. The goal of psychoanalysis is to establish intrapsychic harmony that expands awareness of the forces of the *id*, reduces overcompliance with the demands of the *superego*, and strengthens the role of the *ego*.

Of central importance to a therapist is to understand the way a patient uses the process of *repression* to handle conflicts. Symptoms are considered to be messages from the unconscious that something is wrong. A psychoanalyst's task is to help a patient bring repressed thoughts to consciousness and to gain *insight* into the relationship between the current symptoms and the repressed conflicts. In this psychodynamic view, therapy succeeds and patients recover when they are "released from repression" established in early childhood. Because a central goal of a therapist is to guide a patient toward discovering insights into the relationships between present symptoms and past origins, psychodynamic therapy is often called **insight therapy**.

Traditional psychoanalysis is an attempt to reconstruct long-standing repressed memories and then work through painful feelings to an effective resolution. The psychodynamic approach includes several techniques to bring repressed conflicts to consciousness and to help a patient resolve them (Luborsky & Barrett, 2006). These techniques include free association, analysis of resistance, dream analysis, and analysis of transference and countertransference.

Free Association and Catharsis The principal procedure used in psychoanalysis to probe the unconscious and release repressed material is called **free association**. A patient, sitting comfortably in a chair or lying in a relaxed position on a couch, lets his or her mind wander freely and gives a running account of thoughts, wishes, physical sensations, and mental images. The patient is encouraged to reveal every thought or feeling, no matter how unimportant it may seem.

Freud maintained that free associations are *predetermined*, not random. The task of an analyst is to track the associations to their source and identify the significant patterns that lie beneath the surface of what are apparently just words. The patient is encouraged to express strong feelings, usually toward authority figures, that have been repressed for fear of punishment or retaliation. Any such emotional release, by this or other processes within the therapeutic context, is called **catharsis**.

Resistance A psychoanalyst attaches particular importance to subjects that a patient does *not* wish to discuss. At some time during the process of free association, a patient will show **resistance**—an inability or unwillingness to discuss certain ideas, desires, or experiences. Such resistances are conceived of as *barriers* between the unconscious and the conscious. This material is often related to an individual's sexual life (which includes all things pleasurable) or to hostile, resentful feelings toward parents. When the repressed material is finally brought into the open, a patient generally claims that it is unimportant, absurd, irrelevant, or too unpleasant to discuss. The therapist believes the opposite. Psychoanalysis aims to break down resistances and enable the patient to face these painful ideas, desires, and experiences.

Dream Analysis Psychoanalysts believe that dreams are an important source of information about a patient's unconscious motivations. When a person is asleep, the superego is presumably less on guard against the unacceptable impulses originating in the id, so a motive that cannot be expressed in waking life may find expression in a dream. In analysis, dreams are assumed to have two kinds of content: *manifest* (openly visible) content that people remember upon awakening and *latent* (hidden) content—the actual motives that are seeking expression but are so painful or unacceptable that they are expressed in disguised or symbolic form. Therapists attempt to uncover these

Why is psychoanalytic therapy, originally practised in Freud's study, often called the "talking cure"?

psychoanalysis The form of psychodynamic therapy developed by Freud; an intensive, prolonged technique for exploring unconscious motivations and conflicts in neurotic, anxiety-ridden individuals.

insight therapy A technique by which the therapist guides a patient toward discovering insights between present symptoms and past origins.

free association The therapeutic method in which a patient gives a running account of thoughts, wishes, physical sensations, and mental images as they occur.

catharsis The process of expressing strongly felt but usually repressed emotions.

resistance The inability or unwillingness of a patient in psychoanalysis to discuss certain ideas, desires, or experiences.

hidden motives by using **dream analysis**, a therapeutic technique that examines the content of a person's dreams to discover the underlying or disguised motivations and symbolic meanings of significant life experiences and desires.

Transference and Countertransference During the course of the intensive therapy of psychoanalysis, a patient usually develops an emotional reaction toward the therapist. Often, the therapist is identified with a person who has been at the centre of an emotional conflict in the past—most often a parent or a lover. This emotional reaction is called **transference**. Transference is called *positive transference* when the feelings attached to the therapist are those of love or admiration and *negative transference* when the feelings consist of hostility or envy. Often, a patient's attitude is ambivalent, including a mixture of positive and negative feelings. An analyst's task in handling transference is a difficult one because of the patient's emotional vulnerability; however, it is a crucial part of treatment. A therapist helps a patient to interpret the present transferred feelings by understanding their original source in earlier experiences and attitudes (Henry, Strupp, Schacht, & Gaston, 1994).

Personal feelings are also at work in a therapist's reactions to a patient. **Countertransference** refers to what happens when a therapist comes to like or dislike a patient because the patient is perceived as similar to significant people in the therapist's life. In working through countertransference, a therapist may discover some unconscious dynamics of his or her own. The therapist becomes a "living mirror" for the patient and the patient, in turn, for the therapist. If the therapist fails to recognize the operation of countertransference, the therapy may not be as effective (Winarick, 1997). Because of the emotional intensity of this type of therapeutic relationship and the vulnerability of the patient, therapists must be on guard against crossing the boundary between professional caring and personal involvement with their patients. The therapy setting is obviously one with an enormous power imbalance that must be recognized, and honoured, by the therapist.

LATER PSYCHODYNAMIC THERAPIES

Freud's followers have retained many of his basic ideas but modified certain of his principles and practices. In general, these therapists place more emphasis than Freud did on (1) a patient's *current* social environment (less focus on the past); (2) the continuing influence of life experiences (not just childhood conflicts); (3) the role of social motivation and interpersonal relations of love (rather than of biological instincts and selfish concerns); (4) the significance of ego functioning and development of the self-concept (less on the conflict between id and superego).

In Chapter 14, we noted two other prominent theorists, Carl Jung and Alfred Adler. To get a flavour of more contempo-

In what ways did the theories of Melanie Klein and Sigmund Freud differ?

rary psychodynamic approaches, here we will look at the work of Harry Stack Sullivan and Melanie Klein (see Ruitenbeek, 1973, for a look at other members of the Freudian circle).

Harry Stack Sullivan, 1892–1949 (1953) felt that Freudian theory and therapy did not recognize the importance of social relationships and a patient's needs for acceptance, respect, and love. Mental disorders, he insisted, involve not only traumatic intrapsychic processes but also troubled interpersonal relationships and even strong societal pressures. Anxiety and other mental ills arise out of insecurities in relations with parents and significant others. Therapy based on this interpersonal view involves observing a *patient's feelings* about the *therapist's attitudes*. The therapeutic interview is seen as a social setting in which each party's feelings and attitudes are influenced by the other's.

Melanie Klein, 1882–1960 (1975) defected from Freud's emphasis on the Oedipus conflict as the major source of psychopathology. Instead of oedipal sexual conflicts as the most important organizing factors of the psyche, Klein argued that a *death instinct* preceded sexual awareness and led to an innate aggressive impulse that was equally important in organizing the psyche. She contended that the two fundamental organizing forces in the psyche are aggression and love, where love *unites* and aggression *splits* the psyche. In Klein's view, conscious love is connected to remorse over destructive hate and potential violence toward those we love. Thus Klein explained, "one of the great mysteries that all people face [is] that love and hate—our personal heaven and hell—cannot be separated from one another" (Frager & Fadiman, 1998, p. 135). Klein pioneered the use of forceful therapeutic interpretations of both aggressive and sexual drives in analytic patients.

In contemporary practice, psychodynamic therapists continue to draw upon the foundational concepts of Freud and his followers. The core focus for most psychodynamic therapies is interpersonal conflict. Against that background, individual therapists may put more or less emphasis on particular processes such as the interpretation of transference (Gibbons,

---

dream analysis The psychoanalytic interpretation of dreams used to gain insight into a person's unconscious motives or conflicts.

transference The process by which a person in psychoanalysis attaches to a therapist feelings formerly held toward some significant person who figured into past emotional conflict.

countertransference Circumstances in which a psychoanalyst develops personal feelings about a client because of perceived similarity of the client to significant people in the therapist's life.

Psychology in Your Life

ARE LIVES HAUNTED BY REPRESSED MEMORIES?

On September 22, 1969, eight-year-old Susan Nason vanished from her northern California neighbourhood. In December 1969, her body was found. For 20 years, no one knew who had murdered her. Then, in 1989, Susan's friend Eileen Franklin-Lipsker contacted county investigators. Eileen told them that with the help of psychotherapy, she had recalled a long repressed, horrifying memory about what had happened to Susan. In the fall of 1990, Eileen testified that, over two decades earlier, she had witnessed her father, George Franklin, sexually assault Susan and then bludgeon her to death with a rock (Marcus, 1990; Workman, 1990). This testimony was sufficient to have George Franklin convicted of first-degree murder. Because of a technical error at the trial, George Franklin was released after five years in jail. In those five years, strong doubts had also accumulated about the validity of his daughter's memories. Still, a jury had initially found the dramatic recovery of 20-year-old memories quite credible.

How, in theory, had these memories remained hidden for 20 years? The answer to this mystery finds its roots in Sigmund Freud's concept of repressed memories. As we just reminded you, Freud (1923) theorized that some people's memories of life experiences become sufficiently threatening to their psychological well-being that the individuals banish the memories from consciousness— they repress them. Clinical psychologists are often able to help clients take control of their lives by interpreting disruptive life patterns as the consequences of repressed memories; an important goal of therapy is to achieve catharsis with respect to these repressed memories.

But not all experiences of repressed memories remain in the therapist's office. The media often reports claims of the dramatic recovery of repressed memories. After long intervals of time, individuals report sudden vivid recollections of horrifying events, such as murders or childhood sexual abuse. Could all these claims be real?

Our review of memory research in Chapter 8—particularly research on eyewitness memories—provided you with grounds for scepticism (Loftus & Davis, 2006). You might recall from that research that people will report as true memories information that was provided from an artificial source. They will do so even when, as witnesses, they have been specifically warned that they have been misled. Thus, being in confident possession of a memory provides no assurance of the ultimate source of that memory.

Clinicians worry that therapists who believe in repressed memories may, through the mechanisms of psychotherapy, implant those beliefs in their patients (Lynn et al., 2003). Therapists who believe in repressed memories may instigate patients' efforts to find these memories—and verbally reward them when the "memories" come to light (de Rivera, 1997).

In one study, researchers recruited 128 participants who all claimed that they had experienced childhood sexual abuse (Geraerts et al., 2007). A majority of the participants (71 of the 128) had continuous memories of the abuse. That is, there were no life periods in which they didn't recall the abuse. The other 57 participants had discontinuous memories; they believed that they had forgotten the abuse for some period of time. Of that group, 16 had recovered memories of abuse in therapy, whereas the other 41 had recovered the memories without any special prompting. The researchers sent interviewers into the field to try to find evidence to corroborate the participants' memories of abuse. This was possible for 45 percent of the participants with continuous memories and 37 percent of the participants who had recovered memories on their own. However, for participants who recovered memories during therapy the interviewers found 0 percent corroborating evidence.

This study confirms that some reports of recovered memories are based on real occurrences. However, the study also demonstrates the potential for processes of psychotherapy to lead people to create false memories. Belief in the recovery of repressed memories may provide a measurable benefit for patients in psychotherapy. Even so, if you come to explore the question of whether repressed memories can help explain present discomfort, you should ensure that you are not passively accepting someone else's version of your life.

Crits-Christoph, & Hearon, 2008). Therapists also differ with respect to how active a role the therapist plays in interpreting the patient's life experiences. Finally, traditional psychoanalysis often takes a long time (several years at least, with as many as five sessions a week). It also requires introspective patients who are verbally fluent, highly motivated to remain in therapy, and willing and able to undergo considerable expense. Newer forms of psychodynamic therapy are making therapy briefer in total duration.

An important goal of psychodynamic therapy is to provide patients with insights into the interpersonal conflicts that lie at the roots of their psychological disorders. Behaviour therapies, to which we turn next, focus their attention more directly on the maladaptive behaviours that define the disorders.

❶ Why is psychodynamic therapy also known as insight therapy?

❷ What is transference?

❸ What role did the death instinct play in Melanie Klein's theory?

Behaviour Therapies

Whereas psychodynamic therapies focus on presumed inner causes, behaviour therapies focus on observable outer behaviours. Behaviour therapists argue that abnormal behaviours are acquired in the same way as normal behaviours—through a learning process that follows the basic principles of conditioning and learning. Behaviour therapies apply the principles of conditioning and reinforcement to modify undesirable behaviour patterns associated with mental disorders.

The terms **behaviour therapy** and **behaviour modification** are often used interchangeably. Both refer to the systematic use of principles of learning to increase the frequency of desired behaviours and/or decrease that of problem behaviours. The range of deviant behaviours and personal problems that typically are treated by behaviour therapy is extensive and includes fears, compulsions, depression, addictions, aggression, and delinquent behaviours. In general, behaviour therapy works best with specific rather than general types of personal problems: It is better for a phobia than for unfocused anxiety.

The therapies that have emerged from the theories of conditioning and learning are grounded in a pragmatic, empirical research tradition. The central task of all living organisms is to learn how to adapt to the demands of the current social and physical environment. When organisms do not learn how to cope effectively, their maladaptive reactions can be overcome by therapy based on principles of learning (or relearning). The target behaviour is not assumed to be a symptom of any underlying process. The symptom itself is the problem. Psychodynamic therapists predicted that treating only the outer behaviour without confronting the true, inner problem would result in *symptom substitution*, the appearance of a new physical or psychological problem. However, research has shown that when pathological behaviours are eliminated by behaviour therapy, new symptoms are not substituted (Kazdin, 1982; Wolpe, 1986). "On the contrary, patients whose target symptoms improved often reported improvement in other, less important symptoms as well" (Sloane, Staples, Cristol, Yorkston, & Whipple, 1975, p. 219).

---

behaviour therapy See behaviour modification.

behaviour modification The systematic use of principles of learning to increase the frequency of desired behaviours and/or decrease the frequency of problem behaviours.

counterconditioning A technique used in therapy to substitute a new response for a maladaptive one by means of conditioning procedures.

exposure therapy A behavioural technique in which clients are exposed to the objects or situations that cause them anxiety.

systematic desensitization A behavioural therapy technique in which a client is taught to prevent the arousal of anxiety by confronting the feared stimulus while relaxed.

Let's look at the different forms of behaviour therapies that have brought relief to distressed individuals.

COUNTERCONDITIONING

Why does someone become anxious when faced with a harmless stimulus, such as a spider, a nonpoisonous snake, or social contact? The behavioural explanation is that the anxiety arises due to the simple conditioning principles we reviewed in Chapters 7 and 15: Strong emotional reactions that disrupt a person's life "for no good reason" are often conditioned responses that the person does not recognize as having been learned previously. In **counterconditioning**, a new response is conditioned to replace, or "counter," a maladaptive response. The earliest recorded use of behaviour therapy followed this logic. **Mary Cover Jones** (1924) showed that a fear could be *unlearned* through conditioning. (Compare with the case of Little Albert in Chapter 7.)

> Her patient was Peter, a three-year-old boy who, for some unknown reason, was afraid of rabbits. The therapy involved feeding Peter at one end of a room while the rabbit was brought in at the other end. Over a series of sessions, the rabbit was gradually brought closer until, finally, all fear disappeared and Peter played freely with the rabbit.

Following in Cover Jones's footsteps, behaviour therapists now use several counterconditioning techniques, including systematic desensitization, flooding, and aversion therapy.

Exposure Therapies The central component of **exposure therapy** is that individuals are made to confront the object or situation that causes anxiety. The therapeutic principle is that exposure permits counterconditioning: People learn to remain relaxed in circumstances that once would have made them highly anxious. Individual exposure therapies differ with respect to the time course and circumstances in which people are exposed to their sources of anxiety.

For example, **Joseph Wolpe** (1958, 1973) observed that the nervous system cannot be relaxed and agitated at the same time because incompatible processes cannot be activated simultaneously. This insight was central to the *theory of reciprocal inhibition* that Wolpe applied to the treatment of fears and phobias. Wolpe taught his patients to *relax* their muscles and then to *imagine* visually their feared situation. They did so in gradual steps that moved from initially remote associations to direct images. Psychologically confronting the feared stimulus while being relaxed and doing so in a *graduated* sequence is the therapeutic technique known as **systematic desensitization**.

Desensitization therapy involves three major steps. First, the client identifies the stimuli that provoke anxiety and arranges them in a hierarchy ranked from weakest to strongest. For example, a student suffering from severe test anxiety constructed the hierarchy in **Table 16.1**. Note that she rated immediate anticipation of an examination (No. 14) as more stressful than taking the exam itself (No. 13). Second, the client is trained in a system of progressive deep-muscle relaxation. Relaxation training requires several sessions in which the client learns to distinguish between sensations of tension and relaxation and to let go of tension in order to achieve a state of physical and

TABLE 16.1	Hierarchy of Anxiety-Producing Stimuli for a Test-Anxious College Student (in order of increasing anxiety)
1.	A month before an examination.
2.	Two weeks before an examination.
3.	A week before an examination.
4.	Five days before an examination.
5.	Four days before an examination.
6.	Three days before an examination.
7.	Two days before an examination.
8.	One day before an examination.
9.	The night before an examination.
10.	The examination paper face down.
11.	Awaiting the distribution of examination papers.
12.	Before the unopened doors of the examination room.
13.	In the process of answering an examination paper.
14.	On the way to the university on the day of an examination.

mental relaxation. Finally, the actual process of desensitization begins: The relaxed client vividly imagines the weakest anxiety stimulus on the list. If it can be visualized without discomfort, the client goes on to the next stronger one. After a number of sessions, the most distressing situations on the list can be imagined without anxiety.

Systematic desensitization represents a gradual course of exposure to stimuli that provoke anxiety. Therapists have explored a variety of other techniques, some of which bring about exposure with less delay. For example, in a technique known as *flooding*, clients agree to be put directly into the phobic situation. A person with claustrophobia is made to sit in a dark closet, and a child with a fear of water is put into a pool. Researchers successfully treated a 21-year-old student's phobia of balloon pops by having him experience three sessions in which he endured hundreds of balloons being popped (Houlihan, Schwartz, Miltenberger, & Heuton, 1993). In the third session, the student was able to pop the last 115 balloons himself. Another form of flooding therapy begins with the use of imagination. In this procedure, the client may listen to a tape that describes the most terrifying version of the phobic fear in great detail for an hour or two. Once the terror subsides, the client is then taken to the feared situation.

When exposure techniques were first created, therapists brought about exposure through mental imagery or actual contact. In recent years, clinicians have turned to virtual reality to provide exposure therapy (Powers & Emmelkamp, 2008). Consider this study that compared virtual reality therapy to standard exposure therapy for individuals with a fear of flying.

A team of researchers recruited 50 people whose fear of flying was of sufficient intensity to qualify as a psychological

disorder (Rothbaum et al., 2006). Half of the group received a standard form of exposure therapy. Much of the treatment took place at an actual airport. Over several sessions, the participants were exposed to aspects of flying that became successively more anxiety provoking—they began by viewing the ticketing area and ended by boarding an airplane. The remainder of the participants experienced exposure through virtual environments. For example, they had virtual experiences of sitting in an airplane, taking off, and landing. As with their peers who went out into the world, they remained in each virtual location until their anxiety had diminished. To measure the effectiveness of each intervention, the researchers assessed the participants' lingering discomfort toward flying on measures such as a fear of flying inventory. Both types of therapies yielded consistent and lasting relief for the participants. In fact, when the researchers invited them to take a post-treatment flight, 76 percent of the participants in each treatment group accepted the invitation compared to only 20 percent of individuals in a control group (who had received no treatment).

Exposure therapies have proved to be highly effective for treating anxiety disorders. Virtual reality techniques hold out the promise of providing powerful exposure experiences without the time and expense of venturing out into the real world.

Exposure therapy has also been used to combat obsessive-compulsive disorders. However, the therapy adds another component: *response prevention*. Not only are clients exposed to what they fear, but they are also prevented from performing the compulsive behaviours that ordinarily reduce their anxiety. Consider a study of 20 children and adolescents with OCD (Bolton & Perrin, 2008). Because each participant had different obsessions and compulsions, the treatment needed to be tailored to each individual. However, the core components remained the same: Each participant was exposed to the objects of his or her obsession while engaging in exercises to prevent the compulsive behaviours. This program of therapy brought about substantial relief.

Aversion Therapy The forms of exposure therapy we have described help clients deal directly with stimuli that are not really harmful. What can be done to help those who are *attracted* to stimuli that *are* harmful? Drug addiction, sexual perversions, and uncontrollable violence are human problems in which deviant behaviour is elicited by tempting stimuli. **Aversion therapy** uses counterconditioning procedures to pair these stimuli with strong noxious stimuli such as electric shocks or nausea-producing drugs. In time, the same negative reactions are elicited by the tempting stimuli, and the person develops an aversion that replaces his or her former desire. For example, aversion therapy has been used with individuals who engage in *self-injurious behaviours*, such as hitting their heads or banging their heads against other objects. When an individual performs such a behaviour, he or she is given a mild electric shock. This treatment effectively eliminates self-injurious behaviours in some, but not all, patients (Duker & Seys, 1996).

---

aversion therapy A type of behavioural therapy used to treat individuals attracted to harmful stimuli; an attractive stimulus is paired with a noxious stimulus in order to elicit a negative reaction to the target stimulus.

In the extreme, aversion therapy resembles torture, so why would anyone submit voluntarily to it? Usually, people do so only because they realize that the long-term consequences of continuing their behaviour pattern will destroy their health or ruin their careers or family lives. They may also be driven to do so by institutional pressures, as has happened in some prison treatment programs. However, use of aversion therapy in institutional rehabilitation programs has become regulated by national ethical guidelines and provincial laws. The hope is that, under these restrictions, it will be therapeutic rather than coercive.

CONTINGENCY MANAGEMENT

Counterconditioning procedures are appropriate when one response can be replaced with another. Other behaviour modification procedures rely on the principles of operant conditioning that arose in the research tradition pioneered by B. F. Skinner. **Contingency management** refers to the general treatment strategy of changing behaviour by modifying its consequences. The two major techniques of contingency management in behaviour therapy are *positive reinforcement strategies* and *extinction strategies*.

Positive Reinforcement Strategies When a response is followed immediately by a reward, the response tends to be repeated and to increase in frequency over time. This central principle of operant learning becomes a therapeutic strategy when it is used to modify the frequency of a desirable response as it replaces an undesirable one. Dramatic success has been obtained from the application of positive reinforcement procedures to behaviour problems.

You might recall from Chapter 7 a technique called *shaping* in which researchers reinforce successive approximations to a desired behaviour. Consider how shaping was used to help smokers reduce the number of cigarettes they smoked (Lamb et al., 2007). The researchers measured the participants' breath carbon monoxide (BCO) to determine initial smoking habits. As the study unfolded, the participants received cash incentives if they were able to get their BCO below particular goal levels (which were set for each smoker). Those goals became more demanding over time—shaping participants toward the desired behaviour of abstinence from smoking. In Chapter 7, we also described *token economies*, in which desired behaviours (e.g., practising personal care or taking medication) are explicitly defined, and token pay-offs are given by institutional staff when the behaviours are performed. These tokens can later be exchanged for an array of rewards and privileges (Kazdin, 1994; Martin & Pear, 1999). These systems of reinforcement are especially effective in modifying patients' behaviours regarding self-care, upkeep of their environment, and frequency of their positive social interactions.

In another approach, therapists differentially reinforce behaviours that are incompatible with the maladaptive behaviour. This technique has been used successfully with individuals in treatment for drug addiction.

Researchers recruited 142 individuals who were seeking treatment for cocaine and opioid (e.g., heroin) dependence into a 12-week study (Petry et al., 2005). All the participants received a standard treatment of a series of counselling sessions that imparted strategies and skills for overcoming dependence. In addition to this standard treatment, one group of 53 participants received vouchers each time they produced a urine specimen that was drug free. The first time participants produced a negative urine specimen, they were given a voucher worth $1. The voucher amounts increased by $1.50 with each negative specimen. A positive specimen reset the voucher amount to $1. Another group of 51 participants was given the opportunity to win prizes, contingent on negative urine specimens. To win the prizes, participants pulled cards from an urn. The majority of the cards (62.8 percent) read "good job, try again," but the remainder provided prizes that valued $1, $20, or $100. For the first negative specimen, participants got to pull one card from the urn. For each subsequent negative specimen, they earned an extra one pull. A positive specimen reduced participants back to a single pull. The researchers assessed the efficacy of each treatment program, for example, by measuring the average number of weeks participants in each group were continuously abstinent. For the group that received only standard treatment, that number was 4.6 weeks. For the voucher group, that number was 7.0 weeks, and for the prize group, that number was 7.8 weeks. Thus both contingency management treatments increased the likelihood that participants would abstain from drugs.

This study verifies that two different programs of contingency management—vouchers and prizes—can be used successfully to treat drug dependence. You might recognize the same philosophy at work here as the one that motivated the counterconditioning procedures we described earlier: Basic principles of learning are used to increase the probability of adaptive behaviours.

Extinction Strategies Why do people continue to do something that causes pain and distress when they are capable of doing otherwise? The answer is that many forms of behaviour have multiple consequences—some are negative, and some are positive. Often, subtle positive reinforcements keep a behaviour going despite its obvious negative consequences. For example, children who are punished for misbehaving may continue to misbehave if punishment is the only form of attention they seem able to earn.

Extinction strategies are useful in therapy when dysfunctional behaviours have been maintained by unrecognized reinforcing circumstances. Those reinforcers can be identified through a careful situational analysis, and then a program can be arranged to withhold them in the presence of the undesirable response. When this approach is possible, and everyone in the situation who might inadvertently reinforce the person's behaviour co-operates, extinction procedures work to diminish the frequency of the behaviour and eventually to eliminate the behaviour completely. Consider a classroom example. A boy with attention-deficit hyperactivity disorder was causing problems for his teachers because he frequently engaged in disruptive off-task behaviours. Researchers discovered that the attention the teachers gave to the student when he engaged in off-task behaviours was positively reinforcing those behaviours (Stahr, Cushing, Lane, & Fox, 2006). When the teachers no longer paid attention to him when he behaved inappropriately, the student's behaviour improved.

---

contingency management A general treatment strategy involving changing behaviour by modifying its consequences.

FIGURE 16.1 Participant Modelling Therapy
The subject shown in the photo first watched a model make a graduated series of snake-approach responses and then repeated them herself. She eventually was able to pick up the snake and let it crawl on her. The graph compares the number of approach responses subjects made before and after receiving participant modelling therapy (most effective) with the behaviour of those exposed to two other therapeutic techniques and a control group.

Albert Bandura, from "Modeling Therapy." Reprinted by permission of Albert Bandura.

Even symptoms of schizophrenia can be maintained and encouraged by unintentional reinforcement. Consider the following circumstances. It is standard procedure in many psychiatric hospitals for the staff to ask patients frequently, as a form of social communication, "How are you feeling?" Patients often misinterpret this question as a request for diagnostic information, and they respond by thinking and talking about their feelings, unusual symptoms, and hallucinations. Such responding is likely to be counterproductive because it leads staff to conclude that the patients are self-absorbed and not behaving normally. In fact, the more bizarre the symptoms and verbalizations, the more attention the staff members may show to the patient, which reinforces continued expression of bizarre symptoms. In a classic study, dramatic decreases in symptoms were observed when hospital staff members were simply instructed to ignore the behaviour and to give attention to the patients only when they were behaving normally (Ayllon & Michael, 1959).

SOCIAL-LEARNING THERAPY

The range of behaviour therapies has been expanded by social-learning theorists who point out that humans learn by observing the behaviour of other people. Often, you learn and apply rules to new experiences through symbolic means, such as watching other people's experiences in life, in a movie, or on TV. **Social-learning therapy** is designed to modify problematic behaviour patterns by arranging conditions in which a client will observe models being reinforced for a desirable form of responding. This vicarious learning process has been of special value in overcoming phobias and building social skills. We have noted in earlier chapters that this social-learning theory was largely developed through the pioneering research of **Albert Bandura** (1977, 1986). Here we will mention only two aspects of his approach: imitation of models and social-skills training.

Imitation of Models Social-learning theory predicts that individuals acquire responses through observation. Thus it should be the case that people with phobias should be able to unlearn fear reactions through imitation of models. For example, in treating a phobia of snakes, a therapist will first demonstrate fearless approach behaviour at a relatively minor level,

perhaps approaching a snake's cage or touching a snake. The client is aided, through demonstration and encouragement, to imitate the modelled behaviour. Gradually, the approach behaviours are shaped so that the client can pick up the snake and let it crawl freely over him or her. At no time is the client forced to perform any behaviour. Resistance at any level is overcome by having the client return to a previously successful, less threatening level of approach behaviour.

The power of this form of **participant modelling** can be seen in research comparing this technique with symbolic modelling, desensitization, and a control condition. In *symbolic modelling therapy*, individuals who had been trained in relaxation techniques watched a film in which several models fearlessly handled snakes; they could stop the film and try to relax whenever a scene made them feel anxious. In the control condition, no therapeutic intervention was used. As you can see in **Figure 16.1**, participant modelling was clearly the most successful of these techniques. Snake phobia was eliminated in 11 of the 12 individuals in the participant modelling group (Bandura, 1970).

Social-Skills Training A major therapeutic innovation encouraged by social-learning therapists involves training people with inadequate social skills to be more effective. Many difficulties arise for someone with a mental disorder, or even just an everyday problem, if he or she is socially inhibited, inept, or unassertive. *Social skills* are sets of responses that enable people to achieve their social goals effectively when approaching or interacting with others. These skills include knowing *what* (content) to say and do in given situations in order to elicit a desired response (consequences), *how* (style) to say and do it, and *when* (timing) to say and do it. To help people acquire such skills, many social-learning therapists recommend **behavioural rehearsal**—visualizing how

---

social-learning therapy A form of treatment in which clients observe models' desirable behaviours being reinforced.

participant modelling A therapeutic technique in which a therapist demonstrates the desired behaviour and a client is aided, through supportive encouragement, to imitate the modelled behaviour.

behavioural rehearsal Procedures used to establish and strengthen basic skills; as used in social-skills training programs; requires the client to rehearse a desirable behaviour sequence mentally.

one should behave in a given situation and the desired positive consequences. Social-skills training has proved successful to help the social functioning of diverse groups such as adults with schizophrenia and adolescents with emotional and/or behavioural disorders (Cook et al., 2008; Kurtz & Mueser, 2008).

GENERALIZATION TECHNIQUES

An ongoing issue of concern for behaviour therapists is whether new behaviour patterns generated in a therapeutic setting will actually be used in the everyday situations faced by their clients (Kazdin, 1994). This question is important for all therapies, because any measure of treatment effectiveness must include maintenance of long-term changes that go beyond a therapist's couch, clinic, or laboratory.

When essential aspects of a client's real-life setting are absent from the therapy program, behavioural changes accomplished through therapy may be lost over time after therapy terminates. To prevent this gradual loss, it has become common practice to build generalization techniques into the therapeutic procedure itself. These techniques attempt to *increase* the similarity of target behaviours, reinforcers, models, and stimulus demands between therapy and real-life settings. For example,

behaviours are taught that are likely to be reinforced naturally in a person's environment, such as showing courtesy or consideration. Rewards are given on a partial reinforcement schedule to ensure that their effect will be maintained in the real world, where rewards are not always forthcoming. Expectation of tangible extrinsic rewards is gradually *faded out* while social approval and more naturally occurring consequences, including reinforcing self-statements, are incorporated.

Behaviour therapists, for example, used a fading procedure with a boy (aged 4 years, 10 months) who refused to drink milk (Tiger & Hanley, 2006). To get the boy to drink his milk, the therapists had his teacher mix a small amount of chocolate syrup into a glass of milk. With the chocolate syrup mixed in, the boy drank the milk. Over the next 48 meals, the teacher slowly decreased the amount of chocolate until the boy was offered only plain milk. At the end of this intervention, the boy consistently drank plain milk. This was also true at home, demonstrating generalization from the classroom to an additional setting.

Before we move on to cognitive therapies, take a few minutes to review the major differences between the two psychotherapies outlined thus far—the psychoanalytic and the behavioural—as summarized in **Table 16.2**.

TABLE 16.2 Comparison of Psychoanalytic and Behavioural Approaches to Psychotherapy		
Issue	**Psychoanalysis**	**Behaviour Therapy**
Basic human nature	Biological instincts, primarily sexual and aggressive, press for immediate release, bringing people into conflict with social reality.	Similar to other animals, people are born with the capacity for learning, which follows similar principles in all species.
Normal human development	Growth occurs through resolution of conflicts during successive stages. Through identification and internalization, mature ego controls and character structures emerge.	Adaptive behaviours are learned through reinforcement and imitation.
Nature of psychopathology	Pathology reflects inadequate conflict resolutions and fixations in earlier development, which leave overly strong impulses and/or weak controls. Symptoms are defensive responses to anxiety.	Problematic behaviour derives from faulty learning of maladaptive behaviours. The *symptom* is the problem; there is no *underlying* disease.
Goal of therapy	Psychosexual maturity, strengthened ego functions, and reduced control by unconscious and repressed impulses are attained.	Symptomatic behaviour is eliminated and replaced with adaptive behaviours.
Psychological realm emphasized	Motives, feelings, fantasies, and cognitions are experienced.	Therapy involves behaviour and observable feelings and actions.
Time orientation	Past conflicts and repressed feelings are discovered and interpreted in light of the present.	Concerned only about client's reinforcement history. Present behaviour is examined and treated.
Role of unconscious material	This is primary in classical psychoanalysis and somewhat less emphasized by neo-Freudians.	There is no concern with unconscious processes or with subjective experience even in the conscious realm.
Role of insight	Insight is central; it emerges in "corrective emotional experiences."	Insight is irrelevant and/or unnecessary.
Role of therapist	The therapist functions as a *detective*, searching out basic root conflicts and resistances. Interaction with the client is detached and neutral, to facilitate transference reactions.	The therapist functions as a *trainer*, helping patients unlearn old behaviours and/or learn new ones. Control of reinforcement is important; interpersonal relationship is minor.

❶ What is the basic principle of counterconditioning?
❷ What learning principle is at work when clinicians allow patients to earn vouchers?
❸ What is likely to take place if someone undergoes social-learning therapy?
❹ How does the therapist's role differ between psychoanalysis and behaviour therapy?

CRITICAL THINKING Recall the study that used vouchers and prizes to treat drug dependence. Why did the prize amount or the number of urn pulls get set back to the minimum when participants produced positive specimens?

Cognitive Therapies

Cognitive therapy attempts to change problem feelings and behaviours by changing the way a client thinks about significant life experiences. The underlying assumption of such therapy is that abnormal behaviour patterns and emotional distress start with problems in *what* people think (cognitive content) and *how* they think (cognitive process). Cognitive therapies focus on changing different types of cognitive processes and providing different methods of cognitive restructuring. We discussed some of these approaches in Chapter 13 as ways to cope with stress and improve health. In this section, we will describe two major forms of cognitive therapy: alteration of false belief systems and cognitive behavioural therapy.

CHANGING FALSE BELIEFS

Some cognitive behaviour therapists have—as their primary targets for change—people's beliefs, attitudes, and habitual thought patterns. These cognitive therapists argue that many psychological problems arise because of the way people think about themselves in relation to other people and the events they face. Faulty thinking can be based on (1) unreasonable attitudes ("Being perfect is the most important trait for a student to have"), (2) false premises ("If I do everything they want me to, then I'll be popular"), and (3) rigid rules that put behaviour on automatic pilot so that prior patterns are repeated even when they have not worked ("I must obey authorities"). Emotional distress is caused by cognitive misunderstandings and by failure to distinguish between current reality and one's imagination (or expectations).

Cognitive Therapy for Depression A cognitive therapist helps a patient to correct faulty patterns of thinking by substituting more effective problem-solving techniques. **Aaron Beck** (1976) has successfully pioneered cognitive therapy for the problem of depression. He states the formula for treatment in simple form: "The therapist helps the patient to identify his warped thinking and to learn more realistic ways to formulate his experiences" (p. 20). For example, depressed individuals may be instructed to write down negative thoughts about themselves, figure out why these self-criticisms are unjustified, and come up with more realistic (and less destructive) self-cognitions.

Beck believes that depression is maintained because depressed patients are unaware of the negative automatic thoughts that they habitually formulate, such as "I will never be as good as my brother"; "Nobody would like me if they really knew me"; and "I'm not smart enough to make it in this competitive school." A therapist then uses four tactics to change the cognitive foundation that supports the depression (Beck & Rush, 1989; Beck, Rush, Shaw, & Emery, 1979):

- Challenging the client's basic assumptions about his or her functioning.
- Evaluating the evidence the client has for and against the accuracy of automatic thoughts.
- Reattributing blame to situational factors rather than to the patient's incompetence.
- Discussing alternative solutions to complex tasks that could lead to failure experiences.

This therapy is similar to behaviour therapies in that it centres on the present state of the client.

One of the worst side effects of being depressed is having to live with all the negative feelings and lethargy associated with depression. Becoming obsessed with thoughts about one's negative mood brings up memories of all the bad times in life, which worsens the depressive feelings. By filtering all input through a darkly coloured lens of depression, depressed people see criticism where there is none and hear sarcasm when they listen to praise—further "reasons" for being depressed. Cognitive therapy has proved successful at arresting depression's downward spiral (Hollon, Stewart, & Strunk, 2006).

Rational-Emotive Therapy One of the earliest forms of cognitive therapy was the **rational-emotive therapy (RET)** developed by **Albert Ellis** (1962, 1995; Windy & Ellis, 1997). RET is a comprehensive system of personality change based on the transformation of irrational beliefs that cause undesirable, highly charged emotional reactions, such as severe anxiety. Clients may have core values *demanding* that they succeed and be approved, *insisting* that they be treated fairly, and *dictating* that the universe be more pleasant.

Rational-emotive therapists teach clients how to recognize the "shoulds," "oughts," and "musts" that are controlling their actions and preventing them from choosing the lives they want. They attempt to break through a client's closed-mindedness by showing that an emotional reaction that follows some event is really the effect of unrecognized beliefs about the event. For example, failure to achieve orgasm during intercourse (event) is followed by an emotional reaction of depression and self-derogation. The belief that is causing the emotional reaction is likely to be "I am sexually inadequate and may be impotent because I failed to perform as expected." In therapy, this belief (and others) is openly disputed through rational confrontation and examination of alternative reasons for the event, such as fatigue, alcohol, false notions of sexual performance, or

---

cognitive therapy A type of psychotherapeutic treatment that attempts to change feelings and behaviours by changing the way a client thinks about or perceives significant life experiences.

rational-emotive therapy (RET) A comprehensive system of personality change based on changing irrational beliefs that cause undesirable, highly charged emotional reactions such as severe anxiety.

Suppose you were learning to knit. Assuming you wanted to get better at it over time, what would be the best internal message to give yourself about the activity?

reluctance to engage in intercourse at that time or with that particular partner. This confrontation technique is followed by other interventions that replace dogmatic, irrational thinking with rational, situationally appropriate ideas.

Rational-emotive therapy aims to increase an individual's sense of self-worth and potential to be self-actualized by getting rid of the system of faulty beliefs that block personal growth. As such, it shares much with humanistic therapies, which we consider later in the chapter.

COGNITIVE BEHAVIOURAL THERAPY

You are what you tell yourself you can be, and you are guided by what you believe you ought to do. This is a starting assumption of **cognitive behavioural therapy**. This therapeutic approach combines the cognitive emphasis on changing false beliefs with the behavioural focus on reinforcement contingencies in the modification of performance (Goldfried, 2003). Unacceptable behaviour patterns are modified by *cognitive restructuring*— changing a person's negative self-statements into constructive coping statements.

A critical part of this therapeutic approach is the discovery by therapist and client of the way the client thinks about and expresses the problem for which therapy is sought. Once both therapist and client understand the kind of thinking that is leading to unproductive or dysfunctional behaviours, they develop new self-statements that are constructive and minimize the use of self-defeating ones that elicit anxiety or reduce self-esteem (Meichenbaum, 1977, 1985, 1993). For example, they might substitute the negative self-statement "I was really boring at that party; they'll never ask me back" with constructive criticism: "Next time, if I want to appear interesting, I will plan some provocative opening lines, practise telling a good joke,

---

cognitive behavioural therapy A therapeutic approach that combines the cognitive emphasis on thoughts and attitudes with the behavioural emphasis on changing performance.

and be responsive to the host's stories." Instead of dwelling on negatives in past situations that are unchangeable, the client is taught to focus on positives in the future.

Cognitive behavioural therapy has been used as a successful treatment for a variety of disorders. Let's see how it was used to treat clients with compulsive buying disorder, which is defined as "excessive and mostly senseless spending or excessive shopping impulses that cause marked distress, interfere with social or occupational functioning, and often result in financial problems" (Mueller et al., 2008, p. 1131).

Researchers randomly assigned 60 people with compulsive buying disorder to cognitive behavioural therapy or to a control group (Mueller et al., 2008). Participants in the treatment group had one therapy session a week over the course of 12 weeks. The therapy had several components (Burgard & Mitchell, 2000). One component of the therapy was for participants to identify the cues (such as social or psychological situations) in their lives that triggered buying behaviour. Once participants identified these cues, the therapists worked with them to develop cognitive strategies to disrupt or avoid the cues' impact. Another component of the therapy was for participants to gain confidence that they could control their behaviour. The researchers encouraged participants to undermine negative self-statements (for example "I cannot control my urge to shop") by gathering evidence against such statements and by generating plans to achieve greater control. This program of therapy led to improvement both at the end of treatment and in follow-up assessment six months after treatment ended.

Note that the researchers needed the control group to demonstrate the effectiveness of the treatment (that is, members of the treatment group showed greater improvement than members of the control group). However, members of the control group were also offered treatment once the study came to an end.

As you can see from this example, cognitive behavioural therapy builds expectations of being effective. Therapists know that building these expectations increases the likelihood that people will behave effectively. Through setting attainable goals, developing realistic strategies for attaining them, and evaluating feedback realistically, you develop a sense of mastery and *self-efficacy* (Bandura, 1992, 1997). As we discussed in Chapter 14, your sense of self-efficacy influences your perceptions, motivation, and performance in many ways. Self-efficacy judgments influence how much effort you expend and how long you persist in the face of difficult life situations (Bandura, 2006). Researchers have demonstrated the importance of self-efficacy in recovery from psychological disorders (Benight, Cieslak, Molton, & Johnson, 2008). Consider a study of 108 women with binge eating disorder (Cassin, von Ranson, Heng, Brar, & Wojtowica, 2008). Women in the control group received a handbook that provided information about the disorder. Women in the treatment group received the handbook but also participated in a therapy session designed to raise self-efficacy. For example, each woman was encouraged to "recall past experiences in which she [had] shown mastery in the face of difficulties and challenges" (p. 421). Sixteen weeks after the treatment, 28 percent of women in the treatment group had refrained from binge eating versus only 11 percent in the control group. Within the treatment group, the women who abstained from binge eating reported higher levels of self-efficacy. This study provides further evidence that cognitive behavioural approaches to therapy can bring relief (R. E. Wood & Bandura, 1989). In the study, types of thoughts like "I can learn to do better" actually allowed the students to become better.

STOP AND REVIEW

❶ What is the underlying assumption of cognitive therapy?

❷ With respect to rational-emotive therapy (RET), what is the origin of highly charged emotional reactions?

❸ Why is increased self-efficacy a goal for cognitive behavioural therapy?

CRITICAL THINKING Recall the study that assessed cognitive behavioural therapy for compulsive buying disorder. Why was it important to identify the cues that triggered buying behaviour?

Humanistic Therapies

Humanistic theories have at their core the concept of a whole person in the continual process of changing and of becoming. Although environment and heredity place certain restrictions, people always remain free to choose what they will become by creating their own values and committing to them through their own decisions. Along with this *freedom to choose*, however, comes the burden of responsibility. Because you are never fully aware of all the implications of your actions, you experience anxiety and despair. You also suffer from guilt over lost opportunities to achieve your full potential. Psychotherapies that apply the principles of this general theory of human nature attempt to help clients define their own freedom, value their experiencing selves and the richness of the present moment, cultivate their individuality, and discover ways of realizing their fullest potential (self-actualization).

In some cases, humanistic therapies also absorbed the lessons of *existentialist* approaches to human experience (May, 1975). This approach emphasizes people's ability to meet or be overwhelmed by the everyday challenges of existence. Existential theorists suggest that individuals suffer from *existential crises*: problems in everyday living, a lack of meaningful human relationships, and an absence of significant goals. A clinical version of existential theory, which integrates its various themes and approaches, assumes that the bewildering realities of modern life give rise to two basic kinds of human maladies. Depressive and obsessive syndromes reflect a retreat from these realities; sociopathic and narcissistic syndromes reflect an exploitation of these realities (Schneider & May, 1995).

The humanistic philosophy also gave rise to the **human-potential movement**, which emerged in North America in the late 1960s. This movement encompassed methods to enhance the potential of the average human being toward greater levels of performance and greater richness of experience. Through this movement, therapy originally intended for people with psychological disorders was extended to mentally healthy people who wanted to be more effective, more productive, and happier human beings.

How might volunteer work help people to maximize their human potential?

Let's examine two types of therapies in the humanistic tradition: client-centred therapy and Gestalt therapy.

CLIENT-CENTRED THERAPY

As developed by **Carl Rogers** (1951, 1977), client-centred therapy has had a significant impact on the way many different kinds of therapists define their relationships to their clients. The primary goal of **client-centred therapy** is to promote the healthy psychological growth of the individual.

The approach begins with the assumption that all people share the basic tendency to self-actualize—that is, to realize their potential. Rogers believed that "it is the inherent tendency of the organism to develop all its capacities in ways which seem to maintain or enhance the organism" (1959, p. 196). Healthy development is hindered by faulty learning patterns in which a person accepts the evaluation of others in place of those provided by his or her own mind and body. A conflict between the naturally positive self-image and negative external criticisms creates anxiety and unhappiness. This conflict, or *incongruence*, may function outside of awareness, so that a person experiences feelings of unhappiness and low self-worth without knowing why.

The task of Rogerian therapy is to create a therapeutic environment that allows a client to learn how to behave in order to achieve self-enhancement and self-actualization. Because people are assumed to be basically good, the therapist's task is mainly to help remove barriers that limit the expression of this natural positive tendency. The basic therapeutic strategy is to recognize, accept, and clarify a client's feelings. This is accomplished within an atmosphere of *unconditional positive regard*—nonjudgmental acceptance and respect for the client. The therapist allows his or her own feelings and thoughts to be transparent to the client. In addition to maintaining this

human-potential movement The therapy movement that encompasses all those practices and methods that release the potential of the average human being for greater levels of performance and greater richness of experience.

client-centred therapy A humanistic approach to treatment that emphasizes the healthy psychological growth of the individual based on the assumption that all people share the basic tendency of human nature toward self-actualization.

genuineness, the therapist tries to experience the client's feelings. Such total empathy requires that the therapist care for the client as a worthy, competent individual—not to be judged or evaluated but to be assisted in discovering his or her individuality (Meador & Rogers, 1979).

The emotional style and attitude of the therapist are instrumental in *empowering* the client to attend once again to the true sources of personal conflict and to remove the distracting influences that suppress self-actualization. Unlike practitioners of other therapies, who interpret, give answers, or instruct, the client-centred therapist is a supportive listener who reflects and, at times, restates the client's evaluative statements and feelings. Client-centred therapy strives to be *nondirective* by having the therapist merely facilitate the client's search for self-awareness and self-acceptance.

Rogers believed that, once people are freed to relate to others openly and to accept themselves, individuals have the potential to lead themselves back to psychological health. This optimistic view and the humane relationship between therapist-as-caring-expert and client-as-person have influenced many practitioners.

GESTALT THERAPY

Gestalt therapy focuses on ways to unite mind and body to make a person whole (recall the Gestalt school of perception, described in Chapter 5). Its goal of self-awareness is reached by helping clients express pent-up feelings and recognize unfinished business from past conflicts that is carried into new relationships and must be completed for growth to proceed. **Fritz Perls** (1969), the originator of Gestalt therapy, asked clients to act out fantasies about conflicts and strong feelings and also to recreate their dreams, which he saw as repressed parts of personality. Perls said, "We have to *re-own* these projected, fragmented parts of our personality, and re-own the hidden potential that appears in the dream" (1969, p. 67).

In Gestalt therapy workshops, therapists encourage participants to regain contact with their "authentic inner voices" (Hatcher & Himelstein, 1996). Among the best-known methods of Gestalt therapy is the *empty chair technique*. To carry out this technique, the therapist puts an empty chair near the client. The client is asked to imagine that a feeling, a person, an object, or a situation is occupying the chair. The client then "talks" to the chair's occupant. For example, clients would be encouraged to imagine their mother or father in the chair and reveal feelings they might otherwise be unwilling to reveal. The clients can then "talk" to the feelings in the chair about the impact they have on the clients' lives. This technique allows clients to confront and explore strong unexpressed feelings that may interfere with psychological well-being.

STOP AND REVIEW

❶ What was the goal of the human-potential movement?

❷ In client-centred therapy, what is meant by unconditional positive regard?

❸ In Gestalt therapy, what is the purpose of the empty chair technique?

Gestalt therapy Therapy that focuses on ways to unite mind and body to make a person whole.

Group Therapies

All the treatment approaches outlined thus far are primarily designed as one-to-one relationships between a patient or client and a therapist. Many people, however, now experience therapy as part of a group. There are several reasons why group therapy has flourished. Some advantages are practical. Group therapy is less expensive to participants and allows small numbers of mental health personnel to help more clients. Other advantages relate to the power of the group setting. The group (1) is a less threatening situation for people who have problems dealing on their own with authority; (2) allows group processes to be used to influence individual maladaptive behaviour; (3) provides people with opportunities to observe and practise interpersonal skills within the therapy session; and (4) provides an analogue of the primary family group, which enables corrective emotional experiences to take place.

Group therapy also poses some special problems (Motherwell & Shay, 2005). For example, some groups establish a culture in which little progress can be made—members create a norm of passivity and limited self-disclosure. In addition, the effectiveness of groups can change dramatically when members leave or join the groups. Both arrivals and departures can change the delicate balance that allows groups to function well as a unit. Therapists who specialize in group therapy must take care to address these group dynamics.

Some of the basic premises of group therapies differ from those of individual therapy. The social setting of group therapies provides an opportunity to learn how one comes across to others, how the self-image that is projected differs from the one that is intended or personally experienced. In addition, the group provides confirmation that one's symptoms, problems, and "deviant" reactions are not unique but often are quite common. Because people tend to conceal from others negative information about themselves, it is possible for many people with the same problem to believe "It's only me." The shared group experience can help to dispel this pluralistic ignorance in which many share the same false belief about their unique failings. In addition, the group of peers can provide social support outside the therapy setting.

What are some strengths of group therapies?

COUPLE AND FAMILY THERAPY

Much group therapy consists of strangers coming together periodically to form temporary associations from which they may benefit. Couple and family therapy brings meaningful existing units into a therapy setting.

Couple therapy for marital problems seeks to clarify the typical communication patterns of the partners and then to improve the quality of their interaction (Snyder, Castellani, & Whisman, 2006). By seeing a couple together, and often by videotaping and replaying their interactions, a therapist can help them appreciate the verbal and nonverbal styles they use to dominate, control, or confuse each other. Each party is taught how to reinforce desirable responding in the other and withdraw reinforcement for undesirable reactions. They are also taught nondirective listening skills to help the other person clarify and express feelings and ideas. Couple therapy has been shown to reduce marital crises and keep marriages intact (Christensen, Atkins, Yi, Baucom, & George, 2006).

In *family therapy*, the client is a whole nuclear family, and each family member is treated as a member of a *system* of relationships (Fishman & Fishman, 2003). A family therapist works with troubled family members to help them perceive what is creating problems for one or more of them. Consider circumstances in which a child has been diagnosed with an anxiety disorder. Research suggests that certain parenting practices may, unfortunately, maintain the child's anxiety (Wood et al., 2003). For example, if parents do not allow their children sufficient autonomy, the children may never gain enough self-efficacy to cope successfully with novel tasks. Under those circumstances, novel tasks will continue to provoke anxiety. Family therapy can focus on both the child's anxiety and the parent's behaviours that may maintain that anxiety.

> Researchers recruited 40 children, ages 6 to 13, to participate in a treatment study (Wood, Piacentini, Southam-Gerow, Chu, & Sigman, 2006). All the children had been diagnosed with an anxiety disorder (e.g., generalized anxiety disorder or social phobia). Half of the children underwent individual cognitive behavioural therapy that included skills training (e.g., strategies for coping with anxiety) as well as exposure to a hierarchy of feared situations. The other half of the children participated in similar activities, but their parents were also involved for much of the therapy sessions. In these family sessions, parents were taught skills, for example, to increase their children's autonomy and self-efficacy. The two groups of children were comparable in their levels of distress before treatment. At the end of therapy, both groups presented lower levels of anxiety. However, the group whose parents were included in the therapy showed greater improvement than their peers who received individual treatment.

This study illustrates the importance of the family therapy approach. By engaging the whole family, the therapeutic intervention changed environmental factors that may have helped maintain the children's levels of anxiety.

Family therapy can reduce tensions within a family and improve the functioning of individual members by helping clients recognize the positive as well as the negative aspects in their relationships. **Virginia Satir** (1967), a developer of family therapy approaches, noted that the family therapist plays many roles, acting as an interpreter and clarifier of the interactions that are taking place in the therapy session and as influence agent, mediator, and referee. Most family therapists assume that the problems brought into therapy represent *situational* difficulties between people or problems of social interaction, rather than *dispositional* aspects of individuals. These difficulties may develop over time as members are forced into or accept unsatisfying roles. Nonproductive communication patterns may be set up in response to natural transitions in a family situation—loss of a job, or a child's going to school, dating, getting married, or having a baby. The job of the family therapist is to understand the structure of the family and the many forces acting on it. Then he or she works with the family members to dissolve "dysfunctional" structural elements while creating and maintaining new, more effective structures (Fishman & Fishman, 2003).

COMMUNITY SUPPORT GROUPS

A dramatic development in therapy has been the surge of interest and participation in *mutual support groups* and *self-help groups*. While there is no accurate estimate of how many self-help groups operate in Canada, there are over 6000 of these groups in the United States, reporting over one million members (Goldstrom et al., 2006). Perhaps the most common type of self-help group is for alcohol and illicit drugs. A recent study estimated that 5 million people over the age of 12 attend these self-help groups in the United States alone (Substance Abuse and Mental Health Services Administration, 2008b). These support group sessions are typically free, especially when they are not directed by a health-care professional, and they give people a chance to meet others with the same problems who are surviving and sometimes thriving. The self-help concept applied to community group settings was pioneered by Alcoholics Anonymous (AA), which was founded in 1935. However, it was the women's consciousness-raising movement of the 1960s that helped extend self-help beyond the arena of alcoholism. Now support groups deal with four basic categories of problems: addictive behaviour, physical and mental disorders, life transition or other crises, and the traumas experienced by friends or relatives of those with serious problems. In recent years, people have begun to turn to the internet as another venue for self-help groups (Barak, Boniel-Nissim, & Suler, 2008). In general, internet self-help groups engage the same range of issues as their physical counterparts (Goldstrom et al., 2006). However, the internet provides a particularly important meeting place for people who suffer from conditions that limit mobility, such as chronic fatigue syndrome and multiple sclerosis: An inability to attend meetings physically no longer denies people the benefits of self-help.

Researchers have begun to investigate what properties of self-help groups can make them most effective. Self-help groups appear to serve a number of functions for their members: For example, they provide people with a sense of hope and control over their problems, they engage social support for people's suffering, and they provide a forum for dispensing and acquiring information about disorders and treatments (Groh, Jason, & Keys, 2008; Schiff & Bargal, 2000). If you consider joining a self-help group, it is important to note that these groups have the most positive impact on people's feelings of well-being when they are satisfied with the group (Schiff & Bargal, 2000). For example, one study found that individuals who affiliated most strongly with AA after treatment for alcoholism showed the lowest levels of continuing substance abuse. Strong affiliation with AA apparently allowed these individuals to maintain their behavioural self-efficacy with respect to the control of their alcoholism (Morgenstern, Labouvie, McCrady, Kahler, & Frey, 1997).

A valuable development in self-help is the application of group therapy techniques to the situations of terminally ill patients. The goals of such therapy are to help patients and their families live lives as fulfilling as possible during their illnesses, to cope realistically with impending death, and to adjust to the terminal illness (Kissane et al., 2004). One general focus of such support groups for the terminally ill is to help patients learn how to live fully until they "say goodbye."

The group therapies are our final examples of types of therapies that are based purely on psychological interventions. We will now analyze how biomedical therapies work to alter the brain in order to affect the mind.

STOP AND REVIEW

❶ How does group therapy help inform participants about the uniqueness of their problems?

❷ What is a common goal for couple therapy?

❸ Under what circumstances are internet self-help groups particularly valuable?

CRITICAL THINKING Recall the study that used family therapy to treat children's anxiety disorders. Why was it important that the two groups of children had comparable anxiety levels before treatment began?

Biomedical Therapies

The ecology of the mind is held in delicate balance. When something goes wrong with the brain, we see the consequences in abnormal patterns of behaviour and peculiar cognitive and emotional reactions. Similarly, environmental, social, or behavioural disturbances, such as drugs and violence, can alter brain chemistry and function. Biomedical therapies most often treat mental disorders as problems in the brain. We will describe four biomedical approaches to alleviating the symptoms of psychological disorders: drug therapies, psychosurgery, electroconvulsive therapy (ECT), and repetitive transcranial magnetic stimulation (rTMS).

DRUG THERAPY

In the history of the treatment of mental disorders, nothing has rivalled the revolution created by the discovery of drugs that can calm anxious patients, restore contact with reality in withdrawn patients, and suppress hallucinations in psychotic patients. This new therapeutic era began in the early 1950s with the introduction of tranquilizing drugs into hospital

---

psychopharmacology The branch of psychology that investigates the effects of drugs on behaviour.

treatment programs, most notably *chlorpromazine*, which was approved for use by the Canadian government in 1957. Emerging drug therapies gained almost instant recognition and status as an effective way to transform patient behaviour. **Psychopharmacology** is the branch of psychology that investigates the effects of drugs on behaviour. Researchers in psychopharmacology work to understand the effect drugs have on some biological systems and the consequent changes in responding.

The discovery of *drug therapies* had profound effects on the treatment of severely disordered patients. No longer did mental hospital staff have to act as guards, putting patients in seclusion or straitjackets; staff morale improved as rehabilitation replaced mere custodial care of the mentally ill (Swazey, 1974). Moreover, the drug therapy revolution had a great impact on the Canadian mental hospital population. Over 66 000 Canadians were living in mental institutions in 1955, staying an average of several years. The introduction of chlorpromazine and other drugs reversed the steadily increasing numbers of patients. By the early 1970s, it was estimated that fewer than half the country's mental patients actually resided in mental hospitals; those who did were institutionalized for an average of only a few months.

The drugs we will describe that alleviate symptoms of various mental disorders are widely prescribed. With health-care costs increasing rapidly in Canada, all provincial governments feel pressure to reduce costs by substituting drug therapies for more expensive forms of psychological therapies. Drugs used to assist those with mental health issues have become the second most prescribed types of drugs in Canada, with over 57 million prescriptions worth over $2.2 billion in sales (Carter & Campeau, 2009). For that reason, it is important to understand the positive and negative features of drug therapies.

Three major categories of drugs are used today in therapy programs: *antipsychotic*, *antidepressant*, and *antianxiety* medications (see **Table 16.3**). As their names suggest, these drugs chemically alter specific brain functions that are responsible for psychotic symptoms, depression, and extreme anxiety.

Antipsychotic Drugs Antipsychotic drugs alter symptoms of schizophrenia such as delusions, hallucinations, social withdrawal, and occasional agitation (Dawkins, Lieberman, Lebowitz, & Hsiao, 1999). Antipsychotic drugs work by reducing the activity of the neurotransmitter dopamine in the brain. The earliest drugs researchers developed, such as *chlorpromazine* (marketed under the brand name *Thorazine*) and *haloperidol* (marketed as *Haldol*), blocked or reduced the sensitivity of dopamine receptors. Although those drugs functioned by decreasing the overall level of brain activity, they were not just tranquilizers. For many patients, they did much more than merely eliminate agitation. They also relieved or reduced the positive symptoms of schizophrenia, including delusions and hallucinations.

There were, unfortunately, negative side effects of these early antipsychotic drugs. Because dopamine plays a role in motor control, muscle disturbances frequently accompany a course of drug treatment. *Tardive dyskinesia* is a particular disturbance of motor control, especially of the facial muscles, caused by antipsychotic drugs. Patients who develop this side effect experience involuntary jaw, lip, and tongue movements.

Over time, researchers created a new category of drugs, called *atypical* antipsychotic drugs, that create fewer motor

TABLE 16.3	Drug Therapies for Mental Illness	
Disorder	**Type of Therapy**	**Examples**
Schizophrenia	Antipsychotic drug	chlorpromazine (Thorazine)
		haloperidol (Haldol)
		clozapine (Clozaril)
Depression	Tricyclic antidepressant	imipramine (Tofranil)
		amitriptyline (Elavil)
	Selective serotonin reuptake inhibitor	fluoxetine (Prozac)
		paroxetine (Paxil)
		sertraline (Zoloft)
	Serotonin and norepinephrine reuptake inhibitor	milnacipran (Dalcipran)
		venlafaxine (Effexor)
	MAO inhibitor	phenelzine (Nardil)
		isocarboxazid (Marplan)
Bipolar disorder	Mood stabilizer	lithium (Eshalith)
Anxiety disorders	Benzodiazepines	diazepam (Valium)
		alprazolam (Xanax)
	Antidepressant drug	fluoxetine (Prozac)

Antidepressant Drugs Antidepressant drugs work by increasing the activity of the neurotransmitters norepinephrine and serotonin (Holmes, 1994). Recall from Chapter 4 that nerve cells communicate by releasing neurotransmitters into synaptic clefts (the small gaps between neurons). *Tricyclics*, such as *Tofranil* and *Elavil*, reduce the reuptake (removal) of the neurotransmitters from the synaptic cleft (see **Figure 16.2**). Drugs such as *Prozac* are known as *selective* serotonin reuptake inhibitors (SSRIs) because they specifically reduce the reuptake of serotonin. The *monoamine oxidase* (MAO) *inhibitors* limit the action of the enzyme monoamine oxidase, which is responsible for breaking down (metabolizing) norepinephrine. When MAO is inhibited, more of the neurotransmitter is left available. Thus each type of drug leaves more neurotransmitters available to bring about neural signals.

Antidepressant drugs can be successful at relieving the symptoms of depression, although as many as 50 percent of patients will not show improvement (Hollon, Thase, & Markowitz, 2002). (Those patients may be candidates for ECT or rTMS, which we discuss later.) Because antidepressant drugs affect important neurotransmitter systems in the brain, they have the potential for serious side effects. For example, people taking SSRIs such as Prozac may experience symptoms such as nausea, insomnia, nervousness, and sexual dysfunction. Tricyclics and MAO inhibitors may cause dry mouth, difficulty sleeping, and memory impairment. Research suggests that most of the major antidepressant drugs are roughly equal, across individuals, in their ability to bring relief (Hollon et al., 2002). For that reason, it is important for each individual to find the drug that yields the fewest side effects for him or her personally.

Researchers also continue to search for drugs that will help alleviate the symptoms of depression with fewer side effects. The newest class of drugs is called *serotonin and norepinephrine reuptake inhibitors*, or *SNRIs*. As that name suggests, these drugs, such as *Effexor* and *Dalcipran*, block the reuptake of both serotonin and norepinephrine. Clinical trials using these drugs indicate that they may be more effective than SSRIs (Stahl,

side effects. The first member of this category, *clozapine* (marketed as *Clozaril*), was approved in Canada in 1991. Clozapine both directly decreases dopamine activity and increases the level of serotonin activity, which inhibits the dopamine system. This pattern of activity blocks dopamine receptors more selectively, resulting in a lower probability of motor disturbance. Unfortunately, *agranulocytosis*, a rare disease in which the bone marrow stops making white blood cells, develops in 1 to 2 percent of patients treated with clozapine.

Researchers have created a range of atypical antipsychotic drugs that act in the brain in a fashion similar to clozapine. Large-scale studies suggest that each of these drugs is effective in relieving the symptoms of schizophrenia—but each also has the potential for side effects (Lieberman et al., 2005). For example, people who take these drugs are at risk for weight gain and diabetes (Nasrallah, 2005; M. Smith et al., 2008). Unfortunately, the side effects often prompt patients to discontinue the drug therapy. The rate of relapse when patients go off the drugs is quite high—75 percent have new symptoms within one year (Gitlin et al., 2001). Even patients who remain on the newer drugs, such as clozapine, have about a 15 to 20 percent chance of relapse (Leucht et al., 2003). Thus antipsychotic drugs do not cure schizophrenia—they do not eliminate the underlying psychopathology. Fortunately, they are reasonably effective at controlling the disorder's most disruptive symptoms.

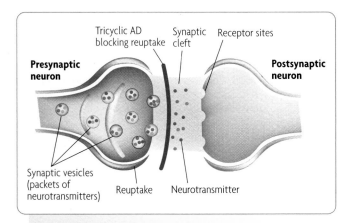

FIGURE 16.2 The Brain Mechanisms of Tricyclic Antidepressants

Tricyclic antidepressants (AD) block the reuptake of norepineprhine and serotonin so that the neurotransmitters remain in the synaptic cleft.

Butcher et al., *Abnormal Psychology*, 13/e, p. 615. Adapted from Gitlin 1996, p. 287.

Grady, Moret, & Briley, 2005). However, researchers still must determine which SNRIs function without serious side effects (Perahia et al., 2008).

In recent years, researchers have examined the important question of whether individuals—and, in particular, children and adolescents—who take antidepressant drugs are at greater risk for suicide. Although conclusions remain controversial, the majority of evidence supports the claim that drug treatment for depression does, in fact, yield a small increase in suicide risk (Möller et al., 2008). The important question is why this is the case. Some researchers believe that the drugs—in particular SSRIs—act in the brain to increase suicidal thoughts. Other researchers suggest that the small increase in suicide risk is an unfortunate consequence of the relief the drugs bring: Because major depressive disorder impairs motivation, people may be able to carry out suicidal behaviours only once their mental health starts to improve. For that reason, people who start drug treatment for major depressive disorder should receive consistent clinical attention to monitor for possible suicidal thoughts or intentions. Note also that many researchers have argued that, because antidepressant drugs bring relief from depression, they prevent many more suicides than they cause; their benefits outweigh their risks (Bridge et al., 2007).

Lithium salts have proven effective in the treatment of bipolar disorders (Thase & Denko, 2008). People who experience uncontrollable periods of hyperexcitement, when their energy seems limitless and their behaviour extravagant and flamboyant, are brought down from their state of manic excess by doses of lithium. In addition, if people continue to take lithium when their symptoms are in remission, they are less likely to have recurrences of the disorder (Biel, Preselow, Mulcare, Case, & Fieve, 2007). However, for those people suffering from bipolar disorders who cycle frequently between manic episodes and depression, lithium appears to be less effective than other treatments such as the drug valproate, which was originally developed as a drug to prevent seizures (Cousins & Young, 2007).

Antianxiety Drugs Like antipsychotic and antidepressant drugs, antianxiety drugs generally produce their effect by adjusting the levels of neurotransmitter activity in the brain. Different drugs are most effective at relieving different types of anxiety disorders (Hoffman & Mathew, 2008). Generalized anxiety disorder is best treated with a *benzodiazepine*, such as *Valium* or *Xanax*, which increases the activity of the neurotransmitter gamma-aminobutyric acid (GABA). Because GABA regulates inhibitory neurons, increases in GABA activity decrease brain activity in areas of the brain relevant to generalized anxiety responses. Panic disorders, as well as agoraphobia and other phobias, can be treated with antidepressant drugs, although researchers do not yet understand the biological mechanism involved. Obsessive-compulsive disorder, which may arise from low levels of serotonin, responds particularly well to drugs like Prozac that specifically affect serotonin function.

As with drugs that treat schizophrenia and mood disorders, benzodiazepines affect a major neurotransmitter system and therefore have a range of potential side effects (Rivas-Vazquez, 2003). People who begin a course of therapy

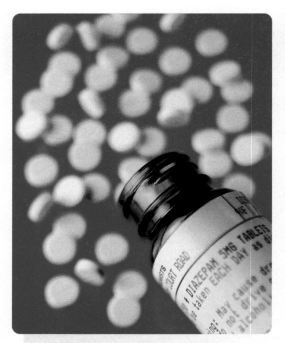

Why should people be cautious when they undertake drug therapies?

may experience daytime drowsiness, slurred speech, and problems with co-ordination. The drugs may also impair cognitive processes such as attention and memory (Stewart, 2005). Furthermore, people who begin treatment with benzodiazepines often experience drug tolerance—they must increase their dosage to maintain a stable effect (see Chapter 6). Discontinuation of treatment might also lead to withdrawal symptoms (O'Brien, 2005). Because of the potential for psychological and physical dependence, people should undertake treatment with antianxiety drugs in careful consultation with a health-care provider.

PSYCHOSURGERY

The headline in the *Los Angeles Times* read, "Bullet in the Brain Cures Man's Mental Problem" (2/23/1988). The article revealed that a 19-year-old man suffering from severe obsessive-compulsive disorder had shot a .22-calibre bullet through the front of his brain in a suicide attempt. Remarkably, he survived, his pathological symptoms were cured, and his intellectual capacity was not affected, although some of the underlying causes of his problems remained.

This case illustrates the potential effects of one of the most direct biomedical therapies: surgical intervention in the brain. Such intervention involves lesioning (severing) connections between parts of the brain or removing small sections of the brain. These therapies are often considered methods of last resort to treat psychopathologies that have proven intractable to other, less extreme forms of therapy. **Psychosurgery** is the general term for surgical procedures performed on brain tissue to alleviate psychological disorders.

psychosurgery A surgical procedure performed on brain tissue to alleviate a psychological disorder.

Electroconvulsive therapy has been very effective in cases of severe depression. Why does it remain controversial as a treatment?

The best-known form of psychosurgery is the **prefrontal lobotomy**, an operation that severs the nerve fibres connecting the frontal lobes of the brain with the diencephalon, especially those fibres of the thalamic and hypothalamic areas. The procedure was developed by neurologist **Egas Moniz**, who, in 1949, won a Nobel Prize for this treatment.

The original candidates for lobotomy were agitated patients with schizophrenia and patients who were compulsive and anxiety ridden. The effects of this psychosurgery were dramatic: A new personality emerged without intense emotional arousal and, thus, without overwhelming anxiety, guilt, or anger. However, the operation permanently destroyed basic aspects of human nature. The lobotomy resulted in inability to plan ahead, indifference to the opinions of others, childlike actions, and the intellectual and emotional flatness of a person without a coherent sense of self. (One of Moniz's own patients was so distressed by these unexpected consequences that she shot Moniz, partially paralyzing him).

Because the effects of psychosurgery are permanent, its negative effects severe and common, and its positive results less certain, its continued use is very limited. Clinicians consider psychosurgery only when other treatments have repeatedly failed. For example, one study evaluated the effectiveness of a procedure called a cingulotomy, in which surgeons create lesions in the limbic system structure called the cingulate gyrus (Shields et al., 2008). The 33 patients in the study had intractable major depression—they had failed to respond to four or more courses of drug treatment as well as other standard treatments. After the surgeries, 75 percent of the patients showed some relief from their symptoms. The cingulotomy procedure has also relieved the symptoms of patients with obsessive-compulsive disorder who were similarly unresponsive to drug treatments (Kim et al., 2003).

ECT AND RTMS

Electroconvulsive therapy (ECT) is the use of electric shock applied to the brain to treat psychiatric disorders such as schizophrenia, mania, and, most often, depression. The technique consists of applying weak electric current (75 to 100 volts) to a patient's temples for a period of time from 1/10 of a second to a full second until a convulsion occurs. The convulsion usually runs its course in 45 to 60 seconds. Patients are prepared for this traumatic intervention by sedation with a short-acting barbiturate and muscle relaxant, which renders the patient unconscious and minimizes the violent physical reactions (Abrams, 1992).

Electroconvulsive therapy has proven quite successful at alleviating the symptoms of serious depression (Lisanby, 2007). ECT is particularly important because it works quickly. Typically, the symptoms of depression are alleviated in a three- or four-day course of treatment, as compared with the one- to two-week time window for drug therapies. Even so, most therapists hold ECT as a treatment of last resort. ECT is often reserved for emergency treatment for suicidal or severely malnourished depressed patients and for patients who do not respond to antidepressant drugs or cannot tolerate their side effects.

If ECT is so effective, why has it so often been demonized? For example, in 1982, the citizens of Berkeley, California, voted to ban the use of electroconvulsive shock in any of their community mental health facilities (the action was later overturned on legal grounds). Scientific unease with ECT centres largely on the lack of understanding of how it works. The therapy was originated when clinicians observed that patients who suffered from both schizophrenia and epilepsy showed improvement in their symptoms of schizophrenia after epileptic seizures. The clinicians conjectured that the same effect could be obtained with artificially induced seizures. Although the conjecture proved correct in part—ECT is much more effective at alleviating depression than alleviating schizophrenia—researchers have yet to fit a definitive theory to this chance observation.

Critics have also worried about the potential side effects of ECT (Breggin, 1979, 1991). ECT produces temporary disorientation and a variety of memory deficits. For example, patients

---

prefrontal lobotomy An operation that severs the nerve fibres connecting the frontal lobes of the brain with the diencephalon especially those fibres in the thalamic and hypothalamic areas; best known form of psychosurgery.

electroconvulsive therapy (ECT) The use of electroconvulsive shock as an effective treatment for severe depression.

Critical Thinking in Your Life

DOES THERAPY AFFECT BRAIN ACTIVITY?

In this chapter, we have made a number of distinctions among types of therapies. However, our most basic distinction has been between psychological and biomedical approaches to treatment. It has often been the practice to use a computer analogy to illustrate this distinction: If we think of the brain as a computer, we can say that mental illness may arise from either the brain's hardware or in the software that programs its actions. With respect to this analogy, biomedical treatments focus on changing the hardware, whereas psychological treatments focus on changing the software. However, cutting-edge research blurs the distinction between hardware and software: There is growing evidence that biomedical and psychological therapies produce many of the same changes in the brain (Frewen, Dozois, & Lanius, 2008).

Consider a study that examined the brain changes that accompanied treatment for social phobia (Furmark et al., 2002). Each of the 10 men and 8 women in the study met *DSM-IV* criteria for the disorder. The researchers placed them into one of three groups. One group of participants was given the drug citalopram (which has the prescription name Celexa). At the end of the nine-week treatment period, the researchers did blood assays to ensure that the participants had adhered to their drug regimen. A second group of participants received eight weekly sessions of therapy. In each three-hour session, participants engaged in simulated exposure to feared situations and cognitive restructuring. The third group of participants was the control group. (After the period of the experiment, they began the drug regimen.)

To assess the impact of the drug and cognitive behavioural therapies,

all the participants were asked to deliver brief speeches while they underwent PET scans. The situation was intended to be quite threatening for individuals with social phobia: An audience of six to eight people surrounded the scanner bed while the participants gave their two-minute speeches. With respect to behavioural measures (e.g., the extent to which participants experienced anxiety during their speeches), both treatment groups showed substantial and roughly equivalent improvement as compared to the control group. Moreover, as shown in the figure, the PET scans demonstrated decreased brain activity (again, relative to the control group) in much the same locations in the brain. Of importance, the decreased activity was in areas of the brain (such as the amygdala) that play a role in emotional responses.

Researchers have now demonstrated the brain impact of psychotherapy for several disorders. For example, after patients underwent psychotherapy for PTSD, brain images showed changes in regions associated with symptoms of the disorder (Lindauer et al., 2008). Similarly,

patients who experienced cognitive behavioural therapy for major depressive disorder showed changes in brain regions that play a causal role in the disorder (Goldapple et al., 2004). In each of these cases, it hasn't been enough to show just that psychotherapies affect particular areas of the brain. Researchers have also argued that changes in those areas are related to the relief that patients experience.

In light of these results, researchers can now shift their attention to *how*. How is it that psychotherapy can restore the brain's balance in the same systems affected by drugs? How, for example, can cognitive therapy have a similar impact on the brain's use of the neurotransmitter serotonin as does a drug that is specifically designated as a selective serotonin reuptake inhibitor (Brody et al., 2002)? These types of questions will help set the research agenda for the first part of the 21st century.

- Why was it important to ensure that the participants in the drug group adhered to the regimen?
- Why did the researchers put a real audience around the scanner?

Cognitive behavioural group therapy (compared to control)

Drug therapy (compared to control)

often suffer amnesia for events in the period of time preceding the treatment as well as difficulty forming new memories (Ingram, Saling, & Schweitzer, 2008). However, most patients recover from these deficits in the first few weeks after treatment. As a way of minimizing even short-term deficits, ECT is now often administered to only one side of the brain so as to reduce the possibility of speech impairment. Such unilateral ECT alleviates some of the cognitive consequences of the treatment and also remains an effective antidepressant (Fraser, O'Carroll, & Ebmeier, 2008).

In recent years, researchers have explored an alternative to ECT called *repetitive transcranial magnetic stimulation (rTMS)*. As you might recall from Chapter 4, people who undergo rTMS receive repeated pulses of magnetic stimulation to the brain. As with ECT, researchers have not yet determined why rTMS can bring relief for major depressive disorder and other forms of psychopathology. However, evidence is mounting that rTMS can be just as effective as some antidepressant drugs (Schutter, 2008). Researchers are working to determine how variables such as the intensity of the magnetic stimulation affect rTMS's ability to bring relief (Daskalakis, Levinson, & Fitzgerald, 2008).

STOP AND REVIEW

❶ What advantages do atypical antipsychotic drugs have over early drug therapies for schizophrenia?
❷ What do SNRIs do in the brain?
❸ What are some effects of a prefrontal lobotomy?
❹ What is the rTMS procedure?

Treatment Evaluation and Prevention Strategies

Suppose you have come to perceive a problem in your life that you believe could be alleviated by interaction with a trained clinician. We have mentioned a great variety of types of therapies. How can you know which one of them will work best to relieve your distress? How can you be sure that *any* of them will work? In this section, we examine the projects researchers undertake to test the effectiveness of particular therapies and make comparisons between different therapies. The general goal is to discover the most efficient way to help people overcome distress. We also consider briefly the topic of *prevention*: How can psychologists intervene in people's lives to prevent mental illness before it occurs?

EVALUATING THERAPEUTIC EFFECTIVENESS

British psychologist Hans Eysenck (1952) created a furor some years ago by declaring that psychotherapy does not work at all! He reviewed available publications that reported the effects of various therapies and found that patients who received no therapy had just as high a recovery rate as those who received psychoanalysis or other forms of insight therapy. He claimed that roughly two-thirds of all people with neurotic problems would recover spontaneously within two years of the onset of the problem.

Researchers met Eysenck's challenge by devising more accurate methodologies to evaluate the effectiveness of therapy. What Eysenck's criticism made clear was that researchers needed to have appropriate control groups. For a variety of reasons, *some* percentage of individuals in psychotherapy *does* improve without any professional intervention. This **spontaneous-remission effect** is one *baseline* criterion against which the effectiveness of therapies must be assessed. Simply put, doing something must be shown to lead to a greater percentage of improved cases than doing nothing.

Similarly, researchers generally try to demonstrate that their treatment does more than just take advantage of clients' own expectations of healing. You may recall our earlier discussions of *placebo* effects: In many cases, people's mental or physical health will improve because they expect that it will improve. The therapeutic situation helps bolster this belief by putting the therapist in the specific social role of *healer* (Frank & Frank, 1991). Although the placebo effects of therapy are an important part of the therapeutic intervention, researchers typically wish to demonstrate that their specific form of therapy is more effective than a **placebo therapy** (a neutral therapy that just creates expectations of healing) (Hyland, Whalley, & Geraghty, 2007).

In recent years, researchers have evaluated therapeutic effectiveness using a statistical technique called meta-analysis. **Meta-analysis** provides a formal mechanism for detecting the general conclusions to be found in data from many different experiments. In many psychological experiments, the researcher asks, "Did most of my participants show the effect I predicted?" Meta-analysis treats experiments like participants. With respect to the effectiveness of therapy, the researcher asks, "Did most of the outcome studies show positive changes?"

Consider **Figure 16.3**, which presents the results of meta-analyses of the research literature on treatments for depression (Hollon et al., 2002). The graph compares results for three types of psychotherapies and medications (averaged across different types of antidepressant drugs) to those for placebo treatments. We described psychodynamic and cognitive behavioural therapies earlier in the chapter. Interpersonal therapy focuses on a patient's current life and interpersonal relationships. As you can see, across all the studies reviewed in the meta-analyses that contributed to this figure, interpersonal therapy, cognitive behavioural therapy, and drug therapies had a consistently larger impact than did placebos. At least for treatment of depression, classic psychodynamic therapy did not fare well. However, research conducted at McGill University suggests that while psychotherapy and medication may both be effective in treating depression, psychotherapy may in fact be more successful in the long run since it involves the development of enhanced resiliency to stressful life events (Hawley, Ringo Ho, Zuroff, & Blatt, 2007).

---

spontaneous-remission effect The improvement of some mental patients and clients in psychotherapy without any professional intervention; a baseline criterion against which the effectiveness of therapies must be assessed.

placebo therapy A therapy independent of any specific clinical procedures that results in client improvement.

meta-analysis A statistical technique for evaluating hypotheses by providing a formal mechanism for detecting the general conclusions found in data from many different experiments.

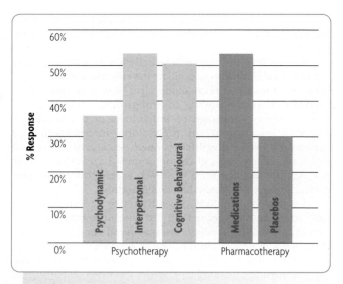

FIGURE 16.3 Treatment Evaluation for Depression

The figure displays the results from meta-analyses of treatments for depression. For each treatment, the figure presents the percentage of patients who typically respond to each category of treatment. For example, about 50 percent of patients taking antidepressant medication experience recognizable symptom relief, whereas 50 percent do not.

Note that these data reflect the impact of each type of treatment alone. Researchers have assessed the effectiveness of psychotherapy alone versus psychotherapy combined with drug therapy. One study found that combination therapy was most able to bring about full remission from chronic depression (Manber et al., 2008). Of participants who completed a course of treatment, 14 percent of the participants who received only drug therapy met the study's criterion for full remission, as did 14 percent of the participants who received only psychotherapy. For participants who received both drug therapy and psychotherapy, 29 percent showed the same level of improvement.

Because of such findings, contemporary researchers are less concerned about asking *whether* psychotherapy works and more concerned about asking *why* it works and whether any one treatment is most effective for any particular problem and for certain types of patients (Goodheart, Kadzin, & Sternberg, 2006). For example, much treatment evaluation has been carried out in research settings that afford reasonable control over patients (often, the studies exclude individuals who have more than one disorder) and procedures (therapists are rigorously trained to minimize differences in treatment). Researchers need to ensure that therapies that work in research settings also work out in community settings in which patients and therapists have more diversity of symptoms and experience (Kazdin, 2008). Another important issue for evaluation research is to assess the likelihood that individuals will complete a course of treatment. In almost all circumstances, some people choose to discontinue treatments (Barrett, Chua, Crits-Christoph, Gibbons, & Thompson, 2008). Researchers seek to understand who leaves treatment and why—with the ultimate hope of creating treatments to which most everyone can adhere.

Figure 16.4 provides a general flowchart for the way theory, clinical observation, and research all play a role in the development and evaluation of any form of treatment (for both mental and physical disorders). It shows the type of systematic research needed to help clinicians discover if their therapies are making the differences that their theories predict. On one side, you see clinical observation—clinicians' own experience with a new procedure. Often, new treatments first get tested without rigorous experimental control. On the other side of the figure, you see a theory being developed. The theory makes predictions about what should work, which may be confirmed in laboratory studies. These two types of insights—clinical and experimental—are combined to yield a new therapy.

In the final section of this chapter, we reflect on an important principle of life: Whatever the effectiveness of treatment, it is often better to prevent a disorder than to heal it once it arises.

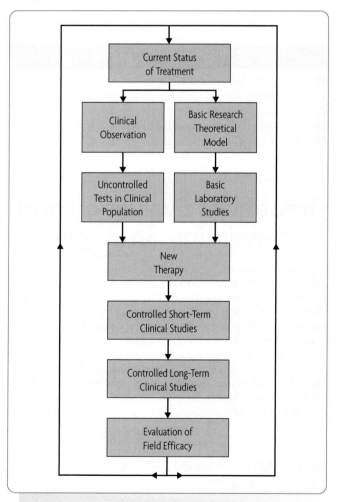

FIGURE 16.4 Building Better Therapies

Flowchart of stages in the development of treatments for mental/physical disorders.

From Weissman et al., *American Journal of Psychiatry,* Vol. 136, p. 558, 1979. Copyright © 1979 American Psychiatric Association.

PREVENTION STRATEGIES

The traditional therapies we have examined in this chapter share the focus of changing a person who is already distressed or disabled. This focus is necessary because, much of the time, people are unaware that they are at risk for psychological disorders. They present themselves for treatment only once they have begun to experience symptoms. However, as we saw in Chapter 15, researchers have identified a number of biological and psychological factors that put people at risk. The goal of prevention is to apply knowledge of those risk factors to reduce the likelihood and severity of distress.

Prevention can be realized at several different levels. *Primary* prevention seeks to prevent a condition before it begins. Steps might be taken, for example, to provide individuals with coping skills so they can be more resilient or to change negative aspects of an environment that might lead to anxiety or depression (Boyd, Diamond, & Bourolly, 2006; Hudson, Flannery-Schroeder, & Kendall, 2004). *Secondary* prevention attempts to limit the duration and severity of a disorder once it has begun. This goal is realized by means of programs that allow for early identification and prompt treatment. For example, based on the study we described for depression, a mental health practitioner might recommend a combination of psychotherapy and drug therapy to optimize secondary prevention (Manber et al., 2008). *Tertiary* prevention limits the long-term impact of a psychological disorder by seeking to prevent a relapse. For example, we noted earlier that individuals with schizophrenia who discontinue drug therapy have a very high rate of relapse (Gitlin et al., 2001). To engage in tertiary prevention, mental health practitioners would recommend that their patients with schizophrenia continue their courses of antipsychotic drugs.

The implementation of these three types of prevention has signaled major shifts in the focus and in the basic paradigms of mental health care. The most important of these paradigm shifts are (1) supplementing treatment with prevention; (2) going beyond a medical disease model to a public health model; (3) focusing on situations and ecologies that put people at risk;

How can prevention strategies encourage people to build "mental hygiene" habits to minimize the need for treatment?

and (4) looking for precipitating factors in life settings rather than for predisposing factors in people.

Preventing mental disorders is a complex and difficult task. It involves not only understanding the relevant causal factors, but also overcoming individual, institutional, and governmental resistance to change. A major research effort will be needed to demonstrate the long-range utility of prevention and a public health approach to psychopathology in order to justify the expense in the face of the many other problems that demand immediate solutions. The ultimate goal of prevention programs is to safeguard the mental health of all members of our society.

STOP AND REVIEW

❶ What conclusions can be drawn from meta-analyses of treatments for depression?

❷ Why has research focused on the probability that people will complete courses of treatment?

❸ What is the goal of primary prevention?

Recapping Main Points

The Therapeutic Context

- Therapy requires that a diagnosis be made and a course of treatment be established.
- Therapy may be medically or psychologically oriented.
- The four major types of psychotherapies are psychodynamic, behavioural, cognitive, and humanistic.
- A variety of professionals practise therapy.
- Harsh early treatment of those with mental illnesses led to a modern movement for deinstitutionalization.
- Unfortunately, many people do not have adequate resources outside the institution, so they may become homeless or be quickly readmitted to institutions.

Visit **MyPsychLab.com** for more review and practice on the following topics:

 Practice: The Therapeutic Context

Psychodynamic Therapies

- Psychodynamic therapies grew out of Sigmund Freud's psychoanalytic theory.
- Freud emphasized the role of unconscious conflicts in the etiology of psychopathology.
- Psychodynamic therapy seeks to reconcile these conflicts.
- Free association, attention to resistance, dream analysis, transference, and countertransference are all important components of this therapy.
- Other psychodynamic theorists place more emphasis on the patient's current social situation and interpersonal relationships.

Behaviour Therapies

- Behaviour therapies use the principles of learning and reinforcement to modify or eliminate problem behaviours.

- Counterconditioning techniques replace negative behaviours, such as phobic responses, with more adaptive behaviours.
- Exposure is the common element in phobia-modification therapies.
- Contingency management uses operant conditioning to modify behaviour, primarily through positive reinforcement and extinction.
- Social-learning therapy uses models and social-skills training to help individuals gain confidence about their abilities.

Visit **MyPsychLab.com** for more review and practice on the following topics:

 Watch: Cognitive Behavioural Therapy

Cognitive Therapies

- Cognitive therapy concentrates on changing negative or irrational thought patterns about the self and social relationships.
- Cognitive therapy has been used successfully to treat depression.
- Rational-emotive therapy (RET) helps clients recognize that their irrational beliefs about themselves interfere with successful life outcomes.
- Cognitive behavioural therapy calls for the client to learn more constructive thought patterns in reference to a problem and to apply the new technique to other situations.

Visit **MyPsychLab.com** for more review and practice on the following topics:

 Research: Albert Ellis

Humanistic Therapies

- Humanistic therapies work to help individuals become more fully self-actualized.
- Therapists strive to be nondirective in helping their clients establish a positive self-image that can deal with external criticisms.
- Gestalt therapy focuses on the whole person—body, mind, and life setting.

Group Therapies

- Group therapy allows people to observe and engage in social interactions as a means to reduce psychological distress.
- Family and marital (couple) therapy concentrates on situational difficulties and interpersonal dynamics of the couple or family group as a system in need of improvement.
- Community and internet self-help groups allow individuals to obtain information and feelings of control in circumstances of social support.

Visit **MyPsychLab.com** for more review and practice on the following topics:

 Explore: Psychotherapy Practitioners and Their Activities

Biomedical Therapies

- Biomedical therapies concentrate on changing physiological aspects of mental illness.
- Drug therapies include antipsychotic medications for treating schizophrenia as well as antidepressants and antianxiety drugs.
- Psychosurgery is rarely used because of its radical, irreversible effects.
- Electroconvulsive therapy and repetitive transcranial magnetic stimulation (rTMS) can be effective with depressed patients.

Treatment Evaluation and Prevention Strategies

- Research shows that many therapies work better than the mere passage of time or than nonspecific placebo treatment.
- Evaluation projects are helping to answer the question of what makes therapy effective.
- Prevention strategies are necessary to stop psychological disorders from occurring and to minimize their effects once they have occurred.

KEY TERMS

aversion therapy (p. 507)
behavioural rehearsal (p. 509)
behaviour modification (p. 506)
behaviour therapy (p. 506)
biomedical therapies (p. 499)
catharsis (p. 503)
client (p. 500)
client-centred therapy (p. 513)
clinical psychologist (p. 500)
clinical social worker (p. 500)
cognitive behavioural therapy (p. 512)
cognitive therapy (p. 511)
contingency management (p. 508)
counselling psychologist (p. 500)

counterconditioning (p. 506)
countertransference (p. 504)
deinstitutionalization (p. 502)
dream analysis (p. 504)
electroconvulsive therapy (ECT) (p. 519)
exposure therapy (p. 506)
free association (p. 503)
Gestalt therapy (p. 514)
human-potential movement (p. 513)
insight therapy (p. 503)
meta-analysis (p. 521)
participant modelling (p. 509)
pastoral counsellor (p. 500)
patient (p. 500)

placebo therapy (p. 521)
prefrontal lobotomy (p. 519)
psychiatrist (p. 500)
psychoanalysis (p. 503)
psychoanalyst (p. 500)
psychopharmacology (p. 516)
psychosurgery (p. 518)
psychotherapy (p. 499)
rational-emotive therapy (RET) (p. 511)
resistance (p. 503)
social-learning therapy (p. 509)
spontaneous-remission effect (p. 521)
systematic desensitization (p. 506)
transference (p. 504)

Practice Test

1. When Sonja begins treatment, her therapist focuses on her inner conflicts, which he believes remain unresolved. It seems that Sonja's therapist takes a —————— approach.
   a. psychodynamic
   b. cognitive
   c. biological
   d. humanistic

2. Which of these topics would you be *least* likely to hear about in a lecture on deinstitutionalization?
   a. homelessness
   b. meta-analysis
   c. readmission rates
   d. violent crime

3. In psychodynamic therapy, —————— refers to a patient's inability or unwillingness to discuss certain topics.
   a. catharsis
   b. transference
   c. countertransference
   d. resistance

4. Research on repressed memories suggests that ——————
   a. recovered memories are never accurate.
   b. people's memories are not subject to therapists' influence.
   c. some memories of abuse are implanted by therapists.
   d. most memories are subject to repression.

5. If Roland undergoes ——————, he should expect to have a strong noxious stimulus paired with stimuli to which he is attracted.
   a. systematic desensitization
   b. behavioural rehearsal
   c. social-learning therapy
   d. aversion therapy

6. Every time Janice provides a urine sample that is drug free, she gets vouchers with which she can purchase items she enjoys. This treatment is a form of ——————
   a. systematic desensitization.
   b. contingency management.
   c. participant modelling.
   d. generalization.

7. People can learn the process of —————— to change negative self-statements into positive coping statements.
   a. social learning
   b. self-efficacy
   c. cognitive restructuring
   d. catharsis

8. You hear a therapist talking about how hard he works to communicate unconditional positive regard. You suspect that he is a —————— therapist.
   a. Gestalt
   b. client-centred
   c. behavioural
   d. psychodynamic

9. In your Introductory Psychology class, you watch a movie clip of an individual in therapy addressing an empty chair as if it were his abusive boss. This clip demonstrates —————— therapy.
   a. Gestalt
   b. client-centred
   c. aversion
   d. social-learning

10. The particular focus of —————— therapy will often be on poor patterns of communication.
    a. Gestalt
    b. client-centred
    c. couple
    d. psychodynamic

11. —————— drugs largely have their impact in the brain by changing the function of the neurotransmitters serotonin and norepinephrine.
    a. Antidepressant
    b. Antianxiety
    c. Antipsychotic
    d. Antimania

12. In clinical research, —————— proven effective at relieving the symptoms of depression.
    a. only ECT has
    b. only rTMS has
    c. neither ECT nor rTMS has
    d. both ECT and rTMS have

13. —————— therapy is the type of treatment *least* likely to provide relief from major depressive disorder.
    a. Placebo
    b. Interpersonal
    c. Cognitive behavioural
    d. Drug

14. When prevention efforts are intended to prevent relapse, it is called —————— prevention.
    a. primary
    b. regulatory
    c. tertiary
    d. secondary

15. You are looking at PET scans of the brain activity of two people who have undergone treatment for social phobia. One received cognitive behavioural therapy and one received drug therapy. You expect —————— to show differences in brain activity in comparison to people who had not received treatment.
    a. only the person who received cognitive behavioural therapy
    b. only the person who received drug therapy
    c. neither person
    d. both people

Essay Questions

1. Why do behaviour therapies target adaptive and maladaptive behaviours?

2. What features of self-help groups make them beneficial to mental health?

3. Why are therapies compared to placebos to evaluate their effectiveness?

Discovering Psychology Viewing Guide

Watch the following video by logging on to MyPsychLab (**www.mypsychlab.com**). After you have watched the video, complete the activities that follow.

Program 22: Psychotherapy

PROGRAM REVIEW

1. What are the two main approaches to therapies for mental disorders?
   a. the Freudian and the behavioural
   b. the client-centred and the patient-centred
   c. the biomedical and the psychological
   d. the chemical and the psychosomatic

2. Vinnie suffers from bipolar disorder, but his mood swings are kept under control because he takes the drug —————
   a. chlorpromazine.
   c. Valium.
   b. lithium.
   d. tetracycline.

3. Imagine you are observing a therapy session in which a patient is lying on a couch, talking. The therapist is listening and asking occasional questions. What is most likely to be the therapist's goal?
   a. to determine which drug the patient should be given
   b. to change the symptoms that cause distress
   c. to explain how to change false ideas
   d. to help the patient develop insight

4. According to Hans Strupp, in what major way have psychodynamic therapies changed?
   a. Less emphasis is now placed on the ego.
   b. Patients no longer need to develop a relationship with the therapist.
   c. Shorter courses of treatment can be used.
   d. The concept of aggression has become more important.

5. In the program, a therapist helped a girl learn to control her epileptic seizures. What use did the therapist make of the pen?
   a. to record data
   b. to signal the onset of an attack
   c. to reduce the girl's fear
   d. to reinforce the correct reaction

6. When Albert Ellis discusses with the young woman her fear of hurting others, what point is he making?
   a. It is the belief system that creates the "hurt."
   b. Every normal person strives to achieve fulfillment.
   c. Developing a fear-reduction strategy will reduce the problem.
   d. It is the use of self-fulfilling prophecies that causes others to be hurt.

7. What point does Enrico Jones make about investigating the effectiveness of different therapies in treating depression?
   a. All therapies are equally effective.
   b. It is impossible to assess how effective any one therapy is.
   c. The job is complicated by the different types of depression.
   d. The most important variable is individual versus group therapy.

8. What is the most powerful antidepressant available for patients who cannot tolerate drugs?
   a. genetic counselling
   b. electroconvulsive therapy
   c. psychoanalysis
   d. family therapy

9. Which style of therapy has as its primary goal to make the client feel as fulfilled as possible?
   a. humanistic
   c. Freudian
   b. cognitive behavioural
   d. social-learning

10. Which psychologist introduced rational-emotive therapy?
    a. Carl Rogers
    c. Albert Ellis
    b. Hans Strupp
    d. Rollo May

QUESTIONS TO CONSIDER

1. Can everyone benefit from psychotherapy, or do you think it is only for people with serious problems?

2. Why is there a stigma sometimes associated with seeking professional help for psychological problems? What might be some effective ways to change that?

3. Should we have any concerns about an overreliance on or abuse of drug therapies?

17

Social Psychology

Imagine circumstances in which you have done everything to get to a job interview on time, but nothing has gone your way. The electricity went off during the night, so your alarm did not wake you. The friend who was supposed to give you a ride had a flat tire. When you tried to get money for a taxi, the ATM ate your card. When you finally get to the office, you know what the manager is thinking: "Why would I give a job to someone this unreliable?" You want to protest, "It's not me, it's the circumstances!" As you have contemplated this scenario, you have begun to enter the world of *social psychology*—that area of psychology that investigates the ways in which individuals create and interpret social situations.

Social psychology is the study of the ways in which thoughts, feelings, perceptions, motives, and behaviour are influenced by interactions and transactions between people. Social psychologists try to understand behaviour within its social context. Defined broadly, the social context includes the real, imagined, or symbolic presence of other people; the activities and interactions that take place between people; the features of the settings in which behaviour occurs; and the expectations and norms that govern behaviour in a given setting (Sherif, 1981).

In this chapter, we explore several major themes of social psychological research. In the first part of the chapter we focus on **social cognition**, which refers to the processes by which people select, interpret, and remember social information. We examine the ways in which people construct social reality and the ways in which attitudes are formed and changed. We also consider circumstances of prejudice and its distressing consequences. We then explore the topic of personal relationships, including two of the most important aspects of human existence: liking and loving. In the last part of the chapter, we extend our analysis of social psychology's relevance beyond the personal to societal concerns. We examine how norms and social roles influence our lives, including factors that promote altruism and aggression. Throughout this chapter, as we illustrate how research in social psychology has immediate applications to your life, we attempt to answer this question: Does psychological knowledge make a difference in the everyday lives of people and society?

Let's look at one classic social psychological example in which people's beliefs led them to view the same situation from different vantage points and make contrary conclusions about what "really happened." The study concerned a football game that took place some years ago between two U.S. Ivy League teams. An undefeated Princeton University team played Dartmouth College in the final game of the season. The game, which Princeton won, was rough, filled with penalties and serious injuries to both sides. After the game, the newspapers of the two schools offered very different accounts of what had happened.

> A team of social psychologists, intrigued by the different perceptions, surveyed students at both schools, showed them a film of the game, and recorded their judgments about the number of infractions committed by each of the teams. Nearly all Princeton students judged the game as "rough and dirty," none saw it as "clean and fair," and most believed that Dartmouth players started the dirty play. In contrast, the majority of Dartmouth students thought both sides were equally to blame for the rough game, and many thought it was "rough, clean, and fair." Moreover, when the Princeton students viewed the game film, they "saw" the Dartmouth team commit twice as many penalties as their own team. When viewing the same film, Dartmouth students "saw" both sides commit the same number of penalties (Hastorf & Cantril, 1954).

This study makes clear that a complex social occurrence, such as a football game, cannot be observed in an objective, unbiased fashion. Social situations obtain significance when observers *selectively encode* what is happening in terms of what they expect to see and want to see. In the case of the football game, people looked at the same activity, but they saw two different games.

To explain how the Princeton and Dartmouth fans came to such different interpretations of the football game returns us to the realm of perception. Recall from Chapter 5 that you often must put prior knowledge to work to interpret ambiguous perceptual objects. The principle is the same for the football game—people bring past knowledge to bear on the interpretation

Constructing Social Reality

To open the chapter, we asked you to imagine everything that could go wrong in advance of a job interview. When you finally arrive at the manager's office you have very different interpretations of the same event. You know you have been a victim of circumstances. However, at least in the short run, the manager judges you only by what is readily apparent: You are late and dishevelled. That's what we mean by *constructing social reality*. The manager considers the evidence you present and makes an interpretation of the situation. If you still wish to get the job, you will have to get the manager to construct a new interpretation.

---

social psychology The branch of psychology that studies the effect of social variables on individual behaviour, attitudes, perceptions, and motives; also studies group and intergroup phenomena.

social cognition The process by which people select, interpret, and remember social information.

Why are fans who watch their favourite team play likely to perceive more instances of unfair play on the part of the opposing team?

of current events—but the objects for perceptual processing are people and situations. **Social perception** is the process by which people come to understand and categorize the behaviours of others. In this section, we will focus largely on two issues of social perception. First, we consider how people make judgments about the forces that influence other people's behaviour—their causal attributions. Next, we discuss how processes of social perception can sometimes bring the world in line with expectations.

THE ORIGINS OF ATTRIBUTION THEORY

One of the most important inferential tasks facing all social perceivers is to determine the causes of events. You want to know the *whys* of life. Why did my girlfriend break off the relationship? Why did he get the job and not I? Why did my parents divorce after so many years of marriage? All such whys lead to an analysis of possible causal determinants for some action, event, or outcome. **Attribution theory** is a general approach to describing the ways the social perceiver uses information to generate causal explanations.

Attribution theory originated in the writings of **Fritz Heider** (1958), who argued that people continually make causal analyses as part of their attempts at general comprehension of the social world. People, he suggested, are all *intuitive psychologists* who try to figure out what people are like and what causes their behaviour, just as professional psychologists do. Heider believed that the questions that dominate most attributional analyses are whether the cause of a behaviour is found in the person (internal or *dispositional* causality) or in the situation (external or *situational* causality). How do people make those judgments?

Harold Kelley (1967) formalized Heider's line of thinking by specifying the variables that people use to make their attributions. Kelley made the important observation that people most often make causal attributions for events under conditions of *uncertainty*. You rarely, if ever, have sufficient information to know for sure what caused someone to behave in a particular way. Kelley believed that people grapple with uncertainty by accumulating information from multiple events and using the *covariation principle*. The **covariation principle** suggests that people should attribute a behaviour to a causal factor if that factor was present whenever the behaviour occurred but was absent whenever it did not occur. Suppose, for example, you are walking down a street and you see a friend pointing at a horse and screaming. What evidence would you gather to decide whether your friend is crazy (a dispositional attribution) or danger is afoot (a situational attribution)?

Kelley suggested that people make this judgment by assessing covariation with respect to three dimensions of information relevant to the person whose acts they are trying to explain: distinctiveness, consistency, and consensus.

- *Distinctiveness* refers to whether the behaviour is specific to a particular situation—does your friend scream in response to all horses?
- *Consistency* refers to whether the behaviour occurs repeatedly in response to this situation—has this horse made your friend scream in the past?
- *Consensus* refers to whether other people also produce the same behaviour in the same situation—is everyone pointing and screaming?

Each of these three dimensions plays a role in the conclusions you draw. Suppose, for example, that your friend was the only one screaming. Would that make you more likely to make a dispositional or a situational attribution?

Thousands of studies have been conducted to refine and extend attribution theory beyond the solid foundation provided by Heider and Kelley (Försterling, 2001; Moskowitz, 2004). Many of those studies have concerned themselves with conditions in which attributions depart from a systematic search of available information. We will describe four types of circumstances in which bias may creep into your attributions.

THE FUNDAMENTAL ATTRIBUTION ERROR

Suppose you have made an arrangement to meet a friend at 7:00. It is now 7:30, and your friend still has not arrived. How might you be explaining this event to yourself?

- I'm sure something really important happened that made it impossible for her to be here on time.
- What a jerk! Couldn't she try a little harder?

We have given you a choice again between a situational and a dispositional attribution. Research has shown that people are more likely, on average, to choose the second type, the dispositional explanation (L. Ross & Nisbett, 1991). This tendency is so strong, in fact, that social psychologist **Lee Ross** (1977) labelled it the fundamental attribution error. The **fundamental attribution error (FAE)** represents the dual tendency for people to overestimate dispositional factors (blame or credit people) and to underestimate situational factors (blame or credit the environment) when searching for the cause of some behaviour or outcome.

Let's look at a laboratory example of the FAE. Ross and his colleagues (Ross, Amabile, & Steinmetz, 1977) created an experimental version of a type of quiz game similar to the TV show *Jeopardy* in which participants became questioners or contestants by the flip of a coin. The questioner was instructed to ask challenging questions to which he or she knew the answers. The contestant tried, often in vain, to answer the questions. At the end of the session, the questioner, the contestant, and observers (other participants who had watched the game) rated the general knowledge of both questioner and contestant. The results are shown in **Figure 17.1**. As you can see, questioners seem to believe that both they and the contestants are average. Both contestants and observers, however, rate the questioner to be much more knowledgeable than the contestant—and contestants even rate themselves to be a bit below average! Is this fair? It should be clear that the situation confers a great advantage on the questioner. The contestants' and observers' ratings ignore the way in which the situation allowed one person to look

social perception The process by which a person comes to know and categorize the personal attributes and behaviours of others.

attribution theory A social-cognitive approach to describing the ways the social perceiver uses information to generate causal explanations.

covariation principle A theory suggesting that people attribute a behaviour to a causal factor if that factor was present whenever the behaviour occurred but was absent whenever it did not occur.

fundamental attribution error (FAE) The dual tendency of observers to underestimate the impact of situational factors and to overestimate the influence of dispositional factors on a person's behaviour.

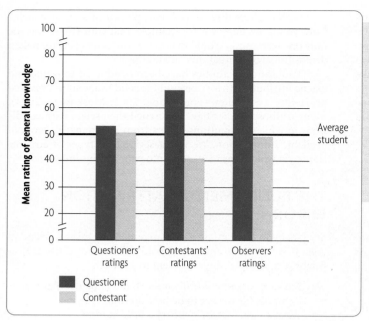

FIGURE 17.1 Ratings of Questioners' and Contestants' General Knowledge
After the quiz game, questioners, contestants, and observers rated each of the participants' general knowledge with respect to a rating of 50 for the average student. Questioners believed that both they and the contestants were average. However, both contestants and observers rated the questioner as much more knowledgeable than the contestant. Furthermore, contestants rated themselves to be a bit below average.

bright and the other to look dull. That is the fundamental attribution error.

You should be on a constant lookout for instances of the FAE. However, this may not always be easy: Situational forces are often invisible, and research has shown that there is a basic difference in the way we make attributions for own behaviours compared to the behaviours of others—a phenomenon called the **actor–observer bias** (Jones & Nisbett, 1971). We often tend to use situational attributions to explain our own behaviour, whereas we tend to overestimate the extent to which disposition affects the behaviours of others. This discrepancy results from our awareness of the many contextual factors that influence the way we act and the lack of similar contextual information when we try to explain others' behaviours. With no knowledge of context, we assume a degree of consistency in their behaviour resulting from personal disposition. With this in mind, what can you do to avoid the FAE? Particularly in circumstances in which you are making a dispositional attribution that is negative ("What a jerk!"), you should take a step back and ask yourself, Could it be something about the situation that is bringing about this behaviour? Think of it as an exercise in "attributional charity."

This advice may be particularly important to those of us who live in Western society, because evidence suggests that the FAE is due, in part, to cultural sources (J. G. Miller, 1984). In Chapter 14, we discussed cultural differences in construals of the self whereby most Western cultures embody *independent construals*, whereas most Eastern cultures embody *interdependent construals* (Markus & Kitayama, 1991). Research demonstrates that, as a function of the culture of interdependence, members of non-Western cultures are less likely to focus on individual actors in situations. Let's see how this cultural difference affects media coverage of Olympic athletes.

---

actor–observer bias The basic difference in the way we make attributions for our own behaviours compared to the behaviours of others.

self-serving bias An attributional bias in which people tend to take credit for their successes and deny responsibility for their failures.

The researchers compiled television and newspaper reports from the United States and Japan that focused on athletes at the 2000 Summer Olympics and the 2002 Winter Olympics (Markus, Uchida, Omoregie, Townsend, & Kitayama, 2006). Research assistants who were unaware of the study's purpose analyzed each media report to determine what categories of explanations were used to discuss an athlete's performance: For example, did the articles mention the athletes' strengths or weaknesses, their level of motivation, or the quality of the other competitors? The results showed that U.S. media coverage focused rather tightly on the personal characteristics of the athletes. The Japanese media considered a broader range of factors. The Japanese reports didn't ignore the athletes' characteristics, but they also discussed other background factors including the extent to which the athletes met others' expectations. In addition, U.S. media reports focused almost entirely on athletes' positive characteristics whereas Japanese reports mentioned both positive and negative.

An impressive feature of this study is that it captures cultural attributional styles as they are represented on TV and in newspapers. The study makes clear one way in which a cultural style of attribution is transmitted and maintained for all those who are exposed to the media in a particular culture (Morling & Lamoreaux, 2008).

SELF-SERVING BIASES

One of the most startling findings in the quiz game study we discussed was the contestants' negative evaluation of their own abilities. This suggests that people will make the FAE even at their own expense. In many circumstances, however, people do just the opposite—their attributions err in the direction of being self-serving. A **self-serving bias** leads people to take credit for their successes while denying or explaining away responsibility for their failures. In many situations, people tend to make dispositional attributions for success and situational attributions for failure (Gilovich, 1991): "I got the prize because of my ability"; "I lost the competition because it was rigged."

These patterns of attribution may be good for short-term self-esteem. However, it may often be more important to have an accurate sense of what causal forces are at work in your life outcomes. Consider how you do in your classes. If you get an A, what attributions do you make? How about if you get a C? Research has demonstrated that students tend to attribute high grades to their own efforts and low grades to factors external to themselves (McAllister, 1996). In fact, professors show the same pattern—they make attributions to themselves for students' successes but not their failures. Can you see what impact this pattern of attributions might have on your GPA? If you do not think about the external causes for your successes (for example, "That first exam was easy"), you might fail to study enough the next time; if you do not think about the dispositional causes for failures (for example, "I shouldn't have stayed so long at that party"), you also might never get around to studying hard enough.

We emphasized earlier that you should strive to avoid the FAE when you think about others' behaviour. Similarly, you might examine attributions about your own behaviour to weed out self-serving biases. In fact, research on the brain activity that accompanies dispositional and situational attributions suggests that people need to expend extra mental effort to avoid a reflexive self-serving bias.

> In the study, participants undertook a test of "facial working memory" (Krusemark, Campbell, & Clementz, 2008). The participants viewed "target" faces on a computer screen. After a series of distractor faces, the participants saw a final face and indicated whether it matched or mismatched the previous target. After participants made that judgment, they received feedback about their performance. However, the feedback wasn't accurate. Because the researchers wanted all the participants to have equal numbers of opportunities to provide attributions for successes and failures, they gave them positive feedback for half the trials and negative feedback for the other half (irrespective of actual performance). After each instance of feedback, participants chose between statements that embodied dispositional attributions ("I am dense") versus situational attributions ("It was hard"). The researchers used EEG (see Chapter 4) to monitor participants' brain activity as they made their judgments. The most distinctive brain activity occurred when participants made judgments that were not self-serving: When they attributed failure to themselves, rather than to the situation, participants were more likely to engage the areas of the brain that are responsible for monitoring intentions and self control.

These data suggest that participants' self-serving judgments arose without much reflection. When, as indicated by their brain activity, participants engaged in greater deliberation, that deliberation was more likely to yield non-self-serving, dispositional attributions for incorrect judgments.

Why does it matter so much what attributions you make? Recall the example of your tardy friend. Suppose that because you do not seek information about the situation, you decide that she is not actually interested in being your friend. Can that incorrect belief actually cause the person to be unfriendly

toward you in the future? To address that question, we turn now to the power of beliefs and expectations in constructing social reality.

EXPECTATIONS AND SELF-FULFILLING PROPHECIES

Can beliefs and expectations go beyond colouring the way you interpret experiences to actually shape social reality? Much research suggests that the very nature of some situations can be modified significantly by the beliefs and expectations people have about them. **Self-fulfilling prophecies** (Merton, 1957) are predictions made about some future behaviour or event that modify behavioural interactions so as to produce what is expected. Suppose, for example, you go to a party expecting to have a great time. Suppose a friend goes expecting it to be boring. Can you imagine the different ways in which the two of you might behave, given these expectations? These alternative ways of behaving may, in turn, alter how others at the party behave toward you. In that case, which of you is actually more likely to have a good time at the party?

One of the most powerful demonstrations of self-fulfilling prophecies took its cue from a play by George Bernard Shaw. In Shaw's *Pygmalion* (popularized as the musical *My Fair Lady*), a street waif is transformed into a proper society lady under the intense training of her teacher, Professor Henry Higgins. The

How do self-fulfilling prophecies affect the likelihood that children will engage in underage drinking?

self-fulfilling prophecy A prediction made about some future behaviour or event that modifies interactions so as to produce what is expected.

effect of social expectancy, or the *Pygmalion effect*, was recreated in a classic experiment by psychologist **Robert Rosenthal** in conjunction with school principal Leonore Jacobson.

Elementary school teachers in Boston were informed by researchers that their testing had revealed that some of their students were "academic spurters." The teachers were led to believe that these particular students were "intellectual bloomers who will show unusual gains during the academic year." In fact, there was no objective basis for that prediction; the names of these late bloomers were chosen randomly. However, by the end of that school year, 30 percent of the children arbitrarily named as spurters had gained an average of 22 IQ points! Almost all of them had gained at least 10 IQ points. Their gain in intellectual performance, as measured by a standard test of intelligence, was significantly greater than that of their control group classmates who had started out with the same average IQ (Rosenthal & Jacobson, 1968).

How did the teachers' false expectations get translated into such positive student performance? Rosenthal (1974) points to at least four processes that were activated by the teachers' expectations. First, the teachers acted more warmly and more friendly toward the "late bloomers," creating a climate of social approval. Second, they put greater demands—involving both quality and level of difficulty—on those for whom they had high hopes. Third, they gave more immediate and clearer feedback (both praise and criticism) about the selected students' performance. Finally, the teachers created more opportunities for the special students to respond in class and be reinforced, thus giving them hard evidence that they were indeed as good as the teachers believed they were.

What is unusual, of course, about this classroom situation is that the teachers were purposefully given false expectations. This methodology allowed Rosenthal and Jacobson to demonstrate the full potential for self-fulfilling prophecies. In most real-world situations, however, expectations are based on fairly accurate social perceptions (Jussim & Harber, 2005). Teachers, for example, expect certain students to do well because those students arrive in the classroom with better qualifications; and those students, typically, do show the best performance. Research has suggested, in fact, that self-fulfilling prophecies have the greatest effect on the lives of low-achieving students (Madon, Jussim, & Eccles, 1997). When teachers expect them to do poorly, they may do even worse; when teachers expect them to do well, that has the potential to turn their school lives around.

Much of the research on self-fulfilling prophecies has focused on school success. However, researchers have found evidence in other domains that people's mistaken beliefs and expectations can have an influence on what actually happens. For example, research suggests that when parents overestimate the amount of alcohol their adolescents will consume, those expectations can become self-fulfilling prophecies (Madon et al., 2008). The data suggest that the adolescents construct a self-image based on their mothers' expectations and consume alcohol to match that self-image.

attitude The learned, relatively stable tendency to respond to people, concepts, and events in an evaluative way.

The research we have described in this section focused on how people explain behaviours with respect to dispositions and situations. In the next section, we provide evidence that people often underestimate the extent to which situations constrain people's actions.

STOP AND REVIEW

❶ What three dimensions did Harold Kelley suggest affect the attribution process?

❷ Why might self-serving biases have a negative impact on a student's grades?

❸ What limits do ordinary classroom practices place on self-fulfilling prophecies?

CRITICAL THINKING Recall the study that examined cross-cultural differences in media reports. Why might the researchers have focused on Olympic athletes?

Attitudes, Attitude Change, and Action

Have you already had a chance today to express an attitude? Has someone asked you, "What do you think of my shirt?" or "Was the steak any good?" An **attitude** is a positive or negative evaluation of people, objects, and ideas. You may have favourable attitudes toward daycare workers, sports cars, and tax cuts, and unfavourable attitudes toward telemarketers, contemporary art, and astrology. This definition of attitude allows for the fact that many of the attitudes you hold are not overt: You may not be consciously aware that you hold certain attitudes. Attitudes are important because they influence your behaviour and how you construct social reality. What are the sources of your attitudes, and how do they affect your behaviours?

ATTITUDES AND BEHAVIOURS

We have already defined attitudes as positive or negative evaluations. We will begin this section by giving you an opportunity to make an evaluation. To what extent do you agree with this statement? (Circle a number.)

I enjoy movies that star Angelina Jolie.

1 —— 2 —— 3 —— 4 —— 5 —— 6 —— 7 —— 8 —— 9
Strongly   Neutral   Strongly
disagree   agree

Let's say that you gave a rating of 3—you disagree somewhat. What is the origin of that judgment? We can identify three types of information that give rise to your attitude (Zanna & Rempel, 1988):

- *Cognitive.* What thoughts do you have in response to "Angelina Jolie"?
- *Affective.* What feelings does the mention of "Angelina Jolie" evoke?
- *Behavioural.* How do you behave when, for example, you have the opportunity to see one of Angelina Jolie's movies?

Some combination of these types of information most likely guided your hand when you circled "3" (or some other number). Your attitudes also generate responses in the same three categories. If you have a somewhat negative attitude toward Angelina Jolie, you might say, "She isn't a serious actor" (cognitive), "She looked better when she first started" (affective), or "After *Sky Captain and the World of Tomorrow*, I'm going to wait to read her reviews before seeing a movie" (behavioural).

It isn't too hard to measure an attitude, but is that attitude always an accurate indication of how people will actually behave? You know from your own life experiences that the answer is "no": People will say they dislike Angelina Jolie but spend good money to see her anyway. At the same time, sometimes people's behaviours *do* follow their attitudes: They say they won't pay to see Angelina Jolie, and they don't. How can you determine when attitudes will or will not predict behaviour? Researchers have worked hard to answer that question—to identify the circumstances in which the link is strongest between people's attitudes and how they act (Ajzen & Fishbein, 2005; Glasman & Albarracín, 2006).

One property of attitudes that predicts behaviour is *accessibility*—the strength of the association between an attitude object and a person's evaluation of that object (Fazio & Roskos-Ewoldsen, 2005). When we asked you about Angelina Jolie, did an answer rush to mind or did you have to consider the question for a while? The more quickly an answer rushed in, the more likely it is that your behaviour will be consistent with that attitude. But how do attitudes become more accessible? Research suggests that attitudes are more accessible when they are based on *direct experience*: You will have a more accessible attitude about Angelina Jolie's movies if you have experienced several of them yourself rather than having heard or read about them indirectly. Attitudes are also more accessible when they have been rehearsed more often: Just as you might expect, the more often you have formulated an attitude about something (consider "chocolate" versus "kiwi"), the more accessible is the attitude. Let's consider a study conducted that illustrates the behavioural consequences of attitude rehearsal.

The researchers were interested in understanding the factors that lead people to make repeated blood donations (Godin, Sheeran, Conner, & Germain, 2008). The study focused on 4672 people in Quebec who had previously donated blood. Prior donors are quite likely to have positive attitudes about the importance of donating blood. The researchers reasoned that they could increase the likelihood that people would donate again if they made those attitudes more accessible. To increase attitude accessibility, the researchers randomly selected 2900 people for the experimental group and mailed a questionnaire that asked them to report their attitudes toward blood donations. Of this group, 2389 people completed the questionnaire. The 1772 people randomly assigned to the control group did not receive the questionnaire. Six months and 12 months after the time the questionnaires went out, the researchers checked to see how many people had made blood donations. The impact of the questionnaire was clear: Members of the experimental group donated more blood. For example, after six months, 8.6 percent more people in the experimental group had registered to give blood.

How does your attitude toward Angelina Jolie affect your willingness to watch her movies?

There are a variety of reasons people might or might not donate blood in six months or a year. However, the very act of rehearsing and reporting their attitudes on a simple questionnaire had a major impact on people's subsequent behaviour.

Attitudes also are better predictors of behaviour when the attitudes remain stable over time. Suppose, for example, we asked you to agree or disagree with the statement "I trust politicians." Your judgment would depend on which politician or politicians came to mind: Was it Pierre Elliot Trudeau, George W. Bush, Jean Chrétien, or Stephen Harper? Now suppose we asked you the same question a week from now. If you called different politicians to mind, your overall attitude toward politicians would likely change (Lord, Paulson, Sia, Thomas, & Lepper, 2004; Sia, Lord, Blessum, Ratcliff, & Lepper, 1997). Only when the "evidence" for your attitude remains stable over time can we expect to find a strong relationship between your evaluation (thoughts) and what you do (actions).

Another way to improve the match between attitudes and behaviours would be to improve attitude measures. In recent years, researchers have created a number of new attitude measures that attempt to capture people's automatic or implicit attitudes—the attitudes they hold toward people, objects, or ideas that often remain outside conscious awareness (Greenwald et al., 2002; Stanley, Phelps, & Banaji, 2008). The claim is these implicit attitudes may allow for predictions of behaviour. Consider a study that focused on a group of undecided voters in an Italian election (Arcuri, Castelli, Galdi, Zogmaister, & Amadori, 2008). Although these voters did not have a conscious preference, many of them revealed an unconscious preference when they underwent a procedure called the *implicit association test*. The political version of the test assessed how easy people found it to categorize the two candidates in association with positive and negative words. When the participants reported their votes after the election, they were consistently more likely to have voted for the candidate with whom they found it easier to associate positive words. Although these voters were not able to reveal conscious preferences, their implicit attitudes were correlated with future behaviour. Across several domains of human experience, researchers continue to examine the ability of implicit measures to predict behaviour. Much of that research focuses on the same issues we identified for explicit attitudes, such as the stability of implicit attitudes over time (Gawronski & LeBel, 2008).

PROCESSES OF PERSUASION

We have just seen that, under appropriate circumstances, attitudes can be relatively good predictors of behaviour. That is good news for all the people who spend time and money to affect your attitudes. But quite often others *cannot* affect your attitudes when they want to do so. For example, you do not change brands of toothpaste each time you see a peppy new commercial with scads of pearly-toothed actors. Many people in your life indulge in **persuasion**—deliberate efforts to change your attitudes. For persuasion to take place, certain conditions must be met. Let's explore some of those conditions.

To begin, we introduce the **elaboration likelihood model**, a theory of persuasion that defines how likely it is that people will focus their cognitive processes to elaborate upon a persuasive message (Petty & Briñol, 2008; Petty, Cacioppo, Strathman, & Priester, 2005). This model makes a critical distinction between *central* and *peripheral* routes to persuasion. The central route represents circumstances in which people think carefully about a persuasive communication so that attitude change depends on the strength of the arguments. When someone is trying to convince you that gasoline should cost $3 a litre, you are likely to process the information in this careful fashion. The peripheral route represents circumstances in which people do not focus critically on the message but respond to superficial cues in the situation. When a sexy model is placed in front of the product someone wishes you to buy, the seller is hoping you will avoid critical thought. That absence of critical thought is called *low* elaboration. The central or peripheral route that people take depends in large part on their *motivation* with respect to the message: Are they willing and able to think carefully about the persuasive content; will they engage in high or low elaboration?

If you take a close look at the messages that surround you, you will quickly come to the conclusion that advertisers often count on you to take the peripheral route. Why do advertisers pay celebrities to sell their products? Do you really believe that Hollywood actors worry enormously about which long-distance phone service will produce bigger savings? Presumably, the advertisers hope that you will not evaluate the arguments too closely—instead, they hope you will let yourself be persuaded by your general feelings of warmth toward the actor hawking the product.

Now ask yourself this question: Under what circumstances are you likely to feel sufficiently motivated to take the central

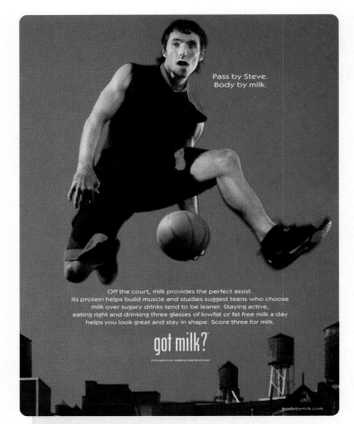

Why do advertisers pay celebrities to endorse their products?

route to persuasion? Researchers have undertaken an enormous amount of research to address that question (Petty et al., 2005). Let's consider a study that illustrates how difficult it is to persuade all of the people all of the time. Research has shown that people often label themselves as a morning person or an evening person. Researchers hypothesized that people are more likely to have the energy and motivation to engage in elaborative processing—the central route to persuasion—when they encounter persuasive messages at their right time of day.

To test their hypothesis, the researchers recruited participants who self-identified their "optimal" time of day as morning or evening (Martin & Marrington, 2005). The study had two sessions: one at 8:30 a.m. and one at 7:00 p.m. Each session included both morning people and evening people. At the start of the session, participants provided attitude ratings (on nine-point scales) on several social issues, including the mercy killing of terminally ill people. Next, the participants read the same set of persuasive statements that argued against mercy killing. Finally, participants listed the thoughts they had while reading the statements and provided a second set of attitude ratings. When the participants' session matched their optimal time of day, they listed more thoughts that were focused on the persuasive statements. In addition, as shown in **Figure 17.2**, people showed more attitude change in the direction of the statements when they read the persuasive statements at the optimal time of day.

---

persuasion Deliberate efforts to change attitudes.

elaboration likelihood model A theory of persuasion that defines how likely it is that people will focus their cognitive processes to elaborate upon a message and therefore follow the central and peripheral routes to persuasion.

FIGURE 17.2 Persuasion at the Optimal Time of Day

When participants read persuasive statements at their optimal time of day, they showed more attitude change in the direction of those statements.

Adapted from Martin & Marrington, *Personality and Individual Differences*, 39, 367–377, 2005.

At their optimal time of day, participants were motivated to elaborate on the persuasive statements. Because the statements provided strong arguments against mercy killing, their attitudes changed in the direction of the statements. If the arguments had been weak, high elaboration should have prevented attitude change.

There are many circumstances in life in which you probably want to resist having your attitudes changed. The elaboration likelihood model suggests that you'll often need to expend some effort to avoid being persuaded. Consider a study in which a researcher asked students to read an essay that argued that university vacations should be shortened to just one month (Burkley, 2008). The essay suggested, for example, that such a change would allow students to graduate more rapidly. Before reading the essay, some participants engaged in a separate task in which they spent five minutes listing thoughts that came to mind—but they were under explicit instructions not to think about a white bear. After doing that task, the participants gave attitude ratings that were more favourable toward the idea of one-month vacations than did control participants. It seemed that the effort they expended trying not to think about white bears had depleted the mental resources they needed to resist the essay's arguments. In your own life, when you know that you're going to face a persuasive appeal, you should try to ensure that you are ready to engage your full mental effort.

PERSUASION BY YOUR OWN ACTIONS

In the last section, we described factors that influence people's ability to change others' attitudes. However, there are forces at work in a number of circumstances that cause people to bring about their own attitude change. Imagine a situation in which you have vowed not to eat any extra calories. You arrive at work, and there is a cake for your boss's birthday. You consume a piece. Did you break your vow? That is, should you have a negative attitude about your own behaviour? Aren't you likely to

think what you did was okay? Why? Let's consider two analyses of self-persuasion: *cognitive dissonance theory* and *self-perception theory*.

Cognitive Dissonance Theory One of the most common assumptions in the study of attitudes is that people like to believe that their attitudes remain consistent over time (Eagly & Chaiken, 1993). This striving for consistency was explored within the field of social psychology in the theory of cognitive dissonance, as developed by **Leon Festinger** (1957). **Cognitive dissonance** is the state of conflict someone experiences after making a decision, taking an action, or being exposed to information that is contrary to prior beliefs, feelings, or values. Suppose, for example, you chose to buy a car against a friend's advice. Why might you be overly defensive about the car? It is assumed that when a person's cognitions about his or her behaviour and relevant attitudes are dissonant—they do not follow one to the next—an aversive state arises that the person is motivated to reduce. Dissonance-reducing activities modify this unpleasant state. In the case of your car, being defensive—overstating its value—makes you feel better about going against your friend's advice. (Dissonance also might lead you to think less well of your friend.)

Dissonance has motivational force—it impels you to take action to reduce the unpleasant feeling (W. Wood, 2000). The motivation to reduce dissonance increases with the magnitude of the dissonance created by a cognitive inconsistency. In other words, the stronger the dissonance, the greater the motivation to reduce it. In a classic dissonance experiment, university students told a lie to other students and came to believe in their lie when they got a small, rather than a large, reward for doing so.

> Stanford University students participated in a very dull task and were then asked (as a favour to the experimenter, because his assistant hadn't shown up) to lie to another participant by saying that the task had been fun and interesting. Half the participants were paid $20 to tell the lie, while the others were paid only $1. The $20 payment was sufficient external justification for lying, but the $1 payment was an inadequate justification. The people who were paid $1 were left with dissonant cognitions: "The task was dull" and "I chose to lie by telling another student it was fun and interesting without a good reason for doing so."
>
> To reduce their dissonance, these $1 participants changed their evaluations of the task. They later expressed the belief that they found "it really was fun and interesting—I might like to do it again." In comparison, the participants who lied for $20 did not change their evaluations—the task was still a bore; they had only lied "for the money" (Festinger & Carlsmith, 1959).

As this experiment shows, under conditions of high dissonance, an individual acts to justify his or her behaviour after the fact and engages in self-persuasion. This analysis says that the way to change attitudes is first to change behaviour.

Hundreds of experiments and field studies have shown the power of cognitive dissonance to change attitudes and

---

cognitive dissonance The theory that the tension-producing effects of incongruous cognitions motivate individuals to reduce such tension.

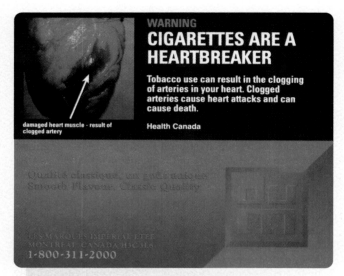

What messages might you give yourself to reduce cognitive dissonance if you are aware of the adverse effects of smoking but continue to smoke?

behaviour (Cooper, 2007). Recently, however, researchers have begun to question whether dissonance effects generalize to other cultures. Consider again the way the concept of *self* changes from culture to culture. As we noted earlier, North Americans typically view themselves as *independent*, distinct from others in the environment; members of Asian cultures typically view themselves as *interdependent*, fundamentally interconnected with others. Does the cultural concept of the self affect the experience of cognitive dissonance?

Groups of Canadian and Japanese participants examined a list of entrées for a Chinese restaurant (Hoshino-Browne et al., 2005). Out of a list of 25 dishes, they chose the 10 that they most liked (in one condition) or that they thought a friend would most like (in a second condition). Next, they rank-ordered those 10 dishes from most to least desirable—again, with respect either to their own or to a friend's preferences. The experimenters then asked the participants to choose between two coupons for free food. The coupons named the participants' fifth- and sixth-ranked choices (for them or their friend). Finally, participants were asked to go through and rate their top 10 choices once again. How might those ratings change from the first to the second time? According to dissonance theory, when you make a tough choice—like the one between your fifth- and sixth-ranked alternatives—you should adjust your attitudes to feel better about the outcome of the choice: "If I chose kung pao chicken [originally no. 5], it really must be a better choice than mu shu pork [originally no. 6]." However, cross-cultural research on the self suggests that

Canadian participants should experience more dissonance with respect to their own choices (because of their independent senses of self), whereas Japanese participants should experience more dissonance with respect to their choices for their friends (because of their interdependent senses of self). The data confirmed those expectations: Canadian participants' attitudes changed considerably more for self-judgments; Japanese participants' attitudes changed considerably more for friend judgments.

This research suggests that people experience cognitive dissonance—they seek to maintain consistency within their self-concept—in ways that are specific to their particular senses of self. If you are ever in circumstances in which you must make decisions jointly with members of other cultures, you will want to reflect on the culture's impact on the way you all think and act after the decision has been made.

Self-Perception Theory Dissonance theory describes one way in which people, at least in Western cultures, allow their behaviours ("I chose that food option") to have an impact on their attitudes ("I must like it much better than my other option"). *Self-perception theory*, developed by **Daryl Bem** (1972), identifies other circumstances in which behaviours inform attitudes. According to **self-perception theory**, you infer what your internal states (beliefs, attitudes, motives, and feelings) are or should be by perceiving how you are acting now and recalling how you have acted in the past in a given situation. You use that self-knowledge to reason backward to the most likely causes or determinants of your behaviour. For example, the self-perceiver responds to the question, "Do you like psychology?" by saying, "Sure, I'm taking the basic course and it's not required, I do all the readings, I pay attention during lectures, and I'm getting a good grade in the course." In other words, you answer a question about personal preferences by a behavioural description of relevant actions and situational factors—rather than undertaking an intense search of thoughts and feelings.

One flaw in the process of gaining self-knowledge through self-perception is that people are often insensitive about the extent to which their behaviour is influenced by situational forces. You can see this if we return a final time to the quiz show experiment. Recall that the participants who laboured unsuccessfully as contestants rated their own general knowledge relatively low. Imagine what it must have been like to be in their position. Over and over you would hear yourself saying, "I don't know the answer to that question." Can you see how observation of this behaviour—the process of self-perception—could give rise to a negative self-evaluation?

Let's return to the attitudes you might express toward yourself if you eat a slice of cake at your boss's birthday party. According to dissonance theory, you need to resolve the inconsistency between your vow ("I won't consume any extra calories") and your behaviour (eating a piece of cake). There are many things you can do to avoid feeling bad: Perhaps you would reason, "I can't afford to have my boss be angry at me by declining a piece of cake." Similarly, according to self-perception theory, you look at your behaviour to calculate your attitude. If you think, "Because I ate cake, my boss's birthday must have been very important," you will also escape

self-perception theory The idea that people observe themselves in order to figure out the reasons they act as they do; people infer what their internal states are by perceiving how they are acting in a given situation.

COMPLIANCE

In this section so far, we have discussed what attitudes are and how they might be changed. It should be clear to you, however, that most often what people want you to do is change your *behaviour*: People wish to bring about **compliance**—a change in behaviour consistent with their direct requests. When advertisers spend a lot of money for TV commercials, they do not just want you to feel good about their products—they want you to march into a store and buy them. Similarly, doctors want you to follow their medical advice. Social psychologists have extensively studied the way in which individuals bring about compliance with their requests (Cialdini, 2009; Cialdini & Goldstein, 2004). We will describe some of those techniques and note how wily salespeople often use them to get you to do things you might not otherwise have done.

Reciprocity One of the rules that dominates human experience is that when someone does something for you, you should do something for that person as well: This is called the **reciprocity norm**. Laboratory research has shown that even very small favours can lead participants to do much larger favours in return (Regan, 1971). Salespeople use reciprocity against you by appearing to do you a favour: "I'll tell you what, I'll take $5 off the price" or "Here's a free sample just for agreeing to talk to me today." This strategy puts you in a position of psychological distress if you do not return the favour and buy the product.

Another compliance technique that arises from the reciprocity norm has often been called the *door-in-the-face technique*: When people say "no" to a large request, they will often say "yes" to a more moderate request.

> In one experiment, students were asked to spend two hours every week for two years as counsellors for juvenile delinquents. They all said "no." Next, they were asked if they would serve as chaperones for some of the delinquents on a trip to the zoo. When they had previously said "no" to the large request, 50 percent of the students agreed to this smaller request. When a different group of students was approached, who had never been asked the large request, only 17 percent of them agreed to serve as chaperones (Cialdini et al., 1975).

How does this technique invoke the reciprocity norm? When people making requests go from the large to the moderate request, they have done something for you: Now you must do something for them—or risk violating the norm. This is why many agree to the smaller request!

Commitment The door-in-the-face technique moves you from a large to a moderate request. Salespeople also know that if they can get you to *commit* yourself to some small concession, they can probably also get you to commit to something larger. In experiments, people who agreed to small requests (for example, signing petitions) were more likely subsequently to agree to a bigger request (for example, putting large signs on their lawn)

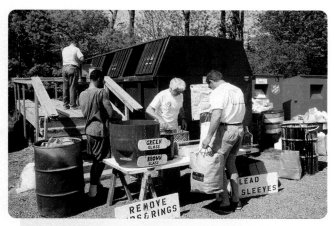

What can you do if you want to increase the probability that your neighbours will recycle?

(Freedman & Fraser, 1966). This is often called the *foot-in-the-door technique*: Once people get a foot in the door, they can use your sense of commitment to increase your later compliance. Salespeople use this technique against you by getting you to make a decision and then subtly changing the deal: "I know this is the car you want to buy, but my manager will only let me give you a $200 discount"; "I know you're the sort of person who buys quality goods, so I know you won't mind paying a little extra." This strategy makes you feel inconsistent or foolish if you do not go through with the purchase.

Scarcity People dislike feeling that they cannot have something (or, from another perspective, people like to have things others can't). How does the principle of scarcity apply in the marketplace? Salespeople know that they can increase the likelihood of your purchase if they make goods seem scarce: "This is the last one I have," or "I have another customer who's planning to get this." This strategy makes you feel as if you are missing a critical opportunity by not buying now.

In explaining these compliance techniques, we have provided a couple of examples of things you might *want* to do (such as buy a car or volunteer). However, much of the time people use these techniques to get you to do things you probably *wouldn't* want to do. How can you defend yourself against salespeople and their kin? Reflect on the various techniques we discussed and try to catch them using these strategies—and resist their efforts. Your knowledge of social psychology can make you an all-round wiser consumer.

In this section we have described attitudes and behaviours and the relationships between them. However, we have not yet touched on circumstances in which attitudes in the form of *prejudice* may lead to destructive behaviours. We turn now to the topic of prejudice and document both how it comes about and procedures that may be effective at reducing or eliminating it.

---

compliance A change in behaviour consistent with a communication source's direct requests.

reciprocity norm Expectation that favours will be returned—if someone does something for another person, that person should do something in return.

① What three components define attitudes?

② What cognitive process discriminates between the central and peripheral routes to persuasion?

③ Why does culture have an impact on processes of cognitive dissonance?

④ Why does the door-in-the-face technique engage the reciprocity norm?

CRITICAL THINKING Recall the study in which experimental participants filled out a questionnaire about their attitudes toward blood donation. Why was it important that people were randomly assigned to the experimental and control groups?

Prejudice

Of all human weaknesses, none is more destructive to the dignity of the individual and the social bonds of humanity than prejudice. Prejudice can demean and destroy the lives of others. **Prejudice** is a learned attitude toward a target object, involving negative feelings (dislike or fear), negative beliefs (stereotypes) that justify the attitude, and a behavioural intention to avoid, control, dominate, or eliminate those in the target group. Nazi leaders, for example, passed laws to enforce their prejudiced beliefs that Jews were subhuman and trying to bring about the downfall of Aryan culture. A false belief qualifies as prejudice when it resists change even in the face of appropriate evidence of its falseness. People display prejudice, for example, when they assert that First Nations people are all lazy despite the fact that many First Nations people are hardworking and successful. Prejudiced attitudes serve as biasing filters that influence the way individuals are perceived and treated once they are categorized as members of a target group.

Social psychology has always put the study of prejudice high on its agenda in an effort to understand its complexity and persistence and to develop strategies to change prejudiced attitudes and discriminatory behaviour (Allport, 1954; Nagda, Tropp, & Paluck, 2006; Nelson, 2006). In this section, we will describe the progress social psychologists have made in their efforts to understand the origins and effects of prejudice, as well as their efforts to help reverse its effects.

---

prejudice A learned attitude toward a target object, involving negative affect (dislike or fear), negative beliefs (stereotypes) that justify the attitude, and a behavioural intention to avoid, control, dominate, or eliminate the target object.

social categorization The process by which people organize the social environment by categorizing themselves and others into groups.

in-groups The groups with which people identify as members.

out-groups The groups with which people do not identify as members.

in-group bias An evaluation of one's own group as better than others.

racism Discrimination against people based on their skin colour or ethnic heritage.

sexism Discrimination against people because of their sex.

ORIGINS OF PREJUDICE

One of the sad truths from the study of prejudice is that it is easy to get people to show negative attitudes toward people who do not belong to the same "group." **Social categorization** is the process by which people organize their social environment by categorizing themselves and others into groups. The simplest and most pervasive form of categorizing consists of an individual determining whether people are like him or her. This categorization results in an "us versus them" orientation: People divide the world into **in-groups**—the groups with which they identify as members—and **out-groups**—the groups with which they do not identify.

The most minimal of distinctive cues is sufficient to trigger the formation of bias and prejudice against those in an out-group. Henry Tajfel and his colleagues (Tajfel, Billig, Bundy, & Flament, 1971) invented a paradigm that demonstrated the impact of what they called *minimal groups*. In one study, students provided estimates of the number of dots in a series of patterns projected on a movie screen. The students were told that, based on their performance, they were "dot overestimators" or "dot underestimators." In reality, the researchers randomly assigned the students to those two groups. Next, each student had the opportunity to allocate monetary rewards to the members of the two groups. The students consistently gave greater rewards to the people who they believed shared their dot estimating tendencies.

Studies of this type illustrate how very easy it is to generate an **in-group bias**: With only a minimal cue to group identity, people begin to favour the members of their own group over the members of other groups (T. D. Nelson, 2006). Many experiments have examined the consequences of in-group versus out-group status (Brewer, 2007; Hewstone, Rubin, & Willis, 2002). This research points to the conclusion that, for the most part, people show favouritism toward those people who are members of their own group rather than bias against members of the other group. For example, people typically rate members of their in-group more highly than they do members of the out-group. However, that is because they have positive feelings toward the in-group and neutral feelings toward the out-group. Thus, one can have an in-group bias without also having the negative feelings that constitute prejudice.

Unfortunately, in some circumstances people's feelings about out-groups are guided by learned prejudices. In those cases, in-group bias may become more purposeful. Prejudice easily leads to **racism**—discrimination against people based on their skin colour or ethnic heritage—and **sexism**—discrimination against people based on their sex. In contemporary times, people are often reluctant to admit to having racist or sexist attitudes. Instead people may express what have been called modern racism and modern sexism. Measures of modern racism, for example, include statements such as "Blacks are demanding too much from the rest of society" and "Over the past few years, blacks have gotten more economically than they deserve" (Henry & Sears, 2002). The implicit attitude measures we introduced earlier also measure less open forms of prejudice (Greenwald et al., 2002). These tests identify people whose explicit attitudes are not racist, but whose automatic responses suggest that they hold negative attitudes toward an out-group. Similarly, these tests identify people who accept claims such as "Blacks are demanding too much," but who do not hold negative implicit attitudes toward other races (Son Hing, Chung-Yan, Hamilton, & Zanna, 2008). To have a complete sense of how individuals will respond to members of other groups, we need to measure both explicit and implicit attitudes.

We have seen so far that people's categorization of the world into "us" and "them" can swiftly lead to prejudice. Let's look at the way in which prejudice functions through applications of stereotypes.

EFFECTS OF STEREOTYPES

We can use the power of social categorization to explain the origins of many types of prejudice. To explain how prejudice affects day-to-day interactions, we must explore the memory structures that provide important support for prejudice: stereotypes. **Stereotypes** are generalizations about a group of people in which the same characteristics are assigned to all members of a group. You are no doubt familiar with a wide range of stereotypes. What beliefs do you have about men and women? Jews, Muslims, and Christians? Asian, Arab, African, Native, or white Canadians? How do those beliefs affect your day-to-day interactions with members of those groups? Do you avoid members of some of these groups based on your beliefs?

Because stereotypes so powerfully encode expectations, they frequently contribute to the types of situations we described earlier in this chapter, in which people construct their own social reality. Consider the potential role stereotypes play to generate judgments about what "exists" in the environment. People are prone to fill in "missing data" with information from their stereotypes: "I'm not going to get in a car with Hiroshi—all Asians are terrible drivers." Those same powerful expectations may cause people to engage in a process called **behavioural confirmation**: Their own actions toward an outgroup individual creates a context in which the individual will produce behaviours consistent with the stereotype (O. Klein & Snyder, 2003). If, for example, someone were noticeably anxious when driving with an Asian friend, that friend might drive less well as a consequence. In addition, to maintain consistency,

people are likely to discount information that is inconsistent with their stereotyped beliefs.

> At the outset of a study, 210 students indicated the extent to which they agreed with the statement "Homosexuality is a legitimate and acceptable sexual orientation" (Boysen & Vogel, 2007). Next, the students read one and a half pages from an introductory psychology textbook that discussed biological evidence for the origins of homosexuality. After they read the text, participants responded to statements such as "How persuasive was the reading on homosexuality in showing that homosexuality is a legitimate and acceptable sexual orientation?" Participants' responses paralleled their prior attitudes. For example, those participants with negative initial attitudes toward homosexuality reported that they did not find the text persuasive with respect to the legitimacy of homosexuality. Participants also indicated whether the text had changed their attitudes. Although they had read the very same words, participants' responses were now more polarized: Participants with negative initial attitudes were likely to report that their attitudes were now even more negative; participants with positive initial attitudes were likely to report that their attitudes were now even more positive.

This experiment suggests why information alone typically can not reduce prejudice: People tend to devalue information that is inconsistent with their prior stereotype. (We will see in the next section more successful methods for overcoming prejudice.)

Let us remind you about another effect of stereotypes that we introduced in the context of intelligence testing. Recall that

---

stereotypes Generalizations about a group of people in which the same characteristics are assigned to all members of a group.

behavioural confirmation The process by which people behave in ways that elicit from others specific expected reactions and then use those reactions to confirm their beliefs.

How does prejudice arise, and why is it so difficult to eradicate?

in Chapter 10, we discussed racial differences among IQ scores. In that section, we reviewed evidence that suggests that members of stereotyped groups suffer from what **Claude Steele** and his colleagues have called *stereotype threat* (Steele, 1997; Steele & Aronson, 1995, 1998). Stereotype threat occurs when people are placed in situations to which negative aspects of stereotypes are relevant. Stereotype threat produces a context in which people are not able to make efficient use of their mental resources (Schmader, Johns, & Forbes, 2008). Although researchers first explored this concept in circumstances of intellectual performance, they have now demonstrated that there is potential for negative effects wherever stereotypes apply. For example, one study examined how a group of women who rated themselves as above-average athletes performed on a golf task (Stone & McWhinnie, 2008). Some of the women were told only that the task was a test of "natural ability." Others were told, in addition, that the task had previously yielded differences between men and women. The instructions continued, "So even though there may be gender differences on this test, we ask that you give 100 percent effort on the task so we can accurately measure your natural skills" (p. 448). Despite this request for 100 percent effort, the women who were reminded about gender differences needed more strokes to complete the eight holes of the golf course. This result illustrates how stereotype threat can impair people's performance across several life domains.

Even if you do not believe yourself to be a prejudiced person, you still are likely aware of the stereotypes that exist in contemporary society. Knowledge of these stereotypes might prompt you to use them in some ways, below the level of conscious awareness (Amodio & Devine, 2006; Trawalter, Todd, Baird, & Richeson, 2008). Even people whose explicit beliefs are not prejudiced may produce automatic acts of prejudice as a function of the messages they have unknowingly internalized from many sources in their current and earlier environments. Consider your best friends: Do they belong to the same ethnic group as you do? If so, why might this be the case?

We have come to the rather troubling conclusion that prejudice is easy to create and difficult to remove. Even so, from the earliest days of social psychology, researchers have attempted to reverse the march of prejudice. Let's now sample some of those efforts.

REVERSING PREJUDICE

One of the classic studies in social psychology was also the first demonstration that arbitrary "us" versus "them" divisions could lead to great hostility. In the summer of 1954, **Muzafer Sherif** and his colleagues (1961/1988) brought two groups of boys to a summer camp at Robbers Cave State Park in Oklahoma. The two groups were dubbed the "Eagles" and the "Rattlers." Each group forged its own camp bonds—for example, the boys hiked, swam, and prepared meals together—in ignorance of the other group for about a week. The groups' introduction to each other consisted of a series of competitive activities like baseball, football, and a tug-of-war. From this beginning, the rivalry between the groups grew violent. Group flags were burned, cabins were ransacked, and a near-riot-like food fight broke out. What could be done to reduce this animosity?

The experimenters tried a propaganda approach, by complimenting each group to the other. That did not work. The experimenters tried bringing the groups together in noncompetitive circumstances. That did not work either. Hostility seethed even when the groups were just watching a movie in the same place. Finally, the experimenters hit on a solution. What they did was to introduce problems that could be solved only through *co-operative action* on *shared goals*. For example, the experimenters arranged for the camp truck to break down. Both groups of boys were needed to pull it back up a steep hill. In the face of mutual dependence, hostility faded away. In fact, the boys started to make "best friends" across group boundaries.

In the intergroup competition phase of the Robbers Cave experiment, the "Eagles" and "Rattlers" pulled apart—but in the end, they pulled together. What general conclusions about contact and prejudice can be drawn from this study?

The Robbers Cave experiment disproved the idea that simple contact between hostile groups alone will reduce prejudice (Allport, 1954). The boys did not like each other any better just by being in each others' company. Instead, the experiment provided evidence for the **contact hypothesis**—a program combating prejudice must foster personal interaction in the pursuit of shared goals (Pettigrew, 2008).

Researchers have carried out studies around the world to determine what types of contact between people lead to reduced prejudice. A review of 515 studies on the contact hypothesis strongly supports the conclusion that contact with out-group members lowers prejudice (Pettigrew & Tropp, 2006). Let's consider a study that adds further weight to that conclusion.

> Although Germany was reunited in October 1990, the inhabitants of the former East and West Germany still show important differences: When social scientists assess the level of prejudice and violence toward foreigners, the data consistently show that East Germans are much more hostile. Researchers tested the hypothesis that an important force that contributes to the ongoing hostility arises from East Germany's historic isolation (Wagner, van Dick, Pettigrew, & Christ, 2003): Fewer foreigners reside in East Germany, providing fewer opportunities for the type of contact that reduces prejudice. A study with 2893 East and West German participants confirmed this hypothesis. Each participant provided information about his or her level of prejudice by responding to statements such as "Foreigners living in Germany are a problem for the social system." Each participant also indicated his or her level of personal contact by responding to questions such as "Are there any foreigners among your friends?" Those individuals who had more foreign friends reported, on average, lower levels of prejudice. Because the inhabitants of East Germany had fewer opportunities to have foreign friends, their prejudice levels remained relatively high.

This study shows the great importance of friendship for prejudice reduction. In fact, people's prejudice is reduced even when the contact is indirect—when they have in-group friends who have out-group friends (Pettigrew, Christ, Wagner, & Stellmacher, 2007; Wright, Aron, McLaughlin-Volpe, & Ropp, 1997). Why are both direct and indirect friendships so effective? Friendships allow people to learn to take the perspective of out-group members and empathize with them. Friendships also reduce the anxiety associated with out-group contacts and make the out-group seem less threatening (Pettigrew, 2008).

We have just considered circumstances in which psychological forces drive individuals apart. In the next section of this chapter, we examine the opposite situations in which people are drawn together in relationships of liking and loving.

STOP AND REVIEW

❶ How does in-group bias affect the distribution of resources?

❷ How does the process of behavioural confirmation support stereotypes?

❸ What has research demonstrated about the impact of contact between members of different groups?

CRITICAL THINKING Recall the study that that looked at people's attitudes on homosexuality. Why might the researchers have used an excerpt from an introductory psychology textbook?

Social Relationships

How do you choose the people with whom you share your life? Why do you seek the company of your friends? Why are there some people for whom your feelings move beyond friendship to feelings of romantic love? Social psychologists have developed a variety of answers to these questions of *interpersonal attraction*. (But don't worry, no one yet has taken all the mystery out of love!)

LIKING

Have you ever stopped to examine how and why you acquired each of your friends? The first part of this answer is straightforward: People tend to become attracted to others with whom they are in close proximity—you see and meet them because they live or work near you. This factor probably requires little explanation, but it might be worth noting that there is a general

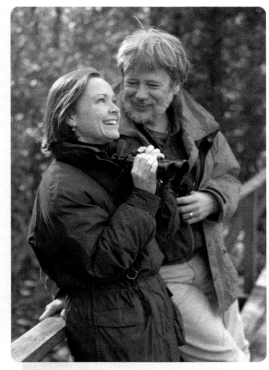

Why does proximity—in physical space or cyberspace—affect liking?

contact hypothesis The prediction that contact between groups will reduce prejudice only if the contact includes features such as co-operation toward shared goals.

tendency for people to like objects and people just by virtue of *mere exposure*: As we explained in Chapter 13, the more you are exposed to something or someone, the more you like it (Zajonc, 1968). This mere exposure effect means that, on the whole, you will come to like more and more the people who are nearby. Many people now maintain relationships over networks of computers. Although a friend may be geographically quite distant, daily messages appearing on a computer screen can make the person seem psychologically very close. Let's look now at other factors that can lead to attraction and liking.

Physical Attractiveness For better or worse, *physical attractiveness* often plays a role in the kindling of friendship. As Kenneth Dion and his colleagues at the University of Toronto noted many years ago (Dion, Berscheid, & Walster, 1972), there is a strong stereotype in Western culture that physically attractive people are also good in other ways. A review of a large number of studies documented the impact of physical attractiveness on a whole range of judgments (Langlois et al., 2000). For example, people rate both children and adults as more socially competent when they are attractive. In addition, attractive children receive higher competence ratings in school, and attractive adults receive higher competence ratings in their occupations. In light of the social basis of the stereotype, it might not surprise you that physical attractiveness plays a role in liking.

In one study, researchers randomly assigned incoming University of Minnesota students to couples as blind dates for a large dance. The researchers collected a variety of information about each student along dimensions of intelligence and personality. On the night of the dance and in later follow-ups, the students were asked to evaluate their dates and indicate how likely they were to see the individual again. The results were clear, and very similar for both men and women. Beauty mattered more than high IQs, good social skills, or good personalities. Only those matched by chance with beautiful or handsome blind dates wanted to pursue the relationship further (Walster, Aronson, Abrahams, & Rottman, 1966).

Physical attractiveness may not have as strong a role in other cultures. For example, students at universities in Ghana and the United States viewed the same photographs of attractive and unattractive people (Anderson, Adams, & Plaut, 2008). They provided ratings of each photograph for several personality traits (such as trustworthy, stable, sensitive, and strong). As you can see in **Figure 17.3**, participants from Ghana did not alter their attributions based on whether the people portrayed were attractive or unattractive. By contrast, participants from the United States made less positive attributions when they viewed unattractive photographs. This finding echoes other results we have described in which people with different cultural construals of the self—independent for the United States and interdependent for Ghana—provide different interpersonal judgments.

Similarity A famous adage on *similarity* suggests that "birds of a feather flock together." Is this correct? Research evidence suggests that, under many circumstances, the answer is yes. Similarity on dimensions such as beliefs, attitudes, and values fosters friendship. Why might that be so? People who are similar

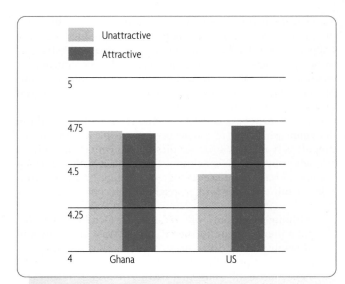

FIGURE 17.3 Cross-Cultural Trait Judgments for Attractive and Unattractive Individuals

Participants in Ghana and the United States made trait judgments based on photographs of attractive and unattractive individuals. Participants from Ghana made nearly the same attributions to attractive and unattractive photographs. U.S. participants made less positive attributions to the unattractive photographs.

From Anderson, S. L., Adams, G., & Plaut, V. C., *Journal of Personality and Social Psychology*, 95, 2008. Copyright © 2008 American Pschological Association. Reprinted with permission.

to you can provide a sense of personal validation, because a similar person makes you feel that the attitudes you hold dear are, in fact, the right ones (Byrne & Clore, 1970). Furthermore, dissimilarity often leads to strong repulsion (Chen & Kenrick, 2002). When you discover that someone holds opinions that are different from yours, you may evoke from memory past instances of interpersonal friction. That will motivate you to stay away—and if you stay away from dissimilar people, only the similar ones will be left in your pool of friends.

Similarity appears to play a role in allowing friendships to endure over time. Consider a study that began in 1983, when researchers assessed similarity between 45 pairs of friends (Ledbetter, Griffin, & Sparks, 2007). In 2002, 58 of the 90 original participants provided information about the state of their friendships after the passage of 19 years. The participants indicated, for example, how much contact they still had with each other. The results suggested that those pairs that had been more similar in 1983 were also more likely to remain in contact in 2002. It is also important to note that, just as similarity may lead to attraction, attraction can lead to perceptions of similarity: People tend to believe that the people they like are more similar than they really are. In one study conducted at the University of Manitoba, students rated themselves and cross-sex friends on the same set of personality traits (Morry, 2007). The students rated their friends as being more similar to them than their friends' self-reports indicated they actually were.

Reciprocity Finally, you tend to like people whom you believe like you. Do you recall our discussion of salespeople's use of *reciprocity*? The rule that you should give back what you receive applies to friendship as well. People give back "liking" to people whom they believe have given "liking" to them (Backman & Secord, 1959; Kenny & La Voie, 1982). Furthermore, because of the way your beliefs can affect your behaviours, believing that someone likes or dislikes you can help bring that relationship about (Curtis & Miller, 1986). Can you predict how you would act toward someone you believe likes you? Toward someone you believe dislikes you? Do you see how your belief could become a self-fulfilling prophecy? This is also true when we look at other people's relationships; if we know that Person A particularly likes Person B, we infer that Person B has the same feelings toward Person A (Kenny, Bond, Mohr, & Horn, 1996).

The evidence we have reviewed suggests that most of your friends will be people you encounter frequently, and people with whom you share the bonds of similarity and reciprocity. But what have researchers found about more intense relationships people call "loving"?

LOVING

Many of the same forces that lead to liking also get people started on the road to love; in most cases, you will first like the people you end up loving. What special factors have social psychologists learned about loving relationships?

The Experience of Love What does it mean to experience *love*? You should take a moment to think how you would

Companionate feelings for someone you were once passionate about do not signal "falling out of love": On the contrary, they are a natural outgrowth of romance and a vital ingredient to most long-term partnerships.

define this important concept. Do you think your definition would agree with your friends' definitions? Researchers have tried to answer this question in a variety of ways, and some consistency has emerged (Reis & Aron, 2008). People's conceptualizations of love cluster into three dimensions (Aron & Westbay, 1996):

- *Passion*—sexual passion and desire
- *Intimacy*—honesty and understanding
- *Commitment*—devotion and sacrifice

Would you characterize all your loving relationships as including all three dimensions? You are probably thinking, "Not *all* of them." In fact, it is important to make a distinction between "loving" someone and being "in love" with someone (Meyers & Berscheid, 1997). Most people report themselves to "love" a larger category of people than the group with whom they are "in love"—who among us has not been heartbroken to hear the words, "I love you, but I'm not *in* love with you"? Being "in love" implies something more intense and special—this is the type of experience that includes sexual passion.

Let us make one final distinction. Many loving relationships start out with a period of great intensity and absorption, which is called *passionate* love. Over time, there is a tendency for relationships to migrate toward a state of lesser intensity but greater intimacy, called *companionate love* (Berscheid & Walster, 1978). When you find yourself in a loving relationship, you may do well to anticipate that transition—so that you do not misinterpret a natural change as a process of falling "out of love." In fact, people who report higher levels of companionate love also generally experience greater satisfaction with their lives (Kim & Hatfield, 2004). Even so, the decline of passionate love may not be as dramatic as the stereotype of long-committed couples suggests. Researchers find a reasonable level of passionate love as much as 30 years into a relationship (Aron & Aron, 1994). When you enter a loving relationship, you can have high hopes that the passion will endure in some form, even as the relationship grows to encompass other needs.

Note that experiences of love are also influenced by cultural expectations (Wang & Mallinckrodt, 2006). At various moments in this chapter, we have alluded to the cultural dimension of independence versus interdependence: Cultures with independent construals of self value the person over the collective; interdependent cultures put greater value on shared cultural goals rather than individual ones. How does this apply to your love life? If you choose a life partner based on your own feelings of love, you are showing preference for your personal goals; if you choose a partner with an eye to how that individual will mesh with your family's structure and concerns, you are being more attuned to collective goals. Cross-cultural research has led to the very strong generalization that members of independent cultures put much greater emphasis on love (Dion & Dion, 1996). Consider the question, "If a man (woman) had all the other qualities you desired, would you marry this person if you were not in love with him (her)?" Only 3.5 percent of a sample of male and female undergraduates in the United States answered yes (we would likely find similar results if the same study were conducted in Canada); 49 percent of a comparable group of students in India answered yes (Levine, Sato, Hashimoto, & Verma, 1995). Members of independent cultures are also more *demanding* of their potential partners. Because people in these

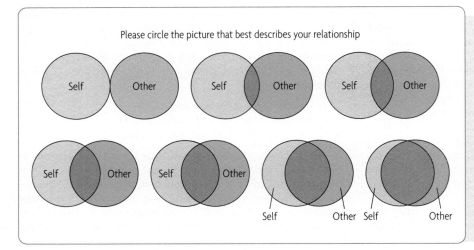

Please circle the picture that best describes your relationship

FIGURE 17.4 The Inclusion of Other in the Self (IOS) Scale

If you are in a romantic relationship, which diagram best captures the interdependence of you and your partner? Research with the IOS scale suggests that people who most perceive the other as included with the self are most likely to stay committed to their relationships.

From Aron, A., Aron, E. N., Smolian, D., IOS Scale, *Journal of Personality and Social Psychology, 63(4), October* 1992, 596–612. Copyright © 1992 American Psychological Association. Reprinted with permission.

cultures have stronger ideas about personal fulfillment within relationships, they also expect more from marriage partners (Hatfield & Sprecher, 1995).

What Factors Allow Relationships to Last? It seems likely that everyone reading this book—and certainly everyone *writing* this book—has been in a relationship that did not last. What happened? Or, to put the question in a more positive light, what can researchers say about the types of situations, and people in those situations, that are more likely to lead to long-term loving relationships?

One theory conceptualizes people in close relationships as having a feeling that the "other" is included in their "self" (Aron et al., 2004). Consider the series of diagrams given in **Figure 17.4**. Each of the diagrams represents a way you could conceptualize a close relationship. If you are in a romantic relationship, can you say which of the diagrams seems to capture most effectively the extent of interdependence between you and your partner? Research has shown that people who perceive the most overlap between self and other—those people who come to view the other as included within the self—are most likely to remain committed to their relationships over time (Aron, Aron, & Smollan, 1992; Aron & Fraley, 1999).

Researchers have also been interested in understanding individual differences in people's ability to sustain loving relationships over an extended period of time. In recent years, attention has often focused on adult attachment style (Fraley, Brumbaugh, & Marks, 2005; Fraley & Shaver, 2000). Recall from Chapter 11 the importance of the quality of a child's attachment to his or her parents for smooth social development. Researchers began to wonder how much impact that early attachment might have later in life, as the children grew up to have committed relationships and children of their own.

What are the types of attachment styles? **Table 17.1** provides three statements about close relationships (Hazan & Shaver, 1987; Shaver & Hazan, 1994). Please take a moment to note which statement fits you best. When asked which of these statements best describes them, the majority of people (55 percent) choose the first statement; this is a secure attachment style. Sizable minorities select the second statement (25 percent, an avoidant style) and the third (20 percent, an anxious–ambivalent style). Attachment style has proven to be an

accurate predictor of relationship quality (Mikulincer, Florian, Cowan, & Cowan, 2002; Tidwell, Reis, & Shaver, 1996). Compared with individuals who chose the other two styles, securely attached individuals had the most enduring romantic relationships as adults. Attachment style also predicts the ways in which individuals experience jealousy in relationships (Sharpsteen & Kirkpatrick, 1997). For example, people with an anxious style tend to experience jealousy more frequently and more intensely than do people with a secure attachment style.

In this section, we have considered some of the factors that influence whether people enter into relationships with each other. We next examine the types of behaviours that emerge within the context of those relationships. We discuss the variety of forces that lead people to harm and help each other.

TABLE 17.1	**Styles of Adult Attachment for Close Relationships**

Statement 1:

I find it relatively easy to get close to others and am comfortable depending on them. I do not often worry about being abandoned or about someone getting too close to me.

Statement 2:

I am somewhat uncomfortable being close to others; I find it difficult to trust them completely, difficult to allow myself to depend on them. I am nervous when anyone gets too close, and often, love partners want me to be more intimate than I feel comfortable being.

Statement 3:

I find that others are reluctant to get as close as I would like. I often worry that my partner doesn't really love me or won't want to stay with me. I want to get very close to my partner, and this sometime scares people away.

STOP AND REVIEW

❶ What effect does similarity have on liking?
❷ Which three dimensions define love?
❸ Which adult attachment style is generally associated with the highest quality relationships?

CRITICAL THINKING Recall the study that examined the impact of physical attractiveness on people's liking for randomly assigned dates. Why was it important to assess the impact of physical attractiveness both on the night of the date and in later follow-ups?

Psychology in Your Life

IN WHAT WAYS ARE YOU LIKE A CHAMELEON?

Here's something you may have noticed: When you interact with other people, you are quite likely to find yourself mimicking them in certain ways. You may, for example, unconsciously match your friends' speech patterns and accents. Social psychologists Tanya Chartrand and John Bargh (1999) labelled this type of mimicry the *chameleon effect*. Chameleons automatically change their colour to blend in with their environment. Chartrand and Bargh suggested that humans also automatically adjust their behaviour to blend with the people around them.

In their original demonstration of the chameleon effect, Chartrand and Bargh had pairs of people interact to describe photographs. However, one member of each pair was actually a confederate of the researchers. Chartrand and Bargh instructed the confederates to perform one of two motor gestures while describing the photographs: Either they rubbed their faces or they shook one foot. If people act like chameleons, we would expect that the experimental participants would mimic those motor gestures. That's exactly what happened. Participants were considerably more likely to rub their faces or shake their feet when the confederates performed those actions.

Chartrand and Bargh speculated that this form of mimicry functions as a type of "social glue." By producing identical motor gestures, people make themselves more similar to the other

individuals around them. Recall from our discussion of social relationships that similarity increases liking. For that reason, Chartrand and Bargh hypothesized that people whose gestures were mimicked by a partner would like that partner better. To test that hypothesis, Chartrand and Bargh conducted a second study in which they instructed their confederates to subtly mimic the actions of the experimental participants. Compared to members of the control group, whose gestures were not mimicked, the mimicked participants consistently reported liking the confederates better. Importantly, only one of the 37 participants was aware of having been mimicked. This strongly suggests that the chameleon effect operates outside of conscious awareness.

Even so, these results might lead you to wonder whether you could do better in some social circumstances by consciously mimicking others' behaviour. To address this question, researchers provided explicit instructions to a subset of students who were about to carry out a negotiation: "Successful negotiators recommend that you should mimic the mannerisms of your negotiation partner to get a better deal. For example, when the other person rubs his/her face, you should too. If he/she leans back or leans forward in the chair, you should too. However, they say it is very important that you mimic subtly enough that the other person does not notice what you are doing,

otherwise this technique completely backfires" (Maddux, Mullen, & Galinsky, 2008, p. 463). The students who received these instructions consistently scored more points in the negotiation than their peers who were not encouraged to mimic.

Of course, there are circumstances in which people might not want to get people to like them more. Suppose someone is already in a romantic relationship. To keep that relationship safe, that individual might want to distance him- or herself from attractive alternatives. That goal might lead to a diminished chameleon effect. To test that hypothesis, researchers recruited some participants who were in romantic relationships and some who were not (Karremans & Verwijmeren, 2008). All the participants interacted with a confederate who rubbed his or her face regularly during a conversation. In support of the hypothesis, participants who were in romantic relationships mimicked the attractive confederate consistently less often. The participants were not aware of their behaviour. The researchers concluded that "the goal to maintain one's current romantic relationship nonconsciously guides an individual's behaviour during an interaction with a potentially relationship-threatening alternative" (p. 947).

Now that you know about the chameleon effect, do you think you will be more aware of how mimicry affects your social relationships?

The Power of the Situation

Throughout *Psychology and Life*, we have noted that psychologists who strive to understand the causes of behaviour consider many different factors when looking for answers. Some look to genetic factors and others to biochemical and brain processes; still others focus on the causal influence of the social environment. Social psychologists believe that the primary determinant of behaviour is the nature of the social situation in which that behaviour occurs. They argue that social situations exert significant control over individual behaviour and attitudes, often dominating personality and a person's past history of learning, values, and beliefs. In this section, and for the rest of the chapter, we will review both classic research and recent studies that together explore the effect of subtle but powerful situational variables on people's behaviours, whether they act individually or in groups.

ROLES AND RULES

What *social roles* are available to you? A **social role** is a socially defined pattern of behaviour that is expected of a person when functioning in a given setting or group. Different social situations make different roles available. When you are at home, you may accept the role of "child" or "sibling." When you are in the classroom, you accept the role of "student." At other times still, you are a "best friend" or "lover." Can you see how these different roles immediately make different types of behaviours more or less appropriate and also available to you?

Situations are also characterized by the operation of **rules**, behavioural guidelines for specific settings. Some rules are *explicitly* stated in signs (do not smoke, no eating in class) or are explicitly taught to children (respect the elderly, never take candy from a stranger). Other rules are *implicit*—they are learned through transactions with others in particular settings: how loud you can play your stereo, how close you can stand to another person, when you can call your teacher or boss by a first name, and what is the suitable way to react to a compliment or a gift. All of these actions depend on the situation. For example, the Japanese do not open a gift in the presence of the giver, for fear of not showing sufficient appreciation; foreigners not aware of this unwritten rule will misinterpret the behaviour as rude instead of sensitive. Next time you get in an elevator, try to determine what rules you have learned about that situation. Why do people usually speak in hushed tones or not at all?

Ordinarily, you might not be particularly aware of the effects of roles and rules, but one classic social psychological experiment, the *Stanford Prison Experiment*, put these forces to work with startling results (Zimbardo, 1975, 2007; replicated in Australia by Lovibond, Adams, & Adams, 1979).

> On a summer Sunday in California, a siren shattered the serenity of college student Tommy Whitlow's morning. A police car screeched to a halt in front of his home. Within minutes, Tommy was charged with a felony, informed of his constitutional rights, frisked, and handcuffed. After he was booked and fingerprinted, Tommy was blindfolded and transported to the Stanford County Prison, where he was stripped, sprayed with disinfectant, and issued a smock-type uniform with an ID number on the front and back. Tommy became Prisoner 647. Eight other college students were also arrested and assigned numbers.
>
> Tommy and his cellmates were all volunteers who had answered a newspaper ad and agreed to be participants in a two-week experiment on prison life. By random flips of a coin, some of the volunteers had been assigned to the role of prisoners; the rest became guards. All had been selected from a large pool of student volunteers who, on the basis of extensive psychological tests and interviews, had been judged as law-abiding, emotionally stable, physically healthy, and "normal-average." The prisoners lived in the jail around the clock; the guards worked standard eight-hour shifts.
>
> What happened once these students had assumed their randomly assigned roles? In guard roles, college students who had been pacifists and "nice guys" behaved aggressively—sometimes even sadistically. The guards insisted that prisoners obey all rules without question or hesitation. Failure to do so led to the loss of a privilege. At first, privileges included opportunities to read, write, or talk to other inmates. Later on, the slightest protest resulted in the loss of the "privileges" of eating, sleeping, and washing. Failure to obey rules also resulted in menial, mindless work such as cleaning toilets with bare hands, doing push-ups while a guard stepped on the prisoner's back, and spending hours in solitary confinement. The guards were always devising new strategies to make the prisoners feel worthless.
>
> As prisoners, psychologically stable students soon behaved pathologically, passively resigning themselves to their unexpected fate. Less than 36 hours after the mass arrest, Prisoner 8412, one of the ringleaders of an aborted prisoner rebellion that morning, began to cry uncontrollably. He experienced fits of rage, disorganized thinking, and severe depression. On successive days, three more prisoners developed similar stress-related symptoms. A fifth prisoner developed a psychosomatic rash all over his body when the Parole Board rejected his appeal.

By the conclusion of the Stanford Prison Experiment, guards' and prisoners' behaviours differed from each other in virtually every observable way (see **Figure 17.5**). However, the figure does not completely reveal the extremes of the guards' behaviour. On many occasions, the guards stripped their prisoners naked. The guards hooded and chained their prisoners. They denied them food and bedding. Does this list of behaviours sound familiar? They are among the abuses the guards committed in 2003 at the Abu Ghraib prison in Iraq. The Stanford Prison Experiment helps shed light on this scandal: Situational forces can lead ordinary people to exhibit horrendous behaviours (Fiske, Harris, & Cuddy, 2004; Zimbardo, 2007).

A critical feature of the Stanford Prison Experiment is that only chance, in the form of random assignment, decided the participants' roles as guards or prisoners. Those roles created status and power differences that were validated in the

---

social role A socially defined pattern of behaviour that is expected of a person who is functioning in a given setting or group.

rules Behavioural guidelines for acting in certain ways in certain situations.

The Stanford Prison Experiment created a new "social reality" in which the norms of good behaviour were overwhelmed by the dynamics of the situation. Why did the student guards and inmates adopt their roles so powerfully?

prison situation. No one taught the participants to play their roles. Without ever visiting real prisons, all the participants learned something about the interaction between the powerful and the powerless (Banuazizi & Movahedi, 1975). The student participants had already experienced such power differences in many of their previous social interactions: parent–child, teacher–student, doctor–patient, boss–worker, male–female. They merely refined and intensified their prior patterns of behaviour for this particular setting. Each student could have played either role. Many students in the guard role reported being surprised at how easily they came to enjoy controlling other people. Just putting on the uniform was enough to transform them from passive college students into aggressive prison guards. What sort of person do *you* become when you slip in and out of different roles? Where does your sense of personal self end and your social identity begin?

How does social psychological research explain some aspects of the guards' behaviours at Abu Ghraib?

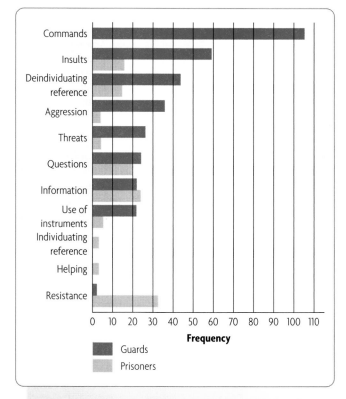

FIGURE 17.5 Guard and Prisoner Behaviour
During the Stanford Prison Experiment, the randomly assigned roles of prisoners and guards drastically affected participants' behaviour. The observations recorded in the six-day interaction profile show that, across 25 observation periods, the prisoners engaged in more passive resistance, while the guards became more dominating, controlling, and hostile.

SOCIAL NORMS

In addition to the expectations regarding role behaviours, groups develop many expectations for the ways their members *should* act. The specific expectations for socially appropriate attitudes and behaviours that are embodied in the stated or implicit rules of a group are called **social norms**. Social norms can be broad guidelines; if you are a member of the New Democratic Party, you may be expected to hold liberal political beliefs, while members of the Young Conservatives will advocate more conservative views. Social norms can also embody specific standards of conduct. For example, if you are employed as a waiter or a waitress, you will be expected to treat your customers courteously no matter how unpleasant and demanding they are to you.

Belonging to a group typically involves discovering the set of social norms that regulates desired behaviour in the group setting. This adjustment occurs in two ways: You notice the *uniformities* in certain behaviours of all or most members, and you observe the *negative consequences* when someone violates a social norm.

Norms serve several important functions. Awareness of the norms operating in a given group situation helps orient members and regulate their social interactions. Each participant can anticipate how others will enter the situation, how they will dress, and what they are likely to say and do, as well as what type of behaviour will be expected of them to gain approval. You often feel awkward in new situations precisely because you may be unaware of the norms that govern the way you ought to act. Some tolerance for deviating from the standard is also part of the norm—wide in some cases, narrow in others. For example, shorts and a T-shirt might be marginally acceptable attire for a religious ceremony; a bathing suit would almost certainly deviate too far from the norm. Group members are usually able to estimate how far they can go before experiencing the coercive power of the group in the form of ridicule, re-education, and rejection.

CONFORMITY

When you adopt a social role or bend to a social norm, you are, to some extent, *conforming* to social expectations. **Conformity** is the tendency for people to adopt the behaviour and opinions presented by other group members. Why do you conform? Are there circumstances under which you ignore social constraints and act independently? Social psychologists have studied two types of forces that may lead to conformity:

- **Informational influence** processes—wanting to be correct and to understand the right way to act in a given situation.
- **Normative influence** processes—wanting to be liked, accepted, and approved of by others.

We will describe classic experiments that illustrate each type of influence.

---

social norms The expectations a group has for its members regarding acceptable and appropriate attitudes and behaviours.

conformity The tendency for people to adopt the behaviours, attitudes, and values of other members of a reference group.

informational influence Group effects that arise from individuals' desire to be correct and to understand how best to act in a given situation.

normative influence Group effects that arise from individuals' desire to be liked, accepted, and approved of by others.

norm crystallization The convergence of the expectations of a group of individuals into a common perspective as they talk and carry out activities together.

Informational Influence: Sherif's Autokinetic Effect

Many life situations in which you must make decisions about behaviours are quite ambiguous. Suppose, for example, you are dining at an elegant restaurant with a large group of people. Each place at the table is set with a dazzling array of silverware. How do you know which fork to use when the first course arrives? Typically, you would look to other members of the party to help you make an appropriate choice. This is *informational influence*.

A classic experiment, conducted by Muzafer Sherif (1935), demonstrated how informational influence can lead to **norm crystallization**—norm formation and solidification.

Participants were asked to judge the amount of movement of a spot of light, which was actually stationary but that appeared to move when viewed in total darkness with no reference points. This is a perceptual illusion known as the *autokinetic effect*. Originally, individual judgments varied widely. However, when the participants were brought together in a group consisting of strangers and stated their judgments aloud, their estimates began to converge. They began to see the light move in the same direction and in similar amounts. Even more interesting was the final part of Sherif's study: When alone in the same darkened room after the group viewing, these participants continued to follow the group norm that had emerged when they were together.

When individuals become dependent on a group—such as a religious cult—for basic feelings of self-worth, they are prone to extremes of conformity. Twenty thousand identically dressed couples were married in this service conducted by the Reverend Sun Myung Moon. More recently, in August 1995, Moon simultaneously married 360 000 "Moonie" couples who were linked by satellite in 500 worldwide locations. Why do people find comfort in such large-scale conformity?

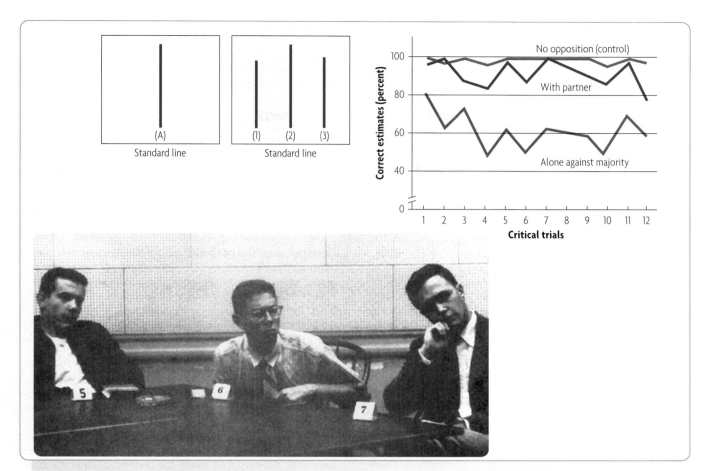

FIGURE 17.6 Conformity in the Asch Experiments
In this photo from Asch's study, it is evident that the naive participant, Number 6, is distressed by the unanimous majority's erroneous judgment. The typical stimulus array is shown at the top left. At top right, the graph illustrates conformity across 12 critical trials when solitary participants were grouped with a unanimous majority, as well as their greater independence when paired with a dissenting partner. A lower percentage of correct estimates indicates the greater degree of an individual's conformity to the group's false estimate.

Once norms are established in a group, they tend to perpetuate themselves. In later research, these autokinetic group norms persisted even when tested a year later and without former group members witnessing the judgments (Rohrer, Baron, Hoffman, & Swinder, 1954). Norms can be transmitted from one generation of group members to the next and can continue to influence people's behaviour long after the original group that created the norm no longer exists (Insko et al., 1980). How do we know that norms can have transgenerational influence? In autokinetic effect studies, researchers replaced one group member with a new one after each set of autokinetic trials until all the members of the group were new to the situation. The group's autokinetic norm remained true to the one handed down to them across several successive generations (Jacobs & Campbell, 1961). Do you see how this experiment captures the processes that allow real-life norms to be passed down across generations?

Normative Influence: The Asch Effect What is the best way to demonstrate that people will sometimes conform because of *normative influence*—their desire to be liked, accepted, and approved of by others? One of the most important early social psychologists, **Solomon Asch** (1940, 1956), created circumstances in which participants made judgments under conditions in which the physical reality was absolutely clear—but the rest of a group reported that they saw that reality differently. Male college students were led to believe they were in a study of simple visual perception. They were shown cards with three lines of differing lengths and asked to indicate which of the three lines was the same length as the standard line (see **Figure 17.6**). The lines were different enough so that mistakes were rare, and their relative sizes changed on each series of trials.

The participants were seated next to last in semicircles of six to eight other students. Unknown to the participants, the others were all experimental confederates—accomplices of the experimenter—who were following a prearranged script. On the first three trials, everyone in the circle agreed on the correct comparison. However, the first confederate to respond on the fourth trial matched two lines that were obviously different. So did all members of the group up to the participant. That student had to decide if he should go along with everyone else's view of the situation and conform or remain independent, standing by what he clearly saw. That dilemma was repeated for the naive participant on 12 of the 18 trials. The participants showed signs of disbelief and obvious discomfort when faced with a majority who saw the world so differently. What did they do?

Roughly one-fourth of the participants remained completely independent—they never conformed. However, between 50 and 80 percent of the participants (in different studies in the research program) conformed with the false majority estimate at least once, while a third of the participants yielded to the majority's wrong judgments on half or more of the critical trials.

Asch describes some participants who yielded to the majority most of the time as "disoriented" and "doubt-ridden"; he states that they "experienced a powerful impulse not to appear different from the majority" (1952, p. 396). In other studies, Asch varied three factors: the size of the unanimous majority, the presence of a partner who dissented from the majority, and the size of the discrepancy between the correct physical stimulus comparison and the majority's position. He found that strong conformity effects were elicited with a unanimous majority of only three or four people. However, giving the naive participant a single ally who dissented from the majority opinion had the effect of sharply reducing conformity, as can be seen in Figure 17.6. With a partner, the participant was usually able to resist the pressures to conform to the majority (Asch, 1955, 1956).

How should we interpret these results? Asch himself was struck by the rate at which participants did *not* conform (Friend, Rafferty, & Bramel, 1990). He reported this research as studies in "independence." In fact, two-thirds of the time, participants gave the correct, nonconforming answer. However, most descriptions of Asch's experiment have emphasized the one-third conformity rate. Accounts of this experiment also often fail to note that not all participants were alike: The number of individuals who never conformed, about 25 percent, was roughly equal to the number who always or almost always conformed. Thus, Asch's experiment teaches two complementary lessons. On the one hand, we find that people are not entirely swayed by normative influence—they assert their independence on a majority of occasions (and some people always do). On the other hand, we find that people will sometimes conform, even in the most unambiguous situations. That potential to conform is an important element of human nature.

Conformity in Everyday Life Although you have almost certainly never faced the exact circumstances of the Asch experiment, you can no doubt recognize conformity situations in your everyday life. Many of these situations are easy to spot. You might notice, for example, that you are wearing certain types of clothes because someone has declared them to be fashionable today. Other behaviours, such as drug and alcohol use, are also strongly affected by the influence of one's peer group.

People often resist the idea that their behaviours are influenced by norms. Consider a study conducted in the United States that examined the types of messages that work most effectively to bring about reductions in people's energy consumption (Nolan et al., 2007). California residents found one of five types of messages hanging on their door knobs. **Table 17.2** provides examples of the types of messages. The researchers later went door-to-door to ask the residents, "How much did the information on these door-hangers motivate you to conserve energy?" Residents' responses could range from 1 (not at all) to 4 (extremely). As you can see in Table 17.2, residents

TABLE 17.2	People Are Unaware of Normative Influence		
Type of Message	**Excerpt from the Message**	**Motivation to Conserve**	**Energy Consumption**
Descriptive Norm	In a recent survey of households in your community, researchers at Cal State San Marcos found that 77% of San Marcos residents often use fans instead of air conditioning to keep cool in the summer.	1.76	16.10
Self-Interest	According to researchers at Cal State San Marcos, you could save up to $54 per month by using fans instead of air conditioning to keep cool in the summer.	1.86	17.45
Environmental Protection	According to researchers at Cal State San Marcos, you can prevent the release of up to 262 lb of greenhouse gases per month by using fans instead of air conditioning to keep cool this summer!	2.07	16.89
Social Responsibility	According to researchers at Cal State San Marcos, you can reduce your monthly demand for electricity by 29% using fans instead of air conditioning to keep cool this summer!	1.99	17.52
Information Only	Summer is here, and the time is right to conserve energy. How can you conserve energy this summer? By using fans instead of air conditioning!	1.94	17.36

Note: Energy consumption is average daily kilowatt hours.

reported that the normative messages (descriptive norm) provided the least motivation. The researchers also read the residents' electricity meters to determine their actual energy consumption one month after the door-hangers were left at their homes. Table 17.2 reveals that the normative message actually yielded the lowest consumption. When you put these pieces together, you'll see why the researchers drew this interesting conclusion: "Despite the fact that participants believed that the behaviour of their neighbours—the descriptive norm—had the least impact on their own energy conservation, results showed that the descriptive norm actually had the strongest effect on participants' energy conservation behaviours" (pp. 920–921).

In the domain of energy conservation, it's easy to be comfortable that people are unknowingly influenced by social norms. However, the strong tendency to succumb to normative influence holds out the possibility of considerably more negative consequences. For example, history has provided several instances of suicide cults—circumstances in which people have internalized group norms that have led them to take their own lives. Consider events that took place in San Diego, California, in March 1997. The members of a group called "Heaven's Gate" committed mass suicide: The police found 39 bodies wearing identical black uniforms and accompanied by travel bags packed for a journey (Balch & Taylor, 2002). Before their suicides, the cult members had accepted a belief system that required them to shed their earthly bodies so they could board a UFO that would take them to the Kingdom of Heaven. That same year, a similar event took place in St. Casimir near Quebec City where five members of the "Solar Temple" cult set fire to their house in an apparent ritual suicide pact. In both of these situations described above, the groups had posted much of their belief system to their official website. Researchers, such as Lorne Dawson and Jeanna Hennebry at the University of Waterloo (2003), worry that the internet will provide a particularly effective means to recruit people into cults and other alternative belief systems. Does this strike you as a legitimate concern? You should consider that question in the context of the Asch experiment and other demonstrations of the ease with which conformity arises.

Minority Influence and Nonconformity Given the power of the majority to control resources and information, it is not surprising that people regularly conform to groups. As we have just seen, majority power even extends to how long it takes people to offer their opinions in private. Yet you know that sometimes individuals persevere in their personal views. How can this happen? How do people escape group domination, and how can anything new (counternormative) ever come about? Are there any conditions under which a small minority can turn the majority around and create new norms?

While researchers in Canada and the United States have concentrated their studies on conformity, in part because conformity is intertwined with the democratic process, some European social psychologists have instead focused on the power of the few to change the majority. **Serge Moscovici** of France pioneered the study of minority influence. In one study where participants were given colour-naming tasks, the majority correctly identified the colour patches, but two of the experimenter's confederates consistently identified a green colour as blue. Their consistent minority opposition had no immediate effect on the majority, but, when later tested alone,

some of the participants shifted their judgments by moving the boundary between blue and green toward the blue side of the colour continuum (Moscovici, 1976; Moscovici & Faucheux, 1972). Eventually, the power of the many may be undercut by the conviction of the dedicated few (Moscovici, 1980, 1985).

You can conceptualize these effects with respect to the distinction we introduced earlier between normative influence and informational influence (Crano & Prislin, 2006; W. Wood et al., 1994). Minority groups have relatively little normative influence: Members of the majority are typically not particularly concerned about being liked or accepted by the minority. On the other hand, minority groups do have informational influence: Minorities can encourage group members to understand issues from multiple perspectives (R. S. Peterson & Nemeth, 1996). Unfortunately, this potential for informational influence is infrequent because majority group members tend to distance themselves from deviant or low-consensus views (W. Wood, 2000).

DECISION MAKING IN GROUPS

If you have ever tried to make a decision as part of a group, you know that it can be quite torturous. Imagine, for example, that you have just seen a movie with a bunch of friends. Although you thought the movie was "OK," by the end of a post-movie discussion you find yourself agreeing that it was "an incredible piece of trash." Is this change after group discussion typical? Are the judgments groups make consistently different from individuals' judgments? Social psychologists have documented specific forces that operate when groups make decisions (Kerr & Tindale, 2004). We will focus on *group polarization* and *groupthink*.

Your post-movie experience is an example of **group polarization**: Groups show a tendency to make decisions that are more extreme than the decisions that would be made by the members acting alone. Suppose, for example, you asked each member of the movie group to provide an attitude rating toward the movie; subsequently, as a group you agree on a single value to reflect your group attitude. If the group's rating is more extreme than the average of the individuals' ratings, that would be an instance of polarization. Depending on the initial group tendency—toward caution or risk—group polarization will tend to make a group more cautious or more risky.

Researchers have suggested that two types of processes underlie group polarization: the *information-influence* model and the *social comparison* model (Liu & Latané, 1998). The information-influence model suggests that group members contribute different information to a decision. If you and your friends each have a different reason for disliking a movie a little bit, all that information taken together would provide the evidence that you should actually dislike the movie a lot. The social comparison model suggests that group members strive to capture their peers' regard by representing a group ideal that is a bit more extreme than the group's true norm. Thus, if you come to decide that everyone was unhappy with a movie, you could try to present yourself as particularly astute by stating a more

---

group polarization The tendency for groups to make decisions that are more extreme than the decisions that would be made by the members acting alone.

extreme opinion. If everyone in a group tries to capture the group's esteem in that same fashion, polarization will result.

Group polarization is one consequence of a general pattern of thought called *groupthink*. **Irving Janis** (1982) coined the term **groupthink** for the tendency of a decision-making group to filter out undesirable input so that a consensus may be reached, especially if it is in line with the leader's viewpoint. Janis's theory of groupthink emerged from his historical analysis of the Bay of Pigs invasion of Cuba in 1960. This disastrous invasion was approved by U.S. President John Kennedy after Cabinet meetings in which contrary information was minimized or suppressed by those advisers to the president who were eager to undertake the invasion. From his analysis of this event, Janis outlined a series of features that he believed would predispose groups to fall prey to groupthink: He suggested, for example, that groups that were highly cohesive, insulated from experts, and operated under directed leadership would make groupthink decisions.

Researchers have attempted to verify Janis's ideas through both further historical analyses and laboratory experiments (Henningsen, Henningsen, Eden, & Cruz, 2006). This body of research suggests that groups are particularly vulnerable to groupthink when they embody a collective desire to maintain a shared positive view of a group (Turner & Pratkanis, 1998). Group members must understand that dissent often improves the quality of a group decision even if it may detract, on the surface, from the group's positive feel.

We have just reviewed some of the situational forces that have an impact on the decisions that groups make. We will focus next on one of the most important decisions people make as individuals: When should you obey authority?

OBEDIENCE TO AUTHORITY

What made thousands of Nazis willing to follow Hitler's orders and send millions of Jews to the gas chambers? Did character defects lead them to carry out orders blindly? Did they have no moral values? How about you? Are there any conditions under which you would blindly obey an order from your religious leader to poison others and then commit suicide? Could you imagine being part of the sexual humiliation and abuse conducted by U.S. soldiers at the Iraqi Prison of Abu Ghraib (Hersh, 2004)? Your answer—as ours used to be—is most likely, "No! What kind of person do you think I am?" After reading this section, we hope you may be more willing to answer, "Maybe. I don't know for sure." Depending on the power of the social forces operating, you might do what other human beings have done in those situations, however horrible and alien their actions may seem—to you and to them—outside that setting.

The most convincing demonstration of situational power over individual behaviour was created by **Stanley Milgram**, (1965, 1974), a student of Solomon Asch, who conducted a series of studies that showed that blind obedience is less a product of dispositional characteristics than the outcome of situational forces that can engulf anyone. Milgram's program of obedience research is one of the most controversial because of its significant implications for real-world phenomena and the ethical issues it raises.

---

groupthink The tendency of a decision-making group to filter out undesirable input so that a consensus may be reached, especially if it is in line with the leader's viewpoint.

The Obedience Paradigm To separate the variables of personality and situation, Milgram used a series of 19 separate controlled laboratory experiments involving more than 1000 participants. Milgram's first experiments were conducted at Yale University, with male residents of New Haven and surrounding communities who received payment for their participation. In later variations, Milgram took his obedience laboratory away from the university. He set up a storefront research unit, recruiting through newspaper ads a broad cross-section of the population, varying widely in age, occupation, and education, and including members of both sexes.

Milgram's basic experimental paradigm involved individual participants delivering a series of what they thought were extremely painful electric shocks to another person. These volunteers thought they were participating in a scientific study of memory and learning. They were led to believe that the educational purpose of the study was to discover how punishment affects memory, so that learning could be improved through the proper balance of reward and punishment. In their *social roles* as *teachers*, the participants were to punish each error made by someone playing the role of *learner*. The major rule they were told to follow was to increase the level of shock each time the learner made an error until the learning was errorless. The white-coated experimenter acted as the *legitimate authority* figure—he presented the rules, arranged for the assignment of roles (by a rigged drawing of lots), and ordered the teachers to do their jobs whenever they hesitated or dissented. The dependent variable was the final level of shock—on a shock machine that went up to 450 volts in small, 15-volt steps—that a teacher gave before refusing to continue to obey the authority.

The Test Situation The study was staged to make a participant think that by following orders, he or she was causing pain and suffering and perhaps even killing an innocent person. Each teacher had been given a sample shock of 45 volts to feel the amount of pain it caused. The learner was a pleasant, mild-mannered man, about 50 years old, who mentioned something about a heart condition but was willing to go along with the procedure. He was strapped into an "electric chair" in the next room and communicated with the teacher via an intercom. His task was to memorize pairs of words, giving the second word in a pair when he heard the first one. The learner soon began making errors—according to a prearranged schedule—and the teacher began shocking the learner. The protests of the victim rose with the shock level. At 75 volts, he began to moan and grunt; at 150 volts, he demanded to be released from the experiment; at 180 volts, he cried out that he could not stand the pain any longer. At 300 volts, he insisted that he would no longer take part in the experiment and must be freed. He yelled out about his heart condition and screamed. If a teacher hesitated or protested delivering the next shock, the experimenter said, "The experiment requires that you continue" or "You have no other choice, you *must* go on."

As you might imagine, the situation was stressful for the participants. Most participants complained and protested, repeatedly insisting they could not continue. Women participants often were in tears as they dissented. That the experimental situation produced considerable conflict in the participants is readily apparent from their protests:

- 180 volts delivered: "He can't stand it! I'm not going to kill that man in there! You hear him hollering? He's hollering.

Milgram's obedience experiment: the "teacher" (participant) with experimenter (authority figure) (left), the shock generator (centre), and the "learner" (the experimenter's confederate) (right). What aspects of the situation affected the likelihood that the teachers would continue to the maximum shock level?

He can't stand it. What if something happens to him? . . . I mean, who is going to take the responsibility if anything happens to that gentleman?" [The experimenter accepts responsibility.] "All right."

- 195 volts delivered: "You see he's hollering. Hear that. Gee, I don't know." [The experimenter says, "The experiment requires that you go on."] "I know it does, sir, but I mean—huh—he don't know what he's in for. He's up to 195 volts" (Milgram, 1965, p. 67).

Even when there was only silence from the learner's room, the teacher was ordered to keep shocking him more and more strongly, all the way up to the button that was marked "Danger: Severe Shock XXX (450 volts)."

Why Do People Obey Authority? When 40 psychiatrists were asked by Milgram to predict the performance of participants in this experiment, they estimated that most would not go beyond 150 volts (based on a description of the experiment). In their professional opinions, fewer than 4 percent of the participants would still be obedient at 300 volts, and only about 0.1 percent would continue all the way to 450 volts. The psychiatrists presumed that only those few individuals who were *abnormal* in some way—sadists who enjoyed inflicting pain on others—would blindly obey orders to continue up to the maximum shock.

The psychiatrists based their evaluations on presumed *dispositional* qualities of people who would engage in such abnormal behaviour; they were, however, overlooking the power of this special situation to influence the thinking and actions of most people caught up in its social context. The remarkable and disturbing conclusion is just how wrong these experts were: *The majority of participants obeyed the authority fully.* No participant quit below 300 volts. Sixty-five percent delivered the maximum 450 volts to the learner. Note that most people *dissented* verbally, but the majority did not *disobey* behaviourally. From the point of view of the victim, that is a critical difference. If you were the victim, would it matter much that the participants said they did not want to continue hurting you (they dissented), if they then shocked you repeatedly (they obeyed)?

The results of the Milgram studies were so unexpected that researchers worked hard to rule out alternative interpretations of the results. But years of research have demonstrated repeatedly that situational cues can overwhelm many people's ability to make independent decisions.

Milgram's research suggests that to understand why people obey authority, you need to look closely at the psychological forces at work in the situation. We saw earlier how often situational factors constrain behaviours; in Milgram's research, we see an especially vivid instance of that general principle. Milgram and other researchers manipulated a number of aspects of the experimental circumstances to demonstrate that the obedience effect is overwhelmingly due to situational variables and not personality variables. **Figure 17.7** displays the level of obedience found in different situations. Obedience is quite high, for example, when a peer first models obedience, when a participant acts as an *intermediary bystander* assisting another person who actually delivers the shock, or when the victim (the learner) is physically remote from the teacher. Obedience is quite low when the learner demands to be shocked, when two authorities give contradictory commands, or when the authority figure is the victim. These findings all point to the idea that the *situation*, and not differences among individual participants, largely controlled behaviour.

When we teach contemporary students about Milgram's research, they often express the strong conviction that, because of cultural changes since the early 1960s, people would no longer obey. To answer this claim, social psychologist Jerry Burger (2009) completed a partial replication of one of Milgram's experiments. Burger modified the experiment to address ethical concerns present in Milgram's original procedure. Specifically, Burger halted participants if they continued to obey after they believed they had delivered a 150-volt shock. As we noted earlier, 150 volts was the point at which the learner demanded to be released from the experiment. Based on Milgram's original data, Burger reasoned that participants who continued after 150 volts would have been quite likely to continue beyond that point. In Milgram's original experiment, 82.5 percent of the participants continued beyond 150 volts; in Burger's replication, 70.0 percent did so. Thus, in the replication, a large majority of participants continued to obey the experimenter. Burger concluded that "the same situational factors that affected obedience in Milgram's participants still operate today" (p. 9).

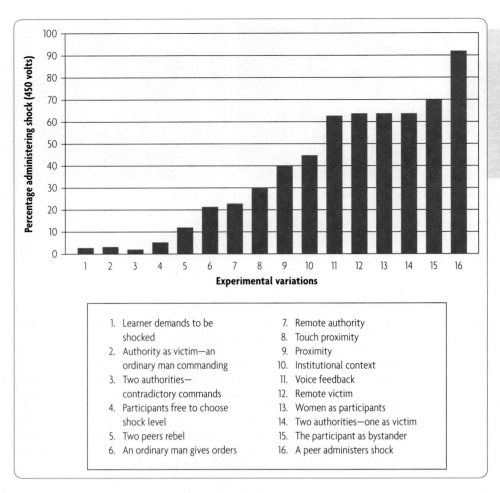

FIGURE 17.7 Obedience in Milgram's Experiments
The graph shows a profile of weak to strong obedience effects across Milgram's many experimental variations.

From *The Obedience Experiments*, by A. G. Miller, 1986, Copyright © 1986 Praeger. Reprinted with permission.

1. Learner demands to be shocked
2. Authority as victim—an ordinary man commanding
3. Two authorities—contradictory commands
4. Participants free to choose shock level
5. Two peers rebel
6. An ordinary man gives orders
7. Remote authority
8. Touch proximity
9. Proximity
10. Institutional context
11. Voice feedback
12. Remote victim
13. Women as participants
14. Two authorities—one as victim
15. The participant as bystander
16. A peer administers shock

Two reasons people obey authority in these situations can be traced to the effects of *normative* and *informational* sources of influence, which we discussed earlier: People want to be liked (normative influence), and they want to be right (informational influence). They tend to do what others are doing or requesting in order to be socially acceptable and approved of. In addition, when in an ambiguous, novel situation—like the experimental situation—people rely on others for cues as to what is the appropriate and correct way to behave. They are more likely to do so when experts or credible communicators tell them what to do. A third factor in the Milgram paradigm is that participants were probably confused about *how* to *disobey*; nothing they said in dissent satisfied the authority. If they had a simple, direct way out of the situation—for example, by pressing a "quit" button—it is likely more would have disobeyed (L. Ross, 1988). Finally, obedience to authority in this experimental situation is part of an *ingrained habit* that is learned by children in many different settings—obey authority without question (R. Brown, 1986). This heuristic usually serves society well when authorities are legitimate and deserving of obedience. The problem is that the rule gets overapplied. Blind obedience to authority means obeying any and all authority figures simply because of their ascribed status, regardless of whether they are unjust or just in their requests and commands.

What is the personal significance to you of this obedience research? Take a moment to reflect on the types of obedience-to-authority situations that might arise in your day-to-day experience. Suppose you were a salesclerk. Would you cheat customers if your boss encouraged such behaviour? Suppose you were a member of Parliament. Would you vote along party lines rather than vote your conscience?

Milgram's obedience research challenges the myth that evil lurks in the minds of evil people—the bad "they" who are different from the good "us" or "you," who would never do such things. Our purpose in recounting these findings is not to debase human nature, but to make clear that even normal, well-meaning individuals are subject to the potential for frailty in the face of strong situational and social forces.

Finally, we wish to add a note on heroism. Suppose the majority of people who are comparable to you yield to powerful group forces. In our view, if you are able to resist, that qualifies you as heroic. The hero is the person who can act mindfully, out of conscience, when others are all conforming, or who can take the moral high road when others are standing by silently, allowing evil deeds to go unchallenged. Perhaps your knowledge of situational forces that make possible the "banality of evil" can nudge you in the direction of heroism.

STOP AND REVIEW

❶ What did the Stanford Prison Experiment demonstrate about social roles?

❷ Why are groups able to have normative influence?

❸ What type of influence are minorities able to exert in a group?

➍ How can you recognize circumstances of group polarization?

➎ How did psychiatrists' predictions compare to participants' actual behaviour in Milgram's experiments?

CRITICAL THINKING Consider the study that looked at conformity in line judgments. Why was it important that the group members all gave the correct answer on the first few trials?

Aggression, Altruism, and Prosocial Behaviour

If you spend a few minutes reviewing the daily news, you'll almost certainly get reports on the extremes of human behaviour. You'll learn both about situations in which people have done each other harm and those in which people have done each other good. In this section, we consider the factors that yield both types of behaviour. We begin with acts of **aggression**: People's behaviours that cause psychological or physical harm to other individuals. Psychologists try to understand the causes of aggression with the goal of using that knowledge to help reduce societal levels of aggression. We then turn our attention to the positive extreme: The **prosocial behaviours** that people carry out with the goal of helping other people. We focus, in addition, on **altruism**—the prosocial behaviours people carry out without considering their own safety or interests. We discuss some personal and situational factors that change the likelihood of these helping behaviours.

INDIVIDUAL DIFFERENCES IN AGGRESSION

One major fact of research on aggression is that some people are consistently more aggressive than others. Why might that be so? One type of research has examined genetic contributions to individual differences in rates of aggression. Researchers have used many of the methods we've illustrated in earlier chapters. They have, for example, compared the similarity of identical (monozygotic, MZ) and fraternal (dizygotic, DZ) twins with respect to aggressive personalities; in other cases, they have estimated the contributions of nature and nurture by examining children raised in adoptive homes.

These studies typically demonstrate a strong genetic component for aggressive behaviour (DiLalla, 2002). For example, MZ twins consistently show higher correlations for aggressiveness than do DZ twins (Haberstick, Schmitz, Young, & Hewitt, 2006). However, research suggests that genetics may play a stronger and weaker role for different types of aggression.

Researchers collected data on 234 six-year-old twins to assess genetic and environmental contributions to individual differences in *physical* and *social* aggression (Brendgen et al., 2005). Physical aggression represents circumstances in which children get into fights or hit, bite, or kick other children. Social aggression represents circumstances in which children spread nasty rumours or try to make others dislike particular classmates. To assess the twins' behaviours for both types of aggression, the researchers obtained ratings from the twins' teachers and their peers. These ratings provided converging evidence that the MZ and DZ twins differed with respect to their similarity levels of aggression. The comparison between MZ and DZ twins suggested that 50 to 60 percent of the variation in physical aggression could be explained by genetic factors. For social aggression, 20 percent of the variation was explained by genetics.

Why might genetics have less influence over social aggression? The researchers speculated that children's inclination to use social aggression might follow from the type of parenting they receive: Parents who use shame or guilt to manipulate their children may provide models for the children's later classroom behaviour. Overall, this study supports the conclusion that some individuals have a greater genetic predisposition toward aggression than do others.

Researchers have also focused attention on brain and hormonal differences that may mark a predisposition toward aggressive behaviour. As we saw in Chapters 4 and 13, several brain structures, such as the amygdala and portions of cortex, play roles in the expression and regulation of emotion. With respect to aggression, it is critical that brain pathways function effectively so that individuals can control the expression of negative emotion. If, for example, people experience inappropriate levels of activation in the amygdala, they may not be able to

Here, students mourn the victims of the shootings at Dawson College in Montreal in 2006. Why do people so often turn to aggression as a solution to their problems?

---

aggression Behaviours that cause psychological or physical harm to another individual.

prosocial behaviours Behaviours that are carried out with the goal of helping other people.

altruism Prosocial behaviours a person carries out without considering his or her own safety or interests.

inhibit the negative emotions that lead to aggressive behaviours (Siever, 2008).

Attention has also focused on the neurotransmitter serotonin. Research suggests that inappropriate levels of serotonin may impair the brain's ability to regulate negative emotions and impulsive behaviour (Siever, 2008). For example, one study demonstrated that men with life histories of more aggression showed decreased response in the serotonin system to a drug (fenfluramine) that typically has a considerable impact on that system (Manuck, Flory, Muldoon, & Ferrell, 2002). Recall from Chapter 15 that researchers have begun to explore consequences of variations in the actual genes that underlie serotonin function. In this study as well, the researchers showed that a particular genetic variation was likely to affect serotonin function in a way that put people at risk for high levels of aggressive behaviour.

Personality research on aggression has pointed to the importance of differentiating categories of aggressive behaviours: People with different personality profiles are likely to engage in different types of aggression. One important distinction separates *impulsive aggression* from *instrumental aggression* (Little, Jones, Henrich, & Hawley, 2003; Ramírez & Andreu, 2006). **Impulsive aggression** is produced in reaction to situations and is emotion-driven: People respond with aggressive acts in the heat of the moment. If you see people get into a fistfight after a car accident, that is impulsive aggression. **Instrumental aggression** is goal-directed (the aggression serves as the *instrument* for some goal) and cognition-based: People carry out acts of aggression, with premeditated thought, to achieve specific aims. If you see someone knock an elderly woman down to steal her purse, that is instrumental aggression. Individuals with high propensities toward one or the other of these types of violence appear to have distinct sets of personality traits (Caprara, Barbaranelli, & Zimbardo, 1996). For example, individuals who reported a propensity toward impulsive aggression were likely, in general, to be characterized as high on the factor of *emotional responsivity*. That is, they were likely, in general, to report highly emotional responses to a range of situations. By contrast, individuals who reported a propensity toward instrumental aggression were likely to score high on the factor of *positive evaluation of violence*. These individuals believed that many forms of violence are justified, and they also did not accept moral responsibility for aggressive behaviours. You learn from this analysis that not all types of aggression arise from the same underlying personality factors.

Most people are not at the extremes of either impulsive or instrumental aggression: They do not lose their tempers at the least infraction or purposefully commit acts of violence. Even so, in some situations, even the most mild-mannered individuals will perform aggressive acts. We look now at the types of situations that may often provide the triggering conditions for aggression.

---

impulsive aggression Emotion-driven aggression produced in reaction to situations.

instrumental aggression Cognition-based and goal-directed aggression carried out with premeditated thought to achieve specific aims.

frustration–aggression hypothesis According to this hypothesis, frustration occurs in situations in which people are prevented or blocked from attaining their goals; a rise in frustration then leads to a greater probability of aggression.

SITUATIONAL INFLUENCES ON AGGRESSION

Take a moment now to think back to the last time you engaged in aggressive behaviour. It may not have been physical aggression: You may just have been verbally abusive toward some other individual, with the intent of causing psychological distress. How would you explain why that particular situation gave rise to aggression?

Consider a situation in which other people made it impossible for you complete some important task. Did you reach a breaking point? This general relationship is captured by the **frustration–aggression hypothesis** (Dollard, Doob, Miller, Mower, & Sears, 1939). According to this hypothesis, frustration occurs in situations in which people are prevented or blocked from attaining their goals; a rise in frustration then leads to a greater probability of aggression. The link between frustration and aggression has obtained a high level of empirical support (Berkowitz, 1993, 1998). For example, children who are frustrated in their expectation that they will be allowed to play with highly attractive toys act aggressively toward those toys when they finally have an opportunity to play (Barker, Dembo, & Lewin, 1941). Researchers have used this relationship to explain aggression at both the personal and societal levels.

Do you recognize this news story? A man gets fired from a job and goes back to kill the boss who fired him, as well as several coworkers. Could this count as an instance of frustration (that is, the frustrated goal of earning a living) leading to aggression? To provide a general answer to this question, a team of researchers examined the relationship between San Francisco's unemployment rate and the rate at which people in that city were committed for being "dangerous to others." This analysis allows for predictions across a whole community: What unemployment rate is likely to lead to the highest levels of violence? The researchers found that violence increased as unemployment increased, but only to a certain point. When unemployment got too high, violence began to fall again. Why might that be? The researchers speculated that people's fears that they too might lose their jobs helped inhibit frustration-driven tendencies toward violence (Catalano, Novaco, & McConnell, 1997, 2002).

This study suggests how individual and societal forces interact to produce a net level of violence. We can predict a certain level of aggression based on the frustration each individual experiences in an economy with rising unemployment. However, as people realize that expressions of aggression may imperil their own employment, violence is inhibited. You can probably recognize these forces in your day-to-day experiences: There are many situations in which you might feel sufficiently frustrated to express aggression, but you also understand that an expression of aggression will work against your long-term best interest.

Frustration does not always lead to aggression. When, for example, the frustration is brought about unintentionally—suppose a child spills juice on his mother's new dress—people are less likely to become aggressive than when the action is intentional (Geen, 1998).

It is not going to surprise you that *direct provocation* will also give rise to aggression. That is, when someone behaves in a way that makes you angry or upset—and you think that behaviour was intentional—you are more likely to respond with some form of physical or verbal aggression (T. E. Johnson & Rule, 1986; Rudolph, Roesch, Greitemeyer, & Weiner, 2004). The effects of direct provocation are consistent with the general idea that situations that produce negative affect will lead to aggression. The intentionality of the act matters because you are less likely to interpret an unintentional act in a negative way. Consider a study that focused on fourth grade children (Nelson, Mitchell, & Yang, 2008). The researchers asked the children to read scenarios and make judgments about the actors' intentions. In one scenario the children were meant to imagine that a peer's basketball rolled under their feet and caused them to fall during a race. The children indicated whether they believed the peer's actions were intentional or accidental. The researchers also gathered information about the extent of the children's actual physical aggression in the classroom. The two types of data revealed interesting relationships. For example, the boys who perceived the most hostile intent in scenarios like the basketball example were also the most physically aggressive. These data remind you why it matters how people construct social reality: When people interpret ambiguous situations as provocations, they are more likely to respond with aggression.

We have been focusing on aspects of particular situations that bring about aggression. In addition, broader social norms also affect the likelihood that people will display aggression (M. H. Bond, 2004). Recall the research discussed in Chapter 7 suggesting that children very readily adopt aggressive behaviours from watching adult models. For example, children who watched adult models punching, hitting, and kicking a large plastic Bobo doll later showed a greater frequency of the same behaviours than did children who had not observed the aggressive models (Bandura, Ross, & Ross, 1963). We also suggested in Chapter 7 that television in North America beams an enormous number of aggressive models directly into children's homes; exposure to violence is highly related to adult levels of aggression (Comstock & Scharrer, 1999; Huesmann, Moise-Titus, Podolski, & Eron, 2003).

Researchers have developed the *general aggression model* to explain the relationship between exposure to violent media (television, movies, and so on) and aggressive behaviour. This model suggests that people acquire a general set of aggression-related knowledge structures through their experiences of media violence: In this view, "each violent media episode is essentially one more trial to learn that the world is a dangerous place, that aggression is an appropriate way to deal with conflict and anger, and that aggression works" (Bushman & Anderson, 2002, p. 1680). Consider a study that examined the short-term impact of violent video games.

> Researchers asked 224 university undergraduates to play either violent video games (for example, Mortal Kombat) or nonviolent video games (for example, 3D Pinball) (Bushman & Anderson, 2002). After playing for 20 minutes, the participants were asked to complete what they believed to be an unrelated task. The participants read incomplete stories and indicated what they thought would happen next. For example, in one story, Todd was rear-ended when he braked quickly at a yellow light. Participants wrote answers to the question, "What happens next?" Those students who played the violent video games gave consistently more aggressive outcomes for the stories. For example, participants suggested that Todd would kick out a window or stab or shoot the other driver.

Why should parents worry that children who play violent video games may be prone to more real-world aggression?

This study illustrates that those students who had just played violent video games versus nonviolent video games were ready to provide much more aggressive responses. Other research has contrasted the physiological responses of college students who have recently played violent or nonviolent video games (Carnagey, Anderson, & Bushman, 2007). The students who had played violent games produced weaker responses (such as lower heart rate) to videos of real-world violence such as stabbings, shootings, and prison fights. These data suggest that the students' game play had desensitized them to the violent images. Thus, exposure to these violent games both makes the world seem more violent and numbs people's response to that violence.

Unfortunately, for many children the world does present real dangers. Children may be exposed to aggressive acts in their homes (Evans, Davies, & DiLillo, 2008). In addition, many children in North America grow up in inner-city communities in which violence is daily and chronic (Berkowitz, 2003; Salzinger et al., 2006). Researchers have only begun to explore the consequences of exposure to violence for children's mental health and their inclination to aggressive behaviour (Bingenheimer, Brennan, & Earls, 2005).

In this section we have described far too many reasons why people might engage in aggressive behaviour. Fortunately, people are also well prepared to provide help to others. We now turn to thee roots of helping behaviour.

THE ROOTS OF PROSOCIAL BEHAVIOUR

On January 12, 2010, an earthquake measuring 7.0 on the Richter scale struck Haiti. This earthquake was the deadliest such event in history, with the number of deaths estimated to be greater than 200 000 people. Soon after this disaster, the media was full of images of the devastation caused by the earthquake. Along with these images were also countless stories of people who risked their lives to save others. People from all around the world converged on Port au Prince, the capital of Haiti, with the hope of aiding survivors. How can we explain why people engage in such prosocial behaviour? Researcher **C. Daniel**

Batson (1994) suggests that there are four forces that prompt people to act for the public good:

- *Altruism.* Acting in response to a motive to benefit others, as in the case of the many people who volunteered to assist the victims of the quake-ravaged city of Port au Prince.
- *Egoism.* Performing prosocial behaviours ultimately in one's own self-interest; someone might perform a helping behaviour to receive a similar favour in return (for example, compliance with a request) or to receive a reward (for example, money or praise).
- *Collectivism.* Performing prosocial behaviours to benefit a particular group; people might perform helping behaviours to improve circumstances for their families, fraternities or sororities, political parties, and so on.
- *Principlism.* Performing prosocial behaviours to uphold moral principles; someone might act in a prosocial manner because of a religious or civic principle.

You can see how each of these motives might apply in different situations.

The same prosocial behaviour can serve more than one motive. For example, many universities now encourage students to participate in service learning: "an educational assignment in which students meet the academic learning goals of a course through an experience working on behalf of others" (Jay, 2008, p. 255). For example, in one service learning project conducted by researchers from Canada and the United States, students who enrolled in a community college course on aging and research served as interviewers of older adults in an effort to assess their needs (Gutheil, Chernesky, & Sherratt, 2006). Because participation in this project enhanced students' educational experience, we might count this as an instance of egoism (that is, the student's reward is greater learning). However, their participation also provided benefits to older adults, so we might also count this instance of service learning as collectivism. In fact, educators who support service learning often hope that the values instilled by service learning will lead students to undertake a lifetime of prosocial behaviour (Tomkovick, Lester, Flunker, & Wells, 2008).

Among these motives for prosocial behaviour, the existence of altruism has sometimes been controversial. To understand why, you must think back to the discussion of evolutionary forces we presented in earlier chapters. According to the evolutionary perspective, the main goal of life is to reproduce so that one can pass on one's genes. How, in that context, does altruism make sense? Why should you risk your life to aid others? There are two answers to this question, depending on whether the "others" are family members or strangers.

For family members, altruistic behaviours make some sense because, even if you imperil your own survival, you aid the general survival of your gene pool (Burnstein, 2005). Researchers have examined the extent to which genetic overlap influences people's altruistic behaviours.

Participants in an experiment had the opportunity to earn money for themselves and for relatives with whom they had 50 percent genetic overlap (for example, siblings and

parents), 25 percent overlap (for example, grandparents, aunts, and nephews), or 12.5 percent overlap (as with cousins) (Madsen et al., 2007). However, to earn the money, the participants had to remain in a painful physical position: The longer they remained in the position, the more money they made for themselves or for their relatives. The participants returned to the laboratory over several days so that the researchers could complete the test for each relatedness category. Participants did not know how long they had held the painful position until the end of each trial. The results demonstrated a clear impact of genetic overlap. On the whole, the greater the genetic overlap, the longer the participants endured the pain. The researchers demonstrated much the same pattern with university students in London and with two South African Zulu populations.

Because the participants endured pain to provide funds to their relatives, their behaviour meets the criteria for altruism. The results strongly suggest that people are more willing to engage in altruistic behaviour for some relatives than for others. However, the researchers acknowledged that other types of social relationships also affect people's behaviours. In fact, some research suggests that people are most willing to help individuals to whom they feel emotionally close, including their circle of friends (Korchmaros & Kenny, 2006; Stewart-Williams, 2007). For most people, their closest emotional attachments are also to their closest kin. Thus, patterns of helping based on emotional closeness indirectly help people's gene pools to survive.

But how about non-kin? Why, for example, is a person who sees someone drowning willing to risk his or her own survival to preserve someone else's genes? To explain altruism toward acquaintances and strangers, theorists have explored the concept of **reciprocal altruism** (Trivers, 1971). This concept suggests that people perform altruistic behaviours because they, in some sense, expect that others will perform altruistic behaviours for them: I will save you when you are drowning with the expectation that you would save me, in the future, if I were drowning.

Note, however, that the concept of reciprocal altruism cannot explain all facets of co-operation in social species (Penner, Dovidio, Piliavin, & Schroeder, 2005). For example, the many people who assisted the victims of the Haitian earthquake surely didn't expect that the Haitian victims would perform similarly altruistic acts in return. To explain acts of this sort, researchers suggest that indirect reciprocity is at work: People perform altruistic behaviours because they believe that, in the future, they will become the recipients of altruistic acts. To put it somewhat more plainly, "I scratch your back, and someone else will scratch mine" (Nowak & Sigmund, 2005, p. 1291). An important component of this concept of indirect reciprocity is that people gain the reputation of being altruistic and trustworthy. For example, in one study, participants played a game that gave them several opportunities to behave altruistically by making monetary donations to other players (Wedekind & Braithwaite, 2002). As the game unfolded, the players' "image scores" were posted as a concrete index of their reputations. In a second phase of the study—in a different game—players with the best reputations for being altruistic were themselves the most likely to be rewarded by altruistic actions. Results of this sort suggest that there is long-term value in having a reputation for being a trustworthy source of altruism.

---

reciprocal altruism The idea that people perform altruistic behaviours because they expect that others will perform altruistic behaviours for them in turn.

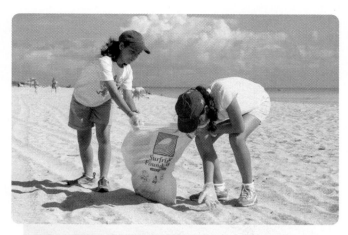

What prosocial motive explains why people band together to protect the environment?

We also cannot dismiss the fact that there often is a social component when people perform altruistic acts toward non-kin. The *empathy-altruism hypothesis* suggests a particular type of relationship: When you feel empathy—feelings of emotional identification—toward another individual, those feelings evoke an altruistic motive to provide help (Batson, 1991). Much research supports this hypothesis. For example, in one study the researchers asked participants to allocate raffle tickets either to a whole group or to individuals within the group (Batson et al., 1999). In one condition of the experiment, the participants read an autobiographical message from someone they were led to believe was a group member; the message revealed that that person had just been dumped by a long-time romantic partner. When participants experienced empathy, they gave extra tickets to the dumped individual. Across humans and other species, researchers have demonstrated quite general links between empathy and altruism (de Waal, 2008).

But are people comfortable with these feelings of compassion? Some research suggests that people who experience a strong sense of compassion often feel the need to inhibit their altruistic feelings.

John Holmes and his colleagues (Holmes, Miller, & Lerner, 2002) have argued that individuals will often recast their compassionate motives as self-interest to match the culturally accepted belief that self-interest is the more sensible option. They suggest that people find ways of reframing their generous action in order to appear more self-interested and to provide a cover for helping.

Participants at a Canadian university were approached to give monetary donations to a charitable organization. The charities represented were all real, but the need of the organization was manipulated from low need to high need. Half the participants were simply asked to give a monetary donation, whereas the other half were asked to purchase either a very inexpensive or moderately expensive set of candles as a means of donation. In all but one condition, participants gave roughly the same amount of money. However, when the need of the organization was high (i.e., participants felt more compassion) and donation was done as an exchange (i.e., to cover up the true act of helping), participants gave more than three times the amount of donation. The authors suggested that when people felt a sense of compassion due to the high need of the organization, the offer of candles increased net donations in that this offer provided not an incentive, but an "excuse" for giving.

You can see why it is important to consider each behaviour in light of the full situation: What looks at first like *anti*social behaviour—for example, violating principles of justice—may turn out, from a different vantage point, to be *pro*social behaviour. And what appears to be an exchange of goods may be a way to resolve the tension associated with strict acts of compassion. A social psychology lesson we emphasized earlier in this chapter was how much people's behaviours are constrained by situations. Next, we describe a classic program of research that demonstrated fully how much people's willingness to help—their ability to follow through on prosocial motives—depends on characteristics of the situation.

THE EFFECTS OF THE SITUATION ON PROSOCIAL BEHAVIOUR

This program of research began with a tragedy. From the safety of their apartment windows, 38 respectable, law-abiding citizens in Queens, New York, for more than half an hour watched a killer stalk and stab a woman in three separate attacks. Two times the sound of the bystanders' voices and the sudden glow of their bedroom lights interrupted the assailant and frightened him off. Each time, however, he returned and stabbed the victim again. Not a single person telephoned the police during the assault; only one witness called the police after the woman was dead (Rosenthal, 1964). This newspaper account of the murder of Kitty Genovese shocked Americans, who could not accept the idea of such apathy or hard-heartedness on the part of its responsible citizenry.

But is it fair to pin the label of "apathetic" or "hard-hearted" on these bystanders? Or can we explain their inaction in terms of situational forces? To make the case for situational forces, **Bibb Latané** and **John Darley** (1970) carried out a

The murder of Kitty Genovese, in a pleasant Queens neighbourhood, shocked America. Why did so many responsible citizens fail to intervene when they heard her cries for help?

classic series of studies. Their goal was to demonstrate that **bystander intervention**—people's willingness to help strangers in distress—was very sensitive to precise characteristics of the situation. They ingeniously created in the laboratory an experimental analogue of the bystander-intervention situation.

> The participants were male university students. Each student, placed in a room by himself with an intercom, was led to believe that he was communicating with one or more students in an adjacent room. During the course of a discussion about personal problems, he heard what sounded like one of the other students having an epileptic seizure and gasping for help. During the "seizure," it was impossible for the participant to talk to the other students or to find out what, if anything, they were doing about the emergency. The dependent variable was the speed with which the participant reported the emergency to the experimenter.
>
> It turned out that the likelihood of intervention depended on the number of bystanders the participant thought were present. The more people he thought were present, the slower he was in reporting the seizure, if he did so at all. As you can see in **Figure 17.8**, everyone in a two-person situation intervened within 160 seconds, but nearly 40 percent of those who believed they were part of a larger group never bothered to inform the experimenter that another student was seriously ill (Darley & Latané, 1968).

This result arises from a **diffusion of responsibility**. When more than one person *could* help in an emergency situation, people often assume that someone else *will* or *should* help—so they back off and do not get involved.

Diffusion of responsibility is only one of the reasons that bystanders may fail to help. Let's explore more of the facets of many emergency situations.

Bystanders Must Notice the Emergency

In the seizure study, the situation was rigged so that participants had to notice what was going on. In many real-life circumstances, however, people who are pursuing their own agendas—who may, for example, be on their way to work or an appointment—may not even notice that there is a situation in which they can help, or they may not have the time to pay attention to the subtle cues that indicate that someone is in need of help. Our ability to help depends on taking the time to evaluate a situation accurately.

Bystanders Must Label Events as an Emergency

Many situations in life are ambiguous. You do not want to embarrass yourself by trying to give mouth-to-mouth resuscitation to someone who is merely asleep. To decide if a situation is an emergency, you typically consider how other people are responding (Latané & Darley, 1970). But often it is hard to decide whether or not you should act—and people around you are in a similar state of uncertainty. Even for someone with a firm grasp on the psychological forces at work, the decision to commit to action when no one else seems to be labelling the situation as an emergency is stressful.

---

bystander intervention Willingness to assist a person in need of help.

diffusion of responsibility In emergency situations, the larger the number of bystanders, the less responsibility any one of the bystanders feels to help.

FIGURE 17.8   Bystander Intervention in an Emergency

The more people are present, the less likely it is that any one bystander will intervene. Bystanders act most quickly in two-person groups.

From Darley & Latané, *Journal of Personality and Social Psychology*, 8(4), 1968. Copyright © 1968 American Psychological Association.

Bystanders Must Feel Responsibility

We have already seen that an important factor in nonintervention is the diffusion of responsibility. If you find yourself in a situation in which you need help, you should do everything you can to cause bystanders to focus responsibility on themselves and overcome this force. You should point directly toward someone and say, "You! I need your help." Consider two studies that involved apparent crimes. In the first study, New Yorkers watched as a thief snatched a women's suitcase in a fast-food restaurant when she left her table. In the second, beachgoers watched as a thief snatched a portable radio from a beach blanket when the owner left it for a few minutes.

> In each experiment, the would-be theft victim (the experimenter's accomplice) asked the soon-to-be observer of the crime either, "Do you have the time?" or "Will you please keep an eye on my bag (radio) while I'm gone?" The first interaction elicited no personal responsibility, and the bystanders simply stood by idly as the thefts unfolded. However, of those who agreed to watch the victim's property, almost every bystander intervened. They called for help, and some even tackled the runaway thief on the beach (Moriarty, 1975).

These experiments suggest that the act of requesting a favour forges a special human bond that involves other people in ways that materially change the situation. This is another instance in which it would be wrong to make an attribution of apathy when people fail to stop the theft. The social psychological power of the small commitment—"Will you watch this for me?"—turned almost every bystander into someone who cared enough to help.

In this section, we have discussed prosocial behaviours—those circumstances in which people come to each others' aid. We have shown that these motivations are complex. We have shown that they are, in some ways, the result of biological propensity. But these general tendencies are often impacted by the social situation that provides important cues about how to act.

STOP AND REVIEW

❶ Why do researchers believe that genetic factors play a role in aggression?

❷ What is the relationship between frustration and aggression?

❸ What is meant by reciprocal altruism?

❹ Why does diffusion of responsibility occur?

CRITICAL THINKING   Recall the experiment that assessed the impact of violent video games. Why was it important for participants to believe that the task in which they provided endings for stories was unrelated to their video game playing?

Recapping Main Points

Constructing Social Reality

- Each person constructs his or her own social reality.
- Social perception is influenced by beliefs and expectations.
- Attribution theory describes the judgments people make about the causes of behaviours.
- Several biases, such as the fundamental attribution error, self-serving biases, and self-fulfilling prophecies, can creep into attributions and other judgments and behaviours.

Visit **MyPsychLab.com** for more review and practice on the following topics:

 Explore: Internal and External Attributions

Attitudes, Attitude Change, and Action

- Attitudes are positive or negative evaluations of objects, events, or ideas.
- Not all attitudes accurately predict behaviours; they must be highly accessible or highly specific.
- According to the elaboration likelihood model, the central route to persuasion relies on careful analyses of arguments, whereas the peripheral route relies on superficial features of persuasive situations.
- Dissonance theory and self-perception theory consider attitude formation and change that arise from behavioural acts.
- To bring about compliance, people can exploit reciprocity, commitment, and scarcity.

Visit **MyPsychLab.com** for more review and practice on the following topics:

Research: Leon Festinger

Prejudice

- Even arbitrary, minimal cues can yield prejudice when they define an in-group and an out-group.
- Stereotypes affect the way in which people evaluate behaviours and information in the world.

- Researchers have eliminated some of the effects of prejudice by creating situations in which members of different groups must co-operate to reach shared goals.
- Cross-cultural studies also suggest that friendship plays an important role in eliminating prejudice.

Social Relationships

- Interpersonal attraction is determined in part by proximity, physical attractiveness, similarity, and reciprocity.
- Loving relationships are defined with respect to passion, intimacy, and commitment.
- Adult attachment style affects the quality of relationships.

Visit **MyPsychLab.com** for more review and practice on the following topics:

Practice: Social Relationships

The Power of the Situation

- Being assigned to play a social role, even in artificial settings, can cause individuals to act contrary to their beliefs, values, and dispositions.
- Social norms shape the attitudes and behaviours of group members.
- Classic research by Sherif and Asch illustrated the informational and normative forces that lead to conformity.
- Minority influence may arise as a consequence of informational influence.
- Milgram's studies on obedience are a powerful testimony to the influence of the situational factors that can lead ordinary people to sanction and participate in organized aggression.

Visit **MyPsychLab.com** for more review and practice on the following topics:

Watch: Stanford Prison Experiment

Aggression, Altruism, and Prosocial Behaviour

- Individual differences in aggressive behaviour reflect genetics, brain function, and personality profiles.
- Frustration and provocation can lead to aggression.

- Different cultures provide different norms for aggressive behaviour.
- Researchers have tried to explain why people engage in prosocial behaviours, particularly altruistic behaviours that do not serve their own interests.
- Evolutionary explanations focus on kinship and reciprocity.

- Bystander intervention studies show that situations largely determine who is likely or unlikely to help in emergencies.

Visit **MyPsychLab.com** for more review and practice on the following topics:

◄●◄ **Simulate:** Helping a Stranger

KEY TERMS

actor–observer bias (p. 530)
aggression (p. 555)
altruism (p. 555)
attitude (p. 532)
attribution theory (p. 529)
behavioural confirmation (p. 539)
bystander intervention (p. 560)
cognitive dissonance (p. 535)
compliance (p. 537)
conformity (p. 548)
contact hypothesis (p. 541)
covariation principle (p. 529)
diffusion of responsibility (p. 560)
elaboration likelihood model (p. 534)
frustration–aggression hypothesis
    (p. 556)

fundamental attribution error (FAE)
    (p. 529)
group polarization (p. 551)
groupthink (p. 552)
impulsive aggression (p. 556)
informational influence (p. 548)
in-group bias (p. 538)
in-groups (p. 538)
instrumental aggression (p. 556)
norm crystallization (p. 548)
normative influence (p. 548)
out-groups (p. 538)
persuasion (p. 534)
prejudice (p. 538)
prosocial behaviours (p. 555)
racism (p. 538)

reciprocal altruism (p. 558)
reciprocity norm (p. 537)
rules (p. 546)
self-fulfilling prophecy (p. 531)
self-perception theory (p. 536)
self-serving bias (p. 530)
sexism (p. 538)
social categorization (p. 538)
social cognition (p. 528)
social norms (p. 548)
social perception (p. 529)
social psychology (p. 528)
social role (p. 546)
stereotypes (p. 539)

Practice Test

1. Becky wants to help her friend Tom avoid the fundamental attribution error. She suggests that he focus on _____ causes of behaviours.
   - a. situational
   - b. distinctive
   - c. dispositional
   - d. consistent

2. Which of these statements is *not* consistent with a self-serving bias?
   - a. I lost because the other guy was probably cheating.
   - b. I lost because it was too hot in the room.
   - c. I won because I am a genius.
   - d. I won because I got lucky.

3. Bruce is about to interview Joan for a job. When he meets her, his first impression is that she is shy. The first question Bruce asks Joan is, "Have you ever had trouble working as part of a group?" It appears that Bruce may be engaging in the process of _____
   - a. self-fulfilling prophecy.
   - b. behavioural confirmation.
   - c. covariation.
   - d. reality construction.

4. When someone hires a celebrity to endorse a product, he or she is likely hoping that most consumers will follow the _____ route to persuasion and engage in _____ elaboration.
   - a. peripheral; low
   - b. peripheral; high
   - c. central; high
   - d. central; low

5. Sam chooses desserts for himself and for his friend Randy. Suppose both desserts turn out to be duds. If Sam has an _____ sense of self, you would expect him to experience the most cognitive dissonance with respect to the dessert he chose for _____.
   - a. independent; Randy
   - b. interdependent; Randy
   - c. interdependent; himself
   - d. dependent; himself

6. Oliver is trying to change his friend Stan's stereotype that woman are not as funny as men. They watch a TV special with a series of women doing comedy routines. Do you think Stan's stereotype will change?
   - a. Yes, because he will appreciate Oliver's effort on his behalf.
   - b. No, because he will discount information that is inconsistent with his stereotype.
   - c. No, because he will convince Stan that the stereotype is true.
   - d. Yes, because he will learn a new stereotype from the TV special.

7. Which of these statements suggests that Carmen is exploiting similarity to get Perry to like her more?
   - a. "Did you know that we're both Libras?"
   - b. "I really enjoy spending time with you."
   - c. "Would you like me to get you the newspaper?"
   - d. "Your new haircut looks terrific."

8. In the Stanford Prison Experiment, the guards often acted in abusive ways toward the prisoners. This result suggests that _____
   - a. people seek situations in which they can indulge their aggressive impulses.
   - b. some people are well suited to take on the role of guards.
   - c. only aggressive people are willing to assume the role of prison guard.
   - d. social roles have an important influence on how people behave.

9. Solomon Asch's experiments on conformity demonstrate the impact of _____ in group situations.
   - a. norm crystallization
   - b. social rules
   - c. normative influence
   - d. informational influence

10. Which statement is *not* correct?
   - a. Companionate love is associated with life satisfaction.
   - b. Most relationships have more passionate love at the outset.
   - c. Companionate love is characterized by less intensity but greater intimacy.
   - d. There is little passionate love in long-term relationships.

11. You are watching a video of Juliet interacting with an attractive man. Because Juliet is mimicking his gestures _____, you guess that she _____ currently in a romantic relationship.
   - a. quite a bit, is
   - b. continuously, is
   - c. very little, is
   - d. infrequently, is not

12. According to the frustration–aggression hypothesis, in which of these situations is Brett most likely to act in an aggressive fashion?
   - a. Brett has an important job interview, but he is stuck in a traffic jam.
   - b. Brett's girlfriend yelled at him all morning for being mean to her.
   - c. Brett does not like the song that is playing on his car radio.
   - d. Brett thinks his boss has been monitoring the websites he visits.

13. Which of these conditions is typically *least* important with respect to bystander intervention?
   - a. Bystanders must notice the emergency.
   - b. Bystanders must label events as an emergency.
   - c. Bystanders must feel responsibility in the situation.
   - d. Bystanders must consider themselves to be helpful people.

14. In Milgram's experiments on obedience, many people protested that they did not want to give any more shocks. After that happened, —————
  a. the experimenter told them the study was over.
  b. most participants asked to leave the experiment.
  c. most participants continued to administer shocks.
  d. the experimenter asked them to shock at a lower level.

15. If you want to increase the likelihood that people will continue to volunteer in the future, which of these measures would you *not* want to try?
  a. Give people T-shirts to recognize their volunteer work.
  b. Have people start to volunteer as a mandatory assignment.
  c. Help people cope with distressing aspects of the volunteer work.
  d. Determine the motives people have for volunteering.

Essay Questions

1. What properties of attitudes increase the correlations between attitudes and behaviours?

2. What impact do stereotypes have on people's behaviour?

3. What situational factors affect the likelihood that people will engage in prosocial behaviours?

Discovering Psychology Viewing Guide

Watch the following videos by logging on to MyPsychLab (**www.mypsychlab.com**). After you have watched the videos, complete the activities that follow.

Program 19: The Power of the Situation

Program 20: Constructing Social Reality

PROGRAM REVIEW

1. Before Stanley Milgram did his experiments on obedience, experts were asked to predict the results. The experts —————
 a. overestimated people's willingness to administer shocks.
 b. underestimated people's willingness to administer shocks.
 c. gave accurate estimates of people's behaviour.
 d. believed most people would refuse to continue with the experiment.

2. Which statement most clearly reflects the fundamental attribution error?
 a. Everyone is entitled to good medical care.
 b. Ethical guidelines are essential to conducting responsible research.
 c. People who are unemployed are too lazy to work.
 d. Everyone who reads about the Milgram experiment is shocked by the results.

3. How did Tom Moriarty get people on a beach to intervene during a robbery?
 a. by creating a human bond through a simple request
 b. by reminding people of their civic duty to turn in criminals
 c. by making the thief look less threatening
 d. by providing a model of responsible behaviour

4. Which leadership style tends to produce hard work when the leader is watching but much less co-operation when the leader is absent?
 a. authoritative   c. democratic
 b. autocratic   d. laissez-faire

5. Typically, people who participated in Milgram's study
—————
 a. appeared to relish the opportunity to hurt someone else.
 b. objected but still obeyed.
 c. refused to continue and successfully stopped the experiment.
 d. came to recruit others into shocking the learner.

6. Psychologists refer to the power to create subjective realities as the power of —————
 a. social reinforcement.   c. cognitive control.
 b. prejudice.   d. the Pygmalion effect.

7. Robert Rosenthal demonstrated the Pygmalion effect in the classroom by showing that teachers behave differently toward students for whom they have high expectations in all of the following ways, except
—————
 a. by punishing them more for goofing off.
 b. by providing them with a warmer learning climate.
 c. by teaching more to them than to the other students.
 d. by providing more specific feedback when the student gives a wrong answer.

8. What happens to low-achieving students in the Jigsaw Classroom?
 a. They tend to fall further behind.
 b. They are given an opportunity to work at a lower level, thus increasing the chance of success.
 c. By becoming "experts," they improve their performance and their self-respect.
 d. By learning to compete more aggressively, they become more actively involved in their own learning.

QUESTIONS TO CONSIDER

1. How is nationalism used to structure social reality? Does this become a more powerful force for people's attitudes and interaction during times of actual war or cold war than it is during times of peace? How might it be affected by phenomena like globalized economics and common languages across borders?

2. Many of the socially undesirable aspects of human behaviour (e.g., violent crime, rudeness, apathy) seem to be more likely in urban than in suburban or rural environments. How can social psychology help to explain this phenomenon?

Answer Appendix

Stop and Review Answers

CHAPTER 1

Stop and Review (p. 6)

1. Psychology is the *scientific* study of the *behaviour* of *individuals* and their *mental* processes.
2. The four goals are to describe, explain, predict, and control behaviour.
3. Researchers regularly try to explain behaviours by identifying underlying causes; successful causal explanations often allow accurate predictions.

Stop and Review (p. 12)

1. Structuralism tries to understand mental experiences as the combination of basic components. Functionalism focuses on the purposes of behavioural acts.
2. The psychodynamic perspective focuses on powerful, instinctive forces, and the behaviourist perspective focuses on how consequences shape behaviours.
3. The humanistic perspective takes this view.
4. Researchers in cognitive neuroscience combine the cognitive and biological perspectives to understand the brain bases of mental activities such as memory and language.
5. The evolutionary perspective focuses on the features that all people share as a consequence of human evolution. The sociocultural perspective focuses on the differences brought about by cultures, against that shared evolutionary background.

Stop and Review (p. 16)

1. Research provides new insights that psychologists then try to apply in real-world settings.
2. Psychologists are most often employed in academic settings (e.g., colleges and universities) and independent practice.

Stop and Review (p. 17)

1. Being an active participant in a course means developing your own understanding of what you hear in lectures and read in the text.
2. In the *Questions* phase you invent questions that direct your attention while you are reading; in the *Read* phase you read the material with an eye to answering your questions.

3. When you attempt to recite explicit answers to questions, you obtain concrete evidence of what you do and do not know.

CHAPTER 2

Stop and Review (p. 32)

1. Theories attempt to explain phenomena. Those explanations should generate new hypotheses—testable consequences of a theory.
2. Researchers can standardize their procedures and provide operational definitions for their variables.
3. Researchers use double-blind controls so that the expectations they bring to the research setting cannot have an impact on their studies' results.
4. When an experiment has a within-subjects design, each participant serves as his or her own control.
5. A correlation coefficient indicates the extent to which two variables are related; it does not give any indication of why that relationship exists.

Stop and Review (p. 34)

1. If a measure is reliable, it means that it yields a comparable value when researchers use it repeatedly. However, that value might still not accurately reflect the psychological variable the researcher is seeking. That is why shoe size would be a reliable but not a valid measure of happiness.
2. Interviewers seek to create a context in which people are willing to provide information through self-reports that might be highly personal or sensitive.
3. The researcher is engaged in naturalistic observation of the children's behaviour.

Stop and Review (p. 37)

1. The purpose of informed consent is to make potential research participants aware of the risks and benefits of an experiment and to advise them of their rights and responsibilities before they agree to engage in the experiment.
2. During debriefing, participants have an opportunity to learn something new about the psychological phenomena that were the topic of the study. In addition, researchers can ensure that participants do not leave the study upset or confused.
3. Ethical considerations support a move toward research in naturalistic or seminaturalistic settings.

CHAPTER 3

Stop and Review (p. 55)

1. Darwin and Wallace proposed the theory of evolution.
2. The two means for selection that Darwin proposed were natural selection and sexual selection.
3. Darwin's theory of sexual selection suggested that females choose mates based on their desirable characteristics.

Stop and Review (p. 59)

1. Sir Francis Galton's contribution to the study of intelligence was that his ideas led people to focus on genes as more important than the environment.
2. Environmental determinism proposes that much of our behaviour results from how we experience our environment. Supporters of this perspective expected recognition of this and a move away from genetic determination.
3. Lorenz, Tinbergen, and von Frisch shared a Nobel prize—Lorenz for imprinting, Tinbergen for proposing a scheme for the division of behaviour by proximate and ultimate causes, and von Frisch for his research in honey bee communication.
4. People become aware of who the cheaters are and try not to be cheated multiple times.

Stop and Review (p. 62)

1. Sociobiological theories tried to explain all human behaviour, but there was little empirical evidence to support them.
2. Buss suggests that there are limits to happiness based on differences between modern and ancestral environments. We evolved in small groups, but recently we have turned to living in bigger urban centres, which include many people. These people are, however, strangers.
3. Harlow's monkeys illustrated that reinforcement from the external environment is not the only determinant of behaviour. Behaviour can also be determined by what is happening in the brain, which is not directly observable.
4. Wilson and Daly have been criticized because their data suggest a role for genes but not for environment.

Stop and Review (p. 64)

1. The *genotype* is the underlying genetic material that helps determine the *phenotype*, the outward appearance and range of behaviours that is the expression of those genes plus their interaction with the environment.
2. Our evolving intelligence depended not on brain size but on the kind of tissue that developed and expanded in the brain.

Stop and Review (p. 69)

1. The two evolutionary advances that were most critical in human evolution were bipedalism and encephalization.
2. Heritability is a measure of the relative influence of genetics in determining an organism's constellation of traits and behaviours.

Stop and Review (p. 74)

1. Though we do not have a comprehensive answer to the question of why language evolved, communication would have conferred many advantages.
2. Communication allows for major advances that produce changes quickly in response to environmental conditions.
3. Yes, gossip could have evolved as a means of sharing information and manipulating the environment.

Stop and Review (p. 75)

1. Language is described as being responsible for cultural evolution, which is the tendency of cultures to respond adaptively, through learning, to environmental change. Cultural evolution has given rise to major advances in toolmaking, agricultural practices, and the development and refinement of industry and technology. The use of language allows our species to make these rapid adjustments to changes in environmental conditions.
2. If depression was well grounded with evolutionary theory, we should see more depressives reviewing their behaviour for a better outcome.

Stop and Review (p. 76)

1. Even without learning them, some behaviours can be potentially advantageous in certain situations. For example, some snakes are poisonous, so fear of snakes could be beneficial. Fear all the time would be better than no fear.
2. Research has shown that wearing red seems to confer a psychological advantage.
3. Red pen has been shown to negatively affect students' performance.

CHAPTER 4

Stop and Review (p. 88)

1. In general, the dendrites receive incoming signals. The soma integrates information from the many dendrites and then passes that information along to the axon.
2. The all-or-none law suggests that, once the threshold for firing has been reached, the strength of an action potential is constant.
3. Neurotransmitters are released into synapses when synaptic vesicles rupture; the neurotransmitters then bind to receptor molecules on the receiving neuron.
4. GABA is the brain's most common inhibitory neurotransmitter.

Stop and Review (p. 106)

1. fMRI allows researchers to make claims about both structures and functions.
2. The autonomic nervous system is divided into the sympathetic and parasympathetic divisions.
3. The amygdala plays a role in emotional control and the formation of emotional memories.
4. For most individuals, the processing style of the left hemisphere is relatively more analytic, whereas the processing style of the right hemisphere is relatively more holistic.
5. The pituitary gland produces hormones that influence the activity of all the other endocrine glands.
6. Neurogenesis is the creation of new neurons.

CHAPTER 5

Stop and Review (p. 117)

1. The proximal stimulus is the optical image on the retina.
2. Psychophysics is the study of the relationship between physical stimuli and the psychological experience of those stimuli.
3. An absolute threshold is defined as the stimulus level at which a sensory signal is detected half the time.
4. Judgments are affected both by sensory processes and by observers' biases.

5. A difference threshold is the smallest physical difference between two stimuli that observers can recognize.
6. Transduction is the conversion of one form of physical energy into another form.

Stop and Review (p. 127)

1. Accommodation is the process by which the thickness of the lens changes so that focus is achieved on both near and far objects.
2. The fovea is 100 percent cones.
3. Complex cells respond to bars in particular orientations, but those bars must also be moving.
4. This experience is explained by opponent-process theory.

Stop and Review (p. 132)

1. You perceive sounds with different frequencies as having different pitches.
2. Hair cells transform the mechanical vibrations of the basilar membrane into nerve impulses.
3. Place theory associates pitch perception with the location of stimulation on the basilar membrane.
4. The sound should reach your right ear before it reaches your left ear.

Stop and Review (p. 138)

1. The olfactory bulb is an important brain structure: Nerve impulses convey odour information to the olfactory bulb.
2. The basic taste qualities are sweet, sour, bitter, saline, and umami.
3. You have separate types of receptors that encode information about warmth and coolness.
4. The vestibular sense provides information about how the body is oriented in space with respect to gravity.
5. Gate-control theory attempts to explain how experiences of pain are affected by psychological context.

Stop and Review (p. 148)

1. Sometimes stimulus features in the environment—like the abrupt change of a spotlight from red to green—will capture your attention.
2. People tend to fill in small gaps to experience objects as wholes.
3. When someone is walking toward you, the size of his or her image on your retina expands.
4. The angle of convergence is larger when an object is closer to you.
5. Shape constancy is your ability to perceive the true shape of an object even as the shape of the retinal image changes.

Stop and Review (p. 150)

1. The overall process of perception includes sensation, perceptual organization, and identification and recognition.
2. A stimulus is ambiguous when more than one object or event in the environment could give rise to the same proximal stimulus.

Stop and Review (p. 152)

1. People use their knowledge of sounds and words to *restore* information that is missing from the auditory signal.
2. In different contexts, you have different expectations of what you are likely to see, hear, and so on.
3. A set is a temporary readiness to perceive or react to a stimulus in a particular way.

CHAPTER 6

Stop and Review (p. 162)

1. A memory is preconscious when it is not currently part of the content of consciousness but could easily become so.
2. Freud suggested that some ideas or motives are sufficiently threatening enough that they become repressed into the unconscious.
3. Researchers ask experimental participants to report their thoughts while they carry out particular tasks.

Stop and Review (p. 164)

1. Consciousness allows you to make explicit decisions about what information you should attempt to commit to memory (storage).
2. A cultural construction of reality is a way of thinking about the world that is shared by most members of a particular group of people.
3. People generally need to use conscious attention to search for objects with a combination of features.

Stop and Review (p. 171)

1. You experience jet lag because your internal circadian rhythm is out of phase with the temporal environment.
2. Early in the night you experience relatively more NREM sleep; late in the night you experience relatively more REM sleep.
3. NREM sleep serves the functions of conservation and restoration.
4. Sleep apnea is a sleep disorder in which a person stops breathing while asleep.
5. The latent content is the underlying meaning that has been hidden by the mind's censors.

Stop and Review (p. 174)

1. The goal of lucid dreaming is for dreamers to become consciously aware that they are dreaming so they can control the content of their dreams.
2. Early twin studies suggested that hypnotizability has a genetic component; researchers have begun to identify specific genes that might underlie this tendency.
3. Some people practise concentrative meditation, whereas others practise mindfulness meditation.

Stop and Review (p. 179)

1. Drug tolerance refers to an individual's requiring greater doses of a drug to yield the same effect.
2. Drugs like heroin bind to the same receptor sites as the brain's endogenous opiates (endorphins).
3. Nicotine is an example of a stimulant.

CHAPTER 7

Stop and Review (p. 186)

1. The learning-performance distinction acknowledges that people's behaviours might not always reflect everything they have learned.
2. He argued that people's private experiences were too subjective to be studied with scientific rigour.
3. Behaviour analysts attempt to discover regularities in learning that occur in all types of animals, including humans.
4. Habituation is a decrease in an organism's behavioural response when a stimulus occurs repeatedly.

Stop and Review (p. 194)

1. Classical conditioning begins with behaviours (such as salivation) that are *reflex* responses to unconditioned stimuli (such as the presentation of food powder).
2. The UCS is the unconditioned stimulus that produces a response prior to conditioning; the CS is the conditioned stimulus that produces a response as a result of conditioning.
3. Stimulus discrimination means that the organism has learned to produce a conditioned response to a more narrow range of conditioned stimuli than would otherwise be the case.
4. It is not enough for the CS and UCS to occur close together in time (an association referred to as contiguous); the UCS must be contingent upon—be predictable from—the CS.
5. The CR is the body's compensatory response to the drug's effects.

Stop and Review (p. 204)

1. The law of effect states that a response followed by satisfying consequences becomes more probable and a response followed by dissatisfying consequences becomes less probable.
2. Reinforcement makes behaviours more likely; punishment makes behaviours less likely.
3. Animals learn that behaviours will have consequences (reinforcement or punishment) only in the context of particular stimuli—those stimuli are the discriminative stimuli.
4. In FR schedules, a reinforcer is delivered each time the organism has made a fixed number of responses. In FI schedules, a reinforcer is delivered when the organism makes the first response after a fixed amount of time.
5. Shaping is a method that allows an organism to learn a behaviour through successive approximations.

Stop and Review (p. 207)

1. Instinctual drift is the tendency, over time, for learned behaviours to drift toward instinctual behaviours.
2. Taste aversion will develop with only one pairing of the CS and UCS and with a long lag between the CS and UCS. It will often be permanent after one experience.

Stop and Review (p. 211)

1. Tolman concluded that his rats developed cognitive maps for the layouts in the mazes.
2. Pigeons can look at photographs of objects and make different responses to categorize them as, for example, "flowers" and "natural stimuli."
3. Clark's nutcrackers were able to use the geometry of an array of food containers to more easily find food.
4. Vicarious reinforcement occurs when an individual's behaviour becomes more probable after he or she observes other people's behaviours being reinforced.
5. Research suggests that children who observe a large number of aggressive acts may learn to be aggressive themselves.

CHAPTER 8

Stop and Review (p. 220)

1. Explicit uses of memory involve conscious effort, whereas implicit uses of memory do not.
2. Your skill relies more on procedural memory.
3. Because you have previously encoded and stored your password, your problem is most likely with retrieval.

Stop and Review (p. 225)

1. Comparisons of the whole- and partial-report procedures indicate that a person's iconic memory has the capacity to give him or her brief access to all the information in a display.
2. Researchers believe that the capacity of STM is in the range of three to five items.
3. Chunking is the process of reconfiguring items into meaningful groups.
4. Working memory includes the phonological loop, the visuospatial sketchpad, and the central executive.

Stop and Review (p. 236)

1. Recognition generally provides more retrieval cues.
2. This would be an example of the primacy effect in serial recall.
3. Transfer-appropriate processing suggests that memory is best when the type of processing carried out at encoding matches the type of processing carried out at retrieval.
4. These circumstances provide an example of retroactive interference because new information has made it harder to remember older information.
5. Beginning with hydrogen, you would associate each element with a position along a familiar route.
6. The familiarity of the retrieval cue and the accessibility of information related to the cue both contribute to feelings-of-knowing.

Stop and Review (p. 243)

1. Concepts are the mental representations you form of categories.
2. The exemplar theory claims that people categorize new objects by comparing them to the exemplars they have stored in memory.
3. Bartlett identified the processes of levelling, sharpening, and assimilating.
4. Loftus and her colleagues demonstrated that people will include incorrect post-event information when they attempt to remember events.

Stop and Review (p. 247)

1. Lashley concluded that the engram did not exist in any localized regions but was widely distributed throughout the brain.
2. Research suggests that important aspects of implicit memory will often be spared in individuals who have amnesia for explicit memories.
3. PET scans reveal that different areas of the brain are disproportionately active for encoding and retrieval—left prefrontal cortex for encoding and right prefrontal cortex for retrieval.

CHAPTER 9

Stop and Review (p. 257)

1. Donders's goal was to determine the speed of mental processes by inventing tasks that differed only by specific processes.
2. Serial processes take place one after the other; parallel processes overlap in time.
3. Automatic processes do not generally require attentional resources.

Stop and Review (p. 267)

1. The co-operative principle is the overarching rule of audience design: It specifies some of the dimensions speakers should consider to design an utterance for a particular listener.

2. Spoonerisms are more likely when the sound exchange yields real words.
3. When representations include more information than the propositions provided by a text, you can conclude that people have encoded inferences.
4. Humans can produce and understand utterances with complex grammatical structures; humans can engage in audience design.
5. Linguistic relativity is the idea that the structure of the language people speak has an impact on the way in which they think about the world.

Stop and Review (p. 270)

1. The consistency of the rate of mental rotation suggests that the processes of mental rotation are very similar to those of physical rotation.
2. Brain-imaging research suggests a large amount of overlap between the brain regions that people use for perception and the regions people use when they create visual images.
3. Research suggests that you find it easier to describe what is in front of you, rather than behind you, in the mental scene.

Stop and Review (p. 278)

1. An algorithm is a step-by-step procedure that guarantees a correct answer for a particular type of problem.
2. You have overcome functional fixedness if you have been able to find a new function for an object that you previously associated with a different purpose.
3. When people succumb to the belief-bias effect, they have judged conclusions based on their real-world believability rather than on their logical relationship to premises.
4. People often engage in inductive reasoning by forming analogies between the features of current circumstances and past experiences in memory.

Stop and Review (p. 286)

1. Heuristics provide people with the shortcuts that allow them to make frequent and rapid judgments.
2. It is likely that you would use the anchoring heuristic—by starting at a plausible anchor (e.g., 100 years old) and adjusting from there.
3. Frames play a large role because they determine, for example, whether people think about the gains or the losses associated with particular circumstances.
4. When making a decision, satisficers often choose the first option that is good enough; maximizers keep evaluating options, trying to find the absolute best one.

CHAPTER 10

Stop and Review (p. 294)

1. To assess split-half reliability, researchers divide a test into two halves. A test with high split-half reliability yields highly similar scores on the two halves.
2. The researcher should determine whether scores on the measure allow for accurate predictions of relevant future outcomes.
3. Norms enable researchers to understand the scores of particular individuals in the context of a broader population's scores.

Stop and Review (p. 299)

1. The original measure of IQ was mental age divided by chronological age.
2. The WAIS currently has subtests that measure verbal IQ and performance IQ.

3. Diagnosis of mental retardation now focuses on both IQ and adaptive skills.
4. The three dimensions are ability, creativity, and task commitment.

Stop and Review (p. 303)

1. Spearman demonstrated that people's performance on a variety of intelligence tests was highly correlated, so he concluded that there was a factor of general intelligence (g).
2. Sternberg's triarchic theory is that people have analytical, creative, and practical intelligence.
3. Gardner defined "spatial" intelligence as the ability to perceive the visual–spatial world and transform one's initial perceptions—these abilities are relevant to sculpture.

Stop and Review (p. 310)

1. Goddard suggested that IQ tests be used to exclude some immigrants as mentally inferior.
2. Heritability estimates do not allow for comparisons between groups of individuals, only within.
3. Research has demonstrated that people who experience quality preschool programs have higher measured IQs and are more likely to graduate from regular high schools and have better paying jobs.
4. People in the United States were more likely to believe that innate ability matters more than hard work; for people in Asia, the beliefs were reversed.

Stop and Review (p. 313)

1. Creativity is often measured by tests that look at divergent thinking—the ability to generate a variety of unusual solutions to a problem.
2. Students with higher IQ have shown greater divergent thinking, which is one measure of creativity. A certain level of intelligence gives a person the opportunity to be creative, but the person may not avail himself or herself of that opportunity.
3. Research suggests that individuals who are exceptionally creative are risk takers, have preparation in their domains, and have intrinsic motivation.

Stop and Review (p. 314)

1. If members of particular groups generally test less well than others, that pattern might prevent equal access to jobs.
2. In many school districts, support is based on test scores—forcing teachers to cover only material that will be tested.
3. When tests are used without flexibility to label people as belonging to certain academic or social tracks, those labels can have broad consequences for an individual's opportunities for development and change.

CHAPTER 11

Stop and Review (p. 322)

1. Developmental age is the chronological age at which most people are able to achieve a particular physical or mental accomplishment.
2. To study individual differences, researchers often measure variation (on some dimension) among people at one age and then re-examine the same participants later in life to examine the consequences of that variation.
3. For some cross-sectional analyses, researchers have to rule out the possibility that what appear to be age-related changes are really differences brought about by the time period in which individuals were born.

Stop and Review (p. 328)

1. Compared to their noncrawling peers, children who have begun to crawl experience fear on the deep end of the visual cliff.
2. Recent studies indicate that the brain continues to mature during adolescence, particularly in areas such as the frontal lobes.
3. As people age, the lenses in their eyes often become yellowed, which is thought to be responsible for diminished colour vision.

Stop and Review (p. 336)

1. Assimilation allows children to fit new information to old schemes; accommodation changes schemes to fit new information.
2. A child who can overcome centration is able to ignore surface aspects of a problem to show deeper understanding of a domain such as number or liquid quantity.
3. By inventing more subtle measures of infants' knowledge, researchers have been able to demonstrate that children show evidence of object permanence by age four months.
4. Vygotsky emphasized the importance of the social context in the way that children's cognitive development unfolds.
5. This approach to successful aging suggests that people should select domains in which they wish to continue to perform at optimal levels by, as necessary, developing strategies that allow them to compensate for losses.

Stop and Review (p. 340)

1. Child-directed speech helps maintain the child's attention as well as helping to forge an emotional bond between the adult and the child.
2. Children form hypotheses for the meanings of new words. On some occasions, their hypotheses are broader than the adult category.
3. Deaf children who have not been exposed to either a spoken language or a formal signed language will sometimes begin to use their own signed languages that share structural features with real languages.
4. If a child is over-regularizing English past-tense constructions, you would expect to hear him or her say words like *doed* and *breaked* rather than *did* and *broke*.

Stop and Review (p. 350)

1. Erikson suggested that the crisis of intimacy versus isolation comes into focus during early adulthood.
2. Research suggests that children who have secure attachments at early ages are, for example, more popular and less socially anxious later in life.
3. Parenting styles are defined by the dimensions of the parent's demandingness and the parent's responsiveness.
4. Adolescents experience peer relationships at the levels of friendships, cliques, and crowds.
5. Research on late adulthood suggests that individuals become more selective in the social partners they choose to satisfy their emotional needs.

Stop and Review (p. 353)

1. Sex differences emerge from biological differences between men and women; gender differences emerge from cultural constructions of different roles for men and women.
2. Research suggests that men and women use somewhat different brain structures to encode and recognize emotional stimuli.
3. Young children prefer the company of peers of the same sex.

Stop and Review (p. 355)

1. The three major levels are preconventional morality, conventional morality, and principled morality.
2. Gilligan argued that men are more focused on justice, whereas women are more focused on caring for others.
3. In general, people in India are more likely to think of interpersonal responsibility as relevant to moral judgments than are people in the United States.

CHAPTER 12

Stop and Review (p. 366)

1. You would probably draw some inference about why the student was running, which relates to the idea that motivational concepts can be links between public acts and private states.
2. Homeostasis is a state of equilibrium with respect to biological states.
3. Research demonstrated a good deal of variability in behaviour between cultures, thereby providing an argument against biological instincts.
4. Heider made a distinction between dispositional and situational forces as explanations for outcomes.
5. Attachment needs relate to people's needs to belong, to affiliate with others, to love, and to be loved.

Stop and Review (p. 372)

1. Sensory-specific satiety refers to circumstances in which an individual has become satiated with respect to a particular flavour of food.
2. The dual-centre model suggested that the VMH was the "satiety centre." However, more recent research suggests that the role of the VMH depends on the type of food.
3. Restrained eaters habitually maintain a low-calorie diet until they become disinhibited, at which point they often will indulge in high-calorie binges.
4. Bulimia nervosa is characterized by the behaviours of bingeing and purging.

Stop and Review (p. 381)

1. In most nonhuman species, all members of the species follow the same predictable pattern of sexual behaviour.
2. Masters and Johnson identified the phases of excitement, plateau, orgasm, and resolution.
3. Men seek more sexual partners because men can impregnate several women in the same period of time, but women can have only one pregnancy at a time.
4. Sexual scripts are socially learned programs of sexual responsiveness that define appropriate forms of sexual activity (e.g., what to do; when, where, and how to do it; with whom or with what to do it; and why it should be done).
5. Concordance rates are higher for MZ twins than for DZ twins, supporting the claim that homosexuality has a genetic component.

Stop and Review (p. 386)

1. *Need for achievement* reflects individual differences in the value people place on planning and working toward goals.
2. People make attributions along the dimensions of internal versus external, global versus specific, and stable versus unstable.
3. Expectancy theory proposes that workers are motivated when they expect their effort and performance will yield desirable outcomes.

CHAPTER 13

Stop and Review (p. 400)

1. Cross-cultural research suggests there are seven facial expressions that people generally recognize around the world.
2. The autonomic nervous system plays an important role in bringing about the physiological aspects of emotions—such as a racing heart and sweaty palms.
3. The Cannon–Bard theory suggests that an emotion stimulus produces concurrently arousal and an emotional feeling.
4. People in negative moods tend to process information in a more detailed and effortful fashion than people in positive moods.
5. Research suggests that good social relationships are the single most important source of happiness.

Stop and Review (p. 414)

1. The three stages of the GAS are the alarm reaction, resistance, and exhaustion.
2. Participants in the 1990s reported more life-change units, suggesting that they were generally experiencing more stress than people in the 1960s.
3. In general, daily hassles have a negative impact on well-being, and daily pleasures have a positive impact.
4. When people engage in emotion-focused coping, they engage in activities that make them feel better but do not directly change the stressor.
5. When people do not believe they have control over a stressful situation, they are at risk for poor physical and psychological adjustment.
6. People are able to identify positive changes that arise from negative life events.

Stop and Review (p. 423)

1. Research comparing MZ and DZ twins for the similarity of their tobacco use indicates that there is a genetic component to people's smoking behaviours.
2. Successful AIDS interventions must provide information, instill motivation, and teach behavioural skills.
3. To produce the relation response, people must find a quiet environment in which they can rest in a comfortable position with their eyes closed and use a repetitive mental device.
4. Researchers who study psychoneuroimmunology seek to understand how psychological states have an impact on the immune system.
5. The aspect of Type A personality that puts people at risk for illness is hostility.
6. Job burnout is a state of emotional exhaustion, depersonalization, and reduced sense of personal accomplishment.

CHAPTER 14

Stop and Review (p. 436)

1. Personality types are defined as all-or-none categories.
2. Neuroticism is defined as a dimension from stable, calm, and contented versus anxious, unstable, and temperamental.
3. To assess the heritability of traits, researchers have conducted studies that compare the trait similarity of monozygotic and dizygotic twins.
4. The consistency paradox refers to the finding that people often give consistent personality descriptions for individuals even though the individuals' behaviour is not consistent across situations.

Stop and Review (p. 442)

1. The individual might engage in oral behaviours such as smoking or overeating; the individual might be overly passive or gullible.
2. The ego is guided by the reality principle to put reasonable choices before the id's demands for pleasure.
3. Leon might be using the defence mechanism of projection—he projects his own motives onto other people.
4. Adler suggested that people are driven to overcome feelings of inferiority.

Stop and Review (p. 443)

1. Self-actualization is a person's constant striving to reach his or her inherent potential.
2. Humanistic theories focus on people's innate qualities that influence their behaviours.
3. A psychobiography uses psychological theories to give a coherent account of the way in which an individual's life unfolds.

Stop and Review (p. 449)

1. People who have an external locus-of-control orientation believe that rewards are largely contingent on environmental factors.
2. Mischel's theory focuses on encodings, expectancies and beliefs, affects, goals and values, and competencies and self-regulatory plans.
3. According to Bandura, the individual's characteristics, the individual's behaviour, and the environment all interact to influence and modify the other components.
4. Social intelligence refers to the expertise people bring to their experiences of life tasks.

Stop and Review (p. 453)

1. Possible selves motivate behaviour by prompting people to consider what behaviours are consistent with the "self" they wish to achieve or wish to avoid.
2. Self-handicapping applies to circumstances in which people engage in behaviours that allow them to attribute their failures to causes besides lack of ability.
3. People who have interdependent construals of self experience themselves as one element of a larger social structure.

Stop and Review (p. 453)

1. Some theories explain individual differences by focusing on each person's genetic endowment, whereas other theories make reference to the life experiences that have shaped individual personalities.
2. Freud's theory stresses the way in which events in early childhood—the past—affect an adult's personality.
3. The relevant dimension of personality theories is consciousness versus unconsciousness.

Stop and Review (p. 457)

1. Each of the MMPI's 10 clinical scales is intended to differentiate people who have a specific clinical disorder from those who do not.
2. The NEO-PI measures the five personality traits defined by the five-factor model of personality.
3. Clinicians assess Rorschach responses for location, content, and determinants.

CHAPTER 15

Stop and Review (p. 469)

1. The most relevant criteria appear to be "distress or disability" (i.e., Jerry's fear causes him personal distress) and "maladaptiveness" (i.e., Jerry's fear prevents him from easily pursuing his goals).
2. Classification can provide a common shorthand language, an understanding of causality, and a treatment plan.
3. Behaviours are interpreted in different ways in different cultures—the same behaviours may seem "normal" or "abnormal" in different cultural contexts.

Stop and Review (p. 474)

1. People who suffer from phobias experience irrational fears in situations that are not objectively dangerous.
2. Obsessions are thoughts, whereas compulsions are acts.
3. Research suggests that the evolutionary history of the human species leaves people "prepared" to experience phobias with respect to certain stimuli.
4. People who are high on anxiety sensitivity are more likely to believe that bodily symptoms will have harmful consequences.

Stop and Review (p. 480)

1. Bipolar disorder is characterized by periods of severe depression alternating with manic episodes.
2. The cognitive triad refers to negative views that people have of themselves, negative views of ongoing experiences, and negative views of the future.
3. Research suggests that women are more likely than men to ruminate on their problems, which has the result of increasing negative feelings.
4. Adolescents are at risk for suicide attempts when they feel depressed, hopeless, or isolated and have negative self-concepts.

Stop and Review (p. 483)

1. People with borderline personality disorder have an intense fear of being abandoned.
2. People with borderline personality disorder are substantially more likely to have experienced childhood sexual abuse.
3. Antisocial personality disorder is characterized by both impulsive behaviours and a disregard for safety, which creates a risk for suicide.

Stop and Review (p. 486)

1. Howard's case fits the definition of hyponchondriasis.
2. Dissociative amnesia is an inability to recall important personal experiences, caused by psychological factors in the absence of any organic dysfunction.
3. Research suggests that nearly all the individuals who develop DID have undergone some form of physical or psychological abuse.

Stop and Review (p. 491)

1. Social withdrawal and flattened emotions are negative symptoms of schizophrenia.
2. Delusions of persecution or grandeur would be symptoms of the paranoid type of schizophrenic disorder.

3. Research suggests that patients who return to families with high expressed emotion are more likely to experience relapses.

Stop and Review (p. 493)

1. ADHD is characterized by degrees of inattention and hyperactivity–impulsivity that are inconsistent with children's levels of development.
2. Many parents start to have concerns only when children fail to meet developmental norms for social interaction or language use starting in the second year.
3. Researchers have suggested that children with autistic disorder fail to develop a standard theory of mind, therefore they fail to develop an understanding that other people have different knowledge, beliefs, and intentions than they do.

Stop and Review (p. 494)

1. Negative attitudes about mental illnesses place people apart as unacceptable.
2. When people enter into treatment, they must often publicly acknowledge that they have a mental illness, creating a context for stigma.
3. Research suggests that contact with people who have mental illnesses serves to reduce stigma.

CHAPTER 16

Stop and Review (p. 502)

1. The goals of the process are to reach a diagnosis, propose a probable etiology, make a prognosis, and carry out a treatment.
2. Psychoanalysts have completed postgraduate training in the Freudian approach to therapy.
3. Research suggests that therapists with greater cultural competence achieve better therapeutic outcomes.
4. Substantial numbers of patients who are released from psychiatric institutions are readmitted after a short amount of time.

Stop and Review (p. 506)

1. Psychodynamic therapy is also known as insight therapy because a central goal is to guide a patient toward insights into the relationships between present symptoms and past conflicts.
2. Transference refers to circumstances in which a patient develops an emotional reaction toward the therapist that often represents an emotional conflict from the patient's life.
3. Klein believed that the death instinct precedes sexual awareness and leads to an innate aggressive impulse.

Stop and Review (p. 511)

1. Treatments using counterconditioning attempt to replace a maladaptive response (such as fear) with a healthy response (such as relaxation).
2. Typically, clinicians use vouchers to provide positive reinforcement for desirable behaviours (such as remaining drug free).
3. In social-learning therapy, clients usually observe models receiving positive reinforcement for desirable forms of responding.
4. In psychoanalysis, the therapist functions as a detective; in behaviour therapy, the therapist functions as a trainer.

Stop and Review (p. 513)

1. The underlying assumption of cognitive therapy is that abnormal behaviour patterns and emotional distress arise from problems in what and how people think.
2. RET suggests that irrational beliefs lead to maladaptive emotional responses.
3. A goal of cognitive behavioural therapy is to change people's behaviours; it is important that they believe they have the efficacy to perform adaptive behaviours.

Stop and Review (p. 514)

1. The goal of the human-potential movement was to enhance individuals' potential toward greater levels of performance and greater richness of experience.
2. A client-centred therapist establishes a setting with unconditional positive regard—nonjudgmental acceptance and respect for the client.
3. In Gestalt therapy, clients imagine that a feeling, person, object, or situation is occupying an empty chair; they talk to the chair's "occupant" to work through issues in their lives.

Stop and Review (p. 516)

1. Group therapy gives participants an opportunity to understand that the types of problems they have may actually be quite common.
2. The goal of couple therapy is often to help partners clarify and improve the quality of their interactions.
3. Internet self-help groups are particularly valuable for individuals with mobility issues, who might not otherwise have access to these groups.

Stop and Review (p. 521)

1. Atypical antipsychotic drugs help alleviate the symptoms of schizophrenia without causing severe problems in motor control.
2. SNRIs inhibit the reuptake of both serotonin and norepinephrine.
3. The procedure fundamentally alters personalities: People become less emotional, but they also lose their sense of self.
4. The rTMS procedure is one in which people receive repeated pulses of magnetic stimulation focused on their brains.

Stop and Review (p. 523)

1. The meta-analyses suggest that many standard treatments for depression (e.g., cognitive behavioural therapy and drug therapy) provide relief beyond a placebo treatment.
2. Even if treatments bring about relief, they are not particularly valuable if people are unwilling or unable to complete the course of treatment.
3. The goal of primary prevention is to implement programs that lower the probability that individuals will experience mental illnesses.

CHAPTER 17

Stop and Review (p. 532)

1. Kelley suggested that people assess distinctiveness, consistency, and consensus when they make attributions.
2. Students are likely to take responsibility for successes and explain away failures—this pattern might prompt them, for example, not to change their study habits when they do poorly on an exam.

3. In most classrooms, teachers have accurate information about their students' potential, which limits the possibility of self-fulfilling prophecies.

Stop and Review (p. 538)

1. Attitudes include cognitive, affective, and behavioural components.
2. The central route to persuasion is marked by high elaboration—careful thought about the persuasive material.
3. Because dissonance reduction reflects the impulse to be self-consistent, cross-cultural differences in sense of self affect the situations in which people experience dissonance.
4. When people make reductions from large to medium requests, they have done something for you. The reciprocity norm requires that you do something for them—by agreeing to their smaller request.

Stop and Review (p. 541)

1. When distributing resources, people tend to give more resources to members of their own in-groups than to members of out-groups.
2. People often interact with others in ways that do not allow them to behave in ways that disconfirm stereotypes.
3. Research suggests that contact with out-group members consistently reduces prejudice.

Stop and Review (p. 545)

1. People tend to like better those individuals who are similar to them.
2. The three dimensions that characterize love are passion, intimacy, and commitment.
3. People with secure attachment styles tend to have the most enduring romantic relationships as adults.

Stop and Review (p. 554)

1. The Stanford Prison Experiment demonstrated how quickly people take up the patterns of behaviours that are defined by social roles.
2. Groups are able to have normative influence because people want to be liked, accepted, and approved of by others.
3. Minorities are able to exert informational influence: They can have an impact because of majority group members' desire to be correct.
4. When a group's joint decision is more extreme than group members would have made on their own, it suggests that processes of group polarization have been at work.
5. Psychiatrists' predictions vastly underestimated the number of people who would continue to administer shocks up to very high levels.

Stop and Review (p. 561)

1. Researchers have used twin studies to demonstrate that MZ twins have a higher concordance for forms of antisocial and aggressive behaviour than do DZ twins.
2. When people are frustrated in pursuit of their goals, they are more likely to engage in aggression.
3. Reciprocal altruism is the idea that people perform altruistic behaviours because they expect, in return, to be the recipients of such behaviours.
4. When groups of people witness an emergency, members of the group most often assume that someone else has taken the responsibility to provide assistance.

Practice Test Answers

CHAPTER 1
1. b
2. b
3. c
4. b
5. c
6. b
7. c
8. c
9. d
10. a
11. a
12. c
13. d
14. b
15. a

CHAPTER 2
1. a
2. b
3. d
4. b
5. d
6. c
7. b
8. d
9. c
10. a
11. b
12. c

CHAPTER 3
1. c
2. b
3. d
4. d
5. a
6. b
7. c
8. b
9. d
10. a

CHAPTER 4
1. d
2. c
3. d
4. c
5. b
6. b
7. a
8. c
9. a
10. b
11. d
12. a

CHAPTER 5
1. a
2. b
3. d
4. b
5. a
6. b
7. d
8. b
9. d
10. d
11. b
12. c
13. c
14. b
15. a
16. c
17. a
18. d
19. c
20. d
21. a
22. c
23. a

CHAPTER 6
1. b
2. a
3. d
4. d
5. d
6. b
7. b
8. d
9. b
10. a
11. c
12. a
13. b
14. d
15. c
16. c
17. b
18. a

CHAPTER 7
1. d
2. b
3. a
4. b
5. c
6. d
7. b
8. a
9. c
10. d
11. b
12. d
13. c
14. d
15. c
16. b
17. b

18. c
19. a
20. a

CHAPTER 8
1. b
2. b
3. c
4. c
5. a
6. a
7. b
8. d
9. b
10. a
11. b
12. d
13. c
14. a
15. d
16. c
17. a
18. b
19. c
20. d

CHAPTER 9
1. c
2. c
3. b
4. a
5. d
6. d
7. b
8. c
9. a
10. c
11. a
12. a
13. c
14. b
15. d
16. d
17. a
18. a

CHAPTER 10
1. d
2. c
3. a
4. b
5. d
6. b
7. b
8. c
9. a
10. c
11. a
12. b
13. a

14. a
15. d
16. c
17. d
18. d
19. c
20. b

CHAPTER 11
1. c
2. b
3. c
4. a
5. d
6. c
7. b
8. a
9. d
10. a
11. d
12. c
13. b
14. d
15. b
16. d
17. a
18. b
19. b
20. a
21. a
22. c
23. d
24. b
25. c

CHAPTER 12
1. c
2. d
3. c
4. d
5. a
6. b
7. b
8. d
9. c
10. b
11. b
12. a
13. c
14. d
15. a

CHAPTER 13
1. a
2. a
3. c
4. d
5. d
6. c
7. c

8. a
9. d
10. d
11. b
12. c
13. a
14. b
15. a
16. d
17. b
18. b

CHAPTER 14

1. b
2. a
3. c
4. c
5. a
6. d
7. c

8. a
9. a
10. c
11. b
12. a
13. d
14. b
15. b

CHAPTER 15

1. d
2. a
3. a
4. d
5. b
6. c
7. d
8. b
9. c
10. b

11. a
12. d
13. d
14. a
15. c

CHAPTER 16

1. a
2. b
3. d
4. c
5. d
6. b
7. c
8. b
9. a
10. c
11. a
12. d
13. a

14. c
15. d

CHAPTER 17

1. a
2. d
3. c
4. a
5. b
6. b
7. a
8. d
9. c
10. d
11. c
12. a
13. d
14. c
15. b

Answers to Program Review Questions and Questions to Consider
(For Discovering Psychology Viewing Guide)

CHAPTER 1

Program Review

1. b, 2. c, 3. b, 4. d, 5. b, 6. b, 7. b, 8. d, 9. c, 10. a,
11. c, 12. b

Questions to Consider

1. The fundamental issues of psychology include the relationship of mind and body, the role of heredity and environment in determining personality and behaviour, the role of the conscious and unconscious in determining behaviour, the influence of individual dispositional and external social and situational forces on behaviour, the influence of early experience on later life, and the significance of individual differences and similarities.

2. Many people are not aware of the many different kinds of work that psychologists do. A popular stereotype is that of the slightly nutty Freudian-style analyst depicted in popular movies of the 1930s and 1940s. As you will learn, the treatment of mental illness is only one part of psychology. Psychologists are scientists who can also help people teach more effectively and learn more efficiently. They help people improve their physical and emotional well-being, enhance communication, find the right job, quit smoking, make decisions, improve social relations, understand child development, promote world peace, and fight poverty and prejudice.

3. Observer bias influences our choice about what is relevant and what isn't. Our values, interests, and expectations can even influence our perceptions, leading us to see things that are not there and overlook things that are.

4. Thinking (perceiving, remembering, imagining) is an accepted focus of psychological study. There have been various approaches to studying thinking behaviour. People are asked to think out loud while solving problems or to report their reactions to internal or external events. Mental processes can also be inferred from such measurable behaviours as reaction times in decision making, problem-solving strategies, speech patterns, eye movements, and changes in brain activity.

CHAPTER 2

Program Review

1. a, 2. d, 3. a, 4. d, 5. a, 6. a, 7. c, 8. d, 9. a

Questions to Consider

1. For every person who is supposedly healed, there are many more who are not. Faith healing is big business, and desperate people are purposely deceived in money-making scams. The sick not only lose money to faith healers for empty promises, but also may not follow proven medical treatments that might help them.

2. Objections to the study of mental processes (dreams, judgment perceptions) include the claim that these sometimes rely on self-reports, are too personal, and cannot be verified. Because mental events cannot be observed directly, these are difficult to study scientifically. But psychologists believe that by defining terms carefully, they can draw inferences from measurable behaviours. Personal experiences, such as sensations, emotions, and reactions to internal and external events, can be inferred from changes in heart rate, brain activity, eye movements, speech patterns, and other behaviours—all of which can be measured.

3. Some studies cannot be run without keeping participants somewhat in the dark about the purpose of the research, since knowledge of the study's goals would be likely to affect their behaviour and make it unlike the actual phenomenon being studied. The goal is always to be as respectful of participants as possible, never to deceive them if it is not necessary to the research, and always to debrief them after their participation is complete so that the deception is removed and any possible distress is dispelled. According to APA guidelines, which hold the participants' welfare as primary, any likely distress must be consented to before the study begins and a study involving deception would threaten the opportunity for truly informed consent. Psychologists acknowledge that this disallows some experiments from being conducted, but we have accepted this limitation and, when possible, we design other, more acceptable studies that address similar questions.

4. Psychology experiments depend largely on introductory college students as their participants, and there is some concern about how broadly the data gathered from this group of people can generalize to the larger population. Although basic studies on how perceptual, biological, and cognitive systems work can generally be applied to humans as a whole, other topics, like cultural values and types of knowledge, may be more specific to individual subpopulations.

CHAPTER 4

Program Review

1. c, **2.** b, **3.** a, **4.** d, **5.** b, **6.** a, **7.** c, **8.** b, **9.** d, **10.** b, **11.** d, **12.** a

Questions to Consider

1. Although we are able to determine which areas of the brain are active and may be able to argue that, for example, verbal activity is involved, there is no indication that we can come any closer to reading or controlling the precise thoughts that people experience.

2. There are several reasons why music might have such a strong effect on people. For example, people are attracted to highly structured patterns, and the tonal patterns and harmonies found in music conform to mathematical patterns that interest and stimulate us. Also, much like intonation and timing in language, music can convey emotional meaning and resolution very effectively. Still, the effects of music remain quite mysterious to us.

3. With an all-or-none response, you have a physical means for detecting stimuli, rather than forcing some higher function to decide whether a neuron has fired with a great enough strength for something to be the case (e.g., there really was a noise, I really did have a memory). You also create a system that allows for the same information to be processed, while protecting the neuron from constantly having to be in some state of firing. As for neurotransmitters, the greater number allows for greater diversity of functioning in the brain and allows for one function to be active while other, less relevant or undesired ones remain inactive.

CHAPTER 5

Program Review

1. d, **2.** c, **3.** a, **4.** c, **5.** c, **6.** c, **7.** b, **8.** d, **9.** a, **10.** a.

Questions to Consider

1. Items on the shelves have labels on them so that it's easy to group by perceptual similarity. Products belonging to the same category are typically stored within the same area of the store, allowing grouping by proximity. At the check-out stand, two different customers will typically leave a perceptible space between their clusters of purchases, allowing the clerk to group the clusters by the principle of proximity. Items moving together on a clerk's conveyor belt can be grouped together by common fate.

2. Perception of similarity, for example, in the quality of two people's voices, involves particular complexity, since it requires perception of two different things and the comparison between the two. Because of this complexity, and because the comparison process depends on what one has experienced in the past, this might vary across people. Other perceptual experiences that might differ between people are those that involve evaluation of pleasantness. One person might perceive a shrill, unpleasant shriek, while another experiences a crisp, pleasant high tone. One person might experience pressure, while another might experience an unpleasant level of pain.

CHAPTER 6

Program Review

1. c, **2.** b, **3.** b, **4.** c, **5.** b, **6.** a, **7.** a, **8.** d, **9.** d

Questions to Consider

1. Filter theory states that there are limits on early stages of perception. Other sensory information is held briefly but not processed. Although attention reduces confusion and sensory overload, it is not an all-or-nothing phenomenon. There is generally some screening of the sensory input for meaningful information and some partial analysis below a level of conscious awareness.

2. Treatment should take into account social and psychological factors, as well as chemical effects and physiological factors. Drug education programs must prepare students to evaluate the social and psychological components of drug use that lead to dependence and addiction. Some drug education programs aimed at children attempt to establish a certain mindset that counteracts peer and cultural pressures and promotes critical thinking about pro-drug messages.

CHAPTER 7

Program Review

1. b, **2.** b, **3.** c, **4.** a, **5.** c, **6.** d, **7.** c, **8.** d, **9.** c, **10.** b, **11.** d

Questions to Consider

1. You could provide positive reinforcement for keeping the school clean. For example, students could receive a sticker for every 50 pieces of litter they pick up. They could also be punished (e.g., with extra homework or reduced break periods) if they are caught littering. You might also try integrating other principles, like modelling, shaping, and ideal reinforcement schedules into your program to increase the likelihood that students' behaviour will conform to your goals.

2. Parents generally don't reward or punish their children's grammar. Instead, they model good grammar for their

children and do what they can to understand whatever utterances their children produce. So the learning of grammar does not depend on operant principles. Parents do, however, reward and punish other linguistic features, such as content (e.g., "That's right; that is a doggy") and politeness (e.g., "Did you say 'thank you?' You're such a good girl").

CHAPTER 8

Program Review

1. c, **2.** b, **3.** b, **4.** a, **5.** b, **6.** b, **7.** d, **8.** a, **9.** d, **10.** a

Questions to Consider

1. The schemas we used as children are very different from the ones we have developed as adults. And because young children are lacking in language, which normally helps us to label and organize memories, we may find that memories from our preverbal days are sparse or nonexistent. There is also evidence that early memories may be lost due to physiological maturation. Nevertheless, many memories, particularly from later childhood, are recoverable through good cues, and most people find that cues, such as family stories or photographs, can help in reconstructing memories.

2. There is substantial controversy over what "leading" questions do to memories. The way a person perceives and recalls an event depends on perceptual and cognitive biases that even the eyewitness may not be aware of. Jury members are subject to their own biases when they hear and judge testimony. Jury members need to be especially alert to leading questions that might introduce details or prompt a witness to report an event in a particular way. The more informed a jury member is about how memory works, the better he or she may be able to weigh the value of testimony.

CHAPTER 9

Program Review

1. d, **2.** b, **3.** b, **4.** c, **5.** a, **6.** d, **7.** b, **8.** a, **9.** b

Questions to Consider

1. Schemas might include types of activities and dress, level of education, achievements, income, social status, family patterns, interests, vacation ideas, restaurant preferences, and health status.

2. Pitfalls of problem solving include the inability to define the problem, the tendency to be illogical in situations in which emotions are involved, and the reluctance to consider opposing points of view. People also depend on certain familiar approaches and strategies and often do not recognize when these are no longer useful. Cognitive bias and mental shortcuts also cause people to draw false conclusions or make bad decisions.

CHAPTER 10

Program Review

1. b, **2.** d, **3.** a, **4.** d, **5.** d, **6.** c, **7.** b, **8.** c, **9.** a, **10.** d

Questions to Consider

1. No. Environment still has an important influence on the expression of any trait or ability. This is obvious from studies of development in enriched and impoverished environments. Impoverished environments lower a person's test performance. Both heredity and environment play a role.

2. Some might say that people already tend to sort and segregate each other according to intelligence, even if judgments are based on informal, personal assessments. If IQs become public knowledge, this might have the largest effect on those at the top and bottom of the scale, leading to institutionalized forms of discrimination.

3. Intelligence tests and psychological assessments attempt to avoid personal bias and to obtain an objective measure of a person's abilities. However, the tests can be used as a shortcut in place of a more thorough and personalized evaluation. Tests are often misunderstood and misapplied. People have an inappropriate reverence for scores. Few people question the authority of a computer printout. Objections to the tests include claims that they are not objective and that they do not measure what they are intended to measure. People often use tests to focus on what is wrong with the individual instead of considering what is wrong with the system. Test scores have been used to argue for the heritability of intelligence, which has important public policy implications for immigration, education, employment, and affirmative action.

CHAPTER 11

Program Review

1. d, **2.** a, **3.** a, **4.** d, **5.** a, **6.** a, **7.** a, **8.** d, **9.** a

Questions to Consider

1. As people age, their interests and activities may need to be modified to fit their capabilities. Their interests may lead them to indoor rather than outdoor activities, and their participation in physical activity may be redirected to watching children play outside. The good news is that, regardless of one's physical limitations, there are plenty of options for occupying one's time and one's mind.

2. Whether gorillas or chimps are truly capable of language is still debated. It really depends on your definition of language. Your textbook definition may include such characteristics as specialization, arbitrariness, displacement, productivity and novelty, and iteration and recursion. Although animals do use symbols, no animal other than humans consistently and naturally organizes symbols according to specific rules. Human language seems to be unique, and humans appear to be uniquely "programmed" to acquire it. Recent research has suggested that gorillas and chimps have higher-level communicative ability, and mothers trained in signs and symbols can transfer their learning to their offspring. The debate goes on.

CHAPTER 12

Program Review

1. d, **2.** b, **3** c, **4.** c, **5.** c, **6.** a, **7.** a, **8.** d, **9.** c, **10.** d

Questions to Consider

1. An individual's sexual script is based on a unique combination of personal, social, and cultural beliefs and attitudes. Scripts are influenced by family role models, the media, and feedback from social experiences. Boys and girls are typically treated differently during development. Cultural stereotypes tend to reinforce some personal choices and not others. Sexual scripts are often not overtly expressed and may be a source of friction and disappointment in a relationship. If couples can talk about mismatched role expectations and values, they may be able to negotiate a shared script. The threat of AIDS and other sexually transmitted infections may change the norms governing sexual activity and thereby

rewrite the social scripts that guide sexual behaviour. Expect to see changes in what characterizes an acceptable mate, dating patterns, and other relationship issues.

2. Armed with this knowledge, you might couple a diet plan with stress management skills, such as meditation, time management courses, exercise, participation in a support group, and/or individual psychotherapy. You might also frame the diet plan so that the dieter doesn't feel deprived or self-restrained and is therefore less tempted by opportunities to binge.

3. People are typically motivated to approach activities or goals that increase pleasure and to avoid those that cause pain. Although food is generally thought of as something pleasurable, even as a reward or incentive, people with certain eating disorders see food as something to avoid. They modify or inhibit their eating behaviour in an attempt to achieve an idealized body shape.

CHAPTER 13

Program Review

1. c, **2.** b, **3.** d, **4.** d, **5.** a, **6.** c, **7.** b, **8.** c, **9.** a, **10.** b

Questions to Consider

1. Friends can help reduce stress in several ways. They can offer practical help. For example, when there is illness or a crisis in a family, friends can relieve temporary concerns about money, child care, food, or transportation needs. They can also offer emotional support, being there to listen and empathize with you about what you are going through and reassuring you that you are not going crazy even when you feel most vulnerable and confused. Friends may also offer advice in an unfamiliar situation, helping you think through decisions. Social support makes people less vulnerable to stress-related problems. Social networks counteract a sense of isolation by providing a sense of belonging. In support groups, individuals help each other by providing a social reference group. They share advice, feelings, and information specific to the situation.

2. Most people use defence mechanisms at times. Some defences help us gain time to adjust to a trauma or other type of problem. Rationalization may be a stress-reducing strategy in the face of frustration or failure. Any defence mechanism can be part of a coping approach, but it may prevent us from confronting and solving our real problems if it becomes habitual.

3. Although the traditional gender roles for running a household have changed over the past several years, men still typically find themselves in more stressful, powerful job situations. Such work conditions are associated with poor lifestyle habits, such as caffeine, nicotine, and alcohol abuse, and with insufficient sleep and lack of exercise. Add to that a cultural tendency to foster aggression in men, and we see that such a combination puts men at risk for cardiovascular disease. Women are also at risk. In the workplace, they may find themselves in situations where they have less control than men do, making them also prone to stress-related health problems, including cardiovascular disease. And as gender roles continue to shift, women become and more vulnerable to the traditional "male" stress-related risks.

CHAPTER 14

Program Review

1. c, **2.** a, **3.** a, **4.** d, **5.** d, **6.** b, **7.** c, **8.** a, **9.** d, **10.** c

Questions to Consider

1. To the extent that standardized tests are used to categorize or place people, they pose some risk for inaccuracy and bias. What is normal or average in the larger population may differ from subculture to subculture. If members of a given subculture are compared to the larger population, they may be judged unfavourably, and this may lead to concrete consequences, such as a greater likelihood of being labelled as abnormal, or fewer job or social opportunities.

2. Your answer is probably yes, different experiences of success or failure can change your sense of efficacy and your level of self-esteem. But success and failure are relative. If a task is too easy, it doesn't help a person with low self-esteem. Also, research has suggested that self-esteem is often affected by a social referent. An extremely attractive person sitting next to you before a job interview might make you feel dissatisfied with yourself, but a dishevelled or unattractive person might make you feel better about yourself.

3. Although the internet exposes us to lots of different kinds of people from all around the world, many of the social skills used with the internet are specific to that particular medium. For people who substitute internet-based interaction with face-to-face interaction, other critical social skills may be underdeveloped or lost over time. Those people may feel isolated, awkward in social situations, and shy. This is becoming particularly important as people find that identities are easy to slip into and out of in an internet-based culture.

CHAPTER 15

Program Review

1. d, **2.** d, **3.** b, **4.** c, **5.** d, **6.** b, **7.** b, **8.** b, **9.** a, **10.** b, **11.** d, **12.** a

Questions to Consider

1. Courts differ on how they deal with the insanity defence. In order for a person to be excused from legal responsibility for criminal actions, the defence must demonstrate severely impaired judgment and lack of self-control. A person is not considered legally responsible if he or she is unable to distinguish right from wrong. The definition may vary from country to country, from state to state, and even from court to court. It is a highly controversial issue.

2. The *Diagnostic and Statistical Manual* has been criticized for inflating disorders, for basing some criteria on myth instead of empirical evidence, and for stigmatizing people. It is also, clearly, a relative assessment guide subject to cultural forces. For example, homosexuality was once characterized as a disorder. Today, the self-defeating personality has been proposed as a disorder to be included. Women's groups and others are very concerned that such a label will lead to a blaming of the victim.

3. Women may be more willing to talk about distress and emotional problems. They are more often denied opportunities for independence and achievement, and may feel angry, hopeless, or helpless, justifiably. There is a general tendency in the psychological and medical professions to bias diagnosis according to traditional concepts of mental health, which define men's more stoic tendencies as most appropriate, and women's openness as problematic.

4. Many psychological problems are just extreme instances of behaviour that most of us exhibit at one time or another. If you are worried about a certain behaviour, if the behaviour is disruptive to relationships, or if it has become a persistent problem, you might consider getting a professional evaluation.

CHAPTER 16

Program Review

1. c, **2.** b, **3.** d, **4.** c, **5.** d, **6.** a, **7.** c, **8.** b, **9.** a, **10.** c

Questions to Consider

1. Program 22 describes therapies that focus on illness and problem solving, as well as on those designed to address life management issues, self-esteem, relationships, and potential. Most people, at some time, could benefit from professional intervention.

2. In North American culture, there is typically a stigma associated with seeking help of any kind. Our culture emphasizes individuality, self-sufficiency, and strength, especially for men. That makes it harder to admit weakness or the need for support. While it may be difficult to change certain aspects of our culture that reduce the likelihood of seeking professional help, educational campaigns that help reduce the stigma associated with psychological problems have been shown to increase the help-seeking behaviour of those who suffer from psychological problems.

3. Although drug therapies can be enormously helpful in correcting abnormal neurochemistry, they cannot fix a marriage or magically raise someone's self-esteem. People who expect too much from drug therapies may fail to do the additional work necessary to make headway on their problems. In addition, people may come to be dependent on or addicted to their prescription drug, creating an additional problem that they will need to address.

CHAPTER 17

Program Review

1 b, **2.** c, **3.** a, **4.** b, **5.** b, **6.** c, **7.** a, **8.** c

Questions to Consider

1. Nationalism can be a source of pride and cohesiveness for a population. However, this is all too often gained at the expense of making certain classes of people into internal or external enemies. These out-groups are used to divert attention from national problems and often become a target for anger. Nationalism can encourage "us versus them" thinking and escalate conflicts. An "us versus them" mentality is simple to create. It depends only on drawing some distinction—relevant or arbitrary—between groups of people. Such opportunities for perceiving differences and exaggerating them are bigger in times of war or cold war, and, since people at war tend not to socialize with each other, negative stereotypes and negative interactions are not easily overridden by positive exchanges. However, globalization might counteract some of these forces, as borders between cultures and economies become blurred.

2. People who are made aware of their identities and responsibilities are more likely to follow cultural norms. The deindividualization and anonymity of big cities foster irresponsible and aggressive behaviour. In addition, in accordance with the principle of diffusion of responsibility, the large number of people who can intervene to help or correct a situation tends to lower the likelihood that anyone will intervene.

Glossary

Abnormal psychology The area of psychological investigation concerned with understanding the nature of individual pathologies of mind, mood, and behaviour.

Absolute threshold The minimum amount of physical energy needed to produce a reliable sensory experience; operationally defined as the stimulus level at which a sensory signal is detected half the time.

Accommodation 1. The process by which the ciliary muscles change the thickness of the lens of the eye to permit variable focusing on near and distant objects. 2. According to Piaget, the process of restructuring or modifying cognitive structures so that new information can fit into them more easily; this process works in tandem with assimilation.

Acquisition The stage in a classical conditioning experiment during which the conditioned response is first elicited by the conditioned stimulus.

Action potential The nerve impulse activated in a neuron that travels down the axon and causes neurotransmitters to be released into a synapse.

Actor–observer bias The basic difference in the way we make attributions for our own behaviours compared to the behaviours of others.

Acute stress A transient state of arousal with typically clear onset and offset patterns.

Addiction A condition in which the body requires a drug in order to function without physical and psychological reactions to its absence; often the outcome of tolerance and dependence.

Aggression Behaviours that cause psychological or physical harm to another individual.

Agoraphobia An extreme fear of being in public places or open spaces from which escape may be difficult or embarrassing.

AIDS Acronym for acquired immune deficiency syndrome, a syndrome caused by a virus that damages the immune system and weakens the body's ability to fight infection.

Algorithm A step-by-step procedure that always provides the right answer for a particular type of problem.

All-or-none law The rule that the size of the action potential is unaffected by increases in the intensity of stimulation beyond the threshold level.

Altruism Prosocial behaviours a person carries out without considering his or her own safety or interests.

Amacrine cells Cells that integrate information across the retina; rather than sending signals toward the brain, amacrine cells link bipolar cells to other bipolar cells and ganglion cells to other ganglion cells.

Ambiguity Property of perceptual object that may have more than one interpretation.

Amnesia A failure of memory caused by physical injury, disease, drug use, or psychological trauma.

Amygdala The part of the limbic system that controls emotion, aggression, and the formation of emotional memory.

Analytic psychology A branch of psychology that views the person as a constellation of compensatory internal forces in a dynamic balance.

Anchoring heuristic An insufficient adjustment up or down from an original starting value when judging the probable value of some event or outcome.

Anorexia nervosa An eating disorder in which an individual weighs less than 85 percent of her or his expected weight but still expresses intense fear of becoming fat.

Anticipatory coping Efforts made in advance of a potentially stressful event to overcome, reduce, or tolerate the imbalance between perceived demands and available resources.

Antisocial personality disorder A disorder characterized by stable patterns of irresponsible or unlawful behaviour that violates social norms.

Anxiety An intense emotional response caused by the preconscious recognition that a repressed conflict is about to emerge into consciousness.

Anxiety disorders Mental disorders marked by psychological arousal, feeling of tension, and intense apprehension without apparent reason.

Archetype A universal, inherited, primitive, and symbolic representation of a particular experience or object.

Assimilation According to Piaget, the process whereby new cognitive elements are fitted in with old elements or modified to fit more easily; this process works in tandem with accommodation.

Association cortex The parts of the cerebral cortex in which many high-level brain processes occur.

Attachment Emotional relationship between a child and the parent or regular caregiver.

Attention A state of focused awareness on a subset of the available perceptual information.

Attention-deficit hyperactivity disorder (ADHD) A disorder of childhood characterized by inattention and hyperactivity–impulsivity.

Attitude The learned, relatively stable tendency to respond to people, concepts, and events in an evaluative way.

Attributions Judgments about the causes of outcomes.

Attribution theory A social-cognitive approach to describing the ways the social perceiver uses information to generate causal explanations.

Audience design The process of shaping a message depending on the audience for which it is intended.

Auditory cortex The area of the temporal lobes that receives and processes auditory information.

Auditory nerve The nerve that carries impulses from the cochlea to the cochlear nucleus of the brain.

Autistic disorder A developmental disorder characterized by severe disruption of children's ability to form social bonds and use language.

Automatic processes Processes that do not require attention; they can often be performed along with other tasks without interference.

Autonomic nervous system (ANS) The subdivision of the peripheral nervous system that controls the body's involuntary motor responses by connecting the sensory receptors to the central nervous system (CNS) and the CNS to the smooth muscle, cardiac muscle, and glands.

Availability heuristic A judgment based on the information readily available in memory.

Aversion therapy A type of behavioural therapy used to treat individuals attracted to harmful stimuli; an attractive stimulus is paired with a noxious stimulus in order to elicit a negative reaction to the target stimulus.

Axon The extended fibre of a neuron through which nerve impulses travel from the soma to the terminal buttons.

Basic level The level of categorization that can be retrieved from memory most quickly and used most efficiently.

Basilar membrane A membrane in the cochlea that, when set into motion, stimulates hair cells that produce the neural effects of auditory stimulation.

Behaviour The actions by which an organism adjusts to its environment.

Behaviour analysis The area of psychology that focuses on the environmental determinants of learning and behaviour.

Behaviour modification The systematic use of principles of learning to increase the frequency of desired behaviours and/or decrease the frequency of problem behaviours.

Behaviour therapy See behaviour modification.

Behavioural confirmation The process by which people behave in ways that elicit from others specific expected reactions and then use those reactions to confirm their beliefs.

Behavioural data Observational reports about the behaviour of organisms and the conditions under which the behaviour occurs or changes.

Behavioural measures Overt actions and reactions that are observed and recorded, exclusive of self-reported behaviour.

Behavioural neuroscience A multidisciplinary field that attempts to understand the brain processes that underlie behaviour.

Behavioural rehearsal Procedures used to establish and strengthen basic skills; as used in social-skills training programs; requires the client to rehearse a desirable behaviour sequence mentally.

Behaviourism A scientific approach that limits the study of psychology to measurable or observable behaviour.

Behaviourist perspective The psychological perspective primarily concerned with observable behaviour that can be objectively recorded and with the relationships of observable behaviour to environmental stimuli.

Belief-bias effect A situation that occurs when a person's prior knowledge, attitudes, or values distort the reasoning process by influencing the person to accept invalid arguments.

Between-subjects design A research design in which different groups of participants are randomly assigned to experimental conditions or to control conditions.

Binge eating disorder (BED) An eating disorder characterized by out-of-control binge eating without subsequent purges.

Biofeedback A self-regulatory technique by which an individual acquires voluntary control over nonconscious biological processes.

Biological constraints on learning Any limitations on an organism's capacity to learn that are caused by the inherited sensory, response, or cognitive capabilities of members of a given species.

Biological perspective The approach to identifying causes of behaviour that focuses on the functioning of genes, the brain, the nervous system, and the endocrine system.

Biomedical therapies Treatments for psychological disorders that alter brain functioning with chemical or physical interventions such as drug therapy, surgery, or electroconvulsive therapy.

Biopsychosocial model A model of health and illness that suggests links among the nervous system, the immune system, behavioural styles, cognitive processing, and environmental domains of health.

Bipolar cells Nerve cells in the visual system that combine impulses from many receptors and transmit the results to ganglion cells.

Bipolar disorder A mood disorder characterized by alternating periods of depression and mania.

Borderline personality disorder A disorder defined by instability and intensity in personal relationships as well as turbulent emotions and impulsive behaviours.

Bottom-up processing Perceptual analyses based on the sensory data available in the environment; results of analysis are passed upward toward more abstract representations.

Brain stem The brain structure that regulates the body's basic life processes.

Brightness The dimension of colour space that captures the intensity of light.

Broca's area The region of the brain that translates thoughts into speech or signs.

Bulimia nervosa An eating disorder characterized by binge eating followed by measures to purge the body of excess calories.

Bystander intervention Willingness to assist a person in need of help.

Cannon–Bard theory of emotion A theory stating that an emotional stimulus produces two co-occurring reactions—arousal and experience of emotion—that do not cause each other.

Case study Intensive observation of a particular individual or small group of individuals.

Catharsis The process of expressing strongly felt but usually repressed emotions.

Central nervous system (CNS) The part of the nervous system consisting of the brain and spinal cord.

Centration A thought pattern common during the beginning of the preoperational stage of cognitive development; characterized by the child's inability to take more than one perceptual factor into account at the same time.

Cerebellum The region of the brain attached to the brain stem that controls motor co-ordination, posture, and balance, as well as the ability to learn control of body movements.

Cerebral cortex The outer surface of the cerebrum.

Cerebral hemispheres The two halves of the cerebrum, connected by the corpus callosum.

Cerebrum The region of the brain that regulates higher cognitive and emotional functions.

Child-directed speech A special form of speech with an exaggerated and high-pitched intonation that adults use to speak to infants and young children.

Chronic stress A continuous state of arousal in which an individual perceives demands as greater than the inner and outer resources available for dealing with them.

Chronological age The number of months or years since an individual's birth.

Chunking The process of taking single items of information and recoding them on the basis of similarity or some other organizing principle.

Circadian rhythm A consistent pattern of cyclical body activities, usually lasting 24 to 25 hours and determined by an internal biological clock.

Classical conditioning A type of learning in which a behaviour (conditioned response) comes to be elicited by a stimulus (conditioned stimulus) that has acquired its power through an association with a biologically significant stimulus (unconditioned stimulus).

Client The term used by clinicians who think of psychological disorders as problems in living, and not as mental illnesses, to describe those being treated.

Client-centred therapy A humanistic approach to treatment that emphasizes the healthy psychological growth of the individual based on the assumption that all people share the basic tendency of human nature toward self-actualization.

Clinical psychologist An individual who has earned a doctorate in psychology and whose training is in the assessment and treatment of psychological problems.

Clinical social worker A mental health professional whose specialized training prepares him or her to consider the social context of people's problems.

Cochlea The primary organ of hearing; a fluid-filled coiled tube located in the inner ear.

Cognition Processes of knowing, including attending, remembering, and reasoning; also the content of the processes, such as concepts and memories.

Cognitive appraisal theory of emotion A theory stating that the experience of emotion is the joint effect of physiological arousal and cognitive appraisal, which serves to determine how an ambiguous inner state of arousal will be labelled.

Cognitive behavioural therapy A therapeutic approach that combines the cognitive emphasis on thoughts and attitudes with the behavioural emphasis on changing performance.

Cognitive development The development of processes of knowing, including imagining, perceiving, reasoning, and problem solving.

Cognitive dissonance The theory that the tension-producing effects of incongruous cognitions motivate individuals to reduce such tension.

Cognitive map A mental representation of physical space.

Cognitive neuroscience A multidisciplinary field that attempts to understand the brain processes that underlie higher cognitive functions in humans.

Cognitive perspective The perspective on psychology that stresses human thought and the processes of knowing, such as attending, thinking, remembering, expecting, solving problems, fantasizing, and consciousness.

Cognitive processes Higher mental processes, such as perception, memory, language, problem solving, and abstract thinking.

Cognitive psychology The study of higher mental processes such as attention, language use, memory, perception, problem solving, and thinking.

Cognitive science The interdisciplinary field of study of the approach systems and processes that manipulate information.

Cognitive therapy A type of psychotherapeutic treatment that attempts to change feelings and behaviours by changing the way a client thinks about or perceives significant life experiences.

Collective unconscious The part of an individual's unconscious that is inherited, evolutionarily developed, and common to all members of the species.

Comorbidity The experience of more than one disorder at the same time.

Comparative cognition The comparative study of the mechanisms and origins of cognition in various species; researchers trace the development of cognitive capabilities across species and the continuity of capabilities from nonhuman to human animals.

Complementary colours Colours opposite each other on the colour circle; when additively mixed, they create the sensation of white light.

Compliance A change in behaviour consistent with a communication source's direct requests.

Concepts Mental representations of kinds or categories of items and ideas.

Conditioned reinforcers In classical conditioning, formerly neutral stimuli that have become reinforcers.

Conditioned response (CR) In classical conditioning, a response elicited by some previously neutral stimulus that occurs as a result of pairing the neutral stimulus with an unconditioned stimulus.

Conditioned stimulus (CS) In classical conditioning, a previously neutral stimulus that comes to elicit a conditioned response.

Cones Photoreceptors concentrated in the centre of the retina that are responsible for visual experience under normal viewing conditions for all experiences of colour.

Conformity The tendency for people to adopt the behaviours, attitudes, and values of other members of a reference group.

Confounding variable A stimulus other than the variable an experimenter explicitly introduces into a research setting that affects a participant's behaviour.

Consciousness A state of awareness of internal events and the external environment.

Conservation According to Piaget, the understanding that physical properties do not change when nothing is added or taken away, even though appearances may change.

Consistency paradox The observation that personality ratings across time and among different observers are consistent while behaviour ratings across situations are not consistent.

Construct validity The degree to which a test adequately measures an underlying construct.

Contact comfort Comfort derived from an infant's physical contact with the mother or caregiver.

Contact hypothesis The prediction that contact between groups will reduce prejudice only if the contact includes features such as co-operation toward shared goals.

Contextual distinctiveness The assumption that the serial position effect can be altered by the context and the distinctiveness of the experience being recalled.

Contingency management A general treatment strategy involving changing behaviour by modifying its consequences.

Control group A group in an experiment that is not exposed to a treatment or does not experience a manipulation of the independent variable.

Control procedures Consistent procedures for giving instructions, scoring responses, and holding all other variables constant except those being systematically varied.

Controlled processes Processes that require attention; it is often difficult to carry out more than one controlled process at a time.

Convergence The degree to which the eyes turn inward to fixate on an object.

Convergent thinking Often considered the opposite of divergent thinking; a single answer is required, generally requiring little creativity to get a correct answer, e.g., most types of multiple-choice questions in a school setting.

Conversion disorder A disorder in which psychological conflict or stress brings about loss of motor or sensory function.

Coping The process of dealing with internal or external demands that are perceived to be threatening or overwhelming.

Corpus callosum The mass of nerve fibres connecting the two hemispheres of the cerebrum.

Correlation coefficient (r) A statistic that indicates the degree of relationship between two variables.

Correlational methods Research methodologies that determine to what extent two variables, traits, or attributes are related.

Counselling psychologist Psychologist who specializes in providing guidance in areas such as vocational selections, school problems, drug abuse, and marital conflict.

Counterconditioning A technique used in therapy to substitute a new response for a maladaptive one by means of conditioning procedures.

Countertransference Circumstances in which a psychoanalyst develops personal feelings about a client because of perceived similarity of the client to significant people in the therapist's life.

Covariation principle A theory suggesting that people attribute a behaviour to a causal factor if that factor was present whenever the behaviour occurred but was absent whenever it did not occur.

Creativity The ability to generate ideas or products that are both novel and appropriate to the circumstances.

Criterion validity The degree to which test scores indicate a result on a specific measure that is consistent with some other criterion of the characteristic being assessed; also known as predictive validity.

Cross-sectional design A research method in which groups of participants of different chronological ages are observed and compared at a given time.

Crystallized intelligence The facet of intelligence involving the knowledge a person has already acquired and the ability to access that knowledge; measured by vocabulary, arithmetic, and general information tests.

Cutaneous senses The skin senses that register sensations or pressure, warmth, and cold.

Dark adaptation The gradual improvement of the eyes' sensitivity after a shift in illumination from light to near darkness.

Date rape Unwanted sexual violation by a social acquaintance in the context of a consensual dating situation.

Debriefing A procedure conducted at the end of an experiment in which the researcher provides the participant with as much information about the study as possible and makes sure that no participant leaves feeling confused, upset, or embarrassed.

Decision aversion The tendency to avoid decision making; the tougher the decision, the greater the likelihood of decision aversion.

Decision making The process of choosing between alternatives; selecting or rejecting available options.

Declarative memory Memory for information such as facts and events.

Deductive reasoning A form of thinking in which one draws a conclusion that is intended to follow logically from two or more statements or premises.

Deinstitutionalization The movement to treat people with psychological disorders in the community rather than in psychiatric hospitals.

Delusions False or irrational beliefs maintained despite clear evidence to the contrary.

Dendrites The branched fibres of neurons that receive incoming signals.

Dependent variable In an experimental setting, a variable that the researcher measures to assess the impact of a variation in an independent variable.

Descriptive statistics Statistical procedures that are used to summarize sets of scores with respect to central tendencies, variability, and correlations.

Determinism The doctrine that all events—physical, behavioural, and mental—are determined by specific causal factors that are potentially knowable.

Developmental age The chronological age at which most children show a particular level of physical or mental development.

Developmental psychology The branch of psychology concerned with interaction between physical and psychological processes and with stages of growth from conception throughout the entire life span.

Diathesis-stress hypothesis A hypothesis about the cause of certain disorders, such as schizophrenia, that suggests that genetic factors predispose an individual to a certain disorder, but that environmental stress factors must impinge in order for the potential risk to manifest itself.

Dichotic listening An experimental technique in which a different auditory stimulus is simultaneously presented to each ear.

Difference threshold The smallest physical difference between two stimuli that can still be recognized as a difference; operationally defined as the point at which the stimuli are recognized as different half of the time.

Diffusion of responsibility In emergency situations, the larger the number of bystanders, the less responsibility any one of the bystanders feels to help.

Discriminative stimuli Stimuli that act as predictors of reinforcement, signaling when particular behaviours will result in positive reinforcement.

Dissociative amnesia The inability to remember important personal experiences, caused by psychological factors in the absence of any organic dysfunction.

Dissociative disorder A personality disorder marked by a disturbance in the integration of identity, memory, or consciousness.

Dissociative fugue A disorder characterized by a flight from home or work accompanied by a loss of ability to recall the personal past.

Dissociative identity disorder (DID) A dissociative mental disorder in which two or more distinct personalities exist within the same individual; formerly known as multiple personality disorder.

Distal stimulus In the processes of perception, the physical object in the world, as contrasted with the proximal stimulus, the optical image on the retina.

Divergent thinking An aspect of creativity characterized by an ability to produce unusual but appropriate responses to problems.

DNA (deoxyribonucleic acid) The physical basis for the transmission of genetic information.

Double-blind control An experimental technique in which biased expectations of experimenters are eliminated by keeping both participants and experimental assistants unaware of which participants have received which treatment.

Dream analysis The psychoanalytic interpretation of dreams used to gain insight into a person's unconscious motives or conflicts.

Dream work In Freudian dream analysis, the process by which the internal censor transforms the latent content of a dream into manifest content.

Drives Internal states that arise in response to a disequilibrium in an animal's physiological needs.

DSM-IV-TR The current diagnostic and statistical manual of the American Psychological Association that classifies, defines, and describes mental disorders.

Echoic memory Sensory memory that allows auditory information to be stored for brief durations.

Ego The aspect of personality involved in self-preservation activities and in directing instinctual drives and urges into appropriate channels.

Ego defence mechanisms Mental strategies (conscious or unconscious) used by the ego to defend itself against conflicts experienced in the normal course of life.

Egocentrism In cognitive development, the inability of a young child at the preoperational stage to take the perspective of another person.

EI The emotional intelligence counterpart of IQ.

Elaboration likelihood model A theory of persuasion that defines how likely it is that people will focus their cognitive processes to elaborate upon a message and therefore follow the central and peripheral routes to persuasion.

Elaborative rehearsal A technique for improving memory by enriching the encoding of information.

Electroconvulsive therapy (ECT) The use of electroconvulsive shock as an effective treatment for severe depression.

Electroencephalogram (EEG) A recording of the electrical activity of the brain.

Emotion A complex pattern of changes, including physiological arousal, feelings, cognitive processes, and behavioural reactions, made in response to a situation perceived to be personally significant.

Emotional intelligence (EI) Type of intelligence defined as the abilities to perceive, appraise, and express emotions accurately and appropriately, to use emotions to facilitate thinking, to understand and analyze emotions, to use emotional knowledge effectively, and to regulate one's emotions to promote both emotional and intellectual growth.

Encoding The process by which a mental representation is formed in memory.

Encoding specificity The principle that subsequent retrieval of information is enhanced if cues received at the time of recall are consistent with those present at the time of encoding.

Endocrine system The network of glands that manufacture and secrete hormones into the bloodstream.

Engram The physical memory trace for information in the brain.

Environmental determinism A theory that the environment, and not genes, contributes to the behaviours exhibited by an individual.

Episodic memories Long-term memories for autobiographical events and the contexts in which they occurred.

Equity theory A cognitive theory of work motivation that proposes that workers are motivated to maintain fair and equitable relationships with other relevant persons; also, a model that postulates that equitable relationships are those in which the participants' outcomes are proportional to their inputs.

Estrogen The female sex hormone, produced by the ovaries, that is responsible for the release of eggs from the ovaries as well as for the development and maintenance of female reproductive structures and secondary sex characteristics.

Ethology The scientific study of animals, often in their natural environment, to understand a behavioural process.

Etiology The causes of, or factors related to, the development of a disorder.

Evolutionary perspective The approach to psychology that stresses the importance of behavioural and mental adaptiveness, based on the assumption that mental capabilities evolved over millions of years to serve particular adaptive purposes.

Evolutionary psychology The study of behaviour and mind using the principles of evolutionary theory.

Excitatory inputs Information entering a neuron that signals it to fire.

Exemplars Members of categories that people have encountered.

Expectancy The extent to which people believe that their behaviours in particular situations will bring about rewards.

Expectancy effects Results that occur when a researcher or observer subtly communicates to participants the kind of behaviour he or she expects to find, thereby creating that expected reaction.

Expectancy theory A cognitive theory of work motivation proposing that workers are motivated when they expect their efforts and job performance to result in desired outcomes.

Experience-sampling method An experimental method that assists researchers in describing the typical contents of consciousness; participants are asked to record what they are feeling and thinking whenever signaled to do so.

Experimental group A group in an experiment that is exposed to a treatment or experiences a manipulation of the independent variable.

Experimental methods Research methodologies that involve the manipulation of independent variables in order to determine their effects on the dependent variables.

Explicit uses of memory Conscious effort to encode or recover information through memory processes.

Exposure therapy A behavioural technique in which clients are exposed to the objects or situations that cause them anxiety.

Extinction In conditioning, the weakening of a conditioned association in the absence of a reinforcer or unconditioned stimulus.

Face validity The degree to which test items appear to be directly related to the attribute the researcher wishes to measure.

Fear A rational reaction to an objectively identified external danger that may induce a person to flee or attack in self-defence.

Fight-or-flight response A sequence of internal activities triggered when an organism is faced with a threat; prepares the body for combat and struggle or for running away to safety; recent evidence suggests that the response is characteristic only of males.

Figure Objectlike regions of the visual field that are distinguished from the background.

Five-factor model A comprehensive descriptive personality system that maps out the relationships among common traits, theoretical concepts, and personality scales; informally called the Big Five.

Fixation A state in which a person remains attached to objects or activities more appropriate for an earlier stage of psychosexual development.

Fixed-interval (FI) schedule A schedule of reinforcement in which a reinforcer is delivered for the first response made after a fixed period of time.

Fixed-ratio (FR) schedule A schedule of reinforcement in which a reinforcer is delivered for the first response made after a fixed number of responses.

Flashbulb memory People's vivid and richly detailed memory in response to personal or public events that have great emotional significance.

Fluid intelligence The aspect of intelligence that involves the ability to see complex relationships and solve problems.

Formal assessment The systematic procedures and measurement instruments used by trained professionals to assess an individual's functioning, aptitudes, abilities, or mental states.

Foundational theories Frameworks for initial understanding formulated by children to explain their experiences of the world.

Fovea Area of the retina that contains densely packed cones and forms the point of sharpest vision.

Frame A particular description of a choice; the perspective from which a choice is described or framed affects how a decision is made and which option is ultimately exercised.

Free association The therapeutic method in which a patient gives a running account of thoughts, wishes, physical sensations, and mental images as they occur.

Frequency distribution A summary of how frequently each score appears in a set of observations.

Frequency theory The theory that a tone produces a rate of vibration in the basilar membrane equal to its frequency, with the result that pitch can be coded by the frequency of the neural response.

Frontal lobe Region of the brain located above the lateral fissure and in front of the central sulcus; involved in motor control and cognitive activities.

Frustration–aggression hypothesis According to this hypothesis, frustration occurs in situations in which people are prevented or blocked from attaining their goals; a rise in frustration then leads to a greater probability of aggression.

Functional fixedness An inability to perceive a new use for an object previously associated with some other purpose; adversely affects problem solving and creativity.

Functional MRI (fMRI) A brain-imaging technique that combines benefits of both MRI and PET scans by detecting magnetic changes in the flow of blood to cells in the brain.

Functionalism The perspective on mind and behaviour that focuses on the examination of their functions in an organism's interactions with the environment.

Fundamental attribution error (FAE) The dual tendency of observers to underestimate the impact of situational factors and to overestimate the influence of dispositional factors on a person's behaviour.

g According to Spearman, the factor of general intelligence underlying all intelligent performance.

Ganglion cells Cells in the visual system that integrate impulses from many bipolar cells in a single firing rate.

Gate-control theory A theory about pain modulation that proposes that certain cells in the spinal cord act as gates to interrupt and block some pain signals while sending others to the brain.

Gender A psychological phenomenon that refers to learned sex-related behaviours and attitudes of males and females.

Gender identity One's sense of maleness or femaleness; usually includes awareness and acceptance of one's biological sex.

Gender roles Sets of behaviours and attitudes associated by society as being male or female and expressed publicly by the individual.

General adaptation syndrome (GAS) The pattern of nonspecific adaptational physiological mechanisms that occurs in response to continuing threat by almost any serious stressor.

Generalized anxiety disorder An anxiety disorder in which an individual feels anxious and worried most of the time for at least six months when not threatened by any specific danger or object.

Generativity A commitment beyond one's self and one's partner to family, work, society, and future generations; typically, a crucial state in development in one's 30s and 40s.

Genes The biological units of heredity; discrete sections of chromosomes responsible for transmission of traits.

Genetic determinism A theory that genes, and not the environment, contribute to the behaviours exhibited by an individual.

Genetics The study of the inheritance of physical and psychological traits from ancestors.

Genocide The systematic destruction of one group of people, often an ethnic or racial group, by another.

Genome The genetic information for an organism, stored in the DNA of its chromosomes.

Genotype The genetic structure an organism inherits from its parents.

Gestalt psychology A school of psychology that maintains that psychological phenomena can be understood only when viewed as organized, structured wholes, not when broken down into primitive perceptual elements.

Gestalt therapy Therapy that focuses on ways to unite mind and body to make a person whole.

Glia The cells that hold neurons together and facilitate neural transmission, remove damaged and dead neurons, and prevent poisonous substances in the blood from reaching the brain.

Goal-directed selection A determinant of why people select some parts of sensory input for further processing; reflects the choices made as a function of one's own goals.

Ground The backdrop or background areas of the visual field, against which figures stand out.

Group polarization The tendency for groups to make decisions that are more extreme than the decisions that would be made by the members acting alone.

Groupthink The tendency of a decision-making group to filter out undesirable input so that a consensus may be reached, especially if it is in line with the leader's viewpoint.

Habituation A decrease in a behavioural response when a stimulus is presented repeatedly.

Hallucinations False perceptions that occur in the absence of objective stimulation.

Health A general condition of soundness and vigour of body and mind; not simply the absence of illness or injury.

Health promotion The development and implementation of general strategies and specific tactics to eliminate or reduce the risk that people will become ill.

Health psychology The field of psychology devoted to understanding the ways people stay healthy, the reasons they become ill, and the ways they respond when they become ill.

Heredity The biological transmission of traits from parents to offspring.

Heritability The relative influence of genetics—versus environment—in determining patterns of behaviour.

Heritability estimate A statistical estimate of the degree of inheritance of a given trait or behaviour, assessed by the degree of similarity between individuals who vary in their extent of genetic similarity.

Heuristics Cognitive strategies, or "rules of thumb," often used as shortcuts in solving a complex inferential task.

Hierarchy of needs Maslow's view that basic human motives form a hierarchy and that the needs at each level of the hierarchy must be satisfied before the next level can be achieved; these needs progress from basic biological needs to the need for self-actualization.

Hippocampus The part of the limbic system involved in the acquisition of explicit memory.

HIV Human immunodeficiency virus, a virus that attacks white blood cells (T lymphocytes) in human blood, thereby weakening the functioning of the immune system; HIV causes AIDS.

Homeostasis Constancy or equilibrium of the internal conditions of the body.

Horizontal cells The cells that integrate information across the retina; rather than sending signals toward the brain, horizontal cells connect receptors to each other.

Hormones The chemical messengers, manufactured and secreted by the endocrine glands, that regulate metabolism and influence body growth, mood, and sexual characteristics.

Hozho A Navajo concept referring to harmony, peace of mind, goodness, ideal family relationships, beauty in arts and crafts, and health of body and spirit.

Hue The dimension of colour space that captures the qualitative experience of the colour of light.

Human behaviour genetics The area of study that evaluates the genetic component of individual differences in behaviours and traits.

Human-potential movement The therapy movement that encompasses all those practices and methods that release the potential of the average human being for greater levels of performance and greater richness of experience.

Humanistic perspective A psychological model that emphasizes an individual's phenomenal world and inherent capacity for making rational choices and developing to maximum potential.

Hypnosis An altered state of awareness characterized by deep relaxation, susceptibility to suggestions, and changes in perception, memory, motivation, and self-control.

Hypnotizability The degree to which an individual is responsive to standardized hypnotic suggestion.

Hypochondriasis A disorder in which individuals are preoccupied with having or getting physical ailments despite reassurances that they are healthy.

Hypothalamus The brain structure that regulates motivated behaviour (such as eating and drinking) and homeostasis.

Hypothesis A tentative and testable explanation of the relationship between two (or more) events or variables; often stated as a prediction that a certain outcome will result from specific conditions.

Iconic memory Memory system in the visual domain that allows large amounts of information to be stored for very brief durations.

Id The primitive, unconscious part of the personality that acts on impulse without considering society's values, standards, and morals; governed by the pleasure principle.

Identification and recognition Two ways of attaching meaning to percepts.

Illusion An experience of a stimulus pattern in a manner that is demonstrably incorrect but shared by others in the same perceptual environment.

Implicit uses of memory Availability of information through memory processes without conscious effort to encode or recover information.

Imprinting A primitive form of learning in which some infant animals physically follow and form an attachment to the first moving object they see and/or hear.

Impulsive aggression Emotion-driven aggression produced in reaction to situations.

Incentives External stimuli or rewards that motivate behaviour although they do not relate directly to biological needs.

Inclusive fitness The sum of the overall direct and indirect fitness effects of an individual's behaviours.

Independent construals of self Conceptualization of the self as an individual whose behaviour is organized primarily by reference to one's own thoughts, feelings, and actions, rather than by reference to the thoughts, feelings, and actions of others.

Independent variable In an experimental setting, a variable that the researcher manipulates with the expectation of having an impact on the value of the dependent variable.

Inductive reasoning A form of reasoning in which a conclusion is made about the probability of some state of affairs, based on the available evidence and past experience.

Inferences Missing information filled in on the basis of a sample of evidence or on the basis of prior beliefs and theories.

Inferential statistics Statistical procedures that allow researchers to determine whether the results they obtain support their hypotheses or can be attributed just to chance variation.

Informational influence Group effects that arise from individuals' desire to be correct and to understand how best to act in a given situation.

In-group bias An evaluation of one's own group as better than others.

In-groups The groups with which people identify as members.

Inhibitory inputs Information entering a neuron that signals it not to fire.

Insanity The legal (not clinical) designation for the state of an individual judged to be legally irresponsible or incompetent.

Insight therapy A technique by which the therapist guides a patient toward discovering insights between present symptoms and past origins.

Insomnia The chronic inability to sleep normally; symptoms include difficulty in falling asleep, frequent waking, inability to return to sleep, and early-morning awakening.

Instincts Preprogrammed tendencies that are essential to a species's survival.

Instinctual drift The tendency for learned behaviour to drift toward instinctual behaviour over time.

Instrumental aggression Cognition-based and goal-directed aggression carried out with premeditated thought, to achieve specific aims.

Intelligence The global capacity to profit from experience and to go beyond given information about the environment.

Intelligence quotient (IQ) An index derived from standardized tests of intelligence; originally obtained by dividing an individual's mental age by chronological age and then multiplying by 100; now directly computed as an IQ test score.

Interdependent construals of self Conceptualization of the self as part of an encompassing social relationship; recognizing that one's behaviour is determined, contingent on, and, to a large extent, organized by what one perceives to be the thoughts, feelings, and actions of others.

Internal consistency A measure of reliability; the degree to which a test yields similar scores across its different parts, such as odd versus even items.

Internalization According to Vygotsky, the process through which children absorb knowledge from the social context.

Interneurons Brain neurons that relay messages from sensory neurons to other interneurons or to motor neurons.

Intimacy The capacity to make a full commitment—sexual, emotional, and moral—to another person.

Introspection People's verbal reports of their own sensations, images, and feelings.

Ion channels The portions of neurons' cell membranes that selectively permit certain ions to flow in and out.

James–Lange theory of emotion A peripheral-feedback theory of emotion stating that an eliciting stimulus triggers a behavioural response that sends different sensory and motor feedback to the brain and creates the feeling of a specific emotion.

Job burnout The syndrome of emotional exhaustion, depersonalization, and reduced personal accomplishment, often experienced by workers in high-stress jobs.

Judgment The process by which people form opinions, reach conclusions, and make critical evaluations of events and people based on available material; also, the product of the mental activity.

Just noticeable difference (JND) The smallest difference between two sensations that allows them to be discriminated.

Kinesthetic sense The sense concerned with bodily position and movement of the body parts relative to one another.

Language-making capacity The innate guidelines or operating principles that children bring to the task of learning a language.

Language production What people say, sign, and write, as well as the processes they go through to produce these messages.

Latent content In Freudian dream analysis, the hidden meaning of a dream.

Law of effect A basic law of learning that states that the power of a stimulus to evoke a response is strengthened when the response is followed by a reward and weakened when it is not followed by a reward.

Learned helplessness A general pattern of nonresponding in the presence of noxious stimuli that often follows after an organism has previously experienced noncontingent, inescapable aversive stimuli.

Learning A process based on experience that results in a relatively permanent change in behaviour or behavioural potential.

Learning disorder A disorder defined by a large discrepancy between individuals' measured IQ and their actual performance.

Learning–performance distinction The difference between what has been learned and what is expressed in overt behaviour.

Lesions Injuries to or destruction of brain tissue.

Levels-of-processing theory A theory suggesting that the deeper the level at which information was processed, the more likely it is to be retained in memory.

Libido The psychic energy that drives individuals toward sensual pleasures of all types, especially sexual ones.

Life-change units (LCUs) In stress research, the measure of the stress levels of different types of change experienced during a given period.

Lightness constancy The tendency to perceive the whiteness, greyness, or blackness of objects as constant across changing levels of illuminations.

Limbic system The region of the brain that regulates emotional behaviour, basic motivational urges, and memory, as well as major physiological functions.

Longitudinal design A research design in which the same participants are observed repeatedly, sometimes over many years.

Long-term memory (LTM) Memory processes associated with the preservation of information for retrieval at any later time.

Loudness A perceptual dimension of sound influenced by the amplitude of a sound wave; sound waves in large amplitudes are generally experienced as loud and those with small amplitudes as soft.

Lucid dreaming The theory that conscious awareness of dreaming is a learnable skill that enables dreamers to control the direction and content of their dreams.

Magnetic resonance imaging (MRI) A technique for brain imaging that scans the brain using magnetic fields and radio waves.

Major depressive disorder A mood disorder characterized by intense feelings of depression over an extended time, without the manic high phase of bipolar depression.

Manic episode A component of bipolar disorder characterized by extreme elation, unbounded euphoria without sufficient reason, and grandiose thoughts or feelings about personal abilities.

Manifest content In Freudian dream analysis, the surface content of a dream, which is assumed to mask the dream's actual meaning.

Maturation The continuing influence of heredity throughout development; the age-related physical and behavioural changes characteristic of a species.

Mean The arithmetic average of a group of scores; the most commonly used measure of central tendency.

Measure of central tendency A statistic, such as a mean, median, or mode, that provides one score as representative of a set of observations.

Measures of variability A statistic, such as a range or standard deviation, that indicates how tightly the scores in a set of observations cluster together.

Median The score in a distribution above and below which lie 50 percent of the other scores; a measure of central tendency.

Meditation A form of consciousness alteration designed to enhance self-knowledge and well-being through reduced self-awareness.

Medulla The region of the brain stem that regulates breathing, waking, and heartbeat.

Memory The mental capacity to encode, store, and retrieve information.

Menarche The onset of menstruation.

Mental age In Binet's measure of intelligence, the age at which a child is performing intellectually, expressed in terms of the average age at which normal children achieve a particular score.

Mental retardation Condition in which individuals have IQ scores of 70 to 75 or below and also demonstrate limitations in their ability to bring adaptive skills to bear on life tasks.

Mental set The tendency to respond to a new problem in the manner used to respond to a previous problem.

Meta-analysis A statistical technique for evaluating hypotheses by providing a formal mechanism for detecting the general conclusions found in data from many different experiments.

Metamemory Implicit or explicit knowledge about memory abilities and effective memory strategies; cognition about memory.

Mnemonics Strategies or devices that use familiar information during the encoding of new information to enhance subsequent access to the information in memory.

Mode The score appearing most frequently in a set of observations; a measure of central tendency.

Mood disorder A mood disturbance such as severe depression or depression alternating with mania.

Morality A system of beliefs and values that ensures that individuals will keep their obligations to others in society and will behave in ways that do not interfere with the rights and interests of others.

Motivation The process of starting, directing, and maintaining physical and psychological activities; includes mechanisms involved in preferences for one activity over another and the vigour and persistence of responses.

Motor cortex The region of the cerebral cortex that controls the action of the body's voluntary muscles.

Motor neurons The neurons that carry messages away from the central nervous system (CNS) toward the muscles and glands.

Narcolepsy A sleep disorder characterized by an irresistible compulsion to sleep during the daytime.

Natural selection Darwin's theory that favourable adaptations to features of the environment allow some members of a species to reproduce more successfully than others.

Need for achievement (*n Ach*) An assumed basic human need to strive for achievement of goals that motivates a wide range of behaviour and thinking.

Negative punishment A behaviour is followed by the removal of an appetitive stimulus, decreasing the probability of that behaviour.

Negative reinforcement A behaviour is followed by the removal of an aversive stimulus, increasing the probability of that behaviour.

Neurogenesis The creation of new neurons.

Neuromodulator Any substance that modifies or modulates the activities of the postsynaptic neuron.

Neuron A cell in the nervous system specialized to receive, process, and/or transmit information from or to other cells.

Neuroscience The scientific study of the brain and of the links between brain activity and behaviour.

Neurotic disorders Mental disorders in which a person does not have signs of brain abnormalities and does not display grossly irrational thinking or violate basic norms but does experience subjective distress; a category dropped from *DSM-III*.

Neurotransmitters The chemical messengers released from neurons that cross the synapse from one neuron to another, stimulating the postsynaptic neuron.

Nonconscious Not typically available to consciousness or memory.

Non-REM (NREM) sleep The period during which a sleeper does not show rapid eye movement (REM); characterized by less dream activity than during REM sleep.

Norm crystallization The convergence of the expectations of a group of individuals into a common perspective as they talk and carry out activities together.

Normal curve The symmetrical curve that represents the distribution of scores on many psychological attributes; allows researchers to make judgments of how unusual an observation or result is.

Normative influence Group effects that arise from individuals' desire to be liked, accepted, and approved of by others.

Normative investigations Research efforts designed to describe what is characteristic of a specific age or developmental stage.

Norms Standards based on measurements of a large group of people; used for comparing the scores of an individual with those of others within a well-defined group.

Object permanence The recognition that objects exist independently of an individual's action or awareness; an important cognitive acquisition in infancy.

Observational learning The process of learning new responses by watching the behaviour of another.

Observer bias The distortion of evidence because of the personal motives and expectations of the viewer.

Obsessive-compulsive disorder (OCD) A mental disorder characterized by obsessions—recurrent thoughts, images, or impulses that recur or persist despite efforts to suppress them—and compulsions—repetitive, purposeful acts performed according to certain rules or in a ritualized manner.

Occipital lobe Rearmost region of the brain; contains primary visual cortex.

Olfactory bulb The centre where odour-sensitive receptors send their signals, located just below the frontal lobes of the cortex.

Operant Behaviour emitted by an organism that can be characterized in terms of the observable effects it has on the environment.

Operant conditioning Learning in which the probability of a response is changed by a change in its consequences.

Operant extinction When a behaviour no longer produces predictable consequences, its return to the level of occurrence it had before operant conditioning.

Operational definition A definition of a variable or condition in terms of the specific operation or procedure used to determine its presence.

Opponent-process theory The theory that all colour experiences arise from three systems, each of which includes two "opponent" elements (red versus green, blue versus yellow, and black versus white).

Optic nerve The axons of the ganglion cells that carry information from the eye toward the brain.

Organizational psychologists Psychologists who study various aspects of the human work environment, such as communication among employees, socialization or enculturation of workers, leadership, job satisfaction, stress and burnout, and overall quality of life.

Out-groups The groups with which people do not identify as members.

Over-regularization A grammatical error, usually appearing during early language development, in which the rules of a language are applied too widely, resulting in incorrect linguistic forms.

Pain The body's response to noxious stimuli that are intense enough to cause, or threaten to cause, tissue damage.

Panic disorder An anxiety disorder in which sufferers experience unexpected, severe panic attacks that begin with a feeling of intense apprehension, fear, or terror.

Parallel forms Different versions of a test used to assess test reliability; the change of forms reduces effects of direct practice, memory, or the desire of an individual to appear consistent on the same items.

Parallel processes Two or more mental processes that are carried out simultaneously.

Parasympathetic division The subdivision of the autonomic nervous system that monitors the routine operation of the body's internal functions and conserves and restores body energy.

Parental investment The time and energy parents must spend raising their offspring.

Parenting practices Specific parenting behaviours that arise in response to particular parental goals.

Parenting style The manner in which parents rear their children; an authoritative parenting style, which balances demandingness and responsiveness, is seen as the most effective.

Parietal lobe Region of the brain behind the frontal lobe and above the lateral fissure; contains somatosensory cortex.

Partial reinforcement effect The behavioural principle that states that responses acquired under intermittent reinforcement are more difficult to extinguish than those acquired with continuous reinforcement.

Participant modelling A therapeutic technique in which a therapist demonstrates the desired behaviour and a client is aided, through supportive encouragement, to imitate the modelled behaviour.

Pastoral counsellor A member of a religious order who specializes in the treatment of psychological disorders, often combining spirituality with practical problem solving.

Patient The term used by those who take a biomedical approach to the treatment of psychological problems to describe the person being treated.

Perceived control The belief that one has the ability to make a difference in the course of the consequences of some event or experience; often helpful in dealing with stressors.

Perception The processes that organize information in the sensory image and interpret it as having been produced by properties of objects or events in the external, three-dimensional world.

Perceptual constancy The ability to retain an unchanging percept of an object despite variations in the retinal image.

Perceptual organization The processes that put sensory information together to give the perception of a coherent scene over the whole visual field.

Peripheral nervous system (PNS) The part of the nervous system composed of the spinal and cranial nerves that connects the body's sensory receptors to the CNS and the CNS to the muscles and glands.

Personality The psychological qualities of an individual that influence a variety of characteristic behaviour patterns across different situations and over time.

Personality disorder A chronic, inflexible, maladaptive pattern of perceiving, thinking, and behaving that seriously impairs an individual's ability to function in social or other settings.

Personality inventory A self-report questionnaire used for personality assessment that includes a series of items about personal thoughts, feelings, and behaviours.

Personality types Distinct patterns of personality characteristics used to assign people to categories; qualitative differences, rather than differences in degree, used to discriminate among people.

Persuasion Deliberate efforts to change attitudes.

PET scans Brain images produced by a device that obtains detailed pictures of activity in the living brain by recording the radioactivity emitted by cells during different cognitive or behavioural activities.

Phantom limb pain Sensations that appear to originate in a limb that has been amputated.

Phenotype The observable characteristics of an organism, resulting from the interaction between the organism's genotype and its environment.

Pheromones Chemical signals released by organisms to communicate with other members of the species; often serve as long-distance sexual attractors.

Phi phenomenon The simplest form of apparent motion: the movement illusion in which one or more stationary lights going on and off in succession are perceived as a single moving light.

Phobia A persistent and irrational fear (of a specific object, activity, or situation) that is excessive and unreasonable, given the reality of the threat.

Phonemes Minimal units of speech in any given language that make a meaningful difference in speech production and reception; |r| and |l| are two distinct phonemes in English but variations of one in Japanese.

Photoreceptors Receptor cells in the retina that are sensitive to light.

Physical development The bodily changes, maturation, and growth that occur in an organism starting with conception and continuing across the life span.

Physiological dependence The process by which the body becomes adjusted to or dependent on a drug.

Pitch Sound quality of highness or lowness; primarily dependent on the frequency of the sound wave.

Pituitary gland Located in the brain, the gland that secretes growth hormone and influences the secretion of hormones by other endocrine glands.

Place theory The theory that different frequency tones produce maximum activation at different locations along the basilar membrane, with the result that pitch can be coded by the place at which activation occurs.

Placebo control An experimental condition in which treatment is not administered, used in cases where a placebo effect might occur.

Placebo effect A change in behaviour in the absence of an experimental manipulation.

Placebo therapy A therapy independent of any specific clinical procedures that results in client improvement.

Plasticity Changes in the performance of the brain; may involve the creation of new synapses or changes in the function of existing synapses.

Pons The region of the brain stem that connects the spinal cord with the brain and links parts of the brain to one another.

Population The entire set of individuals about which generalizations will be made based on an experimental sample.

Positive psychology A movement within psychology that applies research to provide people with the knowledge and skills that allow them to experience fulfilling lives.

Positive punishment A behaviour is followed by the presentation of an aversive stimulus, decreasing the probability of that behaviour.

Positive reinforcement A behaviour is followed by the presentation of an appetitive stimulus, increasing the probability of that behaviour.

Possible selves The ideal selves that a person would like to become, the selves a person could become, and the selves a person is afraid of becoming; components of the cognitive sense of self.

Post-traumatic stress disorder (PTSD) An anxiety disorder characterized by the persistent re-experience of traumatic events through distressing recollections, dreams, hallucinations, or dissociative flashbacks; develops in response to rape, life-threatening events, severe injury, and natural disasters.

Preconscious memories Memories that are not currently conscious but that can easily be called into consciousness when necessary.

Predictive validity The degree to which test scores indicate a result on a specific measure that is consistent with some other criterion of the characteristic being assessed; commonly known as criterion validity.

Prefrontal lobotomy An operation that severs the nerve fibres connecting the frontal lobes of the brain with the diencephalon, especially those fibres in the thalamic and hypothalamic areas; best known form of psychosurgery.

Prejudice A learned attitude toward a target object, involving negative affect (dislike or fear), negative beliefs (stereotypes) that justify the attitude, and a behavioural intention to avoid, control, dominate, or eliminate the target object.

Primacy effect Improved memory for items at the start of a list.

Primary reinforcers Biologically determined reinforcers such as food and water.

Priming In the assessment of implicit memory, the advantage conferred by prior exposure to a word or situation.

Proactive interference Circumstances in which past memories make it more difficult to encode and retrieve new information.

Problem solving Thinking that is directed toward solving specific problems and that moves from an initial state to a goal state by means of a set of mental operations.

Problem space The elements that make up a problem: the initial state (the incomplete information or unsatisfactory conditions the person starts with); the goal state (the set of information or state the person wishes to achieve); and the set of operations (the steps the person takes to move from the initial state to the goal state).

Procedural memory Memory for how things get done; the way perceptual, cognitive, and motor skills are acquired, retained, and used.

Projective test A method of personality assessment in which an individual is presented with a standardized set of ambiguous, abstract stimuli and asked to interpret their meanings; the individual's responses are assumed to reveal inner feelings, motives, and conflicts.

Prosocial behaviours Behaviours that are carried out with the goal of helping other people.

Prototype The most representative example of a category.

Proximal stimulus The optical image on the retina; contrasted with the distal stimulus, the physical object in the world.

Psychiatrist An individual who has obtained an MD degree and also has completed postdoctoral specialty training in mental and emotional disorders; a psychiatrist is authorized to prescribe medications for the treatment of psychological disorders.

Psychic determinism The assumption that mental and behavioural reactions are determined by previous experiences.

Psychoactive drugs Chemicals that affect mental processes and behaviour by temporarily changing conscious awareness of reality.

Psychoanalysis The form of psychodynamic therapy developed by Freud; an intensive, prolonged technique for exploring unconscious motivations and conflicts in neurotic, anxiety-ridden individuals.

Psychoanalyst An individual who has earned either a PhD or an MD degree and has completed postgraduate training in the Freudian approach to understanding and treating mental disorders.

Psychobiography The use of psychological (especially personality) theory to describe and explain an individual's course through life.

Psychodynamic personality theories Theories of personality that share the assumption that personality is shaped by, and behaviour is motivated by, inner forces.

Psychodynamic perspective A psychological model in which behaviour is explained in terms of past experiences and motivational forces, and actions are viewed as stemming from inherited instincts, biological drives, and attempts to resolve conflicts between personal needs and social requirements.

Psychological assessment The use of specified procedures to evaluate the abilities, behaviours, and personal qualities of people.

Psychological dependence The psychological need or craving for a drug.

Psychological diagnosis The label given to a psychological abnormality by classifying and categorizing the observed behaviour pattern into an approved diagnostic system.

Psychology The scientific study of the behaviour of individuals and their mental processes.

Psychometric function A graph that plots the percentage of detections of a stimulus (on the vertical axis) for each unit of stimulus intensity (on the horizontal axis).

Psychometrics The field of psychology that specializes in mental testing.

Psychoneuroimmunology The research area that investigates interactions between psychological processes, such as responses to stress, and the functions of the immune system.

Psychopathological functioning Disruptions in emotional, behavioural, or thought processes that lead to personal distress or block one's ability to achieve important goals.

Psychopharmacology The branch of psychology that investigates the effects of drugs on behaviour.

Psychophysics The study of the correspondence between physical simulation and psychological experience.

Psychosocial stages Proposed by Erik Erikson, successive developmental stages that focus on an individual's orientation toward the self and others; these stages incorporate both the sexual and social aspects of a person's development and the social conflicts that arise from the interaction between the individual and the social environment.

Psychosomatic disorders Physical disorders aggravated by or primarily attributable to prolonged emotional stress or other psychological causes.

Psychosurgery A surgical procedure performed on brain tissue to alleviate a psychological disorder.

Psychotherapy Any of a group of therapies used to treat psychological disorders that focuses on changing faulty behaviours, thoughts, perceptions, and emotions that may be associated with specific disorders.

Psychotic disorders Severe mental disorders in which a person experiences impairments in reality testing manifested through thought, emotional, or perceptual difficulties; no longer used as diagnostic category after *DSM-III*.

Psychotropic drugs Substances that are used to alter behaviour, mood, or thought, which have been used for recreational purposes and for treatment of mental illness.

Puberty The process through which sexual maturity is attained.

Punisher Any stimulus that, when made contingent upon a response, decreases the probability of that response.

Racism Discrimination against people based on their skin colour or ethnic heritage.

Random assignment A procedure by which participants have an equal likelihood of being assigned to any condition within an experiment.

Range The difference between the highest and the lowest scores in a set of observations; the simplest measure of variability.

Rapid eye movements (REM) A behavioural sign of the phase of sleep during which the sleeper is likely to be experiencing dreamlike mental activity.

Rational-emotive therapy (RET) A comprehensive system of personality change based on changing irrational beliefs that cause undesirable, highly charged emotional reactions such as severe anxiety.

Reasoning The process of thinking in which conclusions are drawn from a set of facts; thinking directed toward a given goal or objective.

Recall A method of retrieval in which an individual is required to reproduce the information previously presented.

Recency effect Improved memory for items at the end of a list.

Receptive field The area of the visual field to which a neuron in the visual system responds.

Reciprocal altruism The idea that people perform altruistic behaviours because they expect that others will perform altruistic behaviours for them in turn.

Reciprocal determinism A concept of Albert Bandura's social-learning theory that refers to the notion that a complex reciprocal interaction exists among the individual, his or her behaviour, and environmental stimuli, and that each of these components affects the others.

Reciprocity norm Expectation that favours will be returned—if someone does something for another person, that person should do something in return.

Recognition A method of retrieval in which an individual is required to identify stimuli as having been experienced before.

Reconstructive memory The process of putting information together based on general types of stored knowledge in the absence of a specific memory representation.

Reflex An unlearned response elicited by specific stimuli that have biological relevance for an organism.

Refractory period The period of rest during which a new nerve impulse cannot be activated in a segment of an axon.

Reinforcement contingency A consistent relationship between a response and the changes in the environment that it produces.

Reinforcer Any stimulus that, when made contingent upon a response, increases the probability of that response.

Relative motion parallax A source of information about depth in which the relative distances of objects from a viewer determine the amount and direction of their relative motion in the retinal image.

Relaxation response A condition in which muscle tension, cortical activity, heart rate, and blood pressure decrease and breathing slows.

Reliability The degree to which a test produces similar scores each time it is used; stability or consistency of the scores produced by an instrument.

Repetitive transcranial magnetic stimulation (rTMS) A technique for producing temporary inactivation of brain areas using repeated pulses of magnetic stimulation.

Representative sample A subset of a population that closely matches the overall characteristics of the population with respect to the distribution of males and females, racial and ethnic groups, and so on.

Representativeness heuristic A cognitive strategy that assigns an object to a category on the basis of a few characteristics regarded as representative of that category.

Repression The basic defence mechanism by which painful or guilt-producing thoughts, feelings, or memories are excluded from conscious awareness.

Resistance The inability or unwillingness of a patient in psychoanalysis to discuss certain ideas, desires, or experiences.

Response bias The systematic tendency as a result of nonsensory factors for an observer to favour responding in a particular way.

Resting potential The polarization of cellular fluid within a neuron, which provides the capability to produce an action potential.

Reticular formation The region of the brain stem that alerts the cerebral cortex to incoming sensory signals and is responsible for maintaining consciousness and awakening from sleep.

Retina The layer at the back of the eye that contains photoreceptors and converts light energy to neural responses.

Retinal disparity The displacement between the horizontal positions of corresponding images in the two eyes.

Retrieval The recovery of stored information from memory.

Retrieval cues Internally or externally generated stimuli available to help with the retrieval of a memory.

Retroactive interference Circumstances in which the formation of new memories makes it more difficult to recover older memories.

Rods Photoreceptors concentrated in the periphery of the retina that are most active in dim illumination; rods do not produce sensation of colour.

Rules Behavioural guidelines for acting in certain ways in certain situations.

Sample A subset of a population selected as participants in an experiment.

Saturation The dimension of colour space that captures the purity and vividness of colour sensations.

Schedules of reinforcement In operant conditioning, the patterns of delivering and withholding reinforcement.

Schemas General conceptual frameworks, or clusters of knowledge, regarding objects, people, and situations; knowledge packages that encode generalizations about the structure of the environment.

Schemes Piaget's term for cognitive structures that develop as infants and young children learn to interpret the world and adapt to their environment.

Schizophrenic disorder Severe form of psychopathology characterized by the breakdown of integrated personality functioning, withdrawal from reality, emotional distortions, and disturbed thought processes.

Scientific method The set of procedures used for gathering and interpreting objective information in a way that minimizes error and yields dependable generalizations.

Selective optimization with compensation A strategy for successful aging in which one makes the most gains while minimizing the impact of losses that accompany normal aging.

Selective social interaction theory The theory that, as people age, they become more selective in choosing social partners who satisfy their emotional needs.

Self-actualization A concept in personality psychology referring to a person's constant striving to realize his or her potential and to develop inherent talents and capabilities.

Self-concept A person's mental model of his or her abilities and attributes.

Self-efficacy The set of beliefs that one can perform adequately in a particular situation.

Self-esteem A generalized evaluative attitude toward the self that influences both moods and behaviour and that exerts a powerful effect on a range of personal and social behaviours.

Self-fulfilling prophecy A prediction made about some future behaviour or event that modifies interactions so as to produce what is expected.

Self-handicapping The process of developing, in anticipation of failure, behavioural reactions and explanations that minimize ability deficits as possible attributions for the failure.

Self-perception theory The idea that people observe themselves in order to figure out the reasons they act as they do; people infer what their internal states are by perceiving how they are acting in a given situation.

Self-report measures The behaviours that are identified through a participant's own observations and reports.

Self-serving bias An attributional bias in which people tend to take credit for their successes and deny responsibility for their failures.

Semantic memories Generic, categorical memories, such as the meanings of words and concepts.

Sensation The process by which stimulation of a sensory receptor gives rise to neural impulses that result in an experience, or awareness, of conditions inside or outside the body.

Sensitization The behavioural response to stimuli opposite to that seen with habitutation.

Sensory adaptation A phenomenon in which receptor cells lose their power to respond after a period of unchanged stimulation; allows a more rapid reaction to new sources of information.

Sensory memory The initial memory processes involved in the momentary preservation of fleeting impressions of sensory stimuli.

Sensory neurons The neurons that carry messages from sense receptors toward the central nervous system (CNS).

Sensory receptors Specialized cells that convert physical signals into cellular signals that are processed by the nervous system.

Serial position effect A characteristic of memory retrieval in which the recall of beginning and end items on a list is often better than recall of items appearing in the middle.

Serial processes Two or more mental processes that are carried out in order, one after the other.

Set A temporary readiness to perceive or react to a stimulus in a particular way.

Sex chromosomes Chromosomes containing the genes that code for the development of male or female characteristics.

Sex differences Biologically based characteristics that distinguish males from females.

Sexism Discrimination against people because of their sex.

Sexual arousal The motivational state of excitement and tension brought about by physiological and cognitive reactions to erotic stimuli.

Sexual scripts Socially learned programs of sexual responsiveness.

Sexual selection Darwin's theory that selecting a mate based on features that are attractive could lead to an increase in those features within a species, whereas unattractive features would decrease.

Shape constancy The ability to perceive the true shape of an object despite variations in the shape of the retinal image.

Shaping by successive approximations A behavioural method that reinforces responses that successively approximate and ultimately match the desired response.

Short-term memory (STM) Memory processes associated with preservation of recent experiences and with retrieval of information from long-term memory; short-term memory is of limited capacity and stores information for only a short length of time without rehearsal.

Shyness An individual's discomfort and/or inhibition in interpersonal situations that interferes with pursuing an interpersonal or professional goal.

Signal detection theory A systematic approach to the problem of response bias that allows an experimenter to identify and separate the roles of sensory stimuli and the individual's criterion level in producing the final response.

Significant difference A difference between experimental groups or conditions that would have occurred by chance less than an accepted criterion; in psychology, the criterion most often used is a probability of less than 5 times out of 100, or $p < .05$.

Size constancy The ability to perceive the true size of an object despite variations in the size of its retinal image.

Sleep apnea A sleep disorder of the upper respiratory system that causes the person to stop breathing while asleep.

Social categorization The process by which people organize the social environment by categorizing themselves and others into groups.

Social cognition The process by which people select, interpret, and remember social information.

Social development The ways in which individuals' social interactions and expectations change across the life span.

Social intelligence A theory of personality that refers to the expertise people bring to their experience of life tasks.

Social-learning theory The learning theory that stresses the role of observation and the imitation of behaviours observed in others.

Social-learning therapy A form of treatment in which clients observe models' desirable behaviours being reinforced.

Social norms The expectations a group has for its members regarding acceptable and appropriate attitudes and behaviours.

Social perception The process by which a person comes to know and categorize the personal attributes and behaviours of others.

Social phobia A persistent, irrational fear that arises in anticipation of a public situation in which an individual can be observed by others.

Social psychology The branch of psychology that studies the effect of social variables on individual behaviour, attitudes, perceptions, and motives; also studies group and intergroup phenomena.

Social role A socially defined pattern of behaviour that is expected of a person who is functioning in a given setting or group.

Social support Resources, including material aid, socioemotional support, and informational aid, provided by others to help a person cope with stress.

Socialization The lifelong process whereby an individual's behavioural patterns, values, standards, skills, attitudes, and motives are shaped to conform to those regarded as desirable in a particular society.

Sociobiology A field of research that focuses on evolutionary explanations for the social behaviour and social systems of humans and other animal species.

Sociocultural perspective The psychological perspective that focuses on cross-cultural differences in the causes and consequences of behaviour.

Soma The cell body of a neuron, containing the nucleus and cytoplasm.

Somatic nervous system The subdivision of the peripheral nervous system that connects the central nervous system to the skeletal muscles and skin.

Somatization disorder A disorder characterized by unexplained physical complaints in several categories over many years.

Somatoform disorder A disorder in which people have physical illnesses or complaints that cannot be fully explained by actual medical conditions.

Somatosensory cortex The region of the parietal lobes that processes sensory input from various body areas.

Somnambulism A disorder that causes sleepers to leave their beds and wander while still remaining asleep; also known as sleepwalking.

Sound localization The auditory processes that allow the spatial origins of environmental sounds.

Specific phobias Phobias that occur in response to specific types of objects or situations.

Split-half reliability A measure of the correlation between test takers' performance on different halves (e.g., odd- and even-numbered items) of a test.

Spontaneous recovery The reappearance of an extinguished conditioned response after a rest period.

Spontaneous-remission effect The improvement of some mental patients and clients in psychotherapy without any professional intervention; a baseline criterion against which the effectiveness of therapies must be assessed.

Standard deviation (SD) The average difference of a set of scores from their mean; a measure of variability.

Standardization A set of uniform procedures for treating each participant in a test, interview, or experiment, or for recording data.

Stereotype threat The threat associated with being at risk for confirming a negative stereotype of one's group.

Stereotypes Generalizations about a group of people in which the same characteristics are assigned to all members of a group.

Stigma The negative reaction of people to an individual or group because of some assumed inferiority or source of difference that is considered unacceptable.

Stimulus discrimination A conditioning process in which an organism learns to respond differently to stimuli that differ from the conditioned stimulus on some dimension.

Stimulus-driven capture A determinant of why people select some parts of sensory input for further processing; occurs when features of stimuli—objects in the environment—automatically capture attention, independent of the local goals of a perceiver.

Stimulus generalization The automatic extension of a conditioned response to similar stimuli that have never been paired with the unconditioned stimulus.

Storage The retention of encoded material over time.

Stress The pattern of specific and nonspecific responses an organism makes to stimulus events that disturb its equilibrium and tax or exceed its ability to cope.

Stress moderator variables Variables that change the impact of a stressor on a given type of stress reaction.

Stressor An internal or external event or stimulus that induces stress.

Structuralism The study of the structure of mind and behaviour; the view that all human mental experience can be understood as a combination of simple elements or events.

Superego The aspect of personality that represents the internalization of society's values, standards, and morals.

Sympathetic division The subdivision of the autonomic nervous system that deals with emergency response and the mobilization of energy.

Synapse The gap between one neuron and another.

Synaptic transmission The relaying of information from one neuron to another across the synaptic gap.

Systematic desensitization A behavioural therapy technique in which a client is taught to prevent the arousal of anxiety by confronting the feared stimulus while relaxed.

Tabula rasa A theory proposed by philosopher John Locke that when we are born, our brains are like a blank tablet of clay that can be written on. As the theory assumes there is no built-in knowledge, the sensory and general experiences one has are what come to form the overall knowledge base.

Taste-aversion learning A biological constraint on learning in which an organism learns in one trial to avoid a food whose ingestion is followed by illness.

Temperament A child's biologically based level of emotional and behavioural response to environmental events.

Temporal lobe Region of the brain found below the lateral fissure; contains auditory cortex.

Tend-and-befriend response A response to stressors that is hypothesized to be typical for females; stressors prompt females to protect their offspring and join social groups to reduce vulnerability.

Terminal buttons The bulblike structures at the branched endings of axons that contain vesicles filled with neurotransmitters.

Test–retest reliability A measure of the correlation between the scores of the same people on the same test given on two different occasions.

Testosterone The male sex hormone, secreted by the testes, that stimulates production of sperm and is also responsible for the development of male secondary sex characteristics.

Thalamus The brain structure that relays sensory impulses to the cerebral cortex.

Thematic Apperception Test (TAT) A projective test in which pictures of ambiguous scenes are presented to an individual, who is encouraged to generate stories about them.

Theory An organized set of concepts that explains a phenomenon or set of phenomena.

Think-aloud protocols Reports made by experimental participants of the mental processes and strategies they use while working on a task.

Three-term contingency The means by which organisms learn that, in the presence of some stimuli but not others, their behaviour is likely to have a particular effect on the environment.

Timbre The dimension of auditory sensation that reflects the complexity of a sound wave.

Tolerance A situation that occurs with continued use of a drug in which an individual requires greater dosages to achieve the same effect.

Top-down processing Perceptual processes in which information from an individual's past experience, knowledge, expectations, motivations, and background influence the way a perceived object is interpreted and classified.

Traits Enduring personal qualities or attributes that influence behaviour across situations.

Transcranial magnetic stimulation (TMS) A technique for stimulating brain regions using magnetic pulses.

Transduction Transformation of one form of energy into another; for example, light is transformed into neural impulses.

Transfer-appropriate processing The perspective that suggests memory is best when the type of processing carried out at encoding matches the processes carried out at retrieval.

Transference The process by which a person in psychoanalysis attaches to a therapist feelings formerly held toward some significant person who figured into past emotional conflict.

Trichromatic theory The theory that there are three types of colour receptors that produce the primary colour sensations of red, green, and blue.

Two-factor theory of emotion The theory that emotional experiences arise from autonomic arousal and cognitive appraisal.

Type A behaviour pattern A complex pattern of behaviours and emotions that includes excessive emphasis on competition, aggression, impatience, and hostility; hostility increases the risk of coronary heart disease.

Type B behaviour pattern As compared to Type A behaviour pattern, a less competitive, less aggressive, less hostile pattern of behaviour and emotion.

Unconditional positive regard Complete love and acceptance of an individual by another person, such as a parent for a child, with no conditions attached.

Unconditioned response (UCR) In classical conditioning, the response elicited by an unconditioned stimulus without prior training or learning.

Unconditioned stimulus (UCS) In classical conditioning, the stimulus that elicits an unconditioned response.

Unconscious The domain of the psyche that stores repressed urges and primitive impulses.

Validity The extent to which a test measures what it was intended to measure.

Variable In an experimental setting, a factor that varies in amount and kind.

Variable-interval (VI) schedule A schedule of reinforcement in which a reinforcer is delivered for the first response made after a variable period of time whose average is predetermined.

Variable-ratio (VR) schedule A schedule of reinforcement in which a reinforcer is delivered for the first response made after a variable number of responses whose average is predetermined.

Vestibular sense The sense that tells how one's own body is oriented in the world with respect to gravity.

Visual cortex The region of the occipital lobes in which visual information is processed.

Volley principle An extension of frequency theory, which proposes that when peaks in a sound wave come too frequently for a single neuron to fire at each peak, several neurons fire as a group at the frequency of the stimulus tone.

Weber's law An assertion that the size of a difference threshold is proportional to the intensity of the standard stimulus.

Wellness Optimal health, the ability to function fully and actively; incorporates the physical, intellectual, emotional, spiritual, social, and environmental domains of health.

Within-subjects design A research design that uses each participant as his or her own control; for example, the behaviour of an experimental participant before receiving treatment might be compared to his or her behaviour after receiving treatment.

Working memory A memory resource that is used to accomplish tasks such as reasoning and language comprehension; consists of the phonological loop, visuospatial sketchpad, and central executive.

Zygote The single cell that results when a sperm fertilizes an egg.

References

Abdallah, R. T., & Simon, J. A. (2007). Testosterone therapy in women: Its role in the management of hypoactive sexual desire disorder. *International Journal of Impotence Research, 19*, 458–463.

Abdel Rahman, R., & Melinger, A. (2007). When bees hamper the production of honey: Lexical interference from associates in speech production. *Journal of Experimental Psychology: Learning, Memory, and Cognition, 33*(3), 604–614.

Abrams, R. (1992). *Electroconvulsive therapy.* New York, NY: Oxford University Press.

Abramson, L. Y., Seligman, M. E. P., & Teasdale, J. D. (1978). Learned helplessness in humans: Critique and reformulation. *Journal of Abnormal Psychology, 87,* 32–48, 49–74.

Adams, J. L. (1986). *Conceptual blockbusting* (3rd ed.). New York, NY: Norton.

Adams, J. S. (1965). Inequity in social exchange. In L. Berkowitz (Ed.), *Advances in experimental social psychology* (Vol. 2, pp. 267–299). New York, NY: Academic Press.

Ader, R., & Cohen, N. (1981). Conditioned immunopharmacological responses. In R. Ader (Ed.), *Psychoneuroimmunology* (pp. 281–319). New York, NY: Academic Press.

Ader, R., & Cohen, N. (1993). Psychoneuroimmunology: Conditioning and stress. *Annual Review of Psychology, 44,* 53–85.

Adler, A. (1929). *The practice and theory of individual psychology.* New York, NY: Harcourt, Brace & World.

Adolphs, R., Tranel, D., Damasio, H., & Damasio, A. (1994). Impaired recognition of emotion in facial expressions following bilateral damage to the human amygdala. *Nature, 372,* 669–672.

Adolphs, R., Tranel, D., Hamann, S., Young, A. W., Calder, A. J., Phelps, E. A., . . . Damasio, A. R. (1999). Recognition of facial emotion in nine individuals with bilateral amygdala damage. *Neuropsychologia, 37,* 1111–1117.

Ahmed, S. H., & Koob, G. F. (2004). Changes in response to a dopamine receptor antagonist in rats with escalating cocaine intake. *Psychopharmacology, 172,* 450–454.

Ainsworth, M. D. S., Blehar, M., Waters, E., & Wall, S. (1978). *Patterns of attachment.* Hillsdale, NJ: Erlbaum.

Ajzen, I., & Fishbein, M. (2005). The influence of attitudes on behavior. In D. Albarracin, B. T. Johnson, & M. P. Zanna (Eds.), *The handbook of attitudes* (pp. 173–221). Mahwah, NJ: Erlbaum.

Akmajian, A., Demers, R. A., Farmer, A. K., & Harnish, R. M. (1990). *Linguistics.* Cambridge, MA: The MIT Press.

Albarracín, D., Durantini, M. R., Earl, A., Gunnoe, J. B., & Leeper, J. (2008). Beyond the most willing audiences: A meta-intervention to increase exposure to HIV-prevention programs by vulnerable populations. *Health Psychology, 27,* 638–644.

Allan, C. A., Forbes, E. A., Strauss, B. J. G., & McLachlan, R. I. (2008). Testosterone therapy increases sexual desire in ageing men with low-normal testosterone levels and symptoms of androgen deficiency. *International Journal of Impotence Research, 20,* 396–401.

Allen, G. E. (1997). The social and economic origins of genetic determinism: A case history of the American Eugenic Movement, 1900–1940 and its lessons for today. *Genetica, 99,* 77–88.

Allen, J. P., & Land, D. (1999). Attachment in adolescence. In J. Cassidy & P. R. Shaver (Eds.), *Handbook of attachment: Theory, research, and clinical applications.* NY: Guilford Press.

Allen, J. P., Porter, M. R., & McFarland, F. C. (2006). Leaders and followers in adolescent close relationships: Susceptibility to peer influence as a predictor of risky behavior, friendship instability, and depression. *Development and Psychopathology, 18,* 155–172.

Allport, G. W. (1937). *Personality: A psychological interpretation.* NY: Holt, Rinehart & Winston.

Allport, G. W. (1954). *The nature of prejudice.* Cambridge, MA: Addison-Wesley.

Allport, G. W. (1961). *Pattern and growth in personality.* New York, NY: Holt, Rinehart & Winston.

Allport, G. W. (1966). Traits revisited. *American Psychologist, 21,* 1–10.

Allport, G. W., & Odbert, H. S. (1936). Trait-names, a psycholexical study. *Psychological Monographs, 47*(1, Whole No. 211).

Amabile, T. M. (1983). *The social psychology of creativity.* New York, NY: Springer-Verlag.

Amaral, D. G., Schumann, C. M., & Nordahl, C. W. (2008). Neuroanatomy of autism. *Trends in Neurosciences, 31,* 137–145.

American Association on Mental Retardation. (1992). *Mental retardation: Definition, classification, and systems of supports* (9th ed.). Washington, DC: American Association on Mental Retardation.

Amodio, D. M., & Devine, P. G. (2006). Stereotyping and evaluation in implicit race bias: Evidence for independent constructs and unique effects on behavior. *Journal of Personality and Social Psychology, 91,* 651–661.

Anderson, J. R. (1987). Skill acquisition: Compilation of weak-method problem-solutions. *Psychological Review, 94,* 192–210.

Anderson, J. R. (1996). ACT: A simple theory of complex cognition. *American Psychologist, 51,* 355–365.

Anderson, S. L., Adams, G., & Plaut, V. C. (2008). The cultural grounding of personal relationship: The importance of attractiveness in everyday life. *Journal of Personality and Social Psychology, 95,* 352–368.

Anderson, V. L., Levinson, E. M., Barker, W., & Kiewra, K. R. (1999). The effects of meditation on teacher perceived occupational stress, state and trait anxiety, and burnout. *School Psychology Quarterly, 14,* 3–25.

Anliker, J. A., Bartoshuk, L., Ferris, A. M., & Hooks, L. D. (1991). Children's food preferences and genetic sensitivity to the bitter taste of 6-*n*-propylthiouracil (PROP). *American Journal of Clinical Nutrition, 54,* 316–320.

Anthony, D. B., Holmes, J. G., & Wood, J. V. (2007). Social acceptance and self-esteem: Tuning the sociometer to interpersonal value. *Journal of Personality and Social Psychology, 92,* 1024–1039.

Appleby, D. C. (2006). Defining, teaching, and assessing critical thinking in introductory psychology. In D. S. Dunn & S. L. Chew (Eds.), *Best practices for teaching introduction to psychology* (pp. 57–69). Mahwah, NJ: Erlbaum.

Appleby, L., Luchins, D. J., & Freels, S. (2006). Homeless admissions and immigration in a state mental hospital. *Psychiatric Services, 57,* 144.

Archbold, G.E., Bouton, M.E., & Nader, K. (2010). Evidence for the persistence of contextual fear memories following immediate extinction. *European Journal of Neuroscience, 1, 31*(7), 1303–1311.

Arcuri, L., Castelli, L., Galdi, S., Zogmaister, C., & Amadori, A. (2008). Predicting the vote: Implicit attitudes as predictors of the future behavior of decided and undecided voters. *Political Psychology, 29,* 369–387.

Arendt, J., & Skene, D. J. (2005). Melatonin as a chronobiotic. *Sleep Medicine Reviews, 9,* 25–39.

Arkin, R. M. (Ed.). (1990). Centennial celebration of the principles of psychology. *Personality and Social Psychology Bulletin, 16*(4).

Arnett, J. J. (1999). Adolescent storm and stress reconsidered. *American Psychologist, 54,* 317–326.

Aron, A., & Aron, E. N. (1994). Love. In A. L. Weber & J. H. Harvey (Eds.), *Perspectives on close relationships* (pp. 131–152). Boston: Allyn & Bacon.

Aron, A., & Fraley, B. (1999). Relationship closeness as including other in the self: Cognitive underpinnings and measures. *Social Cognition, 17,* 140–160.

Aron, A., & Westbay, L. (1996). Dimensions of the prototype of love. *Journal of Personality and Social Psychology, 70,* 535–551.

Aron, A., Aron, E. N., & Smollan, D. (1992). Inclusion of other in the self scale and the structure of interpersonal closeness. *Journal of Personality and Social Psychology, 63,* 596–612.

Aron, A., Mashek, D., McLaughlin-Volpe, T., Wright, S., Lewandowski, G., & Aron, E. N. (2004). Including close others in the cognitive structure of self. In M. W. Baldwin (Ed.), *Interpersonal cognition* (pp. 206–232). NY: Guilford Press.

Aruguete, M. S., DeBord, K. A., Yates, A., & Edman, J. (2005). Ethnic and gender differences in eating attitudes among black and white college students. *Eating Behaviors, 6,* 328–336.

Asch, S. E. (1940). Studies in the principles of judgments and attitudes: II. Determination of judgments by group and by ego standards. *Journal of Social Psychology, 12,* 433–465.

Asch, S. E. (1952). *Social psychology.* Englewood Cliffs, NJ: Prentice Hall.

Asch, S. E. (1956). Opinions and social pressure. *Scientific American, 193*(5), 31–35.

Asch, S. E. (1956). Studies of independence and conformity: A minority of one against a unanimous majority. *Psychological Monographs, 70*(9, Whole No. 416).

Aserinsky, E., & Kleitman, N. (1953). Regularly occurring periods of eye mobility and concomitant phenomena during sleep. *Science, 118,* 273–274.

Atwood, M. (2003). *Oryx and crake.* NY: O.W. Toad, Ltd.

Atwood, M. (2009). *The year of the flood.* NY: O.W. Toad, Ltd..

Ayduk, O., Rodriguez, M. L., Mischel, W., Shoda, Y., & Wright, J. (2007). Verbal intelligence and self-regulatory competencies: Joint predictors of boys' aggression. *Journal of Research in Personality, 41,* 374–388.

Ayllon, T., & Michael, J. (1959). The psychiatric nurse as a behavioral engineer. *Journal of the Experimental Analysis of Behavior, 2,* 323–334.

Baars, B. J. (1992). A dozen completing-plans techniques for inducing predictable slips in speech and action. In B. J. Baars (Ed.), *Experimental slips and human error: Exploring the architecture of volition* (pp. 129–150). NY: Plenum Press.

Baars, B. J., Motley, M. T., & MacKay, D. G. (1975). Output editing for lexical status in artificially elicited slips of the tongue. *Journal of Verbal Learning and Verbal Behavior, 14,* 382–391.

Baas, M., De Creu, C. K. W., & Nijstad, B. A. (2008). A meta-analysis of 25 years of mood-creativity research: Hedonic tone, activation, or regulatory focus? *Psychological Bulletin, 134,* 779–806.

Back, M. D., Schmukle, S. C., & Egloff, B. (2008). How extraverted is honey.bunny77@hotmail.de? *Journal of Research in Personality, 42,* 1116–1122.

Backman, C. W., & Secord, P. F. (1959). The effect of perceived liking on interpersonal attraction. *Human Relations, 12,* 379–384.

Baddeley, A. D. (2002). Is working memory still working? *European Psychologist, 7,* 85–97.

Baddeley, A. D. (2003). Working memory: Looking back and looking forward. *Nature Reviews Neuroscience, 4,* 829–839.

Bahrick, H. P., Bahrick, P. O., & Wittlinger, R. P. (1975). Fifty years of memory for names and faces: A cross-sectional approach. *Journal of Experimental Psychology: General, 104,* 54–75.

Bailey, B. A., & Sokol, R. J. (2008). Pregnancy and alcohol use: Evidence and recommendations for prenatal care. *Clinical Obstetrics and Gynecology, 51*(2), 436–444.

Bailis, D. S., & Chipperfield, J. G. (2002). Compensating for losses in perceived personal control over health: A role for collective self-esteem in healthy aging. *Journal of Gerontology Series B: Psychological Sciences and Social Sciences, 57*(6), 531–539.

Balch, R. W., & Taylor, D. (2002). Making sense of the Heaven's Gate suicides. In D. G. Bromley & J. G. Melton (Eds.), *Cults, religion, and violence* (pp. 209–228). Cambridge, United Kingdom: Cambridge University Press.

Baldwin, A. L., & Baldwin, C. P. (1973). Study of mother–child interaction. *American Scientist, 61,* 714–721.

Ballenger, J. C. (1999). Current treatments of the anxiety disorders in adults. *Biological Psychiatry, 46,* 1579–1594.

Baltes, P. B. (1993). The aging mind: Potential and limits. *The Gerontologist, 33,* 580–594.

Baltes, P. B., & Staudinger, U. M. (1993). The search for a psychology of wisdom. *Current Directions in Psychological Science, 2,* 75–80.

Baltes, P. B., Smith, J., & Staudinger, U. M. (1992). Wisdom and successful aging. In T. B. Sonderegger (Ed.), *The Nebraska Symposium on Motivation: Vol. 39. The psychology of aging* (pp. 123–167). Lincoln, NE: University of Nebraska Press.

Bandelow, B., Krause, J., Wedekind, D., Broocks, A., Hajak, G., & Rüther, E. (2005). Early traumatic life events, parental attitudes, family history, and birth risk factors in patients with borderline personality disorder and healthy controls. *Psychiatry Research, 134,* 169–179.

Bandura, A. (1970). Modeling therapy. In W. S. Sahakian (Ed.), *Psychopathology today: Experimentation, theory and research.* Itasca, IL: Peacock.

Bandura, A. (1977). *Social learning theory.* Englewood Cliffs, NJ: Prentice-Hall.

Bandura, A. (1986). *Social foundations of thought and action: A social cognitive theory.* Englewood Cliffs, NJ: Prentice-Hall.

Bandura, A. (1992). Exercise of personal agency through the self-efficacy mechanism. In R. Schwarzer (Ed.), *Self-efficacy: Thought control of action* (pp. 3–38). Washington, DC: Hemisphere.

Bandura, A. (1997). *Self-efficacy: The exercise of control.* New York, NY: Freeman.

Bandura, A. (1999). Social cognitive theory of personality. In L. A. Pervin & O. P. John (Eds.), *Handbook of personality: Theory and research* (2nd ed., pp. 154–196). New York, NY: Guilford Press.

Bandura, A. (2006). Toward a psychology of human agency. *Perspectives on Psychological Science, 1,* 164–180.

Bandura, A., Ross, D., & Ross, S. A. (1963). Imitation of film-mediated aggressive models. *Journal of Abnormal and Social Psychology, 66,* 3–11.

Banks, S., & Dinges, D. F. (2007). Behavioral and physiological consequences of sleep restriction. *Journal of Clinical Sleep Medicine, 3,* 519–528.

Banks, W. C. (1990). *In Discovering Psychology, Program 16* [PBS video series]. Washington, DC: Annenberg/CPB Program.

Banuazizi, A., & Movahedi, S. (1975). Interpersonal dynamics in a simulated prison: A methodological analysis. *American Psychologist, 30,* 152–160.

Banyai, E. I., & Hilgard, E. R. (1976). Comparison of active-alert hypnotic induction with traditional relaxation induction. *Journal of Abnormal Psychology, 85,* 218–224.

Barak, A., Boniel-Nissim, M., & Suler, J. (2008). Fostering empowerment in online support groups. *Computers in Human Behavior, 24,* 1867–1883.

Bárez, M., Blasco, T., Fernández-Castro, J., & Viladrich, C. (2007). A structural model of the relationships between perceived control and the adaptation to illness in women with breast cancer. *Journal of Psychosocial Oncology, 25,* 21–43.

Barha, C. K., & Galea, L. A. M. (in press) Motherhood alters the cellular response to estrogens in the hippocampus later in life. *Neurobiology of Aging.* doi:10.1016/j.neurobiolaging. 2009.12.004

Barha, C. K., Lieblich, S. E., & Galea, L. A. M. (2009). Different forms of oestrogens rapidly upregulate hippocampal cell proliferation in the dentate gyrus of young female rats. *Journal of Neuroendocrinology, 21,* 155–166.

Bar-Hillel, M., & Neter, E. (1993). How alike is it versus how likely is it: A disjunction fallacy in probability judgments. *Journal of Personality and Social Psychology, 65,* 1119–1131.

Barinaga, M. (1993). Carbon monoxide: Killer to brain messenger in one step. *Science, 259,* 309.

Barkataki, I., Kumari, V., Das, M., Taylor, P., & Sharma, T. (2006). Volumetric structural brain abnormalities in men with schizophrenia and antisocial personality disorder. *Behavioural Brain Research, 169,* 239–247.

Barker, L. M., Best, M. R., & Domjan, M. (Eds.). (1978). *Learning mechanisms in food selection.* Houston, TX: Baylor University Press.

Barker, R., Dembo, T., & Lewin, D. (1941). Frustration and aggression: An experiment with young children. *University of Iowa Studies in Child Welfare, 18*(1).

Barlett, C. P., Vowels, C. L., & Saucier, D. L. (2008). Meta-analyses of the effects of media images on men's body-image concerns. *Journal of Social and Clinical Psychology, 27*(3), 279–310.

Baron-Cohen, S. (2008). Theories of the autistic mind. *The Psychologist, 21,* 112–116.

Barondes, S. H. (1994). Thinking about Prozac. *Science, 263,* 1102–1103.

Barrett, L. F., Tugade, M. M., & Engle, R. W. (2004). Individual differences in working memory capacity and dual-process theories of mind. *Psychological Bulletin, 130,* 553–573.

Barrett, M. S., Chua, W.-J., Crits-Christoph, P., Gibbons, M. B., & Thompson, D. (2008). Early withdrawal from mental health treatment: Implications for psychotherapy practice. *Psychotherapy Theory, Research, Practice, Training, 45,* 247–267.

Bartlett, C. W., Gharani, N., Millonig, J. H., & Brzustowicz, L. M. (2005). Three autism candidate genes: A synthesis of human genetic analysis with other disciplines. *International Journal of Developmental Neuroscience, 23,* 221–234.

Bartlett, F. C. (1932). *Remembering: A study in experimental and social psychology.* Cambridge, United Kingdom: Cambridge University Press.

Barton, N. (2000). The rapid origin of reproduction isolation. *Science, 290,* 462–463.

Bartoshuk, L. (1990). Psychophysiological insights on taste. *Science Agenda,* 12–13.

Bartoshuk, L. M. (1993). The biological basis of food perception and acceptance. *Food Quality and Preference, 4,* 21–32.

Bartoshuk, L. M., & Beauchamp, G. K. (1994). Chemical senses. *Annual Review of Psychology, 45,* 419–449.

Bartz, J. A., & Hollander, E. (2006). The neuroscience of affiliation: Forging links between basic and clinical research on neuropeptides and social behavior. *Hormones and Behavior, 50*(4), 518–528.

Basso, E. B. (1987). The implications of a progressive theory of dreaming. In B. Tedlock (Ed.), *Dreaming: Anthropological and psychological interpretations* (pp. 86–104). Cambridge, United Kingdom: Cambridge University Press.

Batson, C. D. (1991). *The altruism question: Toward a social-psychological answer.* Hillsdale, NJ: Erlbaum.

Batson, C. D. (1994). Why act for the public good? Four answers. *Personality and Social Psychology Bulletin, 20,* 603–610.

Batson, C. D., Ahmad, N., Yin, J., Bedell, S. J., Johnson, J. W., Templin, C. M., & Whiteside, A. (1999). Two threats to the common good: Self-interested egoism and empathy-induced altruism. *Personality and Social Psychology Bulletin, 25,* 3–16.

Baudry, M., Davis, J. L., & Thompson, R. F. (Eds.). (1999). *Advances in synaptic plasticity.* Cambridge, MA: MIT Press.

Baumeister, R. F. (2000). Gender differences in erotic plasticity: The female sex drive as socially flexible and responsive. *Psychological Bulletin, 126,* 347–374.

Baumeister, R. F., & Twenge, J. M. (2002). Cultural suppression of female sexuality. *Review of General Psychology, 6,* 166–203.

Baumeister, R. F., Campbell, J. D., Krueger, J. I., & Vohs, K. D. (2003). Does high self-esteem cause better performance, interpersonal success, happiness, or healthy lifestyles? *Psychological Science in the Public Interest, 4,* 1–44.

Baumgartner, T., Heinrichs, M., Vonlanthen, A., Fischbacher, U., & Fehr, E. (2008). Oxytocin shapes the neural circuitry of trust and trust adaptation in humans. *Neuron, 58,* 639–650.

Bayley, N. (1956). Individual patterns of development. *Child Development, 27,* 45–74.

Beauchaine, T. P., Webster-Stratton, C., & Reid, M. J. (2005). Mediators, moderators, and predictors of 1-year outcomes among children treated for early-onset conduct problems: A latent growth curve analysis. *Journal of Counseling and Clinical Psychology, 73,* 371–388.

Beaupré, M. G., & Hess, U. (2005). Cross-cultural emotion recognition among Canadian ethnic groups. *Journal of Cross-Cultural Psychology, 36*(3), 355–370.

Beck, A. T. (1976). *Cognitive therapy and emotional disorders.* New York, NY: International Universities Press.

Beck, A. T. (1983). Cognitive theory of depression: New perspectives. In P. J. Clayton & J. E. Barrett (Eds.), *Treatment of depression: Old controversies and new approaches* (pp. 265–290). New York, NY: Raven Press.

Beck, A. T. (1985). Cognitive therapy. In H. I. Kaplan & J. Sandock (Eds.), *Comprehensive textbook of psychiatry* (4th ed.). Baltimore: Williams & Wilkins.

Beck, A. T. (1988). Cognitive approaches to panic disorders: Theory and therapy. In S. Rachman & J. D. Maser (Eds.), *Panic: Psychological perspectives.* New York, NY: Guilford Press.

Beck, A. T., & Emery, G. (1985). *Anxiety disorders and phobias: A cognitive perspective.* New York, NY: Basic Books.

Beck, A. T., & Rush, A. J. (1989). Cognitive therapy. In H. I. Kaplan & B. Sadock (Eds.), *Comprehensive textbook of psychiatry* (Vol. 5). Baltimore: Williams & Wilkins.

Beck, A. T., Rush, A. J., Shaw, B. F., & Emery, G. (1979). *Cognitive therapy of depression.* New York, NY: Guilford Press.

Beck, C. A., Metz, L. M., Svenson, L. W., & Patten, S. B. (2005). Regional variation of multiple sclerosis prevalence in Canada. *Multiple Sclerosis, 5,* 516–519.

Becker, M. W., Pashler, H., & Anstis, S. M. (2000). The role of iconic memory in change-detection tasks. *Perception, 29,* 273–286.

Becker, S. W., & Eagly, A. H. (2004). The heroism of women and men. *American Psychologist, 59,* 163–178.

Behrman, A. (2002). *Electroboy.* New York, NY: Random House.

Beïque, J-C., Imad, M., Mladenovic, L., Gingrich, J. A., & Andrade, R. (2007). Mechanism of the 5-hydroxytriptamine 2A receptor-mediated facilitation of synaptic activity in the prefrontal cortex. *PNAS Proceedings of the National Academy of Sciences of the United States of America, 104*(23), 9870–9875

Beiser, M., & Gotowiec, A. (2000). Accounting for native/nonnative differences in IQ scores. *Psychology in the Schools, 37,* 237–252.

Belicki, K., & Cuddy, M. (1996). Identifying sexual trauma histories from patterns of sleep and dreams. In D. Barrett (Ed.), *Trauma and dreams* (pp. 46–55). Cambridge, MA: Harvard University Press.

Bell, D. C. (2001). Evolution of parental caregiving. *Personality and Social Psychology Review, 5,* 216–229.

Bem, D. (2000). The exotic-becomes-erotic theory of sexual orientation. In J. Bancroft (Ed.), *The role of theory in sex research* (pp. 67–81). Bloomington: Indiana University Press.

Bem, D. J. (1972). Self-perception theory. In L. Berkowitz (Ed.), *Advances in experimental social psychology* (Vol. 6, pp. 1–62). New York, NY: Academic Press.

Bem, D. J. (1996). Exotic becomes erotic: A developmental theory of sexual orientation. *Psychological Review, 103,* 320–335.

Bem, S. L. (1974). The measurement of psychological androgyny. *Journal of Consulting and Clinical Psychology, 42,* 155–162.

Bem, S. L. (1981). *The Bem Sex Role Inventory: Professional manual.* Palo Alto, CA: Consulting Psychology Press.

Benedetti, F., Mayberg, H. S., Wager, T. D., Stohler, C. S., & Zubieta, J. K. (2005). Neurobiological mechanisms of the placebo effect. *Journal of Neuroscience, 25,* 10390–10402.

Benedict, R. (1938). Continuities and discontinuities in cultural conditioning. *Psychiatry, 1,* 161–167.

Benedict, R. (1959). *Patterns of culture.* Boston: Houghton Mifflin.

Benenson, J. F., & Heath, A. (2006). Boys withdraw from one-on-one interactions, whereas girls withdraw more in groups. *Developmental Psychology, 42,* 272–282.

Benenson, J. F., Apostoleris, N. H., & Parnass, J. (1997). Age and sex differences in dyadic and group interaction. *Developmental Psychology, 33,* 538–543.

Benhamou, S., & Poucet, B. (1996). A comparative analysis of spatial memory processes. *Behavioural Processes, 35,* 113–126.

Benight, C. C., Cieslak, R., Molton, I. R., & Johnson, L. E. (2008). Self-evaluative appraisals of coping capability and posttraumatic distress following motor vehicle accidents. *Journal of Consulting and Clinical Psychology, 76,* 677–685.

Benjamin, A. S. (2005). Response speeding mediates the contributions of cue familiarity and target retrievability to metamnemonic judgments. *Psychonomic Bulletin & Review, 12,* 874–879.

Benjet, C., & Kazdin, A. E. (2003). Spanking children: The controversies, findings, and new directions. *Clinical Psychology Review, 23,* 197–224.

Bennett, D. S., Bendersky, M., & Lewis, M. (2008). Children's cognitive ability from 4 to 9 years old as a function of prenatal cocaine exposure, environmental risk, and maternal verbal intelligence. *Developmental Psychology, 44*(4), 919–928.

Benson, H. (2000). *The relaxation response* (Updated ed.). New York, NY: HarperCollins.

Benson, H., Rauch, S. L., Moore, C. I., & Fischl, B. (2005). Meditation experience is associated with increased cortical thickness. *NeuroReport, 16,* 1893–1897.

Bergman, E. T., & Roediger, H. L., III. (1999). Can Bartlett's repeated reproduction experiments be replicated? *Memory & Cognition, 27,* 937–947.

Bering, J. M., & Bjorklund, D. F. (2007). The serpent's gift: Evolutionary psychology and consciousness. In P. D. Zelazo, M. Moscovitch, & E. Thompson (Eds.), *The Cambridge handbook of consciousness* (pp. 597–629). New York, NY: Cambridge University Press.

Berkowitz, L. (1993). *Aggression: Its causes, consequences, and control.* New York, NY: McGraw-Hill.

Berkowitz, L. (1998). Affective aggression: The role of stress, pain, and negative affect. In R. G. Geen & E. Donnerstein (Eds.), *Human aggression: Theories, research, and implications for public policy* (pp. 49–72). San Diego, CA: Academic Press.

Berkowitz, S. J. (2003). Children exposed to community violence: The rationale for early intervention. *Clinical Child and Family Psychology Review, 6,* 293–302.

Berlin, B., & Kay, P. (1969). *Basic color terms: Their universality and evolution.* Berkeley: University of California Press.

Berlyne, D. E. (1960). *Conflict, arousal, and curiosity.* New York, NY: McGraw-Hill.

Bernard, L. L. (1924). *Instinct.* New York, NY: Holt, Rinehart & Winston.

Berndt, T. J. (1992). Friendship and friends' influence in adolescence. *Current Directions in Psychological Science, 1,* 156–159.

Bernstein, I. L. (1991). Aversion conditioning in response to cancer and cancer treatment. *Clinical Psychology Review, 11,* 185–191.

Berscheid, E., & Walster, E. H. (1978). *Interpersonal attraction* (2nd ed.). Reading, MA: Addison-Wesley.

Bersoff, D. N. (2008). *Ethical conflicts in psychology* (3rd ed.). Washington, DC: American Psychological Association.

Bhuvaneswar, C. G., & Gutheil, T. G. (2008). E-mail and psychiatry: Some psychotherapeutic and psychoanalytic perspectives. *American Journal of Psychotherapy, 62,* 241–261.

Bickerton, D. (1990). *Language and species.* Chicago, IL: University of Chicago Press.

Biederman, J., & Faraone, S. V. (2005). Attention-deficit hyperactivity disorder. *The Lancet, 366,* 237–248.

Biederman, J., Faraone, S. V., & Monteaux, M. C. (2002). Differential effect of environmental adversity by gender: Rutter's index of adversity in a group of boys and girls with and without ADHD. *American Journal of Psychiatry, 159,* 1556–1562.

Biehl, M., Matsumoto, D., Ekman, P., Hearn, V., Heider, K., Kudoh, T., & Ton, V. (1997). Matsumoto and Ekman's Japanese and Caucasian facial expressions of emotion (JACFEE): Reliability data and cross-national differences. *Journal of Nonverbal Behavior, 21,* 3–21.

Biel, M. B., Preselow, E., Mulcare, L., Case, B. G., & Fieve, R. (2007). Continuation versus discontinuation of lithium in recurrent bipolar illnesss: A naturalistic study. *Bipolar Disorders, 9,* 435–442.

Bielak, A. A. M., Hughes, T. F., Small, B. J., & Dixon, R. A. (2007). It's never too late to engage in lifestyle activities: Significant concurrent but not change relationships between lifestyle activities and cognitive speeed. *Journal of Gerontology: Psychological Sciences, 62B,* P331–339.

Biglan, A. (1991). Distressed behavior and its context. *Behavior Analyst, 14,* 157–169.

Billings, A. G., & Moos, R. H. (1982). Family environments and adaptation: A clinically applicable typology. *American Journal of Family Therapy, 20,* 26–38.

Binet, A. (1911). *Les idées modernes sur les enfants.* Paris, France: Flammarion.

Bingenheimer, J. B., Brennan, R. T., & Earls, F. J. (2005). Firearm violence exposure and serious violent behavior. *Science, 308,* 1323–1326.

Black, D. N., Seritan, A. L., Taber, K. H., & Hurley, R. A. (2004). Conversion hysteria: Lessons from functional imaging. *Journal of Neuropsychiatry and Clinical Neurosciences, 16,* 245–251.

Black, J. E., Polinsky, M., & Greenough, W. T. (1989). Progressive failure of cerebral angiogenesis supporting neural plasticity in aging rats. *Neurobiological Aging, 10*(4), 353–358. Review.

Black, J. E., Greenough, W. T., Anderson, B. J., & Isaacs, K. R. (1987). Environment and the aging brain. *Canadian Journal of Psychology, 41*(2), 111–130. Review.

Blatter, K., & Cajochen, C. (2007). Circadian rhythms in cognitive performance: Methodological constraints, protocols, theoretical underpinnings. *Physiology & Behavior, 90*(2–3), 196–208.

Bleuler, M. (1978). The long-term course of schizophrenic psychoses. In L. C. Wynne, R. L. Cromwell, & S. Mattysse (Eds.), *The nature of schizophrenia: New approaches to research and treatment* (pp. 631–636). New York, NY: Wiley.

Blond, A. (2008). Impacts of exposure to images of ideal bodies on male body dissatisfaction: A review. *Body Image, 5,* 244–250.

Bloom, K., Delmore-Ko, P., Masataka, N., & Carli, L. (1999). Possible self as parent in Canadian, Italian, and Japanese young adults. *Canadian Journal of Behavioural Science, 31,* 198–207.

Blos, P. (1965). *On adolescence: A psychoanalytic interpretation.* New York, NY: The Free Press.

Blumberg, H. P., Leung, H. C., Skudlarski, P., Lacadie, C. M., Fredericks, C. A., Harris, B. C., . . . Peterson, B. S. (2003). A functional magnetic resonance imaging study of bipolar disorder. *Archives of General Psychiatry, 60,* 601–609.

Blustein, D. L. (2008). The role of work in psychological health and well-being: A conceptual, historical, and public policy perspective. *American Psychologist, 63,* 228–240.

Boardman, J. D., Saint Onge, J. M., Haberstick, B. C., Timberlake, D. S., & Hewitt, J. K. (2008). Do schools moderate the genetic determinants of smoking? *Behavioral Genetics, 38,* 234–246.

Bock, K. (1990). Structure in language: Creating form in talk. *American Psychologist, 45,* 1221–1236.

Bock, K., Dell, G. S., Chang, F., & Onishi, K. H. (2007). Persistent structural priming from language comprehension to language production. *Cognition, 104*(3), 437–458.

Bogaert, A. F., & Purves, D. (Eds.). (2006). Biological versus nonbiological older brothers and men's sexual orientation. *Proceedings of the National Academy of Sciences of the United States of America, 103*(28), 10771–10774.

Bogaert, A. G., Blanchard, R., & Crosthwait, L. E. (2007). Interaction of birth order, handedness, and sexual orientation in the Kinsey interview data. *Behavioral Neuroscience, 121*(5), 845–853.

Bogle, K. A. (2008). *Hooking up: Sex, dating, and relationships on campus.* New York, NY: New York University Press.

Bohannon, J.N., III, Gratz, S., & Cross, V.S. (2007). The effects of affect and input and source on flashbulb memories. *Applied Cognitive Psychology, 21,* 1023–1036.

Bohlin, G., Hagekull, B., & Rydell, A.-M. (2000). Attachment and social functioning: A longitudinal study from infancy to middle childhood. *Social Development, 9,* 24–39.

Boivin, D. B., Tremblay, G. M., & James, F. O. (2007). Working on atypical schedules. *Sleep Medicine, 8,* 578–589.

Boldizar, J. P., Wilson, K. L., & Deemer, D. K. (1989). Gender, life experiences, and moral judgment development: A process-oriented approach. *Journal of Personality and Social Psychology, 57*(2), 229–238.

Bolino, M. C., & Turnley, W. H. (2008). Old faces, new places: Equity theory in cross-cultural contexts. *Journal of Organizational Behavior, 29,* 29–50.

Bolton, D., & Perrin, S. (2008). Evaluation of exposure with response-prevention for obsessive compulsive disorder in childhood and adolescence. *Journal of Behavior Therapy and Experimental Psychiatry, 39,* 11–22.

Bolton, J. M., Belik, S.-L., Enns, M. W., Cox, B. J., & Sareen, J. (2008). Exploring the correlates of suicide attempts among individuals with major depressive disorder: Findings from the national epidemiologic survey on alcohol and related conditions. *The Journal of Clinical Psychiatry, 69,* 1139–1149.

Bonanno, G. A., & Mancini, A. D. (2008). The human capacity to thrive in the face of potential trauma. *Pediatrics, 121,* 369–375.

Bond, C. F., Jr., Pitre, U., & van Leeuwen, M. D. (1991). Encoding operations and the next-in-line effect. *Personality and Social Psychology Bulletin, 17,* 435–441.

Bond, L. (1995). Unintended consequences of performance assessment: Issues of bias and fairness. *Educational Measurement: Issues and Practices, 14*(4), 21–24.

Bond, M. H. (2004). Culture and aggression—from context to coercion. *Personality and Social Psychology Review, 8,* 62–78.

Bornstein, M. H., & Arterberry, M. E. (2003). Recognition, discrimination and categorization of smiling by 5-month-old infants. *Developmental Science, 6,* 585–599.

Bostrom, N. (2005). In defense of posthuman dignity. *Bioethics, 19,* 202–214.

Bouchard, T. J., Jr. (2004). Genetic influence on human psychological traits: A survey. *Current Directions in Psychological Science, 13,* 148–151.

Bouchard, T. J., Jr., & Loehlin, J. C. (2001). Genes, evolution, and personality. *Behavior Genetics, 31,* 243–273.

Boutin, P., & Frougel, P. (2005). GAD2: A polygenic contribution to genetic susceptibility for common obesity? *Pathologie Biologie, 53,* 305–307.

Bovbjerg, D. H., Montgomery, G. H., & Raptis, G. (2005). Evidence for classically conditioned fatigue responses in patients receiving chemotherapy treatment for breast cancer. *Journal of Behavioral Medicine, 28,* 231–237.

Bowden, E. M., & Beeman, M. J. (1998). Getting the right idea: Semantic activation in the right hemisphere may help solve insight problems. *Psychological Science, 9,* 435–440.

Bowden, E. M., & Beeman, M. J. (2003). Normative data for 144 compound remote associates problem. *Behavior Resarch Methods, Instruments, and Computers, 35,* 634–639.

Bowers, J. S., & Marsolek, C. J. (Eds.). (2003). *Rethinking implicit memory.* London, United Kingdom: Oxford University Press.

Bowlby, J. (1969). *Attachment and loss, Vol. 1. Attachment.* New York, NY: Basic Books.

Bowlby, J. (1973). *Attachment and loss, Vol. 2. Separation, anxiety and anger.* London, United Kingdom: Hogarth.

Boyd, R. C., Diamond, G. S., & Bourolly, J. N. (2006). Developing a family-based depression prevention program in urban community mental health clinics: A qualitative investigation. *Family Process, 45,* 187–203.

Boysen, G. A., & Vogel, D. L. (2007). Biased assimilation and attitude polarization in response to learning about biological explanations of homosexuality. *Sex Roles, 57,* 755–762.

Braginsky, B. M., & Braginsky, D. D. (1967). Schizophrenic patients in the psychiatric interview: An experimental study of their effectiveness at manipulation. *Journal of Consultation Psychology, 31,* 543–547.

Brainerd, C. J. (1996). Piaget: A centennial celebration. *Psychological Science, 7,* 191–195.

Bramlett, M. D., & Mosher, W. D. (2001). *First marriage dissolution, divorce, and remarriage: United States.* Washington, DC: Centers for Disease Control and Prevention.

Brans, R. G. H., van Haren, N. E. M., van Baal, C. M., Schnack, H. G., Kahn, R. S., & Hulshoff, H. E. (2008). Heritability of changes in brain volume over time in twin pairs discordant for schizophrenia. *Archives of General Psychiatry, 65,* 1259–1268.

Braun, K. A., Ellis, R., & Loftus, E. F. (2002). Make my memory: How advertising can change our memories of the past. *Psychology & Marketing, 19,* 1–23.

Breedlove, S. M. (1994). Sexual differentiation of the human nervous system. *Annual Review of Psychology, 45:* 389–418.

Breggin, P. R. (1979). *Electroshock: Its brain disabling effects.* New York, NY: Springer.

Breggin, P. R. (1991). *Toxic psychiatry.* New York, NY: St. Martin's Press.

Breland, K., & Breland, M. (1951). A field of applied animal psychology. *American Psychologist, 6,* 202–204.

Breland, K., & Breland, M. (1961). A misbehavior of organisms. *American Psychologist, 16,* 681–684.

Brendgen, M., Dionne, G., Girard, A., Boivin, M., Vitaor, F., & Pérusse, D. (2005). Examining genetic and environmental effects on social aggression: A study of 6–year-old twins. *Child Development, 76,* 930–946.

Bretherton, I. (1996). Internal working models of attachment relationships as related to resilient coping. In G. G. Noam & K. W. Fischer (Eds.), *Development and vulnerability in close relationships* (pp. 3–27). Mahwah, NJ: Erlbaum.

Brewer, M. B. (2007). The importance of being we: Human nature and intergroup relations. *American Psychologist, 62,* 728–738.

Bridge, J. A., & Barbe, R. P. (2004). Reducing hospital readmission in depression and schizophrenia: Current evidence. *Current Opinion in Psychiatry, 17,* 505–511.

Bridge, J. A., Iyengar, S., Salary, C. B., Barbe, R. P., Birmaher, B., Pincus, H. A., . . . Brent, D. A. (2007). Clinical response and risk for reported suicidal ideation and suicide attempts in pediatric antidepressant treatment: A meta-analysis of randomized controlled trials. *JAMA, 297,* 1683–1696.

Brisson, B., & Jolicoeur, P. (2007). A psychological refractory period in access to visual short-term memory and the deployment of visual-spatial attention: Multitasking processing deficits revealed by event-related potentials. *Psychophysiology, 44*(2), 323–333.

Brody, A. L., Saxena, S., Stoessel, P., Gillies, L. A., Fairbanks, L. A., Alborzian, S., . . . Baxter, L. R., Jr. (2002). Regional brain metabolic changes in patients with major depression treated with either paroxetine or interpersonal therapy. *Archives of General Psychiatry, 58,* 631–640.

Broman, S. H., Nichols, P. I., & Kennedy, W. A. (1975). *Preschool IQ: Prenatal and early developmental correlates.* Hillsdale, NJ: Erlbaum.

Bronfenbrenner, U. (Ed.). (2004). *Making human beings human: Bioecological perspectives on human development.* Thousand Oaks, CA: Sage Publications.

Brown, F. B., & Klute, C. (2003). Friendships, cliques, and crowds. In G. R. Adams & M. D. Berzonsky (Eds.), *Blackwell handbooks of developmental psychology* (pp. 330–348). Malden, MA: Blackwell Publishing.

Brown, N. R., & Siegler, R. S. (1992). The role of availability in the estimation of national populations. *Memory & Cognition, 20,* 406–412.

Brown, R. (1976). Reference: In memorial tribute to Eric Lenneberg. *Cognition, 4,* 125–153.

Brown, R. (1986). *Social psychology: The second edition.* New York, NY: The Free Press.

Brown, R. J. (2004). Psychological mechanisms in medically unexplained symptoms: An integrative conceptual model. *Psychological Bulletin, 130,* 793–812.

Brown, R., & Kulik, J. (1977). Flashbulb memories. *Cognition, 5,* 73–99.

Bruni, O., Ferri, R., Novelli, L., Finotti, E., Miano, S., & Guilleminault, C. (2008). NREM sleep instability in children with sleep terrors: The role of slow wave activity interruptions. *Clinical Neurophysiology, 119*(5), 985–992.

Brunyé, T. T., Rapp, D. N., & Taylor, H. A. (2008). Representational flexibility and specificity following spatial descriptions of real-world environments. *Cognition, 108,* 418–443.

Buboltz, W. C., Jr., Soper, B., Brown, F., & Jenkins, S. (2002). Treatment approaches for sleep difficulties in college students. *Counselling Psychology Quarterly, 15,* 229–237.

Buchner, A., & Wippich, W. (2000). On the reliability of implicit and explicit memory measures. *Cognitive Psychology, 40,* 227–259.

Buckner, J. C., Mezzacappa, E., & Beardslee, W. R. (2003). Characteristics of resilient youths living in poverty: The role of self-regulatory processes. *Development and Psychopathology, 15,* 139–162.

Buckworth, J., Lee, R. E., Regan, G., Schneider, L. K., & DiClemente, C. C. (2007). Decomposing intrinsic and extrinsic motivation for exercise: Application to stages of motivational readiness. *Psychology of Sport and Exercise, 8,* 441–461.

Buffardi, L. E., & Campbell, W. K. (2008). Narcissism and social networking web sites. *Personality and Social Psychology Bulletin, 34,* 1303–1314.

Burchinal, M. R., Roberts, J. E., Riggin, R., Jr., Zeisel, S. A., Neebe, E., & Bryant, D. (2000). Relating quality of center-based child care to early cognitive and language development longitudinally. *Child Development, 71*(2), 339–357.

Burgard, M., & Mitchell, J. E. (2000). Group cognitive behavioral therapy for buying disorder. In A. L. Benson (Ed.), *I shop therefore I am: Compulsive buying and the search for self* (pp. 367–397). Northvale, NJ: Jason Aronson.

Burger, J. M. (2009). Replicating Milgram: Would people still obey today? *American Psychologist, 64,* 1–11.

Burkley, E. (2008). The role of self-control in resistance to persuasion. *Personality and Social Psychology Bulletin, 34,* 419–431.

Burnett, R. C., Medin, D. L., Ross, N. O., & Blok, S. V. (2005). Ideal is typical. *Canadian Journal of Experimental Psychology, 59,* 3–10.

Bushman, B. J., & Anderson, C. J. (2002). Violent video games and hostile expectations: A test of the general aggression model. *Personality and Social Psychology Bulletin, 28,* 1679–1686.

Buss, D. M. (1995). Evolutionary psychology: A new paradigm for psychological science. *Psychological Inquiry, 6,* 1–30.

Buss, D. M. (2000). The evolution of happiness. *American Psychologist, 55,* 15–23.

Buss, D. M. (2004). *Evolutionary psychology: The new science of mind* (2nd ed.). Boston, MA: Allyn & Bacon.

Buss, D. M. (2008). *Evolutionary psychology: The new science of mind* (3rd ed.), Boston, MA: Allyn & Bacon.

Butcher, J. N., & Rouse, S. V. (1996). Personality: Individual differences and clinical assessment. *Annual Review of Psychology, 47,* 87–111.

Butcher, J. N., Graham, J. R., Ben-Porath, Y. S., Tellegen, A., Dahlstrom, W. G., & Kaemmer, B. (2001). *Minnesota Multiphasic Personality Inventory-2 (MMPI-2): Manual for administration and scoring* (2nd ed.). Minneapolis, MN: University of Minnesota Press.

Butcher, J. N., Mineka, S., & Hooley, J. M. (2008). *Abnormal psychology* (13th ed.). Boston, MA: Allyn & Bacon.

Byers, S. E., Purdon, C., & Clark, D. A. (1998). Sexual intrusive thoughts of college students. *Journal of Sex Research, 35*(4), 359–369.

Bykov, K. M. (1957). *The cerebral cortex and the internal organs.* New York, NY: Academic Press.

Byrne, D., & Clore, G. L. (1970). A reinforcement model of evaluative processes. *Personality: An International Journal, 1,* 103–128.

Cabeza, R. (2002). Hemispheric asymmetry reduction in older adults: The HAROLD model. *Psychology and Aging, 17,* 85-100.

Cabeza, R., & Nyberg, L. (2000). Imaging cognition II: An empirical review of 275 PET and fMRI studies. *Journal of Cognitive Neuroscience, 12,*1–47.

Cabeza, R., Daselaar, S. M., Dolcos, F., Prince, S. E., Budde, M., & Nyberg, L. (2004). Task-independent and task-specific age effects on brain activity during working memory, visual attention and episodic retrieval. *Cerebral Cortex, 14,* 364–375.

Cahill, L., Uncapher, M., Kilpatrick, L., Alkire, M. T., & Turner, J. (2004). Sex-related hemispheric lateralization of amygdala function in emotionally influenced memory: An fMRI investigation. *Learning & Memory, 11,* 261–266.

Cahn, B. R., & Polich, J. (2006). Meditation states and traits: EEG, ERP, and neuroimaging studies. *Psychological Bulletin, 132,* 180–211.

Caird, J. K., Edwards, C. J., Creaser, J. I., & Horrey, W. J. (2005). Older driver failures of attention at intersections: Using change blindness methods to assess turn decision accuracy. *Human Factors, 47*(2), 235–249.

Callaghan, T., Rochat, P., Lillard, A., Claux, M. L., Odden, H., Itakura, S., . . . Singh, S. (2005). Synchrony in the onset of mental-state reasoning: Evidence from five cultures. *Psychological Science, 16*(5), 378–384.

Cameron, C. L., Cella, D. C., Herndon, E. E., II, Kornblith, A. B., Zucerkman, E., Henderson, E., . . . Holland, J. C. (2001). Persistent symptoms among survivors of Hodgkin's disease: An explanatory model based on classical conditioning. *Health Psychology, 20,* 71–75.

Campbell, L., & Ellis, B. J. (2005). Commitment, love, and mate retention. In D. M. Buss (Ed.), *The handbook of evolutionary psychology* (pp. 419–442). Hoboken, NJ: John Wiley & Sons.

Campos, J. J., Bertenthal, B. I., & Kermoian, R. (1992). Early experience and emotional development: The emergence of wariness of heights. *Psychological Science, 3,* 61–64.

Camras, L. A., Oster, H., Bakeman, R., Meng, Z., Ujiie, T., & Campos, J. L. (2007). Do infants show distinct negative facial expressions for fear and anger? Emotional expression in 11-month-old European American, Chinese, and Japanese infants. *Infancy, 11,* 131–155.

Camras, L. A., Oster, H., Campos, J., Campos, R., Ujiie, T., Miyake, K., . . . Meng, Z. (1998). Production of emotional facial expressions in European American, Japanese, and Chinese infants. *Developmental Psychology, 34,* 616–628.

Canadian ADHD Resource Alliance (CADDRA). (2007). Retrieved from http://www.caddra.ca/english/educators.html

Canadian Council on Animal Care. (1993). *Guide to the care and use of experimental animals.* Retrieved from http://www.ccac.ca/en/CCAC_Programs/Guidelines_Policies/GUIDES/ENGLISH/toc_v1.htm

Canadian Institute for Health Information (CIHI). (2007). *Improving the health of Canadians: Mental health and homelessness*. Retrieved from http://intraspec.ca/mental_health_report_aug22_2007_e.pdf

Canadian Psychological Association (CPA). (2009b). *Health anxiety*. Retrieved from http://www.cpa.ca/publications/yourhealthpsychologyworksfactsheets/healthanxiety

Canadian Psychological Association. (2000a). *Canadian code of ethics for psychologists (3*rd edition). Ottawa.

Canadian Psychological Association. (2009a). *Annual report 2008–2009*. Retrieved from http://www.cpa.ca/cpasite/userfiles/Documents/aboutcpa/annual_reports/Annual_Report_2009.pdf

Canli, T., Desmond, J. E., Zhao, Z., & Gabrieli, J. D. E. (2002). Sex differences in the neural basis of emotional memories. *Proceedings of the National Academy of Sciences, 99,* 10789–10794.

Canli, T., Desmond, J. E., Zhao, Z., Glover, G., & Gabrieli, J. D. E. (1998). Hemispheric asymmetry for emotional stimuli detected with fMRI. *NeuroReport, 9,* 3233–3239.

Canli, T., Sivers, H., Whitfield, S. L., Gotlib, I. H., & Gabrieli, J. D. E. (2002). Amygdala response to happy faces as a function of extraversion. *Science, 296,* 2191.

Cannon, W. B. (1927). The James-Lange theory of emotion: A critical examination and an alternative theory. *American Journal of Psychology, 39,* 106–124.

Cannon, W. B. (1929). *Bodily changes in pain, hunger, fear, and rage* (2nd ed.). New York, NY: Appleton-Century-Crofts.

Cannon, W. B. (1934). Hunger and thirst. In C. Murchison (Ed.), *A handbook of general experimental psychology.* Worcester, MA: Clark University Press.

Cannon, W. B., & Washburn, A. L. (1912). An explanation of hunger. *American Journal of Physiology, 29,* 441–454.

Cantor, N., & Kihlstrom, J. R. (1987). *Personality and social intelligence.* Englewood Cliffs, NJ: Prentice Hall.

Caprara, G. V., Barbaranelli, C., & Zimbardo, P. G. (1996). Understanding the complexity of human aggression: Affective, cognitive, and social dimensions of individual differences in pro-pensity toward aggression. *European Journal of Personality, 10,* 133–155.

Carazo, P., Sanchez, E., Font, E., & Desbilis, E. (2004). Chemosensory cues allow male *Tenebrio molitor* beetles to assess the reproductive status of prospective mates. *Animal Behaviour, 68,* 123–129.

Carducci, B. J., & Zimbardo, P. G. (1995). Are you shy? *Psychology Today, 28,* 34–40.

Carey, S. (1978). The child as word learner. In M. Hale, J. Bresnan, & G. A. Miller (Eds.), *Linguistic theory and psychological reality* (pp. 265–293). Cambridge, MA: MIT Press.

Carey, S. (1985). *Conceptual change in childhood.* Cambridge, MA: MIT Press.

Carlier, P., & Jamon, M. (2006). Observational learning in C57BL/6j mice. *Behavioural Brain Research, 174*(1), 125–131.

Carnagey, N. L., Anderson, C. A., & Bushman, B. J. (2007). The effect of video game violence on physiological desensitization to real-life violence. *Journal of Experimental Social Psychology, 43,* 489–496.

Caron, S. L., & Moskey, E. G. (2002). Changes over time in teenage sexual relationships: Comparing the high school class of 1950, 1975, and 2000. *Adolescence, 37,* 515–526.

Carroll, J. (1998). Steven Pinker's cheesecake for the mind. *Philosophy and Literature, 22,* 478–485.

Carroll, M. E., & Overmier, J. B. (Eds.). (2001). *Animal research and human health: advancing human welfare through behavioral science.* Washington, DC: American Psychological Association.

Carskadon, M. A. (2002). *Adolescent sleep patterns: Biological, social, and psychological influences.* New York, NY: Cambridge University Press.

Carskadon, M. A., Acebo, C., & Jenni, O. G. (2004). Regulation of adolescent sleep: Implications for behavior. *Annals of New York Academy of Science, 1021,* 276–291.

Carstensen, L. L. (1991). Selectivity theory: Social activity in life-span context. In K. W. Schaie (Ed.), *Annual review of geriatrics and gerontology* (Vol. 11). New York, NY: Springer.

Carstensen, L. L. (1998). A life-span approach to social motivation. In J. Heckhausen & C. S. Dweck (Eds.), *Motivation and self-regulation across the life span* (pp. 341–364). New York, NY: Cambridge University Press.

Carstensen, L. L., & Freund, A. M. (1994). The resilience of the aging self. *Developmental Review, 14,* 81–92.

Carstensen, L. L., & Pasupathi, M. (1993). Women of a certain age. In S. Matteo (Ed.), *American women in the nineties: Today's critical issues* (pp. 66–78). Boston, MA: Northeastern University Press.

Carter, B., & Campeau, L. (2009). The top Rx drugs in Canada: Our annual look at what's topping the chart in prescriptions. *Pharmacy Practice, April/May, 30–38.* Retrieved from: http://www.pharmacygateway.ca/pdfs/2009/04/PPR200904-05TopDrugs.pdf

Carter, J. H. (1982). The effects of aging on selected visual functions: Color vision, glare sensitivity, field of vision, and accommodation. In R. Sekuler, D. Kline, & K. Dismukes (Eds.), *Aging and human visual function* (pp. 121–130). New York, NY: Liss.

Carter, S. J., & Cassaday, H. J. (1998). State-dependent retrieval and chlorpheniramine. *Human Psychopharmacology, 13,* 513–523.

Caspi, A., Sugden, K., Moffitt, T. E., Taylor, A., Craig, I. W., Harrington, H., . . . Poulton, R. (2003). Influence of life stress on depression: Moderation by a polymorphism in the 5–HTT gene. *Science, 301,* 386–389.

Cassel, J.-C., Riegert, C., Rutz, S., Koenig, J., Rothmaier, K., Cosquer, B., . . . Jackisch, R. (2005). Ethanol, 3,4–methylenedioxymethamphetamine (ecstasy) and their combination: Long-term behavioral, neurochemical and neuropharmacological effects in the rat. *Neuropsychopharmacology, 30,* 1870–1882.

Cassin, S. E., von Ranson, K. M., Heng, K., Brar, J., & Wojtowica, A. E. (2008). Adapted motivational interviewing for women with binge eating disorder: A randomized controlled trial. *Psychology of Addictive Behaviors, 22,* 417–425.

Catalano, R., Novaco, R. W., & McConnell, W. (2002). Layoffs and violence revisited. *Aggressive Behavior, 28,* 233–247.

Catalano, R., Novaco, R., & McConnell, W. (1997). A model of the net effect of job loss on violence. *Journal of Personality and Social Psychology, 72,* 1440–1447.

Caterina, M. J., Leffler, A., Malmberg, A. B., Martin, W. J., Trafton, J., Petersen-Zeitz, K. R., . . . Julius, D. (2000). Impaired nociception and pain sensation in mice lacking the capsaicin receptor. *Science, 288,* 306–313.

Cattell, R. B. (1963). Theory of fluid and crystallized intelligence: A critical experiment. *Journal of Educational Psychology, 54,*1–22.

Cattell, R. B. (1979). *Personality and learning theory.* New York, NY: Springer.

Ceci, S. J. (1999). Schooling and intelligence. In S. J. Ceci & W. M. Williams (Eds.), *The nature-nurture debate: The essential readings* (pp. 168–175). Oxford, United Kingdom: Blackwell.

Centers for Disease Control and Prevention. (2007, February 9). Prevalence of autism spectrum disorders—Autism and Developmental Disabilities Monitoring Network, 14 Sites, United States, 2002. *Morbidity and Mortality Weekly Report, 56,* 12–28. Retrieved from http://www.cdc.gov/mmwr/PDF/ss/ss5601.pdf

Centre for Addiction and Mental Health. (2004). *Post traumatic stress disorder.* Retrieved from http://www.camh.net/About_Addiction_Mental_Health/Mental_Health_Information/ptsd_photonov.pdf

Ceschi, G., van der Linden, M., Dunker, D., Perroud, A., & Brédart, S. (2003). Further exploration memory bias in compulsive washers. *Behaviour Research and Therapy, 41,* 737–748.

Chambers, A. P., Koopmans, H. S., Pittman, Q. J., & Sharkey, K. A. (2006). AM 251 produces sustained reductions in food intake and body weight that are resistant to tolerance and conditioned taste aversion. *British Journal of Pharmacology, 147*(1), 109–116.

Chambers, A. P., Sharkey, K. A., & Koopmans, H.S. (2004). CB1 receptor antagonist, AM251, causes sustained reduction of daily food intake in the rat. *Physiology and Behavior, 82,* 863–869.

Champoux, M., Boyce, W. T., & Suomi, S. J. (1995). Biobehavioral comparisons between adopted and nonadopted rhesus monkey infants. *Journal of Developmental and Behavioral Pediatrics, 16,* 6–13.

Chan, A. Y., & Wethington, E. (1998). Factors promoting marital resilience among interracial couples. In H. I. McCubbin, E. A. Thompson, A. I. Thompson, & J. E. Fromer (Eds.), *Resiliency in Native American and immigrant families* (pp. 71–87). Thousand Oaks, CA: Sage.

Chao, S. J., & Cheng, P. W. (2000). The emergence of inferential rules: The use of pragmatic reasoning schemas by preschoolers. *Cognitive Development, 15,* 39–62.

Chapman, P. D. (1988). *Schools as sorters: Lewis M. Terman, applied psychology, and the intelligence testing movement, 1890–1930.* New York, NY: New York University Press.

Chartrand, T. L., & Bargh, J. A. (1999). The chameleon effect: The perception–behavior link and social interaction. *Journal of Personality and Social Psychology, 76,* 893–910.

Chase, W. G., & Ericsson, K. A. (1981). Skilled memory. In J. R. Anderson (Ed.), *Cognitive skills and their acquisition.* Hillsdale, NJ: Erlbaum.

Chaudhari, N., Landin, A. M., & Roper, S. D. (2000). A metabotropic glutamate receptor variant functions as a taste receptor. *Nature Neuroscience, 3,* 113–119.

Chaves, J. F. (1999). Applying hypnosis in pain management: Implications of alternative theoretical perspectives. In I. Kirsch, A. Capafons, E. Cardeña-Buelna, & S. Amigó (Eds.), *Clinical hypnosis and self-regulation: Cognitive-behavioral perspectives* (pp. 227–247). Washington, DC: American Psychological Association.

Chen, F. F., & Kenrick, D. T. (2002). Repulsion or attraction? Group membership and assumed attitude similarity. *Journal of Personality and Social Psychology, 83,* 111–125.

Chen, S., Boucher, H. C., & Tapias, M. P. (2006). The relational self revealed: Integrative conceptualization and implications for interpersonal life. *Psychological Bulletin, 132,* 151–179.

Chen, Z., & Cowan, N. (2005). Chunk limits and length limits in immediate recall: A reconciliation. *Journal of Experimental Psychology: Learning, Memory and Cognition, 31,* 1235–1249.

Cheney, D. L., & Seyfarth, R. M. (1990). *How monkeys see the world.* Chicago, IL: University of Chicago Press.

Cheng, P. W., & Holyoak, K. J. (1985). Pragmatic reasoning schemas. *Cognitive Psychology, 17,* 391–416.

Cherry, E. C. (1953). Some experiments on the recognition of speech, with one and with two ears. *Journal of the Acoustical Society of America, 25,* 975–979.

Chiappe, D., Brown, A., Dow, B., Koontz, J., Rodriguez, M., & McCulloch, K. (2004). Cheaters are looked at longer and remembered better than cooperators in social exchange situations. *Evolutionary Psychology, 2,* 108–120.

Chomsky, N. (1965). *Aspects of a theory of syntax.* Cambridge, MA: MIT Press.

Chomsky, N. (1975). *Reflections on language.* New York, NY: Pantheon Books.

Christensen, A. J., & Johnson, J. A. (2002). Patient adherence with medical treatment regimens: An interactive approach. *Current Directions in Psychological Science, 11,* 94–97.

Christensen, A., Atkins, D. C., Yi, J., Baucom, D. H., & George, W. H. (2006). Couple and individual adjustment for 2 years following a randomized clinical trial comparing traditional versus integrative behavioral couple therapy. *Journal of Consulting and Clinical Psychology, 74,* 1180–1191.

Christensen, B. T., & Schunn, C. D. (2007). The relationship of analogical distance to analogical function and preinventive structure: The case of engineering design. *Memory & Cognition, 35*(1), 29–38.

Christie, B. R., & Cameron, H. A. (2006). Neurogenesis in the adult hippocampus. *Hippocampus, 16,* 199–207.

Cialdini, R. B. (2009). *Influence: Science and practice* (5th ed.). Boston, MA: Allyn & Bacon.

Cialdini, R. B., & Goldstein, N. J. (2004). Social influence: Compliance and conformity. *Annual Review of Psychology, 55,* 591–621.

Cialdini, R. B., Vincent, J. E., Lewis, S. K., Catalan, J., Wheeler, D., & Darby, B. L. (1975). Reciprocal concessions procedure for inducing compliance: The door-in-the-face technique. *Journal of Personality and Social Psychology, 31,* 206–215.

Clark, E. V. (2003). *First language acquisition.* Cambridge, United Kingdom: Cambridge University Press.

Clark, H. H. (1996). *Using language.* Cambridge, United Kingdom: Cambridge University Press.

Clark, H. H., & Clark, E., V. (1977). *Psychology and language: An introduction to psycholinguistics.* New York, NY: Harcourt Brace Jovanovich.

Clark, H. H., & Van Der Wege, M. M. (2002). Psycholinguistics. In H. Pashler & D. Medin (Eds.), *Stevens' handbook of experimental psychology: Vol. 3. Memory and cognitive processes* (pp. 209–259). New York, NY: Wiley.

Clark, M. D., & Carroll, M. H. (2008). Acquaintance rape scripts of women and men: Similarities and differences. *Sex Roles, 58,* 616–625.

Clarke-Stewart, K. A. (1991). A home is not a school: The effects of child care on children's development. *Journal of Social Issues, 47,* 105–123.

Clarke-Stewart, K. A. (1993). *Daycare.* Cambridge, MA: Harvard University Press.

Clopton, N. A., & Sorell, G. T. (1993). Gender differences in moral reasoning: Stable or situational? *Psychology of Women Quarterly, 17,* 85–101.

Clore, G. L., & Huntsinger, J. R. (2007). How emotions inform judgment and regulate thought. *Trends in Cognitive Sciences, 11,* 393–399.

Coan, J. A., Schaefer, H. S., & Davidson, R. J. (2006). Lending a hand: Social regulation of the neural response to threat. *Psychological Science, 17,* 1032–1039.

Coates, T. J., & Szekeres, G. (2004). A plan for the next generation of HIV prevention research: Seven key policy investigative challenges. *American Psychologist, 59,* 747–757.

Coe, C. L. (1999). Psychosocial factors and psychoneuroimmunology within a lifespan perspective. In D. P. Keating & C. Hertzman (Eds.), *Developmental health and the wealth of nations: Social, biological, and educational dynamics* (pp. 201–219). New York, NY: Guilford Press.

Cohen, A., & Avrahami, A. (2005). Soccer fans' motivation as a predictor of participation in soccer-related activities: An empirical examination in Israel. *Social Behavior and Personality, 33,* 419–434.

Cohen, P., Chen, H., Gordon, K., Johnson, J., Brook, J., & Kasen, S. (2008). Socioeconomic background and the developmental course of schizotypal and borderline personality disorder symptoms. *Development and Psychopathology, 20,* 633–650.

Cohen, S., Tyrrell, D. A. J., & Smith, A. P. (1993). Negative life events, perceived stress, negative affect, and susceptibility to the common cold. *Journal of Personality and Social Psychology, 64,* 131–140.

Cole, D. A., Ciesla, J. A., Dallaire, D. H., Jacquez, F. M., Pineda, A. Q., LaGrange, B., . . . Felton, J. W. (2008). Emergence of attributional style and its relation to depressive symptoms. *Journal of Abnormal Psychology, 117,* 16–31.

Collins, D. W., & Kimura, D. (1997). A large sex difference on a two-dimensional mental rotation task. *Behavioral Neuroscience, 111*(4), 845–849.

Collins, M. A., & Amabile, T. M. (1999). Motivation and creativity. In R. J. Sternberg (Ed.), *Handbook of creativity* (pp. 297–312). Cambridge, United Kingdom: Cambridge University Press.

Collins, W. A., Maccoby, E. E., Steinberg, L., Hetherington, E. M., & Bornstein, M. H. (2000). Contemporary research on parenting: The case for nature and nurture. *American Psychologist, 55,* 218–232.

Comstock, G., & Scharrer, E. (1999). *Television: What's on, who's watching, and what it means.* San Diego, CA: Academic Press.

Congdon, E., & Canli, T. (2006). The endophenotype of impulsivity: Reaching consilience through behavioral, genetic, and neuroimaging approaches. *Behavioral and Cognitive Neuroscience, 4,* 1–20.

Cook, C. R., Gresham, F. M., Kern, L., Barreras, R. B., Thornton, S., & Crews, S. D. (2008). Social skills training for secondary students with emotional and/or behavioral disorders: A review and analysis of the meta-analytic literature. *Journal of Emotional and Behavioral Disorders, 16,* 131–144.

Cook, M., & Mineka, S. (1990). Selective associations in the observational conditioning of fear in rhesus monkeys. *Journal of Experimental Psychology: Animal Behavior Processes, 16,* 372–389.

Coolidge, F. L., Thede, L. L., & Jang, K. L. (2001). Heritability of personality disorders in childhood: A preliminary investigation. *Journal of Personality Disorders, 15,* 33–40.

Cooper, J. (2007). *Cognitive dissonance: Fifty years of a classic theory.* Thousand Oaks, CA: Sage Publications.

Cooper, J. O., Heron, R. E., & Heward, W. L. (2007). *Applied behavior analysis.* Upper Saddle River, NJ.: Prentice-Hall.

Coren, S. (1996). Daylight savings time and traffic accidents. *New England Journal of Medicine, 334*(14), 924–925.

Coren, S., Ward, L. M., & Enns, J. T. (1999). *Sensation and perception* (5th ed.). Fort Worth, TX: Harcourt Brace.

Corina, D. P., & McBurney, S. L. (2001). The neural representation of language in users of American Sign Language. *Journal of Communication Disorders, 34,* 455–471.

Corr, P. J., & Gray, J. A. (1996). Attributional style as a personality factor in insurance sales performance in the UK. *Journal of Occupational and Organizational Psychology, 69,* 83–87.

Corso, J. F. (1977). Auditory perception and communication. In J. E. Birren & K. W. Schaie (Eds.), *Handbook of the psychology of aging* (pp. 535–553). New York, NY: Van Nostrand Reinhold.

Costa, P. T., Jr., & McCrae, R. R. (1985). *The NEO Personality Inventory manual.* Odessa, FL: Psychological Assessment Resources.

Costa, P. T., Jr., & McCrae, R. R. (1992). Four ways five factors are basic. *Personality and Individual Differences, 13,* 653–665.

Cota, D., Marsicano, G., Lutz, Z. B., Vicennati, V., Stalla, G. K., Pasquali, R., & Pagotto. U. (2003). Endogenous cannabinoid system as a modulator of food intake. *International Journal of Obesity, 27,* 289–301.

Cota, D., Tschöp, M. H., Horvath, T. L., & Levine, A. S. (2006). Cannabinoids, opioids and eating behavior: The molecular face of hedonism? *Brain Research Reviews, 51,* 85–117.

Council, J. R., & Green, J. P. (2004). Examining the absorption-hypnotizability link: The roles of acquiescence and consistency motivation. *International Journal of Clinical and Experimental Hypnosis, 52,* 364–377.

Cousins, D. A., & Young, A. H. (2007). The armamentarium of treatments for bipolar disorder: A review of the literature. *International Journal of Neuropsychoparmacology, 10,* 411–431.

Couture, S., & Penn, D. (2003). Interpersonal contact and the stigma of mental illness: A review of the literature. *Journal of Mental Health, 12,* 291–306.

Cowan, C. P., & Cowan, P. (2000). *When partners become parents: The big life change for couples.* Mahwah, NJ: Erlbaum.

Cowan, C. P., Cowan, P. A., Heming, G., Garrett, E., Coysh, W. S., Curtis-Boles, H., & Boles, A. J., III. (1985). Transitions to parenthood: His, hers, and theirs. *Journal of Family Issues, 6,* 451–481.

Cowan, N. (2001). The magical number 4 in short-term memory: A reconsideration of mental storage capacity. *Behavioral and Brain Sciences, 24,* 87–185.

Cowan, P., & Cowan, C. P. (1998). New families: Modern couples as new pioneers. In M. A. Mason, A. Skolnick, & S. D. Sugarman (Eds.), *All our families: New policies for a new century.* New York, NY: Oxford University Press.

Cowan, W. M. (1979, September). The development of the brain. *Scientific American, 241,* 106–117.

Cowles, J. T. (1937). Food tokens as incentives for learning by chimpanzees. *Comparative Psychology Monographs, 74,* 1–96.

Craik, F. I. M. (1994). Memory changes in normal aging. *Current Directions in Psychological Science, 3,* 155–158.

Craik, F. I. M., & Lockhart, R. S. (1972). Levels of processing: A framework for memory research. *Journal of Verbal Learning and Verbal Behavior, 11,* 671–684.

Crano, W. D., & Prislin, R. (2006). Attitudes and persuasion. *Annual Review of Psychology, 57,* 345–374.

Crockett, L. J., & Silbereisen, R. K. (Eds.). (2000). *Negotiating adolescence in times of social change.* New York, NY: Cambridge University Press.

Crowder, R. G. (1992). Eidetic imagery. In L. R. Squire (Ed.), *Encyclopedia of learning and memory* (pp. 154–156). New York, NY: Macmillan.

Crowder, R. G., & Morton, J. (1969). Precategorical acoustic storage (PAS). *Perception and Psychophysics, 8,* 815–820.

Cryder, C. H., Kilmer, R. P., Tedeschi, R. G., & Calhoun, L. G. (2006). An exploratory study of posttraumatic growth in children following a natural disaster. *American Journal of Orthopsychiatry, 76,* 65–69.

Cuddy L. L., & Duffin, J. (2005). Music, memory, and Alzheimer's disease: Is music recognition spared in dementia, and how can it be assessed? *Medical Hypotheses, 64*(2), 229–235.

Cummins, D.D. (1996). Evidence of deontic reasoning in 3- and 4-year-old children. *Memory & Cognition, 24,* 823–829.

Cummins, D.D. (1999). Cheater detection is modified by social rank: The impact of dominance on the evolution of cognitive functions. *Evolution and Human Behavior, 20,* 229–248.

Curci, A., & Luminet, O. (2006). Follow-up of a cross-national comparison on flashbulb and event memory for the September 11th attacks. *Memory, 14*(3), 329–344.

Curt, G. A., Breitbart, W., Cella, D., Groopman, J. E., Horning, S. J., Itri, L. M., . . . Vogelzang, N. J. (2000). Impact of cancer-related fatigue on the lives of patients: New findings from the Fatigue Coalition. *Oncologist, 5,* 353–360.

Curtis, R. C., & Miller, K. (1986). Believing another likes or dislikes you: Behaviors making the beliefs come true. *Journal of Personality and Social Psychology, 51,* 284–290.

Cutting, J. C., & Proffitt, D. (1982). The minimum principle and the perception of absolute, common and relative motions. *Cognitive Psychology, 14,* 211–246.

Cvengros, J. A., Christensen, A. J., Hillis, S. L., & Rosenthal, G. E. (2007). Patient and physician attitudes in the health care context: Attitudinal symmetry predicts patient satisfaction and adherence. *Annals of Behavioral Medicine, 33,* 262–268.

Czeisler, C. A., Duffy, J. F., Shanahan, T. L., Brown, E. N., Mitchell, J. F., Rimmer, D. W., . . . Kronauer, R. E. (1999). Stability, precision, and near-24-hour period of the human circadian pacemaker. *Science, 284,* 2177–2181.

D'Augelli, A. R., Grossman, A. H., & Starks, M. T. (2005). Parents' awareness of lesbian, gay, and bisexual youths' sexual orientation. *Journal of Marriage and Family, 67,* 474–482.

D'Augelli, A. R., Grossman, A. H., Salter, N. P., Vasey, J. J., Starks, M. T., & Sinclair, K. O. (2005). Predicting the suicide attempts of lesbian, gay, and bisexual youth. *Suicide and Life-Threatening Behavior, 35,* 646–660.

D'Augelli, A. R., Hershberger, S. L., & Pilkington, N. W. (2001). Suicidality patterns and sexual orientation-related factors among lesbian, gay, and bisexual youths. *Suicide and Life-Threatening Behavior, 31,* 250–264.

Dahlman, I., & Arner, P. (2007). Obesity and polymorphisms in genes regulating human adipose tissue. *International Journal of Obesity, 31,* 1629–1641.

Dahlstrom, W. G., Welsh, H. G., & Dahlstrom, L. E. (1975). *An MMPI handbook, Vol. 1: Clinical interpretation.* Minneapolis, MN: University of Minnesota Press.

Daly, M., & Wilson, M. (1985). Child abuse and other risks of not living with both parents. *Ethology and Sociobiology, 6,* 197–210.

Daly, M., & Wilson, M. (2001). Risk-taking, intrasexual competition, and homicide. *Nebraska Symposium on Motivation, 47,* 1–36.

Daly, M., & Wilson, M., (2005). The "Cinderella effect" is no fairy tale. *Trends in Cognitive Science, 9,* 507–508.

Damasio, H., Grabowski, T., Frank, R., Galaburda, A. M., & Damasio, A. R. (1994). The return of Phineas Gage: Clues about the brain from the skull of a famous patient. *Science, 264,* 1102–1105.

Daneman, M., & Carpenter, P. A. (1980). Individual differences in working memory and reading. *Journal of Verbal Learning and Verbal Behavior, 19,* 450–466.

Danzer, H., Brausein, G.D., Rasor, J., Forsythe, A., & Wade, M.E. (1980). Maternal serum human chorionic gonadotropin concentrations and fetal sex prediction. *Fertility and Sterility, 34,* 336–340.

Darley, J., & Latané, B. (1968). Bystander intervention in emergencies: Diffusion of responsibility. *Journal of Personality and Social Psychology, 8,* 377–383.

Darling, N., & Steinberg, L. (1993). Parenting style as context: An integrative model. *Psychological Bulletin, 113,* 487–496.

Darwin, C. (1965). *The expression of emotions in man and animals.* Chicago, IL: University of Chicago Press. (Original work published 1872)

Daselaar, S. M., Rice, H. J., Greenberg, D. L., Cabeza, R., LaBar, K. S., & Rubin, D. C. (2008). The spatiotemporal dynamics of autobiographical memory: Neural correlates of recall, emotional intensity, and reliving. *Cerebral Cortex, 18*(1), 217–229.

Daskalakis, Z. J., Levinson, A. J., & Fitzgerald, P. B. (2008). Repetitive transcranial magnetic stimulation for major depressive disorder: A review. *Canadian Journal of Psychiatry, 53,* 555–566.

Davidson, R. J., Jackson D.C., & Kalin, N. H. (2000). Emotion, plasticity, context, and regulation: Perspectives for affective neuroscience. *Psychological Bulletin, 126,* 890–909.

Davis, C., & MacDonald, S. (2004). Threat appraisals, distress and the development of positive life changes after the September 11th in a Canadian sample. *Cognitive Behaviour Therapy, 2,* 68–78.

Davis, J. L., Byrd, P., Rhudy, J. L., & Wright, D. C. (2007). Characteristics of chronic nightmares in a trauma-exposed treatment-seeking sample. *Dreaming, 17*(4), 187–198.

Dawkins, K., Lieberman, J. A., Lebowitz, B. D., & Hsiao, J. K. (1999). Antipsychotics: Past and future. *Schizophrenia Bulletin, 25,* 395–405.

Dawkins, R., (1976). *The selfish gene.* New York, NY: Oxford University Press.

Dawson, L. L., & Hennebry, J. (2003). New religions and the Internet: Recruiting in a new public space. In L. L. Dawson (Ed.), *Cults and new religious movements* (pp. 271–291). Oxford, United Kingdom: Blackwell.

De Bellis, M. D., Keshavan, M. S., Beers, S. R., Hall, J., Frustaci, K., Masalehdan, A., Noll, J., & Boring, A. M. (2001). Sex differences in brain maturation during childhood and adolescence. *Cerebral Cortex, 11*, 552–557.

De Cock, R., & Matthysen, E. (2005). Sexual communication by pheromones in a firefly, *Phosphaenus hemipterus* (Coleoptera: Lampyridae). *Animal Behaviour, 70*, 807–818.

De Oliveira Alvares, L., Genro, B. P., Diehl, F., & Quillfeldt, J. A. (2008). Differential role of the hippocampal endocannabinoid system in the memory consolidation and retrieval mechanism. *Neurobiology of Learning and Memory, 90*(1), 1–9.

De Pascalis, V., Cacace, I., & Massicolle, F. (2008). Focused analgesia in waking and hypnosis: Effects on pain, memory, and somatosensory event-related potentials. *Pain, 134*(1–2), 197–208.

de Rivera, J. (1997). The construction of false memory syndrome: The experience of retractors. *Psychological Inquiry, 8*, 271–292.

De Santis, M., Cavaliere, A. F., Straface, G., Di Gianantonio, E., & Caruso, A. (2006). Inherited and acquired thrombophilia: Pregnancy outcome and treatment. *Reproductive Toxicology, 22*(2), 227–233.

De Valois, R. L., & Jacobs, G. H. (1968). Primate color vision. *Science, 162*, 533–540.

de Waal, F. B. M. (2008). Putting the altruism back into altruism: The evolution of empathy. *Annual Review of Psychology, 59*, 279–300.

Deacon, T. (1997). *The symbolic species: The coevolution of language and the human brain.* Hammondsworth, England: Allen Lane.

Dean, K. L., Viglione, D. J., Perry, W., & Meyer, G. J. (2007). A method to optimize the response range while maintaining Rorschach comprehensive system validity. *Journal of Personality Assessment, 89*, 149–161.

Deaux, K., Bkmen, N., Gilkes, A., Ventuneac, A., Joseph, Y., Payne, Y. A., & Steele, C. A. (2007). Becoming American: Sterotype threat effects in Afro-Caribbean immigrant groups. *Social Psychology Quarterly, 70*, 384–404.

DeCasper, A. J., & Prescott, P. A. (1984). Human newborns' perception of male voices: Preference, discrimination, and reinforcing value. *Developmental Psychology, 17*, 481–491.

Dejin-Karlsson, E., Hanson, B. S., Oestergren, P.-O., Sjoeberg, N. O., & Karel, M. (1998). Does passive smoking in early pregnancy increase the risk of small-for-gestational-age infants? *American Journal of Public Health, 88*, 1523–1527.

DeLamater, J. D., & Sill, M. (2005). Sexual desire in later life. *Journal of Sex Research, 42*(2), 138–149.

Delgado, M. R., Olsson, A., & Phelps, E. A. (2006). Extending animal models of fear conditioning to humans. *Biological Psychology, 73*(1), 39–48.

Dell, G. S. (2004). Speech errors in language production: Neuropsychological and connectionist perspectives. In B. H. Ross (Ed.), *The psychology of learning and motivation* (Vol. 44, pp. 63–108). New York, NY: Elsevier.

Delprato, D. J., & Midgley, B. D. (1992). Some fundamentals of B. F. Skinner's behaviorism. *American Psychologist, 47*, 1507–1520.

Dennett, D. C. (1987). Consciousness. In R. L. Gregory (Ed.), *The Oxford companion to the mind* (pp. 160–164). New York, NY: Oxford University Press.

Department of Justice, Government of Canada. (2007). *Methamphetamine report for Federal-Provincial-Territorial ministers responsible for justice.* Retrieved from http://www.justice.gc.ca/eng/dept-min/pub/meth/p3.html

DePaulo, B. M., Ansfield, M. E., Kirkendol, S. E., & Boden, J. M. (2004). Serious lies. *Basic and Applied Social Psychology, 26*, 147–167.

DePaulo, B. M., Lindsay, J. J., Malone, B. E., Muhlenbruck, L., Charlton, K., & Cooper, H. (2003). Cues to deception. *Psychological Bulletin, 129*, 74–118.

Després, J-P., Golay, A., & Sjöström, L. (2005). Effects of rimonabant on metabolic risk factors in overweight patients with dyslipidemia. *The New England Journal of Medicine, 353*, 2121–2134.

Dew, M. A., Hoch, C. C., Buysse, D. J., Monk, T. H., Begley, A. E., Houck, P. R., . . . Reynolds, C. F. (2003). Healthy older adults' sleep predicts all-cause mortality at 4 to 19 years of follow-up. *Psychosomatic Medicine, 65*, 63–73.

Dewsbury, D. A. (1981). Effects of novelty on copulatory behavior: The Coolidge effect and related phenomena. *Psychological Bulletin, 89*, 464–482.

Dhawan, N., Roseman, I. J., Naidu, R. K., Thapa, K., & Rettek, S. I. (1995). Self-concepts across two cultures: India and the United States. *Journal of Cross-Cultural Psychology, 26*, 606–621.

Di Marzo, V., & Cristino, L. (2008). Why endocannabinoids are not all alike. *Nature Neuroscience, 11*, 124–126.

Dickens, W. T., & Flynn, J. R. (2006). Black Americans reduce the racial IQ gap: Evidence from standardization samples. *Psychological Science, 17*(10), 913–920.

Dietrich, A. (2004). The cognitive neuroscience of creativity. *Psychonomic Bulletin & Review, 11*, 1011–1026.

Digman, J. M. (1990). Personality structure: Emergence of the five-factor model. *Annual Review of Psychology, 41*, 417–440.

Dijkstra, P. D., & Preenen, P. T. Y. (2007). No effect of blue on winning contests in judo. *Proceedings of the Royal Society B, 275*(1639), 1157–1162. doi:10.1098/rspb.2007.1700

DiLalla, L. F. (2002). Behavior genetics of aggression in children: Reviews and future directions. *Developmental Review, 22*, 593–622.

DiMatteo, M. R. (2004). Social support and patient adherence to medical treatment: A meta-analysis. *Health Psychology, 23*, 207–218.

DiMatteo, M. R., Haskard, K. B., & Williams, S. L. (2007). Health beliefs, disease severity, and patient adherence: A meta-analysis. *Medical Care, 45*, 521–528.

Dion, K. K., & Dion, K. L. (1996). Cultural perspectives on romantic love. *Personal Relationships, 3*, 5–17.

Dion, K., Berscheid, E., & Walster, E. (1972). What is beautiful is good. *Journal of Personality and Social Psychology, 24*, 285–290.

DiPietro, J. A., Hodgson, D. M., Costigan, K. A., & Johnson, T. R. B. (1996). Fetal antecedents of infant temperament. *Child Development, 67*, 2568–2583.

Dirkzwager, A. J. E., Bramsen, I., & van der Ploeg, H. M. (2003). Social support, coping, life events, and posttraumatic stress symptoms among former peacekeepers: A prospective study. *Personality and Individual Differences, 34*, 1545–1559.

Dixon, R. A. (2003). Themes in the aging of intelligence: Robust decline with intriguing possibilities. In R. J. Sternberg, J. Lautrey, & T. I. Lubart (Eds.), *Models of intelligence: International perspectives* (pp. 151–167). Washington, DC: American Psychological Association.

Dixon, R. A., & de Frias, C. M. (2004). The Victoria longitudinal study: From characterizing cognitive aging to illustrating changes in memory compensation. *Aging Neuropsychology and Cognition, 11,* 346–376.

Do, A. M., Rupert, A. V., & Wolford, G. (2008). Evaluations of pleasurable experiences: The peak-end rule. *Psychonomic Bulletin & Review, 15,* 96–98.

Docherty, N. M., St-Hilaire, A., Aakre, J. M., & Seghers, J. P. (2008). Life events and high-trait reactivity together predict psychotic symptom increases in schizophrenia. *Schizophrenia Bulletin, 34,* 1095–1105.

Dollard, J., Doob, L. W., Miller, N., Mower, O. H., & Sears, R. R. (1939). *Frustration and aggression.* New Haven, CT: Yale University Press.

Domhoff, G. W. (1999). Drawing theoretical implications from descriptive empirical findings on dream content. *Dreaming, 9,* 201–210.

Domhoff, G. W. (2005). Refocusing the neurocognitive approach to dreams: A critique of the Hobson versus Solms debate. *Dreaming, 15,* 3–20.

Donnellan, M. B., Trzesniewski, K. H., Conger, K J., & Conger, R. D. (2007). A three-wave longitudinal study of self-evaluations during young adulthood. *Journal of Research in Personality, 41,* 453–472.

Donnellan, M. B., Trzesniewski, K. H., Robins, R. W., Moffitt, T. E., & Caspi, A. (2005). Low self-esteem is related to aggression, antisocial behavior, and delinquency. *Psychological Science, 16,* 328–335.

Douglas, K. S., & Skeem, J. L. (2005). Violence risk assessment: Getting specific about being dynamic. *Psychology, Public Policy, and Law, 11,* 347–383.

Downing, P. E., Jiang, Y., Shuman, M., & Kanwisher, N. (2001). A cortical area selective for visual processing of the human body. *Science, 293,* 2470–2473.

Drake, C. L., Schwartz, J. R. L., & Roth, T. (2008). The evolution of insomnia in relation to comorbidity. *Psychiatric Annals, 38*(9), 621–626.

Drayna, D., Manichaikul, A., deLange, M., Snieder, H., & Spector, T. (2001). Genetic correlates of musical pitch recognition in humans. *Science, 291,* 1969–1972.

DSM-IV. (1994). *Diagnostic and statistical manual of mental disorders* (4th ed.). Washington, DC: American Psychiatric Association.

DSM-IV-TR. (2000). *Diagnostic and statistical manual of mental disorders* (4th ed., Text revision). Washington, DC: American Psychiatric Association.

DuBois, P. H. (1970). *A history of psychological testing.* Boston, MA: Allyn & Bacon.

Dubrowski, A., Proteau, L., & Carnahan, H. (2004). Practice effects on the use of visual and haptic cues during grasping. *Journal of Motor Behavior, 36*(3), 327–338.

Dudycha, G. J. (1936). An objective study of punctuality in relation to personality and achievement. *Archives of Psychology, 204,* 1–53.

Duffy, K. R., Murphy, K. M., & Jones, D. G. (1998). Analysis of the postnatal growth of visual cortex. *Visual Neuroscience, 15*(5), 831–839.

Duker, P. C., & Seys, D. M. (1996). Long-term use of electrical aversion treatment with self-injurious behavior. *Research in Developmental Disabilities, 17,* 293–301.

Dunbar, R. I. M. (1996). *Grooming, gossip, and the evolution of language.* London, United Kingdom: Faber & Faber.

Duncker, D. (1945). On problem solving. *Psychological Monographs, 58* (No. 270).

Durkin, S. J., & Paxton, S. J. (2002). Predictors of vulnerability to reduced body image satisfaction and psychological well-being in response to exposure to idealized female media images in adolescent girls. *Journal of Psychosomatic Research, 53,* 995–1005.

Dusek, J. A., Hibberd, P. L., Buczynski, B., Chang, B.-H., Dusek, K. C., Johnston, J. M., . . . Zusman, R. M. (2008). Stress management versus lifestyle modification on systolic hypertension and medication elimination: A randomized trial. *The Journal of Alternative and Complementary Medicine, 14,* 129–138.

Dutton, D. G., & Aron, A. P. (1974). Some evidence for heightened sexual attraction under conditions of high anxiety. *Journal of Personality and Social Psychology, 30,* 510–517.

Duvarci, S., Nader, K., & LeDoux, J. E. (2008). De novo mRNA synthesis is required for both consolidation and reconsolidation of fear memories in the amygdala. *Learning and Memory, 15*(10), 747–755.

Dweck, C. S. (1975). The role of expectations and attributions in the alleviation of learned helplessness. *Journal of Personality and Social Psychology, 31,* 674–685.

Eagly, A. H., & Chaiken, S. (1993). *The psychology of attitudes.* Fort Worth, TX: Harcourt Brace Jovanovich.

Eastwick, P. W., Eagly, A. H., Glick, P., Johannesen-Schmidt, M. C., Fiske, S. T., Blum, A. M. B., . . . Volpato, C. (2006). Is traditional gender ideology associated with sex-typed mate preferences? A test in nine nations. *Sex Roles, 54,* 603–614.

Ebbinghaus, H. (1973). *Psychology: An elementary text-book.* New York, NY: Arno Press. (Original work published 1908)

Eckensberger, L. H., & Zimba, R. F. (1997). The development of moral judgment. In J. W. Berry, P. R. Dasen, & T. S. Saraswathi (Eds.), *Handbook of cross-cultural psychology: Vol. 2. Basic processes and human development* (pp. 299–338). Boston, MA: Allyn & Bacon.

Edinger, J. D., Fins, A. I., Glenn, D. M., Sullivan, R. J., Jr., Bastian, L. A., Marsh, G. R., . . . Vasilas, D. (2000). Insomnia and the eye of the beholder: Are there clinical markers of objective sleep disturbances among adults with and without insomnia complaints? *Journal of Consulting and Clinical Psychology, 68,* 593–596.

Edvardsen, J., Torgersen, S., Røysamb, E., Lygren, S., Skre, I., Onstad, S., & Øien, P. A. (2008). Heritability of bipolar spectrum disorders. Unity or heterogeneity. *Journal of Affective Disorders, 106,* 229–240.

Ekman, P. (1972). Universal and cultural differences in facial expressions of emotion. In J. Cole (Ed.), *Nebraska symposium on motivation.* Lincoln, NE: University of Nebraska Press.

Ekman, P. (1984). Expression and the nature of emotion. In K. R. Scherer & P. Ekman (Eds.), *Approaches to emotion.* Hillsdale, NJ: Erlbaum.

Ekman, P. (1994). Strong evidence for universals in facial expressions: A reply to Russell's mistaken critique. *Psychological Bulletin, 115,* 268–287.

Ekman, P., & Friesen, W. V. (1971). Constants across cultures in the face and emotion. *Journal of Personality and Social Psychology, 17,* 124–129.

Ekman, P., & Friesen, W. V. (1986). A new pan-cultural facial expression of emotion. *Motivation and Emotion, 10,* 159–168.

Elbert, T., Pantev, C., Wienbruch, C., Rockstroh, B., & Taub, E. (1995). Increased cortical representation of the fingers of the left hand in string players. *Science, 270,* 305–307.

Elias, S. M., & MacDonald, S. (2007). Using past performance, proxy efficacy, and academic self-efficacy to predict college performance. *Journal of Applied Social Psychology, 37,* 2518–2531.

Elliot, A. J., Maier, M. A., Moller, A. C., Friedman, R., & Meinhardt, J. (2007). Color and psychological functioning: The effect of red on performance attainment. *Journal of Experimental Psychology: General, 136*(1), 154–168.

Ellis, A. (1962). *Reason and emotion in psychotherapy.* New York, NY: Lyle Stuart.

Ellis, A. (1995). *Better, deeper, and more enduring brief therapy: The rational emotive behavior therapy approach.* New York, NY: Brunner/Mazel.

Elms, A. C. (1988). Freud as Leonardo: Why the first psychobiography went wrong. *Journal of Personality, 56,* 19–40.

Elsabagh, S., Hartley, D. E., Ali, O., Williamson, E. M., & File, S. E. (2005). Differential cognitive effects of *Ginkgo biloba* after acute and chronic treatment in healthy young volunteers. *Psychopharmacology, 179,* 437–446.

Endler, N. S., Macrodimitris, S. D., & Kocovski, N. L. (2000). Controllability in cognitive and interpersonal tasks: Is control good for you? *Personality & Individual Differences, 29,* 951–962.

Epley, N., & Gilovich, T. (2006). The anchoring-and-adjustment heuristic. *Psychological Science, 17,* 311–318.

Epstein, L. H., Nandley, E. A., Dearing, K. K., Cho, D. D., Roemmich, J. N., Paluch, R. A., . . . Spring, B. (2006). Purchases of food in youth: Influence of price and income. *Psychological Science, 17,* 82–89.

Ericsson, K. A., & Chase, W. G. (1982). Exceptional memory. *American Scientist, 70,* 607–615.

Ericsson, K. A., & Simon, H. A. (1993). *Protocol analysis: Verbal reports as data* (Rev. ed.). Cambridge, MA: MIT Press.

Erikson, E. (1963). *Childhood and society.* New York, NY: Norton.

Ervik, S., Abdelnoor, M., Heier, M. S., Ramberg, M., & Strand, G. (2006). Health-related quality of life in narcolepsy. *Acta Neurologica Scandinavica, 114,* 198–204.

Eshbaugh, E. M., & Gute, G. (2008). Hookups and sexual regret among college women. *The Journal of Social Psychology, 148,* 77–89.

Espelage, D. L., Aragon, S. R., Birkett, M., & Koenig, B. W. (2008). Homophobic teasing, psychological outcomes, and sexual orientation among high school students: What influence do parents and schools have? *School Psychology Review, 37,* 202–216.

Espie, C. A. (2002). Insomnia: Conceptual issues in the development, persistence, and treatment of sleep disorder in adults. *Annual Review of Psychology, 53,* 215–243.

Estrada, C. A., Isen, A. M., & Young, M. J. (1994). Positive affect improves creative problem solving and influences reported source of practice satisfaction in physicians. *Motivation and Emotion, 18,* 285–299.

Evans, E., Hawton, K., Rodham, K., & Deeks, J. (2005). The prevalence of suicidal phenomena in adolescents: A systematic review of population-based studies. *Suicide and Life Threatening Behavior, 35,* 239–250.

Evans, J. St. B. T. (2008). Dual-processing accounts of reasoning, judgment, and social cognition. *Annual Review of Psychology, 59,* 255–278.

Evans, J. St. B.T., & Curtis-Holmes, J. (2005). Rapid responding increases belief bias: Evidence for the dual-process theory of reasoning. *Thinking & Reasoning, 11,* 382–389.

Evans, S. E., Davies, C., & DiLillo, D. (2008). Exposure to domestic violence: A meta-analysis of child and adolescent outcomes. *Aggression and Violent Behavior, 13,* 131–140.

Exner, J. E., Jr. (1974). *The Rorschach: A comprehensive system.* New York, NY: Wiley.

Exner, J. E., Jr. (2003). *The Rorschach: A comprehensive system* (4th ed.). New York, NY: Wiley.

Exner, J. E., Jr., & Weiner, I. B. (1994). *The Rorschach: A comprehensive system: Vol. 3. Assessment of children and adolescents* (2nd ed.). New York, NY: Wiley.

Eysenck, H. J. (1952). The effects of psychotherapy: An evaluation. *Journal of Consulting Psychology, 16,* 319–324.

Eysenck, H. J. (1973). *The inequality of man.* London, United Kingdom: Temple Smith.

Eysenck, H. J. (1990). Biological dimensions of personality. In L. A. Pervin (Ed.), *Handbook of personality theory and research* (pp. 244–276). New York, NY: Guilford Press.

Fabian, J. M. (2006). A literature review of the utility of selected violence and sexual violence risk assessment instruments. *The Journal of Psychiatry & Law, 34,* 307–350.

Fagan, J. F., & Holland, C. R. (2007). Racial equality in intelligence: Predictions from a theory of intelligences as processing. *Intelligence, 35,* 319–334.

Fagot, B. I., & Hagan, R. (1991). Observations of parent reactions to sex-stereotyped behaviors: Age and sex effects. *Child Development, 62,* 617–628.

Fahey, C. D., & Zee, P. C. (2006). Circadian rhythm sleep disorders and phototherapy. *Psychiatric Clinics of North America, 29,* 989–1007.

Fakhoury, W., & Priebe, S. (2002). The process of deinstitutionalization: An international overview. *Current Opinion in Psychiatry, 15,* 187–192.

Fantz, R. L. (1963). Pattern vision in newborn infants. *Science, 140,* 296–297.

Farina, A., Gliha, D., Boudreau, L. A., Allen, J. G., & Sherman, M. (1971). Mental illness and the impact of believing others know about it. *Journal of Abnormal Psychology, 77,* 1–5.

Farmer, T. A., Anderson, S. E., & Spivey, M. J. (2007). Gradiency and visual context in syntactic garden-paths. *Journal of Memory and Language, 57,* 570–520.

Farooqi, I. S., & O'Rahilly, S. (2007). Genetic factors in human obesity. *Obesity Reviews, 8* (suppl. 1), 37–41.

Farrell, M., & Gibson, S. (2007). Age interacts with stimulus frequency in the temporal summation of pain. *Pain Medicine, 8*(6), 514–520.

Fattore, L., Spano, M. S., Deiana, S., Melis, V., Cossu, G., Fadda, P., & Fratta, W. (2007). An endocannabinoid mechanism in relapse to drug seeking: A review of animal studies and clinical perspectives. *Brain Research Reviews, 53*(1), 1–16.

Fazio, R. H., & Roskos-Ewoldsen, D. R. (2005). Acting as we feel: When and how attitudes guide behavior. In T. C. Brock & M. C. Green (Eds.), *Persuasion: Psychological insights and perspectives* (2nd ed., pp. 41–62). Thousand Oaks, CA: Sage.

Feather, N. T. (1961). The relationship of persistence at a task to expectation of success and achievement related motives. *Journal of Abnormal and Social Psychology, 63*, 552–561.

Fechner, G. T. (1966). *Elements of psychophysics* (H. E. Adler, Trans.). New York, NY: Holt, Rinehart & Winston. (Original work published 1860)

Fernald, A., & Morikawa, H. (1993). Common themes and cultural variations in Japanese and American mothers' speech to infants. *Child Development, 64*, 637–656.

Fernandez-Ballesteros, R. (2002). Social support and quality of life among older people in Spain. *Journal of Social Issues, 58*, 645–659.

Ferrari, M. C., & Chivers, D. P. (2008). Latent inhibition of predator recognition by embryonic amphibians. *Biology Letters, 5*(2), 160–162.

Ferster, C. B., & Skinner, B. F. (1957). *Schedules of reinforcement.* New York, NY: Appleton-Century-Crofts.

Festinger, L. (1957). *A theory of cognitive dissonance.* Stanford, CA: Stanford University Press.

Festinger, L., & Carlsmith, J. M. (1959). Cognitive consequences of forced compliance. *Journal of Abnormal and Social Psychology, 58*, 203–211.

Fields, R. D., & Stevens-Graham, B. (2002). New insights into neuro-glia communication. *Science, 298*, 556–562.

Fillmore, M. T., Blackburn, J. S., & Harrison, E. L. R. (2008). Acute disinhibiting effects of alcohol as a factor in risky driving behavior. Drug and Alcohol Dependence, 95(1–2), 97–106.

Fink, P., Hansen, M. S., & Oxhøj, M. L. (2004). The prevalence of somatoform disorders among internal medical inpatients. *Journal of Psychosomatic Research, 56*, 413–418.

Fiore, M. C., Jaén, C. R., & Baker, T. B. (2008). *Treating tobacco use and dependence: 2008 update.* Rockville, MD: U.S. Department of Health and Human Services. Public Health Service.

Fisher, B. S., Cullen, F. T., & Turner, M. G. (2000). *The sexual victimization of college women.* Washington, DC: National Institute of Justice.

Fisher, L. (1998). Besieged by stress. *Maclean's, 111*(41), 24.

Fisher, R. (1992). *Contact and conflict: Indian–European relations in British Columbia, 1774–1890.* Vancouver, BC: UBC Press.

Fishman, H. C., & Fishman, T. (2003). Structural family therapy. In G. P. Sholevar & L. D. Schwoeri (Eds.), *Textbook of family and couples therapy: Clinical applications* (pp. 35–54). Washington, DC: American Psychiatric Publishing.

Fiske, S. T., Harris, L. T., & Cuddy, A. J. C. (2004). Why ordinary people torture enemy prisoners. *Science, 306*, 1482–1483.

Fitch, W. T., & Hauser, M. D. (2004). Computational constraints on syntactic processing in a nonhuman primate. *Science, 303*, 377–380.

Flavell, J. H. (1985). *Cognitive development* (2nd ed.). Englewood Cliffs, NJ: Prentice Hall.

Flavell, J. H. (1996). Piaget's legacy. *Psychological Science, 7*, 200–203.

Fleming, I. (1959). From a view to a kill. In *For your eyes only* (pp. 1–30). New York, NY: Charter Books.

Foa, E. B., & Riggs, D. S. (1995). Posttraumatic stress disorder following assault: Theoretical considerations and empirical findings. *Current Directions in Psychological Science, 4*, 61–65.

Folkard, S. (2008). Do permanent night workers show circadian adjustment? A review based on the endogenous melatonin rhythm. *Chronobiology International, 25*(2–3), 215–224.

Folkman, S. (1984). Personal control and stress and coping processes: A theoretical analysis. *Journal of Personality and Social Psychology, 46*, 839–852.

Forbes, S. (1997). The evolutionary biology of spontaneous abortion in humans. *Trends in Ecology and Evolution, 12*, 446–450.

Forbes, S. (2002). Pregnancy sickness and embryo quality. *Trends in Ecology and Evolution, 17*, 115–120.

Ford, C. S., & Beach, F. A. (1951). *Patterns of sexual behavior.* New York, NY: Harper & Row.

Forgas, J. P. (2008). Affect and cognition. *Perspectives on Psychological Science, 3*, 94–101.

Forgas, J. P., & East, R. (2008). On being happy and gullible: Mood effects on skepticism and detection of deception. *Journal of Experimental Social Psychology, 44*, 1362–1367.

Forman, R., Klein, J., Meta, D., Barks, J., Greenwald, M., & Koren, G. (1993). Maternal and neonatal characteristics following exposure to cocaine in Toronto. *Reproductive Toxicology, 7*(6), 619–622.

Förster, J., Friedman, R. S., & Liberman, N. (2004). Temporal construal effects on abstract and concrete thinking: Consequences for insight and creative cognition. *Journal of Personality and Social Psychology, 87*, 177–189.

Försterling, F. (2001). *Attributions: An introduction to theories, research and applications.* New York, NY: Psychology Press.

Foster, R. G., & Wulff, K. (2005). The rhythm of rest and excess. *Nature Reviews Neuroscience, 6*(5), 407–414.

Foucault, M. (1975). *The birth of the clinic.* New York, NY: Vintage Books.

Foulkes, D. (1962). Dream reports from different states of sleep. *Journal of Abnormal and Social Psychology, 65*, 14–25.

Fowler, H. (1965). *Curiosity and exploratory behavior.* New York, NY: Macmillan.

Frager, R., & Fadiman, J. (1998). *Personality and personal growth.* New York, NY: Longman.

Fraley, R. C., & Shaver, P. R. (2000). Adult romantic attachment: Theoretical developments, emerging controversies, and unanswered questions. *Review of General Psychology, 4*, 132–154.

Fraley, R. C., Brumbaugh, C. C., & Marks, M. J. (2005). The evolution and function of adult attachment: A comparative and phylogenetic analysis. *Journal of Personality and Social Psychology, 89*, 731–746.

Frank, J. D., & Frank, J. B. (1991). *Persuasion and healing: A comparative study of psychotherapy* (3rd ed.). Baltimore, MD: Johns Hopkins University Press.

Frank, M. E., & Nowlis, G. H. (1989). Learned aversions and taste qualities in hamsters. *Chemical Senses, 14*, 379–394.

Franklin, N., & Tversky, B. (1990). Searching imagined environments. *Journal of Experimental Psychology: General, 119*, 63–76.

Frans, Ö., Rimmö, P. A., Åberg, L., & Fredrikson, M. (2005). Trauma exposure and post-traumatic stress disorder in the general population. *Acta Psychiatrica Scandinavica, 111*, 291–299.

Fraser, L. M., O'Carroll, R. E., & Ebmeier, K. P. (2008). The effect of electroconvulsive therapy on autobiographical memory: A systematic review. *The Journal of ECT, 24*, 10–17.

Freedman, J. L., & Fraser, S. C. (1966). Compliance without pressure: The foot-in-the-door technique. *Journal of Personality and Social Psychology, 4,* 195–202.

Fresco, D. M., Williams, N. L., & Nugent, N. R. (2006). Flexibility and negative affect: Examining the associations of explanatory flexibility and coping flexibility to each other and to depression and anxiety. *Cognitive Therapy and Research, 30,* 201–210.

Freud, A. (1946). *The ego and the mechanisms of defense.* New York, NY: International Universities Press.

Freud, A. (1958). Adolescence. *Psychoanalytic Study of the Child, 13,* 255–278.

Freud, S. (1915). Instincts and their vicissitudes. In S. Freud, *The collected papers.* New York, NY: Collier.

Freud, S. (1923). *Introductory lectures on psycho-analysis* (J. Riviera, Trans.). London, United Kingdom: Allen & Unwin.

Freud, S. (1957). Leonardo da Vinci and a memory of his childhood. In J. Strachey (Ed. and Trans.), *The standard edition of the complete psychological works of Sigmund Freud* (Vol. 11, pp. 59–137). London, United Kingdom: Hogarth Press. (Original work published 1910)

Freud, S. (1965). *The interpretation of dreams.* New York, NY: Avon. (Original work published 1900)

Freund, A. M., & Baltes, P. B. (1998). Selection, optimization, and compensation as strategies of life management: Correlations with subjective indicators of successful aging. *Psychology and Aging, 13,* 531–543.

Frewen, P. A., Dozois, D. J. A., & Lanius, R. A. (2008). Neuroimaging studies of psychological interventions for mood and anxiety disorders: Empirical and methodological review. *Clinical Psychology Review, 28,* 228–246.

Friedman, M., & Rosenman, R. F. (1974). *Type A behavior and your heart.* New York, NY: Knopf.

Friend, R., Rafferty, Y., & Bramel, D. (1990). A puzzling misinterpretation of the Asch "conformity" study. *European Journal of Social Psychology, 20,* 29–44.

Fromkin, V. A. (Ed.). (1980). *Errors in linguistic performance: Slips of the tongue, pen, and hand.* New York, NY: Academic Press.

Furman, W., & Buhrmester, D. (1992). Age and sex differences in perceptions of networks of personal relationships. *Child Development, 63,* 103–115.

Furmark, T., Tillfors, M., Marteinsdottir, I., Fischer, H., Pissiota, A., Långström, B., & Fredrikson, M. (2002). Common changes in cerebral blood flow in patients with social phobia treated with citalopram or cognitive-behavioral therapy. *Archives of General Psychiatry, 59,* 425–433.

Furnham, A., Crump, J., & Whelan, J. (1997). Validating the NEO Personality Inventory using assessor's ratings. *Personality & Individual Differences, 22,* 669–675.

Furniss, E. (1997–1998). Pioneers, progress and the myth of the frontier: The landscape of public history in rural British Columbia. *BC Studies, 115/116,* 7–44.

Gaines, S. O., Jr., & Agnew, C. R. (2003). Relationship maintenance in intercultural couples: An interdependence analysis. In D. Canary & M. Dainton (Eds.), *Maintaining relationships through communication: Relational, contextual, and cultural variations* (pp. 231–253). Mahwah, NJ: Erlbaum.

Gale, C. R., Batty, G. D., & Deary, I. J. (2008). Locus of control at age 10 years and health outcomes and behaviors at age 30 years: The 1970 British Cohort Study. *Psychosomatic Medicine, 70,* 397–403.

Galef, B. G. (1992). Ontogeny and social transmission of food preferences in mammals: Basic and applied research. *Appetite, 19*(3), 309–311.

Galef, B. G., Jr., & Whiskin, E. E. (1995). Learning socially to eat more of one food than of another. *Journal of Comparative Psychology, 109*(1), 99–101.

Galef, B. G., Jr., Whiskin, E. E., & Bielavska, E. (1997). Interaction with demonstrator rats changes observer rats' affective responses to flavors. *Journal of Comparative Psychology, 111*(4), 393–398.

Gallo, L. C., & Matthews, K. A. (2003). Understanding the association between socioeconomic status and physical health: Do negative emotions play a role? *Psychological Bulletin, 129,* 10–51.

Galton, F. (1907). *Inquiries into human faculty and its development.* London, United Kingdom: Dent Publishers. (Original work published 1883)

Ganis, F., Thompson, W. L., & Kosslyn, S. M. (2004). Brain areas underlying visual imagery and visual perception: An fMRI study. *Cognitive Brain Research, 20,* 226–241.

Ganor-Stern, D., Tzelgov, J., & Ellenbogen, R. (2007). Automaticity of two-digit numbers. *Journal of Experimental Psychology: Human Perception and Performance, 33*(2), 483–496.

Gao, Q., & Horvath, T. L. (2007). Neurobiology of feeding and energy expenditure. *Annual Review of Neuroscience, 30,* 367–398.

Garb, H. N., Wood, J. M., Lilienfeld, S. O., & Nezworski, M. T. (2005). Roots of the Rorschach controversy. *Clinical Psychology Review, 25,* 97–118.

Garcia, J. (1990). Learning without memory. *Journal of Cognitive Neuroscience, 2,* 287–305.

Garcia, J., & Koelling, R. A. (1966). The relation of cue to consequence in avoidance learning. *Psychonomic Science, 4,* 123–124.

Gardner, H. (1983). *Frames of mind.* New York, NY: Basic Books.

Gardner, H. (1993). *Creating minds.* New York, NY: Basic Books.

Gardner, H. (1999). *The disciplined mind.* New York, NY: Simon & Schuster.

Gardner, M., & Steinberg, L. (2005). Peer influence on risk taking, risk preference, and risky decision making in adolescence and adulthood: An experimental study. *Developmental Psychology, 41,* 625–635.

Gardner, R. A., & Gardner, B. T. (1969). Teaching sign language to a chimpanzee. *Science, 165,* 664–672.

Gassió, R., Artuch, R., Vilaseca, M. A., Fusté, E., Boix, C., Sans, A., & Campistol, J. (2005). Cognitive functions in classic phenylketonuria and mild hyperphenylalaninaemia: Experience in a paediatric population. *Developmental Medicine & Child Neurology, 47,* 443–448.

Gauthier, S., Bouchard, R., Bacher, Y., Bailey, P., Bergman, H., Carrier, L., . . . et al. (1989). Progress report on the Canadian Multicentre Trial of tetrahydroaminoacridine with lecithin in Alzheimer's disease. *Canadian Journal of Neurological Science, 16*(4 Suppl), 543–546.

Gawronski, B., & LeBel, E. P. (2008). Understanding patterns of attitude change: When implicit measures show change, but explicit measures do not. *Journal of Experimental Social Psychology, 44*, 1355–1361.

Gazzaniga, M. (1970). *The bisected brain.* New York, NY: Appleton-Century-Crofts.

Gazzaniga, M. S. (1985). *The social brain.* New York, NY: Basic Books.

Geen, R. G. (1998). Aggression and antisocial behavior. In D. T. Gilbert, S. T. Fiske, & G. Lindzey (Eds.), *Handbook of social psychology* (4th ed., Vol. 2., pp. 317–356). NewYork, NY: McGraw-Hill.

Gelman, S. A. (2003). *Origins of essentialism in everyday thought.* London, United Kingdom: Oxford University Press.

Gelman, S. A., & Raman, L. (2002). Folk biology as a window into cognitive development. *Human Development, 45*, 61–68.

Gelman, S. A., & Wellman, H. M. (1991). Insides and essences: Early understandings of the non-obvious. *Cognition, 38*, 213–244.

Gentner, D., & Goldin-Meadow, S. (Eds.) (2003). *Language in mind: Advances in the study of language and thought.* Cambridge, MA: MIT Press.

Geraerts, E., Schooler, J. W., Merckelbach, H., Jelicic, M., Hauer, B. J. A., & Ambadar, Z. (2007). The reality of recovered memories: Corroborating continuous and discontinuous memories of childhood sexual abuse. *Psychological Science, 18*, 564–568.

Gergen, K. J., Gulerce, A., Lock, A., & Misra, G. (1996). Psychological science in a cultural context. *American Psychologist, 51*, 496–503.

Gerrig, R. J., & O'Brien, E. J. (2005). The scope of memory-based processing. *Discourse Processes, 39*, 225–242.

Gershkoff, E. T., & Bitensky, S. H. (2007). The case against corporal punishment for children: Converging evidence from social science research and international human rights law and implications for U.S. Public Policy. *Psychology, Public Policy, and Law, 13*, 231–272.

Giambra, L. M., & Arenberg, D. (1993). Adult age differences in forgetting sentences. *Psychology and Aging, 8*, 451–462.

Gibbons, A. (2002). Hot spots of brain evolution. *Science, 296*, 837.

Gibbons, M. B. C., Crits-Christoph, P., & Hearon, B. (2008). The empirical status of psychodynamic therapies. *Annual Review of Clinical Psychology, 4*, 93–108.

Gibson, E. J., & Walk, R. D. (1960). The "visual cliff." *Scientific American, 202*, 64–71.

Gibson, E. S., Powles, A. C. P., Thabane, L., O'Brien, S., Sirriani Molnar, D., Trajanovic, N., . . . Chilcott-Tanser, L. (2006). "Sleepiness" is serious in adolescence: Two surveys of 3235 Canadian students. *BMC Public Health, 6*, 116–125.

Gibson, J. J. (1979). *An ecological approach to visual perception.* Boston: Houghton Mifflin.

Gidron, Y., Davidson, K., & Bata, I. (1999). The short-term effects of a hostility-reduction intervention on male coronary heart disease patients. *Health Psychology, 18*, 416–420.

Gigerenzer, G. (2008). Why heuristics work. *Perspectives on Psychological Science, 3*, 20–29.

Gilbert, D. T., Morewedge, C. K., Risen, J. L., & Wilson, T. D. (2004). Looking forward to looking backward: The misprediction of regret. *Psychological Science, 15*, 346–350.

Gilligan, C. (1982). *In a different voice: Psychological theory and women's development.* Cambridge, MA: Harvard University Press.

Gilovich, T. (1991). *How we know what isn't so: The fallibility of human reason in everyday life.* New York, NY: The Free Press.

Gitlin, M., Nuechterlein, K., Subotnik, K. L., Ventura, J., Mintz, J., Fogelson, D. L., Bartzokis, G., & Aravagiri, M. (2001). Clinical outcome following neuroleptic discontinuation in patients with remitted recent-onset schizophrenia. *American Journal of Psychiatry, 158*, 1835–1842.

Glasman, L. R., & Albarracín, D. (2006). Forming attitudes that predict behavior: A meta-analysis of the attitude-behavior relation. *Psychological Bulletin, 132*, 778–822.

Gleaves, D. H., May, M. C., & Cardeña, E. (2001). An examination of the diagnostic validity of dissociative identity disorder. *Clinical Psychology Review, 21*, 577–608.

Gleitman, L. R., & Rozin, P. (1973). Teaching reading by use of syllabary. *Reading Research Quarterly, 8*, 447–483.

Gleitman, L. R., & Rozin, P. (1977). Structure and the acquisition of reading. I. Relations between orthographies and the structure of language. In A. S. Reber and D. Scarborough (Eds.), *Toward a psychology of reading* (pp. 1–53). Potomac, MD: Erlbaum.

Goddard, H. H. (1914). *The Kallikak family: A study of the heredity of feeble-mindedness.* New York, NY: Macmillan.

Goddard, H. H. (1917). Mental tests and the immigrant. *Journal of Delinquency, 2*, 243–277.

Godden, D. R., & Baddeley, A. D. (1975). Context-dependent memory in two natural environments: On land and under water. *British Journal of Psychology, 66*, 325–331.

Godin, G., Sheeran, P., Conner, M., & Germain, M. (2008). Asking questions changes behavior: Mere measurement effects on frequency of blood donation. *Health Psychology, 27*, 179–184.

Goel, V. (2007). Anatomy of deductive reasoning. *Trends in Cognitive Sciences, 11*(10), 435–441.

Goldapple, K., Segal, Z., Garson, C., Lau, M., Bieling, P., Kennedy, S., & Mayberg, H. (2004). Modulation of cortical-limbic pathways in major depression. *Archives of General Psychiatry, 61*, 34–41.

Goldfried, M. R. (2003). Cognitive-behavior therapy: Reflections on the evolution of a therapeutic orientation. *Cognitive Therapy and Research, 27*, 53–69.

Goldfried, M. R., & Davila, J. (2005). The role of relationship and technique in therapeutic change. *Psychotherapy: Theory, Research, Practice, Training, 42*, 421–430.

Goldin-Meadow, S. (2003). *The resilience of language: What gesture creation in deaf children can tell us about how all children learn language.* New York, NY: Psychology Press.

Goldin-Meadow, S., & Mylander, C. (1990). Beyond the input given: The child's role in the acquisition of language. *Language, 66*, 323–355.

Goldrick, M., & Larson, M. (2008). Phonotactic probability influences speech production. *Cognition, 107*(3), 1155–1164.

Goldstein, E. B. (1999). *Sensation & perception* (5th ed.). Pacific Grove, CA: Brooks/Cole.

Goldstein, J. M., Seidman, L. J., Horton, N. J., Makris, N., Kennedy, D. N., Caviness, V. S., Jr., . . . Tsuang, M. T. (2001). Normal sexual dimorphism of the human brain assessed by in vivo magnetic resonance imaging. *Cerebral Cortex, 11*, 490–497.

Goldstein, R. B., Compton, W. M., Pulay, A. J., Ruan, W. J., Pickering, R. P., Stinson, F. S., & Grant, B. F. (2007). Antisocial behavioral syndromes and *DSM-IV* drug use disorders in the

United States: Results from the National Epidemiologic Survey on Alcohol and Related Conditions. *Drug and Alcohol Dependence, 90,* 145–158.

Goldstrom, I. D., Campbell, J., Rogers, J. A., Lambert, D. B., Blacklow, B., Henderson, M. J., & Manderscheid, R. W. (2006). National estimates for mental health support groups, self-help organizations, and consumer-operated services. *Administration and Policy in Mental Health and Mental Health Services Research, 33,* 92–103.

Goodall, J. (1986). *The chimpanzees of Gombe: Patterns of behavior.* Cambridge, MA: Harvard University Press.

Goodall, J. (1990). *Through a window: My thirty years with the chimpanzees of Gombe.* Boston, MA: Houghton Mifflin.

Goodheart, C. D., Kadzin, A. E., & Sternberg, R. J. (2006). *Evidence-based psychotherapy: Where practice and research meet.* Washington, DC: American Psychological Association.

Gotlib, I. H., & Hamilton, J. P. (2008). Neuroimaging and depression: Current status and unresolved issues. *Current Directions in Psychological Science, 17,* 159–163.

Gottesman, I.I. (1991). *Schizophrenia genesis: The origins of madness.* New York, NY: Freeman.

Gottfredson, L. S. (1997). Mainstream science on intelligence: An editorial with 52 signatories, history, and bibliography. *Intelligence, 24,* 13–23.

Gottfredson, L. S. (2002). Where and why g matters: Not a mystery. *Human Performance, 15,* 25–46.

Gottfredson, L. S. (2005). What if the hereditarian hypothesis is true? *Psychology, Public Policy, and Law, 11,* 311–319.

Gottman, J. M., & Levenson, R. W. (2000). The timing of divorce: Predicting when a couple will divorce over a 14-year period. *Journal of Marriage and the Family, 62,* 737–745.

Gouin, J.-P., Kielcolt-Glaser, J. K., Malarkey, W. B., & Glaser, R. (2008). The influence of anger expression on wound healing. *Brain, Behavior, and Immunity, 22,* 699–708.

Gould, E., & Gross, C. G. (2002). Neurogenesis in adult mammals: Some progress and problems. *Journal of Neuroscience, 22,* 619–623.

Gould, S. J. (2002). *The structure of evolutionary theory.* Cambridge, MA: Belknap Press.

Government of Canada. (2006). *The Human face of mental health and mental illness in Canada 2006.*

Grady, C. L., & Craik, F. I. (2000). Changes in memory processing with age. *Current Opinion in Neurobiology, 10*(2), 224–231. Review.

Grady, C. L., McIntosh, A. R., & Craik, F. I. M. (2005). Task-related activity in prefrontal cortex and its relation to recognition memory performance in young and old adults. *Neuropsychologia, 43,* 1466–1481.

Grady, C. L., Springer, M. V., Hongwanishkul, D., McIntosh, A. R., & Winocur, G. (2006). Age-related changes in brain activity across the adult lifespan. *Journal of Cognitive Neuroscience, 18,* 227–241.

Granic, I., & Patterson, G. R. (2006). Toward a comprehensive model of antisocial development: A dynamic systems approach. *Psychological Review, 113*(1), 101–131.

Grant, A. M. (2008). The significance of task significance: Job performance effects, relational mechanisms, and boundary conditions. *Journal of Applied Psychology, 93,* 108–124.

Grant, B. R., & Grant, P. (1989). *Evolutionary dynamics of a natural population.* Princeton: Princeton University Press.

Grant, P. R., & Grant, B. R. (2002). Unpredictable evolution in a 30-year study of Darwin's finches. *Science, 296,* 707–711.

Gray, M. R., & Steinberg, L. (1999). Unpacking authoritative parenting: Reassessing a multidimensional construct. *Journal of Marriage and the Family, 61,* 574–587.

Greaves, N., Prince, E., Evans, D. W., & Charman, T. (2006). Repetitive and ritualistic behaviour in children with Prader-Willi syndrome and children with autism. *Journal of Intellectual Disability Research, 50,* 92–100.

Green, D. M., & Swets, J. A. (1966). *Signal detection theory and psychophysics.* New York, NY: Wiley.

Greenberg, S. T., & Schoen, E. G. (2008). Males and eating disorders: Gender-based therapy for eating disorder recovery. *Professional Psychology: Research and Practice, 39,* 464–471.

Greene, J. D., Morelli, S. A., Lowenberg, K., Nystrom, L. E. & Cohen, J. D. (2008). Cognitive load selectively interferes with utilitarian moral judgment. *Cognition, 107*(3), 1144–1154.

Greene, J. D., Sommerville, R. B., Nystrom, L. E., Darley, J. M., & Cohen, J. D. (2001). An fMRI investigation of emotional engagement in moral judgment. *Science, 293,* 2105–2108.

Greenfield, P. M. (1997). You can't take it with you: Why ability assessments don't cross cultures. *American Psychologist, 52,* 1115–1124.

Greenwald, A. G., Banaji, M. R., Rudman, L A., Farnham, S. D., Nosek, B. A., & Mellott, D. S. (2002). A unified theory of implicit attitudes, stereotypes, self-esteem, and self-concept. *Psychological Review, 109,* 3–25.

Greenwald, A. G., Spangenber, E. R., Pratkanis, A. R., & Eskenazi, J. (1991). Double-blind tests of subliminal self-help audiotapes. *Psychological Science, 2,* 119–122.

Grice, H. P. (1968). Utterer's meaning, sentence-meaning, and word-meaning. *Foundations of Language, 4,*1–18.

Grice, H. P. (1975). Logic and conversation. In P. Cole & J. L. Morgan (Eds.), *Syntax and semantics: Vol. 3. Speech acts* (pp. 41–58). New York, NY: Academic Press.

Grieger, T. A., Waldrep, D. A., Lovasz, M. M., & Ursano, R. J. (2005). Follow-up of Pentagon employees two years after the terrorist attack of September 11, 2001. *Psychiatric Services, 56,* 1374–1378.

Grigorenko, E. L. (2000). Heritability and intelligence. In R. J. Sternberg (Ed.), *Handbook of intelligence* (pp. 53–91). Cambridge, United Kingdom: Cambridge University Press.

Grigorenko, E. L., Meier, E., Kipka, J., Mohatt, G., Yanez, E., & Sternberg, R. J. (2004). Academic and practical intelligence: A case study of the Yup'ik in Alaska. *Learning and Individual Differences, 14,* 183–207.

Grilo, C. M., Hrabosky, J. I., White, M., Allison, K. C., Stunkard, A. J., & Masheb, R. M. (2008). Overvaluation of shape and weight in binge eating disorder and overweight controls: Refinement of a diagnostic construct. *Journal of Abnormal Psychology, 117,* 414–419.

Grodner, D., Gibson, E., & Watson, D. (2005). The influence of contextual contrast on syntactic processing: Evidence for strong-interaction in sentence comprehension. *Cognition, 95*(3), 275–296.

Groh, D. R., Jason, L. A., & Keys, C. B. (2008). Social network variables in alcoholics anonymous: A literature review. *Clinical Psychology Review, 28,* 430–450.

Grohol, J. M. (1998). Future clinical directions: Professional development, pathology, and psychotherapy on-line. In

J. Gackenbach (Ed.), *Psychology and the internet: Intrapersonal, interpersonal, and transpersonal implications* (pp. 111–140). San Diego, CA: Academic Press.

Grüsser, S. M., Thalemann, C. N., Platz, W., Gölz, J., & Partecke, G. (2006). A new approach to preventing relapse in opiate addicts: A psychometric evaluation. *Biological Psychiatry, 71,* 231–235.

Guéraud, S., Tapiero, I., & O'Brien, E. J. (2008). Context and the activation of predictive inference*s. Psychonomic Bulletin & Review, 15,* 351–365.

Guilford, J. P. (1961). Factorial angles to psychology. *Psychological Review, 68,* 1–20.

Guilford, J. P. (1985). The Structure-of-Intellect model. In B. B. Wolman (Fd.), *Handbook of intelligence.* New York, NY: Wiley.

Guilleminault, C., Poyares, D., Aftab, F., & Palombini, L. (2001). Sleep and wakefulness in somnambulism: A spectral analysis study. *Journal of Psychosomatic Research, 51,* 411–416.

Gur, R. C., Gunning-Dixon, F., Bilker, W. B., & Gur, R. E. (2002). Sex differences in temporo-limbic and frontal brain volumes of healthy adults. *Cerebral Cortex, 12,* 998–1003.

Gutheil, I. A., Chernesky, R. H., & Sherratt, M. L. (2006). Influencing student attitudes toward older adults: Results of a service-learning collaboration. *Educational Gerontology, 32,* 771–784.

Gutierrez, P. M., Watkins, R., & Collura, D. (2004). Suicide risk screening in an urban high school. *Suicide and Life-Threatening Behavior, 34,* 421–428.

Haas, S. M. (2003). Relationship maintenance in same-sex couples. In D. Canary & M. Dainton (Eds.), *Maintaining relationships through communication: Relational, contextual, and cultural variations* (pp. 209–230). Mahwah, NJ: Erlbaum.

Haas, S. M., & Stafford, L. (1998). An initial examination of maintenance behaviors in gay and lesbian relationships. *Journal of Social and Personal Relationships, 15,* 846–855.

Haberstick, B. C., Schmitz, S., Young, S. E., & Hewitt, J. K. (2006). Genes and developmental stability of aggressive behavior: Problems at home and school in a community sample of twins aged 7–12. *Behavior Genetics, 36,* 809–819.

Habib, R., Nyberg, L., & Tulving, E. (2003). Hemispheric asymmetries of memory: the HERA model revisited. *TRENDS in Cognitive Sciences, 7,* 241–245.

Haddock, G. (2002). It's easy to like or dislike Tony Blair: Accessibility experiences and the favourability of attitude judgments. *British Journal of Psychology, 93,* 257–267.

Haffenden, A. M., & Goodale, M. A. (2000). The effect of learned perceptual associations on visuomotor programming varies with kinematic demands. *Journal of Cognitive Neuroscience, 12,* 950–964.

Hagemann, N., Strauss, B. & Leissing, J. (2008). When the referee sees red. . . . *Psychological Science, 19,* 769.

Haier, R. J., Jung, R. E., Yeo, R. A., Head, K., & Alkire, M. T. (2004). Structural variation and general intelligence. *NeuroImage, 23,* 425–433.

Hamilton, M., & Rajaram, S. (2001). The concreteness effect in implicit and explicit memory tests. *Journal of Memory and Language, 44,* 96–117.

Hammond, D., Costello, M.-J., Fong, G. T., & Topham, J. (2006). Exposure to tobacco marketing and support for the tobacco control policies. *American Journal of Health Behavior, 30*(6), 700–709.

Hammond, D., Fong, G. T., McDonald, P. W., Brown, K. S., & Cameron, R. (2004). Graphic Canadian cigarette warning labels and adverse outcomes: Evidence from Canadian smokers. *American Journal of Public Health, 94*(8), 1442–1445.

Hammond, D., Fong, G. T., Zanna, M. P., Thrasher, J. F., & Borland, R. (2006). Tobacco denormalization and industry beliefs among smokers from four countries. *American Journal of Preventive Medicine, 31*(3), 225–232.

Han, J.-S. (2004). Acupuncture and endorphins. *Neuroscience Letters, 361,* 258–261.

Harbluk, J. L., Noy, Y. I., Trbovich, P. L., & Eizenman, M. (2007). An on-road assessment of cognitive distraction: Impacts on drivers' visual behavior and braking performance. *Accident Analysis and Prevention, 39,* 372–379.

Harder, J. W. (1991). Equity theory versus expectancy theory: The case of major league baseball free agents. *Journal of Applied Psychology, 76,* 458–464.

Hardoon, K. K., Baboushkin, H. R., Derevensky, J. L., & Gupta, R. (2001). Underlying cognitions in the selection of lottery tickets. *Journal of Clinical Psychology, 57*(6), 749–763.

Hardy, J., & Selkoe, D. J. (2002). The amyloid hypothesis of Alzheimer's disease: Progress and problems on the road to therapeutics. *Science, 297,* 353–356.

Hare, B. (2007). From nonhuman to human mind: What changed and why? *Current Directions in Psychological Science, 16,* 60–64.

Hargadon, R., Bowers, K. S., & Woody, E. Z. (1995). Does counterpain imagery mediate hypnotic analgesia? *Journal of Abnormal Psychology, 104,* 508–516.

Harlow, H. F. (1965). Sexual behavior in the rhesus monkey. In F. Beach (Ed.), *Sex and behavior.* New York, NY: Wiley.

Harlow, H. F., & Suomi, S. J. (1971). Social recovery by isolation-reared monkeys. *Proceedings of the National Academy of Science of the United States of America, 68,* 1534–1538.

Harlow, H. F., & Zimmerman, R. R. (1958). The development of affectional responses in infant monkeys. *Proceedings of the American Philosophical Society, 102,* 501–509.

Harlow, J. M. (1868). Recovery from the passage of an iron bar through the head. *Publications of the Massachusetts Medical Society, 2,* 327–347.

Harris, B. (1979). Whatever happened to Little Albert? *American Psychologist, 34,* 151–160.

Hart, J. T. (1965). Memory and the feeling-of-knowing experience. *Journal of Educational Psychology, 56,* 208–216.

Hart, S. D., & Roesch, R. (2007). Mental disorder and the law. In P. Firestone & D. J. A. Dozois (Eds.), *Abnormal Psychology* (3rd ed., Chapter 19, pp. 453–472). Toronto, ON: Pearson Prentice-Hall.

Hartshorne, H., & May, M. A. (1928). *Studies in the nature of character: Vol. 1. Studies in deceit.* New York, NY: Macmillan.

Hartsuiker, R. J., Schriefers, H. J., & Kikstra, G. M. (2003). Morphophonological influences on the construction of subject-verb agreement. *Memory & Cognition, 31,* 1316–1326.

Hartup, W. H. (1996). The company they keep: Friendships and their developmental significance. *Child Development, 67,* 1–13.

Hasson, U., Furman, O., Clark, D., Dudai, Y., & Davachi, L. (2008). Enhanced intersubject correlations during movie viewing correlate with successful episodic encoding. *Neuron, 57*(3), 452–462.

Hastorf, A. H., & Cantril, H. (1954). They saw a game: A case study. *Journal of Abnormal and Social Psychology, 49,* 129–134.

Hatcher, C., & Himelstein, P. (Eds.). (1996). *The handbook of Gestalt therapy.* Northvale, NJ: Jason Aronson.

Hatfield, E., & Sprecher, S. (1995). Men's and women's preferences in marital partners in the United States, Russia, and Japan. *Journal of Cross-Cultural Psychology, 26,* 728–750.

Hathaway, S. R., & McKinley, J. C. (1940). A multiphasic personality schedule (Minnesota): I. Construction of the schedule. *Journal of Psychology, 10,* 249–254.

Hathaway, S. R., & McKinley, J. C. (1943). *Minnesota Multiphasic Inventory manual.* New York, NY: Psychological Corporation.

Hauser, M. D., Chomsky, N., & Fitch, W. F. (2002). The faculty of language: What is it, who has it, and how did it evolve? *Science, 298,* 1569–1579.

Hawley, L. L., Ringo Ho, M.-H., Zuroff, D. C., & Blatt, S. J. (2007). Stress reactivity following brief treatment for depression. *Journal of Consulting and Clinical Psychology, 75*(2), 244–256.

Hazan, C., & Shaver, P. (1987). Romantic love conceptualized as an attachment process. *Journal of Personality and Social Psychology, 52,* 511–524.

Hazeltine, E., & Ivry, R. B. (2002). Can we teach the cerebellum new tricks? *Science, 296,* 1979–1980.

Health Canada. (2005a). *Canada food guide to healthy eating.* Retrieved from http://www.hc-sc.gc.ca/fn-an/food-guide-aliment/index_e.html

Health Canada. (2005b). *Canadian tobacco use monitoring survey (CTUMS) 2005.* Retrieved from http://www.hc-sc.gc.ca/hl-vs/pubs/tobac-tabac/ctums-esutc-2005/wave-phase-1_summary-sommaire_e.html

Health Canada. (2007). *Canada's guide to healthy eating and physical activity.* Retrieved from http://www.phac-aspc.gc.ca/guide/index_e.html

Hearst, E. (1988). Fundamentals of learning and conditioning. In R. C. Atkinson, R. J. Herrnstein, G. Lindzey, & R. D. Luce (Eds.), *Stevens' handbook of experimental psychology: Vol. 2. Learning and cognition* (2nd ed., pp. 3–109). New York, NY: Wiley.

Heatherington, L., & Lavner, J. A. (2008). Coming to terms with coming out: Review and recommendations for family systems-focused research. *Journal of Family Psychology, 22,* 329–343.

Hebb, D. O. (1949). *The organization of behavior.* John Wiley & Sons Inc.

Hebl, M. R., & Heatherton, T. F. (1998). The stigma of obesity in women: The difference is black and white. *Personality and Social Psychology Bulletin, 24,* 417–426.

Heider, F. (1958). *The psychology of interpersonal relationships.* New York, NY: Wiley.

Hektner, J. M., & Csikszentmihalyi, M. (2002). The experience sampling method: Measuring the context and the content of lives. In R. B. Bechtel & A. Churchman (Eds.), *Handbook of environmental psychology* (pp. 233–243). New York, NY: Wiley.

Helgeson, V. S., Reynolds, K. A., & Tomich, P. L. (2006). A meta-analytic review of benefit finding and growth. *Journal of Consulting and Clinical Psychology, 74,* 797–816.

Heller, M. A., Bracket, D. D., Salik, S. S., Scroggs, E., & Green, S. (2003). Objects, raised lines, and the haptic horizontal-vertical illusion. *Quarterly Journal of Experimental Psychology, 56A,* 891–907.

Henningsen, D.D., Henningsen, M. L. M., Eden, J., & Cruz, M. G. (2006). Examining the symptoms of groupthink and retrospective sensemaking. *Small Group Research, 37,* 36–64.

Henry, P. J., & Sears, D. O. (2002). The symbolic racism 2000 scale. *Political Psychology, 2,* 253–283.

Henry, W. P., Strupp, H. H., Schacht, T. E., & Gaston, L. (1994). Psychodynamic approaches. In A. E. Bergin & S. L. Garfield (Eds.), *Handbook of psychotherapy and behavior change* (4th ed., pp. 467–508). New York, NY: Wiley.

Herek, G. M. (2002). Gender gaps in public opinion about lesbians and gay men. *Public Opinion Quarterly, 66,* 40–66.

Herman, C. P., Roth, D. A., & Polivy, J. (2003). Effects of the presence of others on food intake: A normative investigation. *Psychological Bulletin, 129,* 873–886,

Herrnstein, R. J., & Murray, C. (1994). *The Bell Curve: Intelligence and class structure in American Life.* New York, NY: Free Press.

Hersh, S. M. (2004, 9 May). Chain of command: How the Department of Defense mishandled the disaster at Abu Ghraib. *The New Yorker,* 9 May. Retrieved from http://www.newyorker.com/fact/content/?040517fa_fact2

Hertwig, R., Herzog, S. M., Schooler, L. J., & Reimer, T. (2008). Fluency heuristic: A model of how the mind exploits a by-product of information retrieval. *Journal of Experimental Psychology: Learning, Memory, and Cognition, 34*(5), 1191–1206.

Hertzog, C., Dixon, R. A., & Hultsch, D. F. (1990). Relationships between metamemory, memory predictions, and memory task performance in adults. *Psychology and Aging, 5,* 215–227.

Hess, T. M. (2005). Memory and aging in context. *Psychological Bulletin, 131,* 383–406.

Hettema, J. M., Neale, M. C., & Kendler, K. S. (2001). A review and meta-analysis of the genetic epidemiology of anxiety disorders. *American Journal of Psychiatry, 158,* 1568–1578.

Hettema, J. M., Prescott, C. A., Myerse, J. M., Neale, M. C., & Kendler, K. S. (2005). The structure of genetic and environmental risk factors for anxiety disorders in men and women. *Archives of General Psychiatry, 62,* 182–189.

Hewstone, M., Rubin, M., & Willis, H. (2002). Intergroup bias. *Annual Review of Psychology, 53,* 575–604.

Hickok, G., Love-Geffen, T., & Klima, E. S. (2002). Role of the left hemisphere in sign language comprehension. *Brain & Language, 82,* 167–178.

Higgie, M., Chenoweth, S., & Blows, M. W. (2000). Natural selection and the reinforcement of mate recognition. *Science, 290,* 519–521.

Higgins, E. T., & Pittman, T. S. (2008). Motives of the human animal: Comprehending, managing, and sharing inner states. *Annual Review of Psychology, 59,* 361–385.

Hilgard, E. R. (1986). *Psychology in America: A historical survey.* San Diego, CA: Harcourt Brace Jovanovich.

Hilgetag, C. C., O'Neill, M. A., & Young, M. P. (1996). Indeterminate organization of the visual system. *Science, 271,* 776–777.

Hill, R. A., & Barton, R. A. (2005). Sporting contests: Seeing red? Putting sportswear into context. *Nature, 435,* 293.

Hills, A. L., Cox, B. J., McWilliams, L. A., & Sareen, J. (2005). Suicide attempts and externalizing psychopathology in a nationally representative sample. *Comprehensive Psychiatry, 46,* 334–339.

Hilsenroth, M. J., Charnas, J. W., Zodan, J., & Streiner, D. L. (2007). Criterion-based training for Rorschach scoring. *Training and Education in Professional Psychology, 1*, 125–134.

Hinshaw, S. P., & Stier, A. (2008). Stigma as related to mental disorders. *Annual Review of Clinical Psychology, 4*, 367–393.

Hobara, M. (2005). Beliefs about appropriate pain behavior: Cross-cultural and sex differences between Japanese and Euro-Americans. *European Journal of Pain, 9*, 389–393.

Hobson, J. A. (1988). *The dreaming brain.* New York, NY: Basic Books.

Hobson, J. A., & McCarley, R. W. (1977). The brain as a dream state generator: An activation-synthesis hypothesis of the dream process. *American Journal of Psychiatry, 134*, 1335–1348.

Hodgkinson, G. P., & Healey, M. P. (2008). Cognition in organizations. *Annual Review of Psychology, 59*, 387–417.

Hoekstra, R. A., Bartels, M., & Boomsma, D. I. (2007). Longitudinal genetic study of verbal and nonverbal IQ from early childhood to young adulthood. *Learning and Individual Differences, 17*, 97–114.

Hoelzle, J. B., & Meyer, G. J. (2008). The factor structure of the MMPI-2 Restructured Clinical (RC) Scales. *Journal of Personality Assessment, 90*, 443–455.

Hoff, T. L. (1992). Psychology in Canada one hundred years ago: James Mark Baldwin at the University of Toronto. *Canadian Psychology, 33*, 683–694.

Hoffman, E. J., & Mathew, S. J. (2008). Anxiety disorders: A comprehensive review of pharmacotherapies. *Mount Sanai Journal of Medicine, 75*, 248–262.

Holahan, C. K., & Sears, R. R. (1995). *The gifted group in later maturity.* Stanford, CA: Stanford University Press.

Holden, C. (1998). No last word on language origins. *Science, 282*, 1455–1458.

Holen, M. C., & Oaster, T. R. (1976). Serial position and isolation effects in a classroom lecture simulation. *Journal of Educational Psychology, 68*, 723–725.

Hollon, S. D., Stewart, M. O., & Strunk, D. (2006). Enduring effects for cognitive behavior therapy in the treatment of depression and anxiety. *Annual Review of Psychology, 57*, 285–315.

Hollon, S. D., Thase, M. E., & Markowitz, J. C. (2002). Treatment and prevention of depression. *Psychological Science in the Public Interest, 3*, 39–77.

Holmbeck, G. N., & O'Donnell, D. (1991). Discrepancies between perceptions of decision making and behavioral autonomy. In R. L. Paikoff (Ed.), *Shared views in the family during adolescence* (pp. 51–69). San Francisco, CA: Jossey-Bass.

Holmes, D. S. (1994). *Abnormal psychology.* New York, NY: HarperCollins.

Holmes, J. G., Miller, D. T., & Lerner, M. J. (2002). Committing altruism under the cloak of self-interest: The exchange fiction. *Journal of Experimental Social Psychology, 38*, 144–151.

Holmes, T. H., & Rahe, R. H. (1967). The social readjustment rating scale. *Journal of Psychosomatic Research, 11*(2), 213–218.

Holyoak, K. J., & Spellman, B. A. (1993). Thinking. *Annual Review of Psychology, 44*, 265–315.

Homer, B. D., Salomon, T. M., Moeller, R. W., Mascia, A., DeRaleau, L., & Halktis, P. N. (2008). Methamphetamine abuse and impairment of social functioning: A review of the underlying neurophysiological causes and behavioral implications. *Psychological Bulletin, 134*, 301–310.

Hooley, J. M. (2007). Expressed emotion and relapse of psychopathology. *Annual Review of Clinical Psychology, 3*, 329–352.

Hopson, J. L. (1979). *Scent signals: The silent language of sex.* New York, NY: Morrow.

Horgen, K. B., & Brownell, K. D. (2002). Comparison of price change and health message interventions in promoting healthy food choices. *Health Psychology, 21*, 505–512.

Horney, K. (1937). *The neurotic personality of our time.* New York, NY: Norton.

Horney, K. (1939). *New ways in psychoanalysis.* New York, NY: Norton.

Horney, K. (1945). *Our inner conflicts: A constructive theory of neurosis.* New York, NY: Norton.

Horney, K. (1950). *Neurosis and human growth.* New York, NY: Norton.

Horton, J. E., Crawford, H. J., Harrington, G., & Downs, J. H., III. (2004). Increased anterior corpus callosum size associated positively with hypnotizability and the ability to control pain. *Brain, 127*, 1741–1747.

Horton, W. S., & Gerrig, R. J. (2005a). Conversational common ground and memory processes in language production. *Discourse Processes, 40*, 1–35.

Horton, W. S., & Gerrig, R. J. (2005b). The impact of memory demands on audience design during language production. *Cognition, 96*, 127–142.

Hoshino-Browne, E., Zanna, A. S., Spencer, S. J., Zanna, M. P., Kitayama, S., & Lackenbauer, S. (2005). On the cultural guises of cognitive dissonance: The case of Easterners and Westerners. *Journal of Personality and Social Psychology, 89*, 294–310.

Hosking, R. D., & Zajicek, J. P. (2008). Therapeutic potential of cannabis in pain medicine. *British Journal of Anaesthesia, 101*, 59–68.

Houghton, J. (1980). One personal experience: Before and after mental illness. In J. G. Rabkin, L. Gelb, & J. B. Lazar (Eds.), *Attitudes toward the mentally ill: Research perspectives* (pp. 7–14). Rockville, MD: National Institutes of Mental Health.

Houlihan, D., Schwartz, C., Miltenberger, R., & Heuton, D. (1993). The rapid treatment of a young man's balloon (noise) phobia using in vivo flooding. *Journal of Behavior Therapy and Experimental Psychiatry, 24*, 233–240.

Howell, R. T., & Howell, C. J. (2008). The relation of economic status to subjective well-being in developing countries: A meta-analysis. *Psychological Bulletin, 134*, 536–560.

Hublin, C., Partinen, M., Koskenvuo, M., & Kaprio, J. (2007). Sleep and mortality: A population-based 22-year follow-up study. *Sleep:Journal of Sleep and Sleep Disorders Research, 30*(10), 1245–1253.

Hudson, J. I., Hiripi, E., Pope, H. G., Jr., & Kessler, R. C. (2007). The prevalence and correlates of eating disorders in the national comorbidity survey replication. *Biological Psychiatry, 61*, 348–358.

Hudson, J. L., Flannery-Schroeder, E., & Kendall, P. (2004). Primary prevention of anxiety disorders. In D. J. A. Dozois, & K. S. Dobson (Eds.), *The prevention of anxiety and depression: Theory, research, and practice* (pp. 101–130). Washington, DC: American Psychological Association.

Huesmann, L. R., Moise-Titus, J., Podolski, C. L., & Eron, L. D. (2003). Longitudinal relations between children's exposure to TV violence and their aggressive and violent behavior in young adulthood: 1977–1992. *Developmental Psychology, 39*, 201–221.

Huey, R. B., Gilchrist, G. W., Carlson, M. L., Berrigan, D., & Serra, L. (2000). Rapid evolution of a geographic cline in size in an introduced fly. *Science, 287,* 308–309.

Huizink, A. C., & Mulder, E. J. (2006). Maternal smoking, drinking or cannabis use during pregnancy and neurobehavioral and cognitive functioning in human offspring. *Neuroscience and Biobehavioral Reviews, 30*(1), 24–41.

Hull, C. L. (1943). *Principles of behavior: An introduction to behavior theory.* New York, NY: Appleton-Century-Crofts.

Hull, C. L. (1952). *A behavior system: An introduction to behavior theory concerning the individual organism.* New Haven, CT: Yale University Press.

Hultsch, D. F., Hertzog, C., Dixon, R. A., & Small, B. J. (1998). *Memory change in the aged.* Cambridge, UK: Cambridge University Press.

Hultsch, D. F., Hertzog, C., Small, B. J., & Dixon, R. A. (1999). Use it or lose it: Engaged lifestyle as a buffer of cognitive decline in aging? *Psychology and Aging, 14*(2), 245–263.

Hume, D. (1951). In L. A. Selby-Bigge (Ed.), *An enquiry concerning human understanding.* London, United Kingdom: Oxford University Press. (Original work published 1748)

Hunt, E., & Carlson, J. (2007). Considerations relating to the study of group differences in intelligence. *Perspectives on Psychological Science, 2,* 194–213.

Hurvich, L., & Jameson, D. (1974). Opponent processes as a model of neural organization. *American Psychologist, 29,* 88–102.

Huston, A. C. (2005). The effects of welfare reform and poverty policies on children and families. In D. B. Pillemer & S. H. White (Eds.), *Developmental psychology and social change: Research, history, and policy* (pp. 83–103). New York, NY: Cambridge University Press.

Hyde, J. S., & Durik, A. M. (2000). Gender differences in erotic plasticity—evolutionary or sociocultural forces? Comment on Baumeister (2000). *Psychological Bulletin, 126,* 375–379.

Hyde, J. S., Mezulis, A. H., & Abramson, L. Y. (2008). The ABCs of depression: Integrating affective, biological, and cognitive models to explain the emergence of the gender difference in depression. *Psychological Review, 115,* 291–313.

Hyland, M. E., Whalley, B., & Geraghty, A. W. A. (2007). Dispositional predictors of placebo responding: A motivational interpretation of flower essence and gratitude therapy. *Journal of Psychosomatic Research, 62,* 331–340.

Hylton, J. H. (1995). Care or control: Health or criminal justice options for the long-term seriously mentally ill in a Canadian province. *International Journal of Law and Psychiatry, 18,* 45–59.

Ingram, A., Saling, M. M., & Schweitzer, I. (2008). Cognitive side effects of brief pulse electroconvulsive therapy: A review. *The Journal of ECT, 24,* 3–9.

Insko, C. A., Thibaut, J. W., Moehle, D., Wilson, M., Diamond, W. D., Gilmore, R., . . . Lipsitz, A. (1980). Social evolution and the emergence of leadership. *Journal of Personality and Social Psychology, 39,* 431–448.

Interagency Secretariat on Research Ethics. (2005). *Tri-Council Policy Statement: Ethical conduct for research involving humans.* Retrieved from http://www.pre.ethics.gc.ca/english/pdf/TCPS%20October%202005_E.pdf

Irvine, J. T. (1990). Registering affect: Heteroglossia in the linguistic expression of emotion. In C. A. Lutz & L. Abu-Lughod (Eds.), *Language and the politics of emotions* (pp. 126–161). Cambridge, United Kingdom: Cambridge University Press.

Ishii-Kuntz, M. (1990). Social interaction and psychological well-being: Comparison across stages of adulthood. *International Journal of Aging and Human Development, 30,* 15–36.

Iyengar, S. S., Wells, R. E. & Schwartz, B. (2006). Doing better but feeling worse: Looking for the "best" job undermines satisfaction. *Psychological Science, 17,* 143–150.

Izard, C. E. (1993). Four systems for emotion activation: Cognitive and noncognitive processes. *Psychological Review, 100,* 68–90.

Izard, C. E. (1994). Innate and universal facial expressions: Evidence from developmental and cross-cultural research. *Psychological Bulletin, 115,* 288–299.

Jackson, V. A., Mack, J., Matsuyama, R., Lakoma, M. D., Sullivan A. M., Arnold, R. M., . . . Block, S. D. (2008). A qualitative study of oncologists' approaches to end-of-life care. *Journal of Palliative Medicine, 11,* 893–906.

Jacobs, R. C., & Campbell, D. T. (1961). The perpetuation of an arbitrary tradition through several generations of a laboratory microculture. *Journal of Abnormal and Social Psychology, 62,* 649–658.

Jacobsen, P. B., Bovbjerg, D. H., Schwartz, M. D., Andrykowski, M. A., Futterman, A. D., Gilewski, T., . . . Redd, W. H. (1993). Formation of food aversions in cancer patients receiving repeated infusions of chemotherapy. *Behaviour Research and Therapy, 31,* 739–748.

Jaffee, S., & Hyde, J. S. (2000). Gender differences in moral orientation: A meta-analysis. *Psychological Bulletin, 126,* 703–726.

Jager, G., de Win, M. M. L., van der Tweel, I., Schilt, T., Kahn, R. S., van den Brink, W., van Ree, J. M., & Ramsey, N. F. (2008). Assessment of cognitive brain function in ecstacy users and contributions of other drugs of abuse: Results from an FMRI study. *Neuropsychopharmacology, 33*(2), 247–258.

Jahnke, J. C. (1965). Primacy and recency effects in serial-position curves of immediate recall. *Journal of Experimental Psychology, 70,* 130–132.

Jain, S., Mills, P. J., von Känel, R., Hong, S., & Dimsdale, J. E. (2007). Effects of perceived stress and uplifts on inflammation and coagulability. *Psychophysiology, 44,* 154–160.

James, S. E., & Murphy, B. C. (1998). Gay and lesbian relationships in a changing social context. In C. J. Patterson & A. R. D'Augelli (Eds.), *Lesbian, gay, and bisexual identities in families: Psychological perspectives* (pp. 99–121). New York, NY: Oxford University Press.

James, W. (1882). Subjective effects of nitrous oxide. *Mind, 7,* 186–208.

James, W. (1892). *Psychology.* New York, NY: Holt.

James, W. (1950). *The principles of psychology* (2 vols.). New York, NY: Holt, Rinehart & Wilson. (Original work published 1890)

Janis, I. (1982). *Groupthink* (2nd ed.). Boston, MA: Houghton Mifflin.

Janis, I. L., & Frick, F. (1943). The relationship between attitudes toward conclusions and errors in judging logical validity of syllogisms. *Journal of Experimental Psychology, 33,* 73–77.

Janowitz, H. D., & Grossman, M. I. (1950). Hunger and appetite: Some definitions and concepts. *Journal of the Mount Sinai Hospital, 16,* 231–240.

January, D., & Kako, E. (2007). Re-evaluating evidence for linguistic relativity: Reply to Boroditsky (2001). *Cognition, 104*(2), 417–426.

Jay, G. (2008). Service learning, multiculturalism, and the pedagogies of difference. *Pedagogy, 8*, 255–281.

Jedrej, M. C. (1995). *Ingessana: The religious institutions of a people of the Sudan-Ethiopia borderland.* Leiden, The Netherlands: Brill.

Jensen, A. R. (1962). Spelling errors and the serial position effect. *Journal of Educational Psychology, 53,* 105–109.

Jensen, A. R. (1995). Psychological research on race differences. *American Psychologist, 50,* 41–42.

Jo, H., Chen, Y. J., Chua, S. C., Jr., Talmage, D. A., & Role, L. W. (2005). Integration of endocannabinoid and leptin signaling in an appetite-related neural circuit. *Neuron, 48,* 1055–1066.

Joh, A. S., & Adolph, K. E (2006). Learning from falling. *Child Development, 77,* 89–102.

Johnson, P. J., McCreary, D. R., & Mills, J. S. (2007). Effects of exposure to objectified male and female media images on men's psychological well-being. *Psychology of Men and Masculinity, 8,* 95–102.

Johnson, T. D., & Gottlieb, G. (1981). Visual preferences of imprinted ducklings are altered by the maternal call. *Journal of Comparative and Physiological Psychology, 95*(5), 665–675.

Johnson, T. E., & Rule, B. G. (1986). Mitigating circumstances, information, censure, and aggression. *Journal of Personality and Social Psychology, 50,* 537–542.

Johnson-Laird, P. N., & Wason, P. C. (1977). A theoretical analysis of insight into a reasoning task. In P. N. Johnson-Laird & P. C. Wason (Eds.), *Thinking* (pp. 143–157). Cambridge, United Kingdom: Cambridge University Press.

Jones, E. (1953). *The life and works of Sigmund Freud.* New York, NY: Basic Books.

Jones, E. E., & Nisbett, R. E. (1971). *The actor and the observer: Divergent perceptions of the causes of behavior.* New York, NY: General Learning Press.

Jones, M. C. (1924). A laboratory study of fear: The case of Peter. *Pedagogical Seminary and Journal of Genetic Psychology, 31,* 308–315.

Jose, P. E., & Brown, I. (2008). When does the gender difference in rumination begin? Gender and age differences in the use of rumination by adolescents. *Journal of Youth and Adolescence, 37,* 180–192.

Joyce, A. S., Ogrodniczuk, J. S., Piper, W. E., & McCallum, M. (2003). The alliance as mediator of expectancy effects in short-term individual therapy. *Journal of Consulting and Clinical Psychology, 71,* 672–679.

Joyce, L. (1990). Losing the connection. *Stanford Medicine,* 19–21.

Jung, C. G. (1959). The concept of the collective unconscious. In *The archetypes and the collective unconscious, collected works* (Vol. 9, Part 1, pp. 54–74.). Princeton, NJ: Princeton University Press. (Original work published 1936)

Jung, C. G. (1973). *Memories, dreams, reflections* (Rev. ed., A. Jaffe, Ed.). New York, NY: Pantheon Books.

Jusczyk, P. W. (2003). Chunking language input to find patterns. In D. H. Rakison & L. M. Oakes (Eds.), *Early category and concept development.* London, United Kingdom: Oxford University Press.

Jusczyk, P. W., & Aslin, R. N. (1995). Infants' detection of the sound patterns of words in fluent speech. *Cognitive Psychology, 29,* 1–23.

Jussim, L., & Harber, K. D. (2005). Teacher expectations and self-fulfilling prophecies: Knowns and unknowns, resolved and unresolved controversies. *Personality and Social Psychology Review, 9,* 131–155.

Just, M. A., Keller, T. A., & Cynkar, J. (2008). A decrease in brain activation associated with driving when listening to someone speak. *Brain Research, 1205,* 70–80.

Kabat-Zinn, J. (1990). *Full catastrophe living: Using the wisdom of your body and mind to face stress, pain, and illness.* New York, NY: Dell.

Kagan, J. (1994). *Galen's prophesy: Temperament in human nature.* New York, NY: Basic Books.

Kagan, J., & Snidman, N. (1991). Infant predictors of inhibited and uninhibited profiles. *Psychological Science, 2,* 40–44.

Kagan, J., & Snidman, N. (2004). *The long shadow of temperament.* Cambridge, MA: Belknap Press.

Kahneman, D. (1992). Reference points, anchors, norms, and mixed feelings. *Organizational Behavior and Human Decision Processes, 51,* 296–312.

Kahneman, D., & Frederick, S. (2002). Representativeness revisited: Attribute substitution in intuitive judgment. In T. Gilovich, D. Griffin, & D. Kahneman (Eds.), *Heuristics and biases: The psychology of intuitive judgment* (pp. 49–81). Cambridge, United Kingdom: Cambridge University Press.

Kahneman, D., & Tversky, A. (1973). On the psychology of prediction. *Psychological Review, 80,* 237–251.

Kahneman, D., Fredrickson, B. L., Schreiber, C. A., & Redelmeier, D. A. (1993). When more pain is preferred to less: Adding a better end. *Psychological Science, 4,* 401–405.

Kallmann, F. J. (1946). The genetic theory of schizophrenia: An analysis of 691 schizophrenic index families. *American Journal of Psychiatry, 103,* 309–322.

Kalueff, A. V., & Nutt, D. J. (2007). Role of GABA in anxiety and depression. *Depression and Anxiety, 24,* 495–517.

Kamil, A. C., & Balda, R. P. (1990). Spatial memory in seed-caching corvids. In G. H. Bower (Ed.), *The psychology of learning and motivation* (Vol. 26, pp. 1–25). San Diego, CA: Academic Press.

Kamil, A. C., Balda, R. P., Olson, D. P., & Good, S. (1993). Returns to emptied cache sites by Clark's nutcrackers, *Nucifraga columbiana*: A puzzle revisited. *Animal Behaviour, 45,* 241–252.

Kamin, L. J. (1969). Predictability, surprise, attention, and conditioning. In B. A. Campbell & R. M. Church (Eds.), *Punishment and aversive behavior* (pp. 279–296). New York, NY: Appleton-Century-Crofts.

Kammrath, L. K., Mendoza-Denton, R., & Mischel, W. (2005). Incorporating if... then... personality signatures in person perception: Beyond the person-situation dichotomy. *Journal of Personality and Social Psychology, 88,* 605–618.

Kane, M. J., Brown, L. H., McVay, J. C., Silvia, P. J., Myin-Germeys, I., & Kwapil, T. R. (2007). For whom the mind wanders, and when: An experience-sampling study of working memory and executive control in daily life. *Psychological Science, 18*(7), 614–621.

Kangas, M., Henry, J. L., & Bryant, R. A. (2005). Predictors of post-traumatic stress disorder following cancer. *Health Psychology, 24,* 579–585.

Kantrowitz, B., & McGinn, D. (2000, June 19). When teachers are cheaters. *Newsweek,* 48–49.

Kaplan, C. A., & Simon, H. A. (1990). In search of insight. *Cognitive Psychology, 22,* 374–419.

Karremans, J. C., & Verwijmeren, T. (2008). Mimicking attractive opposite-sex others: The role of romantic relationship status. *Personality and Social Psychology Bulletin, 34,* 939–950.

Kassebaum, N. L. (1994). Head Start: Only the best for America's children. *American Psychologist, 49,* 1123–1126.

Kazdin, A. E. (1982). The token economy: A decade later. *Journal of Applied Behavior Analysis, 15,* 431–445.

Kazdin, A. E. (1994). *Behavior modification in applied settings* (5th ed.). Pacific Grove, CA: Brooks/Cole.

Kazdin, A. E. (2008). Evidence-based treatment and practice: New opportunities to bridge clinical research and practice, enhance the knowledge base, and improve patient care. *American Psychologist, 63,* 146–159.

Kazdin, A. E., & Benjet, C. (2003). Spanking children: Evidence and issues. *Current Directions in Psychological Science, 12,* 99–103.

Keiger, D. (1993, November). Touched with fire. *Johns Hopkins Magazine, 45*(4), 38, 40–44.

Kelley, H. H. (1967). Attribution theory in social psychology. In D. Levine (Ed.), *Nebraska symposium on motivation* (Vol. 15). Lincoln, NE: University of Nebraska Press.

Kellough, J. L., Beevers, C. G., Ellis, A. J., & Wells, T. T. (2008). Time course of selective attention in clinically depressed young adults: An eye tracking study. *Behaviour Research and Therapy, 46,* 1238–1243.

Kelly, D. M. (2010). Features enhance the encoding of geometry. *Animal Cognition, 13*(3), 453–462.

Kelly, D.M., Kamil, A.C., & Cheng, K. (2010). Landmark use by Clark's nutcrackers (*Nucifraga columbiana*): Influence of disorientation and cue rotation on distance and direction estimates. *Animal Cognition, 13*(1), 175–188.

Kempermann, G. (2002). Why new neurons? Possible functions for adult hippocampal neurogenesis. *Journal of Neuroscience, 22,* 635–638.

Kempermann, G. (2008). The neurogenic reserve hypothesis: What is adult hippocampus neurogenesis good for? *Trends in Neurosciences, 31,* 163–169.

Kendler, H. H. (1987). *Historical foundations of modern psychology.* Chicago, IL: Dorsey Press.

Kendler, K. S., Gatz, M., Gardner, C. O., & Pedersen, N. L. (2006). A Swedish national twin study of lifetime major depression. *American Journal of Psychiatry, 163,* 109–114.

Kendler, K. S., Kuhn, J. W., & Prescott, C. A. (2004). Childhood sexual abuse, stressful life events and risk for major depression in women. *Psychological Medicine, 34,* 1475–1482.

Kendler, K. S., Myers, J., Prescott, C. A., & Neale, M. C. (2001). The genetic epidemiology of irrational fears and phobias in men. *Archives of General Psychiatry, 58,* 257–265.

Kendler, K. S., Thornton, L. M., Gilman, S. E., & Kessler, R. C. (2000). Sexual orientation in a U.S. national sample of twin and nontwin sibling pairs. *American Journal of Psychiatry, 157,* 1843–1846.

Kennedy, R. E., & Craighead, W. E. (1988). Differential effects of depression and anxiety on recall of feedback in a learning task. *Behavior Therapy, 19,* 437–454.

Kenny, D. A., & La Voie, L. (1982). Reciprocity of interpersonal attraction: A confirmed hypothesis. *Social Psychology Quarterly, 45,* 54–58.

Kenny, D. A., Bond, C. F., Jr., Mohr, C. D., & Horn, E. M. (1996). Do we know how much people like one another? *Journal of Personality and Social Psychology, 71,* 928–936.

Keren, G. (2007). Framing, intentions, and trust-choice incompatibility. *Organizational Behavior, and Human Decision Processes, 103,* 238–255.

Kermer, D. A., Driver-Linn, E., Wilson, T. D., & Gilbert, D. T. (2006). Loss aversion is an affective forecasting error. *Psychological Science, 17,* 649–653.

Kerr, N. L., & Tindale, R. S. (2004). Group performance and decision making. *Annual Review of Psychology, 55,* 625–655.

Kesebir, P., & Diener, E. (2008). In pursuit of happiness: Empirical answers to philosophical questions. *Perspectives on Psychological Science, 3,* 117–125.

Keshavan, M. S., Tandon, R., Boutros, N. N., & Nasrallah, H. A. (2008). Schizophrenia, "Just the Facts": What we know in 2008. Part 3: Neurobiology. *Schizophrenia Research, 106,* 89–107.

Kessel, N. (1989). Genius and mental disorder: A history of ideas concerning their conjunction. In P. Murray (Ed.), *Genius: The history of an idea* (pp. 196–212). London, United Kingdom: Basil Blackwell.

Kessler, R. C., Adler, L., Barkley, R., Biederman, J., Conners, C. K., Demler, O., . . . Zaslavsky, A. M. (2006). The prevalence and correlates of adult ADHD in the United States: Results from the National Comorbidity Survey Replication. *American Journal of Psychiatry, 163,* 716–723.

Kessler, R. C., Berglund, P., Demler, O., Jin, R., Merikangas, K. R., & Walters, E. E. (2005a). Lifetime prevalence and age-of-onset distributions of *DSM-IV* disorders in the National Comorbidity Survey Replication. *Archives of General Psychiatry, 62,* 593–602.

Kessler, R. C., Chiu, W. T., Demler, O., & Walters, E. E. (2005b). Prevalence, severity, and comorbidity of 12-month *DSM-IV* disorders in the National Comorbidity Survey Replication. *Archives of General Psychiatry, 62,* 617–627.

Kessler, R. C., McGonagle, K. A., Zhao, S., Nelson, C. B., Hughes, M., Eshleman, S., . . . Kendler, K. S. (1994). Lifetime and 12-month prevalence of *DSM-III-R* psychiatric disorders in the United States. *Archives of General Psychiatry, 51,* 8–19.

Kiecolt-Glaser, J. K., Marucha, P. T., Malarkey, P. T., Mercado, A. M., & Glaser, R. (1995). Slowing of wound healing by psychological stress. *Lancet, 346,* 1194–1196.

Kiecolt-Glaser, J. K., McGuire, L., Robles, T. F., & Glaser, R. (2002). Psychoneuroimmunology: Psychological influences on immune function and health. *Journal of Consulting and Clinical Psychology, 70,* 537–547.

Kihlstrom, J. F. (2005). Dissociative disorders. *Annual Review of Clinical Psychology, 1,* 227–253.

Kihlstrom, J. F. (2007). Consciousness in hypnosis. In P. D. Zelazo, M. Moscovitch, & E. Thompson (Eds.), *The Cambridge handbook of consciousness* (pp. 445–479). New York, NY: Cambridge University Press.

Kihlstrom, J. F., & Cantor, N. (2000). Social intelligence. In R. J. Sternberg (Ed.), *Handbook of intelligence* (pp. 359–369). New York, NY: Cambridge University Press.

Killen, M., & Hart, D. (Eds.). (1999). *Morality in everyday life: Developmental perspectives.* New York, NY: Cambridge University Press.

Kilpatrick, D. G., Ruggiero, K. J., Acierno, R., Saunders, B. E., Resnick, H. S., & Best, C. L. (2003). Violence and risk of PTSD, major depression, substance abuse/dependence, and comorbidity: Results from a national survey of adolescents. *Journal of Consulting and Clinical Psychology, 71,* 692–700.

Kilpatrick, L A., Zald, D. H., Pardo, J. V., & Cahill, L. F. (2006). Sex-related differences in amygdala functional connectivity during resting conditions. *NeuroImage, 30,* 452–461.

Kim, C.-H., Chang, J. W., Koo, M.-S., Kim, J. W., Suh, H. S., Park, I. H., & Lee, H. S. (2003). Anterior cingulotomy for refractory obsessive-compulsive disorder. *Acta Psychiatrica Scandinavica, 107,* 283–290.

Kim, H. S., Sherman, D. K., & Taylor, S. E. (2008). Culture and social support. *American Psychologist, 63,* 518–526.

Kim, J., & Hatfield, E. (2004). Love types and subjective well-being: A cross-cultural study. *Social Behavior and Personality, 32,* 173–182.

Kim, J. J., Jung, M. W. (2006). Neural circuits and mechanisms involved in Pavlovian fear conditioning: A critical review. *Neuroscience and Biobehavioral Reviews, 30*(2), 188–202.

Kimura, D. (1999). *Sex and cognition.* Cambridge, MA: MIT Press.

Kimura, D., & Clarke, P. G. (2002). Women's advantage on verbal memory is not restricted to concrete words. *Psychological Reports, 91*(3 Pt 2), 1137–1142.

King, S. A., & Moreggi, D. (1998). Internet therapy and self-help groups—The pros and cons. In J. Gackenbach (Ed.), *Psychology and the internet: Intrapersonal, interpersonal, and transpersonal implications* (pp. 77–109). San Diego, CA: Academic Press.

Kinsey, A. C., Martin, C. E., & Pomeroy, W. B. (1948). *Sexual behavior in the human male.* Philadelphia, PA: Saunders.

Kinsey, A. C., Pomeroy, W. B., Martin, C. E., & Gebhard, R. H. (1953). *Sexual behavior in the human female.* Philadelphia, PA: Saunders.

Kintner, C. (2002). Neurogenesis in embryos and in adult neural stem cells. *Journal of Neuroscience, 22,* 639–643.

Kintsch, W. (1974). *The representation of meaning in memory.* Hillsdale, NJ: Erlbaum.

Kirkham, T. C. (2005). Endocannabinoids in the regulation of appetite and body weight. *Behavioural Pharmacology, 16,* 297–313.

Kirkpatrick, S. I., & Tarasuk, V. (2008). Food insecurity is associated with nutrient inadequacies among Canadian adults and adolescents. *Journal of Nutrition, 138*(3), 604–12.

Kirkpatrick, S., & Tarasuk, V. (2003). The relationship between low income and household food expenditure patterns in Canada. *Public Health Nutrition, 6*(6), 589–597.

Kisilevsky, B. S., & Low, J. A. (1998). Human fetal behavior: 100 years of study. *Developmental Review, 18,* 1–29.

Kisilevsky, B. S., Hains, S. M., Lee, K., Xie, X., Huang, H., Ye, H. H., . . . Wang, Z. (2003). Effects of experience on fetal voice recognition. *Psychological Science, 14,* 220–224.

Kissane, D. W., Grabsch, B., Clarke, D. M., Christie, G., Clifton, D., Gold, S., Hill, C., Morgan, A., McDermott, F., & Smith, G. C. (2004). Supportive-expressive group therapy: The transformation of existential ambivalence into creative living while enhancing adherence to anticancer therapies. *Psycho-Oncology, 13,* 755–768.

Kitamura, C., Thanavishuth, C., Burnham, D., & Luksaneeyanawin, S. (2002). Universality and specificity in infant-directed speech: Pitch modifications as a function of infant age and sex in a tonal and non-tonal language. *Infant Behavior & Development, 24,* 372–392.

Kitayama, S., Markus, H. R., & Lieberman, C. (1995). The collective construction of self-esteem: Implications for culture, self, and emotion. In J. A. Russell, J. Fernandez-Dols, T. Manstead, & J. Wellenkamp (Eds.), *Everyday conceptions of emotion* (pp. 523–550). Dordrecht, The Netherlands: Kluwer.

Kleim, J. A., Bruneau, R., VandenBerg, P., MacDonald, E., Mulrooney, R., & Pocock, D. (2003). Motor cortex stimulation enhances motor recovery and reduces peri-infarct dysfunction following ischemic insult. *Neurology Research, 5*(8), 789–793.

Kleim, J. A., Chan, S., Pringle, E., Schallert, K., Procaccio, V., Jimenez, R., & Cramer, S. C. (2006). BDNF val66met polymorphism is associated with modified experience-dependent plasticity in human motor cortex. *Nature Neuroscience, 9*(6), 735–737.

Klein, D. N. (2008). Classification of depressive disorders in *DSM-V:* Proposal for a two-dimension system. *Journal of Abnormal Psychology, 117,* 552–560.

Klein, K. E., & Wegmann, H. M. (1974). The resynchronization of human circadian rhythms after transmeridian flights as a result of flight direction and mode of activity. In L. E. Scheving, F. Halberg, & J. E. Pauly (Eds.), *Chronobiology* (pp. 564–570). Tokyo: Igaku.

Klein, M. (1975). *The writings of Melanie Klein* (Vols. 1–4). London, United Kingdom: Hogarth Press and the Institute of Psychoanalysis.

Klein, O., & Snyder, M. (2003). Stereotypes and behavioral confirmation: From interpersonal to intergroup perspectives. In M. P. Zanna (Ed.), *Advances in experimental social psychology* (Vol. 35, pp. 153–234). New York, NY: Academic Press.

Klump, K. L., Burt, A., McGue, M., & Iacono, W. G. (2007). Changes in genetic and environmental influences on disordered eating across adolescence. *Archives of General Psychiatry, 64,* 1409–1415.

Knickmeyer, R., Baron-Cohen, S., Raggatt, P., & Taylor, K. (2005). Foetal testosterone, social relationships, and restricted interests in children. *Journal of Child Psychology and Psychiatry, 46,* 198–210.

Kobiella, A., Grossmann, T., Reid, V. M., & Striano, T. (2008). The discrimination of angry and fearful facial expressions in 7-month-old infants: An event-related potential study. *Cognition and Emotion, 22,* 133–146.

Koffka, K. (1935). *Principles of Gestalt psychology.* New York, NY: Harcourt Brace.

Kohlberg, L. (1964). Development of moral character and moral ideology. In M. L. Hoffman & L. W. Hoffman (Eds.), *Review of child development research* (Vol. 1). New York, NY: Russell Sage Foundation.

Kohlberg, L. (1981). *The philosophy of moral development.* New York, NY: Harper & Row.

Köhler, W. (1947). *Gestalt psychology.* New York, NY: Liveright.

Kolb, B. (1989). Development, plasticity, and behavior. *American Psychologist, 44,* 1203–1212.

Kolb, B. (1995). *Brain plasticity and behavior.* Mahwah, NJ: Lawrence Erlbaum Associates, Inc.

Kolb, B., Cioe, J., & Whishaw, I. Q. (2000a). Is there an optimal age for recovery from motor cortex lesions? II. Behavioral and anatomical consequences of unilateral motor cortex lesions in perinatal, infant, and adult rats. *Restorative Neurology and Neuroscience, 17*(2–3), 61–70.

Kolb, B., Cioe, J., & Whishaw, I. Q. (2000b). Is there an optimal age for recovery from motor cortex lesions? I. Behavioural and anatomical sequelae of bilateral motor cortex lesions in rats on postnatal days 1, 10, and in adulthood. *Brain Research, 882*(1–2), 62–74.

Kong, L. L., Allen, J. J. B., & Glisky, E. L. (2008). Interidentity memory transfer in dissociative identity disorder. *Journal of Abnormal Psychology, 117,* 686–692.

Korchmaros, J. D., & Kenny, D. A. (2006). An evolutionary and close-relationship model of helping. *Journal of Social and Personal Relationships, 23,* 21–43.

Koriat, A., & Fischoff, B. (1974). What day is today? An inquiry into the process of time orientation. *Memory & Cognition, 2,* 201–205.

Koriat, A., & Levy-Sadot, R. (2001). The combined contributions of cue-familiarity and accessibility heuristics to feelings of knowing. *Journal of Experimental Psychology: Learning, Memory, and Cognition, 27,* 34–53.

Kortegaard, L. S., Hoerder, K., Joergensen, J., Gillberg, C., & Kyvik, K. O. (2001). A preliminary population-based twin study of self-reported eating disorder. *Psychological Medicine, 31,* 361–365.

Kosslyn, S. M., Pascual-Leone, A., Felician, O., Camposano, S., Keenan, J. P., Thompson, W. L., Ganis, G., Sukel, K. E., & Alpert, N. M. (1999). The role of area 17 in visual imagery: Convergent evidence from PET and rTMS. *Science, 284,* 167–170.

Kotovsky, K., & Simon, H. A. (1990). What makes some problems really hard: Explorations in the problem space of difficulty. *Cognitive Psychology, 22,* 143–183.

Kotovsky, K., Hayes, J. R., & Simon, H. A. (1985). Why are some problems hard? Evidence from Tower of Hanoi. *Cognitive Psychology, 17,* 248–294.

Kousta, S. T., Vinson, D. P., & Vigliocco, G. (2008). Investigating linguistic relativity through bilingualism: The case of grammatical gender. *Journal of Experimental Psychology: Learning, Memory, and Cognition, 34*(4), 843–858.

Kowal, M. A., Watson, G. M. W., & Madak, P. R. (1990). Concurrent validity of the test of nonverbal intelligence with referred suburban and Canadian Native children. *Journal of Clinical Psychology, 46,* 632–636.

Kraepelin, E. (1921). *Manic-depressive disorder and paranoia.* London, United Kingdom: Churchill Livingstone.

Krahé, B., Bieneck, S., & Scheinberger-Olwig, R. (2007). Adolescents' sexual scripts: Schematic representations of consensual and nonconsensual heterosexual interactions. *Journal of Sex Research, 44,* 316–327.

Krämer, N. C., & Winter, S. (2008). Impression management 2.0: The relationship of self-esteem, extraversion, self-efficacy, and self-presentation within social networking sites. *Journal of Media Psychology, 20,* 106–116.

Krohne, H. W., & Slangen, K. E. (2005). Influence of social support on adaptation to surgery. *Health Psychology, 24,* 101–105.

Krueger, J., & Stanke, D. (2001). The role of self-referent and other-referent knowledge in perceptions of group characteristics. *Personality & Social Psychology Bulletin, 27,* 878–888.

Kruger, J., Wirtz, D., & Miller, D. T. (2005). Counterfactual thinking and the first instinct fallacy. *Journal of Personality and Social Psychology, 88,* 725–735.

Krusemark, E. A., Campbell, W. K., & Clementz, B. A. (2008). Attributions, deception, and event related potentials: An investigation of self-serving bias. *Psychophysiology, 45,* 511–515.

Kuhn, M. H., & McPartland, T. S. (1954). An empirical investigation of self-attitudes. *American Sociological Review, 19,* 68–76.

Kujawski, J. H., & Bower, T. G. R. (1993). Same-sex preferential looking during infancy as a function of abstract representation. *British Journal of Developmental Psychology, 11,* 201–209.

Kuperberg, G. R., Broome, M. R., McGuire, P. K., David, A. S., Eddy, M., Ozawa, F.,... Fischl, B. (2003). Regionally localized thinning of the cerebral cortex in schizophrenia. *Archives of General Psychiatry, 60,* 878–888.

Kuppens, P., Realo, A., & Diener, E. (2008). The role of positive and negative emotions in life satisfaction judgment across nations. *Journal of Personality and Social Psychology, 95,* 66–75.

Kurtz, M. M., & Mueser, K. T. (2008). A meta-analysis of controlled research on social skills training for schizophrenia. *Journal of Consulting and Clinical Psychology, 76,* 491–504.

LaBerge, S. (2007). Lucid dreaming. In D. Barrett & P. McNamara (Eds.), *The new science of dreaming: Volume 2. Content, recall, and personality correlates. Praeger perspectives.* (pp. 307–328). Westport, CT: Praeger Publishers/Greenwood Publishing Group.

LaBerge, S., & Levitan, L. (1995). Validity established of DreamLight cues for eliciting lucid dreaming. *Dreaming: Journal of the Association for the Study of Dreams, 5,* 159–168.

LaBerge, S., & Rheingold, H. (1990). *Exploring the world of lucid dreaming.* New York, NY: Ballantine Books.

LaBerge, S., Nagle, L., Dement, W., & Zarcone, V. (1981). Lucid dreaming verified by volitional communication during REM sleep. *Perceptual & Motor Skills, 52,* 727–732.

Lachman, M. E. (2004). Development in midlife. *Annual Review of Psychology, 55,* 305–331.

Lachman, R., Lachman, J. L., & Butterfield, E. C. (1979). *Cognitive psychology and information processing.* Hillsdale, NJ: Erlbaum.

Lam, R. W., Levitt, A. J., Levitan, R. D., Enns, M. W., Morehouse, R., Michalak, E. E., & Tam, E. M. (2006). The Can-SAD study: A randomized controlled trial of the effectiveness of light therapy and fluoxetine in patients with winter seasonal affective disorder. *American Journal of Psychiatry, 163*(5), 805–812.

Lamb, R. J., Morral, A. R., Kirby, K. C., Javors, M. A., Galbicka, G., & Iguchi, M. (2007). Contingencies for change in complacent smokers. *Experimental and Clinical Psychopharmacology, 15,* 245–255.

Lambert, T. A., Kahn, A. S., & Apple, K. J. (2003). Pluralistic ignorance and hooking up. *The Journal of Sex Research, 40,* 129–133.

Lampinen, J. M., Copeland, S. M., & Neuschatz, J. S. (2001). Recollections of things schematic: Room schemas revisited. *Journal of Experimental Psychology: Learning, Memory, and Cognition, 27,* 1211–1222.

Lander, E. S., & Weinberg, R. A. (2000). Genomics: Journey to the center of biology. *Science, 287,* 1777–1782.

Lang, F. R., & Carstensen, L. L. (1994). Close emotional relationships in late life: Further support for proactive aging in the social domain. *Psychology and Aging, 9,* 315–324.

Langlois, J. H., Kalakanis, L., Rubenstein, A. J., Larson, A., Hallam, M., & Smoot, M. (2000). Maxims or myths of beauty? A meta-analytic and theoretical review. *Psychological Bulletin, 126,* 390–423.

Lanius, R. A., Williamson, P. C., Hopper, J., Densmore, M., Boksman, K., Gupta, M. A., . . . Menon, R. S. (2003). Recall of emotional states in posttraumatic stress disorder: An fMRI investigation. *Biological Psychiatry, 53*, 204–210.

Larner, A. J., Moss, J., Rossi, M. L., & Anderson, M. (1994). Congenital insensitivity to pain: A 20–year follow up. *Journal of Neurology, Neurosurgery & Psychiatry, 57*, 973–974.

Lashley, K. S. (1929). *Brain mechanisms and intelligence.* Chicago, IL: University of Chicago Press.

Lashley, K. S. (1950). In search of the engram. In *Physiological mechanisms in animal behavior: Symposium of the Society for Experimental Biology* (pp. 454–482). New York, NY: Academic Press.

Latané, B., & Darley, J. M. (1970). *The unresponsive bystander: Why doesn't he help?* New York, NY: Appleton-Century-Crofts.

Lau, I. Y., Chiu, C., & Hong, Y. (2001). I know what you know: Assumptions about others' knowledge and their effects on message construction. *Social Cognition, 19*, 587–600.

Lau, J. Y. F., & Eley, T. C. (2008). Attributional style as a risk marker of genetic effects for adolescent depressive symptoms. *Journal of Abnormal Psychology, 117*, 849–859.

Lauronen, E., Veijola, J., Isohanni, I., Jones, P. B., Nieminen, P., & Isohanni, M. (2004). Links between creativity and mental disorder. *Psychiatry, 6*, 81–98.

Lay, C. H. (1986). At last my research article on procrastination. *Journal of Research in Personality, 20*, 474–495.

Lazar, S. W., Kerr, C. E., Wasserman, R. H., Gray, J. R., Greve, D. N., Treadway, M. T., . . . & Wasserman, E. A. (2004). Pigeons concurrently categorize photographs at both basic and superordinate levels. *Psychonomic Bulletin & Review, 11*, 1111–1117.

Lazarus, R. S. (1981, July). Little hassles can be hazardous to your health. *Psychology Today, 15*, 58–62.

Lazarus, R. S. (1984a). On the primacy of cognition. *American Psychologist, 39*, 124–129.

Lazarus, R. S. (1984b). Puzzles in the study of daily hassles. *Journal of Behavioral Medicine, 7*, 375–389.

Lazarus, R. S. (1991). Cognition and motivation in emotion. *American Psychologist, 46*, 352–367.

Lazarus, R. S. (1993). From psychological stress to the emotions: A history of changing outlooks. *Annual Review of Psychology, 44*, 1–21.

Lazarus, R. S. (1995). Vexing research problems inherent in cognitive-mediational theories of emotion-and some solutions. *Psychological Inquiry, 6*, 183–196.

Lazarus, R. S., & Folkman, S. (1984). *Stress, appraisal, and coping.* New York, NY: Springer.

Lazarus, R. S., & Lazarus, B. N. (1994). *Passion and reason: Making sense of our emotions.* New York, NY: Oxford University Press.

Leaper, C. (2000). The social construction and socialization of gender during development. In P. H. Miller & E. K. Scholnick (Eds.), *Toward a feminist developmental psychology* (pp. 127–152). New York, NY: Routledge.

Leatherdale, S. T., & Shields, M. (2009). Smoking cessation: Intentions, attempts and techniques. *Health Reports, 20*(3), 46–60.

Ledbetter, A. M., Griffin, E., & Sparks, G. S. (2007). Forecasting "friends forever": A longitudinal investigation of sustained closeness between best friends. *Personal Relationships, 14*, 343–350.

Lee, H. S., & Holyoak, K. J. (2008). The role of causal models in analogical inference. *Journal of Experimental Psychology: Learning, Memory, and Cognition, 34*(5), 1111–1122.

Lee, M., Zimbardo, P., & Bertholf, M. (1977, November). Shy murderers. *Psychology Today, 11*, 68–70, 76, 148.

Leen-Feldner, E. W., Feldner, M. T., Reardon, L. E., Babson, K. A., & Dixon, L. (2008). Anxiety sensitivity and posttraumatic stress among traumatic event-exposed youth. *Behaviour Research and Therapy, 46*, 548–556.

Leger, D. (1992). *Biological foundations of behavior: An integrative approach.* New York, NY: HarperCollins.

Legrand, D. (2007). Pre-reflective self-as-subject from experiential and empirical perspectives. *Consciousness and Cognition, 16*(3), 583–599.

Leiter, M. P., & Maslach, C. (2005). *Banishing burnout: Six strategies for improving your relationship with work.* San Francisco: Jossey-Bass.

Lennon, R. T. (1985). Group tests of intelligence. In B. B. Wolman (Ed.), *Handbook of intelligence* (pp. 825–847). New York, NY: Wiley.

Lenzenweger, M. F., Lane, M. C., Loranger, A. W., & Kessler, R. C. (2007). *DSM-IV* personality disorders in the National Comorbidity Survey Replication. *Biological Psychiatry, 62*, 553–564.

Lesku, J. A., Bark, R. J., Martinez-Gonzalez, D., Rattenbord, N. C., Amlaner, C. J., & Lima, S. L. (2008). Predator-induced plasticity in sleep architecture in wild-caught Norway rats (*Rattus norvegicus*). *Behavioural Brain Research, 189*(2), 298–305.

Leucht, S., Barnes, T. R. E., Kissling, W., Engel, R. R., Correll, C., & Kane, J. M. (2003). Relapse prevention in schizophrenia with new-generation antipsychotics: A systematic review and exploratory meta-analysis of randomized, controlled trials. *American Journal of Psychiatry, 160*, 1209–1222.

Leung, A. K.-Y., Maddux, W. W., Galinsky, A. D., & Chin, C.-Y. (2008). Multicultural experience enhances creativity: The when and how. *American Psychologist, 63*, 169–181.

Levenson, R. W., Carstensen, L. L., & Gottman, J. M. (1993). Long-term marriage: Age, gender, and satisfaction. *Psychology and Aging, 8*, 301–313.

Levenson, R. W., Ekman, P., Heider, K., & Friesen, W. V. (1992). Emotion and autonomic nervous system activity in the Minangkabau of West Sumatra. *Journal of Personality and Social Psychology, 62*, 972–988.

Leventhal, A. M., Martin, R. L., Seals, R. W., Tapia, E, & Rehm, L. P. (2007). Investigating the dynamics of affect: Psychological mechanisms of affective habituation to pleasurable stimuli. *Motivation and Emotion, 31*, 145–157.

Leventhal, H. (1980). Toward a comprehensive theory of emotion. In L. Berkowitz (Ed.), *Advances in experimental social psychology* (Vol. 13, pp. 139–207). New York, NY: Academic Press.

Leventhal, T., & Brooks-Gunn, J. (2000). The neighborhoods they live in: The effects of neighborhood on child and adolescent outcomes. *Psychological Bulletin, 126*, 309–337.

Levine, R., Sato, S., Hashimoto, T., & Verma, J. (1995). Love and marriage in eleven cultures. *Journal of Cross-Cultural Psychology, 26*, 544–571.

Levitin, D. (2006). *This is your brain on music: The science of human obsession.* New York, NY: Penguin Group.

Levitin, D. (2008). *The world in six songs: How the musical brain created human nature.* New York, NY: Penguin Group.

Levitin, D. J., & Menon, V. (2005). The neural locus of temporal structure and expectancies in music: Evidence from functional neuroimaging at 3 Tesla. *Music Perception, 22*(3), 563–575.

Levy, B., & Langer, E. (1994). Aging free from negative stereotypes: Successful memory in China and among the American deaf. *Journal of Personality and Social Psychology, 66,* 989–997.

Levy, G. D., & Fivush, R. (1993). Scripts and gender: A new approach for examining gender-role development. *Developmental Review, 13,* 126–146.

Lewin, K. (1936). *Principles of topological psychology.* New York, NY: McGraw-Hill.

Lewinsohn, P. M. (1975). The behavioral study and treatment of depression. In M. Hersen, R. M. Eisler, & P. M. Miller (Eds.), *Progress in behavior modification* (pp. 19–64). New York, NY: Academic Press.

Lewinsohn, P. M., Hoberman, H. M., Teri, L., & Hautzinger, M. (1985). An integrative theory of depression. In S. Reiss & R. Bootzin (Eds.), *Theoretical issues in behavior therapy* (pp. 331–359). San Diego, CA: Academic Press.

Lewis, R. J., Derlega, V. J., Clarke, E. G., & Kuang, J. C. (2006). Stigma consciousness, social constraints, and lesbian well-being. *Journal of Counseling Psychology, 53,* 48–56.

Li, M., Chen, L., Lee, D. H. S., Yu, L.-C., & Zhang, Y. (2007). The role of intracellular amyloid b in Alzheimer's disease. *Progress in Neurobiology, 83,* 131–139.

Liang, C. T. H., & Alimo, C. (2005). The impact of white heterosexual students' interactions on attitudes toward lesbian, gay and bisexual people: A longitudinal study. *Journal of College Student Development, 46,* 237–250.

Liao, S. M. (2005). The ethics of using genetic engineering for sex selection. *Journal of Medical Ethics, 31,* 116–118.

Licata, S. C., & Rowlett, J. K. (2008). Abuse and dependence liability of benzodiazepine-type drugs: GABA$_A$ receptor modulation and beyond. *Pharmacology, Biochemistry and Behavior, 90*(1), 74–89.

Lieb, K., Zanarini, M. C., Schmahl, C., Linehan, M. M., & Bohus, M. (2004). Borderline personality disorder. *The Lancet, 364,* 453–461.

Lieberman, J. A., Stroup, T. S., McEvoy, J. P., Swartz, M. S., Rosenheck, R. A., Perkins, D. O., . . . Hsiao, J. K. (2005). Effectiveness of antipsychotic drugs in patients with chronic schizophrenia. *New England Journal of Medicine, 353,* 1209–1223.

Lieberman, L. (2001). How "caucasoids" got such big crania and why they shrank. *Current Anthropology, 42,* 69–95.

Lilienfeld, S. O., & Lynn, S. J. (2003). Dissociative identity disorder: Multiple personalities, multiple controversies. In S. O. Lilienfeld, S. J. Lynn, & J. M. Lohr (Eds.), *Science and pseudoscience in clinical psychology* (pp. 109–142). New York, NY: Guilford Press.

Lilienfeld, S. O., Wood, J. M., & Garb, H. N. (2001). The scientific status of projective techniques. *Psychological Science in the Public Interest, 1,* 27–66.

Lim, M. M., Young, L. J. (2006). Neuropeptidergic regulation of affiliative behavior and social bonding in animals. *Hormones and Behavior, 50*(4), 506–517. Review. Erratum (2007) in: *Hormones and Behavior, 51*(2), 292–293.

Lin, H., Tian, W., Chen, C., Liu, T., Tsai, S., & Lee, H. (2006). The association between readmission rates and length of stay for schizophrenia: A 3-year population-based study. *Schizophrenia Research, 83,* 211–214.

Lindau, S. T., Schumm, L. P., Laumann, E. O., Levinson, W., O'Muircheartaigh, C. A., & Waite, L. J. (2007). A study of sexuality and health among older adults in the United States. *The New England Journal of Medicine, 357,* 762–775.

Lindauer, R. J. L., Booij, J., Habraken, B. A., van Meijel, E. P. M., Uylings, H. B. M., Olff, M., . . . Gersons, B. P. R. (2008). Effects of psychotherapy on regional cerebral blood flow during trauma imagery in patients with post-traumatic stress disorder: A randomized clinical trial. *Psychological Medicine, 38,* 543–554.

Lindsay, D. S. (1990). Misleading suggestions can impair eyewitnesses' ability to remember event details. *Journal of Experimental Psychology: Learning, Memory, and Cognition, 16,* 1077–1083.

Lindsay, D. S., Allen, B. P., Chan, J. C. K., & Dahl, L. C. (2004). Eyewitness suggestibility and source similarity: Intrusions of details from one event into memory reports of another event. *Journal of Memory and Language, 50,* 96–111.

Link, B. G., Struening, E. L., Rahav, M., Phelan, J. C., & Nuttbrock, L. (1997). On stigma and its consequences: Evidence from a longitudinal study of men with dual diagnoses of mental illness and substance abuse. *Journal of Health and Social Behavior, 38,* 177–190.

Lipkus, I. M., Barefoot, J. C., Williams, R. B., & Siegler, I. C. (1994). Personality measures as predictors of smoking initiation and cessation in the UNC Alumni Heart Study. *Health Psychology, 13,* 149–155.

Lisanby, S. H. (2007). Electroconvulsive therapy for depression. *New England Journal of Medicine, 357,* 1939–1945.

Little, T. D., Jones, S. M., Henrich, C. C., & Hawley, P. H. (2003). Disentangling the "whys" from the "whats" of aggressive behavior. *International Journal of Behavioral Development, 27,* 122–123.

Littlewood, R. A., Venable, P. A., Carey, M. P., & Blair, D. C. (2008). The association of benefit finding to psychosocial and health behavior adaptation among HIV+ men and women. *Journal of Behavioral Medicine, 31,* 145–155.

Liu, Z.-Q., Paterson, A. D., Szatmari, P., & The Autism Genome Project Consortium. (2008). Genome-wide linkage analyses of quantitative and categorical autism subphenotypes. *Biological Psychiatry, 64,* 561–570.

Livesley, W. J., & Jang, K. L. (2005). Differentiating normal, abnormal, and disordered personality. *European Journal of Personality, 19,* 257–268.

Lloyd-Jones, T. J., & Luckhurst, L. (2002). Effects of plane rotation, task, and complexity on recognition of familiar and chimeric objects. *Memory & Cognition, 30,* 499–510.

Lobo, I. A., & Harris, R. A. (2008). GABA$_A$ receptors and alcohol. *Pharmacology, Biochemistry and Behavior, 90*(1), 90–94.

LoBue, V., & DeLoache, J. (2008). Detecting the snake in the grass: Attention to fear-relevant stimuli by adults and young children. *Psychological Science, 19,* 284–289.

Locher, P., Frens, J., & Overbeeke, K. (2008). The influence of induced positive affect and design experience on aesthetic responses to new product designs. *Psychology of Aesthetics, Creativity, and the Arts, 2,* 1–7.

Locke, J. (1975). *An essay concerning human understanding.* Oxford, United Kingdom: P. H. Nidditch. (Original work published 1690)

Lockhart, R. S., & Craik, F. I. M. (1990). Levels of processing: A retrospective commentary on a framework for memory research. *Canadian Journal of Psychology, 44,* 87–122.

Loftus, E. F. (1979). *Eyewitness testimony.* Cambridge, MA: Harvard University Press.

Loftus, E. F. (2005). Planting misinformation in the human mind: A 30-year investigation of the malleability of memory. *Learning & Memory, 12,* 361–366.

Loftus, E. F., & Davis, D. (2006). Recovered memories. *Annual Review of Clinical Psychology, 2,* 469–498.

Loftus, E. F., & Palmer, J. C. (1974). Reconstruction of automobile destruction: An example of the interaction between language and memory. *Journal of Verbal Learning and Verbal Behavior, 13,* 585–589.

Loftus, E. F., Miller, D. G., & Burns, H. J. (1978). Semantic integration of verbal information into a visual memory. *Journal of Experimental Psychology: Human Learning and Memory, 4,* 19–31.

Logan, G. D. (2002). Parallel and serial processes. In H. Pashler & J. Wixted (Eds.), *Stevens' handbook of experimental psychology: Vol 4. Methodology in experimental psychology* (pp. 271–300). New York, NY: Wiley.

Logue, A. W. (1991). *The psychology of eating & drinking: An introduction* (2nd ed.). New York, NY: Freeman.

Loomis, A. L., Harvey, E. N., & Hobart, G. A. (1937). Cerebral states during sleep as studied by human brain potentials. *Journal of Experimental Psychology, 21,* 127–144.

Lord, C. G., Paulson, R. M., Sia, T. L., Thomas, J. C., & Lepper, M. R. (2004). Houses built on sand: Effects of exemplar stability on susceptibility to attitude change. *Journal of Personality and Social Psychology, 87,* 733–749.

Lourenço, O., & Machado, A. (1996). In defense of Piaget's theory: A reply to 10 common criticisms. *Psychological Review, 103,* 143–164.

Lovibond, S. H., Adams, M., & Adams, W. G. (1979). The effects of three experimental prison environments on the behavior of nonconflict volunteer subjects. *Australian Psychologist, 14,* 273–285.

Luborsky, L., & Barrett, M. S. (2006). The history and empirical status of key psychoanalytic concepts. *Annual Review of Clinical Psychology, 2,* 1–19.

Lucas, R. E. (2007). Adaptation and the set-point model of subjective well-being: Does happiness change after major life events? *Current Directions in Psychological Science, 16,* 75–79.

Luchins, A. S. (1942). Mechanization in problem solving. *Psychological Monographs, 54* (No. 248).

Luo, M., Fee, M. S., & Katz, L. C. (2003). Encoding pheromonal signals in the accessory olfactory bulb of behaving mice. *Science, 299,* 1196–1201.

Luong, A., & Rogelberg, S. G. (2005). Meetings and more meetings: The relationship between meeting load and daily well-being of employees. *Group Dynamics: Theory, Research, and Practice, 9,* 58–67.

Lynch, D. J., McGrady, A., Alvarez, E., & Forman, J. (2005). Recent life changes and medical utilization in an academic family practice. *The Journal of Nervous and Mental Disease, 193,* 633–635.

Lynch, J. W., Kaplan, G. A., & Shema, S. J. (1997). Cumulative impact of sustained economic hardship on physical, cognitive, psychological, and social functioning. *New England Journal of Medicine, 337,* 1889–1895.

Lynch, W. C., Heil, D. P., Wagner, E., & Havens, M. D. (2008). Body dissatisfaction mediates the association between body mass index and risky weight control behaviors among White and Native American adolescent girls. *Appetite, 51,* 210–213.

Lynn, R. (2005). *Race differences in intelligence: An evolutionary analysis.* Augusta, GA: Washington Summit Books.

Lynn, R., Meisenberg, G., Mikk, J., & Williams, A. (2007). National IQs predict differences in scholastic achievement in 67 countries. *Journal of Biosocial Science, 39,* 861–874. doi:10.1017/S0021932007001964

Lynn, S. J., & Kirsch, I. (2006). *Essentials of clinical hypnosis: An evidence-based approach.* Washington, DC: American Psychological Association.

Lynn, S. J., Lock, T., Loftus, E. F., Krackow, E., & Lilienfeld, S. O. (2003). The remembrance of things past: Problematic memory recovery techniques in psychotherapy. In S. O. Lilienfeld, S. J. Lynn, & J. M. Lohr (Eds.), *Science and pseudoscience in clinical psychology* (pp. 205–239). New York, NY: Guilford Press.

Lyons, N. (1983). Two perspectives: On self, relationships, and morality. *Harvard Educational Review, 53,* 125–146.

Lytton, H., & Romney, D. M. (1991). Parents' differential socialization of boys and girls: A meta-analysis. *Psychological Bulletin, 109,* 267–296.

Lyubomirsky, S., King, L., & Diener, E. (2005). The benefits of frequent positive affect: Does happiness lead to success? *Psychological Bulletin, 131,* 803–855.

Ma, V., & Schoeneman, T. J. (1997). Individualism versus collectivism: A comparison of Kenyan and American self-concepts. *Basic and Applied Social Psychology, 19,* 261–273.

Macchi Cassia, V., Turati, C., & Simion, F. (2004). Can a nonspecific bias toward top-heavy patterns explain newborns' face preference? *Psychological Science, 15,* 379–383.

Maccoby, E. E. (1998). *The two sexes: Growing up apart, coming together.* Cambridge, MA: Harvard University Press.

Maccoby, E. E., & Martin, J. A. (1983). Socialization in the context of the family: Parent-child interaction. In E. M. Hetherington (Ed.), *Handbook of child psychology: Vol. 4. Socialization, personality, and social development* (pp. 1–101). New York, NY: Wiley.

MacGregor, J. N., Ormerod, T. C., & Chronicle, E. P. (2001). Information processing and insight: A process model of performance on the nine-dot and related problems. *Journal of Experimental Psychology: Learning, Memory, and Cognition, 27,* 176–201.

Maddux, W. W., Mullen, E., & Galinsky, A. D. (2008). Chameleons bake bigger pies and take bigger pieces: Strategic behavioral mimicry facilitates negotiation outcomes. *Journal of Experimental Social Psychology, 44,* 461–468.

Madon, S., Guyll, M., Buller, A. A., Scherr, K. C., Willard, J., & Spoth, R. (2008). The mediation of mothers' self-fulfilling effects on their children's alcohol use: Self-verification, informational conformity, and modeling processes. *Journal of Personality and Social Psychology, 95,* 369–384.

Madon, S., Jussim, L., & Eccles, J. (1997). In search of the powerful self-fulfilling prophecy. *Journal of Personality and Social Psychology, 72,* 791–809.

Madsen, E. A., Tunney, R. J., Gieldman, G., Plotkin, H. C., Dunbar, R. I. M., Richardson, J.-M., & McFarland, D. (2007). Kinship and altruism: A cross-cultural experimental study. *British Journal of Psychology, 98*, 339–359.

Maguen, S., Floyd, F. J., Bakeman, R., & Armistead, L. (2002). Developmental milestones and disclosure of sexual orientation among gay, lesbian, and bisexual youths. *Applied Developmental Psychology, 23*, 219–233.

Mahowald, M. W., & Schenck, C. H. (2005). Insights from studying human sleep disorders. *Nature, 437*, 1279–1285.

Maier, N. R. F. (1931). Reasoning in humans: II. The solution of a problem and its appearance in consciousness. *Journal of Comparative Psychology, 12*, 181–194.

Maier, S. F., & Seligman, M. E. P. (1976). Learned helplessness: Theory and evidence. *Journal of Experimental Psychology, 105*, 3–46.

Malinowski, B. (1927). *Sex and repression in savage society.* London, United Kingdom: Routledge & Kegan Paul.

Manber, R., Kraemer, H. C., Arnow, B. A. Trivedi, M. H., Rush, A. J., Thase, M. E., . . . Keller, M. E. (2008). Faster remission of chronic depression with combined psychotherapy and medication than with each therapy alone. *Journal of Consulting and Clinical Psychology, 76*, 459–467.

Mandel, D. R., Jusczyk, P. W., & Pisoni, D. B. (1995). Infants' recognition of the sound patterns of their own names. *Psychological Science, 5*, 314–317.

Manoussaki, D., Dimitriadis, E. K., & Chadwick, R. S. (2006). Cochlea's graded curvature effect on low frequency waves. *Physical Review Letters, 96*, 088701.

Manuck, S. B., Flory, J. D., Muldoon, M. F., & Ferrell, R. E. (2002). Central nervous system serotonergic responsivity and aggressive disposition in men. *Physiology & Behavior, 77*, 705–709.

Marcus, A. D. (1990, December 3). Mists of memory cloud some legal proceedings. *Wall Street Journal,* p. B1.

Marian, V., & Kaushanskaya, M. (2007). Language context guides memory content. *Psychonomic Bulletin & Review, 14*(5), 925–933.

Marin, A. (2001). *Systemic treatment of CF forces with PTSD. Special Report to the Minister of National Defence.* Retrieved from http://www.ombudsman.forces.gc.ca/rep-rap/sr-rs/pts-ssp/doc/pts-ssp-eng.pdf

Markman, K. D., Lindberg, M. J., Kray, L. J., & Galinsky, A. D. (2007). Implications of counterfactual structure for creative generation and analytic problem solving. *Personality and Social Psychology Bulletin, 33*, 312–324.

Markovitz, H., & Nantel, G. (1989). The belief-bias effect in the production and evaluation of logical conclusions. *Memory & Cognition, 17*, 11–17.

Markowitsch, H. J. (2000). Neuroanatomy of memory. In E. Tulving & F. I. M. Craik (Eds.), *The Oxford handbook of memory* (pp. 465–484). Oxford, United Kingdom: Oxford University Press.

Markus, H. R., & Kitayama, S. (1991). Culture and the self: Implications for cognition, emotion, and motivation. *Psychological Review, 98*, 224–253.

Markus, H. R., Mullally, P. R., & Kitayama, S. (1997). Selfways: Diversity in modes of cultural participation. In U. Neisser & D. A. Jopling (Eds.), *The conceptual self in context* (pp. 13–61). Cambridge, United Kingdom: Cambridge University Press.

Markus, H. R., Uchida, Y., Omoregie, H., Townsend, S. S. M. & Kitayama, S. (2006). Going for the gold: Models of agency in Japanese and American contexts. *Psychological Science, 17*, 103–112.

Markus, H., & Nurius, P. (1986). Possible selves. *American Psychologist, 41*, 954–969.

Marshall, G. D., & Zimbardo, P. G. (1979). Affective consequences of inadequately explained physiological arousal. *Journal of Personality and Social Psychology, 37*, 970–988.

Martin, G., & Pear, J. (1999). *Behavior modification: What it is and how to do it* (6th ed.). Upper Saddle River, NJ: Prentice Hall.

Martin, P. Y., & Marrington, S. (2005). Morningness-eveningness orientation, optimal time-of-day and attitude change: Evidence for the systematic processing of a persuasive communication. *Personality and Individual Differences, 39*, 367–377.

Martinez-Taboas, A., Canino, G., Wang, M. Q., Garcias, P., & Bravo, M. (2006). Prevalence of victimization correlates of pathological dissociation in a community sample of youths. *Journal of Traumatic Stress, 19*, 439–448.

Martin-Fardon, R., Lorentz, C. U., Stuempfig, N. D., & Weiss, F. (2005). Priming with BTCP, a dopamine reuptake blocker, reinstates cocaine-seeking and enhances cocaine cue-induced reinstatement. *Pharmacology, Biochemistry, and Behavior, 92*, 46–54.

Maslach, C. (1979). Negative emotional biasing of unexplained arousal. *Journal of Personality and Social Psychology, 37*, 953–969.

Maslach, C., & Leiter, M. (2008). Early predictors of job burnout and engagement. *Journal of Applied Psychology, 93*, 498–512.

Maslow, A. H. (1968). *Toward a psychology of being* (2nd ed.). Princeton, NJ: Van Nostrand.

Maslow, A. H. (1970). *Motivation and personality* (Rev. ed.). New York, NY: Harper & Row.

Mason, L. E. (1997, August 4). Divided she stands. *New York Magazine,* 42–49.

Mason, M. A., Skolnick, A., & Sugarman, S. D. (Eds.). (1998). *All our families: New policies for a new century.* New York, NY: Oxford University Press.

Mason, R. A., & Just, M. A. (2007). Lexical ambiguity in sentence comprehension. *Brain Research, 1146*, 115–127.

Mason, T. B. A., II, & Pack, A. I. (2007). Pediatric parasomnias. Sleep: *Journal of Sleep and Sleep Disorders Research, 30*(2), 141–151.

Masters, W. H., & Johnson, V. E. (1966). *Human sexual response.* Boston, MA: Little, Brown.

Masters, W. H., & Johnson, V. E. (1970). *Human sexual inadequacy.* Boston, MA: Little, Brown.

Masters, W. H., & Johnson, V. E. (1979). *Homosexuality in perspective.* Boston, MA: Little, Brown.

Matheson, F. I., Moineddin, R., Dunn, J. R., Creatore, M. I., Gozdyra, P., & Glazier, R.H. (2006). Urban neighborhoods, chronic stress, gender and depression. *Social Science Medicine, 63*(10), 2604–2616.

Matheson, K., Kelly, O., Cole, B., Tannenbaum, B., Dodd, C., & Anisman, H. (2005). Parental bonding and depressive affect: The mediation role of coping resources. *British Journal of Social Psychology, 44*(3), 371–395.

Maurer, D., Lewis, T. L., Brent, H. P., & Levin, A. V. (1999). Rapid improvement in the acuity of infants after visual input. *Science, 286*, 108–110.

Maxwell, J. S., & Davidson, R. J. (2007). Emotion as motion: Asymmetries in approach and avoidant actions. *Psychological Science, 18,* 1113–1119.

May, R. (1975). *The courage to create.* New York, NY: Norton.

Mayer, J. D., Roberts, R. D., & Barsade, S. G. (2008a). Human abilities: Emotional intelligence. *Annual Review of Psychology, 59,* 507–536.

Mayer, J. D., Salovey, P., & Caruso, D. R. (2008b). Emotional intelligence: New ability or eclectic traits? *The American Psychologist, 63*(6), 503–517.

Mays, V. M., Cochran, S. D., & Barnes, N. W. (2007). Race, race-based discrimination, and health outcomes among African Americans. *Annual Review of Psychology, 58,* 201–225.

McAdams, D. P. (1988). Biography, narrative, and lives: An introduction. *Journal of Personality, 56,* 1–18.

McAdams, D. P. (2001). The psychology of life stories. *Review of General Psychology, 5,* 100–122.

McAdams, D. P., & de St. Aubin, E. (Eds.). (1998). *Generativity and adult development: How and why we care for the next generation.* Washington, DC: American Psychological Association.

McAdams, D. P., Bauer, J. J., Sakaeda, A. R., Anyidoho, N. A., Machado, M. A., Magrino-Failla, K., . . . Pals, J. L. (2006). Continuity and change in the life story: A longitudinal study of autobiographical memories in emerging adulthood. *Journal of Personality, 74,* 1371–1400.

McAllister, H. A. (1996). Self-serving bias in the classroom: Who shows it? Who knows it? *Journal of Educational Psychology, 88,* 123–131.

McCarthy, A., & Lee, K. (2009). Children's knowledge of deceptive gaze cues and its relation to their actual lying behavior. *Journal of Experimental Child Psychology, 103*(2), 117–134.

McClelland, D. C. (1961). *The achieving society.* Princeton, NJ: Van Nostrand.

McClelland, D. C. (1971). *Motivational trends in society.* Morristown, NJ: General Learning Press.

McClelland, D. C., & Franz, C. E. (1992). Motivational and other sources of work accomplishments in mid-life: A longitudinal study. *Journal of Personality, 60,* 679–707.

McClelland, D. C., Atkinson, J. W., Clark, R. A., & Lowell, E. L. (1953). *The achievement motive.* New York, NY: Appleton-Century-Crofts.

McClelland, D. C., Atkinson, J. W., Clark, R. A., & Lowell, E. L. (1976). *The achievement motive* (2nd ed.). New York, NY: Irvington.

McClelland, J. L., & Elman, J. L. (1986). The TRACE model of speech perception. *Cognitive Psychology, 18,* 1–86.

McConaghy, N., Hadzi-Pavlovic, D., Stevens, C., Manicavasagar, V., Buhrich, N., & Vollmer-Conna, U. (2006). Fraternal birth order and ratio of heterosexual/homosexual feelings in women and men. *Journal of Homosexuality, 51*(4), 161–174.

McCrae, R. R., & Costa, P. T., Jr. (1997). Personality trait structure as a human universal. *American Psychologist, 52,* 509–516.

McCrae, R. R., & Costa, P. T., Jr. (1999). A five-factor theory of personality. In L. A. Pervin & O. P. John (Eds.), *Handbook of personality: Theory and research* (2nd ed., pp. 139–153). New York, NY: Guilford Press.

McCrae, R. R., Costa, P. T., Jr., & Martin, T. A. (2005). The NEO-PI-3: A more readable revised NEO Personality Inventory. *Journal of Personality Assessment, 84,* 261–270.

McCrae, R. R., Costa, P. T., Jr., Martin, T. A., Oryol, V. E., Rukavishnikov, A. A., Senin, I. G., Hřebíčková, M., & Urbánek, T. (2004). Consensual validation of personality traits across cultures. *Journal of Research in Personality, 38,* 179–201.

McCrae, R. R., Costa, P. T., Jr., Ostendorf, F., Angleitner, A., Hřebíčková, M., Avia, M. D., . . . Smith, P. B. (2000). Nature over nurture: Temperament, personality, and life span development. *Journal of Personality and Social Psychology, 78,* 173–186.

McCrae, S. M., & Hirt, E. R. (2001). The role of ability judgments in self-handicapping. *Personality & Social Psychology Bulletin, 27,* 1378–1389.

McCrae, S. M., Hirt, E. R., & Milner, B. J. (2008). She works hard for the money: Valuing effort underlies gender differences in behavioral self-handicapping. *Journal of Experimental Social Psychology, 44,* 292–311.

McCreary, D. R., Hildebrandt, T., Heinberg, L. J., Boroughs, M., & Thompson, J. K. (2007). A review of body image influences on men's fitness goals and nutritional supplement use. *American Journal of Men's Health, 1,* 307–316.

McDonald, R. J. & White, N. M. (1993). A triple dissociation of memory systems: hippocampus, amygdala, and dorsal striatum. *Behavioral Neuroscience, 107*(1), 3–22.

McGovern, K., & Baars, B. J. (2007). Cognitive theories of consciousness. In P. D. Zelazo, M. Moscovitch, & E. Thompson (Eds.), *The Cambridge handbook of consciousness* (pp. 177–205). New York, NY: Cambridge University Press.

McGregor, H. A., & Elliott, A. J. (2002). Achievement goals as predictors of achievement-relevant processes prior to task engagement. *Journal of Educational Psychology, 94,* 381–395.

McGue, M., Elkins, I., Walden, B., & Iacono, W. G. (2005). Perceptions of the parent–adolescent relationship: A longitudinal investigation. *Developmental Psychology, 41,* 971–984.

McKenzie, I. A., Biernaskie, J., Toma, J. G., Midha, R., & Miller, F. D. (2006). Skin-derived precursors generate myelinating Schwann cells for the injured and dysmyelinated nervous system. *Journal of Neuroscience, 26*(24), 6651–6660.

McNeil, B. J., Pauker, S. G., Sox, H. C., Jr., & Tversky, A. (1982). On the elicitation of preferences for alternative therapies. *New England Journal of Medicine, 306,* 1259–1262.

McPherson, K. S. (1985). On intelligence testing and immigration legislation. *American Psychologist, 40,* 242–243.

Mead, M. (1928). *Coming of age in Samoa.* New York, NY: Morrow.

Mead, M. (1939). *From the South Seas: Studies of adolescence and sex in primitive societies.* New York, NY: Morrow.

Meador, B. D., & Rogers, C. R. (1979). Person-centered therapy. In R. J. Corsini (Ed.), *Current psychotherapies* (2nd ed., pp. 131–184). Itasca, IL: Peacock.

Meece, J. L., Anderman, E. M., & Anderman, L. H. (2006). Classroom goal structure, student motivation, and academic achievement. *Annual Review of Psychology, 57,* 487–503.

Meichenbaum, D. (1977). *Cognitive-behavior modification: An integrative approach.* New York, NY: Plenum.

Meichenbaum, D. (1985). *Stress inoculation training.* New York, NY: Pergamon Press.

Meichenbaum, D. (1993). Changing conceptions of cognitive behavior modification: Retrospect and prospect. *Journal of Consulting and Clinical Psychology, 61,* 202–204.

Meier, R. P. (1991). Language acquisition by deaf children. *American Scientist, 79,* 60–70.

Meissner, K. K., Kirkham, D. L., & Doering, L. C. (2005). Transplants of neurosphere cell suspensions from aged mice are functional in the mouse model of Parkinson's. *Brain Research, 1057*(1–2), 105–112.

Meldrum, L. (2002). September 11 and its impacts on people around the globe. In S. N. Gold and J. Faust (Eds.), *Trauma practice in the wake of September 11, 2001* (pp. 63–81). New York, NY: Haworth Press.

Melzack, R. (1973). *The puzzle of pain.* New York, NY: Basic Books.

Melzack, R. (1980). Psychological aspects of pain. In J. J. Bonica (Ed.), *Pain.* New York, NY: Raven Press.

Melzack, R. (1999). From the gate to the neuromatrix. *Pain, Suppl. 6,* S121–126.

Melzack, R. (2001). Pain and the neuromatrix in the brain. *Journal of Dental Education, 65*(12), 1378–1382.

Melzack, R. (2005). Evolution of the neuromatrix theory of pain. The Prithvi Raj Lecture: Presented at the Third World Congress of World Institute of Pain, Barcelona 2004. *Pain Practice, 5*(2), 85–94.

Melzack, R., Coderre, T. J., Katz, J., & Vaccarino, A. L. (2001). Central neuroplasticity and pathological pain. *Annals of the New York Academy of Science, 933,* 157–174. Review.

Menec, V. H., Shooshtari, S., & Lambert, P. (2007). Ethnic differences in self-rated health among older adults: A cross-sectional and longitudinal analysis. *Journal of Aging Health. 19*(1), 62–86.

Merton, R. K. (1957). *Social theory and social structures.* New York, NY: The Free Press.

Mesquita, B., & Leu, J. (2007). The cultural psychology of emotion. In S. Kitayama & D. Cohen (Eds.), *Handbook of cultural psychology* (pp. 734–759). New York, NY: Guilford Press.

Metcalfe, J. (2000). Metamemory: Theory and data. In E. Tulving & F. I. M. Craik (Eds.), *The Oxford handbook of memory* (pp. 197–211). Oxford, United Kingdom: Oxford University Press.

Meyer, R. G. (2003). *Case studies in abnormal behavior* (6th ed.). Boston, MA: Allyn & Bacon.

Meyers, S. A., & Berscheid, E. (1997). The language of love: The difference a preposition makes. *Personality and Social Psychology Bulletin, 23,* 347–362.

Michael, R. T., Gagnon, J. H., Laumann, E. O., & Kolata, G. (1994). *Sex in America: A definitive survey.* Boston, MA: Little, Brown.

Middlebrooks, J. C., & Green, D. C. (1991). Sound localization by human listeners. *Annual Review of Psychology, 42,* 135–159.

Miklowitz, D. J., & Tompson, M. C. (2003). Family variables and interventions in schizophrenia. In G. P. Sholevar & L. D. Schwoeri (Eds.), *Textbook of family and couples therapy: Clinical applications* (pp. 585–617). Washington, DC: American Psychiatric Publishing.

Mikulincer, M., Florian, V., Cowan, P. A., & Cowan, C. P. (2002). Attachment security in couple relationships: A systematic model and its implications for family dynamics. *Family Process, 41,* 405–434.

Milgram, S. (1965). Some conditions of obedience and disobedience to authority. *Human Relations, 18,* 56–76.

Milgram, S. (1974). *Obedience to authority.* New York, NY: Harper & Row.

Miller Chenier, N. (1995). Suicide among Aboriginal people: Royal Commission report. Retrieved from http://www.parl.gc.ca/information/library/PRBpubs/mr131–e.htm

Miller N. E. (1978). Biofeedback and visceral learning. *Annual Review of Psychology, 29,* 373–404.

Miller, G. A. (1956). The magic number seven plus or minus two: Some limits in our capacity for processing information. *Psychological Review, 63,* 81–97.

Miller, J. G. (1984). Culture and the development of everyday social explanation. *Journal of Personality and Social Psychology, 46,* 961–978.

Miller, J. G., & Bersoff, D. M. (1992). Culture and moral judgment: How are conflicts between justice and interpersonal responsibilities resolved? *Journal of Personality and Social Psychology, 62,* 541–554.

Miller, J. G., Bersoff, D. M., & Harwood, R. L. (1990). Perceptions of social responsibilities in India and in the United States: Moral imperatives or personal decisions? *Journal of Personality and Social Psychology, 58,* 33–47.

Miller, M. A., & Rahe, R. H. (1997). Life changes scaling for the 1990s. *Journal of Psychosomatic Research, 43,* 279–292.

Mineka, S. & Cook, M. (1986). Immunization against the observational conditioning of snake fear in rhesus monkeys. *Journal of Abnormal Psychology, 95,* 307–318.

Mineka, S. Davidson, M., Cook, M., & Keir, R. (1984). Observational conditioning of snake fear in rhesus monkeys. *Journal of Abnormal Psychology, 93,* 355–372.

Mineka, S., & Keir, R. (1983). The effects of flooding on reducing snake fear in rhesus monkeys: 6-month follow-up and further flooding. *Behavioral Research Therapy, 21,* 527–535.

Miranda, J., Bernal, G., Lau, A., Kohn, L., Hwang, W.-C., & LaFromboise, T. (2005). State of the science on psychosocial interventions for ethnic minorities. *Annual Review of Clinical Psychology, 1,* 113–142.

Mischel, W. (1968). *Personality and assessment.* New York, NY: Wiley.

Mischel, W. (1973). Toward a cognitive social learning reconceptualization of personality. *Psychological Review, 80,* 252–283.

Mischel, W. (2004). Toward an integrative science of the person. *Annual Review of Psychology, 55,* 1–22.

Mischel, W., & Shoda, Y. (1995). A cognitive-affective system theory of personality: Reconceptualizing situations, dispositions, dynamics, and invariance in personality structure. *Psychological Review, 102,* 246–268.

Mischel, W., & Shoda, Y. (1999). Integrating dispositions and processing dynamics within a unified theory of personality: The cognitive-affective personality system. In L. A. Pervin & O. P. John (Eds.), *Handbook of personality: Theory and research* (2nd ed., pp. 197–218). New York, NY: Guilford Press.

Mishra, J., & Backlin, W. (2007). The effects of altering environmental and instrumental context on the performance of memorized music. *Psychology of Music, 35,* 1–20.

Mitchell, K. J., & Johnson, M. K. (2000). Source monitoring: Attributing mental experiences. In E. Tulving & F. I. M. Craik (Eds.), *The Oxford handbook of memory* (pp. 179–195). London, United Kingdom: Oxford University Press.

Mithen, S. (2005). *The singing Neanderthals: The origins of music, language, mind and body.* London, United Kingdom: Weidenfeld and Nicolson.

Modirrousta, M., & Fellows, L. K. (2008). Medial prefrontal cortex plays a critical and selective role in 'feeling of knowing' metamemory judgments. *Neuropsychologia, 46*(12), 2958–2965.

Mogil, J. S., & Chanda, M. L. (2005). The case for the inclusion of female subjects in basic science studies of pain. *Pain, 117*(1–2), 1–5.

Mohamed, F. B., Faro, S. H., Gordon, N. J., Platek, S. M., Ahmad, H., & Williams, J. M. (2006). Brain mapping of deception and truth telling about an ecologically valid situation: Functional MR imaging and polygraph investigation—initial experience. *Radiology, 238*, 679–688.

Mojtabai, R., & Olfson, M. (2006). Treatment seeking for depression in Canada and the United States. *Psychiatric Services, 57*(5), 631–639.

Möller, J.-J., Baldwin, D. S., Goodwin, G., Kasper, S., Okasha, A., Stein, D. J., . . . the WPA section on Pharmacopsychiatry. (2008). Do SSRIs or antidepressants in general increase suicidality? WPA Section on Pharmacopsychiatry: Consensus statement. *European Archives of Psychiatry and Clinical Neuroscience, 258* (Suppl. 3), 3–23.

Moncrieff, R. W. (1951). *The chemical senses.* London, United Kingdom: Leonard Hill.

Morgan, A. H., Hilgard, E. R., & Davert, E. C. (1970). The heritability of hypnotic susceptibility of twins: A preliminary report. *Behavior Genetics, 1*, 213–224.

Morgenstern, J., Labouvie, E., McCrady, B. S., Kahler, C. W., & Frey, R. M. (1997). Affiliation with Alcoholics Anonymous after treatment: A study of its therapeutic effects and mechanisms of action. *Journal of Consulting and Clinical Psychology, 65*, 768–777.

Moriarty, T. (1975). Crime, commitment and the responsive bystander: Two field experiments. *Journal of Personality and Social Psychology, 31*, 370–376.

Morin, S. F., & Rothblum, E. D. (1991). Removing the stigma: Fifteen years of progress. *American Psychologist, 46*, 947–949.

Morling, B., & Lamoreaux, M. (2008). Measuring culture outside the head: A meta-analysis of individualism-collectivism in cultural products. *Personality and Social Psychology Review, 12*, 199–221.

Morris, J. A., Jordan, C. L., & Breedlove, S. M. (2004). Sexual differentiation of the vertebrate nervous system. *Nature Neuroscience, 7*, 1034–1039.

Morris, J. S., Frith, C. D., Perrett, D. I., Rowland, D., Young, A. W., Calder, A. J., & Dolan, R. J. (1996). A differential neural response in the human amygdala to fearful and happy facial expressions. *Nature, 383*, 812–815.

Morrison, M. A., Morrison, T. G., & Franklin, R. (2009). Modern and old-fashioned homonegativity among samples of Canadian and American university students, *Journal of Cross-Cultural Psychology, 40*(4),523–542.

Morry, M. M. (2007). The attraction-similarity hypothesis among cross-sex friends: Relationship satisfaction, perceived similarities, and self-serving perceptions. *Journal of Social and Personal Relationships, 24*, 117–138.

Moscovici, S. (1976). *Social influence and social change.* New York, NY: Academic Press.

Moscovici, S. (1980). Toward a theory of conversion behavior. In L. Berkowitz (Ed.), *Advances in experimental social psychology* (Vol. 13, pp. 209–239). New York, NY: Academic Press.

Moscovici, S. (1985). Social influence and conformity. In G. Lindzey & E. Aronson (Eds.), *The handbook of social psychology* (3rd ed., pp. 347–412). New York, NY: Random House.

Moscovici, S., & Faucheux, C. (1972). Social influence, conformity bias, and the study of active minorities. In L. Berkowitz (Ed.), *Advances in experimental social psychology* (Vol. 6). New York, NY: Academic Press.

Moskowitz, B. A. (1978). The acquisition of language. *Scientific American, 239*(11), 92–108.

Moskowitz, G. B. (2004). *Social cognition: Understanding self and others.* New York, NY: Guilford Press.

Motherwell, L., & Shay, J. J. (2005). (Eds.). *Complex dilemmas in group therapy.* New York, NY: Brunner-Routledge.

Mueller, A., Mueller, U., Silbermann, A., Reinecker, H., Bleich, S., Mitchell, J. E., & de Zwaan, M. (2008). A randomized, controlled trial of group cognitive-behavioral therapy for compulsive buying disorder: Posttreatment and 6-month follow-up results. *Journal of Clinical Psychiatry, 69*, 1131–1138.

Mulvaney, M. K., & Mebert, C. J. (2007). Parental corporal punishment predicts behavior problems in early childhood. *Journal of Family Psychology, 21*, 389–397.

Munafò, M. R., & Johnstone, E. C. (2008). Genes and cigarette smoking. *Addiction, 103*, 893–904.

Munsterberg, H. (1908). *On the witness stand.* New York, NY: McClure.

Murata, P. J., McGlynn, E. A., Siu, A. L., & Brook, R. H. (1992). *Prenatal care.* Santa Monica, CA: The Rand Corporation.

Murphy, G. L. (2002). *The big book of concepts.* Cambridge, MA: MIT Press.

Murphy, K. J., Troyer, A. K., Levine, B., & Moscovitch, M. (2008). Episodic, but not semantic, autobiographical memory is reduced in amnestic mild cognitive impairment. *Neuropsychologia, 46*(13), 3116–3123.

Murphy, K. M., & Mitchell, D. E. (1986). Bilateral amblyopia after a short period of reverse occlusion in kittens. *Nature, 323*(6088), 536–538.

Murphy, K. M., & Mitchell, D. E. (1987). Reduced visual acuity in both eyes of monocularly deprived kittens following a short or long period of reverse occlusion. *Journal of Neuroscience, 7*(5), 1526–1536.

Murphy, K. M., & Mitchell, D. E. (1991). Vernier acuity of normal and visually deprived cats. *Vision Research, 31*(2), 253–266.

Murphy, K. M., Duffy, K. R., & Jones, D. G. (2004). Experience-dependent changes in NMDAR1 expression in the visual cortex of an animal model for amblyopia. *Visual Neuroscience, 21*(4), 653–670.

Murphy, K. M., Duffy, K. R., Jones, D. G., & Mitchell, D. E. (2001). Development of cytochrome oxidase blobs in visual cortex of normal and visually deprived cats. *Cerebral Cortex, 11*(2), 122–135.

Murphy, M. C., & Archer, J. (1996). Stressors on the college campus: A comparison of 1985–1993. *Journal of College Student Development, 37*, 20–28.

Murray, H. A. (1938). *Explorations in personality.* New York, NY: Oxford University Press.

Murray, J. B. (1995). Evidence for acupuncture's analgesic effectiveness and proposals for the physiological mechanisms involved. *Journal of Psychology, 129*(4):443–461.

Mussweiler, T., & Bodenhausen, G. V. (2002). I know you are, but what am I? Self-evaluative consequences of judging in-group and out-group members. *Journal of Personality and Social Psychology, 82*, 19–32.

Nagda, B. A., Tropp, L. R., & Paluck, E. L. (Eds.) (2006). Reducing prejudice and promoting social inclusion: Integrating research, theory, and practice on intergroup relations. *Journal of Social Issues, 62*(3), 439–631.

Narayan, V. M., Narr, K. L., Phillips, O R., Thompson, P. M. Toga, A. W., Szeszko, P. R. (2008). Greater regional cortical gray matter thickness in obsessive-compulsive disorder. *NeuroReport, 19,* 1551–1555.

Nash, J. R., Sargent, P. A., Rabiner, E. A., Hood, S. D., Argyropoulos, S. V., Potokar, J. P.,... Nutt, D. J. (2008). Serotonin 5-HT$_{1A}$ receptor binding in people with panic disorder: Positron emission tomography study. *The British Journal of Psychiatry, 193,* 229–234.

Nasrallah, H. A. (2005). Factors having impact on the tolerability of antipsychotic agents. *Journal of Clinical Psychiatry, 66,* 131–133.

National Institute on Aging. (2008). *Progress report on Alzheimer's Disease.* Retrieved from http://www.nia.nih.gov/Alzheimers/Publications/ADProgress2008

National Sleep Foundation. (2000). *2000 Omnibus Sleep in America poll.* Retrieved from http://www.sleepfoundation.org/publications/2000poll.html

National Sleep Foundation. (2005). *Summary findings: 2005 Sleep in America poll.* Retrieved from http://www.sleepfoundation.org/sites/default/files/2005_summary_of_findings.pdf

Neath, I., & Crowder, R. G. (1990). Schedules of presentation and temporal distinctiveness in human memory. *Journal of Experimental Psychology: Learning, Memory, and Cognition, 16,* 316–327.

Neath, I., & Surprenant, A. M. (2003). *Human memory: An introduction to research, data, and theory* (2nd ed.). Belmont, CA: Wadsworth.

Neath, I., Brown, G. D. A., McCormack, T., Chater, N., & Freeman, R. (2006). Distinctiveness models of memory and absolute identification: Evidence for local, not global, effects. *Quarterly Journal of Experimental Psychology, 59,* 121–135.

Neiss, M. B., Sedikides, C., & Stevenson, J. (2006). Genetic influences on level and stability of self-esteem. *Self and Identity, 5,* 247–266.

Neisser, U. (1967). *Cognitive psychology.* New York, NY: Appleton-Century-Crofts.

Neisser, U., Boodoo, G., Bouchard, T. J., Jr., Boykin, A. W., Brody, N., Ceci, S. J., . . . Urbina, S. (1996). Intelligence: Knowns and unknowns. *American Psychologist, 51,* 77–101.

Nelson, D. A., Mitchell, C., & Yang, C. (2008). Intent attributions and aggression: A study of children and their parents. *Journal of Abnormal Child Psychology, 36,* 793–806.

Nelson, R. E., & Craighead, W. E. (1977). Selective recall of positive and negative feedback, self-control behaviors and depression. *Journal of Abnormal Psychology, 86,* 379–388.

Nelson, T. D. (2006). *The psychology of prejudice* (2nd ed.). Boston, MA: Allyn & Bacon.

Nes, R. B., Røysamb, E., Tambs, K., Harris, J. R., & Reichborn-Kjennerud, T. (2006). Subjective well-being: Genetic and environmental contributions to stability and change. *Psychological Medicine, 36,* 1033–1042.

Nesse, R. M., & Berridge, K. C. (1997). Psychoactive drug use in evolutionary perspective. *Science, 278,* 63–66.

Nettle, D. (2006). The evolution of personality variation in humans and other animals. *American Psychologist, 61,* 622–631.

Nettlebeck, T., & Wilson, C. (2005). Intelligence and IQ: What teachers should know. *Educational Psychology, 25,* 609–630.

Nevéus, T., Cnattingius, S., Olsson, U., & Hetta, J. (2001). Sleep habits and sleep problems among a community sample of schoolchildren. *Acta Paediatrica, 90,* 1450–1455.

Newcomb, T. M. (1929). *The consistency of certain extrovert-introvert behavior traits in 50 problem boys* (Contributions to Education, No. 382). New York, NY: Columbia University Press.

Newell, A., & Simon, H. A. (1972). *Human problem solving.* Englewood Cliffs, NJ: Prentice Hall.

Newman, T. K., Syagailo, Y. V., Barr, C. S., Wendland, J. R., Champoux, M., Grassele, M., . . . Lesch, K.-P. (2005). Monoamine oxidase A gene promoter variation and rearing experiences influence aggressive behavior in rhesus monkeys. *Biological Psychiatry, 57,* 167–172.

Niaura, R., Todaro, J. F., Stoud, L., Sprio, A., III, Ward, K. D., & Weiss, S. (2002). Hostility, the metabolic syndrome, and incident coronary heart disease. *Health Psychology, 21,* 588–593.

Niccols, A. (2007). Fetal alcohol syndrome and the developing socio-emotional brain. *Brain and Cognition, 65*(1), 135–142.

Nielsen, B. D., Pickett, C. L., & Simonton, D. K. (2008). Conceptual versus experimental creativity: Which works best on convergent and divergent thinking tasks? *Psychology of Aesthetics, Creativity and the Arts, 2,* 131–138.

Nielsen, T. A., & Stenstrom, P. (2005). What are the memory sources of dreaming? *Nature, 437,* 1286–1289.

Nigg, C. R., Borrelli, B., Maddock, J., & Dishman, R. K. (2008). A theory of physical activity maintenance. *Applied Psychology: An International Review, 57,* 544–560.

Nisbett, R. E. (2005). Heredity, environment and race differences in IQ: A commentary on Rushton and Jensen (2005). *Psychology, Public Policy, and Law, 11,* 302–310.

Noack, P. (2004). The family context of preadolescents' orientations toward education: Effects of maternal orientations and behavior. *Journal of Educational Psychology, 96,* 714–722.

Nock, M. K., Borges, G., Bromet, E. J., Cha, C. B., Kessler, R. C., & Lee, S. (2008). Suicide and suicidal behavior. *Epidemiologic Reviews, 30,* 133–154.

Nolan, J. M., Schultz, P. W., Cialdini, R. B., Goldstein, N. J., & Griskevicius, V. (2007). Normative social influence is under-detected. *Personality and Social Psychology Bulletin, 34,* 913–923.

Nolen-Hoeksema, S. (2002). Gender differences in depression. In I. H. Gotlib & C. L. Hammen (Eds.), *Handbook of depression* (pp. 492–509). New York, NY: Guilford Press.

Nolen-Hoeksema, S., Larson, J., & Grayson, C. (1999). Explaining the gender difference in depressive symptoms. *Journal of Personality and Social Psychology, 77,* 1061–1072.

Nooteboom, S., & Quené, H. (2008). Self-monitoring and feedback: A new attempt to find the main cause of lexical bias in phonological speech errors. *Journal of Memory and Language, 58,* 837–861.

Norcross, J. C., Karpiak, C. P., & Lister, K. M. (2005). What's an integrationist? A study of self-identified and (occasionally) eclectic psychologists. *Journal of Clinical Psychology, 61,* 1587–1594.

Norman, G. J., Velicer, W. F., Fava, J. L., & Prochaska, J. O. (1998). Dynamic topology clustering within the stages of change for smoking cessation. *Addictive Behaviors, 23,* 139–153.

Norman, G. J., Velicer, W. F., Fava, J. L., & Prochaska, J. O. (2000). Cluster subtypes within stage of change in a representative sample of smokers. *Addictive Behaviors, 25,* 183–204.

Norman, W. T. (1963). Toward an adequate taxonomy of personality attributes: Replicated factor structure in peer nomination personality ratings. *Journal of Abnormal and Social Psychology, 66,* 574–583.

Norman, W. T. (1967). *2,800 personality trait descriptors: Normative operating characteristics for a university population* (Research Rep. No. 08310–1–T). Ann Arbor, MI: University of Michigan Press.

Norris, S., Paré, J.-R., & Starky, S. (2006). *Childhood autism in Canada: Some issues relating to behavioural intervention.* Parliamentary Information and Research Service. Library of Parliament. Retrieved from http://www.parl.gc.ca/information/library/PRBpubs/prb0593–e.htm#increase

Nosofsky, R. M., & Stanton, R. D. (2005). Speeded classification in a probabilistic category structure: Contrasting exemplar-retrieval, decision-boundary, and prototype models. *Journal of Experimental Psychology: Human Perception and Performance, 31,* 608–629.

Novick, L. R., & Bassok, M. (2005). Problem solving. In K. J. Holyoak & R. G. Morrison (Eds.), *Cambridge handbook of thinking and reasoning* (pp. 321–349). New York, NY: Cambridge University Press.

Nowak, M. A., & Sigmund, K. (2005). Evolution of indirect reciprocity. *Nature, 437,* 1291–1298.

Nrugham, L., Larsson, B., & Sund, A. M. (2008). Predictors of suicidal acts across adolescence: Influences of family, peer and individual factors. *Journal of Affective Disorders, 109,* 35–45.

Nyberg, L., & Cabeza, R. (2000). Brain imaging of memory. In E. Tulving & F. I. M. Craik (Eds.), *The Oxford handbook of memory* (pp. 501–519). Oxford, United Kingdom: Oxford University Press.

O'Brien, C. P. (2005). Benzodiazepine use, abuse, and dependence. *Journal of Clinical Psychiatry, 66* (Suppl. 2), 28–33.

O'Connor, M. G., & Lafleche, G. (2005). Amnesic syndromes. In P. J. Snyder, P. D. Nussbaun, & D. L. Robins (Eds.), *Clinical neuropsychology: A pocket handbook for assessment* (2nd ed., pp. 463–488). Washington, DC: American Psychology Association.

O'Regan, J. K. (1992). Solving the "real" mysteries of visual perception: The world as an outside memory. *Canadian Journal of Psychology, 46,* 461–488.

Offord, D. R., Boyle, M. H., Campbell, D., Goering, P., Lin, E., Wong, M., & Racine, Y. A. (1996). One-year prevalence of psychiatric disorder in Ontarians 15 to 64 years of age. *Canadian Journal of Psychiatry, 41,* 559–563.

Öhman, A., & Mineka, S. (2001). Fears, phobias, and preparedness: Toward an evolved module of fear and fear learning. *Psychological Review, 108,* 483–522.

Okamoto-Barth, S., Call, J., & Tomasello, M. (2007). Great apes' understanding of other individuals' line of sight. *Psychological Science, 18*(5), 462–468.

Olsson, I. A. S., Hansen, A. K., & Sandøe, P. (2007). Ethics and refinement in animal research. *Science, 317*(5845), 1680.

Olszewski-Kubilius, P., & Lee, S. Y. (2004). The role of participation in in-school and outside-of-school activities in the talent development of gifted students. *Journal of Secondary Gifted Education, 15,* 107–123.

Olton, D. S. (1992). Tolman's cognitive analyses: Predecessors of current approaches in psychology. *Journal of Experimental Psychology: General, 121,* 427–428.

Oman, D., Hedberg, J., & Thoresen, C. E. (2006). Passage meditation reduces perceived stress in health professionals: A randomized, controlled trial. *Journal of Consulting and Clinical Psychology, 74*(4), 714–719.

Oppenheimer, D. M., & Frank, M. C. (2008). A rose in any other font would not smell as sweet: Effects of perceptual fluency on categorization. *Cognition, 106*(3), 1178–1194.

Orbuch, T. L., Veroff, J., Hassan, H., & Horrocks, J. (2002). Who will divorce: A 14-year longitudinal study of black couples and white couples. *Journal of Social and Personal Relationships, 19,* 179–202.

Orth, U., Robins, R. W., & Roberts, B. W. (2008). Low self-esteem prospectively predicts depression in adolescence and young adulthood. *Journal of Personality and Social Psychology, 95,* 695–708.

Otis, N., & Pelletier, L. G. (2005). A motivational model of daily hassles, physical symptoms, and future work intentions among police officers. *Journal of Applied Social Psychology, 35*(10), 2193–2214.

Owen, M. J., & O'Donovan, M. C. (2003). Schizophrenia and genetics. In R. Plomin, J. C. DeFries, I. W. Craig, & P. McGuffin (Eds.), *Behavioral genetics in the postgenomic era* (pp. 463–480). Washington, DC: American Psychological Association.

Owens, K. M. B., Asmundson, G. J. G., Hadjistavropoulos, T., & Owens, T. J. (2004). Attentional bias toward illness threat in individuals with elevated health anxiety. *Cognitive Therapy and Research, 28,* 57–66.

Ozer, D. J., & Reise, S. P. (1994). Personality assessment. *Annual Review of Psychology, 45,* 357–388.

Pachankis, J. E. (2007). The psychological implications of concealing a stigma: A cognitive-affective-behavioral model. *Psychological Bulletin, 133,* 328–345.

Packer, I. K. (2008). Specialized practice in forensic psychology: Opportunities and obstacles. *Professional Psychology: Research and Practice, 39,* 245–249.

Pagani, L., Derevensky, J. L., & Japel, C. (2009). Predicting gambling behavior in sixth grade from kindergarten impulsivity: A tale of developmental continuity. *Archives of Pediatrics & Adolescent Medicine, 63,* 238–243.

Pagel, J. F. (2008). The burden of obstructive sleep apnea and associated excessive sleepiness. *Journal of Family Practice, 57,* S3–S8.

Pagnoni, G., & Cekic, M. (2007). Age effects on gray matter volume and attentional performance in Zen meditation. *Neurobiology of Aging, 28,* 1623–1627.

Paivio, A. (2006). *Mind and its evolution: A dual coding theoretical interpretation.* Mahwah, NJ: Lawrence and Associates, Inc.

Paller, K. A., & Voss, J. L. (2004). Memory reactivation and consolidation during sleep. *Learning & Memory, 11,* 664–670.

Pandi-Perumal, S. R., Srinivasan, V., Spence, D. W., & Cardinali, D. P. (2007). Role of the melatonin system in the control of sleep: Therapeutic implications. *CNS Drugs, 21,* 995–1018.

Papafragou, A., Li, P., Choi, Y., & Han, C. H. (2007). Evidentiality in language and cognition. *Cognition, 103*(2), 253–299.

Paris, J. (2003). *Personality disorders over time: Precursors, course, and outcome.* Washington, DC: American Psychiatric Publishing.

Parker, A., Ngu, H., & Cassaday, H. J. (2001). Odour and Proustian memory: Reduction of context-dependent forgetting and multiple forms of memory. *Applied Cognitive Psychology, 15,* 342–350.

Parr, W. V., & Siegert, R. (1993). Adults' conceptions of everyday memory failures in others: Factors that mediate the effects of target age. *Psychology and Aging, 8,* 599–605.

Parsons, L. M., & Osherson, D. (2001). New evidence for distinct right and left brain systems for deductive versus probabilistic reasoning. *Cerebral Cortex, 11,* 954–965.

Pasternak, T., Bisley, J. W., & Calkins, D. (2003). Visual processing in the primate brain. In M. Gallager & R. J. Nelson (Eds.), *Handbook of psychology: Biological psychology* (Vol. 3, pp. 139–185). New York, NY: Wiley.

Patel A. D., Iversen, J. R., Bregman, M. R. & Schulz, I. (2009). Experimental evidence for synchronization to a musical beat in a nonhuman animal. *Current Biology, 19*(10), 827–830.

Patterson, C. J. (2002). Lesbian and gay parenthood. In M. H. Bornstein (Ed.), *Handbook of parenting: Vol. 3. Being and becoming a parent* (2nd ed., pp. 317–338). Mahwah, NJ: Erlbaum.

Patterson, G. R. (2002). The early development of coercive family process. In J. B. Ried, G. R. Patterson, & J. J. Snyder (Eds.), *Antisocial behavior in children and adolescents: A developmental analysis and the Oregon model for intervention* (pp. 25–44). Washington, DC: American Psychological Association.

Patterson, M., Sommers, J., McIntosh, K., Sheill, A., & Frankish, C. J. (2008). *Housing and supports for adults with severe addictions and/or mental illness in British Columbia.* Retrieved from: http://www.carmha.ca/publications/index.cfm?contentID=29

Paul, M. A., Miller, J. C., Love, R. J., Lieberman, H., Blazeski, S., & Arendt, J. (2009). Timing light treatment for eastward and westward travel preparation. *Chronobiology International, 26*(5), 867–890.

Pauli, P., Dengler, W., Wiedemann, G., Montoya, P., Flor, H., Birbaumer, N., & Buchkremer, G. (1997). Behavioral and neuropsychological evidence for altered processing of anxiety-related words in panic disorder. *Journal of Abnormal Psychology, 106,* 213–220.

Paus, T. (2005). Mapping brain maturation and cognitive development during adolescence. *Trends in Cognitive Sciences, 9,* 60–68.

Pavlov, I. P. (1927). *Conditioned reflexes* (G. V. Anrep, Trans.). London, United Kingdom: Oxford University Press.

Pavlov, I. P. (1928). *Lectures on conditioned reflexes: Twenty-five years of objective study of higher nervous activity (behavior of animals)* (Vol. 1, W. H. Gantt, Trans.). New York, NY: International Publishers.

Pederson, D. R., & Moran, G. (1996). Expressions of the attachment relationship outside of the strange situation. *Child Development, 67,* 915–927.

Penick, S., Smith, G., Wienske, K., & Hinkle, L. (1963). An experimental evaluation of the relationship between hunger and gastric motility. *American Journal of Physiology, 205,* 421–426.

Penke, L., Denissen, J. J. A., & Miller, G. F. (2007). The evolutionary genetics of personality. *European Journal of Personality, 21,* 549–587.

Penn, D. L., Guynan, K., Daily, T., Spaulding, W. D., Garbin, C. P., & Sullivan, M. (1994). Dispelling the stigma of schizophrenia: What sort of information is best? *Schizophrenia Bulletin, 20,* 567–578.

Penn, D. L., Kommana, S., Mansfield, M., & Link, B. G. (1999). Dispelling the stigma of schizophrenia: II. The impact of information on dangerousness. *Schizophrenia Bulletin, 25,* 437–446.

Pennebaker, J. W. (1990). *Opening up: The healing power of confiding in others.* New York, NY: Morrow.

Pennebaker, J. W. (1997). Writing about emotional experiences as a therapeutic process. *Psychological Science, 8,* 162–166.

Penner, L. A., Dovidio, J. F., Piliavin, J. A., & Schroeder, D. A. (2005). Prosocial behavior: Multilevel perspectives. *Annual Review of Psychology, 56,* 365–392.

Perahia, D. G. S., Pritchett, Y. L, Kajdasz, D. K., Bauer, M., Jain, R., Russell, J. M., . . . Thase, M. E. (2008). A randomized, double-blind comparison of duloxetine and venlafaxine in the treatment of patients with major depressive disorder. *Journal of Psychiatric Research, 42,* 22–34.

Peretz, I., Brattico, E., Järvenpää, M., & Tervaniemi, M. (2009). The amusic brain: In tune, out of key, and unaware. *Brain, 132*(Pt 5), 1277–1286.

Peretz, I., Cummings, S., Dubé, M. P. (2007). The genetics of congenital amusia (tone deafness): A family-aggregation study. *American Journal of Human Genetics, 81*(3), 582–588. Retrieved from http://www.cell.com/AJHG

Perkins, D. N. (1988). Creativity and the quest for mechanism. In R. J. Sternberg & E. E. Smith (Eds.), *The psychology of human thought* (pp. 309–336). Cambridge, United Kingdom: Cambridge University Press.

Perls, F. S. (1969). *Gestalt therapy verbatim.* Lafayette, CA: Real People Press.

Peters, M. (1995a). Does brain size matter? A reply to Rushton and Ankney. *Canadian Journal of Experimental Psychology, 49,* 570–576.

Peters, M. (1995b). Race differences in brain size: Things are not as clear as they seem to be. *American Psychologist, 50,* 947–948.

Peterson, C., & Seligman, M. E. P. (1984). Causal explanations as a risk factor for depression: Theory and evidence. *Psychological Review, 91,* 347–374.

Peterson, C., & Vaidya, R. S. (2001). Explanatory style, expectations, and depressive symptoms. *Personality and Individual Differences, 31,* 1217–1223.

Peterson, D., & Goodall, J. (1993). *Visions of Caliban: On chimpanzees and people.* Boston, MA: Houghton Mifflin.

Peterson, L. R., & Peterson, M. J. (1959). Short-term retention of individual verbal items. *Journal of Experimental Psychology, 58,* 193–198.

Peterson, R. S., & Nemeth, C. J. (1996). Focus versus flexibility: Majority and minority influence can both improve performance. *Personality and Social Psychology Bulletin, 22,* 14–23.

Petitto, L. A., Katerelos, M., Levy, B. G., Gauna, K., Tetreault, K., & Ferraro, V. (2001). Bilingual signed and spoken language acquisition from birth: Implications for the mechanisms underlying early bilingual language acquisition. *Journal of Child Language, 28*(2), 453–496.

Petrie, K. J., Booth, R. J., & Pennebaker, J. W. (1998). The immunological effects of thought suppression. *Journal of Personality and Social Psychology, 75,* 1264–1272.

Petrie, K. J., Fontanilla, I., Thomas, M. G., Booth, R. J., & Pennebaker, J. W. (2004). Effect of written emotional expression on immune function in patients with human immunodeficiency virus infection: A randomized trial. *Psychosomatic Medicine, 66,* 272–275.

Petry, N. M., Alessi, S. M., Marx, J., Austin, M., & Tardif, M. (2005). Vouchers versus prizes: Contingency management treatment of substance abusers in community settings. *Journal of Consulting and Clinical Psychology, 73,* 1005–1014.

Pettigrew, T. F. (2008). Future directions for intergroup contact theory and research. *International Journal of Intercultural Relations, 32,* 187–199.

Pettigrew, T. F., & Tropp, L. R. (2006). A meta-analytic test of intergroup contact theory. *Journal of Personality and Social Psychology, 90,* 751–783.

Pettigrew, T. F., Christ, O., Wagner, U., & Stellmacher, J. (2007). Direct and indirect intergroup contact effects on prejudice: A normative interpretation. *International Journal of Intercultural Relations, 31,* 41–425.

Petty, R. E., & Briñol, P. (2008). Persuasion: From single to multiple to metacognitive processes. *Perspectives on Psychological Sciences, 3,* 137–147.

Petty, R. E., Cacioppo, J. T., Strathman, A. J., & Priester, J. R. (2005). To think or not to think: Exploring two routes to persuasion. In T. C. Brock & M. C. Green (Eds.), *Persuasion: Psychological insights and perspectives* (2nd ed., pp. 81–116). Thousand Oaks, CA: Sage.

Pfeifer, M., Goldsmith, H. H., Davidson, R. J., & Rickman, M. (2002). Continuity and change in inhibited and uninhibited children. *Child Development, 73,* 1474–1485.

Phillips, D. P. (1993). Representation of acoustic events in primary auditory cortex. *Journal of Experimental Psychology: Human Perception and Performance, 19,* 203–216.

Piaget, J. (1929). *The child's conception of the world.* New York, NY: Harcourt, Brace.

Piaget, J. (1954). *The construction of reality in the child.* New York, NY: Basic Books.

Piaget, J. (1965). *The moral judgment of the child* (M. Gabain, Trans.). New York, NY: Macmillan.

Piaget, J. (1977). *The development of thought: Equilibrium of cognitive structures.* New York, NY: Viking Press.

Piccione, C., Hilgard, E. R., & Zimbardo, P. G. (1989). On the degree of stability of measured hypnotizability over a 25–year period. *Journal of Personality and Social Psychology, 56,* 289–295.

Pilcher, J. J., & Walters, A. S. (1997). How sleep deprivation affects psychological variables related to college students' cognitive performance. *Journal of American College Health, 46,* 121–126.

Pilkonis, P. A., & Zimbardo, P. G. (1979). The personal and social dynamics of shyness. In C. E. Izard (Ed.), *Emotions in personality and psychopathology* (pp. 131–160). New York, NY: Plenum Press.

Pines, A., & Zimbardo, P. G. (1978). The personal and cultural dynamics of shyness: A comparison between Israelis, American Jews and Americans. *Journal of Psychology and Judaism, 3,* 81–101.

Pinker, S. (1994). *The language instinct: How the mind creates language.* New York, NY: Morrow.

Pinker, S. (2007). *How the mind works.* New York, NY: W. W. Norton & Company.

Pinker, S., & Jackendoff, R. (2005). The faculty of language: What's special about it? *Cognition, 95,* 201–236.

Piotrowski, C., Keller, J. W., & Ogawa, T. (1993). Projective techniques: An international perspective. *Psychological Reports, 72,* 179–182.

Pischke, C. R., Scherwitz, L., Weidner, G., & Ornish, D. (2008). Long-term effects of lifestyle changes on well-being and cardiac variables among coronary heart disease patients. *Health Psychology, 27,* 584–592.

Pitts, D. G. (1982). The effects of aging on selected visual functions: Dark adaptation, visual acuity, stereopsis, and brightness contrast. In R. Sekuler, D. Kline, & K. Dismukes (Eds.), *Aging and human visual function* (pp. 131–159). New York, NY: Liss.

Plazzi, G., Vertugno, R., Provini, F., & Montagna, P. (2005). Sleepwalking and other ambulatory behaviours during sleep. *Neurological Sciences, 26,* s193–s198.

Plomin, R., & Petrill, S. A. (1997). Genetics and intelligence: What's new? *Intelligence, 24,* 53–77.

Plomin, R., & Spinath, F. M. (2004). Intelligence: Genetics, genes, and genomics. *Journal of Personality and Social Psychology, 86,* 112–129.

Plomin, R., DeFries, J. C., Craig, I. W., & McGuffin, P. (2003). Behavioral genetics. In R. Plomin, J. C. DeFries, I. W. Craig, & P. McGuffin (Eds.), *Behavioral genetics in the postgenomic era* (pp. 3–15). Washington, DC: American Psychological Association.

Polivy, J., & Herman, C. P. (1999). Distress and eating: Why do dieters overeat? *International Journal of Eating Disorders, 26,* 153–164.

Porter, L. W., & Lawler, E. E. (1968). *Managerial attitudes and performance.* Homewood, IL: Irwin.

Poucet, B. (1993). Spatial cognitive maps in animals: New hypotheses on their structure and neural mechanisms. *Psychological Review, 100,* 163–182.

Poulos, C. X., & Cappell, H. (1991). Homeostatic theory of drug tolerance: A general model of physiological adaptation. *Psychological Review, 98,* 390–408.

Powers, M. B., & Emmelkamp, P. M. G. (2008). Virtual reality exposure therapy for anxiety disorders: A meta-analysis. *Journal of Anxiety Disorders, 22,* 561–569.

Pratt, M. W., Golding, G., Hunter, W., & Norris, J. (1988). From inquiry to judgment: Age and sex differences in patterns of adult moral thinking and information-seeking. *International Journal of Aging and Human Development, 27,* 109–124.

Preckel, F., Hollin, H., & Wiese, M. (2006). Relationship of intelligence and creativity in gifted and non-gifted students: An investigation of threshold theory. *Personality and Individual Differences, 40,* 159–170.

Premack, D. (1965). Reinforcement theory. In D. Levine (Ed.), *Nebraska symposium on motivation* (pp. 128–180). Lincoln, NE: University of Nebraska Press.

Premack, D. (1971). Language in chimpanzee? *Science, 172,* 808–822.

Pressman, L. J., Loo, S. K., Carpenter, E. M., Asarnow, J. R., Lynn, D., McCracken, J. T., McGough, J. J., Lubke, G. H., Yang, M. H., & Smalley, S. L. (2006). Relationship of family environment and parental psychiatric diagnosis to impairment in ADHD. *Journal of the American Academy of Child and Adolescent Psychiatry, 45,* 346–354.

Price, D. D. (2000). Psychological and neural mechanisms of the affective dimension of pain. *Science, 288,* 1769–1772.

Price, R. (1980). *Droodles.* Los Angeles, CA: Price/Stern/Sloan. (Original work published 1953)

Prosser, D., Johnson, S., Kuipers, E., Szmukler, G., Bebbington, P., & Thornicroft, G. (1997). Perceived sources of work stress and satisfaction among hospital and community mental health staff, and their relation to mental health, burnout, and job satisfaction. *Journal of Psychosomatic Research, 43,* 51–59.

Public Health Agency of Canada. (2002a). *A report on mental illnesses in Canada. Chapter 1: An overview.* Retrieved from http://www.phac-aspc.gc.ca/publicat/miic-mmac/chap_1_e.html

Public Health Agency of Canada. (2002b). *A report on mental illness in Canada. Chapter 4: Anxiety Disorders.* Retrieved from http://www.phac-aspc.gc.ca/publicat/miic-mmac/chap_4_e.html

Public Health Agency of Canada. (2002c). *A report on mental illness in Canada. Chapter 2: Mood Disorders.* Retrieved from http://www.phac-aspc.gc.ca/publicat/miic-mmac/chap_2_e.html

Public Health Agency of Canada. (2002d). *A report on mental illness in Canada. Chapter 5: Personality Disorders.* Retrieved from http://www.phac-aspc.gc.ca/publicat/miic-mmac/chap_5_e.html

Public Health Agency of Canada. (2002e). *A report on mental illness in Canada. Chapter 3: Schizophrenia.* Retrieved from http://www.phac-aspc.gc.ca/publicat/miic-mmac/chap_3_e.html

Public Health Agency of Canada. (2003). *Canada's physical activity guide for healthy living.* Retrieved from http://www.phac-aspc.gc.ca/pau-uap/paguide/index.html

Quine, W. V. O. (1960). *Word and object.* Cambridge, MA: The MIT Press.

Quittner, A. L., Modi, A., Lemanek, K. L., Ievers-Landis, C. E., & Rapoff, M. A. (2008). Evidence-based assessment of adherence to medical treatments in pediatric psychology. *Journal of Pediatric Psychology, 33,* 916–936.

Rachlin, H. (1990). Why do people gamble and keep gambling despite heavy losses? *Psychological Science, 1,* 294–297.

Rae-Grant, Q. (Ed.) (2001). *Psychiatry in Canada: 50 years (1951 to 2001).* Ottawa, ON: Canadian Psychiatric Association.

Rahman, Q., & Wilson, G. D. (2003). Born gay? The psychobiology of human sexual orientation. *Personality and Individual Differences, 34,* 1337–1382.

Rajaram, S., & Roediger, H. L., III. (1993). Direct comparison of four implicit memory tests. *Journal of Experimental Psychology: Learning, Memory, and Cognition, 19,* 765–776.

Raleigh, M. J., McGuire, M.T., Brammer, G. L., & Yuwiler, A. (1984). Social and environmental influences on blood serotonin concentration in monkeys. *Archives of General Psychology, 41:*405–410.

Ramírez, J. M., & Andreu, J. M. (2006). Aggression, and some related psychological constructs (anger, hostility, and impulsivity): Some comments from a research project. *Neuroscience and Biobehavioral Reviews, 30,* 276–291.

Rao, S. C., Rainer, G., & Miller, E. K. (1997). Integration of what and where in the primate prefrontal cortex. *Science, 276,* 821–824.

Rapoport, J. L. (1989, March). The biology of obsessions and compulsions. *Scientific American, 260,* 83–89.

Rasmussen, T., & Milner, B. (1977). The role of early left-brain injury in determining lateralization of cerebral speech functions. *Annals of the New York Academy of Sciences, 299,* 355–369.

Ratcliff, R., & McKoon, G. (1978). Priming in item recognition: Evidence for the propositional structure of sentences. *Journal of Verbal Learning and Verbal Behavior, 17,* 403–418.

Rau, H., Bührer, M., & Wietkunat, R. (2003). Biofeedback of R-wave-to-pulse interval normalizes blood pressure. *Applied Psychophysiology and Biofeedback, 28,* 37–46.

Rawson, R. A., Maxwell, J., & Rutkowski, B. (2007). OxyContin abuse: Who are the users? *The American Journal of Psychiatry, 164*(11), 1634–1636.

Ray, W. J., Keil, A., Mikuteit, A., Bongartz, W., & Elbert, T. (2002). High resolution EEG indicators of pain responses in relation to hypnotic susceptibility and suggestion. *Biological Psychology, 60,* 17–36.

Raynor, H. A., & Epstein, L. H. (2001). Dietary variety, energy regulation, and obesity. *Psychological Bulletin, 127,* 325–341.

Raz, A. (2005). Attention and hypnosis: Neural substrates and genetic associations of two converging processes. *International Journal of Clinical and Experimental Hypnosis, 53,* 237–258.

Reb, J. (2008). Regret aversion and decision process quality: Effects of regret salience on decision process carefulness. *Organizational Behavior and Human Decision Processes, 105,* 169–182.

Redelmeier, D. A., & Tibshirani, R. J. (1997). Association between cellular-telephone calls and motor vehicle collisions. *New England Journal of Medicine, 336,* 453–458.

Regan, R. T. (1971). Effects of a favor and liking on compliance. *Journal of Experimental Social Psychology, 7,* 627–639.

Reis, H. T., & Aron, A. (2008). Love: What is it, why does it matter, and how does it operate? *Perspectives on Psychological Science, 3,* 80–86.

Renzulli, J. S. (2005). The three-ring conception of giftedness: A developmental model for promoting creative productivity. In R. J. Sternberg & J. E. Davidson (Eds.), *Conceptions of giftedness* (2nd ed., pp. 246–279). New York, NY: Cambridge University Press.

Rescorla, R. A. (1988). Pavlovian conditioning: It's not what you think it is. *American Psychologist, 43,* 151–160.

Reti, I. M., Samuels, J. F., Eaton, W. W., Bienvenu, O. J., III, Costa, P. T., Jr., & Nestadt, G. (2002). Adult antisocial personality traits are associated with experiences of low paternal care and maternal overprotection. *Acta Psychiatrica Scandinavica, 106,* 126–133.

Reyna, C., & Weiner, B. (2001). Justice and utility in the classroom: An attributional analysis of the goals of teachers' punishment and intervention strategies. *Journal of Educational Psychology, 93,* 309–319.

Reynolds, A. J., Temple, J. A., Robertson, D. L., & Mann, E. A. (2001). Long-term effects of an early childhood intervention on educational achievement and juvenile arrest: A 15-year follow up of low-income children in public schools. *Journal of the American Medical Association, 285,* 2339–2346.

Reynolds, J. S., & Perrin, N. A. (2004). Mismatches in social support and psychosocial adjustment. *Health Psychology, 23,* 425–430.

Rhode, L., & Marotta, J. J. (2006). Specificity differences for learned sensorimotor and perceptual associations. *Journal of Vision, 5*(1), 1–9.

Ribeiro, S. C., Kennedy, S. E., Smith, Y. R., Stohler, C. S., & Zubieta, J. K. (2005). Interface of physical and emotional stress regulation through the endogenous opioid system and μ-opioid receptors. *Progress in Neuro-Psychopharmacology & Biological Psychiatry, 29,* 1264–1280.

Richards, M. H., Crowe, P. A., Larson, R., & Swarr, A. (1998). Developmental patterns and gender differences in the experience of peer companionship during adolescence. *Child Development, 69,* 154–163.

Rinck, M., Hähnel, A., Bower, G. H., & Glowalla, U. (1997). The metrics of spatial situation models. *Journal of Experimental Psychology: Learning, Memory, and Cognition, 23,* 622–637.

Riordan, T. (2004). *The Pathways to Homelessness study as referenced by Riordan, T. (2004). Exploring the circle: Mental illness, homelessness and the criminal justice system in Canada.* Retrieved from http://www2.parl.gc.ca/Content/LOP/ResearchPublications/prb0402–e.htm

Ritchie, P. L.-J. (2004). Annual report of the International Union of Psychological Science (IUPsyS). *International Journal of Psychology, 39,* 231–240.

Rivas-Vazquez, R. A. (2003). Benzodiazepines in contemporary clinical practice. *Professional Psychology: Research and Practice, 34,* 424–428.

Roberts, A. H., Kewman, D. G., Mercier, L., & Hovell, M. (1993). The power of nonspecific effects in healing: Implications for psychosocial and biological treatments. *Clinical Psychology Review, 13,* 375–391.

Roberts, A., Cash, T. F., Feingold, A., & Johnson, B. T. (2006). Are Black–White differences in females' body dissatisfaction decreasing? A meta-analytic review. *Journal of Consulting and Clinical Psychology, 74,* 1121–1131.

Rochlen, A. B., Zack, J. S., & Speyer, C. (2004). Online therapy: Review of relevant definitions, debates, and current empirical support. *Journal of Clinical Psychology, 60*(3), 269–283.

Rodd, J. M., Davis, M. H., & Johnsrude, I. S. (2005). The neural mechanisms of speech comprehension: fMRI studies of semantic ambiguity. *Cerebral Cortex, 15,* 1261–1269.

Rode, J. C., Mooney, C. H., Arthaud-Day, M. L., Near, J. P., Baldwin, T. T., Rubin, R. S., & Boomer, W. H. (2007). Emotional intelligence and individual performance: Evidence of direct and moderated effects. *Journal of Organizational Behavior, 28,* 399–421.

Roediger, H. L., III, Gallo, D. A., & Geraci, L. (2002). Processing approaches to cognition: The impetus from the levels-of-processing framework. *Memory, 10,* 319–332.

Roesch, R., Ogloff, J. R. P., Hart, S. D., Dempster, R. J., Zapf, P. A., & Whittemore, K. E. (1997). The impact of Canadian Criminal Code changes on remands and assessments of fitness to stand trial and criminal responsibility in British Columbia. *Canadian Journal of Psychiatry, 42,* 509–514.

Roese, N. J., & Summerville, A. (2005). What we regret most . . . and why. *Personality and Social Psychology Bulletin, 31,* 1273–1285.

Rogers, C. R. (1947). Some observations on the organization of personality. *American Psychologist, 2,* 358–368.

Rogers, C. R. (1951). *Client-centered therapy: Its current practice, implications and theory.* Boston, MA: Houghton Mifflin.

Rogers, C. R. (1959). A theory of therapy, personality, and interpersonal relationships, as developed in the client-centered framework. In S. Koch (Ed.), *Psychology: A study of a science* (Vol. 3). New York, NY: McGraw-Hill.

Rogers, C. R. (1977). *On personal power: Inner strength and its revolutionary impact.* New York, NY: Delacorte.

Rogers, S. (1993). How a publicity blitz created the myth of subliminal advertising. *Public Relations Quarterly, 37,* 12–17.

Rogoff, B. (1990). *Apprenticeship in thinking: Cognitive development in social context.* New York, NY: Oxford University Press.

Rogoff, B. (2003). *The cultural nature of human development.* London, United Kingdom: Oxford University Press.

Rogoff, B., & Chavajay, P. (1995). What's become of research on the cultural basis of cognitive development? *American Psychologist, 50,* 859–877.

Rohrer, J. H., Baron, S. H., Hoffman, E. L., & Swinder, D. V. (1954). The stability of autokinetic judgment. *Journal of Abnormal and Social Psychology, 49,* 595–597.

Roid, G. (2003). *Stanford–Binet intelligence scale* (5th ed.). Itasca, IL: Riverside Publishing.

Rollman, G. B. (2004). Ethnocultural variations in the experience of pain. In T. Hadjistavropoulos and K. D. Craig (Eds.), *Pain: Psychological perspectives* (pp. 155–178). Mahwah, NJ: Lawrence Erlbaum.

Rolls, E. T. (2000). Memory systems in the brain. *Annual Review of Psychology, 51,* 599–630.

Romach, M. K., Sellers, E. M., Somer, G. R., Landry, M., Cunningham, G. M., Jovey, R. D., . . . Ryan, D. (2002). Naltrexone in the treatment of alcohol dependence: A Canadian trial. *Canadian Journal of Clinical Pharmacology, 9*(3), 130–136.

Romer, M., Lehrner, J., Wymelbeke, V. V., Jiang, T., Deecke, L. & Brondel, L. (2006). Does modification of olfacto-gustatory stimulation diminish sensory-specific satiety in humans? *Physiology & Behavior, 87,* 469–477.

Rorschach, H. (1942). *Psychodiagnostics: A diagnostic test based on perception.* New York, NY: Grune & Stratton.

Rosch, E. H. (1973). Natural categories. *Cognitive Psychology, 4,* 328–350.

Rosch, E. H. (1978). Principles of categorization. In E. Rosch & B. B. Lloyd (Eds.), *Cognition and categorization* (pp. 27–48). Hillsdale, NJ: Erlbaum.

Rosch, E. H., Mervis, C. B., Gray, W. D., Johnson, D. M., & Boyes-Braem, P. (1976). Basic objects in natural categories. *Cognitive Psychology, 8,* 382–439.

Rosch, E., & Mervis, C. B. (1975). Family resemblances: Studies in the internal structure of categories. *Cognitive Psychology, 7,* 573–605.

Rose, A. J., & Rudolph, K. D. (2006). A review of sex-differences in peer relationship processes: Potential trade-offs for the emotional and behavioral development of girls and boys. *Psychological Bulletin, 132,* 98–131.

Rose, M. E., & Grant, J. E. (2008). Pharmacotherapy for methamphetamine dependence: A review of the pathophysiology of methamphetamine addiction and the theoretical basis and efficacy of pharmacotherapeutic interventions. *Annals of Clinical Psychiatry, 20,* 145–155.

Rosenfield, S. (1997). Labeling mental illness: The effects of received services and perceived stigma on life satisfaction. *American Sociological Review, 62,* 660–672.

Rosenhan, D. L. (1973). On being sane in insane places. *Science, 179,* 250–258.

Rosenhan, D. L. (1975). The contextual nature of psychiatric diagnoses. *Journal of Abnormal Psychology, 84,* 462–474.

Rosenkoetter, L. I. (1999). The television situation comedy and children's prosocial behavior. *Journal of Applied Social Psychology, 29,* 979–993.

Rosenthal, A. M. (1964). *Thirty-eight witnesses.* New York, NY: McGraw-Hill.

Rosenthal, R. (1974). *On the social psychology of the self-fulfilling prophecy: Further evidence for Pygmalion effects and their mediating mechanisms.* New York, NY: MSS Modular Publications.

Rosenthal, R., & Fode, K. L. (1963). The effect of experimenter bias on the performance of the albino rat. *Behavioral Science, 8,* 183–189.

Rosenthal, R., & Jacobson, L. F. (1968). *Pygmalion in the classroom: Teacher expectations and intellectual development.* New York, NY: Holt.

Rosenzweig, M. R. (1996). Aspects of the search for neural mechanisms of memory. *Annual Review of Psychology, 47,* 1–32.

Rosenzweig, M. R. (1999). Effects of differential experience on brain and cognition throughout the life span. In S. H. Broman & J. M. Fletcher (Eds.), *The changing nervous system: Neurobehavioral consequences of early brain disorders* (pp. 25–50). New York, NY: Oxford University Press.

Ross, L. (1977). The intuitive psychologist and his shortcomings. In L. Berkowitz (Ed.), *Advances in experimental social psychology* (Vol. 10, pp. 173–220). New York, NY: Academic Press.

Ross, L. (1988). Situational perspectives on the obedience experiments. [Review of the obedience experiments: A case study of controversy in social science]. *Contemporary Psychology, 33,* 101–104.

Ross, L., & Nisbett, R. E. (1991). *The person and the situation: Perspectives of social psychology.* New York, NY: McGraw-Hill.

Ross, L., Amabile, T., & Steinmetz, J. (1977). Social roles, social control and biases in the social perception process. *Journal of Personality and Social Psychology, 37,* 485–494.

Rothbaum, B. O., Anderson, P., Zimand, E., Hodges, L., Lang, D., & Wilson, J. (2006). Virtual reality exposure therapy and standard (in vivo) exposure therapy in the treatment of fear of flying. *Behavior Therapy, 37,* 80–90.

Rothman, D. J. (1971). *The discovery of the asylum: Social order and disorder in the new republic.* Boston, MA: Little, Brown.

Rotter, J. B. (1954). *Social learning and clinical psychology.* Englewood Cliffs, NJ: Prentice-Hall.

Rotter, J. B. (1966). Generalized expectancies for internal versus external locus of control of reinforcement. *Psychological Monographs, 80* (Whole No. 609).

Rouse, S. V., Greene, R. L. Butcher, J. N., Nichols, D. S., & Williams, C. L. (2008). What do the MMPI-2 Restructured Clinical Scales reliably measure? Answers from multiple research settings. *Journal of Personality Assessment, 90,* 435–442.

Roussi, P. (2002). Discriminative facility in perceptions of control and its relation to psychological distress. *Anxiety, Stress, & Coping: An International Journal, 15,* 179–191.

Roussi, P., Krikeli, V., Hatzidimitriou, C., & Koutri, I. (2007). Patterns of coping, flexibility in coping and psychological distress in women diagnosed with breast cancer. *Cognitive Therapy and Research, 31,* 97–109.

Rowe, D. C. (1997). A place at the policy table? Behavior genetics and estimates of family environmental effects on IQ. *Intelligence, 24,* 133–158.

Rozin, P., & Fallon, A. E. (1987). A perspective on disgust. *Psychological Review, 94,* 23–41.

Rozin, P., Millman, L., & Nemeroff, C. (1986). Operation of the laws of sympathetic magic in disgust and other domains. *Journal of Personality and Social Psychology, 50,* 703–712.

Rubin, D. C., & Kontis, T. C. (1983). A schema for common cents. *Memory & Cognition, 11,* 335–341.

Rubin, J. Z., Provenzano, F. J., & Luria, Z. (1974). The eye of the beholder: Parents' views on sex of newborns. *American Journal of Orthopsychiatry, 44,* 512–519.

Ruch, R. (1937). *Psychology and life.* Glenview, IL: Scott, Foresman.

Rudd, M. D., Berman, A. L., Joiner, T. E., Jr., Nock, M. K., Silverman, M. M., Mandrusiak, M., Van Orden, K., & Witte, T. (2006). Warning signs for suicide: Theory, research, and clinical applications. *Suicide and Life-Threatening Behavior, 36,* 255–262.

Rudolph, U., Roesch, S. C., Greitemeyer, T., & Weiner, B. (2004). A meta-analytic review of help giving and aggression from an attributional perspective: Contributions to a general theory of motivation. *Cognition & Emotion, 18*(6), 815–848.

Ruitenbeek, H. M. (1973). *The first Freudians.* New York, NY: Jason Aronson.

Rule, N. O., & Ambady, N. (2008). The face of success: Inferences from chief executive officers' appearance predict company profits. *Psychological Science, 19,* 109–111.

Runco, M. A. (1991). *Divergent thinking.* Norwood, NJ: Ablex.

Runco, M. A. (2007). *Creativity: Theories and themes: Research, development, and practice.* San Diego, CA: Elsevier Academic Press.

Runco, M. A. (2008). Commentary: Divergent thinking is not synonymous with creativity. *Psychology of Aesthetics, Creativity and the Arts, 2,* 93–96.

Rundle, H. D., Nagel, L., Boughman, J. W., & Schluter, D. (2000). Natural selection and parallel speciation in sympatric sticklebacks. *Science, 287,* 306–308.

Rushton, J. P. & Jensen, A. R. (2005). Thirty years of research on race differences in cognitive ability. *Psychology, Public Policy, and Law, 11,* 235–294.

Rushton, J. P. (1991). Mongoloid-caucasoid differences in brain size from military samples. *Intelligence, 15,* 351–359.

Rushton, J. P. (1992). Contributions to the history of psychology: XC.Evolutionary biology and heritable traits (with reference to oriental-white-black differences). *Psychological Reports, 71,* 811–821.

Rushton, J. P. (1995). *Race evolution & behavior.* New Brunswick, NJ: Transaction Publishers.

Rushton, J. P. (1998). The new enemies of evolutionary science. *Liberty, 4,* 31–35.

Rushton, J. P. (1999). *Race evolution & behavior (Special abridged edition).* New Brunswick, NJ: Transaction Publishers.

Russo, F. A., & Thompson, W. F. (2005). An interval size illusion: The influence of timbre on the perceived size of melodic intervals. *Perception & Psychophysics, 67,* 559–568.

Russo, N. F., & Denmark, F. L. (1987). Contributions of women to psychology. *Annual Review of Psychology, 38,* 279–298.

Rutter, P. A., & Behrendt, A. E. (2004). Adolescent suicide risk: Four psychosocial factors. *Adolescence, 39,* 295–302.

Ryder, R. D. (2006). Speciesism in the laboratory. In P. Singer (Ed.), *In defense of animals: The second wave.* (pp. 87–103). Malden, MA: Blackwell Publishing.

Ryff, C. D. (1989). In the eye of the beholder: Views of psychological well-being among middle-aged and older adults. *Psychology and Aging, 4,* 195–210.

Sachdev, P., Mondraty, N., Wen, W., & Gulliford, K. (2008). Brains of anorexia nervosa patients process self-images differently from non-self-images: An fMRI study. *Neuropsychologia, 46,* 2161–2168.

Sagi, A., Koren-Karie, N., Gini, M., Ziv, Y., & Joels, T. (2002). Shedding further light on the effects of various types and quality of early child care on infant-mother attachment relationship: The Haifa Study of Early Child Care. *Child Development, 73,* 1166–1186.

Sak, U. (2004). A synthesis of research on psychological types of gifted adolescents. *Journal of Secondary Gifted Education, 15,* 70–79.

Salihu, H. M., & Wilson, R. E. (2007). Epidemiology of prenatal smoking and perinatal outcomes. *Early Human Development, 83*(11), 713–720.

Salloway, S., Mintzer, J., Weiner, M. R., & Cummings, J. L. (2008). Disease-modifying therapies in Alzheimer's disease. *Alzheimer's & Dementia, 4,* 65–79.

Salvy, S.-J., Jarrin, D., Paluch, R., Irfan, N., & Pliner, P. (2007). Effects of social influence on eating in couples, friends and strangers. *Appetite, 49,* 92–99.

Salvy, S.-J., Kieffer, E., & Epstein, L. H. (2008). Effects of social context on overweight and normal-weight children's food selection. *Eating Behaviors, 9,* 190–196.

Salzinger, S., Ng-Mak, D. S., Feldman, R. S., Kam, C. M., & Rosario, M. (2006). Exposure to community violence: Processes that increase the risk for inner-city middle school children. *Journal of Early Adolescence, 26,* 232–266.

Samuel, A. G. (1981). Phonemic restoration: Insights from a new methodology. *Journal of Experimental Psychology: General, 110,* 474–494.

Samuel, A. G. (1991). A further examination of attentional effects in the phonemic restoration illusion. *Quarterly Journal of Experimental Psychology: Human Experimental Psychology, 43A,* 679–699.

Samuel, A. G. (1997). Lexical activation produces potent phonemic percepts. *Cognitive Psychology, 32,* 97–127.

Sanderson, C. A., Rahm, K. B., & Beigbeder, S. A. (2005). The link between pursuit of intimacy goals and satisfaction in close same-sex friendships: An examination of the underlying processes. *Journal of Social and Personal Relationships, 22,* 75–98.

Sandstrom, M. J., & Cramer, P. (2003). Girls' use of defense mechanisms following peer rejection. *Journal of Personality, 71,* 605–627.

Sapir, E. (1964). *Culture, language, and personality.* Berkeley, CA: University of California Press. (Original work published 1941)

Sapolsky, R. M. (1994). *Why zebras don't get ulcers: A guide to stress, stress-related disease, and coping.* New York, NY: Freeman.

Satir, V. (1967). *Conjoint family therapy* (Rev. ed.). Palo Alto, CA: Science and Behavior Books.

Saucier, D. M., Green, S. M., Leason, J, MacFadden, A., Bell, S., & Elias, L. J. (2002). Are sex differences in navigation caused by sexually dimorphic strategies or by differences in the ability to use the strategies? *Behavioral Neuroscience, 116*(3), 403–410.

Savage-Rumbaugh, S., Shanker, S. G., & Taylor, T. J. (1998). *Apes, language, and the human mind.* New York, NY: Oxford University Press.

Savic, I., & Lindström, P. (2008). PET and MRI show differences in cerebral asymmetry and functional connectivity between homo- and heterosexual subjects. *PNAS, 105,* 9403–9408.

Scarborough, E., & Furumoto, L. (1987). *Untold lives: The first generation of American women psychologists.* New York, NY: Columbia University Press.

Scarr, S. (1998). American child care today. *American Psychologist, 53,* 95–108.

Scarr, S., & Eisenberg, M. (1993). Child care research: Issues, perspectives, and results. *Annual Review of Psychology, 44,* 613–644.

Schachter, S. (1971a). Some extraordinary facts about obese humans and rats. *American Psychologist, 26,* 129–144.

Schachter, S. (1971b). *Emotion, obesity and crime.* New York, NY: Academic Press.

Schaie, K. W. (2005). *Developmental influences on adult intelligence: The Seattle longitudinal study.* New York, NY: Oxford University Press.

Schalock, R. L., Luckasson R. A., Shogren, K. A., Borthwick-Duffy, S., Bradley, V., Buntinx, W. H., . . . Yeager, M. H. (2007). The renaming of mental retardation: Understanding the change to the term intellectual disability. *Intellectual and Developmental Disabilities, 45*(2), 116–124.

Schiff, M., & Bargal, D. (2000). Helping characteristics of self-help and support groups: Their contribution to participants' subjective well-being. *Small Group Research, 31,* 275–304.

Schlenger, W. E., Caddell, J. M., Ebert, L., Jordan, B. K., Rourke, K. M., Wilson, D., . . . Kulka, R. A. (2002). Psychological reactions to terrorist attacks: Findings from the National Study of Americans' reactions to September 11. *JAMA, 288,* 581–588.

Schlitz, M. (1997). *Dreaming for the community: Subjective experience and collective action among the Anchuar Indians of Ecuador.* Research proposal. Marin, CA: Institute of Noetic Sciences.

Schmader, T., Johns, M., & Forbes, C. (2008). An integrated process model of stereotype threat effects on performance. *Psychological Review, 115,* 336–356.

Schmitt, D. P. (2003). Universal sex differences in desire for sexual variety: Tests from 52 nations, 6 continents, and 13 islands. *Journal of Personality and Social Psychology, 85,* 85–104.

Schneider, K., & May, R. (1995). *The psychology of existence: An integrative, clinical perspective.* New York, NY: McGraw-Hill.

Scholnick, E. K., Nelson, K., Gelman, S. A., & Miller, P. H. (1999). *Conceptual development: Piaget's legacy.* Mahwah, NJ: Erlbaum.

Scholz, U., Schüz, B., Ziegelmann, J., Lippke, S., & Schwarzer, R. (2008). Beyond behavioural intentions: Planning mediates between intentions and physical activity. *British Journal of Health Psychology, 13,* 479–494.

Schousboe, K., Visscher, P. M., Erbas, B., Kyvik, K. O., Hopper, J. L., Henriksen, J. E., . . . Sørensen, T. I. A. (2004). Twin study of genetic and environmental influences on adult body size, shape, and composition. *International Journal of Obesity, 28,* 39–48.

Schredl, M., & Erlacher, D. (2008). Relation between waking sport activities, reading, and dream content in sport students and psychology students. *Journal of Psychology: Interdisciplinary and Applied, 142*(3), 267–275.

Schultz, R., Braun, R. G., & Kluft, R. P. (1989). Multiple personality disorder: Phenomenology of selected variables in comparison to major depression. *Dissociation, 2,* 45–51.

Schutter, D. J. L. G. (2008). Antidepressant efficacy of high-frequency transcranial magnetic stimulation over the left dorsolateral prefrontal cortex in double-blind sham-controlled designs: A meta-analysis. *Psychological Medicine, 39,* 65–75.

Schützwohl, A. (2006). Sex differences in jealousy: Information search and cognitive preoccupation. *Personality and Individual Differences, 40,* 285–292.

Schwab, C., Bugnyar, T., & Kotrschal, K. (2008). Preferential learning from non-affiliated individuals in jackdaws (*Corvus monedula*). *Behavioural Processes, 79*(3), 148–155.

Schwartz, B., Ward, A., Monterosso, J., Lyubomirsky, S., White, K., & Lehman, D. R. (2002). Maximizing versus satisficing: Happiness is a matter of choice. *Journal of Personality and Social Psychology, 83,* 1178–1197.

Schwarz, N., Bless, H., Wänke, M., & Winkielman, P. (2003). Accessibility revisited. In G. V. Bodenhausen & A. J. Lambert (Eds.), *Foundations of social cognition: A festschrift in honor of Robert S. Wyer* (pp. 51–77). Mahwah, NJ: Erlbaum.

Schweinhart, L. J. (2004). *The High/Scope Perry preschool study through age 40: Summary, conclusions, and frequently asked questions.* Retrieved from http: //www.highscope.org/Research/PerryProject/PerryAge40SumWeb.pdf

Sciutto, M. J., & Eisenberg, M. (2007). Evaluating the evidence for and against the overdiagnosis of ADHD. *Journal of Attention Disorders, 11,* 106–113.

Scott, D., Scott, L. M., & Goldwater, B. (1997). A performance improvement program for an international-level track and field athlete. *Journal of Applied Behavior Analysis, 30,* 573–575.

Scott, S. K., Young, A. W., Calder, A. J., Hellawell, D. J., Aggleton, J. P., & Johnsons, M. (1997). Impaired auditory recognition of fear and anger following bilateral amygdala lesions. *Nature, 385*(6613), 254–257.

Scoville, W. B., & Milner, B. (1957). Loss of recent memory after bilateral hippocampal lesions. *Journal of Neurology, Neurosurgery and Psychiatry, 20,* 11–21.

Scull, A. (1993). *A most solitary of afflictions: Madness and society in Britain 1700–1900.* London, United Kingdom: Yale University Press.

Seal, D. S., Smith, M., Coley. B., Perry, J., & Gamez, M. (2008). Urban heterosexual couples' sexual scripts for three shared sexual experiences. *Sex Roles, 58,* 626–638.

Sealy, P., & Whitehead, P. C. (2004). Forty years of deinstitutionalization of psychiatric services in Canada: An empirical assessment. *Canadian Journal of Psychiatry, 49*(4), 249–257.

Seamon, J. G., Philbin, M. M., & Harrison, L. G. (2006). Do you remember proposing marriage to the Pepsi machine? False recollections from a campus walk. *Psychonomic Bulletin & Review, 13*(5), 752–756.

Sear, R., & Mace, R. (2008). Who keeps children alive? A review of the effects of kin on child survival. *Evolution and Human Behavior, 29,* 1–18.

Searle, J. R. (1979). Literal meaning. In J. R. Searle (Ed.), *Expression and meaning* (pp. 117–136). Cambridge, United Kingdom: Cambridge University Press.

Sears, S. R., Stanton, A. L., & Danoff-Burg, S. (2003). The yellow brick road and the Emerald City: Benefit finding, positive reappraisal coping, and posttraumatic growth in women with early-stage breast cancer. *Health Psychology, 22,* 487–497.

Sedikides, C., & Gregg, A. P. (2008). Self-enhancement: Food for thought. *Perspectives on Psychological Science, 3,* 102–116.

Sedikides, C., Gaertner, L., & Toguchi, Y. (2003). Pancultural self-enhancement. *Journal of Personality and Social Psychology, 84,* 60–79.

Segerstrom, S. C. (2005). Optimism and immunity: Do positive thoughts always lead to positive effects? *Brain, Behavior, and Immunity, 19,* 195–200.

Segerstrom, S. C. (2006). How does optimism suppress immunity? Evaluation of three affective pathways. *Health Psychology, 25,* 653–657.

Segerstrom, S. C. (2007). Stress, energy, and immunity. *Current Directions in Psychological Science, 16,* 326–330.

Seidenberg, M. S., & Petitto, L. A. (1979). Signing behavior in apes: A critical review. *Cognition, 7,* 177–215.

Seidler, R. D., Purushotham, A., Kim S. G., Ugurbil, K., Willingham, D., & Ashe, J. (2002). Cerebellum activation associated with performance change but no motor learning. *Science, 296,* 2043–2046.

Sekuler, R., & Blake, R. (2001). *Perception* (4th ed.). New York, NY: McGraw-Hill.

Selfridge, O. G. (1955). Pattern recognition and modern computers. *Proceedings of the Western Joint Computer Conference.* New York, NY: Institute of Electrical and Electronics Engineers.

Seligman, M. E. P. (1975). *Helplessness: On depression, development, and death.* San Francisco, CA: Freeman.

Seligman, M. E. P. (1991). *Learned optimism.* New York, NY: Norton.

Seligman, M. E. P., & Maier, S. F. (1967). Failure to escape traumatic shock. *Journal of Experimental Psychology, 74,* 1–9.

Seligman, M. E. P., Steen, T. A., Park, N., & Peterson, C. (2005). Positive psychology progress: Empirical validation of interventions. *American Psychologist, 60,* 410–421.

Selye, H. (1976a). *Stress in health and disease.* Reading, MA: Butterworth.

Selye, H. (1976b). *The stress of life* (2nd ed.). New York, NY: McGraw-Hill.

Serpell, R. (2000). Intelligence and culture. In R. J. Sternberg (Ed.), *Handbook of intelligence* (pp. 549–577). Cambridge, United Kingdom: Cambridge University Press.

Serpell, R., & Boykin, A. W. (1994). Cultural dimensions of cognition: A multiplex, dynamic system of constraints and possibilities. In R. J. Sternberg (Ed.), *Handbook of perception and cognition: Vol. 2. Thinking and problem solving* (pp. 369–408). Orlando, FL: Academic Press.

Sevdalis, N., & Harvey, N. (2007). Biased forecasting of postdecisional affect. *Psychological Science, 18,* 678–681.

Shafir, E. (1993). Choosing versus rejecting: Why some options are both better and worse than others. *Memory & Cognition, 21,* 546–556.

Sharpsteen, D. J., & Kirkpatrick, L. A. (1997). Romantic jealousy and adult romantic attachment. *Journal of Personality and Social Psychology, 72,* 627–640.

Shaver, P. R., & Hazan, C. (1994). Attachment. In A. L. Weber & J. H. Harvey (Eds.), *Perspectives on close relationships* (pp. 110– 130). Boston, MA: Allyn & Bacon.

Shaw, M., & Black, D. W. (2008). Internet addiction: Definition, assessment, epidemiology and clinical management. *CNS Drugs, 22*, 353–365.

Shaywitz, B. A., Shaywitz, S. E., Pugh, K. R., Constable, R. T., Skudlarski, P., Fulbright, R. K., . . . Gores, J. C. (1995). Sex differences in the functional organization of the brain for language. *Nature. 373*(6515): 607–609.

Sheehan, E. P. (1993). The effects of turnover on the productivity of those who stay. *Journal of Social Psychology, 133*, 699–706.

Sheehy, R., & Horan, J. J. (2004). Effects of stress inoculation training for 1st-year law students. *International Journal of Stress Management, 11*, 41–55.

Sheets, V. L., & Lugar, R. (2005). Sources of conflict between friends in Russia and the United States. *Cross-Cultural Research, 39*, 380–398.

Sheldon, W. (1942). *The varieties of temperament: A psychology of constitutional differences.* New York, NY: Harper.

Shepard, R. N. (1978). Externalization of mental images and the act of creation. In B. S. Randhawa & W. E. Coffman (Eds.), *Visual learning, thinking, and communicating.* New York, NY: Academic Press.

Shepard, R. N. (1984). Ecological constraints on internal representation: Resonant kinematics of perceiving, imagining, thinking and dreaming. *Psychological Review, 91*, 417–447.

Shepard, R., & Cooper, L. (1982). *Mental images and their transformations.* Cambridge, MA: MIT Press.

Sheppard, L. D., & Vernon, P. A. (2008). Intelligence and speed of information-processing: A review of 50 years of research. *Personality and Individual Differences, 44*, 535–551.

Sher, K. J., Bartholow, B. D., & Wood, M. D. (2000). Personality and substance use disorders: A prospective study. *Journal of Consulting and Clinical Psychology, 68*, 818–829.

Sherif, C. W. (1981, August). *Social and psychological bases of social psychology.* The G. Stanley Hall Lecture on social psychology, presented at the annual convention of the American Psychological Association, Los Angeles, 1961.

Sherif, M. (1935). A study of some social factors in perception. *Archives of Psychology, 27*(187), 1–60.

Sherif, M., Harvey, O. J., White, B. J., Hood, W. R., & Sherif, C. W. (1988). *The Robbers Cave experiment: Intergroup conflict and cooperation.* Middletown, CT: Wesleyan University Press. (Original work published 1961)

Shettleworth, S. J. (1993). Where is the comparison in comparative cognition? *Psychological Science, 4*, 179–184.

Shevlin, M., Houston, J. E., Dorahy, M. J., & Adamson, G. (2008). Cumulative traumas and psychosis: An analysis of the National Comorbidity Study and the British Psychiatric Morbidity Survey. *Schizophrenia Bulletin, 34*, 8193–199.

Shi, J., Gershon, E. S., & Liu, C. (2008). Genetic associations with schizophrenia: Meta-analyses of 12 candidate genes. *Schizophrenia Research, 104*, 96–107.

Shields, D. C., Asaad, W., Eskandar, E. N., Jain, F. A., Cosgrove, G. R., Flaherty, A. W., . . . Dougherty, D. D. (2008). Prospective assessment of stereotactic ablative surgery for intractable major depression. *Biological Psychiatry, 64*, 449–454.

Shields, M. (2006). Overweight and obesity among children and youth. *Health Report, 17*(3), 27–42.

Shiffrar, M. (1994). When what meets where. *Current Directions in Psychological Science, 3*, 96–100.

Shiffrin, R. M. (2003). Modeling memory and perception. *Cognitive Science, 27*, 341–378.

Shiffrin, R. M., & Schneider, W. (1977). Controlled and automatic human information processing: II. Perceptual learning, automatic attending, and a general theory. *Psychological Review, 84*, 127–190.

Shih, J. H., Eberhart, N. K., Hammen, C. L., & Brennan, P. A (2006). Differential exposure and reactivity to interpersonal stress predict sex differences in adolescent depression. *Journal of Clinical Child and Adolescent Psychology, 35*, 103–115.

Shimamura, A. P., Berry, J. M., Mangels, J. A., Rusting, C. L., & Jurica, P. J. (1995). Memory and cognitive abilities in university professors: Evidence for successful aging. *Psychological Science, 6*, 271–277.

Shneidman, E. S. (1987, March). At the point of no return. *Psychology Today*, 54–59.

Shoda, Y., Mischel, W., & Wright, J. C. (1993a). The role of situational demands and cognitive competencies in behavior organization and personality coherence. *Journal of Personality and Social Psychology, 65*, 1023–1035.

Shorter, L., Brown, S. L., Quinton, S. J., & Hinton, L. (2008). Relationships between body-shape discrepancies with favored celebrities and disordered eating in young women. *Journal of Applied Social Psychology, 38*, 1364–1377.

Sia, T. L., Lord, C. G., Blessum, K. A., Ratcliff, C. D., & Lepper, M. R. (1997). Is a rose always a rose? The role of social category exemplar change in attitude stability and attitude-behavior consistency. *Journal of Personality and Social Psychology, 72*, 501–514.

Siegel, J. M. (2005). Clues to the functions of mammalian sleep. *Nature, 437*, 1264–1271.

Siegel, P. H., Schraeder, M., & Morrison, R. (2008). A taxonomy of equity factors. *Journal of Applied Social Psychology, 38*, 61–75.

Siegel, S. (1984). Pavlovian conditioning and heroin overdose: Reports by overdose victims. *Bulletin of the Psychonomic Society, 22*, 428–430.

Siegel, S., & Ramos, B. M. (2002). Applying laboratory research: Drug anticipation and the treatment of drug addiction. *Experimental Clinical Psychopharmaology, 10*(3), 162–183. Review.

Siegel, S., Hinson, R. E., Krank, M. D., & McCully, J. (1982). Heroin "overdose" death: The contribution of drug-associated environmental cues. *Science, 216*, 436–437.

Siever, L. J. (2008). Neurobiology of aggression and violence. *American Journal of Psychiatry, 165*, 429–442.

Sigmon, S. T., Pells, J. J., Edenfield, T. M., Hermann, B. A., Scharter, J. G., LaMattina, S. M., & Boulard, N. E. (2007). Are we there yet? A review of gender comparisons in three behavioral journals through the 20th century. *Behavior Therapy, 38*, 333–339.

Silasi, G., Hamilton, D. A., & Kolb, B. (2008). Social instability blocks functional restitution following motor cortex stroke in rats. *Behavioural Brain Research, 188*, 219–226.

Silventoinen, K., Pietiläinen, K. H., Tynelius, P., Sørensen, T. I. A., Kaprio, J., & Rasmussen, F. (2007). Genetic and environmental factors in relative weight from birth to age 18: The Swedish young male twins study. *International Journal of Obesity, 31*, 615–621.

Silventoinen, K., Posthuma, D., van Beijsterveldt, T., Bartels, M., Boomsma, D. I. (2006). Genetic contributions to the association between height and intelligence: Evidence from Dutch twin data from childhood to middle age. *Genes, Brain and Behavior, 5,* 585–595.

Simmons, J. A., Ferragamo, M. J., & Moss, C. F. (1998). Echo-delay resolution in sonar images of the big brown bat, *Eptesicus fuscus. Proceedings of the National Academy of Sciences of the United States, 95,* 12647–12652.

Simon, H. A. (1973). The structure of ill-structured problems. *Artificial Intelligence, 4,* 181–202.

Simon, H. A. (1979). *Models of thought* (Vol. 1). New Haven, CT: Yale University Press.

Simon, H. A. (1989). *Models of thought* (Vol. 2). New Haven, CT: Yale University Press.

Simons, D. J. (1996). In sight, out of mind: When object representations fail. *Psychological Science, 7,* 301–305.

Simons, D. J., & Ambinder, M. S. (2005). Change blindness: Theory and consequences. *Current Directions in Psychological Science, 14,* 44–48.

Sinclair, R. C., Hoffman, C., Mark, M. M., Martin, L. L., & Pickering, T. L. (1994). Construct accessibility and the misattribution of arousal: Schachter and Singer revisited. *Psychological Science, 5,* 15–19.

Singer, D. G., & Singer, J. L. (1990). *The house of make-believe.* Cambridge, MA: Harvard University Press.

Singer, L. T., Arendt, R., Minnes, S., Farkas, K., Salvator, A., Kirchner, H. L., & Kliegman, R. (2002). Cognitive and motor outcomes of cocaine-exposed infants. *Journal of the American Medical Association, 287,* 1952–1960.

Singer, T., Verhaegen, P., Ghisletta, P., Lindenberger, U., & Baltes, P. B. (2003). The fate of cognition in very old age: Six-year longitudinal findings in the Berlin Aging Study (BASE). *Psychology & Aging, 18,* 318–331.

Sireteanu, R. (1999). Switching on the infant brain. *Science, 286,* 59–61.

Skinner, B. F. (1938). *The behavior of organisms.* New York, NY: Appleton-Century-Crofts.

Skinner, B. F. (1953). *Science and human behavior.* New York, NY: Macmillan.

Skinner, B. F. (1966). What is the experimental analysis of behavior? *Journal of the Experimental Analysis of Behavior, 9,* 213–218.

Skinner, B. F. (1990). Can psychology be a science of mind? *American Psychologist, 45,* 1206–1210.

Skodol, A. E., Pagano, M. E., Bender, D. S., Shea, M. T., Gunderson, J. G., Yen, S., . . . McGlashan, T. H. (2005). Stability of functional impairment in patients with schizotypal, borderline, avoidant, or obsessive-compulsive personality disorder over two years. *Psychological Medicine, 35,* 443–451.

Slivia, P. J. (2008a). Another look at creativity and intelligence: Exploring higher-order mental models and probable confounds. *Personality and Individual Differences, 44,* 1012–1021.

Slivia, P. J. (2008b). Discernment and creativity: How well can people identify their most creative ideas? *Psychology of Aesthetics, Creativity and the Arts, 2,* 139–146.

Sloane, R. B., Staples, F. R., Cristol, A. H., Yorkston, N. J., & Whipple, K. (1975). *Psychotherapy versus behavior therapy.* Cambridge, MA: Harvard University Press.

Slobin, D. I. (1982). Universal and particular in the acquisition of language. In E. Wanner & L. Gleitman (Eds.), *Language acquisition: The state of the art* (pp. 128–170). Cambridge, United Kingdom: Cambridge University Press.

Slobin, D. I. (1985). Crosslinguistic evidence for the language-making capacity. In D. Slobin (Ed.), *The crosslinguistic study of language acquisition: Vol. 2. Theoretical issues* (pp. 1157–1256). Hillsdale, NJ: Erlbaum.

Slobin, D. I., & Aksu, A. (1982). Tense, aspect, and modality in the use of the Turkish evidential. In P. J. Hopper (Ed.), *Tense-aspect: Between semantics & pragmatics* (pp. 185–200). Amsterdam, The Netherlands: Benjamins.

Sloman, S. A., Hayman, C. A. G., Ohta, N., Law, J., & Tulving, E. (1988). Forgetting in primed fragment completion. *Journal of Experimental Psychology: Learning, Memory, and Cognition, 14,* 223–239.

Slovic, P. (1995). The construction of preference. *American Psychologist, 50,* 364–371.

Smetana, J. G., Campione-Barr, N., & Metzger, A. (2006). Adolescent development in interpersonal and societal contexts. *Annual Review of Psychology, 57,* 255–284.

Smith, C. T., Nixon, M. R., & Nader, R. S. (2004). Posttraining increases in REM sleep intensity implicate REM sleep in memory processing and provide a biological marker of learning potential. *Learning & Memory, 11,* 714–719.

Smith, M. A., Wise, I. L., & Lamb, R. J. (2004). Sex ratios of *Sitodiplosis mosellana* (Diptera: Cecidomyiidae): Implications for pest management in wheat (Poaceae). *Bulletin of Entomology Research, 94*(6), 569–575.

Smith, M. S., Kish, B. L., & Crawford, C. B. (1987). Inheritance of wealth as human kin investment. *Ethology and Sociobiology, 8,* 171–182.

Smith, M., Hopkins, D., Peveler, R. C., Holt, R. I. G., Woodward, M., & Ismail, K. (2008). First- v. second-generation antipsychotics and risk for diabetes in schizophrenia: Systematic review and meta-analysis. *The British Journal of Psychiatry, 192,* 406–411.

Smith, S. L., & Donnerstein, E. (1998). Harmful effects of exposure to media violence: Learning of aggression, emotional desensitization, and fear. In R. G. Geen & E. Donnerstein (Eds.), *Human aggression: Theories, research, and implications for public policy* (pp. 167–202). San Diego, CA: Academic Press.

Smith, T. W., & Ruiz, J. M. (2002). Psychosocial influences on the development and course of coronary heart disease: Current status and implications for research and practice. *Journal of Consulting and Clinical Psychology, 70,* 548–568.

Smoller, J. W., Biederman, J., Arbeitman, L., Doyle, A. E., Fagerness, J., Perlis, R. H., Sklar, P., & Faraone, S. V. (2006). Association between the 5HT1B receptor gene (*HTR1B*) and the inattentive subtype of ADHD. *Biological Psychiatry, 59,* 460–467.

Sniehotta, F. F., Scholz, U., & Schwarzer, R. (2006). Action plans and coping plans for physical exercise: A longitudinal study in cardiac rehabilitation. *British Journal of Health Psychology, 11,* 23–37.

Snowden, L. R., & Yamada, A.-M. (2005). Cultural differences in access to care. *Annual Review of Clinical Psychology, 1,* 143–166.

Snyder, D. K., Castellani, A. M., & Whisman, M. A. (2006). Current status and future directions in couple therapy. *Annual Review of Psychology, 57,* 317–344.

Solomon, A. (2001). *The noonday demon*. New York, NY: Scribner.

Sommer, W., Heinz, A., Leuthold, H., Matt, J., & Schweinberger, S. R. (1995). Metamemory, distinctiveness, and event-related potentials in recognition memory for faces. *Memory & Cognition, 23*, 1–11.

Sommerville, J. A., Woodward, A. L., & Needham, A. (2005). Action experience alters 3-month-old infants' perception of others' actions. *Cognition, 96*, B1–B11.

Son Hing, L. S., Chung-Yan, G. A., Hamilton, L. K., & Zanna, M. P. (2008). A two-dimensional model that employs explicit and implicit attitudes to characterize prejudice. *Journal of Personality and Social Psychology, 94*, 971–987.

Sonnad, S. S., Moyer, C. A., Patel, S., Helman, J. I., Garetz, S. L., & Chervin, R. D. (2003). A model to facilitate outcome assessment of obstructive sleep apnea. *International Journal of Technology Assessment in Health Care, 19*, 253–260.

Sonnadara, R. R., & Trainor, L. J. (2005). Perceived intensity effects in the octave illusion. *Perception & Psychophysics, 67*, 648–658.

Spangler, W. D. (1992). Validity of questionnaire and TAT measures of need for achievement: Two meta-analyses. *Psychological Bulletin, 112*, 140–154.

Spearman, C. (1927). *The abilities of man*. New York, NY: Macmillan.

Spence, M. J., & DeCasper, A. J. (1987). Prenatal experience with low-frequency maternal-voice sounds influences neonatal perception of maternal voice samples. *Infant Behavior and Development, 10*, 133–142.

Spence, M. J., & Freeman, M. S. (1996). Newborn infants prefer the maternal low-pass filtered voice, but not the maternal whispered voice. *Infant Behavior and Development, 19*, 199–212.

Sperling, G. (1960). The information available in brief visual presentations. *Psychological Monographs, 74*, 1–29.

Sperling, G. (1963). A model for visual memory tasks. *Human Factors, 5*, 19–31.

Sperry, R. W. (1968). Mental unity following surgical disconnection of the cerebral hemispheres. *The Harvey Lectures*, Series 62. New York, NY: Academic Press.

Spitz, R. A., & Wolf, K. (1946). Anaclitic depression. *Psychoanalytic Study of Children, 2*, 313–342.

Spooner, A. L., Evans, M A., & Santos, R. (2005). Hidden shyness in children: Discrepancies between self-perceptions and the perceptions of parents and teachers. *Merrill-Palmer Quarterly, 51*(4), 437–466.

Springer, M. V., McIntosh, A., Wincour, G., & Grady, C. L. (2005). The relation between brain activity during memory tasks and years of education in young and older adults. *Neuropsychology, 19*, 181–192.

Spritzer, M. D., Weinberg, A., Viau, V., & Galea, L. A. M. (2009). Prior sexual stimulation increases hippocampal cell proliferation and risk assessment behavior in response to acute predator odor stress in the male rat. *Behavioral Brain Research, 200*(1): 106–112.

Stahl, S. M., Grady, M. M., Moret, C., & Briley, M. (2005). SNRIs: Their pharmacology, clinical efficacy, and tolerability in comparison with other classes of antidepressants. *CNS Spectrums, 109*, 732–747.

Stahr, B., Cushing, D., Lane, K., & Fox, J. (2006). Efficacy of a function-based intervention in decreasing off-task behavior exhibited by a student with ADHD. *Journal of Positive Behavior Interventions, 8*, 201–211.

Stams, G. J. J. M., Juffer, F., & van IJzendoorn, M. H. (2002). Maternal sensitivity, infant attachment, and temperament in early childhood predict adjustment in middle childhood: The case of adopted children and their biologically unrelated parents. *Developmental Psychology, 38*, 806–821.

Stanley, D., Phelps, E., & Banaji, M. (2008). The neural basis of implicit attitudes. *Current Directions in Psychological Science, 17*, 164–170.

Stanton, A. L., Revenson, T. A., & Tennen, H. (2007). Health psychology: Psychological adjustment to chronic disease. *Annual Review of Psychology, 58*, 565–592.

Starace, F., Massa, A., Amico, K. R., & Fisher, J. D. (2006). Adherence to antiretroviral therapy: An empirical test of the information-motivation-behavioral skills model. *Health Psychology, 25*, 153–162.

Statistics Canada. (2002b). Alcohol and illicit drug dependence. *The Daily*. Retrieved from http://www.statcan.ca/Daily/English/041209/d041209b.htm

Statistics Canada. (2004a). Health reports: Use of cannabis and other illicit drugs. *The Daily*. Retrieved from http://www.statcan.ca/Daily/English/040721/d040721a.htm

Statistics Canada. (2004b). *Supplement to Health Report, Volume 15*. Statistics Canada Catalogue 82-003. Retrieved from http://www.statcan.ca/english/freepub/82-003-SIE/2004000/pdf/82-003-SIE20040007443.pdf

Statistics Canada. (2005a). *Adult obesity in Canada: Measured in heights and weights*. Retrieved from http://www.statcan.ca/english/research/82-620-MIE/2005001/articles/adults/aobesity.htm#1

Statistics Canada. (2009). *Ten leading causes of death by selected age groups, by sex, Canada—all ages*. Retrieved from http://www.statcan.gc.ca/pub/84-215-x/2009000/tbl/t001-eng.htm

Statistics Canada. (2010). *Suicides and suicide rates, by sex and by age groups*. CANSIM, table 102-0551 and Catalogue no. 84F0209X. Retrieved from http://www40.statcan.ca/l01/cst01/hlth66a-eng.htm

Steel, P. (2007). The nature of procrastination: A meta-analytic and theoretical review of quintessential self-regulatory failure. *Psychological Bulletin, 133*(1), 65–94.

Steele, C. M. (1997). A threat in the air: How stereotypes shape intellectual identity and performance. *American Psychologist, 6*, 613–629.

Steele, C. M., & Aronson, J. (1995). Stereotype threat and the intellectual test performance of African Americans. *Journal of Personality and Social Psychology, 69*, 797–811.

Steele, C. M., & Aronson, J. (1998). Stereotype threat and the test performance of academically successful African Americans. In C. Jencks & M. Phillips (Eds.), *The black-white test score gap* (pp. 401–427). Washington, DC: Brookings Institution Press.

Steger, M. F., Hicks, B. M., Kashdan, T. B., Krueger, R. F., & Bouchard, T. J., Jr. (2007). Genetic and environmental influences on positive traits of the values in action classification, and biometric covariance with normal personality. *Journal of Research in Personality, 41*, 524–539.

Stein, M. B., Jang, K. L., Taylor, S., Vernon, P. A., & Livesley, W. J. (2002). Genetic and environmental influences on trauma exposure and posttraumatic stress disorder symptoms: A twin study. *American Journal of Psychiatry, 159*, 1675–1681.

Steinberg, L. (2008). A social neuroscience perspective on adolescent risk-taking. *Developmental Review, 28*(1), 78–106.

Steinberg, L., Lamborn, S. D., Dornbusch, S. M., & Darling, N. (1992). Impact of parenting practices on adolescent achievement: Authoritative parenting, school involvement, and encouragement to succeed. *Child Development, 63,* 1266–1281.

Stern, M., & Karraker, K. H. (1989). Sex stereotyping of infants: A review of gender labeling studies. *Sex Roles, 20,* 501–522.

Stern, W. (1914). The psychological methods of testing intelligence. *Educational Psychology Monographs* (No. 13).

Sternberg, R. J. (1986b). *Intelligence applied.* San Diego, CA: Harcourt Brace Jovanovich.

Sternberg, R. J. (1994). Intelligence. In R. J. Sternberg (Ed.), *Handbook of perception and cognition: Vol. 2. Thinking and problem solving* (pp. 263–288). Orlando, FL: Academic Press.

Sternberg, R. J. (1999). The theory of successful intelligence. *Review of General Psychology, 3,* 292–316.

Sternberg, R. J. (2007). Who are the bright children? The cultural context of being and acting intelligent. *Educational Researcher, 36,* 148–155.

Sternberg, R. J., & Grigorenko, E. L. (2003). Teaching for successful intelligence: Principles, procedures, and practices. *Journal for the Education of the Gifted, 27,* 207–228.

Sternberg, R. J., & Grigorenko, E. L. (2007). The difficulty of escaping preconceptions in writing an article about the difficulty of escaping preconceptions: Commentary on Hunt and Carlson (2007). *Perspectives on Psychological Science, 2,* 221–226.

Sternberg, R. J., Grigorenko, E. L., & Kidd, K. K. (2005). Intelligence, race, and genetics. *American Psychologist, 60,* 46–59.

Sternberg, R. J., & Lubart, T. I. (1996). Investing in creativity. *American Psychologist, 51,* 677–688.

Sternberg, R. J., & Lubart, T. I. (1999). The concept of creativity: Prospects and paradigms. In R. J. Sternberg (Ed.), *Handbook of creativity* (pp. 3–15). Cambridge, United Kingdom: Cambridge University Press.

Stevens, J. A., Fonlupt, P., Shiffrar, M., & Decety, J. (2000). New aspects of motion perception: Selective neural encoding of apparent human movements. *Neuroreport, 11,* 109–115.

Stevenson, H. W., Chen, C., & Lee, S. Y. (1993). Mathematics achievement of Chinese, Japanese, and American children: Ten years later. *Science, 259,* 53–58.

Stewart, S. A. (2005). The effects of benzodiazepines on cognition. *Journal of Clinical Psychiatry, 66* (Suppl. 2), 9–13.

Stewart-Williams, S. (2007). Altruism among kin vs. nonkin: Effects of cost of help and reciprocal exchange. *Evolution and Human Behavior, 28,* 193–198.

Stone, J., & McWhinnie, C. (2008). Evidence that blatant versus subtle stereotype threat cues impact performance through dual processes. *Journal of Experimental Social Psychology, 44,* 445–452.

Stone, J., Zeman, A., Simonotto, E., Meyer, M., Azuma, R., Flett, S., & Sharpe, M. (2007). fMRI in patients with motor conversion symptoms and controls with simulated weakness. *Psychosomatic Medicine, 69,* 961–969.

Storbeck, J., & Clore, G. L. (2007). On the interdependence of cognition and emotion. *Cognition and Emotion, 21,* 1212–1237.

Story, L. B., & Bradbury, T. N. (2004). Understanding marriage and stress: Essential questions and challenges. *Clinical Psychology Review, 23,* 1139–1162.

Strauch, I. (2005). REM dreaming in transition from late childhood to adolescence: A longitudinal study. *Dreaming, 15,* 155–169.

Strauch, I., & Lederbogen, S. (1999). The home dreams and waking fantasies of boys and girls between ages 9 and 15: A longitudinal study. *Dreaming, 9,* 153–161.

Straus, M. A., & Stewart, J. H. (1999). Corporal punishment by American parents: National data on prevalence, chronicity, severity, and duration, in relation to child and family characteristics. *Clinical Child and Family Psychology Review, 2,* 55–70.

Strayer, D. L., & Drews, F. A. (2007). Cell-phone-induced driver distraction. *Current Directions in Psychological Science, 16,* 128–131.

Strayer, D. L., Drews, F. A., & Johnston, W. A. (2003). Cell-phone-induced failures of visual attention during simulated driving. *Journal of Experimental Psychology: Applied, 9,* 23–32.

Striegel-Moore, R. H., & Bulik, C. M. (2007). Risk factors for eating disorders. *American Psychologist, 62,* 181–198.

Striegel-Moore, R. H., & Franko, D. L. (2008). Should binge eating disorder be included in *DSM-V*? A critical review of the state of the evidence. *Annual Review of Clinical Psychology, 4,* 305–324.

Striegel-Moore, R. H., Dohm, F. A., Kraemer, H. C., Taylor, C. B., Daniels, S., Crawford, P. B., & Schreiber, G. B. (2003). Eating disorders in white and black women. *American Journal of Psychiatry, 160,* 1326–1331.

Studenski, S., Carlson, M. C., Fillit, H., Greenough, W. T, Kramer, A., & Rebok, G. W. (2006). From bedside to bench: Does mental and physical activity promote cognitive vitality in late life? *Science of Aging Knowledge Environment, 2006*(10), pe21. Review.

Substance Abuse and Mental Health Services Administration (SAMHSA). (2008b). *Results from the 2007 national survey on drug use and health: National findings.* Retrieved from http://www.oas.samhsa.gov/nsduh/2k7nsduh/2k7results.pdf

Sue, S. (2006). Cultural competency: From philosophy to research and practice. *Journal of Community Psychology, 34,* 237–245.

Sullivan, H. S. (1953). *The interpersonal theory of psychiatry.* New York, NY: Norton.

Sullivan, R. J., & Hagen, E. H. (2001). Psychotropic substance-seeking: Evolutionary pathology or adaptation? *Addiction, 97,* 389–400.

Sulloway, F. J. (1996). *Born to rebel: Birth order, family dynamics, and creative lives.* New York, NY: Pantheon.

Summerville, A., & Roese, N. J. (2007). Dare to compare: Fact-based versus simulation-based comparison in daily life. *Journal of Experimental Social Psychology, 44,* 664–671.

Suomi, S. J. (1999). Developmental trajectories, early experiences, and community consequences: Lessons from studies with rhesus monkeys. In D. P. Keating & C. Hertzman (Eds.), *Developmental health and the wealth of nations: Social, biological, and educational dynamics* (pp. 185–200). New York, NY: Guilford Press.

Suzuki, L. A., & Aronson, J. (2005). The cultural malleability of intelligence and its impact on the racial/ethnic hierarchy. *Psychology, Public Policy, and Law, 11,* 320–327.

Suzuki, L. A., & Valencia, R. R. (1997). Race-ethnicity and measured intelligence: Educational implications. *American Psychologist, 52,* 1103–1114.

Suzuki, M., Hagino, H., Nohara, S., Zhou, S., Kawasaki, Y., Takahashi, T., . . . Kurachi, M. (2005). Male-specific volume expansion of the human hippocampus during adolescence. *Cerebral Cortex, 15,* 187–193.

Swann, W. B., Chang-Schneider, C., & McClarty, K. L. (2007). Do people's self-views matter? Self-concept and self-esteem in everyday life. *American Psychologist, 62,* 84–94.

Swazey, J. P. (1974). *Chlorpromazine in psychiatry: A study of therapeutic innovation.* Cambridge, MA: MIT Press.

Szasz, T. S. (1974). *The myth of mental illness* (Rev. ed.). New York, NY: Harper & Row.

Szasz, T. S. (2004). *Faith in freedom: Libertarian principles and psychiatric practices.* Somerset, NJ: Transaction Publishers.

Tacón, A. M., McComb, J., Caldera, Y., & Randolph, P. (2003). Mindfulness meditation, anxiety reduction, and heart disease; A pilot study. *Family and Community Health, 26,* 25–33.

Tajfel, H., Billig, M., Bundy, R., & Flament, C. (1971). Social categorization and intergroup behavior. *European Journal of Social Psychology, 1,* 149–178.

Talarico, J. M., & Rubin, D. C. (2003). Confidence, not consistency, characterizes flashbulb memories. *Psychological Science, 14*(5), 455–461.

Talarico, J. M., & Rubin, D. C. (2007). Flashbulb memories are special after all: In phenomenology, not accuracy. *Applied Cognitive Psychology, 21,* 527–578.

Tandon, R., Keshavan, M. S., & Nasrallah, H. A. (2008). Schizophrenia, "Just the Facts": What we know in 2008. 2. Epidemiology and etiology. *Schizophrenia Research, 102,* 1–18.

Tanofsky-Kraff, M., Wilfley, D. E., & Spurrell, E. (2000). Impact of interpersonal and ego-related stress on restrained eaters. *International Journal of Eating Disorders, 27,* 411–418.

Tarbox, S. I., & Pogue-Geile, M. F. (2008). Development of social functioning in preschizophrenic children and adolescents: A systematic review. *Psychological Bulletin, 34,* 561–583.

Taylor, C. B., & Luce, K. H. (2003). Computer- and internet-based psychotherapy interventions. *Current Directions in Psychological Science, 12,* 18–22.

Taylor, M. G. (1996). The development of children's beliefs about social and biological aspects of gender differences. *Child Development, 67,* 1555–1571.

Taylor, S. E. (2006). Tend and befriend: Biobehavioral bases of affiliation under stress. *Current Directions in Psychological Science, 15,* 273–277.

Taylor, S. E., Klein, L. C., Lewis, B. P., Gruenewald, T. L., Gurung, R. A. R., & Updegraff, J. A. (2000). Biobehavioral responses to stress in females: Tend-and-befriend, not fight-or-flight. *Psychological Review, 107,* 411–429.

Tedeschi, R. G., & Calhoun, L. G. (2004). Posttraumatic growth: Conceptual foundations and empirical evidence. *Psychological Inquiry, 15,* 1–18.

Tedlock, B. (1992). The role of dreams and visionary narratives in Mayan cultural survival. *Ethos, 20,* 453–476.

Tellegen, A., & Ben-Porath, Y.S. (2008). *MMPI-2-RF Technical Manual.* Minneapolis: University of Minnesota Press.

Templin, M. (1957). Certain language skills in children: Their development and interrelationships. *Institute of Child Welfare Monograph,* Series No. 26. Minneapolis, MN: University of Minnesota Press.

Tennen, H., Affleck, G., Armeli, S., & Carney, M. A. (2000). A daily process approach to coping: Linking theory, research, and practice. *American Psychologist, 55,* 626–636.

Teplin, L. A., McClelland, G. M., Abram, K. M., & Weiner, D. A. (2005). Crime victimization in adults with severe mental illness. *Archives of General Psychiatry, 62,* 911–921.

Terman, L. M. (1916). *The measurement of intelligence.* Boston, MA: Houghton Mifflin.

Terman, L. M. (1925). *Mental and physical traits of a thousand gifted children. Vol. 1. Genetic studies of genius* (2nd ed.). Stanford, CA: Stanford University Press.

Terman, L. M., & Merrill, M. A. (1937). *Measuring intelligence.* Boston, MA: Houghton Mifflin.

Terman, L. M., & Merrill, M. A. (1960). *The Stanford-Binet intelligence scale.* Boston, MA: Houghton Mifflin.

Terman, L. M., & Merrill, M. A. (1972). *Stanford-Binet intelligence scale-manual for the third revision, Form L-M.* Boston, MA: Houghton Mifflin.

Terrace, H. S., & Metcalfe, J. (2005). *The missing link in cognition: Origins of self-reflective consciousness.* Oxford, United Kingdom: Oxford University Press.

Tetlock, P. E. (2005). *Expert political judgment: How good is it? How can we know?* Princeton, NJ: Princeton University Press.

Thase, M. E., & Denko, T. (2008). Pharmacotherapy of mood disorders. *Annual Review of Clinical Psychology, 4,* 53–91.

The Correctional Investigator. (2004–2005). *Annual report of the Correctional Investigator.* Ottawa: Government of Canada. Retrieved from http://www.oci-bec.gc.ca/reports/AR200405_download_e.asp

Theeuwes, J., Kramer, A. F., Hahn, S., & Irwin, D. E. (1998). Our eyes do not always go where we want them to go: Capture of the eyes by new objects. *Psychological Science, 9,* 379–385.

Thomas, A., & Chess, S. (1977). *Temperament and development.* New York, NY: Brunner/Mazel.

Thomas, E. L., & Robinson, H. A. (1972). *Improving reading in every class: A sourcebook for teachers.* Boston, MA: Allyn & Bacon.

Thomas, E., & Wingert, P. (2000, June 19). Bitter lessons. *Newsweek,* 50, 51–52.

Thompson, P. M., Vidal, C., Giedd, J. N., Gochman, P., Blumenthal, J., Nicolson, R., . . . Rapoport, J. L. (2001). Mapping adolescent brain change reveals dynamic wave of accelerated gray matter loss in very early-onset schizophrenia. *PNAS, 98,* 11650–11655.

Thorndike, E. L. (1898). Animal intelligence. *Psychological Review Monograph Supplement, 2*(4, Whole No. 8).

Thorndike, R. L., Hagen, E. P., & Sattler, J. M. (1986). *Stanford-Binet intelligence scale* (4th ed.). Chicago, IL: Riverside.

Tice, D. M., & Baumeister, R. F. (1997). Longitudinal study of procrastination, performance, stress, and health: The costs and benefits of dawdling. *Psychological Science, 8,* 454–458.

Tidwell, M. C. O., Reis, H. T., & Shaver, P. R. (1996). Attachment, attractiveness, and social interaction: A diary study. *Journal of Personality and Social Psychology, 71,* 729–745.

Tiger, J. H., & Hanley, G. P. (2006). Using reinforcer pairing and fading to increase the milk consumption of a preschool child. *Journal of Applied Behavior Analysis, 39,* 399–403.

Tijus, C. A., & Reeves, A. (2004). Rapid iconic erasure without masking. *Spatial Vision, 17*(4–5), 483–495.

Timberlake, W., & Allison, J. (1974). Response deprivation: An empirical approach to instrumental performance. *Psychological Review, 81,* 146–164.

Tjepkema, M. (2005). Insomnia. *Health Reports / Statistics Canada, Canadian Centre for Health Information, 17*(1), 9–25.

Todd, J. T., & Morris, E. K. (1992). Case histories in the great power of steady misrepresentation. *American Psychologist, 47,* 1441–1453.

Todd, P. M., & Gigerenzer, G. (2007). Environments that make us smart: Ecological rationality. *Current Directions in Psychological Science, 16,* 167–171.

Todrank, J., & Bartoshuk, L. M. (1991). A taste illusion: Taste sensation localized by touch. *Physiology & Behavior, 50,* 1027–1031.

Tolman, E. C. (1948). Cognitive maps in rats and men. *Psychological Review, 55,* 189–208.

Tolman, E. C., & Honzik, C. H. (1930). "Insight" in rats. *University of California Publications in Psychology, 4,* 215–232.

Tombu, M., & Jolicoeur, P. (2005). Testing the predictions of the central capacity sharing model. *Journal of Experimental Psychology: Human Perception and Performance, 31,* 790–802.

Tomkins, S. (1962). *Affect, imagery, consciousness* (Vol. 1). New York, NY: Springer.

Tomkins, S. (1981). The quest for primary motives: Biography and autobiography of an idea. *Journal of Personality and Social Psychology, 41,* 306–329.

Tomkovick, C., Lester, S. W., Flunker, L., & Wells, T. A. (2008). Linking collegiate service-learning to future volunteerism: Implications for nonprofit organizations. *Nonprofit Management and Leadership, 19,* 3–26.

Tomoyasu, N., Bovbjerg, D. H., & Jacobsen, P. B. (1996). Conditioned reactions to cancer chemotherapy: Percent reinforcement predicts anticipatory nausea. *Physiology & Behavior, 59,* 273–276.

Tong, S. T., Van Der Heide, B., Langwell, L., & Walther, J. B. (2008). Too much of a good thing? The relationship between number of friends and interpersonal impressions on Facebook. *Journal of Computer-Mediated Communication, 13,* 531–549.

Torgersen, S., Lygren, S., Øien, P. A., Skre, I., Onstad, S., Edvardsen, J., Tambs, K., & Kringlen, E. (2000). A twin study of personality disorders. *Comprehensive Psychiatry, 41,* 416–425.

Torrance, E. P. (1974). *The Torrance tests of creative thinking: Technical-norms manual.* Bensenville, IL: Scholastic Testing Services.

Trainor, L. J., Austin, C. M., & Desjardins, R. N. (2000). Is infant-directed speech prosody a result of the vocal expression of emotion? *Psychological Science, 11,* 188–195.

Trainor, L. J., Shahin, A., & Roberts, L. E. (2003). Effects of musical training on the auditory cortex in children. *Annals of the New York Academy of Science, 9,* 506–513. Review.

Trawalter, S., Todd, A. R., Baird, A. A., & Richeson, J. A (2008). Attending to threat: Race-based patterns of selective attention. *Journal of Experimental Social Psychology, 44,* 1322–1327.

Trescot, A. M., Datta, S., Lee, M., & Hansen, H. (2008). Opioid pharmacology. *Pain Physician, 11,* S133–S153.

Triandis, H. C. (1990). Cross-cultural studies of individualism and collectivism. In J. Berman (Ed.), *Nebraska Symposium on Motivation, 1989* (pp. 41–133). Lincoln, NE: University of Nebraska Press.

Triandis, H. C. (1994). *Culture and social behavior.* New York, NY: McGraw-Hill.

Triandis, H. C. (1995). *Individualism and collectivism.* Boulder, CO: Westview.

Trivers, R. L. (1971). The evolution of reciprocal altruism. *Quarterly Review of Biology, 46,* 35–57.

Tropepe, V., Coles, B. L., Chiasson, B. J., Horsford, D. J., Elia, A. J., McInnes, R. R., & van der Kooy, D. (2000). Retinal stem cells in the adult mammalian eye. *Science, 287*(5460), 2032–2036.

Trzesniewski, K. H., Donnellan, M. B., Moffitt, T. E., Robins, R. W., Poulton, R., & Caspi, A. (2006). Low self-esteem during adolescence predicts poor health, criminal behavior, and limited economic prospects during adulthood. *Developmental Psychology, 42,* 381–390.

Tulving, E., & Thomson, D. M. (1973). Encoding specificity and retrieval processes in episodic memory. *Psychological Review, 80,* 352–373.

Tupes, E. G., & Christal, R. C. (1961). *Recurrent personality factors based on trait ratings* (Tech. Rep. No. ASD-TR-61-97). Lackland Air Force Base, TX: U.S. Air Force.

Turk, D. C., & Okifuji, A. (2003). Psychological factors in chronic pain: Evolution and revolution. *Journal of Consulting and Clinical Psychology, 70,* 678–690.

Turner, C. F., Villarroel, M. A., Chromy, J. R., Eggleston, E., & Rogers, S. M. (2005). Same-gender sex among U.S. adults: Trends across the twentieth century and during the 1990s. *Public Opinion Quarterly, 69,* 439–462.

Turner, M. E., & Pratkanis, A. R. (1998). A social identity maintenance model of groupthink. *Organizational Behavior and Human Decision Processes, 73,* 210–235.

Tversky, A., & Kahneman, D. (1973). Availability: A heuristic for judging frequency and probability. *Cognitive Psychology, 5,* 207–232.

Tversky, A., & Shafir, E. (1992). Choice under conflict: The dynamics of deferred decision. *Psychological Science, 3,* 358–361.

Tyler, L. E. (1965). *The psychology of human differences* (3rd ed.). New York, NY: Appleton-Century-Crofts.

Ullman, S. E., Filipas, H. H., Townsend, S. M., & Starzynski, L. L. (2007). Psychosocial correlates of PTSD symptom severity in sexual assault survivors. *Journal of Traumatic Stress, 20,* 821–831.

Underwood, B. J. (1948). Retroactive and proactive inhibition after five and forty-eight hours. *Journal of Experimental Psychology, 38,* 28–38.

Underwood, B. J. (1949). Proactive inhibition as a function of time and degree of prior learning. *Journal of Experimental Psychology, 39,* 24–34.

Urban, J., Carlson, E., Egeland, B., & Stroufe, L. A. (1991). Patterns of individual adaptation across childhood. *Development and Psychopathology, 3,* 445–460.

Urbszat, D., Herman, C. P., & Polivy, J. (2002). Eat, drink, and be merry, for tomorrow we diet: Effects of anticipated deprivation on food intake in restrained and unrestrained eaters. *Journal of Abnormal Psychology, 111,* 396–401.

Vaillant, G. E. (1977). *Adaptation to life.* Boston, MA: Little, Brown.

Valencia, R. R., & Suzuki, L. A. (2001). *Intelligence testing and minority students: Foundations, performance factors and assessment issues.* Thousand Oaks, CA: Sage.

van Dijk, E., & Zeelenberg, M. (2005). On the psychology of 'if only': Regret and the comparison between factual and counterfactual outcomes. *Organizational Behavior and Human Decision Processes, 97*, 152–160.

Van Gelder, R. N. (2003). Making (a) sense of non-visual ocular photoreception. *Trends in Neurosciences, 26*(9), 458–461.

Van IJzendoorn, M. H., & Kroonenberg, P. M. (1988). Cross-cultural patterns of attachment: A meta-analysis of the Strange Situation. *Child Development, 59*, 147–156.

Vansteensel, M. J., Stephan, M., & Meijer, J. H. (2008). Organization of cell and tissue circadian pacemakers: A comparison among species. *Brain Research Reviews, 58*(1), 18–47.

Vartanian, L. R., Herman, C. P., & Wansink, B. (2008). Are we aware of the external factors that influence our food intake? *Health Psychology, 27*, 533–538.

Velicer, W. F., Redding, C. A., Sun, X., & Prochaska, J. O. (2007). Demographic variables, smoking variables, and outcome across five studies. *Health Psychology, 26*, 278–287.

Vemuri, V. K., Janero, D. R., & Makriyannis, A. (2008). Pharmacotherapeutic targeting of the endocannabinoid signaling system: Drugs for obesity and the metabolic syndrome. *Physiology & Behavior, 93*(4–5), 671–686.

Verfaelli, M., Martin, E., Page, K., Parks, E., & Keane, M. M. (2006). Implicit memory for novel conceptual associations in amnesia. *Cognitive, Affective, and Behavioral Neuroscience, 6*, 91–101.

Vezina, P., McGehee, D. S., Green, W. N. (2007). Exposure to nicotine and sensitization of nicotine-induced behaviors. *Progress in Neuro-Pharmacology & Biological Psychiatry, 31*, 1625–1638.

Viding, E., Blair, J. R., Moffitt, T. E., & Plomin, R. (2005). Evidence for substantial genetic risk for psychopathy in 7-year-olds. *Journal of Child Psychology and Psychiatry, 46*, 592–597.

Vignoles, V. L., Regalia, C., Manzi, C., Golledge, J., & Scabini, E. (2006). Beyond self-esteem: Influence of multiple motives on identity construction. *Journal of Personality and Social Psychology, 90*, 308–333.

Vohs, K. D., & Schooler, J. W. (2008). The value of believing in free will: Encouraging a belief in determinism increases cheating. *Psychological Science, 19*(1), 49–54.

Vokey, J. R. (2002). Subliminal messages. In J. R. Vokey and S. W. Allen (Eds.), *Psychological sketches* (6th ed., pp.223–246). Lethbridge, AB: Psyence Ink.

Vonnegut, M. (1975). *The Eden express.* New York, NY: Bantam.

Vonofakou, C., & Hewstone, M., & Voci, A. (2007). Contact with out-group friends as a predictor of meta-attitudinal strength and accessibility of attitudes toward gay men. *Journal of Personality and Social Psychology, 92*, 804–820.

Voorspoels, W., Vanpaemel, W., & Storms, G. (2008). Exemplars and prototypes in natural language concepts: A typicality-based evaluation. *Psychonomic Bulletin & Review, 15*(3), 630–637.

Voss Horrell, S. C. (2008). Effectiveness of cognitive-behavioral therapy with adult ethnic minority clients: A review. *Professional Psychology: Research and Practice, 39*, 160–168.

Voss, J. L., & Paller, K. A. (2008). Brain substrates of implicit and explicit memory: The importance of concurrently acquired neural signals of both memory types. *Neuropsychologia, 46*(13), 3021–3029.

Vouloumanos, A., & Werker, J. F. (2007). Listening to language at birth: Evidence for a bias for speech in neonates. *Developmental Science, 10*(2), 159–164.

Vroom, V. H. (1964). *Work and motivation.* New York, NY: Wiley.

Vu, H., Kellas, G., Metcalf, K., & Herman, R. (2000). The influence of global discourse on lexical ambiguity resolution. *Memory & Cognition, 28*, 236–252.

Wade, T. D., Tiggemann, M., Bulik, C. M., Fairburn, C. G., Wray, N. R., & Martin, N. G. (2008). Shared temperament risk factors for anorexia nervosa: A twin study. *Psychosomatic Medicine, 70*, 239–244.

Wagner, U., van Dick, R., Pettigrew, T. F., & Christ, O. (2003). Ethnic prejudice in East and West Germany: The explanatory power of intergroup contact. *Group Processes & Intergroup Relations, 6*, 23–37.

Wahlsten, D. (1997). *Leilani Muir versus the Philosopher King: Eugenics on trial in Alberta.Genetica, 99*(2–3), 185–198. doi: 10.1023/A:1018370806190

Walach, H., Nord, E., Zier, C., Dietz-Waschkowski, B., Kersig, S., & Schüpbach, H. (2007). Mindfulness-based stress reduction as a method for personnel development: A pilot evaluation. *International Journal of Stress Management, 14*(2), 188–198.

Walker, M. P., & Stickgold, R. (2006). Sleep, memory, and plasticity. *Annual Review of Psychology, 57*, 139–166.

Wallace, A. R. (1858). On the tendency of varieties to depart indefinitely from the original type. *Linnean Society of London, 3*, 53–62. With editorial commentary by Charles H. Smith. Retrieved from http://www.wku.edu/~smithch/Wallace/S043.htm

Wallach, M. A., & Kogan, N. (1965). *Modes of thinking in young children.* New York, NY: Holt, Rinehart & Winston.

Wallis, D. J., & Hetherington, M. M. (2004). Stress and eating: The effects of ego-threat and cognitive demand on food intake in restrained and emotional eaters. *Appetite, 43*, 39–46.

Walster, E., Aronson, V., Abrahams, D., & Rottman, L. (1966). Importance of physical attractiveness in dating behavior. *Journal of Personality and Social Psychology, 5*, 508–516.

Walton, G. M., & Cohen, G. L. (2007). A question of belonging: Race, social fit, and achievement. *Journal of Personality and Social Psychology, 92*, 82–96.

Wang, C., & Mallinckrodt, B. S. (2006). Differences between Taiwanese and U.S. cultural beliefs about ideal adult attachment. *Journal of Counseling Psychology, 53*, 192–204.

Wang, P. S., Berglund, P., Olfson, M., Pincus, H. A., Wells, K. B., & Kessler, R. C. (2005). Failure and delay in initial treatment contact after first onset of mental disorders in the national comorbidity survey replication. *Archives of General Psychiatry, 62*, 603–613.

Wang, S., Baillargeon, R., & Brueckner, L. (2004). Young infants' reasoning about hidden objects: Evidence from violation-of-expectation tasks with test trials only. *Cognition, 93*, 167–198.

Wann, D. L., Royalty, J. L., & Rochelle, A. R. (2002). Using motivation and team identification to predict sport fans' emotional responses to team performance. *Journal of Sport Behavior, 25*, 207–216.

Ward, C. D., & Cooper, R. P. (1999). A lack of evidence in 4-month-old human infants for paternal voice preference. *Developmental Psychobiology, 35*, 49–59.

Warker, J. A., & Dell, G. S. (2006). Speech errors reflect newly learned phonotactic constraints. *Journal of Experimental Psychology: Learning, Memory, & Cognition, 32*, 387–398.

Warren, R. M. (1970). Perceptual restoration of missing speech sounds. *Science, 167,* 392–393.

Wasserman, E. A., & Zentall, T. R. (Eds.). (2006). *Comparative cognition: Experimental explorations of animal intelligence.* New York, NY: Oxford University Press.

Waterhouse, J., Reilly, T., Atkinson, G., & Edwards, B. (2007). Jet lag: Trends and coping strategies. *The Lancet, 369*(9567), 1117–1129.

Watson, J. B. (1913). Psychology as the behaviorist views it. *Psychological Review, 20,* 158–177.

Watson, J. B. (1919). *Psychology from the standpoint of a behaviorist.* Philadelphia, PA: Lippincott.

Watson, J. B., & Rayner, R. (1920). Conditioned emotional reactions. *Journal of Experimental Psychology, 3,* 1–14.

Wax, M. L. (2004). Dream sharing as social practice. *Dreaming, 14,* 83–93.

Wearden, A. J., Tarrier, N., Barrowclough, C., Zastowny. T. R., & Rahill, A. A. (2000). A review of expressed emotion research in health care. *Clinical Psychology Review, 20,* 633–666.

Webster, G. D. (2004). Human kin investment as a function of genetic relatedness and lineage. *Evolutionary Psychology, 2,* 120–141.

Wechsler, D. (1997). *Manual for the Wechsler Adult Intelligence Scale-III.* San Antonio, TX: Psychological Corporation.

Wechsler, D. (2002). *WPPSI-III manual.* San Antonio, TX: Psychological Corporation.

Wechsler, D. (2003). *WISC-IV manual.* San Antonio, TX: Psychological Corporation.

Wedekind, C., & Braithwaite, V. A. (2002). The long-term benefits of human generosity in indirect reciprocity. *Current Biology, 12,* 1012–1015.

Weeks, J. W., Heimberg, R. G., Rodebaugh, T. L., & Norton, P. J. (2008). Exploring the relationship between fear of positive evaluation and social anxiety. *Journal of Anxiety Disorders, 22,* 386–400.

Weinberger, L. E., Sreenivasan, S., Garrick, T., & Osran, H. (2005). The impact of surgical castration on sexual recidivism risk among sexually violent predatory offenders. *The Journal of the American Academy of Psychiatry and the Law, 33,* 16–36.

Weiner, B. (2006). *Social motivation, justice, and the moral emotions: An attributional approach.* Mahwah, NJ: Erlbaum.

Weiner, J. (1994). *The beak of the finch.* New York, NY: Knopf.

Weinfield, N. S., Ogawa, J. R., & Sroufe, L. A. (1997). Early attachment as a pathway to adolescent peer competence. *Journal of Research on Adolescence, 7,* 241–265.

Weisberg, R. W. (1986). *Creativity: Genius and other myths.* New York, NY: Freeman.

Weiss, A., Bates, T., C., & Luciano, M. (2008). Happiness is a personal(ity) thing: The genetics of personality and well-being in a representative sample. *Psychological Science, 19,* 205–210.

Weissenborn, R., & Duka, T. (2000). State-dependent effects of alcohol on explicit memory: The role of semantic associations. *Psychopharmacology (Berl), 149*(1), 98–106.

Wellman, H. M., & Inagaki, K. (1997). *The emergence of core domains of thought.* San Francisco, CA: Jossey-Bass.

Wells, G. L., & Loftus, E. F. (2003). Eyewitness memory for people and events. In A. M. Goldstein (Ed.), *Handbook of psychology: Forensic psychology* (Vol. 11, pp. 149–160). New York, NY: Wiley.

Werker, J. F. (1991). The ontogeny of speech perception. In I. G. Mattingly & M. Studdert-Kennedy (Eds.), *Modularity and the motor theory of speech perception* (pp. 91–109). Hillsdale, NJ: Erlbaum.

Werker, J. F., & Lalond, F. M. (1988). Cross-language speech perception: Initial capabilities and developmental change. *Developmental Psychology, 24,* 672–683.

Werker, J. F., & Tees, R. C. (1999). Influences on infant speech processing: Toward a new synthesis. *Annual Review of Psychology, 50,* 509–535.

Wertheimer, M. (1923). Untersuchungen zur lehre von der gestalt, II. *Psychologische Forschung, 4,* 301–350.

Wever, E. G. (1949). *Theory of hearing.* New York, NY: Wiley.

Whaley, A. L., & Davis, K. E. (2007). Cultural competence and evidence-based practice in mental health services. *American Psychologist, 62,* 563–574.

Whishaw, I. Q., & Kolb, B. (1988). Sparing of skilled forelimb reaching and corticospinal projections after neonatal motor cortex removal or hemidecortication in the rat: Support for the Kennard doctrine. *Brain Research, 451*(1–2), 97–114.

Whishaw, I. Q., Alaverdashvili, M., & Kolb, B. (2008). The problem of relating plasticity and skilled reaching after motor cortex stroke in the rat. *Behavioural Brain Research, 192,* 124–136.

White, L., & Edwards, J. N. (1990). Emptying the nest and parental well-being: An analysis of national panel data. *American Sociological Review, 55,* 235–242.

White, N. M., & McDonald, R. J. (2002). Multiple parallel memory systems in the brain of the rat. *Neurobiology of Learning and Memory, 77*(2), 125–184.

Whittlesea, B. W., & Leboe, J. P. (2000). The heuristic basis of remembering and classification: Fluency, generation, and resemblance. *Journal of Experimental Psychology: General, 129*(1), 84–106.

Whorf, B. L. (1956). In J. B. Carroll (Ed.), *Language, and reality: Selected writings of Benjamin Lee Whorf.* Cambridge, MA: MIT Press.

Widom, C. S., Dutton, M. A., Czaja, S. J., & DuMont, K. A. (2005). Development and validation of a new instrument to assess lifetime trauma and victimization history. *Journal of Traumatic Stress, 18,* 519–531.

Wiggins, J. S. (1973). *Personality and prediction: Principles of personality assessment.* Reading, MA: Addison-Wesley.

Wiggins, J. S., & Pincus, A. L. (1992). Personality: Structure and assessment. *Annual Review of Psychology, 43,* 473–504.

Williams, C. (2001). You snooze, you lose? Sleep patterns in Canada. *Canadian Social Trends, 60,* 10–14. Retrieved from http://www.statcan.ca/english/freepub/11-008-XIE/0040011-008-XIE.pdf

Williams, C. (2008). *Work-life balance of shift-workers.* Statistics Canada. Retrieved from http://www.statcan.gc.ca/pub/75-001-x/2008108/article/10677-eng.htm

Williams, T., Connolly, J., Pepler, D., & Craig, W. (2003). Questioning and sexual minority adolescents: High school experiences of bullying, sexual harassment and physical abuse. *Canadian Journal of Community Mental Health. Special Issue: Disrupting Normalcy: Lesbian, Gay, Queer Issues and Mental Health, 22*(2), 47–58.

Williamson, P., McLeskey, J., Hoppey, D., & Rentz, T. (2006). Educating students with mental retardation in general education classrooms. *Exceptional Children, 72,* 347–361.

Wilson, D. R., & Hare, J. F. (2004). Ground squirrel uses ultrasonic alarms. *Nature, 430*, 523.

Wilson, M., & Daly, M. (2004). Do pretty women inspire men to discount the future? *Proceedings of the Royal Society of London, Biology Letters (Supplement) 271*, S177–179.

Wilson, R. I., & Nicoll, R. A. (2002). Endocannabinoid signaling in the brain. *Science, 296*, 678–682.

Wilson, S. I., & Edlund, T. (2001). Neural induction: Toward a unifying mechanism. *Nature Neuroscience, 4*, 1161–1168.

Wilson, T. D., Houston, C. E., Etling, K. M., & Brekke, N. (1996). A new look at anchoring effects: Basic anchoring and its antecedents. *Journal of Experimental Psychology: General, 125*, 387–402.

Winarick, K. (1997). Visions of the future: The analyst's expectations and their impact on the analytic process. *American Journal of Psychoanalysis, 57*, 95–109.

Windy, D., & Ellis, A. (1997). *The practice of rational emotive behavior therapy.* New York, NY: Springer.

Winner, E. (2000). The origins and ends of giftedness. *American Psychologist, 55*, 159–169.

Wismer Fries, A. B., Ziegler, T. E., Kurian, J. R., Jacoris, S., & Pollak, S. D. (2005). Early experience in humans is associated with changes in neuropeptides critical for regulating social behavior. *Proceedings of the National Academy of Sciences, 102*, 17237–17240.

Witt, J. K., & Proffitt, D. R. (2005). See the ball, hit the ball: Apparent ball size is correlated with batting average. *Psychological Science, 16*, 937–938.

Witt, S. D. (1997). Parental influence of children's socialization to gender roles. *Adolescence, 32*, 253–259.

Witte, K., & Noltemeier, B. (2002). The role of information in mate-choice copying in female sailfin mollies (*Poecilia latipinna*). *Behavioral Ecology and Sociobiology, 52*, 194–202.

Wolcott, S., & Strapp, C. M. (2002). Dream recall frequency and dream detail as mediated by personality, behavior, and attitude. *Dreaming, 12*, 27–44.

Wolfe, J. M. (2003). Moving towards solutions to some enduring controversies in visual search. *Trends in Cognitive Science, 7*, 70–76.

Wolfe, J. M., Friedman-Hill, S. R., & Bilsky, A. B. (1994). Parallel processing of part-whole information in visual search tasks. *Perception & Psychophysics, 55*, 537–550.

Wolpe, J. (1958). *Psychotherapy by reciprocal inhibition.* Stanford, CA: Stanford University Press.

Wolpe, J. (1973). *The practice of behavior therapy* (2nd ed.). New York, NY: Pergamon Press.

Wolpe, J. (1986). Misconceptions about behaviour therapy: Their sources and consequences. *Behaviour Change, 3*, 9–15.

Wong, S. C. P., & Gordon, A. (2006). The validity and reliability of the violence risk scale: A treatment-friendly violence risk assessment tool. *Psychology, Public Policy, and Law, 12*, 279–309.

Wood, J. J., McLeod, B. D., Sigman, M., Hwang, W. C., & Chu, B. C. (2003). Parenting and childhood anxiety: Theory, empirical findings, and future directions. *Journal of Child Psychology and Psychiatry, 44*, 134–151.

Wood, J. J., Piacentini, J. C., Southam-Gerow, M., Chu, B. C., & Sigman, M. (2006). Family cognitive behavioral therapy for child anxiety disorders. *Journal of the American Academy of Child and Adolescent Psychiatry, 45*, 314–321.

Wood, N., & Cowan, N. (1995a). The cocktail party phenomenon revisited: How frequent are attention shifts to one's name in an irrelevant auditory channel? *Journal of Experimental Psychology: Learning, Memory, and Cognition, 21*, 255–260.

Wood, N., & Cowan, N. (1995b). The cocktail party phenomenon revisited: Attention and memory in the classic selective listening procedure of Cherry (1953). *Journal of Experimental Psychology: General, 124*, 243–262.

Wood, R. E., & Bandura, A. (1989). Impact of conceptions of ability on self-regulatory mechanisms and complex decision making. *Journal of Personality and Social Psychology, 56*, 407–415.

Wood, S. J., Pantelis, C., Velakoulis, D., Yücel, M., Fornito, A., & McGorry, P. D. (2008). Progressive changes in the development toward schizophrenia: Studies in subjects at increased symptomatic risk. *Schizophrenia Bulletin, 34*, 322–329.

Wood, W. (2000). Attitude change: Persuasion and social influence. *Annual Review of Psychology, 51*, 539–570.

Wood, W., Lundgren, S., Ouellette, J. A., Busceme, S., & Blackstone, T. (1994). Minority influence: A meta-analytic review of social influence processes. *Psychological Bulletin, 115*, 323–345.

Workman, B. (1990, December 1). Father guilty of killing daughter's friend, in '69. *San Francisco Examiner-Chronicle*, 1, 4.

World Health Organization. (2002). *World report on violence and death.* (E. G. Krug, L. L. Dahlberg, J. A. Mercy, A. B. Zwi, and R. Lozano, Eds.). Geneva, Switzerland: Author.

World Health Organization. (2007). Depression. Retrieved from http://www.who.int/mentalhealth/management/depression/definition/en

World Health Organization. (2008). *The global burden of disease: 2004 update.* Retrieved from http://www.who.int/healthinfo/global_burden_disease/GBD_report_2004update_full.pdf

Worthington, R. L., Soth-McNett, A. M., & Moreno, M. V. (2007). Multicultural counseling competencies research: A 20-year content analysis. *Journal of Counseling Psychology, 54*, 351–361.

Wright, M. J., & Myers, C. R. (1982). *History of academic psychology in Canada.* Toronto, ON: C. J. Hogrefe.

Wright, S. C., Aron, A., McLaughlin-Volpe, T., & Ropp, S. A. (1997). The extended contact effect. *Journal of Personality and Social Psychology, 73*, 73–90.

Yamagata, S., Suzuki, A., Ando, J., Ono, Y., Kijima, N., Yoshimura, K., . . . Jang, K. L. (2006). Is the genetic structure of human personality universal? A cross-cultural twin study from North America, Europe, and Asia. *Journal of Personality and Social Psychology, 90*, 987–998.

Yang, Y., Raine, A., Lencz, T., Bihrle, S., Lacasse, L., & Coletti, P. (2005). Prefrontal white matter in pathological liars. *British Journal of Psychiatry, 187*, 320–325.

Yantis, S. (1993). Stimulus-driven attentional capture. *Current Directions in Psychological Science, 2*, 156–161.

Yantis, S., & Jonides, J. (1996). Attentional capture by abrupt onsets: New perceptual objects or visual masking? *Journal of Experimental Psychology: Human Perception and Performance, 22*, 1505–1513.

Yegneswaran, B., & Shapiro, C. (2007). Do sleep deprivation and alcohol have the same effects on psychomotor performances? *Journal of Psychosomatic Research, 63*(6), 569–572.

Young, J. A, Critelli, J. W., & Keith, K. W. (2005). Male age preferences for short-term and long-term mating. *Sexualities, Evolution & Gender, 7,* 83–93.

Zadra, A., & Donderi, D. C. (2000). Nightmares and bad dreams: Their prevalence and relationship to well-being. *Journal of Abnormal Psychology, 109,* 273–281.

Zahn-Waxler, C., Shirtcliff, E. A., & Marceau, K. (2008). Disorders of childhood and adolescence: Gender and psychopathology. *Annual Review of Clinical Psychology, 4,* 275–303.

Zajonc, R. B. (1968). Attitudinal effects of mere exposure. *Journal of Personality and Social Psychology. Monograph Supplement, 9* (2, Part 2), 1–27.

Zajonc, R. B. (2000). Feeling and thinking: Closing the debate over the independence of affect. In J. P. Forgas (Ed.), *Feeling and thinking: The role of affect in social cognition* (pp. 31–58). New York, NY:Cambridge University Press.

Zajonc, R. B. (2001). Mere exposure: A gateway to the subliminal. *Current Directions in Psychological Science, 10,* 224–228.

Zanna, M. P., & Rempel, J. K. (1988). Attitudes and attitude change. *Annual Review of Psychology, 38,* 575–630.

Zaslow, M. J. (1991). Variation in child care quality and its implications for children. *Journal of Social Issues, 47,* 125–138.

Zeanah, C. H., Smyke, A. T., Koga, S. F., & Carlson, E. (2005). Attachment in institutionalized and community children in Romania. *Child Development, 76,* 1015–1028.

Zeineh, M. M., Engel, S. A., Thompson, P. M., & Bookheimer, S. Y. (2003). Dynamics of the hippocampus during encoding and retrieval of face–name pairs. *Science, 299,* 577–580.

Zelazo, P. D., Helwig, C. C., & Lau, A. (1996). Intention, act, and outcome in behavioral prediction and moral judgment. *Child Development, 67,* 2478–2492.

Zelinski, E. M., Gilewski, M. J., & Schaie, K. W. (1993). Individual differences in cross-sectional and 3-year longitudinal memory performance across the adult life span. *Psychology and Aging, 8,* 176–186.

Zenderland, L. (1998). *Measuring minds: Henry Herbert Goddard and the origins of American intelligence testing.* Cambridge, United Kingdom: Cambridge University Press.

Zimbardo, P. G. (1975). On transforming experimental research into advocacy for social change. In M. Deutsch & H. Hornstein (Eds.), *Applying social psychology: Implications for research, practice and training.* Hillsdale, NJ: Erlbaum.

Zimbardo, P. G. (1991). *Shyness: What it is, what to do about it* (Rev. ed.). Reading, MA: Addison-Wesley. (Original work published 1977)

Zimbardo, P. G. (2007). *The Lucifer effect: Understanding how good people turn evil.* New York, NY: Random House.

Zimbardo, P. G., & Montgomery, K. D. (1957). The relative strengths of consummatory responses in hunger, thirst, and exploratory drive. *Journal of Comparative and Physiological Psychology, 50,* 504–508.

Zimmerman, B. J., Bandura, A., & Martinez-Pons, M. (1992). Self-motivation for academic attainment: The role of self-efficacy beliefs and personal goal setting. *American Educational Research Journal, 29,* 663–676.

Zuckerman, M. (2007). *Sensation seeking and risky behavior.* Washington, DC: American Psychological Association.

Zwaan, R. A., & Radvansky, G. A. (1998). Situation models in language comprehension and memory. *Psychological Bulletin, 123,* 162–185.

Zwaigenbaum, L., Bryson, S., Rogers, T., Roberts, W., Brian, J., & Szatmari, P. (2005). Behavioral manifestations of autism in the first year of life. *International Journal of Developmental Neuroscience, 23,* 143–152.

Name Index

McGrady, A., 406
McGregor, H.A., 385
McGue, M., 346, 371
McGuffin, P., 65
McGuire, M.T., 75
McIntosh, A., 336
McIntosh, A.R., 335
McKenzie, I.A., 105
McKinley, J.R., 455
McKoon, G., 263
McLachlan, R.I., 374
McLaughlin-Volpe, T., 541
McLeskey, J., 298
McNeil, B.J., 283
McPartland, T.S., 451
McPherson, K.S., 304
McQueen, A., 480
McWhinnie, C., 540
McWilliams, L.A., 483
Mead, M., 346, 364
Meador, B.D., 514
Mebert, C.J., 202
Medin, D.L., 237
Meece, J.L., 385
Meichenbaum, D., 411–412, 512
Meier, R.P., 337
Meijer, J.H., 164, 337
Meinhardt, J, 75
Meissner, K.K., 105
Meldrum, L., 407
Melinger, A., 260
Melzack, R., 82, 136
Mendel, G., 62
Mendoza-Denton, R., 435
Menec, V.H., 334
Menon, V., 71
Mercado, A.M., 420
Mercier, L., 26
Merrill, M.A., 296
Merton, R.K., 531
Mervis, C.B., 237
Mesquita, B., 393
Metcalf, K., 161
Metcalfe, J., 162, 236
Metz, L.M., 85
Metzger, A., 346
Meyer, G.J., 455, 457
Meyer, R.G., 492
Meyers, S.A., 543
Mezulis, A.H., 478
Mezzacappa, E., 411
Michael, J., 509
Michael, R.T., 372, 379
Middlebrooks, J.C., 131
Midgley, B.D., 186
Midha, R., 105
Mikk, J., 305
Miklowitz, D.J., 490
Mikulincer, M., 544
Milgram, S., 36, 552–553, 554*f*
Miller, A.G., 554
Miller Chenier, N., 480
Miller, D.G., 242
Miller, D.T., 279, 559
Miller, E.K., 120
Miller, F., 105
Miller, F.D., 105
Miller, G., 222

Miller, G.F., 433
Miller, J.G., 355, 530
Miller, K., 543
Miller, M.A., 406
Miller, N., 418, 556
Miller, N.E., 37
Miller, P.H., 330
Millman 192
Mills, J.S., 372
Milner, B., 96, 102
Milner, B.J., 16, 450, 451
Miltenberger, R., 507
Mineka, S., 75, 464, 473
Mintzer, J., 244
Miranda, J., 501
Mischel, W., 434, 435, 445–446, 445*t*
Misenberg, G., 305
Mishra, J., 228
Misra, G., 11
Mitchell, C., 557
Mitchell, D., 121
Mitchell, J.E., 512
Mitchell, K.J., 240
Mithen, S., 72
M'Naghten, D., 467
Modirrousta, M., 246
Moffitt, T.E., 483
Mogil, J.S., 136
Mohamed, F.B., 266
Mohr, C.D., 543
Moir, S., 135
Moise-Titus, J., 210, 557
Mojtabai, R., 476
Moller, A.C., 75
Möller, J.-J., 518
Molton, I.R., 512
Moncrieff, R.W., 133
Mondraty, N., 371
Moniz. E., 519
Montagna, P., 168
Monteaux, M.C., 492
Montgomery, G.H., 197
Montgomery, K.D., 363
Moon, S.M., 548
Moos, R.H., 410
Moran, G., 343
Moreggi, D., 500
Moreno, M.V., 501
Moret, C., 517–518
Morewedge, C.K., 400
Morgan, A.H., 173
Morgenstern, J., 516
Moriarty, T., 560
Morikawa, H., 338
Morin, S.F., 380
Morling, B., 530
Morris, E.K., 207
Morris, J.A., 351
Morris, J.S., 394
Morrison, M.A., 380
Morrison, R., 384
Morrison, T.G., 380
Morry, M.M., 542
Morton, J., 222
Moscovitch, M., 246
Moscovivi, S., 551
Mosher, W.D., 349
Moskey, E.G., 377

Moskowitz, B.A., 338
Moskowitz, G.B., 529
Moss, C.F., 132
Moss, J., 135
Motherwell, L., 514
Motley, M.T., 260
Movahedi, S., 547
Mower, O.H., 556
Mueller, A., 512
Mueller, U., 512
Mueser, K.T., 510
Muir, L., 298
Mulcare, L., 518
Mulder, E.J., 298
Muldoon, M.F., 556
Mullally, P.R., 451
Mullen, E., 545
Mulvaney, M.K., 202
Munafò, M.R., 416
Munsterberg, H., 24
Murata, P.J., 323
Murphy, D., 74
Murphy, G.L., 237
Murphy, K., 121, 246, 348
Murphy, K.M., 121, 325
Murphy, M.C., 170
Murray, C., 305–306
Murray, H.A., 381, 457
Murray, J.B., 88
Mussweiler, T., 449
Musty, R.E., 190
Myers, C.R., 15
Myers, J., 473
Mylander, C., 339

Nader, K., 193
Nader, R.S., 166
Nagda, B.A., 538
Nagel, L., 54
Nagle, L., 171
Nantel, G., 275
Narayan, V.M., 473
Nash, J.R., 473
Nasrallah, H.A., 488, 489, 517
National Institute On Aging, 244
National Sleep Foundation, 170
Neale, M.C., 473, 481
Neath, I., 221, 228, 230
Needham, A., 332
Neiss, M.B., 450
Neisser, U., 220, 309
Nelson. D.A., 557
Nelson, K., 330
Nelson, R.E., 477
Nelson, T.D., 538
Nemeroff, 192
Nemeth, C.J., 551
Nes, R.B., 399
Nesse, R.M., 76
Neter, E., 280
Nettle, D., 433
Nettlebeck, T., 309
Neuschatz, J.S., 239
Nevéus, T., 164
Newcomb, T.M., 434
Newell, A., 272
Newman, T.K., 69
Nezworski, M.T., 457

Ngu, H., 228
Niaura, R., 421
Niccols, A., 323
Nichols, P.I., 307
Nicoll, C.S., 37
Nicoll, R.A., 176
Nicolson, R., 490
Nielsen, B.D., 310
Nielsen, T.A., 170
Nigg, C.R., 419
Nijstad, B.A., 398
Nisbett, R.E., 305, 530
Nixon, M.R., 166
Noack, P., 344
Nock, M.K., 479
Nolan, J.M., 550
Nolen-Hoeksema, S., 478
Noltemeier, B., 373
Nooteboom, S., 260
Norcross, J.C., 499
Nordahl, C.W., 492
Norman, G.J., 416
Norman, W.T., 433
Norris, J., 354
Norris, S., 492
Norton, P.J., 471
Nosofsky, R.M., 239
Novaco, R., 556
Novick, L.R., 274
Nowak, M.A., 558
Nowlis, G.H., 134
Noy, Y.I., 139
Nrugham, L., 480
Nugent, N.R., 410
Nurius, P., 449
Nutt, D.J., 473
Nyberg, L., 92, 246
Nystrom, L.E., 398

Oaster, T.R., 235
O'Brien, C.P., 518
O'Brien, E.J., 263
O'Carroll, R.E., 521
O'Connor, M.G., 245
Odbert, H.S., 432
O'Donovan, M.C., 488
Oestergren, P.-O., 323
Offord, D.R., 482
Ogawa, J.R., 343
Ogawa, T., 456
Ogrodniczuk, J.S., 500
Öhman, A., 473
Ohta, N., 231
Okamoto-Barth, S., 264
Okifuji, A., 136
Olfson, M., 476
Olson, D.P., 208
Olsson, A., 192
Olsson, I.A.S., 37
Olsson, U., 164, 168
Olszewski-Kubilius, P., 299
Olton, D.S., 208
Oman, D., 174
Omoregie, H., 530
O'Neill, M.A., 124
Onishi, K.H., 260
Oppenheimer, D.M., 279
O'Rahilly, S., 368

Subject Index

Note: Entries for tables and figures are followed by "*t*" and "*f*," respectively.

cell phones, 139
central executive, 224
central nervous system (CNS), 92–94, 93f, 394–395
central responses, 367
central sulcus, 97
central traits, 431
centralist theory of emotion, 395
centration, 330
cerebellum, 96, 243, 245f
cerebral cortex, 97, 98f, 243, 245f, 395
cerebral hemispheres, 97, 98f
   see also brain
cerebrum, 97, 100
challenges to objectivity
   alternative explanations, 25–28
   observer bias, 23–25, 25f
chameleon effect, 545
change blindness, 142, 142f
characteristic patterns of behaviour, 429
Chartrand, Tanya, 545
Cheney, Dorothy, 264
child-directed speech, 338
childhood development
   attachment, 343
   cognitive development, 330–334
   concrete operations stage, 330
   contact comfort/social experience, 345–346
   daycare and, 345
   Erikson's psychosocial stages, 341–342, 341t
   formal operations stage, 330
   foundational theories, 332–333
   growth and maturation, 325–326, 325f, 326f
   human deprivation, 346
   parenting styles/practices, 344, 344f
   Piaget's stages of cognitive development, 329–330, 329t
   preoperational stage, 330
   sensorimotor stage, 329
   socialization, 342
   spanking, 202
   Strange Situation Test, 343
   temperament, 342
   vision problems in, 121
childhood psychological disorders
   attention-deficit hyperactivity disorder (ADHD), 491–492
   autistic disorder, 492
chlorpromazine (Thorazine), 516
Chomsky, Noam, 339
chromosomes, 63, 65, 65f
chronic stress, 401, 404–405, 404f, 407–408
chronological age, 295, 320
chunking, 223–224

cigarette smoking, 416–417
Cinderella effect, 60
cingulotomy, 519
circadian rhythms, 164
Clark, Herbert, 259
Clarke-Stewart, Alison, 345
classical conditioning
   acquisition, 187–189, 188f, 191–192
   applications of, 192–194
   basic features of, 188f
   cancer treatment and, 197
   conditioned response, 187
   conditioned stimulus, 187
   contingency, 191–192, 191f, 192f
   defined, 186
   drug addiction, 194
   emotions/preferences, 192–194
   extinction, 187–189, 188f
   fear conditioning, 192–193
   Ivan Pavlov, 186–187, 187f
   processes of, 187–191
   reflex, 187
   spontaneous recovery, 189
   stimulus discrimination, 190–191
   stimulus generalization, 189–190, 190f
   unconditioned response, 187
   unconditioned stimulus, 187
   variations of CS-UCS temporal arrangement, 189f
client, 500
client-centred therapy, 513–514
clinical psychologist, 14, 500
clinical social worker, 500
closure, law of, 141
clozapine (Clozaril), 517
CNS. See central nervous system (CNS)
co-operative principle, 258, 258t
Coates, Thomas, 417
cocaine, 179
cochlea, 129
cochlear nucleus, 129
cocktail party phenomenon, 140
coercion model, 199
cognition
   see also cognitive processes
   cognitive maps, 207–208, 208f
   comparative, 207–209
   conceptual behaviour, 208–209
   defined, 207, 253
   influences on learning, 207–211
   mental resources, 254–257
   observational learning, 209–211
   study of, 254–257
cognitive-affective theory, 445–446, 445t
cognitive appraisal, 409, 409t, 411–412
cognitive appraisal theories of emotion, 396–397, 396f

cognitive behavioural therapy, 512–513
cognitive development
   in adulthood, 334–336
   assimilation/accommodation, 329
   concrete operations stage, 330
   conservation, 330, 331f
   contemporary perspectives on early, 330–334
   defined, 328
   formal operations stage, 330
   foundational theories, 332–333
   infant cognition, 330–332
   intelligence, 334–336
   internalization, 333–334
   memory, 336
   nature vs. nurture, 328
   object permanence, 330–332, 332f
   Piaget's insights into, 328–330
   Piaget's stages of, 329–330, 329t
   preoperational stage, 330
   schemes, 328–329
   sensorimotor stage, 329
   social/cultural influences, 333–334
cognitive dissonance theory, 535–536
cognitive maps, 207–208, 208f
cognitive neuroscience, 10
cognitive perspectives
   on aggression, 12
   on anxiety disorders, 474
   comparison, 12
   defined, 10
   mood disorders, 477–478, 478f
   on motivation, 365
   overview, 10
   on psychological disorders, 468
cognitive processes
   see also cognition
   automatic processes, 256–257, 257t
   break down of high-level, 255f
   controlled processes, 256–257
   decision making, 278, 281–285, 282t, 283t, 284t
   defined, 253
   judgment, 278–281, 280f
   language and. See language use
   mental processes, 254–257, 254t
   parallel processes, 254–255
   problem solving, 270–272, 271f, 272f, 274f, 274t
   reasoning, 270–271, 275–277, 275f, 277f
   serial processes, 254–255
   visual. See visual cognition
cognitive psychologist, 13–14
cognitive psychology, 253, 253f
cognitive restructuring, 512
cognitive science, 2, 253, 253f
cognitive sets theory, 477

creativity (*continued*)
  increasing, 312
  link to intelligence, 310–311
  madness and, 313
  making judgments about, 311*f*
  overview, 310
criterion validity (predictive validity), 293
cross-cultural differences
  attachment, 343
  in cognitive development, 334
  moral reasoning, 355, 355*f*
  study of, 11
  trait judgments, 542, 542*f*
cross-fostering, 346
cross-sectional design, 321–322
cross-situational consistency, 434
"crying baby" dilemma, 163
crystallized intelligence, 300, 334
CS (conditioned stimulus), 187
CSHA (Canadian Study of Health and
      Aging), 334
Cuddy, Marion, 168
cue familiarity hypothesis, 236
cultural constructions of reality, 162
cultural evolution, 70
culture
  basic emotions and, 391–394
  cognitive development and, 333–334
  construction of self, 451–452,
      452*f*, 452*t*
  eating and, 368
  fundamental attribution error
      and, 530
  moral reasoning and, 354–355
  shyness and, 437
  thought and language, 265–267
  validity of IQ tests and, 308–310, 309*f*
cupboard theory of attachment,
      345–346
Curie, Marie (and daughters), 307
cutaneous senses, 134–135
cyberspace, 454

daily hassles, 408–409
Dali, Salvador, 148–149
Dallaire, Roméo (Major General), 472
dark adaptation, 119
Darley, John, 559–560
Darwin, Charles, 52–55, 391
Darwinian theory, 62–64
data analysis, 23
  see also statistics
data, behavioural, 3
data-driven processing, 150–151
date rape, 378
Dawson College, 555
daycare, 345
death, leading causes of, 415*t*

debriefing, 36
deception, 36
decibels, measures of, 129*f*
decision aversion, 284, 284*t*
decision making
  consequences of, 284–285
  decision aversion, 284, 284*t*
  defined, 278
  frame, 282–284, 283*t*
  in groups, 551–552
  overview, 278, 281–282
  predictions and, 285
  psychological factors, 282*t*
  reference points, 283
  regret, 284
  stages in stable, 409*t*
declarative memory, 218–219
deductive reasoning, 275–276, 277*f*
defence mechanisms, 439, 440, 440*t*
deinstitutionalization, 502
delay conditioning, 189, 189*f*
delusions, 488
dendrites, 81
denial of reality, 440*t*
dependence, 175–176
dependent construals of self, 530
dependent variable, 24, 25
depressants, 177–179
depression
  see also mood disorders
  attentional biases in, 478*f*
  characteristics of, 475*t*
  cognitive therapies for, 511
  described, 475–476
  evolutionary theory of, 75
  gender differences, 478–479, 479*f*
  treatment evaluation for, 522*f*
depth perception
  binocular/motion cues, 143–144
  convergence, 144, 144*f*
  interposition (occlusion), 145, 145*f*
  linear perspective (Ponzo illusion),
      114–145, 145*f*
  pictorial cues, 145
  relative motion parallax, 144
  relative size, 145, 145*f*
  retinal disparity, 143–144*f*
  texture gradients, 145, 146*f*
Descartes, René, 80, 159
descriptive statistics
  correlation, 47
  frequency distributions, 44, 44*t*
  graphs, 44–45*f*
  measures of central tendency, 45, 46
  overview, 44
  variability, 46, 46*t*
desensitization therapy, 506–507, 507*t*
determinism, 22

development
  aging successfully, 355–356
  cognitive. *See* cognitive development
  cross-sectional design, 321–322
  gender identity/roles, 351–352
  language acquisition, 336–340
  life span, 320*t*
  longitudinal design, 321, 321*f*
  moral, 353–355
  physical. *See* physical development
  sex differences, 350–351
  social. *See* social development
  study of, 320–322
developmental age, 320
developmental psychologist, 15
developmental psychology, 320
deviation score, 46
Dewey, John, 7
Diagnostic and Statistical Manual of Mental
      Disorders (DSM). *See* DSM-IV-TR
diathesis-stress hypothesis, 489–490
dichotic listening, 140, 140*f*
dieting, 368–370, 370*f*
difference thresholds, 116–117
differential reinforcement, 203
diffusion of responsibility, 560
direct observation, 33
direct provocation, 556–557
discriminative stimulus, 198–199
disorganized type of schizophrenia,
      487–488
displacement, 440*t*
dispositional approach, 443
dispositional forces, 365
dissociative amnesia, 485
dissociative disorders
  causes of, 485–486, 486*f*
  defined, 484
  dissociative amnesia, 485
  dissociative fugue, 485
  dissociative identity disorder, 485
dissociative fugue, 485
dissociative identity disorder (DID), 485
distal stimuli, 112–113, 112*f*
distinctiveness, 529
distractor task, 223
divergent thinking, 310, 311
diversity, of psychological inquiry, 13–15
Dix, Dorothea, 502
DNA (deoxyribonucleic acid), 64, 65*f*
Doctors of the World, 34
Donders, F.C. 254, 254*t*
door-in-the-face technique, 537
dopamine, 86–88
double-blind control, 27
Down syndrome, 298
dream analysis, 503–504
dream work, 169

exam preparation, 235
excitatory inputs, 83
exemplars, 239
exercise, 419
exhaustion stage, 404
existential crises, 513
existential humanistic tradition, 499
expectancy, 385–386, 444
expectancy effects, 26
expectancy theory (Rotter), 384–386,
    444–445, 444t
expectations, 151–152, 152f, 365, 531–532
experience, 184
experience-sampling method, 161, 161t
experimental analysis, 195–196
experimental group, 27
experimental methods
    alternative explanations, problem of, 25,
        26–27
    between-subjects design, 27
    confounding variable, 26
    control procedures, 26–27
    defined, 25
    double-blind control, 27
    elements of experiment, 25f
    expectancy effects, 26
    placebo effects, 26
    population (research), 27
    representative sample, 27
    sample, 27
    within-subjects design, 28, 28f
explanation, of behaviour, 4
explanatory style model, 477
explicit memory, 217–218, 226–227, 230, 245
exposure therapies, 506–507, 507t
*The Expression of Emotions in Man and
    Animals* (Darwin), 391
extension, 339
external control orientation, 444–445, 444t
external ear (pinna), 129
extinction, 187–189, 188f
extraversion, 432, 432f, 433, 433f
eye. *See* human eye
eyewitness memory, 242–243
Eysenck, Hans, 432, 521
Eysenck's personality circle, 432, 432f

face validity, 293
factor analysis, 299
FAE (fundamental attribution error),
    529–531, 530f
family therapy, 515
fantasy, 440t
Fantz, Robert, 325
fatigue, 408
fear, 74, 471
fear conditioning, 192–193
Fechner, Gustav, 114

Festinger, Leon, 535
fight-or-flight response, 401
figure, 141, 141f
filter theory, 140
five-factor model, 432–433, 432t
fixation, 438
fixed-interval (FI) schedules, 203
fixed-ratio (FR) schedules, 203
flashbulb memories, 241–242
flooding, 507
fluid intelligence, 300, 334
fluoxetine, 88
fMRI. *See* functional MRI (fMRI)
foot-in-the-door technique, 537
forensic psychologists, 5
forgetting, 232–233, 232f, 233f
forgetting curve, 232f
formal assessment
    defined, 292
    norms/standardization, 294
    reliability, 292
    validity, 293–294
formal operations stage, 330
foundational theories, 332–333
fovea, 119
frame, 282–284, 283t
Franklin, George, 505
Franklin-Lipsker, Eileen, 505
free association, 503
frequency distributions, 44, 44t
frequency theory, 131
Freud, Anna, 346
Freud, Sigmund, 160, 364, 468
Freudian psychoanalysis
    anxiety, 439, 440
    behaviour therapies *vs.*, 510t
    catharsis, 503
    countertransference, 504
    defined, 503
    dream analysis, 503–504
    of dreams, 169
    drives, 436
    ego, 439
    ego defence, 439, 440, 440t
    evaluation of, 440–441
    free association, 503
    human mind/unconscious, 438f
    id, 439
    insight therapy, 503
    libido, 436
    overview, 436, 503
    psychic determinism, 438–439
    psychosexual development, 437–438, 438t
    repressed memories, 505
    repression, 439, 440
    resistance, 503
    structure of personality, 439
    superego, 439

transference, 504
    unconscious, 438–439
Freudian slip, 438–439
Friedman, Meyer, 420
friendship, 13
frontal lobe, 98
frustration-aggression hypothesis, 556
functional fixedness, 274
functional MRI (fMRI), 92, 123f,
    246–247, 247f
functionalism, 7, 8
fundamental attribution error (FAE),
    529–531, 530f

g (general intelligence), 299, 299f
GABA (gamma-aminobutyric acid), 86,
    177, 518
Gage, Phineas, 89
Galen, 429
Galton, Sir Francis, 56, 291
ganglion cells, 119, 122f
Garcia, John, 205–206
Gardner, Howard (*Multiple Intelligences*),
    302, 303t, 312
gate-control theory, 136
Gazzaniga, Michael, 101
gender, 351
gender differences
    brain, 351
    brain lateralization, 102
    colour blindness, 125–126
    in depression, 478–479, 479f
    in jealousy, 376, 376f, 376t
    moral reasoning, 354–355
    self-handicapping, 450, 451f
gender identity, 351–352
gender roles, 351–352
general adaptation syndrome (GAS),
    404–405, 404f
general aggression model, 557
general intelligence (g), 299, 299f
General Procrastination Scale, 406
generalization, 198–199
generalization gradient, 190–190f
generalization techniques, 510
generalized anxiety disorder, 469
generation heuristic, 281
generativity, 342, 349–350t
genes
    behaviour and, 65–69, 67f
    defined, 64–65
genetic determinism, 56
genetic engineering, 68
genetics
    aggression and, 555
    basic, 64–65, 65f
    defined, 64
    ethical issues in, 67–68

humanistic perspective, 9, 10
  on aggression, 12
  comparison, 12
  defined, 9
humanistic theories, 442–443
humanistic therapies
  client-centred therapy, 513–514
  existentialist crises, 513
  Gestalt therapy, 514
  human potential movement, 513
  overview, 513
  unconditional positive regard, 513–514
Hume, David, 204
humours, 429–430
Huntington's disease, 65
Hurvich, Leo, 126–127
hyperactivity, 491–492
hypercomplex cells, 123
hypnosis
  defined, 172
  effects of, 173
  hypnotic induction, 172
  hypnotizability, 172f, 173
  overview, 172
hypnotic analgesia, 173
hypnotic induction, 172
hypnotizability, 172f, 173
hypochondriasis, 484
hypothalamus, 97, 104, 104t, 367, 401–402
hypothesis, 22
hypothesis-driven processing, 150–151
hysteria, 484

ICD (International Classification of
    Diseases), 466
iconic memory, 220–222
id, 439
identification, 440t
identification and recognition processes,
    111, 113f
  bottom-up processing, 150–151
  contexts/expectations, 151–152, 152f
  phonemic restoration, 150–151, 151f
  set, 152
  top-down processing, 150–151, 151f
identity, 342
if . . . then personality signatures, 435, 435f
illusions, 149, 149f, 150
imaging brain activity, 92, 246–247, 247f
Immigration Restriction Act, 304
immune function, 421, 422f
implicit association test, 533–534
implicit memory, 217–218, 218f, 231–232,
    231f, 238, 245–246
imprinting, 57, 343
impulsive aggression, 556
impulsivity, 66, 491–492

in-group bias, 538
in-groups, 538
inattention, 491–492
inattention blindness, 142, 142f
inborn bias, 206, 206f
incentives, 363–364
inclusion of other (IOS) scale, 544f
inclusive fitness, 58
independent construls of self, 451–452, 530
independent variable, 24
indirect reciprocity, 558
individual differences, 291
individualistic culture, 451–452
individuals, 2, 3
inductive reasoning, 276–278, 277f
industrial-organizational psychologist,
    13–14
infant cognition, 330–332
infant development, 324–325, 325f
inferences, 263, 264t
inferential statistics
  defined, 44
  normal curve, 47–48, 47f
  overview, 47
  statistical significance, 48–49
information-influence model, 551
information processing, 217
informational influence processes, 548, 549
informed consent, 36
inhibitory inputs, 83
initiative, 342
inner ear, 129
insanity, 467–468
insight therapy, 503
  see also psychodynamic therapies
insomnia, 167
instincts, 364–365
instinctual drift, 204–205
institutional treatment, 501–502
instrumental aggression, 556
instrumentality, 385–386
intellectual disabilities, 298–298t
intelligence
  aging and, 334–336
  analytical, 301–301t
  creative, 302
  creativity and, 310–311, 311f
  crystallized, 300, 334
  defined, 294
  emotional, 302–303
  environments and, 307–308, 308f
  extremes of, 297–299
  fluid, 300, 334
  general intelligence (g), 299, 299f
  giftedness, 298–299
  group comparisons of, 304–305
  heredity and, 305–306, 306f

intellectual disabilities/learning disorders,
    297f, 298–298t
  multiple intelligences, 302, 303t
  politics of, 303–310
  practical, 302
  race and, 304–305
  structure of, 301f
intelligence assessment
  on Internet, 300
  IQ tests, 295–297
  mental age, 295
  origins of, 295
  overview, 294–295
  Stanford-Binet Intelligence Scale,
    295–296
  Wechsler Intelligence Scales,
    296–297, 296t
intelligence quotient (IQ)
  defined, 295
  distribution of scores, 297f
  environments and, 307–308, 308f
  heredity and, 305–306, 306f
intelligence theories
  emotional intelligence, 302–303
  Gardner's multiple intelligences,
    302, 303t
  psychometric theories, 299–300
  Sternberg's triarchic theory, 301–302
intentional deception, 36
interactionist perspective, 469
Interagency Secretariat on Research
    Ethics, 35
interdependent construls of self, 451–452
interference, 233, 233f
intermediary bystander, 553
internal consistency, 292
internal control orientation, 444–445, 444t
internal working model, 343
internalization, 333–334
International Classification of Diseases
    (ICD), 466
International Union of Psychological
    Science, 14
Internet
  evaluating psychological information, 38
  intelligence assessment, 300
  online therapy, 500
  personality conveyed, 454
interneurons, 81–82
interpersonal responsibility, 355, 355f
interposition, 145, 145f
The Interpretation of Dreams (Freud), 169
interval schedule, 203
interventions, 6
interview, 33
intimacy, 348–349, 348f
intimacy goals, 448

intrapsychic events, 436
intrinsic motivation, 313
Introduction to Psychology (Atkinson), 117
introspection, 7, 185
ion channels, 84
IOS (inclusion of other) scale, 544f
IQ. *See* intelligence quotient (IQ)
IQ tests, 295–297, 297f, 308–310
iris, 118
isolation, 440t

James-Lange theory of emotion, 395, 396f
James, William, 55, 159, 175, 364, 395, 449
Jameson, Dorothea, 126–127
Janis, Irving, 552
jealousy, 376, 376f, 376t
jet lag, 164
job burnout, 421–422
John Hopkins University, 6
Johnson, Virginia, 374–375
Jolie, Angelina, 532–533
Jones, Mary Cover, 506
judgment
    anchoring heuristic, 281
    availability heuristic, 279–280
    defined, 278
    heuristics and, 278–281
    impact of mood on, 398–399t
    overview, 278
    representativeness heuristic,
        280–281, 280f
Jung, Carl, 441
just noticeable difference (JND),
    116–117, 116f
justice, 354–355, 559

Kagan, Jerome, 342
Kahneman, Daniel, 278
Kelley, Harold, 529
Kennedy, John F. 241
Kiecolt-Glaser, Janet, 420
Kimura, Doreen, 268
kinesthetic sense, 135
Kinsey, Alfred, 377
Klein, Melanie, 504
knowledge compilation, 219
Koelling, Robert, 205–206
Koffka, Kurt, 141
Kohlberg, Lawrence, 353
Kohlberg's stages of moral reasoning,
    353–354, 354t
Köhler, Wolfgang, 141
Kolb, Bryan, 106
Kraepelin, Emil, 466

LaBerge, Stephen, 171
Lamarck, Jean Pierre Antoine de Monet de, 51
Lange, Carl, 395

language
    evolution and, 263–265
    evolution of, 69–71
    production. *See* language production
    speaking written words, 100, 100f
    structure, 264, 337t
language acquisition
    child-directed speech, 338
    grammar acquisition, 338–340, 340f
    language-making capacity, 339
    over-regularization, 339
    phonemes, 337
    speech perception, 337–338
    word meanings, 338, 338f
    word perception, 337–338
language-making capacity, 339
language production
    audience design, 258–259
    defined, 257–258
    Grice's maxims, 258t
    overview, 257–258, 257f
    speech execution/errors, 259–260,
        260f, 260t
language understanding
    ambiguity resolution, 261–263, 261f, 262f
    inferences, 263, 264t
    products of, 263
    propositions, 263
language use
    evolution and, 263–265
    language production, 257–260, 257f, 260f
    language understanding, 261–263,
        261f, 262f
    lies and truth-telling, 266
    thought and culture, 265–267
Lashley, Karl, 243
Latané, Bibb, 559–560
latency stage, 438t
latent content, 169
lateral fissure, 97
law of closure, 141
law of common fate, 141
law of effect, 195
law of good continuation, 141
law of proximity, 141
law of similarity, 141
Lazarus, Richard, 397, 409
lazy eye, 121
LCUs (life-change units), 405–406
leading causes of death, 415t
learned helplessness, 477
learning
    behaviour analysis, 186
    behaviourism, 185–186
    biological constraints on, 204
    biology and, 204–207
    change in behaviour/behaviour
        potential, 184

classical conditioning and. *See* classical
    conditioning
cognitive influences on, 207–211, 208f
consistent change, 184–185
defined, 184
disorders, 297–298
experience-based process, 184
habituation, 185
innate laws of behaviour *vs.* 453
instinctual behaviours and, 364
instinctual drift, 204–205
observational, 209–211
operant conditioning and. *See* operant
    conditioning
sensitization, 185
study of, 184–185
taste-aversion learning, 205–207, 206f
learning-performance distinction, 184
legal system, 5
legitimate authority, 552
lens, 118
leptin, 368
lesions, 89–90
levels of analysis, 3, 4f
levels-of-processing theory, 230
lexical ambiguity, 261
lexical meaning, 337
libido, 436
lies, in language use, 266
life-change units (LCUs), 405–406
life span development, 320t
lightness constancy, 147–147f
liking
    mere exposure effect, 542
    physical attractiveness, 542, 542f
    reciprocity, 543
    similarity, 542
limbic system, 96–97, 97f
linear perspective (Ponzo illusion),
    114–145, 145f
linguistic relativity, 265–267
lithium salts, 518
Little Albert, 192–193
lobotomy, 519
Locke, John, 160, 328
Loftus, Elizabeth, 242
long-term memory (LTM), 229f
    see also memory
    context, 227–230
    contextual distinctiveness, 228–230, 229f
    defined, 226
    encoding/retrieval processes, 230–232
    encoding specificity, 227–228
    implicit memory, 231, 231f
    levels-of-processing theory, 230
    overview, 226
    primacy effect, 228–230
    priming, 231, 231f

psychodynamic perspective, 477
suicide, 479–480
moods, 391, 398
Moon, Reverend Sun Myung, 548
moral behaviour, 353
moral development, 353–355
cultural perspective, 355, 355f
gender perspective, 354–355
Kohlberg's stages of moral reasoning, 353–354, 354t
moral reasoning problems, 399t
moral reasoning, stages of, 353–354, 354t
morality, 353
morpheme, 337
morphine, 176
Moscovici, Serge, 551
motion cues, 143–144
motion perception, 143
motion sickness, 135
motivation
academic achievement and, 385
defined, 362
drives, 363
eating and, 366–372
expectations/cognitive approaches, 365
functions of motivational concepts, 362–363
hierarchy of needs, 365–366, 366f
homeostasis, 363
incentives, 363–364
instincts and learning, 364
personal achievement, 381–385
social-learning theory, 365
sources of, 363–365
motor cortex, 98, 99f
motor homunculus, 90, 99f
motor neurons, 81
motor set, 152
MRI. See magnetic resonance imaging (MRI)
Muir, Leilani, 298
multiple personality disorder, 485
multiple sclerosis (MS), 85
Munroe, Marilyn, 371
Munsterberg, Hugo, 23–24
Murphy, Kathy, 121
Murray, Henry, 381, 457
music, 71–73
mutual support groups, 515–516
myelin sheath, 82

naloxone, 88
naltrexone, 88
naming explosion, 338, 338f
narcolepsy, 167
Nason, Susan, 505
Natural Sciences and Engineering Research Council, 35

natural selection, 53–54, 63f
naturalistic observation, 33, 34
nature vs. nurture, 51, 69–328, 453, 481
Necker cube, 148, 148f
need for achievement (n Ach), 381–382, 382f
negative correlations, 29–29f
negative punishment, 198
negative reinforcement, 196–198
NEO Personality Inventory (NEO-PI), 456
nerve deafness, 130
nervous system
action potentials, 83–85
autonomic nervous system, 94–95
central nervous system, 92–94, 93f
neurons. See neurons
neurotransmitters, 86–88
peripheral nervous system, 92, 93f, 94
somatic nervous system, 94
synaptic transmission, 85–86, 85f
neuro-cultural theory, 393
neurogenesis, 104–106
neuromatrix theory of pain, 136
neuromodulators, 88
neurons
action potentials, 83–85
axon, 81
blood-brain barrier, 83
dendrites, 81
described, 81–83
electrical changes in, timetable for, 84f
glia, 82, 83
interneurons, 81–82
major structures of, 81f
motor, 81
myelin sheath, 82
pain withdrawal reflex, 82, 82f
sensory, 81
soma, 81
terminal buttons, 81
two types of, 80f
neuroscience, 10, 80–81, 89–92
see also brain
neurotic disorders, 467
neuroticism, 432, 432f
neurotransmitters
acetylcholine, 86
additional types of signals, 88
defined, 85
dopamine, 86–88
endorphins, 88
GABA, 86
norepinephrine, 86–88
serotonin, 86–88
in synaptic transmission, 85
Newton, Sir Isaac, 124
next-in-line effect, 234

nicotine, 179
nicotine replacement therapy, 416–417
night terrors, 168
nightmares, 167
nitrous oxide, 88
nodes of Ranvier, 85
noise, 128
Nolen-Hoeksema, Susan, 478
non-REM (NREM) sleep, 164–165
nonconformity, 551
nonconscious processes, 159–160
nontaster, 137
norepinephrine, 86–88
norm crystallization, 548
normal curve (distribution), 47–48
normative influence processes, 548, 549–550, 549f
normative investigations, 320
norms, 294, 377–378
see also social norms
nurture vs. nature. See nature vs. nurture

obedience to authority
obedience paradigm, 552
overview, 552
reasons for, 553–554, 554f
test situation, 552–553
obesity, 368–370
object permanence, 330–332, 332f
objective tests, 454–456
objectivity, 4, 464–465
see also challenges to objectivity
observable behaviour, 185
observation, 33–34
observational learning, 209–211
observer bias
defined, 23
remedy for, 24–25, 25f
in research, 23–24
obsessions, 472
obsessive-compulsive disorder (OCD), 471–472
occipital lobe, 98
occlusion, 145, 145f
Oedipus complex, 437
olfactory bulb, 131f, 132
olfactory cilia, 132, 133f
operant, 195
operant chamber, 196–196f
operant conditioning
defined, 195
experimental analysis of behaviour, 195–196
law of effect, 195
operant chamber, 196–196f
reinforcement contingencies, 196–200
reinforcers, properties of, 200–201
schedules of reinforcement, 201–203, 201f

infant, 324–325, 325*f*
    prenatal, 322–324, 323*f*
physical punishment, 202
physiological dependence, 175
physiology
    of eating, 366–367
    of emotions, 394–395
    of hearing, 128–132
    of stress, 401–405, 403*f*
physique, 429
Piaget, Jean, 328–330, 353
Piaget's stages of cognitive development,
        329–330, 329*t*
Pinel, Philippe, 465–502
pinna (external ear), 129
pitch, 128
pitch perception, 67, 67*f*, 130–131
pituitary gland, 103*f*, 104, 402
PKU (phenylketonuria), 298
place theory, 130
placebo control, 27
placebo effects, 26
placebo therapy, 521
plasticity, of the brain, 104–106
pleasure principle, 439
politics of intelligence
    culture/validity of IQ tests, 308–310, 309*f*
    environments and IQ, 307–308, 308*f*
    group comparisons, 304–305
    heredity and IQ, 305–306, 306*f*
    overview, 303–304
Polivy, Janet, 369
pons, 96
Ponzo illusion, 114–145, 145*f*
population (research), 27
positive correlations, 29–29*f*
positive evaluation of violence, 556
positive psychology, 399
positive punishment, 198
positive reappraisal, 413–414
positive reinforcement, 196–198
positive reinforcer, 200–201
positron-emission tomography.
        See PET scans
possible selves, 449–450
post-event information, 242
post-traumatic growth, 414
post-traumatic stress disorder (PTSD),
        406–472
postsynaptic membrane, 85
practical intelligence, 302
pragmatic reasoning schema, 276
pragmatics, 337
preconscious memories, 160
preconventional morality, 354*t*
prediction(s), 4–6, 285
predictive validity, 293

preferences, 192–194
prefrontal cortex, 246, 246*f*
prefrontal lobotomy, 519
prejudice
    behavioural confirmation, 539
    contact hypothesis, 541
    defined, 538
    in-group bias, 538
    in-groups, 538
    origins of, 538–539
    out-groups, 538
    overview, 538
    racism/sexism, 538
    reversing, 540–541
    social categorization, 538
    stereotypes, 539–540
prenatal development, 322–324, 323*f*
preoperational stage, 330
preparedness hypothesis, 473
preschool intervention, 308*f*
presynaptic membrane, 85
prevention strategies, 523
primacy effect, 228–230
primary appraisal, 409, 409*t*
primary prevention, 523
primary reinforcer, 200
priming, 231, 231*f*
principled morality, 354*t*
Principles of Physiological Psychology
        (Kendler), 6
The Principles of Psychology (James), 6
proactive interference, 233, 233*f*
problem-directed coping, 410, 410*t*
problem solving
    algorithms and, 272–273
    analogical, 276
    defined, 271
    functional fixedness, 274
    heuristics, 272–273
    improving, 273–274
    monk puzzle, 274, 274*f*, 274*t*
    overview, 270–271, 271*f*, 272*f*
    problem spaces/processes, 271–273
    think-aloud protocols, 273
problem spaces, 271–273
procedural memory, 218–219
procrastination, 406, 406*f*
progressive education, 7
projection, 440*t*
projective tests, 456–457
propositions, 263
prosocial behaviours
    bystander intervention, 560–560*f*
    defined, 555
    diffusion of responsibility, 560
    effects of situation on, 559–561
    roots of, 557–559

prototypes, 239
Provincial Training School for Mental
        Defectives, 298
proximal stimuli, 112–113, 112*f*
proximity, law of, 141
Prozac, 517
psychedelics, 176
psychiatrist, 500
psychic determinism, 438–439
psychoactive drugs
    defined, 175
    dependence/addiction, 175–176
    depressants, 177–179
    hallucinogens, 176
    medical uses of, 175*t*
    opiates, 176
    overview, 175
    stimulants, 179
    varieties of, 176–179
psychoanalysis, 15
psychoanalyst, 500
psychobiography, 443
psychodynamic approach. *See*
        psychodynamic perspective
psychodynamic personality theories
    Adler's theory, 441
    defined, 436
    extensions of, 441
    Freudian psychoanalysis, 436–441
    Horney's theory, 441
    Jung's theory, 441
psychodynamic perspective, 8
    on aggression, 12
    on anxiety disorders, 473–474
    comparison, 12
    defined, 8
    on mood disorders, 477
    on psychological disorders, 468
psychodynamic therapies
    defined, 499, 503
    later therapies, 504–505
    psychoanalysis, 503–504
psychological assessment
    defined, 291
    ethical issues, 313
    formal assessment, 292–294
    history of, 291
    society and, 313–314
psychological dependence, 176
psychological diagnosis, 465
psychological dimensions of sound,
        127–128
psychological disorders
    abnormality, criteria for, 463–464
    anxiety disorders, 469–474
    behavioural approach, 468
    biological approach, 468

participant modelling, 509, 509f
social-skills training, 509
social networking, 454
social norms, 548
   see also norms
social perception, 528–529
social phobias, 471
social psychologist, 13–14
social psychology
   aggression. *See* aggression
   altruism, 555, 557–559
   attitudes, 532–537
   construction of social reality, 528–532
   defined, 528
   prejudice, 538–541
   prosocial behaviours, 555, 557–561, 560f
   situation, power of, 546–554
   social relationships, 541–544
Social Readjustment Rating Scale (SRRS),
      405–406
social reality. *See* construction of social reality
social relationships
   chameleon effect, 545
   cross-cultural trait judgments, 542f
   inclusion of other (IOS) scale, 544f
   liking, 542–543
   loving, 543–544, 544f, 544t
   styles of attachment, 544t
social roles, 546–547, 547f
social sciences, 2
Social Sciences and Humanities Research
      Council, 35
social-skills training, 509
social support, 412–413, 412f
socialization, 342
society
   homosexuality and, 379–380
   psychological assessment and, 313–314
sociobiology, 60–61
sociocultural perspective
   on aggression, 12
   comparison, 12
   defined, 11
   overview, 11–12
   on psychological disorders, 468
soma, 81
somatic nervous system, 94
somatization disorder, 484
somatoform disorders
   causes of, 484
   conversion disorder, 484
   defined, 483–484
   hypochondriasis, 484
   somatization disorder, 484
somatosensory cortex, 99, 99f
somnambulism (sleepwalking), 168

sound
   decibel levels of familiar, 129f
   localization, 131–132, 131f
   loudness, 128, 129f
   noise, 128
   physics of, 127
   pitch, 128
   psychological dimensions of, 127–128
   pure tone, 128
   sine waves, 128f
   timbre, 128
sound localization, 131–132, 131f
sound shadow, 131
spanking, 202
spatial integration, 141–142, 142f
spatial mental models, 269–270, 270f
speaker meaning, 257
Spearman, Charles, 299
specific phobias, 471
speech errors, 259–260, 260t
speech execution, 259–260, 260f
speech perception, 337–338
Spencer, Herbert, 55–56
Sperry, Roger, 101
split-brain patients, 100–101, 101f, 102f
split-half reliability, 292
split personality, 485
spontaneous recovery, 189, 198
spontaneous-remission effect, 521
spoonerism, 259–260
SRRS (Social Readjustment Rating Scale),
      405–406
SSRIs (selective serotonin reuptake
      inhibitors), 517
standard deviation (SD), 46, 46t
standardization, 24, 294
Stanford-Binet Intelligence Test, 47f, 48,
      295–296
Stanford Hypnotic Susceptibility Scale, 172
Stanford Prison Experiment, 546–547, 547f
Stanford Shyness Survey, 43
state-dependent memory, 228
statistical significance, 48–49
statistics
   data analysis, 43–43t
   descriptive statistics, 43t, 44–47, 44t,
      45f, 46t
   inferential statistics, 47–49, 47f
   misuse of, 49
   overview, 42–43
Statistics Canada, 175, 177
STD (signal detection theory), 115–116
Steele, Claude, 309, 540
stem cells, 105
stereotype threat, 309–310, 309f, 540
stereotypes, 539–540

Sternberg, Robert (triarchic theory of
      intelligence), 301–302
Stevenson, Harold, 310
stigma of mental illness, 493–494
stimulants, 179
stimulus categorization, 254
stimulus dimensions, 117t
stimulus discrimination, 190–191
stimulus-driven capture, 138
stimulus generalization, 189–190, 190f
stimulus-response connection, 195
stirrup, 129
STM. *See* short-term memory (STM)
storage, memory, 219
storm-and-stress theory, 346
Strange Situation Test, 343
stress
   acute, 401
   chronic, 401, 404–405, 407–408
   cognitive appraisal of, 409, 409t
   coping with, 409–413
   daily hassles, 408–409
   defined, 401
   emergency reactions to acute threats,
      401–404
   eustress, 413
   fight-or-flight response, 401
   general adaptation syndrome (GAS),
      404–405, 404f
   hypothalamus and, 401–402
   major life events, 405–406
   model of, 402f
   physiological reaction to, 401–405, 403f
   positive effects of, 413–414
   post-traumatic stress disorder (PTSD),
      406–407
   procrastination, 406, 406f
   psychological reactions, 405–409
   psychosomatic disorders, 404
   September, 11, 2001 events, 407, 407t
   Student Stress Scale, 405t
   tend-and-befriend response, 402
   traumatic events, 406–407
stress inoculation, 411–412
stress moderator variables, 409
stressor, 401
striatum, 243, 245f
structural ambiguity, 261
structuralism, 7
Student Stress Scale, 405t
subjective insomnia, 167
subjective reality, 10
subjective well-being, 399–400
subjective workload, 408
subjectivity, 4
sublimation, 440t

visual cliff, 325, 325*f*
visual cognition
    brain bases of visual imagery, 269*f*
    spatial mental models, 269–270, 270*f*
    verbal/visual representations combined, 269–270
    visual representations, 267–269, 267*f*, 268*f*
visual cortex, 100
visual representations, 267–269, 267*f*, 268*f*
visual system
    blind spot, 120, 120*f*
    brain processes, 120–124, 122*f*
    childhood amblyopia, 121
    colour, 124–127, 125*f*, 126*f*
    cortical regions, 123–123*f*
    human eye, 118, 118*f*
    neural pathways for information, 101, 101*f*
    pupil/lens, 118
    receptive fields, 120, 122*f*
    retina, 118–120, 119*f*
visuospatial sketchpad, 224
vitreous humour, 118
vocabulary development, 338, 338*f*
volley principle, 131
von Békésy, Georg, 130
von Helmholtz, Hermann, 126

Vonnegut, Mark, 486–487
Vygotsky, Lev, 333–334

Walk, Richard, 325
Washburn, A.L., 367
Wason selection task, 275–276, 275*f*
Watson, John, 57, 185, 192–193
wavelengths, 124–126
Weber, Ernst, 116–117
Weber's law, 116, 116*f*, 117, 117*t*
Wechsler Adult Intelligence Scale (WAIS-IV), 296, 296*t*
Wechsler, David, 296–297
Wechsler Intelligence Scale for Children (WISC-IV), 296–297, 296*t*
Wechsler Intelligence Scales, 296–297
Wechsler Preschool and Primary Scale of Intelligence (WPPSC-III), 296–297, 296*t*
well-being, 348*f*, 399–400
wellness, 415, 416*t*
Werker, Janet, 337
Wernicke's area, 100, 100*f*
Wertheimer, Max, 141
Whishaw, Ian, 106
whole-report procedure, 221
Whorf, Benjamin Lee, 265

Wiesel, Torsten, 120
Wilson, Edward O., 60
within-subjects design, 28, 28*f*
Wolpe, Joseph, 506
women
    see also gender differences
    contributions to psychology, 15
    menarche, 327
    menopause, 106
    tend-and-befriend response, 402
Woodworth Personal Data Sheet, 455
words
    meanings of, 338, 338*f*
    perception of, 337–338
    speaking written, 100, 100*f*
work settings, of psychologists, 15
working memory, 224–225, 225*t*
workplace motivation, 384–386
World Wide Web. *See* Internet
Wundt, Wilhelm, 159

The Year of the Flood (Atwood), 68
Young-Helmholtz trichromatic theory, 126
Young, Sir Thomas, 126

Zajonc, Robert, 397
zygote, 322

Photo Credits

Chapter 1:

Page 1: © Photodisc/Jupiter Images; p. 3 (top-left): Myrleen Ferguson Cate/ Photo Edit, (top-right): Tony Savino/The Image Works, (bottom-left): David Young-Wolff/Photo Edit, (bottom-right): Michael Schwarz/The Image Works; p. 4: George S. Seurat, Bathers at Asnieres. National Gallery, London. Copyright Erich Lessing/Art Resource, NY; p. 5: Jeff Greenberg/Photo Edit; p. 7: Archives of the History of American Psychology/University of Akron; p. 8 (left): Michael Newman/Photo Edit, (right): The Granger Collection; p. 9: Benjamin Harris, PhD; p. 10: Roger Ressmeyer/Corbis; p. 11 (top): Wolfgang Kaehler/Corbis, (bottom): STR/AFP/Getty Images; p. 15 (top): David Kelly Crow/Photo Edit, (bottom): Archives of the History of American Psychology/University of Akron; p. 16: Montreal Neurological Institute and Hospital, McGill University.

Chapter 2:

Page 21: Scott Camazine & Sue Trainor/Photo Researchers, Inc.; p. 25: The Canadian Press/Ryan Remiorz; p. 26: Edouard Berne/Stone/Getty Images; p. 29: David Young-Wolff/Alamy; p. 33: Dan McCoy/Rainbow; p. 34: Michael K. Nichols/National Geographic Image Collection; p. 36: Richard T. Nowitz/Phototake; p. 37: Ethan Miller/Getty Images.

Chapter 3:

Page 50: © Bloomimage/Corbis; p. 52 (top-left): © Jim Zukerman/Corbis, (top-right): Science Photo Library/Photo Researchers, Inc., (bottom): © Hulton-Deutsch Collection/Corbis; p. 53 (right): The Bridgeman Art Library/Getty Images; p. 54 (left): © Yann Arthus-Bertrans/Corbis, (right): Dorling Kindersley Media Library; p. 55 (left): Tammy Ivanco, (right): © Shutterstock; p. 56 (left): © Hulton-Deutsch Collection/Corbis, (right): © Bettmann/Corbis; p. 57: © Bettmann/Corbis; p. 59: © Photodisc/Getty Images; p. 62: Martin Rogers/Stone/Getty Images; p. 63: Dan McCoy/Rainbow; p. 66 (left) © Radius Images/Jupiter Images, (centre) © Shutterstock, (right) Ian O'Leary © Dorling Kindersley; p. 69 (left): © Rick Friedman/Corbis, (right): © Wally McNamee; p. 70: © Brooks Kraft/Sygma/Corbis; p. 71: Kenneth Love/National Geographic/Getty Images; p. 72: Photo by Owen Egan/McGill University; p. 73: Photo courtesy: Irena Schulz of Bird Lovers Only Rescue; p. 76: © Shutterstock.

Chapter 4:

Page 79: © Mads Abildgaard/iStockPhoto; p. 80: D. W. Fawcett/Komuro/Photo Researchers, Inc.; p. 86: Tim Maylon and Paul Biddle/SPL/Photo Researchers, Inc.; p. 88: AP Images/Joe Marquette; p. 89: Reprinted with permission from Damasio H, Grabowski T, Frank R, Galaburda, AM, Damasio AR: The Return of Phineas Gage: Clues about the brain from a famous patient. *Science*, 264:1102–1105, © 1994, American Association for the Advancement of Science. Photo courtesy of H. Damasio, Human Neuroanatomy and Neuroimaging Laboratory, Department of Neurology, University of Iowa; p. 90 (left): © Jiang Jin/Superstock; (right): © The Natural History Museum, London; p. 91: Courtesy of Marcus E. Raichle, M.D., Washington University School of Medicine; p. 92: Stone/UHB Trust/Getty Images; p. 102: AP Images/Roadell Hickman/The Plain Dealer.

Chapter 5:

Page 110: MedioImages/Getty Images; p. 111: Christina Kennedy/Getty Images; p. 114: David Kelly Crow/Photo Edit; p. 115: Stefan May/Stone/Getty Images; p. 118: W. E. Harvey/Photo Researchers, Inc.; p. 121: Norbert Schäfer/Masterfile; p. 124: Alan Levanson/Stock Boston; p. 129: Richard T. Nowitz/Corbis; p. 131: Norbert Schwerin/The Image Works; p. 132 (top) Juniors Bildarchiv/Alamy, (bottom) Norbert Schwerin/The Image Works; p. 134: David Ball/Index Stock; p. 135: The Canadian Press/Paul Chiasson; p. 136: Fuji Photos/The Image Works; p. 137 (left and right): Scott Foresman; p. 143: Shutterstock; p. 145 (left): Andy Levin/Photo Researchers, Inc., (right): Michael Dwyer/Stock Boston; p. 146: William J. Herbert/Stone Allstock/Getty Images; p. 147 (top): David Wells/The Image Works, (bottom): Bob Rowan/Corbis; p. 148: Slave Market with the Disappearing Bust of Voltaire (1940). Oil on Canvas. $18 \times 25^3/_8$ inches. Collection of the Salvador Dali Museum, St. Petersburg, Florida. © 2004 Gala-Salvador Dali Foundation, Figueres (Artists Rights Society [ARS]) New York. © 2004 Salvador Dali Museum, Inc.

Chapter 6:

Page 158: Stockdisc/Getty Images; p. 159: David Young-Wolff/Photo Edit; p. 160 (left): Bonnie Kamin/Photo Edit, (top-right): N. Durrell/McKenna/Photo Researchers, Inc., (bottom-right): Ulrike Welsche/Photo Edit; p. 168: Spencer Grant/Photo Edit; p. 172: Courtesy of Dr. Philip G. Zimbardo; p. 174: Peter Hvizdak/The Image Works; p. 176: Photofusion Picture Library/Alamy; p. 177 (left): Doug Menuez/Getty Images, (right): Ace Stock Limited/Alamy.

Chapter 7:

Page 183: David Robbins/Getty Images; p. 184: Topham/The Image Works; p. 185: Ken Heyman/Woodfin Camp & Assoc.; p. 186: © Bettman/Corbis; p. 190: Richard Heinzen/SuperStock; p. 193 (top): Archives of the History of American Psychology, (bottom-left): Bill Aron/Photo Edit, (bottom-right): Maya Barnes/The Image Works; p. 196: SuperStock; p. 200: Cindy Charles/Photo Edit; p. 201: Yerkes Regional Primate Research Center, Emory University; p. 205 (top left): Gerald Davis/Woodfin Camp & Assoc., (bottom-right): John Warden/Stone/Getty Images; p. 207 (all): Courtesy Dr. Stuart R. Ellins, California State University, San Bernadino; p. 209: © iStockphoto/Thinkstock; p. 210: Courtesy Dr. Albert Bandura, Stanford University.

Chapter 8:

Page 216: Roy Mehta/Getty Images; p. 217: AP Images; p. 219: Corbis Royalty-Free; p. 223: Corbis Royalty-Free; p. 224: Marty Heitner/The Image Works; p. 225: Frank Chmura/Alamy; p. 227: Jeff Greeberg/Photo Edit; p. 228: The Canadian Press/The Brockville Recorder and Times-Darcy Cheek; p. 234: Josef Polleross/The Image Works; p. 237: Hemera Technologies/Alamy; p. 240: OnRequest Images, Inc./Alamy; p. 243: Lon C. Diehl/Photo Edit.